KT-173-652

Archae

WITHDRAWN

Archaeology

Theories Methods and Practice

N 0162550 0

COLIN RENFREW PAUL BAHN

Archaeology

Theories Methods and Practice

THIRD EDITION

with over 600 illustrations

NEWMAN UNIVERSITY
COLLEGE
BARTLEY GREEN
BIRMINGHAM B32 3NT

CLASS	930·1
BARCODE	01625500
AUTHOR	REN

Thames & Hudson

Any copy of this book issued by the publisher as a
paperback is sold subject to the condition that it shall not
by way of trade or otherwise be lent, resold, hired out or
otherwise circulated without the publisher's prior consent
in any form of binding or cover other than that in which it
is published and without a similar condition including
these words being imposed on a subsequent purchaser.

First published in the United Kingdom in 1991 by
Thames & Hudson Ltd, 181A High Holborn,
London WC1V 7QX

www.thamesandhudson.com

© 1991, 1996 and 2000 Thames & Hudson Ltd, London
Text © 1991, 1996 and 2000 Colin Renfrew and Paul Bahn

Second edition 1996
Third edition 2000
Reprinted 2001

All Rights Reserved. No part of this publication may be
reproduced or transmitted in any form or by any means,
electronic or mechanical, including photocopy, recording
or any other information storage and retrieval system,
without prior permission in writing from the publisher.

British Library Cataloguing-in-Publication Data
A catalogue record for this book is available from the
British Library

ISBN 0-500-28147-5

Printed and bound in the United States of America by
R.R. Donnelley and Sons Company

Contents

Preface   9

Introduction
The Nature and Aims of Archaeology   11

PART I
The Framework of Archaeology   17

1 The Searchers
The History of Archaeology   19

The Speculative Phase   20
The Beginnings of Modern Archaeology   24
Classification and Consolidation   34
A Turning Point in Archaeology   38
World Archaeology   40
Summary   48
Further Reading   48

BOX FEATURES
Pompeii: Archaeology Past and Present   22
The Impact of Evolutionary Thought   26
19th-century Pioneers of
   North American Archaeology   28
The Development of Field Techniques   31
Women Pioneers of Archaeology   36
Processual Archaeology: Key Concepts   39
Interpretive or Postprocessual Archaeologies   42
Interpretive Archaeologies at Çatalhöyük   44

2 What is Left?
The Variety of the Evidence   49

Basic Categories of Archaeological Evidence   49
Formation Processes   52
Cultural Formation Processes –
   How People Have Affected What Survives
   in the Archaeological Record   54

Natural Formation Processes – How Nature Affects
   What Survives in the Archaeological Record   55
Summary   70
Further Reading   70

BOX FEATURES
Experimental Archaeology   53
Wet Preservation: The Ozette Site   60
Dry Preservation: The Tomb of Tutankhamun   62
Cold Preservation 1: The Barrow Site   65
Cold Preservation 2: The Iceman   66

3 Where?
Survey and Excavation of Sites and Features   71

Discovering Archaeological Sites and Features   72
Assessing the Layout of Sites and Features   89
Excavation   106
Summary   116
Further Reading   116

BOX FEATURES
Regional Survey on Melos   75
Sampling Strategies   76
Archaeological Aerial Reconnaissance   80
Teotihuacán Mapping Project   90
Surface Investigation at Abu Salabikh   92
Underwater Archaeology   95
The Red Bay Wreck: Discovery and Excavation   96
Geophysical Survey at Roman Wroxeter   100
Measuring Magnetism   102
Controlled Archaeological Test Site   104

4 When?
Dating Methods and Chronology   117

RELATIVE DATING   118
Stratigraphy   118
Typological Sequences   120
Linguistic Dating   124
Climate and Chronology   125

ABSOLUTE DATING 128
Calendars and Historical Chronologies 129
Annual Cycles: Varves and Tree-Rings 133
Radioactive Clocks 137
Trapped Electron Dating Methods 150
Calibrated Relative Methods 155
Chronological Correlations 161
World Chronology 162
Summary 170
Further Reading 170

BOX FEATURES
The Maya Calendar 130
The Principles of Radioactive Decay 137
The Publication of Radiocarbon Dates 139
How to Calibrate Radiocarbon Dates 140
Dating Our African Ancestors 148
Dating the Thera Eruption 160

PART II
Discovering the Variety of Human Experience

171

5 How Were Societies Organized? Social Archaeology

173

Establishing the Nature and Scale
   of the Society 174
Further Sources of Information
   for Social Organization 182
Techniques of Study for Mobile
   Hunter-Gatherer Societies 190
Techniques of Study for Segmentary
   Societies 194
Techniques of Study for Chiefdoms
   and States 203
The Archaeology of the Individual
   and of Identity 215
Investigating Gender 218
The Molecular Genetics of
   Social Groups and Lineages 222
Summary 224
Further Reading 224

BOX FEATURES
Settlement Patterns in Mesopotamia 180
Ancient Ethnicity and Language 189
Space and Density in Hunter-Gatherer Camps 193
Factor Analysis and Cluster Analysis 197
Early Wessex 198

Maya Territories 205
Multi-Dimensional Scaling (MDSCAL) 206
Social Analysis at Moundville 212
Gender Relations in Early Intermediate Period Peru 220

6 What Was the Environment? Environmental Archaeology

225

Investigating Environments on
   a Global Scale 225
Studying the Landscape 232
Reconstructing the Plant Environment 239
Reconstructing the Animal Environment 247
Reconstructing the Human Environment 255
Summary 268
Further Reading 268

BOX FEATURES
Reconstructing Climates from
   Sea and Ice Cores 227
Climatic Cycles: El Niño 228
Cave Sediments 234
Pollen Analysis 240
Elands Bay Cave 254
Site Catchment Analysis 258
Mapping the Ancient Environment:
   Cahokia and GIS 260
Ancient Gardens at Kuk Swamp 262

7 What Did They Eat? Subsistence and Diet

269

What Can Plant Foods Tell Us About Diet? 270
Information from Animal Resources 282
Investigating Diet, Seasonality,
   and Domestication from Animal Remains 286
How Were Animal Resources Exploited? 301
Assessing Diet from
   Human Remains 305
Summary 310
Further Reading 310

BOX FEATURES
Paleoethnobotany: A Case Study 272
Butser Experimental Iron Age Farm 274
Investigating the Rise of Farming
   in Western Asia 280
Taphonomy 284
Quantifying Animal Bones 288

The Study of Animal Teeth 291
Bison Drive Sites 292
Farming Origins: A Case Study 296
Shell Midden Analysis 300

8 How Did They Make and Use Tools?
Technology 311

Unaltered Materials: Stone 315
Other Unaltered Materials 327
Synthetic Materials 335
Archaeometallurgy 339
Summary 349
Further Reading 350

BOX FEATURES
Artifacts or "Geofacts" at Pedra Furada 314
Raising Large Stones 318
Refitting and Microwear Studies at the Meer Site 324
Woodworking in the Somerset Levels 330
Metallographic Examination 341
Copper Production in Peru 344
Early Steelmaking: An Ethnoarchaeological
Experiment 348

9 What Contact Did They Have?
Trade and Exchange 351

The Study of Interaction 351
Discovering the Sources of Traded Goods:
Characterization 358
The Study of Distribution 367
The Study of Production 373
The Study of Consumption 377
Exchange and Interaction:
The Complete System 378
Summary 384
Further Reading 384

BOX FEATURES
Modes of Exchange 354
Materials of Prestige Value 356
Analysis of Artifact Composition 360
Lead Isotope Analysis 364
Trend Surface Analysis 369
Fall-off Analysis 370
Distribution: The Uluburun Wreck 374
Production: Greenstone Artifacts in Australia 376
Interaction Spheres: Hopewell 383

10 What Did They Think?
Cognitive Archaeology, Art, and Religion 385

Investigating How Human Symbolizing Faculties
Evolved 387
Working with Symbols 391
From Written Source to Cognitive Map 391
Establishing Place:
The Location of Memory 397
Measuring the World 399
Planning: Maps for the Future 402
Symbols of Organization and Power 404
Symbols for the Other World:
The Archaeology of Religion 406
Depiction: Art and Representation 412
Summary 420
Further Reading 420

BOX FEATURES
Indications of Early Thought 390
Paleolithic Cave Art 392
Paleolithic Portable Art 394
The Megalithic Yard 401
Maya Symbols of Power 406
Recognizing Cult Activity at Chavín 410
Identifying Individual Artists
in Ancient Greece 414
Conventions of Representation
in Egyptian Art 416
The Interpretation of Swedish Rock Art:
Archaeology as Text 418
A Question of Style 419

11 Who Were They? What Were They Like?
The Archaeology of People 421

Identifying Physical Attributes 422
Assessing Human Abilities 432
Disease, Deformity, and Death 438
Assessing Nutrition 451
Population Studies 452
Ethnicity and Evolution 455
Summary 459
Further Reading 460

BOX FEATURES
Spitalfields:
Determining Biological Age at Death 426
How to Reconstruct the Face 430
Looking Inside Bodies 440

Life and Death Among the Inuit 444
Lindow Man: The Body in the Bog 448
Genetics and Languages 454
Studying the Origins of New World Populations 456

12 Why Did Things Change?
Explanation in Archaeology 461

Migrationist and Diffusionist Explanations 463
The Processual Approach 465
The Form of Explanation: General or Particular 474
Attempts at Explanation: One Cause or Several? 476
Postprocessual or Interpretive Explanation 483
Cognitive-Processual Archaeology 491
Summary 495
Further Reading 496

BOX FEATURES
Diffusionist Explanation Rejected:
    Great Zimbabwe 464
Language Families and Language Change 467
Molecular Genetics and Population Dynamics:
    Europe 468
The Origins of Farming:
    A Processual Explanation 471
Marxist Archaeology: Key Features 473
Origins of the State 1: Peru 478
Origins of the State 2: The Aegean 480
The Classic Maya Collapse 484
Explaining the European Megaliths 488
The Individual as an Agent of Change 492

PART III
The World of Archaeology 497

13 Archaeology in Action
Four Case Studies 499

The Oaxaca Projects: The Origins and Rise
    of the Zapotec State 500
Research Among Hunter-Gatherers:
    Kakadu National Park, Australia 509
Khok Phanom Di: The Origins of
    Rice Farming in Southeast Asia 516
York and the Public Presentation of Archaeology 522
Further Reading 532

14 Whose Past?
Archaeology and the Public 533

The Meaning of the Past:
    The Archaeology of Identity 533
Who Owns the Past? 536
The Uses of the Past 542
Conservation and Destruction 546
Who Interprets and Presents the Past? 558
Archaeology and Public Understanding 559
Summary 563
Further Reading 564

BOX FEATURES
The Politics of Destruction 1:
    The Bridge at Mostar 535
The Politics of Destruction 2:
    The Mosque at Ayodyha 537
Applied Archaeology: Farming in Peru 544
The Practice of CRM in the United States 547
Conservation: The Great Temple of
    the Aztecs in Mexico City 552
Destruction and Response: Mimbres 554
"Collectors Are the Real Looters" 556
Archaeology and the Internet 560
Archaeology at the Fringe 562

Glossary 565

Notes and Bibliography 574

Acknowledgments 619

Index 622

Preface

The dynamic pace of research in archaeology is illustrated by the rapid evolution of this book: first published in 1991, a second edition came out in 1996, and now a third in 2000. There are plenty of indications that the subject continues to change, not only in terms of dramatic new discoveries, but also in terms of theories, methods, and practice.

Developing *methods* continue to open new perspectives. The investigation of individual sites by remote sensing techniques, including satellite imagery, and also by Ground Penetrating Radar, produces ever more sophisticated results. Methods of dating are becoming more reliable and precise – for instance the potential and limitations of radiocarbon have been greatly clarified – and every few years a new technique, such as Chlorine-36 dating, opens up new possibilities.

One of the most rapidly developing fields is the application of molecular genetics to human population history. The contributions of ancient DNA have so far been few, but in at least one case spectacular – the brilliant achievement of extracting and sequencing mitochondrial DNA from Neanderthal remains some 40,000 years old has contributed important new insights into human evolution, which is now beginning to be understood at the molecular level. But so far it is mainly DNA from living populations that has begun to inform us about population events, some of them dating back beyond 10,000 years ago into the Pleistocene era, the time of the Upper Paleolithic.

In recording and trying to see what is significant among these new advances in methodology one has a sense of the excitement of a rapidly moving discipline. For instance, it is clear that insights into population histories offered by molecular genetics may carry important implications for the histories of the language families of the world. Yet at the same time there is the serious risk of jumping to premature conclusions. The methodologies needed in relating two such disparate and complex disciplines are so novel that it is not at present clear where theory ends and method begins. Many of the methods described in this book may now

be recognized as routine science; others, and the interpretive methods of molecular genetics are among them, are still pioneering initiatives.

In the realm of archaeological *theory* it would seem that some sort of truce has been established between the interpretive archaeologists (postprocessual archaeologists) and others who continue to develop the processual tradition. Indeed there is some convergence of interest. "The Archaeology of Identity" is a term which may be used to describe a "bottom-up" approach, focusing on the individual. This contrasts with the "top-down" approach of those studying whole societies and their hierarchies. Gender archaeology continues to develop within this framework, transcending the simple vigor of early feminist archaeology, and the rather basic polarity between male and female, to a much more complex approach, where sexualities are seen as interacting with age, status, and other variables. The notion of ethnicity is at last being regarded not as some essentialist ingredient of existing societies and their ancestors, but rather as a product of the decisions of individuals in their own time.

Interpretive and cognitive-processual archaeologies converge also in the new and widespread interest in the landscape as a product of human activity and belief, with the evolution of the landscape seen as something to be analyzed in terms of changing human perceptions and assumptions. Underlying all this, however, are philosophical positions which should be examined and if possible made clear – whether it is the methodological individualism of the processual approach, or the phenomenology advocated by some of the interpretive archaeologists. It is our task in this book to seek to make some of these distinctions clear, without becoming so far wrapped up in jargon that the subject becomes totally impenetrable. We hold the optimistic view that it is possible to do archaeology quite effectively without being a specialist in the philosophical works of Heidegger or Derrida – without denying that insights in archaeology may come from unexpected quarters. Perhaps by the fourth edition of this book some current philosophical fashions may seem unprofitable, sterile even. But others will be seen to open the way to new and fruitful patterns of thought. We hope that our approach to new modes of thought has been constructive, even when we are not yet entirely persuaded.

The *practice* of archaeology has also changed significantly over the past decade. The interactions in this respect between the politics of archaeology, the growing heritage industry (increasingly seen as a fundamental part of the tourist industry), and the academic status of the discipline are becoming clearer and at the same time more problematic. Just about every nation in the world now uses its past, as revealed in its material culture, to provide symbols of nationhood. Some of these are a blatant misuse of the archaeological past. Others may seem legitimate – but who precisely is to judge? The role of museums in the display of objects from the past has a worthy antiquity, but the continuing practice of the acquisition of unprovenienced antiquities by certain institutions is now the subject of fierce ethical debate. Are such institutions living up to their public responsibilities ?

And where does the boundary come in the heritage industry between effective and informed popularization (as exemplified by the York Archaeological Trust) and the unscrupulous exploitation of the past for commercial gain? With the growing popularity of archaeology these are questions which are becoming more prominent. Archaeology today is a global undertaking, and its research methods have a universal application, just as its problems are everywhere felt. We have tried to keep in view the underlying unity of our discipline.

Once more we have attempted to keep pace with developments in all aspects of this diverse discipline and this has involved a great number of people all over the world. We approached numerous specialists and course tutors to comment on the previous edition, and the list of those to whom we are grateful continues to grow. Those who helped in the two previous editions are credited at the end of the book; here we would like to extend our thanks to the following who provided detailed comments, information, or illustrations.

Janet Ambers (British Museum); Arthur Aufderheide (University of Minnesota); Mike Baillie (Queen's University, Belfast); Ofer Bar-Yosef (Harvard); George Bass and Cemal Pulak (Institute of Nautical Archaeology, College Station, Texas); Bob Bewley; Steve Bourget (University of East Anglia); Neil Brodie (University of Cambridge); Simon Buteux (University of Birmingham); Martin Carver (University of York); Robin Coningham (University of Bradford); Larry Conyers & Dean Goodman (University of Birmingham); Andrew David (English Heritage); Simon Davis (English Heritage); Heather Dawson (York Archaeological Trust); Jenny Doole (University of Cambridge); Leo Dubal (Virtual Archaeometry Laboratory); Brian Fagan (University of California); Chris Gaffney & Vince Gaffney (University of Birmingham); David Gill (University College of Swansea); David Goldstein (University of Oxford); Jack Golson (Australian National University); Richard Hall (York Archaeological Trust); Charles Higham (University of Otago); Ian Hodder (University of Cambridge); Rachel Hood; John Isaacson (Los Alamos National Laboratory); Hiroji Kajiwara (Tohoku Fukushi University); Tony Legge (University of London); Peter Lewin (Hospital for Sick Children, Toronto); Paul Linford (University of Birmingham); Gary Lock (Institute of Archaeology); Caroline Malone (University of Cambridge); Vincent Megaw (Flinders University of South Australia); Simon Martin; James Mellaart; Lynn Meskell (Columbia University); George Milner (Pennsylvania State University); Theya Molleson (Natural History Museum, London); Elisabeth Moore (School of Oriental and African Studies); S.P. Needham (British Museum); Mark Nesbitt (University College London); Rog Palmer (Air Photo Services, Cambridge); Mike Parker Pearson (University of Sheffield); Mark Pollard (University of Bradford); Jeremy Sabloff (University of Pennsylvania Museum); Chris Scarre (University of Cambridge); Pamela Smith (University of Cambridge); Ann Stone (University of New Mexico); Zofia Stos-Gale (University of Oxford); Ann Stone (University of New Mexico); Roger White (University of Birmingham); Michael Wiant (Illinois State Museum); Richard Wilshusen (University of Colorado); Karen Wise (Natural History Museum, Los Angeles County); Rebecca Yamin (John Milner Associates).

Archaeology: Theories, Methods, and Practice is intended fundamentally for the student and for teaching at university level. But it is a work designed as well for the use of the professional archaeologist. For that reason the notes and bibliography have again been enlarged and updated. It is also meant to be read with enjoyment by all who share an enthusiasm for discovering the great variety of ways of looking at the past. Errors of fact or emphasis no doubt remain, and, as always, we would be delighted to hear from anyone who feels sufficiently provoked or stimulated to write suggesting improvements.

Colin Renfrew
Paul Bahn

Introduction
The Nature and Aims of Archaeology

Archaeology is partly the discovery of the treasures of the past, partly the meticulous work of the scientific analyst, partly the exercise of the creative imagination. It is toiling in the sun on an excavation in the deserts of Iraq, it is working with living Inuit in the snows of Alaska. It is diving down to Spanish wrecks off the coast of Florida, and it is investigating the sewers of Roman York. But it is also the painstaking task of interpretation so that we come to understand what these things mean for the human story. And it is the conservation of the world's cultural heritage – against looting and against careless destruction.

Archaeology, then, is both a physical activity out in the field, and an intellectual pursuit in the study or laboratory. That is part of its great attraction. The rich mixture of danger and detective work has also made it the perfect vehicle for fiction writers and film-makers, from Agatha Christie with *Murder in Mesopotamia* to Steven Spielberg with Indiana Jones. However far from reality such portrayals may be, they capture the essential truth that archaeology is an exciting quest – the quest for knowledge about ourselves and our past.

But how does archaeology relate to disciplines such as anthropology and history that are also concerned with the human story? Is archaeology itself a science? And what are the responsibilities of the archaeologist in today's world, where the past is manipulated for political ends and "ethnic cleansing" is accompanied by the deliberate destruction of the cultural heritage?

Archaeology as Anthropology

Anthropology at its broadest is the study of humanity – our physical characteristics as animals, and our unique non-biological characteristics that we call *culture*. Culture in this sense includes what the anthropologist Edward Tylor usefully summarized in 1871 as "knowledge, belief, art, morals, law, custom and any other capabilities and habits acquired by man as a member of society." Anthropologists also use the term culture in a more restricted sense when they refer to the culture of a particular society, meaning the non-biological characteristics unique to that society which distinguish it from other societies. (An "archaeological culture" has a specific and somewhat different meaning, as explained in Chapter 3.) Anthropology is thus a broad discipline – so broad that it is generally broken down into three smaller disciplines: biological anthropology, cultural anthropology, and archaeology.

Biological anthropology, or physical anthropology as it used to be called, concerns the study of human biological or physical characteristics and how they evolved.

Cultural anthropology – or social anthropology – analyzes human culture and society. Two of its branches are *ethnography* (the study at first hand of individual living cultures) and *ethnology* (which sets out to compare cultures using ethnographic evidence to derive general principles about human society).

Archaeology is the "past tense of cultural anthropology." Whereas cultural anthropologists will often base their conclusions on the experience of actually living within contemporary communities, archaeologists study past societies primarily through their material remains – the buildings, tools, and other artifacts that constitute what is known as the *material culture* left over from former societies.

Nevertheless, one of the most challenging tasks for the archaeologist today is to know how to interpret material culture in human terms. How were those pots used? Why are some dwellings round and others square? Here the methods of archaeology and ethnography overlap. Archaeologists in recent decades have developed *ethnoarchaeology*, where like ethnographers they live among contemporary communities, but with the specific purpose of understanding how such societies use material culture – how they make their tools and weapons, why they build their settlements where they do, and so on.

Moreover archaeology has an active role to play in the field of conservation. *Heritage studies* constitute a developing field, where it is realized that the world's cultural heritage is a diminishing resource, and one which holds different meanings for different people. The presentation of the findings of archaeology to the public cannot avoid difficult political issues, and the museum curator and the popularizer today have responsibilities which some can be seen to have failed.

Archaeology as History

If, then, archaeology deals with the past, in what way does it differ from history? In the broadest sense, just as archaeology is an aspect of anthropology, so too is it a part of history – where we mean the whole history of humankind from its beginnings over 3 million years ago. Indeed for more than 99 percent of that huge span of time archaeology – the study of past material culture – is the only significant source of information, if one sets aside physical anthropology, which focuses on our biological rather than cultural progress. Conventional historical sources begin only with the introduction of written records around 3000 BC in western Asia, and much later in most other parts of the world (not until AD 1788 in Australia, for example). A commonly drawn distinction is between *prehistory* – the period before written records – and history in the narrow sense, meaning the study of the past using written evidence. In some countries, "prehistory" is now considered a patronizing and deroga-

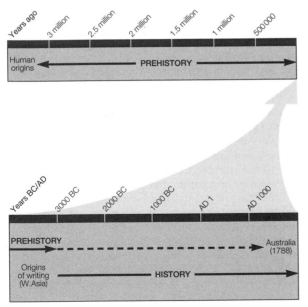

tory term which implies that written texts are more valuable than oral histories, and which classifies their cultures as inferior until the arrival of western ways of recording information. To archaeology, however, which studies all cultures and periods, whether with or without writing, the distinction between history and prehistory is a convenient dividing line that simply recognizes the importance of the written word in the modern world, but in no way denigrates the useful information contained in oral histories.

As will become abundantly clear in this book, archaeology can also contribute a great deal to the understanding even of those periods and places where documents, inscriptions, and other literary evidence do exist. Quite often, it is the archaeologist who unearths such evidence in the first place.

Archaeology as a Science

Since the aim of archaeology is the understanding of humankind, it is a humanistic discipline, a humane study. And since it deals with the human past it is a historical discipline. But it differs from the study of written history – although it uses written history – in a fundamental way. The material the archaeologist finds does not tell us directly what to think. Historical records make statements, offer opinions, pass judgments (even if those statements and judgments themselves need to be interpreted). The objects that archaeologists discover, on the other hand, tell us nothing directly in themselves. It is *we* today who have to make sense of these things. In this respect the practice of archaeology is rather like that of the scientist. The scientist collects data (evidence), conducts experiments, formulates a hypothesis (a proposition to account for the data), tests the hypothesis against more data, and then in conclusion devises a model (a description that seems best to summarize the pattern observed in the data). The archaeologist has to develop a picture of the past, just as the scientist has to develop a coherent view of the natural world. It is not found ready made.

Archaeology, in short, is a science as well as a humanity. That is one of its fascinations as a discipline: it reflects the ingenuity of the modern scientist as well as the modern historian. The technical methods of archaeological science are the most obvious, from radiocarbon dating to studies of food residues in pots. Equally important are scientific methods of analysis, of inference. Some writers have spoken of the need to define a separate "Middle Range Theory," referring to a distinct body of ideas to bridge the gap between raw archaeological evidence and the general

The vast timespan of prehistory compared with the relatively short period for which we have written records ("history"). Before c. 3000 BC, material remains are our only evidence.

observations and conclusions to be derived from it. That is one way of looking at the matter. But we see no need to make a sharp distinction between theory and method. Our aim is to describe clearly the methods and techniques used by archaeologists in investigating the past. The analytical concepts of the archaeologist are as much a part of that battery of approaches as are the instruments in the laboratory.

The Variety and Scope of Archaeology

Today archaeology is a broad church, encompassing a number of different "archaeologies" which are nevertheless united by the methods and approaches outlined in this book. We have already highlighted the distinction between the archaeology of the long prehistoric period and that of historic times. This chronological division is accentuated by further subdivisions so that archaeologists specialize in, say, the earliest periods (the Old Stone Age or Paleolithic, before 10,000 years ago) or the later ones (the great civilizations of the Americas and China; Egyptology; the Classical archaeology of Greece and Rome). A major development in the last two or three decades has been the realization that archaeology has much to contribute also to the more recent historic periods. In North America and Australia historical archaeology – the archaeological study of colonial and postcolonial settlement – has expanded greatly, as has medieval and postmedieval archaeology in Europe. So whether we are speaking of colonial Jamestown in the United States, or medieval London, Paris, and Hamburg in Europe, archaeology is a prime source of evidence.

Cutting across these chronological subdivisions are specializations that can contribute to many different archaeological periods. Environmental archaeology is one such field, where archaeologists and specialists from other sciences study the human use of plants and animals, and how past societies adapted to the ever-changing environment. Underwater archaeology is another such field, demanding great courage as well as skill. In the last 30 years it has become a highly scientific exercise, yielding time capsules from the past in the form of shipwrecks that shed new light on ancient life on land as well as at sea.

Ethnoarchaeology, too, as we discussed briefly above, is a major specialization in modern archaeology. We now realize that we can only understand the archaeological record – that is to say, what we find – if we understand in much greater detail how it came about, how it was formed. Formation processes are now a focus of intensive study. It is here that ethnoarchaeology has come into its own: the study of living

peoples and of their material culture undertaken with the aim of improving our understanding of the archaeological record. For instance, the study of butchery practices among living hunter-gatherers, undertaken by Lewis Binford among the Nunamiut Eskimo of Alaska gave him many new ideas about the way the archaeological record may have been formed, allowing him to re-evaluate the bone remains of animals eaten by very early humans elsewhere in the world. Nor are these studies confined to simpler communities or small groups. Contemporary material culture has now become a focus of study in its own right, and the archaeology of the 20th century ranges from the design of Coca-Cola bottles and beer cans to the garbage of Tucson, Arizona (where the Garbage Project set up by William L. Rathje studied the refuse of different sectors of the city to give insights into the patterns of consumption of the modern urban population). Such "actualistic studies" are increasingly in vogue. Sites such as airfields and gun emplacements from World War II (1939–45) are now being preserved as ancient monuments: there are plans to preserve the shell of the National Picture Theatre at Hull (in the United Kingdom) as a ruinous "bomb site" – a building destroyed in 1941 during the bombing raids of the blitz. The Nevada Test Site, established in 1950 as a continental location for United States nuclear weapons testing is now the subject of archaeological research and conservation. The archaeology of the 20th century even has its looters: artifacts raised from the wreck of the *Titanic* have been sold for large sums to private collectors. The archaeology of the 21st century will soon be upon us.

Aims and Questions

If our aim is to learn about the human past, there remains the major issue of what we hope to learn. Traditional approaches tended to regard the objective of archaeology mainly as reconstruction: piecing together the jigsaw. But today it is not enough simply to re-create the material culture of remote periods, or to complete the picture for more recent ones.

A further objective has been termed "the reconstruction of the lifeways of the people responsible for the archaeological remains." We are certainly interested in having a clear picture of how people lived, and how they exploited their environment. But we also seek to understand *why* they lived that way: why they had those patterns of behavior, and how their lifeways and material culture came to take the form they did. We are interested, in short, in *explaining* change. This interest in the processes of cultural change came to

The diversity of modern archaeology. Top row (Near right)
Working in the laboratory on finds from Çatalhöyük in
Turkey, including study of micromorphological sections.
(Second right) Two archaeologists at the site of Batán
Grande in Peru trace frescoes in position, evidence for a
major pre-Inca civilization. (Far right) A triumph of salvage
archaeology: the rescuing of pharaoh Ramesses II's temples
at Abu Simbel, Egypt, in advance of the rising waters of the
Aswan Dam. Bottom row (Below left) Urban archaeology:
excavation of a Roman site in the heart of London, with St.
Paul's Cathedral in the background. (Below center) An
ethnoarchaeologist in the field in Alaska, sharing and
studying the lives of modern Eskimo as they hunt caribou.
(Below center right) Underwater archaeology: divers
recording finds on the Bronze Age wreck at Uluburun, off
the coast of Turkey. (Below far right) Conservation of a
mosaic at London's Institute of Archaeology.

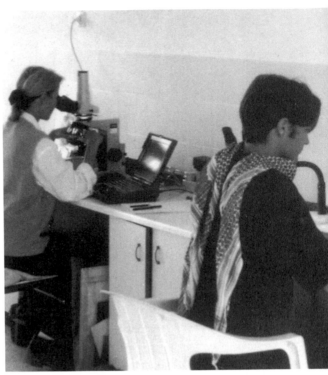

define what is known as *processual archaeology*. Processual archaeology moves forward by asking a series of questions, just as any scientific study proceeds by defining aims of study – formulating questions – and then proceeding to answer them. The symbolic and cognitive aspects of societies are also important areas emphasized by recent approaches, often grouped together under the term *postprocessual* or *interpretive archaeology*, although the apparent unity of this perspective has now diversified into a variety of concerns. It is persuasively argued that in the "post-modern" world different communities and social groups have their own interests and preoccupations, that each may have its voice and its own distinctive construction of the past, and that in this sense there are many archaeologies.

There are many big questions that preoccupy us today. We want to understand the circumstances in which our human ancestors first emerged. Was this in Africa and only in Africa, as currently seems the case? Were these early humans proper hunters or merely scavengers? What were the circumstances in which our own subspecies *Homo sapiens sapiens* evolved? How do we explain the emergence of Paleolithic art? How did the shift from hunting and gathering to farming come about in western Asia, in Mesoamerica, and in other parts of the world? Why did this happen in the course of just a few millennia? How do we explain the rise of cities, apparently quite independently in different parts of the world? The list of questions goes on, and after these general questions there are more specific ones. We wish to know why a particular culture took the form it did: how its particularities emerged, and how they influenced developments. This book does not set out to review the provisional answers to all these questions – although many of the impressive results of archaeology will emerge in the following pages. In this book we examine rather the *methods* by which such questions can be answered.

Plan of the Book

The methods of archaeology could be surveyed in many different ways. We have chosen to think in terms of the many kinds of *questions* to which we wish to have answers. Indeed the form of the question is often crucial. It could be argued that the whole philosophy of archaeology is implied in the questions we ask and the form in which we frame them.

Part I reviews the whole field of archaeology, looking first at the history of the subject, and then asking three specific questions: how are materials preserved, how are they found, and how are they dated?

Part II sets out further and more searching questions – about social organization, about environment, and about subsistence; about technology and trade, and about the way people thought and communicated. We then ask what they were like physically. And finally the interesting question is posed: *why* things changed.

Part III is a review of archaeology in practice, showing how the different ideas and techniques can be brought together in field projects. Four such projects are chosen as case studies: from southern Mexico and northern Australia, from Thailand, and from urban York in England. In conclusion there is a chapter on public archaeology, which discusses the uses and abuses of archaeology in the modern world, and the obligations these things have placed on the archaeologist and on all those who exploit the past for gain or for political purposes. In this way we plan that the book should give a good overview of the whole range of methods and ideas of archaeological investigation.

FURTHER READING

The following books give an indication of the rich variety of archaeology today. Most of them have good illustrations:

Bahn, P.G. (ed.). 2000. *The Penguin Archaeology Guide.* Penguin: London.

Bahn, P.G. (ed.). 2000. *The World Atlas of Archaeology.* Facts on File: New York.

Delgado, J.P. (ed.). 1997. *The British Museum Encyclopedia of Underwater and Maritime Archaeology.* British Museum Press: London; Yale Univ. Press: New Haven.

Fagan, B.M. (ed.). 1996 *The Oxford Companion to Archaeology.* Oxford University Press: Oxford & New York.

Forte, M. & Siliotti, A. (eds.). 1997. *Virtual Archaeology.* Thames & Hudson: London; Abrams: New York.

Gowlett, J. 1993. *Ascent to Civilization: The Archaeology of Early Humans.* (2nd ed.). McGraw-Hill: London & New York.

Scarre, C. (ed.). 1988. *Past Worlds: The Times Atlas of Archaeology.* Times Books: London; Hammond: Maplewood, NJ.

Scarre, C. (ed.). 1999. *The Seventy Wonders of the Ancient World. The Great Monuments and How they were Built.* Thames & Hudson: London & New York.

Schofield, J. (ed.). 1998. *Monuments of War. The Evaluation, Recording and Management of Twentieth-Century Military Sites.* English Heritage: London.

PART I
The Framework of Archaeology

Archaeology is concerned with the full range of past human experience – how people organized themselves into social groups and exploited their surroundings; what they ate, made, and believed; how they communicated and why their societies changed. These are the engrossing questions we address later in the book. First, however, we need a framework in space and time. It is little use beginning our pursuit of ideas and methods concerning the past without knowing what materials archaeologists study, or where these might be found and how they are dated. Indeed, we also want to know how far previous generations of archaeologists have traveled and along which roads before setting off on our own journey of discovery.

Part I therefore focuses on the fundamental framework of archaeology. The first chapter looks at the history of the discipline, showing in particular how successive workers have redefined and enlarged the questions we ask about the past. Then we pose the first question: "What?" – what is preserved, and what is the range of archaeological materials that have come down to us? The second question, "Where?," addresses methods for finding and surveying sites, and principles of excavation and preliminary analysis. Our third question, "When?," considers the human experience of time and its measurement, and assesses the huge battery of techniques now available to help the archaeologist date the past. On this basis we are able to set out a chronology summarizing the human story, as a conclusion to Part I and a prelude to Part II.

1 The Searchers
The History of Archaeology

The history of archaeology is commonly seen as the history of great discoveries: the tomb of Tutankhamun in Egypt, the lost Maya cities of Mexico, the painted caves of the Old Stone Age, such as Lascaux in France, or the remains of our human ancestors buried deep in the Olduvai Gorge in Tanzania. But even more than that it is the story of how we have come to look with fresh eyes at the material evidence for the human past, and with new methods to aid us in our task.

It is important to remember that just a century and a half ago, most well-read people in the Western world – where archaeology as we know it today was first developed – believed that the world had been created only a few thousand years earlier (in the year 4004 BC according to the then-standard interpretation of the Bible), and that all that could be known of the remote past had to be gleaned from the surviving pages of the earliest historians, notably those of the ancient Near East, Egypt, and Greece. There was no awareness that any kind of coherent history of the periods before the development of writing was possible at all. In the words of the Danish scholar Rasmus Nyerup (1759–1829):

> Everything which has come down to us from heathendom is wrapped in a thick fog; it belongs to a space of time which we cannot measure. We know that it is older than Christendom, but whether by a couple of years or a couple of centuries, or even by more than a millennium, we can do no more than guess.

Today we can indeed penetrate that "thick fog" of the remote past. This is not simply because new discoveries are being made all the time. It is because we have learnt to ask some of the *right questions*, and have developed some of the *right methods* for answering them. The material evidence of the archaeological record has been lying around for a long time. What is new is our awareness that the methods of archaeology can give us information about the past, even the prehistoric past (before the invention of writing). The history of archaeology is therefore in the first instance a history of *ideas*, of theory, of ways of looking at the past. Next it is a history of developing research methods, employing those ideas and investigating those questions. And only thirdly is it a history of actual discoveries.

We can illustrate the relationship between these aspects of our knowledge of the past with a simple diagram:

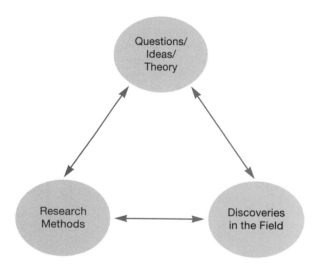

In this chapter and in this book it is the development of the questions and ideas that we shall emphasize, and the application of new research methods. The main thing to remember is that every view of the past is a product of its own time: ideas and theories are constantly evolving, and so are methods. When we describe the archaeological research methods of today we are simply speaking of one point on a trajectory of evolution. In a few decades or even a few years time these methods will certainly look old-fashioned and out of date. That is the dynamic nature of archaeology as a discipline.

THE SPECULATIVE PHASE

Humans have always speculated about their past, and most cultures have their own foundation myths to explain why society is how it is. The Greek writer Hesiod, for instance, who lived around 800 BC, in his epic poem Works and Days envisaged the human past as falling into five stages: the Age of Gold and the Immortals, who "dwelt in ease and peace upon their lands with many good things"; the Age of Silver, when humans were less noble; the Age of Bronze; the Age of Epic Heroes; and lastly his own time, the Age of Iron and Dread Sorrow, when "men never rest from labor and sorrow by day and from perishing by night."

Most cultures, too, have been fascinated by the societies that preceded them. The Aztecs exaggerated their Toltec ancestry, and were so interested in Teotihuacán, the huge Mexican city abandoned hundreds of years earlier which they mistakenly linked with the Toltecs, that they incorporated ceremonial stone masks from that site in the foundation deposits of their own Great Temple (see box, pp. 552–53). A rather more detached curiosity about the relics of bygone ages developed in several early civilizations, where scholars and even rulers collected and studied objects from the past. Nabonidus, last native king of Babylon (reigned

555–539 BC), took a keen interest in antiquities. In one important temple he dug down and discovered the foundation stone which had been laid some 2200 years before. He housed many of his finds in a kind of museum at Babylon.

During the revival of learning in Europe known as the Renaissance (14th to 17th centuries), princes and people of refinement began to form "cabinets of curiosities" in which curios and ancient artifacts were displayed somewhat haphazardly alongside exotic minerals and all manner of specimens illustrative of what was called "natural history." During the Renaissance also scholars began to study and collect the relics of Classical antiquity. And they began too in more northern lands, far from the civilized centers of ancient Greece and Rome, to study the local relics of their own remote past. At this time these were mainly the field monuments – those conspicuous sites, often made of stone, which immediately attracted attention, such as the great stone tombs of northwestern Europe, and such impressive sites (which we should now call prehistoric) as Stonehenge, or Carnac in Brittany. Careful scholars, such as the Englishman William Stukeley (1687–1765), made systematic studies of some of these

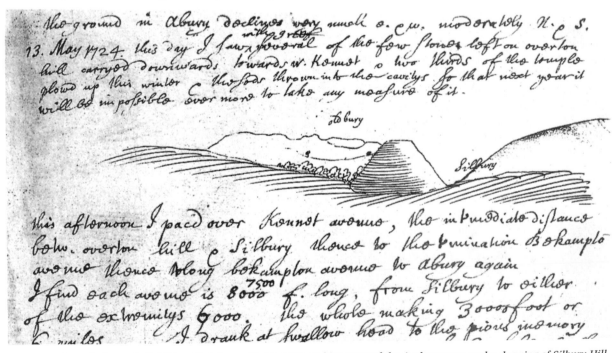

An extract from the journal of William Stukeley, with his notes on his survey of the Avebury area and a drawing of Silbury Hill.

monuments, with accurate plans which are still useful today. In the same period, around 1675, the first archaeological excavation of the New World – a tunnel dug into Teotihuacán's Pyramid of the Moon – was carried out by Carlos de Sigüenza y Góngora.

The First Excavations

In the 18th century more adventurous researchers initiated excavation of some of the most prominent sites. Pompeii in Italy was one of the first of these, with its striking Roman finds, although proper excavation did not begin there until the 19th century (see box overleaf). And in 1765, at the Huaca de Tantalluc on the coast of Peru, a mound was excavated and an offering was discovered in a hollow; the mound's stratigraphy was well described. Nevertheless, the credit for conducting what has been called "the first scientific excavation in the history of archaeology" traditionally goes to Thomas Jefferson (1743–1826), later in his career third President of the United States, who in 1784 dug a trench or section across a burial mound on his property in Virginia. Jefferson's work marks the beginning of the end of the Speculative Phase.

In Jefferson's time people were speculating that the hundreds of unexplained mounds known east of the Mississippi river had been built not by the indigenous American Indians, but by a mythical and vanished race of Moundbuilders. Jefferson adopted what today we should call a scientific approach, that is, he tested ideas about the mounds against hard evidence – by excavating one of them. His methods were careful enough to allow him to recognize different layers in his trench, and to see that the many human bones present were less well preserved in the lower layers. From this he deduced that the mound had been reused as a place of burial on many separate occasions. Although Jefferson admitted, rightly, that more evidence was needed to resolve the Moundbuilder question, he saw no reason why ancestors of the present-day Indians themselves could not have raised the mounds.

Jefferson was ahead of his time. His sound approach – logical deduction from carefully excavated evidence, in many ways the basis of modern archaeology – was not taken up by any of his immediate successors in North America. In Europe, meanwhile, extensive excavations were being conducted, for instance by the Englishman Richard Colt Hoare (1758–1838), who dug into hundreds of burial mounds in southern Britain during the first decade of the 19th century. None of these excavations, however, did much to advance the cause of knowledge about the distant past, since their interpretation was still within the biblical framework, which insisted on a short span for human existence.

Early excavations: Colt Hoare and William Cunnington direct a dig north of Stonehenge in 1805.

POMPEII: ARCHAEOLOGY PAST AND PRESENT

In the history of archaeology, the sites of Pompeii and Herculaneum, lying at the foot of Mount Vesuvius in the Bay of Naples, Italy, hold a very special place. Even today, when so many major sites have been systematically excavated, it is a moving experience to visit these wonderfully preserved Roman cities.

Pompeii's fate was sealed on the momentous day in August AD 79 when Vesuvius erupted, a cataclysmic event described by the Roman writer, the younger Pliny. The city was buried under several meters of volcanic ash, many of the inhabitants being asphyxiated in their houses. Herculaneum nearby was engulfed in volcanic mud. There the complete cities lay, known only from occasional chance discoveries, until the advent of antiquarian curiosity in the early 18th century.

In 1710 the Prince of Elboeuf, learning of the discovery of worked marble in the vicinity, proceeded to investigate by shafts and tunnels what we now know to be the site of Herculaneum. He had the good luck to discover the ancient theater – the first complete Roman example ever found – but he was mainly interested in works of art for his collection. These he removed without any kind of record of their location.

Following Elboeuf, clearance resumed in a slightly more systematic way in 1738 at Herculaneum, and in 1748 Pompeii was discovered. Work proceeded under the patronage of the King and Queen of Naples, but they did little more than quarry ancient masterpieces to embellish their royal palace. Shortly afterwards, on the outskirts of Herculaneum, the remains of a splendid villa were revealed, with statues and an entire library of carbonized papyri that have given the complex its name: the Villa of the Papyri. The villa's dimensions were closely followed by J. Paul Getty in the construction of his museum at Malibu, California.

The first catalog of the royal collection was published in 1755. Seven years later the German scholar Johann Joachim Winckelmann, often regarded as the father of Classical archaeology, published his first Letter on the discoveries at Herculaneum. From that time onward the finds from both cities attracted enormous international attention, influencing styles of furniture and interior decoration, and inspiring several pieces of romantic fiction.

Not until 1860, however, when Giuseppe Fiorelli was put in charge of the work at Pompeii, did well-recorded excavations begin. Buildings were consolidated and where necessary roofed, and wall paintings for the first time left in place. In 1864 Fiorelli devised a brilliant way of dealing with the cavities in the ash within which skeletons were found: he simply filled

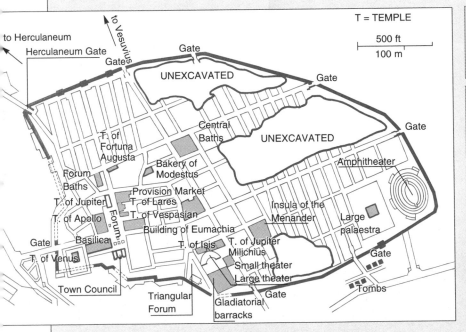

Sketch plan of Pompeii, showing the excavated areas.

1 Pumice and ash bury a victim in AD 79.

2 The body gradually decays, leaving a hollow.

3 Archaeologists find the hollow, and pour in wet plaster.

4 The plaster hardens, allowing the pumice and ash to be chipped away.

How a body shape is retrieved.

them with plaster of Paris. The ash around the cavity acted as a mold, and the plaster took the accurate shape of the decayed body. (In a recent technique, the excavators pour in transparent glass fiber. This allows bones and artifacts to be visible.)

During the present century, Amedeo Maiuri excavated at Pompeii between 1924 and 1961, revealing extensive remains of earlier phases of the town beneath the AD 79 ground level. In recent years his work has been supplemented by limited excavations carried out by Paul Arthur. Another project under the direction of Roger Ling focused on the detailed analysis of one insula, or city block, the Insula of the Menander. The project revealed changes in the property boundaries and uses of different parts of the insula that have thrown much new light on the social and economic development of Roman Pompeii.

Pompeii remains the most complete urban excavation ever undertaken. The town plan is clear in its essentials, and most of the public buildings have been investigated, along with innumerable shops and private houses. Yet the potential for further study and interpretation is enormous.

Today it is not difficult for the visitor to Pompeii to echo the words of Shelley in his Ode to Naples, written more than a century and a half ago:
"I stood within the city disinterred; / And heard the autumn leaves like light footfalls/Of spirits passing through the streets; and heard/The mountain's slumberous voice at intervals/Thrill through those roofless halls."

A view along the Street of the Tombs, Pompeii (top left), an engraving of 1824. In the wall painting from the House of the Vettii, Pompeii (center left), gazelles draw the god of love, Cupid, in a chariot. A plaster cast (left) recreates the shape of a Pompeian struck down in flight. Conditions of preservation at Pompeii are remarkable: for example, many carbonized loaves of bread have survived (right).

THE BEGINNINGS OF MODERN ARCHAEOLOGY

It was not until the middle of the 19th century that the discipline of archaeology became truly established. Already in the background there were the significant achievements of the newly developed science of geology. The Scottish geologist James Hutton (1726–1797), in his *Theory of the Earth* (1785), had studied the stratification of rocks (their arrangement in superimposed layers or strata), establishing principles which were to be the basis of archaeological excavation, as foreshadowed by Jefferson. Hutton showed that the stratification of rocks was due to processes which were still going on in seas, rivers, and lakes. This was the principle of "uniformitarianism." It was argued again by Charles Lyell (1797–1875) in his *Principles of Geology* (1833): that geologically ancient conditions were in essence similar to, or "uniform with," those of our own time. This idea could be applied to the human past also, and it marks one of the fundamental notions of modern archaeology: that in many ways the past was much like the present.

The Antiquity of Humankind

These ideas did much to lay the groundwork for what was one of the significant events in the intellectual history of the 19th century (and an indispensable one for the discipline of archaeology): the establishment of the antiquity of humankind. It was a French customs inspector, Jacques Boucher de Perthes (1788–1868), working in the gravel quarries of the Somme river, who in 1841 published convincing evidence for the association there of human artifacts (of chipped stone, what we would today call "hand-axes" or "bifaces") and the bones of extinct animals. Boucher de Perthes argued that this indicated human existence for a long time before the biblical Flood. His view did not at first win wide acceptance, but in 1859 two leading British scholars, John Evans and Joseph Prestwich, visited him in France and returned persuaded of the validity of his findings.

It was now widely agreed that human origins extended far back into a remote past, so that the biblical notion of the creation of the world and all its contents just a few thousand years before our own time could no longer be accepted. The possibility of a prehistory of humankind, indeed the *need* for one, was established (the term "prehistory" itself came into general use after the publication of John Lubbock's book *Prehistoric Times* in 1865, which went on to become a bestseller).

The Concept of Evolution

These ideas harmonized well with the findings of another great scholar of the 19th century, Charles Darwin (1809–1882), whose fundamental work, *On the Origin of Species*, published in 1859, established the concept of evolution as the best explanation for the origin and development of all plants and animals. The idea of evolution itself was not new – earlier scholars had suggested that living things must have changed or evolved through the ages. What Darwin demonstrated was *how* this change occurred. The key mechanism was, in Darwin's words, "natural selection," or the survival of the fittest. In the struggle for existence, environmentally better-adapted individuals of a particular species would survive (or be "naturally selected") whereas less well-adapted ones would die. The surviving individuals would pass on their advantageous traits by heredity to their offspring and gradually the characteristics of a species would change to such an extent that a new species emerged. This was the process of evolution. Darwin's other great work, *The*

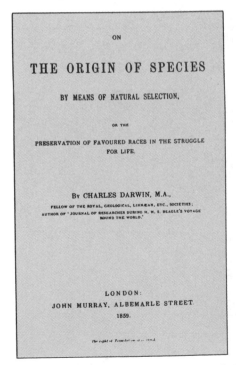

The title page of Darwin's book; his ideas about evolution proved highly influential, not least in archaeology.

Descent of Man, was not published until 1871, but already the implications were clear: that the human species had emerged as part of this same process. The search for human origins in the material record, by the techniques of archaeology, could begin.

The Three Age System

As we have noted, some of these techniques, notably in the field of excavation, were already being developed. So too was another conceptual device which proved very useful for the progress of European prehistory: the Three Age System. In 1836 the Danish scholar C.J. Thomsen (1788–1865) published his guidebook to the National Museum of Copenhagen which appeared in English in 1848 with the title, *A Guide to Northern Antiquities*. In it he proposed that the collections could be divided into those coming from a Stone Age, a Bronze Age, and an Iron Age, and this classification was soon found useful by scholars throughout Europe. Later a division in the Stone Age was established between the Paleolithic or Old Stone Age and the Neolithic or New Stone Age. These terms were less applicable to Africa, where bronze was not used south of the Sahara, or to the Americas, where bronze was less important and iron was not in use before the European conquest. But it was conceptually significant. The Three Age System established the principle that by studying and classifying prehistoric artifacts one could produce a chronological ordering, and say something of the periods in question. Archaeology was moving beyond mere speculation about the past, and becoming instead a discipline involving careful excavation and the systematic study of the artifacts unearthed.

These three great conceptual advances – the *antiquity of humankind*, Darwin's *principle of evolution,* and the *Three Age System* – at last offered a framework for studying the past, and for asking intelligent questions about it. Darwin's ideas were influential also in another way. They suggested that human cultures might have evolved in a manner analogous to plant and animal species. Soon after 1859, British scholars such as General Pitt-Rivers (whom we shall meet again below) and John Evans were devising schemes for the evolution of artifact forms which gave rise to the whole method of "typology" – the arrangement of artifacts in chronological or developmental sequence – later greatly elaborated by the Swedish scholar Oscar Montelius (1843–1921).

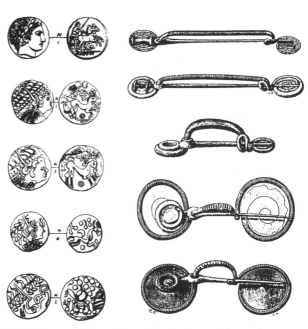

The influence of Darwin is evident in these early typologies. (Left) John Evans sought to derive the Celtic British coinage, bottom, from the gold stater of Philip of Macedon, top. (Right) Montelius' arrangement of Iron Age fibulae (cloak pins), showing their evolution.

C.J. Thomsen shows visitors around the Danish National Museum, arranged according to his Three Age System.

THE IMPACT OF EVOLUTIONARY THOUGHT

The idea of evolution has been of central significance in the development of archaeological thinking. In the first place it is associated with the name of Charles Darwin, whose *On the Origin of Species* (1859) effectively explained the problem of the origin and development of the plant and animal species, including humankind. It did so by insisting that within a species there is variation (one individual differs from another), that the transmission of physical traits is by heredity alone, and that natural selection determines survival. Darwin certainly had precursors, among whom Thomas Malthus was influential with his notion of competition through population pressure, and the geologist Charles Lyell with his insistence upon gradual change.

Darwin's work had an immediate impact on archaeologists such as Pitt-Rivers, John Evans, and Oscar Montelius, laying the foundations for the study of the typology of artifacts. His influence on social thinkers and anthropologists was even more significant: among them was Karl Marx (Marx was also influenced by the American anthropologist, Lewis Henry Morgan – see main text).

The application of the principles of evolution to social organization does not always follow the detailed mechanisms of hereditary transmission which apply to the biologically defined species. For culture can be *learned*, and passed on between generations more widely than between parents and their children. Often, indeed, the term "evolutionary" applied to an argument or an explanation simply means "generalizing." Here it is important to be aware of the great swing in anthropology at the end of the 19th century away from the broad generalizations of L.H. Morgan and E.B.Tylor in favor of a much more detailed, descriptive approach, often termed "historical particularism," and associated with the name of the anthropologist Franz Boas. In the years

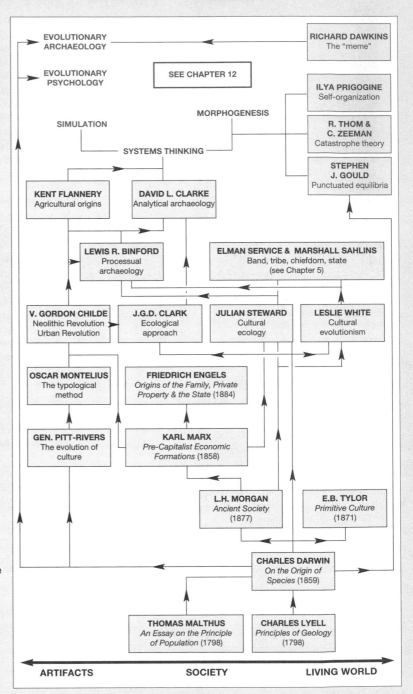

EVOLUTIONARY ARCHAEOLOGY

EVOLUTIONARY PSYCHOLOGY

SEE CHAPTER 12

RICHARD DAWKINS
The "meme"

ILYA PRIGOGINE
Self-organization

MORPHOGENESIS

SIMULATION

R. THOM & C. ZEEMAN
Catastrophe theory

SYSTEMS THINKING

STEPHEN J. GOULD
Punctuated equilibria

KENT FLANNERY
Agricultural origins

DAVID L. CLARKE
Analytical archaeology

LEWIS R. BINFORD
Processual archaeology

ELMAN SERVICE & MARSHALL SAHLINS
Band, tribe, chiefdom, state
(see Chapter 5)

V. GORDON CHILDE
Neolithic Revolution
Urban Revolution

J.G.D. CLARK
Ecological approach

JULIAN STEWARD
Cultural ecology

LESLIE WHITE
Cultural evolutionism

OSCAR MONTELIUS
The typological method

FRIEDRICH ENGELS
Origins of the Family, Private Property & the State (1884)

GEN. PITT-RIVERS
The evolution of culture

KARL MARX
Pre-Capitalist Economic Formations (1858)

L.H. MORGAN
Ancient Society (1877)

E.B. TYLOR
Primitive Culture (1871)

CHARLES DARWIN
On the Origin of Species (1859)

THOMAS MALTHUS
An Essay on the Principle of Population (1798)

CHARLES LYELL
Principles of Geology (1798)

ARTIFACTS   SOCIETY   LIVING WORLD

Ethnography and Archaeology

Another important strand in the thought of the time was the realization that the study by ethnographers of living communities in different parts of the world could be a useful starting point for archaeologists seeking to understand something of the lifestyles of their own early native inhabitants who clearly had comparably simple tools and crafts. Scholars such as Daniel Wilson and John Lubbock made systematic use of such an ethnographic approach.

And at the same time ethnographers and anthropologists were themselves producing schemes of human progress. Strongly influenced by Darwin's ideas about evolution, the British anthropologist Edward Tylor (1832–1917), and his American counterpart Lewis Henry Morgan (1818–1881), both published important works in the 1870s arguing that human societies had evolved from a state of *savagery* (primitive hunting) through *barbarism* (simple farming) to *civilization* (the highest form of society). Morgan's book, *Ancient Society* (1877), was partly based on his great knowledge of living North American Indians. His ideas – particularly the notion that people had once lived in a state of primitive communism, sharing resources equally – strongly influenced Karl Marx and Friedrich Engels, who drew on them in their writings about pre-capitalist societies, thus influencing many later Marxist archaeologists.

Discovering the Early Civilizations

By the 1880s, then, many of the ideas underlying modern archaeology had been developed. But these ideas themselves took shape against a background of major 19th-century discoveries of ancient civilizations in the Old World and the New.

The splendors of ancient Egyptian civilization had already been brought to the attention of an avid public after Napoleon's military expedition there of 1798–1800. It was the discovery by one of his soldiers of the Rosetta Stone that eventually provided the key to understanding Egyptian hieroglyphic writing. Inscribed on the stone were identical texts written in both Egyptian and Greek scripts. The Frenchman Jean-François Champollion (1790–1832) used this bilingual inscription finally to decipher the hieroglyphs in 1822, after 14 years' work. A similar piece of brilliant scholarly detection helped unlock the secrets of cuneiform writing, the script used for many languages in ancient Mesopotamia. In the 1840s the French and British, under Paul Emile Botta (1802–1870) and Austen Henry Layard (1817–1894) respectively, had vied with

Charles Darwin in a cartoon from the London Sketch Book, *of the 1860s.*

before and after World War II American anthropologists like Leslie White and Julian Steward were therefore innovators in rejecting Boas and seeking to generalize, to find explanations for long-term change. White was for many years the only protagonist of what may be termed cultural evolutionism, with books such as *The Evolution of Culture* (1959). White and Steward strongly influenced the New Archaeologists of the 1960s and 1970s, in particular Lewis Binford, Kent Flannery, and D.L. Clarke.

In the past 15 years three lines of thinking from the sciences have been influential in reminding us that evolutionary change need not always be gradual: these concepts of punctuated equilibrium, catastrophe theory, and self-organizing systems are discussed further in Chapter 12. Darwin's own work has inspired two new approaches to the understanding of human behavior and human material culture: evolutionary psychology and evolutionary archaeology, the latter sometimes drawing on Richard Dawkins' concept of the "meme" and Ben Cullen's "Cultural Virus," also discussed in Chapter 12.

19th-CENTURY PIONEERS OF NORTH AMERICAN ARCHAEOLOGY

Squier *Haven* *Powell* *Thomas* *Putnam* *Holmes*

Two themes dominate the study of North American archaeology in the 19th century: the enduring belief in a vanished race of Moundbuilders; and the search for "glacial man" – the idea, sparked off by Boucher de Perthes' Somme river discoveries in mid-century, that human fossils and Stone Age tools would be found in the Americas in association with extinct animals, as they had been in Europe. One way to gain insight into these issues is to view them through the work of some of the main protagonists.

Caleb Atwater (1778–1867)
The newly formed American Antiquarian Society's first Transactions, *Archaeologia Americana* (1820), contained a paper by Atwater, a local

Plan of Serpent Mound, Ohio, as prepared by Squier and Davis in 1846.

postmaster, on burial mounds and earthworks around Circleville, Ohio. His survey work is valuable since the mounds he studied were already disappearing fast, and are now gone. But he took little interest in their contents, and his interpretations were idiosyncratic. Atwater divided the mounds into three periods – modern European, modern American Indian, and those built by the original Moundbuilder people whom he believed to have been Hindus from India who later moved on to Mexico.

Ephraim Squier (1821–1888)
Squier was an Ohio newspaperman who later became a diplomat. He is best known for his work on the prehistoric mounds with Edwin Davis, an Ohio physician. Between 1845 and 1847 they excavated over 200 mounds, and accurately surveyed many other earthworks. Their landmark volume of 1848, *Ancient Monuments of the Mississippi Valley,* was the first publication of the newly founded Smithsonian Institution, and is still useful. It recorded hundreds of mounds, including many being destroyed as settlers moved westward, gave cross-sections and plans, and adopted a simple classification system which inferred function in a general way (burial places, building platforms, effigies, fortifications/defense, etc.).

Like most of their contemporaries, Squier and Davis considered the mounds to be beyond the capabilities

of any Indians, who were "hunters averse to labor," and so they maintained the myth of the intrusive race of Moundbuilders.

Samuel Haven (1806–1881)
As Librarian of the American Antiquarian Society, Haven built up an encyclopedic knowledge of publications on American archaeology. From this wealth of reading he produced a remarkable synthesis in 1856, *The Archaeology of the United States,* published by the Smithsonian Institution, which is considered a foundation stone of modern American archaeology.

In it, Haven argued persuasively that the native Americans were of great antiquity, and, through cranial and other physical characteristics, he pointed to their probable links with Asiatic races. Disagreeing strongly with Atwater and Squier, he concluded that the mysterious mounds had been built by the ancestors of living American Indians. The controversy continued to rage, but Haven's rigorous approach paved the way for the resolution of the issue by John Wesley Powell and Cyrus Thomas.

John Wesley Powell (1834–1902)
Raised in the Midwest, Powell spent much of his youth digging into mounds and learning geology. He became famous for canoeing down the Colorado and shooting the rapids. Eventually Powell was appointed

Part of a 348-ft long painting used by lecturer Munro Dickeson in the 19th century to illustrate his mound excavations.

director of the U.S. Geographical and Geological Survey of the Rocky Mountain region. He published a wide range of information on the rapidly dwindling native American cultures. Moving to Washington, this energetic scholar headed not only the Geological Survey but also his own brainchild, the Bureau of American Ethnology, an agency set up to study the North American Indians. A fearless campaigner for native American rights, he recommended the setting up of reservations, and also began the recording of tribal oral histories.

In 1881 Powell recruited Cyrus Thomas to head the Bureau's archaeology program, and to settle the Moundbuilder question once and for all. After 7 years of fieldwork and the investigation of thousands of mounds, Thomas proved that the Moundbuilder race had never existed: the monuments had been erected by the ancestors of modern native Americans.

But that was not the only controversial issue confronting Powell's Bureau. In 1876, a New Jersey physician named Charles Abbott showed his collection of flaked stone tools to Harvard archaeologist Frederic Putnam, who thought they must be Paleolithic specimens, resembling as they did Stone Age tools found in France. The issue of the "paleoliths" was brought to a head in 1887 when another archaeologist, Thomas Wilson, fresh from a period in France, embarked on a campaign to prove there had been Stone Age occupation of North America. Powell hired William Henry Holmes to look into the question.

William Henry Holmes (1846–1933)
Holmes began his career as a geological illustrator, a training that stood him in good stead when he later turned to archaeology. At Powell's request he spent 5 years studying the "paleolith" question. He collected innumerable specimens and proved that they were not Stone Age tools at all but simply "the refuse of Indian implement making" from recent times. He even manufactured identical "paleoliths" himself. Abbott, Putnam, and Wilson had been deceived into making false comparisons with the French stone tools by superficial similarities.

Holmes' systematic methods also helped him to produce brilliant survey classifications of aboriginal pottery of the eastern United States, and studies of ruins in the Southwest and Mexico. He eventually succeeded Powell as head of the Bureau of American Ethnology. But his obsession with facts rather than theories made it difficult for him to accept the possibility that humans had after all reached North America in the Old Stone Age, as new discoveries at the end of his career in the 1920s began to suggest.

Putnam mistakenly compared prehistoric stone axes from France (left) with Charles Abbott's "paleoliths" (right), which Holmes subsequently proved to be of recent date.

one another using crude "excavations" to see which side could obtain from the Mesopotamian ruins the "largest number of works of art with the least possible outlay of time and money." Layard wrote bestselling books and became famous for his discoveries, which included huge Assyrian sculptures of winged bulls, and a great library of cuneiform tablets from the site of Küyünjik. But it was only the final decipherment of cuneiform by Henry Rawlinson (1810–1895) in the 1850s, building on the work of others, that proved that Küyünjik was biblical Nineveh. Rawlinson spent 20 years copying and studying a 6th-century BC trilingual inscription located on an inaccessible cliff-face between Baghdad and Tehran before cracking the code of cuneiform.

Egypt and the Near East also held a fascination for the American lawyer and diplomat John Lloyd Stephens (1805–1852), but it was in the New World that he was to make his name. His travels in Yucatán, Mexico, with the English artist Frederick Catherwood, and the superbly illustrated books they produced together in the early 1840s, revealed for the first time to an enthusiastic public the ruined cities of the ancient Maya. Unlike contemporary researchers in North America, who continued to argue for a vanished white race of Moundbuilders as the architects of the earthworks there (see box, pp. 28–29), Stephens rightly believed that the Maya monuments were, in his own words, "the creation of the same races who inhabited the country at the time of the Spanish conquest." Stephens also noted that there were similar hieroglyphic inscriptions at the different sites, which led him to argue for Maya cultural unity – but no Champollion or Rawlinson was to emerge to decipher the glyphs until the 1960s (box, pp. 406–07).

If the Bible was one of the main inspirations behind the search for lost civilizations in Egypt and the Near East, it was Homer's account of the Trojan Wars in his narrative poem the *Iliad* that fired the imagination of the German banker Heinrich Schliemann (1822–1890), and sent him on a quest for the city of Troy. With remarkable luck and good judgment he successfully identified it in a series of field campaigns at Hissarlik, western Turkey, in the 1870s and 1880s. Not content with that achievement, he then also dug at Mycenae in Greece and revealed – as he had at Troy – a hitherto unknown prehistoric civilization. Schliemann's methods of excavation have been criticized as crude and cavalier, but few were very rigorous in his day, and he demonstrated how interpretation of the stratigraphy of a mound site could be used to reconstruct the remote past. Nevertheless it fell to the next generation of archaeologists, led by General Pitt-Rivers

and Flinders Petrie, to establish the true basis of modern field techniques (see box).

It is somewhat ironic that the piecemeal approach towards the investigation of the past in Europe was to be surpassed by the creation of the Archaeological Survey of India in 1862. This body was funded by the Government of India because, in the words of Lord Canning, the Governor General, "It will not be to our credit, as an enlightened ruling power, if we continue to allow such fields of investigation … to remain without more examination." In 1922, Sir John Marshall (1876–1958), the Director General of the Survey, was to discover the last of the great Old World civilizations, that of the Indus. Such was the quality of his enormous excavations at both Bronze Age Mohenjodaro (where 8 ha (2 acres) of the city were exposed) and historic Taxila that his reports are still used today for spatial reanalyses at these sites.

Frederick Catherwood's accurate, if somewhat romantic, drawing of Stela D and its "altar" at Copán; at the time of his travels Maya glyphs had not been deciphered.

THE DEVELOPMENT OF FIELD TECHNIQUES

It was only in the late 19th century that a sound methodology of scientific excavation began to be generally adopted. From that time, and during the 20th century, major figures stand out who in their various ways have helped create the modern field methods we use today.

General Augustus Lane-Fox Pitt-Rivers (1827–1900)
For much of his life a professional soldier, Pitt-Rivers brought long experience of military methods, survey, and precision to impeccably organized excavations on his estates in southern England. Plans, sections, and even models were made, and the exact position of every object was recorded. He was not concerned with retrieving beautiful treasures, but with recovering all objects, no matter how mundane. He was a pioneer in his insistence on total recording, and his four privately printed volumes, describing his excavations on Cranborne Chase from 1887 to 1898, represent the highest standards of archaeological publication.

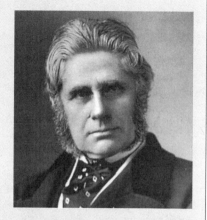

General Pitt-Rivers, excavator of Cranborne Chase, and pioneer in recording techniques.

Excavation in progress at Wor Barrow, Cranborne Chase (above). The barrow was eventually removed.

A view (below) of the Wor Barrow ditch during Pitt-Rivers' excavation at the site in the mid-1890s.

An example (below) of Pitt-Rivers' meticulous records: his plan of Barrow 27 at Cranborne Chase.

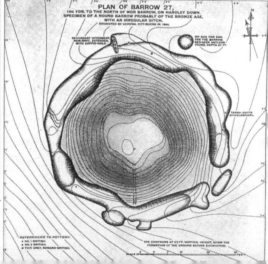

Sir William Flinders Petrie (1853–1942)
A younger contemporary of Pitt-Rivers, Petrie was likewise noted for his meticulous excavations and his insistence on the collection and description of everything found, not just the fine objects, as well as on full publication. He employed these methods in his exemplary excavations in Egypt, and later in Palestine, from the 1880s until his death. Petrie also devised his own technique of seriation or "sequence dating," which he used to bring chronological order to the 2200 pit graves of the Naqada cemetery in Upper Egypt (see Chapter 4).

Petrie (above) at the Egyptian site of Abydos in 1922.

Sir Mortimer Wheeler (1890–1976)
Wheeler fought in the British army in both world wars and, like Pitt-Rivers, brought military precision to his excavations, notably through techniques such as the grid-square method (Chapter 3). He is particularly well known for his work at British hillforts, notably Maiden Castle.

Equally outstanding, however, was his achievement from 1944 to 1948 as Director-General of Archaeology in India, where he held training schools in modern field methods, and excavated at the important sites of Harappa, Taxila, Charsadda and Arikamedu, one of his most famous excavations. However, subsequent excavations at Maiden Castle, Arikamedu and Charsadda have inevitably caused many of his fundamental assumptions to be refuted.

Sir Mortimer Wheeler (above), and his excavation (below) at Arikamedu, India, 1945.

Dorothy Garrod (1892–1968)
In 1937 Dorothy Garrod became the first woman professor in any subject at Cambridge, and probably the first woman prehistorian to achieve professorial status anywhere in the world. Her excavations at Zarzi in Iraq and Mount Carmel in Palestine provided the key to a large section of the Near East, from the Middle Paleolithic to the Mesolithic, and found fossil human remains crucial to our knowledge of the relationship between Neanderthals and *Homo sapiens sapiens*. With her discovery of the Natufian culture, the predecessor of the world's first farming societies, she posed a series of new problems still not fully resolved today.

Dorothy Garrod (above), one of the first to study the prehistoric Near East systematically.

Max Uhle (1856–1944)

Scientific archaeology in South America owes much to the work of Uhle, a German scholar who trained as a philologist and then turned to archaeology and ethnography. His excavation of Pachacamac, a coastal site just south of Lima, in the 1890s became the first important step in establishing an area-wide chronology for Peru. Uhle's concentration on graves and the careful recording of grave-good associations recall Petrie's early work in Egypt.

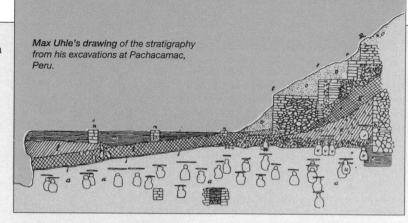

Max Uhle's drawing of the stratigraphy from his excavations at Pachacamac, Peru.

Alfred Kidder (1885–1963)

Kidder was the leading Americanist of his time. As well as being a major figure in Maya archaeology, he was largely responsible for putting the Southwest on the archaeological map with his excavations at Pecos Ruin, a large pueblo in northern New Mexico, from 1915 to 1929. His survey of the region, *An Introduction to the Study of Southwestern Archaeology* (1924) has become a classic.

Kidder was one of the first archaeologists to use a team of specialists to help analyze artifacts and human remains. He is also important for his "blueprint" for a regional strategy: (1) reconnaissance; (2) selection of criteria for ranking the remains of sites chronologically; (3) seriation into a probable sequence; (4) stratigraphic excavation to elucidate specific problems; followed by (5) more detailed regional survey and dating.

Alfred Kidder (above) and his cross-sectional drawing of the stratigraphy at the Pecos Pueblo site.

Fieldwork after 1960

Since 1960, archaeological fieldwork has developed in several new directions. One of these is underwater archaeology, which began as a serious method of research in 1960 with the work of George Bass at the Bronze Age Gelidonya shipwreck off the south coast of Turkey. This was the first ancient vessel ever excavated in its entirety on the sea bed. Bass and his team invented or developed many now standard underwater techniques (see boxes, Underwater Archaeology, p. 95; The Uluburun Wreck, pp. 374–75).

On dryland, the economic boom of the 1960s led to construction of new roads and buildings, which threatened and destroyed many archaeological sites and led to a new emphasis on managing the cultural heritage (Culture Resource Management, or CRM), either by preservation, or by recording and excavation prior to destruction (see box, p. 546).

In Europe, the redevelopment of historic city centers led to highly complex excavations spanning many periods and demanding new techniques of analysis. Finally, in recent years, the application of computerization in fieldwork has offered powerful new tools to help us recover and understand the remains left by past societies.

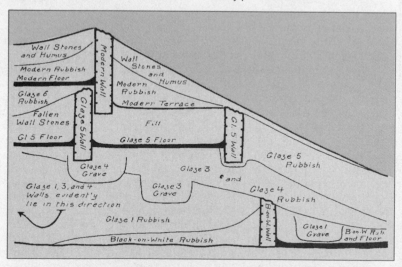

CLASSIFICATION AND CONSOLIDATION

Thus, well before the end of the 19th century, many of the principal features of modern archaeology had been established and many of the early civilizations had been discovered. There now ensued a period, which lasted until about 1960, which Gordon Willey and Jeremy Sabloff in their *A History of American Archaeology* have described as the "classificatory-historical period." Its central concern, as they rightly characterize it, was chronology. Much effort went into the establishment of regional chronological systems, and the description of the development of culture in each area.

In regions where early civilizations had flourished new research and discoveries filled out the chronological sequences. Alfred Maudslay (1850–1931) laid the real scientific foundations of Maya archaeology, while the German scholar Max Uhle (1856–1944) began to establish a sound chronology for Peruvian civilization with his excavation in the 1890s at the coastal site of Pachacamac, Peru. The meticulous work of Flinders Petrie (1853–1942) in Egypt was followed up by the spectacular discovery in the 1920s of Tutankhamun's tomb by Howard Carter (1874–1939) (see box, pp. 62–63). In the Aegean area, Arthur Evans (1851–1941) revealed a previously unknown civilization, that he called Minoan, on the island of Crete; the Minoans proved to be even earlier than Schliemann's Mycenaeans. And in Mesopotamia Leonard Woolley (1880–1960) excavated at Ur, the biblical city of Abraham's birth, and put the Sumerians on the map of the ancient world.

It was, however, scholars studying primarily the prehistoric societies of Europe and North America who made some of the most significant contributions during the first half of the 20th century. Gordon Childe (1892–1957), a brilliant Australian based in Britain, was the leading thinker and writer about European prehistory and Old World history in general. In the United States there was a close link between anthropologists and archaeologists studying the American Indians. The anthropologist Franz Boas (1858–1942) reacted against the broad evolutionary schemes of his predecessors Morgan and Tylor and demanded much greater attention to the collection and classification of information in the field. Huge inventories of cultural traits, such as pot and basket designs or types of moccasins, were built up. This tied in with the so-called "direct historical approach" of the archaeologists, who attempted to trace modern Indian pottery and other styles "directly" back into the distant past. The work of Cyrus Thomas and later W.H. Holmes (see box pp.

28–29) in the east was complemented by that of A.V. Kidder (1885–1963), whose excavations at Pecos Pueblo in the Southwest from 1915 to 1929 established a chronological framework for that region (box p. 33). James A. Ford (1911–1968) later developed the first major framework for the Southeast. By the 1930s the number of separate regional sequences was so great that a group of scholars led by W.C. McKern devised what became known as the "Midwestern Taxonomic System," which correlated sequences in the Midwest by identifying similarities between artifact collections. This was applied to other areas.

Gordon Childe, meanwhile, had almost single-handedly been making comparisons of this sort between prehistoric sequences in Europe. Both his methods and the Midwestern Taxonomic System were designed to order the material: to answer the question, To what period do these artifacts date? and also, With which other materials do they belong? This latter question usually carried with it an assumption which Gordon Childe made explicit: that a constantly recurring collection or "assemblage" of artifacts (a "culture" in his terminology, or an "aspect" in that of McKern) could be taken as the material equipment of a particular group of people. This approach thus offered the hope of answering, in a very general sense, the question, Who did these artifacts belong to? The answer would be in terms of a named people, even if the name for a prehistoric people would be a modern one, not the original name. (There are now seen to be dangers in this approach, as we shall discuss in Chapter 12.)

But in his great works of synthesis, such as *The Dawn of European Civilization* (1925) and *The Danube in Prehistory* (1929), Childe went beyond merely describing and correlating the culture sequences and attempted to account for their origin. In the late 19th century scholars such as Montelius had looked at the richness of the early civilizations then being uncovered in the Near East, and argued that all the attributes of civilization, from stone architecture to metal weapons, had spread or "diffused" to Europe from the Near East by trade or migration of people. With the much greater range of evidence available to him, Childe modified this extreme diffusionist approach and argued that Europe had undergone some indigenous development – but he nevertheless attributed the major cultural changes to Near Eastern influences.

In his later books, such as *Man Makes Himself* (1936), Childe went on to try and answer the much more difficult question: why had civilization arisen in the Near East? Himself influenced by Marxist ideas and the relatively recent Marxist revolution in Russia, he proposed that there had been a Neolithic Revolution which gave rise to the development of farming, and later an Urban Revolution which led to the first towns and cities. Childe was one of the few archaeologists of his generation bold enough to address this whole broad issue of why things happened or changed in the past. Most of his contemporaries were more concerned with establishing chronologies and cultural sequences. But after World War II scholars with new ideas began to challenge conventional approaches.

The Ecological Approach

One of the most influential new thinkers in North America was the anthropologist Julian Steward (1902–1972). Like Childe he was interested in explaining cultural change, but he brought to the question an anthropologist's understanding of how living cultures work. Moreover he highlighted the fact that cultures do not interact simply with one another but with the environment as well. The study of ways in which adaptation to the environment could cause cultural change Steward christened "cultural ecology." Perhaps the most direct archaeological impact of these ideas can be seen in the work of Gordon Willey, one of Steward's graduate associates, who carried out a pioneering investigation in the Virú Valley, Peru, in the late 1940s. This study of 1500 years of pre-Columbian occupation involved a combination of observations from detailed maps and aerial photographs (see box, pp. 80–81), survey at ground level, and excavation and surface potsherd collection to establish dates for the hundreds of prehistoric sites identified. Willey then plotted the geographical distribution of these sites in the valley at different periods – one of the first settlement pattern studies in archaeology (see Chapters 3 and 5) – and set them against the changing local environment.

Quite independently of Steward, however, the British archaeologist Grahame Clark (1907–1995) developed an ecological approach with even more direct relevance for archaeological fieldwork. Breaking away from the artifact-dominated culture-historical approach of his contemporaries, he argued that by studying how human populations adapted to their environments we can understand many aspects of ancient society. Collaboration with new kinds of specialists was essential: specialists who could identify animal bones or plant remains in the archaeological record to help build up a picture not only of what prehistoric environments were like, but what foods

Gordon Willey in a test pit at Barton Ramie during the Belize Valley project studying Maya settlement patterns, 1953–60.

prehistoric peoples ate. Clark's landmark excavation at Star Carr in northeast Britain in the early 1950s demonstrated just how much information could be gleaned from what appeared to be an unpromising site without stone structures and dating to just after the end of the Ice Age. Careful environmental analysis and recovery of organic remains showed that this had been a camp on the edge of a lake, where people had hunted red deer and eaten a wide variety of wild plant foods. Nor need the insights from an ecological approach be confined to individual sites or groups of sites: in a remarkable work of synthesis, *Prehistoric Europe: the Economic Basis* (1952), Clark provided a panoramic view of the varying human adaptations to the European landscape over thousands of years.

Out of this early ecological research has grown the whole field of environmental and dietary reconstruction discussed in Chapters 6 and 7.

The Rise of Archaeological Science

The other striking development of the period immediately after World War II was the rapid development of scientific aids for archaeology. We have already seen how pioneers of the ecological approach forged an alliance with specialists from the environmental sciences. Even more important, however, was the application to archaeology of the physical and chemical sciences.

The greatest breakthrough came in the field of dating. In 1949 the American chemist Willard Libby (1908–1980) announced his invention of radiocarbon (C14) dating. It was not until well over a decade later

WOMEN PIONEERS OF ARCHAEOLOGY

The story of many early women archaeologists was one of exclusion and lack of recognition or promotion – or even employment. Furthermore, many brilliant academic women accepted that, after marriage, their career would no longer be a professional one, and supported the academic work of their husband with little public recognition.

This has remained so until the present time, so the achievements of the following pioneers, spanning the 19th and 20th centuries, stand out all the more.

Harriet Boyd Hawes (in 1892), discoverer of the Minoan town site of Gournia, Crete.

Harriet Boyd Hawes (1871–1945)

This well-educated American majored in Classics and was fluent in Greek. Just after graduating, in her early twenties, she spent several seasons riding around Crete on muleback, in dangerous territory, alone or in the company of a woman friend, looking for prehistoric sites. In 1901 she discovered the Bronze Age site of Gournia – the first Minoan town site ever unearthed – which she excavated

for the next three years, supervising a hundred local workmen. She published her findings in exemplary fashion in a lavishly illustrated report that is still consulted today. It is noteworthy for its classification of artifacts according to potential function, drawing on ethnographic parallels from Cretan rural life of the time.

Gertrude Caton-Thompson – her work at Great Zimbabwe confirmed that the site was the work of a major African culture.

Gertrude Caton-Thompson (1888–1985)

A wealthy British researcher who followed courses in prehistory and anthropology at Cambridge, Caton-Thompson subsequently became well known for her pioneering interdisciplinary project of survey and excavation in the Fayum of Egypt; and later, perhaps most famously, at Great Zimbabwe, where her excavations in 1929 unearthed datable artifacts from a stratified context, and confirmed that the site represented a major culture of African origin (see box, pp. 464–65). The violent reaction from the white community in Rhodesia (as Zimbabwe was then called) to her findings so upset her that she refused to undertake further work in southern Africa and returned to Egypt and Arabia.

Anna O. Shepard (1903–1973)

An American who studied archaeology as well as a wide range of hard sciences, Shepard subsequently became a specialist in ceramics, as well as Mesoamerican and Southwestern archaeology. She was one of the pioneers of petrographic analysis of archaeological pottery (see pp. 358–59), focusing on sherd paste, paint, and temper. She published extensively on the technology of New World pottery, and wrote a standard work, *Ceramics for the Archaeologist*. She carried out most of her work in a laboratory at home, in relative isolation, rarely going into the field, but nevertheless carved out a unique niche for herself in the profession.

Anna O. Shepard was an acknowledged expert in the ceramics of the American Southwest and Mesoamerica.

Kathleen Kenyon (1906–1978)

A formidable British archaeologist, daughter of a director of the British Museum, who trained on Roman sites in Britain under Mortimer Wheeler (see box, p. 32), thus adopting his method, with its close control over stratigraphy. Kenyon subsequently applied this approach in the Near East at two of the most complex and most excavated sites in Palestine: Jericho and Jerusalem. At Jericho, in 1952–58, she

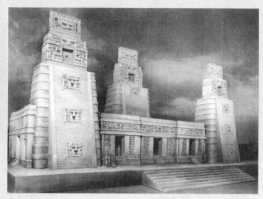

Kathleen Kenyon (above left) was a great excavator and worked at two of the most important and complex sites in the Near East, Jericho and Jerusalem. Tatiana Proskouriakoff (above, center), trained as an architect and worked originally as a museum artist – this is her reconstruction of the Maya site of Xpuhil. Her work on Maya glyphs contributed greatly to their final decipherment.

found evidence that pushed back the date of occupation to the end of the Ice Age, and uncovered the walled village of the Neolithic farming community, commonly referred to as "the earliest town in the world."

Tatiana Proskouriakoff (1909–1985)

Born in Siberia, Proskouriakoff moved with her family to Pennsylvania in 1916. Unemployed after graduating as an architect in 1930, she ended up working as a museum artist in the University of Pennsylvania. A visit to the Maya site of Piedras Negras led her to devote the rest of her life to Maya architecture, art, and hieroglyphs. A skilled artist, she produced numerous plans of the architecture of Chichén Itzá and Copán, and a definitive book entitled *A Study of Classic Maya Sculpture*. She also worked alone till her death on the complex problems of Maya hieroglyphic writing, challenging the notion that the inscriptions contained only calendrical and astronomical information and putting forward the pioneering notion that the Maya were also recording their political and dynastic histories (box, pp. 464–65), work that contributed to the breakthrough in the decipherment of Maya hieroglyphs.

Mary Leakey worked for almost half a century at various early hominid sites in East Africa, transforming our knowledge of human development.

Mary Leakey (1913–1996)

A cigar-smoking, whisky-drinking, British archaeologist who, together with her husband Louis (see p. 40), transformed their chosen field. They worked for almost half a century at many sites in East Africa, carrying out meticulous excavations, most notably at Olduvai Gorge, Tanzania, where in 1959 Mary unearthed the skull of an adult australopithecine, *Zinjanthropus boisei*, of 1.79 million years ago; and at Laetoli, where she excavated the famous trails of fossilized hominid footprints, made 3.7 million years ago. She also painstakingly recorded a large amount of Tanzanian rock art.

A splendid insight into the careers and personalities of women as well as male archaeologists in Greece in the early years of the 20th century is given in

Faces of Archaeology in Greece (Hood 1998), with a wonderful series of portrait caricatures by Piet de Jong, who was the chief illustrator for Sir Arthur Evans at his excavations at Knossos in Crete. Among the well-known archaeologists are Winifred Lamb (1894–1963), the excavator of Thermi in Lesbos (contemporary with early Troy); Hetty Goldman (1881–1972), excavator of Early Bronze Age Eutresis; and Virginia Grace (1901–1994), a world authority on the Roman amphora trade. None of these married. It is clear that the women scholars who did marry, and thus ended their professional careers – such as Vivian Wade-Gery (1897–1988) or Josephine Shear (1901–1967) – were just as brilliant academically.

Virginia Grace (above left) and Hetty Goldman (above right) both working in Greece in the early 20th century, as depicted by Piet de Jong. They had long and very distinguished careers in archaeology.

that the full impact of this momentous technical achievement began to be felt (see below), but the implications were clear: here at last archaeologists might have a means of directly determining the age of undated sites and finds anywhere in the world without recourse to complicated cross-cultural comparisons with areas already dated by historical methods (usually written records). Thus, traditionally, prehistoric Europe had been dated by virtue of supposed contacts with early Greece and hence (indirectly) with ancient Egypt, which could itself be dated historically. The radiocarbon method now held the prospect of providing a completely independent chronology for ancient Europe. Chapter 4 discusses dating methods in general, and radiocarbon in particular.

The growth in archaeological applications for scientific techniques was such that by 1963 a volume entitled *Science in Archaeology*, edited by Don Brothwell

and Eric Higgs (1908–1976), could be published which ran to nearly 600 pages, with contributions from 55 experts, not merely on dating techniques and plant and animal studies, but methods for analyzing human remains (see Chapter 11) and artifacts (Chapters 8, 9).

Artifact studies, for instance, could contribute to an understanding of early trade: it proved possible to identify the raw materials of certain artifacts and the sources from which they had come through the technique of trace-element analysis (the measurement of elements present in the material only in very small amounts). As with many of the new methods, research stretched back to the 1930s, when the Austrian archaeologist Richard Pittioni had begun to apply trace-element analysis to early copper and bronze artifacts. Nevertheless it was not until the postwar years that this and a number of other newly developed scientific techniques really began to make an impact on archaeology.

A TURNING POINT IN ARCHAEOLOGY

The 1960s mark a turning point in the development of archaeology. By this time various dissatisfactions were being expressed with the way research in the subject was being conducted. These dissatisfactions were not so much with excavation techniques, or with the newly developed scientific aids in archaeology, but with the way conclusions were drawn from them. The first and most obvious point concerned the role of dating in archaeology. The second went beyond this: it focused on the way archaeologists explain things, on the procedures used in archaeological reasoning.

With the advent of the radiocarbon method, dates could in many cases be assigned very rapidly, and without the long and laborious framework of cross-cultural comparisons which had been needed previously. To establish a date was no longer one of the main end products of research. It was still important, but it could now be done much more efficiently, allowing the archaeologist to go on to ask more challenging questions than merely chronological ones.

The second and perhaps more fundamental cause for dissatisfaction with the traditional archaeology was that it never seemed to explain anything, other than in terms of migrations of peoples and supposed "influences." Already in 1948 the American archaeologist Walter W. Taylor had in his *A Study of Archaeology* formulated some of these dissatisfactions. He had argued for a "conjunctive" approach, in which the full range of a culture system would be taken into consideration. And in 1958, Gordon Willey and Philip Phillips in their *Method and Theory in American Archaeology*

had argued for a greater emphasis on the social aspect, for a broader "processual interpretation" or study of the general processes at work in culture history. They also spoke of "an eventual synthesis in a common search for sociocultural causality and law."

That was all very well, but what would it mean in practice?

The Birth of the New Archaeology

In the United States the answer was provided, at least in part, by a group of younger archaeologists, led by Lewis Binford, who set out to offer a new approach to the problems of archaeological interpretation, which was soon dubbed by its critics and then by its supporters "the New Archaeology." In a series of articles, and later in an edited volume, *New Perspectives in Archaeology* (1968), Binford and his colleagues argued against the approach which tried to use archaeological data to write a kind of "counterfeit history." They maintained that the potential of the archaeological evidence was much greater than had been realized for the investigation of social and economic aspects of past societies. Their view of archaeology was more optimistic than that of many of their predecessors.

They also argued that archaeological reasoning should be made explicit. Conclusions should be based not simply on the personal authority of the scholar making the interpretation, but on an explicit framework of logical argument. In this they relied on current ideas within the philosophy of science, where conclusions, if they are to be considered valid, must be open to testing.

Within the spirit of processual archaeology advocated by Willey and Phillips, they sought to *explain* rather than simply to describe, and to do so, as in all sciences, by seeking to make valid generalizations.

In doing this they sought to avoid the rather vague talk of the "influences" of one culture upon another, but rather to analyze a culture as a system which could be broken down into subsystems. This led them to study subsistence in its own right, and technology, and the social subsystem, and the ideological subsystem, and trade and demography and so forth, with much less emphasis on artifact typology and classification. In this way they had been partly anticipated by the ecological approach of the 1950s, which was already studying what one might call "the subsistence subsystem" in very much these terms.

In order to fulfill these aims, the New Archaeologists to a large extent turned away from the approaches of history towards those of the sciences. Very similar developments were under way in Britain at the same time, well exemplified by the work of David L. Clarke (1937–1976), particularly in his book *Analytical Archaeology* (1968), which reflected the great willingness of the New Archaeologists to employ more sophisticated quantitative techniques, where possible computer-aided, and to draw on ideas from other disciplines, notably geography.

It must be admitted that in their enthusiasm to seize on and utilize a battery of new techniques, the New Archaeologists drew also on a range of previously unfamiliar vocabularies (drawn from systems theory, cybernetics etc.), which their critics tended to dismiss as jargon. Indeed in recent years, several critics have reacted against some of those aspirations to be scientific, which they have categorized as "scientistic" or "functionalist." Much of the emphasis of early processual archaeology was indeed upon functional or ecological explanation, and it is now possible to regard its first decade as representing a "functional-processual" phase, which has been followed in recent years by a "cognitive-processual" phase, which seeks more actively to include the consideration of symbolic and cognitive aspects of early societies into the program of research. Many of these points are considered in Chapter 12. But there can be no doubt that archaeology will never be the same again. Most workers today, even the critics of the early New Archaeology, implicitly recognize its influence when they agree that it is indeed the goal of archaeology to explain what happened in the past as well as to describe it. Most of them agree too that in order to do good archaeology it is necessary to

PROCESSUAL ARCHAEOLOGY: KEY CONCEPTS

In the early days of the New Archaeology, its principal exponents were very conscious of the limitations of the older, traditional archaeology. The following contrasts were among those which they often emphasized:

THE NATURE OF ARCHAEOLOGY:
Explanatory *vs* Descriptive
Archaeology's role was now to *explain* past change, not simply to reconstruct the past and how people had lived. This involved the use of *explicit theory*.

EXPLANATION: Culture process *vs* Culture history
Traditional archaeology was seen to rely on historical explanation: the New Archaeology, drawing on the *philosophy of science*, would think in terms of *culture process*, of how changes in economic and social systems take place. This implies *generalization*.

REASONING: Deductive *vs* Inductive
Traditional archaeologists saw archaeology as resembling a jigsaw puzzle: the task was one of "piecing together the past." Instead, the appropriate procedure was now seen as formulating *hypotheses*, constructing *models*, and deducing their consequences.

VALIDATION: Testing *vs* Authority
Hypotheses were to be tested, and conclusions should not be accepted on the basis of the authority or standing of the research worker.

RESEARCH FOCUS:
Project design *vs* Data accumulation
Research should be designed to answer specific *questions* economically, not simply to generate more information which might not be relevant.

CHOICE OF APPROACH:
Quantitative *vs* Simply qualitative
The benefits were seen of quantitative data, allowing computerized statistical treatment, with the possibility of *sampling* and *significance testing*. This was often preferred to the purely verbal traditional approach.

SCOPE: Optimism *vs* Pessimism
Traditional archaeologists often stressed that archaeological data were not well suited to the reconstruction of *social organization* or *cognitive systems*. The New Archaeologists were more positive and argued that one would never know how hard these problems were until one had tried to solve them.

make explicit, and then to examine, our underlying assumptions. That was what David Clarke meant when he wrote in a 1973 article of "the loss of innocence" in archaeology.

WORLD ARCHAEOLOGY

The questioning approach of the New Archaeology and the demand for explicit and quantitative procedures led to new developments in field research, many of which built on or coincided with the programs of field-work already being conducted by archaeologists who would not necessarily have thought of themselves as followers of the new school of thought.

In the first place, there was a much greater emphasis on field projects with well-defined research objectives – projects which set out to answer specific questions about the past. In the second place, the new insights yielded by the ecological approach made it clear that satisfactory answers to many major questions would only be forthcoming if whole regions and their environments were looked at, rather than single sites in isolation. And the third development, very much linked to the first and second, was the realization that in order to carry out these objectives effectively, new techniques needed to be introduced of intensive field survey and selective excavation, coupled with statistically based sampling procedures and improved recovery methods, including screening (sieving) of excavated material. These are the key elements of modern field research, discussed in detail in Chapter 3. Here we should observe that their widespread application has begun to create for the first time a true world discipline: an archaeology that reaches geographically right round the globe, and an archaeology that reaches back in time to the beginnings of human existence and right up to the modern period.

The Search for Origins

Among the pioneers of well-focused project design was Robert J. Braidwood, of the University of Chicago, whose multi-disciplinary team in the 1940s and 1950s systematically sought out sites in the Iraqi Kurdistan region that would provide evidence for the origins of agriculture in the Near East (see Chapter 7). Another American project, headed by Richard MacNeish, did the same for the New World: their research in the 1960s in the Tehuacán Valley of Mexico moved our understanding of the long-drawn-out development of maize farming an immense step forward.

If the origins of farming have been the subject of much well-targeted research in recent decades, the rise of complex societies, including civilizations, has been another. In particular, two American field projects have been outstandingly successful: one in Mesopotamia led by Robert Adams (with much use of aerial photography as well as field survey), and the other in the Valley of Oaxaca, Mexico, led by Kent Flannery and Joyce Marcus (see Chapter 13).

However, the credit for the most determined pursuit of a project with a clear archaeological objective in the whole history of archaeology should perhaps go to Louis Leakey (1903–1972) and Mary Leakey (1913–1996), who between them pushed back the known dates for our immediate ancestors by several million years. As long ago as 1931 they began their search in the Olduvai Gorge, East Africa, for fossil human bones, but it was not until 1959 that their extraordinary perseverance was rewarded and Mary Leakey (see box, p. 37) made the first of many fossil hominid (early human) finds in the Gorge. Africa has now become the great focus of study for the early phases of humankind, and has seen crucial theoretical debate between Lewis Binford, C.K. Brain, Glynn Isaac (1937–1985), and others over the likely hunting and scavenging behavior of our ancestors (Chapters 2, 7).

Human origins: Louis and Mary Leakey spent almost three decades working in Olduvai Gorge, East Africa, before making the first of many crucial finds there of fossil bones belonging to our earliest ancestors.

Revealing Australia's past: archaeologist John Mulvaney at the Shelter 2 site, Fromm's Landing, South Australia. In 1956, during his first season of fieldwork here, Mulvaney excavated some 5000 years of occupation deposit.

The Archaeology of Continents

Research in Africa exemplifies the pushing back of archaeology's frontiers in both time and space. The quest for human origins has been one success story, but so too has been the rediscovery through archaeology of the achievements and history of the Iron Age peoples of Africa, including the building of Great Zimbabwe (box, pp. 464–65). By 1970 archaeological knowledge of the whole continent was sufficiently advanced for J. Desmond Clark, one of the leading researchers, to produce the first synthesis, *The Prehistory of Africa*. Meanwhile, in another equally little-studied continent, Australia, John Mulvaney's excavations in the early 1960s at Kenniff Cave, South Queensland, produced radiocarbon dates proving occupation there during the last phase of the Ice Age – thus establishing Australasia as one of the most fruitful regions for new archaeological research in the world.

Work in Australia highlights two further important trends in modern archaeology: the rise of ethno-archaeology or "living archaeology"; and the increasing worldwide discussion about who should control or "own" monuments and ideas about the past.

The Living Past

From its beginnings the New Archaeology placed great emphasis on explanation – in particular explaining how the archaeological record was formed, and what excavated structures and artifacts might mean in terms of human behavior. It came to be realized that one of the most effective ways of addressing such questions would be to study the material culture and behavior of living societies. Ethnographic observation itself was nothing new – anthropologists had studied the American Indians and Australian Aborigines since the 19th century. What was new was the archaeological focus: the new name, ethnoarchaeology, emphasized this. The work of Richard Gould among the Aborigines in Australia, Richard Lee among the !Kung San of southern Africa, and Lewis Binford among the Nunamiut Eskimo has established ethnoarchaeology – discussed in more detail in Chapter 5 – as one of the most significant recent developments in the whole discipline.

However, the increasing involvement of archaeologists with living societies, and the simultaneous rise among such societies of an awareness of their own heritage and their own claims to it, have brought to the fore the question: Who should have access to, or ownership of, the past? It is clear, for example, that the only inhabitants of Australia before European settlement were the Aborigines. Should it therefore be the Aborigines themselves who control archaeological work on their forebears, even those dating back 20,000 years or more? This important issue is explored further in Chapter 14.

Archaeologists such as John Mulvaney and Rhys Jones have stood shoulder to shoulder with the Aborigines in the fight to prevent destruction by developers of parts of Australia's precious ancient heritage, for instance in Tasmania. Inevitably, though, as the pace of worldwide economic development has quickened in the last 30 years, archaeologists everywhere have had to adapt and learn to salvage what they can about the past in advance of the bulldozer or plow. Indeed the massive upsurge of this salvage or rescue archaeology, much of it government-funded, has given a new impetus to the archaeology of our towns and cities – to what in Europe is known as medieval or postmedieval archaeology, and what in the United States and elsewhere is called historical archaeology.

INTERPRETIVE OR POSTPROCESSUAL ARCHAEOLOGIES

For its early proponents, notably Ian Hodder in Britain and Mark Leone in the United States, postprocessual archaeology represented so radical a critique of the New Archaeology (i.e. processual archaeology), as to establish a fresh beginning in archaeological theory, which avoids the positivist philosophy and the "scientistic" outlook of Lewis Binford, David Clarke, and their colleagues.

For its more severe critics, the initiative, while making a number of valid criticisms, simply developed some of the ideas and theoretical problems introduced by the New Archaeology. To these critics it brought in a variety of approaches from other disciplines, so that the term "postprocessual," while rather neatly echoing the epithet "postmodern" in literary studies, was a shade arrogant in presuming to supersede what it might quite properly claim to complement. Michael Shanks and Ian Hodder suggested that "interpretive archaeologies" (plural) may be a more positive label than "postprocessual."

Among the influences which contributed to interpretive or postprocessual archaeology are neo-Marxism, the post-positivist school of thought in the philosophy of science, the hermeneutic or interpretational approach of a number of contemporary thinkers and the phenomenology of Heidegger. The theoretical arguments can become rather heavy at times, and those wishing to investigate these philosophical influences more thoroughly or to come to terms with structuration theory and post-structuralism will need to turn to more specialized books, such as that edited by Ian Bapty and Tim Yates.

The *neo-Marxist* element carries with it a strong commitment to social awareness: that it is the duty of the archaeologist not only to describe the past, but to use such insights to change the present world. This contrasts quite strikingly with the aspirations toward objectivity of many processual archaeologists.

The *post-positivist* approach rejects the emphasis on the systematic procedures of scientific method which are such a feature of processual archaeology, sometimes seeing modern science as hostile to the individual, as forming an integral part of the systems of domination by which, it is argued, the forces of capitalism exert their hegemony. There are clear political overtones here which are made explicit in the writings of some interpretive archaeologists, for instance Michael Shanks and Christopher Tilley.

The *phenomenological* approach lays stress on the personal experiences of the individual or actor and of the way in which encounters with the material world and with the objects in it shape our understanding of the world and hence our construction of our own world view. This has encouraged a new approach, for instance to landscape archaeology, where the archaeologist sets out to experience or re-experience the humanly shaped landscape as it has been modified and formed by such human activities as cultivation, forest clearance, and the creation of monuments. The phenomenological approach has yet to be applied consistently to the artifacts of early cultures, but already one may glimpse how the introduction of metallurgy and hence of new classes of prestige goods may have led to new dimensions in such concepts as commodity and value, and how the creation of new forms of weapon, for instance, may have impacted on the nature of warfare and the social status of warriors.

The *praxis* approach lays stress upon the central role of the human agent or actor and upon the primary significance of human actions or action (*praxis*) in shaping social experience, social reality, and hence social structure. The theory of "structuration" of the sociologist Anthony Giddens has influenced archaeologists' notions of the way social norms and social structures are established and shaped by habitual experience, and the notion of *habitus* introduced by the French sociologist Pierre Bourdieu (see pp. 216–16) similarly refers to the strategy-generating principles employed by the individual which mediate between structure and practice. The role of the individual as a significant agent is thus emphasized.

The *hermeneutic* (or interpretive) view rejects the attempts toward generalization, another feature of processual archaeology. Emphasis is laid, rather, upon the uniqueness of each society and culture and on the need to study the full context of each in all its rich diversity. A related view, derived from modern critical theory, would stress that there can be no single correct interpretation: each observer or analyst is entitled to their own opinion about the past. There will therefore be a diversity of opinions, and a wide range of perspectives – which is why the emphasis is on interpretive archaeologies (plural).

Within this varied body of thought there is room for a further range of perspectives, and feminist archaeologies have found the intellectual environment conducive for the development of their field and of gender studies in general.

One of the strengths of the interpretive approach is to bring into central focus the actions and thoughts of individuals in the past, which is also the goal of cognitive-processual archaeology (see Chapter 12). But it goes beyond the methodological individualism of the latter, arguing that in order to understand and interpret the past, it is necessary to employ an empathetic approach, to "get inside the minds" and think the thoughts of the people in question. This might seem a logical goal when examining symbolic systems (for example figurative works – paintings, sculptures, etc. – employing a complex iconography) but there is in reality no easy way to get into other people's minds, especially past minds, and the methodology of the empathetic approach is not clear.

Another notable feature, as we have seen, was the argument that there can be no single, correct way to undertake research. However, this well-justified critique of the scientism of the early New Archaeology sometimes overlooks more recent developments in the methodology of post-positivist science, and can lead to charges of relativism, where one person's view has to be regarded as good as another's, and where, in interpretive matters, "anything goes."

The postprocessual approach has proved particularly relevant in matters of interpretation and of choice exercised now, in the present – whether in choosing what elements to emphasize in a museum display, or in learning the "lessons" of the past. For there subjectivity is inevitable, and decisions about meaning and significance are indeed made in the present. The implications of this are considered in Chapter 14.

Whatever the methodological problems, the consequence of the various debates has been to broaden the range of archaeological theory in a positive manner and to emphasize the symbolic and the cognitive aspects of human endeavor in a way which the early New Archaeology failed to do. The diversity of postprocessual archaeology was one of its strengths and can be expected to lead on to many further insights in the interpretive archaeologies of the future.

Who Are the Searchers?

The growth of salvage work also leads us to ask: Who today actually are the searchers in archaeology? A century ago they were often wealthy individuals, who had the leisure to speculate about the past, and to undertake excavations. Or in other cases, they were travelers who had reason to be in remote places, and used the opportunity to undertake researches in what was effectively their spare time. Thirty years ago the searchers in archaeology tended to be university scholars, or the representatives of museums seeking to enlarge their collections, or the employees of learned societies and academic institutions (like the Egypt Exploration Society), nearly all of them based in the more prosperous capitals of Europe and the United States.

Today most countries in the world have their own government archaeological or historical services. The scope of current public archaeology is reviewed in Chapter 14. But it is worth noting here that today a "searcher" (i.e. a professional archaeologist) is more likely to be an employee, often directly or indirectly a government employee, on a salvage project than a more independent research worker. How this shift in the center of gravity of archaeological activity will affect the questions asked, and hence the future growth of the discipline of archaeology, remains to be seen.

The Postprocessual Debate of the 1980s and 1990s

Post-modernist currents of thought in the 1980s and 1990s, drawn first from architectural theory and literary studies, and then from wider social and philosophical fields, encouraged a great diversity of approaches to the past. While many field archaeologists were relatively untouched by theoretical debates, and the processual tradition established by the New Archaeology rolled on, there were several new approaches, sometimes collectively termed postprocessual, which dealt with interesting and difficult questions (see box). Influential arguments, some of them first advanced by Ian Hodder and his students in Cambridge, have stressed that there is no single, correct way to undertake archaeological inference, and that the goal of objectivity is unattainable. Even the archaeological data are "theory laden," and as many "readings" are possible as there are research workers. But in their more extreme form these arguments have led to charges of "relativism," or a research style where "anything goes," and where the borderlines between archaeological research and fiction (or science-fiction) may be difficult to define.

INTERPRETIVE ARCHAEOLOGIES AT ÇATALHÖYÜK

TURKEY
● Çatalhöyük

The history of research at this important early farming site in Turkey well illustrates the changing approaches to archaeology in the second half of the 20th century.

Original Excavations

The site was discovered by James Mellaart in 1958, in the course of a survey of the fertile Konya Plain in south-central Turkey which began in 1951. He started excavating the site in 1961, and the dramatic nature of his discovery soon became clear. The 15 m (50 ft) high mound cloaked the remains of an early Neolithic (early farming) town 13 ha (32 acres) in extent with an "agglomerate" plan (see p. 402) and with deeply stratified levels going back at least to 7200 BC. The well-preserved rooms had plastered walls, some with wall paintings and plaster decorations incorporating bull skulls, and the finds included terracotta figures, several of them female, suggesting to certain

scholars a "mother goddess" cult. Well-preserved remains of textiles (linen) and of plants and animals were recovered, and the obsidian of which the abundant tools were made proved on trace-element analysis (see p. 372) to derive from local sources. In 1964 the excavation was interrupted, leaving many questions unanswered. In particular it was not clear whether Mellaart's excavations at the southwest part of the site had revealed a "shrine quarter," or whether the high frequency of rooms with painted walls and other symbolic materials would be repeated on other parts of the mound.

Aim of the New Researches

Ian Hodder, the most influential figure in the postprocessual movement of the 1980s and 1990s, has taken up the challenge offered by the site, beginning surface research in 1993 and excavation in 1995. One aim of the project was to use modern field

techniques to investigate the structure of the site and the functioning of its buildings and so to answer one of the central questions left unresolved by Mellaart. Also a falling water table in the area made urgent the investigation of the lower, unexcavated parts of the site which were known to have well-preserved organic remains, such as wood, wooden artifacts, baskets, and perhaps unfired clay tablets, necessitating a 6- to 8-month excavation season in 1999.

But Hodder also set himself two yet more ambitious objectives appropriate to the "interpretive" approach arising from the postprocessual debate. The first was to develop a more flexible and open approach to stratigraphic excavation, using the opportunities offered by on-site computer recording to allow more interactive stratigraphic interpretations. In this way he set out deliberately to avoid the early division by the excavation director of the observed strata into closely defined "phases" and "units" – the more standard practice – with the director thus taking ultimate responsibility for the stratigraphic interpretation (a practice which some postprocessual critics have seen as authoritarian).

The second objective was similarly to allow more open-ended and multivocal approaches to the interpretation of the site as a whole, allowing not only different specialists to have a voice, but also the local inhabitants, and indeed visitors, not least those considering (with the late Marija Gimbutas) the site to be important for the emergence of a cult of the "Mother Goddess" (see pp. 46–47, 218–19 and 413).

The decision to make data from the excavation available on the project's website (http://catal.arch.cam.ac.uk) thus goes beyond a simple intention to publish the findings promptly: it furthers the postprocessual or interpretive wish for multiple and alternative interpretations by all those choosing to take part, deliberately denying to the excavators the privilege of pronouncing on such matters with special authority, and instead allowing a relativist approach.

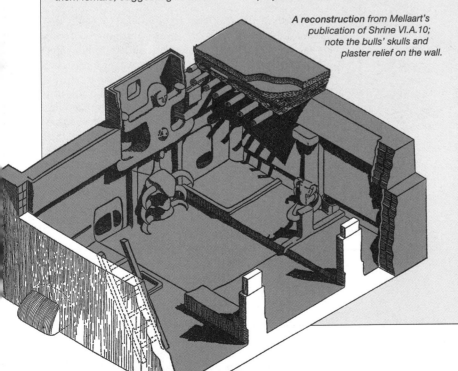

A reconstruction from Mellaart's publication of Shrine VI.A.10; note the bulls' skulls and plaster relief on the wall.

The accompanying anthropological project focuses on the local community living in the surrounding villages – some of whom are hired at the site – on domestic and foreign tourists visiting the site, on Goddess groups and worshippers, on the local and central government officials, and on the fashion designers interested in the site. This "multi-sited" ethnography is seen as an integral part of the "reflexive methodology" being used at Çatalhöyük.

In the same spirit there are four semi-independent excavation teams, one operating in the "Mellaart area" at the southwest, two on the north of the mound including a team of Berkeley archaeologists, and a fourth investigating a separate mound to the west. All four, and the social anthropology / cultural heritage project, as well as the Museum and Interpretive Public Programs (involving the newly-constructed Visitor Center), operate under the general direction of Ian Hodder as project leader.

Early Results

The excavation so far has investigated some rooms at the north of the site in great detail, using techniques of soil micromorphology to study the functioning of different parts of each room. A collapsed roof reveals a fire installation showing the roof area to have been used intensively for domestic and other purposes. The rooms in this area do seem to have features similar to those in the "Mellaart area," calling into question the notion that the latter had a specially religious character.

Of course the project is in its early stages and it is too early yet to assess the extent to which the use of a reflexive methodology will give insights which differ from those of 35 years ago.

Hodder's approach has its critics, yet this does appear to hold the promise of being one of those influential projects where a different and coherent theoretical approach actually does have a significant impact on archaeological practice.

A large clay figurine of a "Mother Goddess" supported by two felines (above), found in Mellaart's excavations.

The new excavations directed by Ian Hodder (left, above and below); and a recent reconstruction showing a room in Building 5.

The writings of Michael Shanks and Christopher Tilley, especially their somewhat provocative "black" and "red" books, initially provoked reactions of this kind. But in their later writings they, and indeed the majority of postprocessual archaeologists, have recently taken a less aggressively anti-scientific tone, and the emphasis has instead been upon the use of a variety of personal and often humanistic insights to develop a range of different fields and interests, recognizing the varied perspectives of different social groups, and accepting the consequent "multivocality" of the post-modern world. The epistemological debate seems over now, with much less rhetorical position-taking and with the recognition that there is no single or coherent postprocessual archaeology, but rather a whole series of interpretive approaches and interests, enriched by the variety of intellectual sources upon which various scholars have drawn.

The various interpretive archaeologies, including those which initially called themselves postprocessual, in general lay stress upon empathetic understanding and interpretation, and hence upon the specific historical context under study. They often reject the tendency toward cross-cultural comparison and the modes of explanation relying upon generalization characteristic of processual archaeology. Some of the most interesting work on themes such as the rise of complex societies thus continues to be undertaken outside the new interpretive or postprocessual tradition, by such scholars as Kent Flannery, Henry Wright, or Tim Earle, who are willing to make cross-cultural comparisons within some more general framework. The study of early human developments in the Paleolithic period also has to operate within a comparative framework where hominid fossils and material culture are compared between continents. Questions relating to the development of human cognitive abilities are certainly being addressed with renewed vigor, but the intellectual context of the discussion remains broadly within the processual (or cognitive-processual) and scientific tradition. In other areas, however, and notably for those periods when archaeology can be text-aided, interpretive approaches are widespread.

The Widening Field: Other Voices

The postprocessual archaeologists are certainly right in arguing that our own interpretation and presentation of the past, as in any museum display, or indeed in the origin myth of almost any modern nation, involve choices which depend less on an objective assessment of the data than on the feelings and opinions of the researchers and of the clients whom they aim to please.

The great national museum in the United States, the Smithsonian Institution in Washington, found it almost impossible to mount an exhibition in 1995 dealing with the destruction of Hiroshima 50 years earlier, without exciting the ire both of ex-servicemen and of liberals sensitive to Japanese sensibilities. The development of indigenous archaeologies raises comparable issues (Chapter 14).

Some of these practical and political issues have been taken up by the World Archaeological Congress, a new international body set up amid controversy in 1986 after the repudiation by the existing international conference (the Union Internationale des Sciences Pré- et Protohistoriques) of the world conference of archaeologists held in Southampton, Britain, that year. The story is a complex one, involving the disinviting (by the WAC) of all archaeologists from South Africa (on anti-apartheid grounds) in a move which irritated many liberals since it prevented the free exchange of ideas between bona fide scholars.

A comparable issue surfaced divisively at the 1994 World Archaeological Congress in New Delhi, India, where pressures were exerted by one Indian faction to prevent any mention at the Congress of the destruction in 1992 by Hindu fundamentalists of the historic mosque at Ayodhya in Uttar Pradesh province (see box, p. 537), and the meetings ended amid fisticuffs. But while disagreements among distinguished academics cannot perhaps escape slightly comical overtones, there is nothing amusing about that particularly virulent aspect of end-of-century nationalism seen in "ethnic cleansing," practiced mainly but not exclusively in the former Yugoslavia, where an integral part of the "cleansing" process involves the destruction of the cultural heritage of the targeted ethnic group (see box, p. 535), and where the ethnic factions seek legitimacy through their own interpretations of their past. Fortunately the 1999 WAC meeting, held at Cape Town in South Africa, proved much more harmonious, with constructive sessions devoted in part to the archaeology of the (former) colonialist world.

It is evident that archaeology cannot avoid being caught up in the issues of the day, social and political as well as intellectual. An example is the influence of feminist thinking (somewhat belatedly in archaeology) and the growth of feminist archaeology, which overlaps with the relatively new field of gender studies (see Chapter 5). A pioneer in the emphasis of the importance of women in prehistory was Marija Gimbutas (1921–1994). Her research in the Balkans led her to create a vision of an "Old Europe" associated with the first farmers whose central focus was (or so she argued) a belief in a great Mother Goddess figure.

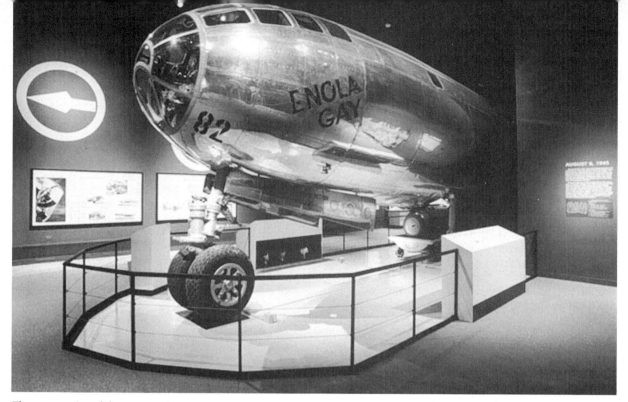

The presentation of the past can be unexpectedly controversial and open to criticisms of lack of objectivity and insensitivity to different views of the past, as shown by an exhibition concerned with Hiroshima at the Smithsonian Institution in 1995.

Although many feminist archaeologists today would take issue with certain aspects of Gimbutas' approach, she has certainly helped foster the current debate on gender roles.

In an article published in 1984, Margaret Conkey and Janet Spector drew attention to the androcentrism (male bias) of the discipline of archaeology. As Margaret Conkey pointed out, there existed a need "to reclaim women's experience as valid, to theorize this experience, and to use this to build a program of political action." However, the questions they raised were not widely explored until the 1990s because it was not until then that a suitable critical climate existed in archaeology. In Britain, this was provided by the theoretical development of postprocessual archaeology (see box pp. 42–43) and much feminist research has been conducted within this framework. In North America, a combination of feminist critique, the growth of historical archaeology, and the keen interest taken by indigenous groups in their own past, formed the intellectual environment for the debate.

The deeply pervasive nature of androcentric thinking in most interpretations of the past should not be underestimated: the gender-specific terminology of "Man the Toolmaker," even when swept away with every reference to "mankind" corrected to "humankind," does in fact conceal further, widely held assumptions or prejudices – for instance that Paleolithic stone tools were mainly made by men rather than women, for which there is little or no evidence. Feminist archaeologists can with justice also point to the imbalances between female and male professionals among archaeologists today, and the goal of "political action" may be seen as justified by current social realities. In the 1990s feminist concern over androcentrism became one voice among many questioning the supposed objectivity and political neutrality of archaeology.

While some aspects of the archaeology of the 1990s were inevitably controversial, they were also in some ways very positive. They emphasized the value and importance of the past for the contemporary world, and they led to the realization that the cultural heritage is an important part of the human environment, and in some ways as fragile as the natural environment. They imply, then, that the archaeologist has an important role to play in achieving a balanced view also of our present world, which is inescapably the product of the worlds which have preceded it. The task of interpretation is now seen as very much more complex than it once seemed: that is all part of the "loss of innocence" which accompanied the New Archaeology more than 20 years ago.

SUMMARY

The history of archaeology, then, is a history of new ideas, methods, and discoveries. Modern archaeology took root in the 19th century with the acceptance of three key concepts: the great antiquity of humanity, Darwin's principle of evolution, and the Three Age System for ordering material culture. Many of the early civilizations, especially in the Old World, had been discovered by the 1880s, and some of their ancient scripts deciphered. This was followed by a long phase of consolidation – of improvements in fieldwork and excavation and the establishment of regional chronologies.

After World War II the pace of change in the discipline quickened. New ecological approaches sought to help us understand human adaptation to the environment. New scientific techniques introduced among other things reliable means of dating the prehistoric past. Spurred on by these developments, the New Archaeology of the 1960s and 1970s turned to questions not just of what happened when, but why they happened, in an attempt to explain processes of change. Meanwhile, pioneer fieldworkers studying whole regions opened up a truly world archaeology in time and space – in time back from the present to the earliest toolmakers, and in space across all the world's continents. More recently a diversity of theoretical approaches, often grouped under the label postprocessual, highlighted the variety of possible interpretations and the sensitivity of their political implications.

Precisely how archaeologists today are continuing to push back the frontiers of knowledge about our planet's human past forms the subject of the remainder of this book.

FURTHER READING

Good introductions to the history of archaeology include:

Bahn, P.G. (ed.) 1996. *The Cambridge Illustrated History of Archaeology*. Cambridge University Press: Cambridge & New York.

Daniel, G. 1967. *The Origins and Growth of Archaeology*. Penguin Books: Harmondsworth and Baltimore. (Quotations from the writings of early archaeologists.)

Daniel, G. 1975. *150 Years of Archaeology*. Duckworth: London.

Daniel, G. & Renfrew, C. 1988. *The Idea of Prehistory*. Edinburgh University Press: Edinburgh; Columbia University Press: New York.

Fagan, B.M. 1996. *Eyewitness to Discovery*. Oxford University Press: Oxford & New York.

Hodder, I. 1991. *Reading the Past: Current Approaches to Interpretation in Archaeology* (2nd ed.) Cambridge University Press: Cambridge & New York.

Lowenthal, D. 1985. *The Past is a Foreign Country*. Cambridge University Press: Cambridge & New York.

Preucel, R.W. & Hodder, I. (eds.). 1996. *Contemporary Archaeology in Theory, a Reader*. Blackwell: Oxford.

Schnapp, A. 1996. *Discovering the Past*. British Museum Press: London; Abrams: New York.

Stiebing, W.H. 1993. *Uncovering the Past. A History of Archaeology*. Oxford University Press: Oxford.

Trigger, B.G. 1989. *A History of Archaeological Thought*. Cambridge University Press: Cambridge & New York.

Willey, G.R. & Sabloff, J.A. 1993. *A History of American Archaeology*. (3rd ed.) Freeman: New York.

2 What is Left?
The Variety of the Evidence

The relics of past human activity are all around us. Some of them were deliberate constructions, built to last, like the pyramids of Egypt, the Great Wall of China, or the temples of Mesoamerica and India. Others, like the remains of the Maya irrigation systems of Mexico and Belize, are the visible relics of activities whose aim was not primarily to impress the observer, but which still command respect today for the scale of the enterprise they document.

Most of the remains of archaeology are far more modest, however. They are the discarded refuse from the daily activities of human existence: the food remains, the bits of broken pottery, the fractured stone tools, the debris that everywhere is formed as people go about their daily lives.

In this chapter we define the basic archaeological terms, briefly survey the scope of the surviving evidence and look at the great variety of ways in which it has been preserved for us. From the frozen soil of the Russian steppes, for instance, have come the wonderful finds of Pazyryk, those great chieftains' burials where wood and textiles and skins are splendidly preserved. From the dry caves of Peru and other arid environments have come remarkable textiles, baskets, and other remains that often perish completely. And by contrast, from wetlands, whether the swamps of Florida or the lake villages of Switzerland, further organic remains are being recovered, this time preserved not by the absence of moisture, but by its abundant presence to the exclusion of air.

Extremes of temperature and of humidity have preserved much. So too have natural disasters. The volcanic eruption that destroyed Pompeii and Herculaneum (box, pp. 22–23) is the most famous of them, but there have been others, such as the eruption of the Ilopango volcano in El Salvador in the 2nd century AD, which buried land surfaces and settlement remains in a large part of the southern Maya area.

Our knowledge of the early human past is dependent in this way on the human activities and natural processes that have formed the archaeological record, and on those further processes that determine, over long periods of time, what is left and what is gone for ever. Today we can hope to recover much of what is left, and to learn from it by asking the right questions in the right way.

BASIC CATEGORIES OF ARCHAEOLOGICAL EVIDENCE

Undoubtedly one of the main concerns of the archaeologist is the study of *artifacts* – objects used, modified, or made by people. But, as the work of Grahame Clark and other pioneers of the ecological approach has demonstrated (Chapter 1), there is a whole category of non-artifactual *organic and environmental remains* – sometimes called "ecofacts" – that can be equally revealing about many aspects of past human activity. Much archaeological research has to do with the analysis of artifacts and these organic and environmental remains that are found together on *sites*, themselves most productively studied together with their surrounding landscapes and grouped together into *regions*.

Artifacts are humanly made or modified portable objects, such as stone tools, pottery, and metal weapons. In Chapter 8 we look at methods for analyzing human technological prowess in the mastery of materials for artifacts. But artifacts provide evidence to help us answer all the key questions – not just technological ones – addressed in this book. A single clay vessel or pot can be the subject of several lines of inquiry. The clay may be tested to produce a date for the vessel and thus perhaps a date for the location where it was found (Chapter 4), and tested to find the source of the clay and thus give evidence for the range and contacts of the group that made the vessel (Chapters 5 and 9). Pictorial decoration on the pot's surface may be used in a

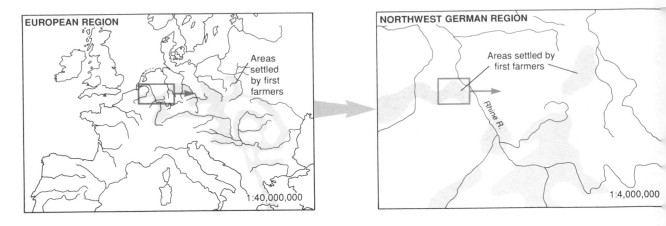

typological sequence (Chapter 3), and tell us something about ancient beliefs, particularly if it shows gods or other figures (Chapter 10). And analysis of the vessel's shape and any food or other residues found in it can yield information about the pot's use, perhaps in cooking, as well as about ancient diet (Chapter 7).

Some researchers broaden the meaning of the term "artifact" to include all humanly modified components of a site or landscape, such as hearths, postholes, and storage pits – but these are more usefully described as *features*, defined in essence as non-portable artifacts. Simple features such as postholes may themselves, or in combination with remains of hearths, floors, ditches, etc., give evidence for complex features or structures, defined as buildings of all kinds, from houses and granaries to palaces and temples.

Non-artifactual organic and environmental remains or ecofacts include animal bones and plant remains, but also soils and sediments – all of which may shed light on past human activities. They are important because they can indicate, for example, what people ate or the environmental conditions under which they lived (Chapters 6 and 7).

Archaeological sites may be thought of as places where artifacts, features, structures, and organic and environmental remains are found together. For working purposes one can simplify this still further and define sites as places where significant traces of human activity are identified. Thus a village or town is a site, and so too is an isolated monument like Serpent Mound in Ohio or Stonehenge in England. Equally, a surface scatter of stone tools or potsherds may represent a site occupied for no more than a few hours, whereas a Near Eastern tell or mound is a site indicating human occupation over perhaps thousands of years. In Chapter 5 we consider the great variety of sites in more detail and look at the ways in which

archaeologists classify them and study them regionally – as part of the investigation of settlement patterns. Here, however, we are more concerned with the nature of individual sites and how they are formed.

The Importance of Context

In order to reconstruct past human activity at a site it is crucially important to understand the *context* of a find, whether artifact, feature, structure, or organic remain. A find's context consists of its immediate *matrix* (the material surrounding it, usually some sort of sediment such as gravel, sand, or clay), its *provenience* (horizontal and vertical position within the matrix), and its association with other finds (occurrence together with other archaeological remains, usually in the same matrix). In the 19th century the demonstration that stone tools were associated with the bones of extinct animals in sealed deposits or matrices helped establish the idea of humanity's high antiquity (Chapter 1). Increasingly since then archaeologists have recognized the importance of identifying and accurately recording associations between remains on sites. This is why it is such a tragedy when looters dig up sites indiscriminately looking for rich finds, without recording matrix, provenience, or associations. All the contextual information is lost. A looted vase may be an attractive object for a collector, but far more could have been learnt about the society that produced it had archaeologists been able to record where it was found (in a tomb, ditch, or house?) and in association with what other artifacts or organic remains (weapons, tools or animal bones?). Much information about the Mimbres people of the American Southwest has been lost forever because looters bulldozed their sites, hunting for the superbly painted – and highly sought after – bowls made by the Mimbres 1000 years ago (box, p. 552).

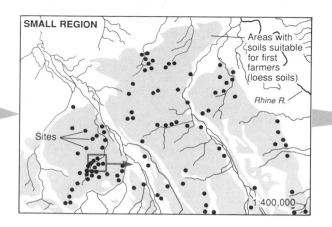

SMALL REGION

Areas with soils suitable for first farmers (loess soils)

Rhine R.

Sites

1:400,000

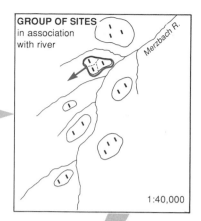

GROUP OF SITES
in association with river

Merzbach R.

1:40,000

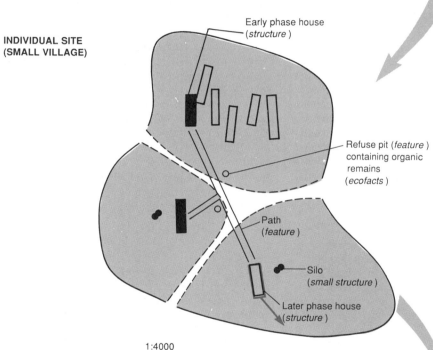

INDIVIDUAL SITE
(SMALL VILLAGE)

Early phase house
(*structure*)

Refuse pit (*feature*)
containing organic
remains
(*ecofacts*)

Path
(*feature*)

Silo
(*small structure*)

Later phase house
(*structure*)

1:4000

*Different scales and terminology used in archaeology,
from the continental region (opposite page, top left) to
the individual structure (right). In this representation
of the pattern of settlement of Europe's first farmers
(5th millennium BC), the archaeologist might study – at
the broader scale – the interesting association between sites
and light, easily worked soils near rivers (see Chapter 7).
At the smaller scale, the association – established by
excavation (Chapter 3) – of houses with other houses
and with structures such as silos for grain storage raises
questions, for example, about social organization and
permanence of occupation at this period.*

INDIVIDUAL STRUCTURE (HOUSE)

Scatter of *artifacts*

Posthole (*feature*)

1:400   Artifacts and features are
found *in association with* the structure

When modern (or ancient) looters disturb a site, perhaps shifting aside material they are not interested in, they destroy that material's *primary context*. If archaeologists subsequently excavate that shifted material, they need to be able to recognize that it is in a *secondary context*. This may be straightforward for, say, a Mimbres site, looted quite recently, but it is much more difficult for a site disturbed in antiquity. Nor is disturbance confined to human activity: archaeologists dealing with the tens of thousands of years of the Old Stone Age or Paleolithic period know well that the forces of nature – encroaching seas or ice sheets, wind and water action – invariably destroy primary context. A great many of the Stone Age tools found in European river gravels are in a secondary context, transported by water action far from their original, primary context.

FORMATION PROCESSES

In recent years archaeologists have become increasingly aware that a whole series of *formation processes* may have affected both the way in which finds came to be buried and what happened to them after they were buried – i.e. their taphonomy (see box pp. 284–85).

The American archaeologist Michael Schiffer has made the useful distinction between *cultural formation processes* (C-transforms) and noncultural or *natural formation processes* (N-transforms). C-transforms involve the deliberate or accidental activities of human beings as they make or use artifacts, build or abandon buildings, plow their fields and so on. N-transforms are natural events that govern both the burial and the survival of the archaeological record. The sudden fall of volcanic ash that covered Pompeii (box, pp. 22–23) is an exceptional N-transform; a more common one would be the gradual burial of artifacts or features by wind-borne sand or soil. Likewise the transporting of stone tools by river action, referred to above, is an example of an N-transform. But the activities of animals on a site – burrowing into them or chewing bones and pieces of wood – are also N-transforms.

At first sight these distinctions may seem of little interest to the archaeologist. In fact they are vital to the accurate reconstruction of past human activities. It may be important, for instance, to know whether certain archaeological evidence is the product of human or non-human activity (the result of C-transforms or N-transforms). If you are trying to reconstruct human woodworking activities by studying cutmarks on timber, then you should learn to recognize certain kinds of marks made by beavers using their teeth and to distin-

Early humans as mighty hunters (left) or mere scavengers (right)? Our understanding of formation processes governs the way in which we interpret associations of human tools with animal bones from the fossil record in Africa.

EXPERIMENTAL ARCHAEOLOGY

One effective way to study formation processes is through long-term experimental archaeology. An excellent example is the experimental earthwork constructed on Overton Down, southern England, in 1960.

The earthwork consists of a substantial chalk and turf bank, 21 m (69 ft) long, 7 m (25 ft) wide, and 2 m (6 ft 7 in) high, with a ditch cut parallel to it. The aim of the experiment has been to assess not only how the bank and ditch alter through time, but also what happens to materials such as pottery, leather, and textiles that were buried in the earthwork in 1960. Sections (trenches) have been – or will be – cut across the bank and ditch at intervals of 2, 4, 8, 16, 32, 64, and 128 years (in real time, 1962, 1964, 1968, 1976, 1992, 2024, and 2088): a considerable commitment for all concerned.

On this timescale, the project is still at a relatively early stage. But preliminary results are interesting. In the 1960s the bank dropped some 25 cm (10 in) in height and the ditch silted up quite rapidly. Since the mid-1970s, however, the structure has stabilized. As for the buried materials, tests after 4 years showed that

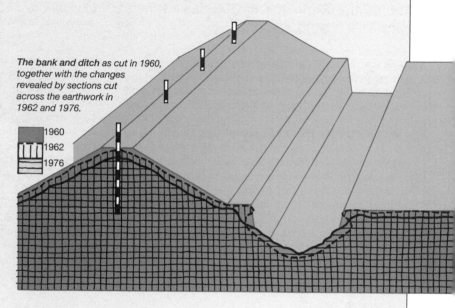

The bank and ditch as cut in 1960, together with the changes revealed by sections cut across the earthwork in 1962 and 1976.

1960
1962
1976

pottery was unchanged and leather little affected, but textiles were already becoming weakened and discolored.

The 1992 excavations revealed that preservation was better in the chalk bank, which is less biologically active, than in the turf core where textiles and some wood had completely disappeared. The structure itself had

changed little since 1976, though there was considerable reworking and transport of fine sediment by earthworms. The experiment has already shown that many of the changes that interest archaeologists occur within decades of burial, and that the extent of these changes can be far greater than had hitherto been suspected.

guish these from cutmarks made by humans using stone or metal tools (Chapter 8).

Let us take an even more significant example. For the earliest phases of human existence in Africa, at the beginning of the Old Stone Age or Paleolithic period, great theoretical schemes about our primitive hunting ability have been based on the association between stone tools and animal bones found at archaeological sites. The bones were assumed to be those of animals hunted and slaughtered by early humans who made the tools. But studies of animal behavior and cutmarks on animal bones by C.K. Brain, Lewis Binford, and others suggest that in many cases the excavated bones are the remains of animals hunted by other predator animals and largely eaten by these. The humans with their stone tools would have come upon the scene as mere scavengers, at the end of a pecking order of differ-

ent animal species. By no means everyone agrees with this scavenging hypothesis. The point to emphasize here is that the issue can best be resolved by improving our techniques for distinguishing between cultural and natural formation processes – between human and non-human activity. Many studies are now focusing on the need to clarify how one differentiates cutmarks on bones made by stone tools from those made by the teeth of animal predators (Chapter 7). Modern experiments using replica stone tools to cut meat off bones are one helpful approach. Other kinds of experimental archaeology can be most instructive about some of the formation processes that affect physical preservation of archaeological material (see box, above).

The remainder of this chapter is devoted to a more detailed discussion of the different cultural and natural formation processes.

CULTURAL FORMATION PROCESSES – HOW PEOPLE HAVE AFFECTED WHAT SURVIVES IN THE ARCHAEOLOGICAL RECORD

One may separate these processes rather crudely into two kinds: those that reflect the original human behavior and activity before a find or site became buried; and those (such as plowing or looting) that came after burial. Now of course most major archaeological sites are formed as the result of a complex sequence of use, burial, and reuse repeated many times over, so that a simple two-fold division of cultural formation processes may not be so simple to apply in practice. Nevertheless, since one of our main aims is to reconstruct original human behavior and activity, we must make the attempt.

Original human behavior is often reflected archaeologically in at least four major activities: in the case of a tool, for example, there may be
1 acquisition of the raw material;
2 manufacture;
3 use; and finally
4 disposal or discard when the tool is worn out or broken. (The tool may of course be reworked and recycled, i.e. repeating stages 2 and 3.)

Similarly a food crop such as wheat will be acquired (harvested), manufactured (processed), used (eaten), and discarded (digested and the waste products excreted) – here one might add a common intermediate stage of storage before use. From the archaeologist's point of view the critical factor is that remains can enter the archaeological record at any one of these stages – a tool may be lost or thrown out as inferior quality during manufacture, a crop may be accidentally burnt and thus preserved during processing. In order accurately to reconstruct the original activity it is therefore crucial to try to understand which of the stages one is looking at. It may be quite easy to identify, say, the first stage for stone tools, because stone quarries can often be recognized by deep holes in the ground with piles of associated waste flakes and

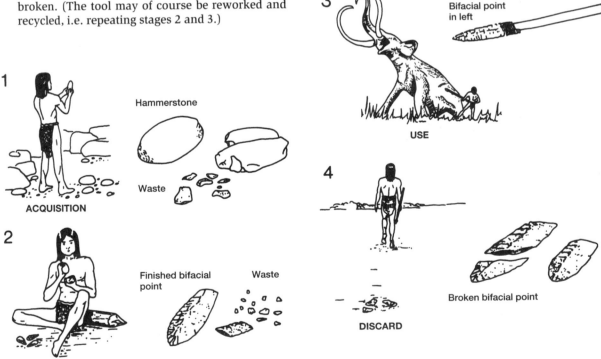

An artifact may have entered the archaeological record at any one of these four stages in its life cycle. The archaeologist's task is to determine which stage is represented by the find in question.

blanks which survive well. But it is much more difficult to know beyond reasonable doubt whether a sample of charred plant remains comes from, say, a threshing floor or an occupation floor – and this may also make it difficult to reconstruct the true plant diet, since certain activities may favor the preservation of certain species of plant. This whole controversial issue is discussed further in Chapter 7.

Deliberate burial of valuables or the dead is another major aspect of original human behavior that has left its mark on the archaeological record. In times of conflict or war people often deposit prized possessions in the ground, intending to reclaim them at a later date but sometimes for one reason or another failing to do so. These *hoards* are a prime source of evidence for certain periods, such as the European Bronze Age, for which hoards of metal goods are common, or later Roman Britain, which has yielded buried treasures of silver and other precious metals. The archaeologist, however, may not find it easy to distinguish between hoards originally intended to be reclaimed and valuables buried perhaps to placate supernatural powers (placed for example at a particularly dangerous part of a crossing over a bog) with no reclamation intended.

How archaeologists set about trying to demonstrate belief in supernatural powers and an afterlife is the subject of Chapter 10. Here we may note that, in addition to hoards, the major source of evidence comes from *burial of the dead*, whether in simple graves, elaborate burial mounds, or giant pyramids, usually with grave-goods such as ceramic vessels or weapons, and sometimes with painted tomb-chamber walls, as in ancient Mexico or Egypt. The Egyptians indeed went so far as to mummify their dead (see below) – to preserve them, they hoped, for eternity – as did the Incas of Peru, whose kings were kept in the Temple of the Sun at Cuzco and brought outside for special ceremonies.

Human destruction of the archaeological record might be caused by burials of the kind just described being dug into earlier deposits. But people in the past deliberately or accidentally obliterated traces of their predecessors in innumerable other ways. Rulers, for instance, often destroyed monuments or erased inscriptions belonging to previous chiefs or monarchs. A classic example of this occurred in ancient Egypt, where the heretic pharaoh Akhenaten, who tried to introduce a new religion in the 14th century BC, was reviled by his successors and his major buildings were torn down for reuse in other monuments. A Canadian team led by Donald Redford has spent many years recording some of these reused stone blocks at Thebes and has successfully matched them with the help of a computerized database in order to reconstruct (on paper), like a giant jigsaw, part of one of Akhenaten's temples.

Some human destruction meant to obliterate has inadvertently preserved material for the archaeologist to find. Burning, for example, may not always destroy. It can often improve the chances of survival of a variety of remains such as of plants: the conversion into carbon greatly increases the powers of resistance to the ravages of time. Clay daubing and adobe usually decay, but if a structure has been fired, the mud is baked to the consistency of a brick. In the same way thousands of clay writing tablets from the Near East have been baked accidentally or deliberately in fires and thus preserved. Timbers too may char and survive in structures, or at least leave a clear impression in the hardened mud.

Today human destruction of the archaeological record continues at a frightening pace, through land drainage, plowing, building work, looting, etc. In Chapter 14 we discuss how this affects archaeology generally and what the potential implications are for the future.

NATURAL FORMATION PROCESSES – HOW NATURE AFFECTS WHAT SURVIVES IN THE ARCHAEOLOGICAL RECORD

We saw above how natural formation processes such as river action can disturb or destroy the primary context of archaeological material. Here we will focus on that material itself, and the natural processes that cause decay or lead to preservation.

Practically any archaeological material can survive in exceptional circumstances. Usually, however, inorganic materials survive far better than organic ones.

Inorganic Materials

The most common inorganic materials to survive archaeologically are stone, clay, and metals.

Stone tools survive extraordinarily well – some are over 2 million years old. Not surprisingly they have always been our main source of evidence for human activities during the Old Stone Age, even though wooden and bone tools (which are less likely to be

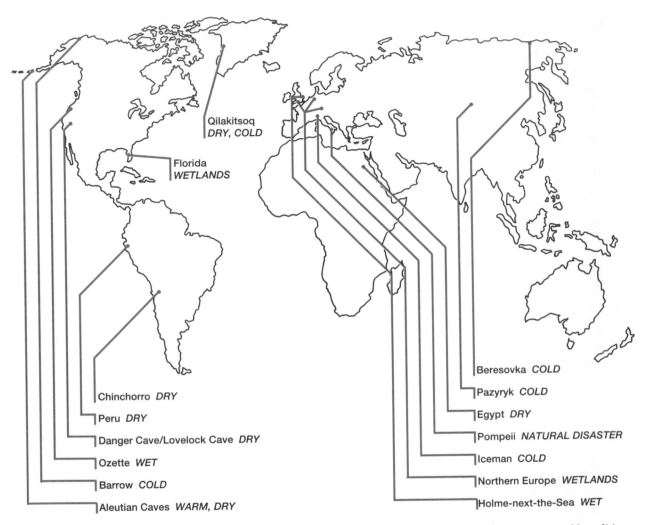

Qilakitsoq *DRY, COLD*

Florida *WETLANDS*

Beresovka *COLD*

Pazyryk *COLD*

Egypt *DRY*

Pompeii *NATURAL DISASTER*

Iceman *COLD*

Northern Europe *WETLANDS*

Holme-next-the-Sea *WET*

Chinchorro *DRY*

Peru *DRY*

Danger Cave/Lovelock Cave *DRY*

Ozette *WET*

Barrow *COLD*

Aleutian Caves *WARM, DRY*

The major sites and regions discussed in this chapter where natural formation processes – from wet to very dry or cold conditions – have led to exceptionally good preservation of archaeological remains.

preserved) may originally have equalled stone ones in their importance. Stone tools sometimes come down to us so little damaged or altered from their primary state that archaeologists can examine microscopic patterns of wear on their cutting edges and learn, for example, whether the tools were used to cut wood or animal hides. This is now a major branch of archaeological inquiry (Chapter 8).

Fired clay, such as pottery and baked mud-brick or adobe, is virtually indestructible if well fired. It is therefore again not surprising that for the periods after the introduction of pottery making (some 16,000 years ago in Japan, and 9000 years ago in the Near East and parts of South America) ceramics have traditionally been the archaeologist's main source of evidence. As we saw at the beginning of this chapter, pots can be studied for their shape, surface decoration, mineral content, and even the food or other residues left inside them. Acid soils can damage the surface of fired clay, and porous or badly fired clay vessels or mud brick can become fragile in humid conditions. However, even disintegrated mud brick can help to assess rebuilding phases in Peruvian villages or Near Eastern tells.

Metals such as gold, silver, and lead survive well. Copper, and bronze with a low-quality alloy, are

Mud brick survives well in the dry conditions of the Near East. Here archaeologists excavate the massive mud-brick wall foundations of the Oval Temple at Khafaje, Iraq, dating from 2650–2350 BC.

attacked by acid soils, and can become so oxidized that only a green deposit or stain is left. Oxidation is also a rapid and powerful agent of destruction of iron, which rusts and may likewise leave only a discoloration in the soil. However, as will be seen in Chapter 8, it is sometimes possible to retrieve vanished iron objects by making a cast of the hollow they have left within the soil or within a mass of corrosion.

The sea is potentially very destructive, with underwater remains being broken and scattered by currents, waves, or tidal action. It can on the other hand cause metals to be coated with a thick, hard casing of metallic salts (such as chlorides, sulphides, and carbonates) from the objects themselves; this helps to preserve the artifacts within. If the remains are simply taken out of the water and not treated, the salts react with air, and give off acid which destroys the remaining metal. But the use of electrolysis – placing the object in a chemical solution and passing a weak current between it and a surrounding metal grill – causes the destructive salts to move slowly from the cathode (object) to the anode (grill), leaving the metal artifact clean and safe. This is a standard procedure in underwater archaeology and is used on all types of objects from cannons (see illus. overleaf) to the finds recently recovered from the *Titanic*.

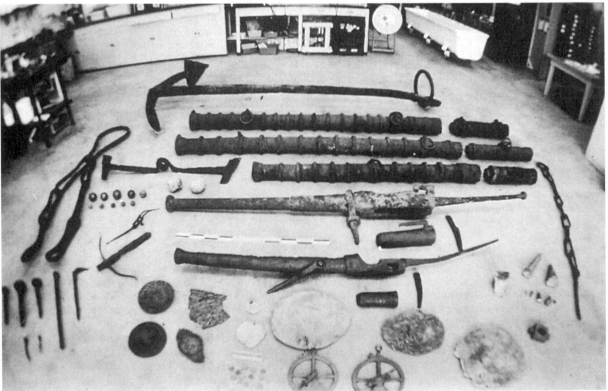

Metal artifacts from a 1554 shipwreck in the Caribbean, before and after conservation. Use of electrolysis (see p. 57) has revealed a unique group of 16th-century armaments, anchors, and navigational instruments.

Organic Materials

Survival of organic materials is determined largely by the matrix (the surrounding material) and by climate (local and regional) – with the occasional influence of natural disasters such as volcanic eruptions, which are often far from disastrous for archaeologists.

The *matrix*, as we saw earlier, is usually some kind of sediment or soil. These vary in their effects on organic material; chalk, for example, preserves human and animal bone well (in addition to inorganic metals). Acid soils destroy bones and wood within a few years, but will leave telltale discolorations where postholes or hut foundations once stood. Similar brown or black marks survive in sandy soils, as do dark silhouettes which used to be skeletons (see Chapter 11).

But the immediate matrix may in exceptional circumstances have an additional component such as metal ore, salt, or oil. Copper can favor the preservation of organic remains, perhaps by preventing the activity of destructive micro-organisms. The prehistoric copper mines of central and southeast Europe have many remains of wood, leather, and textiles. Organic packing material found between copper ingots on the 14th-century BC Uluburun shipwreck, off the coast of southern Turkey (box, pp. 374–75), also survived for the same reason.

Salt mines such as those of Iron Age Hallstatt, Austria, have helped preserve organic finds. Even more remarkably, a combination of salt and oil ensured the preservation of a woolly rhinoceros at Starunia, Poland, with skin intact, and the leaves and fruits of tundra vegetation around it. The animal had been carried by a strong current into a pool saturated with crude oil and salt from a natural oil seep, which prevented decomposition: bacteria could not operate in these conditions, while salt had permeated the skin and preserved it. Similarly, the asphalt pits of La Brea, Los Angeles, are world famous for the prodigious quantities and fine condition of the skeletons of a wide range of prehistoric animals and birds recovered from them.

Climate plays an important role too in the preservation of organic remains. Occasionally one can speak of the "local climate" of an environment such as a cave. Caves are natural "conservatories" because their interiors are protected from outside climatic effects, and (in the case of limestone caves) their alkaline conditions permit excellent preservation. If undisturbed by floods or the trampling feet of animals and people, they can preserve bones and such fragile remains as footprints, and sometimes even plant fibers such as the short length of rope found in the Upper Paleolithic decorated cave of Lascaux, France.

More usually, however, it is the regional climate that is important. *Tropical climates* are the most destructive, with their combination of heavy rains, acid soils, warm temperatures, high humidity, erosion, and wealth of vegetation and insect life. Tropical rainforests can overwhelm a site remarkably quickly, with roots that dislodge masonry and tear buildings apart, while torrential downpours gradually destroy paint and plasterwork, and woodwork rots away completely. Archaeologists in southern Mexico, for example, constantly have to battle to keep back the jungle. From one field season to the next, primary growth of more than 2 m (6 ft 7 in) in height may appear in areas that had been totally cleared the year before. On the other hand, one can also look on jungle conditions as benign, in that they hinder looters from easily reaching even more sites than they do already.

Temperate climates, as in much of Europe and North America, are not beneficial, as a rule, to organic materials; their relatively warm but variable temperatures and fluctuating precipitation combine to accelerate the processes of decay. In some circumstances, however, local conditions can counteract these processes. At the Roman fort of Vindolanda, near Hadrian's Wall in northern England, over 1300 letters and documents, written in ink on wafer-thin sheets of birch and alderwood, have been found by the archaeologist Robin Birley. The fragments, dating to about AD 100, have survived because of the soil's unusual chemical condition: clay compacted between layers in the site created oxygen-free pockets (the exclusion of oxygen is vital to the preservation of organic materials), while chemicals produced by bracken, bone, and other remains effectively made the land sterile in that locality, thus preventing disturbance by vegetation and other forms of life.

A different example of freak preservation in temperate conditions occurred at Potterne, a Late Bronze Age refuse heap in southern England dating to about 1000 BC. Whereas bones normally become mineralized through the percolation of groundwater, in this site bones – as well as unburnt seeds and pottery – have been preserved because a mineral called glauconite (a mica) has translocated from the greensand bedrock and entered into a stable compound with the organic materials.

Natural disasters sometimes preserve sites, including organic remains, for the archaeologist. The most common are violent storms, such as that which covered the coastal Neolithic village of Skara Brae, Orkney Islands, with sand, the mudslide that engulfed the prehistoric village of Ozette on America's Northwest Coast (box, overleaf), or volcanic eruptions such as that of

WET PRESERVATION: THE OZETTE SITE

Ozette

UNITED STATES

A special kind of waterlogging occurred at the Ozette site, Washington, on the U.S. Northwest Coast. About AD 1750, a huge mudslide buried part of a whale-hunting settlement. The village lay protected for two centuries – but not forgotten, for the descendants of the village kept the memory of their ancestors' home alive. Then the sea began to strip away the mud, and it seemed as if the site would fall prey to looters. Local people called on the government to excavate the site and to protect the remains. Richard Daugherty was appointed to organize the excavation. As the mud was cleared with high-pressure hoses, a wealth of organic material came to view.

Several cedarwood long houses, up to 21 m (68 ft 3 in) in length and 14 m (45 ft 6 in) wide, were found, with adzed and carved panels (painted with black designs including wolves and thunderbirds), roof-support posts, and low partition walls. These houses contained hearths, cooking platforms, sleeping benches, and mats.

Over 50,000 artifacts were recovered in a fine state of preservation – almost half in wood or other plant material. The most spectacular was a block of red cedar, a meter high, carved in the form of a whale's dorsal fin. Even ferns and cedar leaves had survived, together with an abundance of whale bones.

The project was an excellent example of cooperation between archaeologists and indigenous peoples. The Makah Indians value the contribution made by archaeologists to the understanding of their past, and have built a museum to display the finds.

PERISHABLE ARTIFACTS FROM OZETTE

Woven material 1330 baskets • 1466 mats • 142 hats • 37 cradles • 96 tump lines • 49 harpoon sheaths

Weaving equipment 14 loom uprights • 14 roller bars • 10 swords • 23 spindle whorls • 6 spools

Hunting equipment 115 wooden bows and fragments • 1534 arrow shafts • 5189 wooden arrow points • 124 harpoon shafts • 22 harpoon finger rests • 161 plugs from seal-skin floats

Fishing equipment 131 bent wood halibut hooks • 607 curved halibut hook shanks • 117 blanks for making hooks • 7 herring rakes • 57 single-barbed hooks • 15 double-barbed hooks

Containers 1001 wooden boxes and fragments • 120 wooden bowls and fragments • 37 wooden trays

Watercraft 361 canoe paddles and fragments • 14 canoe bailers • 14 canoe fragments

Miscellaneous 40 game paddles • 45 carved miniature items (canoes, figurines, etc.) • 52 carved wooden clubs • 1 carved effigy of a whale fin inlaid with sea-otter teeth

General view from the south of the area around the Ozette site. Vancouver Island lies on the horizon.

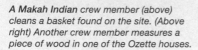

A Makah Indian crew member (above) cleans a basket found on the site. (Above right) Another crew member measures a piece of wood in one of the Ozette houses.

Richard Daugherty (below) with the carved cedar representation of the dorsal fin of a whale. It was inlaid with over 700 sea-otter teeth arranged in the shape of a thunderbird holding a serpent in its claws.

Wooden clubs from the site. (Above, left to right) Head of a seal club; an owl head on a shaman's club; a face on the handle end of a seal club.

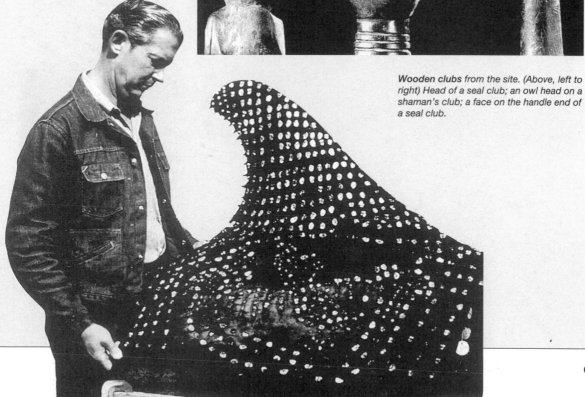

DRY PRESERVATION: THE TOMB OF TUTANKHAMUN

EGYPT

Thebes

FINDS FROM TUTANKHAMUN'S TOMB

Archery equipment • Baskets • Beds • Bier • Boat models • Boomerangs and throwsticks • Botanical specimens • Boxes and chests • Canopic equipment • Chairs and stools • Chariot equipment • Clothing • Coffins • Cosmetic objects • Cuirass • Divine figures • Fans • Foodstuffs • Gaming equipment • Gold mask • Granary model • Hassocks • Jewelry, beads, amulets • Lamps and torches • Mummies • Musical instruments • Portable pavilion • Regalia • Ritual couches • Ritual objects • Royal figures • Sarcophagi • Shabti figures and related objects • Shields • Shrines and related objects • Sticks and staves • Swords and daggers • Tools • Vessels • Wine jars • Writing equipment

The arid conditions that prevail in Egypt have helped preserve a wide range of ancient materials, ranging from numerous written documents on papyrus (made of the pith of a Nile water plant) to two full-size wooden boats buried beside the Great Pyramid at Giza. But the best-known and most spectacular array of objects was that discovered in 1922 by Howard Carter and Lord Carnarvon in the tomb at Thebes of the pharaoh Tutankhamun, dating to the 14th century BC.

Tutankhamun had a short reign and was relatively insignificant in Egyptian history, a fact reflected in his burial, a poor one by pharaonic standards. But within the small tomb, originally built for someone else, was a wealth of treasure. For Tutankhamun was buried with everything he might need in the next life. The entrance corridor and the four chambers were crammed with thousands of individual grave-goods. They include objects of precious metal, like the jewelry and famous gold mask, and food and clothing. But wooden objects, such as statues, chests,

shrines, and two of the three coffins, make up a large part of the tomb's contents. The human remains – the mummies of the king and his two stillborn children – have been the subject of scientific analysis more than once. A lock of hair found separately among the grave-goods has been analyzed and is thought to come from a mummy in another tomb believed to be Tiye, the young king's grandmother.

The grave furniture was not all originally intended for Tutankhamun. Some of it had been made for other members of his family, and then hastily adopted when the young king died unexpectedly. There were also touching items, such as a chair the king had used as a child, and a simple reed stick mounted in gold labeled as "A reed which His Majesty cut with his own hand." Even wreaths and funerary bouquets had survived in the dry conditions, left on the second and third coffins by mourners.

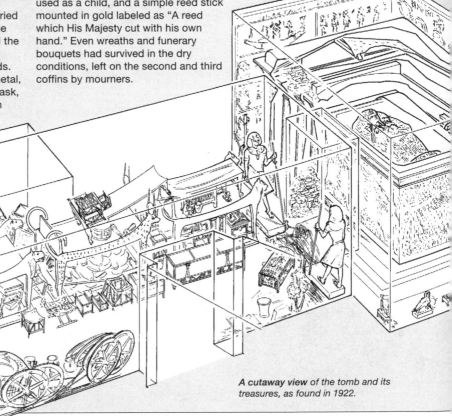

A cutaway view of the tomb and its treasures, as found in 1922.

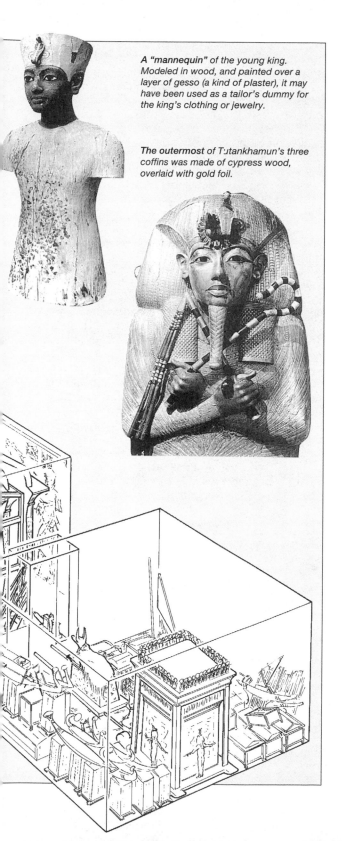

A "mannequin" of the young king. Modeled in wood, and painted over a layer of gesso (a kind of plaster), it may have been used as a tailor's dummy for the king's clothing or jewelry.

The outermost of Tutankhamun's three coffins was made of cypress wood, overlaid with gold foil.

Vesuvius which buried and preserved Roman Pompeii under a blanket of ash (box, pp. 22–23). Another volcanic eruption, this time in El Salvador in about AD 595, deposited a thick and widespread layer of ash over a densely populated area of Maya settlement. Work here by Payson Sheets and his associates has uncovered a variety of organic remains at the site of Cerén, including palm and grass roofing, mats, baskets, stored grain and even preserved agricultural furrows. As will be seen in Chapter 6, volcanic ash has preserved part of a prehistoric forest at Miesenheim, in Germany.

Apart from these special circumstances, the survival of organic materials is limited to cases involving extremes of moisture: that is, arid, frozen, or waterlogged conditions.

Preservation of Organic Materials: Extreme Conditions

Dry Environments. Great aridity or dryness prevents decay through the shortage of water, which ensures that many destructive micro-organisms are unable to flourish. Archaeologists first became aware of the phenomenon in Egypt (see Tutankhamun box), where much of the Nile Valley has such a dry atmosphere that bodies of the predynastic period (before 3000 BC) have survived intact, with skin, hair, and nails, without any artificial mummification or coffins – the corpses were simply placed in shallow graves in the sand. Rapid drying out or desiccation, plus the draining qualities of the sand, produced such spectacular preservative effects that they probably suggested the practice of mummification to the later Egyptians of the dynastic period.

The pueblo dwellers of the American Southwest (*c.* AD 700–1400) buried their dead in dry caves and rockshelters where, as in Egypt, natural desiccation took place: these are not therefore true, humanly created mummies, although they are often referred to as such. The bodies survive, sometimes wrapped in fur blankets or tanned skins, and in such good condition that it has been possible to study hair styles. Clothing (from fiber sandals to string aprons) also remains, together with a wide range of goods such as basketry, feathered ornaments, and leather. Some far earlier sites in the same region also contain organic remains: Danger Cave, Utah (occupied from 9000 BC onward), yielded wooden arrows, trap springs, knife handles, and other wooden tools; Lovelock Cave, Nevada, had nets; while caves near Durango, Colorado, had preserved maize cobs, squashes, and sunflower and mustard seeds. Plant finds of this type have been crucial in helping to reconstruct ancient diet (Chapter 7).

The coastal dwellers of central and southern Peru lived – and died – in a similarly dry environment, so that it is possible today to see the tattoos on their desiccated bodies, and admire the huge and dazzlingly colorful textiles from cemeteries at Ica and Nazca, as well as basketry and featherwork, and also maize cobs and other items of food. In Chile, the oldest deliberately made mummies have been found at Chinchorro, preserved again by the aridity of the desert environment (see p. 427).

A slightly different phenomenon occurred in the Aleutian Islands, off the west coast of Alaska, where the dead were kept and naturally preserved in volcanically warmed caves that were extremely dry. Here the islanders seem to have enhanced the natural desiccation by periodically drying the bodies by wiping or suspension over a fire; in some cases they removed the internal organs and placed dry grass in the cavity.

Cold Environments. Natural refrigeration can hold the processes of decay in check for thousands of years. Perhaps the first frozen finds to be discovered were the numerous remains of mammoths encountered in the permafrost (permanently frozen soil) of Siberia, a few with their flesh, hair, and stomach contents intact. The unlucky creatures probably fell into crevices in snow, and were buried by silt in what became a giant deep-freeze. The best known are Beresovka, recovered in 1901, and baby Dima, found in 1977. Preservation can be still so good that dogs find the meat quite palatable and they have to be kept well away from the carcasses.

The most famous frozen archaeological remains are undoubtedly those from the burial mounds of steppe nomads at Pazyryk in the Altai, southern Siberia, dating to the Iron Age, about 400 BC. They comprise pits dug deep into the ground, lined with logs, and covered with a low cairn of stones. They could only have been dug in the warm season, before the ground froze solid. Any warm air in the graves rose and deposited its moisture on the stones of the cairn; moisture also gradually infiltrated down into the burial chambers, and froze so hard there during the harsh winter that it never thawed during subsequent summers, since the cairns were poor conductors of heat and shielded the pits from the warming and drying effects of wind and sun. Consequently, even the most fragile materials have survived intact – despite the boiling water that had to be used by the Soviet excavator, Sergei Rudenko, to recover them.

The Pazyryk bodies had been placed inside log coffins, with wooden pillows, and survived so well that their spectacular tattoos can still be seen. Clothing included linen shirts, decorated caftans, aprons, stockings, and headdresses of felt and leather. There were also rugs, wall-coverings, tables laden with food, and horse carcasses complete with elaborate bridles, saddles, and other trappings. A further well-preserved burial has been found in the region, containing a female accompanied by six horses and grave-goods including a silver mirror and various wooden objects.

Similar standards of preservation have also been encountered in other circumpolar regions such as Greenland and Alaska. The Barrow site is a good case in point (see box). Another Alaskan example comes from St. Lawrence Island, where the permafrost has yielded the body of an Inuit woman with tattooed arms

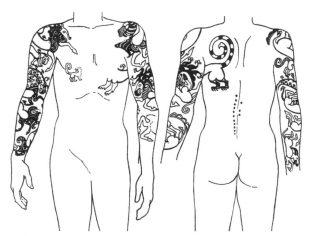

Frozen conditions of southern Siberia helped to preserve the remarkable finds from burial mounds of steppe nomads at Pazyryk dating from about 400 BC. (Left) Tattoo pattern on the torso and arms of a chieftain. (Right) Drawing of part of a Pazyryk wall-hanging in appliquéd felt, showing a horseman approaching an enthroned figure.

COLD PRESERVATION 1: THE BARROW SITE

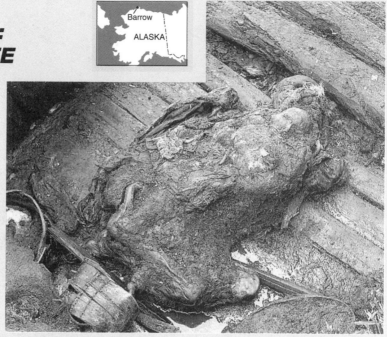

Many former living sites of Inuit, such as those of the Thule culture north of Hudson Bay, have fragile materials in a good state of preservation: wood, bone, ivory, feathers, hair, and eggshell. In the early 1980s, a driftwood-and-sod house was excavated by Albert Dekin and his colleagues at Utqiagvik, modern Barrow, on Alaska's north coast.

Built by Inupiat about 500 years ago, the house had been destroyed one winter's night by a storm which brought a mass of ice crashing down on its sleeping occupants. Like the Pazyryk tombs (see main text), the ruined house had been infiltrated by summer meltwater, which then froze permanently. Inside the solid earth, the excavators found the intact bodies of two women, while the bones of three youngsters lay nearer the surface (and thus had not been permanently frozen). Dekin and his colleagues also found clothing of caribou and sealskin; implements in a wide range of materials, including a wooden bucket; and tools and weapons arranged in kits according to function and season. Winter hunting equipment, for example – including snow goggles, ice picks, and harpoons – was stored in skin bags.

An autopsy on the two women – carried out with the permission of the modern community, to which all the bodies were later returned for reburial – showed that they had been adequately nourished in life, but had suffered from anthracosis (black lungs, from breathing smoke and oil-lamp fumes during the long winters) and also atherosclerosis (a narrowing of the arteries caused by deposits of cholesterol and fat, the result of a diet rich in whale and seal blubber). The older woman had recovered from pneumonia, but may also have suffered from trichinosis, a painful parasite infection of the muscles, perhaps caused by eating raw polar-bear meat.

One of the two female bodies (above; below) found on the house floor. KEY: a, wood snow-goggles; b, skin-wrapped arrowpoints; c, skin bag with weights; d, hide fragment; e, whalebone ice pick; f, polar-bear-hide mitten; g, ivory comb; h, baleen comb; i, wood shaft; j, wood buckets; k, wood ladle; l, hide blanket; m, skin bag used as pillow; n, boots; o, gut bag; p, antler arrowpoint; q, baleen container; r, skin bag with sewing kit; s, bird-skin bag; t, slate blade; u, wood slat; v, walrus hide; w, ceramic pot.

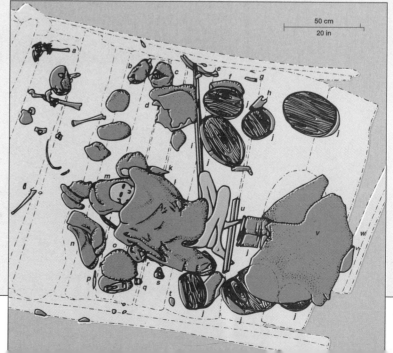

COLD PRESERVATION 2: THE ICEMAN

Ötztaler Alps
ITALY

The world's oldest fully preserved human body was found in September 1991 by German hikers near the Similaun glacier, in the Ötztaler Alps of South Tyrol. They spotted a human body, its skin yellowish-brown and desiccated, at an altitude of 3200 m (10,500 ft). It was four days before the body and its accompanying objects were removed by Austrian authorities and taken to Innsbruck University. There were already suspicions that the corpse might be old, but nobody had any idea just how ancient. The Iceman is the first prehistoric human ever found with his everyday clothing and equipment, and presumably going about his normal business; other

similarly intact bodies from prehistory have been either carefully buried or sacrificed. He brings us literally face to face with the remote past.

The body was handed to the Innsbruck Anatomy department for treatment, after which it was placed in a freezer at -6° C (21° F) and 98 percent humidity. Subsequent investigation determined that the corpse – called Similaun Man, Ötzi, or simply the "Iceman" – had lain *c.* 90 m (300 ft) inside Italy, and he was returned there, to a museum in Bolzano, in 1998. Considerable work has been carried out on the objects that accompanied the Iceman but, apart from scans of his body and radiocarbon dating, very little

has yet been done with the corpse. Fifteen radiocarbon dates have been obtained from the body, the artifacts, and the grass in the boots: they are all in rough agreement, falling in a range of 3365–2940 BC, averaging at 3300 BC.

According to the investigators, the Iceman was probably overcome by exhaustion on the mountain – perhaps caught in a fog or a blizzard. After death, he was dried out by a warm autumn wind, before becoming encased in ice. Since the body lay in a depression, it was protected from the movement of the glacier above it for 5300 years, until a storm from the Sahara laid a layer of dust on the ice that absorbed sunlight and finally thawed it out.

What Did He Look Like?
He was a dark-skinned male, aged in his mid- to late 40s, with a cranial capacity of 1500–1560 cc. Only about 1.56–1.6 m (5ft 2 in) tall, his stature and

The Iceman, the oldest fully preserved human, as found in 1991, emerging from the melting ice that had preserved him for over 5000 years.

morphology fit well within the measurement ranges of Late Neolithic populations of Italy and Switzerland. Preliminary analysis of his DNA confirms his links to northern Europe.

The corpse currently weighs only about 54 kg (120 lb). His teeth are very worn, especially the front incisors, suggesting that he ate coarse ground grain, or that he regularly used them as a tool; there are no wisdom teeth, which is typical for the period, and he has a marked gap between his upper front teeth.

When found he was bald, but hundreds of curly brownish-black human hairs, about 9 cm (3.5 in) long, were recovered from the vicinity of the body and on the clothing fragments. These had fallen out after death and it is possible he had a beard. His right earlobe still retains traces of a pit-like, sharp-edged rectangular depression, indicating that he once probably had an ornamental stone fitted there.

A body scan has shown that the brain, muscle tissues, lungs, heart, liver, and digestive organs are in excellent condition, though the lungs are blackened by smoke, probably from open fires, and he has hardening of the arteries and blood vessels. The isotopic composition of his hair (see p. 309) suggested that he had been a strict vegetarian for the last few months of his life, but traces of meat have been found in his colon, and his final meal appears to have consisted of meat (probably ibex), wheat, plants, and plums.

Traces of chronic frostbite were noted in one little toe and 8 of his ribs were fractured, though these were healed or healing when he died. A fracture to left arm and severe damage to the left pelvic area occurred during his recovery from the ice.

Groups of tattoos, mostly short parallel vertical blue lines were discovered on both sides of his lower spine, on his left calf and right ankle, and a blue cross on his inner right knee. These marks may be therapeutic, aimed at relieving the arthritis which he had in his neck, lower back, and right hip.

His nails had dropped off, but one fingernail was recovered. Its analysis revealed not only that he undertook manual labor, but also that he experienced periods of reduced nail growth corresponding to episodes of serious illness – 4, 3, and 2 months before he died. The fact that he was prone to periodic crippling disease may help explain how he fell prey to adverse weather and froze to death.

The items found with him constitute a unique "time-capsule" of everyday life, many made of organic materials that were preserved by the cold and ice. An great variety of woods and a range of sophisticated techniques of working with leather and grasses were used to create the collection of 70 objects, which add a new dimension to our knowledge of the period.

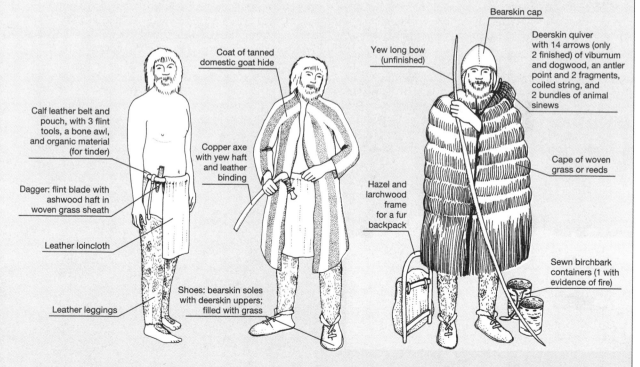

The equipment and clothing of the Iceman are a virtual time-capsule of everyday life – over 70 objects were found associated with him.

dating to the early centuries AD. More southerly regions can produce the same effect at high altitude, for instance the Inca-period tomb at Cerra El Plomo in the Andes, which contained the naturally freeze-dried corpse of a boy wearing a camelid-wool poncho; or the 5300-year-old Iceman found preserved in the ice in the Alps near the border between Italy and Austria (see box, pp. 66–67).

In Greenland, the Inuit bodies of Qilakitsoq, dating to the 15th century AD, had also undergone natural freeze-drying in their rock-overhang graves protected from the elements; their tissue had shrunk and become discolored, but tattoos were still visible (see box, pp. 444–45), and their clothes were in particularly fine condition.

A more modern example of natural refrigeration can be found in the Arctic graves of three British sailors who died in 1846 on the expedition of Sir John Franklin. The bodies were perfectly preserved in the ice of northern Canada's Beechey Island. In 1984 a team led by the Canadian anthropologist Owen Beattie simply removed samples of bone and tissue for an autopsy, before reburying the corpses.

Waterlogged Environments. A useful distinction in land archaeology (as opposed to archaeology beneath the sea) can be drawn between dryland and wetland sites. The great majority of sites are "dry" in the sense that moisture content is low and preservation of organic remains is poor. Wetland sites include all those found in lakes, swamps, marshes, fens, and peat bogs. In these situations organic materials are effectively sealed in a wet and airless (anaerobic or, more correctly, anoxic) environment which favors their preservation, as long as the waterlogging is more or less permanent up to the time of excavation. (If a wet site dries out,

even only seasonally, decomposition of the organic materials can occur.)

One of the pioneers of wetland archaeology in Britain, John Coles, estimates that on a wet site often 75–90 percent, sometimes 100 percent, of the finds are organic. Little or none of this material, such as wood, leather, textiles, basketry, and plant remains of all kinds, would survive on most dryland sites. It is for this reason that archaeologists are turning their attention more and more to the rich sources of evidence about past human activities to be found on wet sites. Growing threats from drainage and peatcutting in the wetlands, which form only about 6 percent of the world's total land area, give this work an added urgency.

Wetlands vary a great deal in their preservative qualities. Acidic peat bogs are kind to wood and plant remains, but may destroy bone, iron, and even pottery. The famous lake sites of the Alpine regions of Switzerland, Italy, France, and southern Germany on the other hand preserve most materials well.

Peat bogs, nearly all of which occur in northern latitudes, are some of the most important environments for wetland archaeology. The Somerset Levels in southern England, for example, have been the scene not only of excavations earlier this century to recover the well-preserved Iron Age lake villages of Glastonbury and Meare, but of a much wider campaign in the last two decades that has unearthed numerous wooden trackways (including the world's "oldest road," a 6000-year-old 1.6-km (1-mile) stretch of track), and many details about early woodworking skills (Chapter 8), and the ancient environment (Chapter 6). On the continent of Europe, and in Ireland, peat bogs have likewise preserved many trackways – sometimes with evidence for the wooden carts that ran along them – and other fragile remains. Other types of European

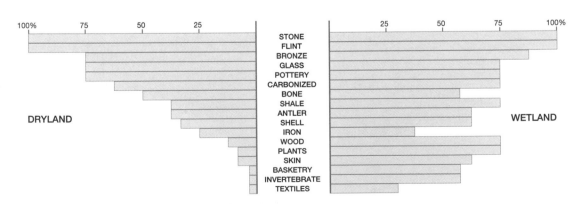

Survival rates for different materials in wet and ordinary dryland sites. Organic remains survive best in wetlands.

In 1998, erosion exposed this amazing monument, in peat levels dating to the Bronze Age, at Holme-next-the-Sea on England's Norfolk coast. An inverted oak tree, pushed into the ground with roots upwards, is surrounded by an oval ring of 54, close-set timber posts, mostly split oaks. Preserved by burial under sand and brine, it is thought to be a ritual structure, perhaps an "altar" for exposing corpses which would then be taken away by the sea. It has recently been tree-ring dated to c. 2050/2049 BC.

wetlands, such as coastal marshes, have yielded dug-out logboats, paddles, even fish-nets and fish-weirs.

Bog bodies, however, are undoubtedly the best-known finds from the peat bogs of northwest Europe. Most of them date from the Iron Age. The degree of preservation varies widely, and depends on the particular conditions in which the corpses were deposited. Most individuals met a violent death and were probably either executed as criminals or killed as a sacrifice before being thrown into the bog (see box, pp. 448–49). The best-preserved examples, such as Denmark's Tollund Man, were in a truly remarkable state, with only the staining caused by bogwater and tannic acid as an indication that they were ancient rather than modern. Within the skin, the bones have often disappeared, as have most of the internal organs, although the stomach and its contents may survive (Chapter 7). In Florida, prehistoric human brains have even been recovered (Chapter 11).

Occasionally, waterlogged conditions can occur inside burial mounds – a temperate-climate version of the Siberian phenomenon. The oak-coffin burials of Bronze Age northern Europe, and most notably those of Denmark dating to about 1000 BC, had an inner core of stones packed round the tree-trunk coffin, with a round barrow built above. Water infiltrated the inside of the mound and by combining with tannin exuding from the tree trunks, set up acidic conditions which destroyed the skeleton but preserved the skin (discolored like the bog bodies), hair, and ligaments of the bodies inside the coffins, as well as their clothing and objects such as birch-bark pails.

A somewhat similar phenomenon occurred with the ships that the Vikings used as coffins. The Oseberg ship in Norway, for example, held the body of a Viking queen of about AD 800, and was buried in clay, covered by a packing of stones and a layer of peat that sealed it in and ensured its preservation.

Lake-dwellings have rivaled bog bodies in popular interest ever since the discovery of wooden piles or house supports in Swiss lakes well over a century ago. The romantic notion of whole villages built on stilts over the water has, thanks to detailed research since the 1940s, given way to the idea of predominantly lake-edge settlements. The range of preserved material is astonishing, not simply wooden structures, artifacts, and textiles but, at Neolithic Charavines in France for example, even nuts, berries, and other fruits.

Perhaps the greatest contribution to archaeology that lake-dwellings and other European wetland sites have made in recent years, however, is to provide abundant well-preserved timber for the study of tree rings, the annual growth rings in trees. In Chapter 4 we explore the breakthrough this has brought about in the establishment of an accurate tree-ring chronology for parts of northern Europe stretching back thousands of years.

One might add that another rich source of water-logged and preserved timbers in land archaeology can be found in the old waterfronts of towns and cities. Archaeologists have been particularly successful in uncovering parts of London's Roman and medieval waterfront, but such discoveries are not restricted to Europe. In the early 1980s New York City archaeologists excavated a well-preserved 18th-century ship that had been sunk to support the East River waterfront there. Underwater archaeology itself, in rivers and lakes and especially beneath the sea, is not surprisingly the richest source of all for waterlogged finds

Reconstruction of Okeechobee burial platform, Florida.

(box, p. 95). Coastal erosion can also reveal once submerged structures, such as the recently discovered prehistoric timber circle on the eastern coast of England.

The major archaeological problem with waterlogged finds, and particularly wood, is that they deteriorate rapidly when they are uncovered, beginning to dry and crack almost at once. They therefore need to be kept wet until they can be treated or freeze-dried at a laboratory. Conservation measures of this kind help to explain the enormous cost of both wetland and underwater archaeology. It has been estimated that "wet archaeology" costs four times as much as "dry archaeology." But the rewards, as we have seen above, are enormous.

The rewards in the future, too, will be very great. Florida, for example, has about 1.2 million ha (3 million acres) of peat deposits, and on present evidence these probably contain more organic artifacts than anywhere else in the world. So far the wetlands here have yielded the largest number of prehistoric watercraft from any one region, together with totems, masks, and figurines dating as far back as 5000 BC. In the Okeechobee Basin, for instance, a 1st-millennium BC burial platform has been found, decorated with a series of large carved wooden totem posts, representing an array of animals and birds. After a fire, the platform had collapsed into its pond. Yet it is only recently that wet finds in Florida have come to us from careful excavation rather than through the drainage that is destroying large areas of peat deposits and, with them, untold quantities of the richest kinds of archaeological evidence.

SUMMARY

The archaeological evidence available to us depends on a number of important factors: first, what people, past and present, have done to it (cultural formation processes); second, what natural conditions such as soil and climate have preserved or destroyed (natural formation processes); and third, our ability to find, recognize, recover, and conserve it. We can do nothing about the first two factors, being at the mercy of the elements and previous human behavior. But the third factor, which is the subject of this book, is constantly improving, as we understand better the processes of decay and destruction, and design research strategies and technical aids to make the most of what archaeological evidence actually survives.

FURTHER READING

Good introductions to the problems of differential preservation of archaeological materials can be found in:

Binford, L.R. 1983. *In Pursuit of the Past: Decoding the Archaeological Record*. Thames & Hudson: London & New York.

Coles, B. & J. 1989. *People of the Wetlands: Bogs, Bodies and Lake-Dwellers*. Thames & Hudson: London & New York.

Dimbleby, G. 1978. *Plants and Archaeology*. Paladin: London. (Chapter 7.)

Nash, D.T. and Petraglia, M.D. (eds.). 1987. *Natural Formation Processes and the Archaeological Record*. British Archaeological Reports, International Series 352: Oxford.

Purdy, B.A. (ed.). 1988. *Wet Site Archaeology*. Telford Press: Caldwell.

Schiffer, M.B. 1976. *Behavioral Archaeology*. Academic Press: New York & London.

Schiffer, M.B. 1996. *Formation Processes of the Archaeological Record*. University of Utah Press: Salt Lake City.

3 Where?
Survey and Excavation of Sites and Features

It has been said that the person with a clear objective and a plan of campaign is more likely to succeed than the person with neither, and this is certainly true of archaeology. The military overtones of the words "objective" and "campaign" are entirely appropriate for archaeology, which often requires the recruitment, funding, and coordination of large numbers of people in complex field projects. It is no accident that two pioneers of field techniques – Pitt-Rivers and Mortimer Wheeler – were old soldiers (box, pp. 31–33). Today, thanks to the impact of such practitioners, and the major influence of the New Archaeology with its desire for scientific rigor, archaeologists try to make explicit at the outset of research what their objectives are and what their plan of campaign will be. This procedure is commonly called devising a *research design*, which broadly has four stages:

1 *formulation* of a research strategy to resolve a particular question or test a hypothesis or idea;
2 *collecting and recording of evidence* against which to test that idea, usually by the organization of a team of specialists and conducting of fieldwork;
3 *processing and analysis* of that evidence and its interpretation in the light of the original idea to be tested;
4 *publication* of the results in articles, books etc.

There is seldom if ever a straightforward progression from stage 1 to stage 4. In real life the research strategy will constantly be refined as evidence is collected and analyzed. All too often, and inexcusably, publication may be neglected (Chapter 14). But in the best planned research the overall objective – the broad question or questions to be answered – will stand even if the strategy for achieving it alters.

In Part II we shall study some of the research strategies archaeologists adopt to answer questions about how societies were organized, what the ancient environment was like, the foods people ate, the tools they made, their trading contacts and beliefs, and indeed *why* societies evolved and changed over time.

Chapter 13 examines 4 projects in detail, to show how research is carried out in practice, from start to finish.

In this chapter, however, we will focus on stage 2 of the research process – on the methods and techniques archaeologists use to obtain evidence against which to test their ideas. It should not be forgotten that suitable evidence can often come from new work at sites already the subject of fieldwork: Ian Hodder's renewal and reappraisal of the Çatalhöyük excavations (box, pp. 44–45) demonstrates this point. Much potentially rich and rewarding material also lies locked away in museum and institution vaults, waiting to be analyzed by imaginative modern techniques. It is only recently, for example, that the plant remains discovered in Tutankhamun's tomb in the 1920s (box, pp. 62–63) have received thorough analysis. Yet it remains true that the great majority of archaeological research is still dependent on the collection of new material by fresh fieldwork.

Traditionally, fieldwork used to be seen almost exclusively in terms of the discovery and excavation of sites. Today, however, while sites and their excavation remain of paramount importance, the focus has broadened to take in whole landscapes, and surface survey at sites in addition to – or instead of – excavation. Archaeologists have become aware that there is a great range of "off-site" or "non-site" evidence, from scatters of artifacts to features such as plowmarks and field boundaries, that provides important information about human exploitation of the environment. The study of entire landscapes by regional survey is now a major part of archaeological fieldwork. Archaeologists are becoming increasingly aware of the high cost and destructiveness of excavation. Site surface survey and subsurface detection using non-destructive remote sensing devices have taken on new importance. We may distinguish between *methods used in the discovery* of archaeological sites and non-site features or artifact scatters, and those employed *once those sites and features have been discovered*, which include detailed survey and selective excavation at individual sites.

DISCOVERING ARCHAEOLOGICAL SITES AND FEATURES

One major task of the archaeologist is to locate and record the whereabouts of sites and features. In this section we will be reviewing some of the principal techniques used in site discovery. But we should not forget that many monuments have never been lost to posterity: the massive pyramids of Egypt, or of Teotihuacán near modern Mexico City, have always been known to succeeding generations, as have the Great Wall of China or many of the buildings in the Forum in Rome. Their exact function or purpose may indeed have aroused controversy down the centuries, but their presence, the fact of their existence, was never in doubt.

Nor can one credit archaeologists with the discovery of all those sites that were once lost. No one has ever made a precise count, but a significant number of sites known today were found by accident, from the decorated caves in France of Lascaux, and more recently Cosquer, the underwater entrance to which was discovered by a deep-sea diver in 1985, to the amazing terracotta army of China's first emperor, unearthed in 1974 by farmers digging for a well, as well as the countless underwater wrecks first spotted by fishermen, sponge-gatherers, and sport-divers. Construction workers building new roads, subways, dams, and office blocks have made their fair share of discoveries too – for example, the *Templo Mayor* or Great Temple of the Aztecs in Mexico City (box, pp. 552–53).

Nevertheless it is archaeologists who have systematically attempted to record these sites, and it is archaeologists who seek out the full range of sites and features, large or small, that make up the great diversity of past landscapes. How do they achieve this?

A practical distinction can be drawn between site discovery conducted at ground level (*ground reconnaissance*) and discovery from the air or from space (*aerial reconnaissance*), although any one field project will usually employ both types of reconnaissance.

Ground Reconnaissance

Methods for identifying individual sites include consultation of documentary sources and place-name evidence, but primarily actual fieldwork, whether the monitoring of building developers' progress in salvage archaeology, or reconnaissance survey in circumstances where the archaeologist is more of a free agent.

Partially buried but never lost: buildings in the Forum of ancient Rome, as depicted in an 18th-century etching by the Italian artist, Piranesi.

The Great Wall of China, over 2000 km (1250 miles) long, was begun in the 3rd century BC. *Like the Forum, it has never been lost to posterity.*

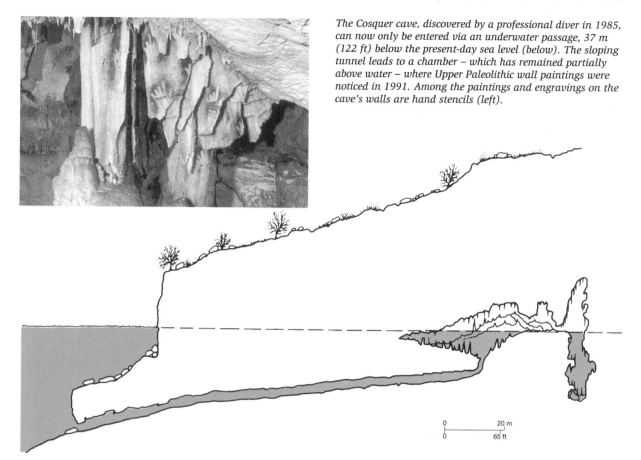

The Cosquer cave, discovered by a professional diver in 1985, can now only be entered via an underwater passage, 37 m (122 ft) below the present-day sea level (below). The sloping tunnel leads to a chamber – which has remained partially above water – where Upper Paleolithic wall paintings were noticed in 1991. Among the paintings and engravings on the cave's walls are hand stencils (left).

0   20 m
0   65 ft

Documentary Sources. In Chapter 1 we saw how Schliemann's firm belief in the historical accuracy of the writings of Homer led directly to the discovery of ancient Troy. A more recent success story of the same kind was the location and excavation by Helge and Anne Stine Ingstad of the Viking settlement of L'Anse aux Meadows in Newfoundland, thanks in large part to clues contained in the medieval Viking sagas. Much of modern biblical archaeology concerns itself with the search in the Near East for evidence of the places – as well as the people and events – described in the Old and New Testaments. Treated objectively as one possible source of information about Near Eastern sites, the Bible can indeed be a rich source of documentary material, but there is certainly the danger that belief in the absolute religious truth of the texts can cloud an impartial assessment of their archaeological validity.

Much research in biblical archaeology involves attempting to link named biblical sites with archaeologically known ones – an effort spurred on in the 1970s by the discovery at Tell Mardikh (ancient Ebla),

Syria, by an Italian team, of Bronze Age writing tablets that refer to biblical cities. Place-name evidence, however, can also lead to actual discoveries of new archaeological sites. In southwest Europe, for example, many prehistoric stone tombs have been found thanks to old names printed on maps that incorporate local words for "stone" or "tomb."

Early maps and old street names are even more important in helping archaeologists work out the former plans of historic towns. In England, for example, it is possible in the better-documented medieval towns to map many of the streets, houses, churches, and castles back to the 12th century AD, or even earlier, using this kind of evidence. These maps then form a reliable basis on which to decide where it would be most profitable to carry out survey work and excavation.

Salvage Archaeology. In this specialized work – discussed more fully in Chapter 14 – the role of the archaeologist is to locate and record as many sites as possible before they are destroyed by new roads, buildings, or

Salvage archaeology: the Aztec temple of Ehecatl-Quetzalcoatl, discovered during the excavation of the Piño Suarez subway station, Mexico City.

dams, or by peatcutting and drainage in wetland environments. Proper liaison with the developer should allow archaeological survey to take place in advance along the projected line of road or in the path of development. Important sites thus discovered may require excavation, and in some cases can even cause construction plans to be altered. Certain archaeological remains unearthed during the digging of subways in Rome and Mexico City were incorporated into the final station architecture.

Reconnaissance Survey. How does the archaeologist set about locating sites, other than through documentary sources and salvage work? A conventional and still valid method is to look for the most prominent remains in a landscape, particularly surviving remnants of walled buildings, and burial mounds such as those in eastern North America or Wessex in southern Britain. But many sites are visible on the surface only as a scatter of artifacts and thus require more thorough survey – what we may call reconnaissance survey – to be detected. Furthermore in recent years, as archaeologists have become more interested in reconstructing the full human use of the landscape, they have begun to realize that there are very faint scatters of artifacts that might not qualify as sites, but which nevertheless represent significant human activity. Scholars such as Robert Dunnell and William Dancey have therefore suggested that these "off-site" or "non-site" areas (that is, areas with a low density of artifacts) should be located and recorded, which can only be done by systematic survey work involving careful sampling procedures (see below). This approach is particularly useful in areas where people leading a mobile way of life have left only a sparse archaeological record, as in much of Africa: see further discussion in Chapter 5.

Reconnaissance survey has become important for another major reason: the growth of regional studies. Thanks to the pioneering researches of scholars such as Gordon Willey in the Virú Valley, Peru, and William T. Sanders in the Basin of Mexico, archaeologists increasingly seek to study settlement patterns – the distribution of sites across the landscape within a given region. The significance of this work for the understanding of past societies is discussed further in Chapter 5. Here we may note its impact on archaeological fieldwork: it is rarely enough now simply to locate an individual site and then to survey it and/or excavate it in isolation from other sites. Whole regions need to be explored, involving a program of survey.

In the last few decades, survey has developed from being simply a preliminary stage in fieldwork (looking for appropriate sites to excavate) to a more or less independent kind of inquiry, an area of research in its own right which can produce information quite different from that achieved by digging. In some cases excavation may not take place at all, perhaps because permission to dig was not forthcoming, or because of a lack of time or funds – modern excavation is slow and costly, whereas survey is cheap, quick, relatively nondestructive, and requires only maps, compasses, and tapes. Usually, however, archaeologists deliberately choose a surface approach as a source of regional data in order to investigate specific questions that interest them and that excavation could not answer.

Reconnaissance survey encompasses a broad range of techniques: no longer just the identification of sites and the recording or collection of surface artifacts, but sometimes also the sampling of natural and mineral resources such as stone and clay. Much survey today is aimed at studying the spatial distribution of human activities, variations between regions, changes in population through time, and relationships between people, land, and resources (see box opposite).

Reconnaissance Survey in Practice. For questions formulated in regional terms, it is necessary to collect data on a corresponding scale, but in a way which provides a maximum of information for a minimum of cost and effort. First, the region to be surveyed needs to be defined: its boundaries may be either natural (such as a valley or island), cultural (the extent of an artifact style), or purely arbitrary, though natural boundaries are the easiest to establish.

The area's history of development needs to be examined, not only to familiarize oneself with previous archaeological work and with the local materials but also to assess the extent to which surface material may have been covered or removed by geomorphological

REGIONAL SURVEY ON MELOS

In 1976 and 1977 a team led by John Cherry undertook a survey on the Greek island of Melos in the eastern Mediterranean. The island's relatively small size (151 sq. km or 94 sq. miles) made it an ideal unit for investigation. The survey aimed to study several questions, including how the number, size, and location of sites have changed through time. The investigation was linked to Colin Renfrew's excavations on the island at the Bronze Age site of Phylakopi, and a major aim was to ascertain whether this was the only settlement site on Melos during most of the 2nd millennium BC.

It was decided to undertake an intensive survey of all parts of the island, but severe constraints on time, funds, and personnel meant that only a 20 percent sample was examined. The survey design was a systematic random sample (see box overleaf) made up of transects, the first chosen at random, the rest at intervals of 5 km (3.1 miles) from it. These transects comprised kilometer-wide strips running north-south across the island. Some areas took up to 3 hours to reach, being inaccessible to vehicles. Each transect was examined by groups of 10 to 12 people walking in parallel lines spaced 15 m to 25 m (49–82 ft) apart. In this way an average of 1.5 to 2 sq. km (0.6–0.8 sq. miles) per day was covered.

The location of sites was plotted on detailed maps prepared from air photographs, and their approximate extent and any noteworthy features were also recorded. Further mapping was undertaken using photographs taken by radio-controlled cameras attached to low-level tethered balloons. Little material was collected in order to minimize disturbance of the spatial patterning on the surface (for example, diagnostic potsherds were identified and photographed but left in the field), and most of the sites were revisited in order to expand the data recorded about them.

As a result of the survey, the total number of sites known on Melos increased from 47 to 130 (of all periods), and the island's overall site density proved to be at least six times greater than had been thought, in part through the recognition and recording of small, low-density scatters of material. No other sites of the same date as Phylakopi were found.

Changes in the number and size of sites through time gave evidence of repeated cycles of aggregation and dispersal of settlement, with notable population peaks in the Late Bronze Age and the late Roman period. Throughout the project, close collaboration was maintained with experts in geology, geomorphology, and historical geography.

The random sample transects selected for intensive study.

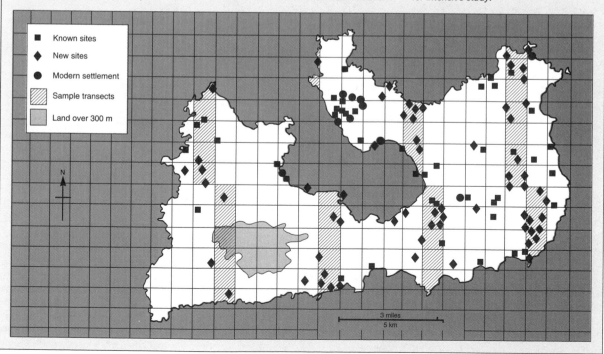

SAMPLING STRATEGIES

Archaeologists cannot usually afford the time and money necessary to investigate fully the whole of a large site or all sites in a given region. So some sort of sample is required. But of what kind?

If the objective is to be able to draw reliable general conclusions about the whole site or region from the small areas sampled, one should try to make use of statistical methods. These employ probability theory, hence the term **probabilistic sampling**. Through mathematical means, they attempt to improve the probability that generalizations from the sample will be correct. This is the technique employed by public opinion polls, which may sample fewer than 2000 people yet will extrapolate from the results to generalize about the opinions of millions. Quite often the polls are proved wrong, yet surprisingly often they are more or less right. As with opinion polls, in archaeological work the larger and better designed the sample, the more likely the results are to be valid.

The alternative is to adopt a non-statistical approach: **non-probabilistic sampling**. Some sites in a given region may be more accessible than others, or more prominent in the landscape, which may prompt a less formally scientific research design. Long years of experience in the field will also give some archaeologists an intuitive "feel" for the right places to undertake work. But in order to judge in any quantitative manner how representative the sample is of a site or region, some form of probabilistic sampling needs to be used.

Types of Probabilistic Sampling
The simplest form is a **simple random sample**, where the areas to be sampled are chosen using a table of random numbers. Research at the small Formative-period hamlet of Tierras Largas in the Oaxaca lowlands, Mexico, can serve as an example. Marcus Winter set out to trace this 3000-year-old site's overall layout and house plans in what was simply a plowed field. First he defined the *sample universe* (the site boundaries) from the area of sherd scatter. Next he chose his *sampling units* (the size of the squares, also called quadrats, in his grid). An initial small test excavation suggested that squares 2 m on a side would be large enough to reveal intelligible features beneath the surface.

Finally, Winter needed to determine how large a *sample fraction* would be sufficient (how many squares to investigate). The greater the number of squares, the more precise the predictions. In this case, Winter estimated from the average size of known Formative houses that they would occupy less than 5 percent of the site's area. With an expected rate of occurrence of less than 5 percent in the

Simple random sample of squares chosen for excavation at Tierras Largas, Mexico.

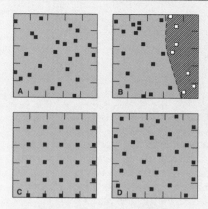

Types of sampling: (A) simple random;
(B) stratified random; (C) systematic;
(D) stratified unaligned systematic.

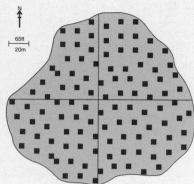

Stratified systematic sample of squares,
5 m on a side, chosen for investigation at
Girik-i-Haciyan, Turkey.

5000 squares of his site grid, he calculated from statistical tables that a sample size of 197 squares would suffice.

The squares were chosen with a table of random numbers. From this sample he was able to estimate the number of houses, pits, burials, and other features which would be found if the entire site were to be exposed.

There are drawbacks to this method. First, it entails defining the site's boundaries beforehand, and these are not always known with certainty. Second, the nature of random numbers results in some areas being allotted clusters of squares, while others remain untouched – the sample is, therefore, inherently biased.

One answer is the **stratified random sample**, where the region or site is divided into its natural zones (strata, hence the technique's name), such as cultivated land and forest, and squares are then chosen by the same random-number procedure, except that each zone has the number of squares proportional to its area. Thus, if forest comprises 85 percent of the area, it must be allotted 85 percent of the squares.

Another solution, **systematic sampling**, entails the selection of a grid of equally spaced locations – e.g. choosing every other square (for an

adaptation, see the box, Regional Survey on Melos, p. 75). By adopting such a regular spacing one runs the risk of missing (or hitting) every single example in an equally regular pattern of distribution – this is another source of potential bias.

A more satisfactory method is to use a **stratified unaligned systematic sample**, which combines the main elements from all three techniques just described. In collecting artifacts from the surface of a large tell or mound site at Girik-i-Haciyan in Turkey, Charles Redman and Patty Jo Watson used a grid of 5 m squares, but orientated it along the site's main N-S/E-W axes, and the samples were selected with reference to these axes. The strata chosen were blocks of 9 squares (3 x 3), and one square in each block was picked for excavation by selecting its N-S/E-W coordinates from a table of random numbers. Not only does this method ensure an unbiased set of samples, more evenly distributed over the whole site, but it also makes it unnecessary to define the boundaries, since the grid can be extended in any direction.

In large-scale surveys, *transects* (linear paths) are sometimes preferable to squares (see box, Regional Survey on Melos, p. 75). This is particularly true in areas of dense vegetation such as

tropical rainforest. It is far easier to walk along a series of paths than to locate accurately and investigate a large number of randomly distributed squares. In addition, transects can easily be segmented into units, whereas it may be difficult to locate or describe a specific part of a square; and transects are useful not merely for finding sites but also for recording artifact densities across the landscape. On the other hand, squares have the advantage of exposing more area to the survey, thus increasing the probability of intersecting sites. A combination of the two methods is often best: using transects to cover long distances, but squares when larger concentrations of material are encountered.

The four probabilistic sampling methods described above have been tested by Stephen Plog on distribution maps from the Valley of Oaxaca, Mexico, in an attempt to assess their comparative efficiency at predicting the total number of sites from a 10 percent sample. He concluded that systematic and stratified systematic sampling were slightly more efficient than the simple or stratified random sampling techniques – but the differences were not statistically significant and therefore archaeologists could in most circumstances use the simpler methods.

Some allowance needs also to be made for the danger that probabilistic sampling, used on its own in regional survey, might easily fail to reveal a major site – a site that may at one time have dominated the whole region. Where there is likely to be a hierarchy of sites, some larger and more dominant than others, it is therefore only prudent to combine probabilistic sampling with conventional survey to discover prominent sites. For further discussion of this point, see Chapter 5.

processes. There is little point, for example, in searching for prehistoric material in sediments only recently laid down by river action. Other factors may have affected surface evidence as well. In much of Africa, for example, great animal herds or burrowing animals will often have disturbed surface material, so that the archaeologist may be able to examine only very broad distribution patterns. Geologists and environmental specialists can generally provide useful advice.

This background information will help determine the intensity of surface coverage of the survey. Other factors to take into consideration are the time and resources available, and how easy it is actually to reach and record an area. Arid (dry) and semi-arid environments with little vegetation are among the best for this type of work, whereas in equatorial rainforest survey may be limited to soil exposures along river banks, unless time and labor permit the cutting of trails to form a survey grid. Many regions, of course, contain a variety of landscapes, and a single survey strategy is often inadequate to cover them. Flexibility of approach is required, with the area "stratified" into zones of differing visibility, and an appropriate technique devised for each. Moreover, it must be remembered that some archaeological phases (with diagnostic artifacts or pottery styles) are more "visible" than others, and that mobile hunter-gatherer or pastoral communities leave a very different – and generally sparser – imprint on the landscape than do agricultural or urban communities (see Chapter 5). All these factors must be taken into account when planning the search patterns and recovery techniques.

Surveying equipment: a Total Station Theodolite, being used on a site in Scotland, records a point in three dimensions and incorporates an Electronic Distance Measurer (EDM).

Another point to consider is whether material should be collected or merely examined for its associations and context (where context is disturbed, as in parts of Africa, mentioned above, collection is often the most sensible option). And should collection be total or partial? Usually, a sampling method is employed (see box, pp. 76–77).

There are two basic kinds of surface survey: the *unsystematic* and the *systematic*. The former is the simpler, involving walking across each part of the area (for example, each plowed field), scanning the strip of ground along one's path, collecting or examining artifacts on the surface, and recording their location together with that of any surface features. It is generally felt, however, that the results may be biased and misleading. Walkers have an inherent desire to find material, and will therefore tend to concentrate on those areas that seem richer, rather than obtaining a sample representative of the whole area that would enable the archaeologist to assess the varying distribution of material of different periods or types.

Most modern survey is done in a systematic way, employing either a grid system or a series of equally spaced traverses or transects. The area to be searched is divided into sectors, and these (or a sample of them, see box, p. 75) are walked systematically. In this way, no part of the area is either under- or over-represented in the survey. This method also makes it easier to plot the location of finds since one's exact position is always known. Even greater accuracy can be attained by subdividing the traverses into units of fixed length, some of which can then be more carefully examined.

Results tend to be more reliable from long-term projects that cover the region repeatedly, since the visibility of sites and artifacts can vary widely from year to year or even with the seasons, thanks to vegetation and changing land-use. In addition, members of field crews inevitably differ in the accuracy of their observations, and in their ability to recognize and describe sites (the more carefully one looks, and the more experience one has, the more one sees); this factor can never be totally eliminated, but repeated coverage can help to counter its effects. The use of standardized recording forms makes it easy to put the data into a computer at a later stage.

Finally, it may be necessary or desirable to carry out small excavations to supplement or check the surface data (particularly for questions of chronology, contemporaneity, or site function), or to test hypotheses which have arisen from the survey. The two types of investigation are complementary, not mutually exclusive. Their major difference can be summarized as follows: excavation tells us a lot about a little of a site, and can only be done once, whereas survey tells us a little about a lot of sites, and can be repeated.

Extensive and Intensive Survey. Surveys can be made more extensive by combining results from a series of individual projects in neighboring regions to produce very large-scale views of change in landscape, land-use, and settlement through time – though, as with individual members of a field crew, the accuracy and quality of different survey projects may vary widely. Outstanding syntheses of regional survey have been produced in parts of Mesoamerica (see Chapter 13) and Mesopotamia, areas which already have a long tradition of this type of work.

In Mesopotamia, for example, the pioneering work by Robert Adams and others, combining surface and aerial survey, has produced a picture of changing settlement size and spacing through time leading to the first cities: scattered agricultural villages became more clustered as population increased, and eventually by the Early Dynastic Period (3rd millennium BC) major centers of distribution had arisen, interconnected by routes of communication. The work has also revealed former watercourses and canals, and even probable zones of cultivation. Alternatively survey can be made more intensive by aiming at total coverage of a single large site or site-cluster – what one might call micro-

regional survey. It is a paradox that some of the world's greatest and most famous archaeological sites have never, or only recently, been studied in this way, since attention has traditionally focused on the grandiose monuments themselves rather than on any attempt to place them within even a local context. At Teotihuacán, near Mexico City, a major mapping project initiated in the 1960s has added hugely to our knowledge of the area around the great pyramid-temples (box, pp. 90–91).

Surface survey has a vital place in archaeological work, and one that continues to grow in importance. In modern projects, however, it is usually supplemented (and often preceded) by reconnaissance from the air, one of the most important advances made by archaeology this century. In fact, the availability of air photographs can be an important factor in selecting and delineating an area for surface survey.

Aerial Reconnaissance

It must be stressed that aerial reconnaissance, particularly aerial photography, is not merely or even predominantly used for the discovery of sites, being more crucial to their recording and interpretation, and to monitoring changes in them through time.

Two early examples of aerial photography. (Left) The first air photograph of Stonehenge (or of any archaeological site) taken from a balloon in 1906. (Right) Crop-marks reveal massive earthworks at Poverty Point, Louisiana, dating from 1500–700 BC.

ARCHAEOLOGICAL AERIAL RECONNAISSANCE

Archaeologists use aircraft to search the ground for traces of former sites and past landscapes. Photographs are usually oblique and taken by hand-held cameras. Such oblique photography is a selective process, involving archaeological judgment, in contrast to the unselective view obtained by vertical survey. Single-frame shots of a site or feature are usual, although stereoscopic pairs of obliques considerably assist subsequent interpretation. Oblique aerial photographs show sites in the context of the landscape and can also be used for preparing archaeological maps.

How Sites Show from the Air

A comprehensive knowledge of the ways in which sites show from the air is essential. Those who take and use aerial photographs must understand the means by which the evidence is made visible in order to determine the type of feature that has been recorded. Conventionally, features photographed from the air are often described according to the way they are revealed, rather than by the archaeological reality they represent, thus "earthworks," "soil marks," or "crop-marks." It is more helpful to extend these descriptions, as, for instance, "earthworks showing the ramparts of an enclosure," or "the soil mark of a leveled burial mound," or "crop-marked ditches of a probable settlement."

Earthworks is a term used to describe banks and associated ditches, or stone-walled features – in fact, any feature that can be seen in relief. These features are usually revealed from the air as *shadow marks* – an effect that is dependent on the lighting and weather conditions at the time of photography. They also show in relief when viewed as a stereoscopic pair. Such features may also be seen by the differences in vegetation supported by banks and ditches, by differential melting or drifting of snow, or by retention of water in ditches in times of flood. Time of day and time of year are thus important in the discovery and recording of such sites.

Soil-marks reveal the presence of buried ditches, banks, or foundations by the changes in subsoil color caused when a plowshare catches and turns over part of the buried feature, bringing it to the surface. Most soil-marked sites are being destroyed by modern cultivation. They are mostly visible in photographs taken in winter months. Bare soil will sometimes also reveal features through differential moisture retention – *damp marks* – or by differences in thermal properties that affect the melting of snow and frost.

Crop-marks develop when a buried wall or ditch either decreases or enhances crop growth by affecting the availability of moisture and nutrients through changing the depth of soil. Suitable crops, such as wheat, barley, and some root vegetables, provide a perfect medium for revealing features in the underlying soil. This response to buried features is very delicate and dependent on variables such as the type and condition of soil, weather during the growing season, crop type, and agricultural practices. Thus features can stand out strongly in one year and be invisible the next. Knowledge of recent and past land-use in an area can be particularly valuable when assessing the potential of apparently blank modern fields. Some features simply do not produce crop-marked evidence.

Earthwork seen from the air: the Iron Age hillfort of Maiden Castle, southern England, whose complex ramparts are thrown into relief by shadows cast by massive earthen banks. The air photograph also highlights an interesting earlier feature: a shallow Neolithic ditch running across the middle of the fort.

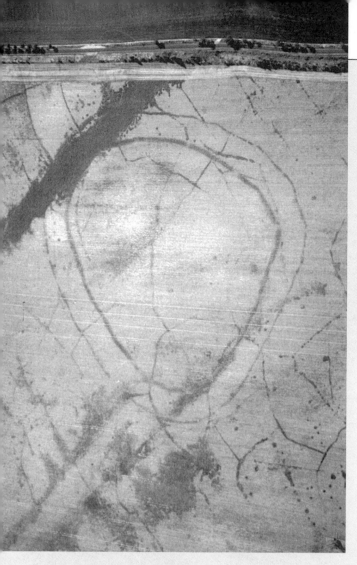

Winter plowing has scraped the chalk foundations of this Gallo-Roman villa in France. This process of destruction has in fact revealed the plan of its main structures against the dark soil.

Crop-marks clearly reveal two concentric rings of ditches defining an enclosure at Merzien, Sachsen-Anhalt, Germany. Both ditch circuits are interrupted and may therefore be of Neolithic date.

Photo Interpretation and Mapping

Interpretation is the process by which features photographed from the air, such as soil-marks, are analyzed in order to deduce the types of archaeological structures causing them. Given that the visibility of features varies from year to year, photos taken over several years need to be studied to compile an accurate plan. Such plans may guide excavation to key points in a structure, place field-collected data in context, or themselves be used as the starting point for new research.

Aerial photos can also be employed to produce a map of known features within a region. Many such records are drawn on to transparent sheets that are overlaid on to maps showing topographical or other information, but more up-to-date systems have converted such information as part of Geographic Information Systems (GIS: see main text).

How crop-marks are formed: crops grow taller and more thickly over sunken features such as ditches (1), and show stunted growth over buried walls (2). Such variations may not be obvious at ground level, but are often visible from the air, as different colored bands of vegetation.

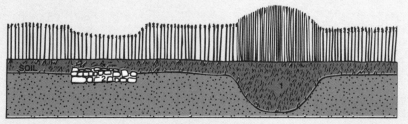

SOIL

Nevertheless, air photography – together with remote sensing from space (see below) – has been responsible for a large number of discoveries, and continues to find more sites every year.

Aerial Photography. The first major archaeological applications of this technique occurred at the start of the century with photographs of the Roman town of Ostia taken from a balloon, and in 1913 when Sir Henry Wellcome took vertical pictures of his excavations in the Sudan by means of a box kite. World War I gave the technique a great impetus when archaeologists such as O.G.S. Crawford in England discovered the clarity that air photographs taken from aircraft and balloons could provide in their plan view of prehistoric monuments.

In Syria, from 1925 onward, Father Antoine Poidebard began tracing ancient caravan routes leading to Roman frontier defenses in the desert; using observation from the air, he discovered many new forts and roads. He also showed that underwater sites could be detected from the air, revealing for the first time the ancient harbor beneath the sea at Tyre, Lebanon – a study which was combined with survey by divers and partial excavation. Poidebard's work was paralleled by that of Erich Schmidt over Iran in the 1930s. His photographs documented his excavations in progress as well as sites he was thinking of digging, and he made reconnaissance flights over previously uncharted areas. Similarly, in 1927, military planes photographed Late Bronze Age oak pile structures through the waters of

Lake Neuchâtel, Switzerland. In the New World, Alfred Kidder flew in 1929 with pioneer aviator Charles Lindbergh over central and eastern Yucatán, in Mexico, and discovered half-a-dozen new sites within a vast and impenetrable jungle landscape. They also made flights over Arizona and New Mexico looking for ancient villages.

From these beginnings aerial photography has developed into one of the archaeologist's most valued aids. New opportunities have arisen in central and eastern Europe since the fall of the Iron Curtain in 1989. Before that time there were restrictions on flying and no archaeological reconnaissance was allowed. Recently, there has been considerable activity in the air over former Soviet areas which has shown that they were as densely occupied as some of the best-known parts of Britain and western Europe. Whole landscapes are beginning to be recorded by projects that integrate aerial and field survey. Recent work by, for example, the aerial photographer Otto Braasch from Germany and landscape archaeologist Martin Gojda in the Czech Republic has marked the beginnings of aerial survey in those regions. The Aerial Archaeology Research Group has run training weekends in Hungary (1996), and Poland (1998) to introduce aerial photography, interpretation, and mapping primarily to ex-Warsaw Pact countries, with great success.

In Britain and Europe aerial photographs are mainly collected in specialist libraries, which may be held regionally or in major national collections, such as the National Library of Air Photographs in England. This

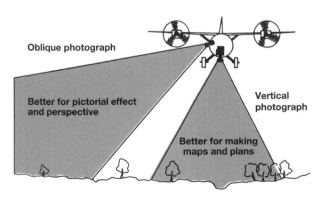

(Above) Aerial photographs are of two types: oblique and vertical. Obliques are easier to view and understand than verticals but may present more difficulty to the interpreter who must transform the information to plan views.

(Right) Aerial photography is also useful in surveying large or inaccessible areas, such as the eastern frontier of the Roman empire; this is a fort or palace at Qasr Bshir, Jordan.

Oblique photograph

Better for pictorial effect and perspective

Vertical photograph

Better for making maps and plans

currently holds 0.75 million specialist oblique prints dating from 1906 to the present, and over 3 million vertical survey photographs spanning the years 1940 to 1979.

How Are Aerial Photographs Used? Photographs taken from the air are merely tools; they are means to an end. Photographs do not themselves reveal sites – it is the photographer and the interpreter who do so, by examination of the terrain and the pictures. These are specialized skills. Long experience and a keen eye are needed to differentiate archaeological traces from other features such as vehicle tracks, old river beds, and canals. Indeed, most military intelligence units during the final years of World War II had archaeologists on their staff as interpreters of air photographs. Glyn Daniel's expertise, for example, proved invaluable to British military photo-intelligence, and he ended the war running a large unit in India.

Aerial photographs are of two types: *oblique* and *vertical*. Each has its advantages and drawbacks, but oblique photographs have usually been taken of sites observed from the air by an archaeologist and thought to be of archaeological significance, whereas most vertical photographs result from non-archaeological surveys (for instance, cartographic). Both types can be used to provide overlapping stereoscopic pairs of prints which enable a scene to be examined in three dimensions and so add confidence to any interpretation. Stereoscopic pictures taken of the ancient city of Mohenjodaro in Pakistan from a tethered balloon, for example, have enabled photogrammetric – accurately contoured – plans to be made of its surviving structures. Similarly, large areas can be surveyed with overlapping photographs, which are then processed into a very accurate photogrammetric base map of all the archaeological evidence identified from the air. Analytical ground survey can then proceed on a much surer basis.

The ways in which sites show from the air and how they are interpreted are discussed in the box (pp. 80–81). Oblique photographs show archaeological features clearly on the whole, while vertical photographs may need to be examined by an interpreter seeking such information. Vertical prints show a near-plan view from which it is relatively easy to take measurements or make maps, although if there is a large amount of information, computer rectification methods are more efficient. These programs were initially developed to help transform the scale and perspective distortions of oblique photographs but can just as readily be used to scale interpretations made from vertical prints. Known points are matched on photograph and map and this enables the archaeological information to be rectified to plan view. Computer rectification (georeferencing in the U.S.) is the usual method for mapping archaeological features from aerial photographs in Britain and could be a useful tool elsewhere. Site-specific mapping at scales of 1:2500 can show considerable detail within a site and is usually accurate to within ± 2 m (6 ft). This allows features to be measured and compared and is essential in providing precise locations so that excavation trenches can be positioned accurately and cost-effectively. Digital terrain modeling can be applied to computer transformations in places where the ground is undulating or has high relief. After computer rectification the resulting plan may be brought to a final form using commercial graphics software or edited and incorporated as a GIS record (Geographic Information Systems – see below).

Mapping of individual sites from aerial photographs is necessary in cases of salvage excavation and also forms the beginning from which landscapes may be mapped and considered. This ability to study large areas is often only possible using aerial resources. In Britain, Roger Palmer used thousands of individual photographs of a 450-sq. km (175-sq. mile) territory around the Iron Age hillfort of Danebury to produce accurate maps which show that the site lay within very complex agricultural landscapes within which there were at least 8 other hillforts. Crop- and soil-marks

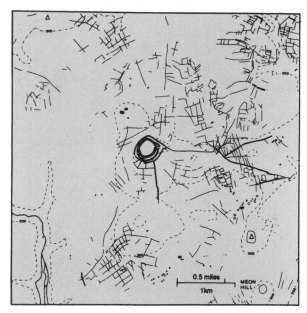

Map of the area around Danebury, an Iron Age hillfort in southern Britain (6th–2nd centuries BC), created from aerial survey, with details of ancient fields, tracks, and enclosures.

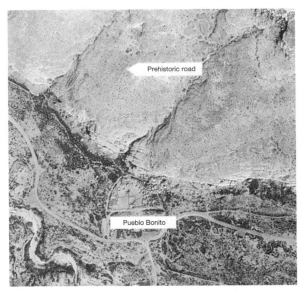

Chaco Canyon and its system of roads, visible from the air.

(see box, pp. 80–81) revealed the presence of 120 ditched farming enclosures, hundreds of acres of small fields, regularly arranged, and 240 km (150 miles) of linear ditches and boundary works, many of which were roughly contemporaneous with Danebury to judge from their forms and/or surface finds.

Although it was known that prehistoric roadways existed within Chaco Canyon in the American Southwest, it was only when a major aerial reconnaissance project was undertaken by the National Park Service in the 1970s that the full extent of the system of roads was appreciated. Using the extensive coverage provided by the aerial photographs a whole network of prehistoric roadways was identified and mapped. This was followed up with selective ground surveys and some archaeological investigation. From the aerial coverage it has been estimated that the network, thought to date to the 11th and 12th centuries AD, extends some 1500 miles (2400 km), though of this only 130 miles (208 km) has been verified by examination at ground level.

Recent Developments in Aerial Photography. New technology is having an impact on aerial photography in different ways. Computer enhancement of pictures can improve their sharpness and contrast. Digital manipulation of images has also been developed and enables a single image, from an oblique or vertical photograph, to be transformed to match the map of the area. Computer programs also exist which allow several images to be transformed and then combined. This is especially useful in cases where a site may lie in two modern fields from which crop-marked information has been recorded in different years. Such plan-form images may help subsequent photo interpretation and mapping. Use of aerial data as a GIS layer may lead to fruitful results from analyses in conjunction with topographic and other archaeological information.

Although black-and-white panchromatic film is still generally used in air photography – because of its cheapness and high resolution – it may be worth employing infrared film as well. This detects radiation just beyond the visible spectrum and has produced some good results over moorland vegetation and in some cereal crops. In Germany false-color infrared film has produced very good results in bare soil conditions by accentuating moisture differences. By contrast, infrared linescan (IRLS) imagery results from equipment that scans from horizon to horizon to detect and record actual temperature differences (thermal prospection) on continuous video tape. Use of IRLS during flights by the British Royal Air Force has led to the identification of a number of new sites, mainly on grass and bare soils in Scotland, but its use is handicapped by the inherent distortion of the image. Computer programs can transform these images to plan views but the resolution cannot match that achieved by conventional photographic films. Recent developments in digital image capture have been advanced by Kodak, who market a system based on a conventional 35mm camera body and lens, but again the achievable resolution is not wholly adequate for capturing the level of detail necessary to record the range of crop- and soil-marked archaeology in Britain and Europe. Most archaeological reconnaissance in these countries is carried out using conventional films, either monochrome or (increasingly) color in order to make high-definition photographs on stock that has good archival permanence.

New World archaeological projects now routinely use the commercially available and cost-effective black-and-white aerial photographs. The 9 × 9 in negatives can be enlarged considerably before showing grain and thus quite small features such as walls, pits, etc. can be clearly seen. Digital cameras may be used to advantage to acquire images of larger-scale structures and systems, more common in arid and jungle zones.

Remote Sensing from High Altitude. Photographs taken from satellites or the space shuttle have a limited application to archaeology, since their scale is often huge, but images from the LANDSAT (Earth Resources Technology) satellites have proved useful. Scanners record the intensity of reflected light and the infrared radiation from the earth's surface, and convert these electronically into photographic images. LANDSAT images have been used to trace large-scale features such as ancient levee systems in Mesopotamia and an ancient riverbed running from the deserts of Saudi Arabia to Kuwait, as well as sediments around Ethiopia's Rift Valley that are likely to contain hominid fossil beds; Space Imaging Radar (which can reveal features beneath 5 m (16 ft) of sand) has been used from the space shuttle to locate ancient riverbeds beneath the deserts of Egypt and hundreds of kilometers of long-abandoned caravan routes in Arabia, many of which converged on a spot in Oman, that may be the lost city of Ubar. Similarly, a radar sensor on the shuttle located ancient watercourses in China's Taklamakan Desert, along which lost settlements can be sought.

In Montana, 8 quarries worked up to 10,000 years ago have been detected by a team from the University of Colorado using the spectral "signatures" of their characteristic geological and vegetational patterns, since different frequencies of radiation detected by satellites provide information about the types of rocks and plants. In Nigeria, Patrick Darling has used both satellite imagery and vertical aerial photographs to carry out major surveys of large areas including swamp forest, tropical rainforest, and savannah, and has identified 1600 walled settlements and more than 16,000 km (10,000 miles) of linear earth boundaries, some surviving to heights of more than 18 m (60 ft) – this has made a huge contribution to the picture of the past that had been put together from piecemeal excavations.

The most remarkable archaeological application so far, however, has been in Mesoamerica. Using false-color LANDSAT imagery, in which natural colors are converted into more sharply contrasting hues, NASA scientists working with archaeologists in 1983 found an extensive network of Maya farmed fields and settlements in the Yucatán peninsula of Mexico. In this expensive experiment, costing $250,000, Maya ruins showed up in false color as tiny dots of blue, pink, and light red – blue for ancient reservoirs cut out of the limestone surface, pink and light red for vegetation on and adjacent to the sites. By looking for examples of blue dots next to pink and light red ones, archaeologists were able to pinpoint 112 sites. They visited 20 by helicopter in order to verify their conclusions.

The project also found an unknown city with twin pyramids, dating to the Classic Maya phase of AD 600–900; and relocated the major city of Oxpemul which had been discovered in the early 1930s but was then lost again in the thick jungle. However, the most important result was the detection of a large network (covering an area 65 km (40 miles) long and 4.8 km (3 miles) wide) of walled fields and house-mounds near

Flores Magón, which effectively destroyed the already discredited theory that Maya civilization was based on a shifting type of agriculture, without regularly maintained fields.

Recent advances in satellite sensors have resulted in much improved resolution. Images from LANDSAT Thematic Mapper (TM) comprise pixels which define the ground in 30 × 30 m blocks – the examples above show that this can have archaeological application. Higher definition is available from the French SPOT satellite which has a panchromatic sensor that can achieve 10 m (33 ft) resolution. LANDSAT TM imagery has recently been used by Chris Cox in Britain to define areas of peat in the wetlands of Cumbria while LANDSAT TM and SPOT were used by a team from Durham University to detect and map part of the system of extinct water courses in the East Anglian Fenland. Elsewhere in Britain, Martin Fowler has tested the resolving power of satellite images in his studies of round barrows and other features in the Stonehenge area. The limitations are mainly due to the resolving power of the imagery which is constantly improving. Recently released Russian military imagery uses multi-spectral sensors with a resolution of 5–7 m (16–23 ft), and their panchromatic sensor has a ground resolution of 2–5 m (6.5–16 ft). The American Central Intelligence Agency has allowed some access to its archives of satellite images but is unlikely to make available that of the highest resolution – speculated to be in the order of 5–10 cm (2–4 in) and therefore offering considerable potential for archaeological studies.

Declassified US images can now be browsed on the web (at edcwww.cr.usgs.gov) and ordered as prints or negatives for about $18 per frame – these excellent high-resolution images are on 70 mm film, and are about 1 m (3 ft) in length. Despite the relatively low cost, however, as long as the resolution remains inferior to that of conventional aerial photography, the latter will continue to play a crucial role. As with conventional aerial photographs, satellite images need to be taken at an appropriate time of year for crop-marks and other such features to stand out, but – as is shown by a Russian image of the Stonehenge area – they can sometimes show a remarkable amount of detail, equal to that on conventional 1:10,000 vertical photos.

Much of this recent use of satellite imagery has identified the known rather than discovering the unknown but it has shown the capabilities of these very high altitude remotely sensed media. Study of an area of Thailand by J.T. Parry compared features interpreted from conventional vertical aerial photographs, at scales between 1:15,000 and 1:50,000, with those that could be identified on color infrared composite

LANDSAT images. Interpretation of the LANDSAT data was undertaken using projected images that were matched to maps at scales of 1:250,000 or zoomed to 1:50,000. Sites identified were large moated sites, for which LANDSAT was excellent, and smaller mounds (some 75 percent were detected), while canals showed only poorly (23 percent) compared to conventional aerial photographs.

Another remote sensing technique, *sideways-looking airborne radar* (SLAR), has also yielded evidence suggesting that Maya agriculture was more intensive than previously imagined. The technique involves recording in radar images the return of pulses of electromagnetic radiation sent out from a flying aircraft. Since radar will penetrate cloud cover and to some extent dense rainforest, Richard Adams and his colleagues were able to use SLAR from a high-flying NASA aircraft to scan 80,000 sq. km (31,200 sq. miles) of the Maya lowlands. The SLAR images revealed not only ancient cities and field systems, but an enormous lattice of grey lines some of which may have been canals, to judge by subsequent inspections by canoe. If field testing – which has scarcely begun – shows that the canals are ancient, it will show that the Maya had an elaborate irrigation and water transport system.

High altitude radar mapping has also helped reveal a hitherto undocumented people in Costa Rica. In 1984–85, Thomas Sever of NASA flew over the area around the volcano of Mount Arenal, which was of interest to archaeologists because local people had found potsherds and tools when roads were cut through the terrain of ash. Sever scanned the area using radar, infrared photographic film, and a device called lidar (light detection apparatus). The resulting images showed roadways radiating from a central graveyard. Subsequent excavation of 62 sites by Payson Sheets revealed that a wandering people had lived in the volcano's shadow since about 11,000 BC, and had settled permanently on the shore of Lake Arenal in 2000 BC. Their campsites, graves, and houses had been buried and protected by a volcanic eruption.

Recently, the vast ruins of the 1000-year-old temple complex of Angkor in northern Cambodia, which cover an area of about 260 sq. km (100 sq. miles) and are shrouded in dense jungle and surrounded by landmines, have been the subject of new studies using high-resolution radar imagery obtained from the space shuttle. The resulting dark squares and rectangles on the images are stone moats and reflecting pools around the temples. The main temple complex of Angkor Wat is readily visible as a small square bounded with black. The most important discovery for archaeologists so far has been the network of ancient canals surrounding

A satellite image of the huge ancient site of Angkor in Cambodia: new temples have been discovered in this way.

the city (visible as light lines) which irrigated rice fields and fed the pools and moats. They were probably also used to transport the massive stones needed for constructing the complex.

In addition, British archaeologist Elisabeth Moore has examined both the satellite images and pictures taken from a DC-8 airplane equipped with AIRSAR (Airborne Synthetic Aperture Radar), which makes a three-dimensional map from stereo-images, and discovered some splendid, hitherto unknown temples and mounds, traces of a city predating the great Khmer capital by two or three centuries. She believes that the finds call into question the traditional concepts of the urban evolution of Angkor.

The application of these exciting new techniques to archaeology is only just beginning. So long as they remain expensive, conventional air photography will, however, continue to dominate aerial reconnaissance. But advanced airborne remote sensing techniques will no doubt become cheaper and more widespread in the future.

Recording and Mapping Sites in Reconnaissance Survey

As already noted in the discussion of air photography, the pinpointing of sites and features on regional maps is an essential next step in reconnaissance survey. To have discovered a site is one thing, but only when it has been adequately recorded does it become part of the sum total of knowledge about the archaeology of a region.

Mapping is the key to the accurate recording of most survey data. For surface features, such as buildings and roads, both topographic and planimetric maps are used. Topographic maps represent differences in elevation or height by means of contour lines and help relate ancient structures to the surrounding landscape. Planimetric maps exclude contour lines and topographic information, concentrating instead on the broad outlines of features, thus making it easier, for example, to understand the relationship of different buildings to each other. On some site maps the two techniques are combined, with natural relief depicted topographically and archaeological features planimetrically.

In addition to plotting a site on a map – including its exact latitude, longitude, and map grid reference – proper recording entails giving the site some kind of locational designation and entering this on a site record form, along with information about who owns the site, its condition, and other details. Locational designations vary in different parts of the world. In the United States they usually consist of a two-digit number for the state, a pair of letters for the county, and a number indicating that this is the 59th (or whatever) site discovered in that county. Thus site 36WH297 designates the 297th site discovered in Washington County (WH), in the state of Pennsylvania (36). This is the locational designation for the famous Paleo-Indian site of Meadowcroft Rockshelter. One of the great values of designating sites using these alpha-numerical systems is that they can be entered easily on computer files, for quick data retrieval, e.g. in salvage archaeology or settlement pattern studies.

Geographic Information Systems

A significant new development in archaeological mapping is the use of GIS (Geographic Information Systems), described in one official report as "the biggest step forward in the handling of geographic information since the invention of the map." A GIS provides a map-based interface to a database; in other words, GIS are designed for the collection, storage, retrieval, analysis, and display of spatial data. GIS developed out of computer-aided design and mapping (CAD/CAM) programs during the 1970s. Some CAD programs, such as AutoCAD, can be linked to commercial databases and have proved valuable in allowing the automatic mapping of archaeological sites held in a computer database. A true GIS, however, also incorporates the ability to carry out a statistical analysis of site distribution, and to generate new information. Given information about slope and distance, for example, a GIS can also be used for *cost-surface analysis*, mapping catchment areas and site territories taking the surrounding terrain into account. The software and digital landscape information are fed into a computer, along with (as a standard measurement) the figure of 1 hour for a 5-km walk on the flat. The software then does the calculations, using built-in data on the energy cost of traversing different kinds of terrain. Therefore GIS have applications far beyond recording and mapping, and we shall return to their analytical capabilities in Chapters 5 and 6.

A GIS will hold information on the location and attributes of each site or point recorded. Spatial data can be reduced to three basic types: point, line, and polygon (or area). Each of these units can be stored along with an identifying label and a number of non-spatial attributes, such as name, date, or material.

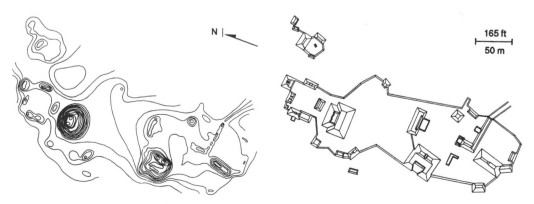

Two ways of presenting survey results, as exemplified by the Maya site of Nohmul, Belize. (Left) A topographic map relating the site to its landscape. (Right) A planimetric map showing the individual features of the site.

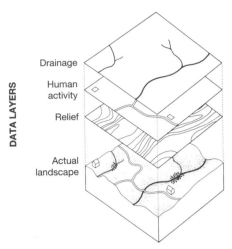

DATA LAYERS

Drainage

Human activity

Relief

Actual landscape

Diagram showing possible GIS data layers.

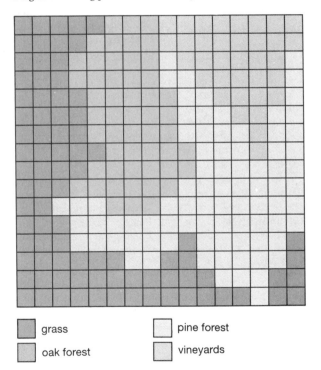

☐ grass   ☐ pine forest

☐ oak forest   ☐ vineyards

Raster representation of a data layer showing vegetation: each cell is coded according to the main vegetation type.

Each map (sometimes described in a GIS as a layer or coverage) may comprise a combination of points, lines, and polygons, along with their non-spatial attributes.

Within a map layer the data may be held in *vector* format, as points, lines, and polygons, or they may be stored as a grid of cells, or *raster* format. A raster layer recording vegetation, for example, would comprise a grid within which each cell contains information on the vegetation present at that point. Originally, GIS were either raster or vector-based systems and were not compatible. Nowadays, however, most commercial systems will allow these different data structures to be mixed.

Topographic maps represent an enormous amount of environmental data on relief, communications, hydrology etc. In order to make use of this within a GIS environment it is normal to divide the information into different map layers, each representing a single variable. Archaeological data may themselves be split into several layers, most often so that each layer represents a discrete time slice. As long as they can be spatially located, many different types of data can be integrated in a GIS. These can include site plans, satellite images, aerial photographs, geophysical survey, as well as maps.

The ability to incorporate satellite and aerial photographs can be particularly valuable for site reconnaissance as they can provide detailed and current land-use information. Many topographic data already exist in the form of digital maps which can be taken directly into a GIS, although considerations of cost, copyright, and the resolution of the data can create obstacles for some GIS projects. Digitizing large numbers of paper maps by hand represents a laborious undertaking. Use can also be made of a handheld Global Positioning System (GPS) to provide a longitude and latitude for a position on the ground, by reference to satellites. These are extremely useful where a region is unmapped, or where the maps are old or inaccurate. Although most archaeological applications have so far focused on landscape survey, there is also no reason why a GIS should not be used at a finer scale to examine spatial relationships within an individual site.

Once data are stored within a GIS it is relatively straightforward to generate maps on demand, and to query the database to select particular categories of site to be displayed. Individual map layers, or combinations of layers, can be selected according to the subject under investigation. The ability of GIS to incorporate archaeological data within modern development plans allows a more accurate assessment of their archaeological impact. In addition, GIS can help in predicting site location by combining data layers that each in some way help determine a site's location.

A single archaeological find might therefore be represented by an easting and northing and a find number, while an ancient road would be recorded as a string of coordinate pairs and its name. A field system could be defined as strings of coordinates following each field boundary, along with reference names or numbers.

One of the earliest, and most widespread, uses of GIS within archaeology has been the construction of *predictive models* of site locations. Most of the development of these techniques has taken place within North American archaeology, where the enormous spatial extent of some archaeological landscapes means that it is not always possible to survey them comprehensively. The underlying premise of all predictive models is that particular kinds of archaeological sites tend to occur in the same kinds of place. For example, certain settlement sites tend to occur close to sources of fresh water and on southerly aspects because these provide ideal conditions in which to live (not too cold, and within easy walking distance of a water source). Using this information it is possible to model how likely a given location is to contain an archaeological site from the known environmental characteristics of that location. In a GIS environment this operation can be done for an entire landscape producing a predictive model map for the whole area.

An example was developed by the Illinois State Museum for the Shawnee National Forest in southern Illinois. It predicts the likelihood of finding a prehistoric site anywhere within the 91 sq. km (35 sq. miles) of the forest by using the observed characteristics of the 68 sites which are known from the 12 sq. km (4.6 sq. miles) which have been surveyed. A GIS database was constructed for the entire area including data themes for elevation, slope, aspect, distance to water, soil type, and depth to the watertable. The characteristics of the known sites were compared with the characteristics of the locations known not to contain sites using a statistical procedure known as logistic regression. This is a probability model whose result is an equation which can be used to predict the probability that any location with known environmental characteristics will contain a prehistoric site.

Recently, the potential value of predictive modeling with GIS has also become apparent outside North America, particularly in the Netherlands and in Britain. Such models can be of value both in understanding the possible distribution of archaeological sites within a landscape, and also for the protection and management of archaeological remains in cultural resource management (see Chapter 14).

Many GIS applications, especially those based on predictive modeling, have been criticized as being environmentally deterministic, and it is easy to see why. Environmental data such as soil types, rivers, altitude, and land use can be measured, mapped, and converted into digital data, whereas cultural and social aspects of landscape are much more problematic In an attempt to escape from these more functionalist analyses, archaeologists have used the GIS function called viewsheds to try to develop more humanistic appreciations of landscape (see p. 200).

ASSESSING THE LAYOUT OF SITES AND FEATURES

Finding and recording sites and features is the first stage in fieldwork, but the next stage is to make some assessment of site size, type, and layout. These are crucial factors for archaeologists, not only for those who are trying to decide whether, where, and how to excavate, but also for those whose main focus may be the study of settlement patterns, site systems, and landscape archaeology without planning any recourse to excavation.

We have already seen how aerial photographs may be used to plot the layout of sites as well as helping to locate them in the first place. What are the other main methods for investigating sites without excavating them?

Site Surface Survey

The simplest way to gain some idea of a site's extent and layout is through a site surface survey – by studying the distribution of surviving features, and recording and possibly collecting artifacts from the surface.

At the site of Teotihuacán (see box, pp. 90–91), careful survey was used to produce detailed maps of the city.

For artifacts and other objects collected or observed during surface survey, it may not be worth mapping their individual locations if they appear to come from badly disturbed secondary contexts. Or there may simply be too many artifacts realistically to record all their individual proveniences. In this latter instance the archaeologist will probably use sampling procedures for the selective recording of surface finds (see box, pp. 76–77). However, where time and funds are sufficient and the site is small enough, collection and recording of artifacts from the total site area may prove possible. For example, Frank Hole and his colleagues picked up everything from the entire surface of a 1.5-ha (3.7-acre) open-air prehistoric site in the Valley of Oaxaca, Mexico, plotting locations using a grid of 5-m squares. They transformed the results into maps with contour lines indicating not differences in elevation, but relative densities of various types of materials and artifacts. It then became clear that, although some objects

TEOTIHUACAN MAPPING PROJECT

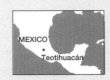

In 1962 the University of Rochester initiated a project, directed by René Millon, to map the pre-Columbian city of Teotihuacán. Located 40 km (25 miles) northeast of Mexico City, the site had been the largest and most powerful urban center in Mesoamerica in its heyday from AD 200 to 650. The layout and orientation of the city had intrigued scholars for decades; however, they considered the grandiose pyramid-temples, plazas, and the major avenue – an area now known as the ceremonial center – to be the entire extent of the metropolis. It was not until the survey conducted by the Teotihuacán Mapping Project that the outer limits, the great east–west axis, and the grid plan of the city were discovered and defined.

Fortunately, structural remains lay just beneath the surface, so that Millon and his team were able to undertake the mapping from a combination of aerial and surface survey, with only small-scale excavation. The survey began with low-altitude aerial photography and preliminary ground reconnaissance to establish a survey grid made up of 147 squares, each 500 m on a side and each with its own map data sheet to be filled in. Using the grid, the city's irregular boundary, enclosing about 20 sq. km (c. 8 sq. miles), was defined by walking the perimeter. The city area itself was then intensively surveyed and mapped, and surface collections made. Individual structures were plotted for each 500-m square, and surface data recorded on special forms. Millions of potsherds were collected, and over 5000 structures and activity areas recorded. Small-scale excavations were also conducted to test the survey results. Eventually Millon and his colleagues combined the architectural interpretation of all this information on to the base map of the whole site, which they then published in conjunction with an explanatory text.

Teotihuacán had been laid out on a regular plan, with four quadrants orientated on the great north–south "Street of the Dead" and another major avenue running east–west across it. Construction had occurred over several centuries, but always following the master plan. The northern quadrant was the oldest residential area, with certain neighborhoods (*barrios*) here and elsewhere in the city apparently reserved for particular craft specialists, as shown by concentrations of obsidian, pottery, and other goods.

Since 1980, a new multi-disciplinary team directed by Rubén Cabrera Castro of the Mexican Institute of Archaeology and History (INAH) has been enlarging the picture, so successfully established by the Teotihuacán Mapping Project. Other teams employed geophysical methods to map a system of caves and tunnels used for extracting construction material, as well as for burials and rituals. Magnetometer and resistivity surveys, undertaken by a team from the National Autonomous University of Mexico led by Linda Manzanilla, were used to create a 3-D reconstruction of subsurface contours.

LEGEND

EXCAVATED ROOM COMPLEX OR OTHER STRUCTURE
UNEXCAVATED ROOM COMPLEX
POSSIBLE ROOM COMPLEX
RM. CMPL. - SOME LIMITS UNCLEAR
TEMPLE PLATFORM
SINGLE STAGE PLATFORM
INSUBSTANTIAL STRUCTURES
MAJOR WALL
WATER COURSE
PROBABLE OLD WATER COURSE
METERS ABOVE MEAN SEA LEVEL
MAPPING PROJECT EXCAVATION

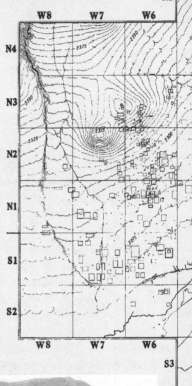

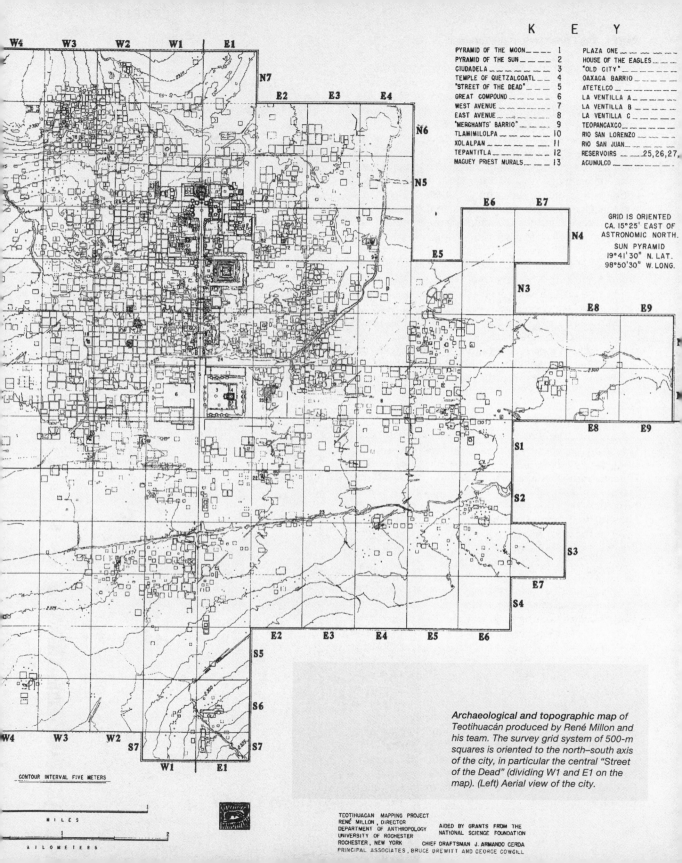

K E Y

PYRAMID OF THE MOON _ _ _ _ 1
PYRAMID OF THE SUN _ _ _ _ 2
CIUDADELA _ _ _ _ _ _ 3
TEMPLE OF QUETZALCOATL _ _ _ 4
"STREET OF THE DEAD" _ _ _ 5
GREAT COMPOUND _ _ _ _ 6
WEST AVENUE _ _ _ _ _ 7
EAST AVENUE _ _ _ _ _ 8
"MERCHANTS' BARRIO" _ _ _ 9
TLAMIMILOLPA _ _ _ _ _ 10
XOLALPAN _ _ _ _ _ _ 11
TEPANTITLA _ _ _ _ _ 12
MAGUEY PRIEST MURALS _ _ _ 13

PLAZA ONE _ _ _ _ _
HOUSE OF THE EAGLES _ _ _
"OLD CITY" _ _ _ _ _
OAXACA BARRIO _ _ _ _
ATETELCO _ _ _ _ _
LA VENTILLA A _ _ _ _
LA VENTILLA B _ _ _ _
LA VENTILLA C _ _ _ _
TEOPANCAXCO _ _ _ _ _
RIO SAN LORENZO _ _ _ _
RIO SAN JUAN _ _ _ _
RESERVOIRS _ 25,26,27,
ACUMULCO _ _ _ _ _

GRID IS ORIENTED
CA. 15°25' EAST OF
ASTRONOMIC NORTH.

SUN PYRAMID
19°41'30" N. LAT.
98°50'30" W. LONG.

CONTOUR INTERVAL FIVE METERS

MILES

KILOMETERS

Archaeological and topographic map of Teotihuacán produced by René Millon and his team. The survey grid system of 500–m squares is oriented to the north–south axis of the city, in particular the central "Street of the Dead" (dividing W1 and E1 on the map). (Left) Aerial view of the city.

TEOTIHUACAN MAPPING PROJECT
RENÉ MILLON, DIRECTOR
DEPARTMENT OF ANTHROPOLOGY
UNIVERSITY OF ROCHESTER
ROCHESTER, NEW YORK
PRINCIPAL ASSOCIATES, BRUCE DREWITT AND GEORGE COWGILL

AIDED BY GRANTS FROM THE
NATIONAL SCIENCE FOUNDATION

CHIEF DRAFTSMAN J. ARMANDO CERDA

such as projectile points were evidently in a secondary context displaced down slopes, others seemed to lie in a primary context and revealed distinct areas for flint-working, seed-grinding, and butchering. These areas served as guides for subsequent excavation.

A similar surface survey was conducted at the Bronze Age city of Mohenjodaro in Pakistan. Here, a team of archaeologists from Pakistan, Germany, and Italy investigated the distribution of craft-working debris and found, to their surprise, that craft activities were not confined to a specific manufacturing zone within the city, but were scattered throughout the site, representing assorted small-scale workshops.

Reliability of Surface Finds. Archaeologists have always used limited surface collection of artifacts as one way of trying to assess the date and layout of a site prior to excavation. However, now that surface survey has become not merely a preliminary to excavation but in some instances a substitute for it – for cost and other reasons, as outlined earlier in this chapter – a vigorous debate is taking place in archaeology about how far surface traces do in fact reflect distributions below ground.

One would logically expect single-period or shallow sites to show the most reliable surface evidence of what lies beneath – an assumption that seems to be borne out by the shallow site of Teotihuacán, or Frank Hole's Oaxaca site mentioned above. Equally one might predict that multi-period, deep sites such as Near Eastern tells or village mounds would show few if any traces on the surface of the earliest and deepest levels. Proponents of the validity of surface survey, while agreeing that there is bound to be a quantitative bias in favor of the most recent periods on the surface, nevertheless point out that one of the surprises for most survey archaeologists is how many of their sites, if collected with care, are truly multi-period, reflecting many phases of a site's use, not just the latest one. The reasons for this are not yet entirely clear, but they certainly have something to do with the kind of formation processes discussed in Chapter 2 – from erosion and animal disturbance to human activity such as plowing.

The relationship between surface and subsurface evidence is undoubtedly complex and varies from site to site. It is therefore wise wherever possible to try to determine what really does lie beneath the ground, perhaps by digging test pits (usually meter squares) to assess a site's horizontal extent, ultimately by more thorough excavation (see below). There are, however, a whole battery of subsurface detection devices that can be brought into play before – or indeed sometimes instead of – excavation, which of course is destructive as well as expensive.

SURFACE INVESTIGATION AT ABU SALABIKH

An effective and simple site investigation strategy has been adopted at Abu Salabikh, Iraq, by Nicholas Postgate. He wanted to study the large-scale layout of an early Mesopotamian city – a considerable challenge, since many of the relevant archaeological deposits lie buried deep within multi-period mounds. However, at Abu Salabikh Postgate found a series of low mounds where occupation layers of a suitably early date lay conveniently just beneath the surface. The site was of a size to daunt most archaeologists (50 ha or 124 acres), but Postgate and his team found that they could obtain good results over wide areas simply by scraping away the shallow topsoil. Exposed immediately beneath were quite clear wall lines which could then be mapped almost as accurately as after actual excavation, and far more quickly.

Potsherds and other artifacts littering the surface were collected, and these were used to suggest earlier or later dates for different parts of the plan. These results could be confirmed by selective excavation.

Surface deposits of a mound on the western side of the site belonged to about 2900 BC, and displayed large, thick-walled, self-contained compounds, each containing separate rectangular houses with courtyards, storerooms, and drainage, as well as fire installations. The main mound, however, revealed houses of c.2500 BC packed tightly side by side, separated by an occasional narrow street. Although only part of the site has been uncovered in this way, it nevertheless represents the largest area of housing known from any 3rd millennium site in southern Iraq.

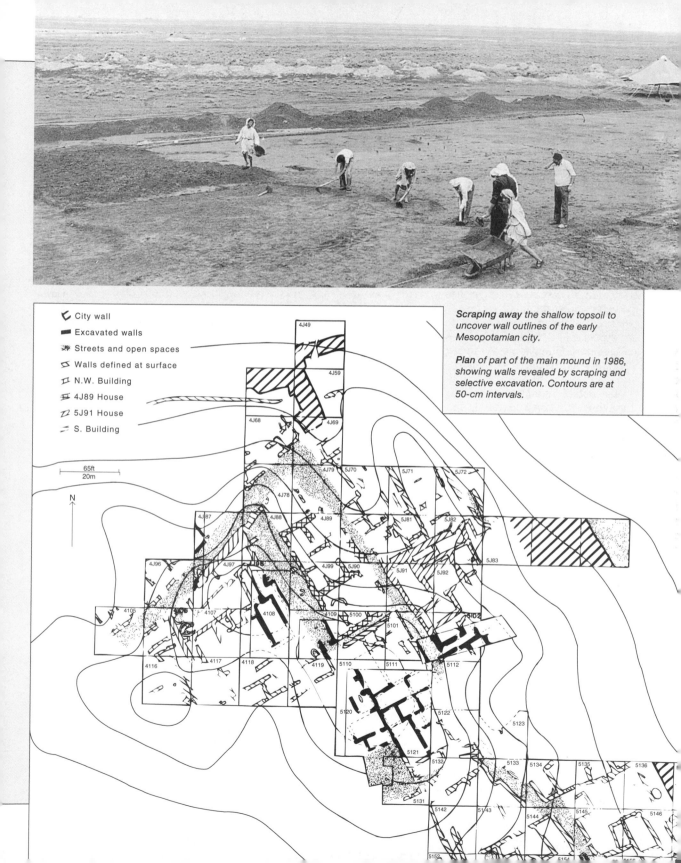

Scraping away the shallow topsoil to uncover wall outlines of the early Mesopotamian city.

Plan of part of the main mound in 1986, showing walls revealed by scraping and selective excavation. Contours are at 50-cm intervals.

Key:

- City wall
- Excavated walls
- Streets and open spaces
- Walls defined at surface
- N.W. Building
- 4J89 House
- 5J91 House
- S. Building

65ft
20m

N

Subsurface Detection

Probes. The most traditional technique is that of probing the soil with rods or borers, and noting the positions where they strike solids or hollows. Metal rods with a T-shaped handle are the most common, but augers – large corkscrews with a similar handle – are also used, and have the advantage of bringing samples of soil to the surface, clinging to the screw. Probing of this type is still employed routinely by some archaeologists – for example, to gauge the depth of the midden at the Ozette site in Washington State (pp. 60–61) or by Chinese archaeologists to plot the 300 pits remaining to be investigated near the first emperor's buried terracotta army. In the mid-1980s, the American archaeologist David Hurst Thomas and his team used over 600 systematically spaced test probes with a gasoline-powered auger in their successful search for a lost 16th-century Spanish mission on St Catherine's Island off the coast of Georgia in the U.S. Augers are also used by geomorphologists studying site sediments. However, there is always a risk of damaging fragile artifacts or features.

One notable advance in this technique was developed by Carlo Lerici in Italy in the 1950s for Etruscan tombs of the 6th century BC. Having detected the precise location of a tomb through aerial photography and soil resistivity (see below), he would bore down into it a hole 8 cm (3 in) in diameter, and insert a long tube with a periscope head and a light, and also a tiny camera attached if needed. Lerici examined some 3500 Etruscan tombs in this way, and found that almost all were completely empty, thus saving future excavators a great deal of wasted effort. He also discovered over 20 with painted walls, thus doubling the known heritage of Etruscan painted tombs at a stroke.

Probing the Pyramids. Modern technology has taken this kind of work even further, with the development of the endoscope (see Chapter 11) and miniature TV cameras. In a project reminiscent of Lerici, a probe was carried out in 1987 of a boat pit beside the Great Pyramid of Cheops (Khufu), in Egypt. This lies adjacent to another pit, excavated in 1954, that contained the perfectly preserved and disassembled parts of a 43-m (141-ft) long royal cedarwood boat of the 3rd millennium BC. The $250,000 probe revealed that the unopened pit does indeed contain all the dismantled timbers of a second boat but that the pit was not airtight – thus dashing hopes of analyzing the "ancient" air to see whether carbon dioxide in the atmosphere had increased over the millennia, and which component of the air preserves antiquities so efficiently.

Projects of this kind are beyond the resources of most archaeologists. But in future, funds permitting, probes of this type could equally well be applied to other Egyptian sites, to cavities in Maya structures, or to the many unexcavated tombs in China.

The Great Pyramid itself has recently been the subject of probes by French and Japanese teams who believe it may contain as yet undiscovered chambers or corridors. Using ultrasensitive microgravimetric equipment – which is normally employed to search for deficiencies in dam walls, and can tell if a stone has a hollow behind it – they detected what they think is a cavity some 3 m (10 ft) beyond one of the passage walls. However, test drilling to support this claim has not been completed and all tests have been stopped by the Egyptian authorities until their potential contribution to Egyptology has been established.

Ground-Based Remote Sensing

Probing techniques are useful, but inevitably involve some disturbance of the site. There are, however, a wide range of non-destructive techniques ideal for the archaeologist seeking to learn more about a site before – or without – excavation. These are geophysical sensing devices which can be either active (i.e. they pass energy of various kinds through the soil and measure the response in order to "read" what lies below the surface); or passive (i.e. they measure physical properties such as magnetism and gravity without the need to inject energy to obtain a response).

Seismic and Acoustic Methods. The simplest way to pass energy through the ground is to strike it. In *bosing* the earth is struck with a heavy wooden mallet or a lead-filled container on a long handle. Recording the resulting sound helps to locate underground features, since a dull sound indicates undisturbed ground, while buried ditches or pits produce a more resonant effect. This crude technique has now been made virtually obsolete through technological advances.

A more refined method, developed by the U.S. Army, has recently been applied to archaeological projects in Japan by Yasushi Nishimura. This *standing wave technique* employs a device which produces and amplifies so-called Rayleigh waves by striking the ground softly and repeatedly. A striker weighing 20 kg (44 lb) can reach depths of 10 m (33 ft), but bigger machines can reach 70 m or even 100 m (230–330 ft). The speed of the waves can be calculated by having two pick-up points a fixed distance apart. Since the waves move fast in hard materials, more slowly in clay or soft materials, features such as buried land surfaces can be detected.

UNDERWATER ARCHAEOLOGY

Underwater archaeology is generally considered to have been given its first major impetus during the winter of 1853–54, when a particularly low water level in the Swiss lakes laid bare enormous quantities of wooden posts, pottery, and other artifacts. From the earliest investigations, using crude diving-bells, it has developed into a valuable complement to work on land. It encompasses a wide variety of sites, including wells, sink holes, and springs (e.g. the great sacrificial well at Chichén Itzá, Mexico); submerged lakeside settlements (e.g. those of the Alpine region); and marine sites ranging from shipwrecks to sunken harbors (e.g. Caesarea, Israel) and drowned cities (e.g. Port Royal, Jamaica).

The invention in recent times of miniature submarines, other submersible craft, and above all of scuba diving gear has been of enormous value, enabling divers to stay underwater for much longer, and to reach sites at previously impossible depths. As a result, the pace and scale of discovery have greatly increased over the last few decades. More than 1000 shipwrecks are known in shallow Mediterranean waters, but recent explorations using deep-sea submersibles have begun to find Roman wrecks at depths of up to 850 m (2790 ft), and two Phoenician wrecks packed with amphorae discovered off the coast of Israel are the oldest vessels ever found in the deep sea.

Underwater Reconnaissance
Geophysical methods are as useful for finding sites underwater as they are for locating land sites (see diagram). For example, in 1979 it was magnetometry combined with side-scan sonar that discovered the *Hamilton* and the *Scourge*, two armed schooners sunk during the War of 1812 at a depth of 90 m (295 ft) in Lake Ontario, Canada.

Nevertheless, in regions such as the Mediterranean the majority of finds have resulted from methods as simple as talking to local sponge-divers, who collectively have spent thousands of hours scouring the seabed.

Underwater Excavation
Excavation underwater is complex and expensive (not to mention the highly demanding post-excavation conservation and analytical work that is also required). Once underway, the excavation may involve shifting vast quantities of sediment, and recording and removing bulky objects as diverse as storage jars (amphorae), metal ingots, and cannons. George Bass, founder of the Institute of Nautical Archaeology in Texas, and others have developed many helpful devices, such as baskets attached to balloons to raise objects, and air lifts (suction hoses) to remove sediment (see diagram). If the vessel's hull survives at all, detailed drawings must be made so that specialists can later reconstruct the overall form and lines, either on paper or in three dimensions as a model or full-size replica (see box, pp. 96–97). In some rare cases, like that of England's *Mary Rose* (16th century AD), preservation is sufficiently good for the remains of the hull to be raised – funds permitting.

Nautical archaeologists have now excavated more than 100 sunken vessels, revealing not only how they were constructed but also many insights into shipboard life, cargoes, trade routes, early metallurgy, and glassmaking. We look in more detail at two projects: the Red Bay Wreck, Canada (pp. 96–97) and the Uluburun Wreck, Turkey (pp. 374–75).

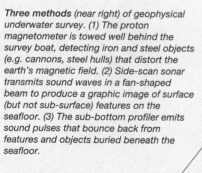

Three methods (near right) of geophysical underwater survey. (1) The proton magnetometer is towed well behind the survey boat, detecting iron and steel objects (e.g. cannons, steel hulls) that distort the earth's magnetic field. (2) Side-scan sonar transmits sound waves in a fan-shaped beam to produce a graphic image of surface (but not sub-surface) features on the seafloor. (3) The sub-bottom profiler emits sound pulses that bounce back from features and objects buried beneath the seafloor.

Underwater excavation techniques (far right): at left, the lift bag for raising objects; center, measuring and recording finds in situ; right, the air lift for removing sediment.

THE RED BAY WRECK: DISCOVERY AND EXCAVATION

Underwater archaeology, in conjunction with archival research and land archaeology, is beginning to yield a detailed picture of whaling undertaken by Basque fishermen at Red Bay, Labrador, in the 16th century AD. The Basques were the largest suppliers to Europe at this time of whale oil – an important commodity used for lighting and in products such as soap.

In 1977, prompted by the discovery in Spanish archives that Red Bay had been an important whaling center, the Canadian archaeologist James A. Tuck began an excavation on the island closing Red Bay harbor. Here he found remains of structures for rendering blubber into whale oil. The next year, the nautical archaeologist Robert Grenier led a Parks Canada team in search of the Basque galleon *San Juan*, which the archives said had sunk in the harbor in 1565.

Structural plan of the wreck on the harbor bottom (2-m grid squares).

Model, at a scale of 1:10, to show how the galleon's surviving timbers may have fitted together.

Project director Robert Grenier (top) examines the remains of an astrolabe (navigational instrument) from Red Bay.

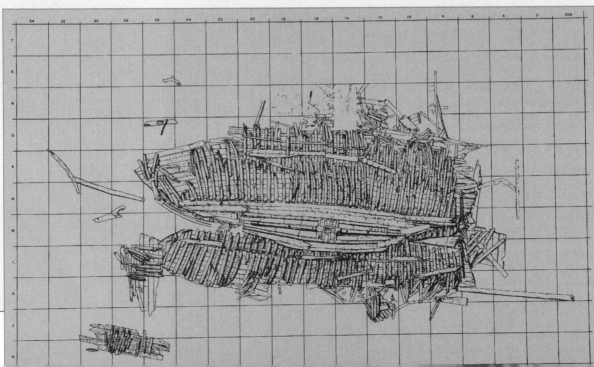

Discovery and Excavation

A wreck believed to be that of the *San Juan* was located at a depth of 10 m (33 ft) in 1978, by a diver towed behind a small boat. A feasibility study carried out the following year confirmed the site's potential, and from 1980 to 1984 Parks Canada undertook a survey and excavation project that employed up to 15 marine archaeologists, backed up by 15–25 support staff, including conservators, draftspersons, and photographers. Two more galleons were discovered in the harbor, but only the supposed *San Juan* was excavated.

The dig was controlled from a specially equipped barge, anchored above the site, that contained a workshop, storage baths for artifacts, a crane for lifting timbers, and a compressor able to run 12 air lifts for removing silt. Salt water was heated on board and pumped down through hoses direct to the divers' suits to maintain body warmth in the near-freezing conditions.

An important technique devised during the project was the use of latex rubber to mold large sections of the ship's timbers in position underwater, thereby reproducing accurately the hull shape and details such as toolmarks and wood grain. The remains of the vessel were also raised in pieces to the surface for precise recording, but the latex molds eliminated the need for costly conservation of the original timbers, which were reburied on-site.

Analysis and Interpretation

On the evidence of the meticulous drawings and molds made during the excavation, a 1:10 scale model was constructed as a research tool to help reveal how the vessel had been built, and what she had looked like. Many fascinating details emerged, for instance that the 14.7-m (48-ft) long keel and bottom row of planks (garboard strakes) had – most unusually for this size of ship – been carved from a single beech tree. Nearly all the rest of the vessel was of oak.

In overview, the research model revealed a whaling ship with fine lines, far removed from the round, tubby shape commonly thought typical of 16th-century merchant vessels.

As the accompanying table (below) indicates, a wealth of artifacts from the wreck shed light on the cargo, navigational equipment, weaponry, and life on board the unlucky galleon.

Thanks to the integrated research design of this Parks Canada project – the largest ever conducted in Canadian waters – many new perspectives are emerging on 16th-century Basque seafaring, whaling, and shipbuilding traditions.

CULTURAL MATERIAL RECOVERED AT RED BAY

THE VESSELS
Whaling ship believed to be the *San Juan:* Hull timbers (more than 3000) • Fittings: capstan, rudder, bow sprit • Rigging: heart blocks, running blocks, shrouds, other cordage • Anchor • Iron nail fragments
Two other whaling ships
Four small boats, some used for whaling
RECOVERED ARTIFACTS
Cargo-Related: Wooden casks (more than 10,000 individual pieces) • Wooden stowage articles: billets, chocks, wedges • Ballast stones (more than 13 tons)
Navigational Instruments: Binnacle • Compass • Sand glass • Log reel and chip • Astrolabe
Food Storage, Preparation, and Serving: Ceramics: coarse earthenware, majolica •

Glass fragments • Pewter fragments • Treen: bowls and platters • Basketry • Copper-alloy spigot key
Food-Related: Cod bones • Mammal bones: polar bear, seal, cow, pig • Bird bones: ducks, gulls, auk • Walnut shells, hazelnut shells, plum pits, bakeapple seeds
Clothing-Related: Leather shoes • Leather fragments • Textile fragments
Personal Items: Coins • Gaming piece • Comb
Weaponry-Related: Verso • Lead shot • Cannonballs • Possible wooden arrow
Tool-Related: Wooden tool handles • Brushes • Grindstone
Building Material: ceramic roof tile fragments
Whaling-Related: Whale bones

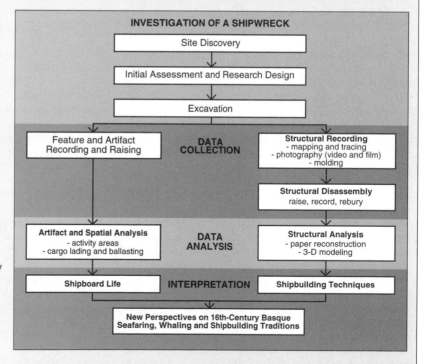

The sections produced can then be transformed into a contour map of the subsurface features.

Other types of echo-sounding, such as sonar, have been employed elsewhere. For example, Kent Weeks and a team from the University of California have systematically mapped tombs in the Valley of the Kings at Thebes in Egypt. Using sonar devices in 1987 they successfully relocated a tomb, the position of which had been lost, only 15 m (49 ft) from that of the pharaoh Ramesses II, which is thought to have belonged to 50 of Ramesses' sons. This has recently revealed itself to be the biggest pharaonic tomb ever found, with at least 67 chambers laid out in a T-shape.

Detection of gravitational anomalies, mentioned in the section on probing the pyramids, can find cavities such as caves. Seismic methods normally used by oil prospectors have helped to trace details of the foundations of St Peter's Basilica in the Vatican in Rome.

One of the most important archaeological applications of echo-sounding techniques, however, is in underwater projects (see box p. 95). For example, after a bronze statue of an African boy was brought up in a sponge diver's net off the Turkish coast, George Bass and his colleagues were able to make a successful search for the Roman ship from which it came by means of echo-location systems.

Electromagnetic Methods. A basically similar method, which employs not sonic but radio pulses, is ground penetrating (or probing) radar (GPR). An emitter sends short pulses through the soil, and the echoes not only reflect back any changes in the soil and sediment conditions encountered, such as filled ditches, graves, walls, etc., but also measure the depth at which the changes occur on the basis of the travel time of the pulses. Three-dimensional maps of buried archaeological remains can then be produced from data processing and image-generation programs (see "time-slices" below).

In the field, the technique usually employs a single surface radar antenna which transmits very short pulses of electromagnetic energy (radar waves) down into the ground. A receiver records reflections from the discontinuities encountered, whether these are natural changes in soil horizons or properties, or buried archaeological features. The time it takes radar waves to travel from the surface source to the discontinuity and back to the receiver is measured in nanoseconds (i.e. billionths of a second), and since the wave velocity can be estimated, this indicates the distance involved.

In archaeological exploration and mapping, the radar antenna is generally dragged along the ground at walking speed in transects, sending out and receiving many pulses per second. In the early years of this method, the reflections were printed on paper and interpreted visually, and thus relied heavily on the experience and ability of the operator who had to guess what the buried feature might be from often indecipherable images. Inevitably this led to uncertainties and inconclusive results, with some notable successes and failures. Now, however, the method has greatly improved, and the reflection data can be stored digitally, which enables sophisticated data processing and analysis to be carried out, producing clean, crisp reflection records which are easier to interpret. Powerful computers and software programs make it possible to store and process large three-dimensional sets of GPR data – e.g. a GPR survey of an area 50 m square can generate 500 megabytes of data – and computer advances now permit automated data and image processing which can help to interpret complicated reflection profiles.

One such advance is the use of "time-slices" or "slice-maps." Thousands of individual reflections are separated into horizontal slices, each of which corresponds to a specific estimated depth in the ground, and can reveal the general shape and location of buried features at each depth. A variety of colors (or shades of grey) are used to make a visual image that the brain can interpret more easily – e.g. areas with little or no subsurface reflection may be colored blue, those with high reflection may be red. Each slice therefore becomes like a horizontal excavation, and illustrates many buried components of the site. In fact, the slices do not need to be horizontal, and can be programmed to follow stratigraphic layers, and to have any orientation or thickness required.

For example, in the Forum Novum, an ancient Roman marketplace located about 100 km (62 miles) north of Rome, British archaeologists from the University of Birmingham and the British School of Archaeology in Rome needed a fuller picture of an unexcavated area than they had been able to obtain from aerial photographs and other techniques such as resistivity (see below). A series of GPR slices of the area revealed a whole series of walls, individual rooms, doorways, courtyards – in short, produced an architectural layout of the site which means that future excavation can be concentrated on a representative sample of the structures, thus avoiding a costly and time-consuming uncovering of the whole area.

Parts of the fourth-largest Roman city in England, that of Wroxeter in Shropshire (see box, pp. 100–01), have recently been studied by GPR; "time-slices" from different depths have revealed the town's changing

Amplitude slice-maps from the Forum Novum site, Italy. The top slice, at 0–10 ns (nanosecond, equivalent to 0–50 cm) reveals a Y-shaped anomaly, reflecting two gravel roads. As the slices go deeper, the Roman walls begin to emerge very clearly, showing a well-organized plan of rooms, doors, and corridors. The deepest slice shows the actual floor levels of the rooms and the objects preserved on them.

history through 400 years. Together with a very extensive magnetometer survey (see box p. 102), this has shown that the town's streets covered a much bigger area than previously thought – more than 60 ha (150 acres) – with a grid street-pattern, and clear outlines of houses, shops, and workshops.

In Japan, a burial mound at Kanmachi Mandara of about AD 350 was protected from excavation by cultural property laws, so GPR was used to locate the burial area within the mound, and determine its structural design. Radar profiles were taken at 50-cm (20-in) intervals across the mound, with pulses that could penetrate about 1 m (3.3 ft) into the ground.

Other electromagnetic methods available to the archaeologist are those employing soil conductivity meters and pulsed induction meters (see box, p. 102).

Electrical Resistivity. A commonly used method that has been employed on archaeological sites for several decades, particularly in Europe, is *electrical resistivity*.

The technique derives from the principle that the damper the soil the more easily it will conduct electricity, i.e. the less resistance it will show to an electric current. A resistivity meter attached to electrodes in the ground can thus measure varying degrees of subsurface resistance to a current passed between the electrodes. Silted up ditches or filled-in pits retain more moisture than stone walls or roads and will therefore display lower resistivity than stone structures.

The technique works particularly well for ditches and pits in chalk and gravel, and masonry in clay. It involves first placing two "remote" probes, which remain stationary, in the ground. Two "mobile" probes, fixed to a frame that also supports the meter, are then inserted into the earth for each reading. A new development is "resistivity profiling," which involves the measurement of earth resistance at increasing depths across a site, by widening the probe spacings and thus building up a vertical "pseudosection". A more sophisticated variant of this method, borrowed from medical science, is electrical tomography, while the future will doubtless see the combination of multiple profiles across a site to create 3-D images of buried surfaces.

One drawback of the technique is that it is rather slow due to the need to make electrical contact with the soil. Mobile resistivity systems, with probe arrays mounted on wheels, have been developed by French geophysicists to increase the speed of survey coverage. Nevertheless, the method is an effective complement to other remote sensing survey methods. Indeed it often replaces magnetic methods (see below) since, unlike some of these, it can be used in urban areas, close to power lines, and in the vicinity of metal. Most things detectable by magnetism can also be found through

Dr Albert Hesse using an experimental automated resistance array at Wroxeter. This should help increase the speed of survey coverage.

GEOPHYSICAL SURVEY AT ROMAN WROXETER

Wroxeter
ENGLAND

Covering an area of nearly 78 ha (193 acres), Roman Wroxeter, or Viroconium Cornoviorum, was the fourth largest urban center in the province of Britannia and the capital of the Cornovii tribe. It is important today because, unlike so many other Roman towns in Britain, Wroxeter has survived largely without damage and no succeeding modern settlement was built over it.

The city has attracted archaeological attention over the last century, with extensive excavations being carried out on the public buildings of the town by antiquarians. Modern large-scale excavations have been undertaken by Graham Webster and Philip Barker. Excavation is not the only source of information for the development of the town, however. Intensive aerial survey over many years has provided important evidence for the layout of the town and its possible development, and has allowed the compilation of a town plan of considerable detail.

A great deal of information is therefore available for the site and its history, from the construction of a fortress for Roman legions XIV and XX by AD 60, and the foundation of the Civitas Cornoviorum during the 90s, through to the intriguing evidence for post-Roman occupation. The information is, however, extremely variable. Modern excavation has only uncovered a very small part of the site, certainly less than 1 percent of the total, while aerial photography is not effective over the whole area, frequently only reflecting the stone buildings, and not even all of these. Consequently, little was known about large parts of the city and indeed perhaps 40 percent of the best-preserved Roman city in Britain was effectively terra incognita.

Surveying the City

The Wroxeter Hinterland Project set out to study the effect of the town on its hinterland, and as part of this work it

was realized that a more complete plan of the interior was essential. It was decided to carry out a geophysical survey of the whole of the available city – given the size of area, a radical solution was required to achieve this. The project was undertaken over several years by an international team of British and foreign geophysicists, including national bodies such as English Heritage and commercial groups including GSB Prospection. Their activities and results are impressive: nearly 63 ha (156 acres) were covered by gradiometer survey, representing over 2.5 million data points, and nearly 15 ha (37 acres) by resistance survey. Over 5 ha (12 acres) of ground penetrating radar data are now available for use in time-slicing software (to provide information on the depth of features, see p. 99), and a myriad other techniques, including seismics, conductivity, and caesium magnetometry, were used. Some techniques were employed to a lesser extent but still provide invaluable comparative results.

Results

The result of this work is the most extensive and complete plan currently available for a Romano-British civitas

The magnetometry data for the area south of the bath insula (left). A large courtyard house and an apsidal building interpreted as a church can be seen.

(Opposite above) A composite plan of the time-sliced radar plot of one building (left) and a web-based virtual reality reconstruction of the apsidal building interpreted as a possible church (right): see also http://www.bufau.bham.ac.uk/ for further examples.

(Opposite below) A detail of the plan of Roman Wroxeter derived from David Wilson's aerial photographic study and the magnetometer survey (left). The team at Wroxeter (right) setting up equipment for a ground penetrating radar survey.

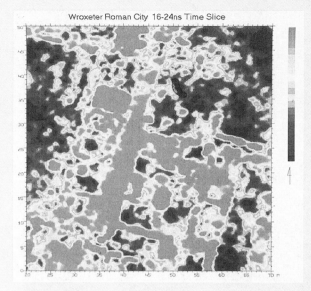

Wroxeter Roman City 16-24ns Time Slice

capital. There is evidence for central areas of elite buildings surrounded by artisan quarters and it is possible to identify specialized industrial areas. Dense pitting in the northwestern quarter of the town may relate to agro-industrial activities, such as tanning. A space in the eastern central area may be interpreted as the *forum boarium* (cattle market).

A number of features deserve specific comment. One large stone building, 27 m (88.5 ft) in length, oriented east–west and with an apse at its eastern end, is possibly a church.

Equally important, among the gradiometer data, is the phenomenon of "reversed" magnetic data in the northeastern quarter of the town. This seems most reasonably interpreted as evidence for a major fire which swept across the town, causing changes in the magnetic properties of the building stone as it was burnt.

Geophysics has also provided a glimpse into the prehistory of the site: a number of ring ditches can be recognized within the survey data, and a small enclosure and associated fields appear to underlie the defenses and

may represent the preceding Iron Age landscape.

The plan derived through geophysics at Wroxeter is exceptional: it is the most detailed of a Roman city ever produced in Britain – but without any expensive and destructive spadework. It is now being used as a basis for a virtual reality reconstruction of the town, which will be available to schools on CD-Rom. However, the study is not important simply because of the extent or even the quality of the data, but because it is an integral part of a larger research program.

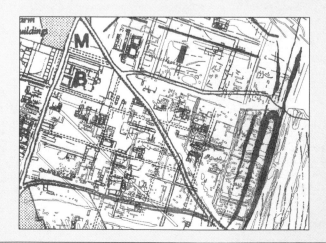

MEASURING MAGNETISM

The main instruments for tracing buried features using magnetic methods are magnetometers. Metal detectors can detect metals and some soil features as well.

The **proton precession magnetometer** consists of a sensor (a bottle of water) encircled by an electrical coil, mounted on a staff and connected by a cable to a small portable box of electronics. The device can detect small but sharp differences in magnetic field intensity caused by buried objects and features.

Proton magnetometers are usually employed using a grid divided into squares 1 m to 3 m on a side. Unfortunately their rate of operation is somewhat slow. Other drawbacks which they share with all other kinds of magnetometer include the fact that the operator cannot wear any iron: all buckles, watches, bootnails, metal pens, etc. must be kept several meters away; there must be no wire fences or corrugated sheeting in the vicinity. Proton magnetometers are also susceptible to interference from overhead cables. In a small, crowded country such as Japan, where one is never far from electrified rail lines or other direct current power lines, two magnetometers have to be used simultaneously (i.e. differential proton magnetometers, using two sensors) in order to overcome the "noise" that causes fluctuations in the magnetic field.

Fluxgate magnetometers have the advantage of sensors which give a continuous reading, but they are more complex to set up and operate – this is a directional instrument, and all measurements must be made with the sensor pointing in precisely the same direction (usually by hanging it vertically).

The most favored type of fluxgate magnetometer, the **fluxgate gradiometer**, uses two sensors in a light, self-contained instrument which produces a continuous output, and

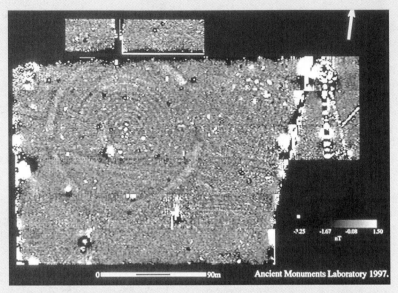

Results of a magnetometer survey of the site of Stanton Drew in Somerset. This revealed the existence of a wooden henge structure consisting of nine concentric rings of timbers that had completely disappeared above ground.

records differences in magnetic intensities on a meter. This can be combined with automatic trace recording and computer processing – consequently it can do fast, accurate surveys of large areas. A survey team using two fluxgate magnetometers can provide detailed coverage of at least two hectares per day. Such rapidity, and the responsiveness of such instruments to a wide range of archaeological features, has led to their increased use in archaeological evaluations, for instance in advance of the building of roads. Along one stretch of the future M3 highway in England, it found 8 sites in 10 km (6.2 miles).

The **caesium magnetometer** is a highly sensitive portable magnetometer that can detect minute magnetic variations, down to about one millionth of the earth's magnetic field. It is being increasingly used to detect weakly magnetized features such as postholes, and more deeply buried sites. Mounted on wheels, it

can achieve rates of ground coverage comparable to fluxgate gradiometer surveys.

Metal detectors employ both magnetism and conductivity – they respond to the high electrical conductivity of all metals and to the high magnetic susceptibility of ferrous metals. There are two main instruments. The **soil conductivity meter** comprises a radio transmitter and receiver in continuous operation, and detects subsurface features by measuring the distortion of the transmitted field caused by changes in the conductivity or susceptibility of the soil. Metals, for example, produce strong anomalies, while pits produce weak ones. The **pulsed induction meter** can find metal objects and magnetic soil anomalies such as pits by applying pulses of magnetic field to the ground from a transmitter coil – the larger the coil, the deeper the penetration. Similar devices are also employed in underwater archaeology (see box, p. 95).

resistivity; and in some field projects it has proved the most successful device for locating features (see box). Techniques based on magnetism are, however, still of great importance to archaeologists.

Magnetic Survey Methods. These are among the most widely used methods of survey, being particularly helpful in locating fired clay structures such as hearths and pottery kilns; iron objects; and pits and ditches. Such buried features all produce slight but measurable distortions in the earth's magnetic field. The reasons for this vary according to the type of feature, but are based on the presence of iron, even if only in minute amounts. For example, grains of iron oxide in clay, their magnetism randomly orientated if the clay is unbaked, will line up and become permanently fixed on the direction of the earth's magnetic field when heated to about 700°C (1292°F) or more. The baked clay thus becomes a weak permanent magnet, creating an anomaly in the surrounding magnetic field. (This phenomenon of thermoremanent magnetism also forms the basis for magnetic dating – see Chapter 4.) Anomalies caused by pits and ditches, on the other hand, occur because the so-called magnetic susceptibility of their contents is greater than that of the surrounding subsoil.

All the magnetic instruments can produce informative site plans which help to delimit archaeological potential (see box). Common means of presentation are contour, dot density, and gray-scale maps, all also used to display resistivity survey results. In the case of magnetic survey, the contour map has contour lines that join all points of the same value of the magnetic field intensity – this successfully reveals separate anomalies, such as tombs in a cemetery. In dot-density mapping, individual magnetometer readings are plotted as dots on a plan, with shading dependent on the magnetic intensity, the blacker areas therefore represent the highest anomalies in the local magnetic field. This makes it easier to pick up regular features, even where changes may be slight.

New developments in image processing by computer make it possible to manipulate geophysical datasets in order to reduce spurious effects and highlight subtle archaeological anomalies. For example, "directional filtering" allows a data "surface" of any chosen vertical scale to be "illuminated" from various directions and elevations to make subtle anomalies visible. Such processing mimics the revealing effects of low sunlight on earthworks, but with the added flexibility of computer manipulation.

An alternative, simpler mapping method has been devised which presents the data as a series of stacked profiles. Each traverse with the equipment is plotted as a curved profile. These are then placed in order, parallel to each other but aligned on an oblique plan, so that one obtains a kind of 3-D image of the site's magnetic variations.

Metal Detectors. These electromagnetic devices are also helpful in detecting buried remains – and not just metal ones. An alternating magnetic field is generated by passing an electrical current through a transmitter coil. Buried metal objects distort this field and are detected as a result of an electrical signal picked up by a receiver coil. Features such as pits, ditches, walls and kilns can also sometimes be recorded with these instruments because of their different magnetic sus-

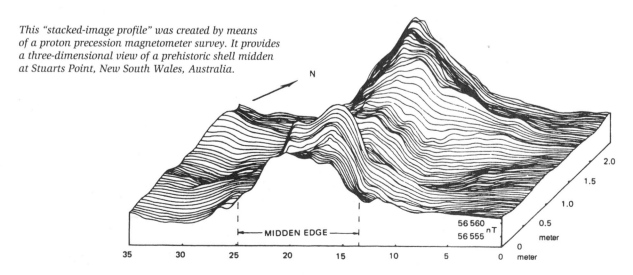

This "stacked-image profile" was created by means of a proton precession magnetometer survey. It provides a three-dimensional view of a prehistoric shell midden at Stuarts Point, New South Wales, Australia.

CONTROLLED ARCHAEOLOGICAL TEST SITE

As this chapter shows, we now have many different ways of "looking" under the ground, but problems start when one tries to interpret what is revealed by the scanners, because an infinity of things could send out the same signal. In an effort to make the assessment of these data more than an educated guess, a Controlled Archaeological Test Site (CATS) has been constructed by the US Army's Construction Engineering Research Labs (CERL) in Urbana, Illinois, for research and training in geophysical applications in archaeology.

This "controlled archaeological test-bed" covers 2500 sq. m (26,910 sq. ft) of land near the campus of the University of Illinois. A meter beneath the surface, four contiguous house floors have been created; there are also hearths, roasting pits, refuse pits, and artifact clusters; mortuary features such as pig and dog burials in mounds, under house floors and in isolated pits; a matrix of clay bricks of various compositions, buried at different depths; an earth oven with remains of cooked chicken and yams inside; clam-shells; and palisades, postholes, ditches, and embankments – the latter in segments of different dimensions and composition. In other words, the site replicates the kind of ephemeral features commonly left in the sub-plowzone by the indigenous cultures of the American Midwest, which are often hard to distinguish from the surrounding soil with the methods outlined in this chapter. There is also a

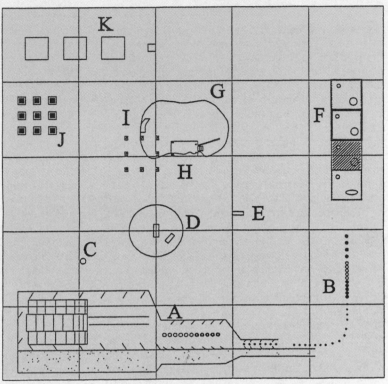

Plan of the CATS, showing the buried features: A ditch and embankment; B palisade; C roasting pit; D mound; E burial; F house complex; G midden; H historical cellar; I limestone piers and brick sidewalk; J brick matrix; K matrix of wood and metal objects.

matrix of wooden rods, metal pipes, and other objects in various configurations and depths.

Since the location and depth of every feature in the CATS are known to within a millimeter, and their geophysical attributes are also known, there is no

need for future excavations to check results. Experiments are now planned to apply non-destructive investigative techniques to the site which should lead to far more precise ways of locating and identifying what lies beneath the soil.

ceptibilities as compared to the surrounding soil or subsoil (see box, p. 102, for types of equipment).

Metal detectors can be of great value to archaeologists, particularly in providing quick general results and locating modern metal objects that may lie near the surface. They are also very widely used by non-archaeologists, most of whom are responsible enthusiasts, but some of whom vandalize sites mindlessly and often illegally dig holes without recording or reporting the finds they make. There are now 30,000 metal detector users in Britain alone.

Other Techniques. There are a few other prospection methods which are not often used but which may become more widely adopted in the future, particularly geochemical analysis, discussed below.

Both *radioactivity* and *neutron scattering* have been tried out in remote sensing tests, but it was found that both work only if the soil cover is very thin. Most soils and rocks have some radioactive content, and, as with resistivity and magnetic surveying, in the radioactivity technique readings measure discontinuity between buried ditches or pits and the surrounding earth. In the neutron method, a probe that is both a source of fast neutrons and a detector of slow ones is inserted into the soil: measurement of their rate of slowing and scattering through the ground is taken. Stone produces a lower count rate than soil, so buried features can sometimes be detected.

Thermal prospection (thermography), which has already been briefly mentioned in the section on aerial photography above, is based on weak variations in temperature (as little as tenths of a degree) which can be found above buried structures whose thermal properties are different from those of their surroundings. The technique has mostly been used from an airplane, but ground-based thermal imaging cameras do exist; these have not yet seen much application to archaeological features, though they can be effective in detecting concealed variations within a building, such as infilled doorways in churches. So far, thermography has been used primarily on very long or massive structures, for instance prehistoric enclosures or Roman buildings.

The mapping and study of the *vegetation* at a site can be very informative about previous work – certain species will grow where soil has been disturbed, and at Sutton Hoo, for example, an expert on grasses was able to pinpoint many holes that had been dug into this mound site in recent years.

Geochemical analysis involves taking samples of soil at intervals (such as every meter) from the surface of a site and its surroundings, and measuring their phosphate (phosphorus) content. It was fieldwork in Sweden in the 1920s and 1930s that first revealed the close correlation between ancient settlement and high concentrations of phosphorus in the soil. The organic components of occupation debris may disappear, while the inorganic ones remain: of these, magnesium or calcium can be analyzed, but it is the phosphates that are the most diagnostic and easily identified. Subsequently, the method was used to locate sites in North America and northwest Europe: Ralph Solecki, for example, detected burials in West Virginia by this means.

Recent phosphate tests on sites in England, examining samples taken at 20-cm (8-in) intervals from the surface downward, have confirmed that undisturbed archaeological features in the subsoil are accurately reflected in the topsoil. In the past, topsoil was considered to be unstratified and hence devoid of archaeological information; it was often removed mechanically and quickly without investigation. Now, however, it is becoming clear that even a site that appears totally plowed-out can yield important chemical information about precisely where its occupation was located. The phosphate method is also invaluable for sites with no apparent internal architectural features. In some cases it may help clarify the function of different parts of an excavated site as well. For example, in a Romano-British farmstead at Cefn Graeanog, North Wales, J.S. Conway took soil samples at 1 m (3 ft 4 in) intervals from the floors of excavated huts and from neighboring fields, and mapped their phosphorus content as contour lines. In one building a high level of phosphorus across the middle implied the existence of two animal stalls with a drain for urine running between them. In another, the position of two hearths was marked by high readings.

Investigations of this type are slow, because one has to lay down a grid, collect, weigh, and analyze the samples. But they are becoming increasingly common in archaeological projects, since they can reveal features not detected by other techniques. Like magnetic and resistivity methods (to which they are complementary), they help to construct a detailed picture of features of special archaeological interest within larger areas already identified by other means such as aerial photography or surface survey.

In concluding this section on subsurface detection, we may refer in passing to a controversial technique that has a few followers. *Dowsing* (in the U.S. witching) – the location of subsurface features by holding out a twig, copper rod, coathanger, pendulum, or some such instrument and waiting for it to move – has been applied to archaeological problems for at least 50 years, but without being taken seriously by most archaeologists.

In the mid-1980s, however, it was used in a project to trace medieval church foundations in Northumberland, England, and the skeptical archaeologists involved became convinced of the technique's validity. While keeping an open mind, most archaeologists remain extremely doubtful. Only excavation can test the predictions made, and in the church project digging confirmed some of the dowser's predictions, but not all of them; this is hardly surprising, since a dowser often has a good chance of being right – either the feature is there or it is not. Tests by the physicist Martin Aitken to find a correlation between dowsing responses and magnetic disturbance in a Romano-British pottery kiln proved entirely negative.

For the moment, therefore, until overwhelming proof of the validity of dowsing and other unconventional methods is forthcoming, archaeologists should continue to put their faith in the ever-growing number of tried-and-trusted scientific techniques for obtaining data about site layout without excavation.

EXCAVATION

So far, we have discovered sites and mapped as many of their surface and subsurface features as possible. But, despite the growing importance of survey, the only way to check the reliability of surface data, confirm the accuracy of the remote sensing techniques, and actually see what remains of these sites is to excavate them. Furthermore, survey can tell us a little about a large area, but only excavation can tell us a great deal about a relatively small area.

Purposes of Excavation

Excavation retains its central role in fieldwork because it yields the most reliable evidence for the two main kinds of information archaeologists are interested in: (1) human activities at a particular period in the past; and (2) changes in those activities from period to period. Very broadly we can say that contemporary activities take place *horizontally in space*, whereas changes in those activities occur *vertically through time*. It is this distinction between horizontal "slices of time" and vertical sequences through time that forms the basis of most excavation methodology.

In the horizontal dimension archaeologists demonstrate contemporaneity – that activities did indeed occur at the same time – by proving to their satisfaction through excavation that artifacts and features are found in association in an undisturbed context. Of course, as we saw in Chapter 2, there are many formation processes that may disturb this primary context. One of the main purposes of the survey and remote sensing procedures outlined in the earlier sections is to select for excavation sites, or areas within sites, that are reasonably undisturbed. On a single-period site such as an East African early human camp site this is vital if human behavior at the camp is to be reconstructed at all accurately. But on a multi-period site, such as a longlived European town or Near Eastern tell, finding large areas of undisturbed deposits will be almost impossible. Here archaeologists have to try to reconstruct during and after excavation just what disturbance there has been and then decide how to interpret it. Clearly, adequate records must be made as excavation progresses if the task of interpretation is to be undertaken with any chance of success. In the vertical dimension archaeologists analyze changes through time by the study of stratigraphy.

Stratigraphy. As we saw in Chapter 1, one of the first steps in comprehending the great antiquity of human-

kind was the recognition by geologists of the process of stratification – that layers or strata are laid down, one on top of the other, according to processes that still continue. Archaeological strata (the layers of cultural or natural debris visible in the side of any excavation) accumulate over much shorter periods of time than geological ones, but nevertheless conform to the same *law of superposition*. Put simply, this states that where one layer overlies another, the lower was deposited first. Hence, an excavated vertical profile showing a series of layers constitutes a sequence that has accumulated through time.

Chapter 4 explores the significance of this for dating purposes. Here we should note that the law of superposition refers only to the sequence of deposition, *not* to the age of the material in the different strata. The contents of lower layers are indeed usually older than those of upper layers, but the archaeologist must not simply assume this. Pits dug down from a higher layer or burrowing animals (even earthworms) may introduce later materials into lower levels. Moreover, occasionally strata can become inverted, as when they are eroded all the way from the top of a bank to the bottom of a ditch.

In recent years, archaeologists have developed an ingenious and effective method of checking that artifacts – so far mostly of stone or bone – discovered in a particular deposit are contemporaneous and not intrusive. They have found that in a surprising number of cases flakes of stone or bone can be fitted back together again: reassembled in the shape of the original stone block or pieces of bone from which they came. At the British Mesolithic (Middle Stone Age) site of Hengistbury Head, for example, reanalysis of an old excavation showed that two groups of flint flakes, found in two different layers, could be refitted. This cast doubt on the stratigraphic separation of the two layers, and demolished the original excavator's argument that the flints had been made by two different groups of people. As well as clarifying questions of stratification, these refitting or conjoining exercises are transforming archaeological studies of early technology (Chapter 8).

Stratigraphy, then, is the study and validating of stratification – the analysis in the vertical, time dimension of a series of layers in the horizontal, space dimension (although in practice few layers are precisely horizontal).

What are the best excavation methods for retrieving this information?

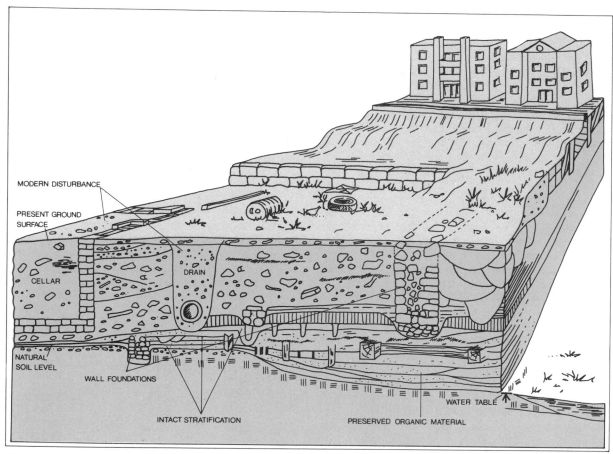

The complexity of stratification varies with the type of site. This hypothetical section through an urban deposit indicates the kind of complicated stratigraphy, in both vertical and horizontal dimensions, that the archaeologist can encounter. There may be few undisturbed stratified layers. The chances of finding preserved organic material increase as one approaches the water table, near which deposits may be waterlogged.

Methods of Excavation

Excavation is both costly and destructive, and therefore never to be undertaken lightly. Wherever possible non-destructive approaches outlined earlier should be used to meet research objectives in preference to excavation. But assuming excavation is to proceed, and the necessary funding and permission to dig have been obtained, what are the best methods to adopt?

This book is not an excavation or field manual, and the reader is referred for detailed information to the texts listed at the end of this chapter and in the bibliography. In fact, a few days or weeks spent on a well-run dig are worth far more than reading any book on the subject. Nevertheless some brief guidance as to the main methods can be given here.

It goes without saying that all excavation methods need to be adapted to the research question in hand and the nature of the site. It is no good digging a deeply stratified urban site, with hundreds of complex structures, thousands of intercutting pits, and tens of thousands of artifacts, as if it were the same as a shallow Paleolithic open site, where only one or two structures and a few hundred artifacts may survive. On the Paleolithic site, for example, one has some hope of uncovering all the structures and recording the exact position, vertically and horizontally – i.e. the *provenience* – of each and every artifact. On the urban site one has no chance of doing this, given time and funding constraints. Instead, one has to adopt a sampling strategy (see box, pp. 76–77) and only key artifacts such as coins (important for dating purposes: see Chapter 4)

107

will have their provenience recorded with three-dimensional precision, the remainder being allocated simply to the layer and perhaps the grid-square in which they were found.

One should note, however, that we have already reintroduced the idea of the vertical and horizontal dimensions. These are as crucial to the methods of excavation as they are to the principles behind excavation. Broadly speaking one can divide excavation techniques into:

1 those that emphasize the vertical dimension, by cutting into deep deposits to reveal stratification;
2 those that emphasize the horizontal dimension, by opening up large areas of a particular layer to reveal the spatial relationships between artifacts and features in that layer.

Most excavators employ a combination of both strategies, but there are different ways of achieving this. All presuppose that the site has first been surveyed and a grid of squares laid down over it to aid in accurate recording.

The *Wheeler box-grid* – developed, as we saw in Chapter 1, from the work of General Pitt-Rivers – seeks to satisfy both vertical and horizontal requirements by retaining intact baulks of earth between the squares of the grid so that different layers can be traced and correlated across the site in the vertical profiles. Once the general extent and layout of the site have been ascertained, some of the baulks can be removed and the squares joined into an open excavation to expose any features (such as a mosaic floor) that are of special interest.

Advocates of *open-area excavation*, such as the English excavator Philip Barker, criticize the Wheeler method, arguing that the baulks are invariably in the wrong place or wrongly orientated to illustrate the relationships required from sections, and that they prevent the distinguishing of spatial patterning over large

Open-area excavation at Sutton Hoo, eastern England. A large area, 32 × 64 m, was uncovered to establish the perimeters of two burial mounds. Detailed stratigraphy was then studied in smaller squares. Immediately below the topsoil lay early medieval features, recorded using overhead color photographs to emphasize soil variations, and plotted on site plans at scales of 1:10 and 1:100.

areas. It is far better, these critics say, not to have such permanent or semi-permanent baulks, but to open up large areas and only to cut vertical sections (at whatever angle is necessary to the main site grid) where they are needed to elucidate particularly complex stratigraphic relationships. Apart from these "running sections," the vertical dimension is recorded by accurate three-dimensional measurements as the dig proceeds and reconstructed on paper after the end of the excavation. The introduction since Wheeler's day of more advanced recording methods, including field computers, makes this more demanding open-area method feasible, and it has become the norm, for instance, in much of British archaeology. The open-area method is particularly effective where single-period deposits lie near the surface, as for instance with remains of Native American or European Neolithic long houses. Here the time dimension may be represented by lateral movement (a settlement rebuilt adjacent to, not on top of, an earlier one) and it is essential to expose large

horizontal areas in order to understand the complex pattern of rebuilding.

Sometimes, if time and money are short, and structures lie sufficiently close to the surface, the topsoil can simply be scraped away over large areas, as has been done to good effect at Tell Abu Salabikh (box, pp. 92–93).

No single method, however, is ever going to be universally applicable. The rigid box-grid, for instance, has rarely been employed to excavate very deep sites, such as Near Eastern tells, because the trench squares rapidly become uncomfortable and dangerous as the dig proceeds downward. One solution commonly adopted is *step-trenching*, with a large area opened at the top which gradually narrows as the dig descends in a series of large steps. This technique was used effectively at the Koster site, Illinois.

Another solution to the problem of dangerously deep excavations, successfully adopted on the salvage excavations at Coppergate, York (see case study,

At the American Indian site of Koster, in the Illinois River Valley, large horizontal areas were uncovered in order to locate living floors and activity zones. However, so that the vertical dimension could also be analyzed at this deep site, vertical sections were cut as steps as the excavation descended. At this complex site 14 occupation levels were identified, stretching from c. 7500 BC to AD 1200.

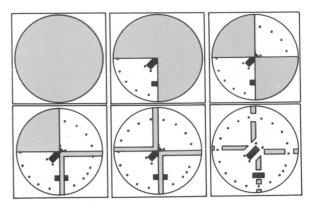

Excavation methods. (Left) Sectioning a burial mound at Moundville, Alabama (see box, pp. 212–13). (Above) Six stages of the quadrant method for excavating burial mounds. The objective is to expose subsurface features while retaining four transverse sections for stratigraphic analysis. (Below) Excavation of 70,000 years of deposits at Boomplaas Cave, South Africa (see Chapter 6), demanded meticulous recording controls, using grid lines attached to the cave roof.

Excavation using a cofferdam: the wreck – visible as air bubbles – of the merchant brig designated YO 88 at Yorktown, Virginia, scuttled during the War of Independence.

Chapter 13) and Billingsgate, London, is to build a *cofferdam* of sheet piling around the area to be dug. Cofferdams have also been used in shipwreck excavations, either simply to control the flow of water – as on a War of Independence wreck at Yorktown, Virginia – or to pump out the water altogether. Cofferdams are expensive and the dig must be well funded.

Whatever the method of excavation – and the accompanying illustrations show other techniques e.g. for the excavation of burial mounds and cave sites – a dig is only as good as its methods of recovery and recording. Since excavation involves destruction of much of the evidence, it is an unrepeatable exercise. Well thought out recovery methods are essential, and careful records must be kept of every stage of the dig.

Recovery and Recording of the Evidence

As we saw above, different sites have different requirements. One should aim to recover and plot the three-dimensional provenience of every artifact from a shallow single-period Paleolithic or Neolithic site, an objective that is simply not feasible for the urban archaeologist. On both types of site, a decision may be made to save time by using heavy mechanical diggers to remove topsoil (but see above, p. 105), but thereafter the Paleolithic or Neolithic specialist will usually want to screen or sieve as much excavated soil as possible in order to recover tiny artifacts, animal bones, and in the case of wet sieving (see Chapter 6), plant remains. The urban archaeologist on the other hand will only be able to adopt sieving much more selectively, as part of a sampling strategy, for instance where plant remains can be expected to survive, as in a latrine or refuse pit.

Once an artifact has been recovered, and its provenience recorded, it must be given a number which is entered in a catalog book or field computer and on the bag in which it is to be stored. Day-to-day progress of the dig is recorded in site notebooks, or on data sheets preprinted with specific questions to be answered (which helps produce uniform data suitable for later analysis by computer).

Unlike artifacts, which can be removed for later analysis, features and structures usually have to be left where they were found (*in situ*), or destroyed as the excavation proceeds to another layer. It is thus imperative to record them, not simply by written description in site notebooks, but by accurately scaled drawings and photography. The same applies to vertical profiles (sections), and for each horizontally exposed layer good overhead photographs taken from a stand or tethered balloon are also essential.

It is the site notebooks, scaled drawings, photographs and computer disks – in addition to recovered artifacts, animal bones, and plant remains – that form the total record of the excavation, on the basis of which all interpretations of the site will be made. This post-

Screening: archaeologists at the Maya site of Cozumel, Mexico, screen excavated dirt through a mesh to recover tiny artifacts, animal bones, and other remains.

The ultimate value of an excavation lies in the records produced during actual fieldwork. Good organization is essential. Here we show the step-by-step methods adopted by the Museum of London. (Right) A flow diagram of procedures for the excavator to follow once a context (deposit) has been identified during the dig. (Below) Recording sheets must be meticulously completed as work proceeds. Most features are excavated and thus destroyed, so post-excavation analysis and layer-by-layer reconstructions of the site depend entirely on accurate field notes. (Opposite) The Roman baths at Huggin Hill in London. A Museum of London archaeologist uses a theodolite to measure the accurate position of a column base on which another archaeologist holds a survey rod (range pole). Their measurements will later form the basis for a detailed plan.

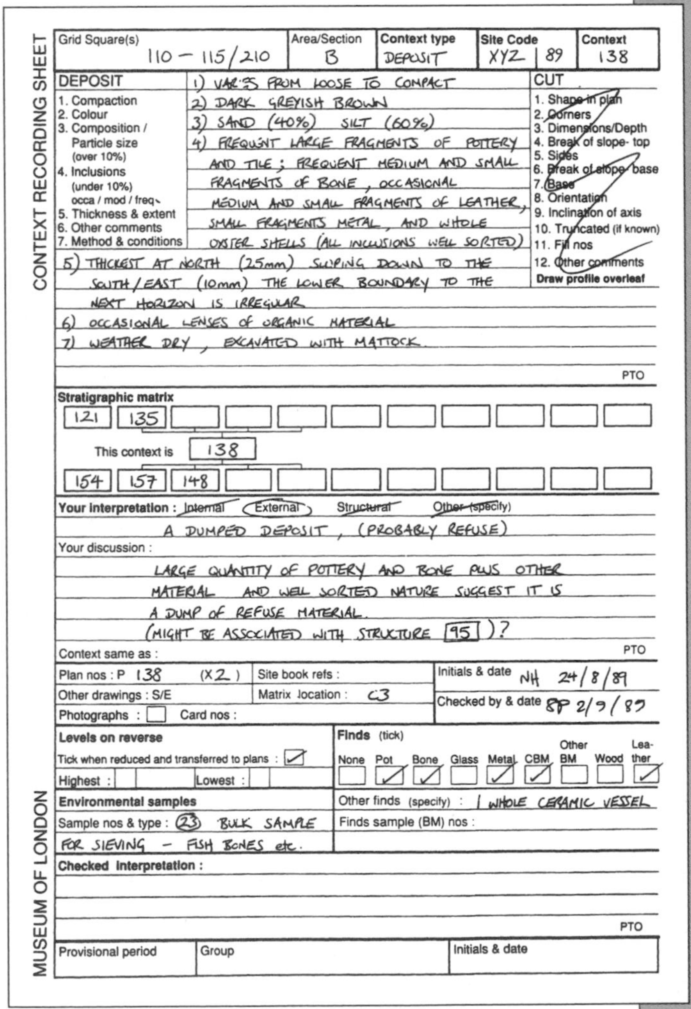

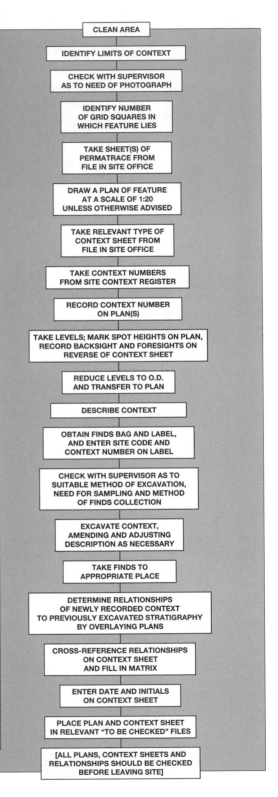

CONTEXT RECORDING SHEET — MUSEUM OF LONDON

Grid Square(s) 110 – 115/210	Area/Section B	Context type DEPOSIT	Site Code XYZ 89	Context 138

DEPOSIT
1. Compaction
2. Colour
3. Composition / Particle size (over 10%)
4. Inclusions (under 10%) occa / mod / freq
5. Thickness & extent
6. Other comments
7. Method & conditions

1) VARIES FROM LOOSE TO COMPACT
2) DARK GREYISH BROWN
3) SAND (40%) SILT (60%)
4) FREQUENT LARGE FRAGMENTS OF POTTERY AND TILE; FREQUENT MEDIUM AND SMALL FRAGMENTS OF BONE, OCCASIONAL MEDIUM AND SMALL FRAGMENTS OF LEATHER, SMALL FRAGMENTS METAL, AND WHOLE OYSTER SHELLS (ALL INCLUSIONS WELL SORTED)
5) THICKEST AT NORTH (25mm) SLOPING DOWN TO THE SOUTH/EAST (10mm) THE LOWER BOUNDARY TO THE NEXT HORIZON IS IRREGULAR
6) OCCASIONAL LENSES OF ORGANIC MATERIAL
7) WEATHER DRY, EXCAVATED WITH MATTOCK

PTO

CUT
1. Shape in plan
2. Corners
3. Dimensions/Depth
4. Break of slope- top
5. Sides
6. Break of slope- base
7. Base
8. Orientation
9. Inclination of axis
10. Truncated (if known)
11. Fill nos
12. Other comments
Draw profile overleaf

Stratigraphic matrix

121 | 135

This context is 138

154 | 157 | 148

Your interpretation : Internal (External) Structural Other (specify)
A DUMPED DEPOSIT, (PROBABLY REFUSE)

Your discussion :
LARGE QUANTITY OF POTTERY AND BONE PLUS OTHER MATERIAL AND WELL SORTED NATURE SUGGEST IT IS A DUMP OF REFUSE MATERIAL.
(MIGHT BE ASSOCIATED WITH STRUCTURE 95)?

PTO

Context same as :		
Plan nos : P 138 (X2)	Site book refs :	Initials & date NH 24/8/89
Other drawings : S/E	Matrix location : C3	Checked by & date BP 2/9/89
Photographs : ☐ Card nos :		

Levels on reverse
Tick when reduced and transferred to plans : ✓
Highest : | Lowest :

Finds (tick)
None | Pot ✓ | Bone ✓ | Glass | Metal ✓ | CBM ✓ | BM | Wood | Other Leather ✓

Environmental samples
Sample nos & type : (23) BULK SAMPLE FOR SIEVING — FISH BONES etc.

Other finds (specify) : WHOLE CERAMIC VESSEL
Finds sample (BM) nos :

Checked interpretation :

PTO

Provisional period	Group	Initials & date

Flow diagram (right):

CLEAN AREA

IDENTIFY LIMITS OF CONTEXT

CHECK WITH SUPERVISOR AS TO NEED OF PHOTOGRAPH

IDENTIFY NUMBER OF GRID SQUARES IN WHICH FEATURE LIES

TAKE SHEET(S) OF PERMATRACE FROM FILE IN SITE OFFICE

DRAW A PLAN OF FEATURE AT A SCALE OF 1:20 UNLESS OTHERWISE ADVISED

TAKE RELEVANT TYPE OF CONTEXT SHEET FROM FILE IN SITE OFFICE

TAKE CONTEXT NUMBERS FROM SITE CONTEXT REGISTER

RECORD CONTEXT NUMBER ON PLAN(S)

TAKE LEVELS; MARK SPOT HEIGHTS ON PLAN, RECORD BACKSIGHT AND FORESIGHTS ON REVERSE OF CONTEXT SHEET

REDUCE LEVELS TO O.D. AND TRANSFER TO PLAN

DESCRIBE CONTEXT

OBTAIN FINDS BAG AND LABEL, AND ENTER SITE CODE AND CONTEXT NUMBER ON LABEL

CHECK WITH SUPERVISOR AS TO SUITABLE METHOD OF EXCAVATION, NEED FOR SAMPLING AND METHOD OF FINDS COLLECTION

EXCAVATE CONTEXT, AMENDING AND ADJUSTING DESCRIPTION AS NECESSARY

TAKE FINDS TO APPROPRIATE PLACE

DETERMINE RELATIONSHIPS OF NEWLY RECORDED CONTEXT TO PREVIOUSLY EXCAVATED STRATIGRAPHY BY OVERLAYING PLANS

CROSS-REFERENCE RELATIONSHIPS ON CONTEXT SHEET AND FILL IN MATRIX

ENTER DATE AND INITIALS ON CONTEXT SHEET

PLACE PLAN AND CONTEXT SHEET IN RELEVANT "TO BE CHECKED" FILES

[ALL PLANS, CONTEXT SHEETS AND RELATIONSHIPS SHOULD BE CHECKED BEFORE LEAVING SITE]

excavation analysis will take many months, perhaps years, often much longer than the excavation itself. However, some preliminary analysis, particularly sorting and classification of the artifacts, will be made in the field during the course of the excavation.

Processing and Classification

Like excavation itself, the processing of excavated materials in the field laboratory is a specialized activity that demands careful planning and organization. For example, no archaeologist should undertake the excavation of a wet site without having on hand team members expert in the conservation of waterlogged wood, and facilities for coping with such material. The reader is referred for further guidance to the many manuals now available that deal with conservation problems confronting archaeologists.

There are, however, two aspects of field laboratory procedure that should be discussed briefly here. The first concerns the cleaning of artifacts; the second, artifact classification. In both cases we would stress the need for the archaeologist always to consider in advance what kinds of questions the newly excavated material might be able to answer. Thorough cleaning of artifacts, for example, is a traditional part of excavations worldwide. But many of the new scientific techniques discussed in Part II make it quite evident that artifacts should *not* necessarily be cleaned thoroughly before a specialist has had a chance to study them. For instance, we now know that food residues are often preserved in pots and possible blood residues on stone tools (Chapter 7). The chances of such preservation need to be assessed before evidence is destroyed.

Nevertheless most artifacts eventually have to be cleaned to some degree if they are to be sorted and classified. Initial sorting is into broad categories such as stone tools, pottery, and metal objects. These categories are then subdivided or classified, so as to create more manageable groups that can later be analyzed. Classification is commonly done on the basis of three kinds of characteristics or *attributes*:

1   surface attributes (including decoration and color);
2   shape attributes (dimensions as well as shape itself);
3   technological attributes (primarily raw material).

Artifacts found to share similar attributes are grouped together into artifact types – hence the term *typology*, which simply refers to the creation of such types.

Typology dominated archaeological thinking until the 1950s, and still plays an important role in the discipline. The reason for this is straightforward. Artifacts make up a large part of the archaeological record, and typology helps archaeologists create order in this mass of evidence. As we saw in Chapter 1, C.J. Thomsen demonstrated early on that artifacts could be ordered in a Three Age System or sequence of stone, bronze, and iron. This discovery underlies the continuing use of typology as a method of dating – of measuring the passage of time (Chapter 4). Typology has also been used as a means of defining archaeological entities at a particular moment in time. Groups of artifact (and building) types at a particular time and place are termed *assemblages*, and groups of assemblages have been taken to define *archaeological cultures*.

As we shall see in Part II, the difficulty comes when one tries to translate this terminology into human terms and to relate an archaeological culture with an actual group of people in the past.

This brings us back to the purpose of classification. Types, assemblages, and cultures are all artificial constructs designed to put order into disordered evidence. The trap that former generations of scholars fell into was to allow these constructs to determine the way they thought about the past, rather than using them merely as one means of giving shape to the evidence. We now recognize more clearly that different classifications are needed for the different kinds of questions we want to ask. A student of ceramic technology would base a classification on variations in raw material and methods of manufacture, whereas a scholar studying the various functions of pottery for storage, cooking etc. might classify the vessels according to shape and size. Our ability to construct and make good use of new classifications has been immeasurably enhanced by computers, which allow archaeologists to compare the association of different attributes on hundreds of objects at once.

In a salvage project in the late 1980s – involving the survey, testing, and excavation of some 500 sites along the 2250-km (1400-mile) route of a pipeline from California to Texas – Fred Plog, David L. Carlson, and their associates developed a computerized system using a video camera for automatic recording of different attributes of artifacts. Four to six people could process 1000–2000 artifacts a day, some 10 times quicker than normal methods. The standardization of recording methods allows rapid and highly accurate comparisons to be made between different artifact types.

In conclusion, it cannot be stressed too strongly that all the effort put into survey, excavation, and post-excavation analysis will have been largely wasted unless the results are published, initially as interim reports and subsequently in a full-scale monograph (see Chapter 14).

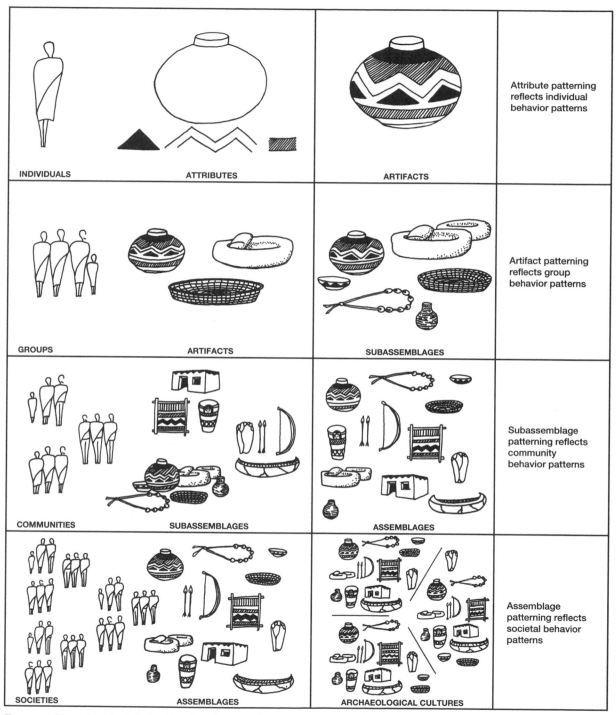

		Attribute patterning reflects individual behavior patterns
INDIVIDUALS	**ATTRIBUTES**	**ARTIFACTS**

Terms used in archaeological classification, from attributes (shape, decoration) of a pot to the complete archaeological culture: a diagram developed by the American archaeologist James Deetz. The columns at left and right give the inferred human meaning of the terms. The extent to which one can draw behavioral inferences from such classification is discussed in Chapter 12.

SUMMARY

Until the present century, individual sites were the main focus of archaeological attention, and the only remote sensing devices used were a pair of eyes and a stick. The developments of aerial photography and reconnaissance techniques have shown archaeologists that the entire landscape is of interest, while geophysical and geochemical methods have revolutionized our ability to detect what lies hidden beneath the soil.

Today archaeologists study whole regions, often employing sampling techniques to bring ground reconnaissance (surface survey) within the scope of individual research teams. Having located sites within those regions, and mapped them using aerial reconnaissance techniques and now GIS, archaeologists can then turn to a whole battery of remote sensing site survey devices able to detect buried features without excavation. The geophysical methods almost all involve either passing energy into the ground and locating buried features from their effect on that energy or measuring the intensity of the earth's magnetic field. In either case, they depend on contrast between the buried features and their surroundings. Many of the techniques are costly in both equipment and time, but they are often cheaper and certainly less destructive than random test-pits or trial trenches. They allow archaeologists to be more selective in deciding which parts of a site, if any, should be fully excavated.

Excavation itself relies on methods designed to elucidate the horizontal extent of a site in space, and the vertical stratification representing changes through time (though time can be represented by horizontal movement of the site as well). Good recording methods are essential, together with a well-equipped field laboratory for processing and classifying the finds. Classification based on selected attributes (decoration, shape, material) of each artifact is the fundamental means of organizing the excavated material, usually into types – hence typology. But classification is only a means to an end, and different schemes are needed for the different questions archaeologists want to address.

However, little of the material retrieved during survey and excavation will be of much use unless it can be dated in some way. In the next chapter we turn to this crucial aspect of archaeology.

FURTHER READING

Useful introductions to methods of locating and surveying archaeological sites can be found in the following:

Allen, K.M.S., Green, S.W. & Zubrow, E.B.W. (eds.). 1990. *Interpreting Space: GIS and Archaeology.* Taylor and Francis: London & New York.

Clark, A. 1996. *Seeing Beneath the Soil: Prospecting Methods in Archaeology.* (2nd ed.) Routledge: London.

Colwell, R.N. (ed.). 1983. *Manual of Remote Sensing.* (2nd ed.) Society of Photogrammetry: Falls Church, Virginia.

Flannery, K.V. (ed.). 1976. *The Early Mesoamerican Village.* Academic Press: New York. (Helpful examples of surface survey.)

Lock, G. & Stančič, Z. (eds.). 1995. *Archaeology and Geographical Information Systems: A European Perspective.* Taylor and Francis: London & Bristol, Penn.

Lyons, T.R. & Avery, T.E. 1977. *Remote Sensing: A Handbook for Archaeologists and Cultural Resource Managers.* U.S. Dept of the Interior: Washington, D.C.

Tite, M.S. 1972. *Methods of Physical Examination in Archaeology.* Seminar Press: London & New York.

Among the most widely used field manuals are:

Barker, P. 1993. *Techniques of Archaeological Excavation.* (3rd ed.) Routledge: London; Humanities Press: New York. (British methods.)

Connah, G. (ed.). 1983. *Australian Field Archaeology. A Guide to Techniques.* Australian Institute of Aboriginal Studies: Canberra. (Australian methods.)

Hester, T.N., Shafer, H.J., & Feder, K.L. 1997. *Field Methods in Archaeology.* (7th ed.) Mayfield: Palo Alto, Calif. (American methods.)

Joukowsky, M. 1980. *A Complete Manual of Field Archaeology.* Prentice-Hall: Englewood Cliffs, N.J. (American methods.)

Scollar, I., Tabbagh, A., Hesse, A. & Herzog, I. (eds.) 1990. *Remote Sensing in Archaeology.* Cambridge University Press: Cambridge and New York.

Spence, C. (ed.). 1990. *Archaeological Site Manual.* (2nd ed.) Museum of London. (British methods.)

And the journal *Archaeological Prospection* (since 1994).

Also useful for beginners, and well illustrated:

McIntosh, J. 1999. *The Practical Archaeologist.* (2nd ed.). Facts on File: New York; Thames & Hudson: London.

4 When?
Dating Methods and Chronology

All human beings experience time. An individual experiences a lifetime of perhaps 70 years or so. That person, through the memories of his or her parents and grandparents, may also indirectly experience earlier periods of time, back over one or two generations. The study of history gives one access – even less directly but often no less vividly – to hundreds of years of recorded time. But it is only archaeology, in particular prehistoric archaeology, that opens up the almost unimaginable vistas of thousands and even a few millions of years of past human existence.

In order to study the past it is not, rather surprisingly, always essential to know precisely how long ago in years a particular period or event occurred. As we saw in Chapter 1, C.J. Thomsen's great achievement in the 19th century was to establish a three-part organization of tools for the Old World into those of stone, bronze, and iron which stratigraphic excavation confirmed was a chronological sequence: stone artifacts came before bronze ones, and iron ones came after. Archaeologists could use this sequence to study, say, changes in tool technology from one stage of the sequence to the next, even without knowing how long each stage lasted or how many years ago such developments took place. This idea that something is older (or younger) relative to something else is the basis of *relative dating*. The initial steps in most archaeological research today still depend crucially on relative dating, on the ordering of artifacts, deposits, societies, and events into sequences, earlier before later.

Ultimately, however, we want to know the full or absolute age in years before the present of the different parts of the sequence – we need methods of *absolute dating* (sometimes called chronometric dating). Absolute dates help us find out how quickly changes such as the introduction of agriculture occurred, and whether they occurred simultaneously or at different times in different regions of the world. Before World War II for much of archaeology virtually the only reliable absolute dates were historical ones – Tutankhamun reigned in the 14th century BC, Caesar invaded Britain in 55 BC. Only in the last 50 years have independent means of absolute dating become available, transforming archaeology in the process.

Measuring Time

How do we detect the passage of time? In our own lives, we observe its passing through the alternating darkness and light of nights and days, and then through the annual cycle of the seasons. In fact, until the development of modern astronomy and nuclear physics, these were the only ways of observing time, other than by the human lifespan. As we shall see, some dating methods still rely on the annual passage of the seasons. Increasingly, however, dating methods in archaeology have come to rely on other physical processes, many of them not observable to the human eye. The most significant of these is the use of radioactive clocks.

Whatever the dating method, we need an agreed measure of time in order to construct a chronology. Most human measuring systems reckon on the basis of years. Thus even age measurements such as radioactive clocks that are independent of annual cycles need to be converted into years. Often when there are dating errors it is the conversion into years rather than the dating method itself that is at fault.

In general the two biggest problems with archaeological dating methods are not the techniques themselves but (1) security of context: i.e. ensuring that the sample we are using does indeed relate securely to the context we are trying to date; and (2) contamination of the sample with more recent (or sometimes older) material. There is also the problem of precision: that many dating methods provide results which form an age-bracket which can stretch over several centuries or even millennia. Misunderstandings can arise when archaeologists have too high an expectation of the precision available from the method which they are using.

Our timescale in years must date from or to a fixed point in time. In the Christian world, this is by convention taken as the birth of Christ, supposedly in the year

AD 1 (there is no year 0), with years counted back before Christ (BC) and forward after Christ (AD or *Anno Domini*, Latin for "In the Year of Our Lord"). In the Muslim world the basic fixed point is the date of the Prophet's departure from Mecca, the Hegira (reckoned at AD 622 in the Christian calendar), whereas many Buddhists take theirs from the date of the Gautama Buddha's death – thus they celebrated his 2500th anniversary in AD 1957. As a result of these differences many scholars use the terms "Before the Common Era" (BCE) and "in the Common Era" (CE) instead of BC and AD to avoid cultural insensitivity.

Scientists who derive dates from radioactive methods, wanting a neutral international system without allegiance to any of the above calendars, have chosen to count years back from the present (BP). But since scientists too require a firm fixed point, they take BP to mean "before 1950" (the approximate year of Libby's establishment of the first radioactive method, radiocarbon). This may be convenient for scientists, but can be confusing for everyone else (a date of 400 BP is not 400 years ago but AD 1550, currently about 450 years ago). It is therefore clearest to convert any BP date for the last few thousand years into the BC/AD system. For the Paleolithic period, however (stretching back two or three million years before 10,000 BC), archaeologists

use the terms "BP" and "years ago" interchangeably, since a difference of 50 years or so between them is irrelevant. For this remote epoch one is dating sites or events at best only to within several thousand years of their "true" date.

Discussion of the Paleolithic makes it evident that our whole conception and interpretation of time and its measurement needs to be adapted to the period being studied. If even the most precise dates for the Paleolithic give us glimpses of that epoch only at intervals of several thousand years, clearly archaeologists can never hope to reconstruct Paleolithic events in the manner of conventional history, peopled with individuals as, for instance, in ancient Egypt during the era of the pharaohs.

On the other hand, Paleolithic archaeologists can gain insights into some of the broad long-term changes that shaped the way modern humans evolved – insights that are denied archaeologists working with shorter periods of time, where in any case there may be too much "detail" for the broader pattern to be easily discernible.

The way in which archaeologists carry out their research is therefore very much dependent on the precision of dating – the sharpness of focus – obtainable for the period of time in question.

RELATIVE DATING

The first, and in some ways the most important, step in much archaeological research involves ordering things into sequences. The things to be put into sequence can be archaeological deposits in a stratigraphic excavation. Or they can be artifacts as in a typological

sequence. Changes in the earth's climate also give rise to local, regional, and global environmental sequences – the most notable being the sequence of global fluctuations during the Ice Age. All these sequences can be used for relative dating.

STRATIGRAPHY

Stratigraphy, as we saw in Chapter 3, is the study of stratification – the laying down or depositing of strata or layers (also called deposits) one above the other. From the point of view of relative dating, the important principle is that the underlying layer was deposited first and therefore earlier than the overlying layer. Thus a succession of layers should provide a relative chronological sequence, from earliest (bottom) to latest (top).

Good stratigraphic excavation at an archaeological site is designed to obtain such a sequence. Part of this work involves detecting whether there has been any human or natural disturbance of the layers since they

were originally deposited. In Chapter 2 we discussed some of these cultural and natural formation processes – such as rubbish pits dug down by later occupants of a site into earlier layers, animals burrowing holes, and floods washing layers away and redepositing them elsewhere in a secondary context. Armed with carefully observed stratigraphic information, the archaeologist can hope to construct a reliable relative chronological sequence for the deposition of the different layers.

But of course what we mostly want to date are not so much the layers or deposits themselves as the humanly generated materials within them – artifacts, structures,

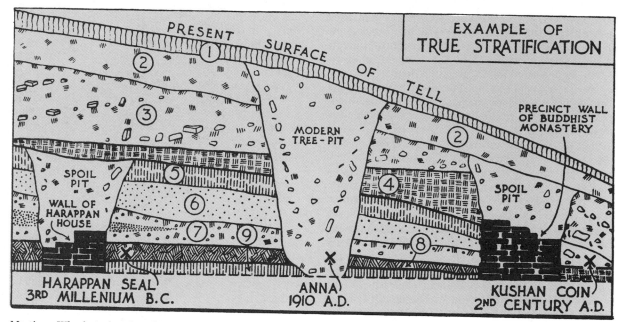

PRESENT SURFACE OF TELL

EXAMPLE OF
TRUE STRATIFICATION

MODERN
TREE-PIT

PRECINCT WALL
OF BUDDHIST
MONASTERY

SPOIL
PIT

WALL OF
HARAPPAN
HOUSE

SPOIL
PIT

HARAPPAN SEAL
3RD MILLENIUM B.C.

ANNA
1910 A.D.

KUSHAN COIN
2ND CENTURY A.D.

Mortimer Wheeler's drawing of a section across a mound or tell in the Indus Valley (modern Pakistan). Pit disturbance makes dating difficult, but the Harappan seal, for example (age known from similar seals found elsewhere), lies in an undisturbed context in layer 8, and can therefore help date that layer and the wall against which the layer abuts.

organic remains – which ultimately (when systematically studied) reveal past human activities at the site. Here the idea of *association*, touched on in Chapter 2, is important. When we say that two objects were found in association within the same archaeological deposit, we generally mean that they became buried at the same time. Provided that the deposit is a sealed one, without stratigraphic intrusions from another deposit, the associated objects can be said to be no later (no more recent) than the deposit itself. A sequence of sealed deposits thus gives a sequence – and relative chronology – for the time of burial of the objects found associated in those deposits.

This is a crucial concept to grasp, because if one of those objects can later be given an absolute date – say a piece of charcoal that can be dated by radiocarbon in the laboratory – then it is possible to assign that absolute date not only to the charcoal but to the sealed deposit and the other objects associated with it as well. A series of such dates from different deposits will give an absolute chronology for the whole sequence. It is this interconnecting of stratigraphic sequences with absolute dating methods that provides the most reliable basis for dating archaeological sites and their contents. The section on radiocarbon dating (see below) illustrates this for the site of Gatecliff Shelter, Nevada.

But there is another important point to consider. So far we have dated, relatively and with luck absolutely, the time of burial of the deposits and their associated material. As we have observed, however, what we want ultimately to reconstruct and date are the past human activities and behavior that those deposits and materials represent. If a deposit is a rubbish pit with pottery in it, the deposit itself is of interest as an example of human activity, and the date for it is the date of human use of the pit. This will also be the date of final burial of the pottery – but it will *not* be the date of human use of that pottery, which could have been in circulation tens or hundreds of years earlier, before being discarded, perhaps buried in another deposit and then dug up with other rubbish to be thrown into the pit. It is necessary therefore always to be clear about which activity one is trying to date, or can reliably date in the circumstances. The cultural formation processes discussed in Chapter 2 all have to be taken into account in any assessment of this question.

Bone Age

A useful method of assessing whether several bones found in association in the same stratigraphic deposit are in fact of the same relative age is chemical dating by studying nitrogen, fluorine, and uranium content.

In the deposit the bone's protein (mainly collagen) content is very gradually reduced by the processes of chemical decay. The most useful index for the amount of protein present is the bone's nitrogen content, which, for modern bone, is around 4 percent. The rate at which the level of nitrogen declines depends on the temperature and the water, chemical, and bacteriological content of the environment in which the bone is buried.

At the same time, percolating ground water has significant effects on the composition of bone. Two elements present in solution in the ground water – fluorine and uranium – are absorbed gradually by the bone. Thus, the content of fluorine and uranium in buried bone gradually increases, and can be measured in the laboratory. Like the rate of decrease in nitrogen, the rates of increase in fluorine and uranium depend strongly on local factors. All these rates of change are thus too variable to form the basis of an absolute dating method, nor can one compare relative ages so derived at one site with those at another site. But on an individual site chemical dating can distinguish bones of different age found in apparent stratigraphic association.

The most famous application of the method was in the case of the Piltdown forgery. In the early 1900s, pieces of human skull, an ape-like jawbone, and some teeth were found in a Lower Paleolithic gravel pit in Sussex, southern England. The discoveries led to claims that the "missing link" between apes and humans had been found. Piltdown Man (*Eoanthropus dawsoni*) had an important place in textbooks until 1953, when it was exposed as a complete hoax. Fluorine, uranium, and nitrogen dating at the British Museum (Natural History) showed that the skull was

Piltdown Man: a reconstruction made shortly before the remains were discovered to be a hoax. Fluorine, uranium, and nitrogen dating of the skull, jawbone, and teeth proved that they were of different relative ages, and not associated.

human but of relatively recent age (it was subsequently dated at about 620 years old); the jawbone came from an orang-utan and was a modern "plant." Both the skull and the jawbone had been treated with pigment (potassium dichromate) to make them look old and associated. Today, many suspect that Charles Dawson, the discoverer, was the hoaxer.

TYPOLOGICAL SEQUENCES

When we look at the artifacts, buildings, and indeed any of the human creations around us, most of us can mentally arrange some of them into a rough chronological sequence. One kind of aircraft looks older than another, one set of clothes looks more "old-fashioned" than the next. How do archaeologists exploit this ability for relative dating?

As we saw in Chapter 3, the form of an artifact such as a pot can be defined by its specific attributes of material, shape, and decoration. Several pots with the same attributes constitute a pot type, and typology groups artifacts into such types. Underlying the notion of relative dating through typology are two other ideas.

The first is that the products of a given period and place have a recognizable style: through their distinctive shape and decoration they are in some sense characteristic of the society that produced them. This point is further discussed in Chapters 5 and 10. The archaeologist or anthropologist can often recognize and classify individual artifacts by their style, and hence assign them to a particular place in a typological sequence.

The second idea is that the change in style (shape and decoration) of artifacts is often quite gradual, or evolutionary. Indeed, this idea came from the Darwinian theory of the evolution of species, and was embraced by 19th-century archaeologists, who realized that here was a very convenient rule, that "like goes with like." In other words, particular artifacts (e.g. bronze daggers) produced at about the same time are often alike, whereas those produced several centuries

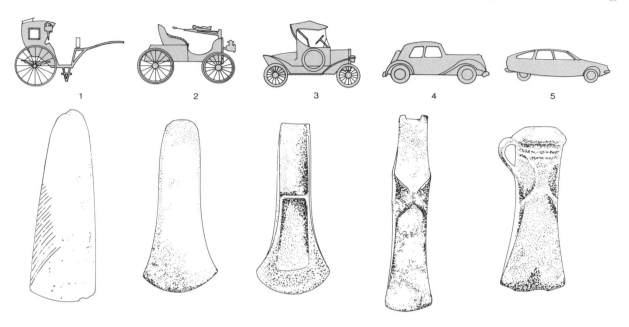

The arrangement of artifact types in a sequence is based on two simple ideas: first, that products of a given period and place have a distinctive style or design; and second, that changes in style are gradual, or evolutionary. Gradual changes in design are evident in the history of the automobile (top) and of the prehistoric European axe (above: (1) stone; (2–5) bronze). However, the rate of change (a century for the automobile, millennia for the axe) has to be deduced from absolute dating methods.

apart will be different as a result of centuries of change. It follows, then, that when one is faced with a series of daggers of unknown date, it is logical first to arrange them in a sequence in such a way that the most closely similar are located beside each other. This is then likely to be the true chronological sequence, because it best reflects the principle that "like goes with like."

Such arguments were developed by many archaeologists, who found that relative chronologies could be established for different classes of artifacts from different regions. The great master of the "typological method" was the 19th-century Swedish scholar Oscar Montelius, who formulated local relative chronologies for many of the regions of Bronze Age Europe, drawing upon bronze tool and weapon forms. These regional sequences could in many cases be confirmed in their outlines by stratigraphic excavations where it was indeed found that the simpler forms were the earliest.

Montelius went on to use the same arguments also in spatial terms to show how the artifact types in one region influenced those in adjacent areas. In this way, making certain assumptions about the direction of influence, he established a relative chronology of tool and weapon forms for the whole of Europe in the Bronze Age. (The assumption about the direction of influence – the famous principle that progress origina-

ted in the Near East and spread out from there – has been challenged and in part overthrown by more recent work. But in other respects the Montelius system for the European Bronze Age, as refined by the German prehistorian Paul Reinecke and others, is effectively still in use.)

For many purposes, it remains true that the best way to assign a relative date to an artifact is to match it with an artifact already recognized within a well-established typological system. In Europe, this is true for Bronze Age artifacts, but it applies, very much more widely, at a world level. In the Paleolithic period, the first approximate (relative) dating of a layer will often come from an examination of the stone tools found within it: hand-axes imply Lower (or to a lesser extent Middle) Paleolithic; blades Upper Paleolithic. In later periods, pottery typologies usually form the backbone of the chronological system. Good examples are the detailed studies on the pottery of Greece in the Mycenaean period by the Danish archaeologist Arne Furumark and his successors, and the ceramic sequence established for the Pueblo Indians of the American Southwest. But nearly every area has its own well-established ceramic succession. If this is tied into a stratigraphic sequence of deposits that can be dated by radiocarbon or other absolute means, then

121

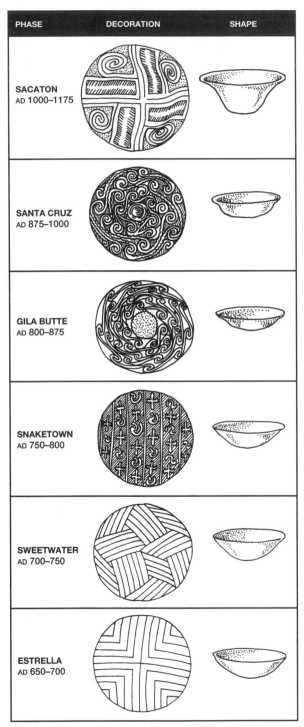

PHASE	DECORATION	SHAPE
SACATON AD 1000–1175		
SANTA CRUZ AD 875–1000		
GILA BUTTE AD 800–875		
SNAKETOWN AD 750–800		
SWEETWATER AD 700–750		
ESTRELLA AD 650–700		

Pottery typology, as exemplified by this 500-year sequence of Hohokam bowl styles from the American Southwest.

the artifacts in the typological sequence can themselves be assigned absolute dates in years.

It is also worth noting that different types of artifact change in style (decoration and shape) at different rates, and therefore vary in the chronological distinctions that they indicate. For example, the changes in decoration of the painted Mycenaean pottery mentioned above may have occurred at intervals of 20 years or so, whereas other types of decorated pottery often lasted more than a century. Undecorated pottery could keep much the same shape for several centuries. By and large, with pottery, surface decoration changes more rapidly than shape and is therefore the most chronologically sensitive attribute to use for a typological sequence. The shape of a vessel or container may in any case be most strongly influenced by a practical requirement, such as water storage, which need not alter for hundreds of years.

Other artifacts, such as metal weapons or tools, can change in style quite rapidly, and so may be useful chronological indicators. By contrast stone tools, such as hand-axes, are often notoriously slow to change in form and therefore rarely make sensitive indicators of the passage of time.

Seriation

The insights of the principle that "like goes with like" have been developed further to deal with associations of finds (assemblages), rather than with the forms of single objects taken in isolation. This technique of seriation allows assemblages of artifacts to be arranged in a succession, or serial order, which is then taken to indicate their ordering in time: it is thus an exercise in relative chronology.

Two versions of the technique have been applied: *contextual seriation* and *frequency seriation*.

Contextual Seriation. Here it is the duration of different artifact styles (shape and decoration) that governs the seriation. The pioneer of the method was Flinders Petrie. Working at Diospolis Parva in Upper Egypt at the very end of the 19th century, he excavated several predynastic graves that could be neither stratigraphically linked to each other nor tied into the historical king-lists of the subsequent dynastic period. Petrie wanted to put the graves into chronological order, so he began by making an inventory of their contents. Each grave was allocated a separate slip of paper listing its artifact types.

Petrie then placed the separate slips parallel to each other, one above the other in a column, and kept rearranging their position up or down the column. He

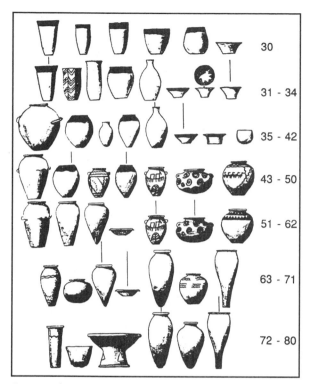

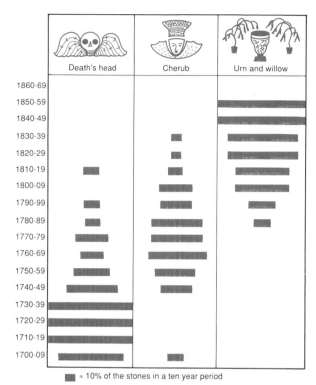

■ = 10% of the stones in a ten year period

Contextual seriation: Flinders Petrie's own serial ordering of predynastic Egyptian pottery from the site of Diospolis Parva. Starting at the top, seven successive stages are identified, each linked to the one before and after by at least one similar shape. At the left of the five lower rows are the "wavy-handled" pots, arranged by Petrie in a sequence of "degradation" – his clue to the order of the whole series. Subsequent research in Egypt has largely supported Petrie's relative chronological sequence.

Frequency seriation: changes in the popularity (or frequency) of three tombstone designs in central Connecticut cemeteries, from 1700 to 1860. Rises and falls in popularity have produced the characteristic battleship-shaped curve for the fluctuating fortunes of each design. As elsewhere in New England, the Death's head design (peak popularity 1710–1739) was gradually replaced by the Cherub (peak 1760–1789) which in turn was replaced by the Urn and willow tree (peak 1840–1859).

believed that the best arrangement would be the one where the greatest number of individual types had the shortest duration across the various slips. In this way he arrived at a sequence of assemblages – and thus of graves – arranged in what he thought was their relative chronological order. Subsequent work in Egypt has largely vindicated Petrie and shown that his serial ordering of the graves does in fact generally reflect their true chronological sequence.

Frequency Seriation. A similar problem – the lack of any external chronological information – was faced by American archaeologists working at Maya sites in the Yucatán in the 1940s. Their material, however, consisted of ceramic collections which had been recovered without stratigraphic context. In this particular case, there was a need to place the ceramic assem-

blages in serial order so as to construct a relative chronology of the buildings and monuments with which they were associated.

The solution was frequency seriation, which relies principally on measuring changes in the proportional abundance, or frequency, of a ceramic style. The two basic assumptions behind the method were set out in a classic paper by W.S. Robinson and another by G.W. Brainerd, both published in *American Antiquity* in 1951. First, they assumed that pottery styles gradually become more popular, reach a peak popularity and then fade away (a phenomenon that diagrammatically produces a shape like a battleship as viewed from above – hence the common term for them, *battleship curves*). Secondly, they argued that at a given time period, a pot style popular at one site would similarly be popular at another. Thus if the style in question

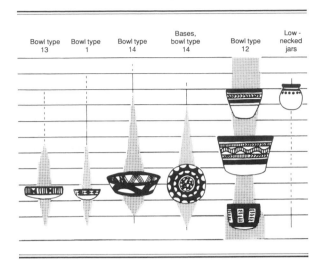

Bowl type 13	Bowl type 1	Bowl type 14	Bases, bowl type 14	Bowl type 12	Low-necked jars

Frequency seriation: Frank Hole's ordering of bowl types representing Susiana Black-on-Buff pottery from sites in the Deh Luran Plain, Iran. The battleship curves are again evident, indicating rises and falls in popularity. Stratigraphic excavation confirmed the validity of these sequences.

represented 18 percent of the total pottery found at site A at a particular period, the pottery from site B for the same period would have a similar proportion or frequency of that style.

Using these two assumptions, Robinson and Brainerd were able to put the assemblages into a sequence so that those with the most similar percentages of certain pot styles were always together. The chronological validity of the method has since been demonstrated by American archaeologists such as James A. Ford working in the American Southeast and Frank Hole in Iran.

Both Ford and Hole studied ceramic assemblages mainly derived from stratigraphic excavations. They were therefore able to compare the sequences obtained using the method of frequency seriation with the true stratigraphic sequences they discovered in their excavations. In both instances there were no serious contradictions.

Nevertheless it should always be borne in mind that seriation by itself does not tell us which end of a given sequence is first and which last – the true chronology has to be determined by other means, for instance by links with excavated stratigraphic sequences.

LINGUISTIC DATING

For completeness, it is appropriate to mention here an interesting approach to questions of chronology, in this case applied not to artifacts but to *language* change, as studied by comparisons in the vocabularies of related languages. Earlier claims suggested that here might be some sort of absolute dating method; these have been widely (and rightly) rejected. However, the method remains of real interest from the standpoint of relative chronology. (And see also box, Language Families and Language Change, p. 467.)

The basic principle is straightforward. If you take two groups of people, speaking the same language, and separate them so that there is no further contact between them, both groups will no doubt continue to speak the same tongue. But in each population, with the passage of time, changes will occur; new words will be invented and introduced whereas others will fall out of use. So, after a few centuries, the two independent groups will no longer be speaking quite the same language; after a few thousand years, the language of one group will probably be almost unintelligible to the other.

The field of *lexicostatistics* sets out to study such changes of vocabulary. A popular method has been to choose a list of either 100 or 200 common vocabulary terms and to see how many of these, in the two lan-

guages being compared, share a common root-word. The positive score, out of 100 or 200, gives some measure of how far the two languages have diverged since the time when they were one.

The rather suspect discipline of *glottochronology* would claim to go further, and use a formula to pronounce, from this measure of similarity and dissimilarity, how long ago in years it is since the two languages under consideration diverged. The American scholar, Morris Swadesh, the principal exponent of the method, concluded that two related languages would retain a common vocabulary of 86 percent of the original after a period of separation of 1000 years. In reality, however, there is no basis for assuming a constant and quantifiable rate of change in this way: many factors influence linguistic change (the existence of literacy among them).

The method is complicated by various other factors, such as the existence of loan-words (borrowed from elsewhere, and not part of the common heritage) in both of the languages under study. But the underlying idea that two languages with a very high score for the common vocabulary are more recently related than those with a low score is itself reasonable, and the approach cannot be excluded from a discussion of methods of relative dating.

CLIMATE AND CHRONOLOGY

So far we have been discussing sequences that can be established stratigraphically for individual sites, or typologically for artifacts. In addition, there is a major class of sequences, based on changes in the earth's climate, that has proved useful for relative dating on a local, regional, and even global scale. Some of these environmental sequences can also be dated by various absolute methods. (The impact of climatic and environmental fluctuations on human life is discussed in detail in Chapter 6.)

Pleistocene Chronology

The idea of a great Ice Age (the Pleistocene epoch), that occurred in the distant past, has been with us since the 19th century. As world temperatures fell, ice sheets – or glaciers – expanded, mantling large parts of the earth's surface and lowering world sea levels (the lost water being quite literally locked up in the ice). Early geologists and paleoclimatologists, studying the clear traces in geological deposits, soon realized that the Ice Age was not one long unbroken spell of colder climate. Instead it had witnessed what they identified as four major *glacials*, or periods of glacial advance (labeled, from earliest to latest, Günz, Mindel, Riss, and Würm in continental Europe; in North America different names were chosen – Wisconsin, for example, being the equivalent of Würm). Punctuating these cold periods were warmer interludes known as *interglacials*. More minor fluctuations within these major phases were called *stadials* and *interstadials*. Until the arrival after World War II of absolute dating methods such as those based on radioactive clocks, archaeologists depended very largely for their dating of the long Paleolithic period on attempts to correlate archaeological sites with this glacial sequence. Far away from the ice sheets, in regions such as Africa, strenuous efforts were made to link sites with fluctuations in rainfall

YEARS AGO	CLIMATE cool warm	GEOLOGICAL PERIODS	GEOLOGICAL EPOCHS	GLACIALS (EUROPE)	GLACIALS (N.AMERICA)	ARCHAEOLOGICAL STAGES
10,000 —			HOLOCENE			
				Würm (Weichsel)	Wisconsin	UPPER PALEOLITHIC
100,000 —			UPPER PLEISTOCENE			MIDDLE PALEOLITHIC
				Riss (Saale)	Illinoian	
			MIDDLE PLEISTOCENE	Mindel (Elster)	Kansan	
780,000 —		QUA-TERNARY		Günz (Menapian)	Nebraskan	LOWER PALEOLITHIC
			LOWER PLEISTOCENE			
	(uncertain)					
1,700,000 —						
		TERTIARY				

Table summarizing the main climatic changes, glacial terminology, and archaeological stages of the Pleistocene epoch.

(*pluvials* and *interpluvials*); the hope was that the fluctuations might somehow themselves be tied in with the glacial sequence.

In recent decades, however, scientists have come to recognize that fluctuations in climate during the Ice Age were much more complex than originally supposed. From the beginning of the Pleistocene, about 1.7 million years ago, down to about 780,000 years ago (the end of the Lower Pleistocene), there were perhaps ten cold periods separated by warmer interludes. Another eight or nine distinct periods of cold climate may have characterized the Middle and Upper Pleistocene, from 780,000 to 10,000 years ago. (The period of warmer climate known as the Holocene covers the last 10,000 years.) Archaeologists no longer rely on complex glacial advances and retreats as the basis for dating the Paleolithic. However, fluctuations in Pleistocene and Holocene climate as recorded in deep-sea cores, ice cores, and sediments containing pollen are of considerable value for dating purposes.

Deep-Sea Cores and Ice Cores

As indicated in Chapter 6, the most coherent record of climatic changes on a worldwide scale is now provided by deep-sea cores, drilled from the ocean bed. These cores contain shells of microscopic marine organisms known as *foraminifera*, laid down on the ocean floor through the slow continuous progress of sedimentation. Variations in the ratio of two oxygen isotopes in the calcium carbonate of these shells give a sensitive indicator of sea temperature at the time the organisms were alive. We now have an accurate temperature sequence stretching back 2.3 million years which reflects climate change on a global scale. Thus the cold episodes in the deep-sea cores relate to glacial periods of ice advance, and the warm episodes to interglacial or interstadial periods of ice retreat. The deep-sea core oxygen isotope record is a framework for a relative chronology for the Pleistocene.

This chronology is invaluable for reconstructing a record of past environmental change, as will be discussed in Chapter 6. Radiocarbon and uranium-series dating (see below) can also be applied to the foraminiferan shells to provide absolute dates for the sequence. In addition, the phenomenon of geomagnetic reversals (reversals in the earth's magnetic field), discussed in a later section of this chapter, can be used to link the sequence to Paleolithic sites in the East African Rift Valley. Such reversals are recorded in both the cores and in the rock strata at the archaeological sites with evidence of early humans (see box, pp. 148–49, Dating Our African Ancestors).

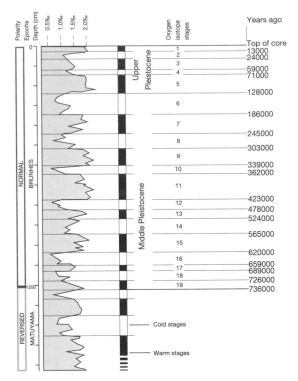

Climatic variations during the Pleistocene as recorded in the differing amounts of the oxygen isotope 18O (tinted area) in the deep-sea core V 28-238, from the Pacific Ocean.

Ice Cores. As with deep-sea cores, cores extracted from the polar ice of the Arctic and Antarctic have been made to yield impressive sequences revealing climatic oscillations. Here again these are most useful for reconstructing ancient environments (Chapter 6), but they have relevance for dating as well.

The layers of compacted ice form annual deposits for the last 2000–3000 years that can be counted – thus giving an absolute chronology for this part of the sequence. As we shall see in the box on Dating the Thera Eruption (pp. 160–61), this has proved useful as one possible means of cross-checking the date of that volcanic explosion, which some scholars believe severely disrupted the Minoan civilization of Crete. For earlier time periods, however – at greater depths – the annual stratification is no longer visible, and dating of the ice cores is much less certain. The Vostok core in Antarctica reached a depth of about 2200 m (7200 ft), and spans a time-range estimated at 160,000 years, an age exceeded in the northern hemisphere by the two Greenland ice cores: GRIP and GISP2. Good correlations have been made with climatic oscillations deduced from the study of the deep-sea cores.

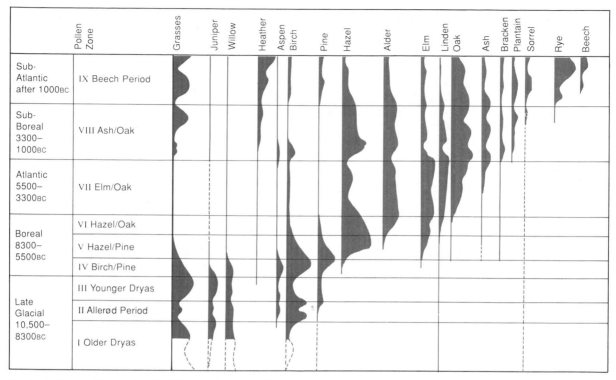

Idealized diagram illustrating the Holocene (postglacial) pollen zone sequence in Jutland, Denmark. Each pollen zone is characterized by rises and falls in pollen of certain plant species, e.g. birch and pine in zone IV, beech in zone IX. Dates are given in uncalibrated radiocarbon years BC (see p. 141).

Pollen Dating

All flowering plants produce the almost indestructible grains called pollen, and their preservation in bogs and lake sediments has allowed pollen experts (palynologists) to construct detailed sequences of past vegetation and climate. These sequences are an immense help in understanding ancient environments, as we shall discuss in Chapter 6. But they have also been – and to a limited extent still are – important as a method of relative dating.

The best-known pollen sequences are those developed for the Holocene (postglacial) of northern Europe, where an elaborate succession of so-called *pollen zones* covers the last 10,000 years. By studying pollen samples from a particular site, that site can often be fitted into a broader pollen zone sequence and thus assigned a relative date. Isolated artifacts and finds such as bog-bodies discovered in contexts where pollen is preserved can also very usefully be dated in the same way. However, it is important to remember that the pollen zones are not uniform across large areas. In any one local region, such as the Somerset Levels of southern England, it is best to work with a specialist who can build up a sequence of pollen zones for that region. The sites and finds in the vicinity can then be linked to it. If tree-ring or radiocarbon dates are available for all or part of the sequence, one has the makings of an absolute chronology for the region.

Thanks to the durability of pollen grains, they can yield environmental evidence even as far back as 3 million years ago for sites in East Africa (Chapter 6). Different interglacial periods in areas such as northern Europe have also been shown to have characteristic pollen sequences, which means that the pollen evidence at an individual site in the area can sometimes be matched to a particular interglacial – a useful dating mechanism given that radiocarbon does not operate at these early time periods.

Faunal Dating

There is a further method of relative dating relevant for the Pleistocene epoch, though this one is not based on the sedimentary processes that lie behind the methods already discussed. This is the old-established technique of faunal dating, which relies on the fact that many mammal species have evolved considerably over the last few million years, new forms emerging and old ones dying out. The changes in each species have been charted to create a rough sequence, for instance of elephants or pigs. In theory, if a similar sequence of pig species is found at two different sites, those sites can be assigned the same relative age. In practice the method is very imprecise for many reasons, including the fact that species extinct in one area may have continued much longer in another.

Nevertheless, its imprecision does not rule out faunal dating altogether as a useful method for the Pleistocene, where an accuracy even only to within the nearest quarter million years can be of value. For instance, faunal dating has proved important in the correlation of the early human sites that have been discovered in East and South Africa. And in Britain, associated mammalian fauna suggested that the human tibia and a tooth found at Boxgrove, southern England, are about 500,000 years old and are thus Britain's oldest human fossils.

ABSOLUTE DATING

Despite the great utility of methods of relative dating, archaeologists ultimately want to know how old sequences, sites, and artifacts are in calendar years. To achieve this they need to use the methods of absolute dating described in the following sections – from traditional historical methods to those which are based on the great variety of modern scientific techniques now available.

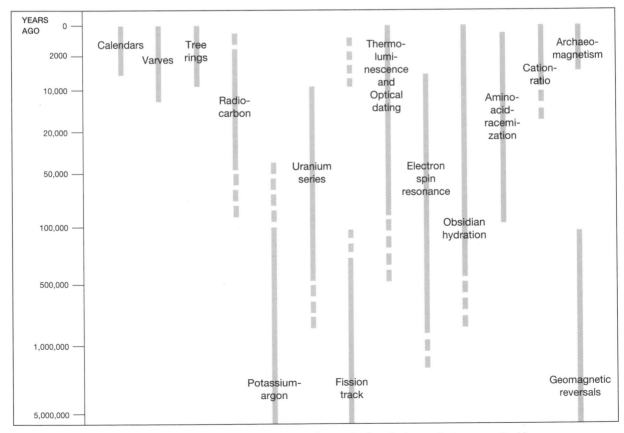

Chronological table summarizing the spans of time for which different absolute dating methods are applicable.

CALENDARS AND HISTORICAL CHRONOLOGIES

Until the development of the first scientific dating techniques around the beginning of this century, dating in archaeology depended almost entirely on historical methods. That is to say, it relied on archaeological connections with chronologies and calendars that people in ancient times had themselves established. Such dating methods are still of immense value today.

In the ancient world, literate societies recorded their own history in written documents. The Romans recorded events in terms of the year of rule of their consuls and emperors, although they sometimes referred events back to the foundation of the city of Rome itself. The Greeks reckoned from the date of the first Olympic Games, today usually set in the year 776 BC. In Egypt, the Near East, and ancient China history was recorded in terms of the successive kings, who were organized in groups of "dynasties." As we shall see, there were also very precise calendrical systems in Mesoamerica.

Archaeologists have to bear in mind three main points when working with early historical chronologies. First, the chronological system requires careful reconstruction, and any list of rulers or kings needs to be reasonably complete. Second, the list, although it may reliably record the number of years in each reign, has still to be linked with our own calendar if it is not to remain merely a "floating chronology." Third, the artifacts, features, or structures to be dated at a particular site have somehow to be related to the historical chronology, perhaps by their association with an inscription referring to the ruler of the time.

These points can be well illustrated by the Egyptian and Maya chronologies. Egyptian history is arranged in terms of 31 dynasties, themselves organized into the Old, Middle, and New Kingdoms. The modern view is a synthesis based on several documents including the so-called Turin Royal Canon. This synthesis gives an estimate of the number of years in each reign, right down to the conquest of Egypt by Alexander the Great, which can be set firmly, using information from Greek historians, in the year 332 BC. So the Egyptian dynasties can be dated by working backward from there, although the exact length of every reign is not known. This system can be confirmed and refined using astronomy. Egyptian historical records describe observations of certain astronomical events that can be dated, quite independently, using current astronomical knowledge and knowledge of where in Egypt the ancient observations were carried out.

Egyptian dates are generally considered to be very reliable after 664 BC. For the New Kingdom (c. 1550–1070 BC), the margin of error may be one or two decades, and by the time one goes back to the beginning of the First Dynasty, around 3000 BC, the accumulated errors might amount to some 200 years or so.

Of the calendrical systems of Mesoamerica, the Maya calendar was the most elaborate (see box overleaf). It does not depend, as do those of Europe and the Near East, on a record of dynasties and rulers. Other areas of Mesoamerica had their own calendrical systems which operated on similar principles.

ANCIENT EGYPTIAN CHRONOLOGY

EARLY DYNASTIC (Archaic) (3000–2575 BC)
Dynasties 1–3

OLD KINGDOM (2575–2134 BC)
Dynasties 4–8

FIRST INTERMEDIATE PERIOD (2134–2040 BC)
Dynasties 9–11

MIDDLE KINGDOM (2040–1640 BC)
Dynasties 11–14

SECOND INTERMEDIATE PERIOD
(1640–1532 BC)
Dynasties 15–17

NEW KINGDOM (1550–1070 BC)
Dynasties 18–20

THIRD INTERMEDIATE PERIOD (1070–712 BC)
Dynasties 21–25

LATE PERIOD (712–332 BC)
Dynasties 25–31

A historical chronology for ancient Egypt. The broad terminology is generally agreed by Egyptologists, but the precise dating of the earlier periods is disputed. Overlapping dates between dynasties/kingdoms (e.g. First Intermediate period and Middle Kingdom) indicate that separate rulers were accepted in different parts of the country.

THE MAYA CALENDAR

The Maya calendar was one of great precision, used for recording dates in inscriptions on stone columns or stelae erected at Maya cities during the Classic period (AD 300–900). The elucidation of the calendar, and the more recent decipherment of the Maya glyphs, mean that a well-dated Maya history is now emerging in a way which seemed impossible a few decades ago.

To understand the Maya calendar it is necessary to comprehend the Maya numerical system, and to recognize the various glyphs or signs by which the various days (each of which had a name, like our Monday, Tuesday, etc.) were distinguished. In addition, it is

necessary to follow how the calendar itself was constructed.

The Maya numerals are relatively straightforward. A stylized shell meant zero, a dot "one," and a horizontal bar "five."

The Maya used two calendrical systems: the Calendar Round and the Long Count.

The **Calendar Round** was used for most everyday purposes. It involved two methods of counting. The first is the Sacred Round of 260 days, which is still used in some parts of the Maya highlands. We should imagine two interlocking cog wheels, one with numbers from 1 to 13, the other with 20 named days. Day 1 (to use our terminology) will be 1 Imix, day 2 is 2 Ik, day 3 is 3 Akbal, and so on until day 13, which is 13 Ben. But then day 14 is 1 Ix, and so the system continues. The sequence coincides again after 260 days and the new Sacred Round begins with 1 Imix once more.

In conjunction with this, the solar year was recorded, consisting of 18

named months, each of 20 days, plus a terminal period of 5 days. The Maya New Year began with 1 Pop (Pop being the name of the month); the next day was 2 Pop, and so on.

These two cycles proceeded simultaneously, so that a given day would be designated in both (e.g. 1 Kan 2 Pop). A specific combination of that kind could occur only once in every 52 years. This calendar was therefore sufficient for most daily purposes, and the 52-year cycle had symbolic significance for the Maya.

The **Long Count** was used for historical dates. Like any unique calendrical system, it needed to have a starting or zero date, and for the Maya this was 13 August 3113 BC (according to a commonly agreed correlation with the Christian calendar). A Long Count date takes the form of five numbers (e.g. in our own numerical notation 8.16.5.12.7). The first figure records the number elapsed of the largest unit, the *baktun* (of 144,000 days or about 400 years). The second is the *katun* (7200

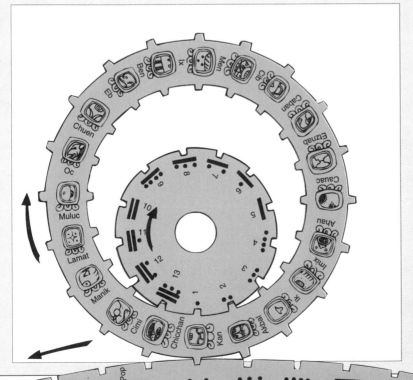

The Calendar Round (left) can be visualized as a set of interlocking cog wheels. The 260-day cycle is created by the interlocking of the two wheels shown above. Meshing with this is the 365-day cycle (part of which is shown below). The specific conjoining of day names given here (1 Kan 2 Pop) cannot return until 52 years (18,980 days) have passed.

The Long Count (right) was used to record historical dates. Here, in Burial 48 at the city of Tikal, the date given – reading from top to bottom – is 9.1.1.10.10 4 Oc, or 9 baktuns, 1 katun, 1 tun, 10 uinals, and 10 kins, with the day name 4 Oc at the bottom. In modern terms this is 19 March AD 457.

days or 20 years), the third a *tun* of 360 days, the fourth a *uinal* of 20 days, and finally the *kin*, the single day.

A positional notation was used, starting at the top with the number of *baktuns*, and proceeding downwards through the lower units. Usually, each number was followed by the glyph for the unit in question (e.g. 8 *baktuns*) so that dates on the stelae can be readily recognized.

The earliest date yet noted on a stela in the Maya area proper is on Stela 29 at Tikal, and reads 8.12.14.8.15. In other words:

8 *baktuns*	1,152,000 days
12 *katuns*	86,400 days
14 *tuns*	5,040 days
8 *uinals*	160 days
15 *kins*	15 days
	or 1,243,615 days

since the zero date in 3113 BC. This is the equivalent of 6 July AD 292. According to the Maya, the end of the present world will come about on 23 December 2012.

Using a Historical Chronology

It is relatively easy for the archaeologist to use a historical chronology when abundant artifacts are found that can be related closely to it. Thus, at major Maya sites such as Tikal or Copán there are numerous stelae with calendrical inscriptions that can often be used to date the buildings with which they are associated. The artifacts associated with the buildings can in turn be dated: for instance, if a pottery typology has been worked out, the finding of known types of pottery in such historically dated contexts allows the pottery typology itself to be dated. Contexts and buildings on other sites lacking inscriptions can be dated approximately through the occurrence of similar pot types.

Sometimes artifacts themselves carry dates, or the names of rulers that can be dated. This is the case with many Classic Maya ceramics that bear hieroglyphic inscriptions. For the Roman and medieval periods of Europe, coins offer a similar opportunity, as they normally carry the name of the issuing ruler, and inscriptions or records elsewhere usually allow the ruler to be dated. To date a coin or an artifact is not the same thing as to date the context in which it is found. The date of the coin indicates the year in which it was made. Its inclusion within a sealed archaeological deposit establishes simply a *terminus post quem* ("date after which"): in other words, the deposit can be no earlier than the date on the coin – but it could be later than that date.

A well-established historical chronology in one country may be used to date events in neighboring and more far-flung lands that lack their own historical records but are mentioned in the histories of the literate homeland. Similarly, archaeologists can use exports and imports of objects to extend chronological linkages by means of *cross-dating*. For instance, Flinders Petrie, in his excavations in 1891–92 at Tell el-Amarna, capital of the heretic pharaoh Akhenaten (now dated in the Egyptian historical chronology to about 1353–1335 BC), discovered pottery that he recognized to be of Aegean origin: Mycenaean pottery in fact. Within the typological system of Mycenaean pottery later established by the Swedish scholar Arne Furumark it can be termed Late Helladic IIIA2 (one of the divisions in a relative chronology). Its presence in a well-dated Egyptian context establishes a *terminus ante quem* ("date before which") for the manufacture in Greece of that pottery: it cannot be more recent than the Amarna context. Likewise, actual Egyptian objects, some with inscriptions allowing them to be accurately dated in Egyptian terms, occur at various Aegean sites, thereby helping to date the contexts in which they are

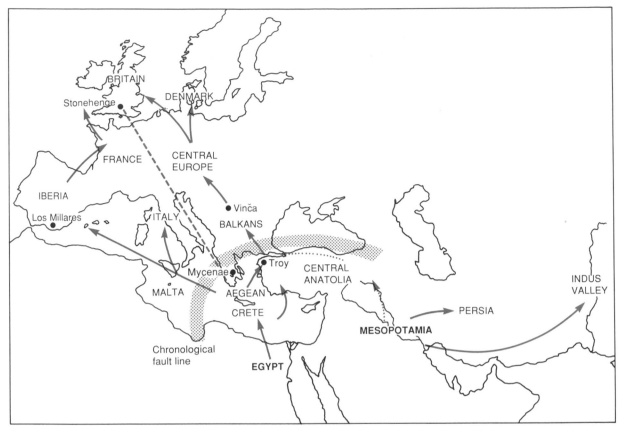

European chronology. Until the 1960s, prehistoric Europe was largely dated by supposed typological links between neighboring lands that rested ultimately on the historical chronology of ancient Egypt. Calibrated radiocarbon dates (p. 141) have shown many of these links to be false ones. Egypt and the Aegean can still be cross-dated by direct exports and imports, but the "fault line" indicates how links have been severed with regions to the north and west, where dates have been pushed back by several centuries.

found. It is this linkage from A to B (Aegean to Egypt), and conversely from B to A, that has given rise to the term cross-dating.

Until 20 or 30 years ago, much of European prehistory was based on this method of dating, with successive links established between neighboring lands. Even the remotest parts of Europe were dated in absolute years BC using a system that rested ultimately on the Egyptian chronology. But the calibration of radiocarbon dates (see below) has brought about the collapse of this precarious chronological edifice.

It is now clear that although the links between Egypt and the Aegean were valid, being based on actual imports and exports, those between the Aegean and the rest of Europe were not. The entire chronology of prehistoric Europe was constructed on false assumptions whose rectification produced (so far as Europe

is concerned) what has come to be called the Second Radiocarbon Revolution (see map).

Dating by historical methods remains the most important procedure for the archaeologist in countries with a reliable calendar supported by a significant degree of literacy. Where there are serious uncertainties over the calendar, or over its correlation with the modern calendrical system, the correlations can often be checked, at least in outline, by the other absolute dating methods to be described below.

Outside the historic and literate lands, however, cross-dating and broad typological comparisons have been almost entirely superseded by the various scientifically based dating methods described below. So that now, all the world's cultures can be assigned absolute dates.

ANNUAL CYCLES: VARVES AND TREE-RINGS

Before the advent of radioactive methods after World War II, the counting of varves and tree-rings provided the most accurate means of absolute dating – but only in two regions of the world: Scandinavia for varves and the American Southwest for tree-rings. Today, while varves remain of restricted use, tree-rings have come to rival radiocarbon as the main method of dating for the last few thousand years in many parts of Europe, North America, and Japan, thanks to painstaking scientific work.

Any absolute dating method depends on the existence of a regular, time-dependent process. The most obvious of these is the system by which we order our modern calendar: the rotation of the earth around the sun once each year. Because this yearly cycle produces regular annual fluctuations in climate, it has an impact on features of the environment which can in certain cases be measured to create a chronology (as well as forming a record of environmental change: see Chapter 6).

Evidence of these annual fluctuations is widespread. For example, the changes in temperature in polar regions result in annual variations in the thickness of polar ice, which scientists can study from cores drilled through the ice (see section above, Climate and Chronology). Similarly, in lands bordering the polar regions, the melting of the ice sheets each year when temperatures rise leads to the formation of annual deposits of sediment, called *varves*, which can be counted. The growth of most species of plant varies annually, which makes possible the principle of *tree-ring dating* (dendrochronology). And growth in many animal species also varies during the year, so that annual variations in tissue deposits can sometimes be detected in skeletons or in shells of, for instance, marine molluscs (Chapter 6).

As with a historical king-list, for absolute dating purposes the sequence needs to be a long one (with no gaps), linked somehow to the present day, and capable of being related to the structures or artifacts one actually wants to date. Annual growth rings on molluscs found at a site can provide good evidence for season of occupation, for example (Chapter 7), but the ring sequence is much too short to form an absolute chronology. Varves and tree-rings, on the other hand, can be counted to produce unbroken sequences stretching back many thousands of years.

Varves and Lake Sediments

In 1878, the Swedish geologist Baron Gerard de Geer noticed that certain deposits of clay were layered in a regular way. He realized that these layers ("varves" in Swedish) had been deposited in lakes around the edges of Scandinavian glaciers by the annual melting of the ice sheets, which had been steadily retreating since the end of the Pleistocene epoch, or last Ice Age. The layers varied in thickness from year to year, a thick layer resulting from a warm year with increased glacial melting, a thin layer indicating colder conditions. By measuring the successive thicknesses of a whole sequence, and comparing the pattern with varves in nearby areas, it proved possible to link long sequences together.

This was the first geochronological method to be developed. Considerable deposits were found, representing thousands of years, stretching (when linked together) from the present back to the beginning of the retreat of the glacial ice sheets in Scandinavia some

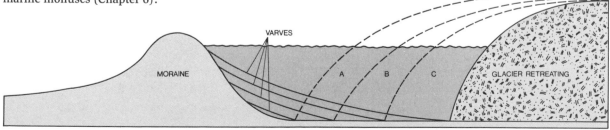

Varves are sediment layers that were deposited in lakes by melting glaciers. When the ice retreated to position A, the sediments contained in the melted waters settled to form the lowermost varve. In successive years (B, C, etc.), more sediments were deposited, each varve extending horizontally to the point where that winter halted the glacier's thaw and representing in thickness the amount of glacial discharge. When varves from several glacial lakes have been recorded they can be correlated, to create a master sequence for an area. Such sequences have been established in Scandinavia and North America.

13,000 years ago. The method allowed, for the first time, a fairly reliable estimate for the date of the end of the last Ice Age, and hence made a contribution to archaeological chronology not only in Scandinavia but in many other parts of the world as well.

Comparable studies have been undertaken in North America, for instance in Wisconsin. But there are problems in correlating the North American and North European (Finnish and Swedish) data. For direct archaeological applications, radiocarbon dating and tree-ring work are in general much more useful. There has however been a significant advance using carbon samples taken from annually laminated sediments from the bottom of Lake Suigetsu in Japan, which can be dated (by direct counting of the annual layers) back to 45,000 years ago. This has, for the first time, permitted the calibration of the radiocarbon calendar back to this very early date.

Tree-Ring Dating

The modern technique of tree-ring dating (dendrochronology) was developed by an American astronomer, A.E. Douglass, in the early decades of this century – although many of the principles had been understood long before that. Working on well-preserved timbers in the arid American Southwest, by 1930

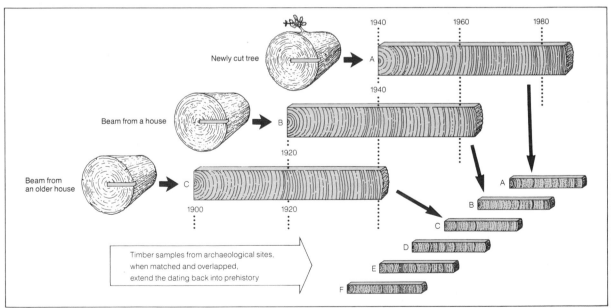

Tree-ring dating. (Top) Section across an Irish oak, the varying thickness of the annual growth rings clearly visible. The inner rings here date to the AD 1550s. (Above) Diagram to show how the annual growth rings can be counted, matched, and overlapped, to build up a master sequence for a particular region.

Douglass could assign absolute dates to many of the major sites there, such as Mesa Verde and Pueblo Bonito. But it was not until the end of the 1930s that the technique was introduced to Europe, and only in the 1960s that the use of statistical procedures and computers laid the foundations for the establishment of the long tree-ring chronologies now so fundamental to modern archaeology. Today dendrochronology has two distinct archaeological uses: (1) as a successful means of calibrating or correcting radiocarbon dates (see below); and (2) as an independent method of absolute dating in its own right.

Basis of Method. Most trees produce a ring of new wood each year and these circles of growth can easily be seen in a cross-section of the trunk of a felled tree. These rings are not of uniform thickness. In an individual tree, they will vary for two reasons. First, the rings become narrower with the increasing age of the tree. Second, the amount a tree grows each year is affected by fluctuations in climate. In arid regions, rainfall above the average one year will produce a particularly thick annual ring. In more temperate regions, sunlight and temperature may be more critical than rainfall in affecting a tree's growth. Here, a sharp cold spell in spring may produce a narrow growth ring.

Dendrochronologists measure and plot these rings and produce a diagram indicating the thickness of successive rings in an individual tree. Trees of the same species growing in the same area will generally show the same pattern of rings so that the growth sequence can be matched between successively older timbers to build up a chronology for an area. (It is not necessary to fell trees in order to study the ring sequence: a usable sample can be extracted by boring without harming the tree.) By matching sequences of rings from living trees of different ages as well as from old timber, dendrochronologists can produce a long, continuous sequence extending back hundreds, even thousands, of years from the present. Thus, when an ancient timber of the same species (e.g. Douglas fir in the American Southwest or oak in Europe) is found, it should be possible to match its tree-ring sequence of, say, 100 years with the appropriate 100-year length of the master sequence or chronology. In this way, the felling date for that piece of timber can usually be dated to within a year.

Applications: (1) The Long Master Sequences and Radiocarbon. Perhaps the greatest contribution so far of dendrochronology to archaeological dating has been the development of long tree-ring sequences, against which it has proved possible to check and calibrate

radiocarbon dates. The pioneering research was done in Arizona on a remarkable species, the California bristlecone pine (*Pinus aristata*), some of which are up to 4900 years old – the oldest living things on earth. By matching samples from these living trees with rings from dead pines preserved in the region's arid environment, the scientists – led by E. Schulman and later C. Wesley Ferguson – built up an unbroken sequence back from the present as far as 6700 BC. Just how this sequence has been used for calibration work will be discussed in the section on radiocarbon below.

The research in the American Southwest has now been complemented by studies in Europe of tree-rings of oak, often well preserved in waterlogged deposits. Two separate oak sequences in Northern Ireland and western Germany both now stretch back unbroken into the distant past, as far as *c.* 5300 BC in the Irish case and *c.* 8500 BC in the German. The scientists who did the work – Michael Baillie in Belfast, the late Bernd Becker in Stuttgart, Marco Spurk from Hohenheim, and their colleagues – have also succeeded in matching the two separate sequences, thus creating a reliable central and west European absolute chronology against which to calibrate radiocarbon dates, as well as to use in direct tree-ring dating.

Applications: (2) Direct Tree-Ring Dating. Where people in the past used timber from a species, such as oak, that today forms one of the dendrochronological sequences, one can obtain an archaeologically useful absolute date by matching the preserved timber with part of the master sequence. This is now feasible in many parts of the world outside the tropics.

Results are particularly impressive in the American Southwest, where the technique is longest established and wood is well preserved. Here Pueblo Indians built their dwellings from trees such as the Douglas fir and piñon pine that have yielded excellent ring sequences. Dendrochronology has become the principal dating method for the Pueblo villages, the earliest dates for which belong to the 1st century BC, although the main period of building came a millennium later.

One brief example from the Southwest will serve to highlight the precision and implications of the method. In his pioneer work, A.E. Douglass had established that Betatakin, a cliff dwelling in northwest Arizona, dated from around AD 1270. Returning to the site in the 1960s, Jeffrey Dean collected 292 tree-ring samples and used them to document not just the founding of the settlement in AD 1267, but its expansion room by room, year by year until it reached a peak in the mid-1280s, before being abandoned shortly thereafter. Estimates of numbers of occupants per room also made

1 1010 – 1009 BC
2 1008 – 1007 BC
3 1005 – 1001 BC
4 996 – 993 BC
5 992 – 989 BC
6 985 BC

50ft
15m

Tree-ring dating of the late Bronze Age settlement of Cortaillod-Est, Switzerland, is remarkably precise. Founded in 1010 BC with a nucleus of four houses (phase 1), the village was enlarged four times, and a fence added in 985 BC.

it possible to calculate the rate of expansion of Beta-takin's population to a maximum of about 125 people. Dendrochronology can thus lead on to wider considerations beyond questions of dating.

In central and western Europe, the oak master sequences now allow the equally precise dating of the development of Neolithic and Bronze Age lake villages such as Cortaillod Est in Switzerland. In the German Rhineland, close to the village of Kückhoven, recently discovered timbers from the wooden supporting frame of a well have provided three tree-ring dates of 5090 BC,

5067 BC, and 5055 BC (see illus. p. 264). The timbers were associated with sherds of the *Linearbandkeramik* culture and thus provide an absolute date for the early practice of agriculture in western Europe. The earliest tree-ring date for the English Neolithic is from the Sweet Track in the Somerset Levels: a plank walkway constructed across a swamp during the winter of 3807/3806 BC, or shortly after (see box, pp. 330–31).

Sometimes local chronologies remain "floating" – their short-term sequences have not been tied into the main master sequences. In many parts of the world, however, master sequences are gradually being extended and floating chronologies fitted into them. In the Aegean area, for example, a master sequence is now available back to early medieval times (the Byzantine period), with earlier floating sequence stretching back in some cases to 7200 BC. In future, the link between them will no doubt be found. Considerable progress is being made toward establishing a long tree-ring chronology for Anatolia by Peter Kuniholm of Cornell.

Limiting Factors. Unlike radiocarbon, dendrochronology is not a worldwide dating method because of two basic limitations:

1 it applies only to trees in regions outside the tropics where pronounced differences between the seasons produce clearly defined annual rings;
2 for a direct tree-ring date it is restricted to wood from those species that (a) have yielded a master sequence back from the present and (b) people actually used in the past, and where (c) the sample affords a sufficiently long record to give a unique match.

In addition, there are important questions of interpretation to consider. A tree-ring date refers to the date of felling of the tree. This is determined by matching the tree-ring sample ending with the outermost rings (the sapwood) to a regional sequence. Where most or all of the sapwood is missing, the felling date cannot be identified. But even with an accurate felling date, the archaeologist has to make a judgment – based on context and formation processes – about how soon after felling the timber entered the archaeological deposit. Timbers may be older or younger than the structures into which they were finally incorporated, depending on whether they were reused from somewhere else, or used to make a repair in a long-established structure. As always, the best solution is to take multiple samples, and to check the evidence carefully on-site. Despite these qualifications, dendrochronology looks set to become the major dating technique alongside radiocarbon for the last 8000 years in temperate and arid lands.

RADIOACTIVE CLOCKS

Many of the most important developments in absolute dating since World War II have come from the use of what one might call "radioactive clocks," based on that widespread and regular feature in the natural world, radioactive decay (see box). The best known of these

THE PRINCIPLES OF RADIOACTIVE DECAY

Carbon-12 atom

Carbon-14 atom

● Neutron
● Proton

Like most elements occurring in nature, carbon exists in more than one isotopic form. It has three isotopes: ^{12}C, ^{13}C, and ^{14}C – the numbers correspond to the atomic weights of these isotopes. In any sample of carbon 98.9 percent of atoms are of ^{12}C type and have six protons and six neutrons in the nucleus, and 1.1 percent are of the ^{13}C type with six protons and seven neutrons. Only one atom in a million millions of atoms of carbon will be that of the isotope ^{14}C with eight neutrons in the nucleus. This isotope of carbon is produced in the upper atmosphere by cosmic rays bombarding nitrogen (^{14}N) and it contains an excess of neutrons, making it unstable. It decays by the emission of weak beta radiation back to its precursor isotope of nitrogen – ^{14}N – with seven protons and seven neutrons in a nucleus. Like all types of radioactive decay the process takes place at a constant rate, independent of all environmental conditions.

The time taken for half of the atoms of a radioactive isotope to decay is called its half-life. In other words, after one half-life, there will be half of the atoms left; after two half-lives, one-quarter of the original quantity remains, and so on. In the case of ^{14}C, the half-life is now agreed to be 5730 years. For ^{238}U, it is 4500 million years. For certain other isotopes, the half-life is a minute fraction of a second. But in every case, there is a regular pattern to the decay.

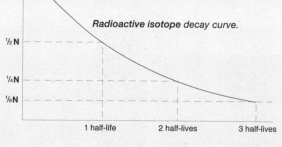

Radioactive isotope decay curve.

½ N

¼ N

⅛ N

1 half-life   2 half-lives   3 half-lives

methods is radiocarbon, today the main dating tool for the last 50,000 years or so. The main radioactive methods for periods before the timespan of radiocarbon are potassium-argon, uranium-series dating, and fission-track dating. Thermoluminescence (TL) overlaps with radiocarbon in the time period for which it is useful, but also has potential for dating earlier epochs – as do optical dating and electron spin resonance – all trapped electron dating methods that rely indirectly on radioactive decay. In the following sections we will discuss each method in turn.

Radiocarbon Dating

Radiocarbon is the single most useful method of dating for the archaeologist. As we shall see, it has its limitations, both in terms of accuracy, and for the time range where it is useful. Archaeologists themselves are also the cause of major errors, thanks to poor sampling procedures and careless interpretation. Nevertheless, radiocarbon has transformed our understanding of the past, helping archaeologists to establish for the first time a reliable chronology of world cultures.

History and Basis of Method. In 1949, the American chemist Willard Libby published the first radiocarbon dates. During World War II he had been one of several scientists studying cosmic radiation, the sub-atomic particles that constantly bombard the earth, producing high-energy neutrons. These neutrons react with nitro-

gen atoms in the atmosphere to produce atoms of carbon-14 (^{14}C), or radiocarbon, which are unstable because they have eight neutrons in the nucleus instead of the usual six as for ordinary carbon (^{12}C) (see box, p. 137). This instability leads to radioactive decay of ^{14}C at a regular rate. Libby estimated that it took 5568 years for half the ^{14}C in any sample to decay – its half-life – although modern research indicates that the more accurate figure is 5730 years (for consistency laboratories still use 5568 years for the half-life; the difference no longer matters now that we have a correctly calibrated radiocarbon timescale: see below).

Libby realized that the decay of radiocarbon at a constant rate should be balanced by its constant production through cosmic radiation, and that therefore the proportion of ^{14}C in the atmosphere should remain the same throughout time. Furthermore, this steady atmospheric concentration of radiocarbon is passed on uniformly to all living things through carbon dioxide. Plants take up carbon dioxide during photosynthesis, they are eaten by herbivorous animals, which in turn are eaten by carnivores. Only when a plant or animal dies does the uptake of ^{14}C cease, and the steady concentration of ^{14}C begin to decline through radioactive decay. Thus, knowing the decay rate or half-life of ^{14}C, Libby recognized that the age of dead plant or animal tissue could be calculated by measuring the amount of radiocarbon left in a sample.

Libby's great practical achievement was to devise an accurate means of measurement. (The traces of ^{14}C are

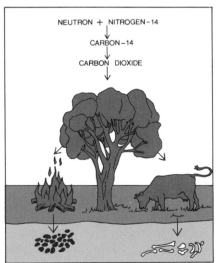

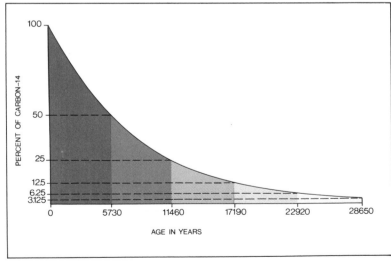

(Left) Radiocarbon (carbon-14) is produced in the atmosphere and absorbed by plants through carbon dioxide, and by animals through feeding off plants or other animals. Uptake of ^{14}C ceases when the plant or animal dies. (Right) After death, the amount of ^{14}C decays at a known rate (50 percent after 5730 years, etc.). Measurement of the amount left in a sample gives the date.

THE PUBLICATION OF RADIOCARBON RESULTS

Radiocarbon laboratories provide an estimate of age based on their measurement of the amount of radiocarbon activity in a sample. The level of activity is converted to an age expressed in number of years between the death of an organism and the present. To avoid confusion caused by the fact that the "present" advances each year, radiocarbon laboratories have adopted AD 1950 as their "present" and all radiocarbon dates are quoted in years BP or years "before the present," meaning before 1950. Thus, in scientific publications, radiocarbon dates are given in the form:

3700 ± 100 BP (P-685)

The first figure is the year BP (i.e. before AD 1950). Next is the associated probable error known as the standard deviation (see below). Finally, in parentheses is the laboratory analysis number. Each laboratory has its own letter code (e.g. P for Philadelphia and Q for Cambridge, England).

As discussed in the main text, various factors prevent the precise measurement of radiocarbon activity in a sample and, consequently, there is a statistical error or standard deviation (which may not have been realistically calculated: see main text) associated with all radiocarbon dates. Thus, when a radiocarbon date is quoted as 3700 ±100 BP this means that there should be a 68 percent probability – two chances in three –

that the correct estimate of age in radiocarbon years lies between 3800 and 3600 BP. Since there is also a one-in-three chance that the correct age does *not* fall within this range, archaeologists are advised to convert the date range to two standard deviations, i.e. to double the size of the standard deviation, so that there should be a 95 percent chance that the age estimate will be bracketed. For example, for an age estimate of 3700 ±100 BP there is a 95 percent chance that the radiocarbon age of the sample will lie between 3900 (3700 +200) and 3500 (3700 -200) BP. Obviously, the larger the standard deviation, the less precise (and for those dealing with later prehistory or historical times, the less useful) the date. For example, the 95 percent probability range of a date of 3700 ±150 BP brackets the period 4000 to 3400 BP, which is 200 years more than a date quoted at ±100 radiocarbon years.

The forms of the dates given above are laboratory determinations. They represent the uncalibrated age estimate of the sample and are based on the assumption, now known to be erroneous, that the levels of radiocarbon produced in the atmosphere have been constant through time. Thus, whenever possible the radiocarbon age should be calibrated to actual calendar years. To make clear whether or not a date has been calibrated, archaeologists often follow one of

	Uncali-brated date	Cali-brated date
"Scientific"	BP	Cal BC/AD
"Historical"	bc/ad	BC/AD

two conventions in their publications: The "scientific" convention (used and promoted by the radiocarbon laboratories) has the merit of being very clear, but has the inconvenience of not providing for the discussion of an uncalibrated date in years bc or ad. The "historical" convention is less cumbersome and is for this reason preferred by many archaeologists. However, the style for distinguishing dates by simply using lower case letters (bc/ad) and upper case ones (BC/AD) is vulnerable to editorial inconsistency and to printing errors. Moreover, it is important (and difficult) to remember that an uncalibrated date of say 3500 bc is not linked to any system of reckoning in calendar years, nor is it a century older than a date of 3400 bc.

Where the archaeologist is discussing absolute chronology generally – perhaps using radiocarbon alongside other methods of dating, including historical ones – it seems logical to employ the simple BC/AD system, provided an attempt has been made to calibrate any radiocarbon dates incorporated in the chronology, and that this is stated clearly at the outset.

minute to start with, and are reduced by half after 5730 years. After 23,000 years, therefore, only one sixteenth of the original tiny concentration of ^{14}C is available to be measured in the sample.) Libby discovered that each atom of ^{14}C decays by releasing beta particles, and he succeeded in counting these emissions using a Geiger counter. This is the basis of the conventional method still employed by many radiocarbon laboratories today. Samples usually consist of organic materials found on archaeological sites, such as charcoal, wood, seeds, and other plant remains, and human or animal bone. The accurate measurement of the ^{14}C activity of a

sample is affected by counting errors, background cosmic radiation, and other factors that contribute an element of uncertainty to the measurements. This means that radiocarbon dates are invariably accompanied by an estimate of the probable error: the plus/minus term (standard deviation) attached to every radiocarbon date (see box above).

One advance on the conventional method came with the introduction in some laboratories in the late 1970s and early 1980s of special gas counters capable of taking measurements from very small samples. In the conventional method one needed some 5 g of pure

HOW TO CALIBRATE RADIOCARBON DATES

Radiocarbon laboratories will generally supply calibrated dates of their samples, but archaeologists may need to calibrate raw radiocarbon dates themselves, generally from a calibration graph.

The tree-ring calibration curve shown in the diagram (below) illustrates the relationship between radiocarbon years (BP) and tree-ring samples dated in actual calendar years (Cal BC/AD). The central line of the curve defines the mean estimate of age while the other two lines indicate the band width of the probable error at one standard deviation. In order to find the calibrated age range of a

radiocarbon sample dated 2200 ±100 BP using this curve, the simplest method would be to draw two horizontal lines (A1 and A2) from the appropriate probability level on the "radiocarbon years" axis to the centre line of the calibration curve, and drop lines (B1 and B2) from these intercept points to the calendar axis. The calibrated date is then quoted as the range – or ranges – enclosed between the vertical lines (one of the problems of a wiggly calibration curve is that a single radiocarbon date will frequently calibrate to two or more possible calendar age ranges). In this instance the result would be an approximately

95 percent chance that the date of the sample falls between c. 405 Cal BC and 5 Cal BC.

Unfortunately, however, this does not truly reflect the information stored in the radiocarbon result. Since a radiocarbon measurement is an estimate of ^{14}C content based on a set of physical measurements, it has a known probability distribution of Gaussian or Normal form, as shown on the radiocarbon axis of the second diagram. Calibrating this probability distribution against the wiggly calibration curve is a complex process, and necessitates the use of a specialized form of statistics, termed Bayesian. This requires the use of a computer program, and is the only way to produce an accurate probability distribution of the resulting calendar age range. An effect of the wildly erratic calibration curve is to produce calendar age ranges with very irregular probability distributions, as clearly shown in this example (the tinted area under the calibration curve). This means that calibrated dates can no longer be expressed as a mean figure with ± error term. Calibrated dates are therefore expressed as possible age ranges, enclosing the most probable results at the required probability level. In this case there is a 95 percent probability that the dated event occurred between 550 Cal BC and 50 Cal AD.

It will be immediately apparent that a calibrated age range of 550 Cal BC to 50 Cal AD is too broad to be useful for most archaeological purposes. Fortunately there are two ways of narrowing the age range: high-precision dates and multiple dates. High-precision dates, obtainable so far from only a handful of the world's radiocarbon laboratories, can offer

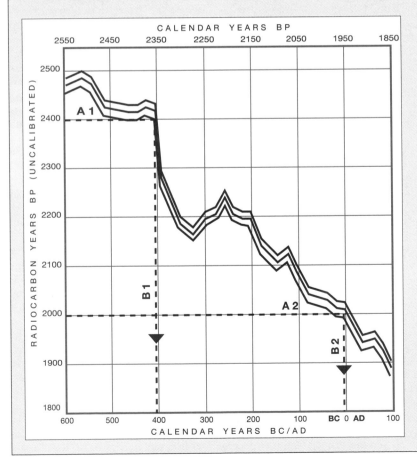

A section of the calibration curve from Stuiver and Pearson (1986) (left) to show the simple intercept method to obtain calibrated dates. Most archaeologists, however, need a more accurate assessment and the diagram (right) shows the probability distribution of the calendar date resulting from the Normal probability distribution of the radiocarbon measurement seen on the 'y'-axis.

dates quoted with a realistic error of ±20 years, which, after calibration, generally allows the sample to be dated within a century or less at the 95 percent probability level. Otherwise one can resort to multiple dates of the same sample to produce mean dates with a smaller standard deviation – hoping that the standard deviations of the dates have been realistically measured by the laboratory.

In the favorable but rare cases where the elapsed time between a series of datable events is known, it is possible to obtain a very precise date by wiggle matching. This is most frequently applied to radiocarbon dates from tree-rings. If high-precision measurements can be made of several radiocarbon samples with a known number of years between them, the resulting pattern of changes in radiocarbon content over time can be directly matched with the wiggles in the calibration curve, giving dates to within 10 or 20 years for the tree-rings included. Alternatively, where other information such as a set of radiocarbon figures linked by stratigraphy exists, it is now possible to use Bayesian statistics to combine all the known data. This was undertaken for the recent re-dating of Stonehenge.

Calibration programs and curves can be obtained directly from the *Radiocarbon* website at www.radiocarbon.org.

carbon after purification, which means an original sample of some 10–20 g of wood or charcoal, or 100–200 g of bone. The special equipment required only a few hundred milligrams (mg) of charcoal.

Several laboratories now use the accelerator mass spectrometry (AMS) method, which requires smaller samples still. AMS counts the atoms of ^{14}C directly, disregarding their radioactivity. The minimum sample size is reduced to as little as 5–10 mg – thus enabling precious organic materials, such as the Turin Shroud (see below), to be sampled and directly dated. Initially it was hoped that the datable timespan for radiocarbon using AMS could be pushed back from 50,000 to 80,000 years, although this is proving difficult to achieve, in part because of sample contamination.

Calibration of Radiocarbon Dates. One of the basic assumptions of the radiocarbon method has turned out to be not quite correct. Libby assumed that the concentration of ^{14}C in the atmosphere has been constant through time; but we now know that it has varied, largely due to changes in the earth's magnetic field. The method that demonstrated the inaccuracy – tree-ring dating – has also provided the means of correcting or calibrating radiocarbon dates.

Radiocarbon dates obtained from tree-rings show that before about 1000 BC dates expressed in radiocarbon years are increasingly too young in relation to true calendar years. In other words, before 1000 BC trees (and all other living things) were exposed to greater concentrations of atmospheric ^{14}C than they are today. By obtaining radiocarbon dates systematically from the long tree-ring master sequences of bristlecone pine and oak (see above), scientists have been able to plot radiocarbon ages against tree-ring ages (in calendar years) to produce calibration curves back to around 8500 BC. The journal *Radiocarbon* publishes the most up-to-date curves which in principle permit the conversion of radiocarbon dates to calibrated dates. Very broadly, radiocarbon ages diverge increasingly from true ages before 1000 BC, so that by 5000 BC in calendar years the radiocarbon age is 900 years too young. Thus an age estimate in radiocarbon years of 4100 BC might well in fact when calibrated be somewhere near 5000 BC. It is this pushing back of many dates that has brought about the Second Radiocarbon Revolution (see above). Recently, comparison of ^{14}C dates and high precision uranium-series dates (see p. 146) from core samples of ancient coral reefs near Barbados has produced a calibration curve for radiocarbon from *c.* 9000 BP (the limit of tree-ring calibration) back to 40,000 BP. It has been found that between 18,000 and 40,000 BP, ^{14}C dates are about 3000 years too young.

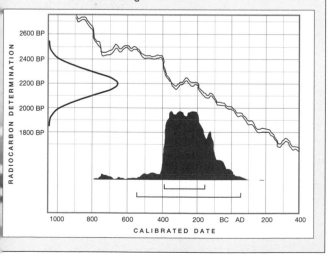

The calibration curve (INTCAL98) recently produced by Minze Stuiver and co-workers combines the available data from tree-rings, uranium-thorium dated corals, and varve-counted marine sediment, to give a curve from 24,000 to 0 Cal BP. There are short-term wiggles in the curve, however, and occasionally, sections of the curve that run so flat that two samples with the same age in radiocarbon years might in reality be 400 years apart in calendar years, a problem that is particularly irksome for the period 800–400 BC in calendar years. To be accurate one needs to calibrate not merely the central radiocarbon date (e.g. 2200 BP) but its error estimate as well (2200 ± 100 BP), which will produce an *age range* in calendar years (see box, pp. 140–41). Some of the ranges will be narrower and more precise than others, depending on where on the curve the radiocarbon date with its error estimate falls.

An age range produced by visual calibration is limited as it contains no statement of probability – it cannot say whether the true age of a dated sample is more likely to be found in one part of the range than in another. To some extent this limitation is overcome by computer calibration. Several programs are now available which use a statistical methodology, termed Bayesian, to generate probability distributions of age estimations for single ¹⁴C dates. Bayesian methods have been used, for instance at Stonehenge, to model complex archaeological event sequences by combining multiple related ¹⁴C dates with associated chronological information such as that derived from stratigraphy.

The crucial point is that in any publication it should be indicated whether or not the radiocarbon determination has been calibrated, and if it has been, by which particular system or curve.

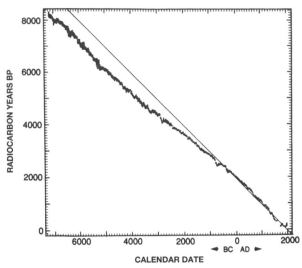

Stuiver and Pearson's calibrated radiocarbon timescale based on Irish oak. The straight line indicates the ideal 1:1 radiocarbon / calendar age timescale.

Contamination and Interpretation of Radiocarbon Samples.
Although radiocarbon dates have certain inescapable levels of error associated with them, erroneous results are as likely to derive from poor sampling and incorrect interpretation by the archaeologist as from inadequate laboratory procedures. The major sources of error in the field are as follows:

1 *Contamination before sampling.* Problems of contamination of the sample within the ground can be serious. For instance, groundwater on waterlogged sites can dissolve organic materials and also deposit them, thus changing the isotopic composi-

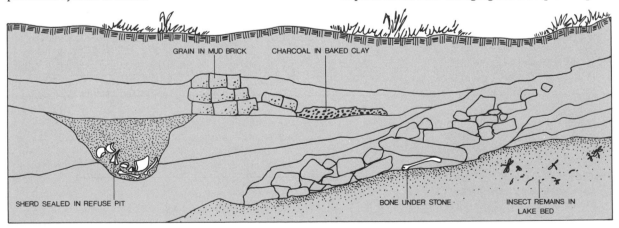

Samples for radiocarbon dating should be obtained, wherever possible, from the kind of contexts shown here – where the material to be dated has been sealed in an immobilizing matrix. The stratigraphic context of the sample must be clearly established by the excavator before the material is submitted to the laboratory for dating.

tion; the formation of mineral concretions around organic matter can bring calcium carbonate entirely lacking in radiocarbon, and thus fallaciously increase the apparent radiocarbon age of a specimen by effectively "diluting" the ^{14}C present. These matters can be tackled in the laboratory.

2 *Contamination during or after sampling.* All radiocarbon samples should be sealed within a clean container such as a plastic bag at the time of recovery. They should be labeled in detail at once on the outside of the container; cardboard labels inside can be a major source of contamination. The container should be placed inside another: one plastic bag, well sealed, inside another bag separately sealed can be a sound procedure for most materials. But wood or carbon samples that may preserve some tree-ring structure should be more carefully housed in a rigid container. Wherever possible exclude any modern carbon, such as paper, which can be disastrous. However, modern roots and earth cannot always be avoided: in such cases, it is better to include them, together with a note for the laboratory, where the problem can be tackled.

Application of any organic material later – such as glue or carbowax – is likewise disastrous (although the laboratory may be able to remedy it). So is continuing photosynthesis within the sample: for this reason, the relevant containers should be stored in the dark. A green mold is not uncommon in sample bags on some projects. It automatically indicates contamination of the sample.

3 *Context of deposition.* Most errors in radiocarbon dating arise because the excavator has not fully understood the formation processes of the context in question. Unless it is appreciated how the organic material found its way to the position where it was found, and how and when (in terms of the site) it came to be buried, then precise interpretation is impossible. The first rule of radiocarbon dating must be that the excavator should not submit a sample for dating unless he or she is sure of its archaeological context.

4 *Date of context.* Too often, it is assumed that a radiocarbon determination, e.g. on charcoal, will give a straightforward estimate for the date of the charcoal's burial context. However, if that charcoal derives from roof timbers that might themselves have been several centuries old when destroyed by fire, then one is dating some early construction, not the context of destruction. There are numerous examples of such difficulties, one of the most conspicuous being the reuse of such timbers or even of fossil wood (e.g. "bog oak") whose radiocarbon

date could be centuries earlier than the context in question. For this reason, samples with a short life are often preferred, such as twigs of brushwood, or charred cereal grains that are not likely to be old at the time of burial.

A strategy for sampling will recall the wise dictum that "one date is no date": several are needed. The best dating procedure is to work toward an internal relative sequence – for instance, in the stratigraphic succession on a well-stratified site such as the Gatecliff Shelter, Monitor Valley, Nevada, excavated by David Hurst Thomas and his associates. If the samples can be arranged in relative sequence in this way with the lowest unit having the earliest date and so on, then there is an internal check on the coherence of the laboratory determinations and on the quality of field sampling. Some of the dates from such a sequence may come out older than expected. This is quite reasonable – as explained above, some of the material may have been

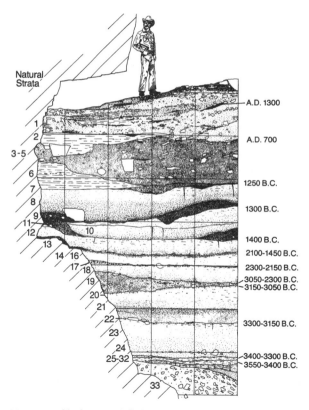

Master profile for Gatecliff Shelter, Nevada, produced by David Hurst Thomas, showing how dates derived from radiocarbon determinations are consistent with the stratigraphic succession.

"old" at the time of burial. But if they come out younger (i.e. more recent) than expected, then there is something wrong. Either some contamination has affected the samples, or the laboratory has made a serious error, or – as not infrequently happens – the stratigraphic interpretation is wrong.

Although many problems with radiocarbon dates may be attributed to the submitter, recent evidence suggests that radiocarbon laboratories themselves may be overestimating the precision of their own dates. In one comparative study, over 30 radiocarbon laboratories dated the same sample. While some estimated their errors within reasonable accuracy others did not, and one laboratory produced systematic errors of 200 years. In general, it was seen that although radiocarbon laboratories might quote levels of precision of ± 50 years, in fact it was safer to assume that their actual errors were ± 80 years or more. As the inter-laboratory study comprised an anonymous sample of the world's radiocarbon laboratories, the archaeological community has no way of knowing how widespread the underestimation of errors is or how systematically biased in their radiocarbon dates some laboratories are. Archaeologists would be best advised to treat radiocarbon laboratories like purveyors of any other service and request evidence that they deliver both the accuracy and the precision they purport to offer. Many laboratories are aware of their past biases and now quote realistic statements of precision which need not be regarded as underestimates. Furthermore, often they may be approached to quote new and more realistic errors for their earlier dates.

Applications: The Impact of Radiocarbon Dating. If we seek to answer the question "When?" in archaeology, radiocarbon has undoubtedly offered the most generally useful way of finding an answer. The greatest advantage is that the method can be used anywhere, whatever the climate, as long as there is material of organic (i.e. living) origin. Thus the method works as well in South America or Polynesia as it does in Egypt or Mesopotamia. And it can take us back 50,000 years – although at the other end of the timescale it is too imprecise to be of much use for the 400 years of the most recent past.

The use of the method on a single site has been illustrated by reference to the Gatecliff Shelter, Nevada. A recent interesting application is the dating of the newly discovered Upper Paleolithic paintings in the Chauvet Cave, southern France. Tiny samples from three paintings done with charcoal were dated, producing a series of results centered around 31,000 BP – far older than anticipated. Two different laboratories also dated sam-

Part of the Turin Shroud, bearing the image of a man's head. Radiocarbon AMS dating has given a calibrated age range for the cloth of AD 1260–1390.

ples of charcoal from the floor, and obtained results of around 29,000 BP, not significantly different from the paintings, and also around 24,000 BP. Torch-marks were analyzed, producing dates of around 26,500 BP. The surprisingly early dates for the paintings show the value of obtaining a series of dates – a single date coming out so early would probably have aroused skepticism. If these still controversial results are valid it seems there were several different phases of use of the cave, each separated by a few thousand years.

On a wider scale radiocarbon has been even more important in establishing for the first time broad chronologies for the world's cultures that previously lacked timescales (such as calendars) of their own. Calibration of radiocarbon has heightened, not diminished, this success. As we saw in the section above on Calendars and Historical Chronologies, calibration has helped assert the validity of an independent radiocarbon chronology for prehistoric Europe, free from false links with the Egyptian historical chronology.

Radiocarbon dating by the AMS technique is opening up new possibilities. Precious objects and works of art can now be dated because minute samples are all that is required. In 1988 AMS dating resolved the long-standing controversy over the age of the Turin Shroud, a piece of cloth with the image of a man's body on it that many genuinely believed to be the actual imprint of the body of Christ. Laboratories at Tucson, Oxford, and Zurich all placed it in the 14th century AD, not from the time of Christ at all, although this remains a matter of controversy. Likewise it is now possible to date a single grain of wheat or a fruit pip. An AMS reading on a grape pip from Hambledon Hill, southern Britain, shows that grapes – and probably vines as well – had reached this part of the world by 3500 BC in calendar years, over 3000 years earlier than had previously been supposed.

Radiocarbon looks set to maintain its position as the main dating tool back to 50,000 years ago for organic materials. For inorganic materials, however, thermoluminescence (p. 151) and other, new, techniques are very useful.

Potassium-Argon (and Argon-Argon) Dating

The potassium-argon (K-Ar) method is used by geologists to date rocks hundreds or even thousands of millions of years old. It is also one of the most appropriate techniques for dating early human (hominid) sites in Africa, which can be up to 5 million years old. It is restricted to volcanic rock no more recent than around 100,000 years.

Basis of Method. Potassium-argon dating, like radiocarbon dating, is based on the principle of radioactive decay: in this case, the steady but very slow decay of the radioactive isotope potassium-40 (^{40}K) to the inert gas argon-40 (^{40}Ar) in volcanic rock. Knowing the decay rate of ^{40}K – its half-life is around 1.3 billion years – a measure of the quantity of ^{40}Ar trapped within a 10 g rock sample gives an estimate of the date of the rock's formation.

A more sensitive variant of the method, which requires a smaller sample, sometimes a single crystal extracted from pumice (single crystal laser fusion), is known as laser-fusion argon-argon dating ($^{40}Ar/^{39}Ar$ dating). A stable isotope of potassium, ^{39}K, is converted to ^{39}Ar by neutron bombardment of the sample to be dated. Both argon isotopes are then measured by mass spectrometry after their release by laser fusion. As the $^{40}K/^{39}K$ ratio in a rock is constant, the age of the rock can be determined from its $^{40}Ar/^{39}Ar$ ratio. As with all radioactive methods, it is important to be clear about

what sets the radioactive clock to zero. In this case, it is the formation of the rock through volcanic activity, which drives off any argon formerly present.

The dates obtained in the laboratory are in effect geological dates for rock samples. Happily, some of the most important areas for the study of the Lower Paleolithic, notably the Rift Valley in East Africa, are areas of volcanic activity. This means that archaeological remains often lie on geological strata formed by volcanic action, and hence suitable for K-Ar dating. In addition, they are often overlain by comparable volcanic rock, so that dates for these two geological strata provide a chronological sandwich, between the upper and lower slices of which the archaeological deposits are set. It has recently been shown, by argon-argon analysis of pumice from the eruption of Vesuvius in AD 79 (giving an age of 1925 ± 94 years), that the method has a good degree of precision even for quite recent eruptions.

Applications: Early Human Sites in East Africa. Olduvai Gorge in Tanzania is one of the most crucial sites for the study of hominid evolution, as it has yielded fossil remains of *Australopithecus* (*Paranthropus*) *boisei*, *Homo habilis*, and *Homo erectus* (see pp. 162–63) as well as large numbers of stone artifacts and bones. Being in the Rift Valley, Olduvai is a volcanic area, and its 2-million-year chronology has been well established by K-Ar dating and Ar-Ar dating of the relevant deposits of hardened volcanic ash (tuff) and other materials between which the archaeological remains are found (see box, pp. 148–49). The K-Ar method has also been immensely important in dating other early East African sites, such as Hadar in Ethiopia.

Limiting Factors. The results of K-Ar dating are generally accompanied by an error estimate, as in the case of other radioactivity-based methods. For example, the date of Tuff IB at Olduvai has been measured as 1.79 ± 0.03 million years. An error estimate of 30,000 years might at first seem a large one, but it is in fact only of the order of 2 percent of the total age. (Note that here, as in other cases, the estimate of error relates to the counting process in the laboratory, and does not seek to estimate also other sources of error arising from varying chemical conditions of deposition, or indeed from uncertainties of archaeological interpretation.)

The principal limitations of the technique are that it can only be used to date sites buried by volcanic rock, and that it is rarely possible to achieve an accuracy of better than ± 10 percent. Potassium-argon dating has nevertheless proved a key tool in areas where suitable volcanic materials are present.

Uranium-Series Dating

This is a dating method based on the radioactive decay of isotopes of uranium. It has proved particularly useful for the period 500,000–50,000 years ago, which lies outside the time range of radiocarbon dating. In Europe, where there are few volcanic rocks suitable for dating by the potassium-argon technique, uranium-series (U-series) dating may be the method of first choice for clarifying when a site was occupied by early humans.

Basis of Method. Two radioactive isotopes of the element uranium (^{238}U and ^{235}U) decay in a series of stages into daughter elements. Two of these daughter elements, thorium (^{230}Th, also called "ionium," a daughter of ^{238}U) and protactinium (^{231}Pa, a daughter of ^{235}U), themselves also decay with half-lives useful for dating. The essential point is that the parent uranium isotopes are soluble in water, whereas the daughter products are

not. This means, for instance, that only the uranium isotopes are present in waters that seep into limestone caves. However, once the calcium carbonate, with uranium impurities, dissolved in those waters is precipitated as travertine onto cave walls and floors then the radioactive clock is set going. At the time of its formation the travertine contains only water soluble ^{238}U and ^{235}U: it is free of the insoluble ^{230}Th and ^{231}Pa isotopes. Thus the quantities of the daughter isotopes increase through time as the uranium decays, and by measuring the daughter/parent ratio, usually $^{230}Th/^{238}U$, the age of the travertine can be determined.

The isotopes are measured by counting their alpha emissions; each isotope emits alpha radiation of a characteristic frequency. In favorable circumstances, the method leads to dates with an associated uncertainty (standard error) of ± 12,000 years for a sample with an age of 150,000 years, and of about ± 25,000 years for a sample of age 400,000 years. These figures can be greatly reduced by using thermal ionization mass spec-

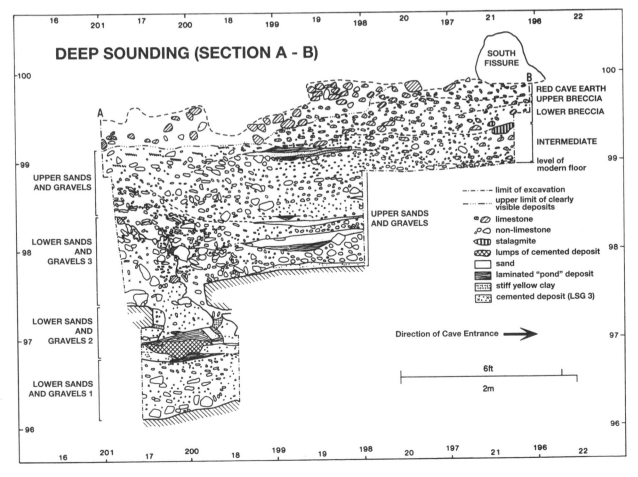

DEEP SOUNDING (SECTION A - B)

SOUTH FISSURE

RED CAVE EARTH
UPPER BRECCIA
LOWER BRECCIA

INTERMEDIATE

level of modern floor

UPPER SANDS AND GRAVELS

UPPER SANDS AND GRAVELS

LOWER SANDS AND GRAVELS 3

LOWER SANDS AND GRAVELS 2

LOWER SANDS AND GRAVELS 1

--·--·-- limit of excavation
———— upper limit of clearly visible deposits
limestone
non-limestone
stalagmite
lumps of cemented deposit
sand
laminated "pond" deposit
stiff yellow clay
cemented deposit (LSG 3)

Direction of Cave Entrance ⟶

6ft
2m

trometry (TIMS) to measure directly the quantities of each isotope present. Such high-precision dates might, for instance, have an associated uncertainty of less than 1000 years for a 100,000-year-old sample.

Applications and Limiting Factors. The method is used to date rocks rich in calcium carbonate, often those deposited by the action of surface or ground waters around lime-rich springs or by seepage into limestone caves. Stalagmites form on cave floors in this way. As early humans used caves and overhanging rocks for shelter, artifacts and bones often became embedded in a layer of calcium carbonate or in another type of sediment between two layers of the calcareous deposit.

The difficulty of determining the correct order of deposition in a cave is one reason why the U-series method is prone to give ambiguous results. For this and other reasons, several layers of deposit in a cave need to be sampled and the geology meticulously examined. The method has nevertheless proved very useful.

At the Pontnewydd Cave in North Wales, the lower breccia which contained the bulk of the archaeological finds there was shown by U-series dating to be at least 220,000 years old. The important site of Bilzingsleben in eastern Germany was also dated by this method, the travertine layer which enclosed the artifacts and human skeletal remains giving an age of around 414,000 years, though some uncertainty remains, as with many U-series determinations.

Teeth can also be dated by this method, because water soluble uranium diffuses into dentine after a tooth has become buried, although there are problems estimating the rate of uranium uptake through time (see section on electron spin resonance dating, pp. 154–55). Nevertheless, TIMS U-series dating has been employed successfully to date mammalian teeth found in association with hominid skeletons in three Israeli caves. Three dates with ages of between 98,000 years and 105,000 years were obtained for strata containing Neanderthal remains at Tabun. The skeletal remains of

Uranium-series dating and Pontnewydd Cave, North Wales (left, deep section; above, measurements being taken in the cave). The lower breccia contained the bulk of the finds at this important Paleolithic site, including the hominid remains such as a tooth of Neanderthal type. A stalagmite on the lower breccia was found by the U-series method to be more than 220,000 years old. The result was confirmed by a TL determination on the same stalagmite, and by another TL reading on a burnt flint core – from a layer immediately underlying the lower breccia – which gave a statistically consistent age of 200,000 ±25,000 years.

early modern humans found at Qafzeh were shown to be between 85,000 and 110,000 years old, while a series of anatomically related skeletons at Skhūl were shown to be between 66,000 and 102,000 years old. Increasingly U-series dates are being used in conjunction with electron spin resonance dates using the same materials. Neanderthal individuals from Krapina in Croatia were dated by both methods using tooth enamel, both methods giving ages of around 130,000 years. However, the proposed dating of *Homo erectus* remains from Ngandong in Java, using both the U-series and ESR methods on samples from animal bones, to the surprisingly recent age of 27,000 years has been questioned – not on the basis of the analyses themselves but the uncertainty of the stratigraphy and the associations of the materials.

Fission-Track Dating

Fission-track dating is another method based on the operation of a radioactive clock. This time, it is the spontaneous fission of an isotope of uranium (^{238}U) present in a wide range of rocks and minerals, in obsidian and other volcanic glasses, in glassy meteorites (tektites), in manufactured glasses, and in mineral inclusions in pottery. As in the case of potassium-argon dating – with whose time range it overlaps – the method produces useful dates from suitable rocks that contain or are adjacent to those containing archaeological evidence.

Basis of Method. As well as decaying naturally to a stable lead isotope, ^{238}U occasionally also divides in half. During this process of spontaneous fission the halves move apart at high speed, coming to a halt only after causing much damage to structures in their path. In materials containing ^{238}U, such as natural glasses, this damage is recorded in the form of pathways called *fission tracks*. The tracks are counted under an optical microscope after the polished surface of the glass has

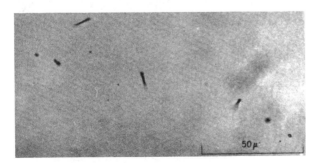

Examples of fission tracks, after etching.

DATING OUR AFRICAN ANCESTORS

In the 19th century, Charles Darwin firmly believed that human origins lay in Africa, and the 20th century has proved him right: Our earliest ancestors have been discovered at several sites in East Africa and southern Africa (see p. 145). One of the greatest triumphs of scientific chronology in the postwar years has been the successful dating and correlating of these sites – particularly those in East Africa – derived from three main methods: potassium-argon (K-Ar), fission-track, and geomagnetic dating. In addition, the relative method of faunal dating has been used to check these results.

Olduvai Gorge
Thanks to the discoveries of early hominid fossils in the gorge by Louis and Mary Leakey, Olduvai is one of the most crucial sites for the study of human evolution. It has proved possible to establish a chronology for the site, particularly on the basis of K-Ar dating of deposits of hardened volcanic ash (tuff), between which the fossil remains lie. For example, the age

Principal early hominid sites in East Africa.

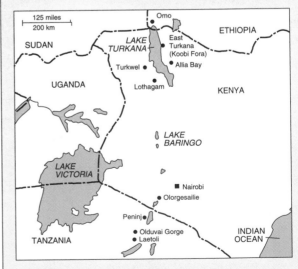

of the important Tuff IB in Bed I was estimated as 1.79 ±0.03 my (million years).

As with all archaeological dating, for a reliable result one should cross-check age estimates derived from one method with those from another. In the case of Bed I laser-fusion argon-argon dating has produced a result of 1.8–1.75 my. A fission-track reading gave a date of 2.03 ±0.28 my, which is within the statistically acceptable confidence limits for the K-Ar estimate.

Another means of checking the K-Ar sequence proved to be geomagnetic dating. As explained on pp. 158–59, there have been periodic reversals in the direction of the earth's magnetic field (the North Pole becoming the South Pole and vice versa). Magnetically charged particles in rocks preserve a record of the sequence of these reversals (from "normal" to "reversed" and back again). It transpired that Beds I–III and part of IV at Olduvai lay within the so-called Matuyama epoch of reversed

polarity, with a significant period of normal polarity 1.87–1.67 million years ago first demonstrated at the site and now known, appropriately, as the "Olduvai event." The discovery of the same sequence of reversals at other East African sites (e.g. East Turkana and Omo) has helped correlate their deposits with those at Olduvai.

A further check on the validity of these sequences is the relative method of faunal dating (biostratigraphy), explained on pp. 127–28. The evolutionary tree for the pig family has proved among the most useful, helping to confirm the correlations among East African sites, including Olduvai, derived from other dating methods.

The KBS Tuff Controversy

Nowhere has the need for extreme care in dating fossil human remains been more evident than in the case of the *Homo habilis* skull, "1470," unearthed by Richard Leakey at East Turkana, Kenya, in 1972. Preliminary K-Ar results from a British laboratory on the so-called KBS tuff above the skull deposit gave a date of *c.* 2.6 my, at least 0.8 my earlier than *H. habilis* finds elsewhere. Could the K-Ar date be right? At first, cross-checking by geomagnetic reversals and fission-track seemed to support it. But there was the worrying fact that pig fossil correlations with other sites implied a date no earlier than 2 my. And in 1974 an American laboratory produced K-Ar readings of *c.* 1.8 my for the tuff.

The controversy dragged on for several years. Eventually one of the scientists who had originally published fission-track dates supporting the older K-Ar readings re-ran fission-track tests and confirmed the younger estimate of *c.* 1.8 my. Finally, to resolve the issue, Leakey commissioned an Australian laboratory to obtain new K-Ar dates. The result was a now generally accepted age for the KBS tuff of 1.88 ±0.02 my.

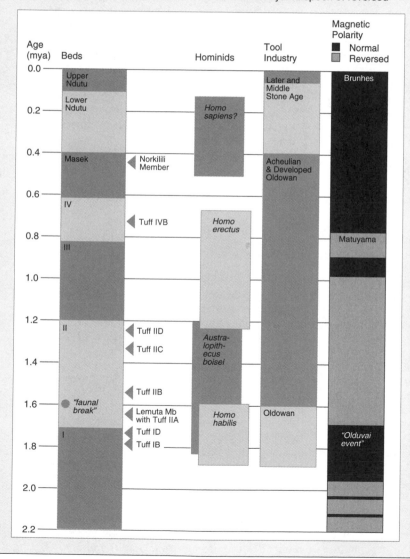

Olduvai Gorge schematic stratigraphy, together with hominids and tool industries from the site, and magnetic reversals.

been etched with acid to improve visibility. The quantity of uranium present in the sample is then determined by counting a second set of tracks created by artificially inducing fission in atoms of ^{235}U. (The ratio of ^{235}U to ^{238}U is known, so that the second count indirectly measures the amount of ^{238}U present.) Knowing the rate of fission of ^{238}U, one arrives at a date – the age since the setting of the clock to zero – by comparing the number of spontaneously induced tracks with the quantity of ^{238}U in the sample.

The radioactive clock is set at zero by the formation of the mineral or glass, either in nature (as with obsidian and tektites) or at the time of manufacture (as with manufactured glass).

Applications and Limiting Factors. The fission-track technique is most useful for early Paleolithic sites, especially where the potassium-argon method cannot be applied. Fission-track also provides independent confirmation of dating results. For example, the date of 2.03 ± 0.28 million years obtained by fission-track analysis for Tuff IB at Olduvai Gorge, Tanzania, falls within the age determination by potassium-argon and other methods of 2.1–1.7 million years for this early hominid site (see box, pp. 148–49). Fission-track also helped to settle the controversy over the date of the KBS Tuff and associated hominid remains and artifacts at the East Turkana sites, Kenya.

The fission-track technique is most easily applied to naturally occurring materials such as pumice and obsidian, but minerals within rock formations (e.g. zircon and apatite which contain high amounts of uranium) can also be dated in this way. The potential time range is considerable: micas from Zimbabwe in Africa have been dated back to more than 2500 million (or 2.5 billion) years ago. Generally, the method is used for geological samples no younger than about 300,000 years old. For more recent material, the method is too time-consuming to operate; here thermoluminescence dating or some other method is generally better.

There are a few exceptions. For example, artificial glass and pottery glazes less than 2000 years old have been dated successfully by the fission-track method. A different application is to obsidian artifacts that have been exposed to fire during manufacture, or during or after use. The heat has the effect of setting the radioactive clock to zero and the tracks left after the fission of ^{238}U can be counted as if this were an artificial glass.

In favorable circumstances, the error associated with the method is of the order of ± 10 percent (one standard deviation), assuming that at least 100 tracks are counted.

TRAPPED ELECTRON DATING METHODS

The following three methods – thermoluminescence dating, optical dating, and electron spin resonance – are also dependent upon radioactive decay, but indirectly, as it is the amount of radiation received by the specimen to be dated which is of interest, not the radiation emitted by the specimen itself. The methods can only be used to date crystalline materials (minerals) and are dependent upon the behavior of electrons within a crystal when exposed to radiation.

When atoms located within a crystal lattice are exposed to nuclear radiation, individual electrons absorb energy and become detached from their parent nuclei and are "trapped" in lattice defects – crystal imperfections caused by missing atoms or the presence of impurities. Provided the amount of radiation (annual dose) remains constant over time then trapped electrons will accumulate at a uniform rate and the size of the trapped electron population will relate directly to the total amount of radiation received by the specimen (total dose), and thus to the total time of exposure. The age of an archaeological specimen can therefore be determined by dividing the total radiation dose by the annual radiation dose.

$$AGE = \frac{TOTAL\ DOSE}{ANNUAL\ DOSE}$$

The annual dose is received mainly from radioisotopes of three elements which occur naturally in geological deposits: uranium, thorium, and a radioactive isotope of potassium, ^{40}K. The radiation emitted by these isotopes consists of alpha particles, beta particles, and gamma rays. Alpha and beta particles have low range and poor penetrability, about 0.02 mm and 2 mm respectively. Gamma rays can travel further, however, up to 20 cm. The isotopes all have long half-lives and their emission is assumed to be constant over the time period for which these dating methods are used. This means that measurement of present-day concentrations of radioisotopes can be used to determine annual dose. Measurement can proceed directly by determining absolute concentrations of uranium and thorium using neutron activation analysis (box, pp. 360–61), and potassium using flame photometry. Alternatively the radiation itself can be counted.

The total dose is determined by measuring the number of trapped electrons, and the different dating methods are distinguished by their different measurement techniques. Accurate determination of the size of the trapped electron population requires that all electron traps were emptied, or set to zero, during the lifetime of the material to be dated. There are various ways in which this can occur, but it is a requirement that limits the range of minerals which are suitable for dating by these methods.

Thermoluminescence Dating

Thermoluminescence (TL) has two advantages over radiocarbon: it can date pottery, the most abundant inorganic material on archaeological sites of the last 10,000 years; and it can in principle date inorganic materials (such as burnt flint) beyond 50,000 years of age, the limit of radiocarbon. But the precision of TL is, in general, poorer than that of radiocarbon.

Basis of Method. It is possible to empty electron traps by the application of heat. Thus TL dating may be performed on minerals which have had their electron

traps set to zero by exposure to high temperature prior to burial. Typically these include ceramics, which are fired during their manufacture, as well as other materials such as flint which may have been deliberately or accidentally burned before discard.

As ceramics are manufactured from a geological material, clay, they contain small amounts of radioactive elements. Thus the annual radiation dose of buried pottery is derived from two sources: externally, from the environment of the pot; and internally from the ceramic material itself. As alpha and beta particles are of such poor penetrative ability their effect on the pot can be eliminated by removing the outer few millimeters. Thus the annual dose may be calculated from the amounts of radioisotopes present within the ceramic fabric and the amount of gamma radiation a pot receives from its surroundings. Ideally the radioactivity of the soil is measured on site by the burial of a small capsule containing a radiation-sensitive material, which is left for about a year. Where this is not possible, a more rapid determination using a radiation counter can be used, or samples of the soil

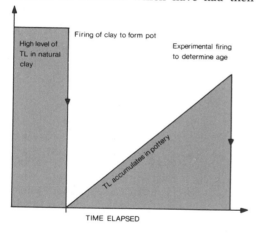

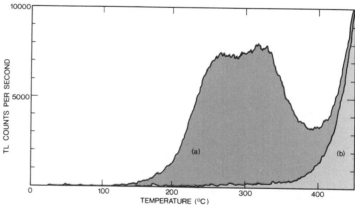

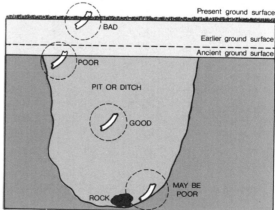

Thermoluminescence dating. (Above left) The TL clock in pottery is set to zero when a vessel is fired. TL accumulates until the pot is heated again in the present day to determine its age. (Above right) Glow-curves observed in the laboratory. Curve (a) displays the light emitted when the sample is first heated. Curve (b) is the non-TL light recorded in a second heating (the red-hot glow observable when any sample is heated). The extra light emitted in the first heating is the TL measured for dating. (Right) Good and bad locations for TL samples. Results will be inaccurate if the subsoil or rock near the sample at the bottom have a measurably different level of radioactivity from that of the filling of the pit or ditch.

collected in plastic bags and dispatched to the laboratory with the object to be dated. Where the radioactivity of the burial context cannot be determined, e.g. for an object not *in situ*, the TL date is much less accurate.

The total radiation dose is determined in the laboratory by heating the material rapidly to 500°C (932°F) or above. Energy lost by electrons as they are evicted from their traps is emitted as light radiation and is termed thermoluminescence. This luminescence is measured and is directly proportional to the number of trapped electrons, and thus to the total radiation dose. It is therefore possible to speak of a mineral accumulating a TL signal as it grows older; or, by analogy with radioactive clocks, of a TL clock.

Applications. A good example of the archaeological application of TL is the dating of the terracotta known as the Jemaa head, from the alluvium of a tin mine near the Jos Plateau of Nigeria. The head and similar examples belong to the Nok culture, but such sculptures could not be dated reliably at the site of Nok itself because of the lack of any plausible radiocarbon dates. A TL reading on the head gave an age of 1520 ± 260 BC, allowing this and similar terracotta heads from the Nok region to be given a firm chronological position for the first time.

Terracotta head from Jemaa, Nigeria, belonging to the Nok culture. A TL reading for the age of the sculpture has provided the first reliable date for this and other terracottas from the Nok region. Height 23 cm.

Of even greater potential is the development of the TL method for dating artifacts made before 50,000 years ago (beyond the basic limit of radiocarbon). Pottery itself is not found at this early time, nor are baked clay artifacts. But the method can be applied to stone (lithic) materials with a crystalline structure, always provided that they were heated at the time of their production as artifacts, or at the time of their use, to a temperature of around 500°C. In this way, geological TL in the stone would be emitted and the TL clock effectively set at zero. Therefore, the measurement of their TL age genuinely dates their archaeological use. In practice, burnt flint has proved a very informative material.

For example, the method has been successfully used in France to date flint tools of so-called Mousterian type found at sites occupied by Neanderthal people (*Homo sapiens neanderthalensis*) in the Middle Paleolithic period. Most of the dates fall between 70,000 and 40,000 years ago. Despite their limited precision, the dates establish a very useful pattern for the tools that has advanced the understanding of the French Middle Paleolithic.

Hélène Valladas and her colleagues have also employed the TL method to date flint tools used at different times by both Neanderthals and the first people of modern appearance (*Homo sapiens sapiens*). Their research at caves in Israel suggests controversially and somewhat surprisingly that Neanderthals were still in the area tens of thousands of years after the arrival of the first anatomically modern humans. At Kebara an age of 60,000 years was indicated for a Neanderthal skeleton, while at Qafzeh results suggested that modern humans were already in the region by about 90,000 years ago.

TL dates can also be obtained from calcium carbonate deposits in caves (e.g. stalagmites and travertines) with which artifacts are associated as TL starts to accumulate from the time the carbonate crystallizes from the solution to form the deposit. TL dating has shown, for instance, that the stalagmitic floor of the Lower Paleolithic cave site of Caune de l'Arago in southern France formed around 350,000 years ago.

There is also a special application of TL dating, its use in the identification of fake pottery and terracotta objects. The TL method can easily distinguish between a genuine antiquity and a forgery made within the last 100 years.

Limiting Factors. Various complications remain with thermoluminescence, and TL dates rarely have a precision of better than ± 10 percent of the age of the sample.

Optical Dating

This method is similar in principle to thermoluminescence, but is used to date minerals which have been exposed to light, rather than heat.

Basis of Method. Most minerals contain a sub-set of electron traps which are emptied, or bleached, by several minutes' exposure to sunlight. This phenomenon has been utilized for dating sedimentary deposits of quartz grains. Their electron traps are bleached during transport but after sedimentation and burial they begin to accumulate electrons once more. After careful sampling the total radiation dose of a sediment may be estimated in the laboratory by directing light of a visible wavelength onto a sample and measuring the resultant luminescence, which is known as optically stimulated luminescence (OSL).

Applications. Artifact-bearing sand sediments in the Nauwalabila I rockshelter in north Australia have been optically dated and shown to be between 53,000 and 60,000 years old – important evidence for an early occupation of this area by humans (see Chapter 13). The general validity of these optically stimulated luminescence results is supported by the good match between radiocarbon dates and optical dates from the Ngarrabullgan Cave in Queensland.

However, the same can certainly not be said for the controversy surrounding the Jinmium rock shelter in the Northern Territory of Australia which hit the headlines in 1996 with claims for human occupation

A section from the Nauwalabila I excavation, north Australia, with luminescence dates (TL and Optical Dating) on the left and calibrated radiocarbon dates on the right. Artifact-bearing sands could be optically dated and produced results of between 53,000 and 60,000 BP, having important implications for the date of the first human occupation of the Australian landmass.

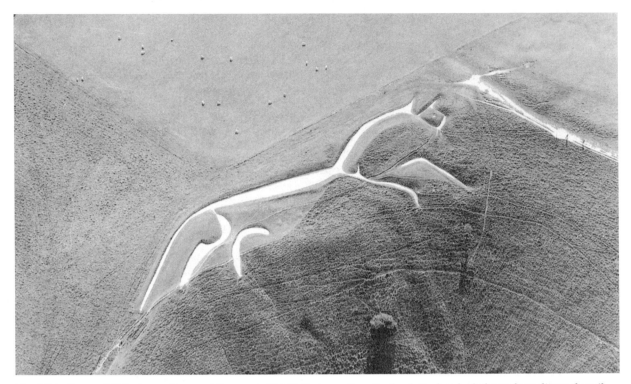

The White Horse of Uffington, a figure cut from a chalk hillside in southern England. Its date had always been disputed until soil samples taken from excavations of part of the figure were optically dated to 1400–600 BC, around 1000 years older than had previously been thought.

prior to 116,000 years ago and artistic activity, inferred from red ocher, before 75,000 years ago and rock-engravings prior to 58,000 years ago, all based on TL dating (where the laboratory analysis, conducted upon quartz grains, effectively sets out to date the time when these were last exposed to sunlight). This was soon criticized on technical grounds (specifically that decaying bedrock retaining the much earlier "geological" TL age signature became incorporated in the sample, thus giving a distorted "early" age). Later work, based on single-grain optical ages, has indicated that the Jinmium deposit is younger than 10,000 years old and confirms that some grains have older optical ages because they received insufficient exposure to sunlight before burial.

The lesson here is that novel dating methods can give misleading results unless a wide range of sources of error are considered: it is always wiser to seek corroboration from other, well-established dating methods before making sweeping claims. To do otherwise is simply scientifically incautious.

In Britain, OSL has been used to date the enigmatic White Horse at Uffington. The only prehistoric equine hill-figure in Britain, the outline of this horse was cut directly into the hillside and then packed with white chalk. On stylistic grounds both Anglo-Saxon and Celtic (late Iron Age) dates had previously been proposed for its delineation; but now three OSL dates obtained from silt laid down in the lowest levels of the horse's belly suggest instead a Bronze Age date, in the range 1400–600 BC. This date accords well with other indications of late Bronze Age activity in the area.

Limiting Factors. Although still in its developmental stage results so far suggest that the method may be used successfully to date aeolian (wind-borne) deposits. The position with alluvial deposits is less clear, however, as it is not certain that the exposure of their constituent grains to sunlight during water transport is sufficient to ensure complete bleaching.

Electron Spin Resonance Dating

Electron spin resonance (ESR) dating is less sensitive than TL, but is suitable for materials which decompose when heated. Its most successful application so far has been for the dating of tooth enamel, which is composed almost entirely of the mineral hydroxyapatite. Newly formed hydroxyapatite contains no trapped electrons, but they begin to accumulate once the tooth is buried and exposed to natural radiation. The precision of the method when used to date tooth enamel is in the order of 10–20 percent.

Basis of Method. For the determination of total dose a sample of the specimen to be dated is powdered and exposed to high frequency electromagnetic radiation (microwaves) in the presence of a strong magnetic field. The field strength may be varied and as it is, the trapped electrons in the sample absorb microwaves of different frequencies and resonate. Maximum resonance occurs at a specific conjunction of microwave frequency and magnetic field strength. The magnitude of resultant microwave absorption can be measured and is directly proportional to the size of the trapped electron population, and thus to the total radiation dose.

Hydroxyapatite does not naturally contain any radioactive isotopes, but it acquires them after burial by uptake of water-soluble uranium, as does its associated dentine. Its annual dose rate therefore increases over time and it is necessary to correct for this by modeling the rate of uranium uptake. Two models are used: the early uptake (EU) model which assumes that the uranium content of the tooth rapidly equilibrates with that of its environment so that uptake diminishes with time; and the linear uptake (LU) model which assumes that uranium uptake proceeds at a uniform rate. As with ceramics, the effect of external alpha and beta emitters can be eliminated by removal of the outer few millimeters of the sample to be dated. For determination of annual dose, therefore, it is necessary to measure the internal concentrations of uranium (and its daughter thorium isotopes) and the external levels of gamma radiation. It is conventional to present results as both EU and LU versions.

Applications. ESR dates from mammalian teeth associated with hominid remains have confirmed dates obtained by U-Series dating and by TL of burnt flints. Thus at Qafzeh dates of 100,000 ± 10,000 BP (EU) or 120,000 ± 8000 BP (LU) and at Skhūl 81,000 ± 15,000 BP (EU) and 101,000 ± 12,000 BP (LU) are associated with the remains of anatomically modern humans, while at Tabun dates in the range of 100,000–120,000 years and at Kebara dates of 60,000 ± 6000 BP (EU) or 64,000 ± 4000 BP (LU) are associated with the remains of Neanderthals. The dates obtained from this series of Israeli caves are important as they demonstrate that all three methods produce data that are compatible. They are also exciting as they suggest that Neanderthal populations must have coexisted in the area with early modern humans for tens of thousands of years, and that therefore the two groups must constitute separate evolutionary lineages. This finding provides support for claims that modern *Homo sapiens* evolved first in Africa and then colonized adjacent continents, replacing earlier *Homo* populations in the process.

Recently it has proved possible to date small dental fragments directly, without first powdering them. This direct ESR dating has been applied to the hominid remains found at the Florisbad spring, South Africa, giving an age of the order of 250,000 years, which was supported by optically stimulated luminescence dating.

Limiting Factors. The age range of ESR dating is limited because ultimately the stability of trapped electrons begins to deteriorate. This deterioration is temperature-dependent so that the electrons are less stable in hot environments than in cold. In theory the age range is in the order of a million years but in practice it may be less. The accuracy of the method is compromised by the need to model uranium uptake. Models have to account for the different rates of uranium uptake by dentine and enamel and also allow for the decay of absorbed uranium and the consequent formation of radioactive daughter isotopes: thorium and uranium. ESR cannot easily be used to date bone as the new minerals which form during fossilization produce consistent under-estimation of age. The behavior of uranium in the more open matrix of bone is also difficult to model.

CALIBRATED RELATIVE METHODS

Radioactive decay is the only completely regular time-dependent process known; it is uninfluenced by temperature or other environmental conditions. There are, however, other natural processes which, while not completely regular, are sufficiently steady over the course of time to be of use to the archaeologist. We have already seen how natural annual cycles produce varves and tree-rings, which of course are immensely useful because they give dates calibrated in years. Other processes that form the basis of the first three techniques described below are not naturally calibrated in years, but in principle they can be made to

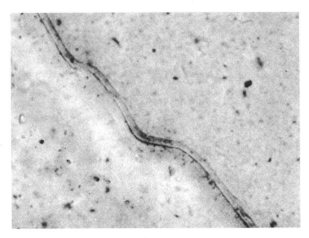

Obsidian hydration dating: a hydration layer visible in an obsidian artifact. The layer increases in thickness as time passes, but there is no universally valid rate of growth.

yield absolute dates if the rate of change inherent in the process can be independently calibrated by one of the absolute methods already discussed. In practice, as we shall see, the calibration for each technique often has to be done afresh for each site or area because of environmental factors that influence the rate of change. This makes these techniques difficult to use as reliable absolute dating methods. They can, however, still prove enormously helpful simply as a means of ordering samples in a relative sequence, in which older is distinguished from younger.

Obsidian Hydration

Basis of Method and Limiting Factors. This technique was first developed by the American geologists Irving Friedman and Robert L. Smith. It is based on the principle that when obsidian (the volcanic glass often used rather like flint to make tools) is fractured, it starts absorbing water from its surroundings, forming a hydration layer that can be measured. In a section through an obsidian tool viewed under the optical microscope, the layer appears as a distinct zone at the surface. It increases in thickness through time.

If the layer increases in thickness in a linear way, then assuming we know the rate of growth and the present thickness, we ought to be able to calculate the length of time elapsed since growth began. The zero moment, when the hydration zone started forming, is the moment when the flake tool was freshly made by removing it from the original obsidian block, or by trimming it. Unfortunately, there is no universally valid rate of growth or hydration rate. For one thing,

the rate is dependent on temperature, and exposure to direct sunlight over long periods increases hydration. Moreover, obsidians from different quarries have different chemical compositions, and this can affect the picture. It is necessary, therefore, to establish separately the hydration rate for the different kinds of obsidian found in a given area, and to keep in mind the temperature factor, which can be allowed for.

To use the method for absolute dating, it has to be calibrated against an established chronological sequence (taking into account the chemical and temperature factors) for the region in question. Samples for dating need to come from one or more well-defined contexts that can be dated securely by other means. A single obsidian artifact cannot be expected to give a reliable date. It is thus safer to use an assemblage of about 10 pieces, so that the date of each one can be separately calculated. In addition to providing direct chronological information, the method can be useful in assessing the relative ages of different strata within a site or region where obsidian is abundant.

Though principally relevant to sites and artifacts of the last 10,000 years (the postglacial period), obsidian hydration has given acceptable dates of around 120,000 years for Middle Paleolithic material from East Africa.

Applications. One of the boldest applications of the method so far has been by one of the pioneers of obsidian dating, Joseph Michels, in his study of the rural hinterland around the important ancient center of Kaminaljuyu in Guatemala. The sites were difficult to date from the pottery found on the surface, which was much abraded, so an attempt was made to date them by measuring the hydration layer on at least four obsidian artifacts from each site. If at least two of the obsidian dates fell within one of the already established chronological phases (ranging from Early Formative *c.* 2500 BC to Late Postclassic *c.* AD 1500), the site was assigned to that phase. In the principal survey area some 70 rural settlements were dated in this way, on the evidence of a total of 288 obsidian samples. The results indicated an increase in the density of rural settlement up to the Early Late Classic period (AD 600–800), then a gradual fall as Kaminaljuyu declined.

Amino-Acid Racemization

This method, first applied in the early 1970s and still at an experimental stage, is used to date bone, whether human or animal (only 10 g are required). Its special significance is that it can be applied to material up to about 100,000 years old, i.e. beyond the time range of radiocarbon dating.

Basis of Method. The technique is based on the fact that amino acids, which make up proteins present in all living things, can exist in two mirror-image forms, termed enantiomers. These differ in their chemical structure, which shows in their effect on polarized light. Those that rotate polarized light to the left are *laevo*-enantiomers or L-amino acids; those that rotate the light to the right are *dextro*-enantiomers or D-amino acids.

The amino acids present in the proteins of living organisms contain only L-enantiomers. After death, these change at a steady rate (they racemize) to D-enantiomers. The rate of racemization is temperature-dependent, and therefore likely to vary from site to site. But by radiocarbon-dating suitable bone samples at a particular site, and measuring the relative proportions (ratio) of the L and D forms in them, one should be able to work out what the local racemization rate is. This calibration is then used to date bone samples from earlier levels at the site beyond the time range of radiocarbon.

L-enantiomers of the stable amino acid isoleucine form D-enantiomers by a rather different process known as epimerization. The rate of isoleucine epimerization has been measured successfully in the proteinaceous residues of ostrich shells and by comparison with ^{14}C dating has been shown to be constant for the past 80,000 years.

Applications and Limiting Factors. Aspartic acid has the fastest racemization rate of the stable amino acids and is the acid usually chosen for dating bone samples. For instance, at the Nelson Bay Cave in Cape Province, South Africa, samples with a D/L aspartic acid ratio of 0.167 gave radiocarbon ages of roughly 18,000 years. This allowed a conversion rate to be calculated, calibrating the racemization rate for that site. Measurements of the ratio were then made on fossil bone samples from the important site of Klasies River Mouth in the same area, giving for the lower levels (18 and 19) D/L aspartic acid ratios of 0.474 and 0.548. From these values, ages of about 90,000 and 110,000 years respectively were estimated. In this case, the "calibration" sample was derived from a different site than the one from which the samples to be dated came. This is less than ideal, because the racemization rates for the different sites, even though geographically the sites are not far apart, could differ to some extent. It now seems that one of the major problems with amino-acid dating has been that amino acids bound up in complex proteins, such as collagen, have very different racemization rates from the same amino acids in their free state. Bone preservation therefore has a huge effect on apparent ages.

As a means of absolute dating the method is of course entirely dependent on the accuracy of its calibration (as are other relative methods). This has led to controversy, particularly as regards the date of fossil human remains from California. Early radiocarbon determinations from skulls found near Los Angeles were used to calibrate aspartic acid racemization rates, which then yielded ages as high as 48,000 years for other remains near San Diego – suggesting human colonization of the Americas much earlier than had been supposed (Chapter 11). More recent radiocarbon dates on the Los Angeles bones by the AMS method have altered the calibration, lowering the oldest age-estimates for the California remains to no earlier than 8000 years.

Cation-Ratios and the Dating of Rock Art

In the 1980s a new technique was developed which, for the first time, seemed to provide direct dates for rock-carvings and engravings, and was also potentially applicable to Paleolithic artifacts with a strong patina caused by exposure to desert dust.

Basis of Method. In desert conditions, a varnish forms on rock surfaces exposed to desert dust. The varnish is composed of clay minerals, oxides, and hydroxides of manganese and iron, minor trace elements, and a small amount of organic matter such as microscopic plant particles. The original dating method depended on the principle that the cations of certain elements (i.e. charged atoms of those elements which combine with oxide and hydroxide ions of opposite charge to form stable compounds) are more soluble than those of certain other elements. They leach out of rock varnish more rapidly than the less-soluble elements and their concentration thus decreases with time. The method simply required the measurement of the ratio of these mobile cations, usually of potassium (K) and calcium (Ca); to the more stable cations of titanium (Ti). The ratio was assumed to decrease exponentially with time (giving a decay curve similar in shape to those of radioactive isotopes discussed above). However, the pioneers of the technique, Ronald Dorn and his associates, do not claim that there is an absolute decay rate (as there is for radioactive decay processes).

Applications and Limiting Factors. Cation-ratio dating was tried out on varnish covering rock-carvings (petroglyphs) in California and in Australia where it produced minimum ages for the images of 6400 years and more than 30,000 years respectively. A detailed debate ensued about the technique's degree of reliability and accuracy. Dorn responded by stressing that CR dating is an experimental method that will always remain a "weaker sister" of other approaches owing to the many environmental influences that have to be allowed for: it is not clear in what climatic conditions the varnish may be damaged or destroyed, nor indeed whether variations in climate might affect the process of cation-ratio reduction. The calibration curves are being revised, but the method is now used primarily as a back-up for other techniques, particularly AMS which can be applied to minute amounts of organic material contained in the rock varnish: for example, dates of 14,000 and 18,000 BP have been obtained by this method for varnish covering petroglyphs in California and Arizona.

These were therefore assumed to be minimal ages for the engravings beneath the varnish; but this whole approach to dating open-air petroglyphs has been called into question by the furore over the rock art of the Côa Valley in northeast Portugal. These images, first reported in 1994 and ascribed by every specialist to the Upper Paleolithic (i.e. more than 10,000 BP), were threatened with inundation by a huge dam. In 1995, an attempt was made by the electricity company building the dam to have a few of the figures dated directly by different methods, all of them highly experimental, including the AMS dating of organic deposits on the images.

Unfortunately, some of the panels chosen had already been much affected by latex molding, chalking, and other damage. The results were mixed, to say the least, but did archaeology a major service by revealing the uncertainty that still surrounds the direct dating of open-air engravings. Unlike organic material extracted from pigments in caves and rockshelters (see below), which is thus in a closed system, organic material trapped in accretions on exposed rocks is part of an open system. Hence, even if the dating of this material is accurate, its source and therefore its chronological relationship with the petroglyphs beneath remain utterly uncertain. For example, a sample taken from the calcareous accretions covering the inscription on a Carthaginian stela, known to be about 2200 years old, recently provided an AMS result of 21,430 years – dead carbonate clearly contaminated the sample, but nobody knows how much of it comes from the underlying stone, from nearby stone, or from the atmosphere. The Côa episode has therefore sent the whole idea of direct dating of petroglyphs back to the drawing board.

As mentioned above, AMS has produced far more reliable results when applied to organic material in prehistoric paintings: for example, apparently sound results have been obtained from 12 French and Spanish Paleolithic caves where charcoal was used as a pigment, from plant fibers in paint in rockshelters in Queensland, and from human blood protein in paint in Wargata Mina cave in Tasmania. Other methods for dating rock art are being explored. For example, layers of calcite that build up on top of images in caves may be datable by radiocarbon and by uranium-thorium; oxalates (salts of oxalic acid, containing organic carbon) also form deposits that are susceptible to radiocarbon dating.

Chlorine-36 Dating

The question of the dating of rock art when no associated artifacts survive has been advanced a little by the ^{36}Cl dating method.

Basis of Method. This method depends upon the accumulation of nuclides at and near the surface of the rock when it is exposed to cosmic radiation. One or two meters of rock will block cosmic radiation. However, where thick slabs of rock spall off to expose fresh faces the accumulation of cosmogenic nuclides will be initiated at the fresh face at the time of the spall event. The concentration of ^{36}Cl in samples taken at and near the surface of the rock is determined using the accelerated mass spectrometer, and is compared with the background concentration present in samples from freshly exposed rock. When the rock exposure is an old one, the concentration is very much higher. It should be clearly understood, however, that the comparison does not given information about the date of a rock engraving as such, but simply about the length of time that the rock surface in question has been exposed since the geological event which led to its exposure.

Applications and Limiting Factors. The method has also been applied to the Côa petroglyphs of Portugal (see above), in the light of the controversy as to whether they were of Pleistocene age (greater than 10,000 BP) or modern. The results suggested exposure ages between 16,000 and 136,000 years. It should be noted that this is an imprecise technique, and the date is for the rock surface, not for the engravings. But at least the result appears to exclude the possibility that the rock surface itself was exposed in relatively recent times, as had earlier been suggested.

Archaeomagnetic Dating

Archaeomagnetic (or Paleomagnetic) dating has so far been of limited use to archaeology, in part because not enough work has been done in different regions.

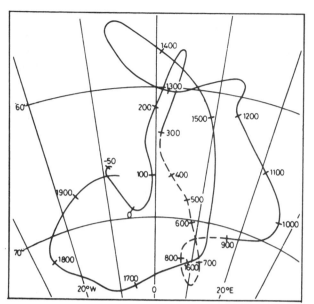
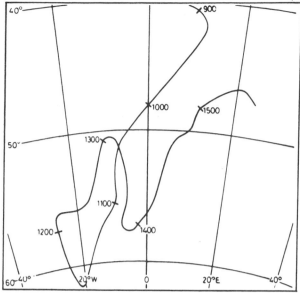

Magnetic direction dating. The changing positions of magnetic north, as plotted here for Britain (left) and the American Southwest (right), can be used to date baked clay structures such as kilns which preserve a record of the direction of magnetic north at the time they were fired.

Basis of Method. The earth's magnetic field is constantly changing in both direction and intensity. Historical records from London, Paris, and Rome have allowed scientists to plot changes in the direction of magnetic north observed there from compass readings over the last 400 years. Scientists have also been able to trace these changes farther back in time in Europe and elsewhere by studying the magnetization at earlier periods of baked clay structures (ovens, kilns, hearths) that have been independently dated, for instance by radiocarbon. (Provided clay is baked to 650–700°C (1202–1292°F) and not reheated, the iron particles in it permanently take up the earth's magnetic direction and intensity at the time of firing. This principle is called thermoremanent magnetism (TRM).) Plots can thus be built up of the variation through time in magnetic *direction* which can be used to date other baked clay structures of unknown age, whose TRM is measured and then matched to a particular point (date) on the master sequence. Different master sequences have to be built up for variations in magnetic *intensity*, which varies independently of magnetic direction.

Applications and Limiting Factors. Regional variations within the global magnetic field mean that a separate master sequence is needed for each region. For magnetic direction these have been created in a few parts of the world such as Britain and the American Southwest

back over the last 2000 years. A baked clay kiln or oven from this time period, measured *in situ* at a site in one of these regions, can be dated quite accurately by the magnetic direction method. Once the structure is moved, however, its ancient magnetic direction can no longer be compared with that of the present day.

Magnetic intensity can be measured when the baked clay is out of context, and so can be applied to pottery unlike the directional method. A recent application to pottery from different provinces of China has yielded a master sequence for the last 4000 years, promising to make it possible to date Chinese pottery of unknown age. But so far the intensity method has proved inherently much less accurate than the directional method.

Geomagnetic Reversals. Another aspect of archaeomagnetism, relevant for the dating of the Lower Paleolithic, is the phenomenon of complete reversals in the earth's magnetic field (magnetic north becomes magnetic south, and vice versa). The most recent major reversal occurred about 780,000 years ago, and a sequence of such reversals stretching back several million years has been built up with the aid of potassium-argon and other dating techniques. The finding of part of this sequence of reversals in the rock strata of African early hominid sites has proved a helpful check on the other dating methods that have been used at those sites (see box, pp. 148–49).

DATING THE THERA ERUPTION

More than 3500 years ago the volcanic island of Thera (also known as Santorini) in the Aegean Sea erupted, burying the prehistoric settlement of Akrotiri on its southern shore. Akrotiri – excavated since the 1960s by the Greek archaeologist Spyridon Marinatos and more recently Christos Doumas – has proved to be a prehistoric Pompeii, with well-preserved streets and houses, some with remarkable wall paintings, all buried beneath many meters of volcanic ash. The eruption itself offers interesting problems and opportunities in dating.

As long ago as 1939, Marinatos suggested that the Thera eruption was responsible for the destruction of the Minoan palaces of Crete (110 km or 69 miles to the south), many of which were abandoned during the Late Bronze Age. This idea sparked off a debate that still continues.

In the first place, the problem can be approached in terms of the **relative chronology** offered by the evolution of pottery styles. There is a well-established stylistic sequence for Minoan pottery, and it was found that the most recent pottery style in the relevant Minoan palaces was Late Minoan IB. This was assigned an absolute date in years by cross-dating between the Minoan sequence and the well-established Egyptian historical chronology. On this basis, the end of Late Minoan IB (and hence the destruction of the Minoan palaces) was dated around 1450 BC.

This date, however, made any link with the destruction of Akrotiri on Thera problematic, because Akrotiri has no Late Minoan IB pottery but abundant material of the Late Minoan IA style. Some scholars thus concluded that the Thera eruption had nothing to do with the destruction of the Minoan palaces, which might well have been a later event. They were therefore happy to date the Thera eruption within the Late Minoan IA period, perhaps (again using the Egyptian-based chronology for Minoan Crete) around 1500 BC.

Other scholars, however, believed that the effects of the Thera eruption would have been widely felt. Here, they were certainly aided by the application of **tephra studies**. Deep-sea coring on the bed of the Mediterranean gave evidence for the Thera ash fall (and the ash was shown by laboratory analysis to be from the appropriate eruption of this particular volcano). Subsequently, traces of ash from the Thera eruption were identified (using refractive index studies) in samples from sites on Minoan Crete, and also from the site of Phylakopi on the Aegean island of Melos. However, this ash has not yet been documented in strata at archaeological sites where there is a clear distinction between the use of Late Minoan IA and Late Minoan IB pottery, so it is premature to speak here of tephrachronology. Nevertheless a major ash layer has been recognized at the archaeological site of Trianda on Rhodes, so the method should offer an answer in due course. Well-stratified pumice found at the Egyptian site of Tell Dab'a has been shown on analysis to derive from the Thera eruption and has been used by some scholars using the accepted Egyptian historical chronology to support a date around 1500 BC.

The problem is one that **radiocarbon dating** should theoretically help resolve, but the distinction between 1500 BC and 1450 BC is a relatively narrow one. However, samples have been analyzed, including short-lived samples (carbonized grain, etc.), that could not have been old at the time of the eruption. The mean date obtained from such short-lived samples is 1615 BC (after calibration). The date range for a single standard deviation, which implies 65 percent probability, is 1630 to 1530 BC. (The range is not symmetrical about the mean date because of irregularities in the calibration curve at this time.) The radiocarbon data thus favor the earlier of the two dates in question.

The matter does not rest there. It has been shown for more recent times that major volcanic eruptions have global effects (since the dust thrown into the atmosphere reduces solar radiation reaching the earth). These can show up as anomalously narrow rings for a year or two in **tree-ring sequences**. Such effects have been sought in the tree-ring record of the California bristlecone pine during the middle of the 2nd millennium BC. One such, firmly dated 1628–1626 BC, has been proposed for

The Thera volcano is still sporadically active, the focus of the eruptions being on this small island in the center of the semi-submerged volcano.

the Thera eruption. A comparable ring has been noted for the tree-ring sequence for Irish oak. A recently developed tree-ring sequence from Anatolia with a markedly anomalous ring has been used to support this early date, but the arguments for associating this ring with the eruption are not conclusive.

It has been similarly shown that ice cores reveal a short peak of high acidity for recently observed major eruptions, when these are on a scale large enough to have global effects. An ice core from Greenland shows such a peak for 1390 BC, and this has been claimed as a possible date for the Thera eruption. More recent work at the Dye 3 site in Greenland has, however, suggested that an acidity maximum in 1645 BC would be more appropriate which could be used to support the tree ring date of 1628 BC. The problem is that there was absolutely nothing in the tree-rings or indeed in the ice cores that allows one major volcanic eruption in one part of the world to be distinguished from another, other than its date in years.

Now, however, a tiny fragment of tephra has been found in the Dye 3 ice core corresponding to the 1645 BC acidity peak – and it proves on analysis not to derive from the Thera eruption, so the early date of 1645 BC (or 1628 BC) is called into question again and the debate continues.

Fresco from Akrotiri called the "Fisherman."

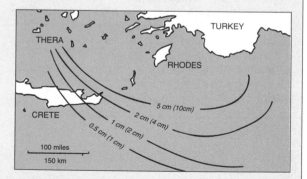

Map indicating isopachs (contours of equal thickness) for tephra fallout from the eruption of Thera, as determined from deep-sea cores. The figures in brackets give an estimate of the corresponding depth of tephra falling on land.

CHRONOLOGICAL CORRELATIONS

One of the most promising avenues for future work in chronology is the correlation of different dating methods. The use of one absolute method in support of another can often bring very powerful results. An excellent example is the way that tree-ring dating has been used to support and indeed calibrate radiocarbon, as a result of which the latter has gained greatly in accuracy and reliability. The same observation is true of the relationship between relative and absolute dating. Although actual dates in years are provided by absolute methods, much of the reliability and internal consistency of those dates (and therefore the possibility of recognizing and weeding out inaccurate absolute age determinations) comes from the framework provided by the relative dating method.

Links between chronological sequences that are geographically remote from each other – "teleconnections" – can present considerable difficulties. The most common are those that depend on the comparison of sequences – for instance of tree-ring widths. This is certainly valid for adjacent trees or for trees within a small area; over a wide region such "teleconnections" must be treated with caution. In the same way, the correlation of varve sequences in Scandinavia and in North America has proved contentious. With such methods there is always the risk of arriving at a "correlation" between sequences which, while initially plausible, is incorrect.

Global Events

One of the most powerful ways of establishing a correlation between sequences is by seeing within them the occurrence of the same significant event, one with wide repercussions geographically, even on a global scale.

Such events are naturally very rare, and are generally catastrophic in their nature. The impact on earth of large meteorites would fall in this category. Much more common are large-scale volcanic eruptions. Close to the volcano these events have striking effects, with mud and lava flows and thick falls of ash, often with devastating consequences for human occupation. At intermediate distances, up to a few hundred kilometers, they can still have a marked effect, with tsunamis ("tidal waves," although they are not in fact tidal) and falls of tephra (volcanic ash). Scientists have sought to correlate earthquake damage at intermediate distances with volcanic eruptions, but the two events are often not connected. Major volcanic eruptions also project significant quantities of tephra into the earth's upper atmosphere, with global effects. Such ash or dust increases the acidity of the snow falling in polar areas, and thus leaves its trace in ice cores. Its effect on tree-rings has also been noted: by reducing the amount of solar radiation reaching the earth (and thus also reducing the temperature) the volcanic dust reduces the growth rate of trees for a short but significant time.

The developing field of tephrachronology is proving useful. Its aim is to distinguish unequivocally, and hence date, the tephra from different volcanic eruptions that may be present in terrestrial deposits, or in deep-sea cores. The products of each eruption are often significantly different, so that measurements of refractive index may be sufficient to distinguish one ash from another. In other cases, analysis of trace elements will separate the two.

When all the sites and objects in an area are buried under a layer of volcanic ash at the same instant – a "freeze-frame" effect – one has a very precise dating method that can be used to correlate the age of all those archaeological materials. Examples include the great eruption of Mount Vesuvius in AD 79 that covered Pompeii, Herculaneum, and other Roman settlements (pp. 22–23); and the eruption of the Ilopango volcano in El Salvador in about AD 175 that buried Early Classic settlements there under 0.5–1 m (1.6–3.3 ft) of volcanic ash. The Ilopango eruption must have disrupted agriculture for several years and interrupted pyramid construction at the site of Chalchuapa, where the break in work can clearly be seen.

Another good example of tephrachronology comes from New Guinea, where various sites have been related chronologically by the presence of up to a dozen identifiable ash falls within them. Australian archaeologists Edward Harris and Philip Hughes were able to relate the horticultural system at Mugumamp Ridge in the Western Highland Province of Papua New Guinea with another at Kuk Swamp, some kilometers to the south, by the characteristics of the volcanic ash overlying both horticultural systems. The ash is thought to derive from the volcanic Mount Hagen some 40 km (25 miles) to the west. A combination of tephrachronology and radiocarbon suggests that horticulture in this area may have begun as early as 7000 BC (see box, pp. 262–63).

The most intensively studied question in the field of tephrachronology, however, is the date of the major eruption of the volcanic island of Thera in the Aegean sometime around the late 17th century or the 16th century BC (see box, pp. 160–61). The eruption buried the Late Bronze Age town of Akrotiri on the island and there were also marked effects on islands nearby.

An important general moral arises from the long dispute over the date of the Thera eruption. It is indeed all too common, when dating evidence is being discussed, to assume long-distance connections without being able to document them. For instance, several writers have tried to link the volcanic eruption of Thera with the Plagues of Egypt reported in the Book of Exodus in the Bible. This is intriguing, and worth investigating. But when it is actually used to date the eruption, as it has been by some, this is no more than a supposed equivalence, a supposition masquerading as a dating.

At the same time, however, there is an important future for the use of several methods in combination to date the eruption. For instance, it is perfectly appropriate to date the eruption approximately using radiocarbon on samples from Thera and then to seek a more precise date, indeed a date in calendar years, from indications in ice cores or tree-rings. The assumptions underlying the correlation – that these different kinds of evidence are telling us about the same event – should not, of course, be forgotten. It would be much more satisfactory if traces of tephra could be found in the ice cores, and if these could be shown by analysis to derive from the eruption in question. Were this to be done, it would be the Greenland or Antarctic ice cores that would, in effect, become responsible for the very precise dating of one important event in the Aegean Late Bronze Age, and hence for a calibration of Aegean Late Bronze Age dating in general. It might even lead to modifications in the Egyptian historical chronology.

WORLD CHRONOLOGY

As a result of the application of the various dating techniques discussed above, it is possible to summarize the world archaeological chronology.

The human story as understood at present begins in East Africa, with the emergence there of the earliest hominids of the genus *Australopithecus*, such as *A. afarensis*, around 4 or 5 million years ago, and the possibly earlier *Ardipithecus*. By around 2 million years ago, there is clear fossil evidence for the first known representative of our own genus, *Homo habilis*, from such sites as Koobi Fora (Kenya) and Olduvai Gorge (Tanzania). The earliest stone tools (from Hadar, Ethiopia) date from about 2.5 million years ago, but it is not known which hominid made them because *Homo habilis* fossils of this age have not yet been found. It is possible that australopithecines also had a tool culture before or during *Homo habilis*'s time. The early toolkits, comprising flake and pebble tools, are called the Oldowan industry, after Olduvai Gorge where they are particularly well represented.

By more than 1.6 million years ago, the next stage in human evolution, *Homo erectus*, had emerged in East Africa. These hominids had larger brains than *Homo habilis*, their probable ancestor, and were makers of the characteristic teardrop-shaped stone tools flaked on both sides called Acheulian hand-axes. These artifacts are the dominant tool form of the Lower Paleolithic. By the time *Homo erectus* became extinct (400,000–200,000 years ago), the species had colonized the rest of Africa, southern, eastern, and western Asia, and central and western Europe.

The Middle Paleolithic period – from about 200,000 to 40,000 years ago – saw the emergence of *Homo sapiens*. Neanderthals, who are generally classed as a subspecies of *Homo sapiens* (*Homo sapiens neanderthalensis*), lived in Europe, and western and central Asia from about 130,000 to 30,000 years ago. Their role in later human evolution is unclear, some specialists believing Neanderthals ultimately evolved into fully modern humans, others that they were an evolutionary dead end. The latter theory is gaining ground now that we have increasing evidence for fully modern people – that is our own subspecies, *Homo sapiens*

sapiens – in Africa by at least 100,000 years ago. They seem to have reached the eastern Mediterranean 100,000–90,000 years ago, and Europe and Asia by at least 40,000 years ago. Australia was colonized by humans at least 50,000 or 60,000 years ago (the date is currently being hotly debated, falling as it does at the very limit of radiocarbon dating). It is uncertain when humans first crossed from northeastern Asia into North America across the Bering Strait, and south to Central and South America. The earliest secure dates for early Americans are around 14,000 years ago, but there is controversial evidence that the continent was populated before then. The Brazilian rockshelter at Pedra Furada (see box, p. 314) has produced disputed evidence for human occupation over 30,000 years ago.

By 10,000 BC, most of the land areas of the world, except the deserts and Antarctica, were populated. The most conspicuous exception is the Pacific, where Western Polynesia does not seem to have been colonized until the first millennium BC, and Eastern Polynesia progressively from *c.* AD 300. By AD 1000 the colonization of Oceania was complete.

Nearly all the societies so far mentioned may be regarded as hunter-gatherer societies, made up of relatively small groups of people (see Chapter 5).

When surveying world history or prehistory at a global level, one of the most significant occurrences is the

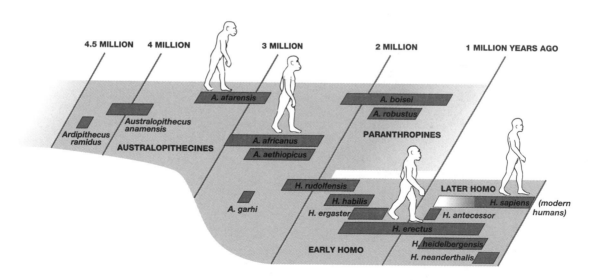

Paleoanthropologists hold strongly differing views on how the fossil remains for human evolution should be interpreted. This family tree presents the evidence as four adaptive radiations: the australopithecines, paranthropines, early Homo, and later Homo (including modern humans).

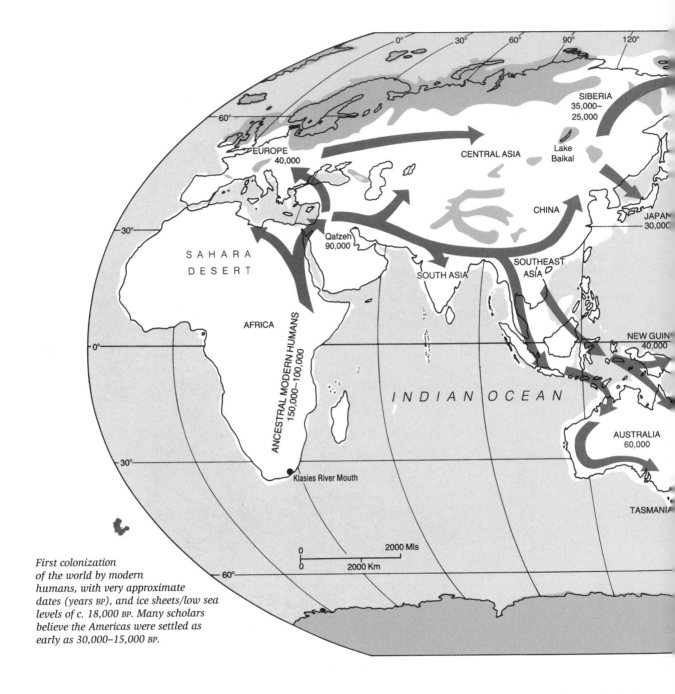

First colonization of the world by modern humans, with very approximate dates (years BP), and ice sheets/low sea levels of c. 18,000 BP. Many scholars believe the Americas were settled as early as 30,000–15,000 BP.

development of food production, based on domesticated plant species and also (although in some areas to a lesser extent) of domesticated animal species as well. One of the most striking facts of world prehistory is that the transition from hunting and gathering to food production seems to have occurred independently in several areas, in each case after the end of the Ice Age, i.e. after c. 10,000 years ago.

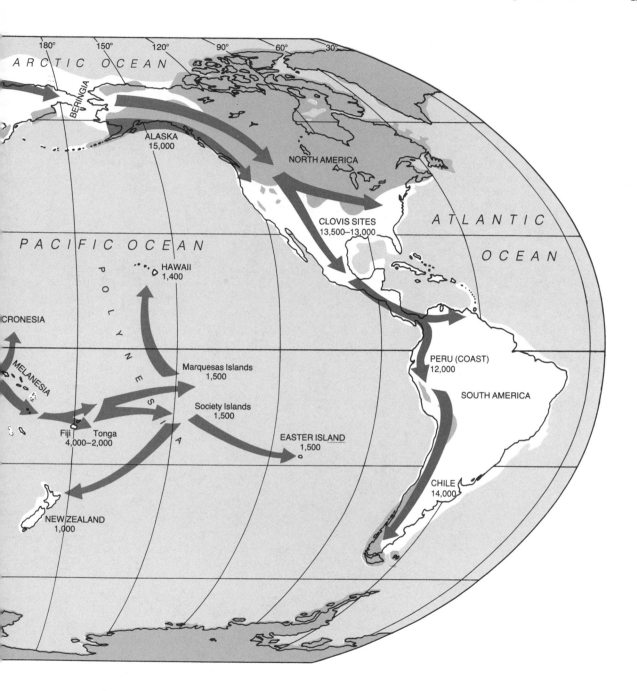

In the Near East, we can recognize the origins of this transition even before this time, for the process may have been gradual, the consequence (as well as the cause) of restructuring of the social organization of human societies. At any rate, well-established farming, dependent on wheat and barley as well as sheep and goats (and later cattle), was under way there by about 8000 BC. Farming had spread to Europe by 6500 BC, and

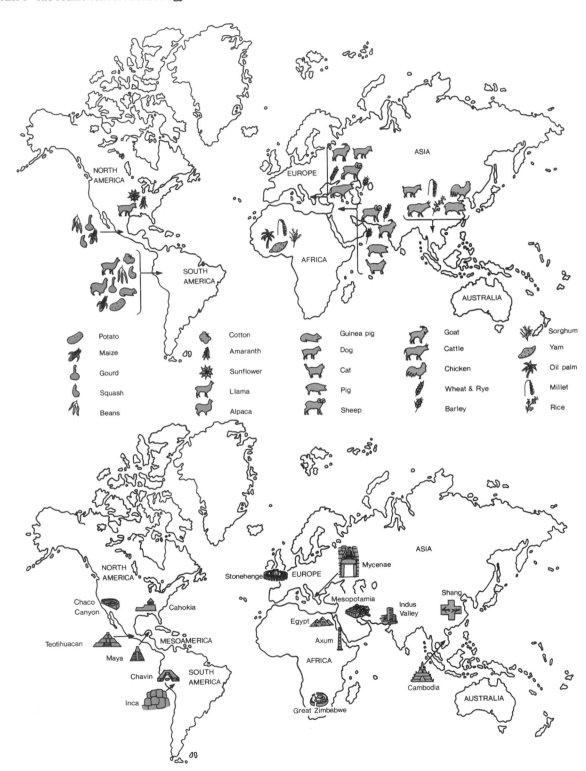

YEARS AD / BC	NEAR EAST	EGYPT & AFRICA	MEDI-TERRANEAN	NORTH EUROPE	SOUTH ASIA	E. ASIA & PACIFIC	MESO-AMERICA	SOUTH AMERICA	NORTH AMERICA
1500		Great Zimbabwe			MUGHAL		AZTEC	INCA	
1000		BYZANTINE EMPIRE		Medieval states	Medieval states	New Zealand settled	TOLTEC	CHIMU	Cahokia / Chaco
500	ISLAM	Towns (Africa) / AXUM			GUPTA	States (Japan)	MAYA / TEOTI-HUACAN	MOCHE	HOPEWELL / PUEBLOS
AD / BC			ROMAN EMPIRE	ROMAN EMPIRE		Great Wall (China)			
500	PERSIA BABYLON ASSYRIA	LATE PERIOD	CLASSICAL GREECE		Writing / MAURYAN / Cities	Cast iron (China)			
1000		NEW KINGDOM	Iron	IRON AGE	Iron / Megaliths	Lapita (Polynesia)		CHAVIN	Maize (Southwest)
1500	HITTITES / Iron	MIDDLE KINGDOM	MYCENAE			SHANG (China)	OLMEC		
2000		OLD (pyramids) KINGDOM	MINOAN	BRONZE / Stonehenge / AGE	Writing		Pottery		Squash, Sunflower, Chenopodium
2500	SUMER	EARLY DYNASTIC			INDUS / Cities	Walled villages (China)		Temple-mounds	Pottery
3000	Writing								
3500	Cities / Wheeled vehicles	Towns (Egypt)			Towns			Llama, cotton	
4000									
4500			Copper (Balkans)	Megaliths	Copper				
5000				Farming, pottery					
5500	Irrigation							Manioc / Maize	
6000					Pottery	Millet (China)	Maize? (Panama)		
6500	Copper	Cattle (N. Africa)	Farming, pottery				Beans, peppers?	Beans, peppers?	
7000	Pottery				Cattle / Farming	Gardens (New Guinea)	Squash		
7500		Pottery (Sudan)						Pottery (Brazil)	
8000	Wheat							Squash? (Ecuador)	
8500	Pigs? (Turkey)							Maize? (Argentina)	
9000	Sheep?								
9500						Rice (China)			
10,000									
11,000	Rye? (Syria)					Pottery (Japan) (14,000 BC)			

The rise of farming and civilization. (Opposite page, above) Locations where major food species were first domesticated. (Opposite page, below) Locations of some of the earliest architecture in various regions of the world. (Above) Chronological chart summarizing worldwide cultural development, including first domestication of certain plants and animals.

is documented in South Asia at Mehrgarh in Baluchistan at about the same time.

A separate development, based at first on the cultivation of millet, seems to have taken place in China, in the valley of the Huang Ho by 5000 BC. Rice cultivation began at about the same time in the Yangzi Valley in China and spread to Southeast Asia. The position in Africa south of the Sahara is more complicated due to the diversity of environments, but millet and sorghum wheat were cultivated by the 3rd millennium BC. The Western Pacific (Melanesian) complex of root and tree crops had certainly developed by that time: indeed, there are indications of field drainage for root crops very much earlier.

In the Americas, a different crop spectrum was available. Cultivation of beans, squash, peppers, and some grasses may have begun by 7000 or even 8000 BC in Peru, and was certainly under way there and in Mesoamerica by the 7th millennium BC. Other South American species, including manioc and potato, were soon added, but the plant with the greatest impact on American agriculture was maize, believed to have been brought into cultivation in Mexico by 5600 years ago, though possibly earlier in northwest Argentina.

These agricultural innovations were rapidly adopted in some areas (e.g. in Europe), but in others, such as North America, their impact was less immediate. Certainly, by the time of Christ, hunter-gatherer economies were very much in the minority.

It is not easy to generalize about the very varied societies of the first farmers in different parts of the world. But in general they may, in the early days at least, be described as *segmentary societies* (see Chapter 5): small, independent sedentary communities without any strongly centralized organization. They seem in the main to have been relatively egalitarian communities. In some cases they were related to their neighbors by tribal ties, whereas in others there was no larger tribal unit.

In each area, following the development of farming, there is much diversity. In many cases, the farming economy underwent a process of intensification, where more productive farming methods were accompanied by an increase in population. In such cases, there was usually increased contact between different areas, associated with developing exchange. Often, too, the social units became less egalitarian, displaying differences in personal status and importance sometimes summarized by anthropologists by the term *ranked societies*. Occasionally, it is appropriate to use the term *chiefdom* (Chapter 5).

These terms are usually restricted, however, to non-urban societies. The urban revolution, the next major transformation that we recognize widely, is not simply a change in settlement type: it reflects profound social changes. Foremost among these is the development of *state societies* displaying more clearly differentiated institutions of government than do chiefdoms. Many state societies had writing. We see the first state societies in the Near East by about 3500 BC, in Egypt only a little later, and in the Indus Valley by 2500 BC. In the Near East, the period of the early Mesopotamian city-states was marked by the rise of famous sites such as Ur, Uruk, and later Babylon, and was followed in the 1st millennium BC by an age of great empires, notably those of Assyria and Achaemenid Persia. In Egypt, it is possible to trace the continuous development of cultural and political traditions over more than 2000 years, through the pyramid age of the Old Kingdom and the imperial power of New Kingdom Egypt.

On the western edge of the Near East, further civilizations developed: Minoans and Mycenaeans in Greece and the Aegean during the 2nd millennium BC, Etruscans and Romans in the 1st millennium BC. At the opposite end of Asia, state societies with urban centers appear in China before 1500 BC, marking the beginnings of the Shang civilization. At about the same time, Mesoamerica saw the rise of the Olmec, the first in a long sequence of Central American civilizations including Maya, Zapotec, Toltec, and Aztec. On the Pacific coast of South America, the Chavín (from 900 BC), Moche, and Chimú civilizations laid the foundations for the rise of the vast and powerful Inca empire that flourished in the 15th century AD.

The further pattern is the more familiar one of literate history, with the

Monuments constructed by state societies around the world: the Lion Gate at Mycenae, Greece, 13th century BC (opposite above); the ziggurat of Ur, in modern Iraq, c. 2000 BC (opposite below); the temple of Ramesses II at Abu Simbel, Egypt, with statues of the pharaoh, c. 1285–1265 BC (left); and a giant Olmec head, possibly a portrait of a ruler, Mexico, c. 1200–600 BC (above).

rise of the Classical world of Greece and Rome as well as of China, and then of the world of Islam, the Renaissance of Europe and the development of the colonial powers. From the 18th century to the present there followed the independence of the former colonies, first in the Americas, then in Asia and in Africa. We are talking now not simply of state societies but of nation states and, especially in colonial times, of empires.

SUMMARY

The answer to the question "When?" in archaeology has two main components. Relative dating methods allow us to determine that something is *relatively* older or younger than something else. Absolute methods make it possible to give a date in years. Archaeological dating is at its most reliable when the two methods are used together, e.g. when the relative order assigned to layers in an excavation can be confirmed by absolute dates for each layer. Wherever possible, results from one absolute method should be cross-checked by those from another, e.g. radiocarbon by tree-ring dating, or uranium-series by TL.

Ultimately the precision of dating attainable for each period helps determine the kinds of questions we ask about the past – for the Paleolithic, questions are about long-term change; for later periods, the questions are more usually concerned with the shorter-term variations in worldwide human development.

FURTHER READING

The following provide a good introduction to the principal dating techniques used by archaeologists:

Aitken, M.J. 1990. *Science-based Dating in Archaeology*. Longman: London & New York.

Aitken, M.J., Stringer, C.B. & Mellars, P.A. (eds.). 1993. *The Origin of Modern Humans and the Impact of Chronometric Dating*. Princeton University Press.

Biers, W.R. 1993. *Art, Artefacts and Chronology in Classical Archaeology*. Routledge: London.

Bowman, S.G.E. 1990. *Radiocarbon Dating*. British Museum Publications: London; University of Texas Press: Austin.

Brothwell, D.R. & Higgs, E.S. (eds.). 1969. *Science in Archaeology*. (2nd ed.) Thames and Hudson: London; Praeger: New York. (Chapters 1–8.)

Parkes, P.A. 1986. *Current Scientific Techniques in Archaeology*. Croom Helm: London & Sydney.

Taylor, R.E. & Aitken, M.J. (eds.). 1997. *Chronometric Dating in Archaeology*. Plenum: New York.

Tite, M.S. 1972. *Methods of Physical Examination in Archaeology*. Seminar Press: London & New York. (Chapters 3–6.)

Wintle, A.G. 1996. Archaeologically relevant dating techniques for the next century. *Journal of Archaeological Science* 23, 123–38.

PART II
Discovering the Variety of Human Experience

In Part I certain basic problems were tackled. The methods were set out by which the space–time framework of the past can be established. We need to know *where* things happened, and *when* they happened. That has always been one of the basic objectives of archaeology, and it remains so.

For traditional archaeology, it was indeed the main task. It seemed sufficient to classify the various finds into different assemblages, which themselves could be grouped to form archaeological cultures, as we saw in Chapter 3. It seemed plausible to Gordon Childe, and to most of those who followed him, that these cultures were the material remains of distinct groups of people, of what we would today call ethnic groups – not in the racial sense, but groups of people with their own distinctive lifestyle and identity. As Childe put it, writing in 1929:

> We find certain types of remains – pots, implements, ornaments, burial sites, house forms – constantly recurring together. Such a complex of regularly associated traits we shall term a "cultural group" or just a "culture." We assume that such a complex is the material expression of what today would be called a "people."

Since the 1960s, however, it has been realized that this conventional way of treating the past is a limiting one. The concept of the archaeological culture is merely a classificatory device that does not necessarily relate to any reality in the archaeological record. And certainly to equate such notional "cultures" with "peoples" is now seen to be extremely hazardous. These issues will be looked at again in Chapter 12.

What archaeologists eventually recognized is that progress comes from asking a different set of questions. These form the basis of the organization of Part II. They have to do with the nature of a society or culture, and how such societies change over time.

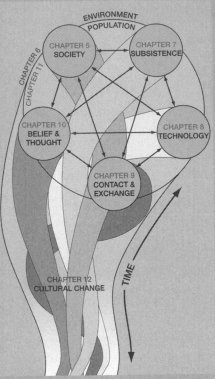

Model of the interrelated parts of a social system, which forms the basis for the organization of Part II.

At its simplest, a society may be viewed as having several interconnecting parts, as indicated in the accompanying diagram. The British archaeologist Christopher Hawkes, writing in 1954, argued that it is easiest in archaeology to find out about technology and diet, and most difficult to discover social organization or what people believed and thought. Archaeologists should therefore start by analyzing aspects of society like technology and diet. This is not an argument we accept. As will be shown in Chapter 5, it is essential first to have some idea about the social organization of the society being studied in order to be able to go on to ask the right questions about other aspects of that society. For example, groups organized as mobile hunter-gatherer groups, subsisting by hunting and gathering food, and constantly on the move, are never in one place long enough to build towns or cities – nor is their population sufficient or their social and economic organization complex enough to support such communities. It would be pointless therefore to expect to find towns or cities among such societies. But equally one must study what mobile hunter-gatherer societies *do* build in the way of structures, and learn what traces these may leave in the archaeological record. Modern observers commonly underestimate the capabilities of simpler societies, believing, for instance – as most archaeologists once did – that the famous monument of Stonehenge in southern England could only have been built by more advanced visitors from the civilization of Mycenae in Greece. (It is explained in Chapter 5 what type of society is now thought to have been responsible for erecting Stonehenge.)

We thus start, in Chapter 5, with the question, "How were societies organized?," and go on in subsequent chapters to consider environment and diet before turning to tools and technology, contact and exchange between societies, the way people thought, and the way people evolved and colonized the world – biological anthropology and population. In Chapter 12 we ask, "Why were things as they were?" and "Why did they change?," and in some ways these are the most interesting questions of all. In their *History of American Archaeology*, Gordon Willey and Jeremy Sabloff have argued that, in the 1960s, archaeology moved on from a period preoccupied with classification, description, and the function of things, and entered an Explanatory Period. Certainly explanation has come to be seen by many as a central goal of archaeological research.

5 How Were Societies Organized?
Social Archaeology

Some of the most interesting questions we can ask about early societies are social. They are about people and about relations between people, about the exercise of power and about the nature and scale of organization.

As is generally the case in archaeology, the data do not speak for themselves: we have to ask the right questions, and devise the means of answering them. There is a contrast here with cultural or social anthropology, where the observer can visit the living society and rapidly form conclusions about its social and power structures before moving on to other matters, such as the details of the kinship system or the minutiae of ritual behavior. The social archaeologist has to work systematically to gain even basic details, but the prize is a rich one: an understanding of the social organization not just of societies in the present or very recent past (like cultural anthropology) but of societies at many different points in time, with all the scope that that offers for studying change. Only the archaeologist can obtain that perspective, and hence seek some understanding of the processes of long-term change.

The first question to address is the size or *scale* of the society. The archaeologist will often be excavating a single site. But was that an independent political unit, like a Maya or Greek city-state, or a simpler unit, like the base camp of a hunter-gatherer group? Or was it, on the other hand, a small cog in a very big wheel, a subordinate settlement in some far-flung empire, like that of the Incas of Peru? Any site we consider will have its own hinterland, its own catchment area for the feeding of its population. But one of our interests is to go beyond that local area, and to understand how that site articulates with others. From the standpoint of the individual site – which is often a convenient perspective to adopt – that raises questions of *dominance*. Was the site politically independent, autonomous? Or, if it was part of a larger social system, did it take a dominant part (like the capital city of a kingdom) or a subordinate one?

If the scale of the society is a natural first question, the next is certainly its internal organization. What kind of society was it? Were the people forming it on a more-or-less equal social footing? Or were there instead prominent differences in status, rank, and prestige within the society – perhaps different social classes? And what of the professions: were there craft specialists? And if so, were they controlled within a centralized system, as in some of the palace economies of the Near East and Egypt? Or was this a freer economy, with a flourishing free exchange, where merchants could operate at will in their own interest?

These questions, however, may all be seen as "top-down" questions, looking at the society from above and investigating its organization. But increasingly an alternative perspective is being followed, looking first at the individual, and at the way the identity of the individual in the society in question is defined. The questions that arise in this "bottom-up" perspective are about the way such important social constructs as gender, status, and even age are constituted – for increasingly archaeologists are coming to realize that these are not "givens," that is they are not unproblematic cross-cultural realities but constructs specific to each different society. These insights are leading to new fields: the archaeology of the individual and the archaeology of identity.

Different kinds of society need different kinds of question. For example, if we are dealing with a mobile group of hunter-gatherers, there is unlikely to be a complex centralized organization. And the techniques of investigation will need to vary radically with the nature of the evidence. One cannot tackle an early hunter-gatherer camp in Australia in the same way as the capital city of a province in China during the Shang Dynasty. Thus, the questions we put, and the methods for answering them, must be tailored to the sort of community we are dealing with. So it is all the more necessary to be clear at the outset about the general nature of that community, which is why the basic social questions are the first ones to ask.

Precisely because the scale of a society is crucial in determining the way many different aspects of its social organization work in practice, this chapter deals first with smaller, simpler societies, building toward larger, more complex ones. Certain questions, such as settlement archaeology or the study of burials, are therefore discussed in the context of each type of society. This involves some repetition between sections but it allows us to deal more coherently with the different social aspects of societies organized on approximately the same scale. We then turn to the "bottom-up" issues, to ask questions about the individual and the archaeology of identity which have general relevance.

ESTABLISHING THE NATURE AND SCALE OF THE SOCIETY

The first step in social archaeology is so obvious that it is often overlooked. It is to ask, what was the scale of the largest social unit, and what kind of society, in a very broad sense, was it?

The obvious is not always easy, and it is necessary to ask rather carefully what we mean by the "largest social unit," which we shall term the *polity*. This term does not in itself imply any particular scale or complexity of organization. It can apply as well to a city-state, a hunter-gatherer band, a farming village, or a great empire. A polity is a politically independent or autonomous social unit, which may in the case of a complex society, such as a state society, comprise many lesser components. Thus, in the modern world, the autonomous nation state may be subdivided into districts or counties, each one of which may contain many towns and villages. The state as a whole is thus the polity. At the other end of the scale, a small group of hunter-gatherers may make its own decisions and recognize no higher authority: that group also constitutes a polity.

Sometimes communities may join together to form some kind of federation, and we have to ask whether those communities are still autonomous polities, or whether the federation as a whole is now the effective decision-making organization. These points are not yet archaeological ones: however, they illustrate how important it is to be clear about what we wish to know about the past.

In terms of research in the field, the question is often best answered from a study of settlement: both in terms of the scale and nature of *individual sites* and in relationships between them, through the analysis of *settlement pattern*. But we should not forget that *written records*, where a society is literate and uses writing, *oral tradition*, and *ethnoarchaeology* – the study from an archaeological point of view of present-day societies – can be equally valuable in assessing the nature and scale of the society under review.

First, however, we need a frame of reference, a hypothetical classification of societies against which to test our ideas.

Classification of Societies

The American anthropologist Elman Service developed a four-fold classification of societies that many archaeologists have found useful, though his terminology has since been amended. Associated with these societies are particular kinds of site and settlement pattern.

Mobile hunter-gatherer groups (sometimes called "bands"). These are small-scale societies of hunters and gatherers, generally of fewer than 100 people, who move

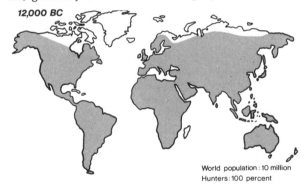

12,000 BC

World population: 10 million
Hunters: 100 percent

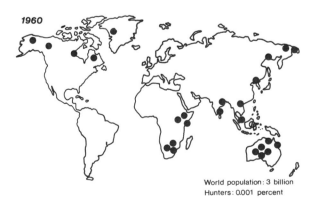

1960

World population: 3 billion
Hunters: 0.001 percent

(Above) Before the advent of farming, all human societies were hunter-gatherer groups; today these scarcely exist. (Right) Classification of societies.

	MOBILE HUNTER-GATHERER GROUPS	SEGMENTARY SOCIETY	CHIEFDOM	STATE
	San hunters, South Africa	Man plowing, Valcamonica, Italy	Horseman, Gundestrup caldron	Terracotta army, tomb of first emperor of China
TOTAL NUMBERS	Less than 100	Up to few 1000	5000–20,000+	Generally 20,000+
SOCIAL ORGANIZATION	Egalitarian Informal leadership	Segmentary society Pan-tribal associations Raids by small groups	Kinship-based ranking under hereditary leader High-ranking warriors	Class-based hierarchy under king or emperor Armies
ECONOMIC ORGANIZATION	Mobile hunter-gatherers	Settled farmers Pastoralist herders	Central accumulation and redistribution Some craft specialization	Centralized bureaucracy Tribute-based Taxation Laws
SETTLEMENT PATTERN	Temporary camps	Permanent villages	Fortified centers Ritual centers	Urban: cities, towns Frontier defenses Roads
RELIGIOUS ORGANIZATION	Shamans	Religious elders Calendrical rituals	Hereditary chief with religious duties	Priestly class Pantheistic or monotheistic religion
ARCHITECTURE	Temporary shelters	Permanent huts Burial mounds Shrines	Large-scale monuments	Palaces, temples, and other public buildings
	Paleolithic skin tents, Siberia	Neolithic shrine, Çatalhöyük, Turkey	Stonehenge, England - final form	Pyramids at Giza Castillo, Chichén Itzá, Mexico
ARCHAEOLOGICAL EXAMPLES	All Paleolithic societies, including Paleo-Indians	All early farmers (Neolithic/Archaic)	Many early metalworking and Formative societies	All ancient civilizations, e.g. in Mesoamerica, Peru, Near East, India and China; Greece and Rome
MODERN EXAMPLES	Inuit San, southern Africa Australian Aborigines	Pueblos, Southwest USA New Guinea Highlanders Nuer and Dinka, E. Africa	Northwest Coast Indians, USA 18th-century Polynesian chiefdoms in Tonga, Tahiti, Hawaii	All modern states

seasonally to exploit wild (undomesticated) food resources. Most surviving hunter-gatherer groups today are of this kind, such as the Hadza of Tanzania or the San of southern Africa. Band members are generally kinsfolk, related by descent or marriage. Bands lack formal leaders, so there are no marked economic differences or disparities in status among their members.

Because bands are composed of mobile groups of hunter-gatherers, their sites consist mainly of seasonally occupied camps, and other smaller and more specialized sites. Among the latter are kill or butchery sites – locations where large mammals are killed and sometimes butchered – and work sites, where tools are made or other specific activities carried out. The base camp of such a group may give evidence of rather insubstantial dwellings or temporary shelters, along with the debris of residential occupation.

During the Paleolithic period (before 12,000 years ago) most archaeological sites seem to conform to one or other of these categories – camp sites, kill sites, work sites – and archaeologists usually operate on the assumption that most Paleolithic societies were organized into bands. Ethnoarchaeology (see below) has devoted much attention to the study of living groups of hunter-gatherers, yielding many insights relevant to the more remote past.

Segmentary societies (sometimes referred to as "tribes"). These are generally larger than mobile hunter-gatherer groups, but rarely number more than a few thousand, and their diet or subsistence is based largely on cultivated plants and domesticated animals. Typically, they are settled farmers, but they may be nomad pastoralists with a very different, mobile economy based on the intensive exploitation of livestock. These are generally multicommunity societies, with the individual communities integrated into the larger society through kinship ties. Although some segmentary societies have officials and even a "capital" or seat of government, such officials lack the economic base necessary for effective use of power.

The typical settlement pattern for segmentary societies is one of settled agricultural homesteads or villages. Characteristically, no one settlement dominates any of the others in the region. Instead, the archaeologist finds evidence for isolated, permanently occupied houses (a *dispersed* settlement pattern) or for permanent villages (a *nucleated* pattern). Such villages may be made up of a collection of free-standing houses, like those of the first farmers of the Danube valley in Europe, *c.* 4500 BC. Or they may be clusters of buildings grouped together – so-called *agglomerate* structures, for example, the pueblos of the American Southwest,

and the early farming village or small town of Çatalhöyük, *c.* 7000 BC, in modern Turkey.

Chiefdoms. These operate on the principle of ranking – differences in social status between people. Different lineages (a lineage is a group claiming descent from a common ancestor) are graded on a scale of prestige, and the senior lineage, and hence the society as a whole, is governed by a chief. Prestige and rank are determined by how closely related one is to the chief, and there is no true stratification into classes. The role of the chief is crucial.

Often, there is local specialization in craft products, and surpluses of these and of foodstuffs are periodically paid as obligations to the chief. He uses these to maintain his retainers, and may use them for redistribution to his subjects. The chiefdom generally has a center of power, often with temples, residences of the chief and his retainers, and craft specialists. Chiefdoms vary greatly in size, but the range is generally between about 5000 and 20,000 persons.

One of the characteristic features of the chiefdom is the existence of a permanent ritual and ceremonial center that acts as a central focus for the entire polity. This is not a permanent urban center (such as a city) with an established bureaucracy, as one finds in state societies. But chiefdoms do give indications that some sites were more important than others (site hierarchy), as discussed later in this chapter. Examples are Moundville in Alabama, USA, which flourished *c.* AD 1000–1500, and the late Neolithic monuments of Wessex in southern Britain, including the famous ceremonial center of Stonehenge (see boxes, below).

The personal ranking characteristic of chiefdom societies is visible in other ways than in settlement patterning: for instance, in the very rich grave-goods that often accompany the burials of deceased chiefs.

Early States. These preserve many of the features of chiefdoms, but the ruler (perhaps a king or sometimes a queen) has explicit authority to establish laws and to enforce them by the use of a standing army. Society no longer depends totally on kin relationships: it is now stratified into different classes. Agricultural workers or serfs and the poorer urban dwellers form the lowest classes, with the craft specialists above, and the priests and kinsfolk of the ruler higher still. The functions of the ruler are often separated from those of the priest: palace is distinguished from temple. The society is viewed as a territory owned by the ruling lineage and populated by tenants who have an obligation to pay taxes. The central capital houses a bureaucratic administration of officials; one of their principal purposes is to collect revenue (often in the form of taxes and tolls) and distribute it to government, army, and craft specialists. Many early states developed complex redistributive systems to support these essential services.

Early state societies generally show a characteristic urban settlement pattern in which *cities* play a prominent part. The city is typically a large population center (often of more than 5000 inhabitants) with major public buildings, including temples and work places for the administrative bureaucracy. Often, there is a pronounced settlement hierarchy, with the capital city as the major center, and with subsidiary or regional centers as well as local villages.

This rather simple social typology, set out by Elman Service and elaborated by William Sanders and Joseph Marino, can be criticized, and it should not be used unthinkingly. For instance, some scholars found the concept of the tribe a rather vague one, and prefer to speak of "segmentary societies." The term "tribe," implying a larger grouping of smaller units, carries with it the assumption that these communities share a common ethnic identity and self-awareness, which is now known not generally to be the case. The term "segmentary society" refers to a relatively small and autonomous group, usually of agriculturalists, who regulate their own affairs: in some cases, they may join together with other comparable segmentary societies to form a larger ethnic unit or "tribe"; in other cases, they do not. For the remainder of this chapter, we shall therefore refer to *segmentary societies* in preference to the term "tribe." And what in Service's typology were called "bands" are now more generally referred to as "mobile hunter-gatherer groups."

Certainly, it would be wrong to overemphasize the importance of the four types of society given above, or to spend too long agonizing as to whether a specific group should be classed in one category rather than another. It would also be wrong to assume that somehow societies inevitably evolve from bands to segmentary societies, or from chiefdoms to states. One of the challenges of archaeology is to attempt to explain why some societies become more complex and others do not, and we shall return to the fundamental issue of explanation in Chapter 12.

Nevertheless, if we are seeking to talk about early societies, we must use words and hence concepts to do so. Service's categories provide a good framework to help organize our thoughts. They should not, however, deflect us from focusing on what we are really looking for: changes over time in the different institutions of a society – whether in the social sphere, the organization of the food quest, technology, contact and exchange, or spiritual life. For archaeology has the unique advantage of being able to study processes of change over thousands of years, and it is these processes we are seeking to isolate. Happily there are sufficiently marked differences between simple and more complex societies for us to find ways of doing this. As we saw above in the description of Service's four types of society, complex societies show in particular an increased specialization in, or separation between, different aspects of their culture. In complex societies people no longer combine, say, the tasks of obtaining food, making tools, or performing religious rites but become specialists at one or other of these tasks, either as full-time farmers, craftspeople, or priests. As technology develops, for example, groups of individuals may acquire particular expertise in pottery-making or metallurgy, and will become full-time *craft specialists*, occupying distinct areas of a town or city and thus leaving distinct traces for the archaeologist to discover. Likewise, as farming develops and population grows, more food will be obtained from a given piece of land (food production will *intensify*) through the introduction of the plow or irrigation. As this specialization and intensification take place, so too does the tendency for some people to become wealthier and wield more authority than others – differences in social status and *ranking* develop.

It is methods for looking at these processes of increasing specialization, intensification, and social ranking that help us identify the presence of more complex societies in the archaeological record – societies here termed for convenience chiefdoms or states. For simpler hunter-gatherer groups or segmentary societies, other methods are needed if we are to identify them archaeologically, as will become apparent in a later section.

Scale of the Society

With this general background in mind one can develop a strategy for answering the first, basic question: what is the scale of the society? One answer may come from an understanding of the settlement pattern, and this can only come from survey (see below).

For a first approximation, however, an elaborate field project may be unnecessary. If, for instance, we are dealing with archaeological remains dating to before about 12,000 years ago, then we are dealing with a society from the Paleolithic period. On present evidence, nearly all the societies known from that enormously long period of time – spanning hundreds of thousands of years – consisted of mobile hunter-gatherers, occupying camps on a seasonal and temporary basis. On the other hand, where we find indications of permanent settlement this will suggest a segmentary society of agricultural villages or something more complex.

At the other end of the scale, if there are major urban centers the society should probably rank as a state. More modest centers, or ceremonial centers without urban settlement, may be indicative of a chiefdom. To use these classificatory terms is a worthwhile first step in social analysis, provided we bear in mind again that these are only very broad categories designed to help us formulate appropriate methods for studying the societies in question.

If it is clear that we are dealing with communities with a mobile economy (i.e. hunter-gatherers, or possibly nomads), highly intensive techniques of survey will have to be used, because the traces left by mobile communities are generally very scanty. If, on the other hand, these were sedentary communities, a straightforward field survey is now called for. It will have as its first objective the establishment of *settlement hierarchy*.

The Survey

The techniques of field survey were discussed in Chapter 3. Surveys can have different purposes: in this case, our aim is to discover the hierarchy of settlement. We are particularly interested in locating the major centers (because our concern is with organization) and in establishing the nature of the more modest sites. This implies a dual sampling strategy. At the intensive level of survey, systematic surface survey of carefully selected transects should be sufficient, although the ideal would be a total survey of the entire area. A random stratified sampling strategy – as outlined in Chapter 3 – taking into account the different environmental areas within the region, should offer adequate data about the smaller sites. However, random sampling of this kind could, in isolation, be misleading and subject to what Kent Flannery has called "the Teotihuacán effect." Teotihuacán is the huge urban site in the Valley of Mexico that flourished in the 1st millennium AD (see box, pp. 90–91). Random stratified sampling alone could easily miss such a center, and would thus ruin any effective social analysis.

The other aim of the strategy must be, therefore, to go for the center. Means must be devised of finding the remains of the largest center in the region, and as many lesser centers as can be located. Fortunately, if it was an urban site, or had monumental public buildings, such a center should become obvious during even a non-intensive survey, so long as a good overview of the

area as a whole is obtained. In most cases the existence of such a prominent site will already be well known to the local population, or indeed recorded in the available archaeological or antiquarian literature. All such sources, including the writings of early travelers in the region, should be scrutinized in order to maximize the chances of finding major centers.

The main centers usually have the most impressive monuments, and contain the finest artifacts. So it is imperative to visit all the major monuments of the period, and to follow up the circumstances of any particularly rich finds in the region. Where appropriate, there is plenty of scope too for remote sensing methods such as were described in Chapter 3.

Settlement Patterning

Any survey will result in a map of the areas intensively surveyed and a catalog of the sites discovered, together with details of each site including size, chronological range (as may be determined from surface remains such as pottery), and architectural features. The aim is then to reach some classification of the sites on the basis of this information. Possible site categories include, for instance, Regional Center, Local Center, Nucleated Village, Dispersed Village, and Hamlet.

The first use we will make of settlement pattern information is to identify the social and political territories around centers, in order to establish the political organization of the landscape. Many archaeological approaches here give prominence to Central Place Theory (see below), which we feel has some limitations. It assumes that the sites in a given region will fall neatly into a series of categories according to variations in site size. All the primary centers should be in one size category, all the secondary centers in the next, etc. This technique cannot cope with the true situation which is that secondary centers in one area are sometimes larger than primary centers in another. More recent work has found a way of overcoming this difficulty (the XTENT technique), but we will deal here with the earlier methods first.

Central Place Theory. This theory was developed by the German geographer Walter Christaller in the 1930s to explain the spacing and functions of cities and towns in modern-day southern Germany. He argued that in a uniform landscape – without mountains or rivers or variations in the distribution of soils and resources – the spatial patterning of settlements would be perfectly regular. Central places or settlements (towns or cities) of the same size and nature would be situated equidistant from each other, surrounded by a constellation

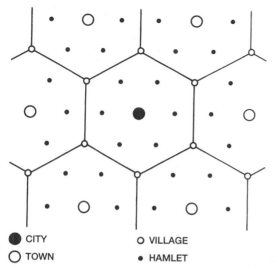

● CITY	○ VILLAGE
○ TOWN	● HAMLET

Central Place Theory: in a flat landscape, with no rivers or variations in resources, a central place (town or city) will dominate a hexagonal territory, with secondary centers (villages or hamlets) spaced at regular intervals around it.

of secondary centers with their own, smaller satellites. Under these perfect conditions, the territories "controlled" by each center would be hexagonal in shape, and the different levels of center would together give rise to an intricate settlement lattice.

Such perfect conditions do not occur in nature, of course, but it is still quite possible to detect the workings of Central Place Theory in the distributions of modern or ancient cities and towns. The basic feature is that each major center will be some distance from its neighbors and will be surrounded by a ring of smaller settlements in a hierarchically nested pattern. In political and economic terms the major center will supply certain goods and services to its surrounding area and will exact certain goods and services in return. Even in an area so far from uniform as Mesopotamia (modern Iraq), Central Place Theory has its uses (see box overleaf).

Site Hierarchy. Despite the reservations we have expressed about Central Place Theory, the analysis of site sizes is a useful basic approach. In archaeological studies, the sites are usually listed in rank order by size (i.e. in a site hierarchy), and then displayed as a histogram. There are normally many more small villages and hamlets in a settlement system than large towns or cities. Histograms allow comparisons to be made between the site hierarchies of different regions, different periods, and different types of society. In band societies, for example, there will usually be only a narrow range of variation in site size and all the sites will be relatively small. State societies, on the other hand, will have both hamlets and farmsteads and large towns and cities. The degree to which a single site is dominant within a settlement system will also be evident from this type of analysis, and the organization of the settlement system will often be a direct reflection of the organization of the society which created it. In a general way, the more hierarchical the settlement pattern, the more hierarchical the society.

Thiessen Polygons. Another relatively simple method that can be used in the study of settlement patterns is the construction of Thiessen polygons. These are simple geometrical shapes that divide an area into a number of separate territories, each focused on a single site. The polygons are created by drawing straight lines between each pair of neighboring sites, then at the mid-point along each of these lines a second series of lines, at right angles to the first. Linking up the second series of lines creates the Thiessen polygons, and in this way the whole of an area can be apportioned among the sites it contains. It should be noted, however, that this procedure takes no account of differences in size or importance of sites; a small site will have as big a polygon as a large site. Thus it is important to use only sites of the same rank in the settlement hierarchy when this technique is being applied. A further question, more difficult to resolve, is contemporaneity, since clearly it would be meaningless to draw Thiessen polygons between sites which were not in occupation at the same time.

XTENT Modeling. One of the shortcomings of Central Place Theory and other approaches is that sites occupying the same level in a settlement hierarchy might not be of the same size. Thus the capital city of a state on the periphery of a distribution could be smaller than a secondary city in the center. We are now able to cope with this using the technique of XTENT modeling. This has the aim of assigning territories to centers according to their scale. To do this, it assumes that a large center will dominate a small one if they are close together. In such a case, of so-called *dominance*, the territory of the smaller site is simply absorbed in the study into that of the larger one: in political terms the smaller site has no independent or autonomous existence. This approach overcomes the limitation of the Thiessen polygon method, where territories are assigned irrespective of the size of the center, and where there are no dominant or subordinate centers.

In XTENT modeling, the size of each center is assumed to be directly proportional to its area of influence. The influence of each center is thought of as analogous to a bell or bell-tent in shape: the greater the size of the center the higher the tent. Centers are considered to be subordinate if their associated bell tents fall entirely within that of a larger center. If they protrude beyond, they will have their own autonomous existence as centers of political units.

SETTLEMENT PATTERNS IN MESOPOTAMIA

Gregory Johnson's work in the Diyala region of Mesopotamia, to the east of Baghdad in modern Iraq, provides a good illustration of the way in which Central Place Theory can be applied to archaeological survey results. Thirty-nine settlements of the Early Dynastic

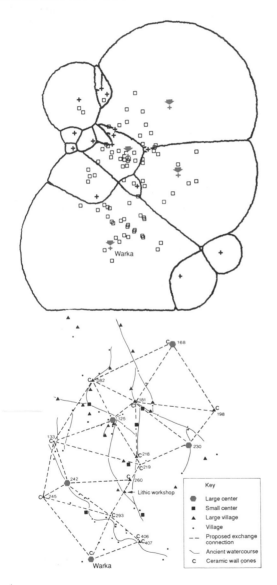

(Top) XTENT model territories, Late Uruk period, Warka area, Mesopotamia. Arrows indicate four centers that emerge as autonomous. Compare Greg Johnson's hierarchy (above) for the same region. Note how four of the five "large centers" correspond with the autonomous ones in the XTENT model.

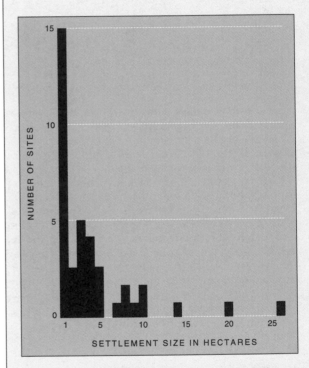

Site hierarchy for 39 settlements in the Diyala region, expressed as a histogram. As is usually the case with such hierarchies, there is a decline in the number of sites as site size increases. There are normally many more small villages and hamlets in a settlement system than large towns or cities. Any analysis of this kind has to make certain assumptions – for instance, that evidence for sites in each category has been uniformly preserved, which may not always be the case.

period (*c.* 2800 BC) are known from this area. They range in size from 25 ha (60 acres) to just over one-tenth of a hectare (0.25 acre), and on this basis Johnson divided them into five categories: large towns, towns, large villages, small villages, and hamlets.

The distribution of sites suggested that there were four lattice cells, each lattice cell being the network of settlements grouped around a first order center or central place. In theory, each cell should have had a large town at the center, towns at each of the four corners, and large villages at the mid-points between the towns and at the

mid-points between the towns and the large towns. Small villages and hamlets completed the pattern to create a model settlement lattice which could be compared with the real pattern as revealed by the Diyala survey. Discrepancies could then be identified and explained.

It is precisely the discrepancies from the expected pattern that are of interest. Johnson found that maximization of usable land (which would have been implied had there been even spacing of settlements) was less significant in determining settlement location than were water

transport networks. Settlements of successively smaller size were located along watercourses – lines of communication – between the larger settlements.

Nevertheless, it was only after considerable modification that the lattice model could be made to fit the Diyala evidence. Several of the predicted primary and secondary centers were lacking, while others were smaller than they were expected to be. Thus, though the exercise was certainly valuable, it highlighted the difficulties of applying Central Place Theory to a real archaeological case.

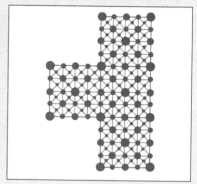

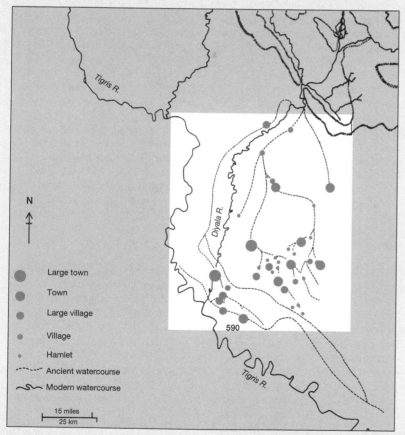

Early Dynastic settlement pattern in the Diyala region of Iraq, based on survey work originally carried out by Robert Adams.

N

●	Large town
●	Town
●	Large village
●	Village
•	Hamlet
----	Ancient watercourse
∿	Modern watercourse

15 miles
25 km

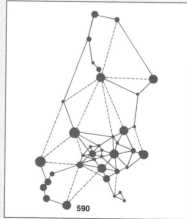

Derivation of the proposed settlement lattice for the Diyala region, from the idealized, regular four lattice cells (top) to the final pattern (above) that seemed best to fit the actual settlement locations on the ground.

Although the XTENT model can never offer more than a simple approximation of the political reality, it does allow a hypothetical political map to be constructed from appropriate survey data (see illustration on p. 180).

By methods such as these, information derived from settlement surveys can be used to produce what is in effect a political and administrative map, even though such maps will always rely on certain basic assumptions that cannot easily be proved. And while the examples given in the box (pp. 180–81) have been drawn from studies of state societies, it is possible to apply similar techniques to the settlement patterns of less complex societies, such as the Neolithic of southern Britain (see box, pp. 198–99). In the Iron Age of southern Britain, more hierarchically organized societies developed, with prominent hillforts dominating the tribal territories. A pioneering analysis by David Clarke interpreted the social position of the Iron Age site of Glastonbury in these terms, as belonging within a territory dominated by such a fortified center.

FURTHER SOURCES OF INFORMATION FOR SOCIAL ORGANIZATION

If the first approach by archaeologists to the study of social organization must be through the investigation of settlement and settlement pattern, this should not exclude other possible avenues of approach, including the use of written records, oral tradition, and ethnoarchaeology.

Here it is appropriate to mention the argument of Lewis Binford, that if we are to bridge the gap between the archaeological remains and the societies those remains represent we need to develop a systematic body of what he terms *Middle Range Theory*. For the moment, however, we believe it is difficult to justify the division of archaeological theory into high, middle, and low. We choose not to use the term Middle Range Theory.

Some scholars also lay great emphasis on the concept of *analogy*. Arguments by analogy are based on the belief that where certain processes or materials resemble each other in some respects, they may resemble each other in other ways also. Thus it may be possible to use details from one body of information to fill the gaps in another body of information from which those details are missing. Some have considered an analogy a fundamental aspect of archaeological reasoning. In our view this emphasis is misplaced. It is true that archaeologists use information from the study of one society (whether living or dead) to help understand other societies they may be interested in, but these are usually in the nature of general observations and comparisons, rather than specific detailed analogies.

Written Records

For literate societies – those that use writing, for instance all the great civilizations in Mesoamerica, China, Egypt, and the Near East – historical records can answer many of the social questions set out at the beginning of this chapter. A prime goal of the archaeologist dealing with these societies is therefore to find appropriate texts. Many of the early excavations of the great sites of the Near East had the recovery of archives of clay writing tablets as their main goal. Major finds of this kind are still made today – for example, at the ancient city of Ebla (Tell Mardikh) in Syria in the 1970s, where an archive of 15,000 clay tablets yielded evidence of a previously unknown language and state of the 3rd millennium BC.

In each early literate society, writing had its own functions and purposes. For instance, the clay tablets of Mycenaean Greece, dating from c. 1200 BC, are almost without exception records of commercial transactions (goods coming in or going out) at the Mycenaean palaces. This gives us an impression of many aspects of the Mycenaean economy, and a glimpse into craft organization (through the names for the different kinds of craftspeople), as well as introducing the names of the offices of state. But here, as in other cases, accidents of preservation may be important. It could be that the Mycenaeans wrote on clay only for their commercial records, and used other, perishable materials for literary or historical texts now lost to us. It is certainly true that for the Classical Greek and Roman civilizations, it is mainly official decrees inscribed on marble that have survived. Fragile rolls of papyrus – the predecessor of modern paper – with literary texts on them, have usually only remained intact in the dry air of Egypt, or buried in the volcanic ash covering Pompeii (see box, pp. 22–23).

An important written source that should not be overlooked is coinage. The findspots of coins give interesting economic evidence about trade (Chapter 9). But the inscriptions themselves are informative about the issuing authority – whether city-state (as in ancient Greece) or sole ruler (as in Imperial Rome, or the kings of medieval Europe).

The decipherment of an ancient language transforms our knowledge of the society that used it. The brilliant work of Champollion in the 19th century in cracking the code of Egyptian hieroglyphs was mentioned in Chapter 1. In recent years, one of the most significant advances in Mesoamerican archaeology has come from the reading of many of the inscribed symbols (glyphs) on the stone stelae at the largest centers. It had been widely assumed that the Maya inscriptions were exclusively of a calendrical nature, or that they dealt with purely religious matters, notably the deeds of deities. But the inscriptions can now in many cases be interpreted as relating to real historical events, mainly the deeds of the Maya kings (see boxes, pp. 130–31 and 406–07). We can also now begin to deduce the likely territories belonging to individual Maya centers (see box, p. 205). Maya history has thus taken on a new dimension. Despite numerous attempts, however, the Indus or Harappan is the last of the great scripts to remain undeciphered.

A more detailed example of the value of written sources for reconstructing social archaeology is Mesopotamia, where a huge number of records of Sumer and Babylon (c. 3000–1600 BC), mainly in the form of clay tablets, have been preserved. The uses of writing in Mesopotamia may be summarized as follows:

Recording information for future use	- Administrative purposes - Codification of law - Formulation of a sacred tradition - Annals - Scholarly purposes
Communicating current information	- Letters - Royal edicts - Public announcements - Texts for training scribes
Communicating with the gods	- Sacred texts, amulets, etc.

The Sumerian king list provides an excellent example of annals recording information for future use. It is extremely useful to the modern scholar for dating purposes, but it also offers social insights into the way the Sumerians conceived of the exercise of power – for example, the terminology of rank that they used. Similarly, inscriptions on royal statues (such as those of Gudea, ruler of Lagash) help us to perceive how the Sumerians viewed the relationship between their rulers and the immortals. This important kind of information concerning how societies thought about themselves and the world – *cognitive* information – is discussed in more detail in Chapter 10.

Of even greater significance for an understanding of the structure of Sumerian society are the tablets associated with the working or organizing centers, which in Sumerian society were often temples. For instance, the 1600 tablets from the temple of Bau at Tello give a close insight into the dealings of the shrine, listing fields and the crops harvested in them, craftspeople, and receipts or issues of goods such as grain and livestock.

Perhaps most evocative of all are the law codes, of which the most impressive example is the law code of Hammurabi of Babylon, written in the Akkadian language (and in cuneiform script) around 1750 BC. The ruler is seen (illus. p. 185) at the top of the stone, standing before Shamash, the god of justice. The laws were promulgated, as Hammurabi states, "so that the strong may not oppress the weak, and to protect the rights of the orphan and widow." These laws cover many aspects of life – agriculture, business transactions, family law, inheritance, terms of employment for different craftspeople, and penalties for crimes such as adultery and homicide.

Impressive and informative as it is, Hammurabi's law code is not straightforward to interpret, and emphasizes the need for the archaeologist to reconstruct the full social context that led to the drafting of a text. As the British scholar Nicholas Postgate has pointed out, the code is by no means complete, and seems to cover only those areas of the law that had proved troublesome. Moreover, Hammurabi had recently conquered several rival city states, and the law code was therefore probably designed to help integrate the new territories within his empire.

Written records undoubtedly contribute greatly to our knowledge of the society in question. But one should not accept them uncritically at face value. Nor should one forget the bias introduced by the accident of preservation and the particular uses of literacy in a society. The great risk with historical records is that they can impose their own perspective, so that they begin to supply not only the answers to our questions, but subtly to determine the nature of those questions, and even our concepts and terminology. A good example is the question of kingship in Anglo-Saxon England. Most anthropologists and historians tend to think of a "king" as the leader of a state society. So when the earliest records for Anglo-Saxon England, *The Anglo-Saxon Chronicle*, which took final shape in about AD 1155, refer to kings around AD 500, it is easy for the historian to think of kings and states at that period. But the archaeology strongly suggests that a full state society did not emerge until the time of King Offa of Mercia in around AD 780, or perhaps

The variety of historical evidence. (Left and above) Scribes were accorded high status in ancient civilizations. Among the Maya, a rabbit god (left) is shown as a scribe on an 8th-century AD painted vase. A scribe from Classical Greek times (above left) is depicted on a 5th-century BC bowl. Egyptian military scribes (above center) record on papyrus rolls the submission of Egypt's New Kingdom foes – a relief carving from Saqqara. The Inca (above right) had no writing system as such, but kept records of accounts and other transactions using knotted ropes called quipu.

Clay tablets and coins. (Left) Some of the 15,000 clay tablets discovered in the royal palace at Ebla (Tell Mardikh in modern Syria), dating from the late 3rd millennium BC. The tablets formed part of the state archives, recording over 140 years of Ebla's history. Originally they were stored on wooden shelving, which collapsed when the palace was sacked. (Below) Hoard of Arabic coins found in Gotland, Sweden, from the Viking period (8th/9th centuries AD). Coin inscriptions can be informative about dating (Chapter 4) and trade (Chapter 9), and also about the issuing authority.

Seals and seal impressions. (Above) Rollout impression from a cylinder seal of c. 500 BC which depicts the Persian king Darius in his chariot hunting lions. The inscription is written in the cuneiform script, like Hammurabi's law code (left). The scene is intended to convey the authority, strength, and dominant status of the king. Such seals were used to mark ownership or authenticity. Many thousands have been recovered from Mesopotamian sites.

Oral tradition. (Below) Scenes from the Hindu epic, the Ramayana, on a late 18th-century AD temple-hanging, Mathura, India. The story describes the exploits of a great ruler (Rama) in his attempt to rescue his consort, carried off to Sri Lanka by a demon king. The legend may have its origins in southward movements of Hindu peoples after 800 BC but – as always with oral tradition – the difficulty comes in disentangling history from myth.

Inscriptions. (Above) The famous law code of the Babylonian king Hammurabi, c. 1750 BC. The laws are carved in 49 vertical columns on a black basalt stela, 2.25 m (7 ft 4 in) high. In this detail the king is seen confronting the seated figure of Shamash, god of justice. See also main text p. 183.

Early medieval documents. (Below) An Anglo-Saxon king and his council depicted in an 11th-century AD manuscript. Historical documents require careful interpretation just as much as archaeological evidence.

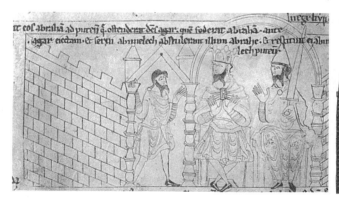

King Alfred of Wessex in AD 871. It is fairly clear that the earlier "kings" were generally less significant figures than some of the rulers in either Africa or Polynesia in recent times, whom anthropologists would term "chiefs."

Thus, if the archaeologist is to use historical records in conjunction with the material remains, it is essential at the outset that the questions are carefully formulated and the vocabulary is well defined.

Oral Tradition

In non-literate societies, valuable information about the past, even the remote past, is often enshrined in oral tradition – poems or hymns or sayings handed on from generation to generation by word of mouth. This can be of quite remarkable antiquity. A good example is offered by the hymns of the *Rigveda*, the earliest Indian religious texts, in an archaic form of the language, which were preserved orally for hundreds of years, before being set down by literate priests in the mid-1st millennium AD. Similarly, the epics about the Trojan War written down by Homer in about the 8th century BC may have been preserved orally for several centuries before that time, and are thought by many scholars to preserve a picture of the Mycenaean world of the 12th or 13th century BC.

Epics such as Homer's *Iliad* and *Odyssey* certainly offer remarkable insights into social organization. But, as with so much oral tradition, the problem is actually to demonstrate to which period they refer – to judge how much is ancient and how much reflects a much more recent world. Nevertheless, in Polynesia, in Africa, and in other areas that have only recently become literate, the natural first step in investigating the social organization of earlier centuries is to examine the oral traditions.

Ethnoarchaeology

Another fundamental method of approach for the social archaeologist is ethnoarchaeology. It involves the study of both the present-day use and significance of artifacts, buildings, and structures within the living societies in question, and the way these material things become incorporated into the archaeological record – what happens to them when they are thrown away or (in the case of buildings and structures) torn down or abandoned. It is therefore an *indirect* approach to the understanding of any past society.

There is nothing new in the idea of looking at living societies to help interpret the past. In the 19th and early 20th centuries European archaeologists often turned for inspiration to researches done by ethnographers among societies in Africa or Australia. But the so-called "ethnographic parallels" that resulted – where archaeologists often simply and crudely likened past societies to present ones – tended to stifle new thought rather than promote it. In the United States archaeologists were confronted from the beginning with the living reality of complex Native American societies, which taught them to think rather more deeply about how ethnography might be used to aid archaeological interpretation. Nevertheless, fully-fledged ethnoarchaeology is a development really of only the last 25 years. The key difference is that now it is archaeologists themselves, rather than ethnographers or anthropologists, who carry out the research among living societies.

A good example is the work of Lewis Binford among the Nunamiut Eskimo, a hunter-gatherer group of Alaska. In the 1960s Binford was attempting to interpret archaeological sites of the Middle Paleolithic of France (the Mousterian period, 180,000–40,000 years ago). He came to realize that only by studying how *modern* hunter-gatherers used and discarded bones and tools, or moved from site to site, could he begin to understand the mechanisms that had created the Mousterian archaeological record – itself almost certainly the product of a mobile hunter-gatherer economy. Between 1969 and 1973 he lived intermittently among the Nunamiut and observed their behavior. For instance, he studied the way bone debris was produced and discarded by men at a seasonal hunting camp (the Mask site, Anaktuvuk Pass, Alaska). He saw that, when sitting round a hearth and processing bone for marrow, there was a "drop zone" where small fragments of bone fell as they were broken. The larger pieces, which were thrown away by the men, formed a "toss zone," both in front and behind them.

Such seemingly trivial observations are the very stuff of ethnoarchaeology. The Nunamiut might not provide an exact "ethnographic parallel" for Mousterian societies, but Binford recognized that there are certain actions or *functions* likely to be common to all hunter-gatherers because – as in the case of the processing of bone – the actions are dictated by the most convenient procedure when seated round a camp fire. The discarded fragments of bone then leave a characteristic pattern round the hearth for the archaeologist to find and interpret. From such analysis, it has proved possible to go on to infer roughly how many people were in the group, and over what period of time the camp site was used. These are questions very relevant to our understanding of the social organization (including the size) of hunter-gatherer groups.

Ethnoarchaeology: the work of Lewis Binford. (Right) From observations among living Nunamiut Eskimo in Alaska, Binford derived this model of bone processing around an outside hearth. Small bone fragments fall in a "drop zone" around the men, while larger pieces are thrown both in front and behind them in two "toss zones." (Below center) At the Paleolithic site of Pincevent, France, dating from about 15,000 years ago, the excavator Leroi-Gourhan interpreted three hearths as being evidence for a complex skin tent (reconstruction, center right). (Below) Binford applied his "outside hearth model" to the three Pincevent hearths, and deduced from the distribution of bones that his model fitted the evidence better than that of Leroi-Gourhan: i.e. that the hearths lay outside, and not within a tent. (Below right) Classic semicircular arrangement around an outside hearth as demonstrated by Nharo Bushmen at Ganzi, Botswana, c. 1969.

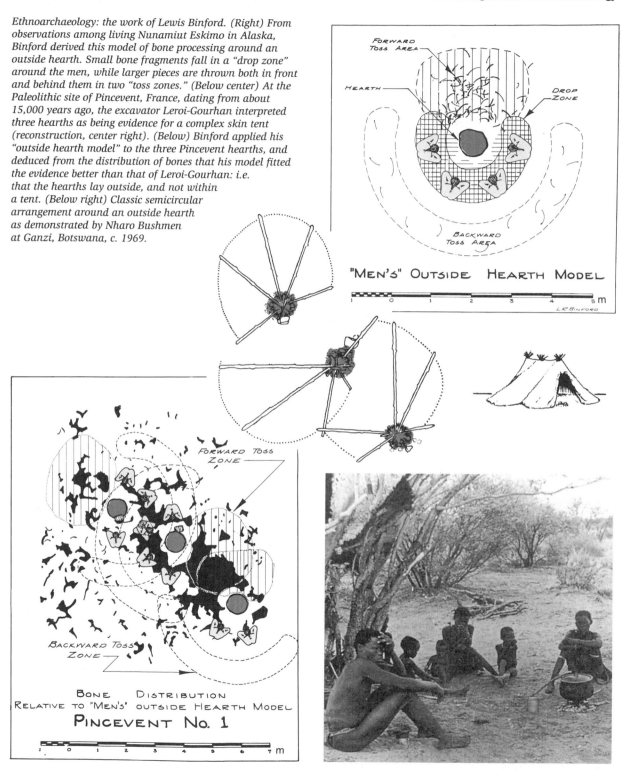

With the benefit of his observations at the Mask site, Binford was able to reinterpret the plan of one habitation at the French Paleolithic site of Pincevent, occupied during the last Ice Age about 15,000 years ago. The excavator, André Leroi-Gourhan, interpreted the remains as indicating a complex skin tent covering three hearths. Binford at the Mask site had noted how when wind direction had changed, people seated outside next to a hearth would swivel round and make up a new hearth downwind so as to remain out of the smoke. The distribution of debris around the Pincevent hearths suggested to Binford that two of them were the result of just such an event, one after the other as wind direction changed and a seated worker rotated his position. He further argued that this kind of behavior is found only with outside hearths, and that therefore the excavator's reconstruction of a covering tent is unlikely. Recent analysis, however, suggests that these hearths had slightly different functions. Work at Pincevent and other similar sites in the Paris Basin is finding useful insights, as well as errors, both in Leroi-Gourhan's focused interpretations and in Binford's generalized observations from ethnoarchaeology.

Ethnoarchaeology is not restricted to observations at the local scale. The British archaeologist Ian Hodder, in his study of the female ear decorations used by different tribes in the Lake Baringo area of Kenya, undertook a regional study to investigate the extent to which material culture (in this case personal decoration) was being used to express differences between the tribes. Partly as a result of such work, archaeologists no longer assume that it is an easy task to take archaeological assemblages and group them into regional "cultures," and then to assume that each "culture" so formed represents a social unit (see Chapter 12). Such a procedure might, in fact, work quite well for the ear decorations Hodder studied, because the people in question chose to use this feature to assert their tribal distinctiveness. But, as Hodder showed, if we were to take other features of the material culture, such as pots or tools, the same pattern would not necessarily be followed. His example documents the important lesson that material culture cannot be used by the archaeologist in a simple or unthinking manner in the reconstruction of supposed ethnic groups.

At this point it is appropriate to move on to consider how one actually sets about systematically searching for evidence of social organization in archaeological remains, using the techniques and sources of information just outlined. Here we will find it useful to look first at mobile hunter-gatherer societies, then segmentary societies, and finally at chiefdoms and states.

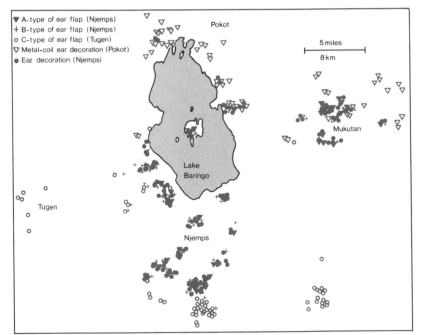

Ethnoarchaeology: the work of Ian Hodder. In the Lake Baringo area of Kenya, East Africa, Hodder studied the female ear decorations worn by the Tugen (right), Njemps, and Pokot tribes, and showed on a map (left) how these ornaments were used to assert tribal distinctiveness. Other features of the material culture (e.g. pots or tools) would reveal a different spatial pattern.

ANCIENT ETHNICITY AND LANGUAGE

Ethnicity (i.e. the existence of ethnic groups, including tribal groups) is difficult to recognize from the archaeological record. For example, the view that Mousterian tool assemblages represented different social groups, as suggested by François Bordes, has been criticized (see discussion in Chapter 10); and the notion that such features as pottery decoration are automatically a sign of ethnic affiliation has been questioned. This is a field where ethnoarchaeology is only now beginning to make some headway.

One field of information, however, once overused by archaeologists, has in recent years been much neglected: the study of languages. For there is no doubt that ethnic groups often correlate with language areas, and that ethnic and linguistic boundaries are often the same. But it should also be remembered that human societies can exist quite well without tribal or ethnic affiliations: there is no real need to divide the social world up into named and discrete groups of people.

Ethnicity should not be confused with race, which insofar as it exists (Chapter 11) is a physical attribute, not a social one. The *ethnos*, the ethnic group, may be defined as "a firm aggregate of people, historically established on a given territory, possessing in common relatively stable peculiarities of language and culture, and also recognizing their unity and difference from other similar formations (self-awareness) and expressing this in a self-appointed name (ethnonym)" (Dragadze 1980, 162).

This definition allows us to note the following factors, all of them relevant to the notion of ethnicity:

1 shared territory or land
2 common descent or "blood"
3 a common language
4 community of customs or culture
5 community of beliefs or religion
6 self-awareness, self-identity
7 a name (ethnonym) to express the identity of the group
8 shared origin story (or myth) describing the origin and history of the group

Ethnicity, however, is a much-abused term, and one that is sometimes used to mask directly political motives. Since 1992, for instance, within the former republic of Yugoslavia, there has been serious fighting between Serbs, Croats, and others (mainly Muslims) over territories. The irony is that there are relatively few underlying differences among the communities involved, the principal distinctions being religious (Orthodox Christian, Roman Catholic, and Muslim respectively). It is sad that blind prejudice along ethnic and religious lines which underlay the horrors of the Holocaust during World War II should once again lead to the mindless slaughter in Yugoslavia termed "ethnic cleansing." The perversion of ethnicity is the curse of our age.

It seems likely that in some cases the scale of the area in which a language came to be spoken was influential in determining the scale of the ethnic group that later came to be formed. For instance, in Greece in the 7th and 6th centuries BC the political reality was one of small, independent city states (and some larger tribal areas). But in the wider area where Greek was spoken there was already an awareness that the inhabitants were together Hellenes (i.e. Greeks). Only Greeks were allowed to compete in the great Panhellenic Games held every 4 years in honor of Zeus at Olympia. It was not until later, with the expansion of Athens in the 5th century BC and then the conquests of Philip of Macedon and his son Alexander the Great in the next century, that the whole territory occupied by the Greeks became united into a single nation. Language is an important component of ethnicity.

In Mesoamerica, Joyce Marcus has drawn on linguistic evidence in analyzing the development of the Zapotec and Mixtec cultures. She notes that their languages belong to the Otomanguean family, and follows the assumption that this relationship implies a common origin. Marcus and Kent Flannery, in their remarkable book *The Cloud People* (1983), seek to trace through time "the divergent evolution of the Zapotec and Mixtec from a common ancestral culture and their general evolution through successive levels of sociopolitical evolution" (Flannery and Marcus 1983, 9). They see in certain shared elements of the two cultures the common ancestry suggested by the linguistic arguments.

Using glottochronology (Chapter 4) Marcus suggests a date of 3700 BC for the beginning of the divergence between the Zapotec and Mixtec; she then seeks to correlate this with archaeological findings.

It is questionable whether glottochronology can be used in this over-precise way. But this criticism in no way undermines the relevance of her introduction of the Zapotec and Mixtec languages into the discussion of the social evolution of the two cultures.

TECHNIQUES OF STUDY FOR MOBILE HUNTER-GATHERER SOCIETIES

In mobile hunter-gatherer societies economic organization and to a large extent political organization are exclusively at a local level – there are no permanent administrative centers. The nature of such societies can be investigated in several ways.

Investigating Activities within a Site

Having identified various sites by employing the methods outlined in Chapter 3, the first approach is to concentrate on the individual site, with an investigation of the variability *within* it. (Off-site archaeology is discussed in the next section.) The aim is to understand the nature of the activities that took place there, and of the social group that used it.

The best approach depends on the nature of the site. In Chapter 3 a site was defined as a place of human activity, generally indicated by a concentration of artifacts and discarded materials. Here we need to be aware that, on sites of sedentary communities (generally, food-producers living in permanent structures), the remains are different in character from the temporary camp sites of mobile communities, whether hunter-gatherers or nomad herders. Sedentary communities are considered in a later section. Our focus in this section is on mobile communities, particularly hunter-gatherers of the Paleolithic period. Here the timescale is so great that the effects of geological processes on sites must be taken into account.

Among mobile communities a distinction can be drawn between *cave sites* and *open sites*. In cave sites, the physical extent of human occupation is largely defined by debris scattered within the cave itself and immediately outside it. Occupation deposits tend to be deep, usually indicating intermittent human activity over thousands or tens of thousands of years. For this reason it is vital to excavate and interpret accurately the stratigraphy of the site – the superimposed layers. Meticulous controls are needed, including the recording in three dimensions of the position of each object (artifact or bone), and the sieving or screening of all soil to recover smaller fragments. Similar observations apply to open sites, except that here one needs to allow for the fact that occupation deposits – without the protection provided by a cave – may have suffered greater erosion.

If it proves possible to distinguish single, short phases of human occupation at a site, one can then look at the distribution of artifacts and bone fragments within and around features and structures (hut foundations, remains of hearths) to see whether any coherent patterns emerge. For the way such debris was discarded can shed light on the behavior of the small group of people who occupied the site at that time. This is where ethnoarchaeology has proved of great value. Lewis Binford's research among the Nunamiut Eskimo, described above, has shown for example that hunter-gatherers discard bone in a characteristic pattern around a hearth. The human behavior documented among the living Nunamiut therefore helps us understand the likely behavior that gave rise to similar scatters of bone around hearths on Paleolithic sites.

Often, it is not possible to distinguish single, short phases of occupation, and the archaeologist recovers instead evidence resulting from repeated activities at the same site over a long period. There may also be initial doubt as to whether the distribution observed is the result of human activity on the spot (*in situ*), or whether the materials have been transported by flowing water and redeposited. In some cases, too, the distribution observed, especially of bone debris, may be the result of the action of predatory animals, not of humans. These are questions to do with formation processes, as discussed in Chapter 2.

The study of such questions requires sophisticated sampling strategies and very thorough analysis. The work of Glynn Isaac's team at the Early Paleolithic sites of Koobi Fora on the eastern shore of Lake Turkana, Kenya, gives an indication of the recovery and analytical techniques involved. The first essential was a highly controlled excavation procedure with, within the areas chosen for detailed sampling, the careful recording of the coordinates of every piece of bone or stone recovered. Plotting the densities of finds was a first step in the analysis. One important question was to decide whether the assemblage was a primary one, *in situ*, or whether it was a secondary accumulation, the result of movement by water in a river or lake. The study of the orientation of the long limb bones proved helpful at Koobi Fora: if the bones had been deposited or disturbed by flowing water, they are likely to show the same orientation. In this case the remains were found to be essentially *in situ*, with only a small degree of post-depositional disturbance.

Isaac's team was also able to fit some fragments of bone back together again. The network of joins could be interpreted as demarcating areas where hominids broke open bones to extract marrow – so-called *activity areas*. (Different techniques had to be applied to try to determine that it was indeed humans and not preda-

Glynn Isaac's research at the Early Paleolithic site of Koobi Fora, Kenya, East Africa. (Top row) Location of bones and stone artifacts plotted at site FxJj 50. (Second row) Lines joining bones and stones that could be fitted back together, perhaps indicating activity areas where bones were broken open to extract marrow, and stone tools were knapped.

tory animals that had broken open the bone. This specialized and important field of study – taphonomy – is discussed in detail in Chapter 6.) A comparable analysis of joins among stone artifacts proved rewarding. Webs of conjoining lines were interpreted as indicating activity areas where stones were knapped. In these ways, the site was made to yield important information about specific human activities.

Broader interpretive questions arise from the consideration of individual camp sites of modern hunter-gatherer communities. One issue is the estimation of population size from camp area. Various models have been proposed, and these have been compared with ethnographic examples among the !Kung San hunter-gatherers of the Kalahari Desert. Another question is the relationship between people (in kinship terms) and space in hunter-gatherer camps: recent studies have shown a strong correlation between kin distance and

the distance between huts. Both questions are discussed in the box overleaf.

These are speculative areas at present, but they are now being systematically researched. Such inferences are bound to become part of the stock-in-trade of the Paleolithic archaeologist.

Investigating Territories in Mobile Societies

The detailed study of an individual site cannot, for a mobile group, reveal more than one aspect of social behavior. For a wider perspective, it is necessary to consider the entire territory in which the group or band operated, and the relationship between sites.

Once again, ethnoarchaeology has helped to establish a framework of analysis, so that one may think in terms of an annual home range (i.e. the whole territory covered by the group in the course of a year) and

191

specific types of site within it, such as a home base camp (for a particular season), transitory camps, hunting blinds, butchery or kill sites, storage caches, and so on. Such concerns are basic to hunter-gatherer archaeology, and a regional perspective is essential if insight is to be gained into the annual life cycle of the group and its behavior. This means that, in addition to conventional sites (with a high concentration of artifacts), one needs to look for sparse scatters of artifacts, consisting of perhaps just one or two objects in every 10-m survey square (this is often referred to as off-site or non-site archaeology – see Chapter 3). One must also study the whole regional environment (Chapter 6) and the likely human use of it by hunter-gatherers.

A good example of off-site archaeology is provided by the work of the British anthropologist Robert Foley in the Amboseli region of southern Kenya. He collected and recorded some 8531 stone tools from 257 sample locations within a study area covering 600 sq. km (232 sq. miles). From this evidence he was able to calculate the rate of discard of stone tools within different environmental and vegetation zones, and interpret the distribution patterns in terms of the strategies and movements of hunter-gatherer groups. In a later study, he developed a general model of stone tool distribution based on a number of studies of hunter-gatherer bands in different parts of the world. One conclusion was that a single band of some 25 people might be expected to discard as many as 163,000 artifacts within their annual territory in the course of a single year. These artifacts would be scattered across the territory, but with significant concentrations at home base camps and temporary camps. According to this model, however, only a very small proportion of the total annual artifact assemblage would be found by archaeologists working at a single site, and it is vitally important that individual site assemblages are interpreted as parts of a broader pattern.

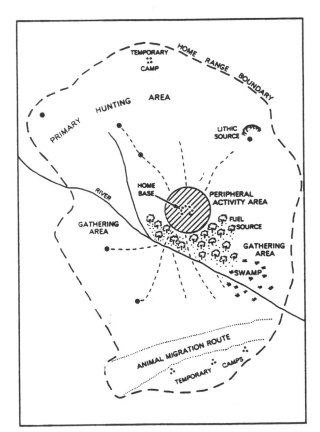 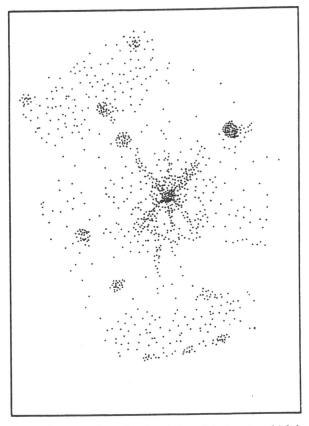

Robert Foley's model (left) of activities within the annual home range of a hunter-gatherer band, and the artifact scatters (right) resulting from such activities. Notice how artifacts appear between the home base/temporary camp sites as well as within them. The home range might be 30 km (19 miles) north–south in tropical environments, but considerably more in higher latitudes.

SPACE AND DENSITY IN HUNTER-GATHERER CAMPS

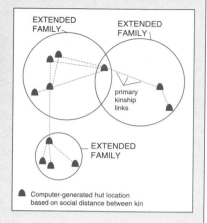

An important question to ask of any settlement site is the size of the population. The interpretation of ethnographic work undertaken by John Yellen among the !Kung San hunter-gatherers of the Kalahari Desert shows how this problem can be tackled. In the dry season, Yellen had noted that large aggregate camps are established for the entire band, ranging from 35 to 60 individuals. In the rainy season, when the band splits up, camps are occupied for just a few days by a single nuclear family, or by several families linked by marriage. Yellen noted that !Kung camp sites are formed of a circle of huts, each of which is a private activity space for a single person, with a shelter, hearth, and hearthside activity area, orientated inward around a central area. Yellen indicated that there is a strong relationship between the area of the camp (established by drawing a line around the perimeter of the hut circle) and its population.

More recently, the Cambridge archaeologist Todd Whitelaw has stressed that this general relationship between camp area and population does not take account of all the relevant factors, including the spacing between huts and the differences between dry and rainy season camps. He took note of the observation that huts and fires belonging to members of the same extended families are close to each other, and he plotted to what extent social distance between kin matched physical distance between huts (measured around the circumference of the camp circle).

Using the data for the two years (1968–69) in which Yellen had observed dry-season camp structure, he obtained a good correlation between closeness of kin and proximity of huts. He then went an interesting step further. Using the

information about kinship distance gathered for two specific camp sites, but not at this stage utilizing any prior information about where the huts were actually located, he constructed a model layout using a non-metric multi-dimensional scaling (MDSCAL) computer routine. This method – described in more detail in a separate box, pp. 206–07 – can be used to construct a spatial structure using only information about relative distance between units.

The hut locations produced by the computer utilizing the model for one dry-season camp are seen in the diagram top right; the actual locations of the huts are shown in the diagram, right. The arrows run from the computer locations to the actual locations. Impressively, in most cases the arrows are quite short; that is, the model produced a good approximation to the actual camp plan, although it was utilizing only data about kinship distance.

This is a good example of the way ethnographic work can enrich a general understanding of a problem, in this case the structure of hunter-gatherer settlement sites. Of course, not all hunter-gatherer settlements are the same. But Whitelaw's study brings out some of the relevant factors, allowing a fresh look at the plans of hunter-gatherer camp sites.

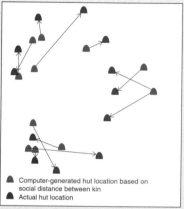

Hut locations in a San dry-season camp. (Top) Todd Whitelaw's model of what the locations might be if one analyzes only the evidence for social relationships using a MDSCAL computer program. (Above) The MDSCAL locations compared with the actual ones.

San hunter-gatherer camp, photographed in about 1927.

TECHNIQUES OF STUDY FOR SEGMENTARY SOCIETIES

Segmentary societies operate on a larger scale than bands. They usually consist of farmers based in villages – permanent sedentary communities. The settlement is therefore the most appropriate aspect of such societies to investigate first. As we shall see, however, the cemeteries, public monuments, and craft specialization evident in these societies also form useful areas of study.

Investigating Settlements in Sedentary Societies

Although a completely excavated settlement from just one period is the ideal case for analysis, it is not often attainable. But much information can be obtained from intensive survey of surface features and from sample excavation. The initial aim is to investigate the structure of the site, and the functions of the different areas recognized. A permanent settlement incorporates a greater range of functions than a temporary hunter-gatherer camp. But the site should not be considered in isolation. As in the hunter-gatherer examples, it is necessary to consider exploitation of the territory as a whole. One means of achieving this is by so-called site catchment analysis, discussed in Chapter 6.

An intensive surface survey of the site can give good indications of the variation in deposits beneath. This was the technique used by Lewis Binford in 1963 at Hatchery West, a Late Woodland occupation site (*c.* AD 250–800) in Illinois. After a local farmer had plowed the topmost surface of the site, and after the summer rains had washed the surface to expose the artifacts, the surface materials were collected from each 6-m square. The resulting distribution maps gave useful indications of the structure of the site below. There were deposits of discarded debris (middens) where there was a high density of potsherds and, between them, houses in areas with a low density of sherds. The patterns indicated by the distribution maps were tested by excavation.

This was a favorable case, where there was a shallow depth of soil, and a close relationship between surface scatter and underlying structures. Remote-sensing techniques can be helpful in revealing site structure, especially aerial photography (Chapter 3). And remote sensing can also be a useful preliminary to excavation. At the Late Neolithic site of Divostin in the former Yugoslavia, Alan McPherron was able to use the proton magnetometer (Chapter 3) to locate the burnt clay floors of the houses in the village, and thus draw an approximate plan before excavation began. Often, however, the conditions are unsuitable for such methods. Furthermore, the site in question may be much larger than Hatchery West (which was less than 2 ha or 4.9 acres) and surface materials, especially pottery, may be abundant. For such sites a survey sampling method, such as random stratified sampling (Chapter 3) may be necessary. On a large site, sampling will also be required in the excavation. There are disadvantages in using small sampling units: they allow one to excavate a wider variety of different parts of the site, but fail to reveal much of the structures (houses, etc.) in question. In other words, there is no substitute for good, wide excavation areas.

For effective analysis of the community as a whole, some structures need to be excavated completely, and the remainder sampled intensively enough to obtain an idea of the variety of different structures (are they repeated household units, or are they more specialized buildings?).

In general, the settlement will be either agglomerate or dispersed. An agglomerate settlement consists of either one or several large units (clusters) of many rooms. A dispersed settlement plan has separate and free-standing house units, usually of smaller size. In the case of agglomerate structures there is the initial problem of detecting repeated social units (e.g. families or households) within them, and the functions of the rooms.

In a now-famous analysis published in 1970 of the agglomerate settlement of Broken K Pueblo, Arizona, in the American Southwest, James Hill undertook a detailed study of the functions of this 13th-century AD site. First he plotted the association of different types of artifact with different rooms. Then, in an ethnographic study of living Pueblo Indians, he identified for the modern period three different types of room – domestic (cooking, eating, sleeping etc.), storage, and ceremonial – and distinctions between rooms used by males and by females. From this ethnographic evidence he derived 16 implications to test against his archaeological evidence, in order to discover whether or not the three room types and male/female distinctions could be identified at Broken K Pueblo itself. His testing suggested that the artifact patterning did indeed indicate the existence of similar distinctions at Broken K.

In recent years there have been criticisms of Hill's conclusions. New work implies that Pueblo architecture, not the artifacts found in them, may be a better guide to room function in prehistoric times. And the

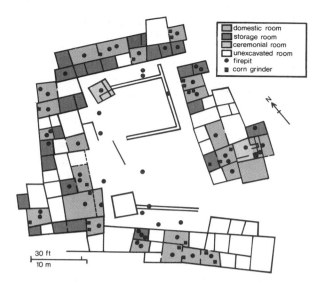

Broken K Pueblo, Arizona: research linked rooms containing firepits and corn grinders with domestic activities; smaller rooms with storage; and two rooms where floors were sunk below ground with ceremonial.

analogy between modern and prehistoric male/female distinctions is not satisfactorily demonstrated here. Cemetery analysis (see below) can provide a better correlation between sex and specific artifact types. But Hill's approach was a pioneering and interesting one in social archaeology, and his methods were commendably explicit, and therefore open to critical appraisal by other scholars (Chapter 12 considers this issue in more detail).

William Longacre undertook similar research at a similar time at the nearby Carter Ranch site in Arizona, with results that have also recently been criticized. To some extent these problems of method – in particular, how to correlate ethnographic with archaeological data – are being solved by the kind of detailed ethno-archaeological research, for instance by Ian Hodder, described in a previous section.

Another informative example of settlement study is offered by Todd Whitelaw's reinterpretation of the Early Minoan site (*c.* 2300 BC) of Myrtos in southern Crete. The excavator, Peter Warren, had suggested that this was a centralized community with a measure of craft specialization (see below). His published report was so commendably thorough as to allow Whitelaw to make a different suggestion – that there was a domestic (household) organization of production rather than craft specialization. By careful study of the function of the rooms (from the remains and features found in them), and their spatial arrangement, he was able to

show that the settlement consisted of 5 or 6 household clusters, each probably with 4–6 individuals. Each cluster had cooking, storage, working, and general domestic areas – there was no evidence of centralization or specialized manufacturing.

The study of sedentary communities is made much easier when separate houses can be identified at the outset. In the 1930s, Gordon Childe excavated the extraordinarily well-preserved Neolithic village of Skara Brae in the Orkney Islands, north of Scotland. He found a settlement, now dated to around 3000 BC, where the internal installations (e.g. beds and cupboards) were still preserved, being made of stone. In such cases, the analysis of the community and the estimation of population size become much easier.

The Study of Ranking from Individual Burials

In archaeology, the individual is seen all too rarely. One of the most informative insights into the individual and his or her social status is offered by the discovery of human physical remains – the skeleton or the ashes – accompanied by artifacts deposited in the grave. Examination of the skeletal remains by a physical anthropologist (Chapter 11) will often reveal the sex and age at death of each individual, and possibly any dietary deficiency or other pathological condition. Communal or collective burials (burials of more than one individual) may be difficult to interpret, because it will not always be clear which grave-goods go with which deceased person. It is, therefore, from single burials that one can hope to learn most.

In segmentary societies, and others with relatively limited differentiation in terms of rank, a close analysis of grave-goods can reveal much about disparities in social status. One must take into account that what is buried with the deceased person is not simply the exact equivalent either of status or of material goods owned or used during life. Burials are made by living individuals, and are used by them to express and influence their relationships with others still alive as much as to symbolize or serve the dead. But there is nevertheless often a relationship between the role and rank of the deceased during life and the manner in which the remains are disposed of and accompanied by artifacts.

The analysis will seek to determine what differences are accorded to males and females in burial, and to assess whether these differences carry with them distinctions in terms of wealth or higher status. The other common factor involved with rank or status is age, and the possibility of age differences being systematically reflected in the treatment of the deceased is an obvious one. In relatively egalitarian societies, achieved status

– that is, high status won through the individual's own achievements (e.g. in hunting) in his or her own lifetime – is something commonly encountered, and often reflected in funerary practice. But the archaeologist must ask, from the evidence available, whether the case in question is one of achieved status, or involves instead status ascribed through birth. To distinguish between the two is not easy. One useful criterion is to investigate whether children are in some cases given rich burial goods and other indications of preferential attention. If so, there may have been a system of hereditary ranking, because at so early an age the child is unlikely to have reached such a status through personal distinction.

Once the graves in the cemetery have been dated, the first step in most cases is simply to produce a frequency distribution (a histogram) of the number of different artifact types in each grave. For further analysis, however, it is more interesting to seek some better indication of wealth and status so that greater weight can be given to valuable objects, and less weight to commonplace ones. This at once raises the problem of the recognition of value (for we do not know in advance what value was given to objects at the time in question). This important subject is discussed in more detail in Chapters 9 and 10.

From the point of view of social questions, the work of the British archaeologist, Susan Shennan, is useful. In an innovative study of burials at the Copper Age cemetery at Brančin Slovakia, she assigned points on a scale of "units of wealth," making the assumption that the valuable objects were those that took a long time to make, or were made of materials brought from a distance or difficult to obtain. This allowed her to produce a diagram of the wealth structure of the cemetery in relation to age and sex. Some individuals, particularly females, had much more elaborate sets of grave-goods than others. She concluded that there was a leading family or families, and status tended to be inherited through the male line, females possibly obtaining their rich artifacts only on marriage.

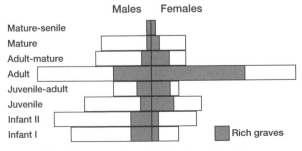

Branč, Slovakia: age and sex distribution of burials.

Sophisticated quantitative techniques can be used to analyze artifact patterning in a cemetery, including factor analysis and cluster analysis (see box).

Ranking is not expressed solely in the grave-goods, but in the entire manner of burial. Some workers, among them Joseph A. Tainter, have developed a more sophisticated approach, seeking to use a much wider range of variables. For instance, in Tainter's study of 512 Middle Woodland burials (*c.* 150 BC–AD 400) from two mound groups in the lower Illinois river valley, he chose 18 variables that each burial might or might not show. He used cluster analysis to investigate relationships between the burials, and concluded from this that there were different social groups. The variables used are worth quoting, as they could be adapted to many different cases:

Checklist of Variables for Burials
1   Uncremated/cremated
2   Articulated/disarticulated
3   Extended/not extended
4   Earthwalls/log walls
5   Ramps/no ramps
6   Surface/sub-surface
7   Log-covered/not log-covered
8   Slab-covered/not slab-covered
9   Slabs in grave/no slabs
10 Interred in central location/not interred in central location
11 Supine/not supine
12 Single/multiple
13 Ocher/no ocher
14 Miscellaneous animal bones/none
15 Hematite/no hematite
16 Imported sociotechnic items (status indicators e.g. royal crown)
17 Locally produced sociotechnic items
18 Technomic items (utilitarian objects e.g. tools)

This list of variables illustrates another important point: that what one is seeking to study is social structure as a whole, not just personal ranking. In life, and in some cases in death, the individual has a whole series of roles and statuses that we seek to detect and understand. To rank individuals in a simple linear order in terms of one variable or a combination of variables may be a considerable oversimplification.

Collective Works and Communal Action

Segmentary societies did not always bury individuals in cemeteries, so archaeologists cannot rely on this

FACTOR ANALYSIS AND CLUSTER ANALYSIS

Both of these techniques are multivariate statistical methods used to isolate patterning in archaeological data. They are alike in that both start with assemblages of artifacts, and these artifacts are listed in terms of types (sometimes referred to as variables). Factor analysis looks for variation among the artifact types within an assemblage. Cluster analysis identifies similarities and differences among complete assemblages, such as assemblages of burial goods from different graves in a cemetery.

Factor Analysis

The basic statistical data needed for a factor analysis is a matrix of correlation coefficients. (Correlation coefficients express, on a scale of from -1 to +1, the degree of correlation between two variables; they must be obtained for each pair of variables considered in the study.) The key concept is that of variance. Variance is of three kinds: common variance (which correlates with other variables), specific variance (which does not), and error variance (caused by errors in sampling, measurement, etc.).

The assumption is that a battery of intercorrelated variables has common factors running through it, and that the scores of any individual variable can be represented more economically in terms of these reference factors. The aim of factor analysis is to identify these factors.

Factor analysis was used by James Hill to study the co-occurrence of pottery types in the different rooms at Broken K Pueblo (see main text, pp. 194–95), and by Lewis and Sally Binford to analyze stone tool types of the Middle Paleolithic in southwest France.

Cluster Analysis

Cluster analysis takes units or assemblages and arranges them in terms of the similarities between them, so that the most similar are grouped (i.e. clustered) together. The similarities are assessed in terms of the occurrence or non-occurrence of specific artifact types in the assemblages. If assemblages have the same types within them occurring in roughly the same quantities, they are obviously very similar and are clustered closely together.

The technique is frequently used in cemetery analysis to investigate the social structure in terms of the grave-goods accompanying the dead. Here the grave-goods listed for each grave represent the individual assemblages to be clustered. The different clusters can then be examined to see which artifacts are taking a predominant role in achieving the clustering. In particular, one may see whether the age and sex of the dead correlate closely with the clustering achieved by considering the grave-goods alone. The occurrence of the graves of each cluster can also be plotted on a map of the cemetery to see whether the clusters as defined by the grave-goods are reflected in the spatial arrangement of the cemetery.

Cluster analysis has been used successfully by John O'Shea for historic-period cemeteries of the Pawnee, Arikara, and Omaha Plains Indians, and by Christopher Peebles at Moundville in Alabama. The accompanying diagram shows the clustering achieved by Peebles. The box later in this chapter (Social Analysis at Moundville) goes on to consider how he deduced information about social organization from it.

Dendrogram produced by Peebles using a cluster analysis of 719 burials from Moundville, Alabama. Divisions were made successively according to the presence or absence of single attributes (- and + on the diagram). For example, the first major division depends on the presence or absence of attribute 2, "plain bowls." Division was terminated when 15 clusters had been defined (Roman numerals at far right). Each cluster box shows the number of burials assigned to it.

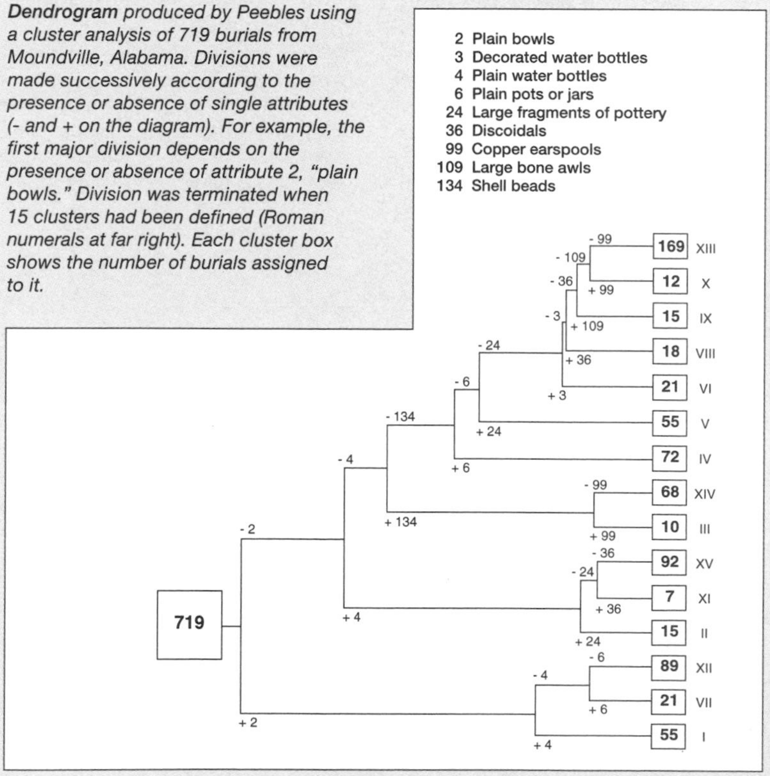

2 Plain bowls
3 Decorated water bottles
4 Plain water bottles
6 Plain pots or jars
24 Large fragments of pottery
36 Discoidals
99 Copper earspools
109 Large bone awls
134 Shell beads

EARLY WESSEX

Prehistoric Wessex (the counties of Wiltshire, Dorset, Hampshire, and Berkshire in southern England) preserves a rich collection of major monuments from the early farming period, but few remains of settlements. Yet the analysis of the scale and the distribution of the monuments does allow the reconstruction of important aspects of social organization, and illustrates one approach to the study of early social relations. This has also been the favoured study area of the early postprocessual archaeologists.

In the **early phase** of monument construction (the earlier Neolithic, *c.* 4000–3000 BC), the most frequent monuments are long earthen burial mounds, termed long barrows, which are up to 70 m (230 ft) in length. They lie mainly on the chalklands of Wessex where the light soils were suitable for early farming.

Excavations show that the monuments usually contained a wooden burial chamber: some of them have a chamber of stone. With each cluster of mounds is associated a larger, circular monument with concentric ditches termed a causewayed camp or enclosure.

Analysis of the spatial distribution and the size of the long barrows suggests a possible interpretation. Lines drawn between them divide the landscape into several possible territories, which are roughly equivalent in size. Each monument seems to have been the focal point for social activities and the burial place of the farming community inhabiting the local territory. A group of 20 people would have needed about 50 working days to construct a long barrow.

The distribution of these long barrows has also been analyzed using GIS to produce viewshed maps of the intervisibility of the monuments (see main text). The first monument builders were constructing a social landscape and thereby a different world from that of the Mesolithic foragers which it replaced.

In the early phase of construction there is little suggestion of the ranking of sites or individuals: this was an egalitarian society. The causewayed enclosures may have served as a ritual focus and periodic meeting place for the larger group of people represented by one whole cluster of long barrows. (The 100,000 hours' labor required to construct one could be achieved in 40 working days by 250 people.) This would have been what anthropologists now term a tribal or segmentary society.

In the **later phase** (the later Neolithic, *c.* 3000–2000 BC), the long barrows and causewayed camps went out of use. In place of the latter, major ritual enclosures are seen. These were large circular monuments delimited by a ditch with a bank usually outside it: they are termed henges. Each would have

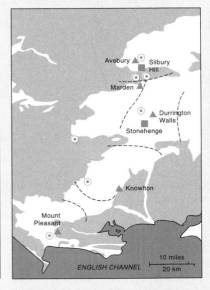

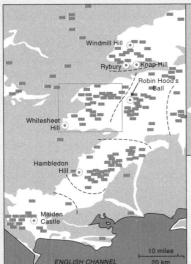

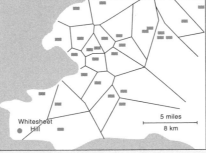

In the early phase, clusters of burial mounds establish a social landscape (left), each cluster with its causewayed enclosure. Analysis indicates (above) that each mound was the territorial focus for a small group of farmers. This was a segmentary society, where no one group was dominant.

In the later phase, the causewayed enclosures were replaced by major henge monuments. Their scale indicates centralized organization, and hence perhaps a chiefdom society. At this time the two great monuments Stonehenge and Silbury Hill were built.

required something of the order of 1 million hours of labor for its construction. The labor input suggests the mobilization of the resources of a whole territory. About 300 people working full time for at least a year would be needed: their food would have to be provided for them unless the process were spread over a very long period.

During this period (*c.* 2800 BC) the great earth mound at Silbury Hill was built. According to its excavator, it required 18 million hours of work, and was completed within 2 years. A few centuries later (*c.* 2100 BC) the great monument at Stonehenge took final shape, with its circle of stones, representing an even greater labor investment, if the transport of the stones is taken into account: a massive corporate endeavor.

Although burials with rich grave-goods directly reflecting the wealth of prominent individuals are not found until the succeeding phase, the Early Bronze Age, the analysis of spatial organization among the monuments, and the consideration of the labor input contributed by their builders, do allow inferences to be drawn about the social organization of the time.

The **postprocessual approach** of the "Neo-Wessex school" of British archaeologists (see p. 216), while accepting much of the above, emphasizes the experience of the individuals moving through the landscape and among the monuments, whose actions and beliefs are shaped thereby, so that new kinds of social relations emerge. This is a constructed landscape which in turn acts upon the *habitus* of individuals in daily life and plays a role in determining the formation of the society in which they live (see also Archaeology of the Individual p. 215 below).

Ethnographic analogy has also recently been used in relation to Stonehenge by Mike Parker Pearson and Ramilisonina to great effect, drawing upon the recent tradition of megalithic funerary monuments in Madagascar where standing stones are still erected and ancestor worship remains very important. By such cross-cultural analogy, they have concluded that the landscape of Wessex was divided into the domain of the living and the domain of the dead.

In this landscape Stonehenge "can be interpreted as belonging to the ancestors, a stone version for the dead of the timber circles used for ceremonials by the living. By extension, Avebury and many other stone monuments of this period can be understood as built for the ancestors in parallel to the wooden monuments constructed for the living." (Parker Pearson & Ramilisonina 1998, 308)

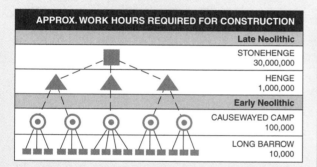

Analysis of the scale of the Wessex monuments *in terms of labor hours needed for their construction suggests the emergence of a hierarchy in the later phase that may mirror a development in social relations and the emergence of a ranked society. Stonehenge, built at this time, is the greatest of the Wessex monuments. In the earlier Neolithic the scale of monuments is commensurate with an egalitarian, segmentary society.*

KEY

■ Stonehenge

▲ Henge

◉ Causewayed camp

■ Long barrow

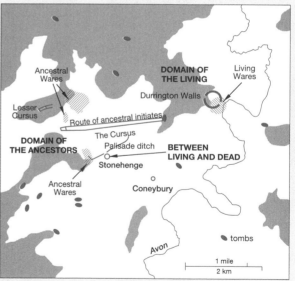

A different way *of viewing the landscape around Stonehenge based on the work of Mike Parker Pearson. He divides it into areas associated with the living and with the dead, reflected in the use of different materials for construction (timber and stone) and different types of pottery.*

source of information being available. Similarly, settlement sites can be difficult to locate, and the remains scanty. The original ground surface may have been destroyed, either by plowing or erosion, so that house floors or structures are not preserved. For instance, all that remains for the early farming period of northern Europe in the way of houses and domestic evidence is often just a few postholes (where timber uprights for house frames were set in the ground) and the lower levels of rubbish pits. In all such cases, the archaeologist in search of social evidence needs to turn to another prime source: public monuments.

We all perhaps have a mental image of such major monuments as the temples of the Maya or the pyramids of Egypt, erected by centrally organized state societies. But a great many simpler societies, at the level of chiefdoms or segmentary groups, have built substantial and conspicuous structures. One thinks of the great stone monuments of western Europe (the so-called "megaliths," see box, pp. 488–89), or the giant stone statues of Easter Island in the Pacific Ocean. Indeed monuments like the Easter Island figures have in the past been interpreted, wrongly, as a sure sign of "civilization." When the indigenous society displays no other characteristics of "civilization," fantastic explanations have been put forward involving long-distance migrations, vanished continents, or even visitors from outer space (see box, p. 562). Such unsubstantiated notions are looked at again in Chapters 12 and 14. For now, we may turn instead to the techniques archaeologists apply when searching for social information from such monuments, particularly among segmentary societies. These involve questions about the size or scale of the monuments; their spatial distribution in the landscape; and clues about the status of individuals buried in certain monuments.

How Much Labor Was Invested in the Monuments? To begin with, the scale of the monument in terms of the number of hours it may have taken to build should be investigated, using evidence not just from the structure itself but also from experimental archaeology of the kind described in Chapters 2 and 8. As explained in the box, in the Wessex region of southern England the largest monuments (so-called causewayed enclosures) of the Early Neolithic period seem to have required some 100,000 hours of work to construct – within the capabilities of 250 people working together for perhaps 6 weeks. This does not suggest a very complex level of organization and might indicate a tribal, segmentary society. But by the Late Neolithic one of the biggest monuments, the great mound of Silbury Hill, demanded 18 million hours, which excavation of the

site showed had been invested over a span of no more than 2 years. The workforce must have been of the order of 3000 individuals over this period of time, which suggests the kind of mobilization of resources indicative of a more centralized, chiefdom society.

How Are the Monuments Distributed in the Landscape? It is also useful to analyze spatial distribution of the monuments in question in relation to other monuments and to settlement and burial remains. For instance, the burial mounds (long barrows) of southern Britain around 3500–2800 BC each represented about 5000–10,000 hours of labor. Their distribution in well-defined regions can be examined by drawing Thiessen polygons around them (see above), and by considering land use, such as the relationship of long barrows to areas of lighter chalk soils most suitable for early agriculture. It has been suggested that each mound was the focal point of the territory of a group of people permanently established there – a symbolic center for the community.

The very act of creating a fixed area for the repeated disposal of the dead implies an element of permanence. The American archaeologist Arthur Saxe has suggested that in those groups where rights to the use of land are asserted by claiming descent from dead ancestors, there will be formal areas maintained exclusively for the disposal of the dead. In this perspective, collective burial in monumental tombs is not simply a reflection of religious beliefs: it has real social significance. Most of the megalithic tombs of western Europe might thus be regarded as the territorial markers of segmentary societies, because the spatial distribution does not suggest any higher level of organization. This and other ideas about the megaliths are more fully discussed in Chapter 12.

A different kind of analysis of the distribution of monuments, in particular their visibility and intervisibility, has been made possible through the use of Geographic Information Systems (see Chapter 3). One such study was undertaken by the British archaeologist David Wheatley of the Neolithic long barrows of prehistoric Wessex (see box, Early Wessex, pp. 198–99). Using GIS he generated a *viewshed* map for each long barrow in the Stonehenge and Avebury groups. These maps showed the locations in a direct line of sight from (and therefore also to) each monument, calculated from a digital elevation model of the landscape. The area of land which might theoretically be visible from each barrow location was then worked out. Wheatley was able to show statistically that, in general, the areas visible from the Stonehenge group tend to be larger than would be expected through the

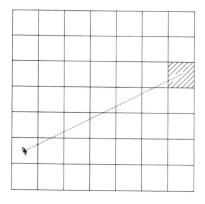

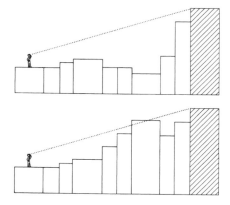

Line of sight: a line is drawn between two cells of a digital elevation model to see whether there is a line of sight or not.

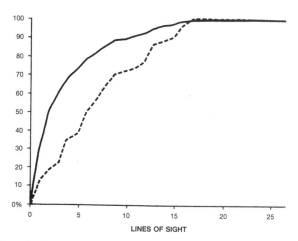

Cumulative viewshed analysis for the intervisibility of barrows of the Stonehenge group: percentages of projected intervisibility (solid line) compared with actual (dotted line). The results suggest that there is greater intervisibility between the barrows in this group than would be expected by chance.

operation of pure chance. The same could not be shown for the Avebury group of barrows. Taking this a stage further, he added together the viewshed maps for each monument, resulting in a *cumulative viewshed* map demonstrating the intervisibility within a defined group of monuments. Another statistical significance test ascertained that the barrows of the Stonehenge group tend to be in locations from which a large number of other barrows in the group are visible; again this could not be shown for the Avebury group.

Although such results are suggestive, they do not conclusively demonstrate that the long barrows on Salisbury Plain were deliberately sited to maximize their visibility or intervisibility, since these might in fact be a by-product of their location rather than a reason for it. Such studies also cannot take into account the effects ancient woodlands would have had on visibility. It is, however, possible that the choice of the location for constructing a barrow was partly guided by the desire to incorporate visual references to existing monuments. Thus, during the burial rituals at the new barrow, the permanence of the prevailing social order would have been visible all around. On the basis of the viewshed analysis of the Stonehenge long barrows, therefore, the monuments might be better interpreted as social foci for entire communities rather than territorial markers for individual distinct family groups (in which case it might be expected that their viewsheds would not overlap very often). Similar interpretations have also been advanced for the arrangement of bones within some chambered tombs, and of the architectural arrangement of chambers and forecourt at the West Kennet barrow.

Which Individuals Are Associated with the Monuments?
Finally it is necessary to investigate the relationship between individuals and monuments. When the monument is associated with a prominent individual, it might indicate that that person held high rank, and might therefore suggest a centralized society. This would not be the case for a monument associated with multiple burials of individuals of apparently similar status. For instance, in the chambered tomb at Quanterness in the Orkney Islands, off the north coast of Scotland, dating to *c.* 3300 BC, remains of a large number of individuals were found, perhaps as many as 390. Males and females were about equally represented, and the age distribution could represent the pattern of deaths in the population at large; that is to say, that the age at death of the people buried in the tomb (46 percent below 20 years, 47 percent aged 20–30 years, and only 7 percent over the age of 30 years) could in proportional terms be the same as that of the whole

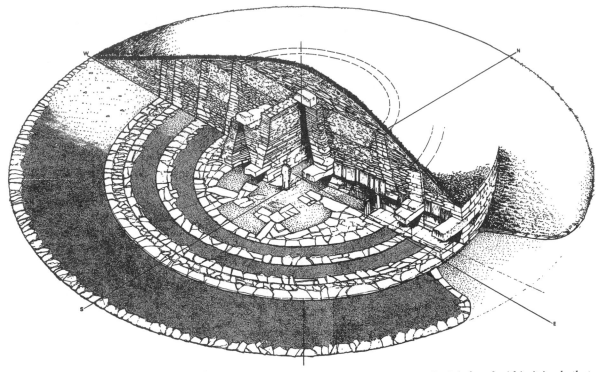

Quanterness, Orkney Islands: reconstruction of a chambered tomb dating to about 3300 BC. Burials found within it imply that this was the product of a segmentary society, not a hierarchical one, despite the sophistication of the architecture.

population. The excavators concluded that this was a tomb equally available to most sectors of the community, and representative of a segmentary society rather than a hierarchical one, which the sophistication of its architecture might at first have suggested.

Similar observations apply to ritual monuments other than tombs, which similarly can give insights into social organization. So, too, can any other major corporate works, whether agricultural or defensive.

Relationships between Segmentary Societies

Segmentary agricultural societies have a whole range of relationships with their neighbors – marriage ties, exchange partnerships, etc. The first step in investigating such relationships archaeologically is to look for the ritual centers that served for periodic meetings of several groups. A study can then be made of the sources of some of the artifacts found at these centers (the techniques are explained in Chapter 9), to indicate the geographical extent of the network of contacts represented at each center.

Some of the major public monuments in southern Britain discussed in the previous section seem to have been just such ritual centers. In particular, the causewayed enclosures of the Early Neolithic have been interpreted as central meeting places – social and ritual centers for the tribal groups in whose territory they lay, and also for larger, periodic meetings with participants from a much greater area. Stone axes at these sites came from far-away sources, hinting at just how broadly based the social interconnections were at this early time.

Similarities and differences in the style and appearance of certain types of artifact – for instance, decorated pottery – can provide important clues to the interactions between societies. However, as we saw in an earlier section, Ian Hodder has shown that while various features of material culture are used to maintain tribal distinctions, others are not patterned in this way. At present archaeologists have not found a reliable way to distinguish in the archaeological record such symbols of ethnic differentiation and to "read" them correctly – for instance, to distinguish them from symbols of rank, or of some other type of specialization, or from mere examples of decorative fashion. Conventions of communication are considered further in Chapter 10.

Farming Methods and Craft Specialists

In segmentary societies the existence of settled villages, cemeteries, public monuments, and ritual centers all indicate greater social complexity than in band societies. One way to try to measure how societies begin to show still greater complexity is to look at farming methods and the growth of craft specialists. Here we shall be concerned with social implications: more detailed questions about how archaeologists look at dietary aspects of farming, and technological aspects of craft production, are considered in Chapters 7 and 8 respectively. The increasing need for communities to exchange goods as craft production developed is the subject of Chapter 9.

As the farming way of life took root in different parts of the world after 10,000 years ago, there is evidence in many areas for a gradual *intensification of food production*, manifested by the introduction of new farming methods such as plowing, terracing, and irrigation, the use of poorer quality land as better land grew scarce, and the exploitation for the first time of so-called "secondary products" such as milk and wool (the meat of domestic animals being the "primary product"). How archaeologists can identify such evidence is discussed in Chapters 6 and 7. What we should note here is that these are all developments requiring a greater expenditure of human effort – they are *labor-intensive* techniques – and new and varied kinds of expertise. For instance, plowing allows once unproductive poor-quality land to be cultivated but it takes more time and effort than cultivating better-quality land without the plow. Moreover, activities like terracing involve cooperative effort on the part of a whole community. These are all activities that can be looked at to measure the likely number of work hours and size of labor force required. As in the case of public monuments, a really significant increase in the effort expended (for instance, on the introduction of irrigation) would suggest some more centralized organization of the workforce, perhaps signaling the transition from a non-hierarchical, segmentary type of society to one that is much more centralized, such as a chiefdom.

If we turn now to *craft specialization* as a source of social information, there is a useful distinction to be drawn here between segmentary societies and centralized ones. In segmentary societies, craft production is mainly organized at the household level – what the American anthropologist Marshall Sahlins in his book *Stone Age Economics* (1972) has termed the Domestic Mode of Production. In more centralized societies such as chiefdoms and states, on the other hand, though the household unit may still play an important role, much of the production will often be organized at a higher, more centralized level.

This distinction is useful at the practical level of survey and excavation. Even small villages in segmentary societies will show signs of household craft production in the form of pottery kilns or perhaps slag from metal-working. But only in centralized societies does one find towns and cities with certain quarters given over almost entirely to specialized craft production. At the 1st millennium AD metropolis of Teotihuacán, near modern Mexico City, for instance, the specialized production of tools from the volcanic glass obsidian took place in designated areas of the city.

Quarries and mines to extract the raw materials for craft production developed with the crafts themselves, and provide another indicator of economic intensification and the transition to centralized social organization. For example, the flint quarries of the first farmers of Britain, around 4000 BC, required less specialized organization than the later flint mine at Grimes Graves in eastern Britain (*c.* 2500 BC), with its 350 shafts up to 9 m (30 ft) deep and complicated network of underground galleries.

TECHNIQUES OF STUDY FOR CHIEFDOMS AND STATES

Most of the techniques of analysis appropriate to segmentary societies remain valid for the study of centralized chiefdoms and states, which incorporate within themselves most of the social forms and patterns of interaction seen in the simpler societies. The investigation of the household and degree of differentiation on the rural village site are just as relevant; so too is the assessment of the degree of intensification of farming. The additional techniques needed arise because of the centralization of society, the hierarchy of sites, and the organizational and communicational devices that characterize chiefdom and state societies. Once again, it is the nature of these devices that interests us, not simply the classification of society into one form or another.

Identifying Primary Centers

Techniques for the study of settlement patterning were discussed earlier in the chapter. As indicated there, the first step, given the results of the field survey, is to consider the size of the site, either in absolute terms, or in terms of the distances between major centers so as to determine which are dominant and which subordinate. This leads to the creation of a map identifying the principal independent centers and the approximate extent of the territories surrounding them.

The reliance on size alone, however, can be misleading, and it is necessary to seek other indications of which are the primary centers. The best way is to try to find out how the society in question viewed itself and its territories. This might seem an impossible task until one remembers that, for most state societies at any rate, written records exist. Their immense value to the

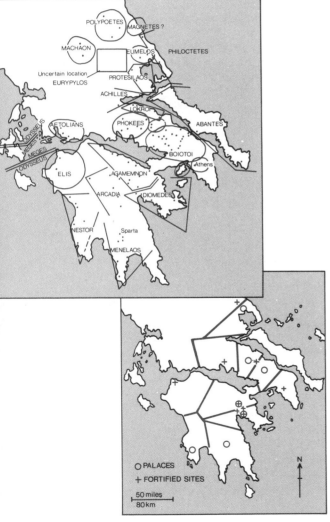

Late Bronze Age Greece: a map of territories derived from Homer's Iliad *(top) compares well with a territorial map (above) based solely on archaeological evidence.*

archaeologist has already been outlined. Here we need to stress their usefulness not so much in understanding what people thought and believed – that is the subject of Chapter 10 – but in giving us clues as to which were the major centers. Written sources may name various sites, identifying their place within the hierarchy. The archaeological task is then to find those named sites, usually by the discovery of an actual inscription including the name of the relevant site – one might for example hope to find such an inscription in any substantial town of the Roman empire. In recent years, the decipherment of Maya hieroglyphs has opened up a whole new source of evidence of this sort (see box, opposite).

In some cases, however, the texts do not give direct and explicit indications of site hierarchy. But place-names within the archive can sometimes be used to construct a hypothetical map by means of multi-dimensional scaling – a computer technique for developing spatial structure from numerical data. The assumption is made that the names occurring together most frequently in the written record are those of sites closest to each other. The British archaeologist John Cherry has developed such a map for the lands of the early Mycenaean state of Pylos in Greece (*c.* 1200 BC) (see box, overleaf).

Even myth and legend can sometimes be used in a systematic way to build up a coherent geographical picture. For instance, the so-called "Catalogue of Ships" in Homer's *Iliad*, which indicates how many ships each of the centers of Greece sent to the Trojan War, was used by Denys Page to draw an approximate political map of the time. It is interesting to compare it with a map drawn using only the hard archaeological data for fortified sites and palace centers in Mycenaean Greece: the archaeological and the historical pictures correlate very well.

Usually, however, site hierarchy must be deduced by more directly archaeological means, without placing reliance on the written word. The presence of a "highest-order" center, such as the capital city of an independent state, can best be inferred from direct indications of central organization, on a scale not exceeded elsewhere, and comparable with that of other highest-order centers of equivalent states.

One indication is the existence of an archive (even without understanding anything of what it says) or of other symbolic indications of centralized organization. For instance, many controlled economies used seals to make impressions in clay as indications of ownership, source, or destination. The finding of a quantity of such materials can indicate organizational activity. Indeed, the whole practice of literacy and of symbolic expression is so central to organization that such indications are of great relevance.

A further indication of central status is the presence of buildings of standardized form known to be associated with central functions of high order. In Minoan Crete, for instance, the "palace" plan around a central court is recognized in this way. Therefore, a relatively small palace site (e.g. Zakros) is accorded a status which a larger settlement lacking such buildings (e.g. Palaikastro) is not.

The same observation holds true for buildings of ritual function, because in most early societies the control of administration and control of religious practice were closely linked. Thus, a large ziggurat in Mesopotamia in Sumerian times, or a large plaza with temple-pyramids in the Maya lowlands, indicates a site of high status.

Failing these conspicuous indicators, the archaeologist must turn to artifacts suggestive of the function of a major center. This is particularly necessary for surface surveys, where building plans may not be clear. Thus, on site surveys in Iraq, workers studying the Early Dynastic period, such as Robert Adams and Gregory Johnson, have used terracotta wall cones as indicators of higher-than-expected status for the smaller sites where they are found. The cones, known to form part of the decoration of temples and other public buildings on larger sites in the region, suggest that such smaller sites may have been specialized administrative centers.

Among other archaeological criteria often used to indicate status are fortifications, and the existence of a mint in those lands where coinage was in use.

Clearly, when settlement hierarchy is under consideration, sites cannot be considered in isolation, but only in relation to each other. The exercise is one of early political geography.

Functions of the Center

In a hierarchically organized society, it always makes sense to study closely the functions of the center, considering such possible factors as kingship, bureaucratic organization, redistribution and storage of goods, organization of ritual, craft specialization, and external trade. All of these offer insights into how the society worked.

Here, as before, the appropriate approach is that of the intensive site survey over the terrain occupied by the center and its immediate vicinity, together with excavation on as large a scale as is practicable. Again, this is a sampling problem, where the objective of comprehensiveness must be balanced against limited

MAYA TERRITORIES

NORTH AMERICA

The Classic Maya lowlands of AD 300–900 were a densely settled area with many large population centers. The first clues to their political organization came with the discovery of "emblem glyphs," hieroglyphic compounds that seemed to identify individual cities. It is now known that these combinations are the titles of Maya kings and describe each as the "divine lord" of a particular polity. The discoveries showed that the lowlands were at this time divided into a dense "mosaic" of numerous small states.

Today, a lively debate continues as to what degree this arrangement reflects the full political landscape. Some scholars think such states were autonomous and of roughly equivalent strength and influence. Others see evidence for a hierarchical ranking between kingdoms, arranged either in a "quadripartite" model of regional states, or a more loosely structured "hegemonic" system, in which dominant powers exercised some control over subject states, without interfering directly in their internal affairs. Increasingly the picture is one of confederations and shifting alliances. These reconstructions give greatest prominence to centers known from surveys such as: Copán, Tikal, Calakmul, Palenque and Caracol.

Copán

Tikal

Calakmul

Palenque

Caracol

Naranjo

Piedras Negras

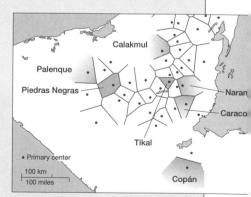

Emblem glyphs (left) of 7 of the most important Classic Maya states, shown also on the map of the arrangement of Classic Maya political territories c. AD 790 (above).

MULTI-DIMENSIONAL SCALING (MDSCAL)

Multi-dimensional scaling (MDSCAL) is a multivariate statistical technique, which, like factor analysis and cluster analysis, seeks to simplify complex information. The main aim is to develop spatial structure from numerical data. The starting point is a series of units, and some way of measuring or estimating the distances between them (often in terms of similarity and difference, where a larger difference is treated as much the same as a larger distance). The method allows one to reach the best arrangement (usually in two dimensions) of the various units in terms of similarities and differences.

One interesting feature of the method is that it does not need fully quantitative measures of similarity and difference: it is sufficient to know, for each unit, which the nearest unit is, and then the next and so on in rank order. For this reason, the method is sometimes called non-metric multi-dimensional scaling.

An ingenious use of the approach, which can serve as an example, was employed by the English archaeologist John Cherry. The problem was to try to reconstruct something of the geography of the Mycenaean kingdom of Pylos in Greece (c.1200 BC). The information for the computer program came entirely from the palace archives recorded on clay tablets found at Pylos. The tablets, which mention many place names, give no direct geographical information whatever, although they contain sufficient hints about the approximate location of some places to have allowed speculative maps to be drawn. Cherry's rather different approach involved just one interesting assumption: that if two or more place names occurred on the same tablet, they were likely to be fairly close to each other in reality. So he studied the frequency with which certain place names were recorded on the tablets, and then compiled a table (or "incidence matrix") showing their co-occurrence on individual tablets. The computer then went to work using the MDSCAL program, and produced as its output a spatial configuration based entirely on these data. Bearing in mind that the MDSCAL map shows relationships rather than distances, Cherry was then able to compare his configuration with the positions of the same sites, suggested by other scholars, on a real geographic map.

While the results remain hypothetical at this stage and have to be tested against further discoveries in the field, there are a number of intriguing similarities between the MDSCAL and geographic maps. For example, the computer was able to separate the towns of the kingdom's two provinces. It also confirmed much of the north-to-south order of the towns in the western province, if one ignores Pylos. Thus, on both MDSCAL and geographic maps, pi-*82 is the most northerly town, followed by me-ta-pa etc. Pylos appears unexpectedly at the top of the MDSCAL map probably because, as the "capital" of the kingdom, its interactions were different in kind from those amongst the satellite towns.

The essential point, however, is that Cherry used information about relationships between pairs of units (in this case places mentioned in the tablets) to produce an ordered spatial configuration of those units. That is the essence of non-metric multi-dimensional scaling.

	a-ke-re-wa	a-pu$_2$-we	e-ra-te-re-we	e-re-e	e-sa-re-wi-ja	ka-ra-do-ro	me-ta-pa	pa-ki-ja-pi	pe-to-no	pi-*82	pu-ro	ra-u-ra-ti-ja	ri-jo	ro-u-so	sa-ma-ra	ti-mi-to a-ke-e	za-ma-e-wi-ja
a-ke-re-wa		1	1	1	0	0	0	0	1	0	0	0	1	1	0	1	0
a-pu$_2$-we			0	0	0	1	0	1	0	0	0	0	0	0	0	0	0
e-ra-te-re-we				0	1	0	1	0	0	1	0	0	0	0	0	1	1
e-re-e					1	0	0	0	0	0	0	0	0	0	0	0	1
e-sa-re-wi-ja						0	0	0	0	0	0	1	0	0	1	1	1
ka-ra-do-ro							0	1	0	0	0	0	1	1	0	0	0
me-ta-pa								0	1	1	0	0	0	0	0	1	0
pa-ki-ja-pi									1	0	1	0	0	1	0	0	0
pe-to-no										0	0	0	0	0	0	0	0
pi-*82											1	0	0	0	0	0	0
pu-ro (=Pylos)												1	0	0	1	0	0
ra-u-ra-ti-ja													0	0	1	1	0
ri-jo														0	0	1	0
ro-u-so															0	0	0
sa-ma-ra																1	0
ti-mi-to a-ke-e																	0
za-ma-e-wi-ja																	

Table ("incidence matrix") showing 17 of the towns recorded on the tablets found at Pylos, and which of these names occur together on the same tablet (1 = link indicated; 0 = no link)

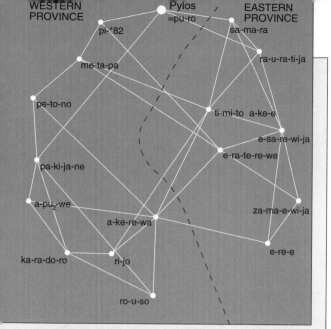

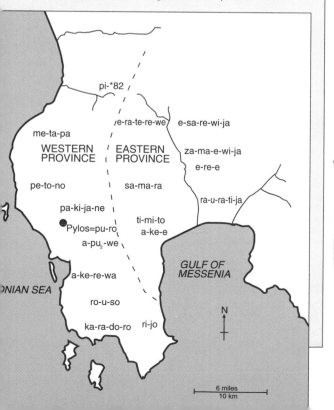

The MDSCAL output or map produced from the information in the incidence matrix, showing general relationships among the towns rather than distances. The computer has successfully reproduced the division of towns into two provinces, with a north-to-south ordering in the western province similar to that on the geographic map.

Geographic map of the Pylos area, with towns positioned approximately by John Chadwick using conventional archaeological and other evidence. The dashed line indicates the known division of the kingdom into two provinces.

resources of time and finance. In the case of smaller centers, just a few hectares in extent, an intensive area survey will be perfectly appropriate. But for very large sites, a different approach is needed.

Abandoned Sites. Many of the most ambitious urban projects have been carried out at abandoned sites, or at sites where the present occupation is not of an urban character, and does not seriously impede the investigation. (The problems of continuously urban sites, i.e. ones that remain major centers today, are considered below.) The first requirement, which may present practical difficulties if the site is forested, is a good topographic map at something like a scale of 1:1000, although this may not be convenient for sites several kilometers in extent. This map will indicate the location of major structures visible on the surface, and some of these will be selected for more careful mapping. On sites where extensive excavations have already been conducted, their results can also be included.

Such topographic maps are among the most cost-effective undertakings of modern archaeology. One of the most interesting examples is Salvatore Garfie's survey of the site of Tell el-Amarna, the capital city of the Egyptian pharaoh Akhenaten, as part of the British project of survey and excavation there. The site was occupied for only 13 years in the 14th century BC, and was then abandoned. The buildings were of mud brick and are not well preserved as surface features, so the map draws heavily on excavations over the course of a century. In the New World, there have been several projects of comparable scale, one of the most notable being the University of Pennsylvania's great mapping project at the Maya city of Tikal, and similar work is now under way at several Maya sites. Perhaps the most ambitious project of all, however, has been the survey at the greatest Mexican urban center, Teotihuacán (see box, pp. 90–91).

The preparation of a topographic map is only the first stage. To interpret the evidence in social terms means that the function of any structures revealed has next to be established. This involves the study of the major ceremonial and public buildings – temples have a social as well as religious function – and other components of the city, such as areas for specialist craft manufacture, and residential structures. Differences in standards of housing will reveal inequalities between rich and poor and therefore an aspect of the social hierarchy.

Quite often, however, the function of large and presumably public buildings is difficult to establish, and there is a temptation to ascribe purposes to them based on guesswork. For instance, the excavator of Knossos on Crete, Sir Arthur Evans, gave names such as "the Queen's Megaron" to some of the rooms there, without any good evidence for the term. Similarly, Sir Mortimer Wheeler allocated terms like "College" and "Assembly Hall" to buildings within the "Citadel" of Mohenjodaro, one of the great Harappan cities, without supporting evidence that they actually served such purposes.

One way to begin studying the city in detail is the intensive sampling of artifact materials from the surface. At Teotihuacán the topographic map (at a scale of 1:2000) was used as the basis for surface sampling on foot. Trained fieldworkers covered the whole site, walking a few meters apart, and collected all the rims, bases, handles, and other special sherds and objects visible to them. The data from Teotihuacán have been processed in an ambitious computer project by George Cowgill. In this way the spatial distribution of specific artifact types can be mapped, and inferences made about the patterns of occupation in different periods.

A stage beyond intensive surface sampling can be the kind of combined surface examination and selective excavation carried out at Tell Abu Salabikh, described in Chapter 3, which revealed the largest area of housing known from any 3rd-millennium BC site in southern Iraq.

Usually, however, excavation on a large scale will be needed for a major center such as a city. Some of the most famous and successful excavations earlier this century have been of this kind, from Mohenjodaro in the Indus Valley in what is now Pakistan to the biblical city of Ur in present-day Iraq.

With luck, the preservation conditions for the last period of occupation will be good. If the site is located in the vicinity of a volcano, this last period may very well be superbly preserved by volcanic ash and lava. Pompeii in southern Italy and Akrotiri on the Greek volcanic island of Thera (Santorini) have been mentioned in earlier chapters as examples of cities buried and preserved for posterity, but there are others: for example, Cuicuilco was the great rival to Teotihuacán in the Valley of Mexico until volcanic eruptions destroyed the city some 2000 years ago. In such extreme circumstances, however, preliminary topographic mapping of the kind just described may not be possible, since structures will be buried too deeply to show up on the surface.

Occupied Sites. The problems are similar, but much more difficult in practice, with continuously urban sites: early centers that remain urban centers to this day and have, therefore, not only a complex strati-

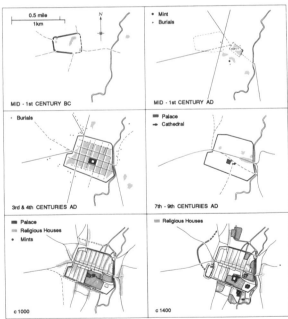

Occupied site: Winchester, southern England. (Top) Excavations in progress beside the cathedral. (Above) The complex development of the city up to AD 1400, based on a decade of excavation and many years of post-excavation analysis. Inhabited areas are shown in color.

graphic succession, but modern buildings on or around the site. For such sites, the approach has to be a longer-term one, taking every opportunity provided by the clearing of a site for new construction, and building up a pattern of finds that eventually take on a coherent shape. This has been very much the story of urban archaeology in Britain and Europe, where the remains of Roman and medieval towns are generally buried beneath modern ones. In a way, this is a kind of sampling, but one where the location from which the sample is taken is not the choice of the research worker but is determined by availability. The work of the Winchester Research Unit in southern England between 1961 and 1971 is a good example. By excavating beside the cathedral, it was possible to trace the history of older structures. Evidence from previous archaeological work, together with the more recent excavations, have provided a good impression of the Roman, Saxon, and medieval towns underlying the present city of Winchester. Another good example is the city of York, discussed in detail in Chapter 13, and the issue of salvage or rescue archaeology in cities and elsewhere threatened with destruction is discussed in Chapter 14.

Administration beyond the Primary Center

Investigation of the mechanisms of organization need not be restricted to the primary, capital center. Outside the main center there may be many clues indicating a centrally organized administration. It is useful, for example, to search for *artifacts of administration*. Perhaps the most obvious of these are the clay sealings found at secondary centers where the redistributive system is administered. Equally useful are other imprints of central authority, such as the imperial seal in any empire, or royal emblems such as the cartouche (the royal name in a distinctive cigar-shaped frame) of an Egyptian pharaoh, or the display of a royal coat of arms. Nor need the existence of a central jurisdiction be indicated by only the actual emblems of power: a Roman milestone on a road, for instance, carries with it the message that it is part of a centrally administered system of imperial highways.

A second approach is to look at *standardization of weights and measures* (see Measuring the World, pp. 399–401). Such standardization is found within most centrally administered economic systems. In many cases, the standard units came to be utilized outside the boundaries of the particular state as well.

The existence of a good *road system* is important to the administration of any land-based empire, although less significant for the smaller nation states that could be crossed by an army on foot in the course of a couple

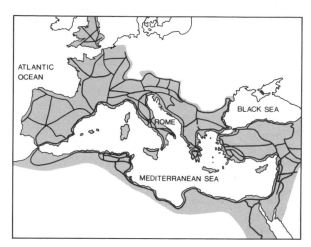

Administration beyond the primary center: the elaborate road network of the Roman empire (shown here in about AD 150) gives a clear indication of central administration.

of days. The road system within the Roman empire gives one of the clearest indications of central administration, and would do so even if written records were unavailable. The Inca road network indicates central organization of a society without such records.

Clear indications of the exercise of military power can give the most direct insight possible into the realities of administration: control of territory often depended heavily on military might. Defensive works on a major scale offer similar insights and mark decisive boundaries. The Great Wall of China, begun in the late 3rd century BC, is perhaps the best-known example.

Investigating Social Ranking

The essence of a centralized society and of centralized government is a disparity between rich and poor in ownership, access to resources, facilities, and status. The study of social organization in complex societies is thus in large measure the study of social ranking.

Elite Residences. Residential structures can indicate marked differences in status. Large and grandiose buildings, or "palaces," are a feature of many complex societies, and may have housed members of the social elite. The difficulty comes in demonstrating that they actually did so. Among the Maya, for example, recent research has shown that the term "palace" is too general, covering a variety of structures that had different functions. Perhaps the best solution is to combine detailed study of the structure itself (architecture, location of different artifacts) with ethnoarchaeological or ethnohistoric research. David Freidel and Jeremy Sabloff did this successfully in their analysis of the island of Cozumel, off the east coast of Mexico's Yucatán peninsula. Using 16th-century Spanish descriptions of elite residences, they were able to identify architecturally similar structures in the pre-Columbian archaeological record dating to a couple of centuries earlier. Test excavations helped clarify the functions of the buildings.

Great Wealth. The very existence of great wealth, if it can be inferred to have been associated with particular individuals, is a clear indication of high status. For instance, the treasures of the Second City at Troy, unearthed (or so he claimed) by Heinrich Schliemann in 1873, must indicate considerable disparity in the ownership of wealth. The treasure included gold and silver jewelry as well as drinking vessels, and there can be little doubt that it was intended for personal use, perhaps on public occasions.

Depictions of the Elite. Perhaps even more impressive than wealth, however, are actual depictions of persons of high status, whether in sculpture, in relief, in mural decoration, or whatever. The iconography of power is further discussed in Chapter 10, but in many ways this is our most immediate approach to social questions. Although such depictions are not often found, it is not uncommon to find symbolic emblems of authority such as Egyptian cartouches, to which may be added artifacts such as royal scepters or swords.

Burials. Undoubtedly, the most abundant evidence of social ranking in centralized societies, just as in non-centralized ones, comes from burial, and from the accompanying grave-goods. As discussed in the section on segmentary societies, a profitable approach is to consider the labor input involved in constructing the burial monuments, and the social implications. The largest and most famous such monuments in the world are the pyramids of Egypt, over 80 of which still exist. At the most straightforward level of analysis they represent the conspicuous display of wealth and power of the highest ranking members of Egyptian society: the pharaohs. But fascinating new research by, amongst others, the British archaeologist Barry Kemp and the American archaeologist Mark Lehner, is beginning to shed further light on the social and political implications of this colossal expenditure of effort – which involved in the case of the Great Pyramid at Giza the shifting of some 2.3 million limestone blocks, each weighing 2.5–15 tons, during the 23-year reign (2589–2566 BC) of pharaoh Cheops (Khufu). As the

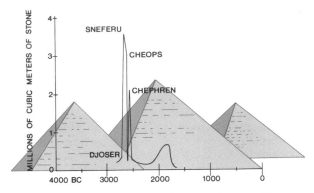

The colossal building effort required to erect the pyramids reflects the centralization of power in the hands of pharaohs such as Djoser, Sneferu, Cheops, and Chephren.

accompanying diagram shows, there was a brief period of the most immense pyramid building activity in Egypt, dwarfing what had gone before and what followed. The peak period of this activity indicates the harnessing of huge resources by a highly centralized state. But what happened afterwards? Kemp has argued that the reduction in pyramid building coincides interestingly with a transfer of social and economic resources to the provinces, away from the main area of the pyramids.

The pyramids and other burial monuments are not the only source of information about social organization and ranking in ancient Egypt. Magnificent grave-goods have often been recovered, most spectacularly those belonging to the boy pharaoh Tutankhamun (box, pp. 62–63). Nor of course were the ancient Egyptians alone in building monuments for their dead rulers and burying the richest artifacts with them. In the New World one thinks, for instance, of the Temple of the Inscriptions at Palenque, which held deep within it the tomb of the Maya city's ruler, Lord Pacal, who died in AD 683 and was buried with his superb jade mosaic mask. Major excavations at Copán, Honduras, likewise revealed a splendid Maya noble's tomb beneath the famous Hieroglyphic Stairway there.

In many early civilizations the ultimate power and rank of the dead ruler were emphasized by the ritual killing of royal retainers, who were interred with the monarch. Such funeral rites have been brought to light in the Sumerian Royal Graves at Ur, in modern Iraq, and among the burials of the Shang dynasty at Anyang in China. The huge army of terracotta warriors buried next to the tomb of the first Chinese emperor, Qin Shi Huangdi, represents a development of this practice, where the life-size terracotta figures take the place of members of the real imperial army.

There are many examples too of elite burials among smaller-scale state societies and chiefdoms. One of the most skillfully conducted excavations in western Germany in recent years has been that of a Celtic chieftain's grave at Hochdorf, dating to the 6th century BC, where Jorg Biel painstakingly recovered the collapsed remains of a wagon, drinking vessels, and many other grave-goods, including the wheeled bronze couch on which the dead chief lay, covered with gold jewelry from head to foot. The Shaft Graves at Mycenae in Greece and the Anglo-Saxon ship burial at Sutton Hoo in England represent similar discoveries by earlier generations of archaeologists.

However, all these remarkable burials are of individuals uniquely powerful in their societies. To obtain a more comprehensive picture of a ranked society it is necessary to consider the burial customs of the society as a whole. In many cases, it has proved possible to discover something about the elites that existed at a level below that of the ruler. Research carried out over many years at Moundville, Alabama, is a good example (see box overleaf).

There is undoubtedly more scope for useful investigations of social structure through cemetery analysis in ranked societies. Up to now, most sophisticated cemetery studies have been devoted to less centralized societies, as reviewed in a previous section. Cemetery data of the early historic period in the Old World have conventionally been studied with a view to illustrating the existing historical texts, or refining typological schemes as an aid to chronology and the study of art history. Only now is the focus shifting toward studies of disparities in social status (see pp. 216–17).

Investigating Economic Specialization

Centralized societies differ from non-centralized ones in a number of important respects. In general, the more centralized structure allows greater economic specialization, and this in turn brings increased efficiency of production. Centralization is often associated with an increased intensification of farming, for not only do centralized societies normally have higher population densities, but they must also produce enough surplus to support full-time (as opposed to part-time) craft specialists. The greater degree of craft specialization is made possible only by the organizing abilities of a more centralized society, which is able to manage and promote an increase in agricultural productivity.

Intensified Farming. The initial development of new farming methods for more intensive food production was discussed above in the section concerned with segmentary societies. In centralized societies the process is taken a stage further, with a still greater emphasis on labor-intensive techniques such as plowing. In addition, major public works such as irrigation canals are often undertaken for the first time, made possible by the coercive, organizing powers of a central authority. Another indicator of growing intensification may be the reorganization of the rural landscape into smaller units, as the population increases and the amount of land available for each farmstead thereby diminishes.

Taxation, Storage, and Redistribution. An important indicator of centralized control of a society is the existence of permanent storage facilities for food and goods, which the central authority will draw on periodically to feed, reward, and thus indirectly control its warriors and the local population. It follows that taxes, for instance in the form of produce to replenish state storehouses, will also be found among centralized societies: without them the controlling authority would have no wealth to redistribute. In chiefdom societies "taxation" may take the form of offerings to the chief, but in more complex societies the obligation is generally formalized. Much of a state's bureaucracy will be devoted to the administration of taxation, and direct indications of bureaucracy, such as recording and accounting systems, in general document it.

Cutaway view of the Temple of the Inscriptions, Palenque, Mexico, showing at the base the hidden burial chamber of Lord Pacal, ruler of this Maya city who died in AD 683, as we know from inscriptions at the site.

SOCIAL ANALYSIS AT MOUNDVILLE

UNITED STATES
Moundville

During its heyday in the 14th and 15th centuries AD, Moundville was one of the greatest ceremonial centers of the Mississippian culture in North America. The site takes its name from an impressive group of 20 mounds constructed within a palisaded area, 150 ha (370 acres) in extent, on the banks of the Black Warrior river in west-central Alabama. Moundville was first dug into as long ago as 1840, but major excavations did not take place until this century, in particular by C.B. Moore in 1905 and 1906, and D.L. DeJarnette in the 1930s. More recently Christopher Peebles and his colleagues have combined systematic survey with limited excavation and reanalysis of the earlier work to produce a convincing social study of the site.

Changing settlement patterns in the Moundville region. In Phase I (AD 1050–1250) Moundville was simply a site with a single mound, like other similar sites in the area. By Phase II, however, it had grown larger, establishing itself as the major regional center. After its heyday in Phase III, Moundville disappeared as a significant site in Phase IV (after 1550), when the region no longer had a dominant center.

Peebles and his team first needed a reliable chronology. This was achieved through an analysis of the pottery by Vincas Steponaitis, using in the first instance a seriation study (see Chapter 4) of whole vessels from a sample of burials at the site. The resultant relative

Slate palette from Moundville incised with a hand-and-eye motif within two entwined horned rattlesnakes. Diameter 32 cm.

chronology was then cross-checked with excavated ceramics from known stratigraphic contexts, whose radiocarbon dating helped convert the scheme into an absolute chronology.

Using this framework, it was now possible to study the development of the site through several phases. Preliminary survey of neighboring sites also established the regional settlement pattern for each phase.

Over 3000 burials have been excavated at Moundville, and Peebles used the technique of cluster analysis (see box, p. 197) to group 2053 of them according to social rank. Peebles observed that the small number of people of highest rank (Segment A: classes IA, IB, and II in the pyramidal diagram) were buried in or near the mounds with artifacts exclusive to them, such as copper axes and earspools. Lower-ranking individuals of Segment B (Classes III, IV) had non-mound burials with some grave-goods but no copper artifacts, while those of Segment C, buried on the periphery, had few or no grave-goods.

Peebles found interesting differences according to age and sex. The 7 individuals in Class IA, the top of the social pyramid, were all adults, probably males. Those of Class IB were adult males and children, while Class II comprised individuals of all ages and both sexes. It seems clear that adult males had the highest status. The presence of children in Class IB suggests that their high status was inherited at birth.

There is much more to say about the work at Moundville. But it should be clear from this summary how the various dimensions of information already examined come together to suggest a regional organization with a well-marked hierarchy of sites, controlled by a highly ranked community at Moundville itself – what Peebles terms a chiefdom society.

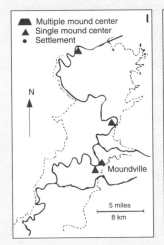

■ Multiple mound center
▲ Single mound center
• Settlement

I

N

5 miles
8 km

Moundville

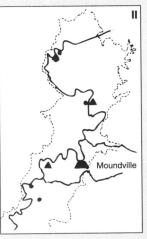

II

Moundville

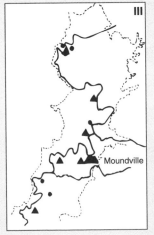

III

Moundville

IV

Moundville

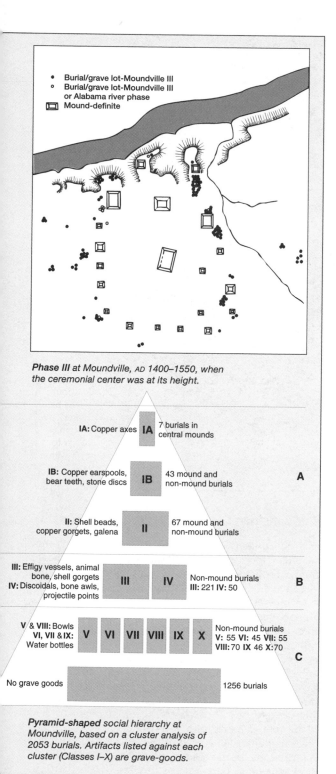

Phase III at Moundville, AD 1400–1550, when the ceremonial center was at its height.

IA: Copper axes — **IA** — 7 burials in central mounds

IB: Copper earspools, bear teeth, stone discs — **IB** — 43 mound and non-mound burials — **A**

II: Shell beads, copper gorgets, galena — **II** — 67 mound and non-mound burials

III: Effigy vessels, animal bone, shell gorgets
IV: Discoidals, bone awls, projectile points — **III IV** — Non-mound burials III: 221 IV: 50 — **B**

V & VIII: Bowls
VI, VII & IX: Water bottles — **V VI VII VIII IX X** — Non-mound burials V: 55 VI: 45 VII: 55 VIII: 70 IX: 46 X: 70 — **C**

No grave goods — 1256 burials

Pyramid-shaped social hierarchy at Moundville, based on a cluster analysis of 2053 burials. Artifacts listed against each cluster (Classes I–X) are grave-goods.

• Burial/grave lot-Moundville III
○ Burial/grave lot-Moundville III or Alabama river phase
▭ Mound-definite

A good example of a research project that has helped clarify this interaction of taxation, storage, and redistribution in one part of the world is the work of the American archaeologist, Craig Morris, at the city of Huánuco Pampa (see illus. p. 214), a provincial capital of the Inca empire high up in the Andes. This city, at one time inhabited by some 10,000–15,000 people, had been built from scratch by the Incas as an administrative center on the royal road to Cuzco, the imperial capital. We know from written accounts by early Spanish chroniclers that Inca rulers exacted taxation in the form of labor on state lands and state construction projects, including building Huánuco Pampa.

Many of the goods thus produced were stored in state warehouses – but to what purpose? Close analysis by Morris of a sample of some 20 percent of the more than 500 warehouses at Huánuco, as well as other structures there, suggested that stored potatoes and maize were used primarily to supply the city at this high altitude, where food production was difficult. But the city itself functioned to accommodate highly organized ceremonies in its huge central plaza, during which feasting and ritual maize-beer drinking took place, thus redistributing much of the stored wealth to the local populace.

As Morris states, this ceremonial aspect of administration seems to have been very important in early state societies. The sharing of food and drink reinforced the idea that participation in the empire was something more than working in state fields or fighting in a distant war.

Craft Specialists. The increased importance of craft specialists is another indicator of a centralized society that can be identified archaeologically. Full-time craft specialists leave well-defined traces, because each craft has its own particular technology and is generally practiced in a different location within the urban area.

Huánuco Pampa again provides a helpful example. Although craft production here was much less developed than in many early cities elsewhere in the world, Morris successfully identified a compound of 50 buildings given over to the making of beer and clothing. Thousands of special ceramic jars and dozens of spindle whorls and weaving implements provided the archaeological clues; the ethnohistoric record linked these with beer and cloth production, more particularly with a special social class of Inca women known as *aklla*, who were kept segregated from the rest of the population.

Morris was able to show from his study that the distinctive architecture of the compound – enclosed by a surrounding wall with a single entrance thus

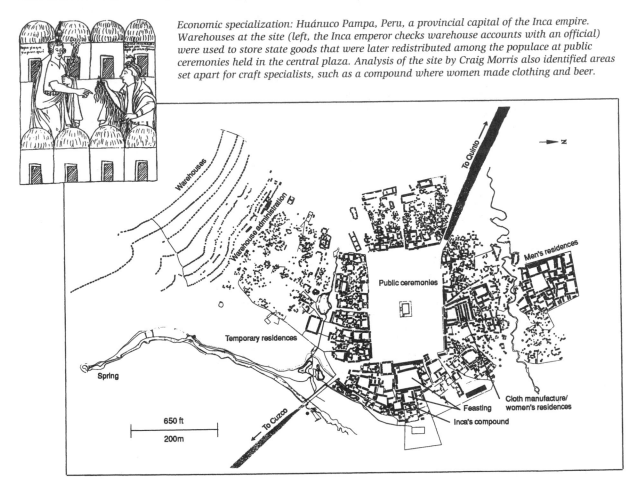

Economic specialization: Huánuco Pampa, Peru, a provincial capital of the Inca empire. Warehouses at the site (left, the Inca emperor checks warehouse accounts with an official) were used to store state goods that were later redistributed among the populace at public ceremonies held in the central plaza. Analysis of the site by Craig Morris also identified areas set apart for craft specialists, such as a compound where women made clothing and beer.

restricting access – and the density of occupational refuse suggested the presence of permanently segregated *aklla* craft specialists.

Detailed archaeological research of this kind is being carried out in many parts of the world, particularly into the specialized production of pottery, metal, glass, and lithic materials such as obsidian (all of which are discussed more fully in Chapter 8). The work of the Italian archaeologist, Maurizio Tosi, at the site of Shahr-i-Sokhta in modern Iran is a case in point, providing as it does an impression of the scale of craft specialization and its relationship to the central administration on the Iranian plateau during the 3rd millennium BC. By studying the evidence of craft production in different parts of the site, Tosi showed that some activities (notably textiles and leather-working) were restricted to residential areas, while others (such as stone tool, lapis lazuli and chalcedony working) were strongly represented in specialist workshop areas.

Relationships between Centralized Societies

External contacts between centralized societies cannot be understood simply in terms of the exchange of goods: they are also social relations. Traditionally, these have been examined, if at all, within the framework of dominance models, where the "influence" of a primary center on outlying secondary areas is considered, often in what has been called the "diffusion" of culture (see Chapter 12). Most interactions between societies, however, take place between neighbors of roughly equal scale and power. These interactions have been termed peer polities. They need to be more carefully considered than has so far been the case in archaeology: one or two broad headings can be listed.

The role of *warfare* in early societies needs further investigation. War need not be undertaken with the objective of permanently occupying the lands of the vanquished in a process of territorial expansion.

The American archaeologist David Freidel made this point in his study of Maya warfare, based on the wall paintings at the site of Bonampak and deductions from early written sources. According to his analysis, the function of Maya warfare was not to conquer new territory, and thus enlarge the frontiers of the state, but instead to give Maya rulers the opportunity of capturing kings and princes from neighboring states, many of whom were later offered as sacrifices to the gods. Warfare allowed rulers to reaffirm their royal status: it had a central role in upholding the system of government, but that role was not one of territorial expansion.

A recent study by Kent Flannery has emphasized the role of charismatic military leaders in the formation of state societies. There is evidence from the Southwest of the United States for endemic warfare, not least in the 11th and 12th centuries AD, and it has been suggested that this may have been accompanied by institutionalized cannibalism (see pp. 286–87).

Competition is a frequent undertaking between societies, sometimes within a ritual framework. The study of places where games were played, or of certain ceremonial areas, may reveal that many interactions between societies took a competitive form. Such seems to be the case for the ball courts of Mesoamerica and was certainly so for the great Panhellenic games of ancient Greece, of which the Olympic Games were the most famous.

One of the most frequent features accompanying competition is *emulation*, where the customs, buildings, and artifacts employed in one society come to adopt the form of those used in neighboring ones. This proves to be so in almost every area, but these issues of style and symbolic form have scarcely been handled yet by archaeologists. In so far as they involve the use of symbols, and hence a consideration of what people think as much as what they do, they are discussed further in Chapter 10.

THE ARCHAEOLOGY OF THE INDIVIDUAL AND OF IDENTITY

The discussion so far in this chapter has started with the concept of the society and its organization. This is a deliberate feature of the structure of this book, where before questions are asked about the variety of human experience it is necessary first to form some view about the scale of society and its complexity – a holistic view. But at the same time this might be criticized as a "top-down" approach, where one begins with questions of organization and of hierarchy, of power and of centralization, and only then turns to the individual who actually lives in society, to that person's role, gender, and status and to what it was really *like* to live there at that time and in that social context.

It would be equally valid to start with the individual and with social relationships, including kinship relations, and to work outward from there: what one might term a "bottom-up" approach. This might involve the consideration of networks of social relationships, and indeed this approach has been developed by Clive Gamble in his work on the Paleolithic period. Gamble contrasts two differing anthropological views of culture: the cognitivist approach, involving mental representations of social structures, and the phenomenological approach, which stresses the active engagement of people with their environment. The latter in particular can be seen to operate at the level of the individual. "The rhythms and gestures of the body during performance of social life, the habitual actions of living, mean that social memory is passed on in non-textual, non-linguistic ways." These experiences are

undergone through individual, inter-personal contacts which are effected through the development of networks. "The elaboration of the extended network through symbolic resources led to the regional social landscape."

This would also be the tendency of many social anthropologists and sociologists, and indeed of economists interested in personal transactions at the micro-economic level. In Chapter 10, "What Did They Think?," this is the outlook from the outset, beginning with a consideration of the cognitive map of the individual, adopting the philosophical standpoint which is there identified as "methodological individualism."

In some ways this approach has initial resemblances with that adopted by interpretive archaeologists of the postprocessual school, although the philosophical background is a different one. They emphasize, following in part the work of the French sociologist Pierre Bourdieu, that social concepts, such as the categories which we habitually use when speaking of age or gender or class, are constructs of our own society and ultimately of ourselves. This point is exemplified below in relation to gender, where the seemingly obvious point is made that biological sex as an objective category is to be distinguished from the social roles which we ascribe to men, to women, to warriors, to midwives etc. which are indeed sex-related but are in fact constructs which are very differently conceived when we compare one specific society with another.

Archaeologists such as Julian Thomas and Roberta Gilchrist have applied Bourdieu's concept of *habitus* (which we might define as socially constituted structuring principles or dispositions operating within each individual) – a rather abstract notion, but still a useful one – to the archaeology and material culture of the Neolithic (early farming period) and the medieval world. A remarkable thing about the archaeological record, with its long time trajectories, is that it allows us to trace the emergence and development in the world of entirely new concepts – e.g. of value and wealth (as discussed in relation to prehistoric Varna in Chapter 10, pp. 404–05), of ownership, of kingship, and indeed many of those by which we organize our very thinking. Bourdieu (1977, 15) speaks of:

a permanent disposition, embedded in the agents' very bodies in the form of mental dispositions, schemes of perception and thought...such as those which divide up the world in accordance with the oppositions between the male and the female, east and west, future and past...etc. and also, at a deeper level, in the form of bodily postures and stances ...ways of standing, sitting, looking, speaking or walking

These things, although they may at first seem to us as natural "givens" are culturally specific: they are developed and adopted by humans in society. One may thus regard *habitus* as an informing ideology that is communicated and reproduced through a process of socialization or enculturation in which material culture plays an active role. Thomas and other archaeologists of the "Neo-Wessex" school have emphasized that conventions and rituals, such as those practiced at the Neolithic monuments of Wessex in the 3rd millennium BC, will have helped to shape the world view, the dispositions, indeed the *habitus* of the early farmers, just as the environment of the medieval nunneries, material as well as spiritual, discussed by Gilchrist, will have shaped the *habitus* of the community of nuns. The buildings in which one lives and their customary use affect the patterns of daily life of the individual, and the individual's experience and expectation of what is normal and commonplace. At a different level, the frequent experience of ritual practice, to the extent that it becomes normal and natural, governs the expectations and assumptions of everyday life. These ideas lead us to see at how deep a level social categories and roles are indeed the constructs of the very societies which use them.

These concepts are not to be taken for granted: indeed the techniques of archaeology allow us to see when such constructs are first given material form (as in the differentiation in dress of ornament of men and women in the European Bronze Age, or the earliest emblems of prestige displayed by an individual whom we might identify as a chief).

There are many dimensions or vectors of identity. As noted below, gender has been the most extensively discussed in recent years. But age and age grades are not unproblematic, and have recently been the subject of attention. The problems of recognizing prestige and high status have been discussed earlier along with the concept of ranking (which belongs as much in a "top-down" discussion as in one taken from the "bottom up"). In recent years ethnicity has come to the fore again (see box p. 189), not least for the misuse of archaeology by political groups for contemporary political ends (see Chapter 14, "Whose Past?").

The theme of the archaeology of social inequality has perhaps not been very comprehensively addressed yet, but in the field of historical archaeology there have been systematic studies of the material culture of some underprivileged groups, including some interesting studies of town areas known from documentary accounts to be considered poor. The infamous Five Points slum area of lower Manhattan, described by early 19th-century writers including Charles Dickens, has been investigated through rescue excavations at the site of a new federal courthouse at Foley Square which give some graphic insights. For instance, the excavated area included the site of a cellar brothel at 12 Baxter Street, historically documented (in the 1843 indictment of its keeper) as a "disorderly house – a nest for prostitutes and others of ill fame and name, where great numbers of characters are in the nightly practice of revelling until late and improper hours of the night." The excavations give further insights based upon the material culture:

The quality of the household goods found in the privy behind 12 Baxter far exceeded that of goods found anywhere else on the block. The prostitutes lived well, at least when they were at work. One attraction was the opportunity to live in a style that seamstresses, laundresses, and maids could not afford. Afternoon tea at the brothel was served on a set of Chinese porcelain that included matching teacups and coffee cups, saucers and plates, a slop bowl and a tea caddie. Meals consisted of steak, veal, ham, soft-shell clams and many kinds of fish. There was a greater variety of artifacts from the brothel than from other excavated areas of the courthouse block.... Other personal items suggested the occupational hazards of prostitution. Two glass urinals,

A view of the rescue excavation of the 19th-century slum area of Five Points in lower Manhattan, New York. The cellar of a brothel was investigated and yielded much information concerning the daily lives of inhabitants. While of a low social rank, the prostitutes at least enjoyed the use of a set of Chinese porcelain (inset) for afternoon tea.

designed especially for women, were probably used when venereal disease confined a prostitute to bed. (Yamin 1997, 51)

Not far from Foley Square another excavation, that of the African Burial Ground, formerly known as the Negros Burial Ground, recorded on a plan of 1755, has proved highly informative and has had wide repercussions. The rescue excavation of 420 skeletons there in 1991 provoked outrage in the African-American community of today, which felt it had not been adequately consulted, and ultimately led to the establishment of a Museum of African and African-American History in New York City. There were no grave markers, and other than wood, coffin nails, and shroud pins, few artifacts were found. The large size of the sample will allow study of nutrition and pathology. Certainly the controversy and the excavation have proved a stimulus toward the development of African-American archaeology, already well-defined through the investigation of plantation sites.

A Yoruba priestess and a Khamite priest perform a libation ceremony for the ancestors over the grave of a person buried in the 17th-century African Burial Ground in lower Manhattan, New York.

INVESTIGATING GENDER

An important aspect of the study of social archaeology, which falls within the scope of the archaeology of identity, is the archaeological investigation of gender. Initially this was felt to overlap with feminist archaeology, which often had the explicit objective of exposing and correcting the androcentrism (male bias) of archaeology (pp. 46–47). There is no doubt that in the modern world the role of women professionals, including archaeologists, has often been a difficult one. For instance, Dorothy Garrod, the first woman professor of archaeology in Britain (see p. 32), was appointed to a Chair in 1937, at a time when female undergraduates in her university (Cambridge) were not allowed to take a degree at the end of their course, as male undergraduates did, but only a diploma. There was – and still is – an imbalance to be rectified in the academic world, and that was one of the early objectives of feminist archaeology. A second was to illuminate the roles of women in the past more clearly, where often they had been overlooked, and to rectify the male bias in so much archaeological writing.

These were sound objectives, but they did not sufficiently define the problems – the early approach has been criticized by later archaeologists of gender as being little more than: "Add women and stir." But the study of gender is much more than simply the study of women. An important central idea soon became the distinction between sex and gender. It was argued that sex – female or male – may be regarded as biologically determined and can be established archaeologically from skeletal remains (Chapter 11). But gender – at its simplest woman or man – is a social construct, involving the sex-related roles of individuals in society. Gender roles in different societies vary greatly both from place to place and through time. Systems of kinship, of marriage (including polygamy, polyandry), inheritance, and the division of labor are all related to biological sex but not determined by it (see box overleaf). These perspectives permitted a good deal of profitable work in the second phase of gender studies in archaeology, but they have now in their turn been criticized by a new "third wave" feminism, as "essentialist," as emphasizing supposedly "inherent" differences between women and men, and emphasizing women's links to the natural world through reproduction.

The work of Marija Gimbutas on the prehistory of southeast Europe is now criticized by more recent workers in the field of gender archaeology as falling into this "essentialist" tendency. In her pioneering work she argued that the predominantly female figu-

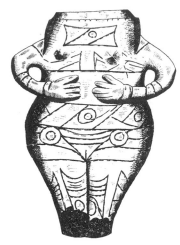

An image symbolizing female power? Neolithic anthropomorphic female vase, from Vidra, Romania.

rines seen in the Neolithic and Copper Age of southeast Europe and in Anatolia demonstrate the important status of women at that time. She had a vision of an Old Europe influenced by feminine values which was to disappear with the succeeding Bronze Age with the dominance of a warlike male hierarchy, supposedly introduced by Indo-European warrior nomads from the east. Such thinking continues to dominate Indo-European studies, where the proposal that proto-Indo-European speech might have been introduced into Europe in Neolithic times (see box p. 467) has been criticized on the grounds that Indo-European society was male-dominated and warlike in character while the iconographic representations from the Neolithic period are claimed as predominantly female.

Marija Gimbutas became something of a cult figure in her own right, and her support for the concept of a great Mother Goddess representing a fertility principle has been embraced by modern "ecofeminist" and New Age enthusiasts. The current excavations at the early Neolithic site of Çatalhöyük in Turkey, where female figurines of baked clay have indeed been found (see box, pp. 44–45), are now visited regularly by devotees of the Goddess whose views are respectfully entertained by the excavators, even though they do not share them. But there are sceptical voices. Ian Hodder has argued instead that "the elaborate female symbolism in the earlier Neolithic expressed the objectification and subordination of women…. Perhaps women rather than men were shown as objects because they, unlike men, had become objects of ownership and male desires." Peter Ucko's careful study of comparable material from the Aegean showed, moreover, that many of these figurines lacked features diagnostic of sex or gender. And Lynn Meskell, in an avowedly feminist critique, has written of "pseudo-feminism" in relation to the Mother Goddess metanarrative, seeing the work of Gimbutas as:

> steeped within the "establishment" epistemological framework of polar opposites, rigid gender roles, barbarian invaders and culture stages which are now regarded as outmoded. It is unfortunate that many archaeologists interested in gender are drawn to historical fiction and emotional narratives. ... At this juncture sound feminist scholarship needs to be divorced from methodological shortcomings, reverse sexism, conflated data and pure fantasy ... (Meskell 1995, 83).

The third phase in the development of gender archaeology, in tune with the "third wave" of feminists of the 1980s, takes a different view of gender in two senses. First, in the narrower sense, and "led by women of colour, lesbian feminists, queer theorists and postcolonial feminists," it recognizes that the field of gender and gender difference is more complex than a simple polarity between male and female, and that other axes of difference have to be recognized. Indeed the very recognition of a simple structural opposition between male and female is itself, even in our own society, an over-simple representation of the way these matters are conceptualized. In many societies children are not regarded as socially male or female until they reach the age of puberty – in the modern Greek language, for instance, while men and women are grammatically male and female in gender, the words for children generally belong to the third, neuter gender.

This leads on to the second point, that gender is part of a broader social framework, part of the social process – in Margaret Conkey's words "a way in which social categories, roles, ideologies and practices are defined and played out." While gender is, in any society, a system of classification, it is part of a larger system which operates simultaneously along a number of vectors of social difference, including age, wealth, religion, ethnicity and so forth. Moreover these are not static constructs but fluid and flexible, constructed and re-constructed in the practice, indeed the *praxis*, of daily life. These experiences come to shape the *habitus* of the individual in relation to that person's own sexuality and gender role, and to their perceptions of the gender roles of others.

The complexities in analyzing burial data with respect to gender are indicated by the study by Bettina Arnold of the so-called "Princess of Vix" burial from east-central France. The grave contained skeletal remains which analysis indicated were female, but the grave-goods consisted of various prestige items normally thought to be indicative of males. This exceptionally rich 5th-century BC burial was initially interpreted as a transvestite priest because it was deemed inconceivable that a woman could be honored in such a way. Arnold's careful reanalysis of the grave-goods supported the interpretation of the burial as an elite female. This may lead to a fresh assessment of the potentially powerful, occasionally paramount role that women played in Iron Age Europe. But this work may yet lead on to a wider consideration of gender distinctions in the Iron Age in a context which may reassess whether in individuals of very high status the traditional bipolar concept of gender is appropriate.

The process of "the construction of gender through appearance" is one which Marie Louise Stig Sørensen has considered in relation to the burials of the Danish Bronze Age. She argues persuasively that in the changing nature of the grave-goods through time we are seeing not simply the reflection of changing gender roles in society, but are obtaining rather some insight into how these roles themselves were constituted or constructed by the changing appearance (in terms of form of dress, of the materials used for clothing, of personal ornaments, and of the use of these together to give a specific ensemble) of the individuals whose roles were defined thereby. Her work involves the gender roles of men as well as of women, and reminds us that a masculinist approach may exist alongside a feminist approach to gender archaeology. Indeed Paul Treherne's study "The warrior's beauty: the masculine body and self-identity in Bronze Age Europe" could be regarded as a "masculinist" study not because his purpose is to exclude the feminine but because he sets out to trace the role of the warrior and the male ideal both during the European Bronze Age and in later representations of that Bronze Age.

The objective of placing gender analysis in archaeology within the wider context of the various dimensions of social life, including age and status, although extolled in programmatic papers in a number of edited volumes devoted to the archaeology of gender, cannot yet be exemplified in many case studies. One such, however, is the analysis by Lynn Meskell of social relations (including gender relations) within the Egyptian workmen's village of Deir el-Medina, built around 1500 BC to facilitate the work of constructing the pharaonic tombs in the Valley of the Kings and in use

GENDER RELATIONS IN EARLY INTERMEDIATE PERIOD PERU

A good example of the appraisal of archaeological evidence within the framework of a study of gender roles is provided by Joan Gero's analysis of Queyash Alto in the highlands of Peru during the Early Intermediate Period (EIP – c. 200 BC–AD 600).

The site of Queyash Alto is located on a narrow terraced ridge and consists of an alignment of rooms and open courtyards. Gero's excavations identified three functionally distinct areas, one domestic and two non-domestic. An upper terrace contained structures and superimposed house floors with evidence for **domestic occupation**, probably high status to judge from the presence of decorated ceramics, imported spondylus (spiny oyster) shells, figurines and copper tupu pins. These pins were used as clothes fasteners exclusively by women in the Andes in Inca times and more recently. Since copper first came into use for making artifacts in the EIP, access to such prestige items is taken to indicate the owners' high status.

Further evidence for the presence of women in this part of the site was suggested by the frequency of spindle whorls. While spinning is not necessarily a female occupation, there is a long record of women being the primary spinners in this region. Only women were buried beneath the lowermost house floors, possibly as progenitors or founding mothers of a matriline.

In contrast to the residential terrace, material from the ridge top suggested **non-domestic activities**, including an area for production and storage of beer and an open courtyard that appears to have been a site for ritual feasts. Abundant remains of serving and drinking vessels were found here, as well as ladles and spoons. Stone tools associated with meat preparation and a profusion of panpipes complete the picture of communal consumption. More copper tupu pins and spindle whorls were also found here, indicating that high-status women were involved in the feasting.

The formal architectural layout of the site, with restrictions on access and movement, indicated that the feasts were more than simply community gatherings to celebrate or appeal for good harvests. Gero suggested rather that they were taking place against a background of an EIP competitive political context which witnessed the emergence of a more ranked society and the consolidation of power in the hands of fewer individuals, perhaps heads of lineages.

It was this appearance of new hierarchical power relations that underpinned the need for feasts at Queyash Alto. A kin group could thus demonstrate that it had sufficient economic resources and status to summon other lineages, to impress them and perhaps repay their labor, and create more obligations. High-status women were participating in these political feasts – probably both as guests and as members of the groups providing the feasts.

To try to illuminate the nature of the women's participation in the feasting, Gero also looked at evidence in the iconography of the EIP Recuay-style pottery associated with the same valley. **Effigy vessels** include models of both women and men, whose clothes and ornaments, although clearly differentiated by gender, are of equal elaboration and prestige. Also, males and females are represented singly, rather than in pairs, except in scenes of ritual copulation, suggesting that the EIP women held rights and authority in

Two of the five copper tupu pins recovered from Queyash Alto (above). The same type of object was still in use in this region for fastening Inca garments (opposite, top right) and into more recent times (left).

High-ranking Inca women wearing tupu pins to fasten their garments (right).

A Recuay effigy vessel (left) showing a prestigious female, apparently also wearing tupu pins.

Queyash Alto: site plan showing the excavated evidence for the functionally distinct areas.

their own right, neither deriving status from, nor sharing power with, a "husband."

The iconography of these vessels allows the identification of separate areas of activity, and perhaps of control or power, for the Recuay men and women. Men are shown with llamas and other animals, weapons, and musical instruments, women with infants held in outstretched arms, or holding ritual items like shells, cups, and mirrors, or standing guard on roofs. From this Gero has argued that it is irrelevant to try to determine whether men's or women's status was "higher," because evidently both men and women participated in a "mosaic" of power.

Both the feasting practices at Queyash Alto and the elaborate Recuay ceramic tradition coincide with an intensification of hierarchical power relations in the north-central highlands of Peru during the EIP. The two strands of evidence can be seen as reiterating themes of power and ritual, inseparably linked with a complex gender system. There seems little doubt also that the intensification of hierarchy required changes in the gender ideology and the high status that women enjoyed at that time.

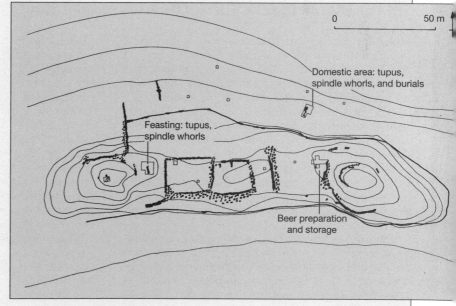

0   50 m

Domestic area: tupus, spindle whorls, and burials

Feasting: tupus, spindle whorls

Beer preparation and storage

for about four centuries. Preservation is excellent, and since this was a literate society there are text-based insights. The village was very much a design-build enterprise with stereotyped house plans, and this regularity aided the analysis of room function, as did a wealth of finds and installations. The first room from the street could be identified as "notionally female-oriented, centered round elite, married, sexually potent, fertile females of the household," while the second room or divan room appeared to be "even more ritually inclined, focusing on the sphere of elite, high-status males" of the household. Meskell was able to give detailed consideration to the use of space in these dwellings, in relation to food processing and other activities, and text references to servants encouraged consideration of differing statuses, even within a village which was, from the standpoint of the pharaoh and his officers, entirely composed of persons of relatively low status. The existence of well-preserved burials, some of them named in inscriptions, gave a further dimension to the analysis, permitting detailed consideration of the life and work of individual craftsmen and their partners.

A house in the village of Deir el-Medina, Egypt, where the workmen who built the tombs of the pharaohs in the Valley of the Kings lived. Lynn Meskell has shown that the plans of the houses followed standard, gender-oriented organization.

THE MOLECULAR GENETICS OF SOCIAL GROUPS AND LINEAGES

Molecular genetics has had an impact upon several branches of archaeology, as reviewed in Chapter 11 (pp. 455–59) and in relation to population dynamics and change in Chapter 12 (see box, pp. 468–69). There are possibilities for social archaeology also, although it is clear that the relationships established are essentially biological: the discussion is not about gender so much as about sex, to use the terminology discussed in the last section.

At present there are two lines of approach: the first to examine genetic relationships at the individual level, the second to examine the long-term genetic history of the wider social group – or "tribe" in cases where that term is applicable.

When the techniques for working with ancient DNA have progressed further, we can expect to see some notable advances in the social archaeology of burial, operating at the family level. A sample of ancient DNA taken from bone can readily be used to determine the sex of a burial, but the potential for studying family relationships goes much further. In the study of royal burials, for instance with the mummies of Egyptian pharaohs, it should be possible to establish whether mummy A is the mother of mummy B, on the basis of mitochondrial DNA (mtDNA), inherited solely from the mother (see p. 457) – although a reliable chronological framework will be needed since the determinations if positive would not exclude the reverse possibility that B is the mother of A. Comparable approaches to paternity, and relationships in general through the male line, are possible using Y-chromosome studies, although the adequate preservation of nuclear DNA may be more problematical than for mtDNA.

While there have so far been no sophisticated cemetery analyses of this kind, using ancient DNA to establish a whole pattern of family (i.e. genetic) relationships, the same logic has been used with Y-chromosome DNA samples from living individuals of the Jewish faith in order to reconstruct relationships of

A study of the DNA of a living population: Mark Thomas and David Goldstein examined the DNA of priests (Cohanim) of the Jewish faith, seen here praying at the Western Wall, Jerusalem. The requirement of the Jewish faith that the priesthood is inherited patrilineally means that the sample of Cohanim examined all shared a Y-chromosomal haplotype and thus enabled the researchers to trace an ancestral mutation dating back to c. 2650 years ago, possibly associated with the First Temple in Jerusalem.

considerable antiquity. Work was undertaken by Mark Thomas, David Goldstein, and their colleagues to investigate with the use of DNA the degree of observance over time of the requirement in the Jewish faith that priests (Cohanim) should follow strictly patrilineal inheritance (descent traced through the male line). Samples were therefore taken from 306 male Jews from Israel, Canada, and the United Kingdom. The Cohanim in the sample all shared a specific Y-chromosomal haplotype, indicative of common ancestry in the male line, and the time at which the Cohen chromosomes were derived from a common ancestral chromosome could be estimated at c. 2650 years ago, a date which the authors suggested might be associated with the historic destruction of the First Temple of Jerusalem in 586 BC and the dispersal of the priesthood. While the dating can hardly be precise enough to warrant a specific association of that kind, the example gives an insight into the potential of the approach.

Of wider application is the study of what may be termed "population-specific polymorphisms," where the DNA is analyzed of members of a social group, for instance a tribal group or an indigenous group defined on the basis of the language of its speakers. Work by Antonio Torroni and his colleagues on samples from group members defined in this way in Central America have found a very high within-group consistency. Since the samples in question were of mtDNA, they imply either a high degree of endogamy within the

group (marriage within the group) or a strict matrilocal residence pattern (marriage partners living with the wife's family).

In Europe it has been observed that, when the distribution within a population of a specific polymorphism is studied, the haplogroup studied in the mtDNA (i.e. in the female line) is in general less spatially localized in the population than are comparable polymorphisms in the Y-chromosome (i.e. in the male line). It is interesting to speculate why this should be. One suggestion has been that a stable and long-term patrilocal residence pattern would, over time, favor local genetic features, and hence spatial diversity, in the Y-chromosomes (and conversely, matrilocality might correlate with spatial diversity in the distribution of mtDNA haplotypes). An alternative explanation would be that, while the mean number of childbirths per male and per female of the population must obviously be approximately the same, the variance is likely to be greater for males, especially in ranked societies where high-ranking males may have preferential access to women.

The most comprehensive analysis of ancient DNA yet undertaken from a prehistoric cemetery comes from the Norris Farms cemetery in Illinois, in the Oneota cultural tradition and dating from c. AD 1300, where 260 skeletons were excavated. The cold, dry conditions favored DNA preservation and Anne Stone and Mark Stoneking were able to obtain mtDNA results from 70 percent of samples, and nuclear DNA (Y-chromosome) data from 15 percent of samples. In addition to undertaking sex identification by means of nuclear DNA, they used the data to reconsider the differing current views on the peopling of the Americas (see p. 456), preferring a "single wave" hypothesis with a date of expansion between 37,000 and 23,000

A study of the DNA of a past population: analysis of skeletons in an Oneota cemetery at Norris Farms, Illinois, has provided a large amount of data.

years ago. Detailed cemetery topography was not reported, but one can see that when excavations reveal what are considered by archaeologists to be "family clusters" of burials, the application of DNA analysis to investigate genetic relationships will be highly interesting and valuable.

SUMMARY

This chapter has shown that a formidable battery of techniques is now available to archaeologists who wish to investigate the social organization of early societies. Only the salient themes have been touched on, but these will have made it clear that the potential for understanding the more complex and highly organized societies represented by states and chiefdoms is especially great.

We can investigate these societies through their site hierarchies and, in the case of state societies, through their urban centers. It should in this way be possible to identify the ruling center using archaeological methods alone, and the extent of the area over which it held jurisdiction.

The study of the buildings and other evidence of administration at the center gives valuable information about the social, political, and economic organization of society, as well as a picture of the life of the ruling elite. We can identify and analyze their palaces and tombs, and the evidence left by craft specialists working under their direction. Road systems and lower-order administrative centers give further information about the social and political structure. The study of the differences in the treatment accorded to different individuals at death, in both the size and wealth of grave offerings, can reveal the complete range of status distinctions in a society. Gender studies are now adding new insight into the structure of society, and molecular genetics can also now be used to illuminate aspects of social archaeology.

As we have seen, similar approaches may be applied to segmentary societies: the study of individual settlements, the evidence for social ranking revealed by burials, and the existence of cooperative communal mechanisms for the construction of major monuments. The small-scale camps of mobile hunter-gatherer societies and the seasonal movement between different sites may also be studied using the methods outlined in this chapter, especially when the insights provided by ethnoarchaeological research on living societies are used in conjunction with direct study of the archaeological record.

We conclude the chapter by indicating the importance in recent studies of a "bottom-up" perspective in social archaeologies: the archaeology of individuals and of identity.

FURTHER READING

The following works illustrate some of the ways in which archaeologists attempt to reconstruct social organization:

Binford, L.R. 1983. *In Pursuit of the Past*. Thames & Hudson: London & New York.

Gero, J.M. & Conkey, M.W. (eds.). 1991. *Engendering Archaeology. Women and Prehistory*. Basil Blackwell: Oxford & Cambridge, MA.

Hodder, I. 1982. *Symbols in Action*. Cambridge University Press: Cambridge & New York.

Jones, S. 1997. *The Archaeology of Ethnicity. Constructing Identities in the Past and Present*. Routledge: London.

Mann, M. 1986. *The Sources of Social Power 1: A History of Power from the Beginning to AD 1760*. Cambridge University Press: Cambridge & New York.

Meskell, L. 1999. *Archaeologies of Social Life: Age, Sex, Class etc. in Ancient Egypt*. Blackwell: Oxford.

O'Shea, J. 1984. *Mortuary Variability. An Archaeological Investigation*. Academic Press: New York & London.

Renfrew, C. 1984. *Approaches to Social Archaeology*. Edinburgh University Press: Edinburgh.

Renfrew, C. & Cherry, J.F. (eds.). 1986. *Peer Polity Interaction and Sociopolitical Change*. Cambridge University Press: Cambridge & New York.

6 What Was the Environment?
Environmental Archaeology

Environmental archaeology is now a well-developed discipline in its own right. It views the human animal as part of the natural world, interacting with other species in the ecological system or *ecosystem*. The environment governs human life: latitude and altitude, landforms and climate determine the vegetation, which in turn determines animal life. And all these things taken together determine how and where humans have lived – or at least they did until very recently.

With a few exceptions, little attention was paid by archaeologists to non-artifactual (ecofactual) evidence until recent decades. Sites were studied more or less as self-contained packages of evidence, rather than in their context within their surrounding landscape. It is now regarded as important to see sites in their setting, and to consider the geomorphological and biological processes occurring in and around them. The environment is seen now as a variable, not as something which is constant or homogeneous through space and time.

The reconstruction of the environment first requires an answer to very coarse-grade questions of chronology and climate. We need to know when the human activities under study took place in terms of the broad world climatic succession. This then is partly a matter of chronology. A reliable date allows us, for instance, to determine whether the context belongs to a glacial or an interglacial phase, and what the temperature is likely to have been in that part of the globe. Sea-level and other questions will be related to this one.

Finer-grade questions will follow, and these are particularly relevant for all postglacial contexts, after about 10,000 years ago. The archaeologist usually turns then to the evidence of the vegetation at the time. Whether from pollen or from other plant remains, information is gained about the vegetation cover, which also contributes yet further useful data about the climate.

The logical next step is to turn to the fauna (animal remains), in the first place to the microfauna, including insects, snails, and rodents, all of which are very sensitive indicators of climatic change. Like some of the plant remains, they are indicators also of the microenvironment – of specific conditions at the site. Some of these conditions, of course, resulted from human activity when people erected structures and otherwise influenced the immediate surroundings to ensure survival and comfort.

Owing to the poor preservation of many forms of evidence, and to the distorted samples we recover, we can never arrive at the "true" facts for past environments. One simply has to aim for the best approximation available. No single method will give an adequate picture – all are distorted in one way or another – and so as many methods as data and funds will allow need to be applied to build up a composite image.

Despite these difficulties, the task of environmental reconstruction is a fundamental one. For if we are to understand how human individuals functioned, and the community of which they formed a part, we have to know first what their world was like.

INVESTIGATING ENVIRONMENTS ON A GLOBAL SCALE

The first step in assessing previous environmental conditions is to look at them globally. Local changes make little sense unless seen against this broader climatic background. Since water covers almost three-quarters of the earth, we should begin by examining evidence about past climates that can be obtained from this area.

In the last few decades, thanks to developments in technology and scientific analysis, it has become possible not only to excavate shipwrecks and submerged sites, but also to extract data from the sea bed that are of great value in reconstructing past environments, particularly for earlier periods.

Evidence from the Oceans

The sediments of the ocean floor accumulate very slowly (a few centimeters every thousand years) and in some areas consist primarily of an ooze made up of microfossils such as the shells of planktonic foraminifera – tiny one-celled marine organisms that live in the surface water masses of the oceans and sink to the bottom when they die. As in an archaeological stratigraphy, one can trace changes in environmental conditions through time by studying cores extracted from the sea bed and fluctuations in the species represented and the morphology (physical form) of single species through the sequence (see box opposite).

Thousands of deep-sea cores have now been extracted and studied, and have produced consistent results that form an invaluable complement to data obtained from land (see below). For example, one 21-m (69-ft) core from the Pacific Ocean has given a climatic record of over 2 million years. In the eastern Mediterranean, analysis by Robert Thunell of foraminifera in sediment samples has enabled him to estimate sea-surface temperatures and salinities (salt levels) at different periods. He has established that about 18,000 years ago, at the height of the last Ice Age, the winter temperature was 6°C (11°F) cooler than now, and the summer temperature was 4°C (7°F) cooler. The Aegean was also 5 percent less saline than at present, probably because cool, low-salinity water was being diverted into the Aegean from the large freshwater lakes that then existed over parts of eastern Europe and western Siberia.

Sea cores also provide climatic information through the analysis of organic molecules in the sediment. Some of these molecules, and especially the so-called fatty lipids, can remain relatively intact, yielding climatic clues because cells adjust the fatty composition of their lipids according to temperature changes. In cold conditions the proportion of unsaturated lipids in marine organisms increases, with a corresponding rise in saturated lipids in warm conditions. Cores of deep-sea sediment have shown variations in the ratio of saturated to unsaturated fatty lipids through time which, according to the British chemist Simon Brassell and his German colleagues, seem to correlate well with changes in ocean temperature over the last half million years known from the oxygen isotope technique (explained in the sea cores box, opposite).

Using a similar technique, cores can also be obtained from stratified ice sheets, and here again the oxygen isotopic composition gives some guide to climatic oscillations. Results from cores in Greenland and the Antarctic, and Andean and Tibetan glaciers are consistent with, and add detail to, those from deep-sea cores.

The Vostok ice-core in the Antarctic has reached a depth of (11,886 ft), and extends back to to 420,000 BP. Oxygen isotope data from GRIP (the Greenland Ice Core Project) and GISP2 (Greenland Ice Sheet Project 2) – two cores 28 km (17 miles) apart and about 3 km (1.9 miles) long, containing at least 200,000 annual growth layers – show that the last glaciation had several cold phases of between 500 and 200 years, all beginning abruptly, perhaps within a few decades, and ending gradually. At first it was thought that they were 12–13°C (21–24°F) colder than at present, but recent analysis of bubbles in ancient methane gas trapped in the ice (resulting from plant decomposition, which is sensitive to temperature and moisture variations) has revealed that the temperatures were twice as severe. A final swing back to glacial cold, in 12,900–11,600 BP (uncalibrated), was followed by a rapid, very abrupt warming – the temperature in Greenland rose by 7°C (13°F) in 50 years. There are some even more violent swings in the cores, when the temperature appears to have risen by up to 12°C (21°F) in only one or two years! The last 10,000 years have been stable apart from the Little Ice Age in the early Middle Ages. The results from the far north and south have been confirmed by the cores from the high Andes, as well as analyses of sediments and coral in other regions, which reveal how the tropics (with half the world's landmass and much of its population) reacted to worldwide climatic changes.

Ancient Winds. Isotopes can be used not merely for temperature studies but also for data on precipitation. And since it is the temperature differences between the equatorial and polar regions that largely determine the storminess of our weather, isotope studies can even tell us something about winds in different periods. As air moves from low latitudes to colder regions, the water it loses as rain or snow is enriched in the stable isotope oxygen 18 with respect to the remaining vapour which becomes correspondingly richer in the other stable isotope of oxygen, oxygen 16. Thus from the ratio between the two isotopes in precipitation at a particular place, one can calculate the temperature difference between that place and the equatorial region.

Using this technique, the changing ratios found over the last 100,000 years in ice cores from Greenland and the Antarctic have been studied. The results show that during glacial periods the temperature difference between equatorial and polar regions increased by 20–25 percent, and thus wind circulation must have been far more violent. Confirmation has come from a deep-sea core off the coast of West Africa, analysis of which led to estimates of wind strength over the last

The stratigraphy of sediment on the ocean floor is obtained from cores taken out of the sea bed. Ships use a "piston-corer" to extract a thin column of sediment, usually about 10–30 m (33–98 ft) in length. The core can then be analyzed in the laboratory.

Dates for the different layers in the core are obtained by radiocarbon, paleomagnetism, or the uranium-series method (Chapter 4). Changing environmental conditions in the past are then deduced by two kinds of

Microscopic fossils of the foraminiferan species Globorotalia truncatulinoides, *which coils to the left during cold periods and to the right during warm ones.*

tests on microscopic fossils of tiny one-celled organisms called foraminifera found in the sediment. First, scientists study the simple presence, absence, and fluctuations of different foraminiferan species. Second, they analyze, by mass spectrometer, fluctuations in the ratio of the stable oxygen isotopes 18 and 16 in the calcium carbonate of the foraminiferan shells. Variations discernible by these two tests reflect not simply changes in temperature, but also oscillations in the continental glaciers. For example, as the glaciers grew, water was drawn up into them, reducing sea levels and increasing the density and salinity of the oceans,

RECONSTRUCTING CLIMATES FROM SEA AND ICE CORES

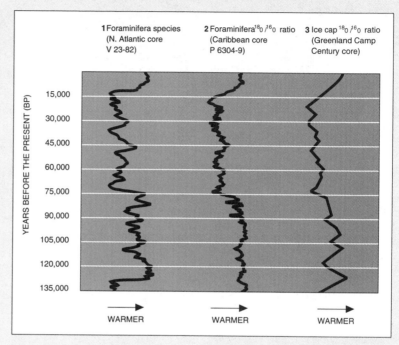

Three climate records compared. Left to right: proportions of different shell species in a deep-sea core; ratio of oxygen 18 to oxygen 16 in shells from a deep-sea core; and oxygen ratios from an ice core. The resemblance of the three records is good evidence that long-term climatic variation has been worldwide.

and thus causing changes in the depths at which certain foraminiferan species lived. At the same time the proportion of oxygen 18 in seawater increased. When the glaciers melted during periods of warmer climate, the proportion of oxygen 18 decreased.

A similar technique can be used to extract cores from present-day ice sheets in Greenland and Antarctica. Here, too, variations in oxygen isotopic composition at different depths of the cores provide some indication of past changes in climate. These results coincide well with those from the deep-sea cores.

700,000 years. Apparently wind "vigor" was greater by a factor of two during each glacial episode than at the present; and wind speeds were 50 percent greater during glacial than interglacial phases. In future, analysis of the minute plant debris in these cores may also add to the history of wind patterns.

Why should archaeologists be interested in ancient winds? The answer is that winds can have a great impact on human activity. For example, it is thought that increased storminess may have caused the Vikings to abandon their North Atlantic sea route at the onset

of a cold period. Similarly, some of the great Polynesian migrations in the southwestern Pacific during the 12th and 13th centuries AD seem to have coincided with the onset of a short period of slightly warmer weather, when violent storms would have been rare. These migrations were brought to an end a few centuries later by the Little Ice Age, which may have caused a sharp increase in the frequency of storms. Had the Polynesians been able to continue, they would probably have gone on from New Zealand to colonize Tasmania and Australia.

CLIMATIC CYCLES: EL NIÑO

It has long been known that the earth's climate moves in cycles, from the annual seasons to the long-term growth and decline of the great ice sheets. Some climatic cycles span several millennia, thus escaping notice in human lifetimes but nevertheless affecting human affairs. Data from the Greenland ice core GISP2 and from marine sediments have exposed a whole range of such cycles, from those of 40,000 and 23,000 years, caused by the tilting and wobbling of the earth's axis, down to cycles of 11,100, 6100, and 1450 years. The 1450-year cycle corresponds with tree-ring records and seems to coincide with abrupt shifts in climate. It may be related to variations in the strength of the sun, though this is uncertain.

The most famous rapid shifts in climate are the tropical Pacific warmings known as El Niño events, named after the Christ child because they occur near Christmastime. They are signalled by a weakening of the trade winds that normally drive warm surface water west from South America's Pacific coast and pull a current of cold water up from the ocean depths to replace it. This incursion of warm tropical waters causes the cold-water fish to decline or head south, thus affecting resource abundance and distribution – tropical species of fish, crustaceans, and some molluscs invade the Peruvian coast for the duration of the event; the Western Pacific and the Andes undergo drought, while coastal Ecuador and Peru are inundated with rain. The monsoon fails in India, droughts occur in Australia and Africa, and storms hit the coasts of California and Mexico.

El Niño events (known as ENSO, or El Niño/Southern Oscillation) show that even a relatively subtle redistribution in sea surface temperature in the tropics can influence climate globally, and these seem to have occurred throughout history, affecting climate, ocean temperatures, and hence coastal species. Evidence has recently been obtained from geoarchaeology and faunal assemblages at sites on the west coast of tropical South America that the modern series of ENSO began with a major climatic change at about 5000 years ago, since sites dating back to 8000 BP contained predominantly warm-water species characteristic of stable, warm tropical water, whereas sites after 5000 BP included temperate species.

It is therefore thought that this onset of ENSO may have helped shape the emergence of civilizations around the Pacific, and notably on the South American coast, with the crop-nourishing rains sparking population increases, temple construction, and more complex societies.

Climate records were recently obtained from sediments at the bottom of Lake Pallcacocha, at an altitude of 4000 m (13,000 ft) in the Ecuadorian Andes. Light, organic-poor layers alternate with dark, organic-rich layers caused by the torrential rains associated with El Niño. The sediments confirm that ENSO was non-existent, or extremely weak, between about 12,000 and 5000 years ago: during the last 5000 years, the lake recorded extreme rains every 2 to 8 years, which is ENSO's current pattern, whereas the preceding seven millennia only had such rains every few decades, or even up to 75 years apart. However, climatic records for even earlier periods, obtained from western Pacific corals and sediments in the Great Lakes, again show ENSO operating much the same as today – hence this phenomenon clearly waxes and wanes over the millennia.

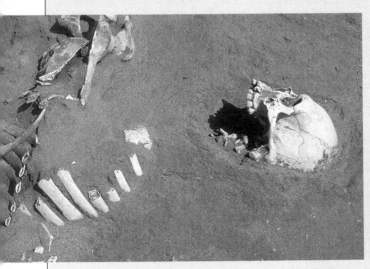

The skeletons of people sacrificed at the Huaca de la Luna, Moche, Peru, during an El Niño event that took place between the late 6th and early 8th century. They were then buried in the mud of the adobe walls of Plaza-3-A which were melted by the torrential rains associated with the event.

Ancient Coastlines

Ancient life at sea is certainly of archaeological interest, but information on past climates is primarily of relevance to archaeology because of what it tells us about the effects on the land, and on the resources that people needed to survive. The most crucial effect of climate was on the sheer quantity of land available in each period, measurable by studying ancient coastlines. These have changed constantly through time, even in relatively recent periods, as can be seen from the Neolithic stone circle of Er Lannic, Brittany, which now lies half submerged on an island (once an inland hill in the Neolithic), or medieval villages in east Yorkshire, England, that have tumbled into the sea in the last few centuries as the North Sea gnaws its way westward and erodes the cliffs. Conversely, silts deposited by rivers sometimes push the sea farther back, creating new land, as at Ephesus in western Turkey, a port on the coast in Roman times but today some 5 km (3 miles) inland.

Nevertheless, for archaeologists concerned with the long periods of time of the Paleolithic epoch there are variations in coastlines of much greater magnitude to consider. The expansion and contraction of the continental glaciers, mentioned above, caused huge and uneven rises and falls in sea levels worldwide. When the ice sheets grew, sea level would drop as water became locked up in the glaciers; when the ice melted, sea level would rise again. Falls in sea level often exposed a number of important *land bridges*, such as those linking Alaska to northeast Asia, and Britain to northwest Europe, a phenomenon with far-reaching effects not only on human colonization of the globe, but also on the environment as a whole – the flora and fauna of isolated or insular areas were radically and often irreversibly affected. Between Alaska and Asia today there lies the Bering Strait, which is so shallow that a fall in sea level of only 46 m (150 ft) would turn it into a land bridge. When the ice sheets were at their greatest extent some 18,000 years ago (the "glacial maximum"), it is thought that the fall here was about 120 m (395 ft), which therefore created not merely a bridge but a vast plain, 1000 km (621 miles) from north to south, which has been called Beringia. The existence of Beringia (and the extent to which it could have supported human life) is one of the crucial pieces of evidence in the continuing debate about the likely route and date of human colonization of the New World (see Chapter 11).

The assessment of past rises and falls in sea level requires study of submerged land surfaces off the coast and of raised or elevated beaches on land. Raised beaches are remnants of former coastlines at higher levels relative to the present shoreline and visible, for instance, along the California coast north of San Francisco (see illus. p. 230). The height of a raised beach above the present shoreline, however, does not generally give a straightforward indication of the height of a former sea level. In the majority of cases, the beaches

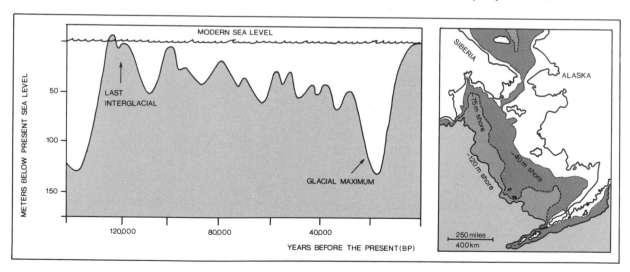

Sea levels and land bridges. (Left) Fluctuations in world sea levels over the last 140,000 years, based on evidence from uplifted coral reefs of the Huon Peninsula, New Guinea, correlated with the oxygen isotope record in deep-sea sediments (see p. 126). (Right) Falls in sea level created a land bridge between Siberia and Alaska known as Beringia. At the coldest period of the last glaciation ("glacial maximum"), some 18,000 years ago, the fall was as much as 120 m.

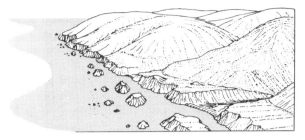

Raised beaches along the California coast north of San Francisco. Such beaches usually lie at a higher level because of isostatic uplift of the land (see right).

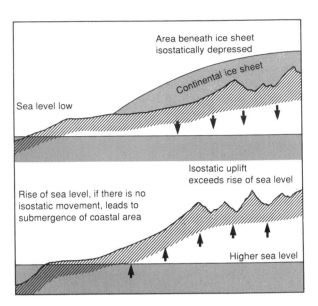

(Above) Principles of isostatic uplift. When sea levels are low and water is locked up in continental glaciers, land beneath the ice sheets is depressed by the weight of the ice. When the glaciers melt, sea level rises, but so too does the land in areas where once it was depressed.

lie at a higher level because the land has literally been raised up through *isostatic uplift* or *tectonic movements*. Isostatic uplift of the land occurs when the weight of ice is removed as temperatures rise, as at the end of an ice age; it has affected coastlines for example in Scandinavia, Scotland, Alaska, and Newfoundland during the postglacial period. Tectonic movements involve displacements in the plates that make up the earth's crust; Middle and Late Pleistocene raised beaches in the Mediterranean are one instance of such movements. The interpretation of raised beaches in connection with past sea levels thus requires specialist expertise. For archaeologists they are equally if not more important as locations where early coastal sites may be readily accessible; coastal sites in more stable or subsiding areas will have been drowned by the rise in sea level.

In addition to the major importance of isostatic uplift and tectonic movements, volcanic eruptions can occasionally affect coastlines. It is thanks to the eruption of AD 79, for example, that the once coastal resorts of Pompeii and Herculaneum now lie some 1.5 km (0.9 miles) from the sea, their former shorelines buried under volcanic lava and mud. Along the coast of northeast Scotland, at an altitude of 8 or 9 m (26–29 ft) above sea level, a layer of coarse white marine sand overlying Mesolithic occupations of the early 8th millennium BP seems to indicate that the area was hit by a tsunami or tidal wave about 7000 years ago.

Tracing Submerged Land Surfaces. The topography of submerged coastal plains can be traced offshore by echo-sounding or the closely related technique of seismic reflection profiling, which in water depths of over 100 m (330 ft) can achieve penetration of more than 10 m (33 ft) into the sea floor. Such acoustic devices are analogous to those used in locating sites (Chapter 3). Using these techniques in the bay in front of the important prehistoric site of Franchthi Cave, Greece, geo-

(Below) Franchthi Cave, Greece. By plotting sea floor depths near Franchthi, and correlating these with known sea level fluctuations (see diagram, p. 229), van Andel and his colleagues produced this map of local changes in coastline.

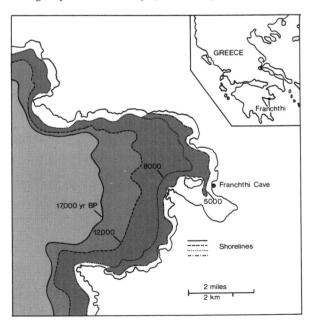

morphologists Tjeerd van Andel and Nikolaos Lianos found that the bay's central shelf is flat, with a series of small scarps (past shoreline positions) at various depths down to one at 118–120 m (387–394 ft) that marks the late glacial shoreline. From this survey it has been possible to reconstruct the coastline for the whole of the sequence represented by the cave's prehistoric occupation (23,000–5000 years ago). As will be seen later (Elands Bay Cave box, pp. 254–55), this kind of reconstruction also enables one to understand changes in the exploitation of marine resources, and to assess the marine molluscs that would have been available for food and ornamentation at different periods by seeing what is present in a range of environments in the Franchthi area today. The lack of seashells in the cave's deposits before 11,000 years ago reflects the distance to the shore at that time. Subsequently, the coast gradually approached the site, and shells accordingly become common in the occupation deposits. During the rise in sea level at the end of the Ice Age, almost half a kilometer of land would have been drowned every millennium, while after 8000 years ago this would have slowed to less than 100 m (330 ft) every millennium. At present, Franchthi is only a few meters from the sea.

Raised Beaches and Middens. Raised beaches often consist of areas of sand, pebbles, or dunes, sometimes containing seashells or middens comprising shells and bones of marine animals used by humans. Indeed, the location of middens can be an accurate indicator of earlier coastlines. In Tokyo Bay, for example, shell mounds of the Jomon period (dated by radiocarbon) mark the position of the shoreline at a time of maximum inundation by the sea (6500–5500 years ago), when, through tectonic movement, the sea was 3–5 m (10 ft–16 ft 5 in) higher in relation to the contemporary landmass of Japan than at present. Analysis of the shells by Hiroko Koike confirms the changes in marine topography, for it is only during this "maximum phase" that subtropical species of mollusc are present, indicating a higher water temperature.

Occasionally, beaches may occur not in a vertical but in a horizontal stratigraphy. At Cape Krusenstern, Alaska, a series of 114 minor relic beach terraces, up to 13 km (8 miles) long, form a peninsula extending into the Chukchi Sea. In 1958, American archaeologist J. Louis Giddings began work here, and his excavations beneath the frozen sod that now covers these ridges revealed settlements and burials dating from prehistoric to historic times. He found that people had abandoned successive beaches as the changing ocean conditions caused a new one to be formed in front of

the old. The modern shoreline is Beach 1, while the oldest dune ridge (no. 114) is now about 4.8 km (3 miles) inland. In this way, six millennia of local occupation are stratified horizontally, with 19th-century AD occupation on Beach 1, Western Thule material (c. AD 1000) about five beaches inland, Ipiutak material (2000–1500 years ago) around Beach 35, an Old Whaling Culture village (c. 3700 years ago) at Beach 53, and so on.

Coral Reefs. In tropical areas, fossil coral reefs provide evidence similar to that of raised beaches. Since coral grows in the upper part of the water, and extends more or less up to sea level, it indicates the position of previous shorelines, and its organisms give information on the local marine environment. For example, the Huon Peninsula, on the northeast coast of Papua New Guinea, has a spectacular shoreline sequence, comprising a stepped series of raised coral terraces produced by an upward tilting of the coast together with falling sea levels during cold glacial periods. The scientists J.M.A. Chappell, Arthur Bloom, and others studied more than 20 reef complexes on the Huon Peninsula dating back over 250,000 years and calculated the sea level at different periods – for instance, 125,000 years ago it was 6 m (20 ft) higher than at present, while 82,000 years ago it was 13 m (43 ft) lower, and 28,000 years ago it was 41 m (134 ft) lower. Measurements of oxygen isotopes provide complementary information on glacial expansion and contraction. The New Guinea results have been found to be in substantial agreement with those from similar formations in Haiti and Barbados.

Rock Art and Shorelines. One interesting technique, useful not so much for accurate shoreline data as for clear indications of change in coastal environments, is the study of rock art devised by George Chaloupka for northern Australia. As the sea rose, it caused changes in the local plants and animals, which in turn produced

Barramundi (giant perch) and saltwater crocodile depicted in northern Australian rock art.

modifications in technology, all of which seem to be reflected in the region's art. The deduced variations in sea level are themselves important in providing a date for the art.

Chaloupka's Pre-Estuarine period, broadly coinciding with the height of the last glaciation, depicts non-marine species including several that have been interpreted as animals now extinct. In the Estuarine period (starting 6000 or 7000 years ago, by which time the postglacial rise in sea level had ceased) one finds images of new species such as the barramundi (giant perch) and the saltwater crocodile, whose presence can be explained by encroaching seawater that had partially filled the shallow valleys and creeks, creating a salt-marsh environment. Contemporaneously, other species, such as small marsupials, that had once occupied the pre-estuarine plains now moved further inland and disappeared from the coastal art, as did the boomerang, the human weapon used to hunt them. Finally, the Freshwater period (about 1000 years ago)

brought another great environmental change when freshwater wetlands developed, supporting species of waterfowl and new food plants such as lilies and wild rice, all of which were depicted in the rock art.

All these sources of evidence – submerged land surfaces, raised beaches, coral reefs, rock art – give us an impressive amount of information about ancient coastlines. But it should be realized that most of this information applies to particular regions only: correlating the evidence over wider areas is difficult, because the dates lack consistency, and there are serious discrepancies in sea-level data worldwide.

This is a common problem in paleoclimatic studies: events do not always happen at the same moment in all areas. Nevertheless attempts have been made at producing paleoclimatic data for the world; one major example is the CLIMAP project, which has published maps showing sea-surface temperatures in different parts of the globe at various periods, based on results from many of the techniques mentioned here.

STUDYING THE LANDSCAPE

Having assessed roughly how much land was available for human occupation in different periods, we should now turn to methods for determining the effects of changing climate on the terrain itself.

Today it would be unthinkable to study any site without a thorough investigation of its sediments and the surrounding landscape. The aim is to achieve the fullest possible reconstruction of the local area (terrain, permanent or periodic availability of water, groundwater conditions, susceptibility to flooding, etc.) and set it in the context of the region, so that one can assess the environment faced by the site's inhabitants in different periods – and also gain some idea of the possible loss of sites through erosion, burial under sediment, or inundation.

Moreover, it is vital to know what happened to a landscape before one can begin to speculate about the possible reasons why it changed and how people adapted to the new conditions. Much of this work is best left to the earth scientist, but in the last few years a number of specialists have urged archaeologists to try to master some of these techniques themselves. Certain major changes in landscape are obvious even to the layman – for example, in cases where former irrigation channels can be seen in areas that are now desert; where well shafts are now exposed above ground through massive erosion of the surrounding sediment; or where volcanic eruptions have covered the land with layers of ash or lava.

Glaciated Landscapes

Some of the most dramatic and extensive effects of global climatic change on landscape were produced by the formation of glaciers. Study of the movements and extent of ancient glaciers rests on the traces they have left behind in areas such as the Great Lakes region in North America, and the Alps and the Pyrenees in Europe. Here one can see the characteristic U-shaped

Glaciated landscape: formerly glaciated valleys at Wasdale Head, Cumbria, northern England. The U-shaped valley in the middle distance is a typical glacial feature.

Glaciers today: like great rivers of ice, two glaciers in Alaska are seen converging and joining into one stream, with so-called moraine deposits at their edges that carry forward rocks and other debris.

valleys, polished and striated rocks, and, at the limits of glacier expansion, the so-called moraine deposits that often contain rocks foreign to the area but carried in by the ice (known as glacial erratics). In some areas the final glaciation obscured traces of its predecessors.

Examples of Ice Age glacial phenomena are readily observable in regions with glaciers today, such as Alaska and Switzerland, while the richness of modern periglacial areas (where part of the ground is permanently frozen in a permafrost layer) gives some idea of the potential resources in the regions at the edge of the ancient glaciers. The distribution of periglacial phenomena such as fossil ice wedges can be a guide to past conditions, since a mean annual temperature of -6°C to -9°C (21.2°F to 15.8°F) is required for ice wedges to form: they are caused when the ground freezes and contracts, opening up fissures in the permafrost that fill with the wedges of ice. The fossil wedges are proof of a past cooling of climate and of the depth of permafrost.

Varves

Among the most valuable periglacial phenomena for paleoclimatic information are varves, discussed as a method of dating in Chapter 4. Deep lakes around the edges of the Scandinavian glaciers received annual layers of sediment deposited after the spring thaw. Thick layers represent warm years with increased glacial melt, thin layers indicate cold conditions. As well as providing dating evidence, the varves often contain pollen which, as will be seen below, complements the climatic information inherent in the sediment. Unfor-

tunately varves are of limited use outside Scandinavia, since most lakes are shallow, and their sediments can be disturbed and new varves created by other factors such as violent storms.

Rivers

So much for frozen water and stationary water: but what are the effects of *flowing* water on the landscape? The reconstruction of past landscapes around major rivers – which tend to be areas of rapid change, through erosion or deposition of sediments along courses and at river mouths – is particularly valuable to archaeology because these environments were frequently the focus of human occupation. In certain cases, such as the Nile, Tigris-Euphrates, and Indus, the floodplains proved crucial to the rise of irrigation agriculture and urban civilization.

Many rivers actually changed their course at different periods, through complex processes of erosion, silting, and varying gradients. The channel of the Indus in modern Pakistan is not incised into the plain like those of most rivers, and therefore has a tendency to change its course from time to time. The lower Indus is shallow, with a gentle gradient, and thus deposits large quantities of alluvial material in its channel, actually raising its bed above the level of the surrounding plain, and frequently breaking out and inundating large areas with fertile silt, vital to early agriculture and, for example, the ancient city of Mohenjodaro.

Similarly, the lower Mississippi Valley is covered with the traces of meander changes over a long period. These abandoned channels have been detected and plotted, by topographic survey and aerial photography (see Chapter 3), for the period AD 1765–1940. Using this information, a pattern of meander changes plotted

Aerial view of the deeply cut meander of the Colorado river, Utah. In some regions, abandoned meander channels have been used to build up a local chronology.

CAVE SEDIMENTS

The sediments that make up the floors of caves are composed of material brought in through entrances and holes in the roof by wind, water, animals, and people. A section through a cave or rockshelter floor usually shows a number of layers, often of differing textures and colors. The contents of these layers can indicate changing temperatures through time. For example, the percolation of water can loosen and break off rounded lumps from wall and roof, a type of weathering associated with a mild, humid climate. In cold conditions, water in rock fissures turns to ice, and this increase in volume puts pressure on the surface rock layer, which can disintegrate into angular, sharp-edged fragments, c. 4–10 cm (1½–4 in) long. Thus, after repeated phases of thawing and freezing, alternating layers of rounded and angular fragments ("rock spalls") will be produced near cave entrances and in rockshelters.

Although there are other potential causes of rubble layers, such as earthquakes, or attack by microbes, it is generally accepted that a study of changes in rubble size can provide information on environmental fluctuations. For example, in Cave Bay Cave, Tasmania, the Australian archaeologist Sandra Bowdler attributed the great accumulation of angular roof detritus between 18,000 and 15,000 years ago to the effects of frost wedging at the height of the last glacial. At the shallow cave of Colless Creek shelter, in tropical Queensland, on the other hand, the marked changes in sediments detectable through the 20 millennia of occupation seem to have been caused by fluctuations in rainfall. The Colless Creek sediments were studied in thin sections under the microscope for micromorphological differences; the lower layers (before

General and detailed sections of a hypothetical cave site.

18,000 years ago) were compacted, and had clearly been modified by the movement of water, which suggested a wetter climate.

Analysis in Practice
In general, analysis is carried out initially by visual examination. Samples need to be taken from several parts of the cave, in view of the microclimates and horizontal variation (e.g. the presence of a large hearth may have had considerable influence on a wall's temperature in some periods). It is often hard to correlate sequences from within a single cave, let alone between caves and regions. Subsequent sieving and laboratory examination of grain size, and of color and texture of sediment, modifies or amplifies the initial assessment. Usually all blocks over 100 mm (4 in) are noted and removed; then the remainder is passed through a series of sieves and differentiated into blocks, granules, gravel, and sand/silt/clay. The more blocks and granules there are in a layer, the more severe the cold in that period.

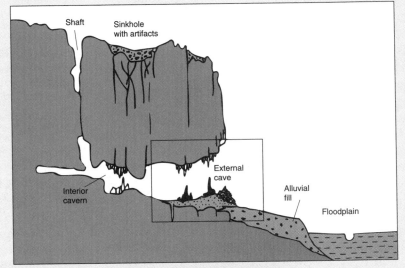

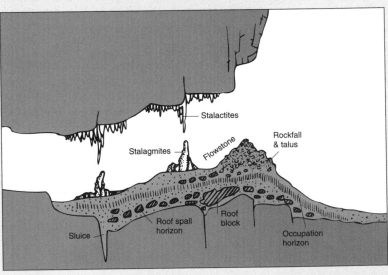

Scholars such as the French archaeologist Yves Guillien have stressed that it is necessary to do experiments on a cave's limestone before attempting to interpret the fill. Laboratory simulation of the natural freeze/thaw successions gives one some idea of the rock's friability under the kind of climatic conditions that caused the real breakage.

Stalagmites and Stalactites

Caves often have layers of stalagmite, and of flowstone (travertine), laid down by water that picks up calcium carbonate in solution as it passes through limestone. Such layers are generally indicative of fairly temperate climatic phases, and sometimes also of humid conditions. Stalagmites and stalactites (collectively known as speleothems) can even be used for accurate assessment of past climate through the oxygen isotope technique. In cross-section, speleothems have a series of concentric growth rings, which can be dated by radiocarbon. Each ring preserves the oxygen isotope composition of the water that formed it, and hence of the average atmospheric precipitation and temperature at which it was deposited. Since the ultimate source of rainwater is the surface of the ocean, this method is a potentially valuable complement to ocean cores.

Scientists have taken samples from speleothems in Soreq cave, Israel, and dated them by the uranium-thorium method. Isotopic analysis has provided a record of eastern Mediterranean rainfall over the past 25,000 years. From 25,000 to 17,000 years ago the region was dry and cool. After that there were some sharp climatic fluctuations until about 6000 years ago, when today's climatic pattern was established.

Since the rate of calcium carbonate deposition per square centimeter on speleothems can be much faster than the deposition of sediment on the ocean bed, this method may achieve more detailed temperature profiles than ocean cores: in fact, it is thought that temperature changes of only 0.2°C may be detectable.

at 100-year intervals has been extrapolated back for the last 2000 years. Like the work on fossil beach lines in Alaska (see above), this sequence has formed the basis for a rough chronology for sites located along particular abandoned channels.

Cave Sites

A different type of abandoned water-channel is represented by the limestone cave, a category of site that has been of tremendous importance to archaeology through its conservation of a wide variety of evidence, not only about human activities but also about local climate and environment.

Caves and rockshelters, although of enormous archaeological interest, are nevertheless special cases. Their importance as places of habitation has always been exaggerated in prehistoric studies at the expense of less well-preserved open sites. What can we learn from the great outdoors where people have spent most of their time?

Sediments and Soils

Investigation of sediments (the global term for material deposited on the earth's surface) and soils (the life-supporting, biologically and physically weathered upper layers of those sediments) can reveal much about the conditions that prevailed when they were formed. The organic remains they may contain will be examined in subsequent sections on plants and animals, but the soil matrix itself yields a wealth of information on weathering, and hence on past soil types and land-use.

Geomorphology (the study of the form and development of the landscape) incorporates specializations such as sedimentology, which itself includes sedimentary petrography and granulometry. These combine to produce a detailed analysis of the composition and texture of sediments, ranging from freely draining gravel and sand to water-retentive clay; the size of constituent particles in sediments, ranging from pebbles to sand or silt; and the degree of consolidation, ranging from loose to cemented. In some cases, the orientation of the pebbles gives some indication of the direction of stream-flow, of slope, or of glacial deposits. As we will see in Chapters 8 and 9, the X-ray diffraction technique can be used to identify specific clay minerals and thus the specific source from which a sediment is derived.

Soil micromorphology – the use of microscopic techniques to study the nature and organization of the components of soils – is becoming an increasingly important part of excavation and site analysis. An intact block sample from a known context is first consolidated with resin and then a thin section is taken from it. This is examined using a polarizing microscope. The observed sequence of soil development may reveal many aspects of a site's or landscape's history not otherwise visible. Three main categories of features can be discerned: those related to the source of the sediment; those which reveal something of the processes of soil formation; and those which are humanly produced or modified, whether deliberately or accidentally. As the environmental archaeologist Karl Butzer recognized, humans have affected soils and sediments found at archaeological sites at a microscopic level.

Butzer has distinguished three groups of cultural deposits. *Primary cultural deposits* are those which accumulate on the surface from human activity, for instance many ash layers or living floors. *Secondary cultural deposits* are primary deposits which have undergone modification, either by physical displacement or because of a change of use of the activity area. *Tertiary cultural deposits* are those which have been completely removed from their original context and may have been reused (for instance to build terracing).

Soil micromorphology can achieve results in two crucial areas. First, it can assist in an environmental reconstruction of ancient human landscapes, both on a regional scale and also at site level. Human effects on soils produced by deforestation and by farming practices are one area of study. Second, it can be used in contextual archaeology – when combined with the traditional approach of the study of artifacts, a much more comprehensive picture of a site and its past activities can be obtained.

Micromorphological investigations have been shown to be highly useful in distinguishing between sediments that are still *in situ* from ones which are no longer in their original situation, and also between human and natural influences on soils and sediments. Study of thin sections has, for example, been able to distinguish natural from man-made accumulations in cave deposits which otherwise look very similar. The absence of evidence of human interference is also very informative – for instance it could demonstrate that artifacts are not in their primary context. Throughout, a comprehensive reference collection of samples is required to allow comparisons to be made between real, experimental, and archaeological situations.

A large range of human activities can now often be recognized from their micromorphological signals in soils and sediments. For instance, it should theoretically be possible when studying a settlement site to identify and distinguish outdoor and indoor fires, cooking and eating zones, activity areas, storage, and passage zones from the examination of thin sections. British environmental archaeologist Wendy Matthews is conducting detailed micromorphological investigations of floor deposits within structures in four Neolithic sites in the Near East. These have indicated the use of space in certain buildings, both before and after their abandonment. Obviously it is not possible to study an entire site in this way and it is necessary for the excavator to make choices as to which soils to sample and which contexts are the most representative for the purposes of analysis. Soil micromorphology is now an integral part of the excavation process.

Soil micromorphology requires a laboratory environment and specialized equipment, but a growing number of archaeologists have gained sufficient field experience to undertake a basic assessment of sediments in the field – simply by rubbing a little of the dry sediment between their fingers, and then testing its plasticity by making it damp and rolling it in the palm. However, for a more accurate assessment the expertise of a specialist is essential. Accurate and standardized descriptions of soil color are also vital, and are usually accomplished by means of the widely adopted Munsell Soil Color Charts (also used for describing archaeological layers).

Accurate analysis of the texture of a soil entails the use of a series of sieves, with mesh sizes decreasing from 2 mm to 0.06 mm for the separation of the sand fraction, and the use of hydrometer or sediograph techniques (for determining the density of liquids) to quantify the proportions of silt and clay fractions comprising the soil/sediment. Similar information may be obtained using micromorphological or thin section techniques. Soil textural analysis provides information on soil type, land-use potential, and susceptibility to erosion, especially when allied with micromorphological and hydrological information. These studies all contribute to the investigation of landscape history.

One technique for close study of sediments, developed before World War II, involved the application of a film of rubber or "lacquer" to the stratigraphy, but modern materials have improved the method enormously. At the open-air Upper Paleolithic camp of Pincevent, near Paris, Michel Orliac has used a thin film of synthetic latex (about 1.5 kg per sq. m or 0.3 lb per sq. ft) painted onto a flat, carefully cleaned section. When dry, the latex preserves an image of the stratigraphy that is far easier than the original to examine in detail. Indeed, the imprint, composed of a very thin film of sediment that adheres to the latex, reveals much more than can be distinguished in the original section. After it has been peeled off, the imprint can be stored

Studying sediments: at Pincevent, France, a film of latex was painted onto a stratigraphic section and peeled off when dry, with an image of the soil profile attached.

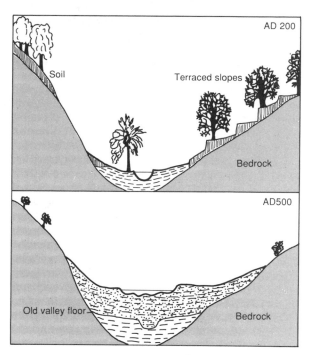

Sediments, erosion, and changing patterns of settlement. A typical Italian valley during the Roman period suffered erosion of hillslope soils under the combined effects of deforestation, intensive agriculture, and overgrazing. Human settlement eventually shifted from hillside to valley bottom.

flat or rolled up, and thus enables the archaeologist to keep or display a faithful record of a soil profile.

Analyses of soils and sediments can provide data on long-term processes of deposition and erosion. For example, the way in which sediments have eroded from hillslopes down into valley bottoms has been widely studied in Mediterranean countries, where the process is associated with shifts in settlement. Hillside farms were abandoned in the face of soil loss, while settlement increased in valley bottoms. Sediment analyses suggest that misuse of the landscape in some Mediterranean areas dates back five millennia, to at least the Early Bronze Age. In Cyprus, for instance, a combination of deforestation, intensive agriculture, and pastoralism destabilized the fragile soil-cover on hillslopes in the Early Bronze Age and led to rapid infilling of sediment along coastal valleys. In the southern Argolid, Greece, a major project conducted by Tjeerd van Andel, Curtis Runnels, and their colleagues has revealed at least four phases of settlement, erosion, and abandonment between 2000 BC and the Middle Ages. At times here, careless land clearance seems to have been to blame, without suitable conservation measures; and on other occasions it was the partial abandonment or neglect of terracing, and hence of soil conservation, that led to soil erosion.

Loess Sediments. A pedologist (soil specialist) can examine a sediment profile, and from its composition and its changing textures and colors can tell whether it was laid down by water, wind, or human action, and can obtain some idea of the weathering it has undergone, and hence of the climatic conditions that existed locally throughout its history. One important wind-blown sediment encountered in certain parts of the world is loess, a yellowish dust of silt-sized particles blown in by the wind and redeposited on land newly deglaciated or on sheltered areas. Loess has been found on about 10 percent of the world's land surface, in Alaska, the Mississippi and Ohio valleys, in northwest and central Europe, and particularly in China, where it covers over 440,000 sq. km (170,000 sq. miles) or about 40 percent of arable land there. It is important to the Paleolithic specialist as an indicator of ancient climate, while all students of Neolithic farming learn to associate it with the first agricultural settlements.

Loess works as a climatic indicator because it was only deposited during periods of relatively cold, dry climate when the fine silt particles were blown off a periglacial steppe-like landscape, with little vegetation or moisture to consolidate the sediment. The loess "rain" stopped in warmer and wetter conditions. Sediment sections taken in areas such as central Europe therefore show loess layers alternating with so-called "forest soils," themselves indicators of climatic improvement and the temporary return of vegetation.

Classic sequences are known at Paudorf and Göttweig in Austria, the former giving its name to the Paudorf Loess Formation (27,000–23,000 years ago) associated with the famous Upper Paleolithic open-air sites of Dolní Věstonice and Pavlov in the Czech Republic. Similarly, in the Paris Basin, François Bordes established a Pleistocene sequence of alternating loess and warmer, more humid levels, associated with different Paleolithic industries, which could be correlated with the known glacial sequence. Studies of climatic oscillations detectable in the extensive sequence available from China have shown a good correlation with the fluctuations of cold-water foraminifera and the oxygen isotope record from deep-sea sediments.

As well as being a good indicator of ancient climate (often containing land snails that provide confirmatory data), loess also played a crucial role in Neolithic farming. Rich in minerals, uniform in structure, and well drained, soils formed in loess provided fertile and easily worked land ideal for the simple technology of the first farming communities. The *Linearbandkeramik* (LBK, i.e. Early Neolithic) sites of central and western Europe have an extremely close association with soils formed in loess: at least 70 percent of LBK sites in a given area are found to be located on loess.

Buried Land Surfaces. Entire land surfaces can sometimes be preserved intact beneath certain kinds of sediment. For example, ancient soils and landscapes have been discovered beneath the peat of the English Fenlands, while at Behy, in Ireland, a Neolithic farming landscape with stone-built banks has emerged from the peat. We shall return to the subject of buried land surfaces below (evidence for plowing section).

By far the most spectacular occurrences of this type are those brought about by volcanic eruptions. The buried cities of Pompeii and Herculaneum in southern Italy, and Akrotiri on the Greek island of Thera, have been referred to in earlier chapters. But, from the point of view of environmental data, volcanically preserved natural landscapes are even more revealing. In 1984, the remains of a prehistoric forest were found at Miesenheim, western Germany. It was already known that

Prehistoric trees and other plant material preserved in a waterlogged layer by a volcanic ash fall some 11,000 years ago at Miesenheim, western Germany. Rare finds such as this give important insights into the character of ancient landscapes.

an eruption about 11,000 years ago had buried the nearby late Upper Paleolithic open-air sites of Gönnersdorf and Andernach under several meters of ash, but the discovery of a contemporaneous forest was a special bonus for the archaeologists. Trees (including willow), mosses, and fungi had been preserved by the ash in a waterlogged layer, 30 cm (11.8 in) thick; mollusc shells, large and small mammals, and even a bird's egg were also present. The forest seems to have been relatively dense, with a thick undergrowth, and this was confirmed by pollen analysis (see box, pp. 240–41); study of the tree-rings will also add information on climatic fluctuations in this period.

Other engulfed trees are also providing climatic information: in California and Patagonia, Scott Stine has examined drowned tree stumps around the edges of lakes, swamps, and rivers. They indicate that water levels in the past were lower, but were followed by flooding. Radiocarbon dating of the trees' outer rings tells him when flooding occurred, and the preceding dry interval can be calculated by counting the earlier rings. His results reveal some sustained droughts, for example in AD 892–1112 and 1209–1350; the latter may be linked with the decline of the Anasazi cliff-dwellers in *c.* 1300 (see below, p. 265).

Tree-Rings and Climate

Tree-rings, like varves (see above), have a growth that varies with the climate, being strong in the spring and then declining to nothing in the winter; the more moisture available, the wider the annual ring. As we saw in

Chapter 4, these variations in ring width have formed the basis of a major dating technique. However, study of a particular set of rings can also reveal important environmental data, for example whether growth was slow (implying dense local forest cover) or fast (implying light forest). Tree growth is complex, and many other external and internal factors may affect it, but temperature and soil moisture do tend to be dominant. For example, a 3620-year temperature record has been obtained from tree-rings in southern Chile, which reveals intervals with above-average and below-average temperatures for the region.

Annual and decade-to-decade variations show up far more clearly in tree-rings than in ice cores, and tree-rings can also record sudden and dramatic shocks to the climate. For example, data from Virginia indicate that the alarming mortality and near abandonment of Jamestown Colony, the first permanent settlement in America, occurred during an extraordinary drought, the driest 7-year episode in 770 years (AD 1606–1612).

The study of tree-rings and climate (dendroclimatology) has also progressed by using X-ray measurements of cell-size and density as an indication of environmental productivity. More recently, ancient temperatures have been derived from tree-rings by means of the stable carbon isotope ($^{13}C/^{12}C$) ratios preserved in their cellulose. A 1000-year-old kauri tree in New Zealand has been analyzed in this way, and the results – confirmed by data from New Zealand speleothems – revealed a series of fluctuations in mean annual temperature, with the warmest phase in the 14th century, followed by a decline and then a recovery to present conditions. Isotopes of carbon and oxygen in the cellulose of timbers of the tamarisk tree, contained in the ramp which the Romans used to overcome the besieged Jewish citadel of Masada in AD 73, have revealed to Israeli archaeologists that the climate at that time was wetter and more amenable to agriculture than it is today.

The importance of tree-rings makes it clear that it is organic remains above all that provide the richest source of evidence for environmental reconstruction. We must now take a detailed look at the surviving traces of plants and animals.

RECONSTRUCTING THE PLANT ENVIRONMENT

Our prime environmental interest in plant studies is to try to reconstruct the vegetation that people in the past will have encountered at a particular time and in a particular place. But we should not forget that plants lie at the base of the food chain. The plant communities of a given area and period will therefore provide clues to local animal and human life, and will also reflect soil conditions and climate. Some types of vegetation react relatively quickly to changes in climate (though less quickly than insects, for instance), and the shifts of plant communities in both latitude and altitude are the most direct link between climatic change and the terrestrial human environment, for example in the Ice Age.

Plant studies in archaeology have always been overshadowed by faunal analysis, simply because bones are more conspicuous than plant remains in excavation. Bones may sometimes survive better, but usually plant remains are present in greater numbers than bones. In the last few decades plants have at last come to the fore, thanks to the discovery that some of their constituent parts are much more resistant to decomposition than was believed, and that a huge amount of data survives which can tell us something about long-dead vegetation. As with so many of the specializations on which archaeology can call, these analyses require a great deal of time and funds.

Some of the most informative techniques for making an overall assessment of plant communities in a particular period involve analysis not of the biggest remains but of the tiniest, especially pollen.

Microbotanical Remains

Pollen Analysis. Palynology, or the study of pollen grains (see box overleaf), was developed by a Norwegian geologist, Lennart von Post, at the beginning of the 20th century. It has proved invaluable to archaeology, since it can be applied to a wide range of sites and provides information on chronology as well as environment – indeed, until the arrival of isotopic chronological methods, pollen analysis was used primarily for dating purposes (Chapter 4).

While palynology cannot produce an exact picture of past environments, it does give some idea of fluctuations in vegetation through time, whatever their causes may be, which can be compared with results from other methods. The best known application of pollen analysis is for the postglacial or Holocene epoch (after 12,000 years ago), for which palynologists have delineated a series of *pollen zones* through time, each characterized by different plant communities (especially trees), although there is little agreement on the numbering system to be used or the total number of zones.

POLLEN ANALYSIS

All hayfever sufferers will be aware of the pollen "rain" that can afflict them in the spring and summer. Pollen grains – the tiny male reproductive bodies of flowering plants – have an almost indestructible outer shell (exine) that can survive in certain sediments for tens of thousands of years. In pollen analysis the exines are extracted from the soil, studied under the microscope, and identified according to the distinctive exine shape and surface ornamentation of different families and genera of plants. Once quantified, these identifications are plotted as curves on a pollen diagram. Fluctuations in the curve for each plant category may then be studied for signs of climatic fluctuation, or forest clearance and crop-planting by humans.

Preservation

The most favorable sediments for preservation of pollen are acidic and poorly aerated peat bogs and lake beds, where biological decay is impeded and grains undergo rapid burial. Cave sediments are also usually suitable because of their humidity and constant temperature. Other contexts, such as sandy sediments or open sites exposed to weathering, preserve pollen poorly.

In wet sites, or unexcavated areas, samples are extracted in long cores, but in dry sites a series of separate samples can be removed from the sections. On an archaeological excavation, small samples are usually extracted at regular stratified intervals. Great care must be taken to avoid contamination from the tools used or from the atmosphere. Pollen can also be found in mud bricks, vessels, tombs, mummy wrappings, the guts of preserved bodies, coprolites (Chapter 7), and many other contexts.

Examination and Counting

The sealed tubes containing the samples are examined in the laboratory, where a small portion of each sample is studied under the microscope in an attempt to identify a few hundred grains in that sample. Each family and almost every genus of plant produce pollen grains distinctive in shape and surface ornamentation, but it is difficult to go further and pinpoint the species. This imposes certain limits on environmental reconstruction, since different species within the same genus can have markedly different requirements in terms of soil, climate, etc.

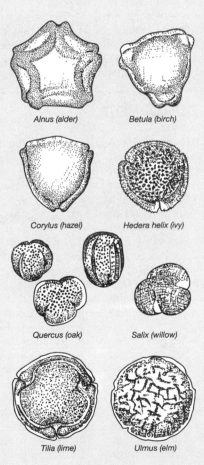

Morphology of a selection of pollen grains, as seen under the microscope.

Alnus (alder) *Betula (birch)*

Corylus (hazel) *Hedera helix (ivy)*

Quercus (oak) *Salix (willow)*

Tilia (lime) *Ulmus (elm)*

Slow and laborious manual counting and identification will probably be replaced in the next few years by an automated technique, in which pollen grains are identified through analysis in the scanning electron microscope of digitized images of the exine's shape and texture.

After identification, the quantity of pollen for each plant-type is calculated for each layer – usually as a percentage of the total number of grains in that layer – and then plotted as a curve. The curves are seen as a reflection of climatic fluctuations through the sequence, using the present-day tolerances of these plants as a guide.

However, adjustments need to be made. Different species produce differing amounts of pollen (pines, for example, produce many times more than oaks), and so may be over- or under-represented in the sample. The mode of pollination also needs to be taken into account. Pollen of lime, transported by insect, is probably from trees that grew nearby, whereas pine pollen, transported by the wind, could be from hundreds of kilometers away. The orientation of sites (and especially of cave-mouths) will also have a considerable effect on their pollen content, as will site location, and length/type of occupation.

It is necessary to ensure there has been no mixing of layers (intrusion is now known to be a common problem), and to assess human impact – samples should be taken from outside the archaeological site as well as within it. In urban archaeological deposits, for instance, pollen from well-fills or buried soils are mostly present through natural transport and deposition, and hence reflect the surrounding countryside. Pollen from urban living areas, on the other hand, derive primarily from food preparation and the many other human uses of plants.

In a study of pollen assemblages from a series of Roman and medieval towns in Britain, James Greig found that the Roman sites were rich in grasses but poor in cereals, whereas the medieval deposits produced the opposite result. The reason is not economic but hygienic – the Romans had a sewerage system for their towns, which were kept clean and, apparently, were surrounded by short grassland which dominates the pollen assemblages. In medieval times, however, garbage was allowed to accumulate in the towns, so that the food refuse remained for the archaeologist to find, and dominated the pollen samples.

As a rule, pollen in soils away from human settlement tends to reflect the local vegetation, while peat bogs preserve pollen from a much wider area. Results from pollen in deep peat-bog successions usefully confirm the long-term climatic fluctuations deduced from deep-sea and ice cores mentioned earlier in the main text.

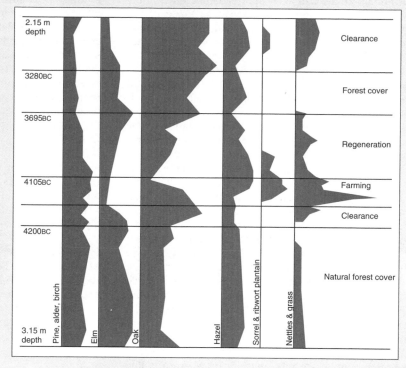

Postglacial pollen core from Fallahogy, Northern Ireland (above right), reveals the impact of the first farmers in the region. Forest clearance is indicated c.4150 BC with a fall in tree pollen and a marked increase in open-country and field species such as grass, sorrel, and ribwort-plantain. The subsequent regeneration of forest cover, followed by a second period of clearance, shows the non-intensive nature of early farming in the area.

Long-term sequences for the Ice Age (right) show the good correlation between a terrestrial pollen core from the Iberian peninsula (at right) and oxygen-isotope curves (at left) derived from deep-sea core SU 8132 extracted in the Bay of Biscay.

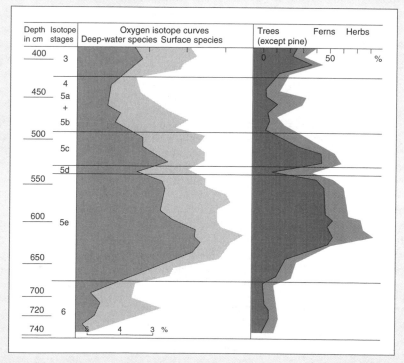

But pollen studies can also supply much-needed information for environments as ancient as those of the Hadar sediments and the Omo valley in Ethiopia around 3 million years ago. It is usually assumed that these regions were always as dry as they are now, but pollen analysis by the French scientist Raymonde Bonnefille has shown that they were much wetter and greener between 3.5 and 2.5 million years ago, with even some tropical plants present. The Hadar, which is now semi-desert with scattered trees and shrubs, was rich, open grassland, with dense woodland by lakes and along rivers. The change to drier conditions, around 2.5 million years ago, can be seen in the reduction of tree pollen in favor of more grasses.

By and large, the fluctuations recorded for the postglacial and especially the historical periods are minor compared with what went before, and where regression of forest is concerned there is the ever-present possibility that climate is not the only cause (see human impact section below). It is also worth noting that the British hydrologist Robert Raikes went much further than most scholars in playing down the significance of climatic changes during the postglacial period. He points out that in Europe variation in rainfall from one year or season to the next is almost certainly greater than rainfall differences generally deduced (though without quantification) from pollen diagrams. Any major climatic change that might have taken place would probably have been ecologically less significant than short-term variation of greater amplitude. Raikes concluded that ecological changes should more probably be ascribed to year-to-year variability of climate and rainfall. The archaeologist, he said, should therefore investigate minor, short-term local changes rather than try to squeeze all the sites in a region into a standardized succession of fixed pollen zones. Most specialists disagree with Raikes' line of argument, but his emphasis on the importance of local environmental reconstruction makes good sense for archaeologists working on individual sites.

Fossil Cuticles. Palynology is particularly useful for forested regions, but the reconstruction of past vegetation in grassy environments such as those of tropical Africa has been much hindered by the fact that grass pollen grains can be virtually indistinguishable from one another, even in the scanning electron microscope (SEM). Fortunately, help is at hand in the form of fossil cuticles. Cuticles are the outermost protective layer of the skin or epidermis of leaves or blades of grass, made of cutin, a very resistant material that retains the pattern of the underlying epidermal cells which have characteristic shapes. The cuticles thus have silica cells

of different shapes and patterns, as well as hairs and other diagnostic features.

The scientist Patricia Palmer has found abundant charred cuticular fragments in core samples from lake sediments in East Africa. The fragments were deposited there as a result of the recurrent natural grass fires common during the dry season, and her samples date back at least 28,000 years. Many of the fragments are large enough to present well-preserved diagnostic features that, under the light microscope or in the SEM, have enabled her to identify them to the level of subfamily or even genus, and hence reconstruct changes in vegetation during this long period. Cuticular analysis is a useful complement to palynology wherever grass material, whole or fragmentary, is to be identified, and it is worth noting that cuticles can also be removed from stomachs or feces.

Phytoliths. A better-known and fast-developing branch of microbotanical studies concerns phytoliths, which were first recognized as components in archaeological contexts as long ago as 1908, but have only been

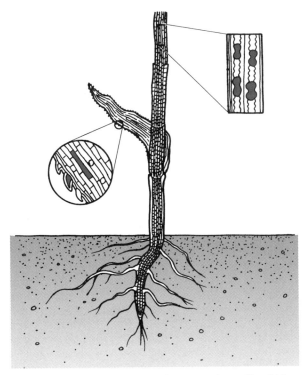

Phytoliths are minute particles of silica in plant cells which survive after the rest of the plant has decomposed. Some are specific to certain parts of the plant (e.g. stem or leaf).

studied systematically in the last few decades. These are minute particles of silica (plant opal) derived from the cells of plants, and they survive after the rest of the organism has decomposed or been burned. They are common in hearths and ash layers, but are also found inside pottery, plaster, and even on stone tools and the teeth of herbivorous animals: grass phytoliths have been found adhering to ungulate teeth from Bronze Age, Iron Age, and medieval sites in Europe.

These crystals are useful because, like pollen grains, they are produced in large numbers, they survive well in ancient sediments, and they have myriad distinctive shapes and sizes that vary according to type, though it is usually difficult to identify their genus or species, even with a SEM. They inform us primarily about the use people made of particular plants, but their simple presence adds to the picture of the environment built up from other sources.

In particular, a combination of phytolith and pollen analysis can be a powerful tool for environmental reconstruction, since the two methods have complementary strengths and weaknesses. The American scholar Dolores Piperno has studied cores from the Gatun Basin, Panama, whose pollen content had already revealed a sequence of vegetation change from 11,300 years ago to the present – from mature tropical forest to mangrove, freshwater swamp, and finally to clearance through swidden (slash-and-burn) agriculture. She found that the phytoliths in the cores confirmed the pollen sequence, with the exception that evidence for agriculture and forest clearance (i.e. the appearance of maize, and an increase in grass at the expense of trees) appeared around 4850 years ago in the phytoliths, about 1000 years earlier than in the pollen. This early evidence is probably attributable to small clearings which do not show up in pollen diagrams because grains from the surrounding forest infiltrate the samples, as well as to the relatively poor production and dispersal of non-arboreal pollen.

Pollen analysis will nevertheless remain the more important technique, if only because of difficulties in phytolith identification.

Diatom Analysis. Another method of environmental reconstruction using plant microfossils is diatom analysis. Diatoms are unicellular algae that have cell walls of silica instead of cellulose, and these silica cell walls survive after the algae die. They accumulate in great numbers at the bottom of any body of water in which the algae live; a few are found in peat, but most come from lake and shore sediments.

Diatoms have been recorded, identified, and classified for over 200 years. The process of identifying and

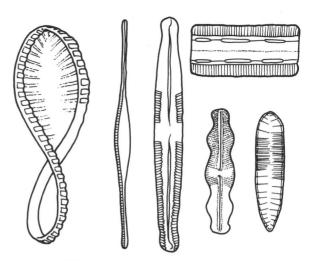

A variety of diatoms, the microscopic single-cell algae, whose silica cell walls survive in many sediments after death. Study of the changing species in a deposit can help scientists reconstruct fluctuations in past environments.

counting them is much like that used in palynology, as is the collection of samples in the field. Their well-defined shapes and ornamentations permit identification to a high level, and their assemblages directly reflect the floristic composition and the productivity of the water's diatom communities, and, indirectly, the water's salinity, alkalinity, and nutrient status. From the environmental requirements of different species (in terms of habitat, salinity, and nutrients), one can determine what their immediate environment was at different periods.

The botanist J.P. Bradbury looked at diatoms from nine lakes in Minnesota and Dakota, and was able to show that the quality of their water had become "eutrophic" (more nutrient) since the onset of European settlement around the lakes in the last century, thanks to the influxes caused by deforestation and logging, soil erosion, permanent agriculture, and the increase in human and animal wastes.

Since diatom assemblages can also denote whether water was fresh, brackish, or salt, they have been used to identify the period when lakes became isolated from the sea in areas of tectonic uplift, to locate the positions of past shorelines, to indicate marine transgressions, and to reveal water pollution. For instance, the diatom sequence in sediments at the site of the former Lake Wevershoof, Medemblick (the Netherlands) suggests that a marine transgression occurred here around AD 800, taking over what had been a freshwater lake and causing a hiatus in human occupation of the immediate area.

Rock Varnishes. Even tinier fragments of plant material can provide environmental evidence. Rock varnishes, which have been formed on late Pleistocene desert landforms in many areas such as North America, the Middle East, and Australia, are natural accretions of manganese and iron oxides, together with clay minerals and organic matter. The organic matter comes from micrometer-sized airborne plant debris that accumulates on rock surfaces and is thus metabolized and cemented into the varnish by bacterial action. Less than 1 percent of the varnish is organic matter, however, so thousands of square centimeters are required for adequate analysis.

The reason for the analysis is that a strong correlation has been found between the ratio of stable carbon isotopes ($^{12}C/^{13}C$) in modern samples and their different local environments (desert, semi-arid, montane-humid, etc.). Therefore, the stable carbon isotope ratios of the organic matter preserved in the different layers of varnish on rocks can provide information about changing conditions, and especially about the abundance of different types of plant in the adjacent vegetation. The American scholars Ronald Dorn and Michael DeNiro have sampled surface and subsurface layers of varnish on late Pleistocene deposits in eastern California, and found that the basal layers formed under more humid conditions than those on the surface, which supports the view that the Southwest of the United States was less arid in the last Ice Age than during the succeeding Holocene. Similarly, samples from the Timna Valley in Israel's Negev Desert revealed a sequence of arid, humid, and arid periods. However, there are difficulties with the technique, primarily because the layers are so thin that distinguishing stratification is not simple. Future work may resolve these problems.

Plant DNA. The tiniest possible fragments of plants are their DNA, and these can now be detected and identified in some contexts: for example, fossilized dung from an extinct ground sloth of about 20,000 years ago, recovered from Gypsum Cave, Nevada, has been chemically analyzed and found to contain a wide variety of plant DNA. This gave clues not only to the sloth's diet (grasses, yucca, grapes, mint, etc.), but also to the vegetation available at that time and place.

All these microbotanical techniques – studies of pollen, cuticles, phytoliths, diatoms, rock varnish, and DNA – are clearly the realm of the specialist. For archaeologists, however, a far more direct contact with environmental evidence comes from the larger plant remains that they can actually see and conserve in the course of excavation.

Macrobotanical Remains

A variety of bigger types of plant remains are potentially retrievable, and provide important information about which plants grew near sites, which were used or consumed by people, and so on. We shall discuss human use in the next chapter; here we shall focus on the crucial contribution of macrobotanical remains to environmental reconstruction. As with microbotanical remains, they cannot assist us in quantifying the vegetation cover except in the most relative fashion, but some of them do provide valuable clues to local environmental conditions.

Retrieval in the Field. Retrieval of vegetation from sediments has been made simpler by the development of screening (sieving) and flotation techniques able to separate mineral grains from organic materials because of their different sizes (screening) and densities (flotation). Archaeologists need to choose from a wide range of available devices in accordance with the excavation's location, budget, and objectives.

Sediments are by no means the only source of plant remains, which have also been found in the stomachs of frozen mammoths and preserved bog bodies; in the coprolites (fossilized feces) of humans, hyenas, giant sloths, etc.; on the teeth of mammoths, etc.; on stone tools; and in residues inside vessels. The remains themselves are varied:

Seeds and Fruits. Ancient seeds and fruits can usually be identified to species, despite changes in their shape caused by charring or waterlogging. In some cases, the remains have disintegrated but have left their imprint behind – grain impressions are fairly common on pottery, leaf impressions are also known, and imprints exist on materials ranging from plaster and tufa to leather and corroded bronze. Identification, of course, depends on type and quality of the traces. Not all such finds necessarily mean that a plant grew locally: grape pips, for example, may come from imported fruit, while impressions on potsherds may mislead since pottery can travel far from its place of manufacture.

Plant Residues. Chemical analysis of plant residues in vessels – primarily by means of chromatograms – will be dealt with in the context of human diet in Chapter 7, but the results can give some idea of what species were available. Pottery vessels themselves may incorporate plant fibers (not to mention shell, feathers, or blood) as a tempering material, and microscopic analysis can sometimes identify these remains – for example, study of early pots from South Carolina and Georgia in the

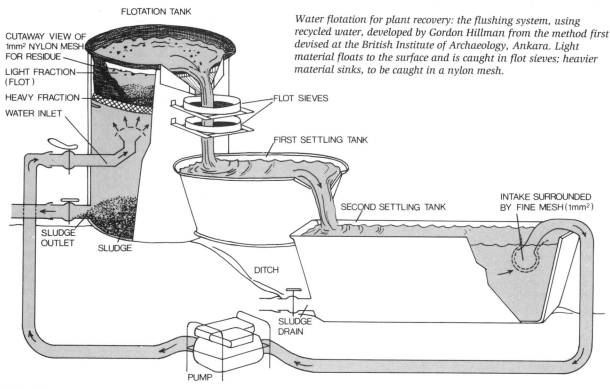

FLOTATION TANK

CUTAWAY VIEW OF
1mm² NYLON MESH
FOR RESIDUE

LIGHT FRACTION
(FLOT)

HEAVY FRACTION

WATER INLET

FLOT SIEVES

FIRST SETTLING TANK

SECOND SETTLING TANK

INTAKE SURROUNDED
BY FINE MESH (1mm²)

SLUDGE
OUTLET

SLUDGE

DITCH

SLUDGE
DRAIN

PUMP

Water flotation for plant recovery: the flushing system, using recycled water, developed by Gordon Hillman from the method first devised at the British Institute of Archaeology, Ankara. Light material floats to the surface and is caught in flot sieves; heavier material sinks, to be caught in a nylon mesh.

United States revealed the presence of shredded stems of Spanish Moss, a member of the pineapple family.

Remains of Wood. Study of *charcoal* (wood that has been burnt for some reason) is making a growing contribution to archaeological reconstruction of environments and of human use of timber. A very durable material, charcoal is usually found and extracted by the archaeologist. Once the fragments have been sieved, sorted, and dried, they can be examined by the specialist under the microscope, and identified (thanks to the anatomy of the wood) normally at the genus level, and sometimes to species. Since no chemicals need to be used, charcoal and charred seeds have also proved the most reliable material from which to take samples for radiocarbon dating (Chapter 4).

Many charcoal samples derive from firewood, but others may come from wooden structures, furniture, and implements burnt at some point in a site's history. Samples therefore inevitably tend to reflect human selection of wood rather than the full range of species growing around the site. Nevertheless, the totals for each species provide some idea of one part of the vegetation at a given time. Quantification is tricky, since charcoal fragments do not come in standard sizes.

Should one compare the number of fragments for each species, or the total mass of each?

Occasionally, charcoal analysis can be combined with other evidence to reveal something not only of local environment but also of human adaptation to it. At Boomplaas Cave, in southern Cape Province (South Africa), excavation of the deep deposits by Hilary Deacon and his team has uncovered traces of human occupation stretching back to about 70,000 years. There is a clear difference between all Ice Age charcoals and those postdating 12,000–14,000 years ago at the site. At times of extreme cold when conditions were also drier, as between 22,000 and c. 14,000 years ago, the species diversity both in the charcoals and the pollen was low, whereas at times of higher rainfall and/or temperature the species diversity increased. A similar pattern of species diversity is seen also in the small mammals.

The vegetation around Boomplaas Cave at the time of maximum cold and drought was composed mainly of shrubs and grass with few fruits and corms that could be used by people. The charcoal samples are dominated by the so-called rhinoceros bush, a small shrub that grows today in relatively dry areas. The larger mammal fauna during the Ice Age was dominated by grazers that included "giant" species of buffalo, horse, and

COLLECTION OF PLANT REMAINS

Kind of remains	Sediment type	Information available from investigation	Method of extraction and examination	Volume to be collected
Soil	All	Detailed description of how the deposit formed and under what conditions	(Best examined *in situ* by environmental staff)	(Column sample)
Pollen	Buried soils, waterlogged deposits	Vegetation, land use	Laboratory extraction and high power (x400) microscopy	0.05 ltr or column sample
Phytoliths	All sediments	As above	As above	As above
Diatoms	Waterlain deposits	Salinity and levels of water pollution	Laboratory extraction and high power (x400) microscopy	0.10 ltr
Uncharred plant remains (seeds, mosses, leaves)	Wet to waterlogged	Vegetation, diet, plant materials used in building crafts, technology, fuel	Laboratory sieving to 300 microns	10–20 ltr
Charred plant remains (grain, chaff, charcoal)	All sediments	Vegetation, diet, plant materials used in building crafts, technology, fuel processing of crops and behavior	Flotation to 300 microns	40–80 ltr
Wood (charcoal)	Wet to waterlogged, charred	Dendrochronology, climate, building materials and technology	Low power microscopy (x10)	Hand or lab. collection

Table summarizing collection methods for microbotanical and macrobotanical plant remains, with an indication of the range of information to be gained for each category.

hartebeest. These became extinct by about 10,000 years ago (the worldwide extinction of big-game is discussed in a later section).

The Boomplaas charcoal directly reflects the gradual change in climate and vegetation which led to the disappearance of the large grazers, and to a corresponding shift in subsistence practices by the cave's occupants. The charcoal analysis also highlights more subtle changes that reflect a shift in the season of maximum rainfall. The woody vegetation in the Cango Valley today is dominated by the thorn tree, *Acacia karroo*, characteristic of large areas in southern Africa where it is relatively dry and rain falls mostly in summer. Thorn tree charcoal is absent in the Ice Age samples at Boomplaas but here and at the nearby site of Buffelskloof it appears from about 5000 years ago and by 2000 years ago is the dominant species. This shift to hot, relatively moist summers after about 5000 years ago in the Cango Valley is traceable also in the carbon isotope analysis of a stalagmite (see box, pp. 234–35) from the nearby Cango Caves. With encroachment of

summer rainfall species the inhabitants of the cave were able to make more use of a new range of fruits; the seeds of some of these are preserved in deposits that postdate 2000 years ago.

By no means all wood subjected to this kind of analysis is charred. Increasing quantities of *waterlogged* wood are being recovered from wet sites in many parts of the world (see below, and Chapters 2 and 8). And in some conditions, such as extreme cold or dryness, *desiccated wood* may survive without either burning or waterlogging; examination of a small slice (less than 1 mm (0.04 in) thick) under the light microscope and in the SEM permits identification of wood in pristine condition.

Other Sources of Evidence. A great deal of information on vegetation in the less remote periods studied by archaeologists can be obtained from art, from texts (e.g. the writings of Pliny the Elder, Roman farming texts, accounts and illustrations by early explorers such as Captain Cook), and even from photographs.

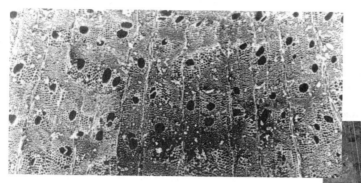

Boomplaas Cave, Cape Province, South Africa. (Left) Scanning electron microscope photograph (×50) of charcoal from the thorn tree Acacia karroo. The appearance of this species at Boomplaas after 5000 years ago indicates a shift to hot, relatively moist summers. (Below) Excavations in progress at the cave in 1978. Compare the photograph on p. 110 taken at an earlier stage of the work.

No single category of evidence can provide us with a total picture of local or regional vegetation, of small-scale trends or long-term changes: each produces a partial version of past realities. Input is needed from every source available, and, as will be seen below, these must be combined with results from the other forms of data studied in this chapter in order to reconstruct the best approximation of a past environment.

RECONSTRUCTING THE ANIMAL ENVIRONMENT

Animal remains were the first evidence used by 19th-century archaeologists to characterize the climate of the prehistoric periods encountered in their excavations. Thus, concepts such as the Mammoth Age, the Aurochs Age, and the Reindeer Age were in common use until the classification of stone tools replaced them. Underlying these terms was the realization that different species were absent, present, or particularly abundant in certain layers and hence also in certain periods, and the assumption that this reflected changing climatic conditions.

Today, in order to use faunal remains as a guide to environment, we need to look more critically at the evidence than did the 19th-century pioneers. We need to understand the complex relationship between modern animals and their environment. We also need to investigate how animal remains arrived at a site – either naturally, or through the activities of carnivores or people (see taphonomy box, pp. 284–85) – and thus how representative they may be of the variety of animals in their period.

Microfauna

Just as tiny plant remains tend to be of greater importance to environmental studies than large ones, so small animals (microfauna) are better indicators of climate and environmental change than are large species,

because they are sensitive to oscillations and adapt relatively quickly, whereas large animals have a relatively wide range of tolerance. In addition, since microfauna tend to accumulate naturally on a site, they reflect the immediate environment more accurately than the larger animals whose remains are often accumulated through human or animal predation. Like pollen, small animals, and especially insects, are also usually found in far greater numbers than larger ones, which improves the statistical significance of their analysis. It is essential to extract a good sample by means of dry and/or wet screening or sieving; huge quantities are otherwise missed in the course of excavation.

A wide variety of microfauna is found on archaeological sites:

Insectivores, Rodents, and Bats. These are the species most commonly encountered. A specialist can obtain a great deal of environmental information from the associations and fluctuations of these seemingly insignificant creatures, since most of them are present in archaeological sites naturally rather than through human exploitation.

It is necessary to ensure as far as possible that the bones are contemporaneous with the layer, and that burrowing has not occurred. One should also bear in mind that, even if the remains are not intrusive, they will not always indicate the *immediate* environment –

if they come from owl pellets, for example, they may have been caught up to a few kilometers from the site (the contents of bird pellets can nevertheless be of great value in assessing local environments).

As with large mammals, certain small species can be indicative of fairly specific environmental conditions. Richard Klein of Stanford University has noted a strong correlation between rainfall and the size of the modern dune mole rat of South Africa – the rats seem to grow larger in response to a general increase in vegetation density brought about by higher rainfall. His analysis of the fauna from Elands Bay Cave, South Africa (see box, pp. 254–55), revealed that the rats from layers dating to between 11,000 and 9000 years ago were distinctly bigger than those of the preceding seven millennia, and this has been taken as evidence of a rise in precipitation at the end of the Pleistocene.

Birds and Fish. Bones of birds and fish are particularly fragile, but are well worth studying. They can for example be used to determine the seasons in which particular sites were occupied (Chapter 7). Birds are sensitive to climatic change, and the alternation of "cold" and "warm" species in the last Ice Age has been of great help in assessing environment, though it is sometimes difficult to decide whether a bird is present naturally or has been brought in by a human or animal predator.

Land Molluscs. The calcium carbonate shells of land molluscs are preserved in many types of sediment, but especially in alkaline contexts where pollen analysis is constrained. They reflect local conditions, and can be responsive to changes in microclimate. But one needs to take into account that many species have a very broad tolerance, and their reaction to change is relatively slow, so that they "hang on" in adverse areas, and disperse slowly into newly acceptable areas.

As usual, it is necessary to establish whether the shells were deposited *in situ*, or washed or blown in from elsewhere. The sample of shells needs to be unbiased – sieving should ensure that not merely the large or colorful specimens that catch an excavator's eye are kept, but the whole assemblage. Quality of preservation is important since shell shape and ornamentation are key elements in identifying species. Once the assemblages have been determined, one can trace changes through time, and hence how the molluscan population has altered in response to environmental oscillations. Temperature and rainfall are the dominant factors; where a species is near the limit of its normal range, it can be a very sensitive indicator of change.

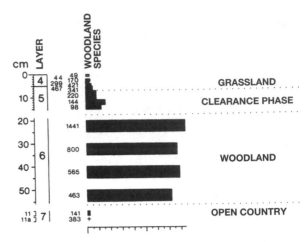

Land mollusc histogram based on excavations at Avebury, southern England. Fluctuating percentages of woodland species of snails reveal a change from open country (tundra) c. 10,000 years ago to woodland and eventually to grassland.

A great deal of work has been done on this topic by the British specialist John Evans and others at a number of prehistoric sites in Britain. For example, snails from sections at the Neolithic monuments of Woodhenge and Durrington Walls show that the area was wooded in that period. At Avebury nearby, the relative percentages of species found in successive layers of soil beneath the site's bank indicate a tundra environment about 10,000 years ago, open woodland 8000–6000 years ago, closed woodland 6000–3000 years ago, followed by a phase of clearance and plowing, and finally grassland.

Marine Molluscs. As we have already seen earlier in this chapter, middens of marine molluscs can sometimes help to delineate ancient shorelines, and their changing percentages of species through time can reveal something of the nature of the coastal microenvironment – such as whether it was sandy or rocky – through study of the modern preferences of the species represented. The climatic change suggested by these alterations in the presence or abundance of different species can be matched with the results of oxygen isotope analysis of the shells – a strong correlation between the two methods has been found by Hiroko Koike in her work on Jomon middens in Tokyo Bay where, for example, the disappearance of tropical species implied a cold phase at 5000 or 6000 years ago, confirmed by an increase in oxygen 18 (and hence a decrease of water temperature) around 5000 years ago. In Chapter 7 we shall see how changes in mollusc shell growth can establish seasonality.

Worms and Insects. Besides molluscs, a narrow range of nematodes (unsegmented worms) and annelids (such as earthworms represented by egg-cases) may be found, especially in waterlogged deposits including cesspits, as well as a wide range of arthropods such as mites and insects, the latter in the form of adults, larvae, and (in the case of flies) puparia. Analyses of fossil assemblages of aquatic midge larvae in cores from lakes in northern North America have shown changes in lake summer surface water temperature over several millennia at the end of the Ice Age. The study of *insects* (paleoentomology) was rather neglected in archaeology until about 30 years ago, since when a great deal of pioneering work has been done, particularly in Britain. Insect exoskeletons can be quite resistant to decomposition, and some assemblages comprise thousands of individuals.

Since we know the distribution and environmental requirements of their modern descendants, it is often possible to use insect remains as accurate indicators of the likely climatic conditions (and to some extent of the vegetation) prevailing in particular periods and local areas. Some species have very precise requirements in terms of where they like to breed and the kinds of food their larvae need. However, rather than use single "indicator species" to reconstruct a microenvironment, it is safer to consider associations of species, as with mammals or plant communities. Hence, the so-called mutual climatic range method is employed: this assumes that the present-day climatic tolerance of each species is the same as in the past, and therefore where several species are found together, the ancient climate must lie within the area of overlap of their tolerance ranges. It follows that the more species present, the more precisely can this area of overlap be determined. Although insects reflect microclimates, it should be remembered that these are in turn largely governed by the overall climate.

In view of their rapid response to climatic changes, insects are useful indicators of the timing and scale of these events, and of seasonal and mean annual temperatures. A few depictions of insects even exist from the Ice Age, and reveal some of the types that managed to survive in periglacial areas.

Coleoptera (beetles and weevils) are particularly useful insects for microenvironmental studies. Their head and thorax are often found well preserved; almost all those known from the Pleistocene still exist; they are sensitive indicators of past climates, responding quickly to environmental change (especially temperature); and they form a varied group with well-defined tolerance ranges – some species are very selective in terms of vegetal environment, and live exclusively on particular plants, such as oak, or on certain fungi.

In one study, the climatic tolerance ranges of 350 coleopteran species that occur as Pleistocene fossils were plotted; the mutual climatic range method was then applied to 57 coleopteran faunas from 26 sites in Britain. It was found that there had been very rapid major warmings at 13,000 and 10,000 years ago, and a prolonged cooling trend from 12,500 years ago (when conditions were the same as now, with average July temperatures around 17°C, 62.6°F) to 10,500 years ago, together with a number of minor oscillations.

Occasionally the discovery of insects in archaeological deposits can have important ramifications. To take a major example, the remains of the beetle *Scolytus scolytus*, found in Neolithic deposits in Hampstead, London, occur in a layer before the sharp decline in elm pollen known just before 5000 years ago in cores from the lake sediments and peats of northwest Europe. This archaeologically famous and abrupt decline was originally attributed to climatic change or degrading soils, and later to clearance by early farmers requiring fodder (see Chapter 12). However, *Scolytus scolytus* is the beetle that spreads the pathogenic fungus causing Dutch elm disease, and thus provides an alternative, natural explanation for the elm decline of 5000 years ago. The recent outbreak of elm disease in Europe has allowed scientists to monitor the disease's effects on the modern pollen record. They have indeed found that the decline in elm pollen is of similar proportions to that in the Neolithic; not only that, but the accompanying increase in weed pollen caused by the opening of the woodland canopy is the same in both

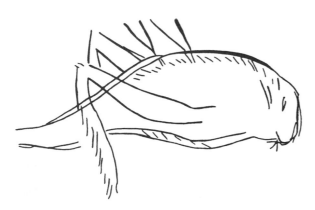

Grasshopper engraved on a bone fragment from the late Ice Age (Magdalenian) site of Enlène, Ariège, France. Insects respond rapidly to climatic change, and are sensitive indicators of the timing and scale of environmental variations.

cases. This fact, together with the known presence of the beetle in Neolithic times, makes a strong case for the existence of elm disease in that period.

Insects have also come to the fore in excavations at York, where some Viking timbers seem to have been riddled with woodworm. A 3rd-century AD Roman sewer in the city was found filled with sludge, which had concentrations of sewer flies in two side channels leading to lavatories. The sewer was known from its position to have drained a military bath-house but remains of grain beetles and golden spider beetles showed that it must also have drained a granary.

Clearly, insects are proving invaluable for the quantity and quality of information they can give archaeologists, not just about climate and vegetation, but about living conditions in and around archaeological sites as well.

Macrofauna

Remains of large animals found on archaeological sites mainly help us build up a picture of past human diet (Chapter 7). As environmental indicators they have proved less reliable than was once assumed, primarily because they are not so sensitive to environmental changes as small animals, but also because their remains will very likely have been deposited in an archaeological context through human or animal action. Bones from animals killed by people or by car-

nivores have been selected, and so cannot accurately reflect the full range of fauna present in the environment. The ideal is therefore to find accumulations of animal remains brought about by natural accident or catastrophe – animals caught in a flash flood perhaps, or buried by volcanic eruption, or mired (as in the case of the wide range of Pleistocene fauna found in the famous tarpits of Rancho La Brea, Los Angeles), or which became frozen in permafrost. But these are by any standards exceptional finds – very different from the usual accumulations of animal bones encountered by archaeologists.

Bone Collection and Identification in the Field. Bones are usually only preserved in situations where they have been buried quickly, thus avoiding the effects of weathering and the activities of scavenging animals. They also survive well, in a softened condition, in non-acidic waterlogged sites. In some cases, they may require treatment in the field before it is safe to remove them without damage. In sediments, they slowly become impregnated with minerals, and their weight and hardness increase, and thus also their durability.

After collection, the first step is to identify as many fragments as possible, both as part of the body and as a species. This is the work of a zoologist or one of the growing number of zooarchaeologists, although every archaeologist should be able to recognize a basic range of bones and species. Identification is made by compar-

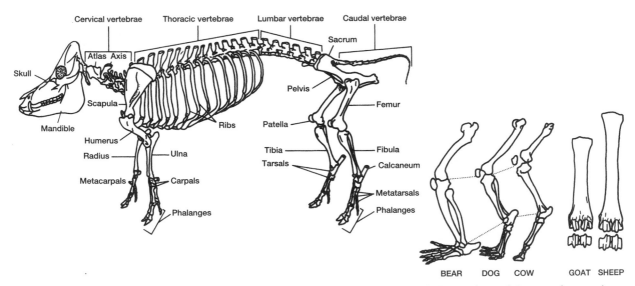

Identifying animal bones. (Left) Bones in the skeleton of a typical domesticated animal, the pig. (Center) Structural comparison of mammal limb bones. In bears (and humans), the whole foot touches the ground, whereas among carnivores such as the dog only the toes do so. Herbivores such as cattle walk on "tiptoe," with only the final phalanges on the ground. (Right) Sheep and goat bones are notoriously difficult to distinguish, although there are subtle differences as in these metacarpals.

COLLECTION OF ANIMAL REMAINS

Kind of remains	Sediment type	Information available from investigation	Method of extraction and examination	Volume to be collected
Small mammal bone	All but very acidic	Natural fauna, ecology	Sieving to 1 mm	75 ltr
Bird bone	As above	See large and small mammal bone	As above	As above
Fish bone, scales, and otoliths	As above	Diet, fishing technology, and seasonal activity	As above	As above
Land molluscs	Alkaline	Past vegetation, soil type, depositional history	Laboratory sieving to 500 microns	10 ltr
Marine molluscs (shellfish)	Alkaline and neutral	Diet, trade, season of collection, shellfish farming	Hand sorting, troweled sediment and sieving	75 ltr
Insect remains (charred)	All sediments	Climate, vegetation, living conditions, trade, human diet	Laboratory sieving and paraffin flotation to 300 microns	10–20 ltr
Insect remains (uncharred)	Wet to waterlogged	As above	As above	As above
Large mammal bone	All but very acidic	Natural fauna, diet, husbandry, butchery, disease, social status, craft techniques	Hand sorting, troweled sediment, and sieving	Whole context troweled except when bulk samples are taken

Table summarizing collection methods for microfauna and macrofauna, with an indication of the variety of information to be gained for each category.

ison with a reference collection. The resulting lists and associations of species can also sometimes help to date Paleolithic sites (see Chapter 4).

Once quantification of the bone assemblage has been completed (see box, pp. 288–89), what can the results tell us about the contemporary environment?

Assumptions and Limitations. The anatomy and especially the teeth of large animals tell us something about their diet and hence, in the case of herbivores, of the type of vegetation they prefer. However, most information about range and habitat comes from studies of modern species, on the assumption that behavior has not changed substantially since the period in question. These studies show that large animals will tolerate – i.e. have the potential to withstand or exploit – a much wider range of temperatures and environments than was once thought. Thus species characteristic today of arctic and temperate regions in fact show a marked overlap in their habitats, and share a very similar minimum-temperature tolerance. This means that we can no longer assume, as archaeologists once did, that Pleistocene species such as the woolly rhinoceros or cave bear necessarily indicate cold climate – the presence of these species should be regarded merely as proof of their ability to tolerate low temperatures.

If it is therefore difficult to link fluctuations in a site's macrofaunal assemblage with changes in *temperature*, we can at least say that changes in *precipitation* may sometimes be reflected quite directly in variations in faunal remains. For example, species differ as to the depth of snow they can tolerate, and this affects winter faunal assemblages in those parts of the world that endure thick snow-cover for much of the winter.

Large mammals are not generally good indicators of *vegetation*, since herbivores can thrive in a wide range of environments and eat a variety of plants. Thus, individual species cannot usually be regarded as characteristic of one particular habitat, but there are exceptions. Ibex, which today are restricted to the higher reaches of mountains, were forced by glaciations to live at lower altitudes, and there were similar latitudinal shifts by other animals and birds. For example, reindeer reached northern Spain in the last Ice Age, as shown not only by bones but also by cave art. Such major shifts clearly reflect environmental change. In the rock art of the Sahara, too, one can see clear evidence for the presence of species such as giraffe and elephant that could not survive in the area today, and thus for dramatic environmental modification.

As will be seen in Chapter 7, fauna can also be used to determine in which seasons of the year a site was occupied. The techniques described there can go some way toward showing how the local environment changed from season to season. It is possible as well to correlate macrofauna and other types of evidence. Many faunal sequences in areas such as Europe or southern Africa display changes of species that are independent of culture change, span thousands of years, and can be correlated with sequences derived from sediment or plant studies.

In coastal sites, including many caves in Cantabrian Spain, or around the shores of the Mediterranean (see Franchthi Cave above), or on the Cape coast of South Africa (see box overleaf), marine resources and herbivore remains may come and go through the archaeological sequence as changes in sea level extended or drowned the coastal plain, thus changing the sites' proximity to the shore and the availability of grazing.

One always has to bear in mind that faunal fluctuations can have causes other than climate or people; additional factors may include competition, epidemics, or fluctuations in numbers of predators. Moreover, small-scale local variations in climate and weather can have enormous effects on the numbers and distribution of wild animals, so that despite its high powers of resistance a species may decline from extreme abundance to virtual extinction within a few years.

Big-game Extinctions. There is clear evidence from many Polynesian islands, as will be seen below, that the first human settlers devastated the indigenous fauna and flora. But in other parts of the world the question of animal extinctions, and whether and how people were involved, still forms a major topic of debate in archaeology. This is particularly true of the big-game extinctions in the New World and Australia at the end of the Ice Age, where losses were far heavier than in Asia and Africa, and included not just the mammoth and mastodon, but species such as the horse in the Americas.

There are two main sides in the big-game extinction debate. One group of scholars, led by the American

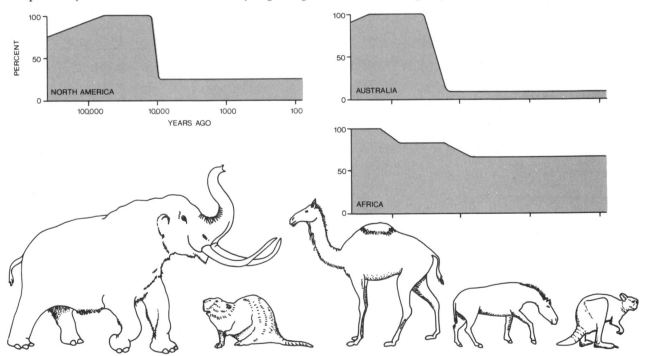

Big-game extinctions. (Top) Diagrams by Paul Martin illustrate the sudden decline of large animal species in North America and Australia around the time of human colonization, by comparison with Africa, where big game had longer to adapt to human predation. Other scholars emphasize the importance of environmental factors as well in the demise of megafauna such as (above, left to right) the mastodon, giant beaver, camel, and horse (all North American), and the Australian giant kangaroo, Sthenurus.

scientist Paul Martin, believes that the arrival of people in the New World and Australia, followed by over-exploitation of prey, caused the extinctions. New data from Australia have provided some support for this view, since dates obtained by amino acid racemization from eggshells of the large flightless bird *Genyornis* from three different climate regions show that it disappeared suddenly, around 50,000 years ago, the time when humans may have arrived in this continent. The simultaneous extinction of *Genyornis* at all sites during a period of modest climate change points to human impact as the major cause of its extinction. This view, however, does not account for the extinction at about the same time of mammal and bird species that were not obvious human prey, or that would not have been vulnerable to hunting. In any case, the precise date of each extinction is not yet known, while the dates of human entry into both continents are still uncertain (Chapter 11) and constantly being pushed back well beyond the extinctions.

The other view, presented by the geologist Ernest Lundelius and others, is that climatic change is the primary cause. But this interpretation does not explain why the many similar changes of earlier periods had no such effect, and in any case many of the species that disappeared had a broad geographic distribution and climatic tolerance.

Extinctions caused by climatic change had occurred previously, but always tended to affect all size classes of mammal equally, and those that disappeared were replaced by migration or the development of new species – this did not happen in the Pleistocene extinctions. All big-game species weighing over 1000 kg (1 ton) as adults (the megaherbivores) disappeared from the New World, Europe, and Australia, as did about 75 percent of the herbivore genera weighing 100–1000 kg (0.1–1 ton), but only 41 percent of species weighing 5–100 kg (11–220 lb), and under 2 percent of the smaller creatures.

A compromise theory that takes these factors into account and links the two main hypotheses has been put forward by the South African scholar Norman Owen-Smith. He believes that it was in the first place human overexploitation that led to the disappearance of the megaherbivores, which in turn caused a change in vegetation that led to the extinction of some medium-sized herbivores.

In view of the tremendous effects that modern elephants in eastern and southern Africa have on vegetation – by felling or damaging trees, opening up clearings for smaller animals, and transforming wooded savanna into grassland – it is certain that the removal of megaherbivores must have radically affected the Pleistocene environment. In one game reserve in Natal Province, South Africa, which has had no elephants for the last 100 years, three species of antelope have also become locally extinct, and open-country grazers such as wildebeest and waterbuck are much reduced in numbers.

Owen-Smith's hypothesis has the merit that it can be tested through a more detailed analysis of vegetation changes and the order in which extinctions took place. Recently, an old notion has been revived – that some kind of epidemic, a mysterious and still totally hypothetical "hyperdisease," wiped out a range of animals. It remains to be seen what evidence can be mustered for this explanation.

Promising New Techniques. Eventually we may be able to extract more specific environmental data from bones using new techniques – for example, information on temperature and moisture histories from isotopic analysis of tooth-enamel and bones of the type described in Chapter 4, or from analysis of the amino acids in bone collagen. Work by M.A. Zeder on trace elements in the bones of sheep and goat from Iran has established that calcium, magnesium, and zinc are found in significantly different concentrations in animals from different environments; it should therefore be possible to obtain information on past environments through similar analyses of ancient bones.

In the same way, Tim Heaton and his colleagues in South Africa have found that the ratio of nitrogen isotopes in bone may be a useful tool for studying past variations in climate. Samples from prehistoric and early historic skeletons of humans and wild herbivores from a variety of habitats and climatic zones in South Africa and Namibia were tested for their $^{15}N/^{14}N$ values. They discovered variations that could not be ascribed to diet: specimens from far inland, or that reflected consumption only of terrestrial plants, produced results similar to those from the coast. In short, the $^{15}N/^{14}N$ ratio seems to be linked to climatic variation, especially in areas such as this where big changes in precipitation have occurred, with increasing aridity being reflected in a rise in ^{15}N.

Other Sources of Animal Evidence. Bones are not the only source of information about macrofauna. Frozen carcasses have already been mentioned, as has art. In some sites, *tracks* have been found. Examples range from the early hominid and animal prints – over 10,000 of them, including birds and insects – at Laetoli in Tanzania; tracks on Bronze Age soils (Chapter 7); and paw-prints on Roman tiles (Chapter 7). Caves are particularly rich in such traces, and the tracks of hyenas

ELANDS BAY CAVE

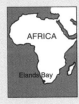

The Verlorenvlei estuary today (above). Elands Bay Cave lies just around the tip of the peninsula seen in the distance.

Located near the mouth of the Verlorenvlei estuary on the southwest coast of Cape Province, South Africa, Elands Bay Cave was occupied for thousands of years and is particularly important for the documentation of changes in coastline and subsistence at the end of the Ice Age. Work at the cave by John Parkington and his associates has demonstrated clearly how, within 6000 or 7000 years, the rise in sea level transformed the site's territory from being inland riverine to estuarine and coastal.

During the period *c.* 13,600–12,000 years ago, subsistence practices remained relatively stable, although the coastline must have approached to about 12 km (7¹/₂ miles) from the site according to present-day offshore sea-bed contours. The faunal remains left by the cave's occupants are dominated by an assemblage of large grazers such as rhinoceroses, equids, buffalo, and eland, suggesting that the local environment was one of fairly open grassland. The very low marine component in the remains reflects the considerable distance to the coast – still beyond the 2-hour distance considered normal for most hunter-gatherers (see box, pp. 258–59), and too far to make it economical to carry shellfish. The birds found are of riverine species, primarily ducks.

By about 11,000 years ago, the coast had approached to some 5–6 km (3.1–3.7 miles) west from the site, well within striking distance for hunter-gatherers. The first thin layers of shellfish now appear in the cave's sequence. In the following three millennia the sea encroached to 2 km (1¹/₄ miles) or so from the site, and gradually drowned the lower reaches of the Verlorenvlei valley, turning them into estuary and then into coastline.

The disappearance of the habitats suited to the large grazers had radical effects on the faunal environment. At least two animals (the giant horse and giant buffalo) became extinct, and other large animals such as the rhinoceros and Cape buffalo are absent or extremely rare in the cave's deposits after 9000 years ago. They are replaced at this site and in other parts of the region by smaller herbivores such as grysbok – browsers rather than grazers, a fact that implies a different plant environment, probably linked to a change in precipitation.

At the same time, there is a clear rise to dominance of marine animals between 11,000 and 9000 years ago, and the cave's sequence changes from a series of brown loams containing thin

Rising sea levels (below) at the end of the Ice Age drowned the coastal plain that once lay to the west of Elands Bay Cave.

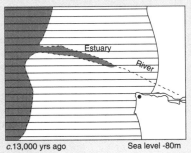

*c.*13,000 yrs ago Sea level -80m

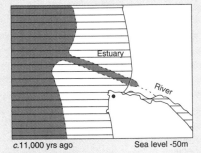

*c.*11,000 yrs ago Sea level -50m

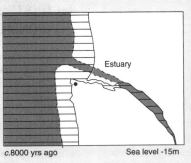

*c.*8000 yrs ago Sea level -15m

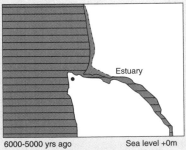

6000-5000 yrs ago Sea level +0m

--·--·-- Ancient shoreline   ‿‿‿ Modern shoreline   ● Elands Bay Cave

6 miles / 10 km

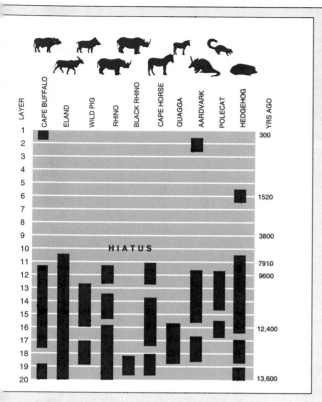

Decline of the grassland animals (above) as reflected in the faunal remains recovered from Elands Bay Cave. By 9000 years ago, when the sea had encroached to within 3 km (1.9 miles) of the site, these animals had virtually ceased to be exploited from the cave.

shell layers to a sequence of true shell middens. In addition there are very high frequencies (in relation to terrestrial species) of cormorants, marine fish, rock lobsters, and seals after 9500 years ago, by which period the coast was a little more than 3 km (1.9 miles) away. The drowning of the valley after 11,000 years ago is reflected in the abundance of hippopotamuses and shallow-water birds such as flamingos and pelicans. At this time the estuary was certainly within exploitable distance. Some 9000–8500 years ago the cave was roughly equidistant between coast and estuary, but after 8000 the coast was nearer, reaching its present position about 6000 years ago.

and cave bears are well known in Europe; one can also find the claw-marks and nest-hollows of the cave bear. Toothmarks of beaver have been found on Neolithic wood from the Somerset Levels, England.

Fossil dung (coprolites) has also survived in many dry caves, and can contain much information about fauna and flora (see above p. 244). Bechan Cave in southeast Utah, for instance, has about 300 cu. m (392 cu. yd) of dehydrated mammoth dung, while many other species left their coprolites in other American caves. Quite apart from revealing which animals were present in different periods, the dung also shows what they ate, and even contributes to the debate on Pleistocene extinctions (see above). Paul Martin, a pioneer of fossil dung analysis, has shown that the contents of the coprolites of the extinct Shasta ground sloth do not change up to the time of its disappearance, and Jim Mead has reached the same conclusion with the dung of mammoths and the extinct mountain goat. These findings therefore suggest that these New World extinctions, at least, were not caused by a change in vegetation or diet. The decline in frequency and the eventual disappearance of the dung of certain species such as the ground sloth provide further (datable) evidence of extinctions even in the complete absence of skeletal material.

Other sources of evidence include horse and reindeer fat identified chemically from residues in sediment, and blood residues of various animals (Chapter 7) found on stone tools. Information can also be extracted from the writings and illustrations of early explorers, or the geographies of Roman writers. Even bone artifacts can sometimes be clear climatic indicators: large numbers of worn and polished bone skates, for instance, have been found in deposits of Anglo-Scandinavian date in York, England, suggesting that winters were harsh enough to freeze the Ouse river.

RECONSTRUCTING THE HUMAN ENVIRONMENT

All human groups have an impact on their environment, both locally and on a wider scale. One of the most important effects of human interference, the domestication of plants and animals, will be examined in Chapter 7. Here we shall concentrate on how people exploited and managed the landscape and natural resources.

The basic feature of the human environment is the site and the factors influencing the selection of a location. Many of these factors are readily detectable, either visually (proximity to water, strategic position, orientation) or by some method of measurement. The climates of caves and rockshelters, for example, can be assessed through the study of temperatures, shade and exposure to sunlight, and exposure to winds in different seasons, since these are the factors that determine their habitability. Site exploitation territory analysis (box overleaf) is one recognized procedure for assessing a site's location and the land around it.

Archaeologists should never forget that sometimes the choice of site will have been dictated by factors that we cannot assess: malevolent spirits, "good" or "bad" places – what Ernest Burch, in his study of the Alaskan Eskimo, has called the Nonempirical Environment.

The Immediate Environment: Human Modification of the Living Area

One of the first ways in which people modified their living places was by the controlled use of fire. Archaeologists have debated for decades just how early fire was introduced. Until recently the earliest contender was Zhoukoudian cave in China at some half a million years ago. In 1988, C.K. Brain and Andrew Sillen discovered pieces of apparently burnt animal bone at the Swartkrans Cave, South Africa, in layers dating to *c.* 1.5 million years ago. Since simple visual analysis cannot reliably differentiate burning from mineral staining on bones, Brain and Sillen carried out experiments with fresh bones, examining the cell structure and chemical changes that occurred when the bones were heated to various temperatures and then cooled slowly. Microscopic analysis showed that the changes were very similar to those in the fossil bones, suggesting that the latter were probably cooked on a wood fire at temperatures of less than 300°C (572°F) up to 500°C (932°F). The bones came from antelope, warthog, zebra, and baboon. Remains of early hominids found in the cave layers give a strong indication as to who tended those fires.

Evidence of actual hearths in early prehistoric campsites has always been hard to find and recognize, but recently, a new technique has been developed for detecting ash in sediments, because different minerals emit characteristic spectra when illuminated with infrared radiation. Hence, ancient hearths can now be detected after they have disintegrated almost completely. Most ash minerals change over time, but about 2 percent stays relatively stable. In this way, fireplaces have been identified in the Israeli cave of Hayonim (250,000 BP) through comparison with clearly defined hearths in the nearby cave of Kebara (70,000 BP). When the technique was applied to Zhoukoudian cave in China, long considered to have the

world's earliest evidence of controlled fire, at 500,000 years ago, the chemical "signature" of ash was not found in the part of the cave that was analyzed. Some bones from the cave are definitely burned, but it remains uncertain whether this was a case of natural or controlled fire.

The presence of fire in a cave is important not only for cooking and human comfort, but also because it affects the cave's microclimates and can accelerate weathering of the walls, as was mentioned in the box on cave sediments on pp. 234–35.

Archaeologists can show that people adapted to cave life in the Upper Paleolithic in other ways too. Visual examination has found evidence for scaffolding in some decorated caves such as Lascaux in France. Excavations elsewhere have unearthed traces of pavements of slabs, and of shelters. Specialized analysis of cave sediments can even unearth proof of bedding and the use of animal skins as floor coverings. Arlette Leroi-Gourhan, for example, has used pollen analysis to show the presence of clusters of grasses in Lascaux, and armfuls of unburnt grasses around a hearth at Fontanet, France, both of which probably indicate bedding. Cave sediments analyzed by Rolf Rottländer at the Upper Paleolithic cave of Geissenklösterle in western Germany showed such a huge proportion of fat that it suggests the floor was probably covered in the skins of large mammals.

Besides caves, archaeologists can investigate evidence from open sites for tents, wind-breaks, and other architectural remains as indicators of the way in which people modified their own immediate environment during the Paleolithic. For later periods, of course, this evidence multiplies enormously and we move into the realm of full-scale architecture and town planning discussed elsewhere in the book (Chapters 5 and 10).

Modification of the immediate environment is certainly fundamental to human culture. But how can we learn something about the varied ways in which people manipulated the world beyond?

Human Exploitation of the Wider Environment

Methods for Investigating Land Use. Examination of the soils around human habitations can be carried out where sections are exposed, or where an original land surface is laid bare beneath a monument. Specialists can go some way to reconstructing human use of the land by a combination of all the methods outlined in earlier sections. However, a different method is needed for cases where the area around the site has to be assessed on the surface.

This kind of off-site analysis was first developed systematically by Claudio Vita-Finzi and Eric Higgs in their work in Israel, and has been widely adopted, albeit with modifications and variations. Two distinct types of investigation are involved – site catchment analysis and site exploitation territory analysis – together with combinations and variations, and these methods are discussed in the box overleaf. Geographic Information Systems (GIS) are now also proving useful in investigating and mapping ancient environments, as, for instance, in George Milner's project at Cahokia, in the United States (see box, pp. 260–61).

Gardens. The archaeology of gardens, whether decorative or food-producing, is a subdiscipline that has only recently come to the fore, devoted to the accurate study, and in some cases the reconstruction, of ancient gardens. Examples include the complexes of mounds, terraces, and walls that constituted the Maori gardens of New Zealand; the formal garden of the 8th-century AD imperial villa at Nara in Japan; and especially those of Roman villas like that at Fishbourne, southern England. The best known are probably those preserved by the volcanic debris at Pompeii and its adjacent settlements. In most cases, as at Nara, a combination of excavation and analysis of plant remains has led to an accurate reconstruction; but at Pompeii, identification of species comes not only from pollen, seeds, and charred wood, but also from the hollows left by tree-roots, casts of which can be taken in the same way as for corpses (see Chapter 11). Such casts can even provide details about gardening techniques: for instance, the base of a lemon tree in a garden of Poppaea's villa at Oplontis, near Pompeii, showed clearly that it had been grafted, a method still used in the region to obtain new lemon trees. Similarly, at the "Mesoamerican Pompeii," the site of Cerén in El Salvador, engulfed by volcanic ash in c. AD 595 (see p. 63), liquid plaster poured into cavities has produced remarkable casts of plants, including corn stalks planted in fields, maize cobs stored in a crib, chili pepper bushes, and an entire household garden of 70 agave plants.

Pollution of Air and Water. Human effects on water resources have not yet received much attention from archaeologists, but recent evidence shows clearly that pollution of rivers is by no means confined to our own epoch. Excavations in the city of York, northeast England, have revealed changes in the composition of freshwater fish over the past 1900 years, with a marked shift from clean-water species such as shad and grayling to species more tolerant of polluted water (such as perch and roach). This change occurs around the 10th century AD, when the Viking town underwent rapid development, apparently intensifying pollution of the river Ouse in the process. The shift is mirrored in remains of freshwater molluscs, which change from species requiring well-oxygenated (i.e. clean) water to others that are less demanding. Air pollution is not a modern phenomenon either: cores from lakes in Sweden and a peat bog in the Swiss Jura Mountains have revealed that lead levels first increased 5500 years ago, when farming increased wind-blown soil, and then far more sharply 3000 years ago, when the Phoenicians started trading in lead mined in Spain, and metal smelting began. Lead pollution continued to increase as the Greeks began releasing lead into the atmosphere through the extraction of silver from ores; and even more so during Roman times, when 80,000 tons of lead were produced every year from European mines. Greenland ice cores not only confirm these data about lead, but also record marked pollution from ancient copper smelting in Roman and medieval times, especially in Europe and China.

Land Management Using Field Systems. Management of land is detectable in several ways. The clearest evidence comprises the various traces visible on the land surface, such as the 300 ha (741 acres) of Maya ridged fields at Pulltrouser Swamp, Belize, linked by a network of canals; the spectacular mountain terraces of the Incas; the *chinampas* (fertile reclaimed land, made of mud dredged from canals) of the Aztecs; or the similar but very much older drainage ditches and fertile garden lands of Kuk Swamp, New Guinea (see box pp. 262–63). Similarly, in Britain archaeologists have discovered Bronze Age stone boundary walls, known as reaves, on Dartmoor, and field systems and lynchets (small banks that build up against field boundaries on slopes) in many areas. In Japan, about 500 ancient rice paddy fields have been discovered, especially from the Yayoi period (400 BC–AD 300), together with their irrigation systems – wooden dams, drainage ditches, and baulks. For example, 10 ha (25 acres) of the 40-ha (100-acre) site of Ikejima-Fukumanji site near Osaka have been excavated, sealed by sandy sediments laid down by floods.

Artifacts and art can also be a valuable source of information about ancient land management. Han dynasty sites in China, for example, have yielded pottery models of paddy fields, some of them with irrigation ponds with a movable gate at the center of a dam, used to regulate the flow of water into the field.

Evidence for Plowing. Investigation of mounds, including their mollusc and pollen content, and especially the

People are geomorphic agents and bring a great deal of varied material into their sites – not just food but also tools, fuel, raw materials, etc. Indeed, the human contribution to a sediment can range from less than 1 percent to almost 100 percent. The catchment of a site is the total area from which the site's contents have been derived. At its simplest, therefore, **site catchment analysis (SCA)** is the attempt to work out the full inventory of a site's contents and their sources.

Site catchment analysis as more widely understood, however, is the technique devised by Eric Higgs and Claudio Vita-Finzi for studying the area around a site that would have been exploited by the site's occupants – hence its more accurate name, analysis of **site exploitation territory (SET)**. The aim is to calculate the proportions within the territory of such resources as arable or pastoral land, so that conclusions can be drawn about the site's nature and function.

SITE CATCHMENT ANALYSIS

The SET technique rests on the assumption that the further the resource area is from the site, the less likely will be its exploitation (the costs in terms of time and effort would simply be too great). Using ethnographic data, it was estimated that hunter-gatherers normally exploit an area of roughly 10 km radius around their base – or, since time rather than distance is the limiting factor, a radius of 2 hours' walk. Most farming communities, on the other hand, normally use an area of 5 km radius, or 1 hour's walk. Thus, modern investigators would walk for either 1 or 2 hours outward from the site in question, and study various aspects of the landscape and soils. The information was drawn up in map form, usually as a circle around the site,

distorted by the effects of topography on the distances covered in the set time, and with different categories of land-use or soil-quality inserted.

Modifications and Assessment
Modifications have been made to the original method, primarily because it took a great deal of time. Some scholars simply draw circles around sites, or take shorter walks (on the assumption that the immediate surroundings of a site were the most crucial to its existence). Others assess the land from a high vantage point, or estimate the shape of the site's territory from detailed contour maps.

When a digital elevation map is available, it is possible to use a GIS (Geographic Information System) to produce a more accurate mapped estimation of the territory within a 1 or 2 hour walk of a particular site using cost-surface analysis (see Chapter 3). These GIS maps are sometimes "calibrated" from the known times taken to walk

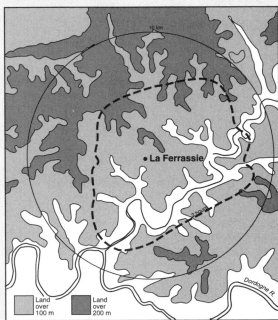

Hunter-gatherer site exploitation territory: the Middle Paleolithic site of La Ferrassie, Périgord, France. The area within 2-hours' walking distance from the site is considerably smaller than the circle of 10 km radius, because of the distortions imposed by hills around the site.

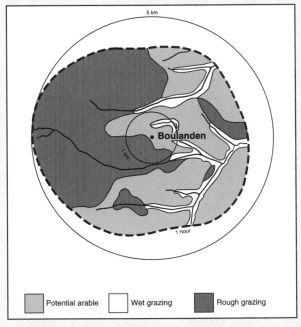

Farming site exploitation territory: the Early Neolithic (Linear pottery) site of Boulanden, Upper Rhine Valley, Germany. The area within 1 hour's walk from the site has been subdivided into three categories of potential land-use (an attempt having been made to reconstruct the likely Neolithic environment).

within the area. This method can be used to generate exploitation territories which take account of the slope of the terrain, and of obstacles such as rivers or walls. GIS can also be used to calculate the proportions of resources which fall within the territory.

Assessment of the area around hunter-gatherer sites is relatively easy, involving a study of the landscape, and the location of water supply, fords, raw materials, natural passages for game, and natural traps and corrals for herds, etc. However, assessment of the area around farming sites is more complex, since it tries to reconstruct the exploitable land in different periods, using different farming technologies. The effects of erosion, irrigation, or terracing need to be taken into account.

Analysis of the soil (see main text) can provide a rough guide to its workability – how much energy is needed to disturb it. Heavy clays, for example, need stronger equipment than loose or sandy soil. Soil potential and fertility are harder to evaluate, and will have altered considerably through time as farming practices changed. Thus, the qualitative assessments from SET analysis tend to be deliberately vague (good arable, potentially arable, good grazing), and geomorphological expertise is required to obtain more detail. As much information as possible needs to be gathered about the area's history of land-use, both from documentation and from what the land and soils can reveal to an expert.

Flannery's Combined Method

A combination of catchment area and exploitation territory analysis has sometimes been employed, most notably by Kent Flannery and his colleagues in Oaxaca (see Chapter 13). Here the starting point is the resources actually found in the site. Investigation then focuses on where the resources probably came from, a task requiring knowledge of resource distribution. The result is a possible zonation of resource use around the site, together with the delineation of a catchment area which is usually larger than the exploitation territory.

This quantitative approach – which enables one to calculate the potential yield of the surrounding area and hence estimate the carrying capacity (the number of people who could live off the land) – avoids the artificiality of a predetermined area of study, but runs the risk of ignoring resources the area could have provided and that have not survived archaeologically. Both methods therefore have advantages and drawbacks. Ultimately it is always wise to combine detailed analyses of the area around particular sites with the more general techniques of regional survey (see Chapter 3), in order to assess how representative the conditions at individual sites really are.

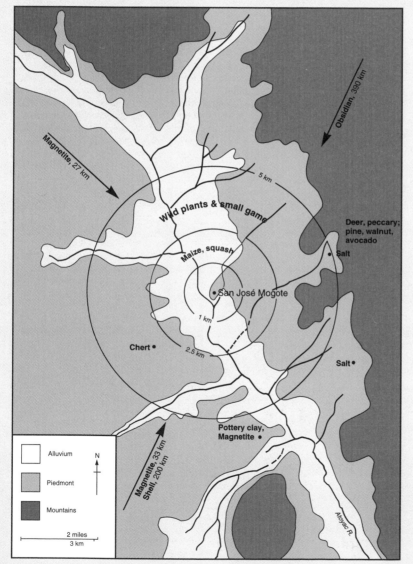

Flannery's analysis of the catchment and exploitation territory around the village of San José Mogote, Oaxaca, Mexico. He concluded that most of the village's agricultural needs would have been satisfied within a 2.5-km radius of the site.

MAPPING THE ANCIENT ENVIRONMENT: CAHOKIA AND GIS

Reconstructing prehistoric human environments requires a detailed knowledge of the natural setting, especially the distribution, productivity, and reliability of edible resources. To handle such complex data, archaeologists are increasingly turning to computer-based mapping systems – Geographic Information Systems (GIS) – when looking at how settlements were distributed in relation to each other and to environmental features such as rivers, topography, soils, and vegetation cover.

The development of GIS makes it possible to organize complex spatial data arranged as a series of separate layers, one for each kind of information – sites, soils, elevation, and so on (see Chapter 3). Relationships between data in various layers can then be analyzed, allowing archaeologists to address questions about human land-use with large numbers of sites and many environmental details.

Mapping Cahokia

One place where such work is underway is the central Mississippi river valley in the United States. This area is uncommonly rich in prehistoric sites, the most impressive of which is Cahokia. Almost a millennium ago, Cahokia was the principal settlement of one of the most complex societies that

ever existed in prehistoric North America. The site once encompassed more than 100 earthen mounds, including an immense 30-m (100-ft) high mound that towered over the surrounding community. Many of these mounds and the remnants of extensive residential areas have survived to modern times. Although a great deal of archaeological work has been undertaken near Cahokia, many questions remain. How many people lived in the area? How was this society organized? Why did people favor some locations but avoid others? How has human land-use changed over time?

Recently George Milner of Pennsylvania State University began a research project in the area. The project has three main objectives:

1 to identify changes in the valley floor that would have caused the destruction or burial of sites;

2 to assess the availability of different resources in different areas;

3 to determine why sites were located where they were.

Work started with the systematic examination of existing site records to determine the locations of known settlements. Diagnostic artifacts in museum collections were studied to identify when these places were occupied. Maps and land surveys up to almost 200 years old were used to

document the movements of the river and the locations of the wetlands that once covered much of the valley floor.

The earliest detailed maps of the river and surrounding landscape were produced by the General Land Office (GLO) surveyors in the early years of the 19th century. The locations of rivers, creeks, and swamps in the GLO notes and maps were plotted, checked against other information about valley landforms, and converted to an electronic GIS format. The paths of later river channels were taken from Corps of Engineers navigation charts.

The natural landscape during Cahokia's heyday is being modeled by focusing first on one of the most important characteristics of the floodplain – the extent, disposition, and nature of the wetlands. By using various sources of information – GLO survey records, other early historical maps and descriptions of the valley, and modern maps and aerial photographs – it is possible to estimate the distribution of resources, and hence the attractiveness of different places.

The spatial arrangement of large and small settlements is being analyzed to identify the natural and social determinants of site positioning. The ecological settings of settlements can be studied by looking at the relative amounts of different kinds of land – dry ground, occasionally inundated areas, and permanent wetlands – within several kilometers of where people lived. For example, the largest sites are for the most part located on well-drained land adjacent to steep banks alongside permanent wetlands. People were therefore able to take advantage of dry land for farming and lakes for fishing. Settlement data complement information on subsistence practices: crops, particularly maize, and fish were mainstays of the diet.

The locations of prehistoric sites in relation to old channel scars indicate that in many places the river has remained within a relatively narrow corridor for the last thousand or more

Reconstruction of the site of Cahokia and its environs, c. AD 1100.

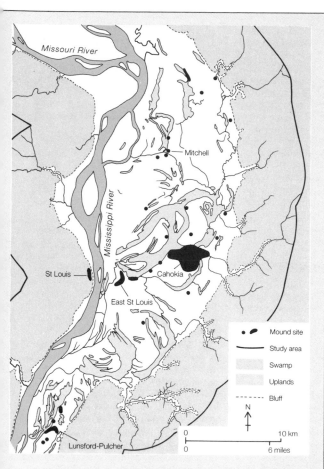

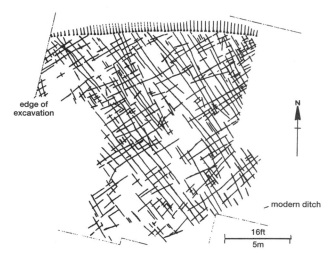

edge of
excavation

modern ditch

16ft

5m

N

A buried land surface revealed beneath the Neolithic burial mound at South Street, southern England. The criss-cross grooves in the soil were made by an ard, an early form of plow that does not turn the soil.

years. Elsewhere, however, the river has taken great bites out of the floodplain, destroying any possible evidence of prehistoric sites. So some gaps in settlement distribution may be nothing more than places where river movement has destroyed sites.

The GIS project has thus helped recreate the landscape of a thousand years ago and indicated the strong wetlands orientation of the settlement pattern of Cahokia's heyday – to be explained by the dietary importance of fish. The initial work is sufficiently encouraging to warrant further systematic study, including new archaeological and geomorphological fieldwork, to gain a better perspective on how the face of the land and the human use of this area changed over many thousands of years.

Cahokia was one of many mound centers scattered across part of the Mississippi floodplain known as the American Bottom. In the past it was covered by water for part or all of the year, the wetlands providing a valuable source of food.

original soils and land surfaces beneath them, can reveal whether there was any cultivation before they were erected. Occasionally, archaeologists are even fortunate enough to uncover buried land surfaces that preserve marks made by plows or ards (ards score a furrow but do not turn the soil). The marks found beneath the Neolithic burial mound at South Street, England, are a good example. Although evidence from prehistoric Danish burial mounds suggest that these marks are not in fact functional (that is, produced in the course of soil cultivation) but are part of the mound-building ritual, they nevertheless provide an indication of the land management techniques available in different periods and on different soils.

Management of Woodland and Vegetation. Many of the techniques for analyzing plant remains, outlined earlier in the chapter, can be used to demonstrate human manipulation of woodland and vegetation generally.

Waterlogged wood, found abundantly in archaeological deposits in the Somerset Levels, England, by John and Bryony Coles, has been used by them to demonstrate the earliest known examples of systematic pollarding and coppicing, dating from about 4000 BC. The evidence consists of remains of thin poles of regular size, produced by cutting trees down to stumps and thus stimulating rapid growth of spring shoots and rods that could be harvested repeatedly. In coppicing, the poles are grown near the ground, while in pollarding the trunks are left some meters high to avoid the effects of grazing animals.

ANCIENT GARDENS AT KUK SWAMP

AUSTRALIA

Kuk Swamp is a 283-ha (700-acre) property in the Wahgi Valley, near Mount Hagen, at an altitude of 1550 m (5084 ft) in the highlands of New Guinea. It contains features that have been interpreted as evidence of some of the world's oldest gardening practices.

The area lay underwater until drainage was begun for a Tea Research Station, giving opportunity in 1972 for a study to begin, led by Jack Golson and his colleagues. Air photographs had revealed that old ditch systems covered virtually the whole swamp. The widely spaced ditches dug for the new plantation, then and in later years, provided the researchers with many kilometers of cross-sections for stratigraphic study. Layers of ash found intermittently in the profiles from volcanic eruptions along the New Guinea north coast could be dated to provide the basis of a chronology. Swamp grasses were also cleared to reveal surface features such as 40 houses (some of which were excavated), and the filled outlines of old channels.

The investigations were seen as providing unequivocal evidence of five separate periods of agricultural use of the swamp back to *c.* 6000 years ago, in the form of large (up to 2 x 2 m or 6.5 x 6.5 ft wide) and long (over 750 m or 2450 ft) drainage channels and of distinctive gardening systems on each of the drained surfaces.

These five drainage episodes lay above a gray clay deposited between *c.* 9000 and *c.* 6000 years ago, which formed part of a fan deposit of sediments

UI, a native New Guinean, displays a paddle-shaped wooden spade excavated from a drainage ditch.

washed in from the southern catchment of the swamp. Beneath this clay was a set of features consisting of hollows, basins, and stakeholes associated with an undeniably artificial channel, which, by analogy, were seen as representing a sixth, older, phase of swamp gardening. Moreover, compared with the previous history of the swamp, the gray clay represented such a dramatic increase in the deposition of eroded materials that it was interpreted as marking the practice of a new dryland

Intersecting drainage ditches of various prehistoric periods.

subsistence mode, that of shifting agriculture. The appearance of these innovations in the immediate wake of the climatic amelioration after the end of the Ice Age suggested that they were introduced fully formed from lower altitude, with a set of tropical cultigens – taro, some kinds of yam, and some of banana – which other evidence indicates were present in the New Guinea region.

Interpreting the Evidence

These interpretations of Kuk must be evaluated in the light of recent results from pollen analysis in the highlands indicating widespread forest disturbance toward the end of the Ice Age associated with fire, and at one archaeological site, Kosipe, with a distinctive type of flake axe designed to be hafted. Together, this evidence is interpreted as indicating the opening up of rainforest to promote the growth of light-demanding plants, particularly the nut-producing *Pandanus*. It has been argued from this that the innovations at Kuk may be seen, not as the result of importations from lower altitudes, but rather as the product of the "forcing" of established strategies because of the rapidly changing climate at the very end of the Ice Age. There are uncertainties about exactly which plants were involved, and at what stage certain cultigens, like taro, yams, and bananas, would have appeared.

Similar uncertainties attach to another proposition – that the Kuk evidence for landscape modification through forest clearance and for swamp use through drainage is consistent with subsistence systems that have reached the stage of agriculture. Such systems include cultivation involving systematic environmental management and possibly domesticated plants, and even

Air view, looking north, showing large prehistoric drainage ditches together with smaller trenches defining a grid of gardens. All these features belong to the most recent systems at Kuk, ending in the 19th century. Two modern parallel drains of the Tea Research Station cut across the landscape from east to west.

Clearing swamp vegetation to expose surface features, such as houses and the outlines of old ditches.

wild-food production involving environmental modification.

The standard interpretation of the evidence from the Kuk project is in fact built around the concept of such an environmental transformation, from forest to grassland. This transformation is seen as having been achieved about 2000 years ago as the result of the progressive deforestation revealed in the pollen record, which put at increasing risk a system of shifting cultivation dependent on forest fallow, with staple crops, assumed to be taro and yams, intolerant of degraded soils. This situation led to a series of innovations in agricultural technology designed to sustain the productivity of dryland cultivation in grassland environments,

together with more continuous and intensive use of the swamp itself, which provided land of sustainable fertility at higher costs in labor. Agricultural production was required not only for humans but also now for pigs, which with deforestation and the loss of forest fauna became important as the major source of protein at the same time that their forest foraging ground was disappearing.

Recent results suggest that there were no pigs in the highlands 6000 years ago as originally thought and that they may have only arrived there following their Lapita-associated introduction into the Bismarck Archipelago *c.* 3500 years ago.

The agricultural sequence at Kuk ends with the arrival of the tropical

American sweet potato in the New Guinea region a few hundred years ago as a result of Iberian explorations in island Southeast Asia. Today it is the dominant staple of most highland communities since it produces better at altitude than older crops, more readily tolerates poorer soils, and is prime pig fodder. It must be implicated, at least in part, in the abandonment of swamp cultivation at Kuk about a hundred years ago.

It was the recent tea-plantation ditches that helped initiate the project, but swamp drainage undertaken for commercial projects of this kind is now threatening the survival – both at Kuk and at similar sites in the region – of some of the world's oldest agricultural remains.

One important aspect of environmental management is the artificial provision of water, whether by storage cisterns, aqueducts, or simple wells. The wooden well-shaft of Kückhoven, Germany, was found on an LBK (Neolithic) site. This box frame of split oak planks, caulked with moss, was dated by dendrochronology to 5090 BC (outer frame) and 5050 BC (inner frame).

Charcoal fragments have been discovered in turves used by Neolithic builders to construct a burial mound at Dalladies in Scotland. The presence of the charcoal indicated that the turves had been cut from grassland formed just after the burning of forest. It is also interesting to reflect on the fact that the farmers could sacrifice 7300 sq. m (8730 sq. yd) of this rich turf in order to build their monument.

Pollen analysis is another highly important method for demonstrating deliberate woodland clearance. The American scholar David Rue has analyzed pollen from cores taken near the Maya city of Copán, Honduras, and managed to trace the process of forest clearance and cultivation in the area. Since there is no evidence for any significant climatic change in the late postglacial of Central America, he could safely attribute the shifts in the pollen record to human activity. Clearings had been made in the forest using swidden (slash-and-burn) techniques and maize agriculture had begun apparently in the preceramic phase at least 4500 years ago. Forest clearance was intensified 1500 years later, and then maintained on a large scale until Copán was abandoned in AD 1200. These findings support not only the early dates from phytolith work (see earlier section) but also the view that ecological stress and soil degradation were probably important in the downfall of cities such as this. (In Chapter 12 we consider more generally the possible reasons for the collapse of cities and civilizations.)

It is known that the vegetation of much of Australia has been changed by the controlled burning practices of the Aborigines, who have managed the landscape in ways that prevent out-of-control bushfires, and create new environments that attract grazing animals with new shoots – although some scholars suspect that this destruction of vegetation could have stopped monsoon rains from penetrating inland, turning much of Australia's heartland into desert. Nevertheless, these techniques – dubbed "fire-stick farming" by the archaeologist Rhys Jones – are being reintroduced in Australian National Parks to prevent uncontrolled fires. There is controversial evidence from pollen that such practices may perhaps be traced back 130,000 years, whereas the earliest archaeological evidence for people in Australia is only about 50,000 years old. Gurdip Singh's studies of sediment cores from Lake George, New South Wales, revealed a period when there was a sudden increase in destructive bush fires, reflected in greatly increased quantities of charcoal, and coinciding with a sudden and dramatic change in vegetation, the first in 750,000 years, when fire-sensitive forests began to be replaced by the fire-tolerant eucalyptus, together with grasses. Singh placed the event at around 130,000 years ago from pollen diagrams in conjunction with results from deep-sea cores. Many scholars find the date – though not the event – archaeologically unacceptable. The archaeologist Richard Wright, for instance, through a simple correlation of age with depth in the lake cores, assigned the vegetation change to 60,000–54,000 years ago, a date far closer to the archaeologically agreed date for the earliest human presence in Australia. However, support for Singh has come from work by Peter Kershaw, who has found similar pollen and charcoal evidence dated to about 140,000 years ago in a 400-m (1300-ft) marine core on the continental shelf off the Queensland coast; the core spans 1.5 million years, and, unlike Lake George, its upper part is well dated. The decline of forest and rise of charcoal particles form the most dramatic change in the whole core, and have been tentatively attributed to human colonization.

Plant macroremains have also been used successfully together with other evidence to indicate woodland clearance. The Anasazi, one of the most advanced pre-Columbian societies in North America, erected buildings in Chaco Canyon, New Mexico, which were the largest and highest in that continent until the advent of the skyscraper. Construction began in the early 10th century AD, and it has been estimated that more than 200,000 pines and firs were needed for the timber. Recently, Julio Betancourt and his colleagues have examined plant macroremains at Chaco cemented into

Human impact on the environment at Chaco Canyon: the large number of trees cut down to build this Anasazi town of Pueblo Bonito brought about the transformation of the local environment and may have contributed to its eventual abandonment.

crystallized urine in ancient packrat middens that can be radiocarbon dated. Since packrats are known to gather plant materials from within 30 m (98 ft) of their dens, these fragments and their associated pollen have permitted the reconstruction of Chaco's vegetational history for the last 11,000 years.

It appears that during the first two centuries of human occupation in Chaco Canyon, the piñon and juniper woodland of the surrounding clifftops was cleared for firewood for a radius of 20 km (12.5 miles). Only relentless woodcutting to meet the fuel demands of a growing population can explain this drastic reduction, because any climatic change in this period was within the range of climatic extremes of earlier millennia, when no such reduction occurred. Study of the timber in the buildings was also instructive: some of the ponderosa pine logs for construction had to be hauled from distances exceeding 40 km (25 miles); and, as the pines declined, the inhabitants began, in AD 1030, to fetch spruce and fir logs from over 75 km (46 miles) away. The environmental damage caused by all this activity was irreversible, and though tree-ring studies have suggested that a drought struck the final blow to the Chaco settlements, the inhabitants were clearly to blame to a large extent. Middens made

by hyraxes (rodents found in Africa and the Middle East) have provided similar evidence that the ancient Byzantine city of Petra, Jordan, collapsed suddenly in AD 900 after centuries of drastic clearance of forests and shrubbery by the inhabitants.

Human Impact on Island Environments

The most devastating human impact on environments can be seen on islands to which settlers introduced new animals and plants. While some of these "transported landscapes" became exactly what the colonists required, others went tragically wrong.

The most notable examples are to be found in Polynesia. The first European explorers who came to these islands assumed that the environments they saw there had remained unchanged, despite the earlier colonization by Polynesians. This view was due in large measure to their paternalistic view of the natives as noble savages, innocents living in harmony with their surroundings like other animals. However, archaeologists can never assume that "what is must always have been so," and work over the last few decades has proved that the Polynesian settlers were only too human in their environmental depredations.

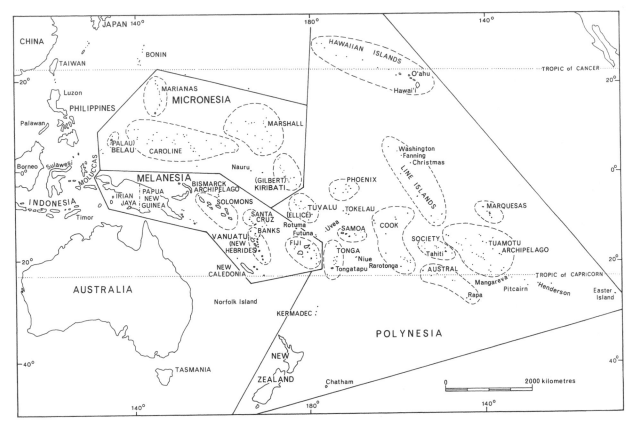

(Top) Human impact on island environments is particularly evident in the Pacific region, where human colonization came relatively late (map pp. 164–65), but often with devastating effect on indigenous plants and animals. Botanical and faunal evidence shows that human predation, deforestation, and newly introduced competitor species caused widespread destruction. (Above) In New Zealand, 13 species of the great flightless moa became extinct (two are shown, right, with the much smaller kiwi that still survives).

A combination of palynology, analysis of plant and animal macro- and micro-remains, and many of the other techniques outlined above has produced a dramatic picture of change. The first arrivals exploited the indigenous resources very heavily during their settling-in phase: the faunal record generally shows an immediate massive reduction in usable meat. For example, Patrick Kirch found that the remains of shellfish and turtle on Tikopia (Solomon Islands) quickly declined in both size and abundance. Most of these resources never recovered, and many were completely wiped out.

The chief cause of extinction was the range of new species introduced to the islands by the settlers. It was certainly necessary for them to bring some, since the islands generally had very few indigenous edible plants and animals. But in addition to the domestic pigs, dogs, and fowl, and the crop plants, they inadvertently brought stowaways such as the Polynesian rat, geckos, and all kinds of weeds and invertebrates (the rat may even have been brought intentionally). These new and highly competitive predators and weeds had drastic effects on the vulnerable island environments.

Rats, for example, must have killed native birds and their eggs, which, combined with human predation for meat and plumage, led to large-scale extinction. In Hawaii, dozens of indigenous bird species were wiped out very rapidly, while in New Zealand about 13 species of the great flightless moa disappeared, together with 16 other kinds of birds.

However, predation was only part of the picture; destruction of habitat was probably the major killer. Pollen, phytoliths, charcoal, and landsnails in Hawaii, New Zealand, and elsewhere combine to reveal a rapid and massive deforestation in the lowlands, producing open grassland in a few centuries. Not only did this have a drastic effect on vegetation and birds, it also eliminated hundreds of molluscan species. In addition, the clearing of vegetation from hillsides to make gardens led to greater erosion: some early sites are covered with meters of alluvium and slopewash.

In other words, people brought their own "landscapes" to these islands, and rapidly altered them both dramatically and irrevocably, both intentionally and accidentally. Analysis of the environmental history of this part of the world makes it plain that (apart from volcanic eruptions) natural catastrophes such as hurricanes, earthquakes, and tidal waves have not affected vegetation to any extent. The changes in landscape and resources have occurred only since the arrival of humans – less than 1000 years ago in New Zealand, 2000 years ago in Hawaii, 3000 years ago in Western Polynesia.

Easter Island. The ultimate example of this process of devastation occurred on Easter Island, the most isolated piece of inhabited land in the world. Here, the settlers wrought environmental damage that is perhaps unique both in its extent and in its cultural and social consequences. Analysis by the British palynologist John Flenley and his colleagues of pollen from cores taken from lakes in the volcanic craters of the island has revealed much of its vegetational history, and in particular the fact that until the arrival of humans in about AD 400 the island was covered with forest. The vegetation was probably dominated by a large palm tree, now extinct but closely related to the Chilean wine palm; not only has its pollen been identified, but a number of ancient endocarps (palm fruits, 820 years old) of this species have been recovered from caves on the island, and its root channels detected in the subsoil.

By the last century, every tree on Easter Island had been cut down, and grassland prevailed. The pollen record shows the decline of forest over the course of a millennium, and since nothing similar had occurred in

Human impact on Easter Island. This remote Pacific island has long been famous for its giant statues (above), but palynologists have only recently discovered that this now treeless environment had forests of large palms before human arrival (top right: palm pollen; top left: palm endocarps).

the pollen record before AD 400 it is clear that people were responsible, even if a local drought or the Little Ice Age may have been contributing factors. It is likely that much of the wood was used for transporting the hundreds of giant statues on the island. In addition, people probably ate the palm fruits; and since those found have all been gnawed by rodents, it is certain that the Polynesian rat, introduced here as elsewhere by the settlers, also ate them. This will have prevented regeneration and thus aided the decline of the tree.

The total loss of timber had several effects. It was probably one of the major reasons for the relatively abrupt termination of statue carving in about AD 1680, because they could no longer be moved. In addition, it was no longer possible to make good canoes, which must have caused a radical decline in exploitation of fish, the main protein source apart from chickens. Deforestation also led to soil erosion (detectable in chemical analysis of the lake-cores) and lower crop yields through the loss of fertile forest soils. The most clearcut case of deforestation in the archaeological record led to starvation and cultural collapse, culminating after AD 1500 in slavery and constant warfare.

SUMMARY

To sum up, humankind has developed from being an inconsequential species at the mercy of the environment to one with a huge influence over its surroundings. The environment is of crucial importance to archaeology. During every period of the past it has played a vital role in determining where and how people could live. Archaeologists now have a battery of techniques to help reconstruct such past environments.

Environmental analysis is no longer undertaken simply to set the scene for particular periods of past human activity, to give some indication of the climate or a site's surroundings. Archaeology now strives to understand former environments in order to assess the key variables that might have influenced the operation of cultural systems. With early farming communities in riverine or estuarine environments, for instance, we need to ascertain not only the basic climate and soil types but also potentially crucial factors such as the extent of the arable area, the frequency of droughts, the pattern of flooding, the rate of silting, and any problems of drainage. The emphasis is no longer on individual sites in isolation, but on site systems, and on changing patterns of land-use through time.

Our present techniques may grant us only a partial and imperfect view of environmental change, but we are steadily developing improved methods, such as the use of Geographic Information Systems, and already we know far more than the early archaeologists could ever have dreamed possible.

FURTHER READING

General introductions to environmental archaeology can be found in the following:

Butzer, K.W. 1982. *Archaeology as Human Ecology*. Cambridge University Press: Cambridge & New York.

Evans, J. & O'Connor, T. 1999. *Environmental Archaeology*. Sutton Publishing: Stroud.

Books on the broad environmental setting include:

Bell, M. & Walker, M.J.C. 1992. *Late Quaternary Environmental Change. Physical and Human Perspectives*. Longman: Harlow.

Brown, A.G. 1997. *Alluvial Geoarchaeology*. Cambridge University Press: Cambridge.

Goudie, A. 1992. *Environmental Change. Contemporary Problems in Geography*. (3rd ed.) Oxford University Press: Oxford & New York.

Limbrey, S. 1975. *Soil Science and Archaeology*. Academic Press: London & New York.

Rapp, G. & Hill, C.L. 1998. *Geoarchaeology: The Earth-Science Approach to Archaeological Interpretation*. Yale University Press: New Haven & London.

Roberts, N. 1998. *The Holocene: An Environmental History* (2nd ed.). Blackwell: Oxford.

Vita-Finzi, C. 1978. *Archaeological Sites in their Setting*. Thames & Hudson: London & New York.

Books on the plant environment include:

Dimbleby, G. 1978. *Plants and Archaeology*. Paladin: London.

For the animal environment, good starting points are:

Davis, S.J.M. 1987. *The Archaeology of Animals*. Batsford: London; Yale University Press: New Haven.

Klein, R.G. & Cruz-Uribe, K. 1984. *The Analysis of Animal Bones from Archaeological Sites*. University of Chicago Press: Chicago.

7 What Did They Eat?
Subsistence and Diet

Having discussed methods for reconstructing the environment, we now turn to how we find out about what people extracted from it. The study of subsistence is one of the most technically developed fields of archaeology. Subsistence is the most basic of all necessities. Although the term sometimes includes fuel and clothing – topics found in Chapter 8 and elsewhere – it is usually taken to mean the quest for food, documented almost everywhere by the waste products of food preparation, both plant and animal. In addition, there have been significant recent developments in the study of human remains, mainly human bone, as a source of information about diet.

In discussing early subsistence, it is useful to make a distinction between *meals*, direct evidence of various kinds as to what people were eating at a particular time, and *diet*, which implies the pattern of consumption over a long period of time.

So far as meals are concerned, the sources of information are varied. Written records, when they survive, indicate some of the things people were eating, and so do representations in art. Even modern ethnoarchaeology helps indicate what they *might* have been eating by broadening our understanding of their range of options. And the actual remains of the foodstuffs eaten can be highly informative.

For the much more difficult question of diet, there are several helpful techniques of investigation. Some methods focus on human bones. As described in this chapter, isotopic analyses of the skeletal remains of a human population can indicate, for example, the balance of marine and terrestrial foods in the diet, and even show differences in nutrition between the more and less advantaged members of the same society.

Most of our information about early subsistence, however, comes directly from the remains of what was eaten. Zooarchaeology (or archaeozoology), the study of past human use of animals, is now big business in archaeology. There can be few excavations anywhere that do not have a specialist to study the animal bones found. The Paleo-Indian rockshelter of Meadowcroft, Pennsylvania, for example, yielded about a million animal bones (and almost 1.5 million plant specimens). On medieval and recent sites, the quantities of material recovered can be even more formidable. Paleoethnobotany (or archaeobotany), the study of past human use of plants, is likewise a growing discipline, with a number of techniques for determining the plant species recovered. In both areas, a detailed understanding of the conditions of preservation on a site (Chapter 2) is a first prerequisite to ensure that the most efficient extraction technique is adopted. The excavator has to decide, for instance, whether a bone requires consolidation before it is removed, or whether plant material can best be recovered by flotation (Chapter 6). In both areas, too, the focus of interest has developed to include not just the species eaten, but the way these were managed. The process of domestication for both plants and animals is now a major research topic.

Interpretation of food remains requires quite sophisticated procedures. We can initially reconstruct the "menu" available in the surrounding environment (Chapter 6), but the only incontrovertible proof that a particular plant or animal species was actually consumed is the presence of its traces in stomach contents or in coprolites (fossilized feces), as will be seen in the section on human remains below. In all other cases, one has to make the inference from the context or condition of the finds: charred grain in an oven, cut or burned bones, or residues in a vessel. Plant remains need to be understood in terms of the particular stage reached in their processing at the time they were deposited. Bone remains have to be considered in terms of butchering practices. Plants that were staples in the diet may be underrepresented thanks to the generally poor preservation of vegetable remains. Fish bones likewise may not survive well.

In addition to these questions, the archaeologist has to consider how far a site's food remains are representative of total diet. Here one needs to assess a site's function, and whether it was inhabited once or frequently, for short or long periods, irregularly or seasonally (season of occupation can sometimes be deduced from plant and animal evidence as well). A long-term settlement is likely to provide more repre-sentative food remains than a specialized camp or kill site. Ideally, however, archaeologists should sample remains from a variety of contexts or sites before making judgments about diet.

WHAT CAN PLANT FOODS TELL US ABOUT DIET?

Macrobotanical Remains

The vast majority of plant evidence that reaches the archaeologist is in the form of macrobotanical remains: they may be desiccated (only in absolutely dry environments such as deserts or high mountains), water-logged (only in environments that have been permanently wet since the date of deposition), or preserved by charring. In exceptional circumstances, volcanic eruption can preserve botanical remains, such as Cerén in El Salvador (see p. 63 and p. 257) where a wide variety have been found carbonized, or as impressions, in numerous vessels. Plant remains can also survive by being partly or wholly replaced by minerals percolating through sediment, a process that tends to occur in places like latrine pits with high concentrations of salts. Charred remains are collected by flotation (Chapter 6), waterlogged remains by wet sieving, desiccated by dry sieving, and mineralized by wet or dry sieving according to context. It is the absence of moisture or fresh air that leads to good preservation by preventing the activity of putrefactive microbes. Plant remains preserved in several different ways can sometimes be encountered within the same site, but in most parts of the world charring is the principal or only cause of preservation on habitation sites.

Occasionally, a single sample on a site will yield very large amounts of material. Over 27 kg (60 lb) of charred barley, wheat, and other plants came from one storage pit on a Bronze Age farm at Black Patch, southern England, for example. This can sometimes give clues to the relative importance of different cereals and legumes and weed flora, but the sample nevertheless simply reflects a moment in time. What the archaeologist really needs is a larger number of samples (each of preferably more than 100 grains) from a single period on the site, and, if possible, from a range of types of deposit, in order to obtain reliable information about what species were exploited, their importance, and their uses during the period of time in question. It is primarily the flotation machine (see p. 245) which makes it possible to obtain these samples.

Having obtained sufficient samples, one needs to quantify the plant remains. This can be done by weight, by number of remains, or by some equivalent of the Minimum Number of Individuals technique used for bones (see below). Some scholars have suggested dispensing with percentages of plant remains in a site, and simply placing them in apparent order of abundance. But numerical frequency can be misleading, as was shown by the British archaeobotanist Jane Renfrew in her study of the material from the Neolithic settlement of Sitagroi, Greece. She pointed out that the most abundant plant in the sample may have been preserved by chance (such as an accident in the course of baking) and thus be overrepresented. Similarly, species that produce seeds or grains in abundance may appear to have an exaggerated importance in the archaeological record: at Sitagroi, 19,000 seeds of *Polygonum aviculare* or knotgrass barely filled a thimble; and it makes little sense to equate an acorn with a cereal grain or a vetch seed. Quite apart from size differences, they make very different contributions to a diet.

Interpreting the Context and the Remains. It is crucial for the archaeologist or specialist to try to understand the archaeological context of a plant sample. In the past attention used to be focused primarily on the botanical history of the plants themselves, their morphology, place of origin, and evolution. Now, however, archaeologists also want to know more about the human use of plants in hunting and gathering economies, and in agriculture – which plants were important in the diet, and how they were gathered or grown, processed, stored, and cooked. This means understanding the different stages of traditional plant processing; recognizing the effect different processes have on the remains; and identifying the different contexts in the archaeological record. In many cases it is the plant remains that reveal the function of the location where they are found, and thus the nature of the context, rather than vice versa.

In a farming economy, there are many different stages of plant processing. For example, cereals have to be threshed, winnowed, and cleaned before consumption, in order to separate the grain from the chaff, straw, and weeds; but seed corn also has to be stored for the next year's crop; and food grain might also be stored unthreshed in order to get the harvested crop

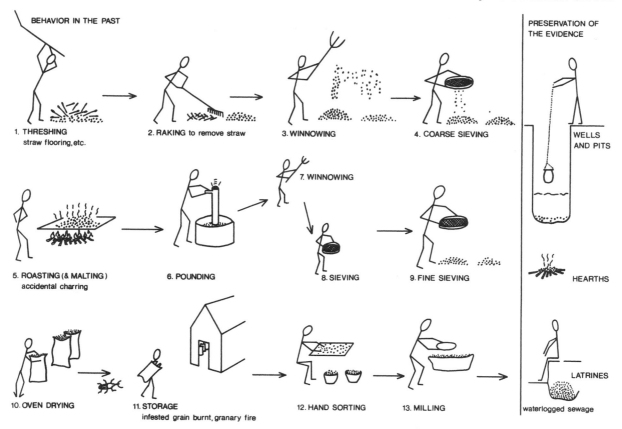

BEHAVIOR IN THE PAST

1. THRESHING
straw flooring, etc.

2. RAKING to remove straw

3. WINNOWING

4. COARSE SIEVING

5. ROASTING (& MALTING)
accidental charring

6. POUNDING

7. WINNOWING

8. SIEVING

9. FINE SIEVING

10. OVEN DRYING

11. STORAGE
infested grain burnt, granary fire

12. HAND SORTING

13. MILLING

PRESERVATION OF THE EVIDENCE

WELLS AND PITS

HEARTHS

LATRINES

waterlogged sewage

Cereal crop processing: waste products from many of these stages may survive as charred or waterlogged remains.

out of the rain, and would then be threshed only when needed. Many of these activities are well documented in our recent agricultural past, before mechanization took over, and they are still observable ethnoarchaeologically in cultures with differing degrees of efficiency and technological capability. In addition, experiments have been carried out in crop processing. From these observations it is known that certain activities leave characteristic residues with which archaeological samples can be compared, whether they are from ovens, living floors, latrines, or storage pits.

There are two main approaches to crop remains. Most archaeobotanists now use "external evidence," and proceed from ethnographic observation of, or experimentation with, plant-processing activities to an examination of the archaeological remains and contexts. In some cases, however, the archaeologist uses an "internal analysis," focusing almost exclusively on the archaeological data: for example, in his study of the plant material from the Bulgarian Neolithic site of Chevdar (6th millennium BC), the British archaeologist Robin Dennell noted that samples from the ovens had

been processed, as one might expect, and were being either dried for storage or cooked when they were accidentally charred. Samples from floors, on the other hand, contained a higher percentage of weed seeds, but no spikelets (small, spike-shaped subdivisions of an ear of grain), suggesting that they were still in the process of being prepared, but had already been threshed and winnowed. The number and variety of weed species present can give clues to the effectiveness of the processing. Most samples show some mixing of different crops, and archaeologists need to bear this in mind when interpreting the data – indeed, the crops may have been mixed at the sowing stage in a fail-safe strategy of growing everything together in the hope that at least something would ripen.

In short, it is desirable, as mentioned earlier, to take samples from as wide an area as possible in the site, and from a variety of contexts. A species that dominates in a number of samples and contexts may be reckoned to have been important in the economy. Change through time can be assessed accurately only by comparing samples from similar contexts and

PALEOETHNOBOTANY: A CASE STUDY

The recovery and identification of plant remains from archaeological contexts are merely the first steps in a wide-ranging series of research issues that make up paleoethnobotany, also known as archaeobotany.

Such issues encompass not only the reconstruction of past environments (Chapter 6) and economies, but also the origins and spread of agriculture (see box, pp. 296–97) and human use of – and impact on – plant communities in

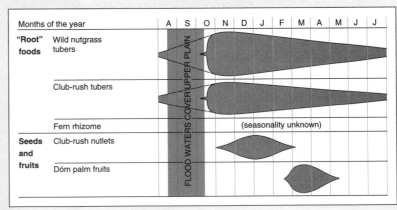

Wild nutgrass (Cyperus rotundus). *Sketch of the living plant, with a few of its edible tubers. (Above left) One of the charred tubers found at Site E-78-3, during excavations at Wadi Kubbaniya.*

Possible seasons of exploitation of major plant foods at Late Paleolithic Wadi Kubbaniya – assuming no storage of food. The varying widths of the bands indicate seasonal variations in the availability (and likely exploitation) of each plant, based on modern growth patterns and known preferences of modern hunter-gatherers. For two months floodwaters probably covered most of the plants, making them inaccessible during that time.

the broadest sense. In addition to studying the plant remains themselves, archaeobotanists can learn a great deal from ethnoarchaeological observation among human groups still practicing traditional methods of plant use or farming, and from assessing the natural potential of the plants in the relevant ecological settings.

A good way to gain an insight into these methods is to look in detail at a recent successful case study.

Wadi Kubbaniya

Four sites dating to between 19,000 and 17,000 years ago were excavated by Fred Wendorf and his associates at this locality northwest of Aswan in Upper Egypt. The sites have produced the most diverse assemblage of food plant remains ever recovered from any Paleolithic excavation in the Old World. The material, which owes its good preservation to rapid burial by sand and the area's great aridity, is concentrated around hearths of wood charcoal, and is dominated by charred fragments of soft vegetable foods, a category of plant that normally has very low archaeological visibility. Flotation (Chapter 6) proved useless for this material, because the fragile, dry remains disintegrated in water; instead, dry sieving had to be employed. Small roasted seeds were also found in what appear to be the feces of human infants.

Analysis of the charred remains by Gordon Hillman and his colleagues at London's Institute of Archaeology has led to the identification of over 20 different types of food-plant brought into the sites, indicating that the occupants' menu was markedly diverse. By far the most abundant food-plants were tubers of wild nutgrass (*Cyperus rotundus*). Other species included different tubers, as well as club-rushes, dóm palm fruits, and various seeds. A study was carried out to ascertain what contribution the nutgrass tubers were likely to have made to the Paleolithic diet.

Investigation of the plant's modern locations, its yields, and its nutritional value suggested that literally tons of tubers could have been obtained easily each year by means of digging sticks. Annual harvesting stimulates the rapid production of abundant young tubers. Since prehistoric people would certainly have noticed this phenomenon, it is by no means impossible that they evolved a system of management, or proto-horticulture, to bring it about consciously.

Ethnographic evidence was available from further afield. Among farming

Months of the year		A	S	O	N	D	J	F	M	A	M	J	J
"Root" foods	Wild nutgrass tubers												
	Club-rush tubers												
	Fern rhizome					(seasonality unknown)							
Seeds and fruits	Club-rush nutlets												
	Dóm palm fruits												

FLOOD WATERS COVER UPPER PLAIN

populations in West Africa, Malaysia, and India nutgrass tubers have become a famine food, eaten when crops fail. In some desert areas of Australia, Aborigine hunter-gatherers exploit the tubers as a staple resource. As long as they are cooked to make them digestible and non-toxic, they can be the principal source of calories during the months when they are available. Ethnographic evidence also shows that tubers are preferred over seeds because they involve less work in processing.

The next step at Wadi Kubbaniya was to use the plant evidence to study whether occupation at the site was seasonal or year-round. Nutgrass tubers were probably available for at least half the year; but they are at their most palatable during the period of active growth, from October to January. Wadi Kubbaniya has no evidence of storage which might have prolonged the tubers' availability, but their growth period together with that of the other species identified at the site would have ensured a food supply for the full year. This does not prove that occupation was not seasonal, but shows that year-round occupation was feasible on the basis of plant resources alone.

Finally, it should be noted that animal-product resources were also in evidence at the site (e.g. fish bones, molluscs), and that many plants prominent in the area today but unrepresented in the remains could have been of importance (e.g. additional palm fruits, rhizomes, leaves, and roots). What is clear, however, is that nutgrass tubers were the dominant resource – the only plant present in all levels at all four sites – and therefore were probably a dietary staple, if not *the* staple resource.

One of the four Wadi Kubbaniya sites (designated E-78-3) under excavation.

processing stages, because the plant remains recovered in a site are not random in composition, and may not necessarily reflect the full crop economy. This is particularly true of charred samples, for many important plant foods may never undergo charring. Plants that are boiled, eaten raw, or used for juices and to make drinks may well not undergo charring, and will therefore be underrepresented or totally absent in an assemblage. If the charring is caused by some accident, the sample may not even be representative of that season's harvest, let alone the site's economy. Indeed, at some sites, such as Abu Hureyra in Syria (pp. 296–97), many of the charred seeds may well come from animal dung being burned as fuel. This again emphasizes the importance of obtaining a variety of samples.

Reconstruction of the crop system that produced the samples is particularly challenging, since entirely different crop systems using the same resources can produce very similar pictures in the archaeological record. Furthermore, it is likely that a great deal of plant refuse was left in the field, used as fuel, or fed to animals. Thus we may never know for certain, without literary evidence, precisely what system of fallow or crop rotation was employed at a particular site. But information about questions of this sort has been obtained from experimental work at Butser Farm in southern England (see box; and similar ones in Denmark, the Netherlands, Germany, and France), where different agricultural techniques are tried out – cultivation with and without manure, various alternations of crops and fallow, etc. This long-term work will take years to provide full results, but already short-term experiments have produced valuable data on crop yields, different types of storage pits, use of sickles, and so on.

Microbotanical Remains

These can also be of help in the reconstruction of diet. Some of the minute particles of silica called *phytoliths* (Chapter 6) are specific to certain parts of a plant (to the root, stem, or flower), and thus their presence may provide clues to the particular harvesting or threshing technique employed on the species. As will be seen below, phytoliths can also help in differentiating wild from domestic species.

The Japanese scientist Hiroshi Fujiwara has found phytoliths of rice (*Oryza sativa*) incorporated in the walls of the latest Jomon pottery of Japan (*c.* 500 BC), which shows that rice cultivation already existed at that time. The same scholar has also located ancient paddy fields through the recovery of rice phytoliths from soil samples, and used quantitative analysis of the phytoliths to estimate the depth and areal extent of

BUTSER EXPERIMENTAL IRON AGE FARM

In 1972 Peter Reynolds established a long-term research project on Butser Hill, Hampshire, in southern England. His aim was to create a functioning version of an Iron Age farmstead dating to about 300 BC: a living, open-air research laboratory on a 6-ha (14-acre) area of land. Results were to be compared with evidence excavated from archaeological sites. The farm has since moved to a nearby location, but the project continues.

All aspects of an Iron Age farm are being explored – structures, craft activities, crops, and domestic animals. Only tools available in this prehistoric period are used. Likewise, prehistoric varieties of crops or their nearest equivalents have been sown, and appropriate livestock brought in.

Several houses of different types have been constructed. The designs have to be inferred from the posthole patterns that are our only clues to the form of Iron Age houses. Much has

Artist's impression of Butser Ancient Farm. Hurdle fences in the foreground enclose sheep pens. Beyond lie the two round houses of the farm itself.

been learned about the quantities of timber required (more than 200 trees in the case of a large house), and about the impressive strength of these structures, whose thatched roofs and walls of rods woven between upright stakes have withstood hurricane-force winds and torrential rain.

The farm is intended to be a long-term project, and results so far are only preliminary. But it has already been established that wheat yields are far beyond what was considered likely for the Iron Age, even in drought years, and this may cause a radical revision of population estimates. In addition, the primitive wheats used, such as einkorn (*Triticum monococcum*), emmer (*Tr. dicoccum*), and spelt (*Tr. spelta*), were found to produce twice as much protein as modern wheats, and to thrive in weed-choked fields without modern fertilizers.

The farm's several fields have been tilled in different ways, such as by an ard (a copy of one found in a Danish peat bog) which stirs up the topsoil but does not invert it. Various systems of crop rotation and fallow are being tested, both with and without manure, and with spring and winter sowing. Also successfully tried out has been a replica of a "vallus," a kind of reaping

machine dating to AD 200 that comprises a two-wheeled vehicle pulled by a draft animal and guided by one person.

Peter Reynolds' team have conducted experiments to assess the effects on grain when stored in different types of pit. One conclusion, supported by ethnographic observations of storage pits in Africa and elsewhere, is that if the seal is impermeable, unparched grain can be stored for long periods without decaying and the germinability maintained.

As for animals, Soay sheep – a type that has remained virtually unaltered for 2000 years – were brought from some Scottish islands. They have proved difficult to keep because of their ability to leap fences. Long-legged Dexter cattle, similar in size and power to the extinct Celtic Shorthorn, have also been installed, and two of them trained for use in traction (pulling the ard).

The Butser Project, which is open to the public, gives us a fascinating glimpse of the Iron Age brought to life, a working interpretation of the past.

Replica Iron Age round house at Butser with its thatched roof.

Dexter cattle being trained as traction animals to pull the Iron Age ard or plow. After training, two men are sufficient, one to guide the cattle and another the ard.

the fields, and even their total yield of rice. Thus, for example, the Itazuke site in Kyushu district, the oldest paddy field in Japan (final Jomon period, mid-1st millennium BC), had a total yield of 1530 kg (1.5 tons), while the Hidaka site in Kanto district (late Yayoi, first centuries AD) yielded 1440 kg (1.4 tons) – the annual yield cannot yet be estimated since we do not know for how long the fields were in use, and it is not yet possible to compare these figures with modern yields.

In addition, phytoliths found adhering to the edges of stone tools may provide information about the plants on which the tools were used, although it must be remembered that such plants may not have figured in the diet, unlike phytoliths extracted from the surface of both animal and human teeth.

Pollen grains often survive in coprolites, but most of them were probably inhaled rather than consumed, and thus they merely add to the picture of the contemporary environment, as shown in Chapter 6.

Chemical Residues in Plant Remains

Various chemicals survive in plant remains themselves which provide an alternative basis for their identification. These compounds include proteins, fatty lipids, and even DNA. The lipids analyzed using infrared spectroscopy, gas liquid chromatography, and gas chromatography mass spectrometry, have so far proved the most useful for distinguishing different cereal and legume species, but always in combination with morphological criteria. DNA offers the prospect of eventually resolving identification at an even more detailed level and of perhaps tracing family trees of the plants and patterns of trade in plant products.

Plant Impressions

Impressions of plant remains are quite common in fired clay (Chapter 6), and do at least prove that the species in question was present at the spot where the clay was worked. Such impressions, however, should not be taken as representative of economy or diet, since they constitute a very skewed sample and only seeds or grains of medium size tend to leave imprints. One has to be particularly careful with impressions on potsherds, because pottery can be discarded far from its point of manufacture, and in any case many pots were deliberately decorated with grain impressions, thus perhaps overemphasizing the importance of a species. Imprints in other objects can be more helpful, such as those in clay bricks from the 3rd millennium BC in Abu Dhabi on the Persian Gulf which represent two-row barley. It is worth noting that large amounts of straw in mudbrick can provide good evidence for local cultivation of cereals.

Turning now from such "passive" evidence, what can be learned from objects that were actually applied to plant materials?

Tools and Other Equipment Used in Plant Processing

Tools can prove or at least suggest that plants were processed at a site, and on rare occasions may indicate the species concerned, and the use that was made of it. In some parts of the world, the mere presence of pottery, sickles, or stone grinders in the archaeological record is taken to prove the existence of cereal farming and settled agricultural life. But in themselves they are inadequate indicators of such features, and require supporting evidence such as remains of domesticated plants. Sickles, for example, may have been used to cut reeds or wild grasses (and a polish or "sickle-sheen" on them is sometimes seen as proof of such a use), while grinders can be employed to process wild plants, meat, cartilage, salt, or pigments. Objects from more recent cultures often have clearer functions – for example, the bread ovens (containing round loaves) at the bakery of Modestus in Pompeii, the flour-grinding mills and wine-presses of the same city, or the great olive-crushers in a Hellenistic house at Praisos, Crete.

Analysis of Plant Residues on Artifacts

Since most tools are fairly mute evidence in themselves, it follows that we can learn far more about their function – or at least their final function before entering the archaeological record – from any residues left on them. Over 65 years ago the German scientist Johannes Grüss was analyzing such residues under the microscope, and identified substances such as wheat beer and mead in two North German drinking horns from a peat bog. Today this sort of analysis is taking on an increased importance.

As we shall see in Chapter 8, microwear analysis of a tool edge can identify broadly whether the tool was used to cut meat, wood, or some other material. Discovery of phytoliths, as mentioned above, can show what type of grasses were cut by a tool. Microscopic study can also reveal and identify plant fibers. Recently it has revealed identifiable starch residues on stone tools from Kilu Cave in the Solomon Islands, Melanesia, some of which date back to 28,700 years ago and constitute the world's oldest evidence for consumption of root vegetables (taro). Another method is chemical analysis of residues on tool edges: certain chemical reagents can provide a means of proving whether plant residues are present on tools or in vessels – thus, potassium iodide turns blue if starch grains are present, and yellow-brown for other plant materials. Starch grains can also be detected by microscope and, for example, have been extracted with a needle from crevices in the surfaces of prehistoric milling stones from the humid tropics of Panama. The grains can be identified to species level, and show that tubers such as manioc and arrowroot – which do not usually leave recoverable fossilized remains – were being exploited here c. 5000 BC.

Chemical investigation of fats preserved in vessels is also making progress, because it has been found that fatty acids, amino acids (the constituents of protein), and similar substances are very stable and preserve well. Samples are extracted from residues, purified, concentrated in a centrifuge, dried, and then analyzed by means of a spectrometer, and by a technique known as chromatography which separates the major constituent components of the fats. Interpretation of the results is made by comparison with a reference collection of "chromatograms" (read-outs) from different substances. By these means, not only the "menu" but even individual "recipes" from the past can sometimes be identified.

For example, the German chemist Rolf Rottländer has identified mustard, olive oil, seed oils, butter, and other substances on potsherds, including specimens from Neolithic lake dwellings. In work on sherds from the German Iron Age hillfort of the Heuneburg, he has been able to prove that some amphorae – storage vessels usually associated with liquids – did indeed contain olive oil and wine, whereas in the case of a Roman amphora the charcoal-like black residue proved to be not liquid but wheat flour. This important technique not only provides dietary evidence, but also helps to define the function of the vessels with which the fats are associated. Ever more refined techniques are currently being developed for identifying food species from protein, lipid, and DNA biochemical analysis of small fragments of plant material.

And from the condition of the starch granules in residues in Egyptian vessels, British scientist Delwen Samuel has been able to reconstruct the malting process used, and hence precisely how the Egyptians brewed beer around 1500 BC. In fact, a British brewery which had helped sponsor the research used her data to produce a beer which turned out to be "delicious, with a long, complex aftertaste." She has also discovered precisely how the ancient Egyptians baked bread from optical and scanning-electron microscopic analysis of starch granules in desiccated original loaves, and has produced very similar bread.

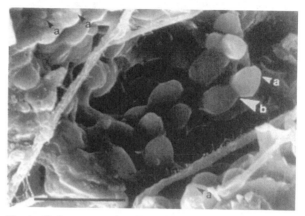

Yeast cells from an ancient Egyptian brewing residue in a pottery vessel from Deir el-Medina, Thebes. Bud scars (a) are visible on some cells and others were budding (b).

Chemical and infrared spectroscopy analysis of a yellowish residue inside a pottery jar from the Neolithic site of Hajji Firuz Tepe, Iran, dating to about 5400–5000 BC, identified it as tartaric acid, found in nature almost exclusively in grapes, and also detected a resin. This has therefore been taken as evidence of a resinated wine, the earliest in the world, 2000 years older than previously thought. Similarly, the tomb of one of Egypt's first kings at Abydos, dating to c. 3150 BC, was found to contain three rooms stocked with 700 jars; chemical analysis of the yellow crusts remaining in them confirmed that they had held wine – a potential total of 5455 litres (1200 gallons).

A further extension of chemical techniques involves isotopic analysis of organic residues, with particular reference to nitrogen and carbon isotope ratios. It is known that beans and other legumes obtain their nitrogen by means of bacterial fixation of atmospheric nitrogen, whereas all other plants obtain it from the soil. Since all legumes are terrestrial, and marine plants do not fix atmospheric nitrogen in this way (but have a distinctive ratio of carbon isotopes), it follows that isotopic analysis can divide plants into three groups: legumes, non-leguminous terrestrial plants, and marine plants.

Through this method, plant residues which were previously unidentifiable can now be characterized. The technique has been applied by Christine Hastorf and Michael DeNiro to prehistoric (200 BC–AD 1000) material from the Upper Mantaro Valley in the central Peruvian Andes which was extracted by flotation but proved to be too burned for normal identification on the basis of morphology. Instead, encrusted organic matter was scraped from some potsherds for examination. Analysis in the scanning electron microscope indicated an absence of bone fragments, which suggested that it was plant material. Isotopic analysis (carbon and nitrogen) was compared with known values for plants from the region, and revealed that the residues came from tubers, including potatoes, which had been boiled and mashed before charring. This accounted for the even distribution of the encrustation on the pots, while the fact that it was limited to the plainest types of pot suggested that such food was probably typical of daily domestic cooking. This is a good instance where, thanks to a new technique, material that was useless to the archaeologist until recently now reveals information on diet and cooking processes. The analysis results corresponded well with modern practices in the same region.

It is not even necessary for actual residues to be visible in a vessel, since we now know that deposits such as oils and resins actually percolate into the clay's fabric and remain there indefinitely. A sherd can be pulverized, and treated with solvents to isolate any trapped organic residues; these are then analyzed by spectrometers and chromatography, which reveal minute amounts of the vessel's contents. Using these techniques, British chemist Richard Evershed and his colleagues have detected the presence of leafy vegetables (probably cabbage) in pots from a Late Saxon/medieval site at West Cotton, Northamptonshire, dating to the 9th–13th centuries AD; and British chemist John Evans may even have discovered traces of opium in a 3500-year-old vase from Cyprus, showing that our Neolithic ancestors were probably as interested in drugs as we are today, and suggesting the existence of a drug trade in the eastern Mediterranean at that time.

Strategies of Plant Use: Seasonality and Domestication

Many plants are only available at certain times of the year, and can therefore provide clues about when a site was occupied. For example, early Neolithic fish traps at Muldbjerg in Denmark were made from willow and hazel twigs less than two years old and cut in early June. Plant remains can also help indicate what was eaten in particular seasons – ripe seeds give an indication of harvest time, and many fruits are limited to certain seasons. Of course, such evidence of *seasonality* has to be extrapolated from modern representatives of the plants in question, and evidence of food storage may indicate that occupation of a site continued beyond the seasons when particular resources were available.

One of the major areas of debate in modern archaeology concerns the question of human management of

Wild and domestic cereals. Left to right: wild and domestic einkorn, domestic maize, extinct wild maize. The wild einkorn is shedding its spikelets, which break off easily thanks to the brittle rachis at each spikelet's base. With a tougher rachis, the domestic form shatters only when threshed.

plants. A prime factor is the status of the species in question, i.e. whether they were wild or *domesticated*. In terms of human behavior the dichotomy is artificial and often irrelevant since many types of cultivation do not change the morphology of the plant, and even in cases where such change occurs we do not know how long it took to appear. But measurement of domestication rates in wild wheats and barleys under primitive cultivation suggests that the transition from wild to domestic could have been complete within only 20 to 200 years – without conscious selection on the farmers' part. Any line drawn between wild and domestic plants does not necessarily correspond to a distinction between gathering and agriculture.

There are nevertheless cases where a clear distinction can be made between wild and fully domestic forms. Macrobotanical remains are of most use here. For example, the American archaeologist Bruce Smith found that 50,000 charred seeds of *Chenopodium* (goosefoot), nearly 2000 years old from Russell Cave, Alabama, exhibited a set of interrelated morphological characteristics reflecting domestication. He was thus able to add this starchy-seed species to the brief list of cultivated plants – including bottle gourd, squash, marsh elder, sunflower, and tobacco – available in the garden plots of the Eastern Woodlands before the introduction of maize in about AD 400.

There has been some debate in recent years about whether wild and domestic legumes can be differentiated on morphological criteria, but archaeobotanical work by the British scholar Ann Butler suggests that there is no foolproof way to do this, even in a scanning electron microscope. Cereals, on the other hand, where well preserved, are more straightforward, and domestication can be identified by clues such as the loss of anatomical features like the brittle rachis that facilitate the dispersal of seed by natural agents. In other words, once people began to cultivate cereals, they gradually developed varieties that retained their seeds until they could be harvested.

Phytoliths can be useful here, since they seem to be bigger in some modern domestic plants than in their wild ancestors. Deborah Pearsall used the appearance of a concentration of very big phytoliths as a criterion for the introduction of domestic maize in Real Alto, Ecuador, by 2450 BC. The large phytoliths were similar to those she had extracted from modern cultivated maize, but were absent from its wild ancestors. This criterion has been supported by macrobotanical remains from other regions, but it is possible that other factors such as climatic change are also involved which might affect the size of phytoliths. Together with Dolores Piperno, Pearsall has also measured maize phytoliths from Panama which imply cultivation there as early as 5700 BC; while squash phytoliths from Vegas Site 80, on the coast of southern Ecuador, revealed a sharp increase in size, suggesting squash domestication here by 10,000 years ago – some 5000 years earlier than had been thought, and rivaling the early squash dates from Guilá Naquitz, Mexico (see p. 502).

Pollen grains are of little use in studies of domestication, since they cannot be used to differentiate wild and domestic categories except for some types of cereal. They can, however, provide indications of the rise of cultivation through time. Fossil buckwheat pollen and a sudden increase of charcoal fragments about 6600 years ago discovered in cores from Ubuka bog, Japan, suggest that agriculture began some 1600 years earlier in this part of the world than had previously been thought.

Molecular genetics is now in a position to make a contribution both to the distinction between wild and domesticated species, and to the question of the origins of domestication. Manfred Heun and his colleagues have conducted an elegant study on wild and domesticated einkorn wheat in Western Asia, using 1362 samples of living wheats, both wild and domesticated. Their investigation showed that the DNA sequences obtained did permit the distinction to be drawn between wild and domesticated einkorn. Moreover, the relationships between the analyses give the clear indication that the inferred ancestral variety could be equated with a variety now growing in the Karacadag mountains of southeast Turkey.

In the future it may prove possible to use ancient DNA from early farming sites to confirm these findings. It is interesting that the use of modern samples has permitted inference to be drawn about the origins of cultivation some 10,000 years ago. Moreover, while many scholars now place the earliest cultivation of cereals in the Levant (Jordan, Israel, and Lebanon), the inference here is that southern Anatolia is also relevant in the case of einkorn.

Meals and Cookery

It is now possible even to estimate at what temperature a plant was cooked. Samples of the material recovered from the stomach of Lindow Man, the British bog body discovered in Cheshire in 1984 (see box, pp. 448–49), were identified by the British archaeobotanist Gordon Hillman as charred bran and chaff, thanks to their characteristic cell patterns under the microscope. They were then subjected to electron spin resonance (Chapter 4), a technique that measures the highest temperature to which the material was subjected in the past. It was discovered some years ago that the burning of organic materials produces a so-called radical carbon which survives a long time, and which reveals not only the maximum temperature of previous heating (it can differentiate boiling at 100°C (212°F) from baking at 250°C (482°F)), but also the duration of that heating and its antiquity. In the case of Lindow Man, the technique revealed that whatever he ate had been cooked on a flat, heated surface for about half an hour, and only at 200°C (392°F). This fact, together with the abundance of barley chaff, suggests that the remains are not derived from porridge, but come from unleavened bread or a griddle cake made using coarse wholemeal flour.

Plant Evidence from Literate Societies

Archaeologists studying the beginnings of plant cultivation, or plant use among hunter-gatherers, have to rely on the kind of scientific evidence outlined above, coupled with the judicious use of ethnoarchaeological research and modern experiments. For the student of diet among literate societies, however, particularly the

INVESTIGATING THE RISE OF FARMING IN WESTERN ASIA

The inception of farming (stock rearing and agriculture) was seen as a decisive step many decades ago by Gordon Childe, who in 1941 coined the term Neolithic Revolution. Our interest here, like Childe's, focuses on Western Asia, but we should not forget that comparable developments occurred independently in other parts of the world.

In the postwar years, a succession of multidisciplinary field expeditions have sought to find evidence for, and to extend, the ideas outlined by Childe. Robert J. Braidwood in Iraq, Frank Hole in Iran, Kathleen Kenyon in Palestine, and James Mellaart in Turkey led what one might call the first wave of research. Together their field projects embraced what Braidwood termed "the hilly flanks of the fertile crescent": the slopes of the Zagros Mountains to the east, the Levant Plain to the west, and to the north the slopes of the Taurus Mountains and beyond. Recently, immense improvements in the recovery and analysis of plant and animal remains have transformed our understanding of the farming revolution.

From Jarmo to Jericho

In 1948 Braidwood, of the Oriental Institute in Chicago, led the first of many expeditions to Iraq which set new standards in problem-orientated field research. Braidwood realized that for farming origins the main issue was domestication. When and where had the principal domesticates (wheat and barley, sheep and goat) developed from their wild prototypes? He correctly reasoned that this could only have taken place in or near areas where the wild forms were available. At that time the best guide to the present-day distribution of such species came from rainfall and vegetation maps. But Braidwood knew that in order to establish the occurrence in prehistory

of wild or domesticated varieties, he would need to excavate stratified deposits at a suitable archaeological site.

After survey and trial excavation, Braidwood selected the site of Jarmo, in northern Iraq. In his initial project, published in 1960, he enlisted the co-operation of several specialists. The first was Fred Matson, who undertook *technical ceramic studies* (pottery thin sections, see Chapters 8 and 9) and was also in charge of the collection of samples for the then new technique of *radiocarbon dating*.

The geomorphologist Herbert E. Wright, Jr. made a *paleoclimatic study*, which at that time was based largely on soil samples. Later the Dutch palynologist W. van Zeist obtained *pollen sequences* from Lake Zeribar which gave a more detailed and comprehensive picture of climatic change. This work allowed the nature of the environment to be established.

A crucial contribution to the Jarmo project came from Hans Helbaek, a specialist in *paleoethnobotany*. He was able to recognize from charred remains not only early domesticated cereal species, but their transitional forms. Charles A. Reed surveyed the evidence on animal domestication in the early Near East, using in part the faunal evidence from Jarmo. *Archaeozoology* was thus added to help shape the emerging picture.

These results were significantly enhanced by work in the Levant – in Jordan, Israel, Syria, and Lebanon. A number of sites were excavated belonging to the immediately pre-farming period (the culture termed "Natufian"). It became clear that here there was already settled village life prior to domestication. At Jericho, Kathleen Kenyon found a large, walled settlement already in early farming times and before pottery was used. Its size carried significant social

implications, while the discovery there of buried skulls, with faces represented in modeled plaster, indicated religious beliefs of a kind beyond those suggested by baked clay figurines found at Jarmo.

Çatalhöyük to Ali Kosh

This impression of a more complex story was reinforced by James Mellaart's excavations in the 1960s at Çatalhöyük (Çatal Hüyük) on the Konya Plain of Turkey, a 13-ha (32-acre) site, which could perhaps be called a town (see box, pp. 44–45). It too was an early farming site, and it too suggested an intense spiritual life with its frescoes and plastered bulls' heads. It was notable for fine objects (including pressure-flaked daggers and polished mirrors) in the volcanic glass obsidian, found locally in Turkey.

Again in the 1960s, the question of farming origins was set in a more coherently *ecological perspective* through the work of Frank Hole and Kent Flannery, who studied the Deh Luran area of Iran, and excavated the site of Ali Kosh there. They laid stress on the evolution of sheep. The archaeozoologist Sandor Bökönyi deduced that the hornless variety found in early levels could be considered a domesticated form. Hans Helbaek also made significant progress here with recovery methods, introducing *flotation techniques* for the lighter components within the soil, notably charred plant remains.

Pushing Back the Frontiers

In the late 1960s the Cambridge archaeologist Eric Higgs argued that too much emphasis was being given to the distinction between wild and domestic, and that what one was studying were long-term changes in the *exploitative relationship* between people and animals, and in the way humans used plants. He suggested

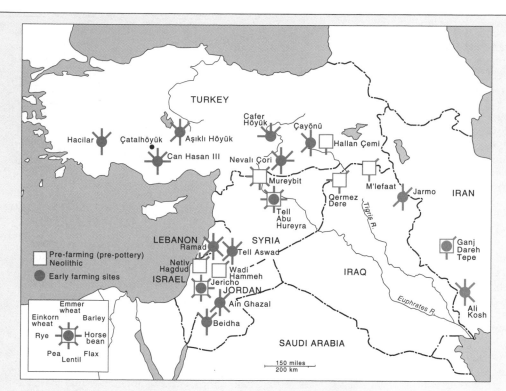

Map showing the location of the principal excavated early farming villages in Western Asia, and the domesticated crops found there.

that several of the important shifts in behavior went much earlier than the Neolithic period. Gazelle, for example, might have been intensively exploited long before sheep and goat became important. Higgs pioneered, with Claudio Vita-Finzi, the technique of *site catchment analysis* (box, pp. 258–59).

Much progress has been made in the last two decades with the investigation of certain key sites. The waterlogged site of Ohalo II, by the Sea of Galilee in Israel, has yielded the world's oldest known cereal grains: hundreds of charred remains of wild wheat and barley dating to 19,000 years ago, together with many other plants and fruits and a rich faunal assemblage indicating a broad-spectrum economy of fishing, hunting, and gathering.

Israeli archaeologist Ofer Bar-Yosef therefore argues that the harvesting of cereals has roots in Natufian times (12,000–10,000 years ago), which gradually intensified into their intentional cultivation (already in 1932

the discoverer of the Natufian culture, Dorothy Garrod, suggested its significance for agricultural origins). Sediments at Jericho and elsewhere already contain evidence of the cultivation of cereals and legumes by the end of that period, and this is confirmed by microwear on stone tools, suggesting the small-scale cultivation of wild-type cereals in the Jordan Valley. As Bar-Yosef has written: "Sedentism was a prerequisite for cereal cultivation and both were essential preconditions for animal husbandry." Animals may have been domesticated by the 9th millennium BC, but large-scale pastoralism did not emerge for at least another thousand years.

Demographic and Symbolic Factors
In a 1968 paper Lewis Binford likewise looked at longer-term trends. He laid stress on *demographic factors*, suggesting that it was the development of settled village life in the pre-farming phase which created

population pressures that led to the intensive use and subsequent domestication of plants and animals (see box, p. 472).

Barbara Bender in 1978 suggested that the motivating impulse was a social one: the competition between local groups who tried to achieve dominance over their neighbors through feasting and the consumption of resources. Jacques Cauvin in recent work has gone further, suggesting that the Neolithic Revolution was fundamentally a *cognitive development*, where new conceptual structures, including religious beliefs, played a significant role in the development of the new sedentary societies which preceded the transition to food production. A range of symbolic finds from the Pre-Pottery Neolithic, including stone masks from Hebron and Nahal Hemar in Israel and the terracotta statues from 'Ain Ghazal in Jordan (p. 408), underline Cauvin's claim that the Neolithic Revolution was a "mental mutation."

great civilizations, there is a wealth of evidence for domestication of plants, as well as for farming practices, cookery, and many other aspects of diet to be found written in documents and in art. If we take the Classical period as an example, Strabo is a mine of information, while the Jewish historian Josephus provides data on the food of the Roman army (bread was the mainstay of the diet). Virgil's *Georgics* and Varro's agricultural treatise allow an insight into Roman farming methods; we have the cookery book of Apicius; and there is a mass of documentary evidence about Greek and Roman cereal production, consumption, pricing, etc. Even the letters found on wooden writing tablets excavated at the fort of Vindolanda, on Hadrian's Wall, written by serving soldiers to their families, mention many kinds of food and drink such as Celtic beer, fish sauce, and pork fat.

Herodotus gives us plenty of information about eating habits in the 5th century BC, notably in Egypt, a civilization for which there is extensive evidence about food and diet. Much of the evidence for the pharaonic period comes from paintings and foodstuffs in tombs, so it has a certain upper-class bias, but there is also information to be found about the diet of humbler folk from plant remains in workers' villages such as that at Tell el-Amarna, and from hieroglyphic texts. In the later Ptolemaic period there are records of corn allowances for workers, such as the 3rd-century BC accounts concerning grain allotted to workers on a Faiyum agricultural estate. Models are also instructive about food preparation: the tomb of Meketre, a nobleman of the 12th dynasty (2000–1790 BC) contained a set of wooden models, including women kneading flour into loaves, and others brewing beer. Three newly deciphered Babylonian clay tablets from Iraq, 3750 years old, present cuneiform texts containing 35 recipes for a wide variety of rich meat stews, and thus constitute the world's oldest cookbook.

On the other side of the Old World, in China, excavations at Luoyang, the eastern capital of the T'ang dynasty (7th–10th centuries AD), have encountered over 200 large subterranean granaries, some containing decomposed millet seeds; on their walls are inscriptions recording the location of the granary, the source

Harvesting and processing a cereal crop: scenes depicted on the walls of a New Kingdom tomb at Thebes in Egypt.

of the stored grain, its variety and quantity, and the date of its storage – thus providing us with data on the economic situation in that period. As will be seen in a later section, the tombs of some Chinese nobles have been found to contain a range of prepared foods in different containers.

In the New World, we owe much of our knowledge of Aztec food crops, fishing practices, and natural history to the invaluable writings of the 16th-century Franciscan scholar Bernardino de Sahagún, based on his own observations and on the testimony of his Indian informants.

It should be remembered, however, that written evidence and art tend to give a very short-term view of subsistence. Only archaeology can look at human diet with a long-term perspective.

Although plant foods may always have constituted the greater part of the diet – except in special circumstances or high latitudes like the Arctic – meat may well have been considered more important, either as food or as a reflection of the prowess of the hunter or the status of the herder. Animal remains are usually better preserved on archaeological sites too so that, unlike plant remains, they have been studied since the very beginnings of archaeology.

INFORMATION FROM ANIMAL RESOURCES

The study of animal bones has evolved in the same way as that of plant remains. What little attention the first archaeologists paid to animal bones was directed primarily to the morphology of different species, and what they could tell us about environment (Chapter 6) or chronology (Chapter 4). But on the question of the interactions between people and animals, few scholars went further than labeling animals as either wild or domestic, and the people as hunters or herders. At best a quantified list of the species found at a site was made.

Since World War II, however, animal remains have achieved such a high degree of importance through the influence of a number of scholars (e.g. Theodore White's analysis of butchering practices in North America, and the work of Grahame Clark and Eric Higgs in England) that archaeozoology or zooarchaeology has become a subdiscipline in its own right. Emphasis is now placed not merely on the identification and quantification of animal species in a site, but also on how the remains got there, and what they can tell us about a wide range of questions such as subsistence, domestication, butchering, and seasonality.

The first question the archaeologist must face when interpreting animal remains is to decide whether they are present through human agency rather than through natural causes or other predators (as in the case of carnivore refuse, owl pellets, burrowing animals, etc.). Animals may also have been exploited at a site for non-dietary purposes (skins for clothing, bone and antler for tools).

As with plant remains, therefore, one must be particularly careful to examine the context and content of faunal samples. This is usually straightforward in sites of recent periods, but in the Paleolithic, especially the Lower Paleolithic, the question is crucial; and in recent years the study of taphonomy – what happens to bones between the time they are deposited and dug up – has begun to provide some firm guidelines (see box overleaf).

Methods for Proving Human Exploitation of Animals in the Paleolithic

In the past, association of animal bones and stone tools was often taken as proof that humans were responsible for the presence of the faunal remains, or at least exploited them. We now know, however, that this is not always a fair assumption (see box overleaf), and since in any case many used bones are not associated with tools, archaeologists have sought more definite proof from the marks of stone tools on the bones themselves. A great deal of work is currently aimed at proving the existence of such marks, and finding ways of differentiating them from other traces such as scratches and punctures made by animal teeth, etching by plant roots, abrasion by sedimentary particles or post-depositional weathering, and indeed damage by excavation tools. This is also part of the search for reliable evidence in the current major debate in Paleolithic studies as to whether early humans were genuine hunters, or merely scavenged meat from carcasses of animals killed by other predators, as Lewis Binford and others maintain.

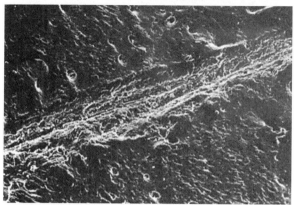

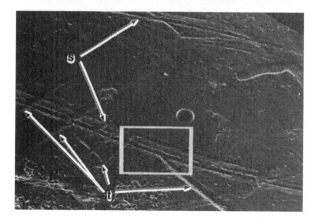

Carnivore marks or toolmarks? Bone surfaces analyzed in the scanning electron microscope by Shipman and Potts. (Top) Round-bottomed groove made on a modern bone by a hyena. (Center) V-shaped groove made on a modern bone by a sharp stone flake. (Below) Fossil bone from Olduvai Gorge that Shipman and Potts believe shows two slicing marks (s) made by a stone flake, and carnivore tooth marks (t) made later.

Much attention has been directed to bones from the famous Lower Paleolithic sites of Olduvai Gorge and Koobi Fora, in East Africa, that are over 1.5 million years old. American archaeologist Henry Bunn claimed to be able to identify cutmarks and hammer fractures, made on some of the bones by stone tools, with nothing more than good light and the naked eye. Cutmarks are v-shaped with straight sides, while carnivore teeth tend to leave broader, u-shaped grooves; roots leave irregular marks; and abrasive particles leave faint, shallow grooves. Bunn supported his findings by comparisons with known butchery marks from more recent periods, and noted that the marks often occurred on bones at key points for butchery.

Pat Shipman and Richard Potts, on the other hand, found that it was necessary at the same sites to use light microscopes and even the scanning electron microscope in order to identify toolmarks, since to the naked eye there were too many similarities with other marks. They even claimed to be able to distinguish different types of tool-use, such as slicing, scraping, and chopping. Their method entails making a high-precision rubber impression of the bone surface, which is then used to produce an epoxy resin replica that can be examined under the microscope. This removes the necessity to handle fragile bones repeatedly, and resin imprints are far easier to transport, to store, and to examine under the microscope.

Like Bunn, Shipman and Potts compared their results with marks produced by known processes on modern bones. They found that many bones from Olduvai had both toolmarks and carnivore scratches, suggesting some competition for the carcass. In some cases, the carnivore marks were clearly superimposed on the toolmarks, but in most cases the carnivores seem to have got there first! Carnivore marks occurred mostly on meat-bearing bones, whereas toolmarks occurred both on these and on non-meat-bearing bones, such as the bottom of horse limbs, indicating a possible use of tendons and skins.

For Shipman and Potts, the diagnostic feature of a cutmark produced by a slicing action is a v-shaped groove with a series of longitudinal parallel lines at the bottom. However, more recent work suggests that very similar marks can be produced by other causes. James Oliver's work in Shield Trap Cave, Montana, indicates that "cutmarks" can be scored on bones through trampling in the cave, producing abrasions by particles, and Kay Behrensmeyer and her colleagues have come to similar conclusions from their analyses. Thus microscopic features alone are not sufficient evidence to prove human intervention. The context of the find and the position of the marks need to be studied too.

TAPHONOMY

Taphonomy is the assessment of what has happened to a bone between its deposition and its discovery. Although bones have a better chance of preservation than plant material in most soils, they nevertheless survive only under special conditions – for example, if they are buried quickly, or deposited in caves. Those that escape destruction by carnivores, weathering, acid soils, etc., and survive long enough, become mineralized through slow percolation by ground water. Many are transported by streams and redeposited in secondary contexts. Much depends on the speed of the water-flow and the density, size, and shape of the bones. Any analysis has also to assume that taphonomic events in the past were the same as those observed today.

Much work is currently in progress concerning the accumulation and fragmentation of bones by carnivores, in the hope that criteria can be found to differentiate bone assemblages produced by humans from those produced by non-humans. This involves ethnoarchaeological observation of different human groups and carnivores, the excavation of animal dens (to study the bones that animals such as hyenas accumulate), and experimental breakage of bones with and without stone tools.

The pioneer of studies of this kind is C.K. Brain, whose work in South Africa has shown not only the effects of carnivores such as leopards, hyenas, and porcupines on animal carcasses, but also that bone fractures previously attributed to early "killer man-apes" were in fact caused by the pressure of overlying rocks and earth in limestone caves in the Transvaal. Indeed, Brain has demonstrated that the early hominids (australopithecines), far from being hunters, were probably

themselves the victims of carnivores at cave sites such as Swartkrans.

Such studies are not confined to Africa. Lewis Binford, for example, has made observations in Alaska and the American Southwest involving the effects of wolves and dogs on bones. He seeks to differentiate human and carnivore interference by means of the relation between the number of bone splinters and the number of intact articular ends. Gnawing animals attack the articular ends first, leaving only bone cylinders and a number of splinters. A bone collection consisting of a high number of bone cylinders and a low number of bones with articular ends intact is therefore probably the result of activity by carnivores or scavengers. John Speth applied these criteria to the bones from the Garnsey site, a 15th-century AD bison-kill complex in New Mexico. The extreme rarity of bone cylinders indicated that there had been minimal destruction by scavengers, and that the bone assemblage could be assumed to be wholly the result of human activity.

One has to be cautious about comparisons of living carnivore behavior with prehistoric assemblages that may have been produced by a different carnivore perhaps now extinct. Since wide variations exist among living species, the behavior patterns of extinct species are far from easy to ascertain. Moreover, animals such as hyenas can produce faunal assemblages similar to those made by human beings, displaying consistent patterning in breakage, and forming similarly shaped fragments. This is not surprising, because the ways in which a bone can break are limited.

These factors may seem discouraging, but they are helping to establish a much sounder basis for the accurate interpretation of bone assemblages.

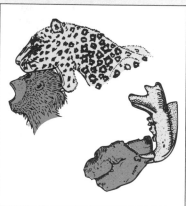

Early hominids as hunters or the hunted? Excavation of the underground cave complex at Swartkrans, South Africa (above), has yielded the remains of over 130 australopithecine individuals, together with those of carnivores and herbivores. Originally it was thought that the hominids had preyed on the other animals. But C.K. Brain matched the lower canines of a leopard jaw found in the cave to the holes in an incomplete australopithecine juvenile cranium (left). This hominid, at any rate, had been more prey than predator.

Brain discovered that modern leopards drag their victims into trees, out of reach of hyenas. Perhaps the remains of the unlucky hominid, once its flesh had been consumed, fell from a tree into the cave.

Studies of this kind are not new – even the pioneer geologist Charles Lyell, in 1863, mentioned the problem of distinguishing cutmarks made by tools on bone from those made by porcupines – but the powerful microscopes now available, together with a greater understanding of taphonomic processes and carnivore behavior, have enabled us to make major advances in recent years. Nevertheless more work still needs to be done before we can be sure of proving early human activity in this way, and also of identifying episodes where our early ancestors were hunters rather than scavengers.

However, there are other types of evidence that can provide proof of human processing of bones. These include artificial concentrations of bones in particular places, such as the stacking of mammoth shoulder blades in the Middle Paleolithic ravine of La Cotte de St Brelade, Jersey, or the use of mammoth bones for the construction of huts in the Paleolithic of central and eastern Europe. Burning of bones is another clear indication of human processing – for bird bones it may be the only proof of human use, because unburnt bone might have been brought to the site by non-human predators, or might be from birds that inhabited the site or its environs (although identification of the species will often answer this point).

Having demonstrated so far as possible that animal remains were indeed produced by human action, the archaeologist then can move on to try to answer the interesting questions such as what did people eat, in which seasons did they eat particular foods, how did they hunt and butcher the animals, and were the animals domesticated?

Human exploitation of bones in the Paleolithic. Reconstruction from excavated remains of a mammoth-bone dwelling at Mezhirich in the Ukraine, dating from about 18,000 years ago. Over 95 mammoth mandibles were used in the structure.

INVESTIGATING DIET, SEASONALITY, AND DOMESTICATION FROM ANIMAL REMAINS

The most abundant and informative residues of animals are the macroremains – bones, teeth, antlers, shells, etc. Numerous techniques are now available to help extract information from data of this type.

As with plant remains, the archaeologist needs to bear in mind that the bones encountered may represent only a fraction of what was originally present. Bones may have been destroyed by weathering or trampling, cleared away out of the site, boiled for stock, used for tools, eaten by dogs or pigs, or even disposed of ritually (some California Indians avoided disrespect to the salmon by never discarding its bones; these were dried, pounded, ground in mortars, and consumed). Other foods such as grubs or the drinking of blood will leave no trace. In addition, our interpretations are clouded by our own culture's tastes. Although herbivores, supplemented by fish and birds, have usually formed the staple animal foods for humans, other creatures such as insects, rodents, and carnivores may all have made a contribution to diet in some cultures.

And should human remains be included on the list of potential resources? In recent years, there has been

a reappraisal (in particular by the anthropologist William Arens) of the archaeological and ethnographic evidence previously interpreted as proof of cannibalism, and all of it has been found open to other explanations. To take one example, the Neanderthal bones from Krapina, Croatia, were found badly broken and scratched, and mixed with animal remains, the flesh assumed to have been cut off the human bones for food. But a reexamination by Mary Russell has shown that the marks on the human bones are quite different from those on defleshed meatbones, but very similar to those found on North American Indian skeletons that have been given secondary burial. In other words, the Krapina bodies were not eaten, but the bones were probably scraped clean for reburial. Recently, however, at the Neolithic cave of Fontbrégoua, southeast France (4000 BC), animal and human bones have been found in different pits, but with definite cutmarks in the same positions; six people were stripped of their flesh with stone tools shortly after death, and their limb bones cracked open. Although there is no direct evidence of consumption of flesh or marrow, Paola Villa and her colleagues have presented this as the most plausible case of prehistoric cannibalism yet discovered. Ethnographic evidence from Australia, on the other hand, suggests that it could well be a mortuary practice. Similarly, a reassessment by German archaeologist Heidi Peter-Röche of numerous claims for cannibalism in the prehistory of Central and Eastern Europe has found absolutely no evidence for the practice, with secondary funerary rituals accounting for all the finds. Recently, dramatic claims have been made for possible cannibalism among the Anasazi of the American Southwest, around AD 1100, but, once again, alternative explanations are readily available for these bone assemblages, involving not only funerary practices but also the extreme violence and mutilation inflicted on enemy corpses in warfare.

Even if cannibalism existed occasionally, the contribution of human flesh to diet must have been minimal and sporadic, paling into insignificance beside that of other creatures, especially the big herbivores.

Analyzing a Macrofaunal Bone Assemblage

In analyzing an assemblage of bones, one has first to identify them (Chapter 6) but then also to quantify them, both in terms of numbers of animals and of meat weight (see box overleaf). The amount of meat represented by a bone will depend on the sex and age of the animal, the season of death, and geographical variation in body size and in nutrition.

A recent illustration of this fact is provided by the Garnsey site, a bison-kill site in New Mexico of the 15th century AD, where John Speth found more male skulls than female, but more female limbs than male. As the kill took place in the spring, when calving and lactating cows are under nutritional stress, the sexual imbalance in the remains suggested that the bones with the most meat and body fat at that time of year (male limbs) were taken away from the site, and the rest were ignored. Seasonal and sexual variation were involved in the nutritional decisions made at this kill site. It follows that where it is necessary to assess the original sex ratio in a collection of bones, the meat-bearing bones are likely to give a misleading picture; only bones with no nutritional value will be accurate.

But if factors of age, sex, and season of death need to be allowed for, how are they established?

Strategies of Use: Deducing Age, Sex, and Seasonality from Large Fauna

Sexing is easy in cases where only the male has antlers (most deer), or large canines (pig), or where a penis bone is present (e.g. dog), or where the female has a different pelvic structure. Measurements of certain bones, such as bovid metapodials (feet), can sometimes provide two distinct clusters of results, interpreted as male (large) and female (small), although in many cases young or castrated males can blur the picture with an intermediate category.

The various mammal species show differing degrees of such sexual dimorphism. In the goat this is very marked, and bone measurements can be used to separate male and female even where the bones are not fully adult. Brian Hesse used this method to show a controlled cull of goats at the site of Ganj Dareh Tepe in Iran, in which most males were killed when still juvenile while females lived well into adult life. This sex and age related difference in survival is a persuasive case for a managed herd under early domestication. In cattle, the separation of males and females by bone measurement can sometimes be good, especially where measurements of later fusing bones are used, though steers can blur the picture. Other mammals like sheep, red deer, and roe deer are more problematic as bone measurements from the two sexes overlap quite significantly. Many of these problems are now under active investigation and it is probable that many of the difficulties will soon be overcome.

The *age* of an animal can be assessed from features such as the degree of closure of sutures in the skull, or, to a certain extent, from the fusion between limb shafts and their epiphyses; the latter factor can be studied more closely by means of X-rays. Age is then estimated by comparison with information on these features in modern populations, though differences in geography or nutrition are hard to allow for. However, estimates of the age at which mammals were killed are usually based on the eruption and wear patterns of the teeth. This may be by the measurement of the crown height of the teeth (see box, p. 291), though this method works best on the high-crowned (hypsodont) teeth of species like horse and antelope. Age estimates for those species that have lower crowned teeth are more usually based on the stage of tooth eruption and the pattern of wear on the biting surface, especially where good modern samples of known age are available for comparison. Interestingly, much new work has been done in this field by archaeologists as veterinary sources are seldom of sufficient detail or accuracy. The mandibles are attributed to one of a series of age classes and the number of specimens in each can be used to construct a "slaughter pattern" (or "survivorship curve"), which will show the age distribution within the cull population. This can be revealing about hunting strategies, and can also tell us much about the ways in which domestic mammals were managed.

Aging gives some insights into dietary preferences and techniques of exploitation, but the *season of death* is also a crucial factor. There are many ways of studying seasonality from animal remains – for example, the identification of species only available at certain times of year, or which shed their antlers in specific seasons. If one knows at what time of year the young of a species were born, then remains of fetuses, or bones of the newly born, can pinpoint a season of occupation (see box, pp. 292–93) – though it should be stressed that, while one can sometimes prove a human presence in some seasons in this way, it is very rare that one can positively disprove a human presence at other times of year (since the consumption of stored food is hard to recognize from archaeological evidence) unless climatic conditions, such as at high altitude, would have made this suicidal.

Methods used for the determination of season of death from animal bones and teeth have advanced much in recent years, and this is one of the most interesting recent contributions from faunal studies. Interpretation depends upon appropriate studies of both animal and plant food evidence along with a consideration of the ecology and behavior of the species, and the setting of the site. The methods employed to determine season of death from mammal bones are very like those used in building up age profiles, but are usually restricted to observation of rapid change in the immature mammal such as stages of tooth eruption, bone shaft growth, or the annual cycle of antler growth and shedding. The bones and teeth of mammals go through marked changes as they mature and these changes can yield important information from an archaeological bone sample.

In young mammals, most bone growth takes place at the ends of the bone shaft (diaphysis) and the articular surfaces of the bones are joined only by cartilage. As adult size is attained, the bone extremities "fuse" to the shaft, the cartilage being replaced by solid bone. This takes place in a known order and at broadly accepted ages in mammal species. The measurement of the shaft length of immature bones can provide valuable information on the season of occupation at an archaeological site. This method, pioneered in Germany in the 1930s, has only recently come back into use. In temperate latitudes most of the larger terrestrial mammals give birth in one short season. In the newborn the limb bones are small and most articular ends are not fused to the shafts. The young grow at broadly similar rates and attain mature size at about the same age. There are good climatic reasons for assuming that species such as deer had seasonal births in the past as now, to ensure the best survival of their young. It follows that length

QUANTIFYING ANIMAL BONES

Animal bones are deposited during the formation of archaeological sites after complex processes of fragmentation and dispersal, caused by both humans and carnivores (see box, pp. 284–85). Careful excavation and recovery are essential so that these activities can be taken into account and the bones quantified accurately. A bone sample retrieved by sieving, for example, is likely to have more small bones than one that was not. Conditions for bone preservation also differ greatly from site to site, and even within the limits of one site, so that bone workers must record the degree of surface erosion of each bone as an aid to understanding any possible causes of additional variation.

When working through a sample, bones are recorded either as fully identified fragments or undiagnostic pieces which might belong to one of several species. Various methods are then used to calculate the relative abundance of the different bones and thus of the species represented.

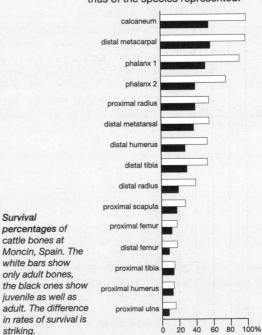

Survival percentages of cattle bones at Moncin, Spain. The white bars show only adult bones, the black ones show juvenile as well as adult. The difference in rates of survival is striking.

The simplest calculation of relative species abundance is based on the **Number of Identified Specimens (NISP)**, where the identified bones of each species are expressed as percentages of the total identified bone sample. Though commonly used, the result obtained may be misleading.

The second level of calculation is the **Minimum Number of Individuals – MNI (or MIND)** – which expresses the least number of animals that were necessary to account for the bone sample. In its simplest form this calculation is based on the most abundant identified bone for each species, either from the right or left side of the body.

Grimes Graves, England

Some of the problems with the NISP type of calculation can be illustrated from the bone sample excavated from the site of Grimes Graves in Norfolk, England. Here extensive Bronze Age middens were dumped into the hollows of Neolithic flint mines, and two recent excavations allow comparison between different bone samples. In both, the bones were carefully recovered and preservation is excellent.

The NISP calculation of the two common species (cattle and sheep) at Grimes Graves shows that these are equally represented in the total bone count, though cattle would obviously be more important because of their greater body size. The MNI calculation was based on the most abundant identified bone – in this case the mandible, since it is very hard and resists gnawing by carnivores. A count of the mandibles showed cattle to be significantly more numerous at 58 percent, while sheep formed 42 percent of the sample. Thus cattle were of greater importance at the site than the proportions of NISP had shown.

Moncin, Spain

An even more striking example of the disparity in results between NISP and MNI can be illustrated from the site of Moncin, Spain. At this Bronze Age village, the inhabitants kept the usual domestic mammals, but also hunted extensively, in particular taking juvenile red deer for their spotted skins. Few

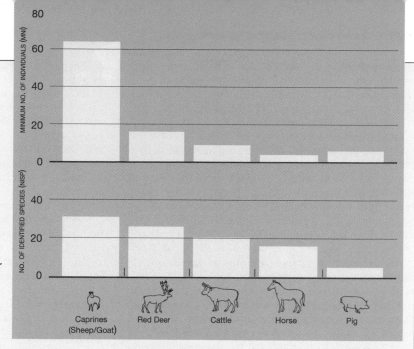

Percentage of species represented at Moncin, Spain, as revealed by MNI and NISP methods.

bones of immature animals survived the attention of dogs and, in consequence, the proportions of mammals shown by the NISP and MNI are very obviously different, as shown in the diagram.

Age, Bone Weight, and Meat Weight

Both NISP and MNI have certain limitations. The MNI figure has little meaning with small samples, and the potential errors in the NISP calculation may be severe when comparing sites with different age profiles, conditions of preservation, or recovery standards.

Some of these difficulties can be overcome by a study of the **ages** at which the different species were killed, as this has a profound effect upon the survival of the bones. Such age profiles are best reconstructed from tooth eruption stages in the young animal and by progressive tooth wear in the adult.

Another method of comparing species abundance utilizes **relative bone weight**. By this means the total weight of identified bone from each species is compared, though the problems of differential bone survival remain. It is important to recognize that the quantification of bones tells us only about the excavated bone sample and this has an unknown relationship to the original fauna at a site. Quantification is

most valuable where sites have long sequences or where groups of sites can be compared. In spite of uncertainties, such comparisons can reveal important faunal trends and regional variations.

The final step in any reconstruction of diet is to try to calculate the actual **weight of meat** represented by the bones in the sample. The average modern meat-weight for each species is a good starting point. Logically one might expect to be able simply to multiply this figure by the relevant MNI, as was done in early analyses. But today it is recognized that one has to take into account the fact that not all parts of the animal will have been used. One cannot assume that every carcass was treated alike, since in cases such as mass drives some will have been partly used, some fully, and others ignored (see box, pp. 292–93). Butchering techniques will have varied according to species, size, purpose, and distance from home. Bones thus represent not full animals but butchering units, or skeletal portions.

Where potential causes of bias have been considered it is probable that a fairly realistic picture is obtained from the MNI calculation, especially with large and well-excavated samples.

measurements of the limb bones from a site that was permanently occupied will show all sizes from newborn to fully adult, while a site occupied only in one season will have limb bone lengths which fall into certain size classes while intermediate sizes are absent.

The site of Star Carr was a pioneering example of the use of bones to interpret the season of occupation. The original interpretation was based upon the presence at the site of both unshed and shed antlers of red deer and elk. In these species the antlers are shed during winter and a new set soon begins to grow. It was argued by Grahame Clark that the site must have been occupied during the winter period so that both unshed and shed antlers could have been collected by the inhabitants. However, later study by a number of archaeologists emphasized that these antlers had been made into artifacts or were the waste from their manufacture. If the red deer and elk antlers are regarded as a raw material like flint, they bear little relation to the season of occupation at the site. The small antlers of roe deer were not used as artifacts and were found in the state representative of summer rather than winter.

Further work on the jaws and bones of the different species by Tony Legge and Peter Rowley-Conwy supported this hypothesis. In smaller mammals such as roe deer the adult dentition is complete in less than 18 months and this allows age at death to be closely determined. The mandibles of roe deer at Star Carr showed a peak of killing at about 1 year of age, which falls in early summer. Besides these specimens, some teeth and bones of red deer, roe deer, and elk were from newborn animals, confirming the pattern of early summer killing. This is the birth season for these species, and the hunters appeared to have targeted the young animals precisely at the point when maternal dependence ends and vulnerability to predation is highest. This reinterpretation also better accommodates the evidence of the few bird bones found at the site, which are also those of summer visitors.

By careful measurement and new analytical techniques one can therefore obtain quite precise data on age, sex, and season of death, which helps greatly in the evaluation of how and when people exploited their resources. Teeth alone can sometimes provide all this information (compare box opposite). The Japanese scholar Noriyuki Ohtaishi has studied 1700 recent specimens of Sika deer (*Cervus nippon*) in order to obtain data on tooth eruption, replacement, and development. He has established an age sequence from the period of eruption and the wear patterns on the cheek teeth, and has determined the age and the season of death by examining the cementum and counting its annual layers. He then applied this information to archaeological specimens. With jaws of the same species from Torihama, an Early Jomon site in Japan (3500 BC), he managed to determine their sex through measurements of jaw depth and of the area from the second premolar to the second molar – these were compared with measurements from specimens of known sex; his wear index provided the age at death; and thin-sections of the cementum layer established the season of death. Around 60 percent of the specimens were from old animals (over 5 years of age), a mortality pattern very similar to that from recent deer populations under protected conditions; whereas jaws from later Jomon sites such as Kidosaku (see box, pp. 300–01), Yahagi (2000 BC), and Sambu-Ubayama (500 BC) came mainly from animals younger than 5 years, a pattern similar to a recent hunted population. He was therefore able to conclude that, with time, hunting pressure increased on this species.

The Question of Animal Domestication

The methods just described help to shed light on the relationship between human beings and their large animal resources, on the composition of herds, and on exploitation techniques. An entirely different set of methods, however, is required to assess the status of the animals – i.e. whether they were wild or domesticated. In some cases this can be obvious, such as where non-indigenous animals have been introduced on to islands by humans – for example, the appearance of cattle, sheep, goat, dog, and cat on Cyprus. One criterion of animal domestication is human interference with the natural breeding habits of certain species, which has led to changes in the physical characteristics of those species from the wild state. But there are other definitions, and specialists disagree about which physical changes in animals are diagnostic of domestication. Too much emphasis on the wild/domestic dichotomy may also mask a whole spectrum of human-animal relationships, such as herd management without selective breeding. Nevertheless, domestication, by any definition, clearly occurred separately in many parts of the world, and archaeologists therefore need to differentiate fully wild from fully domestic animals, and to investigate the process of domestication. How is this done?

Bones and teeth are the most abundant kind of animal remains found on archaeological sites, and specialists have traditionally attempted to determine domestication through morphological changes such as a reduction in jaw size and the increased crowding of teeth. However, these have not proved wholly reliable criteria, because as yet we have no idea how long it

THE STUDY OF ANIMAL TEETH

Teeth survive more successfully than bones, and quite accurate assessments of an animal's age are possible from them. Growth rings around a tooth can be counted (see below), but this involves destruction of the specimen, and mineralization can blur the rings. Most assessments therefore rely on eruption and wear.

Investigation of the presence or absence of milk teeth in a jawbone makes it possible to assign a rough age by reference to the eruption sequence in a modern population. Where permanent dentition is concerned, however, only the degree of wear can provide evidence, once again through comparison with a series of jaws from animals of known age.

One drawback to this method is that assessments of degree of wear tend to be subjective. Complete or nearly complete jaws are also required, and these may not exist in some sites. Moreover, tooth wear will depend on the diet, and does not occur at a constant rate. Young, rough teeth wear down more quickly than older, blunted teeth, so that there is no simple correlation between age and degree of wear.

The American paleontologist Richard Klein has devised a more objective method, relying on measurement of cumulative wear, and widely applicable since it can be used on single teeth. A measurement is taken of the tooth's "crown height," the distance between the occlusal (biting) surface and the "cervical line" that separates the enamel from the dentine of the root. Using data for each species concerning the age when a crown is unworn and when it is fully worn away, the age of the tooth's owner at death can be estimated. Klein and Kathryn Cruz-Uribe have developed a BASIC computer program that uses these measurements to generate a mortality profile of the teeth in a site. In theory there are two fundamental patterns. The first is a **catastrophic age profile**, corresponding to what is thought to be a "natural" age distribution (the older the age group the fewer individuals it has). Such a pattern would be found in natural contexts – e.g. flash floods, epidemics, or volcanic eruptions – where a whole population has been destroyed. Where it is found in an archaeological context, it suggests the use of mass drives.

The second pattern, an **attritional age profile**, has an over-representation of young and old animals in relation to their numbers in live populations. In natural contexts it would suggest death by starvation, disease, accident, or predation. In an archaeological context it suggests scavenging, or hunting by humans of the most vulnerable individuals.

Klein has encountered both types of profile in the Middle Stone Age of Klasies River Mouth Cave, in Cape Province, South Africa, where the eland – easily driven – displayed a catastrophe profile, while the more dangerous Cape buffalo had an attrition profile.

Season of Death

Teeth can also provide clues to season of death through analysis of their growth rings. For example, the archaeozoologist Daniel Fisher studied the tusks and molars of mastodons (primitive, elephant-like animals) that had been killed or at least butchered by Paleo-Indians in southern Michigan in the 11th millennium BC. The layers of dentine formation enabled him to determine, to within a month or two, that the animals had been killed in mid-to-late fall.

In some mammals, annual rings of cementum, a mineralized deposit, form around the tooth roots below the gumline. When a thin-section is taken and placed under the microscope, the layers appear as a series of

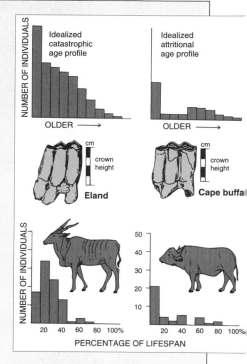

Ages at death deduced from crown heights of lower third molars by Richard Klein. (Top row) Idealized catastrophic age profile and attritional age profile. (Bottom row) Evidence from the cave site of Klasies River Mouth, South Africa, showing a catastrophic profile for the eland and an attritional profile for the Cape buffalo. (Postdepositional leaching may have selectively destroyed teeth for the youngest age band, which would account for the lower than expected number of individuals estimated in that group.)

translucent and opaque bands, representing alternating seasons of want and plenty which cause variation in the rate of deposition. The American scholar Arthur Spiess applied this technique to reindeer teeth from the Upper Paleolithic site of Abri Pataud, France, and proved that the animals were killed between October and March. Computer image enhancement now enables the layers to be distinguished and counted more accurately.

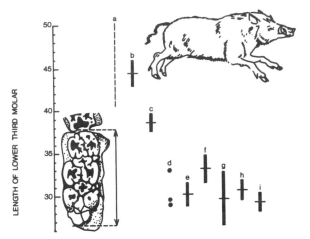

Decreasing tooth size as an indicator of pig domestication: a diagram based on the work of the British zooarchaeologist Simon Davis. Measurements (scale in millimeters) for (a) and (b) are from Late Pleistocene wild boars in the Levant; (c) represents modern Israeli wild boar. The size difference between (a/b) and (c) suggests an environmentally caused reduction in size at the end of the Ice Age. A further size reduction linked to domestication is suggested by the yet smaller size of domestic pig molars (d–i) from the eastern Mediterranean, as compared with the wild boar molars. (Individual measurements are given as circles, samples as mean averages with their ±95 percent confidence limits.)

took for such changes to take effect after humans began the process of domestication, and intermediate stages have not yet been recognized. Some species have certainly decreased in size through domestication (as suggested, for example, by archaeozoologist Richard Meadow for cattle at the Neolithic site of Mehrgarh in Pakistan), but environmental factors may have played a role here, as many wild species have also undergone a size decrease since the last Ice Age. Furthermore, we do not know the range of variation in wild populations, and there must have been a great deal of contact between early domestic and wild groups, with transmission of genes.

Some changes brought about by domestication occur in features such as skin or fleece that very occasionally survive archaeologically. For example, the arrangement of wool and hair is quite different in the skins of wild and domestic sheep. The British scholar Michael Ryder has been able to identify breeds of sheep from the range and distribution of fibers from skins in Viking textiles and medieval costumes.

In South America, the transition from hunting to herding is difficult to trace, because so few post-cranial skeletal features can distinguish domesticated camelid from wild forms. Since many sites, especially ones at

Mapping bones at the Boarding School site.

Excavation of a group of bison skulls at Gull Lake.

292

BISON DRIVE SITES

The driving of bison over bluff or cliff edges was an important periodic hunting method for thousands of years in North America. Much was known from accounts by Indian informants recorded in the first decades of this century, but the picture needed filling out through archaeological investigation of actual drive sites.

The Boarding School Site
One of the first of such excavations was undertaken by Thomas Kehoe in the 1950s at the Boarding School site, Montana. The work was carried out with the help of the local Blackfoot Tribe. Boarding School was not a cliff, but one of the more common, lower but abrupt drops that led to a natural enclosure. In a deep stratigraphy, three main bone layers were found, with well-preserved bison remains that gave insights into the size and composition of the herd, and hence into the seasons of the drives. Bison numbers were assessed using the minimum number of individuals technique (box, pp. 288–89). Ages of the animals came from the eruption sequence and degree of wear on the teeth (box, p. 291), and from bone-fusion, while sex was established on the basis of size and pelvic shape.

The site proved to have been used intermittently for a long period as a temporary camp. Then c. AD 1600 (according to radiocarbon dating of charred bone) a herd of about 100 bison was driven over the bluff. Their remains formed the "3rd bone layer," which included a fetal bone but no mature bulls, implying a late fall or winter drive of a herd composed of cows, calves, and young bulls. A season or two later, another herd of 150 were driven in, forming the "2nd bone layer." This had remains of mature bulls, and together with the lack of fetal or new-born calves it indicated a drive of a "cow-and-bull" herd in the rutting season, between July and September, when pemmican (dried meat) had to be prepared for the winter.

A much later drive (probably just before historic contact), produced the "1st bone layer." Here the remains of 30 bison were subjected to light butchering, probably for transport to a distant camp: much of what was left behind was in articulated units. In the earlier two layers, butchery techniques were similar but far more of each animal was utilized, and much was processed on the spot. Clearly, the distance to the home base was shorter than in the case of the later drive. The lack of pottery at the site emphasized its role as strictly a kill and meat-processing station. Traces of corral poles were found and the total of 440 projectile points suggested an average of 4 or 5 arrows used on each animal.

The Gull Lake Site
In the early 1960s Kehoe carried out a similar excavation at the Gull Lake site, over the border in southwest Saskatchewan. Here too, bison had been driven over a bluff into a depression serving as a corral. Five bone layers were encountered, one of them (c. AD 1300) perhaps representing the remains of as many as 900 bison.

The drives began in the late 2nd century AD, and show little processing of bone: many limb bones and even spinal columns are intact. In the later drives, however, processing was far more thorough, with few articulated bones, and extensive scattering and burning of scrap, indicating a utilization for grease and pemmican.

Surveying excavation trenches down the bluff slope at the Gull Lake site.

Gull Lake *bison drive (right).*

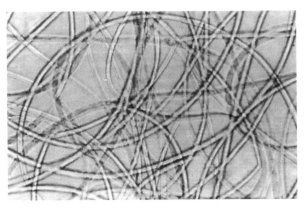 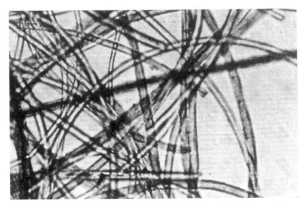

Microscopic analysis of the fibers of archaeological and modern camelid hairs from South America is being used to distinguish wild from domesticated camelid species. A sample from a present-day vicuña (above left), compared with an archaeological sample (above right) attributed to vicuña, from the site of Inca Cueva, Cueva 4, level 2, dated to around 10,000 years ago.

high altitude, are extremely arid, normally perishable items such as cordage, textiles, and fleece often survive, and Argentinian researcher Carmen Reigadas has undertaken microscopic analysis of fibers and follicles in these. Domestication brings about a decrease in the size of the coarse outer-coat hairs and an increase in the number of the underwool hairs. Measurements of prehistoric fibers compared with those from the four modern camelid types have enabled her to confirm osteological clues to the appearance of domestic forms around 3400 years ago at the cave of Huachichocana III. Fiber analysis is thus proving a useful aid in sites where bone remains are absent or too fragmentary to be of use.

Another approach has been to study changes in animal populations rather than individuals. The introduction of domestic animals into areas where their wild ancestors were not indigenous is a criterion of human interference that is often applied, but our knowledge of the original distribution of wild species is inadequate, made more complex by the frequent development of feral (i.e. former domesticated animals which have run wild) populations. More telling would be a radical shift from one slaughter pattern to another in a short space of time; this would certainly make a strong case for domestication, especially if combined with evidence of incipient morphological change. Here again, however, the theory is not so easy to demonstrate in practice. In the past, it was assumed that a high number of immature or juvenile herd animals in a bone assemblage represented human interference, and differed radically from a supposed "normal" wild population. But now it is known that sex ratios or percentages of juveniles can vary enormously in a wild herd. Furthermore, all predators (not just human ones) hunt selectively, con-

centrating on the more vulnerable individuals. It follows that a high proportion of immature animals is insufficient evidence in itself for domestication.

A herd's age and sex structure can nevertheless be a guide as to whether the animals were kept primarily for meat or for dairying purposes. A meat herd will contain a high number of adolescent and young adult animals, whereas a dairy herd will consist mostly of adult females.

Certain tools may indicate the presence of domesticated animals – for example, plows, yokes, and horse trappings. An unusual context can also be informative – for instance, a 12,000-year-old human burial found at Ein Mallaha in Israel contains the remains of a puppy, indicating the close links that were forged early on between humans and dogs.

Artistic evidence suggests even earlier possible attempts to control animals. As shown by Paul Bahn, some images from the end of the last Ice Age hint strongly at control of individual animals – most notably the Upper Paleolithic engraving of a horse's head from La Marche, France, with some form of bridle depicted. There is similar evidence from bones: for example the French Alpine rockshelter of La Grande-Rivoire has yielded remains of a brown bear in Mesolithic deposits. A grooved space between the teeth at both sides of its jaw suggests that this animal had been captured as a young cub, 7000 years ago, and wore a muzzle which restricted the growth of its molars. In other words, this was a tamed bear, perhaps even a pet.

In later times art is particularly informative about domestication, ranging from Greek, Roman, and Mesopotamian depictions of their domestic animals, to the Egyptian murals featuring not only farming but also some sort of domestication of more exotic species.

Deformities and disease can provide convincing evidence for domestication. When used for traction, horses, cattle, and camels all sometimes suffer osteoarthritis or strain-deformities on their lower limbs – a splaying of the bone, or outgrowths. Many archaeological examples are known, such as cattle bones from medieval Norton Priory in England. In horses the condition known as spavin has the same cause, and involves a proliferation of new bone around the tarsal bones and the metatarsal, resulting in fusion. Some diseases can be an indication of mismanagement of herds: rickets, for example, indicates a deficient diet or poor pasture, while close-herding and overstocking predispose animals to parasitic gastroenteritis.

Certain diseases may be a direct proof of domestication. In a study of Telarmachay, a prehistoric site in the Peruvian Andes, Jane Wheeler found that at a certain point in the stratigraphy, around 3000 BC, there was a significant increase in remains of fetal and newborn camelids such as llamas and alpacas. From a normal figure of 35 percent there was a jump to 73 percent. It is highly unlikely that these were young wild animals hunted and brought to the site by humans. No hunter would have found it worthwhile to pursue such small creatures, which might in any case have grown into more productive game. It is far more likely that these were domesticated animals, because mortality is very high among domestic llamas and alpacas, where the main cause of death is a kind of diarrhoea probably brought about by the spread of pathogens in dirty, muddy corrals, and not known to occur among wild species. If the massive mortality at Telarmachay was indeed caused in this way, evidence of this type may prove to be a useful indicator of domestication.

Great progress is therefore being made in studies of domestication. Some of the traditional criteria for demonstrating domestication – such as a reduction in size – may have proved to be less conclusive than was once thought. But these traditional approaches are being placed on a much sounder footing, and new scientific techniques, such as microscopic analysis of fibers, as well as studies of deformity and disease, open up promising new ways of looking at the question of animal domestication.

Currently, work is progressing on tracing the history of domestication through DNA (see pp. 431–32), on species from camelids to chickens. For example, DNA from cattle on three continents has already shaken the well-entrenched idea that their domestication spread from one center in the Near East; instead, Irish biologist Daniel Bradley and his colleagues have found evidence for at least two separate domestications of wild oxen, in southwest Turkey and east of the Iranian desert, with a possible third event in Africa. Since the genetic differences between the groups were too great for them to share a common ancestor 10,000 years ago, they must result from independent domestications of different races of wild ox. DNA has also begun to be used to distinguish the bones of sheep from those of goats in archaeological assemblages, which can be difficult on morphology alone.

Small Fauna: Birds, Fish, and Molluscs

Modern excavation techniques and screening or sieving have greatly improved retrieval of the fragile remains of small species. Identification requires the expertise of a specialist, since remains of the different species can be very similar, as indeed can those of some large species, such as sheep and goat (see above), camelids (see p. 292), or bison, buffalo, and cattle.

Birds. Remains of birds consist not only of bones but also guano, feathers, mummified birds in Egypt, footprints, and even eggshell that has survived at several Upper Paleolithic sites in Europe such as Pincevent, France. In some cases, it is possible to examine the shell in the scanning electron microscope and identify the species from the distribution of its pores.

Birds were often exploited for their feathers rather than their meat, and the particular species involved may settle the point. The enormous flightless moa in New Zealand were clearly exploited for meat, as shown by the numerous sites yielding evidence for moa butchery and cookery, with rows of ovens and bone dumps. At Hawksburn, for instance, a site of about AD 1250, Athol Anderson found the remains of over 400 moa; most had been brought in as leg joints, with the less meaty parts of the carcass abandoned at the kill sites. Such mass exploitation and waste helps to explain the extinction of this and other species in the Pacific (see Chapter 6).

Where small birds are concerned, however, it is often likely that their bones were brought to the site by a non-human predator or, in some cases, that they inhabited the site or its environs themselves. Here again, identification of the species involved may help one to solve the issue, but it is necessary to apply certain criteria in order to determine whether the birds were hunted by humans. A bone collection with a bias in favor of certain bones which differs from that in naturally occurring bone assemblages may suggest human intervention. Burning of the extremities of long bones is also a clue, though it will depend on the particular

FARMING ORIGINS: A CASE STUDY

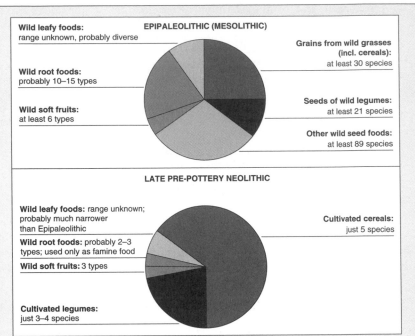

Pie charts comparing Epipaleolithic and Neolithic plant remains from Abu Hureyra. In the earlier period, 90 percent of the plant-based diet came from 160 species. By the later pre-pottery Neolithic, just 8–9 species supplied a similar proportion of the diet.

An outstanding example of how different types of evidence can be integrated into a rounded picture of a subsistence economy is to be found in the study of Tell Abu Hureyra, a site in Syria excavated by Andrew Moore in the early 1970s, and subsequently drowned beneath an artificial lake. The site's great interest lies in its remarkable assemblages of plant and animal remains from a region and a period crucial to the origins of farming in the Near East.

Abu Hureyra is a large mound, 11.5 ha (28 acres) in extent and with an 8-m (26-ft) stratigraphy. The site is located at the edge of the Euphrates valley, and was occupied by perhaps 200 or 300 people in the Epipaleolithic period (Mesolithic; 10th/9th millennia BC), and again in the Neolithic (after 7500 BC) by a population ten times larger. Flotation produced a diverse assemblage of charred plant remains, while dry sieving helped to retrieve over 60,000 identifiable bone fragments. In addition, the charred remains of what are probably the coprolites of infants were recovered.

Plant Remains

Analysis of the varied plant remains by Gordon Hillman and his colleagues at London's Institute of Archaeology involved the collection and study of modern seeds and fruits from the region in order to improve criteria of identification, and to learn about their present distribution and ecology. It was found that even the earliest (pre-pottery) Neolithic levels had fully domesticated cereals. By contrast, the Epipaleolithic layers had only morphologically "wild" forms (e.g. "wild" einkorn and rye). The absence in

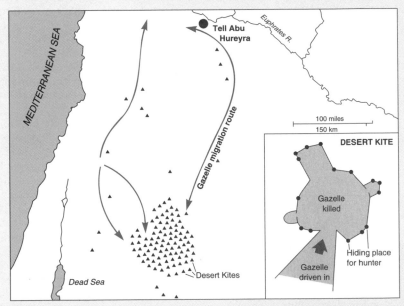

Likely gazelle migration routes, reconstructed largely on the basis of the distribution of desert kites, where gazelle may have been slaughtered. In late spring the animals moved north toward the area around Abu Hureyra, where the young were born. At the end of the summer they returned south.

The site of Abu Hureyra in northern Syria: spoilheaps and an archaeological trench from the excavations are visible in the distance. (The buildings to the right are modern.)

the Epipaleolithic period of all the common, toxic-seeded weeds (abundant in Neolithic levels) and the admixture of seeds of plants with which the wild-type cereals would have grown only in wild (natural) vegetation, indicates that the Epipaleolithic cereals were gathered from wild stands and were not under cultivation.

As for seasonality, the Epipaleolithic plant resources would have been available from late April until at least late October. And since seeds can be stored (although the site has no artifactual evidence of storage until the Neolithic), it is possible that there was year-round occupation here, based on a broad-spectrum plant economy, even before the emergence of agriculture. In whatever way the transition to cultivation came about, it seems to have taken only a few centuries. Once farming was fully established, the spectrum of seed-based foods dropped from 150 species down to a mere 8, which may represent a marked deterioration in dietary quality.

Animal Remains

In the faunal assemblage, studied by Tony Legge and Peter Rowley-Conwy, 80 percent of the bones belonged to gazelle, not only in the Epipaleolithic but in the Early Neolithic as well. Although most were adults, there were also (on the basis of tooth analysis and bone fusion) many very young animals,

including yearlings and newborn, which suggests that some annual killing took place around April or May when the young were born. Entire herds may have been driven to their deaths in specially built stone enclosures known as "desert kites" (from the shape of their ground-plan – see map), although their date is often uncertain, and some are even thought to be fairly recent structures.

If one relies on the evidence of bones alone, therefore, Abu Hureyra looks like a seasonal camp for gazelle hunting; but the size of the mound and, as shown above, the varied plant foods imply that permanent occupation was quite feasible.

The bones of sheep and goat (whether wild or domestic cannot be ascertained) constitute only 10 percent of the Epipaleolithic assemblage, and the same in the Early Neolithic, when cereal cultivation was underway. Analysis of the animals' teeth suggests that, unlike gazelle, they were killed throughout the year, as one might expect of domestic animals. But they remained of little importance while gazelle were available. In the 7th millennium BC there was an abrupt change, with sheep/goats increasing to 80 percent and gazelles declining to

only 20 percent of the bones. The cause may have been overkill of the gazelle, reflected in the proliferation of desert kites which perhaps disrupted the animals' migratory patterns.

Conclusions

An important conclusion is that for at least a thousand years after the first cultivation of morphologically domesticated plants at Abu Hureyra, hunting still played a crucial part in the site's economy. In this region, as in many other parts of the world, farming did not suddenly appear as an all-in-one package, but as a series of steps, adapting to changing circumstances over an extended period.

This example underlines the importance of analyzing all available evidence concerning subsistence. Plants or bones alone may give a distorted view. An integrated approach incorporating paleoethnobotany, archaeology and, where possible, direct dietary clues from human remains, together with archaeological and geomorphological evidence about land-use, will provide the fullest possible picture of subsistence.

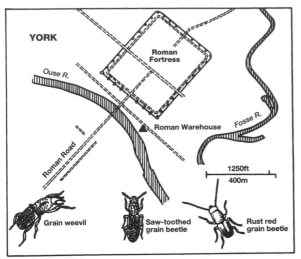

Insects and Roman York: grain beetles and other pests were found in huge numbers in the remains of a Roman grain store, which had evidently become infested.

methods of cooking used. Identification of cutmarks under magnification gives evidence on butchery; while if the quantity of bird bones at a site fluctuates through time independently of the fluctuations in microfauna, this suggests that they were not brought in by birds of prey.

Fish. As with the bones of mammals, methods have been devised for calculating the weight of fish from their bones, and hence assessing their contribution to diet. Different types of fish can provide data on the fishing methods utilized – the bones of deep-sea species, for example, indicate open-sea fishing. Salted fish are often well preserved in Egyptian sites, and indeed certain fish were mummified in that civilization, like so many other animals. The Romans, for their part, had fish-ponds and cultivated oysters.

Microfauna and Insects. Remains of *microfauna* such as rodents, or frogs and toads, are poor indicators of diet, since so many of them came into sites through their own burrowing activities or through the attentions of other predators – owl pellets are even known in the Lower Paleolithic cave sediments at Swartkrans, South Africa.

Insects were occasionally eaten – for example, locusts have been found in a special oven in the rock-shelter of Ti-n-Hanakaten, Algeria, dating to 6200 years ago – and in cases where their remains survive, they can provide important data on diet and seasonality. Wasp nests, for example, broken open to extract

the larvae, have been found in some abundance in refuse layers at the Allen site in Wyoming, which not only points to consumption of larvae but also to summer occupation. At Pueblo Bonito, the well-known pueblo settlement in Chaco Canyon, New Mexico, some pots in graves contained fly pupae and fragments of a beetle whose larvae attack stored cereals; thus the insects revealed the vanished contents of the vessels. Similarly, a grave at Playa de los Gringos, Chile, contained a wooden vessel in which were found pupae cases of a type of fly that lives on meat. And, as mentioned in Chapter 6, the presence of the grain beetle and the golden spider beetle in a Roman sewer at York was sufficient to indicate that it drained a granary; indeed, the remains of a warehouse by the river at York were identified as a grain store because of a soil layer containing an astonishing quantity of grain beetles. Hardly any remains of cereal were found, indicating the damage these pests had caused. So great was the infestation that it caused the Romans to dismantle the store, and to cover its remains and the beetles with a thick clay dump. A replacement store was then built; cereal grains but few beetles were recovered from it, demonstrating that the pest-control policy had been successful.

Molluscs. Midden sites, almost by definition, provide far more direct clues to diet since humans were clearly responsible for most of the material deposited in them. Apart from occasional surviving remnants of crustaceans and echinoderms (the spines of sea-urchins, starfish, etc.), the bulk of marine material in coastal middens usually consists of mollusc shells, together with the bones of whichever animals, birds, and fish were exploited. Similarly, in terrestrial middens, the shells of snails or freshwater molluscs generally vastly outnumber bones. Their predominance is made even greater by the fact that shells survive far more successfully than bones. For this reason, in the past, these ratios were taken to mean that molluscs had formed a staple resource for the occupants at such sites. However, in recent years, studies of the energy yield in calories of different species have revealed that the numerically inferior vertebrate resources were in fact the mainstay of the diet, and that molluscs were often only a crisis or supplementary resource, easy to gather when needed. One calculation showed that a single carcass of a red deer was the equivalent in calories of 52,267 oysters or 156,800 cockles!

In view of the vast amount of shells in most middens – a single cubic meter can contain a ton of material and 100,000 shells – only samples can be analyzed. These are screened (sieved), sorted, and identified, and the meat they represent then calculated from the ratio (which varies with species) of shell to flesh weight. The proportion by flesh weight of different species helps indicate their relative importance in the diet, but it is the calculation of their calorific value that provides the real evidence of their dietary contribution (see box overleaf). It has been found that one person would need to consume 700 oysters or 1400 cockles every day in order to "live by shellfish alone." Such figures, when seen against the timespan of a site's occupation, reveal that the numbers consumed per year could not have supported a large group of people. Calculations of this sort underline the dominant role of other resources in the diet.

Nevertheless, the molluscs present in a midden indicate what people were selecting from the range available. Changes in shell-size through time may reflect environmental fluctuations, but in many cases can reveal overexploitation by humans. The first occupants of the Polynesian island of Tikopia consumed giant shellfish, as well as turtles and wild flightless birds; within a few centuries the birds were extinct, and the turtles and shellfish were far smaller and fewer, and the diet had to be supplemented with other resources.

In sites other than middens, shells may be present in small quantities, and in many cases may not have been food at all. Snails, for example, may have lived in or around the site; and people often collected seashells to use as money, trinkets, or jewelry. Many of the seashells found in Upper Paleolithic sites in Europe are from small and inedible species.

Strategy of Use: Deducing Seasonality from Small Fauna

Some species of migratory birds, rodents, fish, and insects are available only at certain times of the year, and thus their simple presence at a site can provide useful information about the seasons in which humans occupied the site.

Although most fish are poor indicators of seasonality, since they can be treated and stored for consumption in lean times, techniques are emerging for extracting data of this type from their remains. Some species such as pike for example have year-rings in their vertebrae, by which one can calculate the season of death.

One new method being developed is the use of fish otoliths (part of the hearing apparatus) as evidence of seasonality. In late Mesolithic (4th millennium BC) shell middens on the island of Oronsay, off the northwest coast of Scotland, 95 percent of the total fishbone

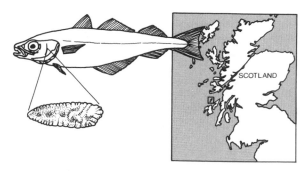

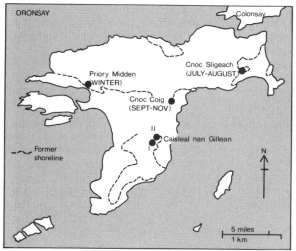

Deducing seasonality from fish otoliths. On the island of Oronsay, Scotland, Mellars and Wilkinson used the varying sizes of coalfish otoliths (top left) from Mesolithic sites to deduce seasons of occupations at those sites (above).

material comes from the saithe or coalfish. A statistical analysis by Paul Mellars and Michael Wilkinson of the sizes of sagittal otoliths (the largest and most distinctive of the three pairs found in the inner ear) has shown that the size distribution gives an accurate indication of the fishes' age at death, and therefore – assuming a standard date of spawning – of the season when they were caught. As usual in studies of this type, they had to assume that we can extrapolate modern rates of growth to the past. Their analysis showed that the coalfish were caught at 1 and 2 years of age. At each of the four sites studied around the island, the size of the fish varied, indicating that they were caught at different seasons of the year. At the site indicating winter occupation, when the fish had left the coast for deeper water, shellfish contributed a much higher percentage of the food than at those sites where coalfish were caught in greater numbers in the warmer seasons.

SHELL MIDDEN ANALYSIS

Over 600 shell mounds of the Neolithic Jomon period are known in the area around Tokyo Bay, Japan, and contain many kinds of food remains. The mound of Kidosaku, on the east coast of the bay and dating from the early 2nd millennium BC, has been analyzed in depth by Hiroko Koike. Her results indicate the wealth of detail about diet, length and season of occupation, and population size that can be obtained from a small shell mound.

Size of population was assessed by studying the 10 circular dwelling pits on the site's terrace. From their overlapping it was established that an average of only 3 had been in use at any one time. The size of the dwellings (11–28 sq. m; 13–33 sq. yd) implies that between 3 and 9 people occupied each house (see Chapter 11), giving a maximum population for the site of 23, and more likely between 12 and 18.

The dwellings appear to have been rebuilt four times, and on that basis (together with pottery evidence for a brief occupation) the site's timespan has been estimated at 20 to 30 years.

On the fringe of the terrace and down a steep slope were 7 concentrations of shells, each up to a meter thick and yielding a total volume of about 450 cu. m (589 cu. yd). Samples proved to contain 22 species of mollusc, all typical of a tidal assemblage from a sandy bottom.

Although the most abundant shell type was a tiny gastropod, it was the dominant bivalve – the clam *Meretrix lusoria* – which was probably the most important mollusc. About 3 million clams were represented in the site. From their shell heights, Koike was able to calculate the wet weight of the living clams, and reached a figure of 30 to 45 tons of clams at the site.

Analysis of growth structures in shells, especially bivalves, can provide important information on the season of exploitation. Under the microscope, one can see that the shell's cross-section has fine striations – these are the daily growth lines. There is seasonal variation in growth, with the thickest

lines in the summer and the thinnest in winter; the temperature of seawater seems to play a major role. The Kidosaku clams had an age composition and a seasonality very similar to those of modern clams collected in the nearby Midori river area, and their modest size indicates a collection pressure as high as that of today. Koike concluded that the Kidosaku clams had been harvested throughout the year as intensively as shellfish are today by modern commercial collectors.

The clams represent only one resource at the site. Apart from the other molluscan species, there were fish remains (retrieved through wet screening) and also mammal bones, dominated by wild boar (minimum no. of individuals 36) and sika deer (MNI 29), together with wild rabbit and raccoon dog. The age composition of the deer suggested that they were subject to high hunting pressure; and Koike has calculated that, with a probable density of 10 per square kilometer, deer could have accounted for 60 percent of the occupant's caloric needs.

Clams, therefore, were an important resource, but by no means the only staple food of the Kidosaku occupants.

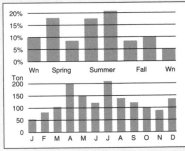

Histograms indicating how the seasonal pattern of clam collection at Kidosaku (top) – with a peak in the summer – is similar to that in the Midori river area today (second row). Collection seasons of the Kidosaku clams were estimated by studying growth lines.

The Kidosaku shell mound terrace (left) under excavation.

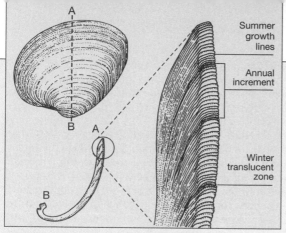

Growth lines in a clam record the time of the year it was harvested. In winter the clam hardly grows at all, whereas in spring and summer thicker growth lines mark a daily growth cycle. By sectioning the shell (A–B) and counting the lines in the last annual increment, the scientist can determine the season of death.

The Kidosaku site (below), showing (A) a plan of the shell deposits and 10 dwelling pits; (B) a section across one of the shell deposits; and (C) a plan of overlapping dwelling pits 1 to 4.

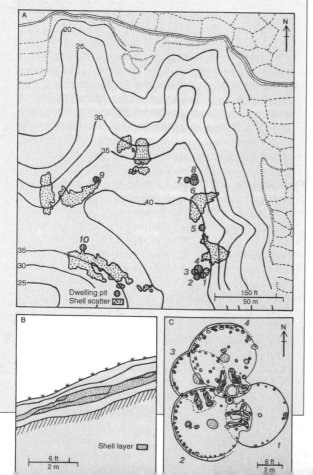

HOW WERE ANIMAL RESOURCES EXPLOITED?

Tools, Vessels, and Residues

Direct proof of human exploitation of animal resources is available in a variety of ways from tools, vessels, and residues.

Evidence for Fishing and Hunting Techniques. Stone Age fish traps are known from Denmark, while one of the earliest known European boats (4th millennium BC from Tybrind Vig in Denmark) was specially adapted for eel-fishing: the stern had a fireplace of sand and small stones, so that fires could be lit to attract them at night.

Working out the function of stone tools is less easy, but experiments on tool usage and microwear are at last providing us with a mass of detailed information (see also Chapter 8). Occasional examples of animal bones with points embedded in them, combined with studies of healed and unhealed wounds in bones and experiments on the efficacy of arrowheads and other projectiles against different materials are providing much evidence on hunting weapons and methods. For example, the Danish zooarchaeologist Nanna Noe-Nygaard has analyzed the skeletons of deer and boar from a number of Mesolithic sites, as well as isolated bog finds, in Denmark. She found that injuries inflicted by humans can usually be distinguished from damage caused naturally in, for example, rutting fights by comparison with marks on modern specimens. Her analysis of the size and outline of the fractures suggested that the bow and arrow, as well as the spear, were used in hunting. On shoulder blades, she noted that the unhealed (and therefore probably fatal) fractures were concentrated in the same part of the bone – the thin area covering vital internal organs – whereas the healed fractures from unsuccessful hunts were scattered all over the bone.

Analysis of microwear polishes is starting to reveal something of the uses of different stone tools. Lawrence Keeley, one of the pioneers in this field, found that tools from Koobi Fora, Kenya, dating to 1.5 million years ago, had a greasy wear similar to the traces produced experimentally by cutting meat and soft animal tissue, and two of the tools had been found near a bovid humerus bone with cutmarks.

Trails of Blood. Until recently it would have been difficult to prove on which species tools had actually been used, except in very rare cases where fragments of feathers or hair adhered to the tool and could be identified. But a new and still somewhat controversial technique, developed by Canadian researcher Thomas Loy, apparently now allows us to identify the species in question from the bloodstains left on stone knives. After use of the tool, the blood dries and fixes quickly; and if the tool is not cleaned well after excavation, this residue can be analyzed. The shape of the crystals of hemoglobin – the oxygen-carrying molecule that is found in red blood cells – varies between animal species, and thus provides a kind of molecular fingerprint. Tools are often buried under conditions that provide the right combination of temperature, moisture, and acidity to preserve the hemoglobin, although a certain amount of blood seeps into the soil.

Loy studied 104 tools of chert, basalt, and obsidian from open sites in coastal British Columbia, dating from 6000 to 1000 years ago, and identified hemoglobin of moose, caribou, grizzly bear, the Californian sealion, and other species. He also obtained radiocarbon dates from some blood residues, using accelerator mass spectrometry (Chapter 4). Stone tools from the Toad River Canyon site, 2180 years old, were found to have blood and hair on them that came from bison, according to microscopy, protein analysis, and DNA analysis.

Loy has recently extended and improved his technique. He has found that blood residues can survive on tools for at least 100,000 years. For example, it has been claimed (but also disputed) that blood has been found on 90,000-year-old stone tools from Tabun Cave, Israel, together with hair and collagen, suggesting that they were used in animal processing. As will be seen in Chapter 11, he has also discovered traces of human blood on a number of artifacts, including one of that remote date.

The blood residue technique, if confirmed by further testing, will prove invaluable on sites where bones are not preserved, and may give more accurate identifications than feather or hair fragments.

Fat and Phosphate Residues. Other residues are identifiable to various degrees by methods already mentioned in the section on plant resources. Chemical investigation of fats, for instance, can reveal the presence of animal products: an example at Geissenklösterle in western Germany was cited in Chapter 6. Horse fat was identified in layers at the Lower Paleolithic cave of Tautavel, southern France, and reindeer bone-oil at the Upper Paleolithic open-air site of Lommersum, southern Germany. Fish fats have also survived in some sites.

Phosphate analysis of soils can point to animal rather than plant husbandry since phosphorus is very abundant in animal and human fats (phospholipids) and

skeletons (phosphates). In some sites, phosphate concentrations can indicate areas of occupation, or places where livestock was concentrated (since phosphate also derives from decomposed dung). This technique is especially valuable for acid soils where the bones have not survived – it can, for example, reveal the former presence of bones in pits – and it underlines the importance of taking adequate soil samples from relevant areas of an excavation. In certain French caves occupied from the Neolithic onward, such as Fontbrégoua, it has been found that the presence of large quantities of so-called calcite spherulites, often associated with phosphate concretions in the floor sediments, is diagnostic evidence for cave-herding, since they represent the mineral residue of the dung of sheep and goats. Archaeological dung deposits can also be identified through the remains of predatory mites, which are characteristic of the droppings of different species: for example, 12 medieval samples from Holland have been found to include specimens from horse.

Use of manure on fields can also be detected. In an experiment carried out at Butser farm (see box pp. 274–75) cow dung was added to part of a field over a period of 13 years, and then the soil was chemically analyzed two years after the last muckspreading. Large quantities of stanols (long-lived fatty molecules which are only made in animal guts) were found in the area which had been manured, and these can sometimes be ascribed to particular species such as cattle or pigs. This experiment has made it possible to tackle remains from the past, such as on the small island of Pseira, off Crete, where Minoan terraces of 2000 BC seem to have been spread with household waste. Stanols were detected here, showing that the older layers were rich in manure, probably from humans or pigs.

Residues in Vessels. Where vessels are concerned, residues can be examined in several ways, as for plants. Investigation under the microscope together with chemical analysis enabled Johannes Grüss to identify a black residue on Austrian potsherds of 800 BC as overcooked milk. Analysis by mass spectrometer provides a record of molecular fragments in a residue, and these fragments can be identified using a reference collection of chromatograms. Employing this technique, Rolf Rottländer has found milk fat and beef suet in Neolithic Michelsberg sherds from Germany, fish fat in sites at Lake Constance, and butter and pork fat in Roman pottery vessels.

Egyptian vessels of the 1st and 2nd dynasties (3rd millennium BC) have been found, through chemical analysis, to contain residues of substances as diverse as cheese, beer, wine, and yeast. In Japan, Masuo

Nakano and his colleagues have identified dolphin fat in Early Jomon potsherds (4000 BC) from the Mauraki site, while the edges of late Paleolithic stone scrapers from the Pirika site (9000 BC) had residues of fat which seemed to come from deer. It is worth noting that his technique, which extracts the fats by "ultrasonic cleaning," can also be used to identify from which species tiny fragments of bone have come, which hitherto would have been completely unidentifiable.

An extension of this technique, gas liquid chromatography, constitutes a very sensitive method of measuring components of complex volatile compounds. It has been applied at the prehistoric coastal midden of Kasteelberg in southwest Cape Province, South Africa, which is less than 2000 years old. Potsherds from the midden had a brown, flaky substance on the inside, resembling burnt food, and the nitrogen content of a sample was so high that it suggested the substance was animal. The chromatography technique was applied in order to determine its composition in terms of fatty acids, and the values obtained were then compared with those of modern species of plants and animals. The results pointed firmly to a marine animal, though not to a precise species. The presence of seal bones in the site makes it probable that the substance came from the boiling of seal meat in jars for food or for extracting blubber.

Animal Prints and Tracks. Another type of residue left by animals are pawprints and animal tracks, as we saw in Chapter 6. Many Ice Age tracks may not have been associated with human beings. More informative are the impressions of sheep or goat feet in mud brick from the Near East and Iran, such as those from the 6th millennium BC at Ganj Dareh Tepe. The English Bronze Age site of Shaugh Moor, Devon, revealed tracks of cattle, sheep or goat, and a badger, preserved at the bottom of a ditch by peat. At the mouth of the Mersey estuary in northwest England, tracks of aurochs (wild cattle), red and roe deer, unshod horse, and crane have been found on the mudflats and date to around 3650 years ago. In Sweden, Bronze Age tracks of unshod horses have also been reported from raised fjord sediments at Ullunda, northwest of Stockholm; while in Japan, the remains of prehistoric paddy fields have often preserved prints of wild animals such as deer.

At Duisburg, western Germany, the remains of the medieval city's market square have been found to comprise successive cobbled surfaces interleaved with thick layers of mud and rubbish in which the tracks of cattle hooves, wagon wheels, and human feet have been preserved by being infilled with gravel to support the next layer of cobbles.

Tracks of aurochs (wild cattle), dating to c. 3650 years ago, in mudflats of the Mersey estuary, northwest England.

However, the best known and most abundant prints are those on Roman roof tiles and bricks – dogs and cats are particularly abundant, as well as birds. Of all the tiles from the Romano-British town of Silchester, no fewer than 2 percent had impressions of this type.

Tools and Art: Evidence for the Secondary Products Revolution

The question of animal domestication, discussed earlier, is one of the key issues in archaeology. British archaeologist Andrew Sherratt looked beyond the initial stage of domestication to ask whether there was not in fact a second and later stage – what he called the Secondary Products Revolution. Sherratt argued that in some parts of the Old World, during the middle and late 4th millennium BC, there was a marked change in the exploitation of domestic animals, no longer solely for the primary products of meat and hides but also for secondary products such as milk and cheese, wool, and animal traction. His evidence consisted to some extent of tools and slaughter patterns of caprines, but primarily of artistic depictions – in Sumerian pictograms from Uruk, Mesopotamian cylinder-seals, in

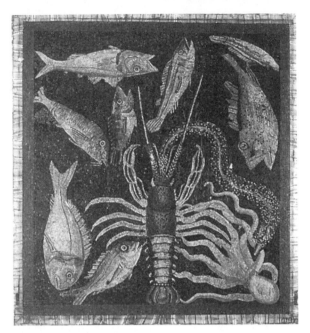

(Left) The Romans liked to eat seafood. Eleven species are shown in this 2nd-century AD mosaic from northern Italy. (Above) Milking scene from a frieze at Ur, Mesopotamia, c. 2900 BC. Use of secondary products may go back to the early Neolithic.

murals and models – that show plowing, milking, and carts (assumed to have been drawn by animals such as oxen). Sherratt argues that the change was a response to population growth and territorial expansion initiated by the origins of agriculture. People found it necessary to penetrate more marginal environments and exploit livestock more intensively.

However, the American archaeologist Peter Bogucki has shown that in the early Neolithic *Linearbandkeramik* culture of temperate Europe the age and sex structure of the cattle, together with ceramic strainers (interpreted as cheese sieves), indicate the presence of dairying as early as 5400 BC. If this is so, then the "revolution" at the end of the Neolithic must be seen not as a beginning but merely as an intensification of an already existing phenomenon. Perhaps before long analysis of residues in early Neolithic vessels will determine whether they held milk, butter, or cheese, and thus help solve the question of the timing and scale of human exploitation of secondary products.

Art and Literature

In addition to providing evidence for use of secondary products, art can be a rich source of other kinds of information. To take just one example, the American scholars Stephen Jett and Peter Moyle have been able to identify 20 species or families of fish depicted accurately on the inside of prehistoric Mimbres pottery from New Mexico (box, p. 554). As most of the fish are

marine types, and the pottery has been found at least 500 km (311 miles) from the nearest sea, it is obvious that the artists had been to the coast and were very familiar with these resources.

Much information can also be obtained from writings, not only of the sort described in the section on plants, but texts dealing with veterinary medicine, which are known in Egypt from 1800 BC on, and in Hittite and Mesopotamian sites of similar date, as well as from Greek and Roman times. As always, history, ethnography, and the experimental methods being applied to crop and animal husbandry (see box, pp. 274–75) help to flesh out the archaeological evidence.

Remains of Individual Meals

One of the most direct kinds of evidence of what people ate at a particular moment in the past comes from occasional finds of actual meals. At Pompeii, for example, meals of fish, eggs, bread, and nuts were found intact on tables, as well as food in shops. Food is often preserved in funerary contexts, as in the desiccated corncobs and other items in Peruvian graves, or at Saqqara, Egypt, where the 2nd-dynasty tomb of a noblewoman contained a huge variety of foodstuffs, constituting a rich and elaborate meal – cereals, fish, fowl, beef, fruit, cakes, honey, cheese, and wine – which, to judge by the tomb paintings, was not unusual. The Han period in China (206 BC–AD 220) has tombs stocked with food: that of the wife of the Marquis of Dai has a unique collection of provisions, herbal medicines, and prepared dishes in containers of lacquer, ceramic, and bamboo, with labels attached, and even inventory slips giving the composition of the dishes!

We should not, however, let the very richness of these finds cloud an objective judgment that meals

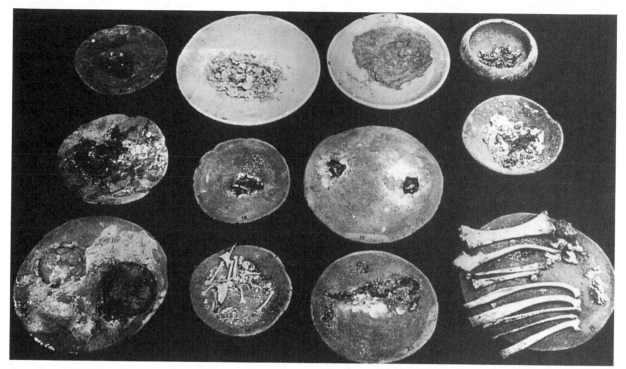

A meal as a funerary offering: the rich and elaborate food remains found in the 2nd-dynasty tomb of a noblewoman at Saqqara, Egypt. These include a triangular loaf of bread (made from emmer wheat); nabk berries (similar in appearance to cherries); cut ribs of beef; a cooked quail; two cooked kidneys; stewed fruit, probably figs; cakes; pigeon stew; a cooked fish. Impressive as such remains are, they are unlikely to be representative of the everyday diet of the ancient Egyptians.

from funerary contexts are unlikely to be representative of everyday diet. Even the meals found so wonderfully preserved at Pompeii are merely a tiny sample from a single day. The only way in which we can really study what people ate habitually is to examine actual human remains.

ASSESSING DIET FROM HUMAN REMAINS

The only incontrovertible evidence that something was consumed by humans is its presence in either stomachs or feces. Both kinds of evidence give us invaluable information about individual meals and short-term diet. The study of human teeth also helps us reconstruct diet, but the real breakthrough in recent years in understanding long-term diet has come from the analysis of bone collagen. What human bones reveal about general health will be examined in Chapter 11.

Individual Meals

Stomach Contents. Stomachs survive only rarely in archaeological contexts, except in bog bodies. It is sometimes possible to retrieve food residues from the alimentary tract of decomposed bodies – the anthropologist Don Brothwell achieved this, for example, by removing the grave earth from the lower abdominal area of some British Dark Age skeletons, and extracting the organic remains by means of flotation; and colon contents have also been obtained from an Anasazi burial of the 13th century AD. Some mummies also provide dietary evidence: the overweight wife of the Marquis of Dai from 2nd-century BC China, mentioned above, seems to have died of a heart attack caused by acute pain from her gallstones an hour or so after enjoying a generous helping of watermelon (138 melon seeds were found in her stomach and intestines).

When stomachs survive in bog bodies, the dietary evidence they provide can be of the greatest interest. Paleobotanist Hans Helbaek's pioneering studies of the stomach contents of Danish Iron Age bogmen showed that Grauballe Man, for instance, had consumed over 60 species of wild seeds, together with one or two cereals and a little meat (as shown by some small bone splinters), while Tollund Man had eaten only plants. But it should be borne in mind that these results, while fascinating, are not necessarily linked to annual diet, since these victims were possibly executed or sacrificed, and thus their last meal – apparently consisting of dense chaff, larger plant fragments, and weed seeds, the residues from sieving in the latter stages of crop processing – may have been out of the ordinary. Such waste crop cleanings were often used as animal feed, as famine food, or were given to condemned criminals.

However, as noted in the section on plant remains, the British Lindow Man (box, pp. 448–49) had consumed a griddle cake before his death, and this rough bread, made of the primary product of crop processing, was nothing out of the ordinary for the period – certainly not a recognizably "ritual" dish.

Fecal Material. Experiments have been done to assess the survival properties of different foodstuffs relevant to the study of ancient diet, and it has been found that many organic remains can survive surprisingly well after their journey through the human digestive tract, to await the intrepid analyst of *coprolites*, or fossilized feces. Coprolites themselves survive only rarely, in very dry sites such as caves in the western United States and Mexico, or very wet sites. But, where they are preserved, they have proved to be a highly important source of information about what individuals ate in the past.

The first step in any study is to attempt to check that the coprolites are indeed of human origin – this can sometimes be done by analysis of fatty molecules such as coprostanol, and of steroids. Once this has been done, what can coprolite contents tell us about food intake? Macroremains can be extremely varied in a human coprolite, in fact this variety is an indication of human origin. Bone fragments, plant fibers, bits of charcoal, seeds, and the remains of fish, birds, and even insects are known. Shell fragments – from molluscs, eggs, and nuts – can also be identified. Hair can be assigned to certain classes of animals by means of its scale pattern, visible under the microscope, and thus help us to know which animals were eaten. Eric Callen analyzed prehistoric coprolites from Tehuacán, Mexico (the valley studied and excavated intensively by Richard MacNeish in the 1960s), and identified hair from gophers, white-tailed deer, cottontail rabbit, and ring-tailed cats. He also managed to ascertain that some millet grains in the feces had been pounded, while others had been rolled on a metate (grinding stone).

Microremains such as pollen are of less help since, as we have already noted, most of the pollen present is inhaled rather than consumed. Pollen does, however, provide data on the surrounding vegetation, and on the season when the coprolite was produced. The fecal material from the Greenland Eskimo mummies (see pp. 444–45) contained pollen of mountain sorrel, which is only available in July and August. Fungal spores, remains of the nematode worm plant parasites, algal remains, and other parasites have also been identified in coprolites.

Exceptional conditions in Lovelock Cave, Nevada, have preserved 5000 coprolites dating from 2500 to 150 years ago, and Robert Heizer's study of their contents yielded remarkable evidence about diet, which seems to have comprised seeds, fish, and birds. Feather fragments were identified from waterfowl such as the heron and grebe; fish and reptile scales, which pass through the alimentary canal unaltered, also led to identification of several species. Fish remains were abundant in some of the coprolites; one, for example, from 1000 years ago, contained 5.8 g (0.2 oz) of fish bone which, it was calculated, came from 101 small chubs, representing a total live weight of 208 g (7.3 oz) – the fish component of a meal for a single person.

Even where feces have not been preserved, we are now sometimes able to detect and analyze residues of digested food by studying sewers, cesspits, and latrines. Biochemical analysis of ditch deposits near latrines at the Roman fort of Bearsden, Scotland, revealed an abundance of coprosterol, a substance typically found in human sewage, as well as a bile acid characteristic of human feces. A low amount of cholesterol showed that there was little meat in the diet. Numerous fragments of wheat bran in the deposit probably formed part of the feces, and no doubt came from defecated bread or some other floury food.

Coprolites and fecal residues represent single meals, and therefore provide short-term data on diet, unless they are found in great quantities, as at Lovelock Cave, and even there the coprolites represent only a couple of meals a year. For human diet over whole lifetimes, we need to turn to the human skeleton itself.

Human Teeth as Evidence for Diet

Teeth survive in extremely good condition, made as they are of the two hardest tissues in the body. Pierre-François Puech is one of a number of scientists to have studied teeth from many periods in an attempt to find some evidence for the sort of food that their owners enjoyed. The method involves a microscopic examination of the abrasions on certain dental surfaces.

To study food intake, one should examine the lateral or side surfaces which best escape abrasion from inorganic particles in the food, and whose wear instead ought to reflect the movement of the organic food itself within the mouth. A replica is made by pouring a thin film of resin onto the tooth-face; when this is peeled off after solidification, it forms a faithful imprint which can be examined under the light microscope or in the scanning electron microscope. Puech began by studying recent teeth from individuals with known dietary habits. The principle involved was that abrasive particles in food leave striations on the enamel whose orientation and length are directly related to the meat or vegetation in the diet and its process of cooking. Modern meat-eating Greenland Eskimos were found to have almost exclusively vertical striations on their lateral surfaces, while largely vegetarian Melanesians had both vertical and horizontal striations, with a shorter average length.

When these results were compared with imprints from fossil teeth, it was found that from the late Lower Paleolithic onward, there is an increase in horizontal and a decrease in vertical striations, and a decrease in average striation length. In other words, less and less effort was needed in the mastication of food, and meat may have decreased in importance as the diet became more mixed: early people crushed and broke down their food with their teeth, but less chewing was required as cooking techniques developed and improved. There are exceptions, such as a *Homo erectus* individual who seems to have been mainly vegetarian, eating thin, chewy vegetable foods, but on the whole the generalization seems sound.

The biting (occlusal) surfaces of human teeth are of limited help in Puech's technique, since much of the wear here is due to the method of food preparation – meat can be exposed to windborne dust, for example, or food may have been cooked on ashes, and the result is the incorporation of extraneous abrasive particles in the food. Furthermore, our ancestors often used teeth not simply for chewing but as a third hand, for cutting, tearing, and so on. All these factors add striations to the biting surfaces. The lower jawbone of the *Homo erectus* (or "archaic" *Homo sapiens*) individual from Mauer, near Heidelberg in western Germany, dating back some half a million years, has marks suggesting that meat was held in the front of the mouth and cut off with a flint tool that left its traces on six front teeth. Wear on Neanderthal teeth reveals that here too teeth were often used in the same way.

Tooth decay as well as wear will sometimes provide us with dietary information. Remains of the California Indians display very marked tooth decay, attributed to their habit of leaching the tannin out of acorns, their staple food, through a bed of sand which caused excessive tooth abrasion. Decay and loss of teeth can also set in thanks to starchy and sugary foods. Dental caries became abundant on the coast of Georgia (USA) in the 12th century AD, particularly among the female population. It was in this period that the transition occurred from hunting, fishing, and gathering to maize agriculture. The anthropologist Clark Larsen believes that the rise in tooth decay over this period, revealed by a study of hundreds of skeletons, was caused by the carbohydrates in maize. Since the women of the group were more subject to the caries than were the men, it is probable that they were growing, harvesting, preparing, and cooking the corn, while the men ate more protein and less carbohydrate. However, not all scientists accept these conclusions, pointing out that women may have suffered from more caries in a period of high population growth because of greater loss of calcium with the higher number of pregnancies.

Finally, as mentioned above (p. 274), direct evidence of diet can be obtained from phytoliths extracted from the surface of human teeth.

Isotopic Methods: Diet over a Lifetime

Recently, a revolution has taken place in dietary studies through the realization that isotopic analysis of human tooth enamel and bone collagen can reveal a great deal about long-term food intake. The method relies on reading the chemical signatures left in the body by different foods – we are what we eat.

Plants can be divided into three groups – two groups of land plants and one of marine plants – based on their differing ratios of the carbon isotopes ^{13}C and ^{12}C. Carbon occurs in the atmosphere as carbon dioxide with a constant ratio of $^{13}C{:}^{12}C$ of about 1:100; in ocean waters, the amount of ^{13}C is slightly higher. When atmospheric carbon dioxide is incorporated into plant tissues through photosynthesis, plants use relatively more ^{12}C than ^{13}C and the ratio is altered. Plants that fix carbon dioxide initially into a three-carbon molecule (called C3 plants) incorporate slightly less ^{13}C into their tissues than do those using a four-carbon molecule (C4 plants). By and large, trees, shrubs, and temperate grasses are C3 plants; tropical and savanna grasses, including maize, are C4 plants. Marine plants photosynthetically fix carbon differently from most land plants, and have a higher $^{13}C/^{12}C$ ratio.

As plants are eaten by animals, these three different ratios are passed along the food chain, and are eventually fixed in human and animal bone tissue. The ratio found in bone collagen by means of a mass spectrometer thus has a direct relation to that in the plants which constituted the main foods. The ratios can show whether diet was based on land or marine plants, and whether on C3 or C4 land plants. Only archaeological evidence, however, can provide more detail about precisely which species of plants or animals contributed to the diet.

Henrik Tauber applied this technique to collagen from prehistoric skeletons in Denmark, and found a marked contrast between Mesolithic people and those of the Neolithic and Bronze Age. In the Mesolithic, marine resources were predominant – even though fish bones were very scarce in the excavated material – whereas in the later period there was a change to reliance on land foods, even in coastal sites.

At coastal sites in other parts of the world, the technique has confirmed a heavy reliance on marine resources. In prehistoric sites on the coast of British Columbia, Brian Chisholm and his associates found that about 90 percent of protein had come from marine foods; little change was apparent over five millennia, and it was noted that adults seemed to eat more food from the sea than did children.

Recently, isotopic analysis of tooth enamel from four *Australopithecus africanus* individuals from Makapansgat, South Africa, revealed that they ate not only fruits and leaves, as had been thought, but also large quantities of carbon-13 enriched food such as grasses or sedges, or the animals which ate those plants, or both. In other words, they regularly exploited fairly open environments (woodlands or grasslands) for food; and since their tooth wear lacks the characteristic scratches of grass-eaters, it is possible that they were indeed already consuming meat, by hunting small animals or scavenging larger ones.

Bone Collagen Studies and the Rise of New World Agriculture.
The carbon isotope bone collagen method is particularly useful for detecting changes in diet, and has revolutionized the study of the rise of food production in the New World. Anna Roosevelt used the technique to assess the diet of the prehistoric inhabitants of the Orinoco floodplain in Venezuela. Analysis of samples from a number of skeletons by her colleagues Nikolaas van der Merwe and John Vogel revealed a dramatic shift from a diet rich in C3 plants such as manioc in 800 BC to one based on C4 plants such as maize by AD 400. Although the technique cannot specify the actual plants consumed, the abundant maize kernels and grinding equipment found in the area's sites from AD 400 confirm the insight provided by isotopic analysis.

The technique is even more crucial in North America, where the rise of agriculture was signaled by the introduction of maize, a C4 food native to Mesoamerica, into a predominantly C3 plant environment (in the Near East, where the first domesticated plants were themselves part of the C3 plant environment, the technique is of less use to studies of the origins of agriculture). In some cases, maize's contribution to a diet can be quantified. In skeletons from southern Ontario, Henry Schwarcz and his colleagues found that the proportion of C4 plants (i.e. maize) in the diet increased between AD 400 and 1650, reaching a maximum of 50 percent by about 1400.

Other Bone Collagen Techniques. Some scholars have attempted to extend the carbon isotope technique to apatite, the inorganic and major constituent of bone, in the hope that it could be applied even in cases where collagen has not survived (it often degrades after 10,000 years); others, however, have found this method unreliable, so that the collagen method is the only one whose validity is confirmed for the present.

Nevertheless there are collagen techniques available involving isotopes of elements other than carbon. Ratios of *nitrogen isotopes* in collagen, for example, can reflect dietary preferences in the same way as carbon. The ^{15}N isotope increases as it passes up the food chain from plants to animals: a low ratio of ^{15}N to ^{14}N points to an agricultural subsistence, while a high ratio points to a marine diet. One anomaly here is caused by coral reef resources such as shellfish, which, because of the way nitrogen is fixed by plants in reefs, give a low nitrogen value. Thus, in cases where a seafood diet seems likely, the carbon isotope method needs to be employed for confirmation.

The two methods have also been applied together to historic and prehistoric material in East and South Africa by Stanley Ambrose and Michael DeNiro. They found it possible to distinguish marine foragers from people using land resources, pastoralists from farmers, camel pastoralists from goat/cattle pastoralists, and even grain farmers from non-grain farmers. Groups that depended on the meat, blood, and milk of domestic animals had the highest ^{15}N values, those dependent mainly on plant foods had the lowest. The results agreed well with ethnographic and archaeological evidence. Comparison of ^{15}N and ^{13}C levels in Preclassic Maya burials and animal bones from the early village site of Cuello, Belize (1200 BC–AD 250), excavated by Norman Hammond and analyzed by him, Nikolaas van der Merwe, and Robert H. Tykot, has also produced interesting results (see diagram).

Measuring the amounts of ^{13}C and ^{15}N in fossilized Neanderthal bones from the cave of Maurillac, Charente, has led French researchers to the conclusion that their diet was almost exclusively carnivorous. The same carbon and nitrogen isotopes have also been analyzed in other kinds of tissue, such as the skin and hair of mummies from the Nubian Desert, dating from 350 BC to AD 350, and suggest that the population ate goats and sheep, cereals and fruit. Since isotopes show up in hair only two weeks after they are consumed (whereas bone shows what was eaten over a lifetime), different segments of the same hair can show changes in diet, the segments closest to the scalp even indicating the season at the time of death. Locks of hair from 2000-year-old Peruvian and Chilean mummies have even been found to contain traces of cocaine consumption from the chewing of coca leaves.

Scientists have also found that concentrations of *strontium*, a stable mineral component of bone, can provide data on diet. Most plants do not discriminate between strontium and calcium, but when animals eat plants, strontium is discriminated against in favor of calcium; most of the strontium is excreted, but a small constant percentage enters the blood stream and becomes incorporated into bone mineral. The contribution of plants to the diet can therefore be assessed through the proportions of strontium and calcium (Sr/Ca) in human bone – the bigger the contribution (e.g. in a vegetarian), the higher the Sr:Ca ratio, whereas a meat-eater's diet gives a low ratio. South African

anthropologist Andrew Sillen has discovered by this technique that *Australopithecus robustus*, formerly thought to have been a vegetarian because of its powerful grinding jaws, did eat some meat and was therefore probably omnivorous.

Analysis by Margaret Schoeninger of strontium levels in bones from the eastern Mediterranean has shown that the proportions of plant and animal foods in the diet did not change radically from the Middle Paleolithic until the Mesolithic, when there was a shift toward a greater use of plant foods. Her results show that people here had a plant-rich diet a considerable time before cereals were domesticated.

Schoeninger has used the same technique to study skeletal material at Chalcatzingo, an Olmec site in central Mexico at its peak around 700–500 BC, where a combination of strontium results and an assessment of grave-goods indicates a ranked society with a differential consumption of meat. She found that the highest-ranked people buried with jade had the lowest bone strontium (and therefore ate plenty of meat); those buried with a shallow dish had a higher strontium level (and thus ate less meat); while a third group lacking any grave-goods had the highest strontium level (and probably ate very little meat).

A different picture emerges where shellfish contributed to diet, because strontium concentrations are far

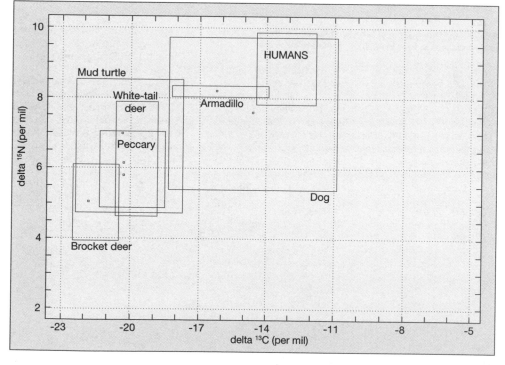

Bone collagen analysis of Preclassic Maya burials and animal bones from the site of Cuello, Belize, showed that maize formed 35–40 percent of the diet of humans, and of dogs bred for food. The wide range of both ¹³C and ¹⁵N for dogs suggests a mixed diet. Forest species, such as deer, and marine turtles ate only C3 plants, and had a lower protein intake, indicated by the ¹⁵N figures. Armadillos have high figures due to eating grubs that themselves eat the roots of maize plants.

higher in molluscs than in plants. Skeletons from an Archaic hunter-gatherer population of around 2500 BC at a northern Alabama site proved to have a higher strontium level, thanks to the molluscs in their diet, than those from an agricultural Mississippian population buried at the same site in about AD 1400.

Recent studies, however, suggest that due to contamination from sediments and ground water in which some bones are buried, strontium values can be misleading and one should keep an open mind until possible pitfalls are better understood. In any case, the technique is only a complement to – not a replacement for – the analysis of carbon isotopes. The Sr:Ca ratio reveals the proportionate amounts of meat and plants in the diet; but isotopic analysis is needed to learn what kinds of plants were being consumed. Archaeology provides the evidence that permits more precise identification of the plant and animal species involved.

SUMMARY

All the methods described in this chapter are providing archaeology with new tools, not to say with "food for thought." The evidence available varies from botanical and animal remains, both large and microscopic, to tools and vessels, plant and animal residues, and art and texts. We can discover what was eaten, in which seasons, and sometimes how it was prepared. We need to assess whether the evidence arrived in the archaeological record naturally or through human agency, and whether the resources were wild or under human control. Occasionally we encounter the remains of individual meals left as funerary offerings or as the contents of stomachs or feces. Finally, the human body itself contains a record of diet in its tooth-wear and in the chemical signatures left in bones by different foods.

Many of the techniques lie in the domain of the specialist, particularly the biochemist, but archaeologists should know how to interpret the results, because the rewards are enormous for our knowledge of what people ate, how they exploited their resources, and in what proportions. Prospects for future research look good. Since we understand increasingly what a good or balanced diet entails, we can now begin to examine past diets in terms of nutritional value and assess the state of health of our ancestors.

FURTHER READING

Most of the sources given at the end of Chapter 6 are appropriate for this chapter as well. In addition, helpful volumes are:

Brothwell, D. & P. 1997. *Food in Antiquity: A Survey of the Diet of Early Peoples*. Johns Hopkins Univ. Press: Baltimore, MD.

Gilbert, R.I. and Mielke, J.H. (eds.). 1985. *The Analysis of Prehistoric Diets*. Academic Press: New York & London.

Harris, D.R. (ed.). 1996. *The Origins and Spread of Agriculture and Pastoralism in Eurasia*. UCL Press: London.

Harris, D.R. & Hillman, G.C. (eds.). 1989. *Foraging and Farming. The Evolution of Plant Exploitation*. Unwin Hyman: London.

Hastorf, C.A. & Popper, V.S. (eds.). 1988. *Current Paleoethnobotany. Analytical Methods and Cultural Interpretations of Archaeological Plant Remains*. University of Chicago Press: Chicago.

Olsen, S.J. 1970. *Osteology for the Archaeologist*. Peabody Museum: Cambridge, Mass.

Pearsall, D.M. 1989. *Paleoethnobotany: A Handbook of Procedures*. Academic Press: New York & London.

Price, T.D. & Gebauer, A.B. (eds.). 1995. *Last Hunters, First Farmers*. School of American Research Press: Santa Fe.

Reitz, E.J. & Wing, E.S. 1999. *Zooarchaeology*. Cambridge University Press: Cambridge.

Smith, B.D. 1995. *The Emergence of Agriculture*. Scientific American Library: New York.

Zohary, D. & Hopf, M. 1999. *Domestication of Plants in the Old World. The Origin and Spread of Cultivated Plants in West Asia, Europe and the Nile Valley*. (3rd ed.). Clarendon Press: Oxford.

8 How Did They Make and Use Tools?
Technology

The human species has often been defined in terms of our special ability to make tools. And many archaeologists have seen human progress largely in technological terms. The 19th-century Danish scholar C.J. Thomsen divided the human past into "ages" of stone, bronze, and iron. His successors further divided the Stone Age into a Paleolithic period (with chipped or flaked stone tools), and a Neolithic period (with polished stone tools). The later addition of the term Mesolithic (Middle Stone Age) carried with it the implication that the very small flint tools, the "microliths," were somehow characteristic of this particular period of human existence.

Even if today we do not place so much emphasis on the particular form of artifacts as a reliable chronological indicator, it remains true that these were and are the basic means by which humans act upon the external world. Modern lasers and computers, guns and electrical appliances all have their origins in the simple tools created by our earliest ancestors. It is the physical remains of humanly made artifacts down the ages that form the bulk of the archaeological record. In other chapters we look at how archaeologists can use artifacts to establish typologies (Chapter 4), learn about diet (Chapter 7), discover past patterns of trade and exchange (Chapter 9), and even recreate systems of belief (Chapter 10). Here, however, we address two questions of fundamental importance: how were artifacts made, and what were they used for?

As we shall see, there are several approaches to these two questions – the purely archaeological, the scientific analysis of objects, the ethnographic, and the experimental. Archaeologists should also seek the advice of modern experts in equivalent technologies. Contemporary craftspeople generally exploit the same materials as their forebears, and often use tools that are little changed. An ancient stone wall will be best understood by a stonemason, a brick building by a bricklayer, and a timber one by a carpenter, although in order to understand a medieval timber building, a modern carpenter will certainly need to know something of the period's materials, tools, and methods. For more recently developed technologies, such as those of the last 200 or 300 years, the growing field of *industrial archaeology* can also make use of eye-witness accounts by living craftspeople or verbal descriptions handed down from one generation to the next, as well as historical and photographic records.

The student of earlier periods has a narrower range of evidence to choose from. Questions of preservation arise, and indeed of how one decides whether an early "tool" is humanly made in the first place (see box, p. 314).

Survival of the Evidence

When assessing ancient technologies, the archaeologist always needs to bear in mind that the sample preserved may well be biased. During the long Paleolithic period implements of wood and bone must surely have rivaled those of stone in importance – as they do in hunting and gathering societies today – but stone tools dominate the archaeological record. As we saw in Chapter 2, fragile objects may sometimes survive on waterlogged, frozen, or dry sites, but these are exceptions. In view of the poor preservative qualities of many types of artifact, it is worth remembering that even those that have totally decayed can occasionally be detected by the hollows, soil-changes, or marks they have left. Examples include the imprint left in sand by the Sutton Hoo boat in eastern England; the imprint of a textile on a mummy; or, as will be seen below, the space within a mass of corroded metal. The vanished wheel of an Iron Age vehicle in a grave at Wetwang, Yorkshire, in northern England, has been successfully investigated by pumping polystyrene foam into the hollow, revealing that the wheel had 12 spokes. In the royal burials at Ur, Leonard Woolley (p. 34) poured plaster into cavities left by the decayed wooden parts of a lyre. Among the plaster casts of plants at El Cerén, El Salvador (see p. 257), one agave was found to have a strand of braided twine of agave

(Left) A hollow left in the ground by an entirely decayed pointed stick and (right) a plaster cast of one end of this "pseudomorph" from the Middle Paleolithic rockshelter of Abric Romani, Spain.

fiber around it, likewise preserved as a cast. At the Middle Paleolithic rockshelter of Abric Romani in northeast Spain, a "pseudomorph" (i.e. hollow) of a decayed pointed wooden stick, 1 m (3.25 ft) long and dating to almost 50,000 years ago, has been found in sediment; a cast made from the hollow is so detailed that striations on its distal end, revealed by the scanning electron microscope, are clearly similar to tool marks made by experimental woodworking.

Implements are also known from artistic depictions, such as boomerangs and axes stenciled on rockshelter walls by Aborigines in a number of regions of Australia. The former presence of some tools can also be detected by their effects – for example, a sword-cut on a skull, or a pick-mark on a quarry wall.

Are They Artifacts at All?

The archaeologist, when studying an object, must first decide whether it was made or used by people in the past. For most periods the answer will be obvious (although one has to beware of fakes and forgeries), but for the Paleolithic, and especially the Lower Paleolithic, judgment can be less straightforward. For many years a vehement debate raged concerning the problem of "eoliths" – pieces of stone found at the beginning of this century in Lower Pleistocene contexts in eastern England and elsewhere and believed by some scholars to have been shaped by early humans, but which other scholars thought were products of nature.

This controversy led to early attempts to establish criteria by which human agency could be recognized, such as the characteristic bulges or "bulbs of percussion" found on pieces of flint purposely struck off (see diagram). Natural fractures caused by factors such as heat, frost, or a fall produce instead irregular scars and no bulb. On this basis the eoliths were pronounced to be of natural origin.

Where the very earliest tools are concerned, however – on which one would expect the traces of human

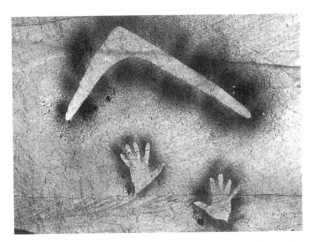

Depictions of tools and weapons are common on rockshelter walls in Australia. This photograph shows the stencil of a V-shaped "killer" boomerang from the Central Queensland Sandstone Belt. Grahame Walsh and his colleagues estimate that there are 10,000 rock art sites in this area alone.

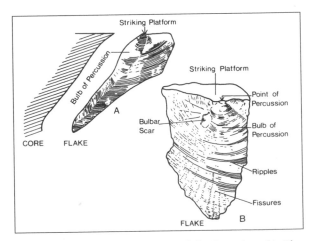

Features of a purposely made stone flake. Two views (A, B) of a flake struck from the edge of a core show the characteristic striking platform and, immediately beneath, the bulb of percussion and ripples produced by the shock waves after the blow has been struck.

work to be minimal – the question is less easy to resolve, since the crudest human working may be indistinguishable from the damage caused by nature. Here the examination of the context of a particular find may help. It is possible that the stone objects were discovered in association with fossil human remains and animal bones that can be studied for signs of human cutmarks made by stone tools, as described in Chapter 7.

It had traditionally been thought that tool-making separated humans from apes, but the past 30 years of field research have revealed that wild chimpanzees make and use tools of wood and stone; in fact American primatologist William McGrew believes that "some artifacts would be unattributable to [human or chimpanzee] species if they lost their museum labels." In particular, chimpanzees use hammers and anvils to crack nuts. This adds an extra uncertainty to the identification of crude humanly made tools, but also offers archaeologists the chance to "observe" some of the possible tool-making, -using, and -discarding behaviors of early hominids.

A complex case is that of the Calico Hills site, California, where thousands of pieces of fractured stone were found in the 1960s and 1970s in geological deposits dating to around 200,000 years ago. The discoverers claim that many of the stones are tools on the basis of their bulbs of percussion, regular shape, and comparison with tools knapped experimentally from local raw materials. If correct, this would suggest human occupation of the New World at least 160,000 years earlier than is indicated by other sites. It is this extraordinarily early date, itself controversial, and lack of supporting evidence from other sites, as well as the crude nature of the "artifacts," that leads most archaeologists to reject the Calico finds as genuine tools.

A similar debate surrounds artifacts from the rockshelter at Pedra Furada, Brazil (see box overleaf). And yet another example of this controversy is represented by a possible quartzite cobble tool discovered on the Potwar plateau of Pakistan. The date of its conglomerate matrix, 1.9 million years ago, suggests that the widely accepted date of 1.6 million years for the colonization of Eurasia by *Homo erectus* from Africa may need revision.

Interpreting the Evidence: the Use of Ethnographic Analogy

If used with care, evidence from ethnography and ethnoarchaeology can shed light on both general and specific questions concerning technology. At the general level, ethnography and common sense together suggest that people tend to use whatever materials are easily and abundantly available for everyday, mundane tasks, but will invest time and effort into making implements they will use repeatedly (though perhaps rarely) and carry around with them. The abundance of a type of tool in the archaeological record is therefore not necessarily a guide to its intrinsic importance in the culture; the tool most frequently found may well have been quickly made, and discarded immediately after use, while the rarer implement was kept and reused ("curated") several times, before eventually being thrown away.

At the specific level of perhaps identifying the precise function of a particular artifact, ethnography can often prove helpful. For example, large winged pendants of polished stone were found in sites of the Tairona Indians of northern Colombia, dating to the 16th century AD. Archaeologists could only assume that these were purely decorative, and had been hung on the chest. However, it was subsequently learnt that the modern Kogi Indians of the area, direct descendants of the Tairona, still use such objects in pairs, suspended from the elbows, as rattles or tinklers during dances!

There are innumerable examples of this sort. The important point is that the identification of tool forms by ethnographic analogy should be limited to cases where there is demonstrable continuity between archaeological culture and modern society, or at least to cultures with a similar subsistence level and roughly the same ecological background.

In recent years, the archaeological and ethnographic aspects of technological studies have been complemented by the ever increasing interest in bringing archaeology to life through experiment. As we shall see, experiments have contributed a great deal to our understanding of how artifacts were made and what they were used for.

For the purposes of the remainder of this chapter, it is convenient to draw a distinction between two classes of raw material used in creating objects – between those that are largely unaltered, such as flint, and those that are synthetic, the product of human activities, such as pottery or metal. Of course even supposedly unaltered materials have often been treated by heat or by chemical reactions in order to assist the manufacturing process. But synthetic materials have undergone an actual change in state, usually through heat treatment. The human use of fire – pyrotechnology – is a crucial factor here. We are becoming increasingly aware of just how precise human control of fire was at an early date.

ARTIFACTS OR "GEOFACTS" AT PEDRA FURADA?

Debate still rages over the dating of the huge sandstone rockshelter of Pedra Furada in northeast Brazil, excavated by Franco-Brazilian archaeologist Nième Guidon from 1978 to 1984, and Italian archaeologist Fabio Parenti from 1984 to 1988. The original goal of the work was to date the rock paintings on the shelter wall, which were confidently assumed to be of Holocene age (i.e. less than 10,000 years old). When radiocarbon dates of Pleistocene age, extending back more than 30,000 years, started to emerge from the stratigraphy, the site and its excavators were thrust into the forefront of the debate about human origins in the Americas (see box, p. 456). One side (primarily North American) insisted that there was no human occupation in the New World before 12,000 or at best 15,000 years ago; the other side accepted far earlier dates from a number of sites in South America and elsewhere. No site had yet met all criteria necessary to convince skeptics that humans had

been in the New World 30,000 years ago, so Parenti set out to tackle the problem.

Parenti's task was made particularly difficult because the sediments of the sandstone shelters of this region of Brazil have destroyed all organic materials (other than charcoal fragments) in pre-Holocene levels. In addition, the Pleistocene levels of Pedra Furada contain tools made only of the quartz and quartzite pebbles from a conglomerate layer above the sandstone cliff, and pebble tools are notoriously difficult to differentiate from naturally broken stones.

Parenti's primary aim, therefore, after erosional, geomorphological, and sedimentary study of the site and its surroundings, was to distinguish between human and natural agencies in terms of the site's contents in general, and of its lithic objects in particular. The stratigraphy comprised mostly sand as well as sandstone plaques that had fallen from the walls, with occasional rubble layers. It was a natural rubble "wall" in front of the shelter that had preserved the sediments within. The site has a series of 54 radiocarbon dates ranging from 5000 to 50,000 years BP.

Where the pebbles are concerned, Parenti conducted a study of 3500 stones fallen from the clifftop, and found that when they break – which is rare – the natural flaking never affects more than one side, never removes more than three flakes, and never

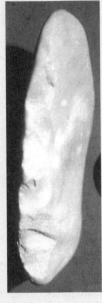

Pebble "tool" from Pedra Furada. Debate continues as to whether these quartzite "artifacts" are natural or humanly-made.

produces "retouch" or "micro-retouch." These observations became his benchmark for recognizing human artifacts at the site. Of some 6000 pieces definitely considered to be tools, 900 came from the Pleistocene layers (quartz and quartzite continued to be worked and used in the same way in the Holocene, but easily identifiable chalcedony pieces account for the high number of definite tools in that period). Thousands more pebbles are ambiguous, and could be either natural or humanly made.

Of the few specialists who have managed to visit this remote site, some remain highly skeptical of all the excavators' claims, including the criteria employed to identify the artifacts, while others are equally certain that the pebbles are definitely tools and that the site was occupied long before the Holocene.

The rockshelter at Pedra Furada (left) where "tools" (top right) were excavated and controversial evidence for occupation dating back 30,000 years has been found.

UNALTERED MATERIALS: STONE

From the first recognizable tools, dating back about 2.5 million years, up to the adoption of pottery-making, dated to 14,000 BC in Japan, the archaeological record is dominated by stone. How were stone artifacts, from the smallest microlith to the greatest megalith, extracted, transported, manufactured, and used?

Extraction: Mines and Quarries

Much of the stone for early tools was probably picked up from streambeds or other parts of the landscape; but the sources most visible archaeologically are the mines and quarries.

The best-known *mines* are the Neolithic and later flint mines in various parts of northern Europe, such as at Spiennes in Belgium, Grimes Graves in England, and Krzemionki in Poland. The basic technology remained fundamentally the same for the later extraction of other materials, such as salt in the Iron Age mines at Hallstatt, Austria, copper at mines such as Rudna Glava and Ai Bunar in former Yugoslavia, and Great Orme in Wales, and silver and gold from mines of later periods.

Excavation has revealed a mixture of open-cast and shaft mining, depending on the terrain and the position of the desirable seams (a high degree of expertise is usually clear from the ignoring of mediocre seams and a concentration on the best material). For example, at Rijckholt in the Netherlands, archaeologists dug an exploratory tunnel for 150 m (490 ft), following the layer of chalk that Neolithic people of the 4th millennium BC had found to be especially rich in flint nodules. No fewer than 66 mine-shafts were encountered, 10–16 m (33–52 ft) deep, each with radiating galleries that had been backfilled with waste chalk. If the archaeologists' tunnel hit a representative sample of shafts, then the Rijckholt area must contain 5000 of them, which could have yielded enough flint for a staggering 153 million axeheads.

There were a variety of clues to the mining techniques at Rijckholt. Impressions in the walls of an excavated shaft indicated that cave-ins were prevented by a retaining wall of plaited branches. Deep grooves in the chalk at the points where the shafts end and the galleries begin imply that ropes were used to raise nodules to the surface. As for the tools used, over 15,000 blunted or broken axeheads were found, suggesting a figure of 2.5 million for the whole mine; in other words, less than 2 percent of the output was expended in extraction. Each shaft had about 350 axeheads – some next to the hollows in the waste chalk

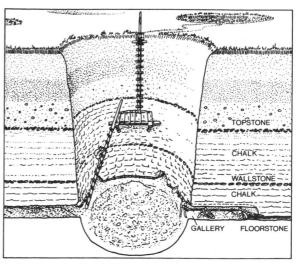

Neolithic flint mine at Grimes Graves, eastern England. Shafts some 15 m (50 ft) deep were sunk to reach the best-quality flint in the floorstone layer. Galleries, once exhausted, were back-filled with rubble from new galleries. Rough estimates suggest that the site could have produced 28 million flint axes.

left by their vanished wooden handles – and it has been estimated that five would have been worn out in removing a single cubic meter of chalk. They were sharpened on the spot, as is shown by the hard hammerstones found with them (one for every 10 or 20 axeheads) and the abundant flakes of flint.

Few antler picks were found at Rijckholt as the chalk there is particularly hard, but they are known from other such mines. Experiments have shown how remarkably effective antler can be against hard rock. Traces of burning in other mines also indicate that rock faces were sometimes initially broken up by heating with a small fire.

Finally, at copper mines in the Mitterberg area of the Austrian Alps some wooden tools have survived – a hammer and wedges, a shovel and torch, a wooden sled for hauling loads, and even a notched tree-trunk ladder. Such finds indicate the range of technological evidence missing from most sites and which we have to rediscover through analysis of clues such as those at Rijckholt.

Where *quarries* are concerned, the archaeologist is often aided in making technological reconstructions by unfinished objects or abandoned stones. The most impressive examples are the statue-quarry on the slopes of the volcano Rano Raraku, Easter Island, and

Stone quarry on Easter Island: one of the giant statues lies flat on its back, unfinished but at an advanced stage of manufacture – yielding clues as to how it was made.

the obelisk quarry at Aswan, Egypt. The Easter Island quarry contains scores of unfinished statues at various stages of manufacture, from a shape drawn on to a rock face to a completed figure attached to the rock only at the base. Discarded hammerstones by the thousand litter the area. Experiments have suggested that six carvers with such stone picks could have shaped a 5-m (16-ft) statue in about a year.

The granite obelisk at Aswan, had it been finished, would have been 42 m (138 ft) high and weighed an immense 1168 tons. The tools used in its initial shaping were heavy balls of dolerite, and experiments indicate that pounding the granite with them for one hour would reduce the level of the obelisk by 5 mm (0.2 in) over each person's work area. At that rate, the monument could have been shaped and undercut in 15 months by 400 workers, giving us some objective indication of the magnitude of Egyptian work of this kind. The pounding marks still visible in the Aswan quarries are very similar to marks on rocks at sites such as Rumiqolqa, Peru. This quarry, the most complete Inca quarry known, has 250 shaped blocks lying abandoned in an enormous pit 100 m (328 ft) long; the blocks had been pounded into shape with hardstone hammers which still bear the traces of the work.

Archaeology, combined with experiments, can thus discover a great deal about stone extraction. The next stage is to ascertain how the material was moved to the place where it was used, erected, or fitted together.

How was Stone Transported?

In certain cases, simple archaeological observation can assist inquiry. At the Inca quarry of Kachiqhata,

near the unfinished site of Ollantaytambo, the Swiss architectural historian Jean-Pierre Protzen's investigations have revealed that slides and ramps were built to enable the workers to move the red granite blocks 1000 m (1094 yd) down the mountain. But discovering the route is one thing – the technique is another. For this, wear patterns need to be studied. At Ollantaytambo itself, Protzen noted drag marks (polishing, and longitudinal striations) on some blocks; and since the marks are found only on the broadest face, it is clear that the blocks were dragged broad-face down.

It is not yet known how the dragging was accomplished, and commentaries by the 16th-century Spanish Conquistadors are of little help on this point. Perhaps the most challenging problem is how the ropes and men could have been arranged. At Ollantaytambo, for example, one block of 140 tons would have required 2400 men to move it, yet the ramp up which it was moved was only 8 m (26 ft) wide. Only experimentation will indicate the most feasible method employed.

The Egyptians faced similar and often greater problems in the transportation of huge blocks. Here, we have some information from an ancient representation showing a 7-m (23-ft) high alabaster statue of Prince Djehutihetep being moved (see illus. p. 417); it must have weighed 60 tons. The statue is tied to a wooden sledge, and 90 men are pulling on ropes. This number was probably insufficient, and must be attributed to artistic licence; but at least depictions of this type serve to counter suggestions that huge statues and blocks could only be moved with the help of visiting astronauts. Calculations by engineers and actual experiments are probably the best way in which we can hope scientifically to solve the enigma of how great stone blocks – like the 300-ton Grand Menhir Brisé in Brittany or the trilithons at Stonehenge, England – were transported and erected (see box overleaf), although debate still rages as to whether the Stonehenge bluestones were brought from Wales by its builders, or were found more locally because they had been transported there by glaciers.

One experiment, in 1955, tackled the great Olmec basalt columns or stelae at La Venta, Mexico, of the 1st millennium BC. Real-life trials proved a 2-ton column was the maximum load that could be lifted by 35 men, using rope slings, and poles on their shoulders. Since the largest La Venta stela weighs 50 tons, it must have required 500 men, at 100 kg (220 lb) per man. But 500 people could not all have got near enough to lift the stela, so it was deduced that the stone must have been dragged instead.

Moving the stones: an experiment at Bougon, western France, in 1979. Three large wooden levers – each maneuvered by a team of 20 people – were used to erect a Neolithic block weighing 32 tons. Supporting wedges held the block as it rose.

How were Stones Worked and Fitted?

Here again, archaeology and experiment combine to provide valuable insights into construction techniques. For example, Inca stonework has always been considered a marvel, and the accuracy with which blocks of irregular shape were joined together once seemed almost fantastic. Jean-Pierre Protzen's work has revealed many of the techniques involved, which, though mundane, by no means detract from the Inca accomplishment. His experiments determined the most effective way to "bounce" hammerstones on the blocks to dress them (see illus. p. 319), and found that one face could easily be shaped in 20 minutes. The bedding joint for each course of stones was cut into the upper face of the course already in place; then the new block was placed on the lower, the required edge outlined, and that shape pounded out of it with a hammerstone.

Protzen found that a fit could be obtained in 90 minutes, especially as practice gave one a keen eye for matching surfaces. His experiments are supported by 16th-century accounts which state that many fits were tried until the stones were correctly adjusted. The Inca blocks also bear traces of the process – their surfaces are covered in scars from the hammerstones, while the finer scars on the edges indicate the use of smaller hammers. In addition, many blocks still have small protrusions which were clearly used when handling them. Similar protruding knobs can also be seen on certain Greek buildings, such as the unfinished temple at Segesta, Sicily.

Until recently we had little knowledge of exactly how Greek architects achieved such precision in both the design and execution of their buildings, since no written accounts or plans have survived. But the German archaeologist Lothar Haselberger has now found "blueprints" in the form of detailed drawings on the walls of the 4th-century BC temple of Apollo at Didyma, Turkey. Thin lines up to 20 m (65 ft) long, forming circles, polygons, and angles, had been etched into the marble with a fine metal gouge. Some drawings were full size while others were scaled down; different parts of the building could be recognized, and, since the walls bearing the drawings should logically have been built before the walls depicted in the drawings, the sequence of construction could thus be determined.

RAISING LARGE STONES

For centuries, scholars have puzzled over the problem of how Stone Age people managed to raise tremendously heavy stones onto the top of high uprights: most famously at Stonehenge, where horizontal lintel stones are accurately fitted on to the top of pairs of uprights to form "trilithons," but also on Easter Island, where many of the statues had *pukao* or topknots (cylinders of red volcanic stone, weighing 8 tons or more) placed on their heads.

It has traditionally been assumed that enormous ramps of earth or imposing timber scaffolds were required – Captain Cook had already suggested these methods in relation to the Easter Island topknots in the

Reconstruction of a possible method used to lift the lintel stones of the trilithons at Stonehenge.

late 18th century. Others have suggested – for both Stonehenge and Easter Island – that the lintels/topknots were lashed to the uprights or statues and the whole unit raised together. However, this is not only very difficult but archaeologically unlikely – the Easter Island topknots were clearly a later addition to the statues. The few that have been placed on to restored statues in modern times have had to be raised by cranes.

Czech engineer Pavel Pavel has found that the feat is actually quite straightforward, requiring just a few people, ropes, and some lengths of timber. He began by working with a clay model of Stonehenge, and, when the method appeared to work, he built a full-size concrete replica of two upright stones and a lintel. Two oak beams were leaned up against the top of the uprights, and two other beams were installed as levers at the other side. The lintel – attached by ropes to the levers – was gradually raised up the sloping beams, which were lubricated with fat. The whole operation was achieved by 10 people in only 3 days.

Pavel has subsequently carried out a similar experiment with a replica Easter Island statue and *pukao*, again finding that the method worked perfectly and with little effort. As with all such experiments, one cannot prove that the Stone Age people used this technique, but the probability is high that something of the kind was employed. The work shows that modern people, so accustomed to using machinery, tend to overestimate the difficulties involved in stone monuments, and underestimate what can be achieved with a little ingenuity, a few people, and simple technology.

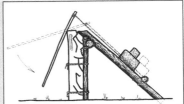

Two stages in the possible method of raising the topknot on the Easter Island statues. Modern experiments have shown that this method works perfectly.

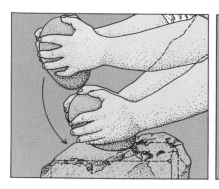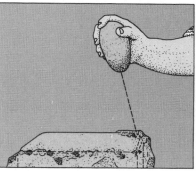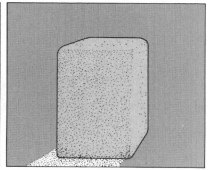

Inca stonework. (Below) The famous 12-angled stone in Cuzco, Peru, part of a wall of accurately fitted blocks built by the Incas. (Above) Diagrams illustrating Jean-Pierre Protzen's experiments to discover how Inca stonemasons may have dressed the blocks. Initially (left) Protzen pounded one face of the stone with a 4-kg (9-lb) hammer which he twisted at the last minute to deliver a glancing blow. Then (center) he used a smaller 560-g (1.2-lb) hammer to prepare the edges of the next face. Having repeated the process for each face, he finally produced a finished block (right) with slightly convex corners, similar to the corners on actual Inca stonework.

Other Greek temples have since been found to contain similar plans, but the Didyma drawings are the most detailed, and survived because the walls never received their customary final polish which would have obliterated the engravings. More recently, a full-size blueprint for part of the façade of Rome's Pantheon of AD 120 has been identified, chiseled into the pavement in front of the Mausoleum of Augustus. In Chapter 10 we consider the importance of plans in terms of the development of human intellectual skills.

So far we have examined the larger end of the lithic spectrum. But how were the smaller stone objects made? And what was their purpose?

Stone Tool Manufacture

For the most part, stone tools are made by removing material from a pebble or "core" until the desired shape of the core has been attained. The first flakes struck off (primary flakes) bear traces of the outer surface (cortex). Trimming flakes are then struck off to achieve the final shape, and certain edges may then be "retouched" by further removal of tiny secondary flakes. Although the core is the main implement thus produced, the flakes themselves may well be used as knives, scrapers etc. The toolmaker's work will have varied in accordance with the type and amount of raw material available.

The history of stone tool technology shows a sporadically increasing degree of refinement. The first recognizable tools are simple choppers and flakes made by knocking pieces off pebbles to obtain sharp edges. The best-known examples are the so-called Oldowan tools from Olduvai Gorge, Tanzania. After hundreds of thousands of years, people progressed to flaking both surfaces of the tool, eventually producing the symmetrical Acheulian hand-axe shape, with its finely worked sharp edges. The next improvement, dating to around 100,000 years ago, came with the introduction of the "Levallois technique" – named after a site in a Paris suburb where it was first identified – where the core was knapped in such a way that large flakes of predetermined size and shape could be removed.

Around 35,000 years ago, with the Upper Paleolithic period, blade technology became dominant in some parts of the world. Long, parallel-sided blades were systematically removed with a punch and hammerstone from a cylindrical core. This was a great advance, not only because it produced large numbers of blanks that could be further trimmed and retouched into a wide range of specialized tools (scrapers, burins, borers), but also because it was far less wasteful of the raw material, obtaining a much greater total length of working edges than ever before from a given amount

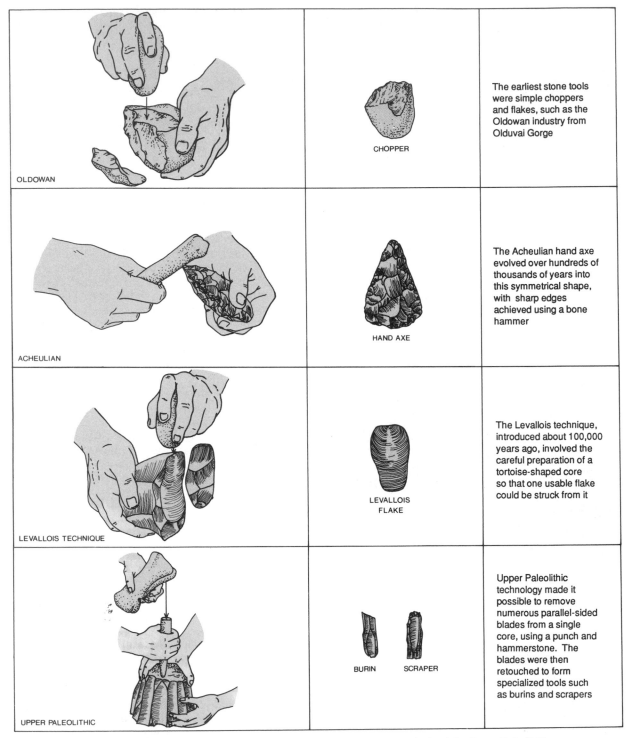

OLDOWAN	**CHOPPER**	The earliest stone tools were simple choppers and flakes, such as the Oldowan industry from Olduvai Gorge
ACHEULIAN	**HAND AXE**	The Acheulian hand axe evolved over hundreds of thousands of years into this symmetrical shape, with sharp edges achieved using a bone hammer
LEVALLOIS TECHNIQUE	**LEVALLOIS FLAKE**	The Levallois technique, introduced about 100,000 years ago, involved the careful preparation of a tortoise-shaped core so that one usable flake could be struck from it
UPPER PALEOLITHIC	**BURIN** **SCRAPER**	Upper Paleolithic technology made it possible to remove numerous parallel-sided blades from a single core, using a punch and hammerstone. The blades were then retouched to form specialized tools such as burins and scrapers

The evolution of stone tools, from the earliest, Oldowan technology to the refined methods of the Upper Paleolithic.

of stone. The stone itself was normally a homogeneous easily worked type such as chert or obsidian. Loren Eiseley has worked out a helpful summary of this increasing efficiency, estimated assuming the use of 500 g (1 lb 1 oz) of high-quality chert:

Technology	Length of Cutting Edge Produced
OLDOWAN	5 cm
ACHEULIAN	20 cm
MOUSTERIAN	
(Middle Paleolithic)	100 cm
GRAVETTIAN	
(Upper Paleolithic)	300–1200 cm

This trend toward greater economy reached its peak in the Mesolithic (Middle Stone Age), around 10,000 years ago, with the rise to dominance of microliths, tiny stone tools many of which were probably used as barbs on composite implements.

The archaeologist has to reconstruct the sequence of manufacturing steps – the *chaîne opératoire* (see p. 388) – a task made easier if the knapping was done in one place and all the waste material (debitage) is still present. The discovery of a network of manufacturing sites also aids analysis. In Japan, the Taku site cluster of over 40 sites in Saga Prefecture, dating to between 15,000 and 10,000 years ago, is located at a stone source and yielded over 100,000 tools, with each site specializing in a different stage of manufacture, from raw material procurement to production of finished artifacts. More commonly, however, the archaeologist will find an industrial site with a full range of waste material and broken tools, but few finished tools since these were mostly removed. Finished tools often turn up in sites far from the stone source. The types of tools found at a site can also provide clues to its function: a hunting kit with projectile points might be expected in a temporary camp, while a wide range of tools would be present in a base camp or a permanent settlement.

Some techniques of manufacture can be inferred from traces left on the tools – e.g. traces of what seems to be a mastic made of heated bitumen found on several stone tools from Umm el-Tlel in Syria suggest that hafting dates back at least to the Middle Paleolithic. Many techniques can still be observed among the few living peoples, such as some Australian Aborigines or highland Maya, who continue to make stone tools. Much ethnoarchaeological work has been done in Australia and Mesoamerica in recent years, most notably by Richard Gould and Brian Hayden. Others have investigated how New Guinea highlanders manufacture stone axes. Artistic depictions can also be of some help, as in the paintings in the tomb of the 12th-

One of the acknowledged masters of stone tool replication: the French Paleolithic specialist, François Bordes. He is seen here in 1975, knapping a piece of stone in order to assess the processes involved and the time and effort expended.

dynasty Egyptian pharaoh Ameny at Beni Hassan, which show the mass production of flint knives under the supervision of foremen.

In most other cases, there are two principal approaches to assessing what decisions the knapper made: replication and refitting.

Stone Tool Replication. This is a type of experimental archaeology that involves making exact copies of different types of stone tool – using only the technology available to the original makers – in order to assess the processes entailed, and the amount of time and effort required. In the past only a handful of experimenters, notably François Bordes in the Old World and Donald Crabtree in the New, reached a high level of expertise, since many years of patient practice are required. Today, however, quite a few archaeologists have become proficient at tool replication, much to the benefit of our knowledge of ancient stone-knapping.

American archaeologist Nicholas Toth, for example, has made and used the entire range of early stone tools, as found at sites such as Koobi Fora, Kenya, and dating to about 1.5 to 2 million years ago – hammerstones, choppers, scrapers, and flakes. His work provides

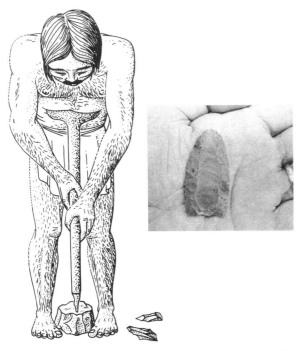

How were Paleo-Indian Folsom points made? Experiments by Donald Crabtree showed that the flakes were pressed from the core using a T-shaped crutch (left). Flintknappers have produced almost perfect replica points (right).

evidence to suggest that simple flakes may have been the primary tools, while the more impressive cores were simply an incidental by-product of flake manufacture. Previously, scholars tended to see the flakes as waste products, and the cores as the intentional end-product.

One specific problem that Donald Crabtree was able to solve through trial and error was how the Paleo-Indians of North America had made their fluted stone tools known as Folsom points, dating to some 11,000–10,000 years ago. In particular, how had they removed the "flute" or channel flake? This had remained a mystery and experiments with a variety of techniques met with disappointing results, until the decisive clue was found in a 17th-century text by a Spanish priest who had seen Aztec Indians make long knife-blades from obsidian. The method, as experiments proved, involves pressing the flake out, downward, by means of a T-shaped crutch placed against the chest; the crutch's tip is forced down against a precise point on the core which is clamped firm.

Another Paleo-Indian specialist, American archaeologist George Frison, wanted to know how the slightly earlier Clovis projectile points were used. He tested replicas, 5–10 cm (2–4 in) long and hafted onto 2-m (6.5-ft) wooden shafts with pitch and sinew, to show that, when thrown from 20 m (65 ft), they penetrated deeply into the back and ribcage of (already mortally wounded) elephants in Africa. Frison discovered that the points could be used up to a dozen times with little or no damage, unless they hit a rib.

Archaeologists can also use replication and experiment to discover whether certain flint tools had been deliberately heated during manufacture, and if so, why. For example, in Florida many projectile points and much chipping debris have a pinkish color and a lustrous surface which suggests thermal alteration. Work by Barbara Purdy and H.K. Brooks has shown that when Florida cherts are slowly heated a color change occurs at 240°C (464°F), while after heating to 350–400°C (662–752°F) flaking leaves a lustrous appearance. Purdy and Brooks investigated the differences between unheated and heated chert. Petrographic thin-sections failed to detect any differences in structure, but in the scanning electron microscope it became clear that heated chert had a far smoother appearance. Furthermore, a study of rock mechanics showed that after heating the chert had an increase in compressive strength of 25–40 percent, but a decrease of 45 percent in the force needed to break it.

Confirmation – and more objective data than a flint's appearance – can be obtained from an entirely different method, electron spin resonance (ESR) spectroscopy, which can identify defects or substitutions within the structure of crystals – in this case within the silica. Heated material has a characteristic ESR signal which is absent from unheated flint, and which remains stable indefinitely. Tests with this method have proved that heat treatment was already present in the French Upper Paleolithic Solutrean culture, about 19,000 years ago. The heating was clearly performed after initial shaping but before final trimming. Experiments by Crabtree on chert indicate that one can obtain larger flakes by pressure flaking after heating. Thermoluminescence (Chapter 4) can also be used to detect heat alteration – and, in some cases, even estimate the temperature – as the amount of TL in a sample relates to the time since firing. A tool not subjected to heat normally yields a high TL reading, while a heated specimen has a far lower reading due to the previous release of trapped electrons.

Replication cannot usually prove conclusively which techniques were used in the past, but it does narrow the possibilities and often points to the most likely method, as in the Folsom example above. *Refitting*, on the other hand, involves working with the original tools and demonstrates clearly the precise chain of actions of the knapper.

Refitting of Stone Tools. This type of work, which can be traced back to F.C.J. Spurrell at the Paleolithic site of Crayford, England, in 1880, has really come into its own in the last couple of decades thanks largely to the efforts of André Leroi-Gourhan at the Magdalenian (late Upper Paleolithic) camp of Pincevent, near Paris, and that of his pupils at similar sites. Refitting, or conjoining as it is sometimes called, entails attempting to put tools and flakes back together again, like a 3-D jigsaw puzzle. The work is tedious and time-consuming, but can produce spectacular results. One refitted stone designated N103 from the Magdalenian site of Etiolles includes 124 pieces, some of which are blades over 30 cm (12 in) long.

Why exactly do archaeologists devote so many hours of hard work to refitting exercises? Very broadly because refitting allows us to follow the stages of the knapper's craft and – where pieces from one core have been found in different areas – even the knapper's (or the core's) movements around the site. Of course, displacement of flakes may have nothing to do with the changing location of the craftsperson: a burin spall, for example, can jump 7 m (23 ft) when struck off. And it should not be assumed automatically that each core was processed in one episode of work: we know from ethnography that a core can be reused after a short or long period of absence.

It is also now known from conjoined pieces that considerable vertical movement can occur through different layers of a site, even where there are no visible traces of disturbance. However, if these factors are allowed for, refitting provides a dynamic perspective on the spatial distribution of tools, and produces a vivid picture of actual movement and activity in an ancient site. Where these observations can be supplemented by information on the functions of the tools, the site really comes to life (see box overleaf, on the site of Meer).

But how can we discover the function of a stone tool? Ethnographic observation often gives valuable clues, as we have already seen, as do residues (p. 302); and experimentation can determine which uses are feasible or most probable. However, a single tool can be used for many different purposes – an Acheulian hand-axe could be used for hacking wood from a tree, for butchering, smashing, scraping, and cutting – and conversely the same task can be done by many different tools. The only direct *proof* of function is to study the minute traces, or microwear patterns, that remain on the original tools.

Stone flakes from the Upper Paleolithic site of Marsangy, France, refitted to show the original core from which they were struck. Such work allows the archaeologist to build up a picture of the different stages of the knapper's craft.

Identifying the Function of Stone Tools: Microwear Studies

Like refitting, microwear studies can be traced back into the 19th century; but the real breakthrough came with the pioneering work, first published in 1957, by Sergei Semenov of the Soviet Union, who had experimented for decades with the microwear on ancient tools. Employing a binocular microscope, he found that even tools of the hardest stone retained traces of their use: primarily a variety of polishes and striations. Subsequent work by Ruth Tringham and others showed that Semenov's striations were not as universal as he had claimed, and attention was focused on microflaking (minute edge-chipping caused by use). Then the work entered a new phase with the introduction of the scanning electron microscope, which enabled Lawrence Keeley, now of the University of Chicago, and others to be far more precise about types of microwear and to record them on photomicrographs.

Describing the wear was all very well, but the different types needed to be identified with specific activities; experimental archaeology proved to be the answer. Different sorts of stone tools were copied, and each was used for a specific task. Study of the traces left by each task on different types of stone allowed Keeley to establish a reference collection with which wear on ancient tools could be compared. He found that different kinds of polish are readily distinguishable, and are very durable, since they constitute a real alteration in the tools' microtopography. Six broad categories of tool use were established: on wood, bone, hide, meat, antler, and non-woody plants. Other traces show the movement of the tool – e.g. in piercing, cutting, or scraping.

The effectiveness of this method was verified in a blind test, in which Keeley was supplied with 15 replicas that had been used for a series of secret tasks. He was able to identify correctly the working portions of the tool, reconstruct the way in which it was used, and even the type of material worked in almost every case. Turning to Lower Paleolithic artifacts from southern England, Keeley found that tools from Clacton (about 250,000 years old) had been used on meat, wood, hide, and bone, while some from Hoxne had also been used on non-woody plants. Sidescrapers seemed to have been used primarily for hide-working.

In a similar study, Johan Binneman and Janette Deacon tested the assumption that the stone adzes from Boomplaas Cave, South Africa, had been used primarily for woodworking (see Chapter 6 for the importance of charcoal at this site). Replicas of the later Stone Age tools were made and then used to chisel and plane wood. When the resulting use-wear was compared with that on 51 tools from the site, dating back to 14,200 years ago, it was found that all the prehistoric specimens had the same polish, thus confirming the early importance of woodworking here.

The Japanese scholar Satomi Okazaki has focused on striations, since she feels that study of their density and direction is more objective than an assessment of degree of polish. In experiments she found that using obsidian produces striations, but no polish: striations parallel to the tool-edge are the results of a cutting motion, while perpendicular striations result from a scraping motion.

Establishing the function of a set of tools can produce unexpected results which transform our picture of activity at a site. For example, the Magdalenian site of Verberie, near Paris (12th millennium BC), yielded only one bone tool; yet studies of microwear on the site's flint tools show the great importance of bone-working: an entire area of the site seems to have been devoted to the working of bone and antler. Some traces adhering to stone tools, such as blood or phytoliths, also provide clues about function (Chapter 7).

As mentioned above, when microwear studies are combined with refitting, they help to produce a vivid picture of prehistoric life. At another French Magdalenian site, Pincevent, the tools and manufacturing waste generally cluster around the hearths; one particular stone core was found to have had a dozen blades removed from it beside one hearth, and eight of the blades had been retouched. The same core was later moved to a different hearth and work recommenced; some of the flakes struck off here were made into tools such as burins (graving implements), all of which were used to work reindeer antler.

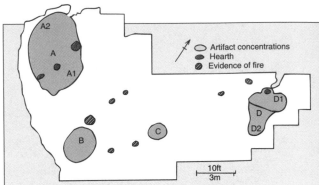

Excavation of the Meer site revealed four concentrations of artifacts – A, B, C, and D; the largest were A and D. Within area A were two "satellite" areas (A₁ and A₂) and 3 hearths. Area D also had two "satellites," but only one hearth.

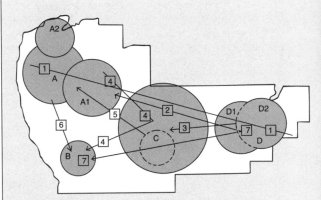

Refitting studies have demonstrated links among the four Meer II concentration areas as shown in the diagram above. Each of these seven links traces one or more artifacts from one area to another.

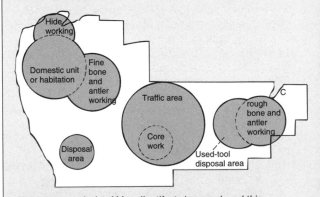

Microwear analysis of Meer II artifacts has produced this plan, showing the breakdown and separation of activities at the site.

REFITTING AND MICROWEAR STUDIES AT THE MEER SITE

The Epipaleolithic (Mesolithic) site of Meer II, Belgium, dates from about 8900 years ago, and was excavated by the Belgian archaeologist Francis Van Noten in 1967–69 and 1975–76. Apart from a few fragments of eroded bone and scraps of charcoal and ocher, the site comprises a scatter of stone tools in a sand dune. There were hammerstones of quartzite and schist, and grinders of sandstone, but 98 percent of the 16,000 stone artifacts were of flint.

Van Noten plotted the horizontal distribution of the tools, which showed marked variation. Some meter squares had over 500 artifacts, others few or none, and there were four particular concentrations (labeled A to D on the site plan). Vertically, the tools were found scattered through a considerable depth of 45 cm (1ft 6 in). Did this mean that the site had been occupied several times, or had the abandoned tools from a single occupation been displaced vertically by natural processes, such as burrowing animals and plant roots?

In order to answer this question, a refitting project was carried out by Daniel Cahen, who succeeded in reconstituting many of the small flint nodules. He found that 18 percent of the artifacts were interrelated, and that there were definite links among the four areas of concentration. The work suggests strongly that occupation was shortlived and that the vertical displacement of tools is indeed due to natural post-depositional factors.

When his results were combined with analysis of microwear traces by Lawrence Keeley, a remarkably detailed picture emerged of some activities at what had, at first, appeared an unpromising site.

For example, out of one group of 15 tools refitted from concentration D, 12 showed microwear. The microwear

indicated that one tool had been used to cut meat, while the others had all been used on bone – 8 as borers, 4 as groovers, and 2 as cutters. From this and other similar evidence, it was deduced that concentration D had been an area where flint tools were prepared for rough work on bone and antler. Furthermore, three of the boring tools in concentration D had done their work by being twisted counter-clockwise, unlike the other borers which had been turned

clockwise. It is therefore very likely that more than two people worked at concentration D, one of whom was left-handed.

At various stages right-handed knappers carried blanks and finished tools from concentration D to concentration A, where they were used for fine work on bone. Other small areas seem to have been used for hide-working and as a refuse dump.

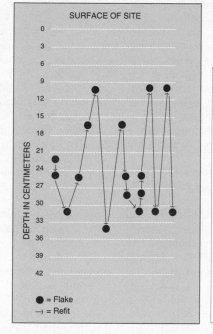

Graph showing how a group of 17 flakes, from varying depths at the site, could be refitted – the arrows indicating refits among flakes struck successively from the same core. This demonstrates that the artifacts, although as much as 24 cm apart in depth, were from the same occupation period at the site. Disturbance of the soil by roots and other natural forces had displaced the flakes vertically through the deposit.

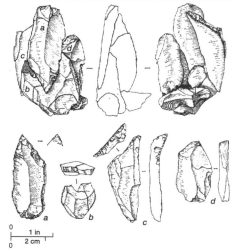

Microwear and refitting studies combined. (Top row) Three views of a refitted block. (Bottom row) Microwear indicated a variety of uses for the flakes: a, borer for use on bone; b, tool for incising grooves in bone; c, another borer for bone; d, tool for graving a u-shaped groove. Borers a and c had been turned counter-clockwise, indicating their use by a left-handed person.

A different category of manufacturing waste has recently been investigated, particularly by Knut Fladmark and other scholars in Canada: that of microdebitage, the "sawdust" of ancient knappers, comprising tiny flakes of rock, less than a millimeter in size, formed during the process of making stone tools. They are recovered by wet sieving or flotation (Chapter 6), and then examined under the microscope to differentiate them from naturally formed dirt particles. Unlike larger waste products, microdebitage was never cleared away, and therefore serves to pinpoint the location of stoneworking at a site.

Identifying Function: Further Experiments with Stone Artifacts

Experimentation can be used in many other ways to help identify stone tool function. Replicas of almost every ancient stone artifact imaginable have been made and tested – from axes and sickles to grinders and arrowheads. For example, the hand axes of the Lower Paleolithic have long been an enigma, being regarded as all-purpose tools but with much speculation and little controlled experimentation to clarify the issue. Recently, a remarkable test was carried out in England, in which nine replica hand axes, made of flint from the quarries around the important Lower Paleolithic site of Boxgrove, were used by a professional butcher on a roe deer carcass. The experiment showed clearly that the hand axe, used by someone with the relevant skills and knowledge, is an outstanding and versatile butchery tool.

In a study of the many varied objects in France claimed to be Upper Paleolithic stone lamps, Sophie de Beaune used experiment, ethnographic observation of Eskimo lamps, and chemical analysis of the residues found in some of the alleged lamps. She found that only 302 objects were potential lamps, and of these only 85 were definite and 31 others probable. The combustion residues analyzed by spectrometry and chromatography (Chapters 6 and 7) proved to be fatty acids of animal origin, while remains of resinous wood clearly came from the wicks.

Sophie de Beaune tried out replica lamps of various types, with different fuels such as cattle lard and horse grease, and a variety of wicks. The tests left traces of use which corresponded with those in the ancient lamps; and the results were confirmed by study of the Eskimo lighting systems. Tests were also undertaken to determine the amount of light given out by the ancient lamps. They were found to be pretty dim, even in comparison with a modern candle. The power of the light depends on the quality and quantity of fuel; the flame is usually unstable and trembling. Experiments with a stone lamp using horse fat produced a flame of one-sixth the power of a candle, according to measurements with a photometer. But it was found that with only one lamp one can move around a cave, read, and even sew if one is close enough to the light – the eye cannot tell that the flame is weaker than a candle.

Other experiments with stone artifacts attempt to assess the time needed for different tasks. Emil Haury studied the minute beads from prehistoric pueblos in Arizona. One necklace, 10 m (33 ft) in length, had about 15,000 beads, which were an average of only 2 mm (0.08 in) in diameter. Replication, with the perforation done with a cactus spine, led to an estimate of 15 minutes per bead, or 480 working days for the whole necklace. Such exercises help to assess the inherent value of an object through the amount of work involved in its creation.

Assessing the Technology of Stone Age Art

In the field of prehistoric art, a number of analyses can be carried out to determine the pigments and binding medium used, and ancient methods of painting and engraving on stone. In the Upper Paleolithic cave art of southern France and northern Spain, for example, the most usual minerals found have proved to be manganese dioxide (black) and iron oxide (red), though recent analyses in a number of decorated caves have detected the use of charcoal as pigment, which has enabled direct dating to be carried out (p. 144). In the Pyrenees, notably in the cave of Niaux, paint analyses by scanning electron microscopy, X-ray diffraction, and proton-induced X-ray emission (Chapter 9) have suggested the use of specific "recipes" of pigments mixed with mineral "extenders" such as talc which made the paint go further, improved its adhesion to the wall, and stopped it cracking. Analyses have also detected traces of binders in the form of animal and plant oils; in Texas, DNA has been extracted from rock paintings 3000–4000 years old, and seems to come from a mammal, probably an ungulate, presumably in the form of an organic binder.

In a few caves the height and inaccessibility of the art show that a ladder or scaffolding must have been used, and the sockets for a platform of beams still survive in the walls of a gallery in the French cave of Lascaux.

Analysis of pigments from prehistoric paintings in Monitor Basin, Nevada, by X-ray diffraction showed that gypsum had been the binding agent, and that reds and yellows had been made by adding various minerals. All the samples were different, suggesting that the paintings accumulated at different times.

Analysis of Stone Age art by experiment: Michel Lorblanchet draws from memory a copy of a frieze in the cave of Pech Merle, France. The exercise suggested that the entire frieze could have been sketched in only one hour.

It is not always apparent exactly how paint was applied in prehistoric times – whether by brush, pad, finger, or by blowing – but ethnographic observation together with experiments can be of great help in narrowing down the possibilities.

Moreover, infrared film now makes it possible for us to distinguish between ocher pigments. Infrared film sees through red ocher as though it were glass, so that other pigments beneath become visible. In addition, impurities in ocher can be detected since they are not transparent, so that different mixes of paint can be identified. Alexander Marshack used this technique to study the famous "spotted horse" frieze in the cave of Pech Merle, France, and to reconstruct the sequence in which the elements of the panel were painted. He found, for example, that the sets of red dots had been made by different types of ochers, and therefore possibly at different times.

A frieze of black paintings in the same cave led Michel Lorblanchet to an analysis by experiment, in an attempt to discover how long it might have taken to create the frieze. Having studied and memorized every stroke of the composition, he sought out a blank wall area of similar dimensions in a different cave, and drew an exact copy of the frieze on it. This exercise indicated that the entire composition could have been made in only one hour, a fact which underlines the view that much rock art was probably done in intensive bursts by talented artists. More recently, he has also replicated the spotted horse frieze by spitting ocher and charcoal from his mouth; this experiment suggests that the whole frieze could be done in 32 hours, though it was clearly built up in at least four episodes.

The binocular microscope can be used to great effect in the study of engravings on stone, since it can determine the type of tool and stroke used, the differences in width and in transverse section of the lines, and sometimes the order in which the lines were made. Léon Pales, in his study of the Upper Paleolithic engraved plaquettes from the French cave of La Marche, also discovered that if one takes a plasticine or silicone relief-imprint of the engraved surface, the impression shows clearly which lines were engraved after which. The technique proved, for instance, that a supposed "harness" was a secondary feature added to a completed horse's head.

Varnish replicas (see below) of engraved surfaces on stone can also be made, examined in the scanning electron microscope, and compared with surface features produced on experimental engravings. By this method one can study the micromorphology of the engraved lines, see exactly how they were created, in what order, and whether by one tool or several. More recently, new computer advances such as image analysis and 3-D optical surface profiling have been applied to this material since the laser scanner removes the need to have any contact with the often delicate objects or to take replicas of them.

Many other methods of analysis used on stone artifacts have also been applied to other unaltered materials such as bone.

OTHER UNALTERED MATERIALS

Bone, Antler, Shell, and Leather

Since there is usually no difficulty in determining how these raw materials were obtained (except for instance when seashells or a sea mammal's bones are found far inland), the archaeologist's attention focuses on the method of manufacture and function. First, however, one has to be sure that they are humanly made tools.

As with stone tools, it is not always easy to differentiate purposely made artifacts of organic material from accidents of nature. Debate continues about the existence of shaped bone tools before the Upper Paleolithic. Common sense suggests that unshaped bones have been used as tools for as long as stones. After all, even in recent times, as in kill sites in North America (see bison drive box, pp. 292–93), entire bones seem to have been used, unworked, as simple expediency tools during the dismemberment of carcasses.

Similarly, fragile objects such as shells may have perforations that are not necessarily artificial. The American scholar Peter Francis carried out experiments with shells in order to find criteria of human workmanship. Using shells beachcombed in western India, he perforated them in a variety of ways with stone tools: by scratching, sawing, grinding, gouging, and hammering. The resulting holes were examined under the microscope, and it was found that the first three techniques left recognizable traces, whereas gouging and hammering left irregular holes which were difficult to distinguish as artificial – in these cases, one would have to rely on the context of the find, and the position of the perforation (which depends on the shape of the shell), to help one decide whether people were responsible. Italian researcher Francesco d'Errico has established microscopic criteria, by means of experimentation, for differentiating perforations in shell made by natural agents and by humans; and also for recognizing the traces left on bone, antler, and ivory objects by long-term handling, transportation, and suspension.

Deducing Techniques of Manufacture. On rare occasions the method of manufacture is clear archaeologically. For example, at the South African site of Kasteelberg, dating to about AD 950, a fabrication area has been discovered where every step in the process of making bone tools can be seen, revealing the complexity, the sequence, and the tools involved. The occupants of this stock-herding site worked in a sheltered spot, using primarily the metapodials (foot bones) of eland and hartebeest. The ends of the bones were removed using a hammerstone and a punch. Next, a groove was pounded along the bone's shaft, and then it was abraded and polished until the shaft was severed. The resulting splinters were shaped with stones (many broken specimens were found discarded), and finally ground and polished into points which are very similar to ethnographic examples known from the San (Bushmen) of the Kalahari Desert.

Microwear studies using the scanning electron microscope combined with experimental archaeology are another successful means of determining methods of bone tool manufacture. Pierre-François Puech and his colleagues have overcome the problem that one cannot place the original tools in the SEM by making varnish replicas of the worked surfaces. A nitrocellulose compound is poured onto the bone, and later peeled off and turned into slide-mounts. They found that experimental marking of bone with various stone tools left characteristic traces which corresponded to marks on prehistoric bone artifacts. Each type of manufacture produced a different pattern of striations. Different methods of polishing bone also left recognizable traces. It is thus becoming possible to reconstruct the history of manufacture of ancient bone artifacts.

Deducing Function. Experimental archaeology and study of wear patterns, either individually or in conjunction with each other, are highly effective in helping us deduce the function as well as the manufacturing techniques of organic artifacts.

One controversial and much-discussed issue is the original function of the perforated antler batons of the European Upper Paleolithic. The orthodox view, based on ethnographic analogy, is that they were arrowshaft-straighteners; but there are at least 40 other hypotheses, ranging from tent pegs to harness pieces. In order to obtain some objective evidence, the French archaeologist André Glory examined the wear patterns in and around the baton perforations. His conclusion was that the wear had definitely been made by the rubbing of a thong or rope of some sort. This result certainly narrows down the list of possible functions. Glory himself used it to bolster his own hypothesis that the batons had been used as handles for slings.

On the other hand, analysis by the American archaeologist Douglas Campana of use-wear in the perforation of a deer shoulder-blade from Mughar et El Wad, Israel, dating to around the 9th millennium BC, suggests that here at any rate a similar if somewhat later perforated object had been employed in straight-

Antler baton from the Upper Paleolithic site of La Madeleine, France. Ethnography suggests that these objects were arrowshaft straighteners, but there are many other theories.

ening wooden shafts. Experimental work supports this conclusion.

Experiments can likewise be used to help resolve all manner of questions about function and efficiency. Copies have been made, for example, of Upper Paleolithic barbed bone or antler points, and they have been hurled against animal carcasses and other objects. In this way M.W. Thompson was able to demonstrate that the small barbed points, with a central perforation, of the so-called Azilian culture at the end of the Ice Age in southwest Europe were probably toggle harpoons which swiveled and became firmly embedded in their prey. Similarly, replicas have been made of antler projectile points from the Lower Magdalenian period of northern Spain, and were found through experimental use on a dead goat to be highly penetrative and extremely durable, indeed far more so than stone points.

In a replication experiment famous in British archaeological circles, John Coles investigated the efficiency of a leather shield from the Bronze Age of Ireland. It was the only one of its kind to have survived, all others of the period being of bronze. It was found that the shield could be hardened by means of hot water and beeswax, although it retained a degree of flexibility. Coles, armed with the leather replica, and a colleague using a copy of a metal shield, then attacked each other with slashing swords and spears of Bronze Age type. The metal shield was cut to ribbons, indicating that those specimens we have were not functional but for prestige or ritual. The leather shield, on the other hand, was barely perforated by the spear, and received only slight cuts on its outer surface from the sword. Its flexibility had absorbed and deflected the blows. This experiment reveals once again the importance to ancient people of the organic materials that so rarely come down to us intact.

Wood

Wood is one of the most important organic materials, and must have been used to make tools for as long as stone and bone. Indeed, as we have seen, many prehistoric stone tools were employed to obtain and work timber. If wood survives in good condition, it may preserve toolmarks to show how it was worked. As with other materials, one has to distinguish genuine toolmarks from those made by other means. John and Bryony Coles have shown how important it is to differentiate toolmarks from the parallel facets left by beaver teeth. A combination of experiment and direct observation of beaver habits has helped them detect the distinction. As a result, a piece of wood from the Mesolithic site of Star Carr in northern England, thought to have been shaped by stone blades, is now known to have been cut by beaver teeth.

A wide range of wooden tools can survive under special conditions, as we saw in Chapter 2. In the dry environment of ancient Egypt, for instance, numerous wooden implements for farming (rakes, hoes, grain-scoops, sickles), furniture, weapons and toys, and carpentry tools such as mallets and chisels have come down to us. Egyptian paintings such as those in the tomb of the nobleman Rekhmire at Thebes sometimes depict carpenters using drills and saws. But it has been waterlogged wood that has yielded the richest information about woodworking skills (see box overleaf).

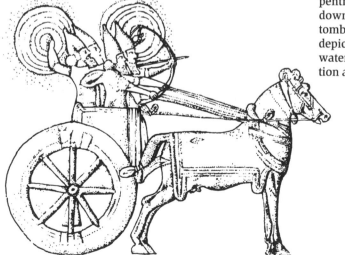

Evidence for the wheel. (Left) In the Old World, the spoked-wheel chariot (Assyrian relief, 7th century BC) evolved from the original solid-wheel cart. (Right) In the pre-Columbian New World, the concept of the wheel was known (wheeled model from Veracruz), but full-size wheeled vehicles only arrived with the Spanish, together with the animals needed to pull them.

WOODWORKING IN THE SOMERSET LEVELS

The wetlands in southwest England known as the Somerset Levels preserve a wide range of organic remains, including ancient wooden trackways. John and Bryony Coles, in their long-term Somerset Levels project, have been able to make a remarkably detailed analysis of the woodworking techniques used in track construction.

The chopped ends of pegs and stakes from the tracks often display facets or cutmarks left by the axes used to shape them. Experiments have shown that stone axes bruise the wood and leave dished facets, whereas bronze axes do not cause bruising, but leave characteristic stepped facets in the cuts. Imperfections in the axes – for example nicks in their edges – can also be identified. Such faults have left their signature with each blow of the axe, allowing archaeologists to pinpoint the use of particular axes on particular pieces of wood.

By this method, John and Bryony Coles have been able to prove that at least 10 different axes were used in the construction of one Bronze Age track in the Somerset Levels. Indeed, they have deduced the exact manner of working from these clues. One piece of wood has three facets – the top one's set of ridges is the reverse of the other two. It is therefore clear that the wood was first held vertically, and the axe came down "backhand"; it was then turned more obliquely to the ground, and the axe came down with a forehand stroke.

The large collections of preserved timber from waterlogged areas such as the Somerset Levels, and Flag Fen in eastern England, are enabling archaeologists for the first time to gain insights into prehistoric techniques for

Experimental felling (below) of an ash tree by John Coles (right) and a colleague, using Neolithic and Bronze Age axes.

splitting, cutting, joining, and piercing wood. It has become apparent that woodcraft changed little through time, even after the arrival of metal tools. For instance, it seems that wood was always split by the wedge-and-mallet method, just as in medieval times.

The Somerset Levels project has also demonstrated that woodlands were being carefully managed at least 5000 years ago. The thin wooden rods used for woven track panels laid flat on the marsh can only have come from the systematic cutting back or coppicing of tree stumps to produce regular crops of young rods.

Chopped ends *of pieces of wood reveal the dished facets produced by a Neolithic stone axe (left), and the angular, stepped facets from a bronze axe (right).*

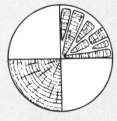

Analysis *of the so-called Sweet Track, nearly 6000 years old, showed that Neolithic woodworkers had split large oaks radially into planks (right), but younger trees – too small to be cut radially – had been split tangentially (left).*

Bronze Age trackway, more than 3500 years old, called the Eclipse Track. The excavated length consisted of over 1000 hurdles, short track sections whose interwoven rods could only have been produced from a managed woodland, where tree stumps were deliberately cut back to encourage young, straight shoots.

Larger wooden objects are not uncommon, such as the Bronze Age tree-trunk coffins of northern Europe, mortuary houses, bridges, waterfront timbers, remains of actual dwellings, and especially a wide range of wheeled vehicles: carts, wagons, carriages, and chariots. Until the Industrial Revolution and the arrival of railways and motor vehicles, all wheeled transport was made of wood, with metal fittings in later periods. A surprising number of vehicles (e.g. entire ox-wagons in the Caucasus) or of recognizable parts (especially wheels) have survived, as well as evidence in models, art, and literature. In the pre-Columbian New World, wheeled models are the only evidence: wheeled vehicles as such were not introduced until the Spanish Conquest, along with the beasts of burden needed to pull them. In the Old World, most finds are vehicles buried in graves. Wheeled vehicles first appeared in the 4th millennium BC in the area between the Rhine and the Tigris; the earliest wheels were solid discs, either single-piece (cut from planks, not transverse slices of tree-trunks) or composite. Spoked wheels were developed in the 2nd millennium for lighter, faster vehicles such as chariots, for instance ones found in Tutankhamun's tomb (see box, pp. 62–63). Wheeled transportation clearly had a huge impact on social and economic development, but nevertheless had a very limited geographical spread when compared with the ubiquitous wooden technology displayed in watercraft.

Investigating Watercraft. Until the 19th century all boats and ships were made predominantly of wood, and in perhaps no other area of pre-industrial technology did the world's craftspeople achieve such mastery as in the building of wooden vessels of all kinds, from small riverboats to great oceangoing sailing ships. The study of the history of this technology is a specialized undertaking, far beyond the scope of the present book to summarize in any detail. But it would be wrong to imagine that the archaeologist has little to contribute to what is already known from historical records. For the prehistoric period such records are of course absent, and even in historic times there are great gaps in knowledge that archaeology is now helping to fill.

The richest source of archaeological evidence is the preserved remains of ships uncovered by underwater archaeology (box, p. 95). In the late 1960s, the excavation of a 4th-century BC Greek ship off Kyrenia, Cyprus, showed that vessels of that period were built with planks held together by mortise-and-tenon joints. The recent excavation by George Bass and his colleagues of a wreck at Uluburun, near Kaş, off the south coast of Turkey (box, pp. 374–75), has now revealed a vessel 1000 years older that uses the same technique.

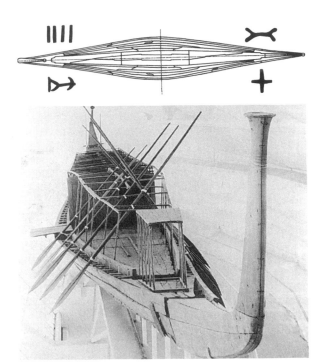

Reconstructing the oldest ship in the world. In 1954 the dismantled parts of a cedarwood boat were found buried in a pit on the south side of the Great Pyramid of King Cheops at Giza, Egypt. (Top left) One important clue to the reconstruction proved to be the four classifying signs, marked on most of the timbers, that indicated to which of the four quarters of the ship the timbers belonged. (Right) Hag Ahmed Youssef used a scale model to help in the task of reconstruction. (Left) After 14 years of work, the 1244 pieces of the ship were finally reassembled.

At the beginning of this chapter we stressed how important it is for archaeologists to obtain the advice of craftspeople in the technology concerned. This is particularly true for the accurate understanding of ship-building. J. Richard Steffy, of the Institute of Nautical Archaeology in Texas, has an unrivaled practical knowledge of the way ships are (or were) put together, a knowledge he has applied to excavated vessels in the Old World and the New. In his judgment the best way to learn how a ship was built and functioned is to refit the excavated timbers in the most likely original shape of the vessel, achieved through analysis of the excavation and painstaking trial and error, with the aid of exact copies at one-tenth scale of the remaining timbers (box, pp. 96–97). This was the procedure adopted by another craftsman, the Egyptian Hag Ahmed Youssef, in his 14-year rebuilding of the dismantled ship of the pharaoh Cheops found at Giza, at 4500 years the oldest known ship in the world.

The next step in any assessment of a ship's construction techniques and handling capabilities is to build either a full-size or a scale replica, preferably one that can be tested on the water. Replicas based on excavated remains, such as the replica Viking *knarr* or cargo ship that sailed around the world in 1984–86, are more likely to produce scientifically accurate results than those built only from generalized artistic depictions, as in the case of replicas of the ships of Columbus. But the building of replicas based on depictions can still be immensely valuable. Until some British scholar-enthusiasts, led by J.F. Coates and J.S. Morrison, actually constructed and tested a replica of an ancient Greek trireme, or warship, in 1987, virtually nothing was known about the practical characteristics of this important seacraft of Classical antiquity.

Another contribution archaeology can make to sea-faring studies is to demonstrate the presence of boats even where no ship remains or artistic depictions exist. The simple fact that people crossed into Australia at least 50,000 years ago – when that continent was cut off from the mainland, even if not by so great a distance as it is today – suggests that they had craft capable of covering 80 km (50 miles) or more. Similarly, the presence of obsidian from the Aegean islands on the Greek mainland 10,000 years ago shows that people at that time had no difficulty in sailing to and from the islands.

Plant and Animal Fibers

The making of containers, fabrics, and cords from skins, bark, and woven fibers probably dates back to the very earliest archaeological periods, but these fragile materials rarely survive. However, as we saw in Chapter 2, they do often survive in very dry or wet conditions. In arid regions, such as Egypt or parts of the New World, such perishables have come down to us in some quantity, and the study of *basketry and cordage* there reveals complex and sophisticated designs and techniques that display complete mastery of these organic materials.

Waterlogged conditions can also yield a great deal of fragile evidence. Well-preserved workshops such as those of Viking York have taught us much about a variety of crafts in England in the 10th century AD. Dyestuffs, including madder root, woad, and quantities of dyer's greenweed were all represented by macrofossils. This interpretation was confirmed by chemical analysis of samples of Viking textiles from the excavations. Chromatography (Chapters 6 and 7) identified a range of dyes in the textiles, again including madder and woad. Original dye colors can be identified from their "absorption spectra," the wavelengths of light they absorb: it has been found that the Romans in Britain often wore purple, while the York Vikings liked red. Clubmoss, also represented by macrofossils,

was probably used as a mordant at York, fixing madder reds and greenweed yellows directly on to the textile fibers. All the animal fibers were wool or silk, while all those of vegetable origin which could be determined were flax. Evidence for the cleaning of sheep's wool came with the discovery of adults and puparia of the sheep ked, a wingless parasitic fly, and also sheep lice.

Analyzing Textiles. Where textiles are concerned, the most crucial question is how they were made, and of what. In the New World, a certain amount of information on pre-Columbian weaving methods is available from ethnographic observation, as well as from Colonial accounts and illustrations, from depictions on Moche pottery, and from actual finds of ancient looms and objects (spindles and shuttles of wood, bone, or bamboo) found preserved in the Peruvian desert. There seem to have been three main types of loom: two were fixed (one vertical, the other horizontal), and used for really big pieces of weaving, while a small portable version was used for items such as clothing or bags.

The richest New World evidence, however, comes from Peruvian textiles themselves, which have survived in an excellent state of preservation thanks to the aridity of much of the country. The Andean cultures mastered almost every method of textile weaving or decoration now known, and their products were often finer than those of today – indeed, were some of the best ever made. By about 3000 BC they had developed cotton textiles, which quickly took over from the previous techniques using fibers (such as reeds and rushes)

New World textiles. Some of the finest woven designs ever made have come from Peru. This scene from the rim of a Moche vase depicts a Peruvian cloth factory. Eight women are shown weaving at their portable, backstrap looms, supervised by the official top right. The meaning of the panel at lower right is not known.

that were far less supple and resistant. The Peruvians also came to use animal fibers from their domesticated camelids, particularly the vicuña and the alpaca. They had an extraordinary range of dyes: the huge textiles from the Nazca culture, dating to the 1st millennium AD, have up to 190 different color tones.

The precise weaving technique can often be deduced through careful observation by specialists. Sylvia Broadbent has studied some painted cotton fabrics of the pre-Hispanic Chibcha culture of Colombia, and has been able to ascertain that they are all woven of "one-ply S-twist cotton in a basic plainweave, single wefts over double warp threads." Counts of the number of threads range from 6 to 12 wefts (side to side) per centimeter, and from 11 to 14 warps (up/down) per centimeter. At the weft edge, the weft threads turn in groups rather than singly, a fact which implies the use of a weaving technique involving multiple shuttles. The end of the weaving was secured by a row of chain-stitch.

It is also thanks to aridity that we have so many surviving textiles from ancient Egypt. Here, as in Peru, we can learn a great deal from surviving equipment and from models such as that found in the tomb of Meketre at Thebes (2000 BC) which shows a weaving workshop with a horizontal or ground loom as well as spindles and other tools. Flinders Petrie's excavation at Kahun, a town site for workers building a pyramid, dating to about 1890 BC, revealed weaver's waste on the floor of some houses: scraps of unspun, spun, and woven threads, colored red and blue. Analysis in the scanning electron microscope proved them to be from sheep's wool, while dye tests showed that madder was used for red, and the blue probably came from the plant *Indigofera articulata*.

The wrappings of a male Egyptian mummy of 170 BC in Pennsylvania University Museum (designated PUM II) also underwent scanning electron microscopy, and proved to be a fabric of fine threads, whose straightness and markings were identical to modern flax fibers: that is, the wrappings were a linen fabric.

But it is not only from Peru and Egypt that we have evidence for textiles. They can survive in waterlogged conditions, as we saw at Viking York, and even where preservation is less good, careful excavation may yield textile remains, as in the Celtic chieftain's tomb at Hochdorf, western Germany, dating to about 550 BC. Here analysis of the remains using a scanning electron microscope showed that the chieftain's death-bed had been covered with woven textiles made from spun and twisted threads of hemp and flax. There were also coverings made of sheep's wool, horse hair, and badger wool, and furs of badger and weasel were present as well. In the SEM, the hair of different species can be identified if the diagnostic cuticle pattern is preserved, as in this case.

The oldest known trace of cloth was found recently in the form of a white linen fragment clinging to the handle of an antler tool from Çayönü, Turkey. Dating to about 7000 BC, it was probably made of flax. However, far older evidence of weaving has been found at Pavlov, Czech Republic, dated to between 25,000 and 27,000 years ago, in the form of impressions of textiles or flexible basketry on fired clay.

Microwear Analysis of Fibers. The analysis of microwear is chiefly associated with stone and bone tools, as shown above; but it has recently been applied with great success to textiles and fibers. Research at the University of Manchester's Department of Textiles using the SEM has shown that different kinds of fracture, damage, and wear leave diagnostic traces on different classes of fibers. Tearing or bursting leave a very different pattern from the prolonged flexing associated with fatigue and breakdown of the fibers – the latter produce longitudinal damage, resulting in the fibers having "brush ends." Cutting of fibers is easy to identify in the SEM, and razor-marks are readily distinguishable from those made by shears or scissors (see also Lindow Man box, pp. 448–49).

In an interesting application of their technique, the Manchester researchers examined two woollen items from the Roman fort of Vindolanda, northern England. For the first, a soldier's leg bandage, they had to determine whether it had been discarded because it was worn out, or whether it had been damaged by its prolonged burial. Analysis showed an abundance of "brush ends" indicating that the bandage had been much used, but there was also evidence of postdepositional damage (transverse fractures). The second item, an insole for a child's shoe, seemed to the naked eye to be in mint condition. However, in the SEM it became clear that there was considerable wear of the surface fibers, implying that the unused insole had been cut from a heavy fabric (perhaps a cloak) that was already quite worn.

This technique obviously holds enormous promise for future analyses of those fabrics that have come down to us. Even where textiles do not survive, they sometimes leave an impression behind, for example on mummies, from which the type of weave can be recognized. And similarly useful information can be derived from the study of imprints of fabrics, cordage, and basketry that are found on fired clay, by far the most abundant of the synthetic materials available to the archaeologist.

SYNTHETIC MATERIALS

Firing and Pyrotechnology

It is possible to consider the whole development of technology, as far as it relates to synthetic materials, in terms of the control of fire: pyrotechnology. Until very recent times, nearly all synthetic materials depended upon the control of heat; and the development of new technologies has often been largely dependent upon achieving higher and higher temperatures under controlled conditions.

Clearly the first step along this path was the mastery of fire, possible evidence for which already occurs in the Swartkrans Cave, South Africa, in layers dating to 1.5 million years ago (Chapter 6). Cooked food and preserved meat then became a possibility, as did the use of heat in working flint (see above), and in hardening wooden implements like the yew spear from the Middle Paleolithic site of Lehringen, Germany.

Terracotta (baked clay) figurines were produced sporadically in the Upper Paleolithic period at sites from the Pyrenees and North Africa to Siberia, but their most notable concentration occurs in the Czech Republic at the open-air sites of Dolní Věstonice, Pavlov, and Předmostí, dating to about 26,000 years ago: they comprise small, well-modeled figurines of animals and humans. Recent analysis reveals that they were modeled in wetted local loess soil, and fired at temperatures between 500°C and 800°C (932–1472°F). The figurines were concentrated in special kilns, away from the living area. Almost all are fragmentary, and the shape of their fractures implies that they were broken by thermal shock – in other words, they were placed, while still wet, in the hottest part of the fire, and thus deliberately caused to explode. Rather than carefully made art objects, therefore, they may have been used in some special ritual.

A significant development of the Early Neolithic period in the Near East, around 8000 BC, was the construction of special ovens used both to parch cereal grains (to facilitate the threshing process) and to bake bread. These ovens consisted of a single chamber in which the fuel was burnt. When the oven was hot the fuel was raked out and the grain or unbaked bread placed within. This represents the first construction of a deliberate facility to control the conditions under which the temperature was raised. We may hypothesize that it was through these early experiences in pyrotechnology that the possibility of making pottery by firing clay was discovered. Initially pottery was made by firing in an open fire. "Reducing" conditions (the removal of oxygen) could be achieved by restricting the flow of air, and by adding unburnt wood.

These simple procedures may well have been sufficient in favorable cases to reach temperatures equivalent to the melting point of copper at 1083°C (1981°F). Given that copper was already being worked by cold hammering, and then by annealing (see below), and some copper ores such as azurite were used as

Pyrotechnology: the control of fire. Initially pottery was made in an open fire. The introduction of the potter's kiln meant higher temperatures could be achieved, also spurring on the development of metallurgy. (Left) Mesopotamian dome-shaped kiln of the early 4th millennium BC, built largely of clay, with an outer wall of stone or mud brick. (Center) Egyptian kiln of c. 3000 BC reconstructed from tomb paintings. The potter may have stood on the small platform to load the kiln. (Right) Greek kiln of c. 500 BC, reconstructed from scenes on Corinthian plaques: the extended fire opening probably improved combustion.

pigments, it was to be expected that the smelting of copper from its ores and the casting of copper would be discovered. Potters' kilns, where there is a controlled flow of air, can produce temperatures in the range of 1000–1200°C (1832–2192°F), as has been documented for such early Near Eastern sites as Tepe Gawra and Susa, Iran, and the link between pottery production and the inception of copper metallurgy has long been noted. Bronze technology subsequently developed with the alloying primarily of tin with copper.

Iron can be smelted from its ores at a temperature as low as 800°C (1472°F), but in order to be worked while hot, it requires a temperature of between 1000 and 1100°C (1832–2012°F). In Europe and Asia, iron technology developed later than copper and bronze technology because of problems of temperature control and the need for stricter control of reducing conditions. In central and southern Africa, however, the technology of bronze does not appear to antedate that of iron. In the New World, iron was not worked in pre-Columbian times. For iron to be cast, as opposed to worked while hot, its melting point has to be reached (1540°C, 2804°F), and this was not achieved until c. 500 BC in China.

There is thus a logical sequence in the development of new materials governed largely by the temperature attainable. In general the production of glass and faience – a kind of "pre-glass," see below – is first seen very much later in an area than that of pottery, since a higher temperature and better control are needed. They appear with the manufacture of bronze.

The study of the technology used to produce synthetic materials such as these naturally requires an understanding of the materials and techniques employed. Traditional crafts, for instance as observed today in many Near Eastern bazaars, can give valuable clues as to the way artifacts may have been made, and to the technical procedures carried out.

Pottery

We saw above that throughout the earlier periods of prehistory containers made of light, organic materials were probably used. This does not mean, as has often been assumed, that Paleolithic people did not know how to make pottery: every fire lit on a cave floor will have hardened the clay around it, and we have already noted that terracotta figurines were sometimes produced. The lack of pottery vessels before the Neolithic period is mainly a consequence of the mobile way of life of Paleolithic hunter-gatherers, for whom heavy containers of fired clay would have been of limited usefulness. The introduction of pottery generally seems to coincide with the adoption of a more sedentary way of life, for which vessels and containers that are durable and strong are a necessity.

The almost indestructible potsherd is as ubiquitous in later periods as the stone tool is in earlier ones – and just as some sites yield thousands of stone tools, others contain literally tons of pottery fragments. For a long time, and particularly before the arrival of absolute dating methods, archaeologists used pottery primarily as a chronological indicator (Chapter 4) and to produce typologies based on changes in vessel shape and decoration. These aspects are still of great importance, for example in assessing sites from surface surveys (Chapter 3). More recently, however, as with stone tools, attention has shifted toward identifying the sources of the raw materials (Chapter 9); the residues in pots as a source of information about diet (Chapter 7); and above all to the methods of manufacture, and the uses to which vessels were put.

Where manufacture is concerned, the principal questions one needs to address can be summarized as: What are the constituents of the clay matrix? How was the pot made? And at what temperature was it fired?

Pot Tempers. Simple observation will sometimes identify the inclusions in the clay that are known as its temper – the filler incorporated to give the clay added strength and workability and to counteract any cracking or shrinkage during firing. The most common materials used as temper are crushed shell, crushed rock, crushed pottery, sand, grass, straw, or fragments of sponge. Experiments by the American scholars Gordon Bronitsky and Robert Hamer have demonstrated the qualities of different tempers. They found that crushed burnt shell makes clay more resistant to heat shock and impact than do coarse sand or unburnt shell; fine sand is the next best. The finer the temper, the stronger the pot; and the archaeological record in parts of the New World certainly shows a steady trend toward finer tempers.

How Were Pots Made? The making or "throwing" of pots on a wheel or turntable was only introduced after 3400 BC at the earliest (in Mesopotamia). The previous method, still used in some parts of the world, was to build the vessel up by hand in a series of coils or slabs of clay. A simple examination of the interior and exterior surfaces of a pot usually allows one to identify the method of manufacture. Wheelthrown pots generally have a telltale spiral of ridges and striations which is absent from handmade wares. These marks are left by the fingertips as the potter draws the vessel up on the turntable. Impressions can also be left on the outer

Evidence for pot-making using a wheel. An Egyptian potter shapes a vessel on the turntable type of wheel in this limestone portrait of c. 2400 BC.

surface of pots by the flat paddles – sometimes wrapped in cloth, which also leaves its mark – which were used to beat the paste to a strong, smooth finish.

How Were Pots Fired? The firing technique can be inferred from certain characteristics of the finished product. For example, if the surfaces are vitrified or glazed (i.e. have a glassy appearance), the pot was fired at over 900°C (1652°F) and probably in an enclosed kiln. The extent of oxidization in a pot (the process by which organic substances in the clay are burned off) is also indicative of firing methods. Complete oxidization produces a uniform color throughout the paste. If the core of a sherd is dark (grey or black), the firing temperature was too low to fully oxidize the clay, or the duration of the firing was insufficient, factors which often point to the use of an open kiln. Open firing can also cause blotchy surface discolorations called "fire clouds." Experimental firing of different pastes at dif-

ferent temperatures and in various types of kiln provides a guide to the colors and effects that can be expected.

An exact approach to firing temperature was used by the American scholars W.D. Kingery and Jay Frierman on a sherd of graphite ware from the Copper Age site of Karanovo, Bulgaria. Their method entailed reheating the specimen until irreversible changes occurred in its microstructure, thus placing a ceiling on the temperature at which it could originally have been fired. Examination by scanning electron microscopy revealed a slight change in microstructure after firing at 700°C (1292°F) in a carbon-dioxide atmosphere; marked changes occurred after one hour at 800°C (1472°F), while the clay vitrified at 900°C (1652°F). They could thus conclude that the graphite ware was originally fired at a temperature below 800°C, and most probably at about 700°C. Such results contribute greatly to our assessment of the technological capabilities of different cultures, particularly as regards their possible mastery of metallurgy (see below).

The archaeology of kiln sites has contributed much to our knowledge of firing procedures. In Thailand, for example, high-fired or "stoneware" ceramics were in mass production from the 11th to the 16th centuries AD, and traded around Southeast Asia and to Japan and western Asia; yet contemporary texts say nothing about the industry. Australian and Thai archaeologists and scientists on this project found that two cities, Sisatchanalai and Sukhothai, were the most important production centers, and excavation of the villages around the former has revealed hundreds of large kilns, often built on earlier collapsed specimens, sometimes to a depth of 7 m (23 ft). This stratigraphy of kiln-types has shown the development of their design and construction – from the early, crude, clay forms to the technically advanced brick ones that could achieve the higher firing temperatures needed for the fine exported wares. The later kilns were built on mounds that kept them away from wet soil, ensuring production throughout the year, and reflecting the increasing demands being made on the industry.

Evidence from Ethnography. Unlike the making of stone tools, the production of pottery by traditional methods is still widespread in the world, so it is profitable to pursue ethnoarchaeological studies not only on the technological aspects but also from the social and commercial points of view. Among many successful projects, one could cite the long-term work of the American archaeologist Donald Lathrap among the Shipibo-Conibo Indians of the Upper Amazon (eastern Peru). Here the modern ceramic styles can be traced back to archaeological antecedents of the 1st millennium AD. Most of the women are potters, each producing vessels primarily for her own household, both for cooking and for other purposes such as storage. The pots are made of local clays, with a variety of tempers including ground-up old potsherds, but other minerals and pigments are imported from neighboring regions for slips and decorative work. The pots are built up with coils of clay. Though a year-round activity, potmaking tends to occur mostly in the dry season, from May to October. Studies such as these are useful for a wide range of questions: not only how pots are made, when, why, and by whom, but also how much time and effort are invested in different types of vessels; how often and in what circumstances they get broken; and what happens to the pieces – in other words, patterns of use, discard, and site-clearance.

Archaeologists can thus derive many valuable insights from ethnoarchaeological work. Historical sources and artistic depictions from a number of cultures provide supplementary data.

Faience and Glass

Glassy materials are relative latecomers in the history of technology. The earliest was *faience* (a French word derived from Faenza, an Italian town), and might be called a "pre-glass"; it was made by coating a core material of powdered quartz with a vitreous alkaline glaze. Originating in predynastic Egypt (before 3000 BC), it was much used in dynastic times for simple beads and pendants. Faience's main importance to archaeology has been in the evidence it can provide for the provenience or source of particular beads, through analysis of their composition, and hence in helping to assess how dependent the technology of prehistoric Europe was on Egypt and the eastern Mediterranean.

Neutron activation analysis (box, pp. 360–61), which can trace elements down to concentrations of a few parts per million, has been applied to Bronze Age faience beads, and proved that those from England had a relatively high tin content which made them clearly different from those from the Czech Republic (which have high cobalt and antimony) and even from those from Scotland. All these groups were distinct from Egyptian beads, thus underlining the existence of local manufacture of this class of artifact.

By about 2500 BC Mesopotamia was making the first beads of real *glass*, which seem to have been highly prized. Once it had been discovered, glass was easy and cheap to make: it simply involves melting sand and cooling it again; the liquid cools without crystallizing, and therefore remains transparent. The problem to be overcome was the high melting point of silica (sand) – 1723°C (3133°F) – but if a "flux" such as soda or potash is added, the temperature is lowered. Soda lowers it to 850°C (1562°F), but the result is rather poor-quality glass. By trial and error, it must have been discovered that also adding lime produces a better result: the optimum mix is 75 percent silica, 15 percent soda, and 10 percent lime. As we have seen, glass can only have been made after the means of generating very high temperatures had been achieved; this occurred in the Bronze Age with the development of charcoal furnaces for smelting metal (see below).

The first real glass vessels have been found in sites of the Egyptian 18th Dynasty, *c.* 1500 BC; the earliest known glass furnace is that at Tell el-Amarna, Egypt,

Roman glass from northern Italy. The Romans introduced the technique of glass-blowing in about 50 BC, and created some of the finest pieces ever made. Their expertise was not matched until Venetian work of Renaissance times.

dating to 1350 BC. Vessels were made using a technique like the lost-wax method (see below): molten glass was fashioned around a clay core, which was scraped out once the glass had cooled. This leaves a characteristic rough, pitted interior. Statuettes and hollow vessels were also made in stone or clay molds.

By 700 BC all the principal techniques of making glass had been developed (producing vessels, figurines, windows, and beads) except for one: glass-blowing, which involves inflating a globule of molten glass with a metal tube, or sometimes blowing it into a mold. This quick and cheap method was finally achieved in about 50 BC by the Romans, whose expertise with glass was not equaled until the heyday of glasswork in Venice during the 15th and 16th centuries AD. Moreover, the Romans' output of glass was not matched until the Industrial Revolution. Why, then, is ancient glass so rare? The answer is not, as one might imagine, because it is fragile – it is often no more fragile than pottery – but because, like metals and unlike pottery, it is a reusable material, with fragments being melted down and incorporated into new glass.

Once again, *composition* and *production* are the keynotes of the archaeological approach to these materials. Until recent decades it was very hard to determine the exact raw materials used, since crystallographic observation provided no clues. In the last 30 years, however, new techniques have enabled specialists to analyze the constituents of a variety of ancient glasses.

E.V. Sayre and R.W. Smith, for example, undertook research to find systematic compositional differences in ancient glasses by analyzing them for 26 elements through a combination of three techniques: flame photometry, colorimetry, and above all optical emission spectrometry (Chapter 9). As a result, several categories of ancient glass were established, each with a different chemical composition. For instance, specimens of the 2nd millennium BC (primarily from Egypt, but also from throughout the Mediterranean area) were a typical soda-lime glass with a high content of magnesium. Specimens of the final centuries BC (from Greece, Asia Minor, and Persia) were rich in antimony, and had a lower content of magnesium and potassium. Roman glass proved to have less antimony and more manganese than the others.

Other methods which have been applied to ancient glass include the electron microbeam probe, which is a refinement of the non-destructive X-ray fluorescence technique (Chapter 9) and which can be used on tiny specimens. Neutron activation analysis can also be used in glass analysis.

Flaws in the glass such as bubbles can sometimes, by their size, shape, orientation, and distribution, inform the specialist how the specimen was handled from crucible to final shaping. By-products, too, can be informative. A "broken bead" from the Iron Age Meare lake village, southwest England, may actually be a mold for making glass beads.

ARCHAEOMETALLURGY

Non-Ferrous Metals

The most important non-ferrous metal – that is one not containing iron – used in early times was copper. In due course it was learnt that a harder, tougher product could be made by alloying the copper with tin to make bronze. Other elements, notably arsenic and antimony, were sometimes used in the alloying process; and in the later Bronze Age of Europe it was realized that a little lead would improve the casting qualities.

Gold and silver were also important, and lead should not be overlooked. Other metals such as tin and antimony were used only rarely in metallic form.

In most areas where copper and bronze were produced there was a natural progression, depending mainly on temperature, analogous to that for synthetic materials in general (see above). A basic understanding of these processes is fundamental to any study of early technology:

1 *Shaping native copper:* Native copper (metallic copper found in that form in nature, in nuggets) can be hammered, cut, polished, etc. It was much used in the "Old Copper" culture (4th–2nd millennium BC) of the Archaic period in the northern United States and Canada, and makes its appearance in the Old World at such early farming sites as Çatalhöyük and Çayönü in Turkey and Ali Kosh in Iran by 7000 BC.

2 *Annealing native copper:* Annealing is simply the process of heating and hammering the metal. Hammering alone causes the metal to become brittle. This process was discovered as soon as native copper began to be worked.

3 *Smelting the oxide and carbonate ores of copper,* many of which are brightly colored.

4 *The melting and casting of copper,* first in a single (open) mold, and later in two-piece molds.

5 *Alloying with tin (and possibly arsenic)* to make bronze.

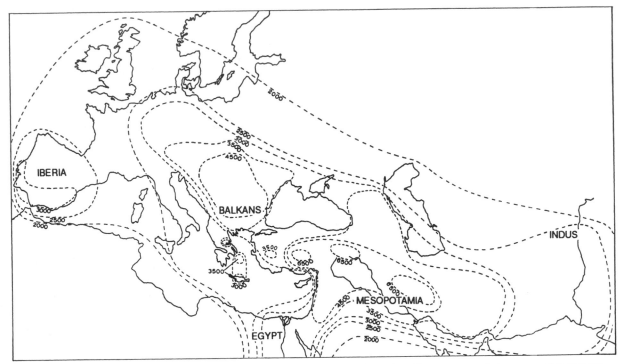

The origins of European copper metallurgy. Traditionally, the techniques of metalworking were seen to have spread to Europe from the more advanced lands of the Near East. But a somewhat different conclusion arises from studies of the early history of copper smelting in the Balkans and elsewhere. If one uses the calibrated radiocarbon chronology to draw a map where lines or "isochrons" indicate the earliest dates for metallurgy in each area, it becomes apparent that there were quite possibly three – not one – independent centers of origin: the Near East, the Balkans, and perhaps Spain and Portugal (Iberia).

6 *Smelting from sulphide ores*, a more complicated process than from carbonate ores.

7 *Casting by the lost-wax ("cire perdue") process* (see below) and use of the casting-on process, where most complicated shapes are produced by casting in several stages.

Lead has a melting point of 327°C (620°F) and is the most easily worked of metals. It can be smelted from its ores at around 800°C (1472°F). Silver melts at 960°C (1760°F), gold at 1063°C (1945°F), and copper at 1083°C (1981°F). So that in general, when craftspeople had mastered copper and bronze technology, they were also adept in working gold and silver and, of course, lead.

The techniques of manufacture of artifacts made from these materials can be investigated in several ways. The first point to establish is *composition*. Traditional laboratory methods readily allow the identification of major constituents. For instance, the alloys present in bronze may be identified in this way. However, in practice it is now more usual to utilize the techniques of trace element analysis which are also used in characterization studies (Chapter 9). For many years optical emission spectrometry (OES) was very widely used, but it has increasingly been superseded by atomic absorption spectrometry. X-ray fluorescence (XRF) is also often utilized, as on ceramic paste or glass. These methods are all reviewed in Chapter 9.

The other essential approach is that of *metallographic examination*, when the structure of the material is examined microscopically (see box opposite). This will determine whether an artifact has been formed by cold-hammering, annealing, casting, or a combination of these methods.

Turning to the sequence of stages outlined above, the use of native copper may be suspected when the copper is very free of impurities. And it can certainly be confirmed when the copper has not been melted and cast, for metallographic examination will then show that the artifact has been shaped only by cold-hammering or annealing. For example, when the American metallurgist Cyril Smith subjected a copper bead of the 7th millennium BC from Tepe Ali Kosh,

METALLOGRAPHIC EXAMINATION

One of the most useful techniques for the study of early metallurgy is that of metallographic examination. It involves the examination under the light microscope of a polished section cut from the artifact, which has been chemically etched so as to reveal the metal structure. Since one cannot make translucent sections, it is necessary to direct reflected light to the object's surface (unlike petrographic study, for instance in the examination of pottery, where a thin section is usually examined in transmitted light).

The microscopic examination of metal structures can be highly informative, not only in distinguishing major phases in the manufacturing history of the artifact (such as casting on), but in the detection of more subtle processes.

In the case of copper, for instance, it is possible to recognize when the artifact has been worked from native copper. The structure will also clearly reveal whether or not the copper has been cold-worked, and whether or not it has been annealed (a process which entails heating and cooling the metal to toughen it and reduce brittleness). Indeed the whole history of the treatment of the material can be revealed, showing successive phases of annealing and cold-working.

Metallographic examination can be just as revealing in the cases of iron and steel. Wrought iron is easily recognizable: crystals of iron and streaks of slag can be clearly seen. The results of carburization – for instance, after part of an iron object has been heated in charcoal to give a hard cutting edge – are also very clear. The dark-etched harder edge is quite distinct from the softer white inner part.

Metallographic examination can thus furnish much information about the manufacturing process, and can reveal the very considerable mastery which many smiths exercised over their craft.

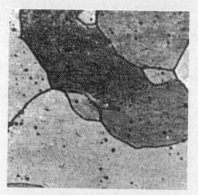

Copper – cast and fully annealed. Magnification x100.

The slip-bands (straight lines) indicate that the copper has been cold-worked (x100).

Copper that has been worked, fully annealed, and cold-worked again (x150).

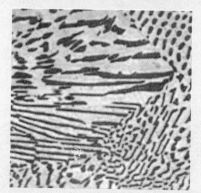

Silver that has been super-saturated with copper (x100).

Wrought iron at x200. The light grain is iron, the darker material slag.

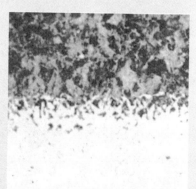

Iron that has been partially hardened. The dark structure is harder than the lighter.

Iran, to microscopic and metallographic examination, he found that a naturally occurring lump of copper had been cold-hammered into a sheet, then cut with a chisel, and rolled to form the bead. If the native copper has been melted and then cast, however, there is no way of distinguishing it with certainty from copper smelted from its ore.

Alloying

The alloying of copper with arsenic or tin represents a great step forward in metallurgical practice. Alloying can have a number of beneficial effects. In the first place arsenical-bronze or tin-bronze are both harder and less brittle than copper. Mainly for this reason the metal blades of weapons – daggers and spears – are generally of bronze, and such weapons that were made of copper were probably of very little use in practice. Certainly the early swords of the Near East and of Europe are of bronze: copper swords would simply be too fragile to be functional.

The addition of arsenic or of tin can also facilitate manufacture in several ways. They can be useful in the casting process by avoiding the formation of bubbles or blow-holes in the copper, and they improve the workability of the object by allowing repeated hammering (with or without heating) without the object becoming brittle. The ideal proportion of tin to copper in tin-bronze is about 1 part in 10.

Naturally the presence of tin or arsenic is an indication that alloying may have taken place. But in the case of arsenic it is probable that arsenic-rich copper ore was used in the first place, and that the arsenic is not a deliberate additive, so that favorable results owed more to luck than to judgment. There is no way of being certain for a single artifact in isolation. But analysis of a series of artifacts can reveal a consistent pattern indicating careful control and hence probably intentional alloying. For example, when applied to Bronze Age material from the Near East by E.R. Eaton and Hugh McKerrell, X-ray fluorescence showed an extensive use of arsenic minerals in the alloys, probably to provide a silver-colored coating on the copper. Indeed, they found that arsenical copper accounts for about one-quarter to one-third of all metal from Mesopotamia over the period 3000 BC to 1600 BC, making it two or three times more important than tin-bronze at that time.

The composition of gold and silver alloys can be deduced by determining their specific gravity. In this way, it has been found that Byzantine coins were debased to a lower silver value between AD 1118 and 1203. An examination of cross-sections of the coins also enabled M.F. Hendy and J.A. Charles to ascertain the method of manufacture, because the microstructure indicated that the coin blanks were cut from sheets (either cold- or hot-worked), rather than stamped from cast droplets.

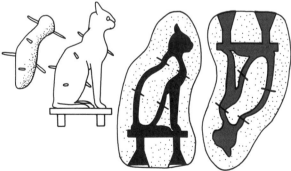

Casting. (Above) The lost-wax method. In this Egyptian example (c. 1500 BC), a clay core is made and then a wax model built around it. The model is encased in a clay mold which is subsequently baked, allowing the melted wax to be poured off. Molten metal is poured into the now hollow mold (colored in the diagram), and finally the clay is broken away to reveal the metal casting. (Left) An Egyptian tomb painting of c. 1500 BC shows foundrymen casting bronze doors. After heating using foot bellows (scene above), the molten metal is poured into a large clay mold (scene below).

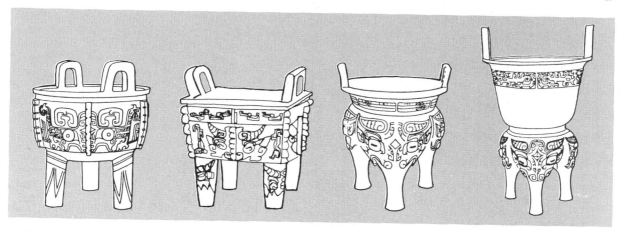

In China, the casting of metal objects in ceramic piece-molds was perfected during the Shang dynasty, c. 1500 BC. In contrast with the technique used in the western Old World, most care went into shaping the mold rather than the model. Large numbers of molds were produced in workshops to supply the foundries. Masterpieces such as these bronze ritual vessels were the result.

Casting

Information on the type of mold used can generally be obtained by the simple inspection of the artifact. If it shows evidence of casting on both upper and lower surfaces, a two-piece mold was presumably used. More elaborate shapes are likely to have required the lost-wax (*cire perdue*) technique which reached a high degree of perfection in the New World (see also Chapter 10). This ingenious and widespread technique involves modeling the desired shape in wax, and then encasing the model in fine clay, but leaving a small channel to the exterior. When the clay is heated, the melted wax can be poured out; thus the clay becomes a hollow mold, and molten metal can be poured into it. After the clay casting is broken away, one is left with a metal copy of the original model. This is, of course, a "one-off" method.

There are several ways in which the technique can be detected in the archaeological record, quite apart from the scanty accounts and illustrations left, for the New World, by Spanish colonists, who mention gold (though not copper) being cast in this way. Apart from surviving molds (see below), evidence exists in the form of black fragments of clay casing which still adhere to a few metal figures. Experiments, sometimes carried out with original unbroken molds, have shown the effectiveness of the lost-wax method.

The examination of sections by metallurgical microscopy (see box p. 341) and electron probe microanalysis can also yield more detailed data on manufacture. The British metallurgist J.A. Charles studied some early copper axes from southeast Europe, and found a great increase in oxygen content toward the upper flat surface: the copper oxide content was 0.15 percent at the lower surface, but 0.4 percent at the upper. This was a clear indication that these Copper Age axes were cast in an open mold.

It should be noted, however, that hammering and annealing can produce results similar to casting. It does not follow that a ribbed dagger was cast in a two-piece mold just because it has a rib on both sides, for this effect can be achieved by hot-working. Metallographic analysis is needed to be sure about the production method.

Detailed evidence of the method of manufacture can be obtained when the by-products of the process are examined, and deductions can also be made from surface traces on some objects. Lumps of excess metal at the ends of figurines were usually removed by the craftsperson, but occasionally they remain attached and thus show in what position it was cast (normally head downward). Similarly unfinished are objects on which the casting seams or "flashes" – where a little metal ran into the join between two halves of a mold – have not been burnished away. On an incense burner from the Quimbaya region of central Colombia, made of a gold-rich alloy in the shape of a human face, one can see a vertical line on the forehead and chin, and a raised seam inside the hollow foot of the pedestal.

Molds can yield much useful information, and since they were often of stone they have frequently survived. Even the broken clay casings of the lost-wax method have occasionally been preserved. Two unbroken specimens have been found in an undated tomb at Pueblo Tapado, in the Quimbaya region of Colombia.

COPPER PRODUCTION IN PERU

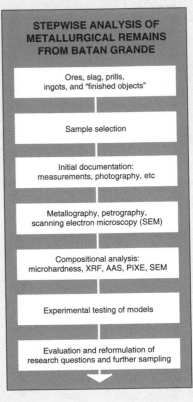

SOUTH
Batán Grande
AMERICA

At Batán Grande in the Central Andean foothills of northern coastal Peru, a team of archaeologists and allied specialists led by Izumi Shimada investigated various aspects of ancient copper alloy production. From 1980 to 1983 they excavated over 50 furnaces at three sites near rich prehistoric copper mines; they estimate there were hundreds more furnaces at these sites. This was copper alloy (copper and arsenic) smelting on an industrial scale, from about AD 900 to 1532 when the Spanish began their conquest of the Inca Empire. The sites provide ample field evidence that Central Andean metalworking was one of the major independent metallurgical traditions of the ancient world.

At one hillside site an entire smelting workshop was revealed, with furnaces, thick layers of crushed slag and charcoal, large grinding stones (*batanes*) up to a meter in diameter, and dozens of *tuyères* (ceramic blowtube tips), as well as food remains and some copper and arsenic-bearing ore. The furnaces, typically about 1 m apart, were in rows of three or four.

Replicative smelting experiments using a 600-year-old furnace and blowtubes have shown that

STEPWISE ANALYSIS OF METALLURGICAL REMAINS FROM BATAN GRANDE

Ores, slag, prills, ingots, and "finished objects"

↓

Sample selection

↓

Initial documentation: measurements, photography, etc

↓

Metallography, petrography, scanning electron microscopy (SEM)

↓

Compositional analysis: microhardness, XRF, AAS, PIXE, SEM

↓

Experimental testing of models

↓

Evaluation and reformulation of research questions and further sampling

Flowchart to indicate how specialists in various fields, using different techniques, worked together to help understand the smelting process. (XRF, AAS, and PIXE are explained pp. 360–61)

Excavated furnaces (left), aligned east–west and north-south, dating to about AD 1000.

Being unbroken, it is clear they were never used, but both were intended for the casting of small ornaments. According to a study done by Karen Bruhns, the molds themselves are shaped like a flattened flask; they have a small hole pierced in the bottom to permit air to escape when the metal was introduced, and thus avoid formation of a bubble.

The study of *slags* can also be informative. Analysis is often necessary to distinguish slags derived from copper smelting from those produced in iron production. It is relevant as well to test for sulphur which is an indicator of sulphide ores. Crucible slags (from the casting process) may be distinguished from smelting slags by their higher concentration of copper.

The microchemical analysis of *residues* in pottery vessels (Chapter 7) has also produced evidence of metalworking. Rolf Rottländer's analysis of small pots from the Iron Age (Hallstatt) hillfort of the Heuneburg

temperatures of 1100°C could be attained (the melting point of copper is 1083°C or 1981°F). Each furnace was lined with a specially prepared "mud" that gave a highly refractory, non-stick, smooth surface capable of withstanding numerous firings. Some furnaces had been relined up to three times.

It appears that copper and arsenic-bearing ore were reduced to slag and metallic copper alloy here, a process experiments suggest would have taken some three hours of high temperatures sustained by continuous blowing. The furnaces could have held 3–5 kg (6.6–11 lb) of copper alloy and partially molten slag. Once the furnace cooled, the slag was cracked and ground up nearby on *batanes* using a smaller rocking stone to release the copper prills (up to 1 cm droplets) from their unwanted slag residue. These prills

were then picked out and remelted in crucibles into ingots. At another part of the site the resultant copper was annealed and forged using faceted stone hammers to produce sheet metal and implements. Prills and implements were all arsenical copper.

Prills extraction existed in the Near East from the 3rd millennium BC onward. The Batán Grande evidence now suggests that it was later

independently invented in the New World. New World metallurgists, however, apparently never had the benefit of bellows, and human lung-power limited the size of furnace and amount of ore smelted at one time.

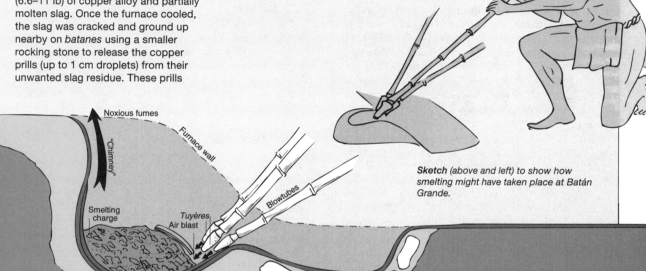

3 people blowing

Sketch (above and left) to show how smelting might have taken place at Batán Grande.

Noxious fumes

"Chimney"

Furnace wall

Smelting charge

Tuyères
Air blast

Blowtubes

Lining

Heat discolored

Stone

on the Upper Danube found that one had been used for melting down copper alloys, while another had traces of gold and two others traces of silver.

A fuller understanding of the technology must come from the thorough examination of the facilities at the *place of manufacture*. Ingots, slag, and other by-products such as molds, fragments of crucibles often with slag inside, broken *tuyères* (the nozzles of pipes for conducting air), failed castings, and scrap metal in

general all provide clues to metallurgical methods. For example, ingots of copper often solidified at the bottom of smelting-furnaces, and their shape thus reveals the shape of the structure's base. One bronze-foundry site, at Hou-Ma, Shaanxi Province, China, dating to 500 BC, has yielded over 30,000 items including piece-molds, clay models, and cores. The Chinese perfected the system of piece-molding quite early on, already at the time of the Shang dynasty around 1500 BC. As with most of the finest early bronze-working, the principle was that of lost-wax casting. Extraordinary works of craftsmanship were produced by the Chinese in this way.

Remains of furnaces, as for instance found at the Peruvian site of Batán Grande, can provide a whole range of information about the technology of the manufacturing process (see box, pp. 344–45).

Silver, Lead, and Platinum

The low melting point of *lead* (327°C or 620°F) allows it to be worked easily, but it is very soft and so was not used for a wide range of purposes. However, figurines are found in this material, and in some areas small clamps of lead were used for mending broken pots.

Lead has a wider significance, however, since lead ores found in nature are often rich in *silver*. The extraction of silver from lead by the process known as cupellation involves the oxidization of lead to litharge (a lead oxide), and other base metals are likewise oxidized. The noble metals, silver and gold, are unaltered while the litharge is absorbed by the hearth or is skimmed off. A shallow hearth is needed so that a considerable surface area is exposed to the oxidizing blast of air that is provided by bellows. Charcoal or wood is used to maintain a temperature of about 1000–1100°C (1832–2072°F).

In Roman Britain, cupellation hearths have been found at the towns of Wroxeter and Silchester. The hearth at Silchester was lined with bone-ash, which is

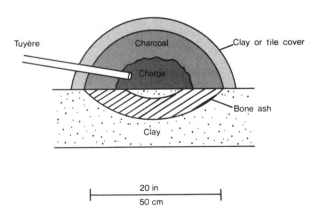

Reconstruction of a cupellation hearth found in the Romano-British town of Silchester. The hearth was probably used to extract silver from coins of debased silver and copper content.

porous and absorbent. Analysis of this hearth suggested that it had been used for the cupellation of copper, since it contained globules which were 78 percent copper. It is likely that it was used to extract silver from coins of very debased silver, with a large copper content.

Slag found in huge quantities (16–20 million tons) at the 8th/7th century BC site in Rio Tinto, Spain, proved on analysis to be primarily from silver metallurgy: the ore seems to have been very rich (600 g per metric ton), but very few metal objects have been found. The distribution of slag and drops of lead in many houses rather than in large piles suggested to the excavators, Antonio Blanco and J.M. Luzón, that the metalworking occurred as a domestic activity instead of in factories.

Platinum (melting point 1800°C or 3277°F) was being worked in Ecuador in the 2nd century BC, though it was unknown in Europe till the 16th century and Europeans only managed to melt it in the 1870s. In Ecuador they clearly liked it for its hardness and resistance to corrosion, and they often used it in combination with gold.

Fine Metalwork

There is no doubt that early craftspeople very soon discovered the full range of techniques which their control over pyrotechnology allowed. By the late Bronze Age of the Aegean, for example, around 1500 BC, as wide a range of techniques was available for working with non-ferrous metals as was used in the Classical or early medieval periods. For instance, the techniques of working sheet metal were well understood, as were those of stamping, engraving, and repoussé working (work in relief executed with hand-controlled punches from the back of sheet metal). Filigree work (open work using wires and soldering) was developed by the 3rd millennium BC in the Near East, and granulation (the soldering of grains of metal to a background usually of the same metal) was used to achieve remarkable effects, notably by the Etruscans.

Astonishing collections of fine metalwork, displaying great skill, have been excavated in recent years at the sites of Sipán and Sicán in Peru. The three royal tombs found at Sipán belong to the Moche period, and probably date to between the 1st and 3rd centuries AD. The Moche metalworkers were accomplished in a variety of techniques (see illustrations opposite).

In general, the method of manufacture can be established in such cases by careful examination, without more sophisticated analysis.

Most of these traditional techniques of manufacture

Gold spider bead – one of 10 that made up a necklace found with the "Old Lord" of Sipán, possibly dating to the 1st century AD. The bead was made up from different parts (right), using a variety of techniques. The three gold spheres in the base of the bead would rattle when the wearer moved.

may still be seen in use in towns of North Africa and in the bazaars of the Near East. There is usually much more to be learnt from careful study of the work of a skilled craftsperson operating with a traditional technology than there is from some less adept attempt at experimental archaeology undertaken by an experimenter who does not have the benefit of generations of experience.

Plating

Plating is a method of bonding metals together, for instance silver with copper, or gold with copper. The ancient Peruvians can be shown to have used methods of electrochemical plating of precious metals once thought to have been invented in late medieval or Renaissance Europe, where iron and steel armor was plated in gold.

Heather Lechtman and her colleagues undertook an analysis of some gold-plated objects of hammered sheet copper from a looted cemetery at Loma Negra, Peru. These dated to the first few centuries AD, the early Moche period, and included human figures, masks, and ear ornaments. Some had very thin gold surfaces that had not been attached mechanically to

the copper. In fact the gold was so thin (0.5 to 2 micrometers) that it could not be seen in cross-section under a microscope at 500× magnification; but its thickness was very even, and it covered the edges of the metal sheets. This was clearly not a simple application of gold leaf or foil.

A zone of fusion between gold and copper indicated that heat had been applied to bind them together. It could not be modern electroplating, which uses an electric current, but its results were similar. Therefore the investigators looked at the possibility of electroplating by chemical replacement. In their experiments they used only chemicals available to the ancient Peruvians, and processes that did not require any external electrical current. They used aqueous solutions of corrosive salts and minerals (common in the deserts of the Peruvian coast and thus available to the Moche) to dissolve and then deposit the gold, and found that it spreads onto clean copper sheeting that is dipped into the solution, if boiling occurs for five minutes during immersion. To achieve a stable bonding, it is necessary to heat the plated sheet for a few seconds at 650–800°C (1202–1472°F). The results were so close to the Loma Negra artifacts that this method – or one very similar – was probably that used by the Moche.

EARLY STEELMAKING: AN ETHNOARCHAEOLOGICAL EXPERIMENT

AFRICA

Haya

Ethnoarchaeological projects that involve detailed observations about manufacturing processes are usually associated with the making of stone tools and ceramics, or with weaving; yet much has also been learned about metalworking by a number of investigators.

One such project, combining ethnography with archaeology and experiment, was carried out in northwest Tanzania by Peter Schmidt and Donald Avery who worked among the Haya, a Bantu-speaking agricultural people living in densely populated villages on the western shore of Lake Victoria. The Haya now use cheap European tools, but had oral traditions concerning their own ancient steelmaking process, which had been used as recently as 60 or 70 years ago. They still have an active blacksmithing tradition, in which scrap iron is employed. Some older men, a few of them smiths, remembered the traditional way in which iron had been smelted, and they were more than willing to recreate the experience.

The Haya were therefore easily persuaded to construct a traditional furnace, which was 1.4 m (4 ft 6½ in) high, cone-shaped, and made of slag and mud, built over a pit, 50 cm (20 in) deep, lined with mud and packed with partially burned swamp grass. These charred reeds provided carbon that combined with molten iron ore to produce steel. Eight ceramic blow tubes (tuyères) extended into the furnace chamber near its base, each one connected to a goatskin bellows outside. These tubes forced preheated air (up to 600°C or 1112°F) into the furnace, which was fueled by charcoal. With this apparatus the Haya could achieve temperatures between 1300° and 1400°C (2372–2552°F), high enough to produce carbon steel.

Archaeological verification of the Haya's claims came from excavations on the lakeshore which uncovered remains of 13 furnaces almost identical to the one built by the modern people. Radiocarbon dates obtained from charcoal showed that they were 1500 to 2000 years old. Iron slag was also found which had a flow temperature of 1350–1400°C (2462–2552°F). Furnaces of similar date have since been found elsewhere in the same region of East Africa.

In short, the Haya had the technology to make medium-carbon steel in preheated forced-draft furnaces some 19 centuries before Europe developed the same capabilities.

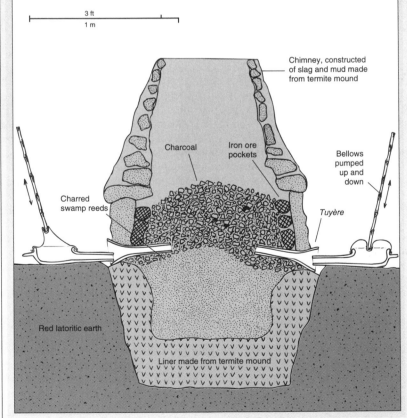

3 ft
1 m

Chimney, constructed of slag and mud made from termite mound

Charcoal

Iron ore pockets

Bellows pumped up and down

Charred swamp reeds

Tuyère

Red latoritic earth

Liner made from termite mound

Idealized profile of a Haya iron smelting furnace, before the addition of the mixed iron ore and charcoal charge. Bellows that were pumped up and down with a stick forced air through tuyères (clay pipes) deep into the center of the furnace.

Iron and Steel

Iron was not used in the New World during pre-Columbian times, and makes its appearance in quantity in the Old World with the inception in the Near East of the Iron Age around 1000 BC. There is evidence, however, that it was worked rather earlier, notably in Hittite Anatolia. Meteoric iron (iron deriving from meteorites, and found naturally in the metallic state) was widely known in the Near East, and cylinder seals and other ornaments are made from it. But there is no evidence that it was extensively worked.

Once the technique of *smelting iron* was well understood, it became very important, not least in Africa, since iron is more widely found in nature than is copper. But it is much more difficult to reduce – i.e. to separate from oxygen with which it is found combined in nature in the form of iron oxides. It requires much more strongly reducing conditions.

Iron may be reduced from pure iron oxide at about 800°C (1472°F) below its melting point of 1540°C (2804°F). But in practice the iron ores also contain other unwanted minerals, called gangue, in addition to the oxides. These must be removed in the smelting process by slagging, where a sufficiently high temperature is reached for the slag to become liquid and to drain away, leaving the iron in a solid state as a sponge or "raw bloom."

The simplest and easiest furnaces for iron smelting were bowl furnaces – hollows in the ground lined with baked clay or bricks. The ore and charcoal were placed in the bowl furnace and the temperature brought up to around 1100°C (2012°F) by the use of bellows.

The next stage is the hot working of the iron by forging, which takes place above ground in the smithy or forge. It is not always easy to distinguish between smelting sites and smithing sites, although if ore is found along with slag, that usually indicates smelting.

The production of *cast iron* requires a sophistication in the construction and operation of furnaces which did not become widespread in Europe until well into the Christian era, more than a thousand years after the production of *wrought iron* (although small statuettes of cast iron appear in Greece as early as the 6th century BC). In China, however, cast iron and wrought iron appear almost together in the 6th century BC, and cast iron was regularly used for making useful tools in China long before it was in the West. Cast iron is a brittle alloy of iron which has a carbon content between 1.5 percent and 5 percent. Its relatively low melting point (around 1150°C or 2102°F), which is lower than that of steel or of wrought iron, allows it to be cast in the molten state. The emphasis in early China is thus upon cast iron rather than wrought iron: in this respect metallurgy in the Far East and in Europe followed very different paths.

Steel is simply iron that contains between about 0.3 and 1.2 percent carbon, and it is both malleable and capable of hardening by cooling. True steel was not produced until Roman times, but a rather similar although less uniform product was made earlier by the process of carburizing (see box opposite): this was achieved by high temperature heating of the iron in contact with carbon. Initially it may have taken place by accident, while the iron was heated in contact with red-hot charcoal by the smith in the process of forging.

The extent to which iron has been carburized, and the processes used, are best assessed by metallographic examination of the artifact in question.

Some apparently featureless lumps of metal may be more than they seem. Corrosion products can "grow" out of an iron object to mineralize and even encase any associated wood. The resulting metal lump may contain a void in the exact shape of an object that has corroded out. X-rays can reveal the hidden shape inside, and, as with the bodies from Pompeii or endocasts of brains (Chapter 11), a cast can be made and extracted.

SUMMARY

In this chapter we have highlighted some basic questions about early technology, and considered how to find answers to them. The examples presented demonstrate the mass of varied technological information that the archaeologist can extract by a combination of excavation, laboratory analysis, ethnographic information, and insight from experimentation. It could even be said that without experiments our knowledge of ancient technology would be minimal.

Ethnography and archaeological context may suggest the function of a stone tool; but only analysis of its microwear can demonstrate its likely use. Microwear studies themselves depend on experiments for categories of wear and to give them meaning. Nevertheless, ethnoarchaeology is proving extremely valuable. Observation of craftspeople in other living cultures by archaeologists who know what kind of information they require has probably arrived just in time, before the final vestiges of many of the ancient processes and traditions die away. No observation made in the present can definitively prove anything for certain about the past. But archaeology deals in degrees of probability, and a hypothesis which has been based on solid evidence from excavation, analysis, ethnography, and experiment is about as close to truth as we can come.

FURTHER READING

There are no up-to-date general accounts that cover all the methods discussed in this chapter. Broad surveys of ancient technology include:

Forbes, R.J. (series) *Studies in Ancient Technology*. E.J. Brill: Leiden.
Hodges, H. 1964. *Artifacts: an Introduction to Early Materials and Technology*. John Baker: London.
Hodges, H. 1971. *Technology in the Ancient World*. Penguin Books: Harmondsworth & Baltimore.
James, P. & Thorpe, N. 1995. *Ancient Inventions*. Ballantine Books: New York; Michael O'Mara: London.
Lambert, J.B. 1997. *Traces of the Past: Unraveling the Secrets of Archaeology through Chemistry*. Helix Books/Addison-Wesley Longman: Reading, Mass.
Rosenfeld, A. 1965. *The Inorganic Raw Materials of Antiquity*. Weidenfeld & Nicolson: London.
White, K.D. 1984. *Greek and Roman Technology*. Thames & Hudson: London; Cornell University Press: Ithaca, NY.

Other important sources are:

Anderson, A. 1984. *Interpreting Pottery*. Batsford: London; Universe: New York 1985.
Coles, J.M. 1979. *Experimental Archaeology*. Academic Press: London & New York.
Keeley, L.H. 1980. *Experimental Determination of Stone Tool Uses*. University of Chicago Press: Chicago.
MacGregor, A. 1985. *Bone, Antler, Ivory, and Horn Technology*. Croom Helm: London.
Orton, C., Tyers, P., & Vince, A. 1993. *Pottery in Archaeology*. Cambridge University Press: Cambridge & New York.
Rice, P.M. 1987. *Pottery Analysis: a Sourcebook*. Chicago University Press: Chicago.
Shepard, A.O. 1985. *Ceramics for the Archaeologist*. Carnegie Institute: Washington, D.C.
Tait, H. (ed.) 1991. *Five Thousand Years of Glass*. British Museum Press: London.
Tite, M.S. 1972. *Methods of Physical Examination in Archaeology*. Seminar Press: London & New York.
Tylecote, R.F. 1987. *The Early History of Metallurgy in Europe*. Longman: London & White Plains, NY.

9 What Contact Did They Have?
Trade and Exchange

The study of exchange and trade in early societies has been one of the growth areas of archaeology in recent years. It was realized that the materials of which artifacts are made can be a far better guide than their style to the place of origin of such artifacts. Whole exchange systems can be reconstructed, or at least the movements of the goods can be investigated, if the materials in question are sufficiently distinctive for their source to be identified. Numerous chemical and other methods now exist for the precise characterization of these materials – that is, the determination of characteristics of specific sources that allow their products to be recognized.

These techniques allow us to tackle the whole question of the production and distribution of traded goods. It is a more ambitious task to try to reconstruct the organization of the trading system as a whole. It is a particularly difficult one if there are no written records to tell us what commodities were traded in exchange for the ones we find in the archaeological record.

Raw materials were not the only items traded, or offered as gifts. Manufactured goods were just as important. Certain prestige goods had symbolic values, with precise meanings that are not always clear to us today, such as the jadeite axes of Neolithic Europe. But some prestige goods were highly significant, and this provides us with another line of investigation to be followed up.

Finds of the actual goods exchanged are the most concrete evidence that the archaeologist can hope to have for determining the contact between different areas, and different societies. But the communication of information, of ideas, may in many ways be more significant. Earlier generations of scholars were too willing to accept similarities between different cultures as a proof of contact, of the flow of ideas, or "diffusion" between the two. Partly in reaction against this tendency, the independent origins of things have been stressed, and the significance of interactions between neighbors somewhat understated. The time is now ripe for a reconsideration of such contacts.

All this relates closely to the social questions discussed in Chapter 5, and no clear separation is possible. Social structure itself may be defined as the pattern of repeated contacts between people, and social organization and exchange are simply different aspects of the same processes.

THE STUDY OF INTERACTION

Exchange is a central concept in archaeology. When referring to material goods, to commodities, it means much the same as trade. But exchange can have a wider meaning, being used by sociologists to describe all interpersonal contacts, so that all social behavior can be viewed as an exchange of goods, non-material as well as material. Exchange in this broader sense includes the exchange of information.

It is necessary, therefore, to consider the exchange transaction in rather more detail. In many exchanges the relationship is more important than what is exchanged. In the Christian tradition, for instance, when presents are exchanged within a family at Christmas, the giving of presents between relatives is generally more important than the actual objects: "it is the thought that counts." There are also different kinds of exchange relationship: some where generosity is the order of the day (as in the family Christmas); others where the aim is profit, and the personal relationship is not emphasized ("Would you buy a used car from this man?"). Moreover, there are different kinds of goods: everyday commodities that are bought and sold, and special goods, valuables, that are suitable for gifts. In all of this we have to consider how exchange works in a non-monetary economy where not only coinage may be lacking, but any medium of exchange.

In the next section we shall consider the ways in which artifacts (traded objects) found by archaeologists can be made to yield information about early trade and exchange. But, first, we must consider further the nature of exchange.

Exchange and Information Flow

Let us imagine two societies, living on islands some tens of miles away from each other. If there was no contact between them they would lie in complete isolation, exploiting their island resources. They may, however, have had boats, and so been in contact with each other. In that case, the archaeologist of the future, in studying the settlements and the artifacts found in them, will recognize on island A objects made from materials that were only available on island B, and will thus be able to document the existence of such contact: there must have been travel between the islands. But what may have been of much more importance to the islanders was the possibility of social contacts, the exchange of ideas, and the possibility of arranging marriage links. These, too, the archaeologist must consider, together with the material goods that were exchanged.

When there is exchange between island A and island B there is a flow of information. Ideas are exchanged, inventions are transmitted, and so are ambitions and aspirations. If the people of island A decide to build a temple of a new kind, those of island B may decide to follow suit. If those of island B develop the techniques of metallurgy, those of island A will not be far behind. There is thus a real equivalence between the

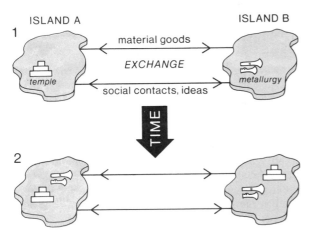

Contact between two islands has the effect that innovations on one (e.g. the building of a temple; metallurgy) may lead to similar developments on the other.

interaction seen as a communications system, and the interaction as a system for the exchange of material goods.

For most of this chapter we shall be dealing with economic aspects of exchange, and with material things. But, at the end, we shall return to this theme of interaction as information exchange: in the long run, it is often more important.

Scale and "World System"

For some purposes it is convenient to distinguish between *internal exchange*, taking place within the specific society we are considering, and *external trade* or *exchange*, where goods are traded over much greater distances, moving from one social unit to another. In using the term "trade," we generally mean external trade – something that takes place with the outside world. But when we consider the interactions within a society, whether involving information or goods, we tend to use the terminology of social organization not of trade. The emphasis in this chapter is on external trade; relations internal to the social unit were dealt with in Chapter 5, where we considered questions of scale and organization of society. But the distinction between the two levels of exchange is not always clear.

Trading systems often have what is almost a life of their own. By definition, they extend widely, over the boundaries of many politically independent societies. But sometimes the different parts of a widespread trading system of this kind can become so dependent on each other commercially that one can no longer think of them as independent entities. This point has been stressed by the American historian Immanuel Wallerstein. He used the term "world system" or "world economy" to designate an economic unit, articulated by trade networks extending far beyond the boundaries of individual political units (e.g. nation states), and linking them together in a larger functioning unit.

Wallerstein's initial example was the relationship that developed between the West Indies and Europe in the 16th century AD, when the economy of the West Indies was indissolubly linked with that of the European parent countries of which they were colonies. (It should be clearly understood that Wallerstein's rather odd term "world system" is not meant to refer to the entire world. He imagines a collection of several world systems, each of which might be conceived as a separate entity: one world system might involve Europe and the West Indies, another China and its Pacific neighbors.)

Wallerstein sees the emergence of the present world system, based on capitalism, as taking place during the Great Transformation of the 16th century AD. But archaeologists and ancient historians have applied the terminology to earlier periods. So that just as Wallerstein speaks of the "core" and the "periphery" of modern world systems, so these historians would like to use this terminology for earlier ages.

In the last section of this chapter we shall see that to adopt this terminology unthinkingly can lead to very dangerous archaeological assumptions. For the moment, it is enough to note that Wallerstein's approach helps us to pose a very important question: What was the scale of the effective functioning economic system in the past? In Chapter 5, we discussed the different approaches that the archaeologist may take to define the scale of the effective social unit. Here, we need to discuss how we can define the scale of the economic system if it is larger than the social system, embracing several politically independent units.

Gift Exchange and Reciprocity

One of the most fundamental advances of anthropological theory was the revelation by the French sociologist, Marcel Mauss, of the nature of gift exchange. He saw that in a range of societies, especially in those lacking a monetary economy, the fabric of social relations was bound by a series of gift exchanges. Individual X would establish or reinforce a relationship with individual Y by means of a gift, a valuable object, which would pass from the hands of X to those of Y. This gift was not a payment: it transcended mere monetary considerations. It was a gesture and a bond, imposing obligations on both parties, especially, of course, on the recipient. For acceptance of the gift implied the obligation of repayment by another, equally munificent presentation.

The anthropologist Bronislaw Malinowski, in his celebrated and influential work *Argonauts of the Western Pacific* (1922), described an exchange network, the *kula*, in which a series of exchange relationships between the inhabitants of some islands in Melanesia was cemented by the exchange of valuable gifts of objects, often of shell. The entire overseas contacts of these islanders centered on the ceremonial exchange with their exchange partners within the *kula*, although within this framework other exchanges of more everyday commodities, such as foodstuffs, took place.

Exchanges such as these, where the transfer of specific objects as gifts is only one part of a relation-

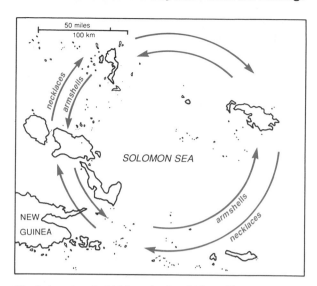

The kula network of Melanesia, in which necklaces were exchanged for armshells and armshells for necklaces in a cycle that cemented relations among the islanders.

ship with other obligations (including friendship) and with other activities (including feasting), are said to take place within a framework of reciprocity. The donor gains in status through the generosity of the scale of the gift. Gifts are often given with maximum publicity and ostentation. Indeed, in some New Guinea societies the position of "Big Man" is achieved by the munificent giving of gifts (often pigs) to exchange partners, and by the accumulation thereby not only of credit (i.e. the obligation of exchange partners to repay), but also what one may term kudos, the immense prestige that comes from being in the creditor position as donor.

The notion of reciprocal exchange of valuables, derived from anthropological studies, including Malinowski's work on the *kula* exchange cycle of Melanesia, has been very influential in shaping the thinking of many archaeologists about trade. For instance, in Britain during the Neolithic period there was clearly an extensive network of trade in stone axes. The methods by which this exchange has been documented, including the petrographic study of thin sections, are discussed below. The long-distance exchange networks that such characterization studies document led the British archaeologist Grahame Clark to suggest that a system of gift exchange was in operation in the British Neolithic. He likened this to the system of exchanging stone axes that operated in Australia into the present century (see boxes p. 369 and 376).

MODES OF EXCHANGE

Exchange, or trade, implies that goods change hands, and that this is a two-way transaction. The American anthropologist Karl Polanyi established that there are three different types or modes of exchange: reciprocity, redistribution, and market exchange.

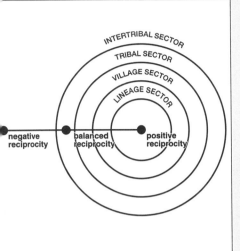

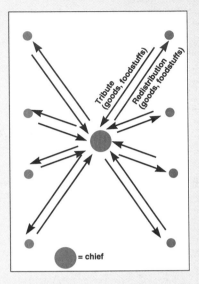

= chief

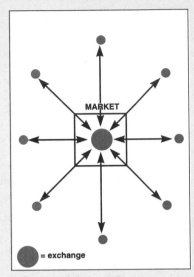

= exchange

Reciprocity refers to exchanges that take place between individuals who are symmetrically placed: that is, they are exchanging more or less as equals. Neither is in a dominant position. In effect, it is the same as gift exchange. One gift does not have to be followed by another at once, but a personal obligation is created that a reciprocal gift will later take place. The American anthropologist Marshall Sahlins has suggested that the generosity or altruism associated with such exchange can be illustrated as positive reciprocity (i.e. generosity) and takes place among close kin. Balanced reciprocity takes place among those well known to each other in a definite social context. And negative reciprocity (i.e. exchange where you try to do better out of it than your exchange partner) operates between strangers or those socially distant from one another.

Redistribution implies the operation of some central organization. Goods are sent to this organizing center, or at least are appropriated by it, and are then redistributed. Sahlins suggested that many chiefdoms in Polynesia operate in this way: the chief redistributes produce, and geographical diversity can thus be overcome. The fisherman receives fruit, and the worker in the plantation gets fish. Such exchange can be much more highly ordered than a series of relatively unstructured reciprocal exchanges between individuals, and it is a feature of more centrally organized societies, such as chiefdoms or states (see Chapter 5). Since it implies the existence of a coherent political organization within which it works, redistribution is a form of internal exchange.

Market exchange implies both a specific central location for exchange transactions to occur (the market-place) and the sort of social relationship where bargaining can occur. It involves a system of price-making through negotiation. Polanyi argued that this kind of bargaining first became the basis of a true market system in ancient Greece, when coinage based on a well-defined monetary system also made its appearance. But other workers have argued that there were markets also in the ancient Near East, as there certainly were in Mesoamerica and China.

Markets are often internal in the socio-political unit – for example, the rural markets of China, or the Greek marketplace (agora). But they do not have to be. The port-of-trade is a place where traders of different nationalities (i.e. belonging to different political units) can freely meet, and where free bargaining and hence price-fixing can take place.

Another instance, perhaps even more comparable to the Melanesian *kula* system, is the exchange of bracelets and other ornaments made of the marine shell *Spondylus gaederopus*, which is a native of the Mediterranean. Such ornaments were distributed right across the Balkans and into central Europe around 4000 BC, and it is clear that a long-distance trade network was in operation then. Just as in the case of the *kula*, handsome marine shells were one of the most conspicuous features of the exchange. But in this case, the exchange was a land-based one. The archaeologist today sees the shell ornaments of that period as fulfilling the role of valuables. Once again, the extent of the trade has to be established through a careful characterization study (to determine the place of origin) before such explanations in terms of reciprocity between exchange partners can be proposed.

When exchange takes place outside close personal relationships, it takes on a different character: the positive reciprocity of the profit motive (see box). And when the symmetrical one-to-one relationship of gift exchange or direct barter gives way to the trader/buyer relationship of the marketplace or to the demands of the tax collector, a different kind of economic relationship is implied (see box, under redistribution and market exchange).

These ideas have become part of the mental toolkit of the student of early trade. In some cases, they can be extended by reference to early documents, such as the inscribed clay tablets from the Assyrian trading colony at Kültepe in Anatolia, dating from the 18th century BC. Here most of the trade was controlled by private merchants in the Assyrian capital of Assur, while the merchants at Kültepe were acting as agents: that may be regarded as redistribution. But in some cases they do seem to have been trading on their own account, for personal gain.

Ethnographic work offers a rich repertoire of examples of trading systems: the markets of West Africa, and those of pre-industrial China have been studied by anthropologists and geographers and provide valuable insights to the archaeologist as to the ways in which exchange can take place.

Valuables and Commodities

In gift exchanges, as observed by anthropologists, the high-prestige gifts that are the focus of attention in any ceremonial exchange are of a special kind. They are valuables, and they are to be distinguished from the commonplace commodities – such as foodstuffs and pots – that may well be exchanged through a more mundane system of barter at the same time.

There are two important concepts here. The first is what the American anthropologist George Dalton has termed *primitive valuables*: the tokens of wealth and prestige, often of specially valued materials (see box overleaf), used in the ceremonial exchanges of non-state societies. Examples include the shell necklaces and bracelets of the *kula* system, and pigs and pearl-shells, and, on the Northwest Coast of America in pre-European times, slaves and fur robes.

Exotic animals were often thought appropriate for royal gifts. Thus, the Near Eastern potentate Haroun al-Rashid presented Charlemagne, the 8th- to 9th-century AD ruler of much of north-central Europe, with an elephant, while a 13th-century Icelandic tale tells how the Icelander Authin presented the King of Denmark with a polar bear from Greenland. Traces of such gifts are sometimes recoverable – for example, the remains of falcons from Greenland have been found on several medieval sites in western Europe.

It should be noted, as Dalton remarks (1977), that "to acquire and disburse valuables in political or social transactions was usually the exclusive prerogative of leaders; or else the valuables were permissibly acquired by leaders in greater quantity or in superior quality than permissibly acquired by small men."

The second important concept is that of the *sphere of exchange*: valuables and ordinary commodities were exchanged quite separately. Valuables were exchanged against valuables in the prestige transactions already noted. Commodities were exchanged against commodities, with much less fuss, in mutually profitable barter transactions.

George Dalton has pointed out that ceremonial exchanges in non-state societies were of two different sorts. The first were ceremonial exchanges to establish and reinforce alliances, such as the *kula* system. The second were competitive exchanges, used to settle rivalries, in which the path to success was to outshine rivals in the richness of one's gifts and the conspicuous nature of public consumption. The potlatch, the ceremonial of the Northwest American Indians, was of this kind. These exchanges involved not only the making of conspicuous gifts of valuables, but also sometimes the actual destruction of valuables in a display of conspicuous wealth.

It is only through an awareness of the social roles that material goods can have, and of the way material exchange can either mask or represent a whole range of social relationships, that we can understand the significance of the exchange of goods. The study of early exchange thus offers many insights not only into the commerce, but also into the structure of early societies.

Nearly all cultures have valuables. Although some of these are useful (e.g. pigs in Melanesia, which can be eaten) most of them have no use at all, other than display. They are simply prestige objects.

Valuables tend to be in a limited range of materials to which a particular society ascribes a high value. For instance, in our own society gold is so highly valued as to be a standard against which all other values are measured. We tend to forget that this valuation is an entirely arbitrary one,

MATERIALS OF PRESTIGE VALUE

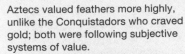

and we speak of gold's *intrinsic* value, as if in some way it were inherent. But gold is not a very useful material (although it is bright, and does not tarnish), nor is it the product of any special skills of the craftsperson. Intrinsic value is a misnomer: the

Aztecs valued feathers more highly, unlike the Conquistadors who craved gold; both were following subjective systems of value.

When we survey the range of materials to which different societies have ascribed intrinsic value we can see that many of them had the qualities of rarity, of durability, and of being visually conspicuous:

• The bright **feathers** favored by the Aztecs and by tribes of New Guinea fulfill two of these qualities.

• **Ivory:** elephant and walrus tusks have been valued since Upper Paleolithic times.

• **Shell**, especially of large marine molluscs, has been highly prized in many cultures for millennia.

• That very special organic material **amber** was valued in Upper Paleolithic times in northern Europe.

• **Jade** is a favored material in many cultures, from China to Mesoamerica, and was valued as long ago as 4000 BC in Neolithic Europe.

• Other naturally hard and **colorful stones** (e.g. rock crystal, lapis lazuli, obsidian, quartz, and onyx) have always been valued.

• **Gemstones** have taken on a special value in recent centuries, when the technique of cutting them to a faceted, light-catching shape was developed.

• **Gold** has perhaps pride of place (certainly in European eyes) among "intrinsically" valuable commodities, followed by **silver**.

• **Copper** and other metals have taken a comparable role: in North America copper objects had a special value.

• With the development of pyrotechnology (Chapter 8) artificial materials such as **faience** (glazed terracotta) and **glass** came into full prominence.

• The finest **textiles** and other clothing materials (e.g. *tapa* in Polynesia) have also always been highly valued, for prestige often means personal display.

Zapotec mask from Monte Albán, Mexico, made of jade, the eyes of shell.

Feathered headdress (above) of the Aztec emperor Motecuhzoma II (Moctezuma). (Above center) The Portland vase, a superb example of 1st-century AD Roman glassworking.

Woven silk robe (above) from the reign of the Chinese emperor Yung Cheng (1723–35), bearing the Imperial dragon.

Upper Paleolithic ivory female figurine (cast) from Lespugue, France (ht. 14.7 cm) (above). (Above center) Gold mask thought by Schliemann to represent King Agamemnon, from a shaft grave at Mycenae, late 16th century BC.

Prestige objects of North America's Mississippian culture (c. AD 900–1450). (Above) Embossed copper face, with typical forked eye motif. (Left) Shell pendant (c. 14 cm) from Texas, showing a panther and bird of prey.

DISCOVERING THE SOURCES OF TRADED GOODS: CHARACTERIZATION

Artifact forms can be imitated, or can resemble each other by chance. So it is not always safe to recognize an import in an archaeological context just because it resembles objects that are known to have been made elsewhere. Much more reliable evidence for trade can be provided if the raw material of which the object is made can be reliably shown to have originated elsewhere. Characterization refers to those techniques of examination by which characteristic properties of the constituent material may be identified, and so allow the source of that material to be determined. Some of the main methods for sourcing of materials by characterization (e.g. petrographic thin section) are described below.

For characterization to work, there must obviously be something about the source of the material that distinguishes its products from those of other sources. Of course, sometimes a material is so unusual and distinctive in itself that it can at once be recognized as deriving from a given source. That used to be thought to be the case with the attractive blue stone called lapis lazuli, for which, in the Old World, only one major source in Afghanistan was known. Now, however, other sources of lapis lazuli in the Indian subcontinent are known, so such claims must be treated with care.

In practice, there are very few materials for which the different sources can be distinguished by eye. Usually, it is necessary to use petrological, physical, or chemical techniques of analysis, which allow a much more precise description of the material. During the past 40 years there have been striking advances in the ability to analyze very small samples with accuracy. A successful characterization, however, does not just depend on analytical precision. The nature of the various sources for the material in question must also be considered carefully. If the sources are very different from each other in terms of the aspects being analyzed, that is fine. But if they are very similar, and so cannot be distinguished, then there is a real problem. For some materials (e.g. obsidian), the sources can be distinguished quite easily; for others (e.g. flint, or some metals), there are real difficulties in detecting consistent differences between sources.

Some materials are not well suited to characterization, because samples from different areas are difficult to distinguish. For example, organic remains, whether of plants or of animals, can present a problem. Of course, if a species is found far from its natural habitat – for instance, shells from the Red Sea in prehistoric

Europe – then we have evidence for trade. But when the species has a widespread distribution, there can be genuine difficulties. However, as we shall see below, even here there may be techniques available, such as oxygen or strontium isotope analysis, to resolve the matter.

An important point to note is that the sourcing of materials by characterization studies depends crucially on our knowledge of the distribution of the raw materials in nature. This derives mainly from the fieldwork of such specialists as geologists. For example, one might have a good series of thin sections cut from a whole range of stone axes, and many of these might be distinctive in the eyes of a petrologist. But this would not help the archaeologist unless one could match those particular kinds of rock with their specific occurrences in nature (i.e. the quarries). Thus, good geological mapping is a necessary basis for a sound sourcing study.

There are two further important points. One is the extent to which the raw material of which the artifact is made may have changed during burial: for instance, some soluble and therefore mobile elements in a clay pot may have leached out into the surrounding soil; or indeed they may leach from the soil into the pot; fortunately this problem is not too severe as it mainly affects poorly fired coarse wares.

A more crucial factor is the extent to which the raw material was changed during the production of the artifact. For objects of stone, this is not a problem. For pottery, one needs to consider the effect of refining the clay, and of adding various possible tempering materials. For metals, however, the problem is serious because there are many significant changes in composition from the ore to the metal artifact. During smelting (Chapter 8), a proportion of the more volatile impurities (e.g. arsenic or bismuth) will be lost. And in the Old World, from the later part of the Bronze Age onward, there is the problem of the reuse of scrap copper and bronze that could have come from more than one source.

Analytical Methods

Visual Examination. Just looking at the material is often the best way to start, whether we are dealing with pottery or a stone object. But while appearance makes an excellent starting-point – it always pays to make a preliminary separation by appearance – it can never be a reliable or authoritative guide.

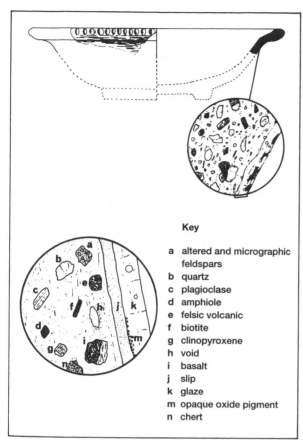

Key

a altered and micrographic feldspars
b quartz
c plagioclase
d amphiole
e felsic volcanic
f biotite
g clinopyroxene
h void
i basalt
j slip
k glaze
m opaque oxide pigment
n chert

Examination of pottery thin section under the microscope: inclusions in the fabric have been used to characterize medieval ceramics from the Yemen, such as this example.

Microscopic Examination of Thin Section. Since the middle of the 19th century techniques have existed for cutting a *thin section* of a sample taken from a stone object or a potsherd to determine the source of the material. It is made thin enough to transmit light and then, by means of petrological examination (studying the rock or mineral structure) with a light microscope, it is usually possible to recognize specific minerals that may be characteristic of a specific source. This part of the work has to be done by someone with petrological training.

This method has been applied to *stone* objects in different parts of the world – to building stones (e.g. the special colored stones used by the ancient Greeks and Romans), monuments (e.g. Olmec heads, Stonehenge), and portable artifacts, such as stone axes (e.g. in Australia, New Guinea, and in Britain). Indeed, the elucidation of the trade in stone axes in Neolithic times

in Britain, which started before 3000 BC, is one of the success stories of characterization studies. It is further discussed in the section on the study of distribution below (box p. 369).

Difficulties are encountered when the stones are insufficiently distinctive: for instance, different kinds of flint are usually difficult to characterize by thin section, and the white marble used for building or statues is so pure and homogeneous that it also does not give good results with this method (see also p. 366).

With *pottery*, the clay itself may be distinctive, but more often it is the inclusions – particles of minerals or rock fragments – that are characteristic. Sometimes the inclusions are naturally present in the clay. In other cases, the inclusions are deliberately added as temper to improve drying and firing qualities, and this can complicate characterization studies, since the pottery fabric may then consist of material from two or more separate sources. Fossil constituents, such as diatoms (Chapter 6) can also be an aid to identification of the source of the raw materials.

Studies of *grain sizes* in the clay itself have also proved useful. In much pottery, the only inclusions present are common minerals such as quartz sand, flint, and calcite/limestone/shell and these are of little help in identifying the sources. In such circumstances, study of the grain size of the quartz, etc. (but not the clay) has also proved useful. *Heavy mineral analysis* is a closely related petrological technique. For this, the body of the pottery sample is broken down using a chemical reagent, and the heavy mineral component (materials such as zircon and tourmaline) is separated from the lighter clay in a centrifuge. These constituent minerals can then be identified under the microscope. Those characteristic of a particular source area may help to identify the place of origin of the clay.

The picture of the prehistoric trade in pottery in Britain that such analyses have documented is quite surprising. Until the thin-section work of David Peacock and his associates it was simply not realized that pottery bowls and other vessels might be traded over quite long distances (of the order of 100 km (62 miles)) in Neolithic times, before 3000 BC. Now that we know the extent of this exchange of pottery, and that of stone axes discussed above, it is clear that many individuals and settlements were linked by quite far-flung exchange systems.

These characterization studies reveal clear evidence of widespread distribution of materials from their geological sources, but the interpretation of this evidence in human terms demands special techniques of spatial analysis and often the use of models based on ethnographic (or ethnoarchaeological) research.

ANALYSIS OF ARTIFACT COMPOSITION

A range of scientific techniques can be used in artifact characterization studies, but they differ in their possibilities, cost, and sample requirements. None of the methods listed below is universal. The archaeologist must carefully match objectives and requirements against the cost and potential of the different techniques. All accurate quantitative analytical methods require the use of standards, that is, specimens of known chemical composition. Some of the methods listed below can detect simultaneously most elements present in the sample and therefore give its qualitative or semi-quantitative composition without the necessity of standardization (XRF and NAA for example, though for quantitative results standards are needed); others (like AAS) need separate tests for each required element.

Modern analytical techniques use the physical properties of atoms for identification and quantification. The methods discussed are listed in groups relying on the same physical principles, but varying in the methods of excitation of the atom, or the detection of the information (energy or wavelength) obtained as a result of excitation.

Optical emission spectrometry (OES) is based on the principle that the outer electrons of the atoms of every chemical element, when excited (e.g. by heating to a high temperature), emit light of a particular wavelength (and hence color) when a sample is burned in a carbon arc. The light given off is composed of different wavelengths, which can be separated into a spectrum when passed through a prism or diffraction grating. The presence or absence of the various elements can be established by looking for the appropriate spectral line of their characteristic wavelengths. The results, expressed as percentages for the commoner elements and in parts per million (ppm) for trace elements, are read off and expressed in tabular form. Generally the method gives an accuracy of only about 25 percent. OES has been more-or-less superseded by **inductively coupled plasma atomic emission spectrometry (ICP-AES)**. This follows the same basic principles, but the sample in solution is atomized and excited in a stream of argon plasma rather than in a carbon arc. Very high temperatures can be reached, which reduces problems of interference between elements. It is suitable for analysis of major and trace elements in most inorganic materials. The sample size needed for elemental analysis is about 10 mg and accuracy is about ±5 percent. ICP-AES is not excessively expensive and a very high rate of sampling can be achieved.

More expensive, but also much more sensitive (many elements can be detected in concentrations in the parts per billion range) is another version of this method – **inductively coupled plasma mass spectrometry (ICP-MS)**. In ICP-MS the sample in solution is again atomized and ionized in a stream of argon plasma, but then the ions are injected into a mass spectrometer where they are divided into their isotopes which can be detected separately and counted, giving the concentration of the elements present.

Atomic absorption spectrometry (AAS) is based on a principle similar to OES – the measurement of energy in the form of visible light. The sample to be analyzed (between 10 mg and 1 g) is dissolved in acid, diluted, and then heated by spraying it onto a flame. Light of a wavelength which is absorbed by the element of interest – and only that element – is directed through the solution. The intensity of the emergent light beam, after it has passed through the solution, is measured with a photomultiplier. The concentration of the particular element is related to the intensity of the beam.

By using different wavelengths of light over 40 elements can be measured, with an accuracy of ±1 percent for major elements and ±15 percent for trace elements. The method has the disadvantage of being slow and it is also destructive. It does, however, have a particular advantage over other methods in detecting metals such as lithium and sodium which have low atomic numbers. AAS has been used archaeologically for analysis of non-ferrous metals (e.g. copper and bronze), flint artifacts, and other materials.

X-ray fluorescence analysis (XRF) is based on the excitation of the inner electrons of the atom. The sample is irradiated with a beam of X-rays which excite electrons in the inner shells (K, L, and M) of all atoms present in the surface layer of a sample. The X-rays bombarding the sample cause the electrons to move up to a higher shell. They instantly revert, however, to their initial positions, and in the process emit specific amounts of energy equal to the difference in energy between the appropriate inner electron shells of the atoms of each element present in the sample (they are called characteristic X-rays). These fluorescent X-ray energies can be measured and their values compared with figures known for each element. In this way the elements present in the sample can be identified. The energy of electromagnetic radiation is directly related to its wavelength. There are two methods of measuring the energy of the characteristic X-rays: the wavelength dispersive XRF method and the energy dispersive XRF method (sometimes also called non-dispersive). The first technique (WD XRF) relies on a measurement of the wavelengths of the X-rays by diffracting them in a crystal of known parameters; the second (ED XRF) relies on the direct measurement of X-ray energy using a semi-conductor detector. In both methods the intensity of the radiation is also measured and can be used to quantify the amount of an element in the sample by comparing the unknown sample with standards.

The measurement geometry of the WD XRF instruments usually requires that the sample is in the form of a pressed powder or glass pellet, and so for many archaeological artifacts this method is not suitable. In contrast, the ED XRF instruments can be constructed in such a way that it is possible to analyze a small area (as small as 1 mm in diameter) on the surface of an object of any size and shape. Also, it is possible to make quantitative and qualitative analyses of small samples taken either from the surface or the interior of the artifact. The effective depth of the XRF analysis is in the range of a millimeter for light materials like glass and pottery, but decreases dramatically for metals. For the analysis of metal artifacts it is advisable either to clean the surface or to take a drilled sample of the unaltered metal from the interior. Detection and measurement of elements present in concentrations below 0.1 percent can be problematic. The accuracy of this technique depends on many factors: it can be as good as 2 percent, but 5–10 percent is more usual. ED XRF is ideal for identifying types of alloys and major components of the fabric of pottery, faience, glass, and glazes, as well as pigments used to color them. There is no need for specific sample preparation for ED XRF (except surface cleaning) and the analysis takes only a few minutes.

Electron probe microanalysis (or **scanning electron microprobe analysis – SEM**) is based on the same physical principle as XRF, but the excitation of the electrons in the atoms is achieved by focusing an energetic beam of electrons from an "electron gun" on to the surface of the sample in a vacuum. The samples for quantitative SEM have to be specially prepared either as thin polished sections or as perfectly flat, carbon- or gold-coated, mounted specimens. The beam can be focused to a spot of a size below 1000th of a millimeter and different layers of a sample (e.g. glaze, underglaze, fabric of

a pot) can be analyzed separately, or the chemical composition of inclusions in the material can be identified one by one. Scanning electron microscopes are present in many archaeological laboratories and this method has been in the last decade a basic tool for the study of metal and ceramic technology.

Proton-induced X-ray emission (PIXE) is a further method based on the emission of characteristic X-rays. PIXE relies on their excitation using a beam of protons from a particle accelerator. The range of analytical possibilities is similar to that of SEM, but PIXE is much better for analyses of very small areas of light materials like layers of pigments, or paper and the soldering of alloys in making jewelry. This method is very good at producing "maps" of elemental concentrations in the samples on the sub-micron scale. PIXE belongs to a group of methods known as **ion beam analysis** (IBA). The same facility (based on an accelerator producing a high energy beam of protons) can be used for analysis based on **particle induced gamma-ray emission (PIGME** or **PIGE)** and **Rutherford backscattering (RBS)**. PIGE relies on excitation of the nucleus rather than the electrons in atomic shells, and on measuring gamma-rays emitted as the nuclei return to their ground-state (unexcited) levels. PIGE is used mostly for the analysis of light elements (below sodium) and employed together with PIXE can provide analysis over the entire periodic table. The facility at the Lucas Heights, Australia, was used for analysis of obsidian artifacts adopting this approach. RBS is based on the recoil of particles in the beam from the nuclei of the atoms in the sample and can be used for major element characterization of the composition of the material (including carbon, oxygen, and nitrogen) and measurement of thickness of layers and diffusion profiles without the necessity of preparing cross-sectional profiles.

There are some laboratories in Europe and North America where PIXE is routinely used for analyses in art and archaeology, notably the facility AGLAE

in the Louvre, Paris. The IBA facility in Oxford has been used for projects using simultaneous PIXE/ PIGME/RBS for the non-destructive analysis of, for example, gemstones (the Ashmolean "Alexander gem"), gilded metal artifacts, and glazed ceramics.

Neutron activation analysis (NAA) – depends on the transmutation of the nuclei of the atoms of a sample's various elements by bombarding them with slow (thermal) neutrons. This process leads to the production of radioactive isotopes of most of the elements present in the sample. The radioactive isotopes, which have characteristic half-lives, decay into stable ones by emitting radiation, often gamma radiation. The energies of these gamma rays are characteristic of the radioactive isotopes, and are measured to identify the elements present. The intensity of radiation of a given energy can be compared with that emitted by a standard which was irradiated together with the sample; hence the quantity of the element in the sample can be calculated. Nuclear reactors are the most efficient source of thermal neutrons, but to some extent other sources of neutrons can also be used for NAA. It is usual to analyze samples of 10–50 mg in the form of powder or drillings, but in the past whole artifacts (mostly coins) were irradiated to provide information about total composition. Unfortunately, all samples and artifacts remain radioactive for many years. Some elements, such as lead and bismuth, cannot be analyzed by NAA, because the isotopes produced by their interaction with thermal neutrons are too long- or short-lived or do not emit detectable gamma rays.

Until recently NAA was the most frequently used method of analysis for trace elements in pottery and metal. It is accurate to about ±5 percent, it can measure concentrations ranging from 0.1ppm to 100 percent, and it can be automated. Because it involves the use of a nuclear reactor it can be used only in certain laboratories, which are becoming rarer as research reactors are being closed down.

Trace-Element Analysis. The basic composition of many materials is very consistent. Obsidian, a volcanic glass used in the manufacture of chipped stone tools in the same manner as flint, is a good example of this. The concentration of the main elements of which obsidian is formed (silicon, oxygen, calcium, etc.) is broadly similar whatever the source of the material. However, the *trace elements* (elements present only in very small quantities, measured in just a few parts per million) do vary according to the source, and there are several useful methods for measuring their concentration.

Optical emission spectrometry, or OES (see box, previous pages), was the first of such methods to be applied to archaeological material. The Austrian archaeologist R. Pittioni and his scientific collaborators used it in the late 1930s in pioneering studies on early metallurgy in the Alpine region. In the 1950s and 1960s, it was used in further studies on early European metallurgy, in the study of faience beads in early Europe, and for the characterization of obsidian. It has now largely been replaced by inductively coupled plasma emission spectrometry (ICPS), as well as by atomic absorption spectrometry (see below).

Neutron activation analysis, or NAA (see box, previous pages), was developed later and came into widespread use in the 1970s. It has been widely used for obsidian, pottery, metals, and other materials. It is particularly useful for coins and other small objects, because it is entirely non-destructive.

Other methods for trace-element analysis include *atomic absorption spectrometry* (AAS), *X-ray fluorescence spectrometry* (XRF), and *PIXE* and *PIGME* (see box, previous pages). The PIXE and PIGME method has recently been automated, and applied to obsidian from the Admiralty Islands in the Pacific, indicating a trade from the Bismarck Archipelago to Vanuatu (for-

Archaeological Material	Means of Characterization	Analytical Techniques
Pottery	Major and trace elemental composition, mineral inclusions distribution patterns	SEM, NAA, AAS, XRF, ICPS/MS, thin section petrology, PIXE&PIGME&RBS
Homogeneous/glassy stone (inc. obsidian and flint)	Major and trace elemental strontium isotope composition	SEM, NAA, AAS, XRF, ICPS/MS, PIXE&PIGME&RBS, TIMS
Gemstones	Major and trace elemental composition, distribution pattern of elements	SEM, NAA, AAS, XRF, ICPS/MS, PIXE&PIGME&RBS
Stone with mineral and biological inclusions	Identification and characterization of inclusions, major and trace elemental composition	Optical microscopy, thin section petrology, SEM, NAA, AAS, XRF, ICPS/MS, PIXE&PIGME&RBS
Marble	Major and trace elemental, oxygen, carbon, and strontium isotope composition	ICPS/MS, NAA, PIXE&PIGME&RBS, Gas MS, TIMS
Marine shell	Oxygen, carbon, and strontium isotope, trace elemental composition	Gas MS, PIXE, NAA, ICP MS, TIMS
Amber	Identification and quantification of organic compounds	Infrared absorption spectroscopy, gas chromatography (GC/MS)
All metals and alloys	Major and trace element, lead isotope composition	SEM, NAA, AAS, XRF, ICPS/MS, PIXE&RBS, TIMS, ICP-MMS
Metal slags	Identification of inclusions, major and trace elements, lead isotope composition	SEM, NAA, AAS, XRF, ICPS/MS, PIXE&RBS, TIMS, ICP-MMS
Ore minerals and pigments	Identification of minerals, major and trace element, lead isotope composition	X-ray diffraction, SEM, NAA, AAS, XRF, ICPS/MS, PIXE&RBS, TIMS, ICP-MMS
Glasses and glazes	Major and trace element, lead (if present) isotope composition	SEM, NAA, AAS, XRF, ICPS/MS, PIXE&RBS, TIMS, ICP-MMS
Pottery decoration	Identification of minerals and technology	X-ray diffraction, Mössbauer spectroscopy, XRF, PIXE&PIGME&RBS

Table summarizing the most appropriate characterization methods for various archaeological materials.

merly the New Hebrides), a distance of 3000 km (1860 miles), over 3000 years ago. Similarly the XRF method has recently demonstrated that finds of Rouletted Ware (first identified at Arikamedu in India by Sir Mortimer Wheeler) from the Indonesian island of Bali share the same geological source as examples found in Sri Lanka and southern India, suggesting the presence of substantial trade networks linking the two areas by the 1st century AD.

These various methods simply produce a table giving the analyses, usually expressed in parts per million (ppm), for each artifact or sample, taking each element in turn. Some of the chemical elements are well-known ones, such as lead or tin, others are less common, such as vanadium or scandium. The problem then arises as to how to interpret them. Obviously, the aim is to match the compositions of the artifacts under examination with those of specific sources. But that can present problems. In the case of pottery, potters' clays are common, so there is little chance of matching specific pots with specific clay beds. Different sources can have similar compositions, thus giving misleading results. For this reason, the trace-element analysis of pottery, or indeed of metal, is not necessarily the best procedure for characterization. In the case of pottery, petrological methods (see above) can be more satisfactory. However, trace-element analysis is more effective than petrology for distinguishing between clay sources near, and therefore similar petrologically, to one another, provided that as many trace elements as possible are considered. (Certainly, if sources are different petrologically it would be most unusual for them to be similar in terms of trace-element analysis.)

In general, rather than considering each sample in turn, with all its constituent elements, it is more satisfactory to group samples according to the concentration of just two or three elements in them. When samples are available from the sources, and the number of sources is limited (as with obsidian), clear results can emerge.

The trace-element analysis of obsidian from sources in Anatolia during the Neolithic period, undertaken by a British team, is a good example. It is described in more detail in the section on the Study of Distribution below. Several methods were employed including NAA, XRF, OES, and fission-track analysis. The results allowed the grouping of samples from the various sources and of artifacts from different excavations.

For any chemical analysis, it is essential to have an interpretive strategy, and to understand the logic underlying the arguments. One of the least successful characterization projects of recent years involved the analysis (by OES) of thousands of copper and bronze objects from the Early Bronze Age of Europe. These were classed into groups on the basis of their composition, without recognizing clearly that very different source areas might produce copper with similar trace-element composition and, furthermore, that changes in the concentration of trace elements had occurred during smelting. From the standpoint of sourcing, the groups were more or less meaningless. The isotopic methods described below have proved much more effective for metal characterization.

Isotopic Analysis. All chemical elements consist of atoms specific for a given element. The mass of an atom is defined by the number of protons and neutrons in the

Element	Isotopes	Archaeological Materials	Information
O – oxygen	^{16}O, ^{17}O, ^{18}O	Bone Marble, shells	Diet Provenience
N – nitrogen	^{14}N, ^{15}N	Bone Ivory	Diet Provenience
C – carbon	^{12}C, ^{13}C	Bone Marble, shells	Diet Provenience
	^{14}C – radioactive	Wood, plants, seeds, charcoal, bone, teeth, shells (pottery, linen fabric)	Dating
Sr – strontium	^{88}Sr, ^{86}Sr, ^{84}Sr ^{87}Sr – radiogenic	Stone (gypsum, marble, obsidian) Bone (ivory)	Provenience
Pb – lead	^{208}Pb, ^{207}Pb, ^{206}Pb – all three radiogenic ^{204}Pb	Ore minerals, pigments in glass, glaze and lead-based paint, metals (silver, copper, lead, and iron)	Provenience
Nd – neodymium	^{142}Nd, ^{143}Nd, ^{144}Nd, ^{145}Nd, ^{146}Nd, ^{148}Nd, ^{150}Nd ^{143}Nd – radiogenic	Rocks, minerals, pottery?, ivory?, marble?	Provenience
U – uranium	^{238}U, ^{235}U, ^{234}U	Calcite materials (speleothems), bone, corals, foraminifera	Dating
Th – thorium	^{232}Th, ^{230}Th	Calcite materials, bone, corals, foraminifera	Dating

Table of isotopes of various elements that are useful in archaeological research.

nucleus. The chemical identity of an element depends on the number of protons in the nucleus, but the number of neutrons can vary. Atoms of the same element, but of different masses (different number of neutrons in the nucleus) are called isotopes. Most elements occurring in nature consist of a number of isotopes. For the great majority of elements the relative proportion of their isotopes (the isotopic composition) is fixed. However, there is a group of elements which due to chemical or biochemical processes are of variable natural isotopic composition (nitrogen, sulphur, oxygen, and carbon). Another group is formed by elements which contain stable (that is non-radioactive) but radiogenic isotopes, formed in part due to radioactive decay of another element (lead, neodymium, and strontium). All isotopic compositions are measured by mass spectrometry. (See table, p. 363, and Chapter 4 for isotopes of carbon, and also some other elements.) The isotopic composition of light elements listed in the first four rows of the table p. 363 can be measured using Gas Source Mass Spectrometers (a ^{14}C accelerator is also a kind of mass spectrometer).

The isotopic compositions of all elements above calcium (mass 20) can in principle be measured by Thermal Ionization Mass Spectrometry (TIMS). The isotope compositions are measured as isotopic ratios and these ratios are used as unique parameters for the isotopic characterization of the samples. High accuracy measurements are necessary for sensitive differentiation. The introduction of multicollector TIMS machines in the late 1980s allows very high accuracy of the TIMS measurements of lead isotopes (overall error less than 0.1 percent). All TIMS measurements are standardized against Pb isotope standard and there are no problems with inter-laboratory comparisons. However, only a small number of elements can be ionized thermally with good efficiency: for example, lead, strontium, and neodymium are very well suited for TIMS, while tin and copper isotopes can be measured by this technique only with difficulty. A recently developed instrument for isotope measurements consists of a plasma source and a multicollector mass spectrometer (ICP-MMS). There are only a few of these machines working at present, but they have the capability for much faster and more accurate isotopic analysis of all elements, combined with far less time-consuming sample preparation procedures. The much more widely available ICP-MS instruments with a quadrupole magnet do not give sufficiently high accuracy of measurements of isotopic ratios for provenance studies.

Isotope geochemistry is now frequently used to investigate metal sources. Analysis of the lead isotopes in metal artifacts and their relation to ore bodies

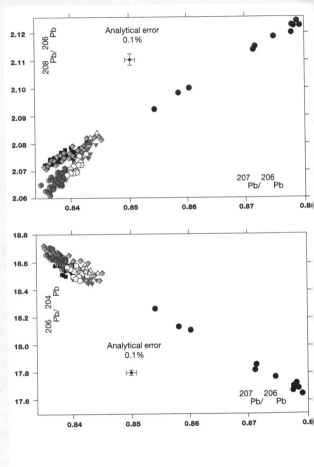

LEAD ISOTOPE ANALYSIS

■ Larnaca ores
△ Limni ores
◇ Limassol Forest ores
▼ Solea ores (includes Apliki)
○ Oxhide ingots found in Cyprus
● Oxhide ingots from Haghia Triadha
◑ Oxhide ingots from Uluburun

Lead isotope compositions of Cypriot copper ores from different regions and oxhide ingots from Cyprus, the Uluburun shipwreck and the Minoan palace of Haghia Triadha, Crete. The diagrams show that the Cretan ingots could not have been made from the copper from any of the known Cypriot sources.

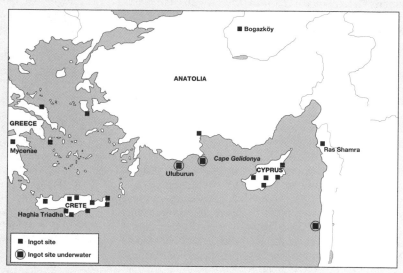

Map showing *finds of copper ingots in the eastern Mediterranean.*

The great majority of the chemical elements occurring in nature have fixed isotopic compositions. There are some, however, whose isotopic composition differs, reflecting the geochemical or biological history of raw materials. One such element is lead which has four isotopes: ^{204}Pb, ^{206}Pb, ^{207}Pb, and ^{208}Pb. The three last isotopes owe their formation in part to the radioactive decay of uranium and thorium, and so the isotopic composition of ore deposits depends on the age of their formation, the initial amount of uranium and thorium, and the subsequent history of the ore deposit. Different lead, silver, and copper sources yield ores containing different proportions of the isotopes of lead. A large analytical program of lead isotope analyses at Oxford of numerous ores from deposits in the British Isles, the Mediterranean, and the Balkans has resulted in a substantial database (published in consecutive issues of *Archaeometry* 1995–8). This shows that ores from these regions have strictly limited and often different lead isotope ratios for each geographic region.

Any metals smelted from these ores retain their isotopic composition unaltered. Thus, in a given region, provided that one has located the main sources of these minerals, and identified their distinctive lead isotope ratios, it is possible to demonstrate that, say, a particular ancient metal artifact or pigment originated from a specific source in this region. Conversely, it can be proved that artifacts excavated on certain sites were made of raw materials not originating from the local sources.

Neither smelting of copper and lead, nor fire refining, nor silver production by cupellation, alters the isotopic composition of lead in the resulting metal. However, errors of interpretation might arise if objects were made of scrap metal originating from several ore sources. Also, some ore deposits, geographically distant or quite close, can have very similar lead isotope compositions and therefore the method is at its best when the isotope characterization of the ore source is based on multiple measurements of different sample ores from each mine, so that statistical evaluation of the data can be applied.

Metal Sources in the Mediterranean
Lead isotope analysis has been extensively applied to the characterization of metal sources in the Mediterranean. Coins of the Classical period made with silver from the mines of Laurion in Attica, Greece, can easily be distinguished from those made of silver from the island of Siphnos or other sources.

Hundreds of Bronze Age metal artifacts from the Aegean have been analyzed in order to discover the main sources of metals used at that time and their movement in this region. This method has been applied by the Oxford-based scientists Noel Gale and Zofia Stos-Gale to the Late Bronze Age copper ingots of the "oxhide" shape from Cyprus and Crete.

Their work has shown that a large group of post-1250 BC oxhide ingots found in regions geographically far apart (e.g. Central Anatolia, Cyprus, Italy) have unique lead isotopic characteristics identical with ore from one Cypriot mining area of Apliki in the Solea region (northern Troodos). However, they argue that a group of ingots found in the Late Minoan I palace of Haghia Triadha, very similar in appearance and metal composition but from a context some 300 years earlier, could not have been made from Cypriot copper (see diagrams: left), and the origin of their copper remains unknown. (Their copper isotope ratios are significantly different from the ingots consistent with an origin from the Apliki mine.)

The cargo of over 350 oxhide ingots carried on the Uluburun shipwreck (see p. 374–75) also appears to have a different origin. Their lead isotope ratios show consistency with copper ores mined in one location which the Gales suggest is most likely a mine neighboring Apliki in Cyprus. This particular lead isotope composition is very rare among many hundreds of other Late Bronze Age artifacts from the Mediterranean, suggesting that this particular mine was not commonly used and that the Uluburun ingots were the main products from it which have come to light.

exploited in antiquity has become an important characterization technique. The four lead isotopes (giving three independent isotope ratios), together with precise methods of analysis and a reasonable range of variation, afford rather good discrimination between different metal sources. The method relies very much on comparisons between the lead isotope characteristics of different ore deposits and their products and so the construction of an "isotope map" of the relevant ore sources, after systematic sampling, is very important. Ambiguities of interpretation occasionally arise as sometimes lead isotope ratios define more than one possible source, but usually these can be resolved by consideration of relevant trace element data.

Lead isotope analysis is of direct use not only for lead artifacts, but also for those of silver, in which lead is usually present as an impurity. Copper sources also contain at least a trace of lead, and it has been shown by experimentation that a large proportion of that lead passes into the copper metal produced during smelting. Here, then, is a characterization method applicable to lead, silver, and copper artifacts. It has been used successfully for the determination of mineral sources of Classical and medieval silver coins, Bronze Age copper and bronze tools, lead weights, as well as lead in pigments of glasses and glazes, and lead-based white paint. The sample of an artifact needed for Thermal Ionization Mass Spectrometry (TIMS) of lead varies from under 1 milligram to about 50 mg, depending on the concentration of lead in the material.

Strontium isotope ratios have been used in the characterization of obsidian artifacts and gypsum and can provide a simple method of distinguishing between marine and elephant ivory. Carbon and oxygen isotopes are widely used in sourcing marble. For a long time, the sourcing of marble had proved very difficult: it was well known that in the Mediterranean in the Classical period, good-quality white marbles were widely exported for sculpture or for building purposes Many of the most important quarries (e.g. on Mount Pendeli and Mount Hymettos near Athens, and on the Aegean islands of Paros and Naxos) had been identified. But attempts at matching the quarry source to a particular building or sculpture using either appearance or petrological methods (for instance, heavy mineral and trace-element analyses) were disappointing.

Analyses using two oxygen isotopes ($^{18}O/^{16}O$) and two carbon isotopes ($^{13}C/^{12}C$) can discriminate between several quarries, albeit with a certain degree of overlap. It is becoming increasingly clear that full characterization of marble sources will require the combined data from three analytical techniques: stable isotope studies, trace-element analysis, and cathodoluminescence.

Oxygen isotope ratios have also proved useful for the characterization of marine shell. As mentioned above, the shell of *Spondylus gaederopus* was widely traded in the form of bracelets and decorations during the Neolithic in southeast Europe. The question at issue was whether it came from the Aegean, or possibly from the Black Sea. As discussed in the section on deep-sea cores in Chapter 4, the oxygen isotopic composition of marine shell is dependent on the temperature of the sea where the organism lives. The Black Sea is much colder than the Mediterranean, and analysis confirmed that the shells in question came from the Aegean.

Other Analytical Methods. Many other analytical methods have been employed for characterization purposes.

X-ray diffraction analysis, used in determining the crystalline structure of minerals, from the angle at which X-rays are reflected, has proved helpful in defining the composition of Neolithic jade and jadeite axes that have been found at several British sites: it seems that the stone may have come from as far away as the Alps. It has also been used extensively in the characterization of pottery.

Infrared absorption spectroscopy has proved the most appropriate method for distinguishing between ambers from different sources: the organic compounds in the amber absorb different wavelengths of infrared radiation passed through them.

Cathodoluminescence segregates white marbles on the basis of colored luminescence emitted after electron bombardment. Calcitic marbles can be divided into two groups: one with an orange luminescence and one with a blue. Dolomitic marbles show a red luminescence. The different colors are caused by impurities or lattice defects within the crystals.

Mössbauer spectroscopy is used in the study of iron compounds, notably in pottery. It involves measuring the gamma radiation absorbed by the iron nuclei, which gives information about the particular iron compounds in the pottery sample and on the conditions of firing when the pottery was made. This was the analytical technique used in the characterization of mirrors made out of different kinds of iron ore (magnetite, ilmenite, and hematite) and widely traded in the Formative period in Oaxaca in Mesoamerica (see p. 378).

Fission-track analysis is mainly a dating method (Chapter 4), but has also been used to distinguish between obsidians from different sources, on the basis of their uranium content and the date of formation of the deposits.

Other dating methods have also been used to discriminate between geological materials of similar composition but different age.

Laser fusion argon-argon dating was successful in showing that a rhyolitic tuff used for making an axe, a fragment of which was found near Stonehenge, came originally from a volcanic source of Lower Carboniferous date in Scotland, not from older formations in South Wales, as had originally been thought. In Japan ESR has been used to differentiate between jasper implements of different sources.

These various analytical methods described enable archaeologists in many cases to identify the sources of the raw materials used in the manufacture of particular artifacts with some precision. How the subsequent movements of these artifacts are to be interpreted in terms of exchange presents a series of other, equally interesting problems, which we shall discuss in the next section.

THE STUDY OF DISTRIBUTION

The study of the traded goods themselves, and the identification of their sources by means of characterization, are the most important procedures in the investigation of exchange. As we shall see below, the investigation of production methods in the source area can also be informative, and so can a consideration of consumption, which completes the story. But it is the study of distribution, or goods on the move, that allows us to get to the heart of the matter.

In the absence of written records it is not easy to determine what were the mechanisms of distribution, or what was the nature of the exchange relationship. However, where such records exist, they can be most informative. The Minoan Linear B tablets from the palace at Knossos in Crete and from Pylos in Mycenaean Greece give a clear picture of the palace economy. They show inventories of material coming in to the palace, and they record outgoings, indicating the existence of a redistributive system. Comparable records of account from centrally administered societies have offered similar insights – for instance, in the Near East. This precise sort of information is, of course, rarely available. Most of what the tablets record relates to internal trade – the production and distribution of goods within the society. But some Egyptian and Near Eastern records, notably in the archive dating to the 15th century BC found at Tell el-Amarna in Egypt, talk of gifts between the pharaoh and other Near Eastern potentates: this was gift exchange between the rulers of early state societies. Examples of such princely gifts survive: one of the treasures of Vienna is the ceremonial headdress of feathers given by the Aztec ruler Motecuhzoma II (Moctezuma) to Cortés as a gift for the King of Spain at the time of the Spanish Conquest of Mexico in the 16th century AD (see box, pp. 356–57).

Earlier evidence from preliterate societies – societies without written records – can, however, give some clear idea of ownership and of the managed distribution of goods. For example, clay sealings, used to stopper jars, to secure boxes, and to seal the doors of storehouses, and distinguished by the impression of a carved seal, are widely found in the preliterate phases in the Near East, and in the Aegean Bronze Age. In the past, these sealstones and their impressions have been studied more for their artistic content than for the light that they might throw on exchange mechanisms. However, if looked for, information about exchange is there, although, once again, it relates mainly to internal exchange. The impressions are only occasionally found at any great distance from their place of origin.

In some cases, however, the traded goods themselves were marked by their owner or producer. For instance, the potters who produced storage containers for liquids (amphorae) in Roman times used to stamp their name on the rim. The map below shows the distribution of amphorae bearing the stamp of the potter Sestius, whose kilns, although not yet located, were probably in the Cosa area of Italy. The general pattern of the export of oil or wine or whatever the amphorae

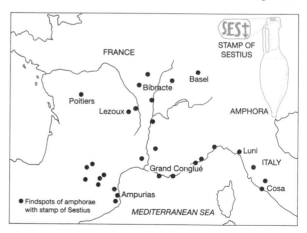

A distribution study. Roman storage containers (amphorae) bearing the stamp of the potter Sestius have been found in northern Italy and widely throughout central and southern France. They and their contents (no doubt wine) were probably made on an estate near Cosa. The distribution map thus indicates the general pattern of the export from the Cosa area of this commodity.

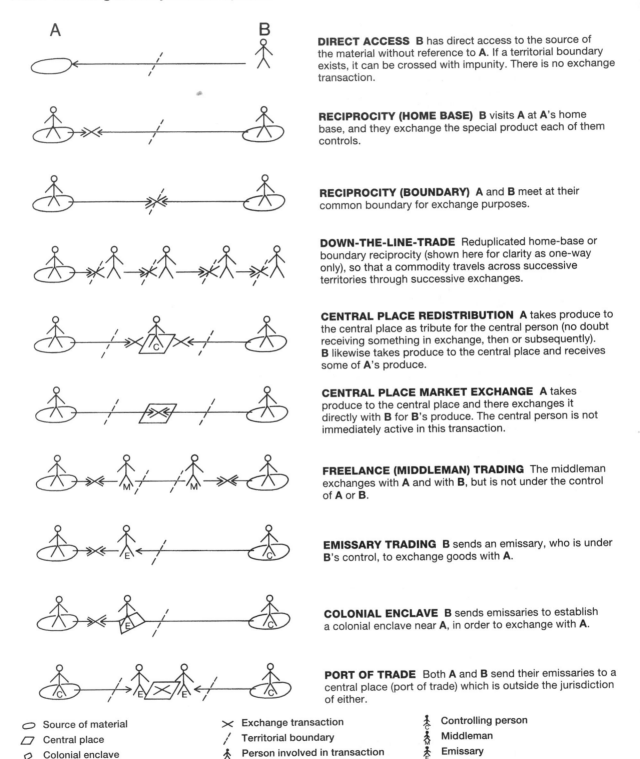

A   **B**

DIRECT ACCESS B has direct access to the source of the material without reference to **A**. If a territorial boundary exists, it can be crossed with impunity. There is no exchange transaction.

RECIPROCITY (HOME BASE) B visits **A** at **A**'s home base, and they exchange the special product each of them controls.

RECIPROCITY (BOUNDARY) A and **B** meet at their common boundary for exchange purposes.

DOWN-THE-LINE-TRADE Reduplicated home-base or boundary reciprocity (shown here for clarity as one-way only), so that a commodity travels across successive territories through successive exchanges.

CENTRAL PLACE REDISTRIBUTION A takes produce to the central place as tribute for the central person (no doubt receiving something in exchange, then or subsequently). **B** likewise takes produce to the central place and receives some of **A**'s produce.

CENTRAL PLACE MARKET EXCHANGE A takes produce to the central place and there exchanges it directly with **B** for **B**'s produce. The central person is not immediately active in this transaction.

FREELANCE (MIDDLEMAN) TRADING The middleman exchanges with **A** and with **B**, but is not under the control of **A** or **B**.

EMISSARY TRADING B sends an emissary, who is under **B**'s control, to exchange goods with **A**.

COLONIAL ENCLAVE B sends emissaries to establish a colonial enclave near **A**, in order to exchange with **A**.

PORT OF TRADE Both **A** and **B** send their emissaries to a central place (port of trade) which is outside the jurisdiction of either.

⬯ Source of material	✕ Exchange transaction	🚶 Controlling person
⬭ Central place	∕ Territorial boundary	🚶 Middleman
⬠ Colonial enclave	🚶 Person involved in transaction	🚶 Emissary

TREND SURFACE ANALYSIS

The aim of trend surface analysis is to highlight the main features of a distribution by smoothing over some of the local irregularities. In this way the important trends can be isolated from the background "noise" more clearly.

The first step is to divide the map into small, uniform areas or "cells." The number of finds within each cell is then noted. The patterning can be smoothed to reduce local irregularities by using not the actual figure of finds per cell but an average calculated from

finds for each individual cell plus all its neighbors. In this way a moving average is produced from which a contour map may be drawn.

The example here shows the distribution density in Britain of so-called Group VI Neolithic stone axes, all of which came ultimately from the Langdale axe factories in northern England. This source was established for each axe by the petrological analysis of thin sections. But to display the distribution in this form may not reveal the mechanism underlying it. Grahame Clark suggested that gift exchange was involved for the British Neolithic axes, analogous to that among the Aborigines in Australia (see box, p. 376).

In a full trend surface analysis the principal trends would be defined by mathematics. This would allow the deviations from the trends (known as residuals) to be isolated and quantified.

Langdale axe.

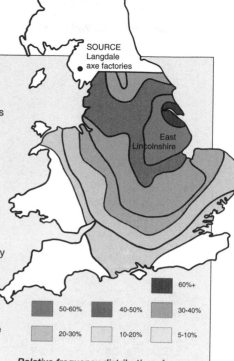

60%+	
50-60%	40-50%	30-40%
20-30%	10-20%	5-10%

Relative frequency distribution of findspots of Group VI Neolithic axes, deriving ultimately from the Langdale axe factories. Out of some 500 axes, well over 50 percent were found in East Lincolnshire.

---

contained (a question that can be decided by analysis of residues in the amphorae: see Chapter 7) can be made clear by the production of a distribution map. But a distribution map must be interpreted if we are to understand the processes that lay behind it, and at this point it is useful to distinguish again between reciprocity, redistribution, and market exchange, and to consider how the spatial distribution of finds may depend on the exchange mechanism.

"Direct access" refers to the situation where the user goes directly to the source of the material, without the intervention of any exchange mechanism. "Down-the-line" exchange refers to repeated exchanges of a reciprocal nature, and is further discussed below. "Freelance (middleman)" trading refers to the activities of traders who operate independently, and for gain: usually the traders work by bargaining (as in market exchange) but instead of a fixed marketplace they are travelers who take the goods to the consumer. "Emissary" trading refers to the situation where the "trader" is a representative of a central organization based in the home country.

Not all of these types of transaction can be expected to leave clear and unequivocal indications in the

archaeological record, although, as we shall see, down-the-line trading apparently does. And a former port of trade ought to be recognizable if the materials found there come from a wide range of sources, and it is clear that the site was not pre-eminent as an administrative center, but specialized in trading activities.

Spatial Analysis of Distribution

Several formal techniques are available for the study of distribution. The first and most obvious technique is naturally that of plotting the distribution map for finds, as in the case of the stamped Roman amphorae mentioned above. Quantitative studies of distributions are also helpful; the size of the dot or some other feature can be used as a simple device to indicate the number of finds on the map. This kind of map can give a good indication of important centers of consumption and of redistribution. The distribution of finds on the map can be further investigated by the technique of trend surface analysis (see box above) to obtain valuable insights into the structure of the data.

Direct use of distribution maps, even when aided by quantitative plotting, may not, however, be the best

FALL-OFF ANALYSIS

The quantity of a traded material usually declines as the distance from the source increases. This is not surprising, because one would expect abundance to decrease with distance. But in some cases there are regularities in the way in which the decrease occurs, and this pattern can inform us about the *mechanism* by which a material reached its destination.

The now-standard way to investigate this is to plot a fall-off curve, in which the quantities of material (on the *y* axis) are plotted against distance from source (on the *x* axis). The first question is precisely what to measure. Simply plotting the number of finds at a site does not take into account the different conditions of preservation and recovery. Some kind of *proportional* method, measuring one class of find against another, can overcome this difficulty. For example, the percentage of obsidian in a total chipped stone industry is a convenient parameter to measure (although it is affected by the availability of other lithic materials).

In the study of Anatolian obsidian discussed in the main text, a plot of the quantity (i.e. percentage) on a *logarithmic scale* against distance (on an ordinary linear scale) produced a fall-off that followed an approximately straight line. That is the equivalent of a fall-off declining exponentially with distance, and it can be shown mathematically to be the equivalent of a "down-the-line" exchange mechanism, explained in the main text. A different exchange mechanism – for example involving central place redistribution – will produce a different fall-off curve (see main text).

Various interesting results come from fall-off analysis. For instance, when a plot was done of the decrease in quantity with distance of Roman pottery made at kilns in the Oxford region in Britain, and when sites that could be reached by water transport were distinguished from those that could not, a clear distinction was visible. Evidently, water transport was a much more efficient distribution method than land transport for this commodity.

In principle, the fact that different models for the mechanism of distribution give different fall-off curves should allow an accurate plotting of the data to reveal which mechanism of distribution was operating. But there are two difficulties. The first is that the quality of the data does not always allow one to decide reliably which fall-off curve is the appropriate one. And the more serious difficulty is that, in some cases, different models for distribution produce the same curve.

Fall-off analysis can be very informative, but these two limitations restrict its usefulness.

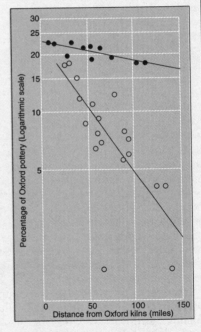

The fall-off in Oxford pottery with increasing distance from the Oxford kilns during the Roman period. Sites with good access to the kilns by water (filled circles) show a much less steep fall-off gradient than those without such easy access, indicating the importance of water transport as a method of distribution at this time.

Distribution map showing the location of sites where Roman pottery from the Oxford kilns has been found.

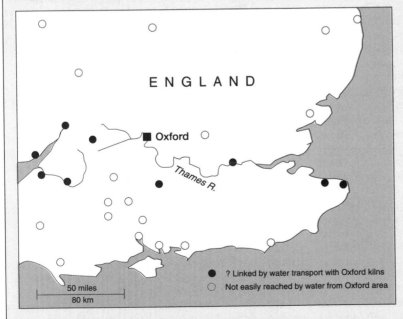

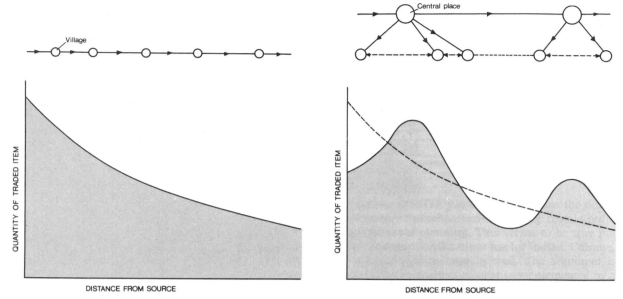

Relationship between settlement organization, type of exchange, and supply, for a commodity traded on land. (Left) Village settlement served by down-the-line exchange (on a basis of reciprocity) leads, in the archaeological record, to an exponential fall-off in abundance. (Right) Central place settlement with directional exchange between centers (and with either redistribution or central market exchange at local regional level) leads to a multi-modal fall-off curve. Note the tendency for lower-order settlements to exchange with the higher-order center, even if the latter lies further from the source than an accessible lower-order settlement.

way of studying the data, and more thorough analysis may be useful. Recently, there has been a considerable focus of interest on fall-off analysis (see box opposite). Although different mechanisms of distribution sometimes produce comparable end-results, the pattern of exponential fall-off is produced only by a down-the-line trading system. For instance, if one village receives its supplies of a raw material down a linear trading network from its neighbor up the line, retains a given proportion of the material (e.g. one-third) for its own use, and trades the remainder to its neighbor down the line, and if each village does the same, an exponential fall-off curve will result. When quantity is plotted on a logarithmic scale, the plot takes the form of a straight line. But a different distribution system, through major and minor centers, would produce a different fall-off pattern. There are many examples where patterns of trade have been investigated using a characterization technique together with a spatial analysis of the distribution of finds. It must be remembered, however, that such techniques rarely reveal the complete trading system, only one component of it.

Distribution Studies of Obsidian. A good example is the obsidian found at Early Neolithic sites in the Near East

(see map p. 372). Characterization studies by Colin Renfrew and colleagues pinpointed two sources in central Anatolia and two in eastern Anatolia. Samples were obtained from most of the known Early Neolithic sites in the Near East, dating from the 7th and 6th millennia BC. A rather clear picture emerged with the central Anatolian obsidians being traded in the Levant area (down to Palestine), while those of eastern Anatolia were mostly traded down the Zagros Mountain range to sites in Iran such as Ali Kosh.

A quantitative distributional study (see box opposite) revealed a pattern of exponential fall-off, which as we have seen is an indicator of down-the-line trade. It could therefore be concluded that obsidian was being handed on down from village settlement to village settlement. Only in the area close to the sources (within 320 km (200 miles) of the sources) – termed the *supply zone* – was there evidence that people were going direct to the source to collect their own obsidian. Outside that area – within what has been termed the *contact zone* – the fall-off indicates a down-the-line system. There is no indication of specialist middleman traders at this time, nor does it seem that there were central places which had a dominant role in the supply of obsidian.

In the early period, the position was as seen on the map below. In the later period, from 5000 to 3000 BC, the situation changed somewhat, with a new obsidian source in eastern Anatolia coming into use. Obsidian was also then traded over rather greater distances. This is a case where it is possible to study the development of the obsidian trade over time.

Obsidian makes a very good material for a characterization and distribution study for several reasons. First, there are relatively few sources of obsidian in the world, because the material is found only at volcanic outcrops of relatively recent geological age. Secondly, it transpires that the different sources are chemically different, so that they can be distinguished by such methods as neutron activation analysis. Thirdly, obsidian was greatly prized in prehistoric times and was used to make chipped stone tools in the same manner as flint, so that it is found at many prehistoric sites.

In the Aegean, obsidian was being collected from the Cycladic island of Melos as early as 10,000 years ago, as finds in the Franchthi Cave on the Greek mainland show. This is the earliest secure evidence for seafaring

The obsidian trade in the Near East. Characterization studies revealed that Early Neolithic villages in Cyprus, Anatolia, and the Levant obtained their obsidian from two sources in central Anatolia, while villages such as Jarmo and Ali Kosh depended on two sources in Armenia (eastern Anatolia). At sites relatively close to the sources (e.g. Çatalhöyük, Tell Shemsharah), obsidian formed 80 percent of the chipped stone tools, suggesting that within this "supply zone" (inner lines on the distribution map) people collected obsidian directly from the source. Beyond this zone there was an exponential fall-off in obsidian abundance (right), indicative of down-the-line trade.

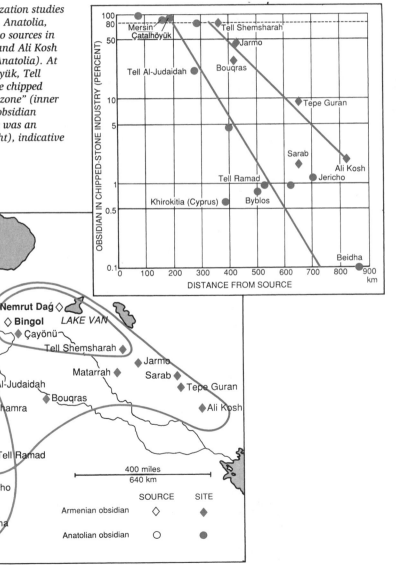

in the Mediterranean. The early trade of obsidian in the Pacific, for instance within the early Lapita culture (Chapter 12), has been documented by similar means. And in Central and North America, several investigations have been conducted of obsidian exchange systems – for example, in the Oaxaca region of Mexico in the Early Formative period (see p. 378).

Trade in Silver and Copper. In the Aegean again the technique of lead isotope analysis (see above) has allowed the sources to be determined for the silver and copper artifacts in use in the 3rd millennium BC. The analyses have shown the operation of the silver mines at Laurion in Greece at a very early date, and have also unexpectedly revealed the importance during the 3rd millennium of a copper source on the island of Kythnos. Lead isotope analyses also appear to indicate the surprising result that copper from Cyprus (in the eastern Mediterranean) was reaching the island of Sardinia (in the western Mediterranean) before 1200 BC. Sardinia has copper sources of its own, so the need for Cypriot imports is puzzling.

Shipwrecks and Hoards: Trade by Sea and Land. A different approach to distribution questions is afforded by the study of transport. Travel by water was often much safer, quicker, and less expensive than travel by land. The best source of information, both for questions of transport and for the crucial question of what commodity was traded against what, and on which scale, is afforded by shipwrecks from prehistoric as well as later times. Probably the best known of these are the wrecks of the treasure ships of the Spanish Main; the artifacts in them give valuable insights into the organization of trade. From earlier times, complete cargoes of the Roman amphorae referred to above have been recovered. Our knowledge of marine trade several centuries before has been greatly extended by George Bass' investigations of two important Bronze Age shipwrecks off the south coast of Turkey, at Cape Gelidonya and Uluburun (see box overleaf).

The terrestrial equivalent of the shipwreck is the trader's cache or hoard. When substantial assemblages of goods are found in archaeological deposits, it is not easy to be clear about the intentions of those who left them there: some hoards evidently had a votive character, but those with materials for recycling, such as scrap metal, may well have been buried by itinerant smiths.

In such cases, particularly with a well-preserved shipwreck, we come as close as we shall ever do to understanding the nature of distribution. Just occasionally, we are lucky enough to see a depiction of traders, together with their exotic goods. Several Egyptian tomb paintings show the arrival of overseas traders: in some cases, for instance in the tomb of Senenmut at Thebes (c. 1492 BC), they can be recognized as Minoans, with characteristic Cretan goods.

THE STUDY OF PRODUCTION

One of the best ways of understanding what was going on in a system involving production, distribution (usually with exchange), and consumption, is to start at the place of production. Whether we are speaking of the place of origin of the raw material, the location where the material was turned into finished products, or the place of manufacture of an artificial material, such a location has much to teach us. We need to know how production was organized. Were craft specialists at work, or did people travel freely to the sources to collect what they wanted? If there were craft specialists, how were they organized, and what was the scale of production? In precisely what form was the product transported and exchanged?

The investigation of quarries and mines is now a well-developed field of archaeology. Detailed mapping of the source area, both in terms of the geological formation and of the distribution of discarded material, is a first step for quarries. The work of Robin Torrence at the obsidian quarries on the Aegean island of Melos offers a good example. The main question that she posed there was whether craft specialists resident on Melos were exploiting this resource, or whether it was utilized by travelers who came in their boats and collected the material when they wanted to do so. Her sophisticated analysis showed that the latter was the case, and that craft specialists had not worked there: this was a direct-access resource.

One of the most interesting techniques for studying production is reconstituting the debris from the production of tool forms. C.A. Singer has done this at felsite quarries in the Colorado Desert of southern California, which have a long history of exploitation from the beginning of the Holocene. He was able to refit flakes and artifacts from one of the quarries (Riverton 1819) with those from an occupation site 63 km (39 miles) away, thus illustrating the movement of the raw material from its source.

This is an area where ethnographic studies, notably at quarries in Australia and Papua New Guinea, have

DISTRIBUTION: THE ULUBURUN WRECK

It is difficult for the archaeologist to learn what commodity was traded against what other commodity, and to understand the mechanics of trade. The discovery of the shipwreck of a trading vessel, complete with cargo, is thus of particular value.

In 1982, just such a wreck, dating from close to 1300 BC, was found at Uluburun, near Kaş, off the south Turkish coast in 43 m (141 ft) to 60 m (198 ft) of water. It was excavated between 1984 and 1994 by George F. Bass and Cemal Pulak of the Institute of Nautical Archaeology in Texas.

The ship's cargo contained about 10 tons of copper in the form of over 350 of the so-called "oxhide" ingots (i.e. shaped like an oxhide) already known from wall paintings in Egypt and from finds in Cyprus, Crete, and elsewhere. The copper for these ingots was almost certainly mined on the island of Cyprus (as suggested by lead-isotope analysis, and trace-element analysis). Also of particular importance are nearly a ton of ingots and other objects of tin found on the sea floor in the remains of the cargo. The source of the tin used in the Mediterranean at this time is not yet clear. It seems evident that at the time

Three striking objects from the wreck: (clockwise, from top) impression of a hematite seal, cut in Mesopotamia c. 1750 BC, with a new scene carved over it some 400 years later; a gold scarab, the first ever found bearing the name of the famous Egyptian queen Nefertiti, who reigned with her consort Akhenaten during the 14th century BC; and gold pendant showing an unknown goddess with a gazelle in each upraised hand.

of the shipwreck, the vessel was sailing westwards from the east Mediterranean coast, and taking with it tin, from some eastern source, as well as copper from Cyprus.

The pottery included jars of the type known as Canaanite amphorae, because they were made in Palestine or Syria (the Land of Canaan). Most held turpentine-like resin from the terebinth tree, but several contained olives, and another glass beads.

Similar jars have been found in Greece, Egypt, and especially along the Levantine coast.

The exotic goods in the wreck included lengths of a wood resembling ebony, which grew in Africa south of Egypt. Then there were Baltic amber beads, which came originally from northern Europe (and which probably reached the Mediterranean overland). There was also ivory in the form of elephant and hippopotamus tusks, possibly from the eastern Mediterranean, and ostrich eggshells that probably came from North Africa or Syria. Bronze tools and weapons from the wreck show a mixture of types that include Egyptian, Levantine, and Mycenaean forms. Among other important finds were several cylinder seals of Syrian and Mesopotamian types, ingots of glass (at that time a special and costly material), and a chalice of gold.

This staggering treasure from the sea bed gives a glimpse into Bronze Age trade in the Mediterranean. Bass and Pulak consider it likely that the trader started his final voyage on the Levantine coast. His usual circuit probably involved sailing across to Cyprus, then along the Turkish coast, past Kaş and west to Crete, or, more likely, to one of the major Mycenaean sites on the Greek mainland, or even further north, as hinted by the discovery on the wreck of spears and a ceremonial scepter/mace from the Danube region of the Black Sea. Then, profiting from seasonal winds, he would head south across the open sea to the coast of North Africa, east to the mouth of the Nile and Egypt, and, finally, home again to Phoenicia. On this occasion, however, he lost his ship, his cargo, and possibly his life at Uluburun.

The map shows the probable route of the ill-fated ship found at Uluburun. Also indicated are likely sources of materials for the various artifacts found on board the wreck.

The thousands of objects from the wreck were drawn on the site plan before the painstaking work of recovery began. (Below) Divers working on the oxhide ingots.

FINDS FROM THE WRECK

Gold 37 pieces: 9 pendants (Canaanite and Syrian?) • 4 medallions with star/ray design • Scarab of Nefertiti • Conical, collared chalice • Ring • Scrap **Silver** 2 bracelets (Canaanite?) • 4 bracelet fragments (scrap) • 3 rings (1 Egyptian) • Bowl fragment and other scrap pieces **Copper** Over 350 oxhide-shaped ingots (c.27kg/60 lb each) • Over 120 complete or partial plano-convex or "bun" ingots • Other ingots **Bronze** Statuette of a female deity partly clad in gold foil • Tools and weapons (Canaanite, Mycenaean, Cypriot, and Egyptian designs): daggers, swords, spearheads, arrowheads, axes, adzes, hoe, sickle blades, chisels, knives, razors, tongs, drill bits, awls, saw • 1 pair finger cymbals • Zoomorphic weights: 2 frogs, 5 bulls, sphinx, duck, waterfowl, calf, fly, lion and lioness, canine (?) head • Balance pans and weights • Figurines of man and 3 calves on lead-filled disk • Bowl and caldron fragments • Rings • Pins • Fishhooks, trident, harpoon **Tin** Over 100 tin ingots and fragments (round bun, oxhide, slab, and sections of large disk shapes) • Mug, pilgrim flask, plate **Lead** Over 1000 fish-net weights • Fish-line weights • Balance-pan weights **Faience** 4 rhyta (ram's head form) • Goblet in shape of woman's head • Tiny discoid beads • Biconical fluted beads • Other bead types **Glass** Over 150 cobalt-blue and light blue disk ingots (Canaanite?) • Beads (many stored in a Canaanite amphora) **Sealstones etc.** 2 quartz cylinder seals (1 with gold caps) • Hematite seal (Mesopotamian) • Gold-framed ?steatite scarab • 8 other scarabs (Egyptian and ?Syrian) • 2 lentoid Mycenaean sealstones • 6 other cylinder seals • Amber beads from Baltic • Small stone plaque with hieroglyphs "Ptah, Lord of Truth" on obverse **Stone** 24 weight-anchors • Ballast stones • Balance-pan weights • Mace heads • Nearly 700 agate beads • Mortar and trays • Whetstones **Pottery** 10 large pithoi (1 with 18 pieces Cypriot pottery inside) • About 150 amphorae (Canaanite) • Mycenaean kylix (Rhodian?), stirrup jars, cup, jugs, dipper, flask • Pilgrim flasks • Syrian jugs • Wide variety of Cypriot pottery **Ivory** 13 hippopotamus teeth • Complete and segment of sawn elephant tusk • 2 duck-shaped cosmetics containers • Ram's-horn shaped trumpet carved from hippopotamus tooth • Scepters, handles, decorative inlay pieces • **Wood** Ship's hull (cedar planks fastened to cedar keel by mortise-and-tenon joints pinned with hardwood pegs) • Logs of African blackwood (Egyptian ebony) • 2 wooden diptychs (writing tablets): 2 wooden leaves joined by 3-piece ivory hinge **Other Organic Materials** Thorny burnet (shrub used as packing around cargo) • Olives stored in amphorae • Pomegranates stored in a pithos • Grapes, figs, nuts, spices • Yellow terebinth resin (?ingredient of perfume or incense) stored in over 100 amphorae • Orpiment (yellow arsenic) stored in amphorae • 1000s of marine mollusc opercula (?ingredient of incense) • Bone astragals • Ostrich eggshells and eggshell beads • 28 sea-shell rings • Over 6 tortoise-shell fragments (?part of soundbox for lute)

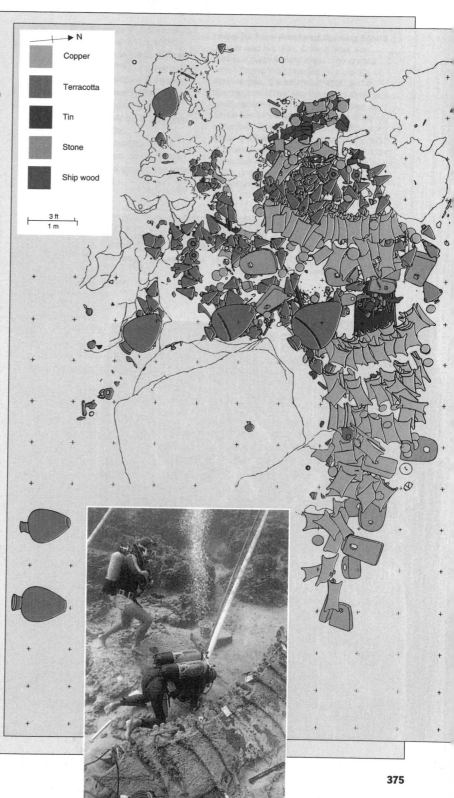

N

	Copper
	Terracotta
	Tin
	Stone
	Ship wood

3 ft
1 m

PRODUCTION: GREENSTONE ARTIFACTS IN AUSTRALIA

One of the most thorough studies of the circumstances of production and distribution yet undertaken is that conducted by Isabel McBryde at the quarry outcrops on Mount William in the ranges north of Melbourne, in southeastern Australia. McBryde started with a large quarry site known from ethnographic accounts to have been an important source for the greenstone used in the manufacture of tomahawks, a basic and universal tool among the Australian Aborigines. She then followed up the quarry's products in museum collections, identifying them in collaboration with petrologist Alan Watchman. Similar-looking greenstone from other quarries could be distinguished by thin-section analysis, supplemented by major- and trace-element analyses.

McBryde mapped and sampled the worked outcrops at the quarry. On the top of the ridge at Mount William, where the outcrop of greenstone is buried, there are strings of quarry pits where the unweathered stone was mined. There are scree slopes of quarried waste around the worked outcrops, and isolated flaking floors indicate the location of the areas where cores and preforms were shaped.

The work also involved the study of the distribution of the artifacts derived from the quarry site. McBryde, drawing on the ethnographic evidence, discovered that access to the quarry was strictly limited, and its stone was available only through those with the kinship or ceremonial affiliations to the "owners" of the site.

In the words of McBryde: "The quarry was still in use when Melbourne was first settled in the 1830s, its operation controlled by strict

Mount William, with its quarried outcrops along the ridge (right), and a map (above right) to show the distribution of artifacts made from the quarry's greenstone.

conventions. The outcrops were owned by a group of Woiwurrung speakers, and only members of a certain family were permitted to work them. The last man responsible for working the quarry, Billi-billeri, died in 1846."

Reed spears were brought from the Goulburn and Murray rivers in exchange. It is recorded that three pieces of Mount William stone would be exchanged for one possum skin cloak, "itself a considerable labor investment in hunting, skin preparation, sewing and decoration, when the skins of many animals might be needed for one garment." Thus the initial exchanges took the axes only to a fairly limited area around the quarry. The wider distribution – up to 500 km – was the result of successive further exchanges with neighboring groups.

Petrologist Alan Watchman takes a rock sample from a greenstone outcrop at the Mount William quarry. Comparison of the rock's composition with that of greenstone axes found elsewhere made it possible to match the artifacts to their quarry source.

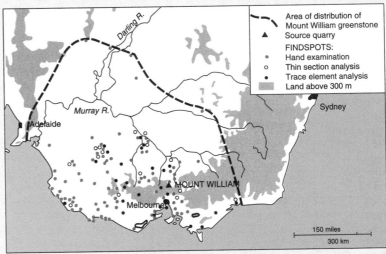

proved very informative: insights are gained not only into the problems of working those and similar production systems, but also into the solutions available to overcome them (see box, left).

The excavation of mines offers special opportunities. For instance, at the Neolithic flint mines at Grimes Graves in Norfolk, eastern England (see p. 315), it was possible for Roger Mercer to calculate the total flint obtained from each mine shaft, and to estimate the amount of work involved in digging the shaft, thus achieving a sort of time and motion study for the actual extraction process.

Studies of the specialist working of raw materials have been undertaken for several materials. One of these is Philip Kohl's study of the production and distribution of elaborately decorated stone bowls, made of green chlorite, in the Sumerian period (2900–2350 BC). He studied two sites in eastern Iran, Tepe Yahya and Shahr-i-Sokhta, and compared the production methods used with modern soft-stone workshops in Meshed. The rapid mass-production of vessels in Meshed, using modern tools such as lathes, contrasts markedly with the much slower production methods employed at Yahya. The distribution of the products also differs, with the ancient chlorite vessels restricted to the upper ruling strata of early urban centers, while the Meshed vessels were sold to a wider range of people. Such comparisons with modern situations can highlight important features of archaeological artifact distributions. The study of village craft specialization in present-day farming societies is another way of learning about techniques of production in the past.

The location of specialist workshops in urban sites is one of the main objectives of survey on such sites. But only the excavation of workshops and special facilities can give adequate insights into the scale of production and its organization. The workshops most commonly found are pottery kilns.

The scale of the installation is sometimes sufficient to imply the nature of the production, and sometimes the products; for instance, bricks referring to the *Classis Britannica*, the fleet of Roman Britain, indicate production under official auspices, as part of the official organization.

THE STUDY OF CONSUMPTION

Consumption is the third component of the sequence that begins with production and is mediated by distribution or exchange. There have been only a few serious studies of the consumption of traded commodities. But such studies are necessary if the nature and scale of the exchange process are to be well understood. The issues soon return to a consideration of formation processes (Chapter 2), because there is no reason to suppose that the quantities of material recovered at a site represent accurately the quantities once traded.

It is necessary to ask first how the materials recovered came to be discarded or lost. Valued objects, carefully curated, are found in excavations less often than less-esteemed everyday ones. Secondly, it is necessary to consider how discarded or lost objects or debris found their way into the archaeological record. On a domestic site, questions of cleanliness and rubbish disposal are important. The study cannot proceed properly without a consideration of both these aspects of formation processes, and also of the timespans involved.

The quantities of material will need estimating very carefully. This means explicit procedures for sampling the site, and standardized recovery procedures. On most excavations it is now standard practice to take samples of the excavated soil, and to sieve or screen it through a fine mesh, often with the aid of water (water sieving). The technique of flotation (Chapter 6) is also used for the recovery of plant residues. A mesh of 3 or 4 mm (0.1–0.15 in) is usually appropriate for the recovery of beads, flint chips, etc., but for pottery a mesh of a larger size is more suitable, so that only pieces above a given length (of say 1 or 2 cm (0.4–0.8 in)) are recovered. (It often makes sense to discard, or at least not to include in the counts, pieces less than about 1 or 2 cm (0.4–0.8 in) long.)

The American archaeologist Raymond Sidrys has attempted to study the pattern of consumption of a specific commodity: obsidian. He set out to see whether consumption of obsidian from source areas in Guatemala and El Salvador during ancient Maya times varied according to different types of site. In the Maya area, as in the Near East (see map, p. 372), the frequency of obsidian finds declines exponentially as the distance from source increases. But, allowing for this decay pattern, was there a marked difference in the amount of obsidian used at different types of site? Sidrys set out to answer this question with two measures of obsidian abundance. First he used a measure of obsidian density (OD), defined as:

$$OD = \frac{\text{Mass of obsidian}}{\text{Excavated volume of earth}}$$

for each site. This measure involved estimating the quantity of soil excavated and weighing the total quantity of obsidian recovered (finished artifacts and waste material) as the soil was passed through the sieve.

The second measure was of obsidian scarcity (OS), defined as:

$$OS = \frac{\text{Number of obsidian artifacts}}{\text{Number of potsherds}}$$

Sidrys' calculations showed clearly that obsidian was less abundant at the minor centers than at the major ceremonial centers.

It is a matter for discussion as to whether this difference between the centers should be attributed to a difference in consumption patterns or to a difference in distribution, but with the major centers acting as the preferential recipients of supplies. The project is in any case a pioneering attempt to consider questions of consumption.

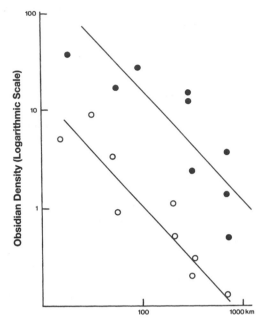

Consumption of Maya obsidian. In this analysis by Sidrys two separate fall-off patterns were revealed, one for minor centers (open circles) and the other for major centers (filled circles).

EXCHANGE AND INTERACTION: THE COMPLETE SYSTEM

The archaeological evidence is rarely sufficient to permit the reconstruction of a complete exchange system. It is extremely difficult, for example, to establish without written records what was traded against what, and which particular values were ascribed to each commodity. Furthermore, exchange in perishable materials will have left little or no trace in the archaeological record. In most cases, all one can hope to do is to fit together the evidence about sources and distribution afforded archaeologically. A good example of such a project is the work of Jane Pires-Ferreira in Oaxaca, Mexico.

An Exchange System in Ancient Mexico. Jane Pires-Ferreira studied five materials used in Oaxaca during the Early and Middle Formative periods (1450–500 BC). The first was *obsidian*, of which some nine sources were relevant. These were characterized by means of neutron activation analysis, and relevant networks were established. She then proceeded to consider exchange networks for *mother-of-pearl shell*, and concluded that two different networks were in operation, one bringing marine material from the Pacific Coast, the other material from freshwater sources in the rivers draining into the Atlantic.

For her next study she considered the *iron ore* (magnetite, ilmenite, and hematite) used to manufacture mirrors in the Formative period. Here the appropriate characterization technique was Mössbauer spectroscopy. Finally, she was able to bring into consideration two classes of *pottery* whose area of manufacture (in Oaxaca and in Veracruz, respectively) could be determined stylistically.

These results were then fitted together onto a single map, showing some of the commodities that linked regions of Mesoamerica in the Early Formative period into several exchange networks. The picture is evidently incomplete, and it does not offer any notion of relative values. But it does make excellent use of the available characterization data, and undertakes a preliminary synthesis that is securely based on the archaeological evidence.

Further Insights into the Exchange System. In a money economy, it may be possible to go further in our analysis, because some measure of the total turnover of the economy may be possible once there is a single, unified measure of value. In the case of coined money, various steps in the economic system can be reconstructed: the circumstances of minting may be examined, and some-

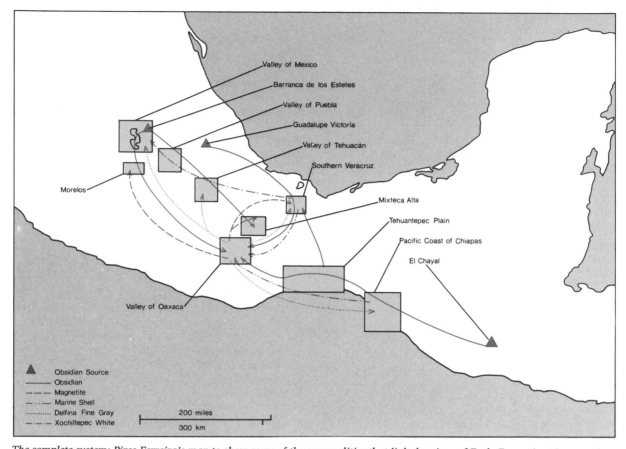

Valley of Mexico
Barranca de los Estetes
Valley of Puebla
Guadalupe Victoria
Valley of Tehuacán
Southern Veracruz
Morelos
Mixteca Alta
Tehuantepec Plain
Pacific Coast of Chiapas
El Chayal
Valley of Oaxaca

▲ Obsidian Source
── Obsidian
─ ─ ─ Magnetite
─ ·· ─ Marine Shell
·········· Delfina Fine Gray
─ · ─ Xochiltepec White

200 miles
300 km

The complete system: Pires-Ferreira's map to show some of the commodities that linked regions of Early Formative Mesoamerica.

thing of the taxation system is sometimes known from other sources.

At a more specific level, coins can often give an accurate indication of the intensity of interactions in space and time because they can usually be dated and because the place of issue is frequently indicated. This is exemplified in the study by the American archaeologist J.R. Clark of the coinage of the Roman period from the site of Dura Europus in Syria. He examined a sample of 10,712 coins found there. These had been minted at 16 different Greek cities in the Near East, and by dividing the coins into four time periods he was able to show how Dura's commercial links with other cities had changed during the period 27 BC–AD 256, with an expansion of trade in the period up to AD 180, and a sharp decrease in the period AD 180–256.

In general, however, the exchange data in themselves are insufficient to document the functioning of the entire exchange system. It is necessary, then, to think of alternative models for describing the system,

as advocated in Chapter 12. The use of such hypothetical models is entirely appropriate provided that the distinction between what has been documented and what is hypothesized is kept clearly in view.

A good example is the Danish archaeologist Lotte Hedeager's study of the "buffer zone" in northern Europe between the frontiers of the Roman empire and the more remote lands of "Free Germany." She drew on literary and philological sources as well as archaeological ones to construct a hypothetical view of the whole system (see illus. p. 380).

Trade as a Cause of Cultural Change

The possible role of trade in the development of a nation state or an empire from the trade interaction of smaller, initially independent units is seen in the illustration p. 381. The city states or other independent units (early state modules, ESMs) trade both at local level and through their capital centers. There are

ROMAN EMPIRE | ROMANIZED CELTIC AREA – BUFFER ZONE | FREE GERMANY

ROMAN FRONTIER

200 km BEYOND FRONTIER

Money & market economy | Market economy & some money use | Moneyless & marketless economy (perhaps moneyless markets)

Pottery, brooches

Bronze, glass, weapons

Gold & silver coins Silver cups

Wine

Goose, soap amber, hides

Wagons

Clothing

Archaeological sources

Writings of Tacitus

Philological sources

Lotte Hedeager studied the exchange system between the Roman empire and "Free Germany." Using archaeological, literary, and philological sources, she concluded that Roman-Germanic trade incorporated three economic systems: (1) the Roman empire, with money and market economy; (2) a "buffer zone," extending c. 200 km (120 miles) beyond the frontier, which lacked independent coinage but maintained a limited money economy, perhaps including markets; and (3) Free Germany, with a moneyless and marketless economy, or perhaps with moneyless markets. Archaeological evidence indicated that the Germanic tribes mainly imported Roman luxury articles (bronze and glass; gold and silver in the form of coins) as prestige items (see Chapter 10). Philological and other evidence suggested that in exchange the Romans imported useful commodities such as soap, hides, wagons, and clothing.

circumstances when these flows of goods can lay the basis for a larger economic unification.

This notion is related to that of the "world system" of Immanuel Wallerstein (see above), which some archaeologists have sought to apply to the pre-capitalist world in a manner that Wallerstein himself did not propose. But there are dangers here of definition being mistaken for explanation. To propose that certain areas were united in an economic "world system" does not of itself prove anything, and it may easily lead the analyst to exaggerate the effects of quite modest trading links.

For it readily casts the discussion in terms of dominance (for the supposed core area) and dependency (for the supposed periphery). Indeed, it can easily lead to the rather unthinking explanation of changes by "dominance" (i.e. diffusion) that processual archaeology has worked hard to overcome.

If exchange systems are to have a central role in explanation, then the model needs to be framed explicitly, and it should show the role of exchange within the system as a whole, and the relationship between the flow of goods and the exercise of power within the system. One good example of such a model is the one offered by Susan Frankenstein and Michael Rowlands for the transition toward a highly ranked society in Early Iron Age France and Germany. They argued that it was the control of the supply of prestige goods from the Mediterranean world exercised by the local chiefs that allowed these individuals to enhance their status. They did so both by using and displaying the finest of these valuables themselves (the use including burial in princely graves, recovered by the archaeologist) and in allocating some of them to their followers. The transition to more prominent ranking was in large measure produced by control of the exchange network by the elite. William L. Rathje has presented a comparable model for the rise of a prominent elite in the Maya lowlands, and hence for the emergence of Classic Maya civilization.

These are models put forward to explain change in the cultural system, and a discussion of their implications belongs in Chapter 12, where the nature of explanation in archaeology is considered. It is appropriate to mention them here, however, as external trade and exchange play integral parts in many explanations proposed for cultural change.

Symbolic Exchange and Interaction

At the beginning of this chapter it was stressed that interaction involves the exchange not only of material goods but of information, which includes ideas, symbols, inventions, aspirations, and values. Modern archaeology has learnt to cope tolerably well with material exchanges, using characterization studies and spatial analyses, but it has been less effective with symbolic aspects of interaction.

As noted above and as further reviewed in Chapter 12, there has been a tendency to label interactions between neighboring areas as simply "diffusion," with one area dominant over another. One response to such dominance models is to think in terms of autonomy: of complete independence of one area from another. But it seems unrealistic to exclude the possibility of

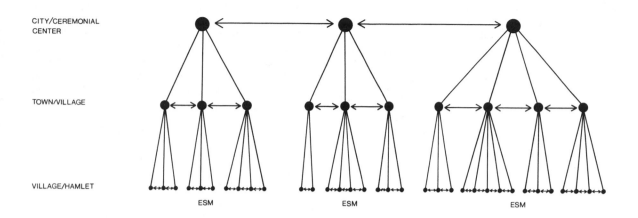

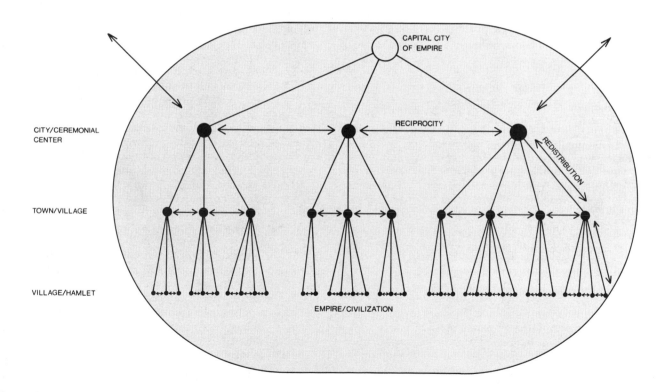

Trade and the development of an empire. (Top) Individual city states or other independent units (early state modules, ESMs) trade both at the local level, within each ESM, and at the higher level through their capital centers. (Above) In certain circumstances these higher-level interactions can lead to the integration of the ESMs within a larger-scale unit, the empire or civilization-state.

significant interactions. The alternative solution is to seek ways of analyzing interactions, including their symbolic components, that do not assume dominance and subordination, core and periphery, but consider different areas as on a more or less equal footing. When discussing such interactions between polities (independent societies) of equal status – known as *peer polities* – it has been found useful to speak of *interaction spheres*, a term first applied to the interaction sphere of the Hopewell people of the eastern United States (see box, opposite) by the late Joseph Caldwell.

Peer-polity interaction takes many forms, some of which have been distinguished:

1 *Competition.* Neighboring areas compete with one another in various ways, judging their own success against that of their neighbors. This often takes a symbolic form in periodic meetings at some major ceremonial centers where representatives of the various areas meet, celebrate ritual, and sometimes compete in games and other enterprises. Such behavior is seen among hunter-gatherer bands, which meet periodically in larger units (at what in Australia are called *corroborees*). It is seen also in the pilgrimages and rituals of state societies, most conspicuously in ancient Greece at the Olympic Games and the other Panhellenic assemblies, when representatives of all the city states would meet.

2 *Competitive emulation.* Related to the foregoing is the tendency for one polity to try to outdo its neighbors in conspicuous consumption. The expensive public feasts of the Northwest Coast American Indians – the institution of the potlatch – was noted earlier. Very similar in some ways is the erection of magnificent monuments at regional ceremonial centers, each outdoing its neighbor in scale and grandeur. One can suspect something of this in the ceremonial centers of Maya cities, and the same phenomenon is seen in the magnificent cathedrals in the capital cities of medieval Europe. The same is also true for the temples of the Greek city states.

A more subtle effect of this kind of interaction is that, although these monuments seek to outdo each other, they end up doing so in much the same way. These different polities in a particular region, at a particular period, come to share the same mode of expression, without its being exactly clear where the precise form originates. Thus it is that in a certain sense all Maya ceremonial centers look the same, just as all Greek temples of the 6th century BC look the same. At a detailed level they are very different, of course, but they undeniably share a common form of expression. This is usually a product of

peer-polity interaction: in most cases, one need not postulate a single innovatory core center, to which other areas are peripheral.

3 *Warfare.* Warfare is, of course, an obvious form of competition. But the object of the competition is not necessarily to gain territory. In Chapter 5 we saw that it might also be used to capture prisoners for sacrifice. It operated under well-understood rules, and was as much a form of interaction as the others listed here.

4 *Transmission of innovation.* Naturally a technical advance made in one area will soon spread to other areas. Most interaction spheres participate in a developing technology, to which all the local centers, the peer polities, make their own contributions.

5 *Symbolic entrainment.* Within a given interaction sphere, there is a tendency for the symbolic systems in use to converge. For instance, the iconography of the prevailing religion has much in common from center to center. Indeed, so does the form of the religion itself: each center may have its own patron deities, but the deities of the different centers somehow function together within a coherent religious system. Thus, in the early Near East, each city state had its own patron deity, and the different deities themselves were sometimes believed to go to war with each other. But the deities were conceived as inhabiting the same divine world, just as mortals occupied different areas of the everyday world. The same comments may be made for the civilizations of Mesoamerica, or ancient Greece.

6 *Ceremonial exchange of valuables.* Although we have emphasized non-material (i.e. symbolic) interactions here, it is certainly the case that between the elites of the peer polities there was also a series of material exchanges, including the kinds already described earlier in this chapter – the transfer of marriage partners and of valuable gifts.

7 *Flow of commodities.* The large-scale exchanges between participating polities of everyday commodities should not, of course, be overlooked. The economies in some cases became linked together. This is precisely what Wallerstein intended by his term "world system." However, it should be noted that in this case there need be no core and periphery, as there is in Wallerstein's colonial case of the 16th century AD, or indeed as there was in the ancient empires. Those, too, are valid cases, but although it is frequently appropriate both to the colonial world and to the ancient empires, these dominance relations should not be made a paradigm for the whole study of interactions in early societies.

INTERACTION SPHERES: HOPEWELL

Among many societies the exchange of valuables far outweighed in importance the exchange of ordinary commodities. Few commodities moved between regions because each region was relatively self-sufficient and bulky goods were hard to transport. One interaction sphere, the Hopewell, operated on a very large scale in what is now the eastern United States during the first two centuries AD.

A number of regions participated in the exchange of valuables, two of which were more central in this exchange – the Scioto region of the Upper Ohio valley and the Havana region of Illinois. Items of marine shell, shark teeth, mica, and other rocks and minerals came from the south; objects of native copper, silver, and pipestone came from the north. Several flints from different regions were commonly used in exchange, and obsidian was obtained far to the west in Wyoming. These materials were made into highly distinctive objects for ritual and costumery. Native copper was

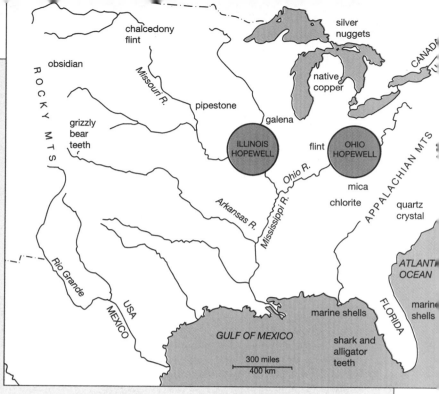

Raven or crow cut from sheet copper, with a pearl eye. Length 38 cm.

hammered into various shapes, including axe and adze heads, large breastplates, headdresses, bicymbal earspools, and jackets for pan pipes. Sheets of mica were cut into geometric figures and naturalistic outlines. Flints, obsidian, and quartz crystal were chipped into large bifaces. Marine shells were made into large cups and beads. Soft carvable stone was used to create distinctively styled pipes for smoking.

The widespread exchange of prestige goods was accompanied by a symbolic system that was adopted in each of the independent regions. Locally made items, including pottery, ornaments, and ritually significant items, conformed to the pan-regional style. Exchange goods were consumed in patterns of mortuary treatment and destruction by fire that are remarkably similar from one region to another. Thus, in a commonality of artifact form and consumptive pattern a veneer of cultural unity was created over the entire interaction area where none had existed before. Nevertheless, at the material level there were significant regional variations. The largest and richest burials are found where the most impressive earthworks were erected. Those in south-central Ohio are the largest and richest of all.

The American archaeologist David Braun has spoken of peer-polity interaction within the Hopewell sphere (while emphasizing that these were relatively simple societies, not states), and has pointed out that competitive emulation and symbolic entrainment may be observed in Hopewell as in the case of other comparable interaction spheres.

Mica ornament in the shape of a human face, found in Ohio.

383

8 *Language and ethnicity.* The most effective mode of interaction is a common language. This point is an obvious one, but it is often not explicitly stated by archaeologists. The development of a shared language, even when initially there was greater linguistic diversity, is one of the features that may be associated with peer-polity interaction. The development of a common ethnicity, and explicit awareness of being one people, is often related to linguistic factors. But archaeologists are only slowly coming to recognize that ethnicity is not something that always existed in the past: rather it came about over time as a result of interactions, which ethnicity itself further influenced.

Such concepts, where as much emphasis is laid on symbolic aspects as on the physical exchange of material goods, can profitably be used to analyze interactions in most early societies and cultures. Systematic analysis of this kind has, however, so far been rare in archaeology.

In Chapter 12, where similar issues are raised in the context of a discussion of explanation in archaeology, it is argued that a new synthesis in archaeological method is emerging, which one may term cognitive-processual archaeology (see p. 491). The analysis of interactions, including those of a symbolic nature, will have a significant role among the methods of that new synthesis.

SUMMARY

The study of exchange has been a growth area in modern archaeology. Scientific techniques of characterization – primarily microscopic examination of thin sections, trace-element analysis, and isotope analysis – now allow us to identify the distinctive characteristics of many materials, such as pottery, stone, and certain metals. Where the sources of raw materials in nature have likewise been identified – as for obsidian – one can then successfully plot on a map the distribution of such materials from source to archaeological findspot. Using techniques of spatial analysis (trend-surface analysis; fall-off analysis), the researcher goes on to investigate this exchange network further. Greater understanding of the network comes from studies of production (mines, quarries, craft workshops) and consumption, leading to as full a reconstruction of the complete exchange system as is possible without the benefit of written records.

Interpretation of exchange systems requires consideration of what the likely mechanism may have been: whether reciprocal exchange, redistribution, or market exchange. Nor should one forget that societies exchanged ideas and other information as well as material goods within a complete interaction sphere.

FURTHER READING

The following works provide a good introduction to the methods and approaches used by archaeologists in the study of trade and exchange:

Earle, T.K. & Ericson, J.E. (eds.). 1977. *Exchange Systems in Prehistory*. Academic Press: New York & London.

Ericson, J.E. & Earle, T.K. (eds.). 1982. *Contexts for Prehistoric Exchange*. Academic Press: New York & London.

Gale, N.H. (ed.). 1991. *Bronze Age Trade in the Mediterranean*. (Studies in Mediterranean Archaeology 90). Åström: Göteborg.

Hodder, I. & Orton, C. 1976. *Spatial Analysis in Archaeology*. Cambridge University Press: Cambridge & New York.

Lambert, J.B. 1997. *Traces of the Past: Unraveling the Secrets of Archaeology through Chemistry*. Helix Books/Addison-Wesley Longman: Reading, Mass.

Parkes, P.A. 1986. *Current Scientific Techniques in Archaeology*. Croom Helm: London & Sydney.

Polanyi, K., Arensberg, M. & Pearson, H. (eds.). 1957. *Trade and Market in the Early Empires*. Free Press: Glencoe, Illinois.

Pollard, A.M. & Heron, C. (eds.). 1996. *Archaeological Chemistry*. Royal Society of Chemistry: Cambridge.

Renfrew, C. & Cherry, J.F. (eds.). 1986. *Peer Polity Interaction and Socio-political Change*. Cambridge University Press: Cambridge & New York.

Sabloff, J. & Lamberg-Karlovsky, C.C. (eds.). 1975. *Ancient Civilization and Trade*. University of New Mexico Press: Albuquerque.

Scarre, C. & Healy, F. (eds.). 1993. *Trade and Exchange in Prehistoric Europe*. Oxbow Monograph 33: Oxford.

10

What Did They Think?
Cognitive Archaeology, Art, and Religion

Cognitive archaeology – the study of past ways of thought from material remains – is in many respects one of the newer branches of modern archaeology. It is true that ancient art and ancient writing, both rich sources of cognitive information, have long been studied by scholars. But too often art has been perceived to be the province of the art historian, and texts that of the narrative historian, and the archaeological perspective has been missing. Moreover for the prehistoric period, where written sources are entirely absent, earlier generations of archaeologists tended in desperation to create a kind of counterfeit history, "imagining" what ancient people must have thought or believed. It was this undisciplined, speculative approach that helped to spark off the New Archaeology, with its pressure for more scientific methods, as described in Chapter 1. But it also led to a general neglect of cognitive studies among the first wave of New Archaeologists, deterred as they were by the seemingly untestable nature of so many ideas about the cognitive past.

In this chapter, we argue that the skepticism of the early New Archaeologists and the sometimes unstructured empathy of the early postprocessual archaeologists can be answered by the development of explicit procedures for analyzing the concepts of early societies and the way people thought. For example, we can investigate how people went about describing and measuring their world: as we shall see, the system of weights used in the Indus Valley civilization can be understood very well today. We can investigate how people planned monuments and cities, since the layout of streets themselves reveals aspects of planning; and in some cases, maps and other specific indications of planning (e.g. models) have been found. We can investigate which material goods people valued most highly, and perhaps viewed as symbols of authority or power. And we can investigate the manner in which people conceived of the supernatural, and how they responded to these conceptions in their cult practice, for example, at the great ceremonial center of Chavín de Huantar in northern Peru (see box, pp. 410–11).

Theory and Method

It is generally agreed today that what most clearly distinguishes the human species from other life forms is our ability to use *symbols*. All intelligent thought and indeed all coherent speech are based on symbols, for words are themselves symbols, where the sound or the written letters stand for and thus represent (or symbolize) an aspect of the real world. Usually, however, meaning is ascribed to a particular symbol in an arbitrary way: there is often nothing to indicate that one specific word or one specific sign should represent a given object in the world rather than another. Take, for instance, the Stars and Stripes. We at once recognize this as the flag representing the United States of America. The design has a history that makes sense, if you know it. But there is nothing in the design itself to indicate which country is represented – or even that this is a flag representing a nation at all. Like many symbols, it is arbitrary.

Moreover, the meaning ascribed to a symbol is specific to a particular cultural tradition. When we look, for example, at a prehistoric Scandinavian rock carving of what appears to us to be a boat, we cannot without further research be certain that it *is* a boat. It might very well perhaps be a sledge in this cold region. But the people who made the carving would have had no

Two people ride in a ship, or is it a sledge? The precise meaning for us of this Bronze Age rock carving from Scandinavia is obscure without additional evidence.

difficulty in interpreting its meaning. Similarly, people speaking different languages use different words to describe the same thing – one object or idea may be expressed symbolically in many different ways. If we were all programmed at birth to ascribe the same meaning to particular symbols, and to speak the same language, the archaeologist's task would be very much easier – but the human experience would be singularly lacking in variety.

It is usually impossible to infer the meaning of a symbol within a given culture from the symbolic form of the image or object alone. At the very least we have to see how that form is used, and see it in the context of other symbols. Cognitive archaeology has therefore to be very careful about specific contexts of discovery: it is the assemblage, the ensemble, that matters, not the individual object in isolation.

Secondly, it is important to accept that depictions and material objects (artifacts) do not directly disclose their meanings to us – certainly not in the absence of written evidence. It is a fundamental of the scientific method that it is the observer, the researcher, who has to offer the interpretation. And the scientist knows that there can be several alternative interpretations, and that these must be evaluated, if necessary against one another, by explicit procedures of assessment or testing against fresh data. This is one of the tenets of processual archaeology, as discussed in Chapter 12. Some processual archaeologists, notably Lewis Binford, argue that it is not useful to consider what people were thinking in the past. They argue that it is the actions not the thoughts of people that find their way primarily into the material record. That, however, is not the position taken here. We start from the assumption that the things we find are, in part, the products of human thoughts and intentions (which the critics of our approach would not deny), and that this offers poten-

tialities as well as problems in their study. They belong, in short, to what the philosopher Karl Popper termed "world 3." As Popper indicated: "If we call the world of things – of physical objects – world 1, and the world of subjective experiences (such as thought processes) world 2, we may call the world of statements in themselves world 3...I regard world 3 as being essentially the products of the human mind." "These...may also be applied to products of human activity, such as houses or tools, and also to works of art. Especially important for us, they apply to what we call 'language', and to what we call 'science'." This insight, however, although a helpful orientation, does not offer us a methodology.

As a first concrete step it is useful to assume that there exists in each human mind a perspective of the world, an interpretive framework, a cognitive map – an idea akin to the mental map that geographers discuss, but one not restricted to the representation of spatial relationships only. For human beings do not act in relation to their sense impressions alone, but to their existing knowledge of the world, through which those impressions are interpreted and given meaning. In the diagram we see the human individual accompanied (in his or her mind) by this personal cognitive map, which allows the recollection of past states in the memory, and indeed the imagining of possible future states in the "mind's eye." Communities of people who live together and share the same culture, and speak the same language often share the same world view or "mind set." To the extent that this is so we can speak of a common cognitive map, although individuals differ, as do special interest groups. This approach is sometimes referred to by philosophers of science as "methodological individualism."

This idea of a cognitive map is a useful one precisely because we can in practice use some of the relevant

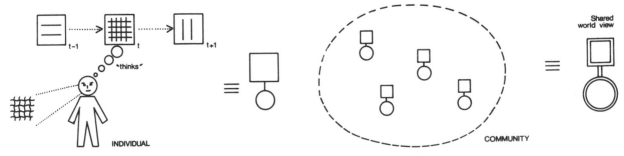

Cognitive maps. (Left) The human individual is accompanied by his or her personal cognitive map (represented by a square). The individual responds both to immediately perceived sense impressions and to this internalized map, which includes a memory of the world in the past (t–1) and forecasts of the world in the future (t + 1). (Right) Individuals who live together in a community share in some sense the same world view. To this extent one can speak of a cognitive map for the whole group.

artifacts from Popper's world 3 to give us insights into the shared cognitive map of a given group. We can hope to gain insight into the way the group used symbols, and sometimes (e.g. in depictions of scenes) the relationships between the individuals making up the group. All of this may sound rather abstract. In the rest of this chapter, however, we discuss specific ways in which we can start putting together this shared cognitive map of a given place and time and social group.

INVESTIGATING HOW HUMAN SYMBOLIZING FACULTIES EVOLVED

We often tend to speak of the human species as if all humans are essentially alike in behavior and cognitive ability. This seems to be true for all living groups of *Homo sapiens sapiens*, if one allows for the fact that within every group there is some variation. In other words, there is no convincing evidence for systematic and significant ability differences between living human "races," however they are defined. So when did these abilities of fully modern humans emerge?

Language and Self-Consciousness

Most physical anthropologists agree, as indicated in Chapter 11, that modern human abilities have been present since the emergence of *Homo sapiens sapiens* some 100,000–40,000 years ago. But as we look earlier, scholars are less united. As the neurophysiologist John Eccles put it: "How far back in prehistory can we recognize the beginning, the origin, the most primitive world 3 existence? As I look at the prehistory of mankind, I would say that we have it in tool culture. The first primitive hominids who were shaping pebble tools for a purpose had some idea of design, some idea of technique." To which Karl Popper replied: "While I agree with what you say, I nevertheless prefer to regard the beginning of world 3 as having come with the development of *language*, rather than *tools*." Some archaeologists and physical anthropologists consider that an effective language may have been developed by *Homo habilis* around 2 million years ago, along with the first chopper tools, but others think that a full language capability developed very much more recently, with the emergence of *Homo sapiens sapiens*. This would imply that the tools made by hominids in the Lower and Middle Paleolithic periods were produced by beings without true linguistic capacities.

As yet there is no clear methodology for determining when language arose (for physical aspects, see Chapter 11). The psychologist Merlin Donald has suggested a series of cognitive evolutionary stages, with a *mimetic* stage for *Homo erectus* (with emphasis upon hominid abilities to imitate behavior), a *mythic* stage for early *Homo sapiens* (emphasizing the significance of speech and narrative), and a *theoretic* stage for more developed societies, with emphasis upon theoretic thought and what Donald terms "external symbolic storage," involving a number of mnemonic mechanisms including writing. This is an important and interesting field, as yet little developed.

The origins of self-consciousness have been debated by scientists and philosophers such as Roger Penrose and Daniel Dennett, but with little tangible conclusion. John Searle has argued that there is no sudden transition, and asserted that his dog Ludwig has a significant degree of self-consciousness. In his book *The Prehistory of the Mind* Steven Mithen draws upon the work of evolutionary psychologists to discuss the issue, but as yet there is little archaeological or neurophysiological evidence adduced to clarify the matter.

There are several lines of approach into other aspects of early human cognitive abilities.

Design in Tool Manufacture

Whereas the production of simple pebble tools – for instance by *Homo habilis* – may perhaps be considered a simple, habitual act, not unlike a chimpanzee breaking off a stick to poke at an ant hill, the fashioning by *Homo erectus* of so beautiful an object as an Acheulian hand-axe seems more advanced.

So far, however, that is just a subjective impression. How do we investigate it further? One way is to measure, by experiment, the amount of time taken in the manufacturing process. A more rigorous quantitative approach, as developed by Glynn Isaac, is to study the range of variation in an assemblage of artifacts. For if the toolmaker has, within his or her cognitive map, some enduring notion of what the end-product should be, one finished tool should be much like another. Isaac distinguished a tendency through time to produce an increasingly well-defined variety or assemblage of tool types. This implies that each person making tools had a notion of different tool forms, no doubt destined for different functions. Planning and design in tool manufacture thus become relevant to our consideration of the cognitive abilities of early hominids, abilities that moreover distinguish them from higher apes such as the chimpanzee.

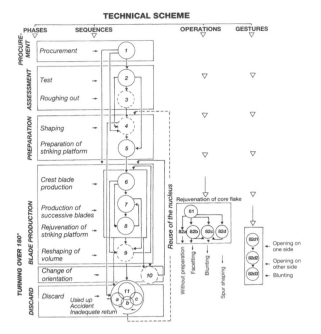

The chaîne opératoire involved in the production of a Magdalenian flint blade. Many manufacturing processes involved sequences of comparable complexity.

The analytical concept of the *chaîne opératoire* (sequence of actions) has been developed to make more explicit the cognitive implications of the complicated and often highly standardized sequence of events necessary for the production of a stone tool, a pot, a bronze artifact, or any product of a well-defined manufacturing process. For early periods, such as the Paleolithic, this approach offers one of the few insights available of the way cognitive structures underlay complex aspects of human behavior. French prehistorians Claudine Karlin and Michèle Julien analyzed the sequence of events necessary for the production of blades in the Magdalenian period of the French Upper Paleolithic (see diagram above); many other production processes can be investigated along similar lines.

Procurement of Materials and Planning Time

Another way of investigating the cognitive behavior of early hominids is to consider planning time, defined as the time between the planning of an act and its execution. For instance, if the raw material used to manufacture a stone tool comes from a specific rock outcrop, but the tool itself is produced some distance away (as documented by waste flakes produced in its manufac-

ture), that would seem to indicate some enduring intention or foresight by the person who transported the raw material. Similarly, the transport of natural or finished objects (so-called "manuports"), whether tools, seashells, or attractive fossils, as has been documented (see Chapter 9), indicates at least a continuing interest in them, or the intention of using them, or a sense of "possession." The study of such manuports, by the techniques of characterization discussed in Chapter 9 and other methods, has now been undertaken in a systematic way.

Organized Behavior: The Living Floor and the Food-sharing Hypothesis

In recent years, as discussed in Chapter 2, a particular focus of research has been the nature of the formation processes by which particular archaeological sites were formed. For the Paleolithic period this is particularly crucial, not only because of the long timespan over which the deposits formed, but also in view of the interpretive care needed in respect of the human behavior. This has proved an area of special controversy at important early hominid sites in Africa and elsewhere – for instance, those at Olduvai Gorge in Tanzania, and Olorgesailie and Koobi Fora in Kenya. Scatters of animal bones, many in fragmentary form, have been found with the stone artifacts at some sites. These sites, dating 2–1.5 million years ago, have been interpreted as activity areas, where the hominids who made the tools (supposedly *Homo habilis*) used them to work on animal carcasses (or parts of them) carried there and to extract marrow from the bones. These have been regarded as occupation sites, or temporary home bases, of small kin groups. Various workers including Glynn Isaac have argued that food-sharing among kin groups was taking place. These ideas have been criticized by Lewis Binford. In his view, these are not occupation sites of early hominids but places where hunting animals killed their prey. The humans used tools to extract marrow only after the animals who killed the game had taken their fill. He opposes the notion that early humans transported meat and marrow bones for processing and storing elsewhere.

Much work is going on at present to test these differing hypotheses. It involves the microscopic examination of the tooth-marks or cut marks on the broken bones (see discussion of taphonomy, Chapter 7), and the detailed analysis of the debris scatters on the supposed "living floors." Binford's argument would imply that no very intelligent behavior is involved, and no impressive social organization. The home-base/food-sharing view, on the other hand, implies a degree of stability in behavior, including social behavior, with more ambitious cognitive implications.

Lithic Assemblages as Functionally or Culturally Determined

When did human groups, inhabiting adjacent areas and exploiting similar resources, first develop behavior and material equipment that was culturally distinctive? This question arises as a major issue when the various Middle Paleolithic stone tool assemblages associated with the Neanderthals (*c.* 180,000–30,000 years ago) are considered: the assemblages generally described as Mousterian. The French archaeologist François Bordes argued in the 1960s that the different artifact assemblages he had identified in southwest France were the material equipment of different groups of people co-existing at that time. These would be an early equivalent of what archaeologists working with later time periods have traditionally termed archaeological "cultures," and equated by some with different ethnic groups. Lewis and Sally Binford, on the other hand, argued that the assemblages represent different tool-kits, used for different functional purposes, by what were essentially the same or similar groups of people. They used factor analysis (see box, p. 197) of the lithic assemblages to document their view. Paul Mellars offered a third explanation, maintaining that there is a consistent chronological patterning among the different finds, so that one phase (with its characteristic tool-kits) followed another.

The argument has not yet been resolved, but there are many who believe that socially distinct groups, roughly equivalent to what one may term ethnic groups, only made their appearance with fully modern humans in the Upper Paleolithic period, and that the Mousterian finds represent something simpler, perhaps along the lines suggested by Binford or Mellars.

Deliberate Burial of Human Remains

From the Upper Paleolithic period there are many well-established cases of human burial, where the body or bodies have been deliberately laid to rest within a dug grave, sometimes accompanied by ornaments of personal adornment. Evidence is emerging, however, from even earlier periods (see box, overleaf). The act of burial itself implies some kind of respect or feeling for the deceased individual, and perhaps some notion of an afterlife (although that point is less easy to demonstrate). The adornment seems to imply the existence of the idea that objects of decoration can enhance the individual's appearance, whether in terms of beauty or

Deliberate burial of the dead: an elderly man buried at Sungir, near Moscow, c. 23,000 years ago, with thousands of ivory beads across his chest and a cap sewn with fox canines.

prestige or whatever. A good Upper Paleolithic example is the discovery made at Sungir, some 200 km (125 miles) northeast of Moscow and dating from *c.* 23,000 years ago: burials of a man and two children together with mammoth ivory spears, stone tools, ivory daggers, small animal carvings, and thousands of ivory beads.

In assessing such finds, one must be sure to understand the formation processes – in particular what may have happened to the burial after it was made. For example, animal skeletons have been discovered alongside human remains in graves. Traditionally this would have been taken as proof that animals were deliberately buried with the humans as part of some ritual act. Now, however, it is thought possible that in certain cases animals scavenging for food found their way into these burials and died accidentally – thus leaving false clues to mislead archaeologists.

Representations

Any object, and any drawing or painting on a surface that can be unhesitatingly recognized as a depiction – that is, a representation of an object in the real world (and not simply a mechanical reproduction of one, as a fossil is) – is a symbol. General questions about representations and depictions for all time periods are discussed in a later section. For the Paleolithic period, there are two issues of prime importance: evaluating the date (and hence in some cases the authenticity), and confirming the status as a depiction. Although it has long been believed that the earliest depictions are of Upper Paleolithic date and produced by *Homo sapiens sapiens*, increasing numbers of earlier examples are forcing us to re-examine this supposition (see box overleaf). The examples given in the box (pp. 392–93)

INDICATIONS OF EARLY THOUGHT

The problem of establishing whether a burial is deliberate or not – and therefore whether it is associated with the idea of respect for the dead – becomes particularly acute when one moves back in time to consider the Neanderthals of the Middle Paleolithic period. On current evidence, the practice of deliberate burial began at this time. The best evidence for the burial of decorative items with the dead comes only from the Upper Paleolithic and later periods, although it has been claimed that a famous Neanderthal burial at Shanidar Cave in Iraq was accompanied by pollen indicating an offering of flowers.

However, there are indications of even earlier rudimentary funerary practices. The Spanish site of Atapuerca, 14 km (8.6 miles) east of Burgos, has revolutionized our knowledge of archaic *Homo sapiens* – a form transitional between *Homo erectus* and Neanderthals in the Middle Pleistocene. Excavation of a limestone cave known as the Sima de los Huesos (Pit of the Bones). Excavation by a team of specialists from Madrid and Tarragona has been going on since 1976.

The site is located at the bottom of a 12-m (39-ft) deep shaft. The bones of over 250 cave bears, which probably died during hibernation, were found in its upper deposits; the lower layers, dated to more than 200,000 years ago, have so far yielded over 2500 human bones from at least 32 individuals (based on teeth), and possibly as many as 50 (thus constituting about 90 percent of all pre-Neanderthal bones known from Europe). The bones are mixed up, with no anatomical connections, but all parts of the body are present. Most are adolescents and young adults of both sexes – in fact *c.*40 percent died between the ages of 17 and 21. Since less than a quarter lived beyond their early 20s, they cannot be representative of a full population, and it is likely the older people were disposed of elsewhere.

Juan-Luis Arsuaga, one of the excavation's directors, believes that the bodies may have been deposited in the shaft, over several generations at least, in a form of mortuary ritual which may point to some embryonic religious belief. The lack of herbivore (food animal) bones and stone tools with them implies that they were not accumulated in the shaft by carnivores and that the cave itself was not an occupation site.

Similarly, sporadic finds are being made which suggest that "art" (or at least non-utilitarian markings) did not start with modern humans, as has traditionally been thought, but stretch back as far as *Homo erectus*. For

Bifaces at the Lower Paleolithic site of Kamitakomuri in Japan, carefully arranged by Homo erectus *and possible evidence of a very early ceremonial act.*

example, a remarkable "figurine" was found by Israeli archaeologists in 1981 at Berekhat Ram on the Golan Heights. Dating to at least 230,000 years ago (the late Acheulian), it is a pebble of volcanic tuff, just over 2.5 cm (1 in) long, whose natural shape is approximately female. Microscopic analysis of the object by the American researcher Alexander Marshack has shown that the groove around the "neck" is definitely humanly made, no doubt with a flint tool, and lighter grooves delineating the "arms" may also be artificial. In other words, the site's occupants not only noticed the pebble's natural resemblance to a human figure, but deliberately accentuated that resemblance with a stone tool. The Berekhat Ram pebble is therefore undeniably an "art object."

Possible evidence for some kind of early ceremony has been found at the Lower Paleolithic Kamitakomuri site in Japan, where three storage pits contained bifaces and other tools; this seems to be evidence of advance planning by *Homo erectus*, while the careful centripetal arrangement of tools in one pit may point to some kind of ritual.

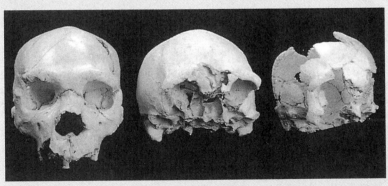

Three skulls from the Sima de los Huesos, or Pit of the Bones, Atapuerca in Spain. This site is producing some of the earliest evidence for deliberate human burial.

indicate some of the important conclusions that are emerging from the application of new research methods to studies of Paleolithic art.

The analysis at the detailed level should not obscure the enormous cognitive significance of the act of depiction itself, in all the vividness seen in the art of Chauvet or Lascaux in France, or Altamira in Spain. To admire this art is one thing; but to develop frameworks of inference that allow us to analyze carefully the cognitive processes involved is much more difficult. This analytic work is as yet in its infancy. Archaeologists have nevertheless made considerable progress in developing techniques and approaches for studying the behavior of our Paleolithic ancestors, and as further advances are made the pattern of early human cognitive development is becoming ever clearer.

WORKING WITH SYMBOLS

In the previous section we looked at ways in which archaeologists can study the emergence of human cognitive abilities. In this and later sections we will be assessing the methods of cognitive archaeology for anatomically fully modern humans. Before going into details, it is worth outlining the scope of cognitive archaeology as it appears to us today, in the very early stage of the development of the discipline.

We are interested in studying *how symbols were used*. Perhaps to claim to understand their meaning is too ambitious, if that implies the full meaning they had for the original users. Without going into a profound analysis, we can define "meaning" as "the relationship between symbols." As researchers today we can hope to establish some, but by no means all, of the original relationships between the symbols observed.

In the pages that follow we shall consider cognitive archaeology in terms of six different uses to which symbols are put.

1   A very basic step is the *establishment of place* by marking and delimiting one's territory and the territory of the community, often with the use of symbolic markers and monuments, thereby constructing a perceived landscape, generally with a sacred as well as a secular dimension, a land of memories.
2   A fundamental cognitive step was the development of symbols of *measurement* – as in units of time, length, and weight – which help us organize our relationships with the natural world.
3   Symbols allow us to cope with the future world, as instruments of *planning*. They help us define our intentions more clearly, by making models for some future intended action, for example plans of towns or cities.
4   Symbols are used to regulate and organize *relations between human beings*. Money is a good example of this, and with it the whole notion that some material objects carry a higher value than others. Beyond this is a broader category of symbols, such as the badges of rank in an army, that have to do with the exercise of power in a society.
5   Symbols are used to represent and to try to regulate *human relations with the Other World*, the world of the supernatural or the transcendental – which leads on to the archaeology of religion and cult.
6   Above all, symbols may be used to describe the world through *depiction* – through the art of representation, as in sculpture or painting.

No doubt there are other kinds of uses for symbols, but this rather simplistic listing will serve to initiate the discussion of how we should set about analyzing them. Symbols of depiction provide us with perhaps our most direct insight into the cognitive map of an individual or a society for pre-literate periods. Among literate communities, however, written words – those deceptively direct symbols used to describe the world – inevitably dominate the evidence. Ancient literature in all its variety, from poems and plays to political statements and early historical writings, provides rich insights into the cognitive world of the great civilizations. But, to use such evidence accurately and effectively, we need to understand something of the social context of the use of writing in different societies. That is the subject of the next section – after which we return to the categories of symbol outlined above.

FROM WRITTEN SOURCE TO COGNITIVE MAP

The very existence of writing implies a major extension of the cognitive map. Written symbols have proved the most effective system ever devised by humans not only to describe the world around them, but to communicate with and control people, to organize society as a whole, and to pass on to posterity the accumulated

PALEOLITHIC CAVE ART

Much has been written about the Ice Age caves of western Europe, decorated with images of animals and with abstract markings. Clustered in specific regions – most notably the Périgord and Pyrenees in southwest France and Cantabria in northern Spain – they span the whole of the Upper Paleolithic, from about 30,000 BC onward. The majority of the art, however, dates to the latter part of the Ice Age, to the Solutrean and especially the Magdalenian period, ending around 10,000 BC.

The cave artists used a great range of techniques, from simple finger tracings and modeling in clay to engravings and bas-relief sculpture, and from hand stencils to paintings using two or three colors. Much of the

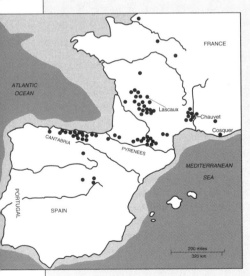

Principal locations of Paleolithic cave art in western Europe.

Position of the major figures (right) in Lascaux's Axial Gallery: mainly horses, aurochs (wild cattle), deer, ibex, and enigmatic dots and rectangles. About 17,000 years old.

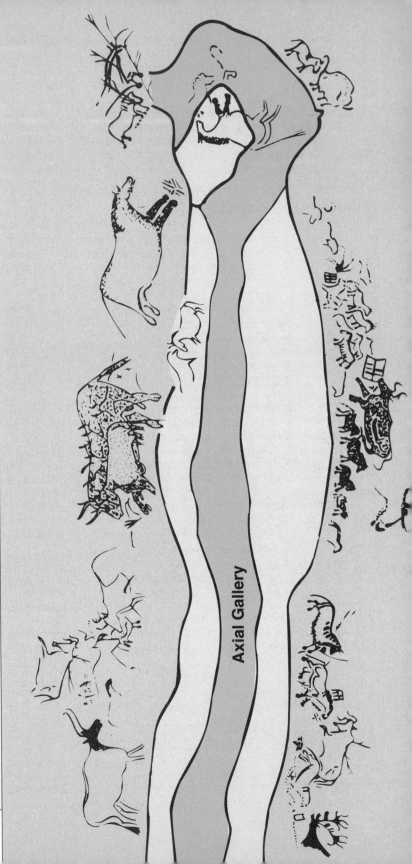

Axial Gallery

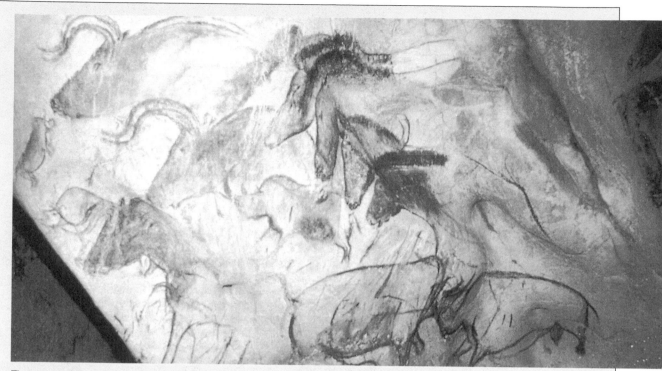

The spectacular paintings of Chauvet Cave, southern France, discovered in 1994, depict over 440 animals.

art is unintelligible – and therefore classified by scholars as "signs" or abstract marks – but of the figures that can be identified, most are animals. Very few humans and virtually no objects were drawn on cave walls. Figures vary greatly in size, from tiny to over 5 m (16½ ft) in length. Some are easily visible and accessible, while others are carefully hidden in recesses of the caves.

The first systematic approach to the study of cave art ("parietal art") was that of the French archaeologist André Leroi-Gourhan, working in the 1960s. Following the lead of Annette Laming-Emperaire, Leroi-Gourhan argued that the pictures formed compositions. Previously they had been seen as random accumulations of individual images, representing simple "hunting magic" or "fertility magic." Leroi-Gourhan studied the positions and associations of the animal figures in each cave. He established that horse and bison are by far the most

commonly depicted animals, accounting for about 60 percent of the total, and that they are concentrated on what seem to be the central panels of caves. Other species (e.g. ibex, mammoth, and deer) are located in more peripheral positions, while less commonly drawn animals (e.g. rhinoceroses, felines, and bears) often cluster in the cave depths. Leroi-Gourhan therefore felt sure he had found the "blueprint" for the way each cave had been decorated.

We now know that this scheme is too generalized. Every cave is different, and some have only one figure whereas others (e.g. Lascaux in southwest France) have hundreds. Nevertheless, Leroi-Gourhan's work established that there is a basic thematic unity – profiles of a limited range of animals – and a clearly intentional layout of figures on the walls. Currently, research is exploring how each cave's decoration was adapted to the shape of its walls, and even to the areas in the cave where

the human voice resonates most effectively.

New finds continue to be made – an average of one cave per year, including major discoveries in France, such as Cosquer Cave (1991) near Marseilles, whose Ice Age entrance is now drowned beneath the sea (see p. 73), and the spectacular Chauvet Cave (1994) in the Ardèche, with its unique profusion of depictions of rhinoceroses and big cats.

However, in the 1980s and 1990s a series of discoveries also revealed that "cave art" was produced in the open air. Indeed this was probably the most common form of art production in the Ice Age, but the vast majority of it has succumbed to the weathering of many millennia, leaving us with the heavily skewed sample of figures that survived more readily inside caves. Only six sites are known so far, in Spain, Portugal, and France, but they comprise hundreds of figures, mostly pecked into rocks, which by their style and content are clearly Ice Age in date.

PALEOLITHIC PORTABLE ART

Ice Age portable ("mobiliary") art comprises thousands of engravings and carvings on small objects of stone, bone, antler, and ivory. The great majority of identifiable figures are animals, but perhaps the most famous pieces are the so-called "Venus figurines," such as the limestone Venus of Willendorf, Austria. These depict females of a wide span of ages and types, and are by no means limited to the handful of obese specimens that are often claimed to be characteristic.

Various research methods have been devised by the American scholar Alexander Marshack. By microscopic examination of the engraved markings on some objects, he claims to have distinguished marks made by different tools, and by different hands on different occasions, producing what he terms

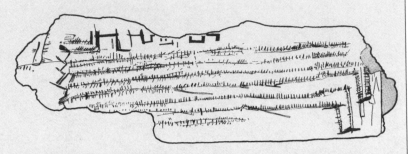

A plaque from Taï, France, with a continuous serpentine accumulation of marks.

"time-factored" compositions (made over a period of time rather than as a single operation). However, experiments using replica tools on stone slabs show that a single implement can produce a wide variety of traces. Only now, with the use of the scanning electron microscope, are scholars beginning to produce criteria by which one can reliably recognize marks made by the same tool (which leaves telltale tiny striations next to the purposely made lines).

Marks on Ice Age objects are sometimes incised in groups or lines. Marshack has long argued that some of these markings, such as a winding series of 69 on an early Upper Paleolithic bone from Abri Blanchard, France, are non-arithmetic "notations," used perhaps in observing the phases of the moon and also other astronomical events. The phases of the moon would certainly have been the principal way Paleolithic people could measure the passage of time.

Marshack has also interpreted a highly complex and cumulative set of more than 1000 short incisions on an Upper Paleolithic bone from the Grotte du Taï in eastern France as a notation, possibly a lunar calendar. Although this view is certainly far more plausible than that of simple decoration, some have remained skeptical of Marshack's claims for notation in the Paleolithic. However,

Italian researcher Francesco d'Errico's analysis of some parallel lines on a late Upper Paleolithic bone from Tossal de la Roca, Spain, has brought strong support for Marshack's view. D'Errico made incisions on bone with different techniques and tools, and produced firm criteria for recognizing how such marks are produced, and whether with one or several tools. He and his Spanish colleague Carmen Cacho then applied these criteria to the Tossal bone, which has four series of parallel lines on each face, and concluded that each set of incisions was made by a different tool, and there were changes in the technique and direction of tool-use between sets, implying that these markings were accumulated over time and may well be a system of notation.

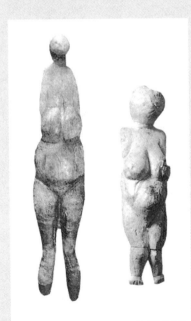

Two "Venus" figurines found in Russia. (Left) Lanky Venus, from Avdeevo. (Right) Kostenki ivory Venus.

One side of the Tossal de la Roca bone, from Spain, possibly with a system of notation.

knowledge of a society. Sometimes it is possible to discern the beginnings of this evolved cognitive map in the form of sign systems that do not yet constitute a fully developed writing system – such as the signs found on pottery of the Vinča culture in southeast Europe before 4000 BC. The rongo-rongo script of Easter Island, which survives as markings on 25 pieces of wood, defied analysis until recently when a key to its structure was discovered which suggests that most of the inscriptions are cosmogonies (creation chants).

Societies with Restricted Literacy

Even where a proper writing system has developed, literacy is never shared by all members of a community, and it may be used for very restricted purposes. In Mesopotamia and Mesoamerica, literacy seems to have been restricted to the scribes and perhaps a few of the elite minority. Mesopotamian writing was discussed in Chapter 5.

In Mesoamerica inscriptions appear mainly on stone panels, lintels, stairways, and stelae, all largely intended as public commemorative monuments (see box, pp. 406–07). In addition, there is the store of Maya knowledge preserved in the codices, but only four of these survive. Inscriptions are found on other objects, such as pottery and jades, but these are all elite items and not evidence for any general spread of literacy among the Maya.

Conceptualizing Warfare. In their study of the Maya center at Caracol in Belize, Diane and Arlen Chase have drawn attention to the existence of four major warfare-related hieroglyphs which, they argue, refer to different kinds of warfare events. There are (1) "capture events," perhaps the capture of individuals for sacrifice; (2) "destruction events," involving the accomplishment of specific objectives; (3) "axe events," which have been interpreted as important battles; and (4) "shell-star" or "star war events" in consequence of which one polity may interrupt succession and exert dominion over another, or break free in a war of independence. An example is offered by the epigraphic record of Caracol in the Late Classic era. Beginning the first episode of widespread war at Caracol is an "axe event," probably a battle initiated by Tikal against Caracol in AD 556. Then in AD 562 came a full-blown "star war" against Tikal. It is followed by the marked absence of hieroglyphic history from Tikal for over 120 years and presumably by the subjugation of Tikal. Apart from its interesting insights into Maya political history, this study illustrates how the increasing understanding of Maya glyphs is allowing us to glimpse the manner in

Maya glyphs identified as referring to warfare (left to right): chuc'ah, *"capture";* ch'ak, *"decapitation", or* batcaba *or* batelba, *"to wield an axe" or "to do battle";* hubi, *"destruction"; and "star-war."*

which the Maya viewed their own history, and how they distinguished between different categories of warfare perhaps more clearly than we do today.

Widespread Literacy of Classical Greece

Against these examples of restricted literacy may be set those cases where literacy was widespread, as in Classical Greece. For extended texts, whether works of literature or accounts, the Greeks wrote on papyrus. Examples of such texts have been found at Pompeii (box, pp. 22–23) and in the very dry conditions of the Faiyum depression in Egypt. For public inscriptions, the Greeks used stone or bronze, although notices that were not of permanent interest were put on display on whitened boards (the simple alphabetic script of the Greeks favored such relatively casual use).

Among the functions of Greek inscriptions carved on stone or bronze were:

- Public decree by the ruling body (council or assembly)
- Award of honors by the ruling body to an individual or group
- Treaty between states
- Letters from a monarch to a city
- List of taxes imposed on tributary states
- Inventories of property and dedications belonging to a deity
- Rules for divination (understanding omens), e.g. from the flight of birds
- Building accounts, records of specifications, contracts, and payments
- Public notices: e.g. list for military service
- Boundary stones and mortgage stones
- Epitaph
- Curse laid on whoever might disturb a particular tomb.

It is clear from this list what an important role writing had within the democratic government of the Greek states.

A better index of literacy and of the role of writing in Greek daily life is given by the various objects bearing

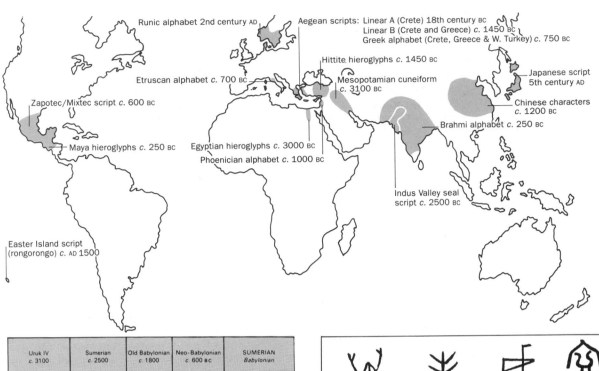

Uruk IV c. 3100	Sumerian c. 2500	Old Babylonian c. 1800	Neo-Babylonian c. 600 BC	SUMERIAN Babylonian
				APIN epinnu plough
				ŠE šeʾu grain
				ŠAR kirû orchard
				KUR šadû mountain
				GUD alpu ox
				KU(A) nunu fish
				DUG karpatu jar

Writing and literacy. (Top) Map to show locations of the world's earliest writing systems. (Left) Evolution of the cuneiform script in Mesopotamia. (Above) Evolution of the Chinese script, using a sentence of classical Chinese composed of four characters "wan pang hsien ming" ("the multitudinous nations have laid down their arms"). First line, oracle bone script; second line, large seal of the Shang dynasty; third line, small seal of the Ch'in dynasty; fourth line, clerical writing of the Han dynasty.

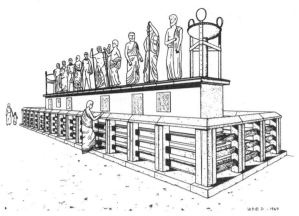

Greek literacy. (Above) In the Agora (marketplace) of Classical Athens, notices were displayed on this public monument. (Right) Potsherds (ostraka) inscribed with two famous Greek names: above, Themistokles; below, Perikles.

inscriptions, and by comments scrawled on walls (graffiti). One type of object, the *ostrakon*, was a voting ticket in the form of a fragment of pottery with the name of the individual – for (or against) whom the vote was being cast – incised on it. Many have been found in Athens where (by the system of "ostracism") public men could, by a vote of the assembly, be driven into exile.

Other Greek uses of writing on a variety of objects were:

- On coins, to show the issuing authority (city)
- To label individuals shown in scenes on wall paintings and painted vases
- To label prizes awarded in competitions
- To label dedications made to a deity
- To indicate the price of goods
- To give the signature of the artist or craftsperson
- To indicate jury membership (on a jury ticket)

Many of these simple inscriptions are very evocative. The British Museum has a black-figure drinking cup of *c.* 530 BC, made in Athens and imported to Taranto, Italy, bearing the inscription: "I am Melousa's prize: she won the maiden's carding contest."

It can be seen from this brief summary that writing touched nearly all aspects of Classical Greek life, private as well as public. The cognitive archaeology of ancient Greece thus inevitably draws to a great extent on the insights provided by such literary evidence – as will become apparent, for example, in our discussion of procedures for identifying supernatural beings in art and individual artists. But we should not imagine that cognitive archaeology is thus *necessarily* dependent on literary sources to generate or test its theories.

Textual evidence is indeed of paramount importance in helping us understand ways of thought among literate societies but, as we saw above for the Paleolithic period and shall shortly see below, there are in addition purely archaeological sources that may be used to create cognitive hypotheses, and purely archaeological criteria to judge their validity. Moreover, as we saw in Chapter 5, literary sources may themselves be biased in ways which need to be fully assessed before any attempt can be made to marry such sources with evidence from the archaeological record.

ESTABLISHING PLACE: THE LOCATION OF MEMORY

One of the fundamental aspects of the cognitive map of the individual is the establishment of place, often through the establishment of a center, which in a permanent settlement is likely to be the hearth of one's home, the *domus* to use the term employed by Ian Hodder. For a community another significant place is likely to be the burial place of the ancestral dead, whether within the house or at some collective tomb or shrine. For a larger community, whether sedentary or mobile, there may be some communal meeting place, a sacred center for periodic gatherings. These are matters of deep significance: as Mircea Éliade has said: "To live in a world one has to establish it.... To install oneself within a territory is equivalent to the foundation of a world." (Éliade 1965, 22) That sacred central place will be the *axis mundi*, the central axis of the world and probably of the cosmos.

These various features, some of them deliberate symbolic constructions, others more functional works which nonetheless are seen to have meaning – the home, the tilled agricultural land, the pasture – together constitute a constructed landscape in which the individual lives. As interpretive archaeologists working in the postprocessual tradition have pointed out, this landscape structures the experience and the world view of that individual. These observations can apply with as much force to small-scale societies as to state societies. As Paul Wheatley pointed out in *The Pivot of the Four Quarters*, many great cities from China to Cambodia and from Sri Lanka to the Maya Lowlands and Peru (see box pp. 410–11) are laid out on cosmological principles, allowing the ruler to ensure harmony between his subjects and the prevailing sacred and supernatural forces. But the sacred center can be important in smaller acephalous societies also, and many of those which appear to have had a corporate structure rather than a powerful central leader, were capable of major public works – the temples of Malta and the megalithic centers of Carnac and of Orkney are good examples, as well as Stone-henge (see box pp. 198–99) and Chaco Canyon (see below and pp. 264–65). Such monuments can also be used to structure time (see Newgrange p. 403) and can operate to facilitate access to the other, sacred world (see below). But these things operate also at a local level, not only at great centers. So the entire countryside becomes a complex of constructed landscapes, with meaning as well as utility – an image well, if poetically, evoked in the case of the Aborigines of Australia by Bruce Chatwin in his book *The Songlines*. The landscape is composed of places bringing memories, and the history of the community is told with reference to its significant places.

Landscape archaeology thus has a cognitive dimension, which takes it far beyond the preoccupation with productive land-use characteristic of a purely materialist approach: the landscape has social and spiritual meaning as well as utility. Building upon earlier traditions of landscape archaeology, these ideas have been well developed in Britain by postprocessual archaeologists of what one may term the "Neo-Wessex school" (Wessex being the area of southern England in which many monuments of the early farming period are situated). Using a variety of approaches, including the phenomenology of Heidegger and the structuration theory of Giddens, they have reconsidered the archaeological approach to the landscape and to the monuments within it, frequently indeed using the

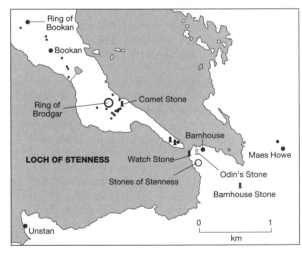

The ceremonial center of Orkney, a ritual landscape in which individuals lived and which in turn shaped their experience and world view. The Ring of Brodgar (left) was one element of a complex and rich sacred landscape (above) which demonstrates that not only large, organized state societies were capable of creating major public works.

monuments of Wessex as their prime example, and this literature (see Bibliography) constitutes the most extensive body of work developed by the postprocessual or interpretive archaeologies of the 1990s (see also The Archaeology of the Individual and of Identity, Chapter 5, p. 215). The landscape and its monuments are seen not simply as reflecting the social structures of society but, by bringing into being new perceptions about the human place in the world, as facilitating the emergence of a new social order. Comparable approaches have been employed in the Classical world: the ancient Greeks sited their earliest temples in ways which structured as well as followed the emergence of the Greek city state.

Even the desert can become a constructed landscape, as the roads around Chaco Canyon in the American Southwest document. Indeed it is very appropriate to see Chaco Canyon (see also pp. 264–65) as a ritual center in what was primarily a symbolic landscape. It has been shown, for example, that the important site of Aztec Ruin lies some 112 km (70 miles) due north, although its heyday came after the decline of Chaco in the 12th century AD. The important site of Casas Grandes, also dating from after the decline of Chaco, lies due south. The Great North Road goes some distance due north from Chaco, although it may not reach as far as Aztec Ruin, and the "roads" (see p. 84), many of which have been rediscovered by aerial photography, are hardly likely to have been constructed for utilitarian purposes: they are processional or ritual ways. Studies have shown that some of the Great Houses at Chaco were aligned to the "standstill" points of the sun and moon. The great circular rooms or *kivas* within them were clearly intended for ceremonial purposes and at Chetro Ketl an impressive range of painted wooden artifacts hints at the decorative and ritual paraphernalia which may have been used, suggesting analogies with the use of the *kivas* in the Pueblo villages of the Southwest which continues to the present.

The lines and figures in the Nazca desert of southern Peru also give us an extraordinary glimpse into the cognitive maps of a vanished people. The archaeological field surveys and the aerial photography of today are directed as much to reinterpreting the experience of the ancient landscape as to reconstructing its practical use.

MEASURING THE WORLD

One aspect of the cognitive map we can readily reconstruct is the way in which it copes with measurement or quantitative description. The development of units was a fundamental cognitive step. In many cases, they can be recovered archaeologically, especially in the case of units of time, length, and weight.

Units of Time

The possibility that time-reckoning developed in the Upper Paleolithic was mentioned in the box on Paleolithic art above. To judge claims for time-reckoning at any period, it is necessary to show either a system of notation with a patterning closely related to that of the movements of heavenly bodies, or clear evidence of astronomical observation. The former is splendidly documented by the calendars of the Mesoamerican civilizations, in the inscriptions on their stelae, and in their codices (see box on the Maya calendar pp. 130–31).

Claims have been made that buildings and monuments in many places were aligned on significant astronomical events such as the rising of the midsummer sun. This was investigated quantitatively by Alexander Thom for the British megalithic circles. Although some of the details of Thom's claims for individual stone circles have been challenged, the cumulative picture argues plausibly for a preoccupation with such calendrical events. In the Americas, the work of the archaeoastronomer Anthony Aveni has done much to demonstrate that the Mesoamerican and Andean civilizations determined the orientation of many of their major buildings in accordance with astronomical alignments. He has shown, for example, that the east–west alignment of the great Teotihuacán street plan (see box, pp. 90–91) is oriented on the heliacal rising of the Pleiades (when these stars first become visible before sunrise), important in Mesoamerican cosmology. The Maya site of Uaxactún provides another example (illus. p. 400), where the arrangement of a suite of three buildings on the east side of the plaza marks the positions of sunrise (as viewed from the west side of the plaza) at midsummer (north), midwinter (south), and the two equinoxes (center) (equinoxes being the midway points of spring and fall).

Units of Length

There are statistical methods for assessing claims that a standard unit of length was used in a particular series of buildings or monuments. The statistical test based on what is known as "Broadbent's criterion" allows

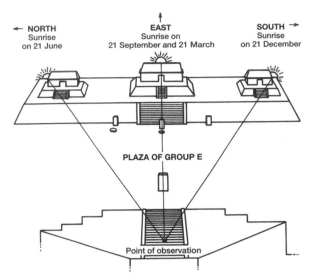

← **NORTH**
Sunrise
on 21 June

EAST
Sunrise on
21 September and 21 March

SOUTH →
Sunrise
on 21 December

PLAZA OF GROUP E

Point of observation

Measuring time: at the Maya site of Uaxactún, Mexico, buildings were positioned so that the rising sun at mid-summer, midwinter, and two equinoxes could be recorded.

such a standard to be sought from the data without knowing or guessing in advance what the unit is. It also gives a measure of the probability that a unit of length discovered in this way is not just a product of chance, without any real existence.

"Broadbent's criterion" has been used to assess the claim by Alexander Thom that a "megalithic yard" was used in the construction of the Neolithic stone circles of the British Isles (see box opposite). Comparable claims have been made for units of measure in the construction of the Minoan palaces, for the Maya, and indeed in many early civilizations. In Egypt, measuring rods have actually been found.

Units of Weight

The existence of measurements of weight can be demonstrated by the discovery of objects of standard form that prove to be multiples of a recurrent quantity (by weight), which we can assume to be a standard unit. Such finds are made in many early civilizations. Sometimes the observations are reinforced by the discovery of markings on the objects themselves, that accurately record how many times the standard the piece in question weighs. Systems of coinage are invariably graded using measurement by weight, as well as by material (gold, silver etc.), although their purpose is to measure differences in value, discussed in a later section. More directly pertinent here are discoveries of actual weights.

An excellent example comes from the site of Mohenjodaro, a major city of the Indus Valley civilization around 2000 BC. Attractive and carefully worked cubes of colored stone were found there. They proved to be multiples of what we may recognize as a constant unit of mass (namely 0.836 g, or 0.03 oz), multiplied by integers such as 1 or 4 or 8 up to 64, then 320 and 1600. One can argue that this simple discovery indicates:

1   that the society in question had developed a concept equivalent to our own notion of weight or mass;
2   that the use of this concept involved the operation of units, and hence the concept of modular measure;
3   that there was a system of numeration, involving hierarchical numerical categories (e.g. tens and units), in this case apparently based on the fixed ratio of 16:1;
4   that the weight system was used for practical purposes (as the finding of scale pans indicates), constituting a measuring device for mapping the world quantitatively as well as qualitatively;
5   that there probably existed a notion of equivalence, on the basis of weight among different materials (unless we postulate the weighing of objects of one material against others of the same material), and hence, it may follow, a ratio of value between them;
6   that this inferred concept of value may have entailed some form of constant rate of exchange between commodities. (This notion of value is further explored in a later section, see below, pp. 404–05)

Items 5 and 6 are more hypothetical than the others. But it seems a good example of the way that superficially simple discoveries can, when subjected to analysis, yield important information about the concepts and procedures of the communities in question.

Units of weight: stone cubes from Mohenjodaro, Pakistan, were produced in multiples of 0.836 g (0.03 oz). Scale pans indicate the practical use to which the cubes were put.

THE MEGALITHIC YARD

The use of units of measure can be documented for several early literate civilizations. It is only since World War II, however, that formal statistical methods have been applied that allow us to look at the evidence from pre-literate societies (those without written sources). The first such application was to a supposed prehistoric unit of length, the "megalithic yard."

In 1955, the Scottish-born Professor of Engineering at the University of Oxford, Alexander Thom, published an article entitled "A statistical examination of megalithic sites in Britain." In this article, Thom measured the diameters of 46 circles of standing stones (megalithic rings), monuments which are first seen in Britain around 3000 BC and continued to be erected for about 1000 years (see box, Explaining the European Megaliths, pp. 488–89). Thom then recorded these diameters on a frequency plot.

The results suggested to him that a unit of measure had been utilized, for the peaks of the frequency distribution seemed to fall at integral multiples of a unit for the diameters of about 5.435 ft (c. 1.657 m). Thom argued that the radius rather than the diameter would have been used in laying out the circles (the circumference perhaps being marked out by a rope fixed to the center of each circle). He therefore proposed

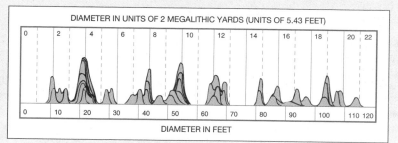

DIAMETER IN UNITS OF 2 MEGALITHIC YARDS (UNITS OF 5.43 FEET)

DIAMETER IN FEET

Histogram (above) of the diameters of 46 megalithic rings (below, the Swinside Stone Circle, northern England), based on Alexander Thom's diagram of 1955. Each peak represents a diameter, measured in feet on the bottom scale. The higher and narrower the peak, the more accurate in Thom's view was the measurement for that diameter. Note how 8 diameters cluster around c.22 ft, 3 diameters around c.44 ft, 5 diameters around c.55 ft etc., suggesting that a standard unit of measure was being employed by the megalith builders. The top scale gives Thom's "best fit" for the unit for the diameters of 5.43 ft. Thom's megalithic yard was half this, i.e. 2.72 ft, since he thought that it would have been the radius of a circle, not its diameter, that was measured out.

that the standard of length in use at the time, the "megalithic yard," was half the diameter, i.e. about 2.72 ft (c. 0.829 m). This is an example of the "quantum hypothesis": that is, that basic units of measure were employed.

Initially, there was no obvious way of assessing this interesting claim. But a paper published by the British statistician, S.R. Broadbent, offered several means of testing whether a given body of data involved the use of a quantum of measure, and these were followed up by another British statistician, D.G. Kendall. These tests show that Thom's 1955 data are significant at about the 1 percent level: that is if we had numerous samples of random data and tried to find the best-fitting unit, it would fit as well as Thom's unit in only 1 sample in about 100.

Thom's work has been criticized, but it is possible that a regular unit of

length was used by the megalith builders. If the accuracy of the layout of the circles was a little higher, it might support the view that measuring rods, 1 megalithic yard in length, were in use throughout Britain in the 3rd millennium BC. But the alternative suggestion has been put forward that the regularity is no more precise than would be expected from the use of a human dimension such as the pace in the layout of the circles.

The outcome of this discussion is not yet certain. What is clear is that statistical methods now exist to allow evaluation of such hypotheses. In cases where the result is shown to be significant at a very fine level, such as 0.1 percent, we may be confident that a regular unit of measure was used, provided always that the data have been fairly sampled, and that appropriate statistical tests have been applied.

PLANNING: MAPS FOR THE FUTURE

The cognitive map that each one of us carries in the "mind's eye" allows us to conceive of what we are trying to do, to formulate a plan, before we do it. Only rarely does the archaeologist find direct material evidence as to how the planning was carried out. But sometimes the product is so complex or so sophisticated that a plan prepared in advance, or a formalized procedure, can be postulated.

It is, of course, difficult to demonstrate purposive planning, if by that is meant the prior formulation of a conscious plan in the construction of some work. At first sight, a village like Çatalhöyük in Turkey (c. 6500 BC), or a sector of an early Sumerian town like Ur (c. 2300 BC), suggest prior planning. But when we look at the operation of various natural processes we can see that effects of very high regularity can occur simply by repetition within a well-defined scheme. There is no need to suggest that the polyps in a coral reef, or the worker bees in a beehive, are operating according to a conscious plan: they are simply getting on with the job, according to an innate procedure. The layouts of Çatalhöyük and Ur may be no more sophisticated than that. To demonstrate prior planning it is necessary to have some clear evidence that the scheme of construction was envisaged at the outset. However, such proof is rarely forthcoming. A few actual maps have come down to us from prehistoric or early historic times; but

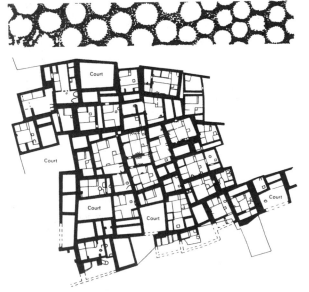

The Çatalhöyük village layout (above) may have been no more consciously planned than the cells in a beehive (top).

most probably represent depictions or representations of existing features, not the planning of future ones. Just occasionally, however, we find models of buildings that may have been constructed before the building itself. There are five or six models of Neolithic temples on the Mediterranean island of Malta that might represent planning in this way: they certainly show close attention to architectural detail.

Such direct projections in symbolic form of the cognitive map of the designer are rare. Sculptor's trial pieces and models, such as have been found in the ancient Egyptian city at Tell el-Amarna, are likewise unusual discoveries.

An alternative strategy is to seek ways of showing that regularities observed in the finished product are such that they could not have come about by accident. That seems to be the case for the passage grave of Newgrange in Ireland, dating from c. 3200 BC. At sunrise on midwinter's day the sun shines directly down the passage and into the tomb chamber. There is only a low probability that the alignment would be by chance in the approximate direction of the sun's rising or setting at one of its two major turning points, in terms of azimuth. But it is unlikely also that, in terms of altitude, the passage of such a tomb would be aligned on the horizon at all. In fact, there is a special "roof box" with a slit in it, over the entrance, which seems to have been made to permit the midwinter sun to shine through.

Often, careful planning can be deduced from the methods used in a particular craft process. Any metal objects produced by the lost-wax method (see Chapter 8) undoubtedly represent the result of a complex, controlled, premeditated sequence, where a version of the desired shape was modeled in wax before the clay mold was constructed round it, which then allowed the shape in question to be cast in bronze or gold. Another example is the standardization in many early metal-using communities of the proportions of different metals in objects made of alloyed metal. The constant level of 10 percent tin in the bronze objects of the European Early Bronze Age is not fortuitous: it is evidently the result of carefully controlled procedures that must themselves have been the result of generations of trial and experiment. The use of a unit of length will also document some measure of planning and was discussed in the box on the megalithic yard. Complete regularity in layout, where there is a grid of streets at right angles, evenly spaced, is also a convincing indication of town planning. Traditionally, it is claimed that the Greek architect Hippodamus of Miletus (in the 6th cen-

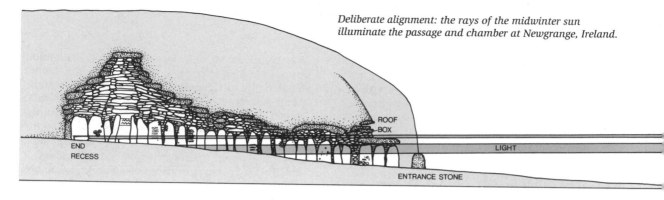

Deliberate alignment: the rays of the midwinter sun illuminate the passage and chamber at Newgrange, Ireland.

tury BC) was the first town planner. But ancient Egypt furnishes much earlier examples – for instance, in the workmen's village at Tell el-Amarna, which dates from the 15th century BC. And the cities of the Indus Valley civilization around 2000 BC show some very regular features. They are not laid out on an entirely rectilinear grid, but the main thoroughfares certainly intersect approximately at right angles. How much of this was deliberate prior planning, and how much was simply unplanned urban growth are questions that have not yet been systematically investigated.

A stronger case for deliberate town planning can be made when the major axis of a city is aligned on an astronomically significant feature, as discussed in the previous section on Measuring the World and the great Mesoamerican and Andean centers. The geographer Paul Wheatley, in his influential book *The Pivot of the Four Quarters* (1971), has emphasized how the desire to harmonize the urban order with the cosmic order influenced town planning. This seems to be true not just for American civilizations but for Indian, Chinese, and Southeast Asian ones as well. The argument is reinforced when the urban order is supplemented by a rich cosmic iconography, as in such cities as Angkor, capital of the Khmer empire, in modern Cambodia.

So far, no archaeologist has sat down to work out in detail the minimum number of procedural steps that must have been planned in advance in undertaking major building works. Of course, like the master craftsmen responsible for many medieval cathedrals, the builders may have relied also on skill and judgment exercised simply as decisions arose, rather than on elaborate forward planning.

There are also some examples of designs being altered during construction. The great Step Pyramid of King Djoser at Saqqara, the first of the major Egyptian pyramids, was clearly the product of several changes or developments of plan by its legendary creator, Imhotep. (His name is found in written texts, but our knowledge of the stages of construction is derived from the study of the monument itself.)

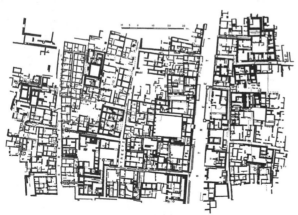

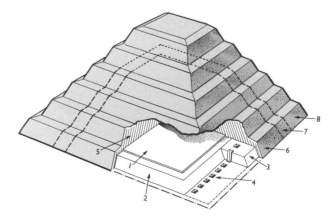

(Above) The regularity in layout of the Indus Valley city of Mohenjodaro – with main streets approximately at right angles – hints at conscious town planning. An example of a change in plan: the Step Pyramid, Saqqara (right): (1–3) pre-pyramid building stages; (4) shafts to subsidiary tombs; (5) buttress walls; (6) pyramid with four steps; (7–8) pyramid enlarged to six steps.

SYMBOLS OF ORGANIZATION AND POWER

Symbols are used for regulating and organizing people as well as the material world. They may simply convey information from one person to another, as with language or, as in the case of archival records, from one point in time to another. But sometimes they are symbols of power, commanding obedience and conformity, for example the giant statues of rulers found in many civilizations.

Money: Symbols of Value and Organization in Complex Societies

In Chapter 5 we referred briefly to the existence of an accounting system as an important indicator of complex social structure. The symbols used in an accounting system – symbols of value such as standardized quantities of precious materials or coins – are both social and cognitive artifacts, reflecting the way in which the controlled elements of the economy are conceptualized within the society's shared cognitive map.

This is nowhere clearer than in the case of money. Money was briefly referred to as a measuring device in an earlier section, but it is something much more than this: it represents the recognition that we live in a world of commodities, which may be quantified and exchanged against one another, often in a marketplace. It represents also the realization that this is most effectively done using an artificial medium of exchange, in terms of gold or silver or bronze (if the money is in the form of coinage), by means of which the values of other commodities may be expressed. Money – and particularly coinage, where the form of the money is determined by an issuing authority – is a form of communication second in its power only to writing. In more recent times, token money, and now stocks and shares, are developments of comparable significance, indispensable to the workings of a capitalist economy.

Identifying Symbols of Value and Power in Prehistory

The existence of scales of value in non-monetary economies is more difficult to demonstrate, although several archaeological studies have sought to establish such scales. Robert Mainfort has used an ethnographic account from the 18th-century AD North American fur trade to aid such an investigation. The account, a list dated 1761 relating to trade at Miami, Ohio, itemized the values of certain goods in terms of beaver pelts (e.g. 1 musket = 6 beaver pelts). On this basis Mainfort assigned values to grave-goods in burials at the Fletcher Site, a historic and roughly contemporary Indian cemetery in Michigan (see also discussion in Chapter 12). This analogy from the ethnographic record assumes, however, that the values operating at the Fletcher Site were the same as those that were recorded several hundred kilometers south in Miami, Ohio. This may be a reasonable assumption, but it does not help us establish a more general methodology for cases where ethnographic or written records are unavailable.

The Gold of Varna. Archaeological evidence on its own can in fact yield evidence of scales of value, as work by Colin Renfrew on the analysis of finds from the late Neolithic cemetery at Varna in Bulgaria, dating from *c.* 4000 BC, has shown. Numerous golden artifacts were discovered in the cemetery, constituting what is the earliest known major find of gold anywhere in the world. But it cannot simply be assumed that the gold is of high value (its relative abundance in the cemetery might imply the converse).

Deducing scales of value: the great worth of the gold from Varna, Bulgaria, is suggested by, among other things, its use to decorate significant parts of the body.

Three arguments, however, can be used to support the conclusion that the gold here was indeed of great worth:

1 Its use for artifacts with evidently symbolic status: e.g. to decorate the haft of a perforated stone axe which, evidently, through its fine work and friability, was not intended for use.

2 Its use for ornaments at particularly significant parts of the body: e.g. for face decorations, for a penis sheath.

3 Its use in simulation: sheet gold was used to cover a stone axe to give the impression of solid gold; such a procedure normally indicates that the material hidden is less valuable than the covering material.

Indicators of this kind need to be developed if the formulation of such concepts of "intrinsic" value (which is a misnomer because the "value" of precious materials is ascribed rather than inherent) are to be better understood. In Chapter 9 we looked at materials other than gold that had prestige value in different societies (box, pp. 356–57).

The demonstration that gold objects were highly valued by society at this time in ancient Bulgaria also implies that the individuals with whom the gold finds were associated had a high social status. The importance of burials as sources of evidence for social status and ranking was discussed in Chapter 5. Here we are more interested in the use of grave-goods like the Varna gold-covered axes, and other discoveries, as *symbols of authority and power*. The display of such authority is not very pronounced in a society like that excavated at Varna, but it becomes more blatant the more hierarchical and stratified the society becomes.

Symbols of Power in Hierarchical Societies

The 6th-century BC chieftain's grave at Hochdorf, western Germany – mentioned in Chapter 5 – was accompanied by a rich array of accoutrements symbolizing his wealth and authority. Near to a comparable princely grave at Glauberg (Frankfurt, Germany) was found a life-size limestone statue of the chief, wearing armrings and neck torque similar to those found in the grave, as well as a sword and shield. Archaeologists today recognize that the grave-goods in a burial are chosen to give a representation or "construction" of the identity of the deceased individual. Here we have a further such construction in the form of a statue, using very similar indicators of rank, perhaps intended to emphasize his heroic status. Even these magnificent burials pale in comparison with some of the treasures buried with the rulers of state societies. It would be difficult, for example, to find a more potent example of royal wealth and power than the tomb of Philip II at Vergina in northern Greece (see box, p. 430), or of Tutankhamun in the Valley of the Kings in Egypt (see box, pp. 62–63).

Indeed, among state societies and empires the symbolism of power goes far beyond merely the burial evidence to suffuse the whole of art and architecture – from the imposing stelae of the Maya (see box overleaf) and the giant statues of Egyptian pharaohs, right up to their later counterparts in Soviet Russia and elsewhere; from the Egyptian pyramids and Mesoamerican temples to the Capitol in Washington.

A study of the art and architecture of the Assyrian palace at Khorsabad, in modern Iraq, provides a good example of symbols designed to impress both native subjects and foreign visitors. At Khorsabad the Assyrian King Sargon II (721–705 BC) built a heavily walled city, with a huge fortified citadel on its northwestern side. Dominating the citadel was Sargon's own palace, its walls decorated with friezes carved in low relief. The subject matter of the reliefs was specifically designed to suit the function of each room. Thus two outer reception rooms – used for receiving visiting delegations – contained scenes of torture and the execution of rebels, whereas inner rooms showed Assyrian military conquests, which reinforced the status and prestige of Assyrian courtiers who used these rooms.

More general questions concerning symbols and art are considered in a later section. Inevitably there is a good deal of overlap between the different categories of symbol isolated for discussion in this chapter. The important point to remember is that these categories are for our convenience as researchers, and do not necessarily indicate any such similar symbolic divisions in the minds of members of the societies that are being studied.

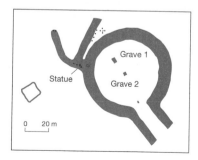

This life-size statue of a chief was found near a 6th-century BC princely grave at Glauberg, Germany. Armrings and a neck torque similar to the ones shown on the statue were found in the grave.

SYMBOLS FOR THE OTHER WORLD: THE ARCHAEOLOGY OF RELIGION

One leading English dictionary defines religion as: "Action or conduct indicating a belief in, or reverence for, and desire to please, a divine ruling power." Religion thus entails a framework of beliefs, and these relate to supernatural or superhuman beings or forces that go beyond or transcend the everyday material world. In other words superhuman beings are conceptualized by humans, and have a place in the shared cognitive map of the world.

But religion is also a social institution, as the French anthropologist Emile Durkheim emphasized in his writings earlier this century. Durkheim pointed out the contribution of religion towards "upholding and reaffirming at regular intervals the collective sentiments and the collective ideas which make its [the social group's] unity and personality." More recently anthropologists such as Roy Rappaport have stressed the same idea, that religion helps regulate the social and economic processes of society. Indeed, more than a century ago Karl Marx argued that the leaders of society can manipulate such belief systems to their own ends.

One problem that archaeologists face is that these belief systems are not always given expression in material culture. And when they are – in what one might term the *archaeology of cult*, defined as the system of patterned actions in response to religious beliefs – there is the problem that such actions are not

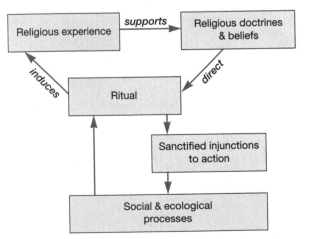

Religion as interpreted by Roy Rappaport: beliefs direct ritual which induces religious experience. Through ritual, religion helps regulate the social and economic processes of society.

MAYA SYMBOLS OF POWER

In the past 30 years our knowledge of the ancient Maya has increased significantly as a result of what has been called "the Last Great Decipherment" of an unknown script. Previously, we knew a good deal about the Maya, not least from their cities and from the stone stelae found there with complicated inscriptions on them.

However, the subject matter of the inscriptions (glyphs) had not been well understood. In 1954, the great Maya scholar Sir Eric Thompson wrote: "so far as is known, the hieroglyphic texts of the Classic period deal entirely with the passage of time and astronomical matters... they do not appear to treat of individuals at all... Apparently no individual of that period is identified by his name glyph." In 1960, however, Tatiana Proskouriakoff (see box, p. 37) of the Carnegie Institution, Washington, published a paper in which she identified rulers of specific Maya dynasties, and from that time, glyphs identifying persons (usually rulers) and places have been increasingly recognized. Indeed, it is possible to reverse Thompson's verdict. *Most Maya stelae are now seen to commemorate events in the reigns of rulers who are almost invariably identified by name.* Moreover, following the insights of the Soviet scholar Yuri Knorosov, we also know that the glyphs have phonetic values: they represent syllables, not concepts (as true ideograms do), and hence, language. Impressive progress is being made.

Maya archaeology has now become fully text-aided archaeology, like Egyptology, or the archaeology of other great civilizations. Previously we had to rely on the documentary evidence of the early Spanish historians in Mexico, such as Diego de Landa. Although writing six centuries after the end of the Classic Maya period, these scholars were able to draw on much knowledge that had survived into the post-Classic era. But now the decipherment of the stelae inscriptions has given us the benefit of a double literacy: that of the Spanish Conquistadors and that of the Classic Maya themselves.

A formidable amount can today be learned about Maya beliefs from the interpretation of a single monument. We may take as an example one of the masterpieces of Maya art, a lintel from the Classic Maya city of Yaxchilán, removed from there by Alfred Maudslay and given by him to the British Museum. This lintel has been analyzed by Proskouriakoff in some detail. It is also one of the works discussed by the American art historians Linda Schele and Mary Ellen Miller in their remarkable book *The Blood of Kings* (1986).

The standing figure is the ruler of Yaxchilán, named Shield Jaguar. He holds aloft a flaming torch, which suggests that the scene lay within a dark interior space. He has feathers at the rear of his head, and "the shrunken head of a past sacrificial victim is tied at the top of his head by a headband, marking Shield Jaguar's largesse in providing sustenance to the gods." In front of him kneels his wife, the Lady K'abal Xoc. She has begun the bloodletting rite in which he will shortly take part, and is pulling a thorn-lined rope through her mutilated tongue. Her cloak is a remarkable representation of Classic Maya weaving.

The inscription gives the names of the ruler and his wife, and indicates a date in the Maya Long Count calendar (see box, pp. 130–31) of 9.13.17.15.12 5 Eb 15 Mac, which is equivalent to 28 October AD 709.

This monument, and others like it, give us insights into a wide variety of fields: for example, they exemplify the use of Maya writing; they use the remarkably precise Maya calendar; they tell us something of the Maya view of the cosmos; and they provide a series of well-dated royal events as a framework to Maya history. In doing so they make major contributions to Maya political geography (see box on Maya Territories, p. 205).

This and other similar depictions are an impressive instance of what the American scholar Joyce Marcus has appropriately termed "the iconography of power." They also indicate sacred rituals of the Maya, where the rulers had an obligation on specified occasions to shed their blood to give sustenance to the gods.

Now that we can interpret these monuments we can see more clearly than ever that this was one of the great art styles of the world.

Lintel 24 from Yaxchilán showing Shield Jaguar and his wife, Lady K'abal Xoc, during a bloodletting ritual. The glyphs which frame their images give details of their names, the calendar date, and a description of the rite. Between them is a bowl containing strips of bark paper on which the blood shed during the ritual is collected. To complete the sacrifice the blood-soaked paper is ceremonially burnt to provide sustenance to the gods, so that water will come to nourish the plants of the earth, providing abundance and sustenance.

5 Eb 15 Mac
9.13.17.15.12
28 Oct.
AD 709

he is letting blood

?

?

4 Katun Lord

Shield Jaguar the captor of

name of captive

Lord of Yaxchilán

she is letting blood

name or titles

Lady K'abal Xoc

Lady Batab

always clearly separated from the other actions of everyday life: cult can be embedded within everyday functional activity, and thus difficult to distinguish from it archaeologically.

The first task of the archaeologist is to recognize the evidence of cult for what it is, and not make the old mistake of classifying as religious activity every action in the past that we do not understand.

Recognition of Cult

If we are to distinguish cult from other activities, such as the largely secular ceremonial that may attend a head of state (which can also have very elaborate symbolism), it is important not to lose sight of the transcendent or supernatural object of the cult activity. Religious ritual involves the performance of expressive acts of worship toward the deity or transcendent being. In this there are generally at least four main components (we will see below how these may then help us draw up a list of aspects that are identifiable archaeologically):

– *Focusing of attention* The act of worship both demands and induces a state of heightened awareness or religious excitement in the human celebrant. In communal acts of worship, this invariably requires a range of attention-focusing devices, including the use of a sacred location, architecture (e.g. temples), light, sounds, and smell to ensure that all eyes are directed to the crucial ritual acts.

– *Boundary zone between this world and the next* The focus of ritual activity is the boundary area between this world and the Other World. It is a special and mysterious region with hidden dangers. There are risks of pollution and of failing to comply with the appropriate procedures: ritual washing and cleanliness are therefore emphasized.

– *Presence of the deity* For effective ritual, the deity or transcendent force must in some sense be present, or be induced to be present. It is the divine as well as human attention that needs to be heightened. In most societies, the deity is symbolized by some material form or image: this need be no more than a very simple symbol – for instance, the outline of a sign or container whose contents are not seen – or it may be a three-dimensional cult image.

– *Participation and offering* Worship makes demands on the celebrant. These include not only words and gestures of prayer and respect, but often active participation involving movement, perhaps eating and drinking. Frequently, it involves also the offering of material things to the deity, both by sacrifice and gift.

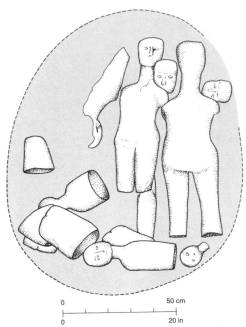

One of two pits containing caches of statues found at the site of 'Ain Ghazal, in Jordan. This is a clear case of the deliberate burial of cultic objects.

The ritual burial of objects of cult significance is one of the earliest attested indications of cult practice. It occurs as early as the 7th millennium BC in the Levant at sites such as 'Ain Ghazal, where it precedes the appearance of recognizable sanctuaries. Extraordinary statues discovered at this site were made of lime plaster modeled over a reed framework and many were decorated with paint. Buried in a pit under the floor of a house, they may represent mythical ancestors.

From this analysis we can develop the more concrete archaeological indicators of ritual listed below, some of which will usually be found when religious rites have taken place, and by which the occurrence of ritual may therefore be recognized. Clearly, the more indicators that are found in a site or region, the stronger the inference that religion (rather than simple feasting, or dance, or sport) is involved.

Archaeological Indicators of Ritual

Focusing of attention:

1 Ritual may take place in a spot with special, natural associations (e.g. a cave, a grove of trees, a spring, or a mountaintop).
2 Alternatively, ritual may take place in a special building set apart for sacred functions (e.g. a temple or church).

3 The structure and equipment used for the ritual may employ attention-focusing devices, reflected in the architecture, special fixtures (e.g. altars, benches, hearths), and movable equipment (e.g. lamps, gongs and bells, ritual vessels, censers, altar cloths, and all the paraphernalia of ritual).

4 The sacred area is likely to be rich in repeated symbols (this is known as "redundancy").

Boundary zone between this world and the next:

5 Ritual may involve both conspicuous public display (and expenditure), and hidden exclusive mysteries, whose practice will be reflected in the architecture.

6 Concepts of cleanliness and pollution may be reflected in the facilities (e.g. pools or basins of water) and maintenance of the sacred area.

Presence of the deity:

7 The association with a deity or deities may be reflected in the use of a cult image, or a representation of the deity in abstract form (e.g. the Christian Chi-Rho symbol).

8 The ritualistic symbols will often relate iconographically to the deities worshiped and to their associated myth. Animal symbolism (of real or mythical animals) may often be used, with particular animals relating to specific deities or powers.

9 The ritualistic symbols may relate to those seen also in funerary ritual and in other rites of passage.

Participation and offering:

10 Worship will involve prayer and special movements – gestures of adoration – and these may be reflected in the art or iconography of decorations or images.

11 The ritual may employ various devices for inducing religious experience (e.g. dance, music, drugs, and the infliction of pain).

12 The sacrifice of animals or humans may be practiced.

13 Food and drink may be brought and possibly consumed as offerings or burned/poured away.

14 Other material objects may be brought and offered (votives). The act of offering may entail breakage and hiding or discard.

15 Great investment of wealth may be reflected both in the equipment used and in the offerings made.

16 Great investment of wealth and resources may be reflected in the structure itself and its facilities.

In practice, only a few of these criteria will be fulfilled in any single archaeological context. A good example is offered by the Sanctuary at Phylakopi on the Aegean island of Melos dating from about 1400 to about 1120 BC. Two adjacent rooms were found, with platforms that may have served as altars. Within the rooms was a rich symbolic assemblage including some human representations. Several of the criteria listed above were thus fulfilled (e.g. 2, 3, 7, and 14). However, although the assemblage was perfectly consonant with a cult usage, the arguments did not seem completely conclusive. It was necessary to compare Phylakopi with some sites in Crete that shared similar features. The Cretan sites could be recognized as shrines precisely because there were *several* of them. One such occurrence might have been attributable to special factors, but the discovery of several with closely comparable features suggested a repeated pattern for which the explanation of religious ritual seemed the only plausible one.

The case for religious ritual can, of course, be more easily proven when there is an explicit iconography in the symbols used. Representations of human, animal, or mythical or fabulous forms offer much more scope for investigation and analysis (see box overleaf). The recognition of offerings can also be helpful. In general, offerings are material goods, often of high value, ritually donated or "abandoned" by their owners for the benefit and use of the deity. Naturally, the fact of abandonment is much easier to establish than its purpose. Yet collections of special objects, often symbolically rich, are sometimes found in buildings in such a way as to make clear that they are not simply being stored there – for example, objects buried in foundations, like the extraordinary caches of jaguar skeletons, jade balls, ceramics and stone masks deposited in layers within the innermost structure of the Great Temple of Aztec Tenochtitlan (see box, pp. 552–53).

Notable assemblages of goods are also found in outdoor contexts – for example, the Iron Age weapons thrown into the river Thames, England, or the impressive hoards of metalwork deliberately deposited in the bogs of Scandinavia around 1000 BC. Individual objects found in this way may, of course, have been lost, or simply buried for safe-keeping, with the intention of later discovery. Sometimes, however, so many valuable objects are found – in some instances with rich symbolic significance, and in others damaged in a way that appears both deliberate and willful if further use were intended – that their ritual discard seems clear. A famous example is offered by the *cenote* or well at Chichén Itzá, the late Maya site in northern Yucatán, into which enormous quantities of symbolically rich goods had been thrown.

Identifying the Supernatural Powers

If the supernatural powers worshipped or served in the practice of cult are to be recognized and distinguished from each other by us, then there have to be distinctions within the archaeological record for us to recognize. The most obvious of these is a developed iconography (representations, often with a religious or ceremonial significance; from the Greek word *eikon* ("image")), in which individual deities are distinguished, each with a special characteristic, such as corn with the corn god, the sun with the sun goddess.

The study of iconography is, for any well-developed system, a specialist undertaking in itself, and one in which the cognitive archaeologist needs to work hand in hand with epigraphers and art historians (see, for example, the box on Maya Symbols of Power, pp. 406–07). Such work is well established for most of those religions that depicted their divine powers frequently. The iconography of Mesoamerica and Mesopotamia generally falls within this category, as does that of Classical Greece. On a painted Maya or Greek vase, for example, it is common to see scenes from their respective mythologies. In the Greek case particularly, we are dependent on literacy for our interpretation. In the first place, it is certainly convenient (although not always necessary if one knows the mythological repertoire) that one often finds the name of a mythic figure actually written on the vase. But the name itself usually has meaning only because it allows us to place the character within the rich corpus of Greek myths and legends known from Classical literature. Without that it is doubtful whether the scenes would in most cases divulge a great deal.

Where literacy and available literary evidence are less widespread – for instance, in Mesoamerica – more emphasis has to be placed on a painstaking study of the different representations, in the hope of spotting recurrent attributes associated in a definable way with specific individuals. Michael Coe has successfully achieved this in his analysis of Classic Maya ceramics. The so-called Popol Vuh manuscript, discovered among the living Maya of the Guatemalan highlands during the 19th century, preserves a fragment of a great 2000-year-old epic concerning the Maya Underworld. Coe's careful research has demonstrated that there are highly explicit pictorial references to this epic on Classic Maya pottery. For example, one of the three divine rulers of the Underworld, God L, can be identified by the fact that he wears an owl headdress and smokes a cigar. His mythical opponents, the Hero Twins, often appear in ceramic scenes distinguished by, respectively, the black spots of death and patches

RECOGNIZING CULT ACTIVITY AT CHAVIN

Two views of the Lanzón or Great Image (top, complete image; above, rollout drawing), depicting a fanged anthropomorphic being.

The great site of Chavín de Huantar, high up in the Andes in north-central Peru, flourished in the years 850–200 BC and has given its name to one of the major art styles of ancient South America. Chavín-style art is dominated by animal motifs represented above all in sculpture, but also on pottery, bone, painted textiles, and worked sheets of gold found at this time in different parts of northern Peru.

First discovered in 1919 by the father of Peruvian archaeology, Julio Tello, Chavín de Huantar itself has long been recognized as a ceremonial center, the focus of a religious cult. But on what grounds?

Excavations in recent years by Luis Lumbreras, Richard Burger, and others have indicated the presence of a substantial settled population, and also helped confirm the existence of cult activity. In the main text we listed 16 separate indicators of ritual that can be identified archaeologically, and at Chavín over half of these have now been established with at least some degree of certainty.

The most immediately obvious feature of the site is its imposing architecture, comprising a complex of stone-faced platforms built in the earliest phase on a U-shaped plan and set apart from living areas at the site – thus fulfilling many of the criteria of archaeological indicators 2 and 16 given in the main text. Ritual involving both conspicuous public display and hidden mysteries (5) is implied by the presence of an open circular sunken plaza that could hold 300 participants, and hidden underground passageways, the most important of which led to a narrow chamber dominated by a 4.5 m (14 ft 9 in) high granite shaft know as the *Lanzón* (Great Image). The carving on this shaft of a fanged anthropomorphic being, its location in a

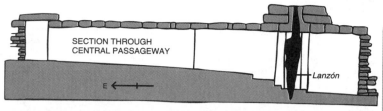

SECTION THROUGH CENTRAL PASSAGEWAY

E ←

Lanzón

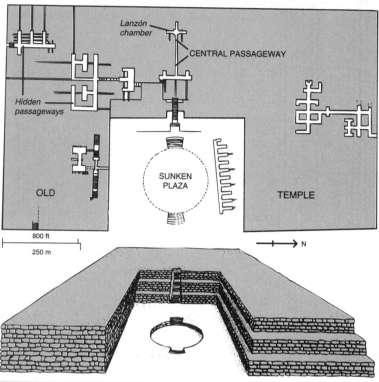

Lanzón chamber

CENTRAL PASSAGEWAY

Hidden passageways

OLD

SUNKEN PLAZA

TEMPLE

800 ft

250 m

N →

Perspective and plan views of the early U-shaped platforms at the site, with a section through the central passageway showing the narrow chamber dominated by the Lanzón or Great Image.

central chamber facing east along the temple's main axis, and its size and workmanship all suggest that this was the principal cult image of the site (7). Moreover, some 200 other finely carved stone sculptures were discovered in and around the temple, the iconography of which was dominated

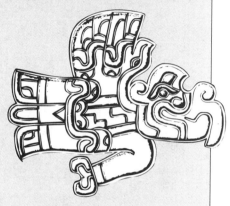

Crested eagle motif from a Chavín ceramic bowl.

by images of caymans, jaguars, eagles, and snakes (4, 8). A cache of over 500 broken high-quality pots containing food found in an underground gallery may have been offerings (13, 14) (though the excavator, Lumbreras, believes they were used for storage). There is iconographic evidence for drug-induced rituals (11) and the possibility that canals beneath the site were used for ritual cleansing (6) and to create roaring sounds to heighten the impact of ceremonies.

The study of Chavín thus demonstrates that a careful archaeological and art historical analysis of different kinds of evidence can produce sound proof of cult activity – even for a site and society concerning which there are no written records whatsoever.

Transformation of a masked shaman (far left) into a jaguar (left). These sculptures were displayed tenoned into the outer wall of the temple, and hint at drug-induced rituals.

Identifying the Maya gods: this scene on a Late Classic Maya vase, probably from Naranjo, Guatemala, has been interpreted by Michael Coe as showing God L, a divine ruler of the Underworld identified by his cigar and headdress.

of jaguar skin over face and body. Through this work Coe has not only enriched our understanding of Maya art and myth, but also in the process convincingly shown that Maya painted ceramics had a funerary function (from the Underworld imagery, backed up by the repeated discovery of such vessels in tombs).

The archaeology of death and burial is an important aspect of the study of religion, as we now discuss.

The Archaeology of Death

Archaeologists have often used burial evidence as the basis for social interpretations, because material possessions buried with individuals offer information about differences in wealth and status within the community. These points were discussed in Chapter 5. But although the living use funerary rituals to make symbolic statements about the importance of themselves

and their deceased relatives and associates, and thus to influence their relationships with others in the society, this is only a part of the symbolic activity. For they are guided also by their beliefs about death and what may follow it.

The deposition of objects with the dead is sometimes assumed to indicate a belief in an afterlife, but this need not follow. In some societies, the deceased's possessions are so firmly associated with him or her that for another to own them would bring ill luck, and there is therefore a need to dispose of them with the dead, rather than for the future use of the dead. On the other hand, when food offerings accompany the deceased, this does more strongly imply the idea of continuing nourishment in the next world. In some burials – for instance, the pharaohs of Egypt or the princes of the Shang and Zhou dynasties in China (and indeed until more recent times) – a whole paraphernalia of equipment accompanied the dead person. As we saw in Chapter 5, in the Shang case, as in the Royal Graves at Ur in Mesopotamia, attendants were slaughtered in order to accompany the deceased in the burial – a practice found in Polynesia too, for example the 40 subjects discovered buried with the 13th-century AD ruler Roy Mata – and here it seems likely that some belief in an afterlife is to be inferred.

In many cultures, special artifacts were made to accompany the dead. The jade suits in which some early Chinese princes were buried, the gold masks in the Mycenaean shaft graves, and the masks of jade and other precious stones accompanying some Mesoamerican burials are artifacts of this kind. Naturally, they had a social significance, but they also carry implications for the way the communities that made them conceived their own mortality, which is an important piece of anybody's cognitive map.

Further inferences can perhaps be drawn from other aspects of funerary rites: cremation as against inhumation or excarnation; collective as against individual burial; the use of major buildings for the purpose, and so on. Again, these are determined in part by the prevailing social system, and the uses to which the living put their ideology. But they are conditioned too by the religious beliefs of the time and the culture involved.

DEPICTION: ART AND REPRESENTATION

We can obtain the greatest insight into the cognitive map of an individual or a community by representation in material form of that map, or at least a part of it. Models and plans are special examples, but a

more general case is that of depiction, where the world, or an aspect of it, is represented so that it appears to the seeing eye much as it is conceived in the "mind's eye."

The Work of the Sculptor

To re-create, in symbolic form and in three dimensions, an aspect of the world, is an astonishing cognitive leap. It is a step that we see first taken in the early Upper Paleolithic period, with the portable or "mobiliary" art mentioned in the box (p. 394). Bas reliefs in stone and some clay models of animals are also known from this period. The latter are smaller than life size, but are much larger than miniatures. More common, however, are representations of the female figure. These are usually carved in stone or ivory, but a series of female figurines modeled in clay, and then baked (in itself quite a complex process) have been found at Dolní Věstonice and Pavlov in the Czech Republic.

Although the relevant abilities may have been latent within all members of our subspecies *Homo sapiens sapiens*, it is nonetheless the case that such Upper Paleolithic sculptural work was limited mainly to Eurasia. In the period of early farming, in many parts of the world, terracotta human figurines, using much the same technology as at Dolní Věstonice and Pavlov many thousands of years earlier, are found. They are widespread in the Early Neolithic of the Near East and of southeast (but not central and western) Europe, and in Mesoamerica. Analysis of these small human figures has illuminated certain details of the dress of the period. Some scholars have also seen in them a representation of a near-universal Great Earth Mother or fertility goddess. But arguments hitherto produced in support of that interpretation of these figurines have been effectively dismissed by Peter Ucko – for instance, by showing that most of them are not even clearly female.

The figurines found in southeast Europe were subjected to iconographic study of the kind described in the previous section by Marija Gimbutas, who claimed to see certain recurrent deities among them (see also pp. 218–19). As she pointed out, some of them do indeed appear to be masked figures. However, the more detailed identifications have not won widespread acceptance.

Sculptures approaching life size were produced in prehistoric Malta and in the Cycladic Islands (see box overleaf) – neither of which could be considered urban societies – and life size, or on a truly monumental, larger-than-life scale, in early dynastic Egypt and Sumer, and in many other civilizations. Each had its own sculptural conventions, requiring specialist expertise to be properly understood and interpreted. Conventions of Egyptian art are discussed in the box, pp. 416–17.

Pictorial Relationships

Painting, drawing, or carving on a flat surface in order to represent the world offers much more scope than the representation in three dimensions of a single figure. For it offers the possibility of showing relationships *between* symbols, between objects in the cognitive map. In the first place, this allows us to investigate how the artist conceived of space itself, as well as the way in which events at different times might be shown. It also allows analysis of the manner or *style* in which the artist depicted the animals, humans, and other aspects of the real world. The word "style" is a difficult one (see box, p. 419). It may be defined as the manner in which an act is carried out. Style cannot exist except as an aspect of an activity, often a functional one. And no intentional activity, or more precisely no series of repeated activities, can be carried out without generating a style. Thus the 7000-year-old paintings in rockshelters in east Spain have similarities that lead us to designate them collectively as the Spanish Levantine style. This seems simplified in contrast to the more representational or naturalistic Upper Paleolithic cave paintings of southwest France and north Spain, some 10,000 or 20,000 years earlier (see box, pp. 392–93). Though the nature of what the act of depiction entails from the cognitive viewpoint has yet to be analyzed satisfactorily, the probable purposes of such art are being profitably studied.

The depictions most successfully analyzed are more complex scenes, for instance in mural paintings. One such is the ship fresco from Akrotiri on Thera, a scene which has been variously interpreted as the homecoming of a victorious fleet, or as a marine celebration or ritual. Another excellent example is offered by some of the Mesoamerican frescoes and sculptural reliefs, where close study has allowed the elucidation of the various pictorial conventions. For instance, Frances R. and Sylvanus G. Morley in 1938 identified a particular class of Maya human representations as captive figures, that is "subsidiary figures, generally though not always bound, in attitudes of degradation ... or of supplication." By a consideration of this convention, Michael Coe and Joyce Marcus have shown convincingly that the enigmatic *danzante* figures, the earliest sculptured reliefs from the site of Monte Albán in the valley of Oaxaca, some 400 km (250 miles) west of the Maya area, are not swimmers or dancers, as had been thought. The distorted limbs, open mouths, and closed eyes indicate that they are corpses, probably chiefs or kings slain by the rulers of Monte Albán (see p. 507).

The rules and conventions for depictions on a flat surface will vary from culture to culture, and require

IDENTIFYING INDIVIDUAL ARTISTS IN ANCIENT GREECE

Artists were much valued in ancient Greek society for their skill. In the case of vase painting it was quite common for the painter (and sometimes the potter also) to sign the vessel in paint before it was fired. This means that numerous vessels are known from the hand of a single painter. For the Attic black-figure style (common in Athens in the 6th century BC, where human figures were shown in black on a red ground), twelve painters are known by name. It was the great work of the British scholar, Sir John Beazley, in the middle years of the 20th century to assign three-quarters of the surviving black-figure vases either to individual artists (in many cases without a name known to us) or to other distinct groups.

When talking of "style" (see box), we must separate the style of a culture and period from the (usually) much more closely defined style of an individual worker within that period. We need to show, therefore, how the works that are recognizable in that larger group (e.g. the Attic black-figure style) divide on

Exekias, the 6th-century BC Greek vase painter, signed many of the vessels he worked on. Above, part of a funerary plaque by Exekias, with two mourners. Below, Achilles and Ajax – Greek heroes of the Trojan War – depicted by Exekias playing a game.

closer examination into smaller, well-defined groups. Moreover, we need to bear in mind that these smaller subgroupings might relate not to individual artists but to different time periods in the development of the style, or to different subregions (i.e. local substyles). Or they might relate to workshops rather than to single artists. In the Athenian case, Beazley was confident that in the main he was dealing with pots painted in Athens, and he was able to consider the chronological development separately. He was also greatly helped by the small number of signed vases, which confirmed the hypothesis that the grouping he arrived at did indeed represent individual painters.

Beazley used both an overall appraisal of the style and composition of the painted decoration on a pot in relation to other pots, and the comparative study of smaller but characteristic details, such as the rendering of drapery or aspects of anatomy. Where the name of the painter was unknown, he would assign an arbitrary name, often taken from a

Two Early Cycladic, female figurines of the folded-arm type, c. 2500 BC, both identified as being by the so-called Goulandris Master. The larger figurine is 63.4 cm (25 in) tall.

collection in which the most notable work was housed (e.g. the Berlin Painter, the Edinburgh Painter). All this sounds highly subjective, but it was also very systematic and the evidence was thoroughly published. Although scholars argue about the attribution of some pieces, there is general agreement that the main outlines of Beazley's system are correct.

But can one, using this procedure, identify individual artists for earlier periods in Greece? Many of the sculptures of the Early Cycladic period (c. 2500 BC) take the form of a standing woman with arms folded across the stomach. This well-defined series has been subdivided into groups, and the American scholar Patricia Getz-Preziosi has proposed that some of these may be assigned to the hands of individual sculptors or "masters," all of whom are inevitably anonymous in this pre-literate period. This proposal meets the criterion that there should be well-defined subgroups within the broader "cultural" style. There is no reason to suggest that these subgroups are chronologically or regionally distinguished. But in order to identify them with a specific "master" rather than, for example, with a larger workshop, it would certainly help to have the key evidence available to Beazley: a few signatures, or at least personal marks, or the discovery of a workshop. Nonetheless, Getz-Preziosi's assignments to individual sculptors are plausible.

detailed study in each case. But similar approaches to those described above may be applied by the cognitive archaeologist to any past society – from the Bronze Age rock carvings of Sweden (compare box, p. 418) and Val Camonica in northern Italy (see box, p. 492), to the medieval wall paintings of Europe or India.

Decoration

Art is not, of course, restricted to the depiction of scenes or objects. The decoration of pottery and other artifacts (including weaving) with abstract patterns must not be overlooked. Various approaches are being developed, of which one of the most useful is *symmetry analysis*. Mathematicians have found that patterns can be divided into distinct groups or symmetry classes: 17 classes for patterns that repeat motifs horizontally, and 46 that repeat them horizontally and vertically. Using such symmetry analysis, Dorothy Washburn and Donald Crowe have argued in their book *Symmetries of Culture* (1989) that choice of motif arrangements within a culture is far from random.

Ethnographic evidence suggests that specific cultural groups prefer designs that belong to specific symmetry classes – often as few as one or two classes. For example, the modern-day Yurok, Korok, and Hupa tribes in California speak different languages, but share patterns in two symmetry classes on baskets and hats – a link confirmed by intermarriage between them. With further work, this may prove a fruitful method for analyzing patterns on artifacts, with a view to assessing objectively from material culture how closely connected different societies were in the past. But the interpretation of symmetry is undoubtedly more problematic than the formal analysis, and does not always tell us the meaning or purpose of a design, though it may reveal something of the cognitive structure which underlies it.

Art and Myth

At different times, anthropologists have tried to analyze what is special to the thinking – the logic – of non-western, non-urban communities on a worldwide scale. This approach often has the unfortunate consequence of proceeding as if western, urbanized, "civilized" ways of thinking are the natural and right ones to help comprehend the world, whereas those others might be lumped together as "primitive" or "savage." In reality, there are many equally valid ways of viewing the world. Nevertheless, such broad researches have led to the realization of the significance of myth in many early societies. This was well brought out in

CONVENTIONS OF REPRESENTATION IN EGYPTIAN ART

All art styles employ conventions: indeed in a sense the conventions define the style. Where decorative motifs and abstract forms are concerned, the conventions may be entirely arbitrary. But when the aim of the artist is *depiction* – the representation of objects in the real world and of relationships between them – the conventions are more closely determined.

These conventions may be so different from our own that we may have real difficulty in "reading" them.

They therefore require careful study. It is useful also to define the range of subjects represented, and to consider those subjects *not* chosen. The conventions of the ancient Egyptians were investigated in this way in 1919

The human body was drawn according to a strictly defined canon. Every body part (forehead, nose, navel, knees, feet, etc.) was at a set point on a standard grid, faces were normally in profile, the torso twisted so that it appeared to be facing forward.

by Heinrich Schäfer in his influential work, *Principles of Egyptian Art*, which can still serve as a model for studies of this kind.

The Egyptians did not organize their wall paintings and reliefs primarily by means of perspective. Rather, each object was shown as it was *known* to be. Thus a chest would be seen, usually, sideways on, and, if there were two, the second would be indicated a little out of line with the first. If it was necessary to show that a jar or a chest contained something, that would be shown protruding or on top of the container. The human body also had its standard conventions. As the Egyptologist Gay Robins puts it: "The human figure was represented by a composite diagram constructed from what was regarded as the typical aspect of each part of the body; yet the whole is immediately recognizable. The head was shown in profile, into which were set at the appropriate place a full-view eye and eyebrow and a half mouth. The shoulders were shown full width from the front, but the boundary

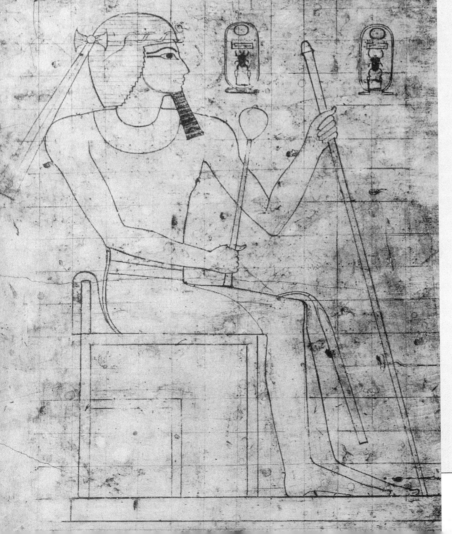

In Egyptian art a single chest was always shown from the long side. To indicate more than one, the chests would be represented slightly out of line with each other.

To show that jars (above) contained incense, the artist has depicted the contents as a ball standing proud of the actual jar. On the left it is entirely visible; on the right partially visible.

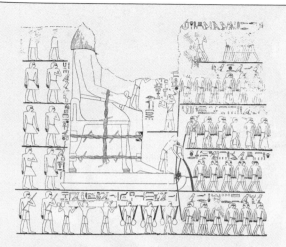

line on the forward side of the body from armpit to nipple or, on a woman, the breast, was in profile, as were the waist, elbows, legs and feet. It was traditional to show both feet from the inside with a single toe and an arch. ... It made perfect sense to have one form symbolizing 'foot' which was then used without differentiation for both near and far feet." (Robins 1986, 12–14.)

The major figure, whether pharaoh or tomb owner (in a tomb painting), was shown at a larger scale than his or her retainers. These minor figures were organized into horizontal registers placed vertically one above another. This was purely a method of ordering; it was not used to indicate spatial relationships or time sequence. But escape from the use of formal registers

Two pictures of a colossal statue being dragged into position by teams of men – one Egyptian (above left), the other Assyrian (above right). The Egyptian rendering is exact in its detail, but the way of depicting the gangs of workers in horizontal registers creates a stilted, artificial effect. The more painterly Assyrian version appears "scenic" to modern eyes.

developed in desert and battle scenes, where forces associated with chaos rather than the ordered world were depicted.

In accordance with the same principles, scenes were shown as much as they were *known* to be as they were *seen* to be, and often a bird's-eye view principle was followed. These principles are admirably brought out by Schäfer in

comparing an Egyptian painting of a colossal statue being dragged with an Assyrian relief of a similar subject (although the latter was carved a

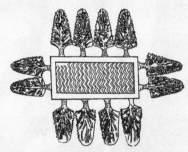

The bird's-eye view principle: the artist has drawn the pool and its surrounding trees as he knew them to be rather than as he actually saw them.

millennium later, around 700 BC). The Egyptian picture depicts with meticulous detail what is known. The Assyrian relief, while it follows its own conventions, appears to us as much more "scenic."

Analysis of this kind is indispensable for a proper understanding of such depictions. Indeed, comparable conventions may be seen in the reliefs, paintings, and codices of Mesoamerica (see, for instance, the box on Maya Symbols of Power pp. 406–07).

In battle scenes, as in nature depictions, the artist could allow the sense of chaos to show in his work.

The Egyptian artist had considerably more freedom when creating scenes of nature, as in this one of desert animal life.

THE INTERPRETATION OF SWEDISH ROCK ART: ARCHAEOLOGY AS TEXT

One of the approaches favored by postprocessual archaeology is to regard the archaeological record as a text composed of meaningful signs, and as Linda Patrik stresses: "all material symbols require a contextual interpretation because their meanings are a function of the specific associations they evoke in a culture and of the actual ways they are combined with other symbols and behavior." One of the most comprehensive attempts to apply this approach to a longstanding and difficult problem, the interpretation of Swedish rock art, has been undertaken by Christopher Tilley. He studied the very rich complex of motifs, generally assigned to the Neolithic and earlier Bronze Age (c. 3500–2000 BC), found carved or pecked on the bare glossy rock surfaces overlooking the river rapids at Nämforsen in northern Sweden.

At first sight the carvings represent an extraordinary jumble, with elks and boats as the preponderant motifs, along with humans, shoe soles, tools, and fish, sometimes occurring together in combination. Tilley undertakes a sustained analysis, breaking down the "text" constituted by the assemblages of carvings, investigating the "grammar," and analyzing the design of elk and boat motifs. His first task he regards as

"reading a material text" and the second "mediating the text" by considering: (1) a structural logic – where the principles linking elks with boats are investigated, leading to the suggestion of a binary class system; (2) a hermeneutics of meaning, where ethnohistorical perspectives are introduced. This follows an earlier suggestion that there may be a long-term continuity between the rock carvings and the designs found on the membranes of historically documented Saami drums in the 18th century AD. He draws also on the beliefs of the Evenk hunter-fisher-gatherer groups of western Siberia relating to Shamanism and the spirit world. Nämforsen is then interpreted in the light of Evenk cosmology, with the notion of a cosmic river, mediating between the different worlds of the cosmos; and (3) an analytics of power, with considerations of social complexity, of exchange and ethnicity, and of domination and the body.

The reader is left with an open-ended array of possibilities, "riddled with contradictions," and no unified and coherent interpretation – not "a painting of a prehistoric social landscape with the carvings positioned in it, but more a painting of different ways of painting this landscape...the reader is intended to

be a participant, not a spectator, however critical, left at the margins."

There is much theoretical discussion, with considerations of assorted thinkers including Saussure, Barthes, Lévi-Strauss, Gadamer, Ricoeur, Marx, and Althusser, and there is no conclusive end-product to the discussion. But Tilley's approach may be described as a strategy of traveling hopefully rather than arriving, and his intellectual journey is rich in unexpected insights – a sustained meditation which offers the reader who possesses the necessary stamina a rich array of concepts and a variety of perspectives.

A herd of elks and a "herd" of boats: two of the rock carvings which can interpreted as archaeological "texts."

Before Philosophy (1946), by Henri Frankfort, one-time Director of the Oriental Institute, Chicago, and his colleagues. They stressed that much of the speculative thought, the philosophy, of many ancient societies took the form of myth. A myth may be described as a narrative of significant past events with such relevance for the present that it needs to be re-told and sometimes re-enacted in dramatic or poetic form.

Mythic thought has its own logic. Most cultures have a story of the creation of the world (and human soci-

ety), which accounts for many features in a single, simple narrative. The Old Testament story of the Creation is one example; the creation story of the Navajo American Indians is another. Thus we should explore oral traditions and written records – where these survive – to help understand the myths and hence the art of such societies. To understand Aztec art, for example, we need to know something of Quetzalcoatl, the plumed serpent, father and creator who brought humans all knowledge of the arts and sciences and is

A QUESTION OF STYLE

The concept of "style" has provoked much discussion among archaeologists and art historians. It is easy for a number of arguments to confuse the issue, and some clarifications are necessary.

Definition Style is *how you do something*. Most writers distinguish between the functional aspect (*what you are doing*) and the stylistic (*how you are doing it*). According to the art historian Ernst Gombrich: "Style is any distinctive and therefore recognizable way in which an act is performed or an artifact made."

Example If we look at any part of the world, we see artifacts made in a distinctive way. The pottery of Mimbres is different from that of the ancient Greeks. Decoration on early Chinese bronzes is different from that on Viking brooches, although both are highly elaborate.

Individual The word "style" derives from the Latin *stylus* (writing implement), referring initially to different styles of handwriting. This reminds us that the term originally referred to the style of the individual (see box pp. 414–15, Identifying Individual Artists in Ancient Greece). The paleographer, working with ancient manuscripts, readily recognizes the different "hands" of a number of scribes. Different hands have been identified in the archives of clay tablets at Knossos in Crete of 1300 BC and written in the Minoan Linear B script, and in comparable archives in the Near East.

Stylistic Area At the beginning of this century, geographers and anthropologists were preoccupied with the definition of stylistic areas in different parts of the globe. Here one is obviously not talking of individual styles but of shared ways of producing and decorating artifacts. A correlation was established between stylistic area and the area occupied by a given ethnic group. Several archaeologists in recent decades have different views:

James Sackett writes as an archaeologist viewing different assemblages of Paleolithic flint tools. He observes that there are longlasting traditions of style, what he terms "passive style," to be contrasted with active and intentional use.

Stephen Plog, in a study of pottery decoration in the American Southwest, has used a related view, where the degree of similarity in the pottery of neighboring areas is seen to be dependent on the degree of social interaction. Stylistic similarity is here dependent upon interaction.

Polly Wiessner undertook an ethnographic study of variation in projectile points among the San people of the Kalahari Desert. She distinguished between *assertive style*, which is personally based and carries information supporting individual identity, and *emblemic style*, which

carries information about group affiliation.

Martin Wobst asserted that "much of what archaeologists label 'stylistic behavior' may be viewed as a strategy for information exchange." Using modern Yugoslavian peasant costume as his example, he showed how variations in dress can convey stylistic messages about status, age, and so forth. Wobst thus firmly links style with the process of information exchange. There is the danger here, however, of confusing the question of style with the whole matter of non-verbal communication effected by visual means. When Wobst speaks in this way, or when Wiessner gives as an example of emblemic style the use of a flag to convey identity, they are losing sight of the original meaning of the word. It is not appropriate to subsume all visual communication under the rubric of "style."

The other distinctions remain valid. It is pertinent to ask whether we are talking of (1) the style of an individual or of the group; or (2) of a consciously adopted mode of decoration (which may well be shared by an ethnic group), or an involuntary similarity brought about by interaction (cf. Plog), or by shared tradition (cf. Sackett).

The analysis by archaeologists of information contained in visual form in artifacts and on representations is still in its infancy. Prehistorians are much less practiced at this kind of study than are art historians and Classical archaeologists. There is much to learn.

---

represented by the morning and evening stars. Similarly, to understand the funerary art of ancient Egypt we have to comprehend Egyptian views of the underworld and creation myths. It is easy to dismiss myths as improbable stories. Instead, we should see them as embodying the accumulated wisdom of societies, in much the same way that all of us, whatever our beliefs, can respect the Old Testament of the Bible as embodying the wisdom of Israel over many centuries down to the late 1st millennium BC.

Aesthetic Questions

The most difficult theme to treat in the study of early art is in a way the most obvious: why is some of it so beautiful? Or, more correctly: why is some of it so beautiful to us?

We can be reasonably confident that many of the objects of display in imperishable and eye-catching materials, such as gold or jade, were attractive to their makers as they are attractive to us. But when it is not so much a matter of material as of the way the material is handled, the analysis is less easy. One important criterion seems to be simplicity. Many of the works that we admire convey their impression with great economy of means. A near life-size head from the Cycladic Islands of Greece from around 2500 BC illustrates this point very well.

Another criterion seems to relate to the coherence of the stylistic convention used. The art of the American Northwest Coast is complex, but is susceptible of very coherent analysis, as Franz Boas, Bill Holm, Claude Lévi-Strauss, and others have shown.

Such questions have been extensively discussed, and will continue to be. They remind us in a useful way that in trying to understand the cognitive processes of these earlier craft workers and artists we are, at the same time, embarking on the necessary program of seeking to understand our own.

SUMMARY

In this chapter we have shown how archaeological evidence can be used systematically to provide insights into the way of thinking of cultures and civilizations long dead. Whether it be evidence for measurement, planning, means of organization and power, cult activity, or the whole field of artistic depiction – there are good archaeological procedures for analyzing and testing cognitive hypotheses about the past. An archaeological project may focus on one aspect of the way ancient people thought (for example, in the search for a possible unit of measurement, the megalithic yard), or it may be much broader (for example, the work at Chavín, which we looked at from the point of view of recognizing cult activity, but which in its way also touches on measurement, planning, symbols of power, and artistic depiction). The two fundamental points to remember are that methods of working need to be rigorous, and that while textual evidence may be of crucial importance in supporting or helping to assess cognitive claims – as in Mesoamerica or Mesopotamia – cognitive archaeology does not depend on literary sources for its validity.

FURTHER READING

The following provide an introduction to the study of the attitudes and beliefs of past societies:

Aveni, A.F. (ed.). 1988. *World Archaeoastronomy.* Cambridge University Press: Cambridge & New York.

Coe, M.D. 1999. *Breaking the Maya Code.* (2nd ed.) Thames & Hudson: London & New York.

Flannery, K.V. & Marcus, J. (eds.). 1983 *The Cloud People. Divergent Evolution of the Zapotec and Mixtec Civilizations.* Academic Press: New York & London.

Frankfort, H., Frankfort, H.A., Wilson, J.A. & Jacobson, T. 1946. *Before Philosophy.* Penguin: Harmondsworth.

Johnson, M. 1999. *Archaeological Theory.* Blackwell: Oxford.

Lévi-Strauss, C. 1966. *The Savage Mind.* Weidenfeld & Nicolson: London; University of Chicago Press: Chicago.

Marshack, A. 1991. *The Roots of Civilization.* (2nd ed.) Moyer Bell: New York.

Renfrew, C. 1982. *Towards an Archaeology of Mind.* Cambridge University Press: Cambridge & New York.

Renfrew, C. 1985. *The Archaeology of Cult. The Sanctuary at Phylakopi.* British School of Archaeology at Athens: London.

Renfrew, C. & Scarre, C. (eds.). 1998. *Cognition and Material Culture: the Archaeology of Symbolic Storage.* McDonald Institute: Cambridge.

Renfrew, C. & Zubrow E.B.W. (eds.). 1994. *The Ancient Mind: Elements of Cognitive Archaeology.* Cambridge University Press: Cambridge & New York.

Schele, L. & Freidel, D. 1990. *A Forest of Kings.* Morrow: New York.

Schele, L. & Miller, M.E. 1986. *The Blood of Kings.* Braziller: New York. (Thames and Hudson: London & New York 1992.)

Wheatley, P. 1971. *The Pivot of the Four Quarters.* Edinburgh University Press: Edinburgh.

11 Who Were They? What Were They Like?
The Archaeology of People

Introductory books on archaeology generally say little or nothing about the archaeology of people themselves – about their physical characteristics and evolution. This seems a strange omission, and one we hope to rectify in this chapter. One of archaeology's principal aims is to recreate the lives of the people who produced the archaeological record, and what more direct evidence can there be than the physical remains of past humanity? Certainly, it is the specialist physical anthropologist rather than the archaeologist who initially analyzes the relevant evidence. But archaeology draws on the skills of a great variety of scientists, from radiocarbon experts to botanists, and the role of the modern archaeologist is to learn how best to use and interpret all this information from the archaeological point of view. Physical anthropology yields a wealth of evidence to enrich the archaeologist's understanding of the past.

A major reason for the lack of integration between archaeology and physical anthropology in the decades immediately after World War II was the question of race. During the 19th and early 20th centuries some scholars (and many politicians) attempted to use physical anthropology to help prove their theories of white racial superiority. This stemmed from their belief that local, indigenous people were incapable of constructing impressive monuments, for instance the burial mounds of the eastern United States. As recently as the 1970s, the white government of Rhodesia maintained that the great monument that today gives the nation its name – Zimbabwe – could not have been the unaided work of the indigenous black population (box, pp. 464–65).

Today, physical anthropologists are much less willing to recognize supposedly different human populations on the basis of a few skeletal measurements. That does not mean that racial distinctions cannot be looked for and studied, but a more robust methodology is needed, supported by well-conceived statistical methods to ensure that any variations observed are not simply of a random nature.

The main thrust of the work today is to use the human remains to show the age and sex of the deceased, to examine the state of health during life, and sometimes to establish family resemblances. In the future, developments in biochemistry and genetics may soon allow much more work to be done at the molecular level, instead of relying mainly on the osteology – the study of bones. There is real hope of approaching once again the whole question of racial distinctions, and how these may correlate with ethnic groups: social groups which regard themselves as separate and distinct.

Perhaps the most interesting field of study, however, is in the origins of the human species. When and how did the uniquely human abilities emerge? What were the processes that led to the development of the first hominids, and then of successive forms up to the emergence of our own species? And what changes have there been in the physical form and in the innate abilities of the human individual since that time?

The Variety of Human Remains

The initial step is to establish that human remains are present, and in what number. This is relatively easy where intact bodies, complete skeletons, or skulls are available. Individual bones and large fragments should be recognizable to competent archaeologists (except for ribs which resemble those of other animals and may therefore require identification by a specialist). Even small fragments may include diagnostic pieces by which human beings can be recognized. In some recent, careful excavations, individual hairs have been recovered which can be identified under the microscope as human. In cases of fragmentary multiple burials or cremations, the minimum number of individuals (see box, pp. 288–89) can be assessed from the part of the body that is most abundant.

As we saw in Chapter 2, purposely made mummies are by no means the only bodies to have survived intact: others have become naturally desiccated, freeze-

The variety of human remains. (Left) At Sutton Hoo, eastern England, the early medieval burials could be recovered only as outlines in the acid sandy soil. (Right) The well-preserved body of a blindfolded girl, drowned in a bog pool at Windeby, north Germany, about 2000 years ago.

being the Iron Age Grauballe Man from Denmark. Sometimes chemical action will alter original hair color, but for mummies fluorescence analysis can often help to establish what that original color was.

Even where the body has disappeared, evidence may sometimes survive. The best-known examples are the hollows left by the bodies of the people of Pompeii as they disintegrated inside their hardened casing of volcanic ash (see box, pp. 22–23). Modern plaster casts of these bodies show not only the general physical appearance, hairstyles, clothing, and posture, but even such fine and moving detail as the facial expression at the moment of death. Foot- and hand-prints are a different kind of "hollow" in the archaeological record, and will be examined later.

Disappeared bodies can also be detected by other means. At Sutton Hoo, England, the acid sandy soil has destroyed most remains, usually leaving only a shadowy stain in the soil – a kind of sand silhouette. If such traces are flooded with ultraviolet light, the "bone" in them fluoresces, and can be recorded photographically. Amino acids and other products of organic decay in the soil may help identify the sex and blood groups of such "invisible" corpses.

In Germany, numerous intact empty pots, buried in the cellars of houses between the 16th and 19th centuries AD, were tested by archaeologist Dietmar Waidelich; samples of sediment from inside them were found, through chromatography, to contain cholesterol which pointed to human or animal tissue, and steroid hormones such as oestrone and oestradiol, so it is virtually certain that the pots had been used to bury human placenta (afterbirth) – according to local folklore, this ensured the children's healthy growth.

Nevertheless the vast majority of human remains are in the form of actual skeletons and bone fragments, which yield a wide range of information, as we shall see. Indirect physical evidence about people also comes from ancient art, and assumes great importance when we try to reconstruct what people looked like.

dried, or preserved in peat. Since so much of our appearance lies in the soft tissues, such corpses can reveal what mere skeletons cannot, namely features such as the length, style, and color of hair, skin color, and marks on the skin such as wrinkles and scars; tattoos (some very clear, as in the 5th-century BC frozen body of a Scythian chieftain); and details such as whether the penis is circumcized. In exceptional circumstances the lines on fingertips that produce fingerprints, and the corresponding lines on the soles of the feet, may survive – the most famous example

IDENTIFYING PHYSICAL ATTRIBUTES

Once the presence and abundance of human remains have been established, how can we attempt to reconstruct physical characteristics – sex, age at death, build, appearance, and relationships?

Which Sex?

Where *intact bodies* and *artistic depictions* are concerned, sexing is usually straightforward from the

genitalia. If these are not present, secondary characteristics such as breasts and beards and moustaches provide fairly reliable indicators. Without such features, the task is more of a challenge – length of hair is no guide, but associated clothing or artifacts may be of help in making a decision. With depictions, one can go no further – for example, in the late Ice Age human figures from La Marche, France, the only definite females have vulvas or breasts, the definite males

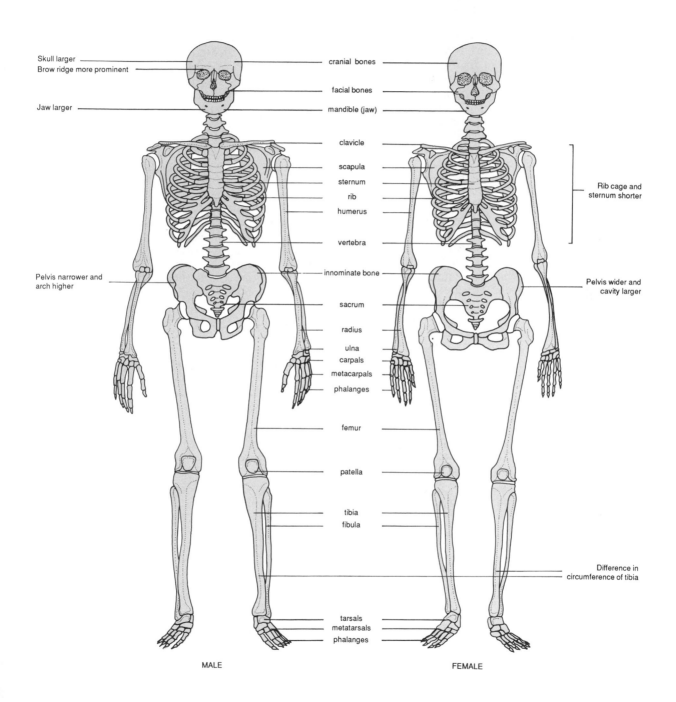

Skull larger
Brow ridge more prominent
cranial bones
Jaw larger
facial bones
mandible (jaw)
clavicle
scapula
sternum
rib
humerus
vertebra
Rib cage and sternum shorter
Pelvis narrower and arch higher
innominate bone
sacrum
Pelvis wider and cavity larger
radius
ulna
carpals
metacarpals
phalanges
femur
patella
tibia
fibula
Difference in circumference of tibia
tarsals
metatarsals
phalanges

MALE
FEMALE

Bones of the human skeleton, with salient differences between the sexes.

423

have male genitalia or beards/moustaches, and the rest of the figures have to be left unsexed.

Where *human skeletons* and *bone remains* without soft tissue are concerned, however, one can go a great deal further. The best indicator of sex is the shape of the pelvis, since males and females have different biological requirements (see diagram, previous page). Not all populations display the same degree of difference between the sexes – for example, it is much less marked in pelvises of Bantu than in those of the San (Bushmen) or Europeans.

Other parts of the skeleton can also be used in sex differentiation. Male bones are generally bigger, longer, more robust, and have more developed muscle markings than those of females, which are slighter and more gracile. The proximal ends of male arm and thigh bones have bigger articular surfaces; females have a shorter chest bone (sternum); and males have bigger skulls, with more prominent brow-ridges and mastoid processes (the bump behind the ear), a sloping forehead, a more massive jaw and teeth, and in some populations a bigger cranial capacity (in Europeans, above 1450 cc tends to indicate a male, below 1300 cc a female). These criteria, used in blind tests on modern specimens, can achieve 85 percent accuracy – but females in certain parts of the world, such as some Polynesians and Australian Aborigines, often have very large skulls.

Anthropologists Yasar Iscan and Patricia Miller-Shaivitz have found that measurement of the circumference of the shin-bone (tibia), about a third of the way down from the knee, can accurately predict sex in 80 percent of samples. But the method is much more accurate for blacks than for whites; the length of bones seems more useful for sexing whites, and thus the method requires prior knowledge of the population involved and, to some extent, of its nutritional level. One should not therefore place too much faith in measurements of any one bone, but combine results from as many sources as possible.

For *children* it is worth noting that, with the exception of preserved bodies and artistic depictions showing genitalia, their remains cannot be sexed with the same degree of reliability as adults, although dental measurements have had some success. Faced with subadult skeletal remains one can often only guess – though the odds of being right are 50:50. Progress has been made in sexing them using discriminant function analysis of measurements of juveniles from Spitalfields, London (see box overleaf), whose sex and age are known from coffin labels. Helgar Schutkowski was able to predict sex with 85 percent accuracy, and found the mandible particularly revealing.

Recently, a new technique has been developed of determining the sex of fragmentary or infant skeletal remains from DNA analysis (see below, p. 432). For example, skeletons of 100 neonates have been recovered in a sewer beneath a Roman bath-house (and probable brothel) at Ashkelon, Israel, most likely the victims of infanticide. Out of 43 left femurs tested for DNA, 19 produced results: 14 were male and 5 female. DNA can also be extracted from coprolites, thanks to cells being sloughed off from the intestines during defecation, and can thus determine the sex of the person who produced them – information which could eventually elucidate gender-based differences in diet. For instance, four coprolites from the La Quinta site, California, and Lovelock Cave, Nevada, were analyzed, and the originators of two were identified as female, one as male, and one remained indeterminate. Experiments on sex determination in coprolites have also been carried out through an analysis of hormones and steroids such as estradiol and testosterone in feces from Salts Cave and Mammoth Cave in Kentucky, which, it turned out, had all been left by men.

How Long Did They Live?

However confidently some scholars may indicate the exact age at death of particular deceased human beings, it should be stressed that what we can usually establish with any certainty is biological age at death – young, adult, old – rather than any accurate chronometric measurement in years and months. The best indicators of age, as with fauna, are the *teeth*. Here one studies the eruption and replacement of the milk teeth; the sequence of eruption of the permanent dentition; and finally the degree of wear, allowing as best one can for the effects of diet and method of food preparation.

A timescale for age at death derived from this kind of dental information in modern people works reasonably well for recent periods, despite much individual variation. But can it be applied to the dentition of our remote ancestors? New work on the microstructure of teeth suggests that old assumptions need to be tested afresh. Tooth enamel grows at a regular, measurable rate, and its microscopic growth lines form ridges that can be counted from epoxy resin replicas of the tooth placed in a scanning electron microscope. In modern populations a new ridge grows approximately each week, and a similar rate of growth has to be assumed in analyses of our hominid ancestors. The method has been shown to be accurate on the Spitalfields juveniles (see box overleaf).

By measuring tooth growth ridges in fossil specimens, Tim Bromage and Christopher Dean have concluded that previous investigators overestimated the age at death of many early hominids. The famous 1–2 million-year-old australopithecine skull from Taung, South Africa, for example, belonged to a child who probably died at just over 3 years of age, not at 5 or 6 as had been believed. These conclusions have been confirmed by analyses of root growth patterns and by independent studies of dental development patterns in early hominids by Holly Smith, and by a recent investigation of the Taung skull's dental development using computerized tomography (see below). All this suggests that our earliest ancestors grew up more quickly than we do, and that their development into maturity was more like that of the modern great apes. This is supported by the biologically known fact that smaller creatures reach maturity sooner than larger ones (our earliest ancestors were considerably shorter than we are – see below).

Bromage and Dean, together with Chris Stringer, have also studied the Neanderthal child from Devil's Tower Cave, Gibraltar, dating to perhaps 50,000 years ago, and changed its age at death from about 5 years to 3 years, a result confirmed by analysis of the temporal bone. Other researchers, however, remain skeptical of this method of aging – tooth ridges are no longer seen as strict indicators of growth, and it is thought there was great variation in Neanderthal populations, making it impossible to generalize from one individual.

Other aspects of teeth can also provide clues to age. After a tooth's crown has erupted fully, its root is still immature and takes months to become fully grown – its stage of development can be assessed by X-ray – and thus, up to the age of about 20, results can be obtained with some accuracy by this means. The fully grown roots of a young adult's teeth have sharp tips, but they gradually become rounded. Old teeth develop dentine in the pulp cavities, and the roots gradually become translucent from the tip upwards. Measurement of the transparent root dentine of an 8000-year-old skeleton from Bleivik, Norway, suggested an age at death of about 60. Accumulated layers of cement around the roots can also be counted to give an age since the tooth erupted.

Bones are also used in age assessment. The fixed sequence in which the articulating ends (epiphyses) of bones become fused to the shafts provides a timescale that can be applied to the remains of young people. One of the last bones to fuse is the inner end of the clavicle (collar bone) at about 26; after that age, different criteria are needed to age bones. Synostosis, the joining of separate pieces of bone, can also indicate age: for instance, the sacrum (base of the spine) unifies between 16 and 23.

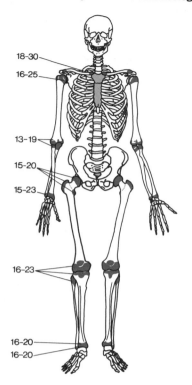

Assessing age: the years at which bone epiphyses fuse (darker color). Areas in lighter color indicate synostosis, the joining of a group of bones (e.g. the sacrum at 16–23 years).

The degree of fusion of the sutures between the plates of the cranial vault (top of the skull) can be an important indicator of age, but the presence of open sutures should not necessarily be taken as an indication of youth: open sutures often persist in old individuals, perhaps because they have a selective advantage. Skull thickness in immature individuals on the other hand does bear a rough relationship to age – the thicker the skull the older the specimen – and in old age all bones usually get thinner and lighter, although skull bones actually get thicker in about 10 percent of elderly people. Ribs can also be used to provide an age at death for adults, since their sternal end becomes increasingly irregular and ragged with advancing age, as the bone thins and extends over the cartilage: this method has been used on the man thought to be Philip of Macedon (Alexander the Great's father) found in a tomb at Vergina, northern Greece (box, p. 430): it suggests he was closer to 45 than 35 (historical evidence indicates that Philip was 46 when murdered).

But what if the bone remains are small fragments? The answer lies under the microscope, in *bone microstructure*. As we get older, the architecture of our

SPITALFIELDS: DETERMINING BIOLOGICAL AGE AT DEATH

London
(Spitalfields)

A rare opportunity to test the accuracy of different methods of aging skeletal material came in 1984–86 with the clearance by archaeologists of almost 1000 inhumations in the crypt of Christ Church, Spitalfields, in east London. No fewer than 396 of the coffins had plates attached giving information on the name, age, and date of death of the occupants, who were all born between 1646 and 1852, and died between 1729 and 1852. Females and males were equally represented, and one third were juveniles. The mean age at death of the adults was 56 for both sexes and the oldest was aged 92.

A range of techniques was used on the material to evaluate apparent age at death, including the closure of cranial sutures, involution of the pubic symphisis, the study of thin-sections of bone tissue, and amino acid racemization in teeth. The results were then compared with the true ages as documented on the coffin plates. It was found that traditional methods of determining age at death are inaccurate. All the methods applied to the Spitalfields skeletons tended to underestimate the age of the old, and overestimate the age of the young, a result that reflects the bias inherent in cemetery material composed of individuals who died of natural causes. Those who die young have presumably failed to achieve their potential and already have "old bones," while those who live to a great age are survivors and have "young" bones at death.

In the Spitalfields population, children were small for their age compared to children today, but the material helped analysts develop and test methods that can give a fairly precise assessment of juvenile age. The Spitalfields adults began aging

later (after 50) and at a slower rate than people today, which should make one cautious in applying data from modern reference samples to skeletal material from the past. As a result of the findings from Spitalfields, it would be rash to try to age an adult more precisely than as biologically young, middle-aged, or old.

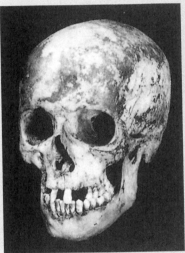

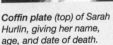

Coffin plate (top) of Sarah Hurlin, giving her name, age, and date of death.

Peter Ogier (1711–75), a master silk weaver, in life and death (above): a portrait compared with his actual skull.

Comparison of the ages at death estimated from bone analysis (shaded) with real ages reveals that many mature adults had been given too high an age because they have "old bones." The cut-off at 75 years old is due to the scale used for the reference population.

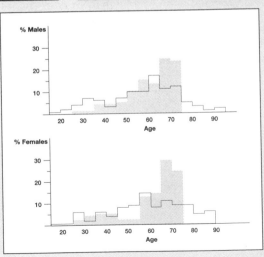

% Males

30

20

10

20 30 40 50 60 70 80 90
Age

% Females

30

20

10

20 30 40 50 60 70 80 90
Age

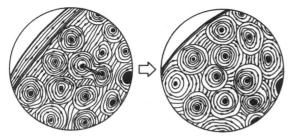

Assessing age: changes in bone structure are visible under the microscope as humans grow older. The circular osteons become more numerous and extend to the edge of the bone.

bones changes in a distinct and measurable way. A young longbone, at about 20, has rings around its circumference, and a relatively small number of circular structures called osteons. With age the rings disappear, and more and smaller osteons appear. By this method, even a fragment can provide an age. Putting a thin section of a femur (thigh bone) under the microscope and studying the stage of development is a technique which, in blind tests with modern specimens, has achieved accuracy to within 5 years. However, on material from Spitalfields (see box) it proved no more accurate than using rib ends or the pubic symphysis.

Akira Shimoyama and Kaoru Harada have applied a new chemical method to a skeleton from a 7th-century AD burial mound in Narita, Japan. They measured the ratio of two sorts of aspartic acid in its dentine. This amino acid has two forms or isomers which are mirror images of each other. The L-isomer is used in building teeth, but converts slowly to the D-isomer during life through the process of racemization (Chapter 4). The D/L ratio increases steadily from the age of 8 to 83, and is therefore directly proportional to one's age. In this case, it was shown that the skeleton was that of a 50-year-old. Since the L-isomer continues to convert to the D-isomer after death, depending on temperature, the burial conditions have to be taken into account in the calculation.

Interpreting Age at Death. Once the ages of a sample of remains have been estimated, one can calculate the average and maximum lifespan within that sample. (It should be realized that calculating these lifespans will not indicate what percentages of people in a particular population lived to those average and maximum ages – if most deaths occur in childhood and old age, this would give an average age at death of around 30, even though few people actually die at that age.) It has been calculated, for instance, that few Neanderthalers reached 50, and most died before 40. By combining age information with sexing results, one can also see

whether men or women lived longer. For example, it seems that women in prehistory were more likely to die before the age of 40 than men, no doubt because of the stresses and dangers of childbirth. Among the prehistoric Chinchorro mummies of Arica, Chile (see p. 64), dating back 4000–7800 years, few individuals lived beyond 50, and the birth-scarred women seem to have died on average two or three years before the men. In 450 skeletons from Roman Cirencester, studied by Calvin Wells, the average male age was 40.8, the female 37.8; both sexes did reach 65 occasionally. In a sample of 40 adults from Wairau Bar, New Zealand, of AD 1150–1450, however, women slightly outlived men on average, although members of both sexes tended to die in their early 20s, and the oldest only reached their 40s.

It must be stressed that one can only calculate average age at death for the bodies and skeletons that have survived and been discovered. Many scholars used erroneously to believe that to dig up a cemetery,

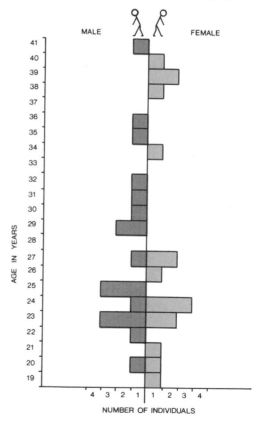

Ages at death of the people of Wairau Bar, New Zealand. Out of a sample of 40 adults dating from AD 1150–1450, the majority died in their early 20s.

and assess the age and sex of its occupants, provided an accurate guide to the life expectancy and mortality pattern of a particular culture. This entails the considerable assumption that the cemetery contains all members of the community who died during the period of its use – that everyone was buried there regardless of age, sex, or status; that nobody died elsewhere; and that the cemetery was not reused at another time. This assumption cannot realistically be made. A cemetery provides a sample of the population, but we do not know how representative that sample might be. Figures on life expectancy and average age in the literature should therefore be looked at critically before they are accepted and used by archaeologists.

But it is not sufficient to have a population broken down by age and sex. We also want to know something of their build and appearance.

What Was Their Height and Weight?

Height is easy to calculate if a body is preserved whole – as long as one allows for the shrinkage caused by mummification or desiccation. But it is also possible to assess stature from the lengths of some individual longbones, especially the leg bones. Tutankhamun's height, for example, was estimated from the mummy and from his intact longbones as 1.69 m (5 ft 6½ in), which corresponded to that of the two wooden guardian statues standing on either side of the burial chamber door.

The formula for obtaining a rough indication of height from the length of longbones is called a regression equation – the metrical relationship of bone length to full body length. However, different populations require different equations because they have differing body proportions. Australian Aborigines and many Africans have very long legs that constitute 54 percent of their stature; but the legs of some Asian people may represent only 45 percent of their height. Consequently, people of the same height can have leg bones of very different lengths. The answer, in cases where the source population of the skeletal material is unknown, is to use a mean femoral stature (an average of the different equations), which will provide an adequate estimate of height, probably accurate to within 5 cm or a couple of inches, which is good enough for archaeological purposes. In Roman Cirencester, people seem to have been a little shorter than today: the average female height was 1.57 m (5 ft 2 in), and the tallest woman was equivalent in height to the average man (1.69 m or 5 ft 6½ in).

Arm bones can also be used where necessary to estimate stature, as in the legless Lindow Man (see box,

Tutankhamun's mummy was unwrapped in 1923, revealing within the bandages a shrunken body. The young king's original height was estimated by measuring the longbones.

pp. 448–49); hand stencils have also occasionally been used. And footprints also give a good indication, since foot length in adult males is reckoned to be equivalent to 15.5 percent of total height; in children under 12 it is thought to be 16 or 17 percent. The Laetoli footprints in Tanzania, which date to 3.6–3.75 million years ago, are 18.5 and 21.5 cm (7.3 and 8.5 in) in length, and were therefore probably made by hominids of about 1.2 and 1.4 m (3 ft 11 in and 4 ft 7 in) in height, assuming that the same calculation is equally valid for premodern people.

Weight is also easy to calculate from intact bodies, since it is known that dry weight is about 25 to 30 percent of live weight. An Egyptian mummy of 835 BC at Pennsylvania University Museum (designated PUM III) was thus reckoned to have weighed between 37.8 and 45.4 kg (83–100 lb) when alive. Simply knowing the height can also be a guide, since from modern data we know the normal range of weight for people of either sex at given heights, who are neither obese nor unusually thin. Therefore, armed with the sex, stature, and age at death of human remains, one can make a reasonable estimate of weight. A single leg bone could thus indicate not only the height but also the sex, age, and bulk of its owner. Where early hominids are concerned, body size is more a matter of conjecture. Nevertheless, because the skeleton of the australopithecine nicknamed "Lucy" (see section on walking, p. 433) is 40 percent complete, it has been possible to reckon that this hominid was about 1.06 m (3 ft 6 in) tall, and weighed about 27 kg (60 lb).

So far, we have a sexed body of known age and size; but it is the human face that really serves to identify and differentiate individuals. How, therefore, can we pull faces out of the past?

What Did They Look Like?

Once again, it is preserved bodies that provide us with our clearest glimpses of faces. Tollund Man, one of the remarkable Iron Age bog bodies from Denmark, is the best-known prehistoric example. Another finely preserved face belongs to the 50-year-old man from Tomb 168 near Jinzhou in China, who was buried in the 2nd century BC and perfectly preserved by a mysterious dark red liquid. Discoveries at Thebes in Egypt in 1881 and 1898 of two royal burial caches have given us a veritable gallery of mummified pharaohs, their faces still vivid, even if some shrinkage and distortion has taken place.

Thanks to artists from the Upper Paleolithic onward, we also have a huge array of portraits. Some of them, such as images painted on mummy cases, are directly associated with the remains of their subject. Others, such as Greek and Roman busts, are accurate likenesses of well-known figures whose remains may be lost for ever. The extraordinary life-size terracotta

army found near Xi'an, China, is made up of thousands of different likenesses of soldiers of the 3rd century BC. Even though only the general features of each are represented, they constitute an unprecedented "library" of individuals, as well as providing invaluable information on hairstyles, armor, and weaponry. From later periods we have many life- or death-masks, sometimes used as the basis for life-size funerary effigies or tomb-figures, such as those of European royalty and other notables from medieval times onward.

Occasionally, one can identify historical individuals by juxtaposing bones and portraits. Belgian scholar Paul Janssens developed a method of superimposing photographs of skulls and portraits. By this means one can confirm the identity of skeletons during the restoration of tombs. For instance, a photo of the skull thought to belong to Marie de Bourgogne, a French duchess of the 15th century AD, was superimposed on a picture of the head from her tomb's sculpture and the match proved to be perfect. Superimposition of photos and skulls was also used to help identify the skulls of Tsar Nicholas II, his wife Alexandra, and their children, murdered in 1918 and excavated a few years ago from the pit in a Russian forest where they had been buried.

There are other ways of proving identity. X-ray investigations in the 1970s of the mummy of an important but unknown Egyptian lady, found in the 1898 royal burial cache at Thebes, showed that her skull resembled that of a woman called Thuya. Thuya was the mother of Queen Tiye who was the wife of Amenophis III and mother of Akhenaten, and probably also Tutankhamun's grandmother – a locket in his tomb was inscribed with Tiye's name and contained a lock of hair. A sample of this hair and a sample from that of the unidentified female mummy were subjected to

Faces from the past. (Far left) Bronze head of the Roman emperor Hadrian (reigned AD 117–138), from the Thames river. (Second left) Moche portrait vase, c. 6th century AD, from Peru. (Second right) Head of Tollund man, the Iron Age bog body from Denmark. (Far right) Mummified head of a man, perhaps the pharaoh Tuthmosis I (1504–1492 BC), from Deir el-Bahri, Egypt.

HOW TO RECONSTRUCT THE FACE

Attempts to reconstruct faces were already being carried out in the 19th century by German anatomists in order to produce likenesses from the skulls of celebrities such as Schiller, Kant, and Bach. But the best-known exponent of the technique in the 20th century was the Russian Mikhail Gerasimov, who worked on specimens ranging from fossil humans to Ivan the Terrible. It is now felt that much of his work represented "inspired interpretation," rather than factual reconstruction. Currently, the process has reached a higher degree of accuracy.

One of the most successful recent reconstructions has been of human remains from Tomb II at Vergina, northern Greece. It was suspected that these remains belonged to Philip II of Macedon, assassinated in 336 BC, who was the father of Alexander the Great. Small family portrait figures in the tomb seemed to support the suspicion.

Richard Neave, John Prag, and their colleagues in Manchester, England, first took casts of the cremated fragments of skull, and fitted them together – a difficult task owing to shrinkage of some of the parts, injury and congenital deformity: the left side of the face proved to be markedly underdeveloped, with compensating overdevelopment of the right. An injury to the right eye socket (a healed fracture, and a notch on the upper edge of the orbit) implied a blow by a missile from above, and tallied with hints from portrait heads as well as with an account by a 1st-century BC author who stated that Philip was hit in the right eye by an arrow at the siege of Methone.

The next step was to insert measuring pegs at 23 key points in

Richard Neave reconstructs a face, perhaps of King Midas, from skull remains found at Gordion, Turkey, where Midas ruled (738–696 BC).

Miniature ivory head thought to represent Philip II, from Tomb II at Vergina.

the skull: the thickness of soft tissue at these points was known from modern specimens. The size and distribution of facial features were largely determined by the skull's structure, and therefore the major muscles could be modeled on. Finally, the superficial layers of muscle and skin were added, though their degree of development was far less accurately determined.

Normally this is as far as the skull will allow one to go, though in the case of Philip a detailed scar was originally added to the right eye based on the study of an almost identical injury received by a present-day Canadian lumberjack! Only after the reconstruction was made was it discovered from reading Pliny's *Natural History* that Philip had received treatment that would have prevented or at least reduced scarring. Other details – hair type/ color/style/length, skin color and condition, facial hair, eye color, and the shape and configuration of nose, lips, and ears – were not totally unknown, and were broadly determined by racial type. Facial hair depends on ethnic type (some lack it); configuration of nose, lips, and position of ears are determined within broad limits by the shape of the skull. In Philip's case, the confirmation of his identity meant that certain of these characteristics could be copied from family portraits (for example, the typical nose shape).

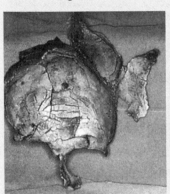
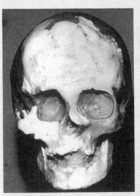
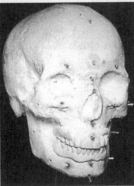
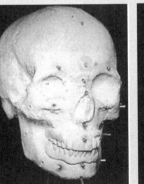

Reconstruction in progress (left to right): the frontal bone of the skull from the Vergina tomb; the skull after laboratory reconstruction; a plaster cast with marker pegs in position for the addition of soft tissue; a wax cast of the reconstructed head, with the eye wound rendered to give the impression of Philip's having received some medical treatment.

scanning electron microprobe analysis by James Harris and his colleagues at the University of Michigan. The almost identical X-ray scatters from these two samples suggested that the lady is indeed Tiye, although more recent work in Germany has cast some doubt on the validity of these results.

A different method has proved to some, if not all, scholars' satisfaction the identity of Philip of Macedon's remains (see box opposite). It involved the reconstruction of the skull, and then the building up of facial tissue. The resulting head was compared with a portrait assumed to be of Philip found in the tomb and with written descriptions of his wounds. Some facial reconstructions are now done with a laser-scanning camera connected to a computer containing information about the skull's muscle-group thickness, and a computer-controlled machine then cuts a 3-D model out of hard foam: this method has been used, for example, to recreate the face of a Viking fisherman at York.

Stereolithography, a technique used for surgical reconstructions, has been used to replicate the skull of Italy's 5300-year-old Iceman (see box, pp. 66–67). Multiple scans (see box, pp. 440–41) enabled a computer to record electronic "slices" of the skull; a second computer then used these data to construct replica skulls by carving plastic with a laser, as in the case of the York Viking. The technique recreates not only the outside of the skull but also its inner surfaces. A complete facsimile skeleton of the Iceman is planned, which will aid its investigation since the actual body can only be examined for 20 minutes every two weeks to avoid deterioration. Fragmentary fossil skulls can also now be restored, measured, and replicated without physical contact through a similar technique. Using a combination of computerized tomography (see box pp. 440–41), computer-assisted reconstruction, and stereolithography, Swiss researchers have turned five fossil fragments of the Neanderthal child from Devil's Tower Cave, Gibraltar (see p. 425), into a solid model of an intact skull; missing areas were restored with mirror images from opposite sides.

Any jewelry or clothing found associated with bodies or skeletons are also invaluable in assessing how these people looked during life. And footprints provide clues about footwear. Nearly all Ice Age prints are barefoot, but one of those in the French late Upper Paleolithic cave of Fontanet seems to have been made by a soft moccasin.

How Were They Related?

We have seen that in certain cases it is possible to assess the relationship between two individuals by comparing skull shape or analyzing the hair. There are other methods of achieving the same result, primarily by study of dental morphology. Some dental anomalies (such as enlarged or extra teeth, and especially missing wisdom teeth) run in families.

Blood groups can be determined from soft tissue, bone, and even from tooth dentine up to more than 30,000 years old, since the polysaccharides responsible for blood groups are found in all tissues, not just in red blood cells, and survive well. Indeed, protein analysis by radioimmunoassay (the detection of reaction to antibodies) can now identify protein molecules surviving in fossils which are thousands or even millions of years old, and can decipher taxonomic relationships of fossil, extinct, and living organisms. In the near future we may obtain useful information on the genetic relationships of early hominids.

One potentially major advance in this direction has emerged from the Canadian Thomas Loy's still somewhat controversial analysis of blood residues on stone tools (see Chapter 7). In cases where identification points to human blood, he uses an immunological testing procedure that gives a positive reaction for the presence of human immunoglobulin. One tool, from the site of Barda Balka in Iraq, dates to 100,000 years ago, and the human blood on it is almost certainly Neanderthal. In Britain, blood has also been detected in Saxon bones more than 1000 years old.

Since blood groups are inherited in a simple fashion from parents, different systems – of which the best known is the A-B-O system in which people are divided into those with blood types A, B, O, AB etc. – can sometimes help clarify physical relationships between different bodies. For example, it was suspected that Tutankhamun was somehow related to the unidentified body discovered in Tomb 55 at Thebes in 1907. The shape and diameter of the skulls were very similar, and when X-rays of the two crania were superimposed there was almost complete conformity. Robert Connolly and his colleagues therefore analyzed tissue from the two mummies, which showed that both had blood of group A, subgroup 2 with antigens M and N, a type relatively rare in ancient Egypt. This fact, together with the skeletal similarities, makes it almost certain that the two were closely related. The exact identity of the mysterious Tomb 55 body is still unresolved, however, some scholars holding that it is Tutankhamun's possible father, Akhenaten, others that it is his possible brother, Smenkhkare.

New work in genetics means that it is now possible to work out family relationships through analysis of DNA (see illustration overleaf). The Swedish scientist Svante Pääbo first succeeded in extracting and cloning

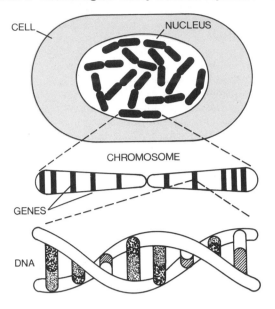

Genes, the organizers of inheritance, are composed of DNA (deoxyribonucleic acid), which carries the hereditary instructions needed to build a body and make it work. Genes are copied or "replicated" with every new generation of living cells; nuclear DNA forms the blueprint for the cells, and is copied every time a new cell is produced. Thus, when cells are cultured in the laboratory, DNA is being grown. Sometimes a segment of nuclear DNA from humans or other animals can be inserted into bacteria and grown in the laboratory. This is called "cloning." The mitochondria (small organelles) within the cell contain relatively small loops of DNA (mitochondrial DNA; abbreviated mtDNA) which have been intensively studied.

mitochondrial DNA from the 2400-year-old mummy of an Egyptian boy. Over such a long time period, the DNA molecules are broken up by chemical action, so there is no question of reconstituting a functioning gene, far less a living body. But information on the DNA sequences of, for example, Egyptian mummies may indicate the relationships between members of royal families, and determine whether members of a dynasty did practice incest, as is commonly believed: an analysis of DNA from six mummies of 2200 BC found at Hagasa, Egypt, has proved that they were a family group. Currently, a databank of thousands of tissue samples is being compiled from mummies all over the world, for future research into everything from the spread of diseases to human migrations.

Genetic material has also been removed from ancient human brain cells in Florida by Glen Doran and his colleagues. Brain material has been recovered from 91 of 177 individuals buried in Windover Pond, a peat bog near Titusville, between 7000 and 8000 years ago. Some of the skulls, when placed in a scanner, proved to contain well-preserved and largely undamaged brains. DNA extracted from them may make it possible to discover whether there are any survivors from this particular Indian group.

Pääbo has also retrieved some DNA molecules from the brain of an Archaic period American Indian (over 7000 years old) preserved in a skull found in 1988 in Little Salt Spring Bog, Florida. The molecules contained a previously unknown mitochondrial DNA sequence which suggests that an additional group of humans entered America (i.e. separate from the three lineages known to have migrated there – see below), but that they died out sometime after their arrival.

It is now possible also to extract the tiny amounts of DNA left in bones and teeth. Researchers at Oxford, using a technique invented in California known as "polymerase chain reaction," have been able to amplify minute amounts of DNA for study. The team has already extracted and copied DNA from fossils over 5000 years old such as a human femur from Wadi Mamed in the Judaean desert, and from the 4000-year-old skull of a child from Maiden Castle, England.

A highly significant breakthrough has been achieved by Matthias Krings, Svante Pääbo, and their colleagues with the extraction of DNA (in this case mtDNA) from hominid fossil remains more than 40,000 years old. As discussed below, this has changed current thinking about the Neanderthals and opens a new era in biological anthropology.

The recent advances in genetic engineering thus open up fascinating possibilities for future work in human evolution and past human relationships.

So far in this chapter we have learnt how one can deduce a great deal about our ancestors' physical characteristics; but the picture is still a static one. The next step is to learn how one reconstructs the way these bodies worked and what they could do.

ASSESSING HUMAN ABILITIES

The human body is a superb machine, capable of performing a great variety of actions, some requiring strength and force, and others involving fine control and specialized skills, but it has not always been able to perform these tasks. How then do we trace the development of various human abilities?

Walking

One of the most basic uniquely human features is the ability to walk habitually on two legs – bipedalism. A number of methods provide insights into the evolution of this trait. Analysis of certain parts of the skeleton, and of body proportions, is the most straightforward method, but skulls are often the only parts of our early ancestors to have survived. One exception is the 40 per-cent complete australopithecine skeleton nick-named "Lucy," dating from around 3.18 million years ago and found by Donald Johanson and his colleagues at Hadar in the Afar region of Ethiopia – hence its scientific name, *Australopithecus afarensis*. Much attention has been focused on the lower half of Lucy's skeleton. The American paleoanthropologists Jack Stern and Randall Susman believe that it could walk, but still needed trees for food and protection – their evidence consists of the long, curved, and very muscular hands and feet, fea-tures that suggest grasping.

Another American researcher, Bruce Latimer, and his colleagues, think that Lucy was a fully adapted biped. They doubt that curved finger and toe bones are proof of a life in trees, and find that the lower limbs were "totally reorganized for upright walking": the orientation of the ankle is similar to that in a modern human, implying that the foot was less flexible in its sideways movements than an ape's. Lucy's propor-tions are not incompatible with bipedalism, but it had not yet achieved the gait of modern humans, since the pelvis was still somewhat like that of a chimpanzee.

Recently, the debate has been exacerbated by analy-sis of "Little Foot", four articulating footbones from a probable *Australopithecus africanus* from Sterk-fontein, South Africa, up to 3.5 million years old. Some specialists believe that, while clearly adapted for bipedalism, the foot also has apelike traits which make it perfect for tree-life. Other specialists insist that these are simply relict anatomical traits, and that these aus-tralopithecines spent all their time on two legs on the ground.

A different type of evidence for upright walking can be found in *skulls*. The position of the hole at their base, for example, where the spinal column enters, tells a great deal about the position of the body during locomotion. Even fossil skulls trapped inside a rock-hard matrix can now be examined through the tech-nique of computerized axial tomography (CAT or CT), in which X-ray scans made at 5-mm intervals produce a series of cross-sections that the computer can refor-mat to create vertical or oblique images as required. A skull can therefore be seen from any angle. The tech-nique is also useful for studying mummies without unwrapping them, and for revealing which organs still remain inside them (see box, pp. 440–41).

Dutch scientists Frans Zonneveld and Jan Wind have used the CAT-scan technique on the very complete skull of *Australopithecus africanus*, 2–3 million years old, from Sterkfontein, South Africa, known as "Mrs Ples." The scans revealed the semicircular canals of the inner ear, entombed inside the solid fossil cranium. This feature is of special interest because it provides an indication of the carriage of the head: the horizontal canal has a relationship with the angle of the head in upright-walking humans. The angle in "Mrs Ples" sug-gested that she walked with her head at a greater forward-sloping angle than in modern humans. Dutch anatomist Fred Spoor and his colleagues have recently studied the canals in a series of different hominids, and found that in australopithecines this feature is decid-edly apelike – supporting the view that they mixed tree-climbing with bipedalism – while *Homo erectus* was similar to modern humans in this respect.

Footprints in Time. A great deal can be learned from the actual traces of human locomotion: the footprints of early hominids. The best known specimens are the remarkable trails discovered at Laetoli, Tanzania, by Mary Leakey. These were left by small hominids around 3.6–3.75 million years ago, according to potas-sium-argon dates of the volcanic tuffs above and below this level. They walked across a stretch of moist vol-canic ash, which was subsequently turned to mud by rain, and then set like concrete.

Observation of the prints' shape revealed to Mary Leakey and her colleagues that the feet had a raised arch, a rounded heel, a pronounced ball, and a big toe which pointed forward. These features, together with the weight-bearing pressure patterns, resembled the prints of upright-walking humans. The pressures exer-ted along the foot, together with the length of stride (average 87 cm, or 34 in), indicated that the hominids (probably early australopithecines) had been walking slowly. In short, all the detectable morphological fea-tures implied that the feet which did the walking were very little different from our own.

A detailed study has been made of the prints using photogrammetry (Chapter 3), which created a drawing showing all the curves and contours of the prints. The result emphasized that there were at least seven points of similarity with modern prints, such as the depth of the heel impression, and the deep imprint of the big toe. Michael Day and E. Wickens also took stereo-photographs of the Laetoli prints, and compared them with modern prints made by men and women in simi-lar soil conditions. Once again, the results furnished

The Laetoli footprints. (Top) One of the remarkable footprint trails left by early hominids 3.6–3.75 million years ago at this East African site. (Above) The contour pattern of one of the Laetoli footprints, left, is strikingly similar to that of a modern male foot impression made in soft ground, right.

possible evidence of bipedalism. Footprints thus provide us not merely with rare traces of the soft tissue of our remote ancestors, but evidence of upright walking that in many ways is clearer than can be obtained from analysis of bones.

The study of fossil prints is by no means restricted to such remote periods. Hundreds of prints are known, for example, in French caves, dating from the end of the last Ice Age. Research by Léon Pales, using detailed silicone resin molds, has revealed details of behavior in these caves: we have already mentioned that most of these prints are barefoot. Many of the prints were made by children, who seem to have had no fear of exploring the dark depths of caves. In the cave of Fontanet one can follow the track of a child who was chasing a puppy or a fox. In the cave of Niaux, the prints show that children's feet were narrower and more arched than today.

More recent prints are known from the surface of ancient Japanese paddy fields, from early Holocene surfaces on the Argentine seashore, and especially from 3600-year-old mud-flats in England's Mersey estuary where 145 footprint trails show a mean adult male height of 1.66 m (5 ft 5 in) and a female height of 1.45 m (4 ft 9 in). Many children are present, moving slowly like the women (perhaps gathering shellfish), while the men moved rapidly. Some of the prints show abnormalities such as toes missing or fused, providing information on medical conditions.

Which Hand Did They Use?

We all know that many more people today are right-handed than left-handed. Can one trace this same pattern far back in prehistory? Much of the evidence comes from stencils and prints found in Australian rockshelters and elsewhere, and in many Ice Age caves in France, Spain, and Tasmania. Where a left hand has been stenciled, this implies that the artist was right-handed, and vice versa. Even though the paint was often sprayed on by mouth, one can assume that the dominant hand assisted in the operation. One also has to make the assumption that hands were stenciled palm-downward – a left hand stenciled palm-upward might of course look as if it were a *right* hand. Of 158 stencils in the French cave of Gargas, to which we shall return later, 136 have been identified as left, and only 22 as right: right-handedness was therefore heavily predominant.

Cave art furnishes other types of evidence of this phenomenon. Most engravings, for example, are best lit from the left, as befits the work of right-handed artists, who generally prefer to have the light source on the left so that the shadow of their hand does not fall on the tip of the engraving tool or brush. In the few cases where an Ice Age figure is depicted holding something, it is mostly, though not always, in the right hand.

Clues to right-handedness can also be found by other methods. Right-handers tend to have longer, stronger, and more muscular bones on the right side, and Marcellin Boule as long ago as 1911 noted that the La Chapelle aux Saints Neanderthal skeleton had a right upper arm bone that was noticeably stronger than the left. Similar observations have been made on other Neanderthal skeletons such as La Ferrassie I and Neanderthal itself, while skeletons of the 11th to 16th centuries AD from the English medieval village of Wharram Percy have been found to have right arms longer than the left in 81 percent of specimens, and the left longer in 16 percent.

Fractures and cutmarks are another source of evidence. Right-handed soldiers tend to be wounded on the left. The skeleton of a 40- or 50-year-old Nabataean warrior, buried 2000 years ago in the Negev Desert, Israel, had multiple healed fractures to the skull, the left arm, and ribs. Pierre-François Puech, in his study of scratches on the teeth of fossil humans (Chapter 7), noted that the Mauer (Heidelberg) jaw of *c.* 500,000 years ago has marks on six front teeth; these were made by a stone tool, and their direction indicates that the jaw's owner was right-handed.

Tools themselves can be revealing. Long-handled Neolithic spoons of yew wood, preserved in Alpine lake villages dating to 3000 BC, have survived; the signs of rubbing on their left side indicate that their users were right-handed. The late Ice Age rope found in the French cave of Lascaux consisted of fibers spiraling to the right, and was therefore tressed by a right-hander.

Occasionally one can determine whether stone tools were used in the right hand or the left, and it is even possible to assess how far back this feature can be traced. In stone toolmaking experiments, Nick Toth, a right-hander, held the core in his left hand and the hammerstone in his right. As the tool was made, the core was rotated clockwise, and the flakes, removed in sequence, had a little crescent of cortex (the core's outer surface) on the side. Toth's knapping produced 56 percent flakes with the cortex on the right, and 44 percent left-orientated flakes. A left-handed toolmaker would produce the opposite pattern. Toth has applied these criteria to the similarly made pebble tools from a number of early sites (before 1.5 million years) at Koobi Fora, Kenya, probably made by *Homo habilis*. At seven sites, he found that 57 percent of the flakes were right-orientated, and 43 percent left, a pattern almost identical to that produced today.

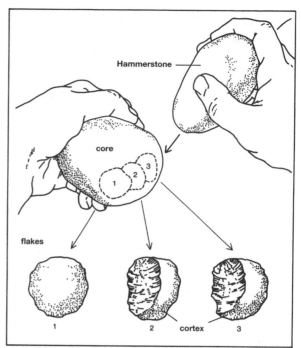

Nick Toth's experiments showed that a right-handed stone toolmaker will typically produce flakes 56 percent of which have the cortex on the right, as here. Tools over 1.5 million years old from Koobi Fora, Kenya, display an almost identical ratio.

About 90 percent of modern humans are right-handed: we are the only mammal with a preferential use of one hand. The part of the brain responsible for fine control and movement is located in the left cerebral hemisphere, and the above findings suggest that the hominid brain was already asymmetrical in its structure and function not long after 2 million years ago. Among Neanderthalers of 70,000–35,000 years ago, Marcellin Boule noted that the La Chapelle aux Saints individual had a left hemisphere slightly bigger than the right, and the same was found for brains of specimens from Neanderthal, Gibraltar, and La Quina.

When Did Speech Develop?

Like fine control and movement, speech is also controlled in the left part of the brain. Some scholars believe we can learn something about early language abilities from **brain endocasts**. These are made by pouring latex rubber into a skull; when set the latex forms an accurate image of the inner surface of the cranium, on which the outer shape of the brain leaves faint impressions. The method gives an estimate of cranial capacity – thus Ralph Holloway has examined two reconstructed skulls from Koobi Fora (KNM-ER 1470 and 1805), and calculated their brain volumes. Skull 1470, dating to about 1.89 million years and usually attributed to *Homo habilis*, had a capacity of either 752 cc or about 775 cc, while 1805, dating to about 1.65 million years and belonging to either *Homo* or *Australopithecus*, had a brain of australopithecine size (582 cc). According to American scholar Dean Falk, 1470's brain endocast shows clearly human features, while 1805 had a brain more like that of a gorilla or chimpanzee.

The speech center of the brain is a bump protruding on the surface of the left hemisphere, which an endocast should theoretically record. Certainly Dean Falk, following on from analyses done by Phillip Tobias, argues that this area of 1470's brain is already specialized for language, and that this hominid was perhaps capable of articulate speech. But by no means all scholars are convinced that features of this type in fossil hominids are ever sufficiently clear for reliable interpretation.

Since fine control and movement are located in the same part of the brain as speech, some scholars go on to argue that the two may be interconnected. From this they develop the thesis that symmetry in tools could be a sign of the sort of intellectual skill needed to understand language. The increasing abundance and perfection of form of the Acheulian hand-axe, or an increase in the number of tool categories, might imply an elevation in intellectual – and therefore language – capacity.

Others, however, deny any correlation between spatial (technological) abilities and linguistic behavior, arguing that toolmaking and language are not conceived or learned in the same way. Much of the apparent standardization of tools, they say, is probably the result of technological constraints in the material and manufacturing process, as well as in our archaeological classifications. Stone tools alone, these scholars conclude, cannot tell us much about language.

Reconstructing the Vocal Tract. Another approach to assessing speech ability is to try to reconstruct the vocal tract in the throat. Philip Lieberman and Edmund Crelin compared the vocal tract of Neanderthalers, chimpanzees, and modern newborn and adult humans, and claimed that the adult Neanderthal upper throat most closely resembles that of modern infants. Neanderthalers, they argue, lacked a modern pharynx (the cavity above the larynx or voice box) and therefore could make only a narrow range of vowel sounds, not fully articulated speech. This claim rests on fragile evidence and has not been widely accepted.

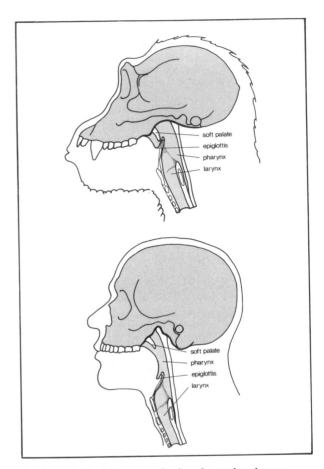

Vocal tracts of a chimpanzee (top) and a modern human (above) compared. The human larynx is lower, and the base of the skull is also more arched – a trait whose origins can be studied in the fossil record.

However, the vocal tract work has received support from Jeffrey Laitman using a different method. He noted that the shape of the base of the skull, which forms a "ceiling" to the throat, is linked to the position of the larynx. In mammals and human infants, the base is flat, and the larynx high, below a small pharynx, but in adult humans the base is curved and the larynx low, with a large pharynx allowing greater modulation of vocal sounds.

Turning to fossil hominids, Laitman found that in australopithecines the base of the skull was flat, and the pharynx therefore small – albeit slightly bigger than in apes. Australopithecines could vocalize more than apes, but probably could not manage vowels. Moreover, like apes and unlike humans, they could still breathe and swallow liquids at the same time. In skulls of *Homo erectus* (1.6 million to 300,000 years ago), the skull-base is becoming curved, indicating that the larynx was probably descending. According to Laitman, full curvature of modern type probably coincides with the appearance of *Homo sapiens*, though he agrees that Neanderthalers (*H. sapiens neanderthalensis*) probably had a more restricted vocal range than modern humans.

Debate about Neanderthal speech abilities was rekindled by the find, at Kebara Cave, Israel, of a 60,000-year-old human hyoid, a small U-shaped bone whose movement affects the position and movement of the larynx to which it is attached. The size, shape, and muscle-attachment marks put the find within the range of modern humans, thus casting more doubt on Lieberman's view and suggesting that Neanderthalers were indeed capable of speaking a language. However, several scholars have pointed out that language is a function of the brain and of mental capacity, and the simple presence of a hyoid is not involved so much as the level of the larynx in the neck.

Recently, however, analysis of the hypoglossal canal, a perforation at the bottom of the skull, where the spinal cord links to the brain, has shown that as long ago as 400,000 years ago these canals were comparable in size to those of modern humans, which suggests that they contained a similar complement of nerves leading to the tongue, and thus that humanlike speech capabilities may have evolved far earlier than had been thought, and certainly long before the Neanderthals.

Identifying Other Kinds of Behavior

Use of Teeth. As we saw in Chapter 7, marks on the teeth of our early ancestors can sometimes suggest that they often used their mouths as a sort of third hand to grip and cut things. In Neanderthalers this is indicated by the extreme wear on the teeth even of fairly young adults, and by the very high incidence of enamel chipping and microfractures.

The history of dental hygiene may seem of remote interest to archaeologists, but it is certainly intriguing to know that science can now indicate use of toothpicks of some kind by our early ancestors. David Frayer and Mary Russell found grooves and striations on the cheek teeth of Neanderthalers from Krapina, Croatia, consistent with regular probing by a small, sharp-pointed instrument. Such marks have been observed on the teeth of *Homo erectus* and *Homo habilis* as well. For a much more recent period, the 16th century AD, analysis in the scanning electron microscope of the front teeth of King Christian III of Denmark revealed striations whose form and direction

indicated that the king had cleaned his teeth with a damp cloth impregnated with abrasive powder.

Use of Hands and Fingers. One can study surviving hands and fingers to assess manual dexterity and labor. Randall Susman has shown that the first (thumb) metacarpal bone has a broad head in relation to its length in humans but not in chimpanzees, and since this bone has a similar configuration in *Homo erectus*, it follows that this hominid must have had a well-muscled thumb capable of generating the force needed for tool use and manufacture; conversely, the thumb of *Australopithecus afarensis* did not have this potential – it could not have grasped a hammer stone with all five fingers, but its hands were still better adapted to tool use than those of apes. Jonathan Musgrave likewise analyzed the hand bones of Neanderthalers and concluded that they gave a somewhat less precise grip than we have between thumb and index finger. The manicured fingernails of Lindow Man (see box, pp. 448–49) suggested that he did not undertake any heavy or rough work.

Stresses on the Skeleton. Human beings repeat many actions and tasks endlessly through their lives, and these often have effects on the skeleton that physical anthropologists can analyze and try to interpret.

Squatting has been suggested by Erik Trinkaus as a habitual trait among Neanderthalers, on the basis of a high frequency of slight flattening of the ends of the thigh bone and other evidence. Squatting facets on the bones of the ankle joints of the female prehistoric Chinchorro mummies from Arica, on the Chilean coast, are also thought to have been caused by working crouched, perhaps opening shellfish on the beach.

Load-carrying can lead to degenerative changes in the lower spine. In New Zealand such changes have been found in both sexes, but in other regions of the world they are predominantly associated with men. On

In Mesoamerica, without beasts of burden, porters like these Aztecs carried loads using straps around the forehead.

the other hand, females seem to have done most of the carrying in Neolithic Orkney. In his analysis of the skeletons from the Orkney chambered tomb of Isbister, Judson Chesterman noted that several skulls had a visible depression running across the top of the cranium; it was associated with a markedly increased attachment of neck muscles to the back of the skull. These features are known from the Congo, Africa, where women get them from carrying loads on their back, held by a strap or rope over the head. In parts of Central and South America, northern Japan, and other regions, the strap goes across the forehead, and can leave a similar depression there. Numerous Aztec codices depict porters carrying goods in this way in pre-Columbian times.

Theya Molleson's analysis of human remains from the early farming settlement of Tell Abu Hureyra, Syria (box, pp. 296–97), reveals that bones in the foot and big toe bore facets attributable to kneeling and pushing with the toes while grinding grain. Arthritic growths around the joints of the big toes would seem to be the consequence of injuries sustained by over-shooting the end of the saddle-quern – an early version of Repetitive Strain Injury. The deformed bones are found predominantly in females, indicating a division of roles.

Hunting activities may also be detectable from human remains. Neolithic skeletons from a hunter-gatherer site in Niger, some 6000–7000 years old, displayed lesions (the technical term for injuries) representing hyperactivity of certain muscles – in this case, an inflammation of the arms and feet probably caused by the use of bows, throwing weapons, and long runs over hard ground. No such traces were found on females at the site.

Midwives assisting at the birth of a child: a scene from a Peruvian vase produced during the Moche period.

Sexual Behavior and Childbirth. Art and literature provide evidence for innumerable human activities in the past, some of which, such as sex, may not be detectable from any other source. The abundant and finely modeled pre-Columbian Moche pottery of Peru gives us a vivid and detailed display of sexual behavior in the period between AD 200 and 700. If it can be taken as an accurate record, it appears that there was a strong predominance of anal and oral sex, with occasional homosexuality and bestiality – were these methods perhaps adopted as a means of contraception rather than out of preference? We also learn from pottery representations the position that Moche women adopted for childbirth.

DISEASE, DEFORMITY, AND DEATH

So far, we have reconstructed human bodies and assessed human abilities. But it is necessary to look at the other, often more negative aspect of the picture: What was people's quality of life? What was their state of health? Did they have any inherited variations? We may know how long they lived, but how did they die?

Where we have intact bodies, the precise cause of death can sometimes be deduced – indeed, in some cases such as the asphyxiated people of Pompeii and Herculaneum it is obvious from the circumstances (the effect of the eruption of the volcano Vesuvius). For the more numerous skeletal remains that come down to us, however, cause of death can be ascertained only rarely, since most afflictions leading to death leave no trace on bone. Paleopathology (the study of ancient disease) tells us far more about life than about death, a fact of great benefit to the archaeologist.

In parallel, physical and forensic anthropologists are increasingly using techniques developed within archaeology to assist them with the recovery and study of human remains. Indeed, a new sub-discipline is now appearing – forensic archaeology – which helps in the recovery and interpretation of murder victims, as well as trying to identify individuals within mass burials, as encountered in Rwanda and former Yugoslavia.

Evidence in Soft Tissue

Since most infectious diseases rarely leave detectable traces in bones, a comprehensive analysis of ancient diseases can only be carried out on bodies with surviving soft tissue. The *surface tissue* can sometimes reveal evidence of illness, such as eczema or similar conditions. It can also reveal certain causes of violent death, such as the slit throats of several bog bodies.

Where *inner tissue* is involved, a number of methods are at the analyst's disposal. X-rays can provide much information, and have been used on Egyptian mummies, but newer, more powerful methods are now available (see box overleaf). Occasionally, one can study soft tissue that is no longer there: the *footprints*, *handprints*, and *hand stencils* mentioned in an earlier section. *Fingerprints* have survived on pieces of fired loess from the Upper Paleolithic site of Dolní Věstonice, the Czech Republic, and on artifacts from many other periods such as Babylonian clay disks and cuneiform tablets from Nineveh (3000 BC), and on ancient Greek vases and sherds, helping to identify different potters.

Some handprints and stencils may supply intriguing pathological evidence. In three or four caves, most notably that of Gargas, France, there are hundreds of late Ice Age hand stencils with apparently severe damage. Some have all four fingers missing. Debate still continues as to whether the stencils were made with the fingers folded, as a kind of sign language, or whether the damage is real but caused by mutilation or disease.

A cast of a finger-end produced by the City of London Police from a hole in a 5000-year-old pot from the Thames, London.

Other forms of art from all periods yield evidence for illnesses. The small figures carved in medieval churches and cathedrals in western Europe illustrate various maladies and ills. The Mexican Monte Albán *danzante* figures carved on stone slabs have sometimes been interpreted as a kind of early medical dictionary, with symptoms and internal organs displayed,

Hand stencils from the late Ice Age cave of Gargas, France. (Left) Photograph of some of the stencils. (Right) Chart showing the numbers of hands found with particular types of "mutilation." Debate still continues as to whether the hands were indeed mutilated, or were shown with the fingers folded.

LOOKING INSIDE BODIES

When examining human remains it is essential to extract the maximum information while causing minimum damage to the remains themselves. In some cases, such as the mummies of the Egyptian pharaohs, the authorities permit examination only under exceptional circumstances. But a considerable amount of knowledge can be gained by simply "seeing" into a body, and modern technology has placed several effective methods at scientists' disposal.

Non-destructive Techniques
Archaeologists are often surprised by what **X-rays** of coffins and wrapped mummies reveal – animal bodies where human remains were anticipated, additional bodies in one coffin, or a mass of unexpected jewelry. **Xeroradiography** goes a step further. This technique is rather like a cross between X-rays and a photocopy, in that it produces electrostatic images through colored powder being blown onto a selenium plate. The result is a much sharper definition than that

produced by normal X-rays; and the wide exposure latitude allows both soft and hard tissue to show clearly on the same image. With "edge enhancement," features are outlined like a pencil drawing. The technique can be used on mummies, either wrapped or in their coffins. When used on the head of the pharaoh Ramesses II, xeroradiography revealed a tiny animal bone inserted by the embalmer to support the nose; and in cavities behind the nose a cluster of tiny beads became apparent.

When the mummy of Ramesses II was taken to Paris for specialized medical treatment in the 1970s, it was subjected to xeroradiography. Revealed for the first time was a tiny animal bone at the front of the king's nose; in the nasal cavities were clusters of tiny beads.

Computed axial tomography using a scanner (hence the abbreviation CT or CAT scanner) is an important method that also allows wrapped mummies and other bodies to be examined in some detail non-destructively. The body is passed into the machine and images produced of cross-sectional "slices" through the body. CAT scanners are more effective at dealing with tissues of different density, enabling soft organs to be viewed as well. New helical scanners move spirally around the body and produce continuous images rather than slices, a much quicker method.

Another technique for looking at internal organs is *Magnetic Resonance Imaging* (MRI), which lines up the body's hydrogen atoms in a strong magnetic field, and causes them to resonate by radio waves. The resulting measurements are fed into a computer which produces a cross-sectional image of the body. However, this method is only suitable for objects containing water, and is thus of limited use in studying desiccated mummies.

By using a fiber-optic endoscope –

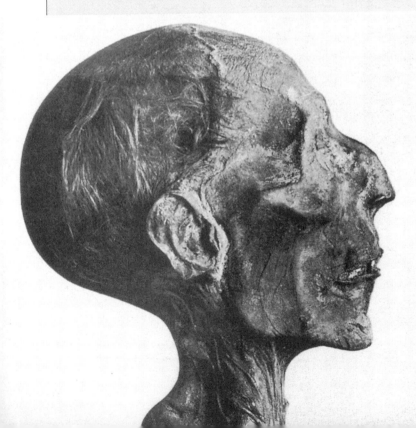

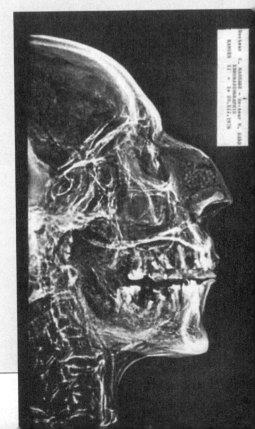

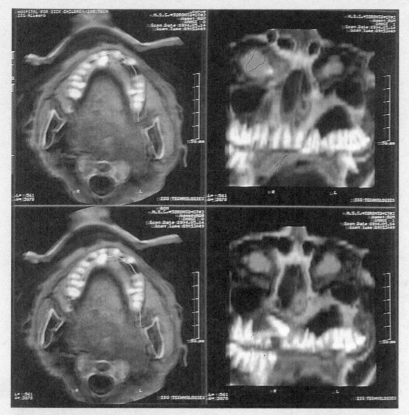

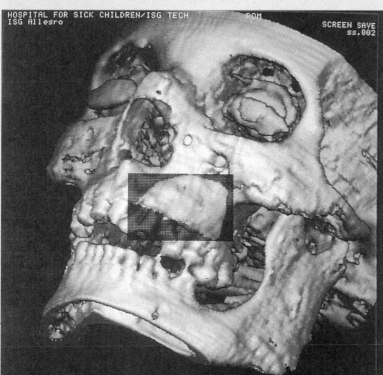

a narrow, flexible tube with a light source – analysts can look inside a body, see what has survived, and in what condition (see box, Lindow Man, pp. 448–49). Endoscopy occasionally reveals details of the mummification process. When inserted into the head of Ramesses V, for example, the fibroscope showed an unexpected hole at the base of the skull through which the brain had been removed (the brain was often broken up and removed through the nose); a cloth had later been put inside the empty skull.

Destructive Techniques

In cases where it is acceptable for the body to have samples taken from it for analysis, there are several techniques at the disposal of the scientist. (It is worth noting that fiber-optic endoscopy (above) is also used in some cases for removing tissue.)

When tissue samples are removed, they are rehydrated in a solution of bicarbonate of soda (becoming very fragile in the process). They are then dehydrated, placed in paraffin wax, and sliced into thin sections which are stained for greater clarity under a microscope. Using this technique on Egyptian mummies, analysts have detected both red and white corpuscles, and have even been able to diagnose arterial disease.

Finally, **analytical electron microscopy** (similar to scanning electron microscopy) permits elements in tissue to be analyzed and quantified. When Rosalie David's Manchester mummy team applied it to one Egyptian specimen, they found that particles in the lung contained a high proportion of silica and were probably sand – evidence of pneumoconiosis in ancient Egypt, where this lung disease was evidently quite a common hazard.

Computed axial tomography scanners allow scientists detailed views of mummies without the need to unwrap them. These CT scan images are of an Egyptian female mummy in the Royal Ontario Museum, Toronto examined by Dr Peter Lewin at the Hospital for Sick Children in Toronto. The unfortunate woman had a huge tooth abscess, visible in the scan.

although the current view is that these figures represent slain or sacrificed captives (see Chapters 10 and 13).

Parasites and Viruses

Where soft tissue survives, one can usually find *parasites* of some sort. The first place to look is in the bodies themselves, and principally in the guts, although body and head lice can also be detected. Parasites can be identified from their morphology by a specialist. A huge diversity of such infestations has been found in Egyptian mummies – indeed, almost all have them, no doubt because of inadequate sanitation, and an ignorance of the causes and means of transmission of diseases. The Egyptians had parasites that caused amoebic dysentery and bilharzia, and they had many intestinal occupants. Pre-Columbian mummies in the New World have eggs of the whipworm, and the roundworm. Grauballe Man in Denmark must have had more or less continuous stomach ache through the activities of the whipworm *Trichuris*, since he had millions of its eggs inside him (see also the Lindow Man box, pp. 448–49).

Another important source of information about parasites is human coprolites (Chapter 7). The parasite eggs pass out in the feces encased in hard shells, and thus survive very successfully. Parasites are known in prehistoric dung from Israel, Colorado, and coastal Peru – but it is worth noting that 50 coprolites from Lovelock Cave, Nevada, proved to have none at all. It is not uncommon for hunter-gatherers in temperate latitudes and open country to be parasite-free. On the other hand some 6000-year-old samples from Los Gavilanes, Peru, analyzed by Raul Patrucco and his colleagues, had eggs from the tapeworm *Diphyllobothrium*, with which one becomes infested from eating raw or partially cooked sea-fish. Coprolites in other parts of the New World have yielded eggs of the tapeworm, pinworm, and thorny-headed worm, as well as traces of ticks, mites, and lice. Parasites can also be detected in medieval cesspits, while sediments from a French Upper Paleolithic cave at Arcy-sur-Cure, dating to between 25,000 and 30,000 years ago, have been found to contain concentrations of the eggs of parasitic intestinal worms, *Ascaris*, that are almost certainly from human excrement.

Certain parasites cause medical conditions that can be recognized if soft tissue survives. Some prehistoric mummies from the Chilean desert, dating from 475 BC to AD 600, had clinical traces of Chagas' disease – notably an inflamed and enlarged heart and gut. The muscles of these organs are invaded by parasites left on the skin in the feces of bloodsucking bugs.

A lump on the lung of a 900-year-old Peruvian mummy was caused by tuberculosis, ascertained by isolating DNA of the disease in the lesion. It proves that TB was not brought to the Americas by the European colonists.

Scabs and *viruses* can also survive in recognizable form in soft tissue, and may possibly even pose problems for the unwary archaeologist. We do not know for certain how long microbes can lie dormant in the ground. Most experts doubt that they pose any danger after a century or two, but there is a claim that anthrax spores survived in an Egyptian pyramid, and infectious micro-organisms may also persist in bodies buried in the Arctic, preserved by the permafrost. The dangers in decaying bone and tissue may be very real – especially as our immunity to vanished or rare diseases has now declined.

A safer approach is provided by genetics, since some diseases leave traces in DNA. Smallpox and polio, for example, are caused by viruses, and a virus is simply DNA, or closely related RNA, in a "protective overcoat" of protein. A virus infects by releasing its DNA into the unfortunate host, and some of the host's cells are then converted to the production of viruses. In this way viral infections can leave traces of the DNA of the virus. Analysis of ancient genetic material may therefore help to trace the history of certain diseases. For example, American pathologist Arthur Aufderheide and his colleagues have isolated fragments of DNA of the tuberculosis bacterium from lesions in the lungs of a 900-year-old Peruvian mummy, thus proving that this microbe was not brought to the Americas by European colonists.

Skeletal Evidence for Deformity and Disease

Skeletal material, as we have seen, is far more abundant than preserved soft tissue, and can reveal a great deal of paleopathological information. Effects on the outer surface of bone can be divided into those caused by violence or accident, and those caused by disease or congenital deformity.

Violent Damage. Where violence or accidents – known as traumas – are concerned, straightforward observation by an expert can often reveal how the damage was caused, and how serious its consequences were for the victim. For example, one of the Upper Paleolithic skeletons of children from Grimaldi, Italy, had an arrowhead buried in its backbone, a wound that was very probably mortal – as was the famous Roman ballista bolt found by Mortimer Wheeler in the spine of an ancient Briton at the Iron Age hillfort of Maiden Castle, southern England. A study by Douglas Scott and Melissa Connor of the skeletal remains at the famous battle of the Little Big Horn, Montana – where General Custer and his entire force of 265 men were wiped out by the Sioux in 1876 – showed the extensive use of clubs and hatchets to deliver a *coup de grâce*. One poor soldier, about 25 years old, had been wounded in the chest by a .44 bullet, then shot in the head with a Colt revolver, and finally had his skull crushed with a war club.

In cases where the bones are masked by soft tissue, X-ray analysis is necessary (see box previous pages).

Individual wounds and fractures, however compelling the personal stories they reveal, are nevertheless of limited interest to medical history. It is their frequency and type that are more useful. A community of hunter-gatherers will have encountered different dangers from those faced by a community of farmers, and their skeletal traumas should therefore be different. The aim should be to study the pathologies of entire groups and communities wherever possible.

As with other kinds of archaeological evidence, one has to be alert to the possibility that changes (in this case damage such as broken or deformed skulls) may have been caused by physical or chemical action after burial in the soil. Some human communities have even deformed skulls deliberately, by binding the brow of growing infants, with or without a board, or by applying pressure at regular intervals to produce a frontal flattening. Analysis of two of the Neanderthalers of Shanidar Cave, Iraq, has led Erik Trinkaus to claim that skull deformation was already practiced at this early date. It also seems to have existed in Pleistocene or early Holocene Australia. Peter Brown compared deliberately deformed Melanesian skulls with normal specimens, in order to identify the changes caused by deformation. He then applied his results to skulls from early Australian sites in Victoria, including Kow Swamp, and established beyond doubt that they had

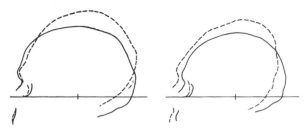

Skull deformation. (Right) Skull outlines of an artificially deformed Melanesian male – dashed line – and a normal male. (Left) A 13,000-year-old skull from Kow Swamp, Australia – dashed line – compared with that of a modern male Aborigine, suggesting that the Kow skull was deformed deliberately.

been artificially deformed. The oldest specimen, Kow Swamp 5, is 13,000 years old.

One of the Shanidar Neanderthalers, a man aged about 40, had suffered a blow to the left eye, making him partially blind. He also had a useless, withered right arm, caused by a childhood injury, a fracture in one foot bone, and arthritis in the knee and ankle. Individuals such as this could only have survived through the help of their fellows.

Other practices besides skull deformation are detectable. Tim White used a scanning electron microscope to analyze the skull of "Bodo," a large male *Homo erectus* or archaic *Homo sapiens* from Ethiopia, about 300,000 years old, and came to the conclusion that it had been scalped. Analysis revealed two series of cutmarks, one on the left cheek under the eye socket, and the other across the forehead. These were made before the bone had hardened and fossilized, and therefore just before or just after death. Pre-Columbian Indian skulls that were scalped – for ritual reasons prior to burial – have similar marks in the same positions.

Identifying Disease from Human Bone. The small number of diseases that affect bone do so in three basic ways – they can bring about erosion, growths, or an altered structure. Each of these phenomena has many possible causes, but some afflictions leave quite clear signs. *Leprosy*, for example, erodes the bones of the face and the extremities in a distinctive manner, and there are clear specimens from medieval Denmark. Recently, DNA from the leprosy bacterium has been isolated from a 1400-year-old skeleton in Israel. Certain cancers also have a noticeable effect on bone (see box overleaf), such as the pathological changes to the leg bones of the elderly Neanderthal man of La Ferrassie 1, France, which are likely to have been caused by lung cancer. Australian archaeologist Dan Potts and his colleagues have discovered the world's earliest known

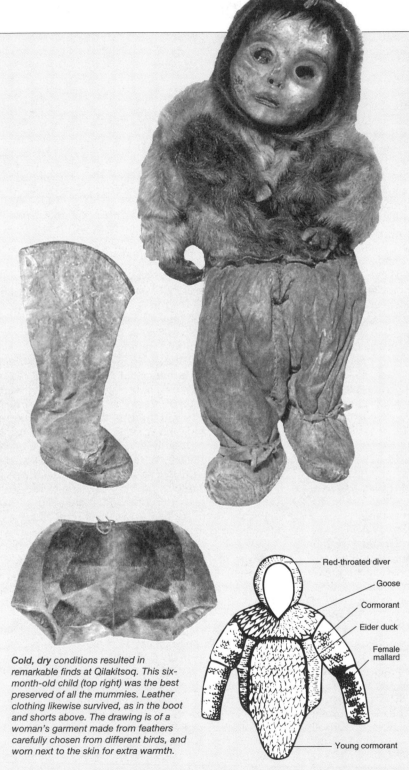

LIFE AND DEATH AMONG THE INUIT

Among the most interesting aspects of the study of human remains are the assessment of the state of health, the quality of life, and the cause of death of the individuals concerned.

In 1972, two collective burials were discovered under an overhanging rock at Qilakitsoq, a small Inuit settlement on the west coast of Greenland dating to about AD 1475. The eight bodies had all been mummified naturally by a combination of low temperature and lack of moisture. In one grave were 4 women and a six-month-old infant; in the other, 2 women and a four-year-old boy. The over- and under-clothing (a total of 78 items including trousers, anoraks, boots) had also survived in perfect condition.

The bodies were sexed by the genitalia of those that were unwrapped, and from X-ray examination of the pelvis and other bones of the mummies left intact; in addition, facial tattoos were usually restricted to adult women in this society.

Aging was done from dental development and other physical features. Three of the women died in their late teens/early 20s, but the other three had reached about 50 – a good age, since even at the turn of this century the average age of death for women in Greenland was only 29.

The young boy and one woman may have been in much pain. X-rays of the boy showed that he had a misshapen pelvis of a kind often associated with Down's Syndrome children. A disorder known as Calvé-Perthe's disease was also destroying the head of a thigh bone, and he may have had to move around on all fours. The woman, one of those aged 50, had broken her left collarbone at some stage; it had never

Cold, dry conditions resulted in remarkable finds at Qilakitsoq. This six-month-old child (top right) was the best preserved of all the mummies. Leather clothing likewise survived, as in the boot and shorts above. The drawing is of a woman's garment made from feathers carefully chosen from different birds, and worn next to the skin for extra warmth.

Red-throated diver
Goose
Cormorant
Eider duck
Female mallard
Young cormorant

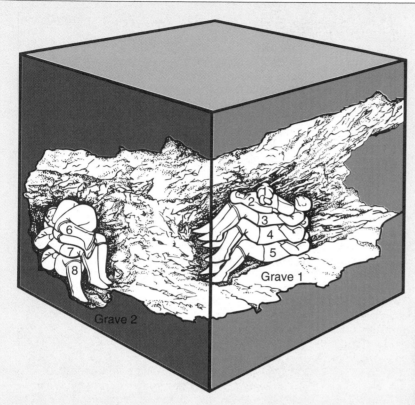

The eight bodies, layers of animal skins between them, lay protected by overhanging rock. Their frozen, moistureless grave resulted in natural mummification.

Finally, analysis was carried out to ascertain the possible relationships among these individuals. Tissue typing established that some were not related at all, while others might have been. Either of two of the younger women could have been the mother of the four-year-old boy buried above them; while two of the women aged about 50 (including the one with cancer) may have been sisters. They also had identical facial tattoos, perhaps by the same artist, which were just like those on the earliest known portrait from this area (c. AD 1654). Another woman had a tattoo so different in style and workmanship that she probably came from a different region and had married into the group.

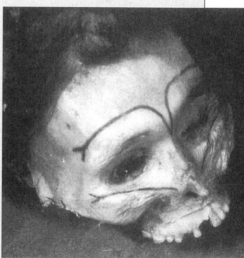

Infrared photography has made the tattoo design on this woman's face clearly visible.

knitted, which perhaps impaired the function of her left arm. In addition, she had naso-pharyngeal cancer (cancer at the back of her nasal passage) which had spread to surrounding areas, causing blindness in the left eye, and some deafness.

Some of her features could be attributed to particular activities: her left thumbnail had fresh grooves on it, caused by cutting sinew against it with a knife (and, incidentally, showing that she was right-handed). She had also lost her lower front teeth, no doubt from chewing skins and using her teeth as a vice, like the Barrow Inuit in Alaska (box, p. 65).

Another similarity with the Alaskan case is that the youngest woman's lungs contained high levels of soot, probably from seal-blubber lamps. On the other hand, hair samples from the mummies showed low levels of mercury and lead, far lower than in the region today.

How these people met their deaths remains a mystery. At any rate, they did not die of starvation. The woman with cancer had Harris lines showing arrested bone growth as a child caused by illness or malnutrition, but she was well nourished when she died. The youngest woman had a sizeable quantity of digested food in her lower intestine. Isotopic analysis of the young boy's skin collagen (p. 307) revealed that 75 percent of his diet came from marine products (seals, whales, fish) and only 25 percent from the land (reindeer, hare, plants).

polio victim in a 4000-year-old grave in the United Arab Emirates; the skeleton of an 18- to 20-year-old girl showed classic symptoms of the condition, such as the small size and inflammation of muscle attachments, thinness of all long bones, one leg 4 cm (1.6 in) shorter than the other, a curved sacrum, and asymmetrical pelvis.

In some diseases, the body produces hard structures distinct from bone – calcium compounds, which form stones in the gallbladder or kidney – and these often survive. Straightforward observation or X-ray analysis is sufficient for most studies of this kind.

Deformity in bone often reveals a congenital abnormality. The tiny mummified fetus of a female, one of two found in the tomb of Tutankhamun, was shown by X-ray analysis to have *Sprengel's deformity* – where the left shoulder blade is congenitally high, and spina bifida is present – which probably explains why the infant, perhaps Tutankhamun's own child, was stillborn. Egypt also provides skeletal evidence of *dwarfism*, a congenital birth condition, and the same has been found among Paleo-Indians in Alabama. However, the earliest known example of a dwarf is a male from the 10th millennium BC, no more than 1.1–1.2 m (3 ft 7 in–3 ft 11 in) tall, who died at the age of about 17 and was buried in the decorated cave of Riparo del Romito, Calabria, Italy.

Calvin Wells' analysis of the 450 skeletons from Roman Cirencester, England, revealed a number of congenital defects in the spine, and five skeletons with evidence of *Spina bifida occulta*. However, the most common ailment was *arthritis*, in most joints of the body, which was found in about half the males. At Mesa Verde, Colorado, in the period AD 550 to 1300, every known individual over 35 suffered from osteoarthritis.

Art may also provide evidence of congenital deformities. The most common motif in the Olmec art of Mexico is an anthropomorphic figure, a child with feline facial features known as the "were-jaguar motif." It often displays a cleft forehead, and a downturned, open mouth, with canine teeth protruding; the body is usually obese and sexless. Carson Murdy suggests that the motif represents congenital deformities, and Michael Coe has argued that the cleft forehead represents spina bifida, which is associated with a number of cranial deformities. Such conditions usually occur only about once in every thousand live births and may therefore have been restricted to a certain social group, or even to a single extended family. Carson Murdy hypothesizes that a chief's family may have used the phenomenon in art and religion to reinforce their status, identifying their children's deformities with the characteristics of the supernatural jaguar. If "jaguar blood" ran in the family, it would be only natural to produce "were-jaguar" offspring.

X-ray analysis of bone may reveal lines of arrested growth known as *Harris lines* (see box pp. 444–45 for a study that detected these lines). These are opaque calcified formations, a few micromillimeters thick, that occur when growth is interrupted during childhood or adolescence because of illness or malnutrition. They are usually clearest in the lower tibia (shin-bone). The number of lines can provide a rough guide to the frequency of difficult periods during growth. If the lines are found in whole groups of skeletons of the same age group and period, they can indicate crises of subsistence, or, in other cases, some social inequality of the sexes. Similarly, *Beau's lines* on finger- and toenails are shallow grooves indicating slowed growth caused by disease or malnourishment; the one surviving fingernail of the Alpine Iceman of 3300 BC has 3 such grooves, suggesting that he had been subject to bouts of crippling disease 4, 3, and 2 months before he died (see box, pp. 66–67).

Lead Poisoning. Analysis of bone can show that the danger of poisoning from toxic substances is by no means confined to our own times. Some of the Roman inhabitants of Poundbury, England, had a remarkably high concentration of lead in their bones, probably thanks to their diet. Lead has also been found in face-powder from a 3000-year-old Mycenaean tomb in Greece, probably used as a cosmetic.

Three British sailors, who died and were buried 140 years ago on Canada's Beechey Island, Northwest Ter-

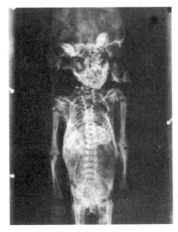

A tiny mummified fetus from Tutankhamun's tomb was shown by X-ray analysis to have Sprengel's deformity, probably explaining why the child, a female, was stillborn.

ritories, had been crew members of the 1845 Franklin expedition attempting to find a navigable Northwest Passage. Their bodies, well preserved in permafrost, were exhumed by the Canadian anthropologist Owen Beattie and his colleagues. Analysis of bone samples revealed an enormously high lead content, enough to cause poisoning if ingested during the expedition. The poisoning probably came from the lead-soldered tins of food, lead-glazed pottery, and containers lined with lead foil. Combined with other conditions such as scurvy, this could have been lethal.

Lead in skeletons has also provided insights into the lives of Colonial Americans. Arthur Aufderheide analyzed bones from burial grounds in Maryland, Virginia, and Georgia, dating from the 17th to 19th centuries. He found that the people there had been exposed to lead from the glaze in their ceramics, and also from pewter containers, which they used for storing, preparing, and serving food and drink. However, only the affluent could afford to poison themselves in this way, and this is the key to obtaining social data from the lead content. In two populations from plantations in Georgia and Virginia, white tenant farmers tended to have more lead than free blacks or slaves, but less than the wealthier plantation owners. On the other hand, white servants usually had low levels, especially those working for white tenant farmers. This suggests sharp segregation from their employers.

Teeth

Food not only affects bones, it also has a direct impact on the teeth, so that study of the condition of the dentition can provide much varied information. Analysis of the teeth of ancient Egyptians such as Ramesses II, for example, shows that the frequently heavy wear and appalling decay was caused not just by sand entering the food, but by the consistency of the food and the presence of hard material in plants. X-ray analysis can in addition reveal dental caries and lesions. The skeletons from Roman Herculaneum had an average of only 3.1 dental lesions each, which indicates a low sugar intake compared with today, as in ancient Egypt, probably helped by a water supply with lots of fluoride.

When analyzing dentitions one needs to remember that healthy teeth were sometimes extracted for ceremonial or aesthetic reasons. This practice was very common in the Jomon period in Japan (especially around 4000 years ago), and was applied to both sexes over the age of 14 or 15. Certain incisors, and occasionally premolars, were removed. Indeed, in the later Jomon (3000–2200 years ago), three different regional styles developed.

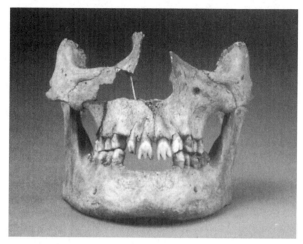

Part of an adult female skull and jawbone from a Jomon-period site in Fujiidera City, Osaka, Japan, with teeth extracted and decorated – presumably for ceremonial or decorative reasons.

In Australia the Aboriginal custom of tooth avulsion – the knocking out of one or two upper incisors as part of a male initiation ceremony – has been found in a burial at Nitchie, New South Wales, dating to around 7000 years ago, while the skull from Cossack, Western Australia, some 6500 years old, also seems to have had a tooth removed long before death.

Finally, there is early evidence of dentistry. The world's oldest filling has been found in Israel, in the tooth of the Nabataean warrior buried 2000 years ago in the Negev Desert, mentioned in an earlier section. Investigation by Joe Zias found that one of his teeth was green because it had been filled with a wire that had oxidized. It is likely that the dentist had cheated him. Instead of inserting a gold wire, he had installed one in bronze, which is corrosive and poisonous. The oldest known false tooth is an iron specimen, precisely fitted to the jaw of a 1900-year-old Gaul from Chantambre, near Paris.

The examination of the skull of Isabella d'Aragona (1470–1524), an Italian noblewoman and possible inspiration for Leonardo da Vinci's Mona Lisa, revealed that her teeth were coated with a black layer which she had tried so desperately to remove that the enamel on her incisors was rubbed away. Analysis of the black layer showed that it was caused by mercury intoxication: inhalation of mercury fumes was common in that period as a treatment for syphilis and other complaints, especially skin conditions. The result of protracted treatment was a serious inflammation of the teeth, and it is probable that Isabella's death was caused by mercury rather than the syphilis.

LINDOW MAN: THE BODY IN THE BOG

In 1984, part of a human leg was found by workers at a peat-shredding mill in northwest England. Subsequent investigation of the site at Lindow Moss, Cheshire, where the peat had been cut revealed the top half of a human body still embedded in the ground. This complete section of peat was removed and later "excavated" in the laboratory by a multi-disciplinary team led by British Museum scientists. The various studies made of the body have yielded remarkable insights into the life and death of this ancient individual, now dated to the late Iron Age or Roman period – perhaps the 1st century AD – although results from radiocarbon have been conflicting.

Age and Sex

Despite the missing lower half, it was obvious from the beard, sideburns, and moustache that this was the body of a male. The age of Lindow Man (as he is now called) has been estimated at around the mid–20s.

Physique

Lindow Man appears to have been well-built, and probably weighed around 60 kg (132 lb or nearly 10 stone). His height, calculated from the length of his humerus (upper arm bone), was estimated to be between 1.68 and 1.73 m (5 ft 6 in to 5 ft 8 in) – average today, but fairly tall for the period.

Appearance

Lindow Man wore no clothing apart from an armband of fox fur. His brown/ginger hair and whiskers were cut, and analysis by scanning electron microscopy indicated that their ends had a stepped surface, implying that they had probably been cut by scissors or shears. His manicured fingernails indicate that he did not do any heavy or rough work – he was clearly not a laborer.

Bright green fluorescence in his hair was thought to be caused by the use of copper-based pigments for body decoration, but in fact is due to a natural reaction of hair keratin with acid in the peat.

The bog acid had removed the enamel from his teeth, but what survived seemed normal and quite healthy – there were no visible cavities.

State of Health

Lindow Man appears to have had very slight osteoarthritis; and computed axial tomography (see box, pp. 440–41) revealed changes in some vertebrae caused by stresses and strains. Parasite eggs show that he had a relatively high infestation of whipworm and maw worm, but these would have caused him little inconvenience. Overall, therefore, he was fairly healthy.

His blood group was found to be O, like the majority of modern Britons. Computed tomography scans showed

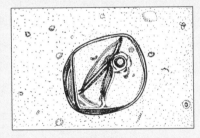

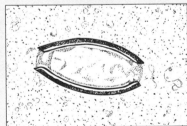

Cereal pollen grain (top) from the small intestine.

Egg of the intestinal worm Trichuris trichiura (above) from Lindow Man.

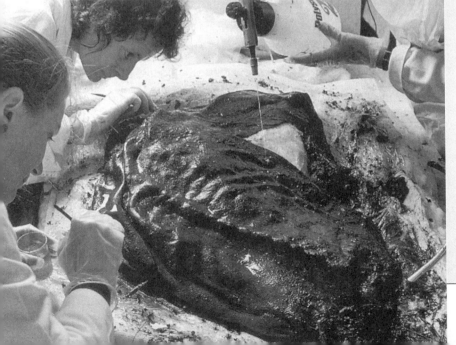

Cleaning the back of Lindow Man in the laboratory. Distilled water is being sprayed to keep the skin moist.

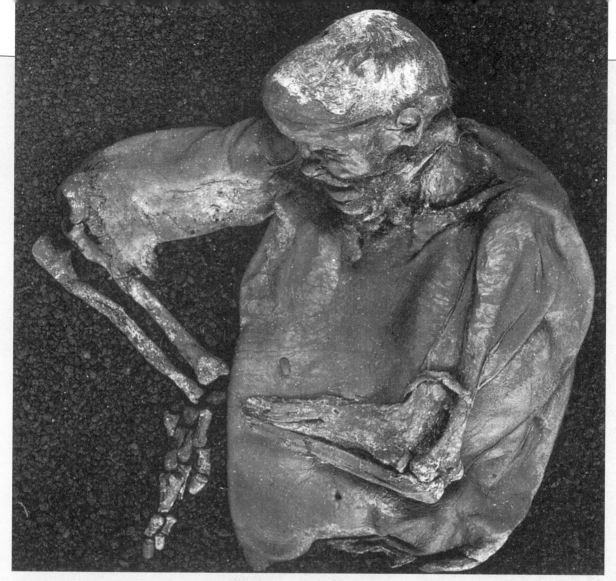

that the brain was still present, but when an endoscope (box, pp. 440–41) was inserted to explore the interior of his skull it became clear that no brain structure remained, only a mass of putty-like tissue. As explained in Chapter 7, the food residues in the part of his upper alimentary tract that survived revealed that his last meal had consisted of a griddle cake.

How Did He Die?

Xeroradiography (box, pp. 440–41) confirmed that his head had been fractured from behind – it revealed splinters of bone in the vault of the

Fully conserved remains of Lindow Man photographed in ultra-violet light to enhance the details.

skull. A forensic scientist deduced from the two lacerated wounds joined together that the skull had been driven in twice by a narrow-bladed weapon. There may also have been a blow (from a knee?) to his back, because xeroradiography showed a broken rib.

The blows to the head would have rendered him unconscious, if not killed him outright, so that he cannot have felt the subsequent garotting or the knife in his throat. A knotted thong of sinew, 1.5

mm thick, around his throat had broken his neck and strangled him, and his throat had been slit with a short, deep cut at the side of the neck that severed the jugular. Once he had been bled in this way, he was dropped face-down into a pool in the bog.

We do not know why he died – perhaps as a sacrifice, or as an executed criminal – but we have been able to learn a great deal about the life and death of Lindow Man, who has been subjected to perhaps the most extensive battery of tests and analyses ever applied to an ancient human being.

Medical Knowledge

Documentary sources are important to our understanding of early medicine. Egyptian literature mentions the use of wire to prevent loss of teeth by holding them together. Roman texts also tell us something about dental treatment. Where general medicine is concerned, there are medical papyri from Egypt, and ample documentary and artistic evidence from Greece and Rome, as well as from later cultures.

The most common and impressive archaeological evidence for medical skill is the phenomenon of trepanation, or trephination, the cutting out of a piece of bone from the skull, probably to alleviate pressure on the brain caused by skull fracture, or to combat headaches or epilepsy. Over 1000 cases are known, and more than half had healed completely – indeed, some skulls have up to seven pieces cut out. Amazingly, this practice dates back at least 7000 or 8000 years.

Other evidence for early medical expertise includes bark splints found with broken forearms dating to the 3rd-millennium BC in Egypt, and the dismembered skeleton of a fetus from the 4th-century AD Romano-British cemetery at Poundbury Camp, Dorset, whose cutmarks correspond precisely to the operation described by Soranus, a Roman doctor, for removing a dead infant from the womb to the save the mother.

Actual examples of surgeons' equipment include large sets of instruments unearthed at Pompeii and a full Roman medical chest with intact contents (including wooden lidded cylinders of medicines) recovered from a shipwreck off Tuscany, Italy. A similar kit was discovered in the wreck of the *Mary Rose*, the 16th-century British ship, and included flasks, jars, razors, a urethral syringe, and knives and saws.

The remains of an 11th-century AD hospital attached to a Buddhist monastery outside the city of Polonnaruva in Sri Lanka contained medical and surgical instruments, and glazed storage vessels, suggesting a sophisticated level of medical care. A set of surgical instruments has also been found in Peru, from the Chimú period, AD 450–750. It consists of scalpels, forceps, bandages of wool and cotton, and, most interesting of all, some metal implements closely resembling modern instruments used to scrape a uterus in order to induce an abortion. It comes as no surprise that the ancient Peruvians had achieved this level of skill – we know from other evidence that they routinely did trepanation, and added artificial parts to support faulty limbs. Their pottery displays detailed medical knowledge, including the different stages of pregnancy and labor. It is also clear from Maya codices and Spanish records of the Aztecs that other peoples of the New World had sophisticated medical know-how, including the use of hallucinogenic fungi.

Archaeologists and paleopathologists thus use a wide variety of methods to provide insights into the health of past peoples. By combining these approaches with data on subsistence (Chapter 7), we can now go on to examine the quality of diet of our ancestors and the likely character and size of their populations.

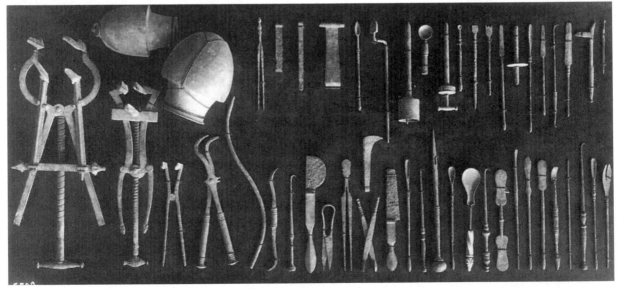

Medical knowledge: an awe-inspiring set of Roman surgical instruments from Pompeii.

ASSESSING NUTRITION

Nutrition can be described as the measure of a diet's ability to maintain the human body in its physical and social environment. We are of course interested to be able to learn that a particular group of people in the past enjoyed good nutrition. In his investigations in northeast Thailand, the archaeologist Charles Higham found that the prehistoric people of 1500–100 BC had abundant food at their disposal, and displayed no signs of ill health or malnutrition; some of them lived to over 50. But in many ways what is more informative is to discover that the diet was deficient in some respect, which may have affected bone thickness and skeletal growth. Furthermore, comparison of nutrition at different periods may significantly add to our understanding of fundamental changes to the pattern of life, as in the transition from hunting and gathering to farming.

Malnutrition

What are the skeletal signs of malnutrition? In the previous section, we mentioned the Harris lines that indicate periods of arrested growth during development, and that are sometimes caused by malnutrition. A similar phenomenon occurs in *teeth*, where patches of poorly mineralized dentine, which a specialist can detect in a tooth-section, reflect growth disturbance brought about by a diet deficient in milk, fish, oil, or animal fats. A lack of vitamin C produces scurvy, an affliction that causes changes in the palate and gums, and has been identified in an Anglo-Saxon individual from Norfolk, England. Scurvy was also common among sailors until the 19th century because of their poor diet.

The general size and condition of a skeleton's bones can provide an indication of aspects of diet. The adult skeletons found at Roman Herculaneum, for example, had leg bones flatter than the modern average, an indi-

cation of a diet poorer in protein than ours. As mentioned earlier, sand in food, or the grit from grindstones, can have drastic effects on teeth. The excessive abrasion of teeth among certain California Indians can be linked to their habit of leaching the tannins out of acorns (their staple food) through a bed of sand, leaving a residue in the food.

Additional evidence for malnutrition can be obtained from *art and literature*. Vitamin B deficiency (beriberi) is mentioned in the *Su Wen*, a Chinese text of the 3rd millennium BC, and Strabo also refers to a case among Roman troops. Egyptian art provides scenes such as the well-known "famine" depicted at Saqqara, dating to around 2350 BC.

Comparing Diets: the Rise of Agriculture

Chemical analysis of bone allows further insights. After bone has been burnt to ash, atomic absorption spectroscopy can reveal the amounts of various elements (strontium, zinc, calcium, sodium, etc.) present in it. Two burial populations from the eastern United States have been compared using this method. One was a group of hunter-gatherers of the Middle Woodland period (AD 400), while the other was a group of maize farmers of the Late Woodland (AD 1200). In the first group, males and females had statistically identical bone composition for every element. Among the maize farmers, on the other hand, there were significant differences between the sexes, in that males had less strontium and calcium, and more zinc, than females.

All of these are diet-related elements, and it therefore appears that there existed dietary differences between the sexes by this period, with perhaps a greater differentiation of roles which may be linked to maize cultivation. The lower concentration of strontium in males indicates that they had more animal protein in their diet than the females, who presumably ate more maize than the men (see also section on analysis of bone collagen, p. 307).

A maize diet can have other effects on the body. In a similar study of two eastern North American populations from a single site, Dickson Mounds in Illinois, John Lallo and Jerome Rose found that through time, from AD 1050 to 1300, there was a growing dependence on maize. This seems to have been accompanied by a rise in population density and hence in social contacts, associated with a marked increase in the frequency and severity of damage from disease in bones. They also found skeletal evidence for a deficiency of iron,

Evidence for malnutrition: detail of a wall relief at Saqqara in Egypt depicting famine victims, c. 2350 BC.

and an increase in dental defects reflecting nutritional stress or an increase in disease. In short, the skeletons showed how economic and social changes can be linked in this case to an increase in disease and nutritional problems.

These findings are supported by Clark Larsen's comparison of some 269 hunter-gatherer skeletons (2200 BC–AD 1150) and 342 agricultural community skeletons (AD 1150–1550) from 33 sites on the Georgia coast (see also Chapter 7). Larsen discovered that through time there was a decline in dental and skeletal health, but also a decrease in the sort of joint disease related to the mechanical stress of being a hunter (men of both periods suffered from this osteoarthritis much more than women).

There was also a reduction in the size of the face and jaws – but only females had a decrease in tooth-size, and it was females who had the greater increase in dental decay and the most marked decrease in cranial and overall skeletal size (probably related to a reduction in protein intake and an increase in carbo-

hydrates). These results suggest that the shift to agriculture affected women more than men, who perhaps carried on hunting and fishing while the women did the field preparation, planting, harvesting, and cooking. Taken together, therefore, the eastern North American data are quite consistent in highlighting the differential effects of maize agriculture on males and females.

At a broader level of analysis, it is difficult to distinguish the effects of different aspects of the adoption of agriculture – not merely a changed diet, but a settled way of life, greater concentrations of population, differential access to resources, and so on. Nevertheless studies of skeletal pathology in many areas are beginning to form a pattern, suggesting that the adoption of agriculture (and its accompanying effects on group size and permanence of settlement) commonly led to increased rates of chronic stress, including infection and malnutrition. As in the case of Georgia, a decrease in mechanical stress was replaced by an increase in nutritional stress.

POPULATION STUDIES

In the preceding sections of this chapter we have looked at individuals or at small groups of people. The time has now come to extend the discussion to larger groups and to entire populations, a field of research known as *demographic archaeology*, which is concerned with estimates from archaeological data of various aspects of populations such as size, density, and growth rates. It is also concerned with the role of population in culture change. Simulation models based on archaeological and demographic data can be used to gain an understanding of the link between population, resources, technology, and society, and have helped clarify the peopling of North America and Australia, and the spread of agriculture into Europe.

An allied field is *paleodemography*, which is primarily concerned with the study of skeletal remains to estimate population parameters such as fertility rates and mortality rates, population structure, and life expectancy. All the techniques mentioned so far can be of assistance here, by helping us to investigate the life-span of both sexes in different periods, or to assess fertility through the number of births. Study of disease or malnutrition can be combined with sex and age data to cast light on differential quality of life. But there remains one fundamental question: how can one estimate the size of population, and hence population densities, from archaeological evidence?

There are two basic approaches. The first is to derive

figures from settlement data, based on the relationship between group size and total site area, roofed area, site length, site volume, or number of dwellings. The second is to try to assess the richness of a particular environment in terms of its animal and plant resources for each season, and therefore how many people that environment might have supported at a certain level of technology (the environment's "carrying capacity"). For our purposes the first approach is the most fruitful. In a single site, it is necessary to establish, as best one can, how many dwellings were occupied at a particular time, and then one can proceed to the calculation. (On waterlogged, or very dry sites as in the American Southwest, remains of timber dwellings can often be tree-ring dated to the exact years when they were built, occupied, and then abandoned. Usually such results indicate that fewer buildings were lived in during a particular phase than archaeologists had previously imagined.) Assessments of occupied floor area are potentially the most accurate means of achieving population figures. The most famous equation is that proposed by the demographer Raoul Naroll. Using data derived from an examination of 18 modern cultures, he suggested that the population of a prehistoric site is equal to one tenth of the total floor area in square meters.

This claim was later refined and modified by a number of archaeologists, who found that it was necessary to take into account the variation in dwelling environments. But just as Naroll's original formula was over-generalized, some more recent equations have perhaps been too narrowly focused on a particular area – for example, "Pueblo population = one third of total floor area in square meters." One useful rule of thumb developed by S.F. Cook and R.F. Heizer, if one is starting with non-metric measurements, is to allow 25 sq. ft (2.325 sq. m) for each of the first 6 people, and then 100 sq. ft (9.3 sq. m) for every other person.

In the case of long houses of the Neolithic *Linearbandkeramik* (LBK) culture in Poland, Sarunas Milisauskas first applied Naroll's formula and obtained a figure of 117 people for a total of 10 houses. He then tried using a colleague's ethnographic evidence, which assumes one family for every hearth in a long house, and thus one family for every 4 or 5 m (13–16 ft) of house length, and he obtained a figure of 200 people for the same houses.

Samuel Casselberry further refined the procedure for multi-family dwellings of this sort. Using data from ethnography he established a formula for New World multi-family houses, claiming that "population = one sixth of the floor area in square meters." Applying this to the Polish LBK houses, he reached a figure of 192 people for the 10 dwellings, which is close enough to Milisauskas' second result to suggest that methods of

this type are steadily achieving greater reliability. The important factor is that the ethnographic data used are from types of dwelling similar to those under investigation in the archaeological record.

Other techniques are possible. For example, in her attempt to assess the population of a *pa* (hillfort) in Auckland, New Zealand, Aileen Fox used ethnographic data which showed that Maori nuclear families were relatively small in the late 18th and early 19th centuries AD. Archaeological evidence indicated an average of one household utilizing two storage pits on the *pa* terraces. A combination of both sets of data led to a formula of six adults to every two storage pits; thus the site's 36 pits indicated 18 households, and 108 people – a far smaller figure than had previously been believed. Population estimates may also be made from the frequency of artifacts or the amount of food remains, though these calculations depend on many assumptions.

It is also ethnography (primarily the !Kung San of the Kalahari Desert and the Australian Aborigines) that has given us the generalized totals of about 25 people in a hunter-gatherer local group or band, and about 500 people in a tribe. Since bands in Australia and elsewhere vary considerably in size through time and with the seasons, often numbering less than 25, it follows that such figures provide only a rough guide. Nevertheless, given that we can never establish exact

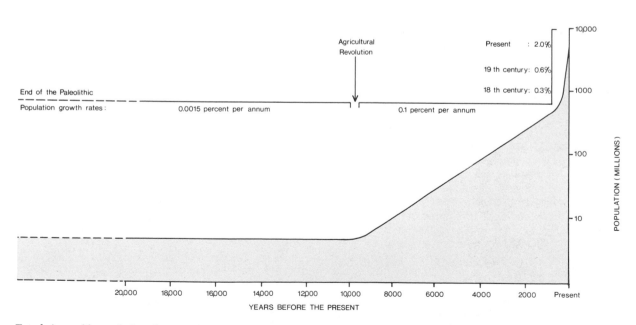

Trends in world population: the rate of growth increased considerably after the farming revolution, and has accelerated dramatically in the last two centuries.

GENETICS AND LANGUAGES

Genetic methods are increasingly being used in conjunction with linguistics to investigate population history. In many parts of the world, the language spoken by a human community is the best predictor of the genetic characteristics (as seen e.g. in blood groups) that community will have. Laurent Excoffier and his colleagues have studied African populations, measuring the frequencies of the varieties of gammaglobulin in the blood of different populations. The frequencies were used to compute similarities and differences between the various populations which were then plotted in tree form. It was found that this classification, based on genetic evidence, actually arranges the populations of Africa into their language families. The genetic classification (based on gammaglobulin frequencies) for example classes together the Bantu-speaking populations. The Afroasiatic speakers of north Africa form another group, and the pygmies, with languages of the Khoisan family, another group again. So striking a correlation between genetic composition and language is impressive.

Luca Cavalli-Sforza and his colleagues have suggested a very widespread correlation between genetic and linguistic classifications, arguing that both are the products of similar evolutionary processes. But language change takes place much more quickly than genetic change, which is governed by the mutation rate for individual genes. Instead, the correlation is partly explained by the processes underlying language replacement (see box, Language Families and Language Change, p. 467).

If a farming dispersal introduces large numbers of a new human population speaking a language new to the territory, language replacement may be accompanied by genetic replacement also.

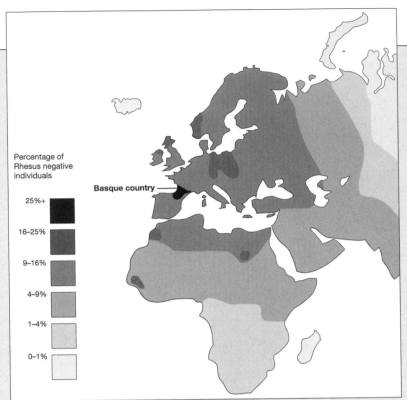

Percentage of Rhesus negative individuals

Basque country

25%+

16–25%

9–16%

4–9%

1–4%

0–1%

A map showing the distribution of the Rhesus negative blood group reveals a high concentration in the Basque region of Spain, coinciding impressively with the distinctive language spoken there.

The Basques

Many of the studies so far conducted employ classical genetic markers (blood groups etc.). One such study highlights the Basque country of northern Spain as distinctive, on the basis of the high incidence here of the rare Rhesus negative gene. Interestingly the Basques are also distinctive in speaking one of the very few non-Indo-European languages now remaining in Europe. The Basque language is generally thought to be a relic of a language family more widely spoken before the coming of Indo-European to Europe. Mitochondrial DNA and Y-chromosome DNA studies have now confirmed the special genetic status of the Basque population (see box Molecular Genetics and Population Dynamics: Europe, pp. 468–69).

DNA and Languages

Increasingly mtDNA (mitochondrial) and Y-chromosome studies are being used to study the affinity of populations defined by the languages they speak. The situation is more complicated when language replacement has taken place by the mechanism of elite dominance (see box, p. 467), since if the immigrant population is small in number the gene flow may not be significant, and in such cases the genetic and the linguistic pictures will no longer correlate.

The application of molecular genetics to population studies and to historical linguistics is still in its early stages, but the information potentially available is vast in quantity, and this is certain to be an expanding field.

There is some evidence from mtDNA studies in the Americas that the speakers of a particular language may have different haplogroup frequencies from those of their neighbors, and indeed that specific haplotypes may be seen to be characteristic of the speakers of a particular language. This phenomenon of "population specific polymorphism" and its relation to specific languages remains to be explored further (see p. 223), but, as we have seen, it seems clear for the Basques and among African populations (where it is language families rather than specific languages which are being contrasted).

Macrofamilies

Russian and Israeli linguists have made the controversial proposal that a number of major language families in the western part of the Old World (namely the Indo-European, Afroasiatic, Uralic, Altaic, Dravidian, and Kartvelian families) can be classified in a single, more embracing (and more ancient) macrofamily, to which the term "Nostratic" has been given. The American linguist Joseph Greenberg has proposed an analogous "Eurasiatic" macrofamily, although he would draw the boundaries differently. In 1963 he classified the various languages of Africa into just four macrofamilies, a proposal which has been widely accepted, but his similar proposal for just three macrofamilies among the native languages of the Americas (Eskimo-Aleut, Na-Dene and "Amerind") has been widely criticized by historical linguists.

Despite this, there is some evidence from molecular genetics which has been taken as support of the Greenberg view, and as we have seen there is a correlation in Africa between his classification and the molecular genetic data there. The whole question is also caught up with that of the peopling of the Americas (see box p. 456) and other continents. At present it is probably wise for the archaeologist to treat concepts such as "Amerind" or "Nostratic" with considerable caution, in view of the reservations of many linguists. Even if the genetic data favor a classification which might correlate well with the linguistic "lumpers" (who favor long-range linguistic connections and macrofamilies, as against the "splitters" who are skeptical of both), there might be other explanations. Caution is in order until the linguistic picture is clearer.

population figures for prehistoric peoples, figures of this sort do provide useful estimates that are certainly of the right order of magnitude.

But what of the population of large areas? Where archaeological evidence is concerned, one can only count the number of sites for each region, assume how many in each cultural phase were occupied at the same time, estimate the population of each relevant site, and then arrive at a rough figure for population density. For historical periods, it is sometimes possible to use written evidence. On the basis of censuses and grain imports and other data, for example, it has been estimated that the population of Classical Attica, Greece, was 315,000 in 431 BC and 258,000 in 323 BC. In another Classical example, this time of a city rather than a region, the population of ancient Rome was recently estimated to be about 450,000 on the basis of the population densities of Pompeii and Ostia, as well as of hundreds of pre-industrial and modern cities.

However, population estimates for wide areas during prehistory are no more than guesses. Estimates for world population in the Paleolithic and Mesolithic vary from 5 million to over 20 million. Perhaps in the future, with improved knowledge of the population densities of different economic groups and the carrying capacities of past environments, we may be able to achieve a more informed guess for the tantalizing question of world population.

ETHNICITY AND EVOLUTION

Finally, we come to the question of identifying the origins and distribution of human populations from human remains. Modern techniques have ensured that such studies are on a sounder and more objective footing than they were before World War II.

Studying Genes: Our Past within Ourselves

Much the best information on early population movements is now being obtained from the "archaeology of the living body," the clues to be found in genetic material. For example, light has recently been cast on the old problem of when people first entered the Americas, and it has come not from archaeological or fossil evidence but from the distribution of genetic markers in modern Native Americans (box overleaf).

It is proving possible to compare ancient DNA, such as that extracted from ancient brains in Florida (see above), with that of modern Native Americans. If the ancient DNA has patterns that no longer exist, this might indicate that the ancient group in question had

STUDYING THE ORIGINS OF NEW WORLD POPULATIONS

Northeast Asia and Siberia have long been accepted as the launching ground for the first human colonizers of the New World. But was there one major wave of migration across the Bering Strait into the Americas, or several? And when did this event or events take place? In recent years new clues have come from research into linguistics, teeth, and genetics.

Evidence from Linguistics
The linguist Joseph Greenberg has since the 1950s argued that all native American languages belong to just three major macrofamilies: Amerind, Na-Dene, and Eskimo-Aleut – a view that has given rise to the idea of three main migrations.

The glottochronologies of the individual macrofamilies might suggest that Eskimo-Aleut languages began to diverge from their ancestral form about 4000 years ago, with the Na-Dene divergence beginning sometime between 9000 and 5000 years ago. These dates for first divergence are thought to time the entry into the Americas of population groups who spoke the proto-language of each macrofamily. The time depth of the Amerind macrofamily is too great for glottochronology to be of any real value, but a date in excess of 11,000 years ago is indicated.

Greenberg is in a minority among fellow linguists, however, most of whom favor the notion of a great many waves of migration to account for the more than 1000 languages spoken at one time or another by American Indians.

The historical linguist Johanna Nichols has used the high degree of linguistic diversity in the Americas to produce a colonization date of 35,000 years ago, but the assumptions underlying her work have been robustly questioned by Daniel Nettle. In the last analysis it is for the archaeologist, using standard radiometric methods, to establish the date of the first human settlement and it is not realistic to expect a more reliable chronology from linguistic arguments.

Evidence from Teeth
Studies of teeth claim to support the hypothesis of three waves of migration. The biological anthropologist Christy Turner is an expert in the analysis of changing physical characteristics in human teeth. He argues that tooth crowns and roots have a high genetic component, minimally affected by environmental and other factors.

According to Turner, the dental evidence ties in with the idea of a Paleo-Indian migration out of northeast Asia which he sets at before 14,000 years ago by calibrating rates of dental microevolution, followed by two later migrations which he equates with Na-Dene and Eskimo-Aleut.

Evidence from Genetics
Antonio Torroni, Douglas Wallace, and their colleagues have examined the mitochondrial DNA (mtDNA) from American Indians belonging to widely separated Native American groups. By analyzing divergences in the sequence variation of mtDNA within and between the groups, they were able to suggest that the first Amerind speakers had entered the Americas sometime between 42,000 and 21,000 years ago, while a population ancestral to the present-day Na-Dene arrived between 16,000 and 5000 years ago. Interestingly, the date for the Amerind migration of 20,000 years ago or more suggests an occupation phase earlier than that attested by the widespread Clovis points, generally dated to about 14,000 years ago.

Their initial picture of four founding female (mtDNA) lineages has however been complicated by the discovery of further haplogroups, and recently by data from Y-chromosomes. Indeed it has now been shown that up to 85 percent of Native American males share a common Y-chromosome marker, leading to talk of a "Native American Adam" living around 20,000 years ago, and to the suggestion that many of the first Americans arrived in a single migration from an ancestral Siberian home. Andrew Merriwether has concluded (1999, 126): "It is much more parsimonious with a single wave of migration with all these types, followed by linguistic and cultural diversification after or during entry." So it can no longer be claimed that the genetic data give clear-cut support for the "three waves" hypothesis initially supported by the mtDNA: the Y-chromosome data currently favors a single migration view. But the pace of research is considerable and matters may be clearer in a few years.

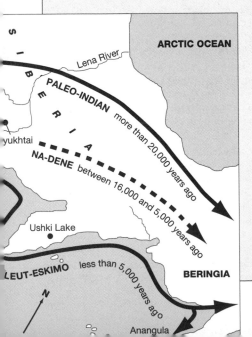

Three possible waves of migration from Siberia to North America using dates initially suggested by Wallace, Torroni and their colleagues: but this is already seen as too simple an account which further research is modifying.

disappeared or greatly changed. The discovery of "Kennewick Man," dated to some 7000 years ago, and according to some anthropologists very different from modern American Indian populations, has underlined that possibility (see p. 541). Adrian Hill has established that certain mutations in DNA occurred in Polynesians, Melanesians, and Southeast Asians, but nowhere else, a fact which supports archaeological and linguistic evidence in casting considerable doubt on theories that Polynesians came from South America. Further work by Erika Hagelberg and John Clegg on this problem, involving mitochondrial DNA (see below) from modern populations and skeletal remains in the Pacific, has helped to trace the migration route of the proto-Polynesian voyagers. Their preliminary results suggest that the earliest inhabitants of the central Pacific may have come from Melanesia rather than Southeast Asia.

Other population movements in the distant past have been reassessed through genetic evidence, as a result of which it appears that Africans were the ancestors of modern humans. This has been deduced by James Wainscoat and his colleagues from mapping part of a human chromosome in eight different populations around the world. Members of the same population all tend to carry similar mutations, and populations that are geographically close have very similar patterns; but African samples differ markedly from non-African. Africans have two unique patterns, and only 5 percent of African samples have the pattern most common among Eurasians. It seems, therefore, that the more "recent" Eurasians have lost, or never had, the predominant patterns of African people, a fact which suggests that the founder population of anatomically modern people was small and highly inbred; that there is a big genetic distance between African groups and the others, interpreted as a mark of great age; and that the strong genetic homogeneity among various non-African peoples points to a common center of origin. So does the origin of *Homo sapiens sapiens* lie in Africa? If so, the founder population could have been as small as 1000 people.

A very similar conclusion was reached by Rebecca Cann, Mark Stoneking, and Allan Wilson by using very different genes. Most of our genetic information in the form of DNA is stored in the nuclei of our cells, but other bodies in our cells (mitochondria) also contain such information. However, mitochondrial DNA (mtDNA) is passed on only by females, because the male sperm's mitochondria do not survive fertilization intact. Since mtDNA is thus inherited solely through the mother, unlike nuclear DNA which is a mixture of both parents' genes, it preserves a family record that is altered over the generations only by mutations.

In a comparable way, Y-chromosome DNA (which is part of the nuclear DNA) is inherited in the male line and likewise does not recombine as the genetic material is passed on to the next generation. Most nuclear DNA does of course recombine, with contributions from the male and female parents, making the inheritance of DNA a complex process: the possibility of studying female (mitochondrial) and male (Y-chromosome) non-recombining DNA is therefore of great importance.

Consequently mtDNA can be used to study the movements of women, and thus provide more information on the origins of modern people. Cann and her colleagues believed that mtDNA mutates at a known and steady rate (about 2–4 percent per million years), so that one can calculate the dates of these movements; and they claimed that we are all descended from one woman who lived in Africa about 200,000 years ago: she was nicknamed "Eve," although it was stressed that she not only had a mother herself but lived at the same time as other people. Indeed, many other males and females must have contributed to her or her children's offspring in order to account for the genetic variability we possess in nuclear DNA.

The important point about Eve, in Cann's formulation, was that she was *not* the first woman, but the ancestor of everyone on earth today. Other females alive at the same time also had descendants, but Eve was the only one who still appears in everyone's genealogy. Some of the other females' descendants will have included generations that produced no children or only males, thus halting the propagation of their mtDNA. This process can still be seen today – it is reckoned that of the French people alive in 1789, only 14 percent have descendants today.

Cann, Stoneking, and Wilson analyzed mtDNA from 147 present-day women from five different geographical populations (Africa, Asia, Europe, Australia, and New Guinea), and concluded that the people of sub-Saharan African descent showed the most differences among themselves, which implied that their mtDNA has had the most time to mutate – hence their ancestors must be the earliest.

To the glee of researchers who support the alternative "Multiregional Hypothesis" (the theory, based primarily on fossils and tools, that *Homo erectus*, having left Africa, evolved separately in different parts of the Old World, and was not simply replaced by a much later migration of anatomically modern humans from Africa), geneticist Alan Templeton subsequently pointed out crucial flaws in the "Mitochondrial Eve Hypothesis." In his view, the analysis was invalid, since it used inappropriate statistical tests and sampling

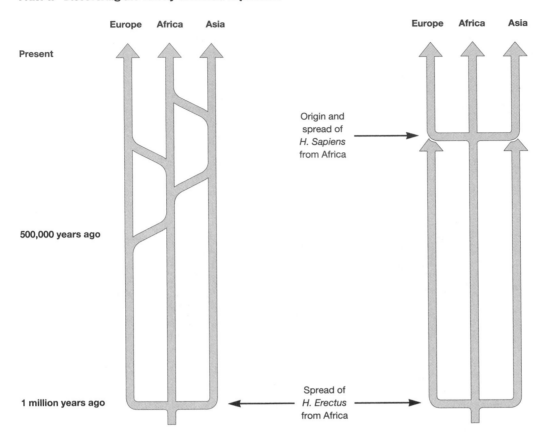

Two views of the origins of modern humans. (Left) The "Multiregional Hypothesis": according to this view, after the migration of Homo erectus *out of Africa around 1 million years ago, people evolved into modern humans independently in different parts of the world. (Right) "Out of Africa": others believe the genetic evidence indicates that modern humans evolved first in Africa, migrating from there into other continents around 100,000 years ago and replacing earlier* Homo erectus *populations.*

methods biased in favor of an African root; its results were dictated by the order in which the information was fed into the computer. Instead of one "family tree" leading back to Africa 200,000 years ago, these data can produce thousands of simpler trees, some of which do not have African roots. Moreover, variation in population sizes may help explain the greater genetic divergence of Africa. Templeton instead argued that a model in which modern humans evolved from many centers would fit all the evidence.

Opinions differ sharply about the reliability of "molecular clocks," and the rate of mutational change in human DNA, in calculating Eve's date. There have also recently been disquieting suggestions that there may sometimes be a male contribution to the inherited mitochondrial DNA which, if confirmed, would invalidate much recent work in this field.

Supporters of the "Out of Africa" model, however, maintain that other lines of fossil and nuclear DNA evidence still point to Africa as the birthplace of modern humans. For example, analysis of part of the Y chromosome in men around the world shows limited variation in its DNA, suggesting a common male ancestor less than 200,000 years ago.

This polarization of views is currently one of the hottest debates in the whole of anthropology, though many believe the truth is likely to lie somewhere between the two extremes, and to be more complex, for example with more than one migration out of Africa, as well as movements in the other direction. With time, the disputes will no doubt be resolved, and the human relationships that modern DNA studies are only just beginning to reveal will be determined with much greater precision. Genetics are also being combined with the study of languages to produce interesting results (see box, pp. 454–55).

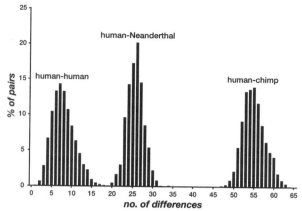

Distributions of pairwise sequence differences among humans, the Neanderthals, and chimpanzees (X axis: number of sequence differences; Y axis: the percentage of pairwise comparisons) showing human-Neanderthal differences to be much more numerous than had been imagined and hence the Neanderthals to be much more remote cousins of the human species.

So far most of the running in the application of molecular genetics has come from the study of samples from living populations. But the contribution of ancient DNA, from the remains of ancient burials and other human remains, will soon prove highly important. The most striking example comes from the study of Neanderthal DNA from one of the original fossils found in the Neander Valley in western Germany in 1856, which gave its name to "Neanderthal Man." Mathias Krings and Svante Pääbo in Munich, with Anne Stone and Mark Stoneking at Pennsylvania State University, were able to extract genetic material and then amplify segments of mtDNA. By using overlapping amplifications they recovered mitochondrial DNA sequences over 360 base pairs in length. When these were compared with the comparable sequences in humans, 27 differences were found. Taking an estimated divergence date between humans and chimpanzees of 4 to 5 million years, and assuming constant mutation rates, a date of 550,000 to 690,000 years ago for the divergence of Neanderthal mtDNA and contemporary human mtDNA was obtained (compared with a divergence date among humans of 120,000 to 150,000 years).

The divergence date for humans corresponds well with current thinking and the Out of Africa hypothesis for human origins. The surprise is that the human-Neanderthal divergence date is so much earlier. The Neanderthals may still just be considered our "cousins," but they are very much more remote cousins than had previously been thought. This conclusion also appears to rule out any direct Neanderthal input to the human genome. It therefore makes a fundamental contribution to the debates concerning human origins.

Genetic research techniques are thus revealing a good deal more about our past than we ever thought possible. This is proving of major assistance to archaeologists and anthropologists. Even the best fossil beds preserve only about one skeleton in every million, but we all carry a record of our history in some of the cells of our bodies. The archaeology of our cells has started to tell us much about ourselves. It must be noted, however, that genetics can only tell us about past populations which left descendants; it can tell us nothing about people who died out.

SUMMARY

Since archaeology studies the relics of the human past, it follows that the archaeologist's ultimate interest must lie in the remains of the very people who produced the archaeological record. Much of the material in this chapter lies within the realm of physical anthropologists, but it is usually archaeologists who provide them with the specimens for study and who derive great benefit from their findings.

A huge range of very varied information can now be extracted from even minor fragments of humanity. We can assess age, sex, height, weight, appearance, inter-relationships; abilities such as walking, talking, and left- or right-handedness; stresses, traumas, and disease; and whether nutritional level was good or inadequate.

Finally, the newest field of inquiry – molecular genetics, forming a genetic history – is "archaeology within the human body," a kind of ethnoarchaeology where observations made in the present can have tremendous influence on our interpretation of the past. Most information comes at present from samples taken from modern populations, but the study of ancient DNA from preserved human remains (and plant and animal residues) is also developing as extraction techniques improve. DNA studies have been adding amazing new insights into our understanding of the history of human populations. In modern archaeology, human remains have thus reached center stage, and rightly so since they were, so to speak, the actors in the play we are trying to reconstruct.

FURTHER READING

The following provide good general introductions to the study of human remains:

Brothwell, D. 1981. *Digging up Bones. The Excavation, Treatment and Study of Human Skeletal Remains.* (3rd ed.) British Museum (Natural History): London; Oxford University Press: Oxford.

Brothwell, D. 1986. *The Bog Man and the Archaeology of People.* British Museum Publications: London; Harvard University Press: Cambridge, Mass.

Larsen, C.S. 1997. *Bioarchaeology: Interpreting Behaviour from the Human Skeleton.* Cambridge University Press: Cambridge & New York.

Mays, S. 1998. *The Archaeology of Human Bones.* Routledge: London.

Ubelaker, D.H. 1984. *Human Skeletal Remains.* (Revised ed.) Taraxacum: Washington.

White, T. 1991. *Human Osteology.* Academic Press: New York.

For the study of disease and deformity, one can begin with:

Brothwell, D.R. & Sandison, A.T. (eds.). 1967. *Diseases in Antiquity.* C.C. Thomas: Springfield, Illinois.

Ortner, D.J. & Putschar, W.G. 1981. *Identification of Pathological Conditions in Human Skeletal Remains.* Smithsonian Institution Press: Washington D.C.

Roberts, C. & Manchester, K. 1995. *The Archaeology of Disease* (2nd ed.) Alan Sutton: Stroud; Cornell University Press: Ithaca.

The standard work on population studies is:

Hassan, F.A. 1981. *Demographic Archaeology.* Academic Press: New York & London.

For the evolution of modern humans see:

Johanson, D. & Edgar, B. 1996. *From Lucy to Language.* Simon & Schuster: New York.

Stringer, C. & Gamble, C. 1994. *In Search of the Neanderthals.* Thames & Hudson: London & New York.

For the application of molecular genetics see:

Cavalli-Sforza, L.L., Menozzi, P., & Piazza, A. 1994. *The History and Geography of Human Genes.* Princeton University Press: Princeton.

Sykes, B. (ed.) 1999. *The Human Inheritance: Genes, Languages and Evolution.* Oxford Univ. Press.

12

Why Did Things Change?
Explanation in Archaeology

To answer the question "why?" is the most difficult task in archaeology. Indeed, it is the most challenging and interesting task in any science or field of knowledge. For with this question we go beyond the mere appearance of things, and on to a level of analysis that seeks in some way to *understand* the pattern of events. Yet this is the goal motivating many who take up the study of the human past, whether we are speaking of archaeology or of history more generally. There is a desire to learn something from a study of what is dead and gone that is relevant for the conduct of our own lives and those of our contemporaries today. Archaeology, which allows us to study early and remote prehistoric periods as well as the more recent historical ones, is unique among the human sciences in offering a considerable time depth. Thus, if there are patterns to be found among human affairs, the archaeological timescale may reveal them.

The eminent French historian Fernand Braudel distinguished three levels of historical events, and of historical analysis. At the surface, so to speak, are the specific occurrences of human history: *l'histoire événementielle*, as he termed it. Beneath these superficial happenings lie slower rhythms, including the cycles identified by economists with a periodicity measured perhaps in decades. Finally, beneath these rhythms are the basic, long-term trends, the *longue durée*, which usually prevail in the end.

That is only one man's view. Even so, it hints at the complexity of trying to explain history. Indeed, there is no agreed and accepted way of setting out to understand the human past. A chapter such as this is therefore bound to be inconclusive, and certain to be controversial. Yet it is a chapter worth writing and worth thinking about, for it is in this area of inquiry that archaeological research is now most active.

The past 30 years have seen the re-emergence of the use of archaeological theory. For several decades, the whole subject of explanation was in the doldrums. However, with the development of the New Archaeology in the 1960s, and the accompanying "loss of inno-cence," came the realization that there was no well-established body of theory to underpin current methods of archaeological inquiry. To a large extent this is still true, although there have been many attempts sparked off by the processual approach of the New Archaeology to provide an underlying body of theory. Today there is a superabundance of approaches to explaining "why?" The archaeological literature is awash with polemical discussions between positivists, Marxists, structuralists, postprocessualists (see box, pp. 42–43), etc., all claiming some special insight.

The early New Archaeology involved the explicit use of theory and of models, and above all of generalization. Subsequently, it was criticized as too "functionalist," too much concerned with ecological aspects of adaptation and with efficiency, and with the purely utilitarian and functional aspects of living. Meanwhile, an alternative perspective, inspired by Marxism, was laying more stress on social relations and the exercise of power. Nevertheless, the processual and Marxist approaches have much in common: they are compatible, as we shall see below, even though they use rather different terminologies (some would say jargons) to express their views.

From the 1970s, in reaction to the processual "functionalists," a structuralist archaeology was proclaimed, then a post-structuralist, and, finally, a postprocessual one. These performed a useful service in stressing that the ideas and beliefs of past societies should no longer be overlooked in archaeological explanation.

In the 1980s, several of the practitioners of processual archaeology sought ways of dealing with the cognitive aspects of past societies in the framework of processual thinking. This "cognitive-processual" approach seeks to enlarge the scope of the now-traditional processual archaeology by stressing social and cognitive aspects, yet without rejecting the value of earlier work. It opens the way, using the theoretical approach known as "methodological individualism," to consider more carefully the place of agency, i.e. the actions of individuals, in processes of change (see box, pp. 492–93). The significant role of the individual has been one of the points stressed by postprocessual archaeologists (especially those advocating "structuration theory") and one can now see some convergence here between the two approaches. We shall therefore discuss approaches to the explanation of the past in these terms, fully realizing that, when so many different schools of thought are in existence, no complete consensus is possible. "Why" questions are significant ones, but the answers depend to a large extent on one's perceptions and preconceptions. In emphasizing the variety displayed in current approaches towards explanation in archaeology, we are perhaps revealing one of contemporary archaeology's greatest strengths – that it is as exciting at the intellectual level as it is rich in its subject material.

What Are We Trying to Explain?

Many of the current debates about archaeological explanation fail to notice that different workers are explaining different things. Pronouncements about valid methods frequently appear contradictory, yet the contradiction may disappear when we realize the vast differences between the individual cases. For instance, an archaeologist seeking to explain the distribution of humankind during the last Ice Age, using timescales that are accurate only to within a few thousand years, will often lean more heavily on climatic and vegetational factors than on other aspects of community affairs. Such explanations at first sight lay themselves open to charges of "ecological determinism" – that changes in the environment automatically determine changes in human society. Certainly, a research worker studying the designs on glazed tile floors of the Middle Ages would propose explanations far removed from the world of Paleolithic hunter-gatherers.

First, therefore, let us distinguish between some of the different things we may be trying to explain: they may, in fact, require different kinds of explanation.

Explaining Specific Conditions of Burial and Preservation. Our concern with a particular find or site may be with the essentially natural processes that have resulted in burial and preservation. These are the kind of processes that the American archaeologist Michael Schiffer has called "N-transforms" (i.e. the work of natural processes) to distinguish them from "C-transforms" (the work of culturally determined processes resulting from human actions) (see Chapter 2). The types of question one might be trying to answer are: How did these animal bones come to be buried with those tools? Why are these textiles so well preserved?

Explaining a Specific Event. Our concern may be to explain why a specific event took place. The philosopher of history R.G. Collingwood used to ask, "Why did Caesar cross the Rubicon?" Archaeology is less often concerned with events in the lives of named individuals, but it will still ask such specific questions as, "What caused the Classic Maya collapse?" or "Why was the Second City at Troy destroyed when it was?" And the answer may well involve the actions and thoughts of individuals, although these are likely to be generic individuals, not those whom we can name or identify from the archaeological record as separate and recognizable people.

Explaining a Specific Pattern of Events. Often, the archaeologist perceives some pattern in the archaeological record, and it is this pattern rather than a single, specific occurrence that seems to require explanation. A good example is offered by the "elm decline" in Neolithic Europe. Pollen sequences in much of northern Europe show that the percentage of elm pollen declined markedly, although the absolute date for the decline is not the same in each area. Why was this? Is the explanation climatic change? Did some pest attack the trees? Or was there a change in the pattern of exploitation by humans? The answer may not yet be clear: what is clear is that there is a pattern in need of explanation. (For a possible explanation of the elm decline, refer to Chapter 6.)

Explaining a Class of Events. Generalization, as we shall see, is still rare in archaeology. Yet some of the most interesting explanations of change concern not just one event or pattern of events, but a whole, more general class of events. For instance, we might regard the development of food production in the Near East at the end of the last Ice Age as constituting a pattern of change over a wide area. We might say the same of the development of food production in Mesoamerica. When we compare the two, and then bring into consideration the inception of food production in China and in Southeast Asia, and then in sub-Saharan Africa, we are dealing with phenomena that may be unconnected. Yet it is remarkable that food production seems to have begun in all these areas within a relatively short time-span in the post-Pleistocene period. Why? Here, then, is a class of events that demands an explanation. (For one proposed explanation, see box, p. 472.)

Another example is the emergence of state societies – of cities and "civilization" – in different parts of the world, when some of these areas were apparently not in significant contact with each other. How do we explain such a phenomenon?

The issue of the rise of complex society is one of the most actively debated in contemporary archaeology and is discussed further below. Another example, the phenomenon of system collapse in early state societies, is likewise looked at in some detail later in the chapter.

Explaining a Process. In some cases, the problem is not to explain a given event or pattern or even a class of events. Instead, insight may be sought into processes at work in society of a continuous and long-enduring nature. The phenomenon of the intensification of agri-cultural production may be of this kind, or the development of ranked society. These processes may be seen as something common to large parts of human-kind, at least under certain conditions. To explain such processes may by no means be an easy task, but their understanding must be one of the essential goals of archaeological and anthropological research.

There are many different kinds of explanation on offer. Some are more suitable for one of these types of problem than for others. This needs bearing in mind.

MIGRATIONIST AND DIFFUSIONIST EXPLANATIONS

The New Archaeology made the shortcomings of trad-itional archaeological explanations much more appa-rent. These shortcomings can be made clearer in an example of the traditional method – the appearance of a new kind of pottery in a given area and period, the pottery being distinguished by shapes not previously recognized and by new decorative motifs. The tradi-tional approach, in its own way a systematic one, will very properly require a closer definition of this pottery style in space and time. The archaeologist will be expected to draw a distribution map of its occurrence, and also to establish its place in the stratigraphic sequence at the sites where it occurs. The next step is to assign it to its place within an archaeological *culture*, defined (following Gordon Childe) as a "constantly recurring assemblage of artifacts." The pottery may itself be one of its most conspicuous features, but there will be others with which it is associated.

Using the traditional approach, it is argued that each archaeological culture is the manifestation in material terms of a specific *people* – that is, a well-defined ethnic group, detectable by the archaeologist by the method just outlined. This is an ethnic classification, but of course the "people," being prehistoric, have to be given an arbitrary name. Usually, they will be named after the place where the pottery was first recognized (e.g. the Mimbres people in the American Southwest or the Windmill Hill people in Neolithic Britain), or some-times after the pottery itself (e.g. the Beaker Folk).

Next it is usual to see if it is possible to think in terms of a folk *migration* to explain the changes observed. Can we locate a convenient homeland for this group of people? Careful study of the ceramic assemblages in adjoining lands may suggest such a homeland, and perhaps even a migration route.

Alternatively, if the migration argument does not seem to work, a fourth approach is to look for specific features of the cultural assemblage that have *parallels* in more distant lands. If the whole assemblage cannot be ascribed to an external source, there may be specific features of it that can. Links may be found with more civilized lands. If such "parallels" can be discovered, the traditionalist would argue that these were the points of origin, of departure as it were, for the features in our assemblage, and were transmitted to it by a pro-cess of cultural *diffusion*. Indeed, before the advent of radiocarbon dating, these parallels could also be used to date the pottery finds in our hypothetical example, because the features and traits lying closer to the heart-lands of civilization would almost certainly already be dated through comparison with the historical chrono-logy of that civilization. The occurrences of these traits may offer a *chronological horizon*, which is of great use in dating the culture.

It would be easy to find many actual examples of such explanations. For instance, in the New World, the very striking developments in architecture and other crafts in Chaco Canyon in New Mexico, and with it Mesa Verde in Colorado, have been explained by comparisons of precisely this kind with the more "advanced" civilizations of Mexico to the south. Simi-larly, for a long time archaeologists in what is now Zimbabwe attempted misguidedly to explain the great stone monuments at the site of Great Zimbabwe in this way, by saying they were built by foreigners, not by the indigenous Shona people (see box overleaf).

Traditional explanations rest, however, on assump-tions that are easily challenged today. First, there is the notion among traditionalists that archaeological "cul-tures" can somehow represent real entities rather than merely the classificatory terms devised for the conven-ience of the scholar. Second is the view that ethnic units or "peoples" can be recognized from the archaeo-logical record by equation with these notional cul-tures. It is in fact clear that ethnic groups do not always stand out clearly in archaeological remains (the point

DIFFUSIONIST EXPLANATION REJECTED: GREAT ZIMBABWE

The remarkable monument of Great Zimbabwe, near Masvingo in modern Zimbabwe, has been the object of intense speculation ever since this region of Africa was first explored by Europeans in the 19th century. For here was an impressive structure of great sophistication, with beautifully finished stonework.

Early scholars followed the traditional pattern of explanation in ascribing Great Zimbabwe to architects and builders from "more civilized" lands to the north. On a visit to the site by the British explorer Cecil Rhodes, the local Karange chiefs were told that "the Great Master" had come "to see the ancient temple which once upon a time belonged to white men." One writer in 1896 took the view that Great Zimbabwe was Phoenician in origin.

The first excavator, J.T. Bent, tried to establish parallels – points of similarity – between the finds and features found in more sophisticated contexts in the Near East. He concluded: "The ruins and the things in them are not in any way connected with any known African race," and he located the builders in the Arabian peninsula. This was thus a migrationist view.

Much more systematic excavations were undertaken by Gertrude Caton-Thompson (p. 36), and she concluded her report in 1931: "Examination of all the existing evidence, gathered from every quarter, still can produce not one single item that is not in accordance with the claim of Bantu origin and medieval date." Despite her carefully documented conclusions, however, other archaeologists continued to follow the typical pattern of diffusionist explanation in speaking of "influences" from "higher centers of culture." Portuguese traders were one favored source of inspiration. But if the date of the monument was to be set earlier than European travelers, then Arab merchants in the Indian Ocean offered an alternative. As late as 1971, R. Summers could write, using a familiar diffusionist argument: "It is not unduly stretching probability to suggest some Portuguese stonemason may have reached Zimbabwe and entered the service of the great chief living there.... Equally probably, although rather less plausible, is that some travelling Arab craftsman may have been responsible."

Subsequent research has backed up the conclusions of Gertrude Caton-Thompson. Great Zimbabwe is now seen as the most notable of a larger class of monuments in this area.

Although the site has an earlier history, the construction of a monumental building probably began there in the 13th century AD, and the site reached its climax in the 15th century. Various archaeologists have now been able to give a coherent picture of the economic and social conditions in the area that made this great achievement possible. Significant influence – diffusion – from more "advanced" areas is no longer part of that picture. Today a processual framework of explanation has replaced the diffusionist one.

An aerial view of the Elliptical Building.

Carved soapstone bird found in the Great Zimbabwe Eastern Enclosure in 1889, and later sold to Cecil Rhodes.

Racism and archaeology: a subservient black slave presents his offering of gold to a ghostly Queen of Sheba in this Rhodesian government poster of 1938.

Site plan: the Elliptical Building, with its series of enclosed areas, platforms, and the conical tower displayed in the poster (shown above).

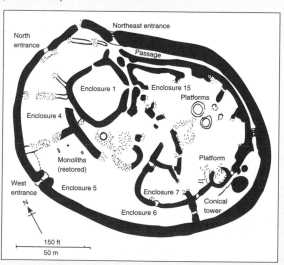

is discussed further in the box, Ancient Ethnicity and Language, p. 189). Third, it is assumed that when resemblances are noted between the cultural assemblages of one area and another, this can be most readily explained as the result of a migration of people. Of course, migrations did indeed occur (see below), but they are not so easy to document archaeologically as has often been supposed.

Finally, there is the principle of explanation through the diffusion of culture. Today, it is felt that this explanation has sometimes been overplayed, and nearly always oversimplified. For although contact between areas, not least through trade, can be of great significance for the developments in each area, the effects of this contact have to be considered in detail: explanation simply in terms of diffusion is not enough.

Nevertheless it is worth emphasizing that migrations did take place in the past, and on rare occasions this can be documented archaeologically. The colonization of the Polynesian islands in the Pacific offers one example. A complex of finds – especially pottery with incised decoration – known as the Lapita culture provides a record of the rapid movement of islanders eastward across a vast uninhabited area, from the northern New Guinea region to as far as Samoa, between 1600 and 1000 BC (see overleaf). Also, innovations are frequently made in one place and adopted in neighboring areas, and it is still perfectly proper to speak of the mechanism as one of diffusion (see illustration of the origins of the Roman alphabet overleaf).

THE PROCESSUAL APPROACH

The processual approach attempts to isolate and study the different processes at work within a society, and between societies, placing emphasis on relations with the environment, on subsistence and the economy, on social relations within the society, on the impact which the prevailing ideology and belief system have on these things, and on the effects of the interactions taking place between the different social units.

In 1967, Kent Flannery summed up the processual approach to change as follows:

Members of the process school view human behavior as a point of overlap (or "articulation") between a vast number of systems each of which encompasses both cultural and non-cultural phenomena – often much more of the latter. An Indian group, for example, may participate in a system in which maize is grown on a river floodplain that is slowly being eroded, causing the zone of the best farmland

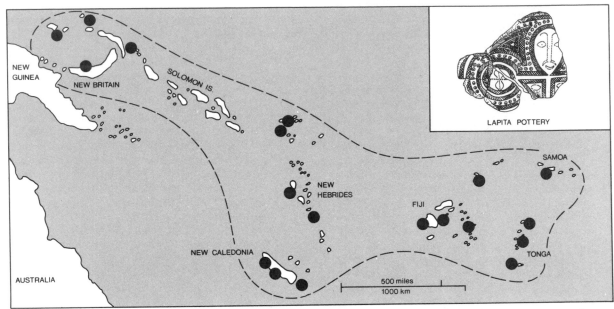

Migration: a positive example. The question of first settlement of the Polynesian islands has apparently been resolved by the discovery of a finds complex known as the Lapita culture, characterized in particular by pottery with incised decoration. Lapita sites were small villages, often with evidence of permanent occupation. They provide a record of the rapid movement of islanders by boat, eastwards from the northern New Guinea region to as far as Samoa in western Polynesia, between 1600 and 1000 BC according to radiocarbon dating. It is generally accepted that the Lapita migrants were the ancestors of the Polynesians, while those (the majority) who remained in Melanesia formed a large part of the ancestry of the present island Melanesians.

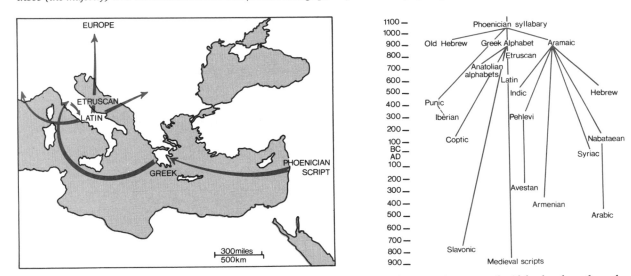

Diffusion: a positive example. One instance where an innovation in one place is known to have spread widely elsewhere through diffusion is that of the alphabet. Around the 12th century BC, on the Levantine coast, the Phoenicians developed a simplified phonetic script to write their Semitic language (a script now believed to derive ultimately from Egyptian hieroglyphic). By the early 1st millennium BC, the script had been adapted by the Greeks to write their language. This ultimately formed the basis for the Roman alphabet used today. (The Phoenician script also gave rise to the Hebrew, Arabic, and many other alphabets.) But of course the Greek alphabet had first to be modified and adopted in Italy, to write the Etruscan language and then Latin, the Roman language. It was through Latin that the Roman alphabet came to much of Europe, and later the rest of the world.

LANGUAGE FAMILIES AND LANGUAGE CHANGE

In 1786, Sir William Jones, a scholar working in India, recognized that many European languages (Latin, Greek, the Celtic languages, the Germanic languages – including English) as well as Old Iranian and Sanskrit (the ancestor of many modern languages of India and Pakistan) have so many similarities in vocabulary and grammar that they must all be related. Together they form what has come to be known as the Indo-European language family.

Since then many language families have been recognized, and it is generally accepted that each family is descended from an ancestral proto-language. Where and when each proto-language was originally spoken is a matter for discussion among historical linguists and prehistoric archaeologists. The origin of the Indo-Europeans has for long been a thorny question in European prehistory and in the 1930s and 1940s took on unpleasant political overtones with the racist claims for "Aryan" (i.e. Indo-European) racial supremacy made then by Adolf Hitler and the National Socialists.

Inevitably, the discussion is rather speculative, since direct evidence is not available until the time that the languages in question were recorded in written form, but archaeologists are beginning to address these problems in a more systematic way.

A specific language can come to be spoken in a given territory by one of four processes: by initial colonization; by divergence, where the dialects of speech communities remote from each other become more and more different, finally forming new languages, as in the case of the various descendants of Latin (including French, Spanish, Portuguese, Italian, etc.); by convergence, where contemporaneous languages influence one another through the borrowing of words, phrases, and grammatical forms; and by language replacement, where one language in the territory comes to replace another.

Language replacement can occur in several ways:

1 by the formation of a trading language or *lingua franca*, which gradually becomes dominant in a wide region;
2 by elite dominance, whereby a small number of incomers secure power and impose their language on the majority;
3 by a technological innovation so significant that the incoming group can grow in numbers more effectively. The best example is farming dispersal.
4 by contact induced language change, where adjacent communities speaking different languages come into more sustained contact

It is now widely accepted that the Bantu languages of Africa took up their vast area of distribution as a result of farming dispersal with other technical innovations (including iron-working), from west Africa.

Another case of farming dispersal is provided by the Austronesian languages of Southeast Asia and the Pacific, including the Polynesian languages. The first Polynesians may have been associated with the spread of Lapita ware as noted on the opposite page, although molecular research now suggests that the picture may be more complicated.

The distribution of the Indo-European languages has generally been regarded as a case of elite dominance (with mounted nomads from north of the Black Sea at the beginning of the Bronze Age constituting the elite), but the alternative view has been advanced that proto-Indo-European came to Europe from Anatolia around 6000 BC with the first farmers.

As noted in Chapter 11 (see box, pp. 454–55), there are correlations between the distribution of language families and of molecular genetic markers which indicate that both have much to teach us about world population history, and this is one of the growth areas of archaeological research.

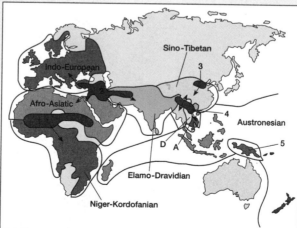

1 sorghum/millet
2 wheat/barley
3 millet
4 Asian rice
5 taro/sweet potato

D Daic
A Austroasiatic

Major areas of primary domestication of selected food plants and distributions of selected language families whose extent may be ascribed to agricultural dispersal. The areas of primary crop domestication are numbered, and Southeast Asian language families are indicated by letters.

MOLECULAR GENETICS AND POPULATION DYNAMICS: EUROPE

Molecular genetic research is now beginning to give significant new information about population histories, and in particular about the first peopling of the continents (see boxes, pp. 454–55, and p. 456). The story of the initial colonization of land masses is inevitably a migrationist one, as the Polynesian case (p. 466) illustrates, although more work needs to be done on the demography of local populations.

The case of early Europe illustrates how the patterns are changing. Initially the map of one genetic marker, the Rhesus negative gene, produced the pattern seen on the map on p. 454. Subsequent work by Luca Cavalli-Sforza and his associates with a principal components of data relating to 32 classical genetic markers produced a map of the first principal component of the variability, seen below. This shows pronounced clines from southeast to northwest. Such a map is a palimpsest, a compound overlay of

the effects of different processes at different times, with no way of disentangling these. However, these workers attributed the pattern to the spread of farming from Anatolia to Europe at the beginning of the Neolithic period around 6500 BC, which they viewed as a demographic "wave of advance," a process of demic diffusion. This would have left the genetic markers of the earlier, Upper Paleolithic population predominating in the northwest, where the demic diffusion process was least pronounced.

The impact of DNA studies has modified this picture significantly. In the first place work on mitochondrial DNA (mtDNA) by Brian Sykes, Martin Richards, and their colleagues suggested that several haplogroups are present in the modern European populations. Moreover, by studying the distribution of each haplogroup in turn it is possible to suggest a date for the initial spread – usually the initial arrival in Europe – for each. This has led them

to suggest that about 20 percent of the modern European gene pool was indeed contributed by the population of first farmers arriving from Anatolia about 8500 years ago (haplogroup J). About 10 percent remains from the initial peopling of Europe by our species from 50,000 years ago, but the largest contribution of 70 percent is contributed by haplogroups whose expansion is dated between 14,000 and 11,000 years ago, again coming to Europe from Anatolia. They agree then with the strong contribution made by Anatolia to the European gene pool, but place the principal processes much earlier, back in the Upper Paleolithic. This view has been criticized by some writers, but is complemented by the work of Antonio Torroni and colleagues, again using mtDNA, and by that of Patrizia Malaspina, Rosaria Scozzari, and Andrea Novelletto and their colleagues working with Y-chromosomal types.

Torroni's conclusion is that a major population expansion from the "Atlantic zone" of southwestern Europe occurred around 15,000 to 10,000 years ago, after the Late Glacial climatic maximum. This expansion is associated with an autochthonous European haplogroup (haplogroup V) which may

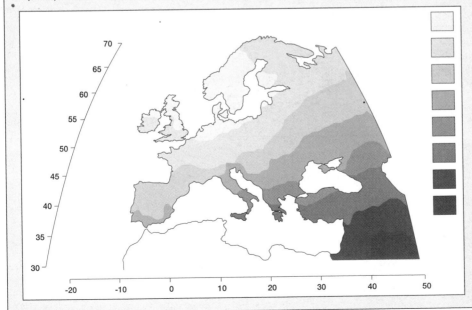

A synthetic map of Europe and western Asia, using the first principal component of the 32 genetic markers: this was interpreted by Cavalli-Sforza et al. as the result of a population "wave of advance" from Anatolia to Europe with the spread of farming. The scale is an arbitrary one, from 1 to 100.

Map of Europe (right) depicting the most likely homeland, 10,000 to 15,000 years ago (shaded area), of haplogroup V and its pattern of diffusion in the aftermath of the glacial maximum.

have originated in north Iberia or southwestern France around 15,000 years ago.

This view finds very strong support from the Y-chromosome studies of Malaspina and her colleagues. Indeed it is clear now that, as Lewis Binford has recently pointed out, climatic factors have to be taken very seriously into account. During the Late Glacial cold maximum in the Younger Dryas period, prior to 15,000 years ago, the population of Europe retreated to rather localized refugia, and in the succeeding millennia Europe was effectively recolonized from these refugia, rather than from Anatolia. Although there are still controversies of interpretation, the mtDNA data and the Y-chromosome data currently seem to support a picture of several colonization episodes from Anatolia, but with other very significant demographic episodes internal to Europe activated by the climatic changes during and after the last glacial period.

More work remains to be done, and already ancient DNA is beginning to play a part: Sykes, Richards, and their colleagues have analyzed mtDNA from early farming burials in central Europe and confirmed the presence in them of haplogroup J, which they had independently predicted would be associated with the early farming population. In ten years time we shall know more: this is a very active field of research.

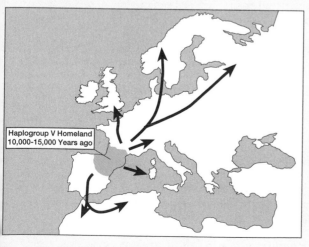

Haplogroup V Homeland
10,000–15,000 Years ago

to move upstream. Simultaneously it may participate in a system involving a wild rabbit population whose density fluctuates in a 10-year cycle because of predators or disease. It may also participate in a system of exchange with an Indian group occupying a different kind of area from which it receives subsistence products at certain predetermined times of the year, and so on. All these systems compete for the time and energy of the individual Indian; the maintenance of his way of life depends on an equilibrium among systems. Culture change comes about through minor variations in one or more systems which grow, displace or reinforce others and reach equilibrium on a different plane.

The strategy of the process school is therefore to isolate each system and study it as a separate variable. The ultimate goal of course is a reconstruction of the entire pattern of articulation, along with all related systems, but such complex analysis has so far proved beyond the powers of the process theorists. (Flannery 1967, 120.)

This statement moves at once into the language of systems thinking, discussed in a later section. But it is not always necessary to use systems language in this context. Moreover, Flannery places great emphasis here on the environment – on what he terms "non-cultural phenomena." Some critics of the New Archaeology in its early days felt that too much emphasis was placed on the economy, especially subsistence, and not enough on other aspects of human experience, including the social and the cognitive. But that does not diminish the force of what processual archaeology at once achieved and has retained: the focus on the analysis of the working of different aspects of societies, and the study of how these fit together to help explain the development through time of the society as a whole.

Another important point was made already in 1958, before the New Archaeology had formally begun at all. Gordon Willey and Philip Phillips wrote then: "In the context of archaeology, processual interpretation is the study of the nature of what is vaguely referred to as the culture-historical process. Practically speaking it implies an attempt to discover regularities in the relationships given by the methods of culture-historical integration." (Willey and Phillips 1958, 5–6.) In other words, explanation involves some element of generalization, and the discovery of "regularities."

As we shall see in the next section, much discussion today concerns the role of generalization in explanation, and how far the historical events we are analyzing were unique and, therefore, cannot be considered as general instances of any underlying process at all.

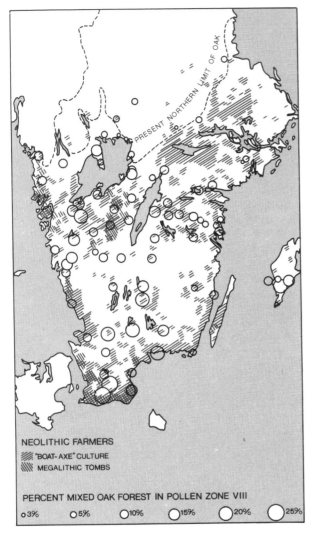

NEOLITHIC FARMERS

- ▨ "BOAT-AXE" CULTURE
- ▧ MEGALITHIC TOMBS

PERCENT MIXED OAK FOREST IN POLLEN ZONE VIII

○3%   ○5%   ○10%   ○15%   ○20%   ○25%

Conjunction of Neolithic farming with deciduous forest in Scandinavia.

Applications

If all this seems rather abstract, it may be useful to give an example from the ecological side of archaeology of the way processual thinking has more to offer than the old school of thought. This is appropriate because the ecological-economic approach was in many ways a precursor of the New Archaeology (see Chapter 1).

In 1952, the British archaeologist Grahame Clark sought to explain the pattern of early farming settlements in Scandinavia, following his own studies of the Mesolithic (hunter-gatherer) period there. He plotted on a map the distribution of finds of the so-called "boat axe" culture – an indicator of the activities of the early farmers – and also the occurrence of megalithic tombs, taken again as an indicator of settled farming communities. On the same map he also plotted, using pollen information then becoming available, the distribution of deciduous (mainly oak) forests in the relevant climatic subdivision, termed in Scandinavia the Subboreal period (*c.* 4000–1500 BC). After some discussion, and with careful reservations, he stated: "the coincidence of economic and ecological zones is sufficiently marked to justify the hypothesis that the northern margins of the deciduous forest in fact determined the limits of the early spread of farming in the countries of northern Europe." (Clark 1952, 21)

Clark thus explained the distribution of early farming cultures in terms of the extent of deciduous forest, making the inference from his data that there was some kind of necessary connection, and that these farming cultures were not adapted to live in the zone of coniferous forests beyond. Now, as we shall see below, it is a matter for discussion just how far the simple demonstration of a correlation between one thing and another actually takes us toward a truly satisfying explanation.

Grahame Clark's outlook in the 1950s, with its emphasis on the efficient adaptation of human society and culture to its environment, has much in common with the subsequent work of Lewis Binford. In 1968 Binford produced one of the first general explanations (where the New Archaeology set out to explain a class of events) of the farming revolution. In his paper, "Post-Pleistocene Adaptations," he gave the sort of generalizing explanation that the New Archaeology set as its goal (see box). Yet, as we shall see below, this general approach could be criticized as taking too "functionalist" a view of human affairs, laying more stress on the environment, demography, and subsistence than on social or cognitive factors.

It is interesting to contrast Binford's approach with that of Barbara Bender in 1978. Working from a broadly Marxist perspective, she argued that, before farming began, there was competition between local groups who tried to achieve dominance over their neighbors through feasting, and the expenditure of resources on conspicuous ritual and on exchange. It was these demands that led to the need to increase subsistence resources and so to a process of intensification in the use of land and the development of food production.

The early processual archaeology may reasonably be termed *functional-processual*. It is notable, and understandable, that many functional-processual explanations are applied to hunter-gatherer and early farming communities, where subsistence questions often seem

THE ORIGINS OF FARMING: A PROCESSUAL EXPLANATION

In 1968, Lewis Binford published an influential paper, "Post-Pleistocene Adaptations," in which he set out to explain the origins of farming, or food production. Attempts to do this had been made by earlier scholars, notably Gordon Childe and Robert Braidwood (see box, pp. 280–81). But Binford's explanation had one important feature that distinguished it from earlier explanations and made it very much a product of the New Archaeology: its generality. For he was setting out to explain the origins of farming not just in the Near East or the Mediterranean – although he focused on these areas – but worldwide. He drew attention to global events at the end of the last Ice Age (i.e. at the end of the Pleistocene epoch, hence the title of his paper).

Binford centered his explanation on demography: he was concerned with population dynamics within small communities, stressing that once a formerly mobile group becomes sedentary – ceases to move around – its population size will increase markedly. For in a settled village the constraints no longer operate that, in a mobile group, severely limit the number of small children a mother can rear. There is no longer the difficulty, for instance, of carrying small children from place to place. Binford thus saw as the nub of the question the fact that in the Near East some communities (of the Natufian culture around 9000 BC) did indeed become sedentary before they were food-producing. He could see that, once settled, there would be considerable population pressure, in view of the greater number of surviving children. This would lead to increasing use of locally available plant foods such as wild cereals that had hitherto been considered marginal and of little value. From the intensive use of cereals, and the

introduction of ways of processing them, would develop the regular cycle of sowing and harvesting, and thus the course of plant-human involvement leading to domestication would be well under way.

But why did these pre-agricultural groups become sedentary in the first place? Binford's view was that rising sea levels at the end of the Pleistocene (caused by the melting of polar ice) had two significant effects. First, they reduced the extent of the coastal plains available to the hunter-gatherers. And second, the new habitats created by the rise in sea level offered to human groups much greater access to migratory fish ("anadromous" species, i.e. fish such as salmon that swim upriver from the sea to spawn) and to migrant fowl. Using these rich resources, rather as the inhabitants of the Northwest Coast of North America have done in more recent times, the hunter-gatherer groups found it possible for the first time to lead a sedentary existence. They were no longer obliged to move.

That encapsulates all too concisely the outline of Binford's explanation. In some respects it is seen today as rather too simple (see box, pp. 280–81). Nevertheless, it has many strengths. For although the focus was on the Near East, the same arguments can equally be applied to other parts of the world. Binford avoided migration or diffusion, and analyzed the position in processual terms.

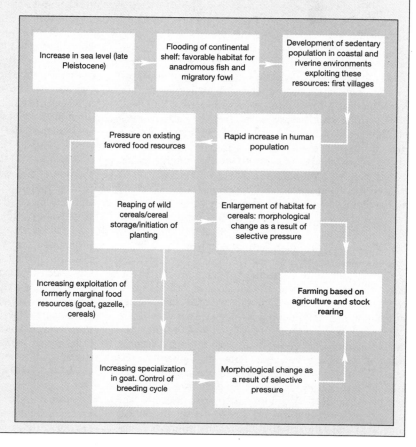

to have had a dominant role. For the study of more complex societies, however, a development of this approach, which we may term the *cognitive-processual*, has recently seemed more promising. For it does not rest solely on the somewhat holistic approach of functional-processual archaeology, but is willing to consider also the thoughts and actions of individuals (even if these can rarely be recognized directly in the archaeological record). In this respect it responds to some of the aims of postprocessual archaeology, but without the anti-scientific rhetoric and the reliance upon unbridled empathy which is sometimes advocated by exponents of the latter.

Marxist Archaeology

Following the upsurge in theoretical discussion that followed the initial impact of the New Archaeology, there has been a reawakening of interest in applying to archaeology some of the implications of the earlier work of Karl Marx, many of which had been re-examined by French anthropologists in the 1960s and 1970s. But it should be remembered that, already in the 1930s, such avowed Marxist archaeologists as Gordon Childe were producing analyses that were broadly in harmony with the principles of Marxist archaeology (described in the box opposite). Childe's book *Man Makes Himself* (1936) is a splendid example, in which he introduced the concepts of the Neolithic (farming) and urban revolutions. Moreover, Soviet archaeologists produced Marxist explanations of change that owed more to traditional Marxism than to French neo-Marxism: a good example is the explanation by Igor Diakonoff for the emergence of state society in Mesopotamia, discussed below.

Even the explanations that have been developed by archaeologists influenced by French neo-Marxism ("structural Marxism"), such as by Antonio Gilman (1981), Michael Rowlands and Susan Frankenstein (1978), and Jonathan Friedman and Michael Rowlands (1978), can often be seen to fit well into the traditional Marxist mold. Examples that do not – where the neo-Marxist emphasis on the ideological and cognitive (on the so-called "superstructure") is particularly significant – are mentioned below.

Gilman's study sets out to explain the shift from egalitarian to ranked society in the Neolithic and Bronze Ages of Spain and Portugal. Some previous explanations had stressed that a society with a partly centralized administration (organized by a chieftain) could in certain ways work more efficiently than an egalitarian society without such a central figure. Gilman, on the other hand, questioned whether the institution of chief-tainship was particularly beneficial to society as a whole. He argued rather that chiefs attained power through conflict and maintained themselves in power by force of arms, living a life of relative comfort through the exploitation of the common people. The notion of the clash of interests, the struggle between classes or sectors of society and the exploitation of the poor by the elite, is a typically Marxist one.

Frankenstein and Rowlands developed a model to explain the emergence of ranking in the central European Iron Age, emphasizing the significance of the importing of prestige goods from the Mediterranean by local chieftains. Once again, chieftains do very well out of their privileged position. They effectively corner the market in imported goods, keeping the best for themselves and handing on other imports to their most trusted henchmen. According to the Marxist model, the chief is seen as perpetrating a "rip-off" rather than acting altruistically as a wise official for the greater good of the community as a whole.

Friedman and Rowlands developed what they call an "epigenetic" model for the evolution of "civilization" of much wider application. In the case of each civilization they locate the prime locus of change among social relations within the society in question, and in the tensions between differing social groups.

There is nothing here that is inappropriate to a processual analysis, and for that reason the two approaches cannot be clearly distinguished. The positive features that these Marxist analyses share with functional-processual archaeology include a willingness to consider long-term change in societies as a whole, and to discuss social relations within them. On the other hand, many such Marxist analyses seem, by comparison with the processual studies of the New Archaeologists, rather short on the handling of concrete archaeological data. The gap between theoretical archaeology and field archaeology is not always effectively bridged, and the critics of Marxist archaeology sometimes observe that since Karl Marx laid down the basic principles a century ago, all that remains for the Marxist archaeologists to do is to elaborate them: research in the field is superfluous. Despite these differences, functional-processual archaeology and Marxist archaeology have much in common. This is all the more clear when they are both contrasted with structuralist and postprocessual approaches.

Evolutionary Archaeology

For some years neo-evolutionary thought and the direct influence of Charles Darwin have been experiencing something of a renaissance in archaeology, with

MARXIST ARCHAEOLOGY: KEY FEATURES

Marxist archaeology, especially in its more traditional form, is based mainly on the writings of Karl Marx and Friedrich Engels, who were influenced by Charles Darwin and Lewis Henry Morgan (see Chapter 1). Several features may be stressed:

1 It is evolutionary: it seeks to understand the processes of change in human history through broad general principles.

2 It is materialist: it sets the starting point of the discussion in the concrete realities of human existence, with emphasis on the production of the necessities of life.

3 It is holistic: it has a clear view of the workings of society as a whole, and of the interrelation of the parts within that whole (see 8 below).

4 Marx constructed a typology of different forms of human societies or "social formations" to which correspond different "modes of production." These include, before the capitalist mode, primitive communism, the ancient (i.e. Greek and Roman), Asiatic, and feudal modes of production.

5 Change within a society comes about mainly from the *contradictions* that arise between the forces of production (including the technology) and relations of production (mainly the social organization). Characteristically these contradictions emerge as a struggle between classes (if this is a society where distinct social classes have already developed). Emphasis on class struggle and internal differences is a feature of most Marxist explanations. This may be described as an *agonistic* view of the world where change comes about through the resolution of internal dissent. It may be contrasted with the *functionalist* view favored by the early New Archaeology where selective pressures towards greater efficiency are seen to operate, and changes are often viewed as mutually beneficial.

6 In traditional Marxism the

ideological superstructure, the whole system of knowledge and belief of the society, is seen as largely determined by the nature of the productive infrastructure, the economic base. This point is disputed by the neo-Marxists (see main text) who regard infrastructure and superstructure as interrelated and mutually influential, rather than one as dominant and the other subordinate. They can point to

passages in the writings of Marx which support this view.

7 Marx was a pioneer in the field of the sociology of knowledge where, as implied above, the belief system is influenced by, and indeed is the product of, the material conditions of existence, the economic base. This implies that as the economic base evolves, so too will the belief system of society, in a systematic way.

8 Marx's view of the internal structure of society may be set out as shown in the chart below. The analysis is applicable to the various different social formations into which human societies may be divided.

9 The systems approach within the mainstream of processual archaeology has a great deal in common with the above analysis. But to embrace the term "Marxist" often carries with it political overtones. Many Marxist archaeologists naturally apply the Marxian analysis of society to present-day societies also, which they see as being involved in a continuing class struggle in which their own alignment is with a proletariat in conflict with a putative capitalist elite. Most processual archaeologists would prefer to separate their own political views as far as possible from their professional work. Many Marxist archaeologists would argue that such a separation is impracticable, and would suspect the motives of those who make such a claim.

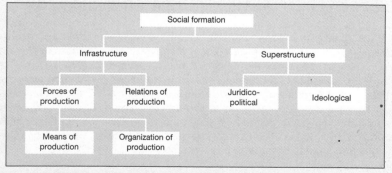

The internal structure of society according to Marx.

the notion that the processes responsible for biological evolution also drive culture change. Three strands of thinking may currently be recognized.

In Britain Richard Dawkins, an evolutionary advocate in the tradition of Thomas Huxley, already in 1976 proposed that cultural evolution is produced by the replication of "memes," the analogue of the genes which are now recognized as the instruments of biological evolution and which take molecular form in DNA. A replicator is an entity that passes on its structure directly in the course of replication, and Dawkins suggested that "examples of memes are tunes, ideas, catch-phrases, clothes fashions, ways of making pots, of building arches." Ben Cullen's preferred replicator was the Cultural Virus, and he saw the process of diffusion through cultural contact as the result of the transmission of Cultural Viruses. Critics have however argued that in the absence of any specific mechanism for the cultural replication process (to compare with DNA as the embodiment of the genes) these are little more than metaphors, offering little further insight into the processes in question.

The evolutionary anthropologists such as John Tooby and Leda Cosmides see the modern mind as the product of biological evolution, and argue that the only way so complex an entity can have arisen is by natural selection. In particular they argue that the human mind evolved under the selective pressures faced by hunter-gatherers during the Pleistocene period, and that our minds remain adapted to that way of life. Several writers have followed this lead, seeking to place the evolution of mind in an explicitly evolutionary framework. Dan Sperber has written of the "modularity of mind," seeing the pre-sapiens mind as functioning with a series of modules for different activities (hunting, planning, social intelligence, natural history intelligence, speech etc.), and Steven Mithen has argued that the "human revolution" which marked the emergence of our species was the result of a new cognitive fluidity which emerged as these specialized cognitive domains came to work together. These are fascinating insights, but they have not yet been supported by any neurological analysis of the hardware of the brain and of its evolution. A critic could suggest that, as in the case of the "meme," the argument is simply a narrative with a metaphorical quality, lacking any precise insights into physiological mechanisms.

The advocates of evolutionary archaeology in the United States do not propose the use of the "meme" or the Cultural Virus as an explanatory mechanism, nor do they embrace evolutionary psychology or evolutionary anthropology. They do however advocate the application of Darwinian evolutionary theory to the archaeological record, and they emphasize the value of the concept of the lineage, defined as "a temporal line of change owing its existence to heritability." They can justifiably point to long-standing cultural traditions in different parts of the world which reflect the inheritance of cultural traits from generation to generation. And they are right to remind us that Darwinian evolution was proposed and widely accepted as explaining the evolution of species long before the work of Mendel clarified the genetic mechanisms of transmission, or the research of Crick and Watson established their molecular basis in the structure of DNA. It could be argued that they have shown how the transmission of human culture can validly be seen in Darwinian evolutionary terms. What is less clear, however, is that to analyze it in those terms offers fresh insights not already available to the archaeologist. Evolutionary archaeology has not yet produced case studies of culture change which explain its processes more coherently or persuasively than hitherto: that is the challenge which it currently faces.

THE FORM OF EXPLANATION: GENERAL OR PARTICULAR

It is now time to ask rather more carefully what we mean by explanation. The different things we might try to explain were reviewed above. It was envisaged that different kinds of problem might require different kinds of explanation. An explanation relating to specific circumstances in the past, or to patterns of events, seeks to make us understand how they came to be that way, and not another. The key is understanding: if the "explanation" adds nothing to our understanding it is not (for us) an explanation.

As a first approximation we can distinguish two diametrically opposite approaches to the problem. The first approach is specific: it seeks to know more and more of the surrounding details. It operates with the belief that if one can establish enough of the antecedent circumstances, of the events leading up to the happening we hope to explain, then that happening itself will become much clearer for us. Such explanation has sometimes been called "historical," although it must be said that not all historians would be happy with that description.

Some historical explanations lay great stress on any insights we can gain into the ideas of the historical people in question, and for that reason are sometimes termed *idealist*. R.G. Collingwood used to say that if you wanted to know why Caesar crossed the Rubicon it was necessary to get inside the mind of Caesar, and thus to know as many of the surrounding details, and as much about his life, as possible.

The New Archaeology laid much more stress on generalization. Willey and Phillips, as we have seen, spoke in 1958 of "regularities," and the early New Archaeologists followed this lead, and turned to the philosophy of science of the time. Unluckily, perhaps, they turned to the American philosopher Carl Hempel, who argued that all explanations should be framed in terms of those most ambitious generalizations: *natural laws*. A lawlike statement is a universal statement, meaning that in certain circumstances (and other things being equal) X always implies Y, or that Y varies with X according to a certain definite relationship. For Hempel, the events or pattern we might be seeking to explain (the "explanandum") could be accounted for by bringing together two things: the detailed antecedent circumstances, and the law which, when applied, would by deductive reasoning allow the forecasting of what actually happened. The lawlike statement and the antecedent statement together form the "explanans." The form of explanation is seen as a *deductive* one, because the outcome is deduced from antecedent circumstances, plus the law. It is also *nomothetic* because it relies on lawlike statements (from Greek *nomos*, "law"). This system of Hempel's is sometimes called the deductive-nomothetic or D-N form of explanation.

Just a few of the second and third generation New Archaeologists then set off to try to write archaeology in the form of universal laws: a notable example is the book by Patty Jo Watson, Steven LeBlanc, and Charles Redman, *Explanation in Archaeology* (1971). Most archaeologists, however, saw that it is very difficult to make universal laws about human behavior that are not either very trivial, or untrue. Traditionalists, such as the Canadian archaeologist Bruce Trigger, then argued for a return to the traditional explanations of history, for a form of explanation one might term *historiographic*. Certainly the initial foray into the philosophy of science by the New Archaeologists did not prove successful. The wilier archaeologists, such as Kent Flannery, saw that the "law and order" school was making a mistake, and producing only "Mickey Mouse laws" of little conceivable value. Flannery's favorite example was: "as the population of a site increases, the number of storage pits will go up." To which he replied, scathingly: "leapin' lizards, Mr. Science!" Some critics of the New Archaeology have seized on this setback to suggest that this school is (or was) in general "scientistic" (i.e. modeling itself unthinkingly

on the hard sciences). And certainly this heavy reliance upon lawlike explanation can be termed positivistic. But one of the positive contributions of the New Archaeology was in fact to follow the scientific convention of making specific and explicit, as far as is possible, the assumptions on which an argument rests.

Scholars writing since the mid-1970s, within the mainstream tradition of processual archaeology, still seek to learn from the philosophy of science, although it is no longer to Carl Hempel that they turn. The work of Karl Popper is much less rigid in its approach, with its insistence that every statement, so far as possible, should be open to testing, to setting up against the data: in this way, untrue statements, and generalizations that do not hold up, can be refuted. Moreover, these writers say, there is nothing wrong with deductive reasoning. It makes very good sense to formulate a hypothesis, establish by deduction what would follow from it if it were true, and then to see if these consequences are in fact found in the archaeological record by testing the hypothesis against fresh data: that is the *hypothetico-deductive* or H-D approach, and it does not carry with it the same reliance on lawlike statements as the D-N approach. It is this willingness to subject one's beliefs and assumptions to the confrontation with harsh reality that distinguishes scientific work from mere uncontrolled exercise of the imagination – or so philosophers of science, and with them processual archaeologists, would argue.

The Individual

More recently, some processual archaeologists, following the approach of Popper (and of free-market economists such as Friedrich von Hayek) have shown themselves more willing to consider the thoughts and actions of individuals, and to seek to recover aspects of the thinking of early societies. Their approach, which has been described as methodological individualism, would claim to be "scientific" (using Popper's concept of refutability as a criterion for science), but it no longer dismisses the attempt to investigate past symbolic systems as "paleopsychology," as some of the earlier New Archaeologists would have done.

The Cambridge archaeologist Ian Hodder has argued that archaeologists should abandon the generalizing approach and the scientific method advocated by the New Archaeology, and seek to return to the idealist-historical outlook of R.G. Collingwood, laying much greater emphasis on the specific past social context (see below). But there is perhaps a middle way between the two extremes, where Lewis Binford (with Carl Hempel in the background) on the one hand stands opposed to

Ian Hodder (with R.G. Collingwood in the background) on the other. Between the two lies the possibility of considering the role of the individual, as indicated by Karl Popper and James Bell, without the positivist extreme of the one approach or the total rejection of scientific method of the other.

This renewed emphasis on the individual as an agent of change within society leads back to a number of lines of argument presented earlier. First it takes us back to the notion of the *cognitive map*, introduced in Chapter 10 and again to the philosophical position of methodological individualism. It relates also to the notion of *individual experience*, considered in the discussion of place and memory, also in Chapter 10, and hence to the phenomenological approach. The individual in society and the notion of *identity* is considered in Chapter 5, and the position of the *individual artist* is treated in Chapter 10. The individual as *agent* or as *actor*, as noted again below (p. 492), has been considered afresh in discussions of the origins of state societies. This is an area where approaches from different perspectives are producing important new insights.

ATTEMPTS AT EXPLANATION: ONE CAUSE OR SEVERAL?

As soon as one starts to address the really big questions in archaeology, matters become complicated. For many of the big questions refer as we have seen not to a single event, but to a class of events. The enigma of the world-wide development of farming at the end of the last Ice Age has already been mentioned as one of these big questions in the main text above. Lewis Binford's attempted explanation was described in the box on the origins of farming. Kent Flannery's approach is discussed below.

Another of the big questions is the development of urbanization and the emergence of state societies. This process apparently happened in different parts of the world independently. Each case was, in a sense, no doubt unique. But each was also, it can be argued, a specific instance (with its own unique aspects) of a more general phenomenon or process. In just the same way, a biologist can discuss (as Darwin did) the process by which the different species emerged without denying the uniqueness of each species, or the uniqueness of each individual within a species.

If we focus now on the origins of urbanization and the state, we shall see that this is a field where many different explanations have been offered.

The Origins of the State

If we look at different explanations in turn, we shall find that some of them are in their way very plausible. Often, however, one explanation works more effectively than another when applied to a particular area – to the emergence of the state in Mesopotamia, for instance, or in Egypt, but not necessarily in Mexico or in the Indus Valley.

The Hydraulic Hypothesis. The historian Karl Wittfogel, writing in the 1950s, explained the origin of the great civilizations in terms of the large-scale irrigation of the alluvial plains of the great rivers. It was, he suggested, this alone that brought about the fertility and the high yields, which led to the considerable density of population in the early civilizations, and hence to the possibility of urbanism. At the same time, however, irrigation required effective management – a group of people in authority who would control and organize the labor needed to dig and maintain irrigation ditches, etc. So irrigation and "hydraulic organization" had to go together, and from these, Wittfogel concluded, emerged a system of differentiated leadership, greater productivity and wealth, and so on.

Wittfogel categorized the system of government characteristic of those civilizations founded on irrigation agriculture as one of "oriental despotism." Among the civilizations to which this line of thinking has been applied are:

- Mesopotamia: the Sumerian civilization from *c.* 3000 BC and its successors
- Ancient Egypt: the Valley of the Nile from *c.* 3000 BC
- India/Pakistan: the Indus Valley civilization from *c.* 2500 BC
- China: the Shang civilization, *c.* 1500 BC, and its successors

Comparable claims have been made for the agriculture (although the irrigation was not based on a major river) both of the Valley of Mexico, and the Maya civilization.

Internal Conflict. In the late 1960s the Russian historian Igor Diakonoff developed a different explanation for state origins. In his model, the state is seen as an organization that imposes order on class conflict, which itself arises from increased wealth. Internal differentiation within the society is here seen as a major causative element, from which other consequences follow.

Warfare. Warfare between adjacent polities is increasingly seen as an agent of change (see p. 395). While in some cases there were cyclical conflicts between peer polities with little long-term effect, in others the result was conquest and the formation of larger, inclusive state societies. Kent Flannery has recently emphasized the historically documented role of individual military leaders in the initial formation of state societies (noting this as an example of the "agency" of the individual which postprocessual writers have sought).

Population Growth. An explanation much favored by many archaeologists focuses on the question of population growth. The 18th-century English scholar, Thomas Malthus, in his *An Essay on the Principle of Population* (1798), argued that human population tends to grow to the limit permitted by the food supply. When the limit or "carrying capacity" is reached, further population increase leads to food shortage, and this in turn leads to increased death rate and lower fertility (and in some cases to armed conflict). That sets a firm ceiling on population.

population growth → food shortage → increased death rate & lower fertility

Esther Boserup, in her influential book *The Conditions of Agricultural Growth* (1965), effectively reversed the position of Malthus. He had viewed food supply as essentially limited. She argued that agriculture will intensify – farmers will produce more food from the same area of land – if population increases. In other words, by shortening the periods during which land is left to lie fallow, or by introducing the plow, or irrigation, farmers can increase their productivity. Population growth can then be sustained to new levels.

population growth → introduction of new farming methods → increase in agricultural production

So increase of population leads to intensification of agriculture, and to the need for greater administrative efficiencies and economies of scale, including the development of craft specialization. People work harder because they have to, and the society is more productive. There are larger units of population, and consequent changes in the settlement pattern. As numbers increase, any decision-making machinery will need to develop a hierarchy. Centralization ensues, and a centralized state is the logical outcome.

These ideas can be made to harmonize very well with the work of the American archaeologist Gregory Johnson, who has used them in the study of smaller-scale societies. From recent ethnographic accounts of !Kung San encampments in southwest Africa he showed that the level of organization rose with the increasing size of the encampment. Whereas in small camps the basic social unit was the individual or the nuclear family of 3–4 individuals, in large camps it was the extended family of around 11 people. In larger-scale societies, such as those of New Guinea, hierarchical social systems were needed in order to control disputes and maintain the efficient functioning of the society as a whole.

Environmental Circumscription. A different approach, although one that uses some of the variables already indicated, is offered by Robert Carneiro (see box overleaf). Taking as his example the formation of state society in Peru, he developed an explanation that laid stress on the constraints ("circumscription") imposed by the environment, and on the role of warfare. Population increase is again an important component of his model, but the model is put together in a different way, and the development of strong leadership in time of war is one of the key factors.

External Trade. The importance of trading links with communities outside the homeland area has been stressed by several archaeologists seeking explanations for the formation of the state. One of the most elaborate of these is the model put forward by the American archaeologist William Rathje for the emergence of state societies in the Maya lowlands. He argued that in lowland areas lacking basic raw materials there will be pressure for the development of more integrated and highly organized communities able to ensure the regular supply of those materials. He used this hypothesis to explain the rise of the Classic Maya civilization in the lowland rainforest.

Multivariate Explanations

All the preceding explanations for the origins of the state lay stress primarily on a chief variable, a principal strand in the explanation, even though there are several strands involved. Explanations, such as Karl Wittfogel's, which emphasize a single factor, are termed *monocausal*. In reality, however, when there are so many factors at work, there is something rather too simplified about monocausal explanations. It is necessary somehow to be able to deal with several factors at once. Such explanations are termed *multivariate*. Of course, none of the explanations summarized above is so naive as to be truly *monocausal*: each involves a number of factors. But these factors are not systematically integrated. Several scholars have thus sought for

ORIGINS OF THE STATE 1: PERU

In a 1970 paper, Robert Carneiro offered an explanation for the origins of the state in coastal Peru, laying stress on the factor of what he termed environmental circumscription (restrictions imposed by the environment). Population growth is also an important component of the explanation (and here his ideas relate to those of Esther Boserup discussed in the main text).

Early villages in coastal Peru were located in about 78 narrow valleys, flanked by desert. These villages grew, but as long as land was available for the settlement of splinter communities, they split from time to time so that they did not become too large. Eventually, a point was reached when all the land in a particular valley was being farmed. When this happened, the land already under cultivation was more intensively worked (with terracing and irrigation), and less suitable land, not previously worked, was brought into cultivation.

Carneiro argued that population growth outstripped the increase in production gained through intensification, and warfare became a major factor. In the past, armed conflict had occurred simply out of a desire for revenge – now it was in response to a need to acquire land.

A village defeated in war became subordinate to the victorious village, and its land was appropriated. Moreover, the defeated population had no means of escape from its valley environment, enclosed by mountains and sea. If it remained on its own land it was as a subordinate tribute payer. In this way, chiefdoms were formed, and the stratification of society into classes began.

As land shortages continued, Carneiro argued, so did warfare, which was now between larger political units – the chiefdoms. As chiefdom conquered chiefdom, the size of political units greatly increased and centralization developed. The result of this process was the formation of the state. Valley-wide kingdoms emerged, then multi-valley kingdoms, until finally all of Peru was unified in a single powerful empire by the Incas.

Carneiro has subsequently argued that the reduction in the number of political units and increase in their size is a process still continuing, one which will ultimately lead to a world state sometime in the future.

Like other so-called "monocausal" (single cause) explanations, this one does, in fact, draw on a series of factors working together. But it is highly selective in its choice of factors. And like all monocausal explanations, it has a "prime mover": a basic process that sets the whole sequence of events going and continues to act as the driving force as they unfold. In this case, the prime mover is population growth.

As is always the case with a prime mover explanation, we are not told what sets it in motion.

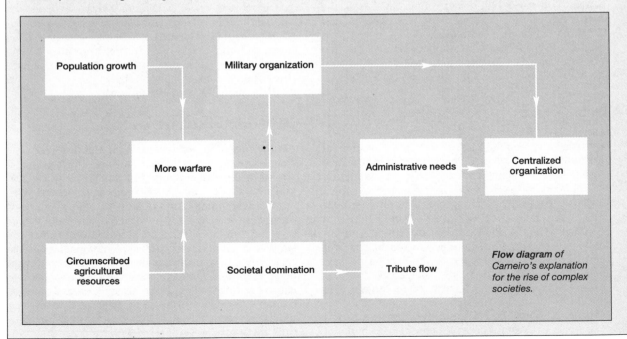

Flow diagram of Carneiro's explanation for the rise of complex societies.

Population growth · Military organization · More warfare · Administrative needs · Centralized organization · Circumscribed agricultural resources · Societal domination · Tribute flow

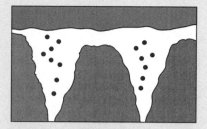

Villages in two valleys, separated by mountains.

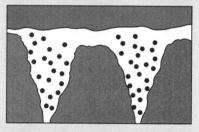

Population growth leads to more villages, with some now on marginal land.

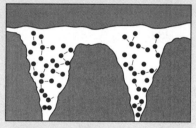

Competition between villages leads to warfare.

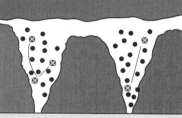

Dominance of some villages over others, making them centers of chiefdoms.

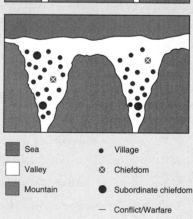

One chiefdom dominates the others: creation of a state.

■ Sea	● Village
□ Valley	⊠ Chiefdom
▓ Mountain	● Subordinate chiefdom
	— Conflict/Warfare

ways of coping with a large number of variables that simultaneously vary. Obviously, this is complicated and it is here that the systems terminology – already introduced in quite simple form in Kent Flannery's 1967 definition of processual archaeology cited in an earlier section – can prove very useful.

The Systems Approach. If the society or culture in question is regarded as a *system*, then it makes sense to consider the different things that are varying within that system, and to try and list these, and be explicit about them. Clearly, the size of population will be one of those *system parameters*. Measures of the settlement pattern, of production of different crops, materials, and so on, and measures of various aspects of social organization will all be parameters of the system. We can imagine the system proceeding over time through a series of successive *system states*, each defined by the values of the system variables at the time in question. The successive system states in sequence establish the *trajectory* of the system.

It is convenient to think of the overall system as broken down into several *subsystems*, reflecting the different activities of the system as a whole (see box overleaf). Each subsystem may be thought of as defined by the kind of activity that it represents: within it will be the humans involved in such activities, the artifacts and material culture involved, and those aspects of the environment that are relevant. Each subsystem will display, in common with all systems, the useful phenomenon of *feedback*. This concept was derived from the field of cybernetics (control theory).

The key notion is that of a system with *input* and *output*. If a portion of that input is channeled back to form a continuing part of the input, then that is known as "feedback." This is important because it means that what is happening to the system at one moment can have an effect on the system state at the next moment.

If the feedback is negative, then a change in the external input produces *negative feedback*, which goes back, as input, to counter the original change. That is very significant because the countering of change makes for stability. All living systems employ negative feedback in this way. For instance, the temperature of the human body acts so that when body temperature rises we sweat: the output is such as to reduce the input

ORIGINS OF THE STATE 2: THE AEGEAN A MULTIVARIATE APPROACH

The palace civilization of Minoan Crete developed around 2100 BC, while that of Mycenaean Greece reached its climax in the centuries following 1600 BC. In *The Emergence of Civilization* (1972), Colin Renfrew outlined an explanation in systems terms for the development of these state societies. The subsystems considered were those listed in the table, which have a general application, together with the metallurgical subsystem. This subsystem was given special treatment in the book because of the considerable importance of early metallurgy in the Aegean.

Each subsystem can be considered in its own right. For instance, in the subsistence subsystem, wheat and barley were the principal crops in the Neolithic period (6500–3000 BC), and sheep and goats with some cattle and pigs, the principal animals. But, Renfrew argued, the new crops (olive and vine) took on a special significance during the Early Bronze Age and played a major part during the heyday of the palaces in the Late Bronze Age. They allowed diversification, and offered individual farmers the possibility of specializing. The exchange of products became necessary, and in this exchange the palaces could play a central redistributive role.

The mutual interactions of the subsystems were indicated by Renfrew in a simple diagram. He did not stress the dominance of any one subsystem: each interacted with all the others.

In the explanation of the rise of state societies in the Aegean, Renfrew emphasized the importance of what is known in systems theory as the multiplier effect: changes or innovations occurring in one field of human activity (in one subsystem of a culture) sometimes act so as to favor changes in other fields (in other subsystems). The multiplier effect is said to operate when these induced changes in one or more subsystems themselves act so as to enhance the original changes in the first subsystem.

For example, we might consider changes in some of the subsystems that favored growth in the metallurgical subsystem. In the craft technology subsystem, it was technical developments, notably the pyrotechnological discoveries of the potter, that made metallurgy possible (see p. 335). Several changes in the social subsystem affected metallurgy. First, there was an increasing need for metal weapons arising from an increase in military hostilities (documented by the construction of fortifications in the Early Bronze Age). Second, a market grew up for objects of display with the production of new objects in gold and silver. And third, the growing custom of burying valuable metal objects with the dead helped to remove such objects from circulation and thus increase demand for them. The external trade subsystem also favored the development of metallurgy, because additional raw materials now became available.

Renfrew's explanation recognized that the essential drive towards growth and change came from the interaction of these various subsystems, through the working of the multiplier effect, and not primarily from any one prime mover. While it was possible to stress the importance of certain processes (e.g. increasing skill in metallurgy, and the development of the vine and olive), the explanatory emphasis was placed on the aggregate of the interactions.

The palace civilization of Mycenaean Greece, as exemplified at Pylos in this reconstruction drawing by Piet de Jong.

TABLE OF SUBSYSTEMS

Subsistence subsystem, whose interactions and activities relate to the production and distribution of food resources

Technological subsystem, defined by human activities that result in the production of material artifacts

Social subsystem, where the defining activities are those that take place between the members of the society (other than those in the two preceding subsystems)

Symbolic or projective subsystem, embracing all those activities, notably religion, art, and science, by which humans express their knowledge, feelings, and beliefs about their relationships with the world

External trade and communications subsystem, defined by all those activities by which information or material goods are transferred across the boundaries of the system

Population, although not defined strictly by human activities, may be thought of as a further subsystem

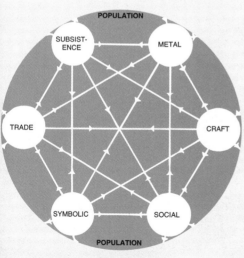

Interactions between the subsystems of the culture system. Sustained positive feedback between them – the multiplier effect – resulted in cultural change and growth.

effect (i.e. the rise in external temperature). When a system is maintained in a constant state through the operation of negative feedback, this is known as *homeostasis* (from the Greek words, *homeo,* "the same", and *stasis,* "standing" or "remaining"). Similarly, all human societies have devices that ensure they carry on much as before: if they did not they would radically change their natures almost every moment of their existence.

However, *positive feedback* can occur. When it does, the change produced (in the output) has a positive effect on the input, thus favoring more of the same. Growth occurs, and with it sometimes change. Positive feedback is one of the key processess underlying progressive growth and change, and ultimately the emergence of totally new forms: this is termed morphogenesis.

It is thus possible to consider the influence of one subsystem on another, looking in turn at the interactions of each pair (see box opposite).

In a 1968 paper, Kent Flannery applied the systems approach to the origins of food production in Mesoamerica during the period 8000–2000 BC. His cybernetic model involved an analysis of the various procurement systems used for the different plant and animal species that were exploited and of what he called "scheduling," namely the choice between the relative merits of two or more courses of action at a particular time. Flannery regarded the constraints imposed by the seasonal variations in the availability of the different species and the need for scheduling as *negative feedback* in his systems model; that is to say, these two factors acted to hinder change and maintain the stability of the existing patterns of food procurement. Over the course of time, however, genetic changes in two minor species, beans and maize, made them both more productive and more easily harvested. The effects of these changes led to a greater and greater reliance on these two species, in a deviation amplifying or *positive feedback* manner. The ultimate consequence of the process thus set in motion – a consequence neither foreseen nor intended by the human population – was domestication. As Flannery concluded in his paper:

> The implications of this approach for the prehistorian are clear: it is vain to hope for the discovery of the first domestic corn cob, the first pottery vessel, the first hieroglyph, or the first site where some other major breakthrough occurred. Such deviations from the preexisting pattern almost certainly took place in such a minor and accidental way that their traces are not recoverable. More worthwhile

would be an investigation of the mutual causal processes that amplify these tiny deviations into major changes in prehistoric culture. (Flannery 1968, 85.)

The systems approach is certainly convenient. It has, however, been criticized. The postprocessual archaeologists (see below) apply to it most of the criticisms that they make of processual archaeology in general: that it is scientist and mechanistic, that it leaves the individual out of account, and that systems thinking subscribes to the system of domination by which the elites of the world appropriate science to control the underprivileged. Criticisms from researchers who are not against scientific explanation in principle are particularly interesting. One of their most telling points is that the approach is ultimately descriptive rather than explanatory: that it imitates the world without really accounting for what happens within it. (But many would reply that to show how the world works is indeed one of the functions of explanation.) The critics also say that it is difficult in many cases to give real values to the various variables. They agree, however, that the approach does offer a practical framework for the analysis of the articulation of the various components of a society. And it does lend itself very readily to computer modeling and simulation (see next section). The models can become complicated, so that it is difficult to see the overall pattern. But that is the penalty when one is dealing with complicated systems like state societies, and difficult issues like the explanation of their emergence.

Simulation

Simulation involves the formulation of a dynamic model: that is, a model concerned with change through time. Simulation studies are of considerable help in the development of explanations. To produce a simulation one must have in mind, or develop, a specific model that leads to a set of rules. One can then feed in some initial data, or some starting conditions, and through the repeated application of the model (generally with the aid of a computer) reach a series of system states, which may or may not carry conviction in relation to the real world.

A simulation is thus an exemplification, a working out (and sometimes a test) of a model that has already taken shape. In reality, of course, no simulation ever works perfectly first time, but from the experience of simulation one can improve the model. That then, is the principal value of simulation: the actual explanation is the model rather than the simulation itself.

As an example, A.J. Chadwick decided to model the development of settlement in Bronze Age Messenia in Greece. He took some very simple rules for the growth and development of settlement, and then used the

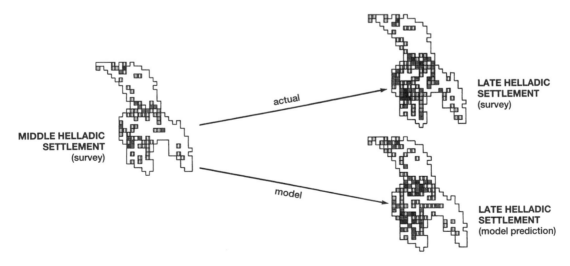

A.J. Chadwick's simulation of settlement growth in Bronze Age Messenia. The University of Minnesota Messenia Expedition had already mapped the distribution of settlement in Middle Helladic and Late Helladic times. The object of Chadwick's study was to see whether he could develop a simulation model which, if given the Middle Helladic pattern as the starting position, would then give rise to the Late Helladic pattern. The diagram shows the actual distribution of Middle and Late Helladic sites discovered by survey, together with the best fit simulation result, using a combination of environmental (e.g. soils) and human (e.g. density of existing occupation) factors. The intensity of shading indicates one, two, or three settlements, respectively, per 2 × 2-km cell.

computer to apply these to the landscape of prehistoric Messenia. The outcome is a set of simulated settlement patterns through time. Moreover, they have interesting resemblances with the real settlement patterns as we know they developed. The simulation thus clearly suggests that Chadwick's generative model was at least in part successful in seizing the essential of the settlement development process.

It is also possible to model the development of entire systems in this way, starting in essence from the systems approach outlined above. Here one analyzes the articulation or interplay of various subsystems. One then has to suggest precisely how these articulations might work in practice, how a change in the value of a parameter in one subsystem would alter the parameters in the other subsystems.

The simulation allows one to go through this in practice, starting from initial values for all the parameters, which one must oneself determine (or take from the real case). The System Dynamics modeling group at the Massachusetts Institute of Technology, led by Jay Forrester, has pioneered this technique in several fields, including the growth of towns and the future of the world economy. This simulation technique is generally in its infancy in archaeology, but there have been a few studies using it. For example, Jeremy Sabloff and his associates employed it to model the collapse of the Classic Maya civilization around AD 900,

building in their own assumptions and constructing their own model. The results were instructive in showing that the model could achieve plausible results (see box overleaf), though there have been new theories.

The American archaeologist Ezra Zubrow modified the Forrester approach and applied it to model the growth of ancient Rome from the period of the emperor Augustus. His aim was not to establish a complete simulated pattern of behavior for Rome, but to test which were the sensitive parameters that would have a crucial effect on growth and on stability. Some of Zubrow's results reveal a pattern of multiple cycles of sudden growth and decline, some three in 200 years. By undertaking different computer runs with different input variables (e.g. by doubling the size of the labor force), it is possible to see which changes would, according to the model, be highly significant. In fact, doubling the labor force did not have a major effect: doubling it again did.

This is an example where simulation is being used as an exploratory tool with which to investigate the behavior of the system. So far, with such simulations, work has been of a preliminary nature, and more has been learnt about the procedures and potentialities of simulation than of the early culture under study. Moreover simulation can set out to model decision-making by individuals, as Steven Mithen has done, and to model multi-agent interactions.

POSTPROCESSUAL OR INTERPRETIVE EXPLANATION

Since the mid-1970s, the early New Archaeology we have termed here functional-processual archaeology has come under criticism from several quarters. For example, early on it was criticized by Bruce Trigger in his book *Time and Tradition* (1978), who found the approach which sought to formulate explanatory laws (the nomothetic approach) too constraining. He preferred the historiographic approach, the broadly descriptive approach of the traditional historian. It was also criticized by Kent Flannery, who was scornful of the trivial nature of some of the so-called laws proposed and felt that more attention should be focused on the ideological and symbolic aspects of societies. Ian Hodder, likewise, felt that archaeology's closest links were with history, and wanted to see the role of the individual in history more fully recognized. Hodder also very validly stressed what he called "the active role of material culture," emphasizing that the artifacts and the material world we construct are not simply the reflections of our social reality that become embodied in the material record (by what Michael Schiffer would

call a C-transform: see Chapter 2). On the contrary, material culture and actual objects are a large part of what makes society work: wealth, for instance, is what spurs many to work in a modern society. Hodder goes on to assert that material culture is "meaningfully constituted," the result of deliberate actions by individuals whose thoughts and actions should not be overlooked.

Out of these criticisms, some archaeologists in Britain (notably Ian Hodder, Michael Shanks, and Christopher Tilley) and in the United States (in particular Mark Leone) formulated new approaches, overcoming some of what they saw as the limitations of functional-processual archaeology (and indeed much of traditional Marxist archaeology also), thereby creating the postprocessual archaeology of the 1990s. The postprocessual debate is largely over now, leaving behind a series of interesting (and sometimes mutually contradictory) approaches which together will shape the interpretive archaeologies of the early 21st century, operating alongside the continuing processual or cognitive-processual tradition. Among the influences

THE CLASSIC MAYA COLLAPSE

Ever since the impressive remains of ancient states and cities were first discovered and studied by western scholars, the collapse of long-gone civilizations has been a focus of debate and inquiry. One of the first attempts to account for such a collapse was Gibbon's famous *Decline and Fall of the Roman Empire* (1776–88), in which he attributed the decline to the undermining effect of Christianity on Classical civilization. In the 1830s the explorations of Stephens and Catherwood in Central America led to the discovery of a then unknown civilization whose demise may have been as spectacular as that of Rome: the Maya.

The last 30 years have witnessed a number of theories seeking to account for the Classic Maya collapse in the 9th century AD, most of them based broadly on the concept of civilization as a system, and seeing collapse as the result of disequilibrium between different parts of the system.

Evidence for a Collapse

The first evidence for a crisis in the Maya lowlands came from the monumental record. Here the cessation of activity at each site could be dated with some accuracy, with the assumption that this represented the collapse of its ruling dynasty. Such failures in the Southern Lowlands began just after AD 800 and, although some centers clung to existence for a time, none survived to erect monuments beyond 909. Subsequent excavation demonstrated that there was a corresponding halt to major construction and building maintenance. The number of formal burials declined and the grave offerings were fewer and of lower quality. Demographic studies consistently showed that political disintegration coincided with a dramatic decline in population. This fall continued until, by the 10th century, the southern lowlands held only a fraction of the millions it once supported. During

the ensuing Postclassic period the homes of the former elite were re-occupied by squatters and simple pole-and-thatch houses were erected on the great ceremonial plazas. For a time there was a renaissance to the north, which saw rising populations and major construction, especially in the Puuc region and cities like Uxmal. However, this was shortlived and by the mid-10th century only Chichén Itzá continued elite traditions on any scale, and by now these were heavily modified by contact with Central Mexico.

Causal Factors

If these were the effects of the collapse, what were the causal factors that lay behind it? In the absence of any definitive data scholars in the 1970s devised a variety of theoretical models, in some cases constructing computer simulations to test them. While early explanations had emphasized single factors, whether epidemic disease, drought, peasant revolt, foreign invasion, etc., there was a growing recognition that the collapse must be viewed as a system failure, with a number of contributing factors. It was also widely accepted that since the highest populations and most conspicuous signs of cultural florescence directly preceded the collapse, the very same processes that had created one had led to the other.

There was a broad division between those modeling a system failure and those emphasizing a greater element of social conflict. In the former, rising populations forced the society into more intensive forms of agriculture. In the short term, yields increased and allowed the rise in population to escalate, but such methods over-exploited the soils and were not sustainable. The result was falling yields exactly when demand was at its greatest. At the very least, a subsistence system under such stress would have been especially vulnerable to crop diseases or drought.

On the social front, a percentage increase of the elite class (who would reproduce more successfully than the less well-nourished peasantry) led to social imbalance and ever greater demands on the lower orders. Competition between elite groups would have expressed itself in larger and more magnificent construction projects and production was increasingly funneled into such activity and away from basic farming. This ultimately led to social strife and disintegration.

There was also work on the impact of trade, seen either in terms of a technological shift from riverine to sea-going transport that took routes away from the southern lowlands, or competition between the Maya and better-organized traders in Mexico. Our very poor understanding of Maya economics hampers any reconstruction of this kind.

Lowe

One of the most recent simulations of the Classic Maya collapse is that by John Lowe (see diagram opposite). His work is based on the chronological patterning of the collapse, as determined from the latest dates of monument construction at different Maya centers. From this Lowe reconstructs a collapse which started in the peripheral areas and moved inward, with sites in the northeast being the last to feel the effects. By correlating this pattern with site density and site hierarchy, Lowe is led to the conclusion that it was population pressure coupled with a top-heavy elite administration which precipitated the collapse.

The basic mechanism was pressure on land creating the need for more intensive agriculture, which in turn

After the collapse of the Southern Lowlands there was a brief florescence to the north, especially at Uxmal and fellow centers in the Puuc region. However, the Northern Lowlands did not escape the crisis that swept the south and these centers were abandoned in the early 10th century. Chichén Itzá (above, the Castillo pyramid) survived for a while longer, though under strong Mexican influence.

placed greater demands on the ruling elites for the regulation of food distribution and the allocation of manpower. Competition within and between the elites themselves placed still further strains on the system, requiring increasing labor inputs for the construction of ceremonial monuments.

The model owes much to earlier work, such as that of Willey and Shimkin, and Hosler, Sabloff, and Runge. It is, however, the most thorough attempt so far to account for the details of the Classic Maya collapse within a systems framework.

Current Understanding

Mayanists have continued to collect relevant data and shape research projects around the collapse problem. In some cases it has been possible to introduce new methodologies and thereby expand the variety of available data. A detailed examination of the energetics of ancient Maya building technology has countered the idea that monumental construction was a major drain on labor and resources. Firm evidence of increased social strife has been produced in the Southern Lowland Petexbatun region, where the last years of occupation show hurriedly built defenses.

While there is some regional variability, many recent studies support the view of ecological over-exploitation. Pollen from lake sediments has provided evidence for deforestation, while changes in the chemical composition of such deposits (reflecting run-off from the surrounding terrain) points to soil erosion and infertility. Skeletal analysis has produced evidence for accompanying malnutrition, disease, and infant mortality. Sediments from the northern Lake Chichancanab have produced shells whose oxygen isotope make-up reveal a severe drought between AD 750 and 900 (the driest period in Central America for 6000 years).

While Maya collapse continues to pose interpretive problems, our understanding is undoubtedly improving. There is much support now for "overshoot," the effect by which a highly successful system reaches and then exceeds its ecological limits. While the evidence for social turmoil is patchy, few doubt that the dying days of the Classic Period were a calamitous time for all.

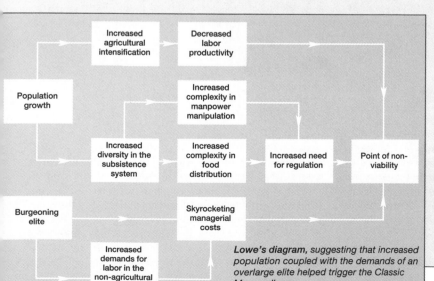

Lowe's diagram, suggesting that increased population coupled with the demands of an overlarge elite helped trigger the Classic Maya collapse.

contributing to these interpretive archaeologies are:

- neo-Marxism (Althusser, Balibar, Lukacs)
- the "post-positivist" (anarchic) view of scientific method advocated by Feyerabend
- the structuralism of Claude Lévi-Strauss
- the phenomenological approach of Ernst Cassirer and Martin Heidegger
- the hermeneutic (interpretational) approach initiated by Dilthey, Croce, and Collingwood and developed more recently by Ricoeur
- Critical Theory as developed by philosophers of the Frankfurt School (Marcuse, Adorno) and by Habermas
- the post-structuralism (deconstructionism) of Barthes, Foucault, and Derrida
- structuration theory as exemplified by Giddens, and the approach of Bourdieu
- feminist approaches to archaeology (pp. 46–47, 218–22).

Structuralist Approaches

Several archaeologists have been influenced by the structuralist ideas of the French anthropologist Claude Lévi-Strauss, and by the advances in linguistics of the American Noam Chomsky. Structuralist archaeologists stress that human actions are guided by beliefs and symbolic concepts, and that the proper object of study is the structures of thought – the ideas – in the minds of human actors who made the artifacts and created the archaeological record. These archaeologists argue that there are recurrent patterns in human thought in different cultures, many of which can be seen in such polar opposites as: cooked/raw; left/right; dirty/clean; man/woman, etc. Moreover, they argue that thought categories seen in one sphere of life will be seen also in other spheres, so that a preoccupation with "boundedness" or boundaries, for instance, in the field of social relations is likely to be detectable also in such different areas as "boundedness" visible in pottery decoration.

The work of André Leroi-Gourhan in the interpretation of Paleolithic cave art (box, pp. 392–93) was a pioneering project using structuralist principles. For this attempt at the interpretation of depictions of animals the approach seems particularly appropriate. In another example, the American archaeologist Dean Arnold has used the structuralist assumption that human thought categories in one field of experience are related to those in others in his study of the village of Quinua, near Ayacucho in Peru. Here he sought to relate the design elements on the pottery produced and used in the village to aspects of social patterning

within the community, and to the community's perception of its own environment. Arnold studied 172 vessels of four different shapes with particular reference to the organization of design elements. He looked at the division of the surface of each pot into areas, and the use of the patterns of symmetry, and the variability of the motifs within the design zones. He then considered the organization of space within the landscape surrounding the village, and the social divisions governed by kinship categories. He was able to summarize the relationship of spatial organization and decorative space as shown in the accompanying table.

It should be noted that like most structuralist arguments the analysis is not concerned with change through time: it is synchronic. A more telling question that the skeptic might pose, however, is whether there is any necessary relationship between the decorative principles detected for pottery, and the other superficially unrelated concepts involved in kinship and in describing the landscape. It is at this point that the processual archaeologist, perhaps to the irritation of the structuralist, would wish to investigate whether there are any hypotheses here that would be open to testing.

Another influential structuralist study is the work of the folklore specialist Henry Glassie on folk housing in Middle Virginia, USA. In it he uses such structuralist dichotomies as human/nature, public/private, internal/external, intellect/emotion, and applies them in a detailed way to the plans and other features of houses mainly of the 18th and 19th centuries AD. As he is working primarily from material culture with only limited reference to written records, his work is certainly relevant to archaeological interpretation. But whether his interpretations would seem so plausible if he were not able to claim that his subject matter belongs to the same cultural tradition as that within which he is working is another matter.

Critical Theory

Critical Theory is the term given to the approach developed by the so-called "Frankfurt School" of German social thinkers, which came to prominence in the 1970s. This stresses that all knowledge is historical, distorted communication, and that any claims to seek "objective" knowledge are illusory. By their interpretive ("hermeneutic") approach these scholars seek a more enlightened view, which will break out of the limitations of existing systems of thought. For they see research workers (including archaeologists) who claim to be dealing in a scientific way with social matters as tacitly supporting the "ideology of control" by which domination is exercised in modern society.

SPATIAL ORIENTATION	COMMUNITY PATTERN	DECORATIVE SPACE	VESSEL SHAPE	
Vertical	Vertical set of ecological zones	Set of vertically arranged decorative zones on vessels with vertically arranged space	*puyñu* *yukupuyñu*	*puyñu*
Horizontal	Division of savannah into upper and lower zones based on the complementary functions of the irrigation system	High frequency use of bilateral symmetry for motifs	All except the *tachu*	
		Bifurcation of space by a vertical plane created by two narrow bands	*tachu*	*yukupuyñu*
		Mirroring of color and shape of framing lines on bands	*tachu*	
		High frequency use of vertical reflection to form band patterns	All except the *tachu*	
		Division of design space into two parts by one band	*plato*	
Vertical	Division of savannah into two barrios based on the irrigation system	Use of horizontal reflection in conjunction with vertical reflection as the second most prominent band pattern	All except the *tachu*	*tachu*
Horizontal	Bilateral membership of individuals (the smallest unit of social space in the community) in each of two descent groups	Predominance of bilateral symmetry for production of motifs (the smallest unit of design space in the community)	All except the *tachu*	
	Social classes: higher class in the village, lower class in the rural area	Inner versus outer spatial organization	*plato*	*plato*

Dean Arnold's structuralist analysis of the relationship of spatial organization and decorative space in Quinua, Peru.

EXPLAINING THE EUROPEAN MEGALITHS

A longstanding issue in European prehistory is that of the so-called megalithic monuments. These are impressive prehistoric structures built of large stones ("megalith" comes from the Greek *megas* [great] and *lithos* [stone]). In general, the stones are arranged to form a single chamber, buried under a mound of earth and entered from one side. The chambers may be large with a long entrance passage. Human remains and artifacts are usually found within these structures, and it is clear that most served as collective burial chambers, i.e. tombs for several people.

Megalithic monuments of various kinds occur widely along the Atlantic coasts of Europe. They are also found inland over most of Spain, Portugal, and France, but in other countries they do not occur more than about 100 km (65 miles) from the coast, and in general they are not present in central and eastern Europe. Most megaliths belong to the Neolithic period – the time of the first farmers. By the beginning of the Bronze Age they were going out of use in most areas.

Many questions arise. How were the Neolithic inhabitants of western Europe able to erect these great stone

Distribution of megalithic monuments in western Europe.

monuments? Why are they not found in other areas? Why were they built at this time and not earlier or later? What is the explanation for the range and variety of forms that they show?

Migrationist and Diffusionist Explanations

In the 19th century megaliths were seen as the work of a single group of people, who had migrated to western Europe. Many of the explanations were offered in racial terms. But even when distinctions of race were not drawn, the explanations remained ethnic: a new population of immigrants was responsible.

In the early 20th century alternative explanations were offered in terms of the influence of the higher civilizations of the eastern Mediterranean on those of the barbarian west. Trading links and other contacts between Crete and Greece on the one hand, and Italy and perhaps Spain on the other were credited with the responsibility for a flow of ideas. Thus the custom of collective burial in built tombs seen in Crete around 3200 BC was thought to have been transmitted to Spain within a couple of centuries. From there it would have spread through the workings of diffusion. This view carried with it the idea that the megaliths of Spain and Portugal and then those of the rest of Europe must be *later* than those of Crete.

Functional-processual Explanation

Radiocarbon dating made it clear that the megalithic tombs of western Europe were in many cases earlier than those of Crete. Now it was suggested that local communities had developed their own practices for the burial of the dead. A good processual explanation had to account for such a development in terms of the local social and economic processes at work.

Renfrew proposed (see box, Early Wessex, pp. 198–99) that in the

Neolithic period in many areas the settlement pattern was one of dispersed egalitarian groups. Each communal tomb would serve as a focal point for the dispersed community, and would help to define its territory. The megaliths were seen as the territorial markers of segmentary societies.

A related idea was introduced by the British archaeologist Robert Chapman, drawing on the work of the American Arthur Saxe: that formal disposal areas for the dead (e.g. tombs) occur in societies where there is competition for land ownership. To be able to display the family tomb containing the bones of ancestors would legitimize one's claim to own and use the ancestral lands within the territory.

This explanation may appropriately be termed "functionalist" because it suggests how the tombs have served a useful function, in social and economic terms, within the society.

Neo-Marxist Explanation

In the early 1980s Christopher Tilley developed an account of the Middle Neolithic megaliths of Sweden, which (like the processual one) emphasized local factors. He saw such monuments as related to the exercise of power within these small societies by individuals who used the rituals associated with megaliths as a means of masking the arbitrary nature of control and of legitimizing inequalities within society. The mixing of body parts of different individuals within a tomb emphasized the organic wholeness of society, taking attention away from the inequalities in power and status which actually existed. The tombs and the rituals made the established order seem normal or natural.

The emphasis in Tilley's explanation on dominance within the group is typically Marxist, while that on ritual and ideology masking the underlying contradictions is typical of neo-Marxist thought.

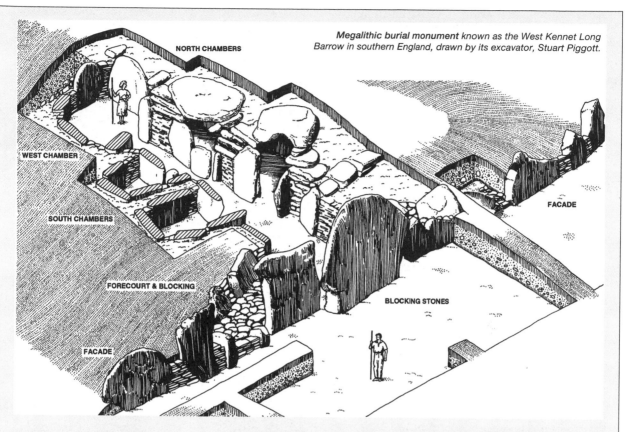

Megalithic burial monument known as the West Kennet Long Barrow in southern England, drawn by its excavator, Stuart Piggott.

NORTH CHAMBERS

WEST CHAMBER

SOUTH CHAMBERS

FORECOURT & BLOCKING

FACADE

FACADE

BLOCKING STONES

Postprocessual Explanation

Ian Hodder, in criticizing both the processual and the neo-Marxist standpoints, has stressed symbolic aspects. He argues that earlier explanations have failed adequately to consider the particularity of the historical contexts in which the megaliths are found. And he argues that without consideration of the specific cultural context one cannot hope to understand the effects of past social actions.

Hodder maintains that many of the chamber tombs of western Europe referred symbolically to earlier and contemporary houses in central and western Europe: "the tombs signified houses." As he puts it: "the way megaliths were involved actively in social strategies in western Europe depended on an existing historical context. The existence of the tombs can only be adequately considered by assessing their value-laden meanings within European society" (Hodder, 1984, p. 53). Hodder brings into the argument a number of further issues, including the role of women in the societies in question. His aim is to arrive at some sort of insight for the meaning that the tomb in a specific context held for those who built it.

Alasdair Whittle has questioned whether the builders of the monuments were farmers, arguing that the impulse which transformed society at this time was not economic or demographic (i.e. farming) but ideational, and that the techniques of farming were widely adopted only later: this might seem to be pushing the postprocessual standpoint to an extreme.

Comparison

The functional-processual, neo-Marxist, and postprocessual explanations all lay greater stress on internal factors. But are they in conflict with one another? We suggest that in fact they are not, and that all three could be operating simultaneously.

The processual idea that the monuments were useful to society in serving as territorial markers, and as the ritual focus of territorial belief and activity, does not necessarily contradict the Marxist view that they were used by the elders to manipulate the members of the society into the continued recognition of their social status.

And neither of these ideas need contradict the view that in particular contexts there were specific meanings for the tombs, and that the rich variety of the megalithic tombs needs to be considered further, as interpretive archaeologists of the "Neo-Wessex school" have continued to do (see p. 216).

This overtly political critique has serious implications for archaeology. For the philosophers of this school stress that there is no such thing as an objective fact. Facts only have meaning in relation to a view of the world, and in relation to theory. Followers of this school are critical of the criterion of testing as used by processual archaeologists, seeing this procedure as merely the importing into archaeology and history of "positivistic" approaches from the sciences. These views have been advanced by Ian Hodder in his book *Reading the Past* (1991) and by Michael Shanks and Christopher Tilley in their work *Re-Constructing Archaeology* (1987). They call into question most of the procedures of reasoning by which archaeology has hitherto operated.

The processualists' response to these ideas is to point out that to follow them seems to imply that one person's view of the past is as good as another's (so-called "relativism"), without any hope of choosing systematically between them. This would open the way to the "fringe" or "alternative" archaeologies discussed in Chapter 14, where explanations can be offered in terms of flying saucers, or extra-terrestrial forces or any phantasms which the human mind may conjure up. It is not entirely clear how the Critical Theorists can answer this criticism.

Neo-Marxist Thought

One feature of neo-Marxist ("structuralist Marxist") thought, as noted earlier, is to stress that the ideological superstructure should not be assumed to be subordinate to the economic base of society. This opens the way to a much greater emphasis on the significance of ideology in shaping change in early societies.

One example is offered by the work of Mark Leone at Annapolis in Maryland, as part of a research project concerned with establishing a deeper historical identity for the area. His example is the 18th-century garden of William Paca, a wealthy landowner: the garden has been studied archaeologically and has now been reconstructed. Leone uses the neo-Marxist concept of ideology: "Ideology takes social relations and makes them appear to be resident in nature or history: which

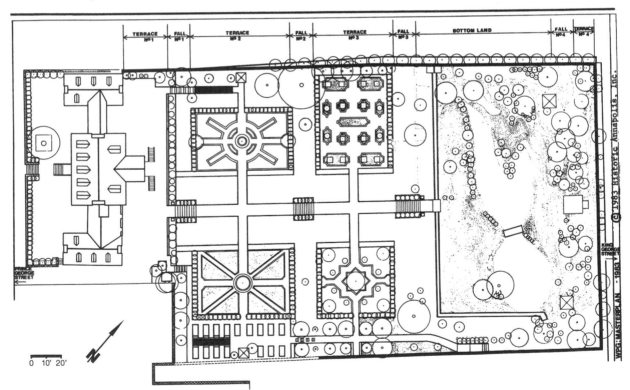

Reconstructed plan of the garden in Annapolis, Maryland, of the 18th-century landowner William Paca. Mark Leone and his colleagues were concerned to show how Paca's position of power "was placed in law and in nature...in practicing law and in gardening." The outlines of the garden are archaeologically derived, but the terraces and most of the plantings are conjectural.

makes them apparently inevitable…. Thus the class or interest group which controls the use of precedent does so to insure its own interests. It is in this sense that the classic Marxist writers have said that history tends to be written for class purposes." (Leone 1987, 26)

Leone examines the Annapolis garden in detail, and emphasizes the contradiction represented between a slave-owning society and one proclaiming independence in order to promote individual liberty, a contradiction seen also in Paca's life. "To mask this contradiction," Leone writes, "his position of power was placed in law and in nature. This was done both in practicing law and in gardening."

This neo-Marxist outlook has its echo in the emerging local archaeologies of some Third World countries, where there is an understandable desire to construct a history (and an archaeology) that lays stress on the local population and its achievements before the colonial era.

But some archaeologists, embracing also the relativist outlook encouraged by Critical Theory, have suggested that the archaeological *methods* used in those countries should also be different. They suggest that the whole framework of archaeological reasoning built up over the past century (and, let us admit, built up mainly in the western world) may have to be set aside. Certainly one must face the reality that different systems of values are at work, as is indicated by the controversy in North American archaeology over whether or not Native Americans should have control over the excavated remains of their ancestors (see Chapter 14).

COGNITIVE-PROCESSUAL ARCHAEOLOGY

During the 1980s and 1990s a new perspective emerged, which transcends some of the limitations of functional-processual archaeology of the 1970s. This new synthesis, while willingly learning from any suitable developments in postprocessual archaeology, remains in the mainstream of processual archaeology. It still wishes to explain rather than merely describe. It still emphasizes the role of generalization within its theoretical structure, and stresses the importance not only of formulating hypotheses but of testing them against the data. It rejects the total relativism that seems to be the end point of Critical Theory, and it is suspicious of structuralist (and other) archaeologists who claim privileged insight into "meaning" in ancient societies, or proclaim "universal principles of meaning." To this extent, it does not accept the revolutionary claims of postprocessual archaeology in rejecting the positive achievements of the New Archaeology. Instead, it sees itself (although its critics will naturally disagree) in the mainstream of archaeological thinking, the direct inheritor of the functional-processual archaeology of 20 years ago (and the beneficiary of Marxist archaeology and various other developments).

Cognitive-processual archaeology differs from its functional-processual predecessor in several ways:

1 It seeks actively to incorporate information about the cognitive and symbolic aspects of early societies into its formulations (see below).
2 It recognizes that ideology is an active force within societies and must be given a role in many explanations, as neo-Marxist archaeologists have argued, and that ideology acts on the minds of individuals.
3 Material culture is seen as an active factor in constituting the world in which we live. Individuals and societies construct their own social reality, and material culture has an integral place within that construction (see box overleaf), as effectively argued by Ian Hodder and his colleagues.
4 The role of internal conflict within societies is a matter to be more fully considered, as Marxist archaeologists have always emphasized.
5 The earlier, rather limited view of historical explanation being entirely related to the human individual, indeed of being often anecdotal, should be revised. This point is well exemplified in the work of the French historian Fernand Braudel, who considered cyclical change and underlying long-term trends.
6 It can take account of the creative role of the individual without retreating into mere intuition or extreme subjectivity by the philosophical approach known as methodological individualism.
7 An extreme "positivist" view of the philosophy of science can no longer be sustained: "facts" can no longer be viewed as having an objective existence independent of theory. It is also now recognized that the formulation of "laws of culture process" as universal laws like those of physics is not a fruitful path towards explanation in archaeology.

This last point needs further discussion. Philosophers of science have long contrasted two approaches to the evaluation of the truth of a statement. One approach evaluates the statement by comparing it with relevant facts, to which, if true, it should correspond (this is

THE INDIVIDUAL AS AN AGENT OF CHANGE

	figure	icon
social maleness	male	dagger
hunting/capture of stag	stag	antlers
plowing/mastery of oxen	ox	horns

Steven Mithen has argued in his *Thoughtful Foragers*, which considers hunter-gatherers, that a "focus on the individual decision makers is the stance for developing adequate explanations in archaeology." John Barrett, in his study of the British Neolithic and Early Bronze Age periods, *Fragments from Antiquity*, stresses that the perceptions and beliefs of individuals are an integral part of the social reality, without which culture change cannot adequately be understood. A cognitive approach (as discussed in Chapter 10) is therefore seen as indispensable to an understanding of change. Kent Flannery has recently stressed the role of the individual as actor in the historical drama with reference to the formation of state societies, drawing upon such historically documented examples as the formation of the Zulu state in South

Africa and of state society in Hawaii under the leadership of Kamehameha I.

A good example of an approach incorporating individual actions and their symbolic context is provided by John Robb's study of change in prehistoric Italy, where indications of personal inequality, in terms of age, of gender, and of prestige are carefully considered, and the evidence for the elaboration of a male gender hierarchy toward the beginning of the Bronze Age is examined.

As he points out, the rock engravings found in the Alps at Monte Bego and Val Camonica (compare the Swedish rock engravings discussed in the box, p. 418) employ images which stand for certain specific concepts: the association and repetition of male hunters, male plowers, cattle, and daggers suggest that these symbols

were primarily used to enact and express male gender.

Robb draws on recent theories of social change which argue that, although an individual's actions are structured by the social system in which they live, specific actions also construct, reconstitute, and change that social system. In other words, social systems are both the medium and the outcome of people's actions.

On the basis of evidence drawn from cult caves, burials, and human representations such as figurines, Robb concluded that during the Neolithic in Italy (c. 6000–3000 BC), society probably contained "balanced, complementary cognitive oppositions between male and female." As Ruth Whitehouse points out, cult caves appear to have been used by both women and men, although only male activities seem to be represented in the innermost areas. Burials are simple inhumations located within villages and without grave-goods. Commonly, however, males are placed on their right side and females on their left. The extant figurines of this period are dominated by female images. Taken together, these strands of evidence suggest that, although gender distinctions were important in Neolithic society, gender hierarchy was not present.

Changes in the Bronze and Iron Age

The balanced gender oppositions of the Neolithic were transformed in the Copper and Bronze Ages (after 3000 BC) into a gender hierarchy which valued male above female. The main evidence for this change is drawn from art. Female figurines disappear; on stelae, monumental stone representations of schematic human figures, males are identified by cultural icons, mainly daggers, while females are identified by breasts. In other art

An example of a rock carving from Val Camonica, northern Italy, showing a stag with prominent antlers being hunted by a male figure holding a spear, and possibly a dog.

forms three new dominant themes appear: weaponry, especially males with daggers; hunting images, particularly stags identified by antlers; and plowing, with oxen identified by horns. This consistent association of male form with male cultural icon – men/daggers; stags/antlers; oxen/horns – builds a symbolic system used to enact and express male gender from which an ideology of male power and vitality is created. At the same time, women, by their lack of representation or association with cultural icons are left naturalized and culturally unvalued. Robb cautions, however, that male gender symbols may be telling only one side of a complex gender situation.

During the Iron Age (after 1000 BC), the gender hierarchy of the Bronze Age became a class-based hierarchy. This was achieved by transforming a generalized ideology of male potency into one of aristocratic warrior prowess complemented by a new female elite. Again art works and burials are the main sources of evidence.

Grave-goods placed in male burials now include swords, shields, and military rather than simple daggers, while stelae and depictions in rock art favor warfare rather than the earlier hunting and plowing imagery. Ornamentation and spindle whorls appear in female graves, and females depicted on stelae are culturally marked by dress and finery – not simply breasts. These finds suggest the expansion also of the female symbolic register to express class distinctions.

Robb in his study does not claim to account for the origins of gender inequality, but he does throw light on the development of society in prehistoric Italy. Drawing on concepts of meaning and social action, he shows how gender symbolisms may have motivated males to participate in diverse and changing institutions such as hunting, warfare, economic intensification, and trade, and how these institutions reproduced gender ideology. He does so without any retreat into relativism and without relying on mere empathetic "understanding."

called the *correspondence* approach). The other approach evaluates the statement by judging whether or not it is consistent with (or coherent with, hence *coherence* approach) the other statements that we believe to be true within our framework of beliefs.

Now, although it might be expected that the scientist would follow the first of these two procedures, in practice any assessment is based on a combination of the two. For it is accepted that facts have to be based on observations, and observations themselves cannot be made without using some framework of inference, which itself depends on theories about the world. It is more appropriate to think of facts modifying theory, yet of theory being used in the determination of facts:

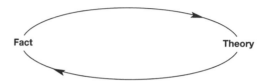

Cognitive-processual archaeologists, like their functional-processual predecessors, believe that theories must be tested against facts. They reject the relativism of the Critical Theory and postprocessual archaeology of the 1990s, which seem to follow entirely a coherence view of truth. But they accept that the relationship between fact and theory is more complicated than some philosophers of science 30 years ago recognized. Cognitive-processual archaeology at present appears to be exploring two main directions: investigation of the role of symbols within processes of change, and exploration of the structure of transformations.

Symbol and Interaction

The point has already been made that the early New Archaeology aspired to investigate social structures, and the progress already made in that direction was reviewed in Chapter 5. But it was slow to explore symbolic aspects of culture, which is why cognitive-processual archaeology is a recent development.

The role of religious ritual within society has been investigated in a new way over the past 20 years by the cultural anthropologist Roy Rappaport. Instead of seeking to immerse himself in the agricultural society in New Guinea under study, becoming totally familiar with the meanings of its symbolic forms, he followed instead a strategy of distancing himself – of looking at the society from the outside, at what it actually does (not what it says it does) in its ritual behavior. This position is a convenient one for the archaeologist who is always outside the society under study, and unable to discuss issues of meaning with its participants. Rappaport has studied the way ritual is used within society and his focus is on the functioning of symbols rather than on their original meaning. His work influenced Kent Flannery, one of the few of the original generation of New Archaeologists to concern himself in detail with symbolic questions. The book written by Joyce Marcus and Kent Flannery, *Zapotec Civilization* (1996), is one of those rare archaeological studies where symbolic and cognitive questions are integrated with subsistence, economic, and social ones to form an integrated view of society. This huge project is described in detail in Chapter 13.

Quite clearly religion and other ideologies such as modern Communism have brought about great changes, not just in the way societies think but in the way they act and behave – and this will leave its mark in the archaeological record. The whole field of official symbolism, and of religious symbolism within it, is now the focus of archaeological research in several parts of the world.

Postprocessual or interpretive archaeology has not shown itself adept at explaining classes of events or general processes (see p. 462, "What are we trying to explain"), since the focus in postprocessual thought is upon the specific conditions of the context in question, and the validity of wider or cross-cultural generalizations is not accepted. Cognitive-processual archaeology on the other hand is very willing to generalize, and indeed to integrate the individual into the analysis as an active agent as Kent Flannery again has done in a recent study.

Two recent works in the mainstream processual tradition exemplify well the emphasis that is now placed upon the cognitive or ideational dimension. Timothy Earle in *How Chiefs Come to Power* (1997), drawing upon the work of the sociologist Michael Mann, devotes successive chapters to economic power, military power, and ideology as a source of power, utilizing three widely separated case studies situated in Denmark, Hawaii, and the Andes. And in a recent collective work devoted to archaic states (Feinman and Marcus, 1998) and likewise treating the subject within a comparative perspective, Richard Blanton has examined the sources of power in early states, contrasting the "cognitive-symbolic base of power" with what he terms the "objective base of power." The terminology may not be entirely appropriate – for who is to adjudicate upon the boundaries of the objective? – but the effect is to integrate the cognitive dimension fully into the analysis, alongside economic issues, rather than treating it as a mere epiphenomenon as was common

in the days of the functional-processual approach. In such works the limitations of the earlier processual archaeology have been transcended and the roots of change are investigated in a generalizing context with full weight being given to the cognitive and the symbolic dimensions.

The Structure of Transformations

The role of symbols within processes of change is one current focus of much research; another, of rather a different kind, is on the processes of change themselves. By what means do social forms change? How is growth sustained? What determines the new structures that emerge?

Contemporary archaeology has sought inspiration from disciplines where questions of growth and form have been systematically considered for some time: for instance from evolutionary biology, from the mathematics of non-linear systems, and from the general study of non-equilibrium systems. It is appropriate here to say a brief word about each.

Positive Feedback. In the early days of systems analysis in archaeology it was argued by some that a functioning system maintained itself in relation to its environment in a position of stability or homeostasis through the operation of negative feedback. Essential changes within the system were thus seen as homeostatic changes (through negative feedback) in response to changes of external origin. As noted above, systems thinking is now very much at home with the notion of positive feedback as a cause of the growth of new forms (morphogenesis).

Punctuated Equilibria. One of the problems within archaeology, as within evolutionary thinking in general, has been to accommodate the notion of sudden change. Much of the thinking of Charles Darwin in *The Origin of Species* (1859) was toward the explanation of changes taking place over long periods of time. It is only relatively recently, notably through the work of Stephen Jay Gould and Niles Eldredge (1977), that it has been accepted that sudden change is not in contradiction to Darwinian thought. It is now believed by many evolutionary biologists that there were long time periods when plant and animal species changed very little, and much shorter periods ("punctuations") when evolution progressed at a very rapid rate.

This general lesson is certainly applicable to archaeology, and the British archaeologist John Cherry has argued, in relation to the emergence of the palace society of Minoan Crete, that a gradualist approach does not seem appropriate. Inspired by the concept of "punctuated equilibria," he maintains that the sudden emergence of palace society may nonetheless be accommodated within an evolutionary perspective; the impact of gradual change over a period of more than a thousand years led to a rapid reordering of Minoan society at the end of the 3rd millennium BC.

Catastrophe Theory and Chaos Theory. Similar lessons are offered by catastrophe theory, a branch of mathematics which is employed to argue that when a number of variables are working together (in a non-linear way), gradual changes in the variables can produce sudden effects. Moreover, René Thom, in his *Structural Stability and Morphogenesis* (1975), was able to show that there are only a limited number of ways in which such changes can take place. These he describes as the elementary catastrophes, of which one has been applied to archaeological cases.

Self-Organization in Non-Equilibrium Systems. Using a related perspective, derived initially from thermodynamic studies in chemistry, the Belgian scientist Ilya Prigogine has stressed that many systems, and specifically those that are not at equilibrium and in which energy is dissipated, have a propensity towards self-organization. That means new and more complex forms emerge quite naturally within them. The paths or trajectories of growth arrive at bifurcation points at which sudden changes may occur.

These ideas, like those of Catastrophe Theory, have been of great interest to theoretical biologists. They have also been applied to the human sphere. For instance, Prigogine's colleague P.M. Allen has simulated the growth of urban centers using this approach, showing how the growth of new and more complex

forms may be predicted. Taking into account such factors as industry, population, and retail trade, he modeled the development of a small town into a city, showing how the location of different activities within the city shifted as population grew and external demands of the industrial and financial sectors expanded.

These various approaches have not yet been comprehensively applied in the field of archaeology, although in each case the application has begun, and they have been applied by van der Leeuw and McGlade to an ambitious field project in the Mediterranean. At present, the models are in general too simple, and most of them fail to take into account the cognitive features to which the cognitive-processual archaeology aspires. Postprocessual archaeologists have argued that such approaches are too mechanistic to account for the richness and complexity of human behavior. In the simple forms in which such models exist at present, that criticism is certainly justified. But already computer scientists such as J.E. Doran are devising simulations where individuals within a community, each with different perceptions of the world, will interact.

One of the aspirations of cognitive-processual archaeology is to develop more effective formal models within which human perceptions and the symbolic side of human society will have a significant role. Modeling of this kind is, however, a specialized field. Most archaeologists will prefer to proceed in the first place from the archaeological material, and to frame their explanations initially in verbal rather than mathematical form.

Cognitive-processual archaeology offers an appropriate framework for the development of such explanations. It is a framework in which the specifically human qualities of the human animal – the symbolic – will play a central role.

SUMMARY

One of the cornerstones of the New Archaeology was an emphasis on the importance of theory in archaeology. For too long scholars had felt it sufficient to explain the past simply in terms of archaeological cultures interpreted as the remnants of distinct groups of people, who experienced change as a result of migrations and diffusion from other cultures. The New Archaeology seriously questioned the equation of cultures with peoples, and challenged the assumption that diffusion – even in the rare cases where it could be proved to have occurred – actually explained the underlying causes of change in societies. New Archaeologists sought to study societies as functioning cultural systems, and to find regularities in the culture-historical process.

In this functional-processual approach, any new hypotheses derived from archaeological evidence were to be tested against fresh evidence – the hypothetico-deductive method. Marxist archaeologists likewise attempted to understand the processes of change in history, but tended to limit their explanations of change in terms of the struggle between social classes.

In any explanation, it is important to be clear about what one is trying to explain – whether a specific event, a class of events, or a more general process. Two classes of events addressed by the New Archaeology have been the rise of agriculture and the origins of the state. Here, the most successful explanations appear to be multicausal ones using the systems approach, which allows the use of computer simulation and modeling.

From the 1970s on structuralists, poststructuralists, and then postprocessualists reacted against the functionalism of the early New Archaeology, advocating greater emphasis on the ideas and the beliefs of past societies, and criticizing the procedure of testing, since all knowledge is subjective. Processualists have responded by reaffirming the importance of testing – how else are we to choose between competing theories? – but have accepted the need to look afresh at ideas and beliefs, at the cognitive aspects of culture and to develop a methodology which can recognize the role of the individual and of agency in the inception of change.

A new cognitive-processual synthesis can thus be seen to have emerged in the 1990s, alongside the interpretive archaeologies which have succeeded the polemic of the early postprocessual archaeology.

FURTHER READING

Bell, J.A. 1994. *Reconstructing Prehistory: Scientific Method in Archaeology*. Temple University Press: Philadelphia. (Chapter 9, for a clear exposition of methodological individualism.)

Daniel, G. & Renfrew, C. 1988. *The Idea of Prehistory*. Edinburgh University Press: Edinburgh; Columbia University Press: New York.

Earle, T. 1997. *How Chiefs Come to Power, the Political Economy in Prehistory*. Stanford Univ. Press.

Feinman, G.M. & Marcus, J. (eds.). 1998. *Archaic States*. School of American Research Press: Santa Fe.

Flannery, K.V. (ed.). 1976. *The Early Mesoamerican Village*. Academic Press: New York. (Book of well-argued case studies which reveals more about the structure of explanation than most works devoted to archaeological theory. Also has an excellent running commentary.)

Hodder, I. 1991. *Reading the Past*. (2nd ed.) Cambridge University Press: Cambridge & New York. (The contextual and postprocessual alternative.)

Mithen, S. 1996. *The Prehistory of the Mind*. Thames & Hudson: London & New York.

Renfrew, C. 1982. Explanation Revisited, in Renfrew, C., Rowlands, M., & Seagraves, B.A. *Theory and Explanation in Archaeology*. Academic Press: New York, 5–24.

Renfrew, C. & Zubrow, E.B.W. (eds.). 1994. *The Ancient Mind: Elements of Cognitive Archaeology*. Cambridge University Press: Cambridge & New York.

Shanks, M. & Tilley, C. 1987. *Social Theory and Archaeology*. Polity Press: Oxford; University of New Mexico Press: Albuquerque 1988.

PART III
The World of Archaeology

The basic materials of archaeology, and the methods available for establishing a space–time framework, were reviewed in Part I of this book. The range of questions we can ask of the past, and the techniques available for answering them, were surveyed in Part II. Here, in Part III, our aim is to see how these various techniques are put into practice. In an actual field project one would like, of course, to answer all the questions at once (no archaeologist ever set out to answer just one of them without at the same time coming up with observations relevant to others).

In Chapter 13, four selected case studies show how several questions can be addressed at once. In a regional study we are concerned with the location of the relevant evidence, with establishing the time sequence of the remains discovered, with the investigation of the environment, with the nature of the society, and indeed with the whole range of issues raised in the various chapters of this book. Any director of a major project has, in a sense, to reach a compromise in order to be able to follow up several avenues of inquiry simultaneously. The aim here is to illustrate with informative examples how such compromises have indeed been reached in practice, with a fair degree of success. Thus we hope to give something of the flavor of archaeological research in practice.

An archaeological investigation, even on a regional scale, cannot, however, be considered in isolation. It is only one part of the world of archaeology, and hence of society as a whole. The last chapter in this book is therefore devoted to public archaeology – to the ethical, practical, and political relationships that relate the archaeologist to society at large. The aim of archaeology, after all, is to provide information, knowledge, and insight into the human past. This is not for the benefit of the archaeologist alone but for society at large. Society finances the archaeologist, and, in the final analysis, society is the consumer. The relationship merits examination.

13 Archaeology in Action
Four Case Studies

In this volume we have sought to examine the various methods and ideas employed by archaeologists. We have tried to stress that the history of archaeology has been the story of an expanding quest, in which the finds made in the field can often be less important for progress than the new questions asked and the new insights gained. The success of an archaeological enterprise thus depends crucially on our learning to ask the right questions, and finding the most productive means of answering them.

It is for this reason that the chapters in this book have been organized around a series of key questions. Inevitably, that has meant focusing chapter by chapter on a number of different themes. But in reality the life of the archaeologist is not quite like that. For when you go out into the field with your research design, with the bundle of questions you would like to answer, you may in fact find something quite different from what you expected, yet obviously very important. The archaeologist excavating a multi-period site may be interested primarily in a single, perhaps early, phase of occupation. But that does not give him or her the right to bulldoze away the overlying levels without keeping any record. Excavation is destruction and (as we shall discuss in the final chapter) this brings to the archaeologist a series of responsibilities, some of them not always welcome, which cannot be avoided. The practice of archaeology, in the hard light of reality, is often very much more complicated – and therefore more challenging – than one might imagine.

This is particularly so at the organizational level. To undertake a project in the field takes money, and it is not the purpose of the present book to examine the funding or organization of such projects. Increasingly, as we review Chapter 14, archaeological sites are protected by law, and a permit from the relevant authorities will be needed in order to undertake fieldwork and to excavate. Then there is the task of recruiting an efficient excavation team. What about transport, lodging, and food? After the excavation, who is to write what part of the excavation report? Are the photo-graphs adequate, have the finds been suitably illustrated by drawings, who will finance publication? These are the practical problems of the field archaeologist.

This book is primarily about how we know what we know, and how we find out – in philosophical terms, about the epistemology of archaeology. To complete the picture, it is important to see something of archaeology in action: to consider a few real field projects where the questions and methods have come together and produced, with the aid of the relevant specialisms, some genuine advance in our knowledge.

The questions we ask are themselves dependent on what, and how much, we already know. Sometimes the archaeologist starts work in archaeologically virgin territory – where little or no previous research has been undertaken – as for instance when the Southeast Asian specialist Charles Higham began his fieldwork in Thailand (see our third case study, Khok Phanom Di: the Origins of Rice Farming in Southeast Asia).

In the Valley of Oaxaca in Mexico, on the other hand – our first case study – when Kent Flannery and his colleagues began work two decades ago, little was understood of the evolution in Mesoamerica of what we would call complex society, although the great achievements of the Olmec and the Maya were already well known. The work of the Flannery team has involved continual formulation of new models. It represents an excellent example of the truism that new facts (data) lead to new questions (and new theories), and these in turn to the discovery of new facts.

Our second case study follows the research project of Rhys Jones and his associates in Kakadu National Park, northern Australia. Here the archaeologists worked closely with the legal owners of the region's sites, the Aborigines – an experience of growing relevance for all researchers in lands occupied by indigenous peoples (Chapter 14).

The transformation in our knowledge of prehistoric Australia and Southeast Asia over the course of the last 30 years has been one of the most exciting developments to have taken place in modern archaeology. The Kakadu and Khok Phanom Di projects, with their close integration of both environmental and archaeological studies, have played an important part in that transformation.

Our fourth case study focuses on the work of the York Archaeological Trust in the English city of York.

This is a project of a very different kind: working under all the constraints of archaeology in a modern urban setting, the York unit has set out to present its findings to the public in a novel and effective way, and the Jorvik Viking Centre has for the past 15 years led the way in this aspect of public archaeology.

THE OAXACA PROJECTS: THE ORIGINS AND RISE OF THE ZAPOTEC STATE

The Valley of Oaxaca in the southern highlands of Mexico is best known for the great hilltop city of Monte Albán, one-time capital of the Zapotecs and famous for its magnificent architecture and carved stone slabs. Here, from 1930 onward, 18 seasons of fieldwork by the great Mexican archaeologist Alfonso Caso first laid the foundations of the region's time sequence. In recent decades, however, research has broadened to encompass the whole valley. There have been two major, long-term and complementary projects. The first, led

by Kent Flannery from 1966 to 1973 and directed by him and Joyce Marcus from 1974 to 1981, has concentrated on the earlier periods – before Monte Albán's heyday – with the aim of elucidating the origins of agriculture and evolution of complex society in the region. The second project, conducted by Richard E. Blanton, Stephen Kowalewski, and Gary Feinman, has focused on the later periods dominated by Monte Albán. In what follows we shall look at the work of both projects down to the end of the Formative period (c. AD 100), and how new light has been cast on the inception of agriculture, the process of state formation in the Valley of Oaxaca, and the emergence of the Zapotec state.

Background

The Valley of Oaxaca is the only broad riverine valley in the southern highlands of Mexico. Shaped like a

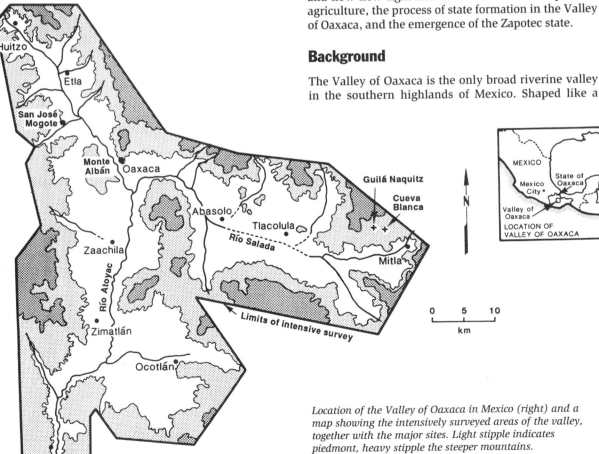

Location of the Valley of Oaxaca in Mexico (right) and a map showing the intensively surveyed areas of the valley, together with the major sites. Light stipple indicates piedmont, heavy stipple the steeper mountains.

wishbone, it is drained by two rivers. Surrounded by mountains, it lies at an altitude of between 1420 and 1740 m (4658 and 5708 ft) and has a semi-arid, semi-tropical environment where rainfall fluctuates markedly – both predictably, between wet and dry seasons, and unpredictably from year to year.

Building on work by Ignacio Bernal, who had already catalogued many sites in the valley through survey, the Flannery-Marcus project began by surveying and locating as many early sites as possible in selected areas, before deciding on those to be excavated. In fact, survey still continues to reveal sites in the area as land clearance and canal building expose buried horizons. Survey from the air has been particularly helpful, since one can see through the sparse vegetation and identify small details almost to the level of individual trees.

Guilá Naquitz and the Origins of Agriculture

One excavation, designed to clarify the transition from foraging to food production, was that of a small rockshelter, Guilá Naquitz (White Cliff).

Survey and Excavation. Surface collection of artifacts from more than 60 caves in the same area suggested that four, including Guilá Naquitz, had enough preceramic material (such as projectile points) and depth

Work in progress inside Guilá Naquitz rockshelter, 1966. Zapotec Indian workmen from Mitla, Oaxaca, are excavating level D (the first level to include evidence of domestic plants).

of deposit (up to 1.2 m or 3 ft 9 in) to warrant full excavation. After access for transport to the site had been improved, test excavations were carried out to determine the stratigraphic sequence, establish whether preceramic levels were present *in situ*, and assess how far back in the sequence plant remains might be preserved. The stratigraphy was complex, but very clear because of dramatic color changes.

It was to be expected that survival of food remains would be good, because the site is located in the driest part of the Valley of Oaxaca. The Flannery-Marcus team indeed found that preservation was outstanding, but the low densities of artifacts meant that all or most of the small cave would have to be dug in order to establish the nature of the tool assemblage. In the end, the entire area of preceramic occupation under the cave's overhang was removed through the excavation of 64 one-meter squares. Thorough screening and sieving techniques ensured that even the smallest items were recovered.

Dating. Radiocarbon dates obtained from charcoal found at Naquitz showed that its preceramic living floors extended from about 8750 to 6670 BC (there was also a little Formative and Postclassic occupation, not yet fully analyzed and published). The date of 8750 BC is close to the supposed transition from the Paleo-Indian period, characterized by extinct Pleistocene fauna, to the early Archaic, with Holocene fauna.

Environment. Analysis of pollen samples from the different levels provided a sequence of change for the area's vegetation with fluctuations in thorn, oak, and pine forest, and the possible utilization of cultivated plant resources from about 8000 BC onward, together with the collection of wild plant resources from the start of the sequence.

The microfauna recovered – rodents, birds, lizards, landsnails – were compared with their modern representatives in the region in order to cast further light on the preceramic environment, which was found to be not vastly different from that in existence today except for humanly induced changes. The present landscape is thus relevant to any interpretation of the past.

Diet. Rodents had been very active in the cave, gnawing nuts and seeds, so that it was vital to establish from the start how many of the food resources had been introduced to the site by people. Burrows were very visible in the living floors, and their contents could be examined. None of the commonly gnawed items such as acorns or nuts were found inside them. In addition, the distribution of plant species on the floors showed

Plant	April	May	June	July	Aug	Sep	Oct	Nov	Dec	Jan	Feb	Mar	No. of grams consumed	No. of Kilocalories represented
acorns													629	1812
agave													140	176
nopales													97	12
guaje seeds													54	19
nanches													30	21
mesquite pods				pods			stored seeds						14	42
hackberries													13	4
opuntia fruits													12	9
susi nuts													5	30
beans			flowers			seeds							3	4
piñon nuts													1	6
wild onions			flowers						bulbs				1	0
cucurbit					flowers		seeds						1	4

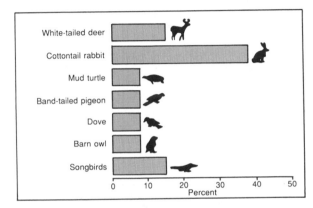

(Top) At Guilá Naquitz plants dominated the diet, especially acorns, agave, and mesquite pods and seeds. The site was occupied mainly from August (mesquite harvest) till early January (end of acorn harvest). (Above) Animals consumed.

a human pattern of large discard areas rather than the small pockets characteristic of rodent caches. Some plant remains also showed signs of food preparation. In short, the researchers could be confident that almost all the food resources in the site had been introduced by people.

Unfortunately, the six coprolites obtained from the preceramic levels all appeared to be from animals (probably coyote or fox). However, these creatures had probably scavenged food from the cave, and so the roasted plant remains (prickly pear and *agave*) in their feces provided clues to the human diet.

Clearer indications of diet were obtained through a combination of methods. These included data on plant and animal remains; modern plant censuses that provided information on the density, seasonality, and annual variations of various species in the area; and an analysis of the foods in the site from a nutritional point of view (calories, protein, fats, carbohydrates). The result was both a hypothetical diet for each living floor

and an estimate of productivity of the Guilá Naquitz environment. Finally, all this information was pooled to reconstruct the "average diet" of the preceramic cave occupants and estimate the area needed to support them.

Over 21,000 identifiable plant remains were recovered, dominated by acorns, with *agave*, and mesquite pods and seeds. Dozens of other species were represented in small quantities. It thus became clear that, despite the wide variety of edible plants available, the occupants had adopted a selected few as staples. Acorns were probably stored after the autumn gathering for use throughout the year, because one of the major factors in life here is the great seasonal variation in the availability of different foods. It was found that the plant remains in each level reflected the harvest of an area from a few to a few hundred square meters.

Recently, some seeds of squash (*Cucurbita pepo*) from the site, which are morphologically domesticated, were directly dated by AMS to between 10,000 and 8000 years ago, which predates other domesticates in Mesoamerica (such as maize, beans, etc) by several millennia.

At least 360 identifiable fragments came from animals hunted or trapped for food. They were counted both as numbers of fragments (with the parts of the body and the position in the cave noted) and as minimum numbers of individuals (in order to estimate the amount of meat consumed or the territory needed to account for the remains). All the species are still common in the area today, or would have been common until the arrival of firearms. The major source of meat seems to have been the white-tailed deer.

The site catchment of Guilá Naquitz was calculated as follows: plant food requirements probably came from no more than 5–15 ha (12–37 acres); the deer from at least 17 ha (42 acres); and raw materials from up to 50 km (31 miles) away.

Technology. Being a small camp, Guilá Naquitz did not contain the full range of stone tools known from the preceramic in the Valley of Oaxaca generally. Of the 1716 pieces of chipped stone recovered from the preceramic levels, no fewer than 1564 lacked any retouch, implying that most had been used "raw," without being worked further. Almost every living floor had evidence for flake production, in the form of cores. Only 7 projectile points were found, setting in perspective the evidence from the animal bones and suggesting that hunting was not a major activity during the season the cave was occupied. Sidescrapers and knives may have been used in butchering or hide preparation. A survey of stone sources showed that the coarse material from which most tools were made was available within a few kilometers, but higher quality chert had occasionally been obtained from sources 25 and 50 km (15 and 31 miles) distant.

It is assumed that most of the grinding stones had been used for plant processing, since remains of food plants were found in the same levels. Textile materials also survived – netting, basketry, and cordage, including the oldest radiocarbon-dated examples from Mesoamerica (before 7000 BC) – and there were a few artifacts of wood, reed, or cactus as well, including materials for firemaking and toolhafting. Fragments of charcoal occurred here and there, and were used by the research team for radiocarbon dating or to determine the woods preferred as fuels by the cave's occupants. It was found that the choice of timber in the preceramic period had been wide-ranging, unlike that of the Formative villagers of the Oaxaca Valley who later showed a marked preference for pine which continued into the Colonial and modern eras and which probably explains the disappearance of that tree from some areas.

Social Organization and the Division of Labor. The distribution of material on the living floors was subjected to three separate computer analyses in order to assess activity areas and the organization of labor. The activity areas – clusters in the distribution – were defined on the basis of association: i.e. showing that an increase in one variable (such as nut hulls or hackberry seeds) is a good predictor of an increase or decrease in other variables. Hence the raw data consisted of the frequencies of different items per meter square of each floor, converted into density contour maps by computer.

When six living floors were analyzed, a number of repetitive patterns emerged that probably reflect regularities in the way tasks had been organized in the cave. These patterns are quite complex, and cannot be divided simplistically into men's and women's workspace. They include areas for light butchering, raw plant eating, toolmaking, meal preparation and cooking, and the discard of refuse. However, ethnographic research suggested some sexual division of work areas. Pathways into and within the cave were also isolated by the analyses.

Flannery and Marcus concluded that Guilá Naquitz was a small microband camp, used by no more than four or five people, perhaps a single family. It was occupied mainly in the fall, between late August/early September (the mesquite harvest season) and December/early January (the end of the acorn harvest season). Collecting wild plants was a major activity here, but hunting was less dominant than at other sites. Toward the end of preceramic occupation, there was a transition to food production. The full picture of activities at this site now has to be compared with results from other sites in this area and with other regions in Mesoamerica in order to assess how representative or unusual they are for their period.

Reconstructed activity areas and pathways of Zone D at Guilá Naquitz. Area I is interpreted as a curving pathway with acorn, hackberry, and flint debris. Another path, Area II, runs between acorn storage and food preparation areas. Area III may have been where animal processing was carried out by one or two people (probably men). Area IV may have been used by one or two people (probably women) to process and cook both seasonally restricted and cactus/agave group plants.

Why Did Things Change? In order to gain further insights into the process of adopting an agricultural way of life, Robert G. Reynolds designed an adaptive computer simulation model, in which a hypothetical microband of five foragers started from a position of ignorance and gradually learned how to schedule the gathering of the 11 major plant foods in the cave's environment by trial and error over a long period of time. At each step of the simulation the foragers were programmed to try to improve the efficiency of their recovery of calories and protein, in the face of an unpredictable sequence of wet, dry, and average years that changed the productivity of the plants.

Information on their past performance was fed back into the memory of the system, and affected their decisions about modifying strategy with each change. When the system reached such a level of efficiency that it could scarcely be improved, agricultural plants were introduced into the simulation and the whole process began again. Priorities were changed, and a new set of strategies developed. Changes in the frequency of wet, dry, and average years were also tried out, as well as alterations in population level.

The results of this model based on artificial intelligence theory, with its built-in feedback relationships, were that the hypothetical foragers developed a stable set of resource collecting schedules (one for dry and average years, the other for wet years) that closely mirrored those at Guilá Naquitz, as did the shifts in resource use that followed the introduction of incipient agriculture. No absolute time units were used in the simulation – we do not know how long a real-life group would actually take to achieve the same strategies. Nor was a "trigger" for agriculture, such as population pressure, introduced into the system. The resources were simply made available – as it were from a neighboring region – and adopted, first in wet years and later, when they proved reliable, in dry and average years.

When the simulated climate changed significantly, or population growth was introduced, the rate at which cultivated plants were adopted into the system actually slowed down. This suggests that neither climatic change nor population growth is necessary to explain the rise of agriculture in the Valley of Oaxaca. Rather, the work implies that a major reason for the adoption of agriculture was to help even out the effects of annual variation in food supplies, and was therefore merely an extension of the strategy already developed in pre-agricultural times.

The research project at Guilá Naquitz was fully published in 1986 in a volume edited by Kent Flannery after more than 15 years of analysis.

Village Life in the Early Formative (1500–850 BC)

Another part of the project's work that has been published in some depth concerns Early Formative villages in the Valley of Oaxaca, the period when true, permanent settlements of wattle-and-daub houses first became widespread in the region. The project's aim was to construct a model of how the early village operated, and to do that it studied them at every level, from features and activity areas within a single house to household units, groups of houses, whole villages, all villages in a valley, and, finally, interregional networks within Mesoamerica.

Settlement and Society. As seen in Chapter 3, the Flannery team took care to obtain as representative a sample as possible for each level, in order to gain a clear idea of the range of variation in artifacts, activities, site-types, etc. Before the Oaxaca project, not a single plan of an Early Formative house had been published. The project has recovered partial or nearly complete plans of 30 houses, along with others from later phases. Using Naroll's formula (see pp. 452–53), it was estimated that these houses (15–35 sq. m or 161–376 sq. ft) were intended for nuclear families.

Activity areas were plotted for each house, and, through ethnographic analogy, tentatively divided into male and female work areas. After detailed analysis household activities were divided into three types:

1   *Universal activities* such as food procurement, preparation, and storage – as revealed by grinding equipment, storage pits, and jars, and food remains recovered by excavation, screening, and flotation; some tool preparation was also classed in this group.

2   Possible *specialized activities* – activities found at only one or two houses, including manufacture of certain kinds of stone and bone tool.

3   Possible *regional specializations* – activities found in only one or two villages within a region; these include production of some shell ornaments, or featherworking; saltmaking was limited to villages such as Fábrica San José near saline springs.

The project also produced the first maps showing the layout of a Formative village (principally that of Tierras Largas). Some evidence for differences in social status emerged, particularly at Santo Domingo Tomaltepec. Here one group of residences – deduced to be of relatively higher status – had not only a house platform built of higher-quality adobe and stone, but a greater quantity of animal bone, imported obsidian, and

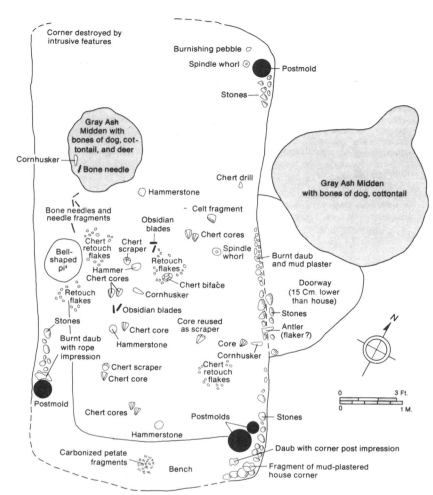

Early Formative Oaxaca. (Left) Plan of a house at Tierras Largas, c. 900 BC, with certain artifacts plotted in position. (Above) Zapotec workmen pour a solution of ash, water, and sodium silicate into a brass carburetor-mesh screen. By "floating" the charcoal fragments out of ash deposits at Early Formative sites such as Tierras Largas, the project was able to recover charred maize kernels, beans, squash seeds, chilli pepper seeds, prickly pear seeds, and other food remains that were invisible to the eye while excavating.

imported marine shell than the area of wattle-and-daub houses deduced to be of lower status. Significantly, locally available (and therefore less prestigious) chert formed a higher proportion of the tools in the lower-status area. Other villages may have had a zone of public buildings, though zonation was less formal than that of Classic and Postclassic sites.

The Early Formative settlements showed considerable variation in size on the basis of site surveys. About 90 percent were small hamlets, of between one and a dozen households, up to 12 ha (29 acres) in size, and with up to 60 people. Most remained stable at that size for centuries, but a few villages grew bigger. San José Mogote reached 70 ha (172 acres) by 850 BC, the largest settlement in the Valley of Oaxaca at that time and the central place for a network of about 20 villages. Flannery and Marcus postulated that the spacing of the villages about 5 km or 3 miles apart was probably

determined socially, to avoid overcrowding, rather than by environmental or agricultural factors, because the available arable land could easily have supported a closer grouping of sites. On the other hand, factors of site catchment determined the precise location for each settlement.

Catchment Areas and Trade. The catchment areas for several sites were assessed. San José Mogote could have satisfied its basic agricultural requirements in a radius of 2.5 km (1.5 miles); its basic mineral resource needs and some important seasonal wild plants within 5 km (3 miles); deer meat, material for house construction, and preferred types of firewood had to be fetched from within 15 km (9.4 miles). Trade with other regions brought in exotic materials largely from a radius of 50 km (30 miles), but sometimes from as far as 200 km (125 miles; see box, pp. 258–59).

Trade in obsidian seems to have taken the egalitarian form of exchange in the Early Formative, with all villages participating. From its various sources, it traveled along chain-like networks of villages, to be distributed among households in each community. Unmodified shell was brought in from the coast, and apparently converted into ornaments in the larger villages by part-time specialists who were also farmers, as suggested by the range of materials on their floors.

What Did They Think? What Were They Like? The Oaxaca Early Formative project also examined the evidence for religion and burial. From a study of context, ritual paraphernalia could be distinguished at three levels: the individual, the household, and the community.

At the *community* level, only certain villages had structures that were evidently public buildings rather than residences, and it is assumed that some of the activities carried out in them were ceremonial in nature, and presumably served the neighboring hamlets as well. Conch-shell trumpets and turtle-shell drums also probably functioned in ritual at the community level (local ethnography supports this view), and were brought in from the coastal lowlands.

At the *household* level, features such as enigmatic shallow, lime-plastered basins within houses have been interpreted as ritual, or at least non-utilitarian, as have figurines of ancestors and dancers in costumes and masks. The excavators now believe, based on ethnographic sources, that the basins were used for divination. After filling them with water, women tossed maize kernels or beans on the surface and interpreted the pattern. Ethnography and ethnohistory suggest that fish spines were used in personal rituals of self-mutilation and bloodletting; spines from marine fish were specially imported to the valley.

At the *individual* level, burials, like houses, suggest that ranking formed a continuum from simple to elaborate, rather than a rigid class system. The cemetery outside the village of Santo Domingo Tomaltepec had over 60 burials of 80 individuals, of whom 55 could be aged and sexed. There were no infants (these were usually buried near the house) and only one child. The oldest person was 50 years of age. Males and females were roughly equal in number, but most women had died between the ages of 20 and 29, while most men had survived into their 30s.

All the burials were face-down, and almost all faced east, most in the fully extended position. But a few males were flexed and, although they constituted only 12.7 percent of the whole cemetery, they had 50 percent of the fine burial vessels, 88 percent of the jade beads, and a high proportion of the graves covered by stone slabs. Clearly, this group had some kind of special status.

Social Developments in the Later Formative (850 BC–AD 100)

The research designs for the two long-term projects initiated by Kent Flannery on the one hand and Richard Blanton on the other had as their ultimate joint goal the identification of the processes leading to the rise of societies with hereditary ranking and to the evolution of the Zapotec state.

Richard Blanton, Stephen Kowalewski, Gary Feinman, and their associates conducted intensive, valley-wide settlement surveys using the survey methods originally pioneered in the Valley of Mexico, and then drew up settlement maps for successive phases. They also carried out a very detailed survey of the major site of Monte Albán. This, it turned out, had been a new foundation sometime around 500 BC, and the site had at once become the principal center in the region. Meanwhile, the excavations by Flannery and his associates already mentioned, at no fewer than nine village sites, provided evidence of the development of houses, storage pits, activity areas, burials, and other features throughout the Formative period. Subsistence was again a special focus of study through work with charred seeds, animal bones, pollen remains, and site catchment analysis.

Social organization was investigated by comparing residences from successive periods, by studying burials, and by considering public buildings in order to document the growth of various Zapotec state institutions out of the more generalized institutions of earlier times. Early Zapotec hieroglyphic writing was an important focus of study. And design element studies on pottery, undertaken by Stephen Plog, suggested that as complex regional networks of sites developed, certain groups of hamlets shared the services of a local civic-ceremonial center.

Already in the Early Formative period, as noted above, the site of San José Mogote had grown to pre-eminence in the valley. It was, however, in the succeeding Middle Formative period (850–500 BC) that a three-tier settlement hierarchy was observed through site survey. The site hierarchy was identified by size, and there are no clear indications of administrative functions. But the ceremonial functions are much clearer. San José Mogote reached its peak development as a chiefly center, a focus for some 20 villages, with a total population of perhaps 1400 persons. It boasted an acropolis of public buildings on a modified natural hill. An important find, from Monument 3, was a

The danzantes ("dancers"), now interpreted as slain captives. (Above left) The origins of danzante carving can be traced to this figure from Monument 3 at San José Mogote, dating to the Rosario phase (600–500 BC). (Above right) San José's largest Rosario phase public building. The workman stands beside structure 28. (Right and below) Photograph of one of the Monte Albán danzantes, and a drawing that reconstructs their probable arrangement on Structure L at that site, c. 500–200 BC.

carved slab showing a sprawled human figure (see illus. above).

The carved slab is one of those discoveries which carries wide implications. For it anticipates 300 or more stone slabs carved with human figures found at Monte Albán in the succeeding phase – the so-called *danzantes*, now interpreted as depicting slain captives. To find a precursor at San José Mogote before 500 BC is therefore of particular interest. In addition it may be taken to imply the sacrifice of captives at this early time. Between the feet of the San José figure are signs that may be interpreted as giving the date or name-day

"One Earthquake." This indicates that the 260-day calendar was already in operation at this time.

Monte Albán. The major site of Monte Albán was founded around 500 BC on a mountain not previously occupied. Richard Blanton has suggested that the site was selected as an administrative center precisely because it was on unoccupied, politically neutral ground in the "no man's land" between different arms of the valley. He suggests that its founding might be seen as the result of a confederacy among previously autonomous, and perhaps even competitive chiefdoms from various parts of the valley.

View south across the central plaza at Monte Albán, with the restored ruins of several temples visible. The site was founded on a mountain top in 500 BC.

This view is supported by the apparent cessation of monument construction at centers such as San José Mogote (the largest of them) and Huitzo at roughly the time that Monte Albán was founded. The deliberate fusing of different chiefdom territories in this way could be seen as the initial formation that later led to a state society, a society which continued without a break with Monte Albán as its capital until the demise of the Classic Zapotec state sometime after AD 700. By the time of Monte Albán phase II (200 BC–AD 100), the evidence for the Zapotec state is clear. Monte Albán had become a city with rulers living in palaces. Temples staffed with priests were to be found both here and at secondary and tertiary centers. Ceremonial inscriptions with multiple columns of texts appeared on buildings. These have been interpreted as listing the more than 40 places subjugated by Monte Albán.

This view of the emergence of the state throws the spotlight on the earlier phase I at Monte Albán, from 500 to 200 BC. But unfortunately at Monte Albán itself the evidence is not altogether clear. It can, however, be established that the site was a large one, ultimately by the end of phase I the home of some 10,000–20,000 people. The 300 *danzante* slabs belong to this phase. Fortunately the evidence from Monte Albán can be supplemented by indications from contemporary secondary centers, such as San José Mogote.

Conclusion

The key to this analysis of the emergence of state society in the valley of Oaxaca has been a sound chronology, based in the first instance on a study of successive pottery styles. Radiocarbon dates later provided an absolute chronology. The successive phases of settlement growth could then be studied.

One component in the success of the Oaxaca projects was the use of *intensive field survey* for settlements. In the end a complete survey of the valley was preferred to any sampling strategy. The second component was the *ecological approach*, most crucial for the earlier periods when agriculture was developing, but important also in later phases, when systems of intensification such as irrigation were introduced. The emphasis on *social organization*, using evidence from settlement hierarchy, differences in residences within settlements, and from burials, was a key feature. So too was modern cognitive-processual archaeology and the emphasis on *religion and symbolic systems*. This is brought out by the books by Kent Flannery and Joyce Marcus and their colleagues: *The Cloud People* (1983) and *Zapotec Civilization* (1996), which also exemplify their commitment to the full and accessible publication of their research. The Oaxaca projects are thus of great interest for their methods as well as their results.

RESEARCH AMONG HUNTER-GATHERERS: KAKADU NATIONAL PARK, AUSTRALIA

In 1981–82, a team led by Rhys Jones of the Australian National University carried out a multidisciplinary research program inside Kakadu National Park in the Northern Territory of Australia. This World Heritage area is a tropical region, close to the north coast, and has been made internationally famous as the main location for the *Crocodile Dundee* movies. Few people realize, however, that in terms of the number of its occupied rockshelters and the profusion and probable antiquity of its rock art, Kakadu can be compared with such classic archaeological regions as southwest France.

Preparatory Work, and Aims of the Project

The project involved site survey and excavation in a variety of environments, building on previous work in this and neighboring areas. The first stage was to review all earlier archaeological studies in the area, from 1926 until 1979. These had included some site surveys, and excavations of rockshelters, shell mounds, and open-air sites, and had resulted in a basic knowledge of the stone-tool industries and the regional chronology. It had been revealed – particularly through the work of Carmel Schrire – that the occupation of tropical Australia could be traced back more than 23,000 years. One of the most startling discoveries had been the existence of edge-ground axes 20,000 years ago: at first, doubts were expressed about them by the international archaeological community, because in Europe the grinding of stone was a phenomenon associated with the much later Neolithic period.

In addition, investigation of the region's rock art by George Chaloupka had led him to the conclusion that the earliest art there (the "dynamic figure style") was as old as the Upper Paleolithic art of Europe. As we saw in Chapter 6, Chaloupka's art sequence is linked to environmental change in the region, and particularly to the progression of the sea up the river estuaries.

The new research program was designed to test and improve the results of previous work. More basic information was required for the stratigraphic and typological sequences, as well as for the chronology, including the date of the earliest occupation. In addition, it was necessary to investigate the relationship of the archaeological sequences to paleoenvironmental conditions, including the impact of the first inhabitants and their fires. It was also hoped to obtain a large amount of ethnographic information from the Aboriginal inhabitants of the area.

Collaboration with the Aborigines. Before any new fieldwork could be planned or carried out, it was imperative to consult the local Aboriginal community (see Chapter 14), explain and discuss the plans, and alter or abandon them if necessary. The Aborigines had traditional ties with the areas and specific sites in question, and were the legal owners. They took a keen interest in the details of the project. It was stressed to them that everything would be done openly and could be scrutinized at all times by members of their community. The Aborigines felt that the work should indeed be "supervised" by one of their number, not out of distrust of the archaeologists but rather to protect the diggers from doing something that could bring practical or ritual danger: the totemic geography of a region contains some "dangerous places," into which archaeologists might stray through ignorance.

The Aborigines emphasized that permission to excavate would depend on their perception of the degree of responsibility and decorum with which the work was carried out. The team planned to limit the extent of its excavations (to extract a maximum of information with a minimum of digging), and, after completion, to refill the pits and return the sites to their original condition. The Aborigines also stipulated that work at one

Kakadu National Park is rich in Aboriginal rock art. This figure comes from the Anbangbang site.

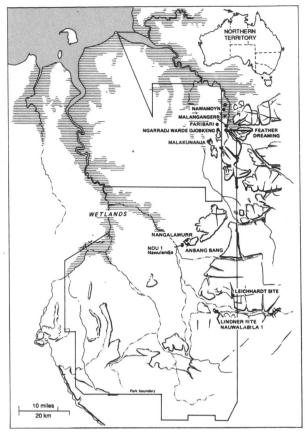

The location and boundaries of Kakadu National Park in Australia's Northern Territory, with the sites studied.

site must be finished before proceeding to another – an admirable dictum for all archaeology!

In order to streamline the work, the excavations were to be integrated not only with the sieving and processing of material but also with preliminary analysis in a field laboratory. Geomorphological work was carried out on the excavated deposits while they were still open. A portable computer was taken into the field, so that data from the worksheets could be entered quickly onto floppy disks. In this way, preliminary analyses could be carried out while still excavation was still continuing, enabling the team to use the results as a guide for formulating the questions about the next phase of excavation and so on. Senior Aborigine men representing the relevant groups accompanied the team on field trips and carefully monitored the excavations, while trainee Aboriginal rangers helped in the laboratory, and were instructed in archaeological procedures.

The Choice of Area and Sites

An area was selected about 60 km (37.5 miles) south of previous foci of investigation, so as to build up a regional pattern of site use. In order to take in a variety of environments, the team chose a transect running NW/SE, from huge open sites on the floodplains and freshwater swamplands of the South Alligator river to the large caves and rockshelters on the edge of a massif, and, finally, to the rockshelters in the inland valley of Deaf Adder Gorge, within the Arnhem Land escarpment. It was hoped that such a transect would provide information on seasonal differences of land use, and also help to contrast freshwater systems with the estuarine areas previously studied to the north.

The project carried out excavations and/or surface collections of artifacts in seven rockshelters. Two of these proved to be of major importance: Anbangbang I for its wealth of preserved organic material, and the Lindner site for its stratified sequence of over 2.5 m (8.2 ft) of sands resting on artifact-bearing rubble that probably dates back 60,000 years according to Optical Dating. A total of 30 radiocarbon determinations have been obtained, two-thirds from archaeological sites and the other third from geomorphological locations designed to resolve archaeological problems: they span a period from 12,000 years ago to modern times.

Anbangbang I Rockshelter

Anbangbang I is a huge rockshelter that seemed suitable for investigation because the material on its ground surface suggested a rich and varied record. It was hoped that this might give a detailed picture of economic activities during the immediate precolonial period, which could in turn be linked with ethnographic information from written sources and from contemporary Aborigines of the area. Another factor was its ease of access from early in the dry season.

Dating and Preservation. It was found that humans started occupying the site considerably before 6000 years ago, and probably in the late Pleistocene (i.e. before 10,000 years ago), judging by the depth and geomorphology of the artifact-bearing gravels. The intensity of occupation (the density of tools and organic remains) increased markedly about 6000 years ago, and then again about 1000 years ago.

The preservation of organic material is remarkable in the site's upper level. Usually, stone tools are the only things to survive in most sandstone rockshelters in tropical Australia – sandy soil conditions generally provide a poor environment for the preservation of anything else. The dry microenvironment at Anbangbang, however, has permitted good preservation, especially at the sheltered rear of the site.

Technology, Diet, and the Division of Labor. Thanks to the good preservation the team was able to assess the relative role of stone as opposed to wood and other organic implements within a "total" toolkit over the last millennium. Stone tools were clearly of less importance than they appear to be in most sites where only inorganic tools survive. There were numerous bone implements (notably large awls), and some had traces of gum resin indicating that they had been barbs, probably hafted onto fishing spears. Almost 40 wooden tools were also recovered, including barbed spearpoints for hunting large game or for fighting.

Numerous slivers and shavings of wood indicated that the manufacture and maintenance of spears were carried out at the rockshelter (by the men, according to ethnography), while women were probably responsible for weaving the string (found in some quantity) from fibers and hair.

Fragments of reeds and bamboo represent the shafts of weapons, and most probably came from the wetlands, at least a day's walk away, perhaps through some system of seasonal trade. Remains of plant resources were so numerous (some of them were retrieved by flotation) that only a sample could be analyzed. Those present through human agency (deduced in part from ethnographic information) had been gathered from the nearby Anbangbang lagoon, no doubt by the women: water-lilies seem to have been exploited intensively, together with tubers and tree-fruits. Women probably also foraged the freshwater turtles, mussels, and crocodile eggs whose remains were recovered. The men, on the other hand, will have foraged the many large fish, as well as the larger animals: over 50 species were hunted. This was, therefore, a broad-spectrum economy.

Not all animals were represented by bones: for example, the echidna's presence was shown only by its quills and feces, suggesting animal intrusion rather than human agency. Proof of human exploitation – as in the case of the large marsupials such as kangaroo

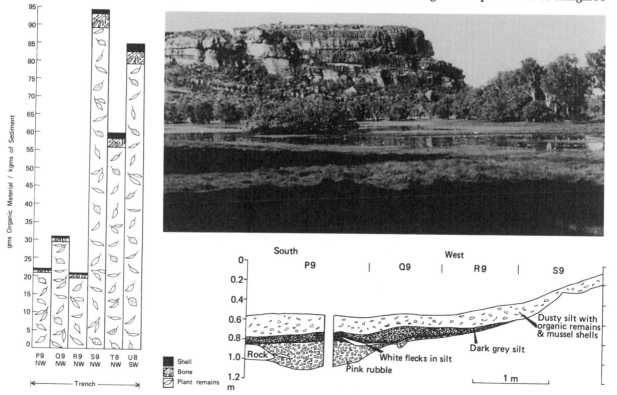

Anbangbang I rockshelter. (Top right) The general area near the site, showing the southwest face of Burrung-gui Cliff, with the Anbangbang lagoon in the foreground. (Left) The relative proportional weight of plant remains, bone, and shell from different trenches excavated at the site. (Above right) Cross-section across trenches P9–S9, showing the stratigraphy.

A sample of the numerous plant remains at Anbangbang I being washed after flotation (Rhys Jones center of picture).

and wallaby – lies in the broken and burnt bones, and in marks of butchering and percussion. The minimum numbers of each mammal species were calculated on the basis of jawbones: the little red flying-fox and the short-nosed bandicoot were most abundant, but the large marsupials provided most meat.

Both plant and animal remains point to a human presence (during the site's final phase, over the last millennium) in the wet season and the early dry season. The site was probably a base camp for a community of men and women, such as a band of perhaps 25 people, who carried out a wide range of domestic activities here. Anbangbang is one of the richest sites in the whole continent.

Lindner Rockshelter

Technology and Art. The Lindner site (Nauwalabila I) is a rockshelter situated within a plateau valley. The meter square excavated to a depth of over 2.5 m (8.2 ft) yielded more than 30,000 stone artifacts – an average of 12,000 per cubic meter, though they were denser at the top of the stratigraphy than below. Only about 1 percent of the material was retouched, showing that quartz and chert tools were fashioned and trimmed on site. In the lower layers, quartzite tools seem to have been brought in ready-made, whereas in the upper layers the final manufacturing of stone spearpoints

was carried out here, with most of the finished products being taken elsewhere. The introduction of these spearpoints occurred between 6200 and 5700 years ago, whereas that of adze/chisels has been dated here to around 3500 years ago. Before these tool types appeared, there were hand-held scrapers and edge-ground axes: flakes from the latter were found down to levels dating to at least 14,000 years ago, which confirm the earlier findings in the region by Carmel Schrire (see above).

No bone material survived, apart from a few small burnt fragments from large mammals. However, one important find was the presence of coloring materials (pieces of red ocher with facets and traces of grinding) throughout the layers, down to a depth of 2.37 m (7 ft 9 in), dated to about 53,000 years ago by Optical Dating of unburnt sediments (see p. 153). Although they may have been used simply for body-painting, they do at least prove some artistic activity in the late Pleistocene, and it is quite probable that these "crayons" were used to prepare pigment for rock art, thus supporting the hypotheses of George Chaloupka about the antiquity of some of the region's depictions.

Thanks to flotation techniques, a sequence of about 200 charcoal samples was retrieved from the stratigraphy, and are now promising a detailed basis for calculating the (apparently steady) rate of accumulation of the deposit, and hence an accurate date for the lowest occupied layers. The Lindner site appears to be one of the oldest habitations in Australia.

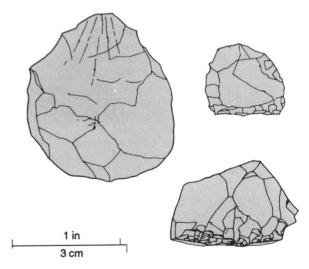

1 in

3 cm

Lindner rockshelter: steep edge scrapers from the lower layers of the site, which yielded more than 30,000 stone artifacts from a meter square excavated to a depth of over 2.5 m (8 ft). Clockwise from top left: quartz, red chert, and pink chert.

The Wetland-Edge Sites

The wetland edges proved to have a series of large, open sites (up to 25,000 sq. m or 269,000 sq. ft in area) mostly on headlands of dry land that were strategically located close to the rich food resources of the swamps. These sites seemed to consist mostly of surface scatters of thousands of artifacts, though one site (Ki'na) consisted of a shallow midden of freshwater mussel shells. The research team sampled each site's scatter by using a line of 1 m squares, 10 m (c. 33ft) apart, along its major axis, thus providing some idea of variation in the density of material, and within-site patterning of different elements. In addition, on each site at least one area, 5 m (just over 16ft) square, was laid out and subdivided into 25 × 1 m squares, from which separate, total collections of surface archaeological material were made, to obtain extra information on configurations of material. The 5-m squares were located arbitrarily, after initial survey, in areas of least disturbance or which seemed to provide as large and varied a sample as possible.

Among the millions of stone flakes and other artifacts – which, it must be remembered, were all carried into the sites by the occupants as there is no stone in the wetlands – there were many of quartz from nearby sources, whereas quartzite had been brought from a distance of 20–40 km (12–25 miles), and chert from over 50 km (31 miles). There were also grinding stones of sandstone and volcanic rock (brought from outcrops a few kilometers away, no doubt for the processing of plant foods), and adze/chisel slugs. Under strong magnification, it was found that some of the slugs had a narrow band of high polish, just a few micrometers wide, together with striations at right angles to the edge, which fit the criteria for wear caused by working hardwoods.

In many wetland sites (but not the inland sites), flakes were found, often unretouched, with a thick silica polish on them, probably caused by plant phytoliths when cutting grasses or reeds. The Japanese researcher Hiroshi Fujiwara processed soil samples from the Ki'na freshwater swamp, and also from archaeological sites (both wetland open sites and from rockshelter excavations) and found phytoliths primarily from wild rice (*Oryza*), as well as from grasses and reeds. The fact that no rice phytoliths were found at Anbangbang suggests that this plant was unavailable at the nearby lagoon.

It is clear, therefore, that in the recent past the wetland edges were densely occupied, most probably specifically in the dry season to take advantage of the wetland resources (especially plants and water birds).

The base of the Ki'na midden was dated to 500 years ago, and it is reckoned that all these sites are of similar age (ranging between 1000 and 500 years). The reason for the increase in settlement at this particular time was established by paleoenvironmental work, to which we now turn.

The Broader Picture: Changes in Environment and Economy

A section of the team studied the past and present landscape around the archaeological sites, attempting to assess how and why it has changed, especially over the last 35,000 years. Soil samples were removed for sedimentary and pollen analysis as well as for radiocarbon dating of organic materials. One of the most crucial dates was that of about 1400 years ago for the base of the freshwater peats, showing that the creation of the freshwater swamps is a fairly recent event.

It was established that the most substantial change came when the postglacial rise in sea-level flooded the Alligator river valleys; these estuarine conditions existed by 6000 or 7000 years ago, a fact that fits well with the worldwide sea-level curve. Saltwater extended well up the valleys, and large areas of saline plains and mudflats evolved. Subsequently, there was a period of infilling of the river valleys, with silt and sand deposits building up into levees; freshwater was ponded up behind them, and eventually within the last 2000 years created the rich and productive freshwater wetlands that were seasonally flooded. It will be recalled (see Chapter 6) that George Chaloupka's theories link the styles of rock art in the region to these same transformations of the landscape. No evidence was found by the project team for great change in the inland vegetation over this period.

The sparse early archaeological material suggests that, before the formation of the freshwater swamps, population density was low, with occupation perhaps sporadic or seasonal. The arrival of the sea around 6000 years ago seems (from the evidence discovered at Anbangbang) to have led to denser occupation; but clearly it was the creation of freshwater swamps about 1000 years ago that transformed the landscape, dramatically increasing the population density and leading the local Aborigines to alter their economy in order to take full advantage of the newly available food resources.

Large groups of people camped at the swamp edges, probably in the dry season, and carried out many maintenance and production activities there. The same groups may have occupied the inland shelters during the dry season; here the effects of the changed land-

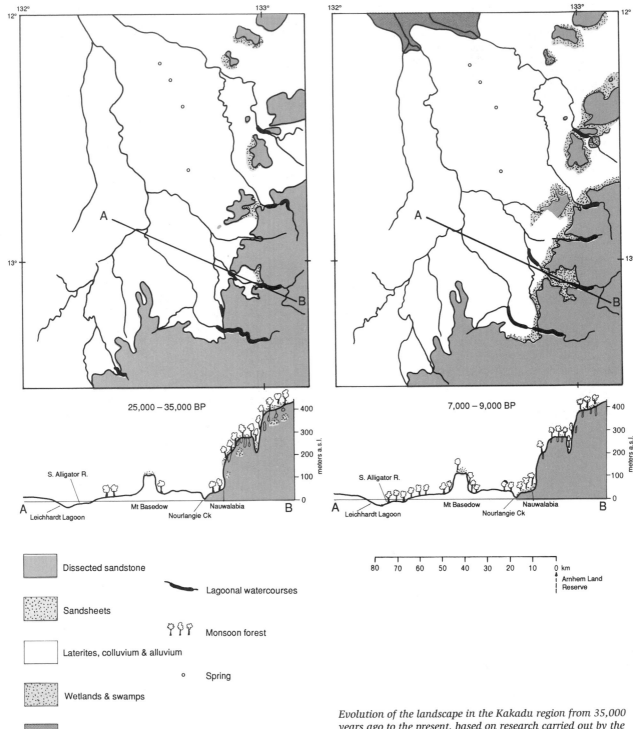

25,000 – 35,000 BP

7,000 – 9,000 BP

Dissected sandstone

Lagoonal watercourses

Sandsheets

Monsoon forest

Laterites, colluvium & alluvium

Spring

Wetlands & swamps

Saline flats & blacksoil plains

Evolution of the landscape in the Kakadu region from 35,000 years ago to the present, based on research carried out by the multidisciplinary project led by Rhys Jones.

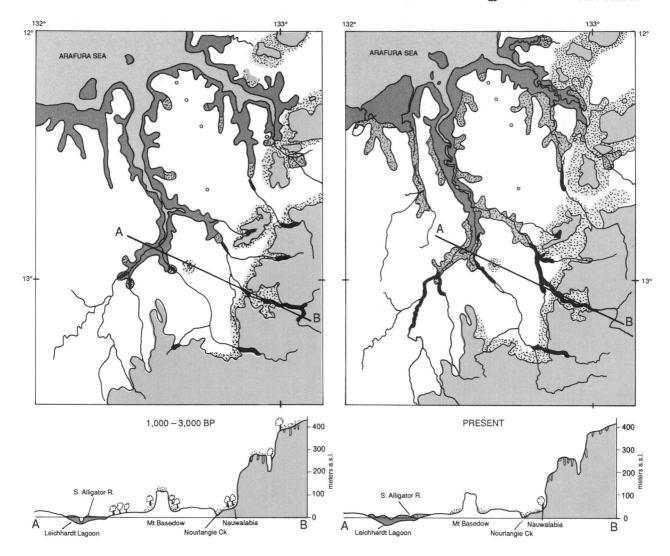

scape are less marked, but still detectable in the archaeological remains.

In addition, the sediments in the shelters provide some clues to the long-term human use of the landscape. Studies suggest that the sediments accumulated largely as a result of human activity in the vicinity. For example, the practice of regular burning caused soil erosion, which built up the sediments. The gradual erosion of the sandstone shelters themselves also contributed to the deposits. Changes in the rate of accumulation thus helped the team to judge how intensely people used the sites and the landscape, and corresponded well with the results obtained from other types of evidence.

Conclusion

The Kakadu project was thus very successful in producing a new and detailed picture of environment, subsistence, population, and technology in this important region of Australia for the past 60 millennia. In particular, it proved that there had been a significant increase in the number of sites, in population density, and in the intensity of site-use that can be closely correlated with the transformation of the landscape and its productivity.

Publication of the work followed swiftly: an interim report was produced by March 1983, and a monograph in 1985.

515

KHOK PHANOM DI: THE ORIGINS OF RICE FARMING IN SOUTHEAST ASIA

Aims of the Project

In 1984–85, the New Zealand archaeologist Charles Higham and Thai archaeologist Rachanie Thosarat excavated a large mound, 12 m (39 ft) high and covering 5 ha (12 acres), situated on a flat plain 22 km (14 miles) from the coast of the Gulf of Siam in central Thailand. The site lies an hour's drive east from modern Bangkok. Its name, Khok Phanom Di, means "good mound," and it is visible for miles around. The rice-growing lowlands here form part of one of the world's richest agricultural ecosystems, but very little was known of their archaeology. So a major aim of the project was to investigate the origins and development of an agricultural system on which a large proportion of humanity depends.

The Searchers

Areas of northeast Thailand had been quite extensively studied in the early 1970s, yielding such major sites as Ban Chiang and Non Nok Tha, the excavation of which by Chester Gorman and others provided evidence for a local tradition of bronze-working dating from about 1500 BC. Central and coastal Thailand, on the other hand, had seen little systematic archaeological work until the onset of the Khok Phanom Di project. The site was discovered by Thai archaeologists in the late 1970s and they took samples in 1978 and dug test squares in 1979 and 1982. The Thai excavator, Damrongkiadt Noksakul, obtained a radiocarbon date for human bone from the oldest burial he had found of 4800 BC. If the new excavation could discover evidence of rice cultivation here at this early date, it would begin to rival the earliest dates for domesticated rice known from China.

What Is Left?

Preservation of some materials was outstanding at the site: some postholes still contained their original wood in place, and the layers were rich in organic remains such as leaves, nuts, rice-husk fragments, and fish scales. No fewer than 154 human burials came to light, with bones and shell ornaments intact – one of the largest and certainly the best provenienced collections of human remains from Southeast Asia. Some graves yielded sheets of a white fabric which proved to be shrouds of unwoven fabric – some of beaten bark, others sheets of asbestos, the earliest such use known use

of this material which occurs naturally in Thailand, and which was highly valued in the ancient world as it was virtually indestructible and fire-resistant. Bodies lay on wooden biers.

Where?

A 10 × 10 m (33 × 33 ft) square – large enough to give adequate information on the spatial dimension at the site – was dug in the central part of the mound, a spot chosen by the Abbot of the local Buddhist temple because it would avoid damaging any of his trees. A roof was built over the square to permit work even in the rainy season, and brick walls were required to prevent water filling the excavation.

After more than seven months of hard and continuous work the excavation came to an end when the natural mud flat layer was finally encountered at the considerable depth of 7 m (23 ft). Many years of laboratory analysis of the tons of excavated material lay ahead.

Before beginning the excavation of Khok Phanom Di, Higham, Thosarat, and three other colleagues had spent six weeks undertaking a site survey in this part of the Bang Pakong Valley. They walked the survey area 20 m (65 ft) apart, studied aerial photographs, and interviewed local villagers and Buddhist priests. The

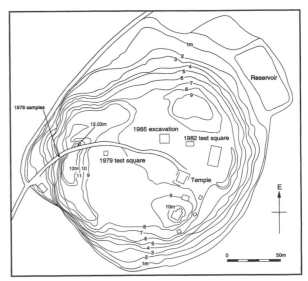

Plan of the almost circular mound of Khok Phanom Di, Thailand, which covers about 5 ha (12 acres). It rises to a maximum of just over 12 m (39 ft) above the flood plain.

The searchers at Khok Phanom Di. In 1984–85 excavations were undertaken by New Zealand and Thai archaeologists, led by Charles Higham and Rachanie Thosarat. (Above) The roof covers the excavation; the site was chosen by the local Buddhist Abbot. (Right) The excavators encountered an extraordinarily deep and detailed stratigraphic sequence.

survey showed, if nothing else, that Khok Phanom Di was not an isolated site, but one of several early villages in the area. In 1991 Higham and Thosarat returned to the valley to begin the excavation of one of these sites: Nong Nor (see pp. 521–22).

When?

It had been assumed, from impressions gained in the field and the dates obtained by earlier excavators from human bone, that Khok Phanom Di had first been settled in the 5th millennium BC. Its numerous hearths provided charcoal samples for radiocarbon dating. First results from six samples studied at a laboratory in Wellington, New Zealand, gave one early date, but the series did not form a coherent pattern. Then the Australian National University laboratory produced an internally consistent series of dates based on 12 samples. Interestingly, however, these ANU results revealed that the site was occupied for a far shorter time than had been thought – a few centuries rather than millennia. Higham and Thosarat concluded that the settlement had been occupied from about 2000 BC for 500 years (after calibration of the dates). Although this was disappointing in some ways (in terms of finding early dates for rice cultivation), it nevertheless meant that the 154 burials from the site might well rep-

resent an unbroken mortuary tradition – a rare occurrence at any site, anywhere in the world. This resulted from the very rapid accumulation of cultural remains which, in effect, kept pace with the successive superimposed interments.

Social Organization

It was quickly noticed that the graves occurred in clusters, with spaces between. Computer graphics were used to plot their concentrations in three dimensions. A very detailed burial sequence was worked out, which provided insights into the community's kinship system over about 20 generations. (Assuming about 20 years per generation, this gave a timespan of about 400 years, satisfactorily close to the 500 years allocated by radiocarbon dating for the duration of the site.) Variations in the presence and quantity of gravegoods – shell jewelry, pottery vessels, clay anvils, and

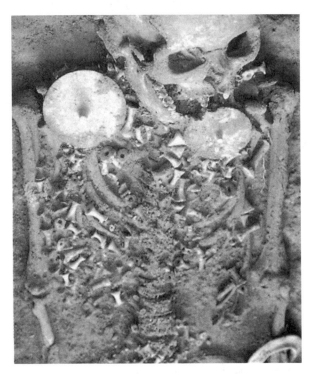

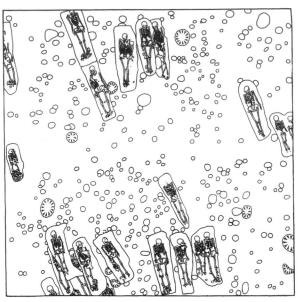

(Left) The "Princess," who was accompanied by a set of shell jewelry, with over 120,000 beads, a headdress, and a bracelet, as well as fine pottery vessels. (Above) In Mortuary Phase 4 the dead were buried individually, in neat rows.

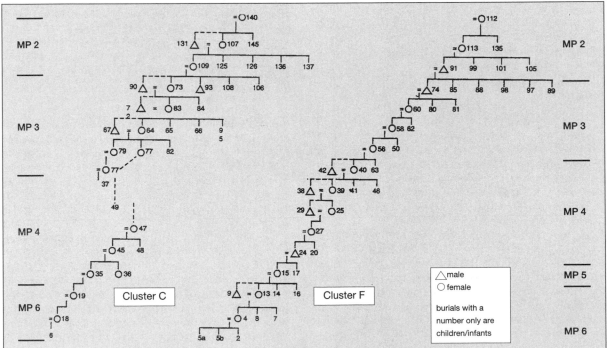

Two prehistoric family trees. Analysis of the skeletal remains from mortuary phases 2 to 6 allowed the archaeologists to suggest two genealogical sequences, C and F. Tracing families down the generations like this is extremely rare in prehistory.

burnishing stones – were analyzed with multivariate statistics, namely cluster analysis (see box, p. 197), principal component analysis, and multidimensional scaling (see box, pp. 206–07). It was found that there was no significant difference in overall wealth between males and females, though in the later phases they displayed variations: clay anvils were found only with females and the young, while turtle-shell ornaments were found only with males. Also in these later phases, there was a predominance of women, some of them buried with considerable wealth – one, nicknamed the "Princess," had over 120,000 shell beads, as well as other objects, a profusion and richness never before encountered in prehistoric Southeast Asia. But the descendants of the "Princess" were buried with very few grave-goods: this was not a society in which social ranking was inherited.

Nevertheless there was a clear link between the wealth of children and the adults with whom they were buried – poor children accompanied poor adults, or both categories were rich; a person's age does not seem to have been a determining factor in the quantity of grave-goods. Infants who failed to survive beyond birth were buried in their own graves or with an adult, though without grave-goods; but those who survived a few months before dying were given the same funerary treatment as adults.

Analysis by the physical anthropologist Nancy Tayles of the human remains (see pp. 520–21) suggested that two main clusters of burials represented successive generations of two distinct family groups. A number of genetically determined hereditary features in skulls, teeth, and bones enabled relationships between some individuals to be established, and these links confirmed that the individual's comprising each cluster were related. Patterns of tooth extraction were found in both sexes: the commonest was the removal of both upper first incisors in men and women, but only women had all the lower incisors removed as well. The consistency of some patterns was compatible with their being markers for successive members of the same family line.

Environment

The site is surrounded by flat rice fields, and is now 22 km (14 miles) east of the sea. However, it used to be located at the mouth of an estuary, on an ancient shoreline formed when the sea was higher than its present level, between 4000 and 1800 BC. This was deduced from radiocarbon dating of charcoal in cores taken by the paleoecologist Bernard Maloney from sediments in the Bang Pakong Valley, 200 m (650 ft) north

of the site. These cores, which document human and natural environments back to the 6th millennium BC, also contained pollen grains, fern spores, and leaf fragments; there were several periods – 5300, 5000, and 4300 BC – showing peaks of charcoal, fern spores, and the pollen of weeds associated today with rice-field cultivation. Although rice cannot be identified directly from pollen, the decline in tree species, rise in burning, and increase in rice-field weeds could reflect agriculture in this area in the 5th millennium BC. Subsequent analysis of the plant phytoliths (see p. 242) from the cores confirmed at least part of this hypothesis. Phytoliths of rice (whether wild or domesticated cannot yet be determined) were discovered together with those of agricultural field weeds at the 5th-millennium BC level – although they disappear shortly after, not to return until about 3000 BC, approximately 1000 years before the first occupation of Khok Phanom Di. The phytoliths however, suggested that the earliest episodes of burning are more likely associated with fuel production than agricultural activity. Thus, while the burning could have been associated with agriculture, burn-offs by hunter-gatherers, or even normal conflagrations might have been involved as well.

The deposits in the excavated square were found to contain ostracodes and forams, minute aquatic creatures with restricted habitats. Their frequencies in successive layers demonstrated that the site used to be on, or near, an estuary, with freshwater marshes behind it. Eventually, however, the sea retreated, and brackish water came to dominate, but with freshwater ponds still nearby.

Organic remains from the excavation were collected by the paleobotanist Jill Thompson using flotation – which yielded charred seeds, fragments of rice, and tiny snails. Some potsherds near the bottom of the site were encrusted with barnacles, indicating that the site had once been low-lying and overrun by seawater during tidal surges. Thousands of fragments of bone were recovered from mammals, fish, birds, and turtles, as well as the remains of crabs and shellfish. Their analysis revealed the presence of crocodile and open-coast birds such as cormorants in early contexts, but marshland and mangrove birds like pelicans and herons in later phases. Finally, marine and riverine species were replaced by birds of woodland and forest, such as crows and broadbills, together with porcupines and bandicoots, animals that prefer dry conditions. Similarly, the fish remains show a predominance of estuarine species in the early phases, but later freshwater fish took over; and the molluscs showed a change from sandy-coast and marine species to mangrove, estuarine, freshwater, and ultimately land species.

It was therefore clear that the site was originally located on a slight elevation by an estuary, near an open coast with some clear sandy areas. The sea gradually retreated as sedimentation increased the site's distance from the shore. Eventually the river itself moved away to the west: this change to a non-estuarine habitat may have involved the formation of an oxbow lake, preventing ready access to the river, or even a major flood which moved the river away from the site.

Diet

The site yielded well over a million shellfish, as well as animal bones and seeds. Since the shells could not all be transported to a laboratory, the commonest species, a cockle, was counted in the field and 10 percent of its shells were kept. This cockle, *Anadara granosa*, is adapted to mudflats and found in estuarine locations. A mere eight species comprised 99.4 percent of the shellfish, all of them sources of food.

However, it appears from food residues and other evidence that fish and rice were the staple diet here, as they are today. In the grave of one woman, who died in her mid-40s, a mass of tiny bones was found in her pelvic area – not a fetus, as first thought, but the remains of her last meal: bones and scales from *Anabas testudineus*, the climbing perch, a small freshwater fish. Tiny pieces of rice chaff were found among the scales, together with stingray teeth. Another grave contained human feces which, under the microscope, revealed many fragments of rice husk whose morphology indicated that the rice was domesticated. Among the husks was a beetle, *Oryzaphilus surinamensis*, which is often found in stored products such as rice, and hair from mice, which may also have haunted the site's rice stores. Finally, some pottery vessels had been tempered with rice chaff before firing; some potsherds had a thin layer of clay on the outside, containing a dense concentration of rice husk fragments; and fragments of rice were recovered from the archaeological deposits.

Clay net-weights provided further evidence for fishing, as did bone fishhooks which became increasingly rare with time. Few large animals were represented – mostly macaques and pigs – showing that they were of little importance as food; it is not clear whether the pigs were domestic or wild. No domestic animal apart from the dog has been positively identified.

Technology

Khok Phanom Di was a center for pottery-making throughout its occupation, being located in an area rich in clay deposits. Thick spreads of ash indicated where people had probably fired their pots, and some graves contained clay anvils, clay cylinders, and burnishing pebbles, implements used in the shaping and decoration of pots. The techniques of pot decoration remained virtually unchanged throughout the centuries of the site's occupation, but new forms and motifs were introduced. The site produced tons of pottery, about 250,000 shell beads, and thousands of other artifacts – many as grave-goods, but others discarded when broken or lost.

Some shells had been modified and apparently used as tools. There were striations and polished areas on their concave surfaces. Experiments with similar shells showed that some of these marks were formed by abrading them with sandstone from the site to sharpen their cutting edge. A series of possible uses were tried out – cutting wild grasses, incising designs on pottery, cutting bark-cloth, and processing fish, taro (a tropical food plant), meat, and hair. The prehistoric and modern experimental specimens were then examined under the scanning electron microscope, and some tasks could be eliminated at once: the prehistoric shells had clearly not been used to decorate pottery, gut fish or cut bark-cloth. By far the most likely function was harvesting a grass such as rice, which not only produced the same pattern of striations and polish but also required frequent sharpening.

Although no remains of woven fabric have survived, the abundance of cord-marked pottery and the existence of fish nets (as shown by the presence of net-weights) indicate the use of twine and cordage. Small bone implements with a chisel-shaped end and a groove down one side have been tentatively interpreted as shuttles, used in weaving cloth.

What Contact Did They Have?

Thin sections taken from some of the site's stone adzes helped to pinpoint likely sources of materials; it was found that the stone quarries must have been in the uplands to the east, where outcrops of andesite and volcanic sand- and siltstones occur. One adze of calcareous sandstone must have come from 100 km (63 miles) to the northeast.

Since the site contains almost no stone flakes, it is probable that the occupants obtained ready-made stone adzeheads in exchange for their fine ceramics and shell ornaments.

What Were They Like?

In Southeast Asia it is unusual for soil conditions to allow the preservation of bone, but at Khok Phanom Di the excavation encountered a "vertical cemetery," an accumulation through time of 154 inhumations. After conservation of the bones and two years of analysis by Nancy Tayles they could be aged and sexed, as far as was possible, and other indicators used – for example, pelvic scarring indicated whether a woman had given birth. In terms of health, it was found that the earliest occupants of the site had been relatively tall with good, strong bone development indicating a sound diet. Nevertheless, they had died in their 20s and 30s, and half had perished at birth or soon after. A thickening of their skulls suggested anemia, probably caused by the blood disorder thalassemia (which may paradoxically have provided some resistance to the malarial mosquito). The adults also suffered some dental disease, and considerable tooth wear owing to the number of shellfish consumed.

In this early group, the men – but not the women – suffered degeneration of the joints, especially on the right side, indicating regular and vigorous use of these limbs, probably from paddling canoes. Men and women also had different diets, as shown by their tooth wear and decay.

A subsequent phase features a notable fall in infant mortality, but men were smaller and less robust than before, with less degeneration of the joints, suggesting they were relatively inactive. They also had healthier teeth, no doubt caused by a different diet incorporating fewer shellfish

The human feces found in one burial contained an egg, probably from the intestinal fluke *Fasciolopsis buski*, which finds its way into the human digestive system through the eating of aquatic plants. However, there is no evidence whatsoever of violence or warfare; there are no injuries or traumas visible in the human bones.

Why Did Things Change?

All these varied categories of evidence form a fairly coherent picture. At first, the occupants had the river close by, and offshore colonies of shellfish suitable for the manufacture of jewelry. Despite high infant mortality and anemia, the men were active and robust, with particular strength on the right, probably caused by canoeing. Some people were buried with considerable wealth. The men were engaged in fishing and obtaining supplies of shell, while the women probably made pots in the dry season and worked in the rice fields during the wet.

It is known from ethnography that environments of this kind can expect a disastrous flood every 50 years or so, with not only inundation but also destruction of

fields and the relocation of rivers. The excavators believe that this is what caused the changes in the environmental and archaeological record at Khok Phanom Di after about 10 generations: the large river burst its banks and relocated to the west. By this time, the sea was already some distance away, and silty water had eliminated many of the shellfish used for jewelry.

Following the change, hardly any shell beads are found with the dead, and pottery was less decorative. The men were less robust, less active; fishhooks and net-weights were no longer made, there were fewer marine and estuarine fish, less shellfish, and teeth show a less abrasive diet. This all suggests that once the flood had occurred, the site no longer had easy access to the coast, so men stopped going out to the estuary or sea in boats.

In the later phase, there was a dramatic rise in wealth, and burials were more elaborate, while pottery vessels became larger and display enormous skill. Women now predominated in the cemetery, and one of them had very well-developed wrist muscles. It has therefore been hypothesized, through ethnographic accounts from the islands of Melanesia, that the rise in wealth, prestige, and power came from exchange activities. There was a development of craft specialization, centered on the women; they made pottery masterpieces, which were traded for the shells that could no longer be obtained locally. Hence their skill was converted into status in the community. The women may have become entrepreneurs, with men in a subservient role; or conversely, the men may have exploited the women's skill to boost their own status, and placed their womenfolk in large graves, accompanied by a great wealth of rare and prestigious shell jewelry.

Conclusion

One of the principal original aims of the project had been to help elucidate the origins and rise of rice agriculture in Southeast Asia. Settlement at the site itself proved to be too late (2000 BC) to overturn the conventional view that rice cultivation began further north in China, in the Yangzi Valley, before 5000 BC and spread south from there. But pollen and phytolith analysis of cores from sediments around Khok Phanom Di provided elusive evidence for at least some agricultural activity involving wild or domesticated rice as early as the 5th millennium BC in this part of Thailand.

The more recent excavations conducted by the same team at Nong Nor, 14 km (9 miles) to the south, have helped clarify this situation. Nong Nor comprises in its first phase a coastal site dating to 2400 BC. Its pottery,

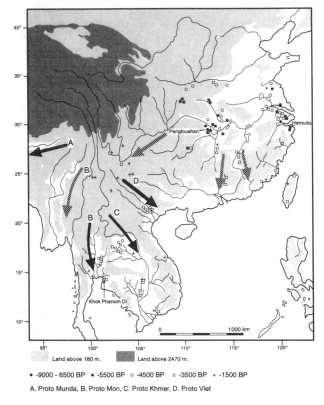

Land above 180 m.   Land above 2470 m.

• -9000 - 6500 BP ■ -5500 BP ○ -4500 BP □ -3500 BP + -1500 BP

A. Proto Munda, B. Proto Mon, C. Proto Khmer, D. Proto Viet

The spread of rice agriculture and languages in Southeast Asia.

bone, and stone industries are virtually identical with those from early Khok Phanom Di. But there is no rice, nor are there any shell harvesting knives or stone hoes. Higham and Thosarat suggest that this represents a coastal hunter-gatherer tradition, and that rice cultivation was introduced into Thailand between 2400 and 2000 BC, ultimately from the Yangzi Valley. In this interpretation, the early inhabitants of Khok Phanom Di would have either adopted the new resource, or perhaps themselves experimented with the plant.

The excavation and analysis of Khok Phanom Di have been exemplary for several reasons. To begin with, they demonstrate just how much information can be obtained from a single burial site with good preservation, using a truly multidisciplinary approach. The many years of analysis of the site's stratigraphy, the human bones, shellfish, charcoal samples, plant remains, and artifacts, have culminated in the publication of a wide range of reports, notably a full-scale four-volume research report (Higham and others 1990–93), with three more volumes planned, and a shorter synthesis by Higham and Thosarat (1994). Above all, the project has shown that well-focused research can both cast new light on an issue of wide general importance – the origins of Southeast Asian agriculture – and also greatly increase our understanding of the local archaeological record in a previously little researched region of the world.

YORK AND THE PUBLIC PRESENTATION OF ARCHAEOLOGY

York is one of the great early cities of Europe, at times in its history it was the most important place in northern England and second in significance only to London; it is also the home of one of Britain's great cathedrals, York Minster. Successively the site of a Roman legionary headquarters, an Anglo-Saxon royal and monastic center, and a major Viking town, York retained its importance in Norman and medieval times and today offers a fine illustration of the complexity of archaeology in a continuously occupied city where the ancient and the modern are in close proximity.

We have chosen here to discuss the work of the York Archaeological Trust (YAT) in particular for two reasons. First, because the story of its origin and development provides a good example of the professional response to the conservation problems of urban archaeology, where the rescue issues are much the same as they would be in Peking, or Delhi, or downtown Manhattan (see pp. 216–17). And second, perhaps more importantly, because the Trust was a pioneer

in techniques seeking actively to engage the interest of a much broader public, and has developed innovative and highly successful approaches to achieve this, most notably the Jorvik Viking Centre (see below).

Background and Aims

From as early as the 1820s the archaeology of York had been of interest to local antiquarians, notably the Yorkshire Philosophical Society. In 1960 the first major survey of York was carried out by the Royal Commission on the Historical Monuments of England (RCHME). This survey highlighted Roman York, but in the course of the 1960s further work by the Commission brought to light York's Anglian and Viking phases, and between 1966 and 1972 excavations by the RCHME under York Minster, which was in danger of collapse, produced a record of continuous occupation from AD 79 to 1080 – one of the most important sequences in Europe.

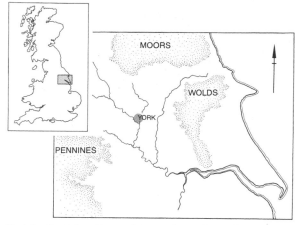

York is situated at the confluence of two rivers, the Ouse and the Foss. (Right) Excavations in progress at Coppergate, before the construction of the shopping complex and Jorvik Viking Centre on the same site.

It was proposals for an inner ring road in the late 1960s, however, which caused alarm bells to ring, coupled with the general awareness at that time of the destructiveness of urban development across Britain. The York Archaeological Trust was formed in 1972 from a consortium of interests and Peter Addyman became its first Director. Its aim was to save archaeological evidence before it was destroyed by development – what has been called "preservation by record" (see p. 550), and Addyman took the decision to excavate only those sites under threat.

Already in that year there were salvage excavations on a number of sites. For instance, beneath the Lloyds Bank building over 5 m (16½ ft) of minutely stratified organic-rich deposits were found, dating from the 9th to the 11th centuries (see illus. p. 526). These had been airtight from the time of their deposition, and a wide range of organic materials of kinds which do not normally survive were preserved due to the anaerobic conditions, such as textiles, leather and wooden objects, industrial waste and coprolites, and biological organisms. It became clear that widespread area excavations in the Pavement-Coppergate area of the city could be expected to reveal in unprecedented detail the layout of a Viking Age town, preserved from that period in Anglo-Saxon history, prior to the Norman Conquest of AD 1066, when Scandinavian invaders dominated the north of England.

In the early days there were difficulties with some developers, whose permission and cooperation was by no means guaranteed. Out of such problems, not least in York itself, came national legislation, "The Ancient Monuments and Archaeological Areas Act" of 1979, as a result of which central York was designated one of the nation's five Areas of Archaeological Importance.

For the next decade excavations were undertaken with the ultimate backing of a four-and-a-half month mandatory period of access, and many such excavations were carried out. But in 1989, through complex circumstances at the site of the Queen's Hotel, it became evident that this provision was insufficient. Similar problems arose in the same year at the site of Shakespeare's Rose theater in London (see p. 550).

Then in 1990 Martin Carver of the University of York and the engineering firm Ove Arup & Partners were commissioned by English Heritage and the City of York to produce a report on the methods and aims of urban archaeology. The report featured a predictive map of York's deposits and a research program whereby sites can be either excavated if they have a research priority or preserved if they do not. Several ideas contained in the report, notably the concept of "evaluation," were incorporated into the document being prepared at this time by the British Government – Planning Policy Guidance paper 16, which brought forward a new philosophy towards archaeology and development. PPG 16 stresses that archaeology is an irreplaceable resource, and makes the presumption in favor of preservation when archaeological deposits are threatened by development; it also stipulates that necessary archaeological work will be carried out at the expense of the developer. This brought about the legal and planning system within which salvage archaeology works in Britain today. From 1990 much of the work carried out by the Trust has been undertaken as paid contractor to developer clients, carrying out projects specified by the City Archaeologist for York.

The objectives of YAT include "a broadly based examination of the whole process of urbanization over the past two millennia," and involve a pragmatic approach to the opportunities which minor works and major developments within the city may offer. Moreover there is a recognition that different classes of evidence must be brought to bear, for instance one objective of the Trust is to integrate the quantities of new archaeological data about medieval York with the evidence derived from place names, documentary sources, and standing buildings. However, one of the special and original aims of the Trust which evolved as a result of opportunities that arose during the course of work, was to present their findings in new and innovative ways to the public (see below).

Although here we are choosing to focus on the work of YAT, it was not, of course, carried out in isolation by the Trust alone. The excavations beneath York Minster by the RCHME – still the largest and most important to have taken place in York – have already been mentioned. A major urban project of this kind is always a cooperative work by a number of organizations, and in addition to the York Archaeological Trust and the Royal Commission, the Department of Archaeology at the University of York, the City of York Council, and the national organization English Heritage have all played major roles. The success of archaeology in York has depended upon such cooperation and indeed it provides an important lesson for urban archaeology everywhere.

Survey, Recording, and Conservation

On an urban site, a certain amount of potentially valuable information inevitably turns up in an uncontrolled way as a result of building activity. Such information can still be incorporated successfully into the whole picture. As Peter Addyman wrote in 1974:

> "Holes of one sort or another are always being dug throughout the city. In 1972 it has been calculated over 1500 were excavated by the Corporation alone. The Trust has therefore adopted the policy whereby chance finds are recorded systematically to help build up evidence for the extent, character, and intensity of settlement in the past."

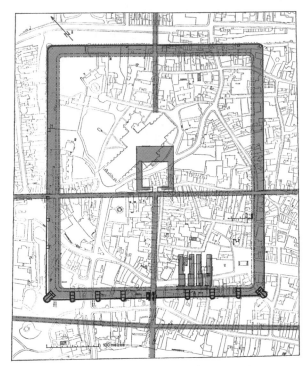

The outline of the Roman legionary fortress at York superimposed on a plan of the modern city.

Skillful use of the available information can also suggest how next to proceed. For instance the indications of the plan of the Roman fortress revealed in the early stages of excavation, or already known, allowed a hypothetical plan to be drawn predicting where other traces would be found. The results of the urban survey of York were integrated into two maps produced in 1988 by the Ordnance Survey (the national British cartographic agency) in collaboration with the Trust and the RCHME. The first summarized what is known of Roman and Anglian York, and the second Viking and Medieval York.

As noted above, during the lifetime of YAT the climate of urban archaeology in Britain has changed, as Addyman recognized in 1992:

> "It seems possible that the era of large-scale excavation may be over. In a certain sense the Trust's first two decades may turn out to have been a golden age for York archaeology, for the large-scale excavations have transformed archaeological knowledge of the city. The 1990s, however, are a more responsible age, in which only a sustainable utilization of the archaeological resources is permitted. The new more selective approach to excavation will demand new

theoretical approaches. There will be emphasis on non-destructive evaluation by remote sensing; for example by radar; correlation of existing data through creation of sites and monuments records; predictive modeling by computer; and the use of GIS."

Such methods have been used at York, and the excavations from the outset began to develop a standardized system of recording, using a pre-printed "context card" for each stratigraphic unit. With the development of low-cost computers a Computer Integrated Finds Record system has been developed to cope with the vast quantities of artifacts, and an Integrated Archaeological Data Base to allow interrogation of the excavation and finds data generated in more than 25 years of continued excavation.

Recording systems have been developed and refined, and photogrammetry, based on measurement from stereoscopically projected pairs of photographs, has been used to produce the primary drawn record by the English Heritage photogrammetry unit, based in York. The definitive record of the Coppergate Anglian helmet (see below) was also achieved by photogrammetry and by holography. In some cases the simpler but useful technique of rectified photography has been used, even for site recording, as at the medieval cemetery at Jewbury. Here rectified vertical photography of each burial enabled the cemetery to be recorded at great speed. The human remains have now been reburied so the photographs form the only source of new information.

Conservation work has also been a major concern and a laboratory for waterlogged materials, including leather and wood, was established in 1981. Among other things, it has had to cope with structural features including 6-m (20-ft) long timbers from the Viking buildings in Coppergate. The Trust laboratory is now one of the main regional conservation centers: the York Archaeological Wood Centre opened at the laboratory in 1993, and is the national wetwood treatment center for English Heritage.

Excavations at York produced a large amount of wood and leather preserved due to the anaerobic conditions. The York Archaeological Trust's laboratory set up to conserve this material is now one of the main regional centers for this type of work.

Alongside this work, Julian Richards and Paul Miller of the Department of Archaeology, University of York, have developed a GIS for York. Data relating to deposits, monuments, as well as accidental finds can be stored in this way and used to create models of surfaces in York at a given period.

History and Dating

The broad historical outline of the Roman conquest, the Anglo-Saxon period, the Scandinavian ("Viking") invasions and the arrival of the Normans in AD 1067 are clearly established for York from historical sources (see below). But the detailed stratigraphic sequences, especially for the Anglo-Saxon and Viking periods, were able to bring a much better definition to the developmental sequence for the pottery and other artifacts.

A computer program is now used to reconcile the recorded relationships of the various site contexts and produce a comprehensive interpretive periodization. For instance, at the site for the new Lloyds Bank, on the street called Pavement, the stratigraphic sequence provided samples for radiocarbon dating, and these as well as coin finds permitted a precise chronological control for the pottery fabrics known as York Ware and Torksey Ware. A series of dendrochronological determinations for the Coppergate site has confirmed and further refined the ceramic chronology.

Phases of Urban Development

The study of deep stratigraphy on an urban site allows special insights into the development of urban life, particularly when there is abundant evidence also from written sources. For each of the main phases of occupation we know the name of the settlement from written texts (and often from locally issued coins). There is also the possibility, at least from the medieval period, of using charters, leases, and other documents relating to land tenure to relate to actual urban plots of land under excavation. Thus "Domesday Book," a national land survey conducted in the late 11th century AD, records two churches, All Saints and St. Crux, in the Coppergate and Pavement area of the City and a deed of AD 1176 relates to "land in Ousegate in the parish of St. Crux." The Shambles is also mentioned in Domesday Book, demonstrating that this street-line at least was already in existence before the Norman Conquest. Insights into successive urban phases have thus been gained, building up the picture of York's development:

Eburacum. Roman York. The legionary fortress and the adjoining Roman town (or *Colonia*) have been

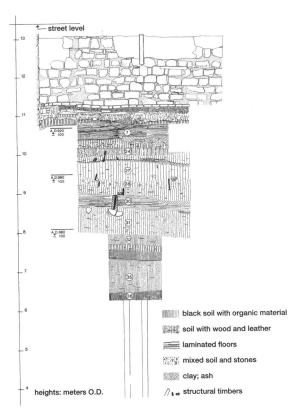

The stratigraphic section at the Lloyds Bank site on the street called Pavement provided the basis for a detailed chronology.

systematically investigated. The remains of the headquarters or *Principia* can be seen under York Minster. One remarkable discovery was the extensive system of stone-built sewers preserved beneath the city, from which organic remains produced valuable samples for study. Also informative was the study of remains thought to have come from warehouses, clearly representing the remains of a large quantity of spoiled grain (see pp. 250, 298). Evidence was also found of a basilica, barrack blocks, centurions' houses, and roads and alleys, making York one of the most fully known legionary headquarters in the Roman empire.

Eoforwic. Anglo-Saxon York. The collapse of the Roman empire at the end of the 4th century AD led to notable depopulation at York, and there are few remains from the succeeding two centuries. Historical records indicate that York was an important royal center in the 7th century and became the seat of an archbishop in AD 735. Not a great deal is yet known of the buildings of Anglian, or Anglo-Saxon York, but they must have contained an archbishop's church, an

Examination of one of the extensive system of Roman sewers still preserved beneath the city.

important monastic school, and almost certainly a royal palace (yet to be located). However, information on the Anglian settlement was found in YAT excavations at Fishergate, at the confluence of the rivers Ouse and Foss, which provides valuable insights into the economy of the period, showing that the site was already a center of trade with northern Europe. A splendid helmet of this period was recovered from Coppergate (see below). When the Vikings took York in AD 866 they would have found not a densely packed city, but a small town consisting of a series of smaller settlements each perhaps serving a different function, scattered around the area of the old Roman city and dominated by the walls of the Roman fortress. As the work in York has vividly shown, the city they created was a very different place.

Jorvik. Viking or Anglo-Scandinavian York. The excavations in the Coppergate area and beyond have given the clearest evidence yet available for a city of the Viking period in England. While the churches of the city were of stone, the houses and workshops were built of timber with thatched roofs. Their preserved remains formed the basis for the reconstruction undertaken at the Jorvik Viking Centre. Remains of the Roman walls would have been familiar to the inhabitants of Anglo-Scandinavian York: parts of the ruined Roman barracks were reused to house light industrial activities such as jet-working, and the *Principia* stub

walls enclosed a wealthy cemetery. Within the old Roman city walls many of the parish churches and graveyards were established at this time.

York. The medieval (and modern) city, from the arrival of the Norman invaders in AD 1067. Extensive excavations have clarified the plan of the medieval city, which until the early 15th century was to remain the second city of England, with a population of between 8000 and 15,000. Building of the Cathedral of St. Peter (York Minster) was begun on its present site in 1070, and fragments of stone houses of 12th-century date survive, along with many timber-framed houses from the 14th century and later. Other impressive remains of medieval York include city walls, traces of two castles, parish churches, and guild halls.

Environment

One of the most interesting features of the York excavations has been the study not only of general climatic issues and of the rural situation on the outskirts, but also of ecological conditions and activities within the town.

Excavations of Roman waterlogged occupation deposits at the Tanner Row site, close to the river Ouse, were highly informative. The plant, invertebrate, and vertebrate remains provided evidence for pre-occupation grazing land traversed by ditches, substantial "landfill" consisting largely of stable manure and other waste, and a range of imported foods. There were indications that the river was cleaner than in the medieval period or today (see p. 257).

The waterlogged levels beneath the fringes of the river Foss provided much interesting evidence relating to Viking Age York. The insect remains at 16–22

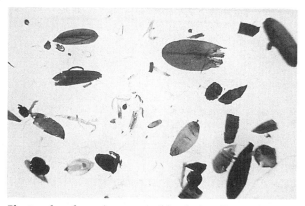

Plant and seed remains recovered by sieving. Excavations at York have provided a wealth of environmental evidence.

Coppergate, especially, permit one to reconstruct a whole series of small-scale urban environments, each the result of a specific human activity which created conditions of temperature and substrate suitable for specific insect communities. For example, there was a distinctive "house fauna," including human fleas and lice, typical of internal floors, while cess pits contained abundant flies and beetles indicating that foul matter had often been exposed for long periods, with consequent danger of infection. The distribution of lice gave indications that some buildings were domestic, others workshops.

The yards around and behind the buildings were pockmarked with pits, whose fills were mainly human feces rich in cereal bran and fruitstones (such as sloes and wild plums) and containing abundant eggs of intestinal parasites. Woodland plants and insects were rather common, probably because they were brought with moss used for sanitary purposes.

The presence of sheep lice indicated the presence of wool preparation and dyeing. Dye plants included madder and woad, and clubmoss from mainland Europe (see p. 333). Waste from the dyebaths formed thick layers in places. Bees were probably kept: they were often found, and were abundant in two deposits; honey presumably helped to make the sour sloes and other wild fruits more palatable. The animal bones and plant food remains have been extensively studied at York as on other urban excavation projects in Britain.

Technology and Trade

The excavations yielded extensive evidence for the practice of urban crafts, including a Roman workshop for the production of window glass. The most notable finds, however, came from the Viking deposits at the Coppergate site. Silverworking was an important industry, and was at its peak in the mid-10th century, although gold, lead tin, and pewter were also worked. Evidence for metal refining was found, both cupellation and parting (the separation of gold and silver), with crucibles and *tuyères*, ingot and object molds, and tools. The contemporary finds of coin dies suggest that much of the silver may have been used for coinage, possibly with moneyers working on the site. The coin dies themselves were made of iron and may be connected with the very extensive iron-working industry of the mid-10th century.

From the same area the abundant finds of textiles, including 221 specimens of fibers, cordage, and textiles of wool, linen, and silk, mainly from the Viking period, have given important insights into the textile industries of the period. Finds of loom weights indicate that the warp-weighted loom was in use. Much of the cloth produced was wool, but linen was also made, probably for bed-linen and undergarments. Dyeing materials such as madder and woad (see above) were recovered. It is clear therefore that the weavers were producing wool and linen cloth of good serviceable quality. The finer textiles may have arrived as a result of trade; the silks certainly were, perhaps brought by Viking traders from Russia, who were in contact with the silk route from China and Central Asia. Some at least of the silks are likely to be Byzantine.

These finds of metalworking and of imported textiles, and other indications including what were once interpreted as "trial stamps" for coins but are now thought to be customs receipts, allow a comprehensive picture to be built up of trading connections in the successive periods at York.

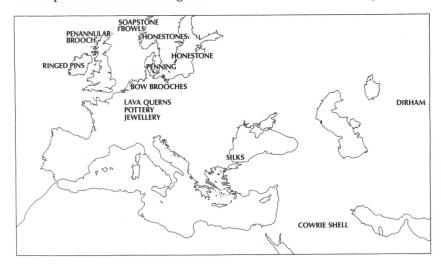

Viking York had extensive trade connections stretching across Europe into Asia. This map shows the principal sources of goods imported to Jorvik.

A coin die (right), lead trial piece, and silver pennies from 10th-century York.

Cognitive Aspects

Since all four periods of urban development at York were periods of literacy, and since written records from each referring to York survive, in addition to the coins and inscriptions found during the course of the excavations, there is abundant evidence concerning the world view and thought processes of the population. Of particular interest were the medieval wax writing tablets found in a 14th-century rubbish pit – the 8 boxwood leaves had 14 waxed faces carrying scribed inscriptions – which turned out to be a risqué poem and a legal document.

One of the 14th-century writing tablets found at York. Each tablet was made of boxwood filled with wax, in which the text was inscribed.

One of the outstanding finds of the excavations is the Coppergate helmet, the focus of a meticulous study by Dominic Tweddle. The helmet dates from the 8th century AD, from the Anglian period, prior to the advent of the Vikings. It is one of a series of display helmets known from Britain and Europe, including one from the celebrated ship burial at Sutton Hoo. It is a work of superb technology – the neck was protected by chain mail and it has been shown that one defective link in the mail was meticulously repaired. It is possible to see this marvellous artifact as an intersection of the technical, social, and cognitive dimensions: supreme technological accomplishment and artistic skill used intelligently to convey and enhance the social status of a pre-eminent individual. The noseguard is a fine example of the animal-art interlace which is so notable a feature of the "Dark Ages" of northern Europe following the end of the Roman empire and of the centuries which followed.

The conservation of this important find was itself an involved process, and today it can be seen in the Yorkshire Castle Museum only a few hundred yards from its

One of the outstanding finds made in York is this 8th-century AD Anglian helmet, found at Coppergate; the noseguard was finely incised with an interlace design.

findspot in Coppergate. (It should be noted that the street names themselves carry a cognitive dimension – "Coppergate" meaning "Cup-makers' street" from the Norse *gata*, not the English "gate").

It is finds like these, and indeed the Sutton Hoo ship burial itself, which give us some of our clearest glimpses into the ethos of the heroic society of Britain and northern Europe in the centuries after Rome.

Whose Past? Public Archaeology in York

The first task of the archaeologist after excavation and initial research is to publish, but unfortunately often years pass before the full findings see the light of day. For that reason many excavators publish fairly full interim reports each year, immediately after the field-work campaign, and this was the approach followed by Peter Addyman following the early excavations undertaken by the Trust. However, he developed a novel approach, since adopted by many other projects, to the big problem of the Final Report. Rather than waiting for all the various specialist reports to come in before the final, heavy excavation volumes could appear, he resolved to publish the individual contributions as they arrived on his desk, in a series of briefer volumes or fascicules. Together these will make up 19 major, composite volumes in *The Archaeology of York*:

1. Sources for York History to AD 1100
2. Historical Sources for York after AD 1100
3. The Legionary Fortress
4. The Colonia (the Roman city, outside the military fortress, but within the city wall)
5. The Roman Cemeteries
6. The Roman Extra-Mural Settlement and Roads
7. Anglian York (AD 410–876) – i.e. the Anglo-Saxon period
8. Anglo-Scandinavian York (AD 876–1066) – i.e. the Viking period, until the Norman Conquest
9. The Medieval Walled City southwest of the Ouse
10. The Medieval Walled City northeast of the Ouse
11. The Medieval Suburbs
12. The Medieval Cemeteries
13. Early Modern York (from *c.* AD 1485 onwards)
14. The Past Environment of York
15. The Animal Bones
16. The Pottery
17. The Small Finds
18. The Coins
19. Principles and Methods

Elements of most of the projected volumes have been published over the past 25 years: including a series of pioneering studies in environmental archaeology.

Probably the most notable feature of the work of the York Archaeological Trust, however, has been its success in involving the public – locals as well as an increasing number of tourists – using exciting new methods. Part funded with public money from local and national government, support has also come from property developers and, notably, from the millions of visitors who have paid to see the Jorvik Viking Centre. This is on the site of the original Coppergate excavation, incorporated at basement level beneath the commercially operated Coppergate Shopping Centre.

The Jorvik Viking Centre was a ground-breaking initiative which introduced innovative ways of communicating the results of archaeology to the public. The visitor first experiences an underground journey on a "timecar" through an authentic re-creation of the 10th-century Viking settlement, complete with skillfully devised sights, sounds, and smells, everything validated by careful research at York or using parallels from Scandinavia. This is followed by a part of the original excavation area and a walk through a small display of finds. In its first year of opening (1984) it had more than 850,000 visitors, and within 4 years the proceeds allowed the repayment (with interest) of the loan which had funded construction. This was pioneer archaeological entrepreneurism, and it has since been followed widely.

Its critics say that the "time capsule" approach of the Jorvik Viking Centre's underground "timecars" comes closer to Disneyland than to serious archaeology. But nearly all those who have undergone the "Jorvik experience," including archaeologists, say that they have enjoyed it and that they have learnt something – even if it is only how unpleasant the backyards of Viking Age York must have smelt.

In 1990 the Trust opened the Archaeological Resource Centre in the converted 15th-century St. Saviour's Church. Here school groups and the public can try hands-on sorting of finds, see researchers at work, and experiment with a variety of early technologies such as weaving and shoemaking. This too has proved very popular and now has 40,000 visitors per year. Finally Barley Hall is a restored and reconstructed medieval hall where visitors gain some experience of what life was like in 15th-century England.

The work of the York Archaeological Trust is a prime example of an archaeological project in an urban setting which is at once commercially and educationally successful, as well as academically productive. The Trust's continuing commitment to communicating the results of its work, and its pre-eminence in devising innovative and effective means to achieve this, are major contributions to public archaeology.

(Top left and right, and above) At the Jorvik Viking Centre visitors are transported by a "timecar" through Viking York, and can experience all the activities, sounds, and smells associated with life in the town at the time. Meticulously researched and based on both actual excavations at York and information from comparable Viking sites in Scandinavia, the Centre presents an authentic replica of 10th-century York. The York Archaeological Trust pioneered this method of presenting archaeology to the public, and it has since been widely emulated.

(Left) At the Archaeological Resource Centre in a specially converted 15th-century church, members of the public and school groups can find out what archaeologists do by sorting finds and watching researchers at work. This is another part of the Trust's innovative program of involving the public in archaeology.

FURTHER READING

The fundamental sources for the four case studies are as follows:

Oaxaca:

Blanton, R.E. 1978. *Monte Albán: Settlement Patterns at the Ancient Zapotec Capital.* Academic Press: New York.

Flannery, K.V. & Marcus, J. (eds.). 1983. *The Cloud People: Divergent Evolution of the Zapotec and Mixtec Civilizations.* Academic Press: New York.

Flannery, K.V. (ed.). 1986. *Guilá Naquitz: Archaic Foraging and Early Agriculture in Oaxaca, Mexico.* Academic Press: New York.

Marcus, J. & Flannery, K.V. 1996. *Zapotec Civilization. How Urban Society Evolved in Mexico's Oaxaca Valley.* Thames & Hudson: London and New York.

Kakadu:

Jones, R. (ed.). 1985. *Archaeological Research in Kakadu National Park.* Australian National Parks and Wildlife Service, Special Publication No. 13. Australian National University: Canberra.

Roberts, R.G. & others. 1994. The human colonisation of Australia: Optical dates of 53,000 and 60,000 years bracket human arrival at Deaf Adder Gorge, Northern Territory. *Quaternary Geochronology (Quaternary Science Reviews)* 13, 575–83.

Khok Phanom Di:

Higham, C. & others. 1990–93. *The Excavation of Khok Phanom Di, a Prehistoric Site in Central Thailand.* Vols. 1–4. Society of Antiquaries: London.

Higham, C. & Thosarat, R. 1994. *Khok Phanom Di: Prehistoric Adaptation to the World's Richest Habitat.* Harcourt Brace College Publishers: Fort Worth.

Kealhofer, L. & Piperno, D.R. 1994. Early agriculture in southeast Asia: phytolith evidence from the Bang Pakong Valley, Thailand. *Antiquity* 68, 564–72.

Thompson, G.B. (ed.). 1996. *The Excavation of Khok Phanom Di, a Prehistoric Site in Central Thailand. Vol. IV. Subsistence and Environment: the Botanical Evidence.* Society of Antiquaries: London.

York:

The main source of information is the series, edited by P.V. Addyman, *The Archaeology of York*, published by the York Archaeological Trust by the Council for British Archaeology.

Addyman, P.V. 1992. *York Archaeological Trust – 21 Years of Archaeology in York.* Annual Report of the Yorkshire Philosophical Society for 1992: York.

Hall, R.A. 1994. *Viking Age York.* Batsford/English Heritage: London.

Hall, R.A. 1996. *York.* Batsford/English Heritage: London.

Phillips, D. & Heywood, B. 1995. *Excavations at York Minster 1: From Roman Fortress to Norman Cathedral.* HMSO: London.

Phillips, D. 1985. *Excavations at York Minster 2: The Cathedral of Archbishop Thomas of Bayeux.* HMSO: London.

14

Whose Past?
Archaeology and the Public

This book is concerned with the way that archaeologists investigate the past, with the questions we can ask and our means of answering them. But the time has come to address much wider questions: Why, beyond reasons of scientific curiosity, do we want to know about the past? What does the past mean to us? What does it mean to others who have different viewpoints? And whose past is it anyway?

These issues very soon lead us to questions of responsibility, public as well as private. For surely a national monument, such as Great Zimbabwe or the Athenian Acropolis, means something special to the modern descendants of its builders? Does it not also mean something to all humankind? If so, should it not be protected from destruction, in the same way as endangered plant and animal species? If the looting of ancient sites is to be deplored, should it not be stopped, even if the sites are on privately owned land? Who owns, or should own, the past?

These very soon become ethical questions – of right and wrong, of appropriate action and reprehensible action. The archaeologist has a special responsibility because, as we saw in Chapter 3, excavation itself entails destruction. Future workers' understanding of a site can never be much more than our own, because we will have destroyed the evidence and recorded only those parts of it we considered important and had the energy to publish properly.

Destruction on a much larger scale comes from another quarter, far exceeding anything suffered in earlier centuries. The earth's surface is now being exploited more exhaustively than ever before, for commercial, industrial, and agricultural purposes, and any fragile vestiges of earlier human activity are liable to be swept away if they hinder that exploitation. Moreover, the very interest that archaeology has generated in our past has created new destructive forces: not only looters and illicit excavators – whose plunder finds its way into private collections and public museums – but also tourists, who by their numbers threaten the sites they seek to enjoy.

The past is big business – in tourism and in the auction rooms. The past is politically highly charged, ideologically powerful, and significant. And the past, or what remains of it, is subject to increasing destruction. What can we do about these problems?

THE MEANING OF THE PAST: THE ARCHAEOLOGY OF IDENTITY

When we ask what the past means, it is implicit in the question that we are asking what the past means for *us*, for clearly it means different things to different people. An Indian, looking at the great monuments of Moghul rule, may see things differently according to whether he or she is a Hindu or a Muslim, and a European tourist will look at one of these buildings with different eyes again. In the same way, an Australian Aborigine may attach a very different significance to fossil human remains from an early site like Lake Mungo or to paintings in the Kakadu National Park, than a white Australian. Different communities have very different conceptions about the past which often draw on sources well beyond archaeology.

At this point we go beyond the question of what actually happened in the past, and of the explanation of why it happened, to issues of meaning, significance, and interpretation. And it is at this point, therefore, that many of the concerns which have become explicit in archaeology over the past couple of decades become entirely relevant. How we interpret the past, how we present it (for instance in museum displays), and what lessons we choose to draw from it, are to a considerable extent matters for subjective decision, often involving ideological and political issues, as the advocates of Critical Theory have argued.

For in a very broad sense, as well outlined by David Lowenthal in *The Past is a Foreign Country* (1985), the past is where we came from. Individually we each have our personal, genealogical past – our parents, grandparents, and earlier kinsfolk from whom we are descended. Increasingly in the western world there is an interest in this personal past, reflected in the enthusiasm for family trees and for "roots" generally. Our personal identity, and generally our name, are in part defined for us in the relatively recent past, even though those elements with which we choose to identify are largely a matter of personal choice. Nor is this inheritance purely a spiritual one. Most land tenure in the world is determined by inheritance, and much other wealth is inherited: the material world in this sense comes to us from the past, and is certainly, when the times comes, relinquished by us to the future.

Nationalism and its Symbols

Collectively our cultural inheritance is rooted in a deeper past, where lie the origins of our language, our faith, our customs. Increasingly archaeology plays an important role in the definition of national identity, and this is particularly the case for those nations which do not have a very long written history, though many consider oral histories of equal value to written ones. The national emblems of many recently emerged nations are taken from artifacts seen as typical of some special and early local golden age: even the name of the state of Zimbabwe comes from the eponymous archaeological site.

Yet the same is true for Egypt or for Greece, for Mexico or Peru, where the ancient past is used in some ways to legitimate the present and is drawn upon to reinforce a sense of national greatness and identity. A major recent crisis related to the name and national emblems adopted by the newly independent Former Yugoslav Republic of Macedonia. For Greece, the name Macedonia refers not only to contemporary provinces (nomes) within Greece, but to the kingdom of that famous Greek leader, Alexander the Great, so that appropriation of the name by a state whose national language is not even Greek was seen as an affront. This was compounded by the use by the FYR Macedonia of a star as a national symbol, drawing on a version from the tomb of Philip of Macedon (father of Alexander), found among the splendid objects from his tomb at Vergina, well within modern Greek territory. Resentment at the appropriation of this image stirred up a great wave of nationalistic feeling within Greece to the extent of disturbing relations between Greece and other member states of the European Union, until an accommodation was reached.

In Israel, too, archaeology is used to serve the cause of national ideology. The excavation by Yigael Yadin in the 1960s of the fortress of Masada resurrected the stirring story of the last stand of the Jewish Zealots against the besieging Romans in AD 73, and how they chose mass suicide instead of surrender. It has become a symbol of Israeli defiance and pride, as well as an important place of tourism. Israel employs archaeology

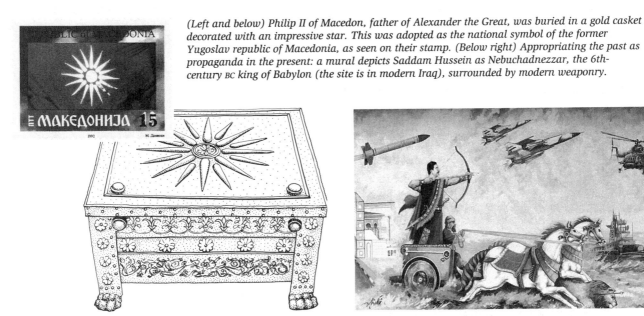

(Left and below) Philip II of Macedon, father of Alexander the Great, was buried in a gold casket decorated with an impressive star. This was adopted as the national symbol of the former Yugoslav republic of Macedonia, as seen on their stamp. (Below right) Appropriating the past as propaganda in the present: a mural depicts Saddam Hussein as Nebuchadnezzar, the 6th-century BC king of Babylon (the site is in modern Iraq), surrounded by modern weaponry.

THE POLITICS OF DESTRUCTION 1: THE BRIDGE AT MOSTAR

FORMER YUGOSLAVIA
• Mostar

On 9 November 1993, the Old Bridge of Mostar, a fine architectural work constructed in 1566 by order of Sultan Suleyman the Magnificent, of great significance to the (mainly Muslim) inhabitants of that city, finally collapsed after months of shelling by Croatian guns. It symbolizes the deliberate destruction of the cultural heritage by the warring ethnic factions of the former state of Yugoslavia.

As John Chapman (1994, 122) remarks:

"In a cultural war, the conquest of territories and the 'ethnic cleansing' of settlements is insufficient. Nothing less than the destruction of past historical identities is needed. If the identities between past nations and their landscapes are best symbolized by their monuments, it is these monuments which have been prime targets in this cultural war. Mosques for Serbs and Croats, Orthodox churches for Muslims and Croats, Catholic monasteries for Serbs and Muslims – each monumental symbol fatally attracts the cultural warriors. Designation of a building for UNESCO Protection marks out buildings for special destruction... the term genocide must now be extended from forced migration to include the disappearance of cultural markers from a territory."

The deliberate destruction of historical and cultural monuments was a notable feature of this war, although the practice has its antecedents in the so-called "Baedecker raids" (named after the excellent series of guidebooks published before the war in Germany) upon historic British cities by the German airforce during World War II.

Indeed even the pharaohs of Egypt practiced the systematic destruction of the monuments (or at least the erasure of the names) of predecessor rulers of whom they disapproved. For instance, monuments of the heretic king, Akhenaten, were completely dismantled and their blocks used to construct new buildings.

But the scale of destruction in Bosnia was notable: over 50 percent of known mosques were damaged or destroyed. Yet even if Serbian forces caused the bulk of the damage, it is said that 146 Serbian Orthodox churches were also destroyed and 111 badly damaged, with the church of the Dormition at Derventa destroyed by explosives on 4 June 1992.

As J.M. Halpern (1993, 50) ironically puts it, we may now anticipate an "ethno-archaeology of architectural destruction."

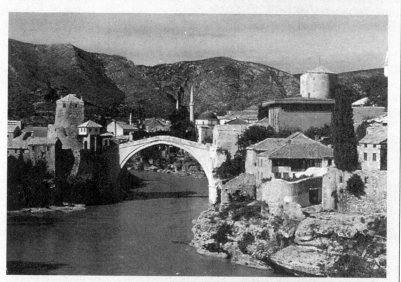

The beautiful bridge at Mostar, dating from the 16th century, before its destruction. *Such important cultural symbols are often targeted in wars.*

	destroyed	damaged	total
mosques	300	162	462
communal-buildings*	250	46	296
cemeteries	33	2	35

*Includes buildings such as the mesjid (small mosque or place of prayer), the medrese (school), the mekteb (place of work), the Imam's house etc.

Destruction of the Bosnian Islamic cultural heritage up to April 1993 (after Chapman).

as a means of underlining historical continuity and hence of justifying her existence. Indeed, while it might have been hoped and expected that the sort of crude ethnic and nationalist concepts which inspired Adolf Hitler's National Socialists in Germany during World War II might have disappeared by the end of the century, the converse seems to be the case. Kosovo has followed Bosnia in the former Yugoslavia as a battleground of "ethnic cleansing" (a concept of the 1990s), and in the states of the former Soviet Union different groups vie with each other for legitimacy by claiming to be the inheritors of a historic past, often misusing archaeological data in the process.

These feelings of "us" and "them" at a national level are often expressions of ethnic identity (see box, Ancient Ethnicity and Language, p. 189). Ethnicity today is a living force, just as strongly as it may have been in earlier times, and it relies upon the past, and upon past material culture, for its (supposed) legitimation, sometimes with sad and destructive results (see boxes, p. 535 and opposite).

Archaeology and Ideology

The legacy of the past extends beyond sentiments of nationalism and ethnicity. Sectarian sentiments often find expression in major monuments, and many Christian churches were built on the site of deliberately destroyed "pagan" temples. In just a few cases they actually utilized such temples – the Parthenon in Athens is one example – and one of the best preserved Greek temples is now the Cathedral in Syracuse. Unfortunately the destruction of ancient monuments for purely sectarian reasons is not entirely a thing of the past, as the case of the Ayodhya mosque shows.

The past, moreover, has ideological roles even beyond the sphere of sectarian religion. In China Chairman Mao used to urge that the past should serve the present, and excavation of ancient sites in China certainly continued even at the height of the Cultural Revolution of the 1960s. Today there is widespread

The Cathedral of St. Lucy in Syracuse, Sicily, preserves the former Doric temple to Athena.

popular concern in that country for its ancient cultural relics. Great emphasis is placed on artistic treasures as products of skilled workers rather than as the property of rulers; they are seen as reflections of the class struggle, while the palaces and tombs of the aristocracy underline the ruthless exploitation of the laboring masses. The Communist message is also conveyed through humbler artifacts. The museum at the Lower Paleolithic site of Zhoukoudian, for example, proclaims that labor, as represented by the making and using of tools, was the decisive factor in our transition from apes to humans.

WHO OWNS THE PAST?

Until recent decades, archaeologists gave little thought to the question of the ownership of past sites and antiquities. Most archaeologists themselves came from western, industrialized societies whose economic and political domination seemed to impart an almost automatic right to acquire antiquities and excavate sites around the world. Since World War II, however, former colonies have grown into independent nation states eager to uncover their own past and assert control over their own heritage. Difficult questions have therefore arisen. Should antiquities acquired for western museums during the colonial era be returned to their lands of origin? And should archaeologists be free to excavate the burials of groups whose modern descendants may object on religious or other grounds?

THE POLITICS OF DESTRUCTION 2: THE MOSQUE AT AYODHYA

Religious extremism is responsible for many acts of destruction. The important mosque, the Babri Masjid, at Ayodhya in Uttar Pradesh, northern India, constructed by the Moghul prince Babur in the 16th century AD, was torn down by Hindu fundamentalists on 6 December 1992. The mosque was situated at a location which has at times been equated with the Ayodhya of the Hindu epic, the *Ramayana*, where it is identified as the birthplace of the Hindu deity/hero Rama.

Excavations had been carried out at the site by B.B. Lal in 1975 and 1976, and did not report medieval finds of any special interest. But in June 1992 stone carvings were allegedly uncovered 3.6 m (12 ft) underground at the site and a group of archaeologists published a booklet, *Ramajamna Bhumi: Ayodhya: New Archaeological Discoveries*, in which it was claimed that Babur's mosque was built over the ruins of a Hindu temple of 11th-century date, a temple which Babur had destroyed. Encouraged by politicians of the influential Bharatiya Janata Party, Hindu fundamentalists proceeded to raze the mosque to the ground.

This act naturally angered the Muslim population of India, although remarkably not all Indian archaeologists condemned so significant a destruction of part of the nation's cultural heritage. Indeed much of the argument has centered less on the morality of destroying a major monument of the 16th century, than on the quality of the archaeological evidence – apparently weak – for the alleged 11th-century temple to Rama.

At the request of the Indian hosts, and to the dissatisfaction of many participants, the subject of the

destruction of the Ayodhya mosque was excluded from discussion at the third meeting of the World Archaeological Congress in New Delhi in 1994 by a resolution of the International Executive Committee of the Congress.

By a process of displacement the argument became centered on the claims (supported by the Hindu fundamentalist faction) that the "Aryans" depicted in the Hymns of the *Rigveda*, the earliest texts at the root of the Hindu tradition, were

indigenous to India. The contrary and indeed conventional view, that of an Aryan invasion which took place at the end of the Indus Valley civilization around 1800 BC, was also reiterated with warmth.

To the uncommitted observer it seemed remarkable that hypothetical events of nearly 4000 years ago were being used to fuel a debate surrounding the recent destruction of a notable historical monument, an action which itself resulted in riots and the loss of many lives.

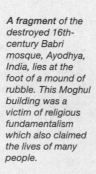

A fragment of the destroyed 16th-century Babri mosque, Ayodhya, India, lies at the foot of a mound of rubble. This Moghul building was a victim of religious fundamentalism which also claimed the lives of many people.

Museums and the Return of Cultural Property

At the beginning of the 19th century Lord Elgin, a Scottish diplomat, removed some of the marble sculptures from the façade of the Parthenon, the great 5th-century BC temple that crowns the Acropolis in Athens. Elgin did so with the permission of the then Turkish overlords of Greece, and later sold the sculptures to the British Museum, where they still reside, finely displayed. The Greeks now want the "Elgin Marbles" back. That in essence is the story so far of perhaps the best-known case where an internationally famous museum is under pressure to return cultural property to the country of origin. But there are numerous other claims directed at European and North American museums. The Berlin Museum, for example, holds the famous bust of the Egyptian queen Nefertiti, which was shipped out of Egypt illegally. The Greek government has officially asked France for the return of the Venus de Milo, the *pièce de résistance* of the Louvre, bought from Greece's Ottoman rulers. And Turkey has recently been successful in recovering art treasures, including the "Lydian Hoard," from New York's Metropolitan Museum, and may now pursue Turkish statuary and objects in European countries, including the British Museum.

The issues are complex. The British Museum's main argument against returning objects is that its trustees are expressly forbidden by British law to dispose of the objects in their charge. But there are ways round this – a fragment of the beard of the great Sphinx of Giza, for example, may perhaps be returned by the museum to Egypt as a reciprocal loan, in exchange for the body of a stone jackal whose head is in London. Furthermore, modern materials and techniques make it feasible to produce virtually perfect casts and replicas. The question then is: should the original or the copy be presented to the country making the request? A crucial factor here is whether the original will be adequately protected and conserved once returned. Many fragile antiquities survive today only because they have been housed in western museums. The Elgin Marbles in the British Museum, despite an unfortunate episode of over-cleaning in 1937–38, are in much better condition than those sections of the Parthenon frieze that were left in place on the Acropolis, exposed to the pollution of Athens. On the other hand, the Greeks plan to build a special museum to safeguard the sculptures if they are returned.

Quite apart from the legal issues, there is certainly a good moral case to be made for the restitution of

Part of the "Elgin Marbles": a horseman from the frieze of the Parthenon in Athens, c. 440 BC.

objects of special religious or cultural significance, such as the kachinas (dolls representing spirits) of the North American Hopi Indians. Artifacts of this kind are not museum pieces but "living" and powerful things within their culture. It might also make sense to reassemble material from particular sites that is now scattered throughout the world's museums, and to repatriate at least a sample of objects that may be over-represented in foreign collections but rare or absent in museums of the country of origin.

At the same time, one can set up the problem in a different way, and ask whether the interest of the great products of human endeavor does not in fact transcend the geographical boundaries of modern-day nationalism. Does it make sense that all the Paleolithic hand-axes and other artifacts from Olduvai Gorge or Olorgesailie in East Africa should remain confined within the bounds of the modern nations where they have been found? Should we not all be able to benefit from the insights they offer? And is it not a profound and important experience to be able, in the course of one day in one of the world's great museums, to be able to walk from room to room, from civilization to civilization, and see unfolded a sample of the whole variety of human experience? Would it not be a greater service, in response to requests to repatriate one nation's antiquities, to offer instead great works belonging to a *different* cultural tradition?

Even if one is willing to operate within a framework of modern national chauvinism, it may be more appropriate for the works of one nation to be seen and appreciated overseas. Nearly all the important products of Minoan civilization remain in Crete, in the Herakleion Museum. In consequence, they are little known other than from glossy picture books and to Hellenic travelers. Are the nationalistic ends of Greek culture better served by the confining of Minoan works of art to Herakleion, or by the dispersal of Classical Greek art throughout the western world? Certainly the Mexican government has recently chosen the path of propagating its cultural image abroad in relation to monuments held in the British Museum, such as the richly carved lintels taken by Alfred Maudslay from the Maya site of Yaxchilán in the 1880s. These are now displayed in a new gallery largely sponsored by the Mexicans.

There are difficult issues to unravel here, as much to do with national and international politics as with modern archaeology.

Excavating Burials: Should We Disturb the Dead? The question of excavating burials can be equally complex. For prehistoric burials the problem is not so great, because we have no direct written knowledge of the relevant culture's beliefs and wishes. For burials dating from historic times, however, religious beliefs are known to us in detail. We know, for example, that the ancient Egyptians and Chinese, the Greeks, Etruscans, and Romans, and the early Christians all feared disturbance of the dead. Yet it has to be recognized that tombs were falling prey to the activities of robbers long before archaeology began. Egyptian pharaohs in the 12th century BC had to appoint a commission to inquire into the wholesale plundering of tombs at Thebes. Not a single Egyptian royal tomb, including that of Tutankhamun, escaped the robbers completely. Similarly, Roman carved gravestones became building material in cities and forts; and at Ostia, the port of ancient Rome, tomb inscriptions have even been found serving as seats in a public latrine!

However, disturbance and plunder by the ignorant and greedy cannot alone justify archaeological investigation, although the scholar certainly benefits more people than the robber. Can archaeology reconcile a respect for the people of the past with deliberate disturbance of their remains, destruction of their tombs, and removal of their bodies and grave-goods against the wishes of modern groups who for religious or other reasons see themselves as the living representatives of the deceased? In Egypt, the mummies of the pharaohs were removed from public view some years ago, in accordance with Islamic respect for the dead; but economic necessity, caused by the drop in tourist revenues because of terrorism, led to their being put back on show recently. Clearly archaeologists must show sensitivity on this issue. Where the modern descendants have a legitimate case, the only way forward lies in negotiation and compromise. In the longer term, archaeology should be made more relevant for, and open to, all sectors of the community.

Archaeology and Judaism. One religion which takes an intense and often hostile interest in archaeology is Judaism. In 1981 the issue erupted when thousands of militant, ultra-orthodox Jews held a demonstration in Jerusalem against the alleged desecration of graves at a major archaeological site in the city. The demonstration led to a heated debate over whether religious or secular law should apply in this case. Similarly, in August 1986, an important archaeological project at Tel Haror in the Negev Desert was vandalized, most probably by members of Atra Kadisha, an ultra-orthodox group dedicated to preserving the sanctity of Jewish cemeteries and which patrols excavation sites and intimidates archaeologists. So far there appears to be no meeting of minds, or satisfactory compromise, between the opposed camps. Indeed recently the study of human evolution has been brought to a virtual halt by an Israeli government ruling (under pressure from ultra-orthodox Jews) stating that no archaeological or scientific examination may henceforth be carried out on human remains, and all such remains, of whatever age or religion, must be handed over to religious Jews for reburial. Truckloads of bones have been removed from Jerusalem's Rockefeller Museum for burial.

The burial issue has also become a political and legal problem in several other countries, including Australia, New Zealand, and the United States.

The Australian Aborigines. In Australia, the present climate of Aboriginal emancipation and increased political power has focused attention on wrongdoings during the colonial period, when anthropologists had little respect for Aboriginal feelings and beliefs. Sacred sites were investigated and published, burial sites desecrated, and cultural and skeletal material exhumed, to be stored or displayed in museums. The Aborigines were thus, by implication, seen as laboratory specimens. Inevitably, the fate of all this material, and particularly of the bones, has assumed great symbolic significance. Unfortunately, here as in other countries, archaeologists are being blamed for the misdemeanors of the non-archaeologists who obtained most of the human remains in question.

Broadly, the view of Aborigines in some parts of Australia is that all human skeletal material (and occasionally cultural material too) must be returned to them, and then its fate will be decided. Since the Aborigines have an unassailable moral case, the Australian Archaeological Association (AAA) is willing to return remains which are either quite modern or of "known individuals where specific descendants can be traced," and for these to be reburied. However, such remains are somewhat the exception. The University of Melbourne's Murray Black Collection consists of skeletal remains from over 800 Aborigines ranging in date from several hundred years to at least 14,000 years old. They were dug up in the 1940s without any consultation with local Aborigines. Owing to a lack of specialists the collection has still by no means been exhaustively studied – but nevertheless it has been returned to the relevant Aboriginal communities. In 1990 the unique series of burials from Kow Swamp, 9000 to 13,000 years old, were handed back to the Aboriginal community and reburied; more recently the first skeleton found at Lake Mungo, the world's oldest known cremation (26,000 years BP), was returned to the custody of the Aborigines of the Mungo area; and Aboriginal elders have announced they may rebury all the skeletal material (up to 30,000 years old) from Mungo.

Archaeologists are understandably alarmed at the prospect of having to hand over material many thousands of years old. Some also point out that the Aborigines – like indigenous peoples elsewhere – tend to forget that not all of their recent forebears took pious care of the dead. But in view of Aboriginal sufferings at European hands, one must certainly look on their claims with sympathy.

This is particularly true of the Australian state of Tasmania, where the government ordered the Crowther Collection of skeletal material from known historical people to be returned to the Aboriginal community to dispose of as it saw fit. The way in which the material had been collected was so appalling that the AAA took the view that any potential scientific value was far outweighed by ethical considerations, and actually urged the Tasmanian government to hand over the material. The Crowther Collection underwent traditional cremation in 1985. Tasmanian Aborigines, backed by a cultural heritage law, have now demanded the return of everything Australian archaeologists have found in recent excavations at sites in the region with occupation dating back 35,000 years; the demand is not only for artifacts but even for animal bones, and it is feared that the as yet unstudied material would simply be thrown in a lake, like some artifacts returned in 1994.

In 1991 a code of ethics was adopted by the AAA that acknowledges members' obligations to respect and consult with the living people whose ancestors' lives are being studied. The future lies in negotiation, compromise, and involvement of Aborigines in archaeological work. Many Aborigines object to displays of skeletal material in museums, and these have now been replaced by casts, or removed altogether. They also demand to be consulted and are prepared to discuss each case on its merits. In parts of Australia, the employment and training of Aborigines as museum curators is underway. Aborigines will thus develop an informed appreciation of their heritage, as the North American Indians have done. This is surely more worthwhile than destruction of material or reburial with no access.

Remarkable progress is being made. In 1982 an indigenous community at Robinvale, on the Murray river, requested that a prehistoric burial site endangered by erosion of the riverbank should undergo a rescue excavation. The dig was carried out with Aboriginal assistance and constant consultation with the local community who were most interested in the data from the site. When excavation revealed a major burial ground, the community halted the work, had the site saved and stabilized by soil conservation experts, and skeletal material reburied after being documented in the field.

New Zealand. In New Zealand, no display of skeletal material now occurs. As elsewhere, there is no single, standard indigenous viewpoint about these problems, but certainly many Maori (the indigenous New Zealanders) dislike the past being examined. The history they pass down among themselves is secret, sacred information, not for public discussion. Where burials are concerned, they often prefer to see them destroyed by nature or even by the impersonal bulldozer than to have them dug up and preserved. Currently, archaeologists in New Zealand (who include a young Maori lecturer) maintain close consultation with local Maori, and as a result there is a great deal of cooperation between the two sides, though, as yet, there is little direct involvement on the part of the indigenous community.

The American Indians. The Indians of North America have expressed their grievances strongly in recent years, and as a result have been able to exert political influence resulting in legal mechanisms to prevent archaeological excavations or calling for the return of collections now in museums to Indian peoples. Archaeology has become a focal point for complaints about wrongdoings of the past. Apart from the question of returning and/or reburying material, sometimes there have been vehement objections to new excavations. The Chumash Indians, for example, refused permission for scientists to remove what may be the oldest human remains in California, even though an offer was made to return and rebury the bones after a year's study. The bones, thought to be about 9000 years old, were eroding out of a cliff on Santa Rosa Island, 100 km (62 miles) west of Los Angeles. Under California's Antiquities Act the fate of the bones lay with their most likely descendants – and the Chumash were angry about past treatment of their ancestors' skeletons, with hundreds of remains scattered in various universities and museums. Like many Maori, they preferred to see the bones destroyed "in accordance with nature's law" than to have other people interfere with them.

As in Australia and New Zealand, there is no single, unified indigenous tradition. American Indians have wide-ranging attitudes toward the dead and the soul. The solution to the problem has been found to lie in acquiescence, compromise, and collaboration. Quite often archaeologists have acquiesced in the return of very recent remains from known individuals or from fairly close ancestors of living objectors. Much material has also been returned that had no archaeological context and was thus of minimal value to science. Reburial of more important material is a difficult issue. Despite resolutions passed by the Society for American Archaeology and other anthropological associations in North America opposing such reburial except where lineal descendants can be traced, there is now a clear trend in favor of negotiated reburial on a large scale. In 1990, the Native American Graves Protection and Repatriation Act (NAGPRA) was passed, requiring some 5000 federally funded institutions and government agencies to return Native American skeletons, funerary and sacred objects, and items of profound cultural importance to American Indian tribes and Native Hawaiians. By 1995 they had to provide detailed inventories of all skeletal remains and funerary goods in their collections, and the next step will be to determine exactly what will be returned. The most difficult problems – apart from defining what key terms in the law, such as "items of profound cultural importance," actually mean – will arise over prehistoric material, as opposed to remains of known individuals, although for some Native Americans – as for some Aborigines – the age is

immaterial and everything is considered ancestral. Indeed, the law explicitly recognizes the validity of oral traditions, so a tribe can claim prehistoric remains if its oral traditions say that its people were created in the same region where the remains were found.

Controversy and a legal battle still dog the bones of "Kennewick Man," found a few years ago in Washington State, and radiocarbon dated to 9300 BP. Eight prominent anthropologists have sued the Army Corps of Engineers, which has jurisdiction over the site, for permission to study the bones, but the Corps wants to hand the skeleton to the local Native American Umatilla Tribe for reburial, in accordance with NAGPRA. The scientists are extremely anxious to run tests, since preliminary examination had suggested that Kennewick Man was a 19th-century white settler, so that its early date raises complex, important and fascinating questions about the peopling of the Americas. The Umatilla, on the other hand, are adamantly against any investigation, insisting that their oral tradition says their tribe has been part of this land since the beginning of time, and so all bones recovered from here are necessarily their ancestors – and must not be damaged for dating or genetic analysis.

Some tribes are taking matters to such extremes that even naturally shed strands of human hair, now being recovered from archaeological sites, are considered as human remains (and hence sacred) and their return has been demanded. Tribal representatives have worked out agreements to reinter extensive collections from several museums, including Stanford University and the American Museum of Natural History. Chicago's Field Museum has given back 62 of its 2000 remains, and expects to return the rest. The Smithsonian Institution has returned 2000 skeletons for reburial, with the remaining 14,000 to follow. And at Wounded Knee, South Dakota, Seminole Indian bones from Florida were reburied by archaeologists and American Indians in 1989 to mark the establishment of a national cemetery for American Indians (see p. 542).

To the relief of researchers, however, who stress the new techniques that can extract hitherto unimagined information from human bone (see Chapter 11), not all tribes want human material returned or are planning to rebury it once it is returned; many have opened or are planning museums of their own, some with small research centers which are staffed with Native American scientists and open to academic researchers willing to work with tribal councils. Moreover, some tribes are willing to let the bones be laser-scanned before reburial – this stores digital data from the specimens, enabling electronic copies or even 3-D facsimiles to be available for study.

Seminole Indian bones from Florida are reburied in 1989 by archaeologists and American Indians at Wounded Knee.

Now that archaeologists have come to recognize Native American rights, working relations have improved, and there are growing numbers of American Indian representatives who appreciate the contribution that archaeology is making to their history and, indeed, to their ethnic identity. But there are still tensions – some archaeologists have had their lives threatened as grave-robbers – so it is important for excavators to be sensitive to the wishes of the local community. One excellent example is the archaeological program at the Zuni Pueblo, New Mexico, begun in 1975, which involved consultation with the local community every step of the way, and which trained some of the Zuni people in archaeology. Although the Zuni abhor the exposure of human remains, let alone the handling of bones, they allowed the archaeologists to take photographs and record data, and in one instance to remove and rebury an eroding burial. Influence was felt in both directions, in that the Zuni acknowledged the importance of new information about their mortuary customs, while some archaeologists experienced a qualitative change in their values and beliefs concerning excavation of such burials. Since then, however, there has been a change at Zuni, and no permits for archaeological excavation are being approved by the tribal council, showing the volatility of such situations.

THE USES OF THE PAST

The uses of the past, and the problems surrounding them, go beyond the specific question of who owns what. They concern ideological and economic issues. The ideological ones are perhaps the more important, ultimately, and they were reviewed above in "The Meaning of the Past: The Archaeology of Identity." But the past has its economic uses, both for tourism and in making available the medical, agricultural and technological experiences of past societies, some of which are relevant to the present.

Making the Past Pay

Tourism now represents a significant part of the economic turnover of many countries of the world, and in many of these the "heritage industry," as it has come to be called, is a highly significant part of the touristic opportunity. Of course the presentation of major sites to the public has for a long time been seen as part of the responsibility of governments, along with the proper conservation of monuments. And particularly in Mexico, Egypt, Greece, and Italy, the ancient monuments have attracted a large tourist trade for over a

century. But increasingly the display of archaeological sites in many lands is being commercialized. Heritage has become big business, and at times it becomes part of the entertainment industry. The success of the Jorvik Viking Centre (see Chapter 13), for instance, has stimulated the development of other "time capsule" experiences, not all of them so carefully researched or so authentically based.

And if the innovative display of the past at Jorvik has had its followers, so has the "recreation" of the past, at projects like Butser Ancient Farm in southern England (see box, pp. 274–75). That project had a serious research objective, within the framework of experimental archaeology, but others have been constructed with the principal objective of attracting a paying public. Increasingly, volunteer participants are used, who dress in appropriate ancient costume, live (at any rate in daylight hours) in reconstructed ancient houses, and sometimes carry out the craft occupations (often with considerable skill) of their early predecessors.

Of course, public awareness and enjoyment of archaeology are crucial to the discipline's survival and development when government money available is often restricted. Peru's new antiquities laws now allow the granting of private concessions to develop and run archaeological monuments as tourist attractions. However, despite the possible financial advantages, many archaeologists and preservationists are worried, since there is already a huge conflict between tourist-driven "reconstruction" and the integrity of archaeological sites – many sites have been "reconstructed" so extensively that it is increasingly difficult to study them. And, as we discuss below, increasing tourism has an inevitable effect on preservation problems at sites like Machu Picchu which attracts 300,000 visitors per year and is in serious risk of permanent damage.

Another potential danger is that the sites, and even the tourists themselves, become targets for terrorism, which can have a major impact on a country's economy. For example, by 1995 attacks by Islamic fundamentalists had cost the Egyptian government at least $2 billion in lost tourist revenues, one of the main sources of hard currency for the country's ailing economy, while the massacre of 58 tourists in Luxor in 1997 has already lost Egypt a further $700 million.

The presentation of the past to the public is now adopting techniques at the cutting edge of modern technology, such as holograms of artifacts. For example, thanks to the massive database of computerized information on Pompeii, visitors to recent exhibitions about the city could take electronic walks through rich houses, moving from room to room, calling up images and a mass of information on their frescoes, mosaics, and artifacts. The French abbey of Cluny, once the greatest church in Christendom, was demolished in 1793 after the French Revolution, but has been "brought back to life" with computer technology. It has been reconstructed inside a computer's memory, and by wearing a virtual reality helmet one can walk electronically through its interior. Already other sites – including existing ones which the public can no longer see (such as Lascaux Cave or the interior of Stonehenge) – have been developed for virtual reality. Eventually, an Internet archive will exist, allowing anyone connected to download a file via a modem and print out a perfect 3-D replica of a fossil or artifact.

There is also a less attractive side to the notion of making the past pay, and that is the looting of archaeological sites so that their contents may be sold to collectors. That issue is discussed below and in the box "Collectors are the Real Looters" (pp. 556–57).

Economic Lessons from the Past

The economic uses of archaeology are not, however, restricted to tourism and collecting. Archaeology shows that in many areas where today the soil is barren agriculture once flourished. Are there lessons to be learnt here for modern farmers?

Nabataeans in the Negev Desert. Israel's Negev Desert is one of the world's most inhospitable places, with temperatures rising above 38°C (100°F), and it receives less than 2 cm (0.79 in) rainfall each year. Yet about 2000 years ago the Nabataeans lived there in cities, growing grapes, wheat, and olives. How did they do it?

It used to be assumed that the climate was lusher and much wetter, but we now know that it remained unaltered since well before these settlements. Aerial photographs reveal a complex pattern of ditches, terraces, and barriers crisscrossing the hills. Evidently the Nabataeans took advantage of the region's rare, violent cloudbursts and flash-floods to utilize the rainwater, which was collected in ditches and then channeled by a system of low walls into terraced fields. The system also supplied drinking water, which was collected in large cisterns dug into limestone ridges. Thousands of such cisterns are known in the Middle East.

Scientists of the Ben-Gurion University of the Negev have used exactly the same methods, without irrigation or new technology, to reconstruct ancient farms such as that near the ruins of the Nabataean town of Avdat, which was an important stopping place for caravans between 300 BC and AD 600. Here they are able to grow a variety of cereals (with very high yields), fruits, vegetables, and nuts, even in years of drought. They have learnt that the runoff technique requires hilly regions from which the water can flow down and where the soil is sufficiently firm to support the drainage channels. The rain-collection area also needs to be 30 times larger than the growing area.

The ancients therefore show that by adapting intelligently to one's environment and natural resources, it should be possible to make fertile land once dismissed as worthless – perhaps 5 percent of all arid land. The techniques are being taught to agriculturalists from developing nations.

Agriculture in the Andes. A similar lesson from the past has emerged in Peru, where the Cusichaca Trust, directed by Ann Kendall, is applying archaeology to the revival of agriculture. The ancient town of Patallacta, located between Cuzco and Machu Picchu on an Inca highway, stands on artificial terraces above the confluence of the Cusichaca and Urubamba rivers. In its heyday it had 115 dwellings and a fortress nearby, and farmland in the area may have supported 5000 people. Until recently most of this land was barren, supporting only 15 families.

The Incas and their predecessors had built stone canals which carried water down from glacier-fed streams to the lower slopes by a winding route which prevented it overflowing or bursting the stonework. The canals were always kept free of rubble and silt – until they were abandoned at the Spanish Conquest. Working with the local community, the Cusichaca Trust has cleared and restored two of these canals. Around 60 ha (150 acres) are now flourishing again under irrigation and the Trust is pursuing similar work in the nearby Patacancha valley.

A similar project around Lake Titicaca has also proved a great success (see box). The latest work of American archaeologist Alan Kolata and his colleagues in Bolivia involves 52 communities in the altiplano, numbering several thousand people, and has 200 ha (495 acres) under raised-field cultivation. Crop yields are about seven times as high as on traditional dry-farmed fields. Development agencies are now supporting various field projects in Peru and Bolivia.

From Building Lessons to the History of Disease. There are other lessons to be learnt from archaeological remains. It is unwise, for example, to build modern settlements or dams in areas known to have been repeatedly damaged in the past by torrents, earthquakes, or volcanic eruptions. All over China, there are ancient stelae and documents that record past earthquakes, and "seismic archaeology" is considered of great importance here. In the Near East, information on ancient earthquakes can be obtained from historical, biblical, and archaeological evidence extending back 10,000 years, including 30 major quakes in the past 2000 years alone.

Human remains can likewise, as was discussed in Chapter 11, yield important information on the history of specific diseases and pathologies, some of which are still a problem today. For example, medical specialists claim that the high incidence of ear-canal pathologies in the skeletons of ancient Australian Aborigines could help to pinpoint the causes of the high rate of chronic middle-ear infections found among modern Aborigine children.

To sum up, the past can serve the present in a variety of ways – ideological, touristic, agricultural, constructional, and medical. Archaeologists could do worse than to lay more emphasis on the practical benefits of their discipline, thereby helping to justify their claim on public and private funds.

There will, however, be little archaeology for future generations to pursue unless the great tide of destruction of our heritage is stemmed and adequate conservation measures are introduced.

APPLIED ARCHAEOLOGY: FARMING IN PERU

In 1980, American archaeologist Clark Erickson, Peruvian agronomist Ignacio Garaycochea and their colleagues set up PACE (Proyecto Agricola de los Campos Elevados, or Raised Field Agricultural Project). The multidisciplinary team's aim was to reintroduce ancient agricultural practices around Lake Titicaca, in Peru and Bolivia.

As in many other parts of tropical Latin America, the ancient cultures constructed raised fields (known locally as *camellones* or *waru-waru*). These elevated planting surfaces are up to 1 m (3 ft) high, 4–10 m (13–33 ft) wide, and up to 100 m (325 ft) long, and made of

The two stages of construction: drawings used in booklets produced by the Raised Fields project to teach the technique and its advantages to local communities.

the soil dug from the canals in between. They combine good drainage and moisture control with excellent soil and growth conditions, and remarkable resistance to night frosts because the canal water stores heat during the day and releases it slowly at night. The canals can be manipulated either to drain excessive water during periods of heavy rainfall or to retain water during periods of drought.

Aerial photography and excavation revealed that the high, flat pampas around Lake Titicaca had at least 82,000 ha (202,620 acres) devoted to this system; it seems to have begun around 1000 BC, and was abandoned after the Inca Conquest about 500 years ago: the Spanish chroniclers make no mention of it at all.

On this altiplano (high plain), at an altitude of nearly 4000 m (13,000 ft), the soils are poor, rainfall is irregular, wet and dry seasons vary unpredictably, and frost and drought are constant threats. At the marshy lake edge fluctuating water levels can cause widespread inundations. Modern

agricultural methods have been introduced, involving heavy machinery, chemical fertilizers, irrigation, and imported crops, in the mistaken belief that the plain was being under-utilized. They have proved unsuccessful, falling prey to the adverse climatic conditions. Consequently, much of the area filled with relic raised fields is classed as of low agricultural potential and used as pasture.

The PACE team cleared and refurbished about 10 ha (25 acres) of abandoned but well-preserved raised fields at Huatta, near Puno (Peru), using only traditional tools, and planted them with potatoes and other traditional tuber crops. The yields were excellent even in dry years. In the 1984/85 season alone potato production was increased by over two-and-a-half to four times.

In addition, the raised fields were unharmed by the severe drought of 1982/83 and by the massive flooding of the 1983/84 and 1985/86 growing seasons, which destroyed crops on land farmed with modern methods.

Likewise, frosts severely damaged nearby fields, but had minimal effect on the raised fields.

It now seems clear that the prehistoric field technologies are an excellent solution to the development of agriculture in this kind of environment. They are perfectly adapted to its climatic factors; the rich organic muck that accumulates in the canals provides the fertilizer for the next growing season, and the only requirements are local labor, and traditional crops, tools, and skills. Initial high labor costs are soon offset by high production yields and low maintenance costs.

The local populace is taking a keen interest, as is the government, and the project has produced well-illustrated booklets, some of them in Quechua (the native language), aimed specifically at teaching the techniques to the local farmers. A videotape in Quechua is also used in the training program.

Peruvian villagers (right) use footplows (chakitaqlla), hoes (rawkana), and carrying cloths (manta) for moving soil to create raised fields. The result of their endeavors are fields like those below, planted with potatoes.

CONSERVATION AND DESTRUCTION

Most nations of the world now recognize that it is the public duty of a government to have some policy with regards to conservation. That policy will apply to natural resources and wildlife, but it will also apply to archaeological remains. So most nations now have some protective legislation – which is not all equally effective – for their ancient sites, minor as well as major, and government programs. In the United States these are organized under the rubric of Cultural Resource Management (CRM; see box opposite), and in other countries under Archaeological Heritage Management.

There are two principal stages in archaeological conservation everywhere. The first is the gathering of information, so that relevant sites and areas may be recognized and properly recorded. The second is the conservation of those sites and areas that can be effectively protected. Sometimes damage or destruction cannot be prevented, in which case one adopts a policy of salvage or rescue archaeology, partially excavating or at least recording the site before it vanishes for good.

There are two main agencies of destruction, both of them human. One is construction of roads, quarries, dams, office blocks, etc. These are conspicuous and the threat is at least easily recognizable. A different kind of destruction – agricultural intensification – is slower but much wider in its extent, thus in the long term much more destructive. Ever increasing areas of the earth, once uncultivated or cultivated by traditional non-intensive methods, are being opened up to mechanized farming. The tractor and the deep plow have replaced the digging stick and the ard. In other areas, forest plantations now cover what was formerly open land, and tree roots are destroying settlement sites and field monuments.

Elsewhere, reclamation schemes are transforming the nature of the environment, so that arid lands are being flooded, and the wetlands of say Florida or the Somerset Levels are being reclaimed through drainage. In each case the result is destruction of remarkable archaeological evidence. More ancient remains have been lost in the last two decades than ever before in the history of the world.

There are two further human agencies of destruction, which should not be overlooked. The first is tourism, which, while economically having important effects on archaeology (see p. 544), makes the effective conservation of archaeological sites more difficult. The second is not new, but has grown dramatically in scale: the looting of archaeological sites by those who dig for monetary gain, seeking only saleable objects and destroying everything else in their search.

Legislative Basis of Conservation

The legislation for the ancient heritage varies considerably from nation to nation.

The Rise of CRM in the United States. Over the past two decades the whole pace and direction of American archaeology has been transformed by the development of public archaeology – archaeology funded primarily from federal or state resources and known, as we have seen, as Cultural Resource Management. The history of the legislation for public archaeology is very relevant to how CRM is practiced today.

The Antiquities Act of 1906 stated the responsibilities of the federal government for "antiquities" and extended these responsibilities to include lands controlled by, as well as owned by, the government. Then in 1935 the Historic Sites Act gave the National Park Service responsibility for identifying and protecting outstanding historic sites. The National Historic Preservation Act of 1966 (amended in 1976 and 1980) was an important milestone. It established a National Register of Historic Places, and provided for grants to state preservation programs. The National Environmental Policy Act of 1969 established the basis for CRM by laying down a firm policy for government land use, requiring federal agencies to consider environmental, historical, and cultural values whenever federally owned land is modified, or federal funds used on private land. The act required the preparation of an Environmental Impact Statement (EIS) for any federal works – thus bringing in archaeologists at an earlier stage – but it did not in itself provide funding for salvage archaeology to mitigate their effects.

In 1971, Executive Order 11593 was issued by President Nixon to unite existing legislation into a more coherent federal policy. This set the framework for the great upsurge of archaeological survey work funded by federal agencies such as the Forest Service, the National Parks Service, and the Army Corps of Engineers in the 1970s. It was, however, the Archaeological and Historic Preservation Act of 1974 that authorized federal agencies to provide funds for the preservation and recovery of archaeological or historic resources when endangered by federal projects. These funds were to be provided by contract – giving rise to the term *contract archaeology* – specifying that up to 1 percent of the cost

THE PRACTICE OF CRM IN THE UNITED STATES

Federal construction projects in the United States – those on federal land, or on private land but federally funded – are legally required to consider environmental, cultural, and historical resources that may be adversely affected. Cultural Resource Management (CRM) has grown out of this requirement. Projects on state land, or funded by the states, are in general similarly protected.

Most projects develop in two phases: assessment, and mitigation. During assessment, the affected land is surveyed and an Environmental Impact Statement prepared. The decision is then made as to what steps need to be taken in "mitigation." Can project plans be altered? What salvage work should be carried out?

One good example is the vast Tennessee-Tombigbee Waterway project. Of the 682 sites revealed by survey, it was determined that 27

would be affected by waterway construction. Of these, 17 had good research potential, and another 24 sites were selected for data recovery. Twelve sites could be preserved by altering the construction program.

Excavation was designed to investigate the evolution of cultures in the area, with emphasis on sampling a good range of sites. The largest site was Lubbub Creek, the only major settlement in the threatened area belonging to the Mississippian culture (AD 900–1450). It includes a major ceremonial mound surrounded by a fortified village. The work undertaken in mitigation of environmental impact gave an excellent opportunity for systematic excavation of both settlement and cemeteries.

Several institutions have established outstanding reputations for salvage archaeology. Among them are the Arkansas Survey and the University of South Carolina. These

reputations are based on the quality of their published reports – reflecting coherent project designs – and on efficient data recovery and clear-minded interpretation.

Not all contract archaeology is of this standard. "Cowboy" operators can be attracted by the large sums of money involved. But the Society of Professional Archaeologists (SOPA) and the American Society for Conservation Archaeology have considered standards of professional qualifications, training, and ethical guidelines. What has been termed "a crisis of quality" may in due course result in a more uniform and higher standard of work.

An aerial view of the Lubbub Creek site on the Tombigbee River, Alabama. The smaller photograph shows two of the salvage archaeologists carefully cleaning a large urn.

of the project might be expended in this way. The legislation thus provided funds for excavation, analysis of finds, and publication of the results (but with no legal obligation to publish fully). Finally, the Archaeological Resources Protection Act of 1979 gave better protection to sites located on federal and Native American lands. This protection of Native American lands was enhanced by the passage of the Native American Graves Protection and Repatriation Act (NAGPRA) in 1990 – see above. Following the federal legislation there have been laws passed at the state and, in some places, city level to protect archaeological and historic resources (these are generally called State (or City) Environmental Quality Review laws). The federal laws are administered for the most part through State Historic Preservation Offices.

Unfortunately, the 1990, 1979, and earlier acts suffer from the great defect of all American heritage legislation: they offer no protection to sites located on privately owned land. Archaeologists Mark Michel and Steven LeBlanc have set up the independent Archaeological Conservancy precisely in order to purchase and protect such vulnerable sites, but the task is a huge one, at present beyond the means of a single private organization. Furthermore, current legislation is completely inadequate to protect the thousands of shipwrecks in American waters. Occasionally there are success stories, such as the World War II battleship USS *Arizona*, sunk in Pearl Harbor in 1941 and now preserved on the sea bed as a National Memorial. All too often, however, historic wrecks have been looted before archaeologists could reach them.

The scale of CRM funding is considerable. A major project may cost in the order of $1 million, whereas a research grant from the National Science Foundation will rarely exceed $100,000. The concern underlying this expenditure is with conservation rather than research. The result, however, has been to fund some very ambitious archaeological projects, where it has proved possible to formulate valid research aims and to advance our knowledge of the past. CRM archaeology is on such a large scale that, not surprisingly, some projects have been less well conducted, and less well published. This has led to tensions between academic and CRM archaeologists. Yet, although some academic criticisms may be justified, there is ample evidence that CRM archaeology can meet the highest scholarly standards (see box, p. 547).

Britain and Denmark. Few other countries in the world have the comprehensive US-style legal provisions that bind the government to consider environmental and cultural factors in the course of government-funded work, and to pay for salvage archaeology where appropriate. On the other hand, many countries do have legislation that prevents the private developer from destroying important archaeological sites on private land.

In Britain, for instance, the official agency English Heritage advises the relevant government department on sites worthy of protection, whether or not these are on private land. If they are regarded as of national importance they are placed on a Schedule of Ancient Monuments. The Schedule includes not simply major sites – often in the care of English Heritage and open to the public – but minor ones as well. There are currently about 13,000 scheduled sites in England alone. When the private owner of a listed site wishes to develop it or the land around it, he or she has to apply for Scheduled Monument Consent. In cases where it is judged that the development should go ahead, English Heritage will usually pay part of the costs of excavation so that the site can be recorded.

In Denmark some 28,000 monuments are included in a "first category." Each of these is fully protected by law against destruction and is surrounded by a 100-m (328-ft) protection zone. All other fixed monuments fall within the "second category" of protection, which is only a legal one: there are over 100,000 of these.

Australia and New Zealand. In both Australia and New Zealand considerable steps have been taken in recent years toward the recording and safeguarding of archaeological sites of all kinds. Only 20 years ago not one Australian state provided statutory protection for any Aboriginal relics or sites, but by 1981 all of them did so. Analogous legislation to protect the European cultural inheritance – material remains of 200 years of European settlement in Australia – lagged behind, but great progress has been made on this issue as well.

The Australian Heritage Commission was established in 1976 and has provided a national focus for the natural and cultural environment. Its first priority was a Register of the National Estate, published in 1981, which listed over 6600 places including many of archaeological importance. The register helps to protect sites from development projects. Preservation of the national heritage is one of the primary functions of the Commission, which also plays a vital role in the identification and documentation of sites, in serving as a planning tool for the government and developers, and in stimulating public consciousness of Australia's rich cultural background.

In New Zealand, the Historic Places Act of 1980 set out to preserve and protect places of historic significance, including archaeological sites associated with human activity over 100 years old, both Maori and European. The 100-year rule, however, does not preclude the Historic Places Trust being involved with much younger sites. Thanks to the 1980 Act, no site can be modified or damaged in any way without the permission of the Trust, and this applies not only to known sites but also to places where there is reasonable cause to suspect the existence of a site.

Increasingly today archaeologists think in terms of entire landscapes rather than simply of single sites. In this respect, the legal systems of protection of many nations are proving inadequate, based as they are on the now rather old-fashioned notion of the single site. In some countries, however, it is proving possible to establish "conservation areas," where monuments are considered in relation to each other and to the landscape of which they form a part.

Recording of New Archaeological Sites

The first task in any program of Cultural Resource Management is that of locating sites and recording them systematically. The appropriate recording techniques are those of remote sensing and surface survey, discussed in Chapter 3. Here the issue is rather one of organization.

Although, as we have seen, most nations have registers of their more important known archaeological sites, few organize comprehensive survey programs in which new sites are methodically sought and recorded. Denmark is one of the most advanced in this field and Canada, too, has been a pioneer, with an early, computerized national archaeological survey.

In Britain, since the beginning of this century, the Royal Commissions on Historical Monuments have been carrying out surveys for each county – each administrative division of the country – publishing the principal sites in handsome inventories. In the early 1900s the national mapping agency, the Ordnance Survey, also set up its own archaeological section to provide information for the national survey of maps. This section produced a remarkable series of maps that treated the archaeology of Britain on a period-by-period basis. Over the past 30 years, most counties have also set up their own County Sites and Monuments Record, to provide a full database for the County Planning Office, so that when some development is proposed, information on known sites within the development area is readily available.

Gradually these various enterprises are being brought together so that there is a unified national database of archaeological remains. In England, for example, this is the responsibility of the Royal Commission on Historical Monuments, which maintains a computerized "National Archaeological Record." Many archaeological agencies have now begun to make use of Geographic Information Systems (see Chapter 3) such as the ARC/INFO system for recording site data. In the United States, GIS have been used extensively within Cultural Resource Management for some years, most notably to generate and test predictive models of archaeological resources (Chapter 3). GRASS (the Geographic Resources Analysis Support System, written by the United States Corps of Engineers), is a GIS system used by the National Park Service, which offers access to information on the environment. These systems offer a number of advantages over existing text-based databases, particularly in that they allow the complete storage and subsequent querying of data about archaeological monuments which have a large spatial extent. GIS also allow planners to store and manipulate archaeological data within the same computer system as other data about the landscape such as landuse, topography, or plant and animal habitats. For this reason, GIS are widely seen as an appropriate means of integrating archaeological planning within a large environmental planning framework.

In one sense a national archaeological record can never be complete, because new sites are being discovered all the time. For this reason, when any major development is proposed, it is necessary that the area in question be surveyed, or re-surveyed, intensively. In the terminology of CRM, it is necessary to produce an Environmental Impact Statement (EIS) – the impact being that of the development on the local archaeological remains. It is then possible to assess what damage will be done.

Threats to Archaeological Sites: Partial Solutions and Unresolved Problems

Damage by Developers. The ideal administrative arrangement, from an archaeological point of view, is that each developer should have to apply for planning and development permission. During the procedures leading to the granting of that permission, the drafting of an Environmental Impact Statement should be mandatory, paid for by the developer. If the EIS indicates that archaeological sites are likely to be damaged, alternative schemes should be devised.

If there is no clear alternative available, some judgment has to be taken as to whether the value of the threatened site or sites outweighs the importance of the proposed development. If it is deemed necessary that the development has to go ahead, then

Threats to our heritage: concrete piles – foundations for a modern office block – have been driven into the ground around the archaeological remains of the Rose theater, where some of Shakespeare's plays were first performed in the 1590s.

archaeological survey, including excavation, should take place in advance of any unavoidable destruction. Such work, and its full publication, should be paid for by the developer.

In reality the situation and the specific threats vary from country to country. In *England*, developer-funding is now the norm, developers paying either for rescue excavation ("preservation by record") or for special foundations which minimize the damage to archaeological deposits. Things can still go wrong, as in the case of the Rose theater in London – where some of Shakespeare's plays were performed in the 1590s – the remains of which were encountered during construction work in 1989. Although the theater's position was approximately known, the actual walls were unearthed only after planning permission had been given and construction was under way; the development had to be halted and a redesign undertaken – a major expense which was largely met by the developer. It was plain that the archaeological profession needed to improve its ability to predict the value of sites before planning permission was given, and a special project was initiated by English Heritage (the state agency) and undertaken by the University of York with Ove Arup, consulting engineers, intended to design a procedure for the management of archaeological resources in towns (see pp. 523–24). The new protocol requires that, for each historic urban area, a research agenda is composed and a deposit model of the buried resource made, the data being entered on a GIS. The potential impact of any development can then be immediately assessed, and this is followed by a detailed on-site evaluation. The planners, in collaboration with the archaeological community and the developer, can then decide the mitigation strategy: to design special "benign" foundations; to make the site available for research; or to allow its destruction. Some of these principles have since been enshrined in the Department of the Environment's Planning Policy Guidance note 16. In the countryside, the chief means of protection is "scheduling," that is, placing the site on a list, or schedule of protected monuments (see above).

In the *United States*, annual expenditure on salvage or contract archaeology is some 10 times greater than in England but, as we saw above, full protection is granted only to federally funded projects, or those on federal lands. There is, furthermore, no legislative provision for full publication of the work undertaken. The results can be notified to the State Historic Preservation Officer simply in the form of a "letter report," which is filed but often never published.

Problems of keeping up with the rate of development are particularly acute in *Japan*. In 1980 alone, more than 6200 sites were recorded as having been destroyed or exposed to destruction by developers. This is why the great majority of archaeological work in Japan has to be devoted to rapid salvage excavations. Processing of the voluminous data cannot keep pace with its extraction from the ground, so there is a mountainous backlog of material to be published. The country now has a critical shortage of storage space, exacerbated by a five-fold increase in (mostly salvage) excavations, during the past 15–20 years (there were 8200 in 1991, which cost 98 billion yen – about $1 billion).

In *Australia*, threats posed by development were made all too clear by the case of the proposed dam on the Franklin river, southwest Tasmania. This would

Salvage excavations in Japan: work in progress at a site in Tama New Town, 1986. The conveyor belts are used to transport spoil from the site.

have destroyed one of the last great natural temperate wilderness areas on earth, as well as some of the richest and most important early inhabited cave sites in Australia. Only an international outcry prevented the hydro-electric scheme from going ahead. The region has now been added to the UNESCO (United Nations) list of World Heritage Areas. Dams all over the world have drowned innumerable archaeological sites, and new ones are constantly being built. It recently proved possible to save the rock art of Portugal's Côa Valley from a major dam (see above, p. 158), and the valley has also been added to UNESCO's World Heritage List; but the huge dam being built on China's Yangzi River is going to destroy countless archaeological sites.

Nevertheless, given that development is an inevitable feature of the world economy, archaeologists have in most cases to learn to cooperate with developers. The fruits of such a policy can be seen in those towns and cities where archaeology is now accorded some importance in urban planning, often involving salvage work and subsequent preservation of important remains. A good example is Mexico City, where the discovery in 1978 of the *Templo Mayor* or Great Temple of the Aztecs led to the initiation of an impressive salvage and preservation project (see box overleaf). Other examples of successful preservation of archaeological remains in towns include the Roman

CONSERVATION: THE GREAT TEMPLE OF THE AZTECS IN MEXICO CITY

When the Spanish Conquistadors under Hernán Cortés occupied the Aztec capital, Tenochtitlan, in 1521, they destroyed its buildings and established their own capital, Mexico City, on the same site.

In 1790 the now-famous statue of the Aztec mother goddess Coatlicue was found, and also the great Calendar Stone, but it was not until the 20th century that more systematic archaeological work took place.

Various relatively small-scale excavations were carried out on remains within the city as they came to light in the course of building work. But in 1975 a more coherent initiative was taken: the institution by the Department of Pre-Hispanic Monuments of the Basin of Mexico Project. Its aim is to halt the destruction of archaeological remains during the continuing growth of the city. In 1977, a Museum of Tenochtitlan Project was begun, with the aim of excavating the area where remains of what appeared to be the Great Temple of the Aztecs had been found in 1948. The project was radically transformed early in 1978 when electricity workers discovered a large stone carved with a series of reliefs.

The Department of Salvage Archaeology of the National Institute of Anthropology and History took charge. Within days, a huge monolith, 3.25 m (10 ft 7 in) in diameter, was revealed depicting the dismembered body of the Aztec goddess Coyolxauhqui who, according to myth, had been killed by her brother, the war god Huitzilopochtli.

The Museum of Tenochtitlan Project, under the direction of Eduardo Matos Moctezuma, became the Great Temple Project, which over the next few years brought to light one of the most remarkable archaeological sites in Mexico.

No one had realized how much would be preserved of the Great Temple. Although the Spaniards had razed the standing structure to the ground in 1521, this pyramid was the last of a series of re-buildings. Beneath the ruins of the last temple the excavations revealed those of earlier temples.

In addition to these architectural remains was a wonderful series of offerings to the temple's two gods, Huitzilopochtli and the rain god Tlaloc – objects of obsidian and jade, terracotta and stone sculptures, and other special dedications, including rare coral and the remains of a jaguar buried with a ball of turquoise in its mouth.

A major area of Mexico City has now been turned into a permanent museum and national monument. Mexico has regained one of its greatest pre-Columbian buildings, and the Great Temple of the Aztecs is once again one of the marvels of Tenochtitlan.

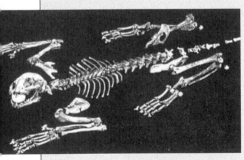

The skeleton of a jaguar from a chamber in the fourth of seven building stages of the Great Temple. The jade ball in its mouth may have been placed there as a substitute for the spirit of the deceased.

The Great Temple excavation site, with stairways visible of successive phases of the monument. The building was originally pyramidal in form, surmounted by twin temples to the war god Huitzilopochtli and the rain god Tlaloc. Conservation work is in progress here on the Coyolxauhqui stone, visible under scaffolding (left of center).

The Great Stone, found in 1978, provided the catalyst for the Great Temple excavations. The goddess Coyolxauhqui is shown decapitated (left, a detail of her head) and dismembered – killed by her brother, the war god Huitzilopochtli.

mosaic in Cologne, Germany; Viking Age timber buildings at York (see Chapter 13); the Roman and medieval foundations in front of Notre Dame in Paris; and the Lower Paleolithic camp of Terra Amata preserved in a museum under an apartment block in Nice, on the French Mediterranean coast.

Agricultural Damage. Although most countries keep some control over the activities of developers and builders, the damage to archaeological sites from farming is much more difficult to assess. The few published studies make sober reading. One of the best, *The Past Under the Plough* (ed. J. Hinchliffe and R.T. Schadla-Hall, 1980), shows that in Britain even those sites that are notionally protected – by being listed on the national Schedule of Ancient Monuments – are not, in reality, altogether safe. The position may be much better in Denmark and in certain other countries, but elsewhere only the most conspicuous sites are protected. The more modest field monuments and open settlements are not, and these are the sites that are suffering from mechanized agriculture.

Damage from Looting and the Market in Illicit Antiquities. The saddest kind of damage is that by clandestine excavators, concerned only to find objects of high saleable value, and quite untroubled by the loss of information when the finds are divorced from their original context. Many of these looters use metal detectors, even on legally protected sites.

One such *clandestino*, Luigi Perticarari, a robber in Tarquinia, published his memoirs in 1986 (*I Segreti di un Tombarolo*) and makes no apology for his trade. He has more first-hand knowledge of Etruscan tombs than any archaeologist, but his activity destroys the chance of anyone sharing that knowledge. He claims to have emptied some 4000 tombs dating from the 8th to the 3rd centuries BC in the past 30 years. So it is that, while the world's store of Etruscan antiquities in museums and private collections grows larger, our knowledge of Etruscan burial customs and social organization does not.

The same is true for the remarkable marble sculptures of the Cycladic islands of Greece, dating to around 2500 BC. We admire the breathtaking elegance of these works in the world's museums, but we have little idea of how they were produced or of the social and religious life of the Cycladic communities that made them. Again, the contexts have been lost.

In the American Southwest, 90 percent of the Classic Mimbres sites (c. AD 1000) have now been looted or destroyed (see box, overleaf). In southwestern Colorado, 60 percent of prehistoric Anasazi sites have been

DESTRUCTION AND RESPONSE: MIMBRES

One of the most melancholy stories in recent archaeology is that of Mimbres. The Mimbres potters of the American Southwest created a unique art tradition in the prehistoric period, painting the inside of hemispherical bowls with vigorous animalian and human forms. These bowls are now much prized by archaeologists and art lovers. But this fascination has led to the systematic looting of Mimbres sites on a scale unequaled in the United States, or indeed anywhere in the world.

The Mimbres people lived along a small river, the Rio Mimbres, in mud-built villages, similar in some respects to those of the later Pueblo Indians. Painted pottery began, as we now know, around AD 550, and reached its apogee in the Classic Mimbres period, from about AD 1000 to 1130.

Systematic archaeological work on Mimbres sites began in the 1920s, but it was not in general well

Funerary bowl of the 10th century AD. *The figures may be male and female, or life and death. The "kill" hole at the base allowed the object's spirit to be released.*

published. Looters soon found, however, that with pick and shovel they could unearth Mimbres pots to sell on the market for primitive art. Nor was this activity necessarily illegal. In United States law there is nothing to prevent excavation of any kind by the owner on private land,

A masked coyote dancer is the subject of this fine Mimbres bowl, dating from AD *1100–1250.*

and nothing to prevent the owner permitting others to destroy archaeological sites in this way.

In the early 1960s, a method of bulldozing Mimbres sites was developed which did not destroy all the pottery. The operators found that by controlled bulldozing they could remove a relatively small depth of soil at a time and extract many of the pots unbroken. In the process sites were of course completely destroyed, and all hope of establishing an archaeological context for the material was lost.

Since 1973 there has at last been a concerted archaeological response. The Mimbres Foundation, under the direction of Steven LeBlanc, was able to secure funding from private sources to undertake excavations in the remains of some of the looted

sites. They also made good progress in explaining to the owners of those sites how destructive this looting process was to any hope of learning about the Mimbres past. From 1975 to 1978 a series of field seasons at several partially looted sites succeeded in establishing at least the outlines of Mimbres archaeology, and in putting the chronology upon a sure footing.

The Mimbres Foundation also reached the conclusion that archaeological excavation is an expensive form of conservation, and decided to purchase a number of surviving (or partially surviving) Mimbres sites in order to protect them. Moreover, this is a lesson that has been learned more widely. Members of the Mimbres Foundation have joined forces with other archaeologists and benefactors to form a national organization, the Archaeological Conservancy. Several sites in the United States have now been purchased and conserved in this way. The story thus has, in some sense, a happy ending. But nothing can bring back the possibility of really understanding Mimbres culture and Mimbres art, a possibility which did exist at the beginning of this century before the wholesale and devastating looting.

Unfortunately, in other parts of the world there are similar stories to tell.

Animalian forms were a popular Mimbres subject, as in this bowl with its depiction of geometric-patterned insects.

vandalized. Pothunters work at night, equipped with two-way radios, scanners, and lookouts. They can be prosecuted under the present legislation only if caught red-handed, which is almost impossible.

The *huaqueros* of Central and South America, too, are interested only in the richest finds, in this case gold – whole cemeteries are turned into fields of craters, with bones, potsherds, mummy wrappings, and other objects smashed and scattered. The remarkable tombs excavated between 1987 and 1990 at Sipán, northwest Peru, of the Moche civilization, were rescued from the plunderers only by the persistence and courage of the local Peruvian archaeologist, Walter Alva.

England, too, has its well-organized gangs of professional treasure hunters. At least three gangs are said to exist in the region of East Anglia alone, feeding the demand from international collectors for antiquities. Nor are the depredations of looters restricted to unpublished sites and unknown finds. Famous Etruscan wall paintings from tombs excavated and published long ago are hacked off and sold in fragments, and the same is true of many Egyptian reliefs. The destruction to Maya stelae is notorious: they are cut into pieces using power saws so as to be more easily transportable. Reliefs in French megalithic tombs have been damaged in this way. Nor are the museums themselves free from such predation. In 1985, the National Museum of Anthropology in Mexico City was raided and some of its most precious smaller objects stolen – thankfully nearly all have been recovered. Many other museums have been raided in recent years, objects often being apparently stolen to order rather than for open sale. Naples Museum has even had to close for a while, because thousands of coins and other objects have disappeared from its storerooms where less than half the stock is catalogued.

The antiquities market in Europe and North America must ultimately take a good deal of the blame for this state of affairs, since antiquities bought without reliable provenience may well have been looted (see box, overleaf). The widespread looting of archaeological sites to provide saleable goods for the antiquities trade is as old as archaeology itself. It certainly flourished in Renaissance Italy, and grew there with the discovery of Pompeii and Herculaneum and of the tombs of the Etruscans, with their abundant Greek painted vases.

In the 20th century, antiquities were seized as the booty of war, and Hitler and Goering, when they plundered the museums of Italy, were only repeating what Napoleon had done more than a century earlier in transporting antique statues to the Louvre. The gold of Troy, which Schliemann had given to the Berlin Museum, was looted by the Russians at the end of World War II and came to light (still remains) in 1994.

There is abundant evidence th[...]ing not only in the homelands of [...]tions – Greece, Turkey, Italy, Ira[...] also in many other parts of the wo[...]tage experts all over the world now consider the theft and smuggling of artworks and antiquities to be second in scale only to the drugs trade in the world of international crime. Despite the threat of execution for offenders, thieves ransacked 40,000 ancient tombs in China in 1989 and 1990 alone, In 1997, Chinese customs seized more than 11,200 smuggled antiquities; conversely, in 1998, 3000 antiquities discovered by British Customs in 1994 were returned to China. In Mesoamerica and South America armed gangs are involved, in Southeast Asia, notably Cambodia, there are links with drug dealing and gun-running. Sadly, looting has now become rampant in West Africa, for instance in Mali, where terracotta figures of the Djenne culture have been looted from many sites, while hardly any have been properly recovered in systematic archaeological excavations.

Public and national morality in these matters has changed significantly, and many nations now recognize the UNESCO Convention of 1970 prohibiting the illicit import and export of antiquities and works of art. For instance, the United States has ratified the Convention, and looted antiquities have been returned to the Mexican and Peruvian governments under its provisions. Britain has not yet ratified the Convention but has passed legislation initiated by the European Community which conforms with some of its provisions. As a result, some of the major auction houses continue to sell antiquities which have been illicitly excavated and exported in those circumstances when to do so is not against British law. On recent occasions they have, despite the protests of the Greek government, publicly sold Cycladic figurines from Keros, a site looted after World War II. (As already noted, it is a melancholy fact that nearly all the larger Cycladic sculptures in existence are from illicit excavations, and as a result almost nothing is known about their original use or significance.) But there is progress. After a television exposé and an ensuing scandal in 1997, the auction house Sotheby's conducted an internal investigation and decided to end their antiquities sales in London.

Also in 1970, the University Museum in Philadelphia, shortly after acquiring artifacts in doubtful circumstances, pronounced the "Philadelphia Declaration." This stated that it would no longer acquire or accept antiquities without a reliable and honest provenience. In Britain, the British Museum and other

COLLECTORS ARE THE REAL LOOTERS"

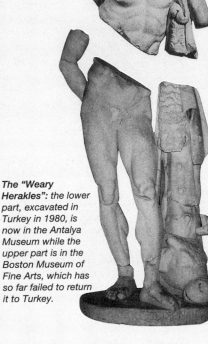

So far as illicit antiquities are concerned, the spotlight has turned upon museums and private collectors. Many of the world's great museums, following the lead of the University Museum of Philadelphia in 1970, now decline to purchase or receive by gift any antiquities which cannot be shown to have been exported legally from their country of origin. But others, such as the Metropolitan Museum of New York, have in the past had no such scruples: Karl Meyer in his disquieting survey *The Plundered Past* (1974) quotes Thomas Hoving, at that time Director of the museum: "We are no more illegal in anything we have done than Napoleon was when he brought all the treasures to the Louvre." The Getty Museum, with its great wealth, has a heavy responsibility in this, and at present its policies are not entirely clear.

Museums like the Metropolitan Museum of Art, which in 1990 put on display the collection of Shelby White and Leon Levy, and the J. Paul Getty Museum which in 1994 exhibited (and then acquired) that of Barbara Fleischman and the late Lawrence Fleischman – both collections with a high proportion of antiquities of unknown provenience – must share some responsibility for the prevalence of collecting in circumstances where much of the money paid inevitably goes to reward dealers who are part of the ongoing cycles of destruction, and thus ultimately the looters. And the responsibility borne by collectors who, in buying such works, indirectly fund the looting process, is now being recognized. Ricardo Elia has argued that "Collectors are the real looters."

The exhibition of the George Ortiz collection of antiquities at the Royal Academy in London in 1994 excited controversy and was felt by many archaeologists to have brought no credit to the Royal Academy. The art critic Robert Hughes has correctly observed that "Part of the story is the renewed cult of the collector as celebrity and of the museum as spectacle, as much concerned with show business as with scholarship."

It remains a real paradox that collectors, who often have a real feeling for the antiquities which they amass, are ultimately funding the looting which is the main threat to the world's archaeological heritage.

Recent cases include:
The "Weary Herakles" Two parts of a Roman marble statue of the 2nd century AD are now separate. The lower part was excavated at Perge in Turkey in 1980 and is in the Antalya Museum, while the joining upper part was purchased by Leon Levy shortly

The "Weary Herakles": the lower part, excavated in Turkey in 1980, is now in the Antalya Museum while the upper part is in the Boston Museum of Fine Arts, which has so far failed to return it to Turkey.

afterwards, and is currently on view at the Boston Museum of Fine Arts, to which Levy has given a half share. The Museum and Levy decline to return the piece to Turkey.

The Getty Kouros The Archaic Greek statue of the 6th century BC was purchased by the J. Paul Getty

A splendid silver dish (left) from the looted Sevso Treasure, one of the major scandals in the recent story of illicit antiquities. (Above) Miniature bronze shields recovered (and now in the British Museum) from the Salisbury Hoard, a massive treasure looted by metal detectorists in 1985.

Museum in 1983 with dubious documentation. Its authenticity is also now widely questioned.

The Lydian Treasure Illicitly excavated in Turkey, and bought privately by the Metropolitan Museum of Art, New York, between 1966 and 1970, but not exhibited publicly until 1984, this important burial group of silver vessels from the 6th century BC was recovered by the Republic of Turkey in 1990, after action in the New York court.

The Sevso Treasure A splendid late Roman assemblage of silver vessels was acquired as an investment by the Marquess of Northampton, but was subsequently claimed in a New York court action by Hungary, Croatia, and Lebanon. Possession was awarded to Lord Northampton, who then found the treasure unsaleable and sued his former legal advisors in London for their advice at the time of purchase; an out-of-court settlement, reportedly in excess of £15 million, was agreed on confidential terms in 1999.

The Aidonia Treasure The treasure, an important collection of Mycenaean antiquities illicitly excavated from tombs in Greece and illegally exported to the USA, was advertised for sale by the New York dealer Michael Ward for $1.5 million in 1993, but was returned to Greece following Greek government action in the New York court.

The Salisbury Hoard A hoard of bronze axes, daggers, and other tools forming a massive assemblage of Bronze Age metalwork was illegally excavated by "nighthawks" (clandestine metal detectorists working at night) near Salisbury in southwest England in 1985. Much of the material was later recovered in a police raid following detective work by Ian Stead of the British Museum.

The Getty kouros, a statue of unknown provenience bought by the Getty Museum in 1985.

members of the Museums' Association now refuse to buy objects without a reliable pedigree. But it has to be said that establishing such a pedigree for certain is no easy matter.

Developers, farmers, and looters are by no means the only threats to archaeological sites. Participants in wars have wrought untold damage over the centuries, and continue to do so. The great Roman site of Baalbek, Lebanon, was the base of the Hizbollah, one of the warring factions in the region; since hostilities ceased, archaeologists have been taking stock of the mass looting of that country's antiquities. Thousands of tons of artifacts were stolen and secretly shipped out by militiamen and unscrupulous dealers; many have turned up on open sale around the world. Angkor Wat in Cambodia deteriorated rapidly during the conflicts that took place in that country, thanks to the prolonged interruption of maintenance, as well as massive looting during Pol Pot's regime. A similar phenomenon has been observed in both Afghanistan and adjoining areas in Pakistan, where Buddhist sculptures and associated artifacts dating to the Kushan period (first half of the 1st millennium AD) have been looted from both archaeological sites and the Kabul Museum, following the withdrawal of the Russians and the subsequent civil war.

Care of Protected Sites

Even though many archaeological sites now receive protection of one sort or another in many countries, the problems do not end there.

In Egypt, for example, many monuments are crumbling through a combination of salt in the building stone and moisture from the ground and air. At Thebes the tomb of Queen Nefertari – the wife of Ramesses II, who lived about 3200 years ago – has magnificent wall paintings that have been pushed off the walls by the build up of salt behind the plaster. A group of tourists in a tomb for an hour can significantly raise the humidity, and such fluctuations encourage more crystallization of salt. By 1950, Nefertari's tomb had deteriorated so much that only dignitaries were allowed in, and by 1983 it was fully closed. Restored at a cost of $2 million by the Getty Conservation Institute, it reopened in 1992, though only to specialists; however, many other famous Egyptian tombs are cracking or in danger of collapse, while in 1994 devastating floods inundated many, including that of Tutankhamun.

Egypt's open-air sites are just as vulnerable. The Nile Valley's climatic extremes make dew condense on the stones on cold nights, which dissolves the salts near the surface. The dew evaporates during the day and the re-forming salt crystals result in crumbling and flaking. The Sphinx at Giza, 4600 years old, is crumbling for this reason and because sewage water from a Cairo slum is seeping into the monument's structure. A fragment recently fell from the Sphinx's right shoulder. The world's best restorers were summoned, but not one of their 16 conservation reports claims the deterioration is reversible. An important program of conservation, however, was completed in 1999.

The rescue and resiting of the temples of Abu Simbel and Philae, which would have been drowned due to the building of the Aswan Dam in 1970, is still a great international triumph of conservation. The annual flooding of certain temples by the Nile was halted; but the permanent availability of water allowed increased irrigation, which has raised the water table. There is thus a constant supply of moisture containing destructive impurities that can seep into the monuments.

There are several remedies for these problems in Egypt. Visitors to the tombs must be banned or strictly controlled, as in the tomb of Nefertari or the Paleolithic decorated caves in western Europe. Air-conditioning should be installed in the tombs to control the temperature and humidity, and a plastic barrier placed between the walls and the plaster. Open-air monuments require pumps to lower the underground water level, and trenches filled with gravel around the bases of walls to stop water seeping into the stone. Finally, silicone compounds can be applied to the stone – these penetrate deeply and bond its molecules together. But all of this will cost a great deal of money.

Egypt is not alone in experiencing difficulties in the care of its ancient monuments. Mohenjodaro, the great early city in Pakistan, is under threat from both a rising water table and corrosion by salts, as well as from erosion by the Indus river. Since 1922 the water table has risen from 8 m (26 ft) below the surface to 4–1.5 m (13–5 ft), depending on the season. Pumping and draining are needed to lower it again, and the walls need cleaning to leach out the accumulated salts. An international conservation campaign is being run by UNESCO, but again the task is a costly one. In Tanzania, after 13 years of neglect, the unique trail of hominid footprints at Laetoli (p. 433) was recently discovered to be under threat from erosion, torrential

The Sphinx at Giza: one of the many monuments in Egypt under threat from encroaching moisture and corrosive salts.

rain and tree roots – half of the reburied 70 footprints were destroyed or damaged – but the Getty Institute has managed to stabilize and preserve the remainder, reburying the trail under geotextiles to prevent root penetration and erosion. In Europe, car pollution, harsh weather and swift droppings have combined to erode and crack the Roman aqueduct in Segovia, Spain, while the marble of the Acropolis in Athens is under attack not only from pollution but also from climatic change which causes a black fungus to grow deep within the stone.

The management of protected sites, therefore, in such a way that natural forces and tourism do not inflict damage, and yet that the public is allowed some sort of access, is now a complex and increasingly specialized field in its own right.

WHO INTERPRETS AND PRESENTS THE PAST?

Some of the ideological questions raised by the public "presentation" of the past were noted earlier: nationalist aims, sectarian objectives, and political agendas are often served by the partisan interpretation and presentation of what is alleged to be the cultural heritage. But there are other issues here beside nationalistic or religious sentiments. In Chapter 1, some of the concerns of feminist archaeology were touched on. And of course one of the reasons that male bias leads to androcentric views in so much archaeological writing is that the majority of the writers, and indeed the majority of professional archaeologists, are men. In the academic world today, while women students in general do have the opportunities which they were formerly denied, it remains the case that there are far fewer women than men among the teaching staff. Up till now – and this is broadly true for the museum profession also – the past has generally been interpreted by men.

Victorian views and interpretations, or at least 19th-century ones, persist in many areas of interpretation and display. This is true in the West and, as noted earlier, most archaeological displays in China are still based almost directly upon the writings of Marx and Engels a century ago.

And while some colonialist and racist preconceptions have been rooted out, more subtle assumptions remain. Minoan Crete, for instance, is still often presented as it appeared to its great discoverer Sir Arthur Evans nearly a century ago. As John Bintliff observes (1984, 35): "Evans's revitalization of a wondrous world of peaceful prosperity, stable divine autocrats and a benevolent aristocracy, owes a great deal to the general political, social and emotional 'Angst' in Europe of his time."

In museum displays, moreover, it is aesthetic concerns that often predominate. This can easily lead to an approach where ancient artifacts are displayed in a situation where they are divorced from all historical context, as "works of art" – thus encouraging a somewhat sanitized quest for beauty ("In Pursuit of the Absolute" was the title of a 1994 public exhibition of the Ortiz collection of largely unprovenienced antiquities). This outlook, where the archaeological context is disregarded, can easily lead on to the ruthless acquisition of "works of art" and to a disregard of ethical standards in archaeology (see box, pp. 556–57).

Museum Studies has, over the past two decades, very properly become a well-established discipline in which the great complexity of the task of interpreting and displaying the past is now being recognized. A few years ago it was estimated that there are now 13,500 museums in Europe, 7000 in North America, 2800 in Australia and Asia, and perhaps 2000 in the rest of the world. But who visits these museums, and at whom are the displays targeted? These are questions which are now systematically being addressed.

ARCHAEOLOGY AND PUBLIC UNDERSTANDING

Archaeologists have a duty, both to colleagues and to the general public, to explain what they are doing and why. Fundamentally this means publishing and disseminating discoveries so that the results are available to other scholars, and can be enjoyed and understood by that wider public which has usually paid the bill for the work, however indirectly. In some cases, such as the successful *Earthwatch* scheme, amateur enthusiasts provide the willing hands and financial support without which many projects could not survive.

Publish or Be Damned

We have already remarked several times in this book that all excavation is to a certain extent destruction – and we make no apology for repeating the point in our closing pages. All excavators have an obligation to record their findings fully and publish them quickly. In practice few do so, or at any rate did so in the past.

Estimates vary, but it has been claimed by the British archaeologist Peter Addyman that up to 60 percent of modern excavations remain unpublished after 10 years, and it is reckoned that only 27 percent of the digs funded by America's National Science Foundation since 1950 have ever reached print. In Israel, for example, it is reckoned that about 39 percent of excavations carried out in the 1960s, 75 percent of those in the 1970s, and an amazing 87 percent of those in the 1980s have yet to produce a site report. There are many reasons for this appalling record. Archaeologists can be lazy or incompetent like people everywhere. They often prefer to dig new sites rather than devote time to laborious post-excavation analysis and publication. They also often fail to allocate a large enough proportion of a project's budget for post-excavation work. Work in the field may sometimes represent only 10 percent of the project's total expenditure. Underwater teams, for example, need to be aware that for every month of diving, about two years need to be spent on conserving, recording, and publishing.

Whatever the reason, deliberate non-publication is a form of theft – in fact a double theft, involving the misuse of other people's money and the withholding of unique information. Some archaeologists compound the felony by hoarding finds, which they consider to be their scientific property, deliberately preventing colleagues from gaining access to the material or from publishing research connected with the site.

One major scandal concerned the Dead Sea Scrolls, the oldest known Hebrew books, written about 2000

ARCHAEOLOGY AND THE INTERNET

The frenetic expansion of the Internet, especially in the guise of the WorldWideWeb (WWW) and e-mail, is changing the way archaeological information is disseminated and the way archaeologists communicate with each other and with the public. This has implications for the future of archaeology – its practice and study, and the control of information.

The WorldWideWeb

Traditionally, archaeological information has been delivered in printed formats. But inevitably such publications, produced for a small, specialized market are often expensive and difficult to obtain. The material in them – text, photographs, plans, drawings, and databases (more often than not already gathered and stored in digital formats) – is ideally suited for electronic publication, particularly on the WWW, the area of the Internet which supports graphics and audio. There it can be presented to a worldwide audience, by anyone with the basic skills and equipment necessary, free from many of the restrictions and costs associated with traditional printing.

A daunting and ever-increasing amount of archaeological material is now available on the WWW, generally free of charge for those who have the equipment to access it. Ranging from site reports to virtual museums, interactive educational resources to digital database archives, this electronic library now constitutes an essential research facility. However, the WWW has developed so rapidly, and in such an unrestricted way, that scholars in particular have voiced concerns about the quality and transient nature of much of the material available.

Feeding an archaeological key-word into a WWW search engine can produce hundreds of thousands of potential information sources to check, so a better place to start is at a **Virtual Library**, which lists and provides access to relevant resources (including news groups and mail lists).

Although many archaeological virtual libraries have been created, the official one for archaeology worldwide is *ArchNet* (archnet.uconn.edu). Maintained by the University of Connecticut, it catalogues thousands of links, according to geographical region and subject. Academic electronic journals and publishers, academic departments, and museums are also listed. The other virtual library for European archaeology, *ARGE* (Archaeological Resource Guide to Europe), divides information by country, subject, or period, and visits and evaluates Web sites before including them. Both facilities offer multilingual access and search facilities.

The Websites of **major archaeological institutes** – the Archaeological Institute of America or the Council for British Archaeology, for instance – or **academic departments**, are also excellent places to begin, since they usually offer extensive lists of links to other sites of interest.

A number of established **journals** have a Web presence, which may range from basic subscription or contact details to whole issues on-line. Many provide indexes of printed volumes, useful for references and often accompanied by tasters and illustrations from selected articles. In recent years electronic archaeological journals, like *Internet Archaeology,* and virtual conference arenas have been launched which aim to provide scholarly information, while making the most of the technical possibilities and sense of immediacy of the WWW.

As yet there seems no danger of pixels totally replacing print. Far from making traditional archaeological publications obsolete, the Web has made it easier, and cheaper, to find and to buy printed works from all over the world, since it hosts gigantic "virtual" bookshops. These stock millions of titles, both popular and academic, which may be otherwise very difficult to get hold of. Ordered over the Internet, the books are delivered to your door.

E-mail

Another aspect of the Internet, e-mail, has made a big impact on archaeology. Instant, cheap, and reliable, it enables archaeologists to communicate anything they might use paper mail or the telephone for: ideas, gossip, data, references, requests, papers. Ease of communication means collaborations are easier, new projects possible, and international barriers are dissolved. Many academic institutions list staff e-mail addresses on their WWW pages, which presents students in particular the opportunity to approach, in a very immediate way, scholars they may never have the chance to meet.

It is also possible to subscribe to a growing number of archaeological e-mail communities – known as "discussion groups" (or "mailing lists") and "newsgroups." Discussion groups have their own e-mail address: anything that someone sends to that address is distributed to all the people on the list, sometimes via a "moderator" (or editor). This creates a conversational environment where hot topics can be discussed, ideas floated, contacts chased, jobs advertised, references exchanged, and bibliographies created. There are specific lists for virtually all aspects of archaeology, in a number of languages. Archives of previous contributions and discussion "threads" are usually available to search through on the WWW. These discussion forums are generally populated by educated and well-informed contributors, both amateur and professional, from around the world. They are immensely useful to the archaeological community.

Newsgroups, operated through Usenet news servers, are another way to have running e-mail conversations. Contributed "articles" are stored at a single location, and grouped according to topic "threads" to be retrieved at the user's wish. Archaeological newsgroups are a good place to track discussions both serious and popular, and sometimes cover more "fringe" issues than the mailing lists.

The Democratization of Knowledge

As Ian Hodder has pointed out (*Internet Archaeology*, Issue 6), the speed, range, and low cost of the Internet have created new possibilities for dissemination and participation in knowledge construction and acquisition. He states that the website for Çatalhöyük (see box pp. 44–45) has rapidly become the most important way of publishing the archaeological site, because it is widely read and can be frequently edited and renewed. Electronic provision of site archives provides interested parties access to raw data from which to form their own conclusions. The website also places the views of specialists and the public side by side, opening up real possibilities for "democratization, participation and erosion of boundaries between specialist and popular archaeology." This could be seen as part of the overall process of a shift from a hierarchical to a networked **structure of archaeological** knowledge, although there is clearly a danger of excluding the un-networked.

For the growing constituency with access to the Internet, however, there exists a vast new world of electronic archaeology there to be explored.

Archaeological Websites

The number of sites is huge and increasing. There is a danger that some disappear or change address, but this list may provide some useful sites:

Archaeology on the Net
www.serve.com/archaeology

Yahoo! Anthropology and Archaeology
dir.yahoo.com/Social_Science/
Anthropology_and_Archaeology/Archaeology/

European Megalithic Monuments
www.stonepages.com/

Underwater Archaeology
www.pophaus.com/underwater/

Mediterranean Archaeology
rome.classics.lsa.umich.edu/

Zooarchaeology
borealis.lib.uconn.edu/

World Wide Ancient Egypt
www.geocities.com/~amenhotep/wwae/

Egyptology Links
guardians.net/egypt
www.newton.cam.ac.uk/egypt

Mesoamerican Archaeology
copan.bioz.unibas.ch/meso.html

Aboriginal Studies
www.ciolek.com/WWWVL-Aboriginal.html

Journals:
Andean Past
kramer.ume.maine.edu/~anthrop/AndeanP.html

Historical Archaeology
sha.org/sha_ha.htm

Radiocarbon
www.radiocarbon.org/

Journal of Near Eastern Studies
www.journals.uchicago.edu/JNES/home.html

Bulletin of the Asia Institute
bulletinasiainstitute.org/

Athena Review
www.athenapub.com/

Biblical Archaeology
www.asor.org/

Archaeology Ireland
www.kerna.ie/archaeology/

Discover Archaeology
www.discoveringarchaeology.com/

Anistorian
users.hol.gr/~dilos/anistor/cover.htm

American Journal of Archaeology
classics.lsa.umich.edu/AJA.html

Bulletin of the American Schools of Oriental Research
www.asor.org/

Organizations and Societies:
Canadian Archaeological Association
www.canadianarchaeology.com/

Center for American Archeology
www.caa-archeology.org/

American Oriental Society
www.umich.edu/~aos/

American Schools of Oriental Research
www.asor.org

Other:
Underwater Archaeology
www.adp.fsu.edu/uwarch.html

Virtual Museum of Nautical Archaeology
nautarch.tamu.edu/ina/vm.htm

Voyage into Archaeology
ted.educ.sfu.ca/people/staff/jmd/archaeology/
voyage1.htm

Archaeological Sampling Strategies
archnet.uconn.edu/archnet/topical/theory/
sampling/sampling.html

Collapse: Why do civilisations fall?
www.learner.org/exhibits/collapse/

Dating Techniques
emuseum.mankato.msus.edu/archaeology/dating/
index.shtml/shtml

Archaeological Fieldwork Server
www.sscnet.ucla.edu/ioa/afs/testpit.html

Satellite Remote Sensing and Archaeology
ourworld.compuserve.com/homepages/mjff/
homepage.htm

The Center for Archaeoastronomy
www.wam.umd.edu/~tlaloc/archastro/index.html

Arctic Circle
arcticcircle.uconn.edu/

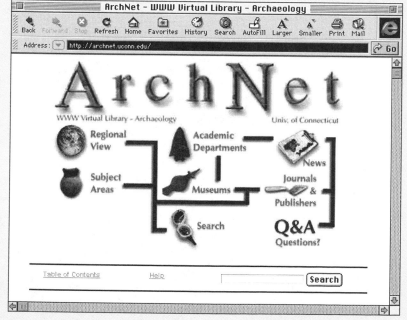

The home page of the ArchNet website.

ARCHAEOLOGY AT THE FRINGE

In the later years of the 20th century "Other Archaeologies" grew up at the fringe of the discipline, offering alternative interpretations of the past to those generally formulated in academic discourse. To the scientist these seem fanciful and extravagant – manifestations of a post-modern age in which horoscopes are widely read, New Age prophets preach alternative life styles, and when many members of the public are willing to believe that "corn circles" and megalithic monuments are alike the work of aliens. Many archaeologists label such populist approaches as "Pseudoarchaeology," and place them on a par with archaeological frauds such as Piltdown Man or Glozel, where deliberate deception can be demonstrated or inferred.

But how does an archaeologist persuade the self-styled Druids who perform their rituals at Stonehenge at the summer solstice (if the governing authority, English Heritage, allows them access) that their beliefs are not supported by archaeological evidence? This issue troubles postprocessual archaeologists, with their relativist position, and brings us back to the central question of this chapter: "Whose Past?" It is not clear that one should question the reality of the Dreamtime of the Australian Aborigines, even if aspects of their belief effectively clash with current scientific interpretations. Where does one distinguish between respect for deeply held beliefs and the role of the archaeologist to inform the public and to dismiss credulous nonsense?

One of the most popular and durable myths concerns a "lost Atlantis," a story narrated by the Greek philosopher Plato in the 5th century BC, and attributed by him to the Greek sage Solon, who had visited Egypt and consulted with priests, the heirs to a long religious and historical tradition. They told him of a legend of the lost continent beyond the Pillars of Hercules (the modern Straits of Gibraltar), hence in the Atlantic Ocean, with its advanced civilization, which vanished centuries earlier "in a night and a day." In 1882 Ignatius Donnelly published *Atlantis, the Antediluvian World*, elaborating this legend. His work was one of the first to seek a simple explanation of all ancient civilizations of the world by a single marvellous means. Such theories often share characteristics:

1 They celebrate a remarkable lost world whose people possessed many skills surpassing those of the present.

2 They account for most of the early accomplishments of prehistoric and early state societies with a single explanation: all were the work of the skilled inhabitants of that lost world.

3 That world vanished in a catastrophe of cosmic proportions.

4 Nothing of that original homeland is available for scientific examination, nor are any artifacts surviving.

The basic structure of Donnelly's argument was repeated with variants by Immanuel Velikovsky (meteors and astronomical events) and recently by Graham Hancock (who sites his lost continent in Antarctica). A popular alternative, elaborated with great financial profit by von Däniken, is that the source of progress is outer space, and that the advances of early civilizations are the work of aliens visiting earth. Ultimately, however, all such theories trivialize the much more remarkable story which archaeology reveals – the history of humankind.

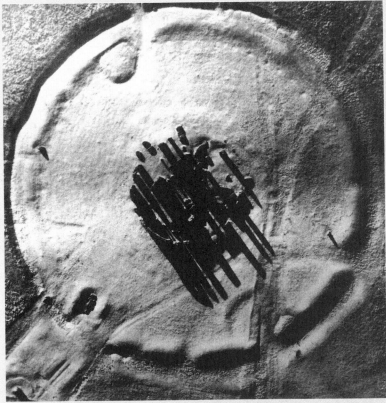

Stonehenge *has generated innumerable theories about its origins and meaning. Several groups, including Druids and New Agers claim it as a monument central to their beliefs.*

years ago. The first scrolls were discovered in Qumran, Palestine, in 1947, but most of the thousands of fragments found still remained unpublished (by the editorial team appointed in 1953 to decipher and edit the material) in 1991, when the monopoly they exercised over the material was breached. In that year microfilm of all texts, published or unpublished, was made available to all bona fide scholars by an American library which had obtained a full set of negatives. It was generally felt that a "scholarly closed shop," denying others legitimate access to important material for an excessive length of time, could no longer be tolerated.

In a controversial comment after the death of the Romano-British specialist Ian Richmond, Mortimer Wheeler lamented that "not more than a quarter of his productive fieldwork can now ever see the light of day ... in spite of the constant entreaties of his colleagues he obstinately declined to keep pace with his digging by the normal method of the interim report." A deceased scholar's disciples can attempt to put something together from the notes and finds left behind – should either survive – but this is a poor substitute for a considered account by the original excavator.

What can be done? It has been suggested that each country should issue a list of those sites whose publication is long overdue, together with the identity of the excavators. In Britain, English Heritage has devoted a high proportion of its archaeological budget to the analysis and publication of old as well as new excavations. However, measures are required to ensure better conduct in the future. Professional bodies such as the Society of Professional Archaeologists in the United States and the Institute of Field Archaeologists in Britain now require their members to abide by a Code of Conduct, which stipulates that continuing membership depends among other things on publication of excavations within a reasonable time.

In addition, the archaeological community ought to establish a fixed period (perhaps 5 to 20 years, depending on the scale of the project) when excavators might be allowed control over finds and results, after which these would become available to all, even if unpublished. Many students would find it more profitable as a research topic to retrieve and write up such material than to embark on digs at sites not under threat.

Finally, all directors of excavations should act as if they expected to die before the project reaches completion. In Italy, for example, a copy of the excavation fieldnotes has to be left with the local authority to guard against such an eventuality. Excavators should ensure that their notes are fully comprehensible to others, that each season's finds are processed before starting the next, and that at least a manuscript report on each season's work is produced. Leaving all the analysis till the end is a recipe for disaster.

The Wider Audience

Although the immediate aim of most research is to answer specific questions, the fundamental purpose of archaeology must be to provide people with a better understanding of the human past. Skillful popularization – site and museum exhibits, books, television, and increasingly the Internet (box, pp. 560–61) – is therefore required, but not all archaeologists are prepared to devote time to it, and few are capable of doing it well.

Excavators often regard members of the public as a hindrance to work on-site. More enlightened archaeologists, however, realize the financial and other support to be gained from encouraging public interest, and they organize information sheets, open days, and on long-term projects even fee-paying daily tours, as at the Bronze Age site of Flag Fen in eastern England. In Japan, on-the-spot presentations of excavation results are given as soon as a dig is completed. Details are released to the press the previous day, so that the public can obtain information from the morning edition of the local paper before coming to the site itself.

We have already seen how archaeologists at York, northern England, not only encouraged visits from the public during excavations, but also presented the results in a hugely successful new museum that paid for itself within five years (see Chapter 13).

Clearly, there is an avid popular appetite for archaeology. In a sense, the past has been a form of entertainment since the early digging of burial mounds and the public unwrapping of mummies in the 19th century. The entertainment may now take a more scientific and educational form, but it still needs to compete with rival popular attractions if archaeology is to thrive.

SUMMARY

World Archaeology and the Human Past

Archaeology can be made to serve many masters. We have seen how it can be used for economic ends, to

make arid lands fertile once again. Or it can be popularized and sold to a willing public, curious to know more of vanished cities and lost civilizations. Or again it can be used for national ends, to provide a sense of national identity by tracing back a link from an uncertain present to a past whose achievements are seen as significant and admirable.

But the ultimate value of archaeology goes beyond these specific and in a certain sense limited concerns. For world archaeology is something in which we can all share. The human origins revealed in Africa are the origins of us all. Archaeology can document the trajectory of growth of the population of every country on earth. Our concern need not be restricted to our own personal line of descent. The archaeology of every land has its own contribution to make to the understanding of human diversity and hence of the human condition. So it is that skeletal remains of the Australian Aborigines of earlier millennia, or of the Native Americas, ought to matter as much to Europeans or white Americans as skeletal remains found in Europe. Modern-day Aborigines and Native Americans should also recognize that their contribution to the human story merits a significant place in the history of the world. Although earlier generations of scholars did indeed behave with flagrant disregard for the feelings and beliefs of native peoples, and some may continue to do so, the interest in these matters today is not some neocolonial attempt further to appropriate the native past. It is, rather, an assertion that this past has a legitimate wider significance, in which others may properly be interested than those who inhabit the areas in question. That is not a negative message, nor a disparaging one.

If we are to have an adequate perception of our place as human beings in the modern world, the past matters. It is where we have come from, and it has determined what we are. For that reason, it is necessary for us to set our faces against the lunatics and the fringe archaeologists who seek (sometimes for their own gain, but sometimes simply from a misguided inability to think straight) to confuse or corrupt our view of the past. Writers such as Erich von Däniken, author of *Chariots of the Gods?*, have written highly readable books purporting to give new insights into the past that differ markedly from those of modern archaeology. In von Däniken's case, the argument is that most of the developments of human civilization are due to the influence of alien beings arriving on earth in flying saucers. The matter would be comic if such views had not been so widely believed (box, p. 562).

The objection to this kind of nonsense is not simply that it differs from the conventional archaeological wisdom. No one has a monopoly of the truth – not even the archaeologist. The objection is that such works gloss over the difficulties, and fail to submit their evidence to the kind of scientific scrutiny that we have been advocating in this volume. Anyone who has read this book, and who understands how archaeology proceeds, will already see why such writings, and others that propose ancient (and undocumented) catastrophes, or lost continents, or long-range migrations by the Lost Tribes of Israel, or the forces of "earth magic" at such sites as Stonehenge, are a snare and a delusion. These misconceptions have been well discussed by Jeremy Sabloff in his *Archaeology, Myth and Reality* (1982). The real antidote is a kind of healthy skepticism: to ask "where is the evidence?" Knowledge advances by asking questions – that is the central theme of the present book, and there is no better way to disperse the lunatic fringe than by asking difficult questions, and looking skeptically at the answers.

FURTHER READING

Cleere, H. (ed.). 1984. *Approaches to the Archaeological Heritage: A Comparative Study of World Cultural Resource Management Systems.* Cambridge University Press: Cambridge & New York.

Darvill, T. 1987. *Ancient Monuments in the Countryside: An Archaeological Management Review.* English Heritage: London. (A British perspective.)

Green, E.L. (ed.). 1984. *Ethics and Values in Archaeology.* Free Press: New York.

Greenfield, J. 1996. (2nd ed.). *The Return of Cultural Treasures.* Cambridge University Press: Cambridge & New York.

Kohl, P.L. & Fawcett, C. (eds.). 1995. *Nationalism, Politics and the Practice of Archaeology.* Cambridge University Press: Cambridge & New York.

Layton, R. (ed.). 1989. *Conflict in the Archaeology of Living Traditions.* Unwin Hyman: London.

Messenger, P. Mauch (ed.). 1989. *The Ethics of Collecting Cultural Property: Whose culture? Whose property?* University of New Mexico Press, Albuquerque.

McBryde, I. (ed.). 1985. *Who Owns the Past?* Oxford University Press: Melbourne, Oxford & New York.

McGimsey, C. 1972. *Public Archaeology.* Seminar Press: New York.

Renfrew, C. 1999. *Loot, legitimacy and ownership: the ethical crisis in archaeology* (The Kroon Lecture for 1999). The Foundation for Anthropology and Prehistory in the Netherlands: Amsterdam.

Tubb, K.W. 1995. *Antiquities Trade or Betrayed. Legal, Ethical and Conservation Issues.* Archetype: London.

Vitelli, K.D. (ed.). 1996. *Archaeological Ethics.* Altamira Press: Walnut Creek.

Glossary

(Terms in *italics* are defined elsewhere in the glossary)

absolute dating The determination of age with reference to a specific time scale, such as a fixed calendrical system; also referred to as chronometric dating. (Chapter 4)

achieved status Social standing and prestige reflecting the ability of an individual to acquire an established position in society as a result of individual accomplishments (*cf. ascribed status*). (Chapter 5)

aerial reconnaissance An important survey technique in the discovery and recording of archaeological sites (see also *reconnaissance survey*). (Chapter 3)

alleles Different sequences of genetic material occupying the same locus on the *DNA* molecule; alleles of the same gene differ by mutation at one or more locations within the same length of DNA. (Chapter 11)

alloying Technique involving the mixing of two or more metals to create a new material, e.g. the fusion of copper and tin to make bronze. (Chapter 8)

amino-acid racemization A method used in the dating of both human and animal bone. Its special significance is that with a small sample (10g) it can be applied to material up to 100,000 years old, i.e. beyond the time range of *radiocarbon dating*. (Chapter 4)

annealing In copper and bronze metallurgy, this refers to the repeated process of heating and hammering the material to produce the desired shape. (Chapter 8)

anthropology The study of humanity – our physical characteristics as animals, and our unique non-biological characteristics we call *culture*. The subject is generally broken down into three subdisciplines: *biological (physical) anthropology, cultural (social) anthropology*, and *archaeology*. (Introduction)

archaeobotany See *paleoethnobotany*.

archaeological culture A constantly recurring *assemblage* of artifacts assumed to be representative of a particular set of behavioral activities carried out at a particular time and place (*cf. culture*). (Chapter 3)

archaeology A subdiscipline of anthropology involving the study of the human past through its material remains. (Introduction)

archaeology of cult The study of the material indications of patterned actions undertaken in response to religious beliefs. (Chapter 10)

archaeomagnetic dating Sometimes referred to as paleomagnetic dating, it is based on the fact that changes in the earth's magnetic field over time can be recorded as remanent magnetism in materials such as baked clay structures (ovens, kilns, and hearths). (Chapter 4)

archaeozoology Sometimes referred to as zooarchaeology, this involves the identification and analysis of faunal species from archaeological sites, as an aid to the reconstruction of human diets and to an understanding of the contemporary environment at the time of deposition. (Chapters 6 & 7)

artifact Any portable object used, modified, or made by humans; e.g. stone tools, pottery, and metal weapons. (Chapter 3)

ascribed status Social standing or prestige which is the result of inheritance or hereditary factors (*cf. achieved status*). (Chapter 5)

assemblage A group of artifacts recurring together at a particular time and place, and representing the sum of human activities. (Chapter 3)

association The co-occurrence of an artifact with other archaeological remains, usually in the same *matrix*. (Chapter 2)

atomic absorption spectrometry (AAS) A method of analyzing artifact composition similar to *optical emission spectrometry* (OES) in that it measures energy in the form of visible light waves. It is capable of measuring up to 40 different elements with an accuracy of *c*. 1 percent. (Chapters 8 & 9)

attribute A minimal characteristic of an artifact such that it cannot be further subdivided; attributes commonly studied include aspects of form, style, decoration, color, and raw material. (Chapter 3)

attritional age profile A mortality pattern based on bone or tooth wear which is characterized by an overrepresentation of young and old animals in relation to their numbers in live populations. It suggests either scavenging of attritional mortality victims (i.e. those dying from natural causes or from non-human predation) or the hunting by humans or other predators of the most vulnerable individuals. (Chapter 7)

augering A *subsurface detection* method using either a hand- or machine-powered drill to determine the depth and character of archaeological deposits. (Chapter 3)

Australopithecus A collective name for the earliest known hominids emerging about 5 million years ago in East Africa. (Chapter 4)

band A term used to describe small-scale societies of hunters and gatherers, generally less than 100 people, who move seasonally to exploit wild (undomesticated) food resources. Kinship ties play an important part in social organization. (Chapter 5)

bifurcation See *self-organization*.

biological anthropology See *physical anthropology*.

bosing A *subsurface detection* method performed by striking the ground with a heavy wooden mallet or a lead-filled container on a long handle. (Chapter 3)

brain endocasts These are made by pouring latex rubber into a skull, so as to produce an accurate image of the inner surface of the cranium. This method gives an estimate of cranial capacity and has been used on early hominid skulls. (Chapter 11)

catastrophe theory A branch of mathematical topology developed by René Thom which is concerned with the way in which nonlinear interactions within systems can produce sudden and dramatic effects; it is argued that there are only a limited number of ways in which such changes can take place, and these are defined as elementary catastrophes. (Chapter 12)

catastrophic age profile A mortality pattern based on bone or tooth wear analysis, and corresponding to a "natural" age distribution in which the older the age group, the fewer the individuals it has. This pattern is often found in contexts such as flash floods, epidemics, or volcanic eruptions. (Chapter 7)

cation-ratio dating This method aspires to the direct dating of rock carvings and engravings, and is also potentially applicable to Paleolithic artifacts with a strong patina caused by exposure to desert dust. It depends on the principle that cations of certain elements are more soluble than others; they leach out of *rock varnish* more rapidly than the less soluble elements, and their concentration decreases with time. (Chapter 4)

cenote A ritual well, for example at the late Maya site of Chichén Itzá, into which enormous quantities of symbolically rich goods had been deposited. (Chapter 10)

central place theory Developed by the geographer Christaller to explain the spacing and function of the settlement landscape. Under idealized conditions, he argued, central places of the same size and nature would be equidistant from each other, surrounded by secondary centers with their own smaller satellites. In spite of its limitations, central place theory has found useful applications in archaeology as a preliminary heuristic device. (Chapter 5)

chaîne opératoire Ordered chain of actions, gestures, and processes in a production sequence (e.g. of a stone tool or a pot) which led to the transformation of a given material towards the finished product. The concept, introduced by André Leroi-Gourhan, is significant in allowing the archaeologist to infer back from the finished artifact to the procedures, the intentionality in the production sequence, and ultimately to the conceptual template of the maker. (Chapter 8)

characterization The application of techniques of examination by which characteristic properties of the constituent material of traded goods can be identified, and thus their source of origin; e.g. petrographic *thin-section analysis.* (Chapter 9)

chiefdom A term used to describe a society that operates on the principle of ranking, i.e. differential social status. Different *lineages* are graded on a scale of prestige, calculated by how closely related one is to the chief. The chiefdom generally has a permanent ritual and ceremonial center, as well as being characterized by local specialization in crafts. (Chapter 5)

chinampas The areas of fertile reclaimed land, constructed by the Aztecs, and made of mud dredged from canals. (Chapter 6)

chronometric dating See *absolute dating.*

classification The ordering of phenomena into groups or other classificatory schemes on the basis of shared attributes (see also *type* and *typology*). (Chapters 1 & 4)

CLIMAP A project aimed at producing paleoclimatic maps showing sea-surface temperatures in different parts of the globe, at various periods. (Chapter 6)

cluster analysis A multivariate statistical technique which assesses the similarities between units or assemblages, based on the occurrence or non-occurrence of specific artifact *types* or other components within them (Chapter 5)

cognitive archaeology The study of past ways of thought and symbolic structures from material remains. (Chapter 10)

cognitive map An interpretive framework of the world which, it is argued, exists in the human mind and affects actions and decisions as well as knowledge structures. (Chapter 10)

cognitive-processual approach An alternative to the materialist orientation of the functional-processual approach, it is concerned with (1) the integration of the cognitive and symbolic with other aspects of early societies; (2) the role of ideology as an active organizational force. It employs the theoretical approach of *methodological individualism*. (Chapters 1 & 12)

computed axial tomography (CAT or CT scanner) The method by which scanners allow detailed internal views of bodies such as mummies. The body is passed into the machine and images of cross-sectional "slices" through the body are produced. (Chapter 11)

conjoining See *refitting.*

conjunctive approach A methodological alternative to traditional normative archaeology, argued by Walter Taylor (1948), in which the full range of a culture system was to be taken into consideration in explanatory models. (Chapter 1)

context An artifact's context usually consists of its immediate *matrix* (the material around it e.g. gravel, clay, or sand), its *provenience* (horizontal and vertical position in the matrix), and its *association* with other artifacts (with other archaeologial remains, usually in the same matrix). (Chapter 2)

contextual seriation A method of *relative dating* pioneered by Flinders Petrie in the 19th century, in which artifacts are arranged according to the frequencies of their co-occurrence in specific contexts (usually burials). (Chapter 4)

contract archaeology Archaeological research conducted under the aegis of federal or state legislation, often in advance of highway construction or urban development, where the archaeologist is contracted to undertake the necessary research. (Chapter 14)

coprolites Fossilized feces; these contain food residues that can be used to reconstruct diet and subsistence activities. (Chapter 6)

core A lithic artifact used as a blank from which other tools or flakes are made. (Chapter 8)

Critical Theory A theoretical approach developed by the so-called "Frankfurt School" of German social thinkers, which stresses that all knowledge is historical, and in a sense biassed communication; thus, all claims to "objective" knowledge are illusory. (Chapter 12)

cultural anthropology A subdiscipline of anthropology concerned with the non-biological, behavioral aspects of society; i.e. the social, linguistic, and technological components underlying human behavior. Two important branches of cultural anthropology are *ethnography* (the study of living cultures) and *ethnology* (which attempts to compare cultures using ethnographic evidence). In Europe, it is referred to as *social anthropology*. (Introduction)

cultural ecology A term devised by Julian Steward to account for the dynamic relationship between human society and its environment, in which *culture* is viewed as the primary adaptive mechanism. (Chapter 1)

cultural evolution The theory that societal change can be understood by analogy with processes underlying the biological evolution of species. (Chapter 1)

cultural group A complex of regularly occurring associated artifacts, features, burial types, and house forms comprising a distinct identity (Chapter 5)

cultural resource management (CRM) The safeguarding of the archaeological heritage through the protection of sites and through salvage archaeology (rescue archaeology), generally within the framework of legislation designed to safeguard the past. (Chapter 14)

culture A term used by anthropologists when referring to the non-biological characteristics unique to a particular society (cf. *archaeological culture*). (Chapter 1)

culture-historical approach An approach to archaeological interpretation which uses the procedure of the traditional historian (including emphasis on specific circumstances elaborated with rich detail, and processes of *inductive* reasoning). (Chapter 12)

deduction A process of reasoning by which more specific consequences are inferred by rigorous argument from more general propositions (cf. *induction*). (Chapter 12)

deductive nomological (D–N) explanation A formal method of explanation based on the testing of hypotheses derived from general laws. (Chapter 12)

deep-sea cores Cores drilled from the sea bed that provide the most coherent record of climate changes on a worldwide scale. The cores contain shells of microscopic marine organisms (foraminifera) laid down on the ocean floor through the continuous process of sedimentation. Variations in the ratio of two oxygen isotopes in the calcium carbonate of these shells give a sensitive indicator of sea temperature at the time the organisms were alive. (Chapter 4)

demography The study of the processes which contribute to population structure and their temporal and spatial dynamics. (Chapter 11)

dendrochronology The study of tree-ring patterns; annual variations in climatic conditions which produce differential growth can be used both as a measure of environmental change, and as the basis for a chronology. (Chapter 4)

diachronic Referring to phenomena as they change over time; i.e. employing a chronological perspective (cf. *synchronic*). (Chapter 12)

diatom analysis A method of environmental reconstruction based on plant microfossils. Diatoms are unicellular algae, whose silica cell walls survive after the algae die, and they accumulate in large numbers at the bottom of rivers and lakes. Their assemblages directly reflect the floristic composition of the water's extinct communities, as well as the water's salinity, alkalinity, and nutrient status. (Chapter 6)

diffusionist approach The theory popularized by V.G. Childe that all the attributes of civilization from architecture to metalworking had diffused from the Near East to Europe. (Chapter 1)

DNA (Deoxyribonucleic acid) The material which carries the hereditary instructions (the "blueprint") which determine the formation of all living organisms. *Genes*, the organizers of inheritance, are composed of DNA. (Chapter 11)

dowsing The supposed location of subsurface features by employing a twig, copper rod, pendulum, or other instrument; discontinuous movements in these instruments are believed by some to record the existence of buried features. (Chapter 3)

echo-sounding An acoustic underwater survey technique, used to trace the topography of submerged coastal plains and other buried land surfaces (see also *seismic reflection profiler*). (Chapter 6)

ecofacts Non-artifactual organic and environmental remains which have cultural relevance, e.g. faunal and floral material as well as soils and sediments. (Chapters 2 & 6)

ecological determinism A form of explanation in which it is implicit that changes in the environment determine changes in human society. (Chapter 12)

electrical resistivity See *soil resistivity*.

electrolysis A standard cleaning process in archaeological conservation. Artifacts are placed in a chemical solution, and by passing a weak current between them and a surrounding metal grill, the corrosive salts move from the cathode (object) to the anode (grill), removing any accumulated deposit and leaving the artifact clean. (Chapter 2)

electron probe microanalysis Used in the analysis of artifact composition, this technique is similar to XRF (*X-ray fluorescence spectrometry*), and is useful for studying small changes in composition within the body of an artifact. (Chapter 9)

electron spin resonance (ESR) Enables trapped electrons within bone and shell to be measured without the heating that *thermoluminescence* requires. As with TL, the number of trapped electrons indicates the age of the specimen. (Chapter 4)

empathetic method The use of personal intuition (in German *Einfühlung*) to seek to understand the inner lives of other people, using the assumption that there is a common structure to human experience. The assumption that the study of the inner experience of humans provides a handle for interpreting prehistory and history is made by

idealist thinkers such as B. Croce, R.G. Collingwood and members of the *postprocessual* school of thought. (Chapter 12)

emulation One of the most frequent features accompanying competition, where customs, buildings, and artifacts in one society may be adopted by neighboring ones through a process of imitation which is often competitive in nature. (Chapters 5 & 9)

environmental archaeology A field of inter-disciplinary research – archaeology and natural science – is directed at the reconstruction of human use of plants and animals, and how past societies adapted to changing environmental conditions. (Chapters 6 & 7)

environmental circumscription An explanation for the origins of the state propounded by Robert Carneiro that emphasizes the fundamental role exerted by environmental constraints and by territorial limitations. (Chapter 12)

eoliths Crude stone pebbles found in Lower Pleistocene contexts; once thought to be the work of human agency, but now generally regarded as natural products. (Chapter 8)

ethnicity The existence of ethnic groups, including tribal groups. Though these are difficult to recognize from the archaeological record, the study of language and linguistic boundaries shows that ethnic groups are often correlated with language areas (see *ethnos*). (Chapter 5)

ethnoarchaeology The study of contemporary cultures with a view to understanding the behavioral relationships which underlie the production of material culture. (Introduction & Chapter 8)

ethnography A subset of *cultural anthropology* concerned with the study of contemporary cultures through first-hand observation. (Introduction)

ethnology A subset of *cultural anthropology* concerned with the comparative study of contemporary cultures, with a view to deriving general principles about human society. (Introduction)

ethnos The ethnic group, defined as a firm aggregate of people, historically established on a given territory, possessing in common relatively stable peculiarities of language and culture, and also recognizing their unity and difference as expressed in a self-appointed name (ethnonym) (see *ethnicity*). (Chapter 5)

evolution The process of growth and development generally accompanied by increasing complexity. In biology, this change is tied to Darwin's concept of natural selection as the basis of species survival. Darwin's work laid the foundations for the study of artifact

typology, pioneered by such scholars as Pitt-Rivers and Montelius. (Chapter 1)

excavation The principal method of data acquisition in archaeology, involving the systematic uncovering of archaeological remains through the removal of the deposits of soil and the other material covering them and accompanying them. (Chapter 3)

experimental archaeology The study of past behavioral processes through experimental reconstruction under carefully controlled scientific conditions. (Chapters 2, 7, 8, & 14)

factor analysis A multivariate statistical technique which assesses the degree of variation between artifact types, and is based on a matrix of correlation coefficients which measure the relative association between any two variables. (Chapter 5)

faience Glass-like material first made in predynastic Egypt; it involves coating a core material of powdered quartz with a vitreous alkaline glaze. (Chapter 8)

fall-off analysis The study of regularities in the way in which quantities of traded items found in the archaeological record decline as the distance from the source increases. This may be plotted as a fall-off curve, with the quantities of material (Y-axis) plotted against distance from source (X-axis). (Chapter 9)

faunal dating A method of *relative dating* based on observing the evolutionary changes in particular species of mammals, so as to form a rough chronological sequence. (Chapter 4)

feature A non-portable *artifact*; e.g. hearths, architectural elements, or soil stains. (Chapter 3)

filigree Fine open metalwork using wires and soldering, first developed in the Near East. (Chapter 8)

fission-track dating A dating method based on the operation of a radioactive clock, the spontaneous fission of an isotope of uranium present in a wide range of rocks and minerals. As with *potassium-argon dating*, with whose time range it overlaps, the method gives useful dates from rocks adjacent to archaeological material. (Chapter 4)

flotation A method of screening (sieving) excavated *matrix* in water so as to separate and recover small *ecofacts* and *artifacts*. (Chapter 6)

fluxgate gradiometer A type of *fluxgate magnetometer*, producing a continuous reading on a meter. (Chapter 3)

fluxgate magnetometer A type of magnetometer used in *subsurface detection*, producing a continuous reading. (Chapter 3)

formation processes Those processes affecting the way in which archaeological materials came to be buried, and their subsequent history afterwards. Cultural formation processes include the deliberate or accidental activities of humans; natural formation processes refer to natural or environmental events which govern the burial and survival of the archaeological record. (Chapter 2)

fossil cuticles Outermost protective layer of the skin of leaves or blades of grass, made of cutin, a material that survives in the archaeological record often in feces. Cuticular analysis is a useful adjunct to *palynology* in environmental reconstruction. (Chapter 6)

fossil ice wedges Soil features caused when the ground freezes and contracts, opening up fissures in the permafrost that fill with wedges of ice. The fossil wedges are proof of past cooling of climate and of the depth of permafrost. (Chapter 6)

frequency seriation A *relative dating* method which relies principally on measuring changes in the proportional abundance, or frequency, observed among finds (e.g. counts of tool types, or of ceramic fabrics). (Chapter 4)

functional-processual approach See *processual archaeology*.

genes The basic units of inheritance, now known to be governed by the specific sequence of the genetic markers within the DNA of the individual concerned. (Chapter 11)

genotype Genetic composition of a cell or individual, as distinct from its *phenotype*. (Chapter 11)

geochemical analysis The investigatory technique which involves taking soil samples at regular intervals from the surface of a site, and measuring their phosphate content and other chemical properties. (Chapter 3)

geomagnetic reversals An aspect of archaeomagnetism relevant to the dating of the Lower Paleolithic, involving complete reversals in the earth's magnetic field. (Chapter 4)

geomorphology A subdiscipline of geography, concerned with the study of the form and development of the landscape, it includes such specializations as *sedimentology*. (Chapter 6)

gift exchange See *reciprocity*.

glottochronology A controversial method of assessing the temporal divergence of two languages based on changes of vocabulary (*lexicostatistics*), and expressed as an arithmetic formula. (Chapters 4 & 5)

granulation The soldering of grains of metal to a background, usually of the same metal, and much used by the Etruscans. (Chapter 8)

ground-penetrating radar A method of *subsurface detection* in which short radio pulses are sent through the soil, such that the echoes reflect back significant changes in soil conditions. (Chapter 3)

ground reconnaissance A collective name for a wide variety of methods for identifying individual archaeological sites, including consultation of documentary sources, place-name evidence, local folklore, and legend, but primarily actual fieldwork. (Chapter 3)

half-life The time taken for half the quantity of a radioactive isotope in a sample to decay (see also *radioactive decay*). (Chapter 4)

hand-axe A Paleolithic stone tool usually made by modifying (chipping or flaking) a natural pebble. (Introduction & Chapter 8)

haplotype A specific combination of *alleles* within a *gene* cluster. (Chapters 5 & 11)

historical archaeology The archaeological study of historically documented cultures. In North America, research is directed at colonial and post-colonial settlement, analogous to the study of medieval and post-medieval archaeology in Europe. (Introduction & Chapter 3)

historical particularism A detailed descriptive approach to anthropology associated with Franz Boas and his students, and designed as an alternative to the broad generalizing approach favored by anthropologists such as Morgan and Tylor. (Chapter 1)

historiographic approach A form of explanation based primarily on traditional descriptive historical frameworks. (Chapter 12)

hoards Deliberately buried groups of valuables or prized possessions, often in times of conflict or war, and which, for one reason or another, have not been reclaimed. Metal hoards are a primary source of evidence for the European Bronze Age. (Chapters 2 & 10)

holism Theoretical approach which, when applied to human societies, sees change as the product of large-scale environmental, economic, and social forces with the assumption that what individual humans wish, desire, believe, or will is not a significant factor. (Chapter 12)

homeostasis A term used in *systems thinking* to describe the action of *negative feedback* processes in maintaining the system at a constant equilibrium state. (Chapter 12)

hunter-gatherers A collective term for the members of small-scale mobile or semi-sedentary societies, whose subsistence is mainly focused on hunting game and gathering wild plants and fruits; organizational structure is based on *bands* with strong kinship ties. (Introduction)

hypothetico-deductive explanation A form of explanation based on the formulation of hypotheses and the establishment from them by *deduction* of consequences which can then be tested against the archaeological data.

ice cores Borings taken from the Arctic and Antarctic polar ice caps, containing layers of compacted ice useful for reconstructing paleoenvironments and as a method of *absolute dating*. (Chapter 4)

iconography An important component of *cognitive archaeology*, this involves the study of artistic representations which usually have an overt religious or ceremonial significance; e.g. individual deities may be distinguished, each with a special characteristic, such as corn with the corn god, and the sun with a sun goddess etc. (Chapter 10)

idealist explanation A form of explanation that lays great stress on the search for insights into the historical circumstances leading up to the event under study in terms primarily of the ideas and motives of the individuals involved. (Chapter 12)

induction A method of reasoning in which one proceeds by generalization from a series of specific observations so as to derive general conclusions (*cf. deduction*). (Chapter 12)

inductively coupled plasma emission spectrometry (ICPS) Based on the same basic principles as OES (*optical emission spectrometry*), but the generation of much higher temperatures reduces problems of interference and produces more accurate results. (Chapter 9)

infrared absorption spectroscopy A technique used in the characterization of raw materials, it has been particularly useful in distinguishing ambers from different sources: the organic compounds in the amber absorb different wavelengths of infrared radiation passed through them. (Chapter 9)

interaction sphere A regional or inter-regional exchange system, e.g. the Hopewell interaction sphere. (Chapter 9)

isostatic uplift Rise in the level of the land relative to the sea caused by the relaxation of Ice Age conditions. It occurs when the weight of ice is removed as temperatures rise, and the landscape is raised up to form *raised beaches*. (Chapter 6)

isotopic analysis An important source of information on the reconstruction of prehistoric diets, this technique analyzes the ratios of the principal isotopes preserved in human bone; in effect the method reads the chemical signatures left in the body by different foods. Isotopic analysis is also used in *characterization* studies. (Chapter 7)

kula ring A system of ceremonial, non-competitive, exchange practiced in Melanesia to establish and reinforce alliances. Malinowski's study of this system was influential in shaping the anthropological concept of *reciprocity*. (Chapter 9)

LANDSAT See *remote sensing*.

landscape archaeology The study of individual features including settlements seen as single components within the broader perspective of the patterning of human activity over a wide area. (Chapter 1)

lexicostatistics The study of linguistic divergence between two languages, based on changes in a list of common vocabulary terms and the sharing of common root words (see also *glottochronology*). (Chapter 4)

lineage A group claiming descent from a common ancestor. (Chapter 5)

loess sediments Deposits formed of a yellowish dust of silt-sized particles blown by the wind and redeposited on land newly deglaciated, or on sheltered areas. (Chapter 6)

macrofamily Classificatory term in linguistics, referring to a group of language families showing sufficient similarities to suggest that they are genetically related (e.g. the Nostratic macrofamily, seen by some linguists as a unit embracing the Indo-European, Afro-Asiatic, Uralic, Altaic, and Kartvelian language families). (Chapters 11 & 12)

market exchange A mode of exchange which implies both a specific location for transactions and the sort of social relations where bargaining can occur. It usually involves a system of price-making through negotiation. (Chapter 9)

Marxist archaeology Based principally on the writings of Karl Marx and Friedrich Engels, this posits a materialist model of societal change. Change within a society is seen as the result of contradictions arising between the forces of production (technology) and the relations of production (social organization). Such contradictions are seen to emerge as a struggle between distinct social classes. (Chapter 12)

material culture The buildings, tools, and other artifacts that constitute the material remains of former societies. (Introduction)

matrix The physical material within which artifacts are embedded or supported. (Chapter 2)

Maya calendar A method employed by the Maya of measuring the passage of time, comprising two separate calendar systems: (1) the Calendar Round, used for everyday purposes; (2) the Long Count, used for the reckoning of historical dates. (Chapter 4)

megalithic yard A metrological unit (*c.* 2.72 ft) proposed by Alexander Thom, and argued by him, on statistical grounds, as the standard unit of length used in the construction of megalithic monuments in Britain and France. (Chapter 10)

Mesolithic An Old World chronological period beginning around 10,000 years ago, between the *Paleolithic* and the *Neolithic*, and associated with the rise to dominance of *microliths*. (Chapter 8)

metallographic examination A technique used in the study of early metallurgy involving the microscopic examination of a polished section cut from an artifact, which has been etched so as to reveal the metal structure. (Chapter 8)

methodological individualism (individualistic method) Approach to the study of societies which assumes that thoughts and decisions do have agency, and that actions and shared institutions can be interpreted as the products of the decisions and actions of individuals. (Chapters 1 & 12)

microlith A tiny stone tool, characteristic of the *Mesolithic* period, many of which were probably used as barbs. (Chapter 8)

microwear analysis The study of the patterns of wear or damage on the edge of stone tools, which provides valuable information on the way in which the tool was used. (Chapter 8)

midden The accumulation of debris and domestic waste resulting from human use. The long-term disposal of refuse can result in stratified deposits, which are useful for *relative dating*. (Chapter 7)

Middle Range Theory A conceptual framework linking raw archaeological data with higher-level generalizations and conclusions about the past which can be derived from this evidence. (Introduction)

Midwestern taxonomic system A framework devised by McKern (1939) to systematize sequences in the Great Plains area of the United States, using the general principle of similarities between artifact *assemblages*. (Chapter 1)

MNI (minimum number of individuals) A method of assessing species abundance in faunal assemblages based on a calculation of the smallest number of animals necessary to account for all the identified bones. Usually calculated from the most abundant bone or tooth from either the left or right side of the animal. (Chapter 7)

mobiliary art A term used for the portable art of the Ice Age, comprising engravings and carvings on small objects of stone, antler, bone, and ivory. (Chapter 10)

monocausal explanation Explanations of culture change (e.g. for *state* origins) which lays stress on a single dominant explanatory factor or "prime mover." (Chapter 12)

Mössbauer spectroscopy A technique used in the analysis of artifact composition, particularly iron compounds in pottery. It involves the measurement of the gamma radiation absorbed by the iron nuclei, which provides information on the particular iron compounds in the sample, and hence on the conditions of firing when the pottery was being made. (Chapter 9)

mtDNA Mitochondrial *DNA*, present in the mitochondria – organelles in the cell

engaged in energy production. MtDNA has a circular structure involving some 16,000 base pairs and is distinct from *nuclear DNA*; mtDNA is not formed by recombination, but is passed on exclusively in the female line. (Chapters 5, 11 & 12)

multi-dimensional scaling (MDSCAL) A multivariate statistical technique which aims to develop spatial structure from numerical data by estimating the differences and similarities between analytical units. (Chapter 5)

multiplier effect A term used in *systems thinking* to describe the process by which changes in one field of human activity (subsystem) sometimes act to promote changes in other fields (subsystems) and in turn act on the original subsystem itself. An instance of *positive feedback*, it is thought by some to be one of the primary mechanisms of societal change. (Chapter 12)

multivariate explanation Explanation of culture change, e.g. the origin of the state, which, in contrast to monocausal approaches, stresses the interaction of several factors operating simultaneously. (Chapter 12)

native copper Metallic copper found naturally in nuggets, which can be worked by hammering, cutting, and *annealing*. (Chapter 8)

negative feedback In *systems thinking*, this is a process which acts to counter or "dampen" the potentially disruptive effects of external inputs; it acts as a stabilizing mechanism (see *homeostasis*). (Chapter 12)

Neolithic An Old World chronological period characterized by the development of agriculture and, hence, an increasing emphasis on sedentism. (Chapter 4)

Neolithic Revolution A term coined by V.G. Childe in 1941 to describe the origin and consequences of farming (i.e. the development of stock raising and agriculture), allowing the widespread development of settled village life. (Chapter 7)

neutron activation analysis (NAA) A method used in the analysis of artifact composition which depends on the excitation of the nuclei of the atoms of a sample's various elements, when these are bombarded with slow neutrons. The method is accurate to about plus or minus 5 percent. (Chapter 9)

neutron scattering A *remote sensing* technique involving placing a probe into the soil in order to measure the relative rates of neutron flows through the soil. Since stone produces a lower count rate than soil, buried features can often be detected. (Chapter 3)

New Archaeology A new approach advocated in the 1960s which argued for an explicitly scientific framework of archaeological method and theory, with hypotheses rigorously tested, as the proper basis for explanation rather than simply description (see also *processual archaeology*). (Introduction & Chapter 1)

NISP (number of identified specimens) A gross counting technique used in the quantification of animal bones. The method may produce misleading results in assessing the relative abundance of different species, since skeletal differences and differential rates of bone preservation mean that some species will be represented more than others. (Chapter 7)

non-equilibrium systems See *self-organization*.

non-probabilistic sampling A non-statistical sampling strategy (in contrast to *probabilistic sampling*) which concentrates on sampling areas on the basis of intuition, historical documentation, or long field experience in the area. (Chapter 3)

nuclear DNA *DNA* present (within the chromosomes in the nucleus of the cell. (Chapters 5 & 11)

obsidian A volcanic glass whose ease of working and characteristically hard flint-like edges allowed it to be used for the making of tools. (Chapters 4, 9, etc.)

obsidian hydration dating This technique involves the absorption of water on exposed surfaces of obsidian; when the local hydration rate is known, the thickness of the hydration layer, if accurately measured, can be used to provide an absolute date. (Chapter 4)

off-site data Evidence from a range of information, including scatters of artifacts and features such as plowmarks and field boundaries, that provides important evidence about human exploitation of the environment. (Chapter 3)

Oldowan industry The earliest toolkits, comprising flake and pebble tools, used by hominids in the Olduvai Gorge, East Africa. (Chapters 4 & 8)

open-area excavation The opening up of large horizontal areas for *excavation*, used especially where single period deposits lie close to the surface as, for example, with the remains of American Indian or European Neolithic long houses. (Chapter 3)

optical emission spectrometry (OES) A technique used in the analysis of artifact composition, based on the principle that electrons, when excited (i.e. heated to a high temperature), release light of a particular wavelength. The presence or absence of various elements is established by examining the appropriate spectral line of their characteristic wavelengths. Generally, this method gives an accuracy of only 25 percent and has been superseded by ICPS (*inductively coupled plasma emission spectrometry*). (Chapter 9)

paleoentomology The study of insects from archaeological contexts. The survival of insect exoskeletons, which are quite resistant to decomposition, is important in the reconstruction of paleo-environments. (Chapter 6)

paleoethnobotany (archaeobotany) The recovery and identification of plant remains from archaeological *contexts*, used in reconstructing past environments and economies. (Chapter 7)

Paleolithic The archaeological period before *c*.10,000 BC, characterized by the earliest known stone tool manufacture. (Chapters 1, 4, 8, etc.)

paleomagnetism See *archaeomagnetic dating*.

palynology The analysis of fossil pollen as an aid to the reconstruction of past vegetation and climates. (Chapters 4 & 6)

paradigmatic view Approach to science, developed by Thomas Kuhn, which holds that science develops from a set of assumptions (paradigm) and that revolutionary science ends with the acceptance of a new paradigm which ushers in a period of normal science. (Chapter 12)

parietal art A term used to designate art on the walls of caves and shelters, or on huge blocks. (Chapter 10)

peer-polity interaction The full range of exchanges taking place – including imitation, emulation, competition, warfare, and the exchange of material goods and information – between autonomous (self-governing) socio-political units, generally within the same geographic region. (Chapter 9)

phenetic dendrogram Tree diagram (dendrogram) showing the relationship of individuals on the basis of observed similarity and difference, generally calculated in terms of taxonomic distance: the tree-form does not necessarily carry phylogenetic implications. (Chapter 11)

phenotype Total appearance of an organism, determined by interaction during development between its genetic constitution (*genotype*) and the environment. (Chapter 11)

phylogenetic tree Tree diagram (dendrogram) representing the descent and ancestry of an individual or group. (Chapters 5 & 11)

phylogeny Evolutionary history (of an individual or group). (Chapters 5 & 11)

physical anthropology A subdiscipline of anthropology dealing with the study of human biological or physical characteristics and their evolution. (Introduction)

phytoliths Minute particles of silica derived from the cells of plants, able to survive after the organism has decomposed or been burned. They are common in ash layers, pottery, and even on stone tools and teeth. (Chapter 6)

pinger (or boomer profiler) An underwater survey device, more powerful than *sidescan sonar*, capable of probing up to 60 m (197 ft) below the seabed. (Chapter 3)

piston corer A device for extracting columns of sediment from the ocean floor. Dates for the different layers are obtained by *radiocarbon*, *archaeomagnetic*, or *uranium series* methods. (Chapter 6)

plating A method of bonding metals together, for instance silver with copper or copper with gold. (Chapter 8)

polity A politically independent or autonomous social unit, whether simple or complex, which may in the case of a complex society (such as a state) comprise many lesser dependent components. (Chapter 6)

pollen analysis See *palynology*.

polymorphism Simultaneous occurrence in a population or social group of two or more discontinuous forms. (Chapter 5)

positive feedback A term used in *systems thinking* to describe a response in which changing output conditions in the system stimulate further growth in the input; one of the principal factors in generating system change or morphogenesis (see also *multiplier effect*). (Chapter 12)

positivism Theoretical position that explanations must be empirically verifiable, that there are universal laws in the structure and transformation of human institutions, and that theories which incorporate individualistic elements, such as minds, are not verifiable. (Chapter 12)

postprocessual explanation Explanation formulated in reaction to the perceived limitations of functional-processual archaeology. It eschews generalization in favor of an "individualizing" approach that is influenced by *structuralism*, *Critical Theory*, and neo-Marxist thought. (Chapter 12)

potassium-argon dating A method used to date rocks up to thousands of millions of years old, though it is restricted to volcanic material no more recent than *c*. 100,000 years old. One of the most widely used methods in the dating of early hominid sites in Africa. (Chapter 4)

prehistory The period of human history before the advent of writing. (Introduction)

prestige goods A term used to designate a limited range of exchange goods to which a society ascribes high status or value. (Chapter 9)

primitive valuables A term coined by Dalton to describe the tokens of wealth and prestige, often of specially valued items, that were used in the ceremonial exchange systems of non-state societies; examples include the shell necklaces and bracelets of the *kula* systems (*cf. prestige goods*). (Chapter 9)

probabilistic sampling Sampling method, using probability theory, designed to draw reliable general conclusions about a site or region, based on small sample areas; 4 types of sampling strategies are recognized: (1) *simple random sampling*; (2) *stratified random sampling*; (3) *systematic sampling*; (4) *stratified systematic sampling*. (Chapter 3)

processual archaeology An approach that stresses the dynamic relationship between social and economic aspects of culture and the environment as the basis for understanding the processes of culture, change. Uses the scientific methodology of problem statement, hypothesis formulation, and subsequent testing. The earlier functional-processual archaeology has been contrasted with *cognitive-processual archaeology*, where the emphasis is on integrating ideological and symbolic aspects. (Introduction & Chapter 12)

proton magnetometer A device used in *subsurface detection* which records variation in the earth's magnetic field. (Chapter 3)

pseudo-archaeology The use of selective archaeological evidence to promulgate nonscientific, fictional accounts of the past. (Chapter 14)

punctuated equilibria Principal feature of the evolutionary theory propounded by Niles Eldredge and Stephen J. Gould, in which species change is represented as a form of Darwinian gradualism, "punctuated" by periods of rapid evolutionary change. (Chapter 12)

pyrotechnology The intentional use and control of fire by humans. (Chapter 8)

radioactive decay The regular process by which radioactive isotopes break down into their decay products with a half-life which is specific to the isotope in question (see also *radiocarbon dating*). (Chapter 4)

radiocarbon dating An absolute dating method that measures the decay of the radioactive isotope of carbon (^{14}C) in organic material (see *half-life*). (Chapter 4)

radioimmunoassay A method of protein analysis whereby it is possible to identify protein molecules surviving in fossils which are thousands and even millions of years old. (Chapter 11)

raised beaches These are remnants of former coastlines, usually the result of processes such as *isostatic uplift* or *tectonic movements*. (Chapter 6)

ranked societies Societies in which there is unequal access to prestige and status e.g. *chiefdoms* and *states*. (Chapter 5)

reaves Bronze Age stone boundary walls, e.g. on Dartmoor, England, which may designate the territorial extent of individual communities. (Chapter 6)

reciprocity A mode of exchange in which transactions take place between individuals who are symmetrically placed, i.e. they are exchanging as equals, neither being in a dominant position. (Chapter 9)

reconnaissance survey A broad range of techniques involved in the location of archaeological sites, e.g. the recording of surface artifacts and features, and the sampling of natural and mineral resources. (Chapter 3)

redistribution A mode of exchange which implies the operation of some central organizing authority. Goods are received or appropriated by the central authority, and subsequently some of them are sent by that authority to other locations. (Chapter 9)

refitting Sometimes referred to as conjoining, this entails attempting to put stone tools and flakes back together again, and provides important information on the processes involved in the knapper's craft. (Chapter 8)

refutationist view Approach which holds that science consists of theories about the empirical world, that its goal is to develop better theories, which is achieved by finding mistakes in existing theories, so that it is crucial that theories be falsifiable (vulnerable to error and open to testing). The approach, developed by Karl Popper, emphasizes the important of testability as a component of scientific theories. (Chapter 12)

relative dating The determination of chronological sequence without recourse to a fixed time scale; e.g. the arrangement of artifacts in a typological sequence, or *seriation* (*cf. absolute dating*). (Chapter 4)

religion A framework of beliefs relating to supernatural or superhuman beings or forces that transcend the everyday material world. (Chapter 10)

remote sensing The imaging of phenomena from a distance, primarily through airborne and satellite imaging. "Ground-based remote sensing" links geophysical methods such as radar with remote sensing methods applied at ground level, such as thermography. (Chapter 3)

rescue archaeology See *salvage archaeology*.

research design Systematic planning of archaeological research, usually including (1) the formulation of a strategy to resolve a particular question; (2) the collection and recording of the evidence; (3) the processing and analysis of these data and their interpretation; and (4) the publication of results. (Chapter 3)

resistivity meter See *soil resistivity*.

rock varnishes Natural accretions of manganese and iron oxides, together with clay minerals and organic matter, which can provide valuable environmental evidence. Their study, when combined with radiocarbon methods, can provide a minimum age for some landforms, and even some types of stone tool which also accumulate varnish. (Chapters 4 & 6)

salvage archaeology The location and recording (usually through excavation) of archaeological sites in advance of highway construction, drainage projects, or urban development. (Chapters 3 & 14)

scientism The belief that there is one and only one method of science and that it alone confers legitimacy upon the conduct of research. (Chapter 12)

sedimentology A subset of *geomorphology* concerned with the investigation of the structure and texture of sediments i.e. the global term for material deposited on the earth's surface. (Chapter 6)

segmentary societies Relatively small and autonomous groups, usually of agriculturalists, who regulate their own affairs; in some cases, they may join together with other comparable segmentary societies to form a larger ethnic unit. (Chapter 5)

seismic reflection profiler An acoustic underwater survey device that uses the principle of *echo-sounding* to locate submerged landforms; in water depths of 100 m, this method can achieve penetration of more than 10 m into the sea-floor. (Chapter 6)

self-organization The product of a theory derived from thermodynamics which demonstrates that order can arise spontaneously when systems are pushed far from an equilibrium state. The emergence of new structure arises at bifurcation points, or thresholds of instability (*cf. catastrophe theory*). (Chapter 12)

seriation A relative dating technique based on the chronological ordering of a group of artifacts or assemblages, where the most similar are placed adjacent to each other in the series. Two types of seriation can be recognized, *frequency seriation* and *contextual seriation*. (Chapters 4 & 5)

sidescan sonar A survey method used in underwater archaeology which provides the broadest view of the sea-floor. An acoustic emitter is towed behind a vessel and sends out sound waves in a fan-shaped beam. These pulses of sonic energy are reflected back to a transducer – return time depending on distance traveled – and recorded on a rotating drum. (Chapter 3)

simple random sampling A type of *probabilistic sampling* where the areas to be sampled are chosen using a table of random numbers. Drawbacks include (1) defining the site's boundaries initially; (2) the nature of random number tables results in some areas being allotted clusters of sample squares, while others remain untouched. (Chapter 3)

simulation The formulation and computer implementation of dynamic models, i.e. models concerned with change through time. Simulation is a useful heuristic device, and can be of considerable help in the development of explanation. (Chapter 12)

site A distinct spatial clustering of *artifacts, features,* structures, and organic and environmental remains – the residue of human activity. (Chapter 2).

site catchment analysis (SCA) A type of *off-site* analysis which concentrates on the total area from which a site's contents have been derived; at its simplest, a site's catchment can be thought of as a full inventory of artifactual and non-artifactual remains and their sources. (Chapter 6)

site exploitation territory (SET) Often confused with *site catchment analysis,* this is a method of achieving a fairly standardized assessment of the area habitually used by a site's occupants. (Chapter 6)

slag The material residue of smelting processes from metalworking. Analysis is often necessary to distinguish slags derived from copper smelting from those produced in iron production. Crucible slags (from the casting process) may be distinguished from smelting slags by their high concentration of copper. (Chapter 8)

SLAR (sideways-looking airborne radar) A *remote sensing* technique that involves the recording in radar images of the return of pulses of electromagnetic radiation sent out from aircraft (*cf. thermography*). (Chapter 3)

social anthropology See *cultural anthropology.*

soil resistivity A method of *subsurface detection* which measures changes in conductivity by passing electrical current through ground soils. This is generally a consequence of moisture content, and in this way, buried features can be detected by differential retention of groundwater. (Chapter 3)

sphere of exchange In non-market societies, prestige valuables and ordinary commodities were often exchanged quite separately i.e. valuables were exchanged against valuables in prestige transactions, while commodities were exchanged against commodities with much less ceremony, in mutually profitable barter transactions. These separate systems are termed spheres of exchange. (Chapter 9)

standing wave technique An acoustic method, similar to *bosing,* used in *subsurface detection.* (Chapter 3)

state A term used to describe a social formation defined by distinct territorial boundedness, and characterized by strong central government in which the operation of political power is sanctioned by legitimate force. In cultural evolutionist models, it ranks second only to the empire as the most complex societal development stage (Chapter 12)

stela (pl. stelae) A free-standing carved stone monument. (Chapter 4)

step-trenching *Excavation* method used on very deep sites, such as Near Eastern *tell* sites, in which the excavation proceeds downwards in a series of gradually narrowing steps. (Chapter 3)

stratification The laying down or depositing of strata or layers (also called deposits) one above the other. A succession of layers should provide a relative chronological sequence, with the earliest at the bottom and the latest at the top. (Chapters 3 & 4)

stratified random sampling A form of *probabilistic sampling* in which the region or site is divided into natural zones or strata such as cultivated land and forest; units are then chosen by a random number procedure so as to give each zone a number of squares proportional to its area, thus overcoming the inherent bias in *simple random sampling.* (Chapter 3)

stratified systematic sampling A form of *probabilistic sampling* which combines elements of (1) *simple random sampling,* (2) *stratified random sampling,* and (3) *systematic sampling,* in an effort to reduce sampling bias. (Chapter 3)

stratigraphy The study and validation of *stratification;* the analysis in the vertical, time dimension, of a series of layers in the horizontal, space dimension. It is often used as a *relative dating* technique to assess the temporal sequence of artifact deposition. (Chapter 3)

structuralist approaches Interpretations which stress that human actions are guided by beliefs and symbolic concepts, and that underlying these are structures of thought which find expression in various forms. The proper object of study is therefore to uncover the structures of thought and to study their influence in shaping the ideas in the minds of the human actors who created the archaeological record. (Chapter 12)

style According to the art historian, Ernst Gombrich, style is "any distinctive and therefore recognizable way in which an act is performed and made." Archaeologists and anthropologists have defined "stylistic areas" as areal units representing shared ways of producing and decorating artifacts. (Chapter 10)

sub-bottom profiler See *underwater reconnaissance.*

subsurface detection Collective name for a variety of remote sensing techniques operating at ground level, and including both invasive techniques (probing, *augering* or coring) and non-invasive techniques (geophysics, geochemistry, *remote sensing, dowsing*). (Chapter 3)

surface survey Two basic kinds can be identified: (1) unsystematic and (2) systematic. The former involves field-walking, i.e. scanning the ground along one's path and recording the location of artifacts and surface features. Systematic survey by comparison is less subjective and involves a grid system, such that the survey area is divided into sectors and these are walked systematically, thus making the recording of finds more accurate. (Chapter 3)

symmetry analysis A mathematical approach to the analysis of decorative style which claims that patterns can be divided into two distinct groups or symmetry classes: 17 classes for those patterns that repeat motifs horizontally, and 46 classes for those that repeat them horizontally and vertically. Such studies have suggested that the choice of motif arrangement within a particular culture is far from random. (Chapter 10)

synchronic Referring to phenomena considered at a single point in time; i.e. an approach which is not primarily concerned with change (*cf. diachronic*). (Chapter 12)

synostosis The joining of separate pieces of bone in human skeletons; the precise timing of such processes is an important indicator of age. (Chapter 11)

systematic sampling A form of *probabilistic sampling* employing a grid of equally spaced locations; e.g. selecting every other square. This method of regular spacing runs the risk of missing (or hitting) every single example if the distribution itself is regularly spaced. (Chapter 3)

systematic survey See *surface survey.*

systems thinking A method of formal analysis in which the object of study is viewed as comprising distinct analytical sub-units. Thus in archaeology, it comprises a form of explanation in which a society or culture is seen through the interaction and interdependence of its component parts; these are referred to as system parameters, and may include such things as population size, settlement pattern, crop production, technology etc. (Chapter 12)

taphonomy The study of processes which have affected organic materials such as bone after death; it also involves the microscopic analysis of tooth-marks or cut marks to assess the effects of butchery or scavenging activities. (Chapter 7)

tectonic movements Displacements in the plates that make up the earth's crust, often responsible for the occurrence of *raised beaches.* (Chapter 6)

tell A Near Eastern term that refers to a mound site formed through successive human occupation over a very long timespan. (Chapter 2)

temper Inclusions in pottery clay which act as a filler to give the clay added strength and workability and to counteract any cracking or shrinkage during firing. (Chapter 8)

tephra Volcanic ash. In the Mediterranean, for example, *deep-sea coring* produced evidence for the ash fall from the eruption of Thera, and its *stratigraphic* position provided important information in the construction of a *relative chronology*. (Chapter 4)

thermal prospection A *remote sensing* method used in *aerial reconnaissance*. It is based on weak variations in temperature which can be found above buried structures whose thermal properties are different from those of their surroundings. (Chapter 3)

thermography A technique which uses thermal or heat sensors in aircraft to record the temperature of the soil surface. Variations in soil temperature can be the result of the presence of buried structures. (Chapter 3)

thermoluminescence (TL) A dating technique that relies indirectly on radioactive decay, overlapping with radiocarbon in the time period for which it is useful, but also has the potential for dating earlier periods. It has much in common with *electron spin resonance* (ESR). (Chapter 4)

Thiessen polygons A formal method of describing settlement patterns based on territorial divisions centered on a single site; the polygons are created by drawing straight lines between pairs of neighboring sites, then at the mid-point along each of these lines, a second series of lines are drawn at right angles to the first. Linking the second series of lines creates the Thiessen polygons. (Chapter 5)

thin-section analysis A technique whereby microscopic thin sections are cut from a stone object or potsherd and examined with a petrological microscope to determine the source of the material. (Chapter 9)

Three Age System A *classification* system devised by C.J. Thomsen for the sequence of technological periods (stone, bronze, and iron) in Old World prehistory. It established the principle that by classifying artifacts, one could produce a chronological ordering. (Chapter 1)

trace element analysis The use of chemical techniques, such as *neutron activation analysis*, or *X-ray fluorescence spectrometry*, for determining the incidence of trace elements in rocks. These methods are widely used in the identification of raw material sources for the production of stone tools. (Chapters 7 & 9)

trajectory In *systems thinking*, this refers to the series of successive states through which the system proceeds over time. It may be said to represent the long-term behavior of the system. (Chapter 12)

tree-ring dating See *dendrochronology*.

trend surface analysis The aim of trend surface analysis is to highlight the main features of a geographic distribution by smoothing over some of the local irregularities. In this way, important trends can be isolated from the background "noise" more clearly. (Chapter 9)

tribes A term used to describe a social grouping generally larger than a *band*, but rarely numbering more than a few thousand; unlike bands tribes are usually settled farmers, though they also include nomadic pastoral groups whose economy is based on exploitation of livestock. Individual communities tend to be integrated into the larger society through kinship ties. (Chapter 5)

tuyère A ceramic blowtube used in the process of smelting. (Chapter 8)

type A class of artifacts defined by the consistent clustering of *attributes*. (Chapters 1 & 4)

typology The systematic organization of artifacts into types on the basis of shared *attributes*. (Chapters 1, 3 & 4)

underwater reconnaissance Geophysical methods of underwater survey include (1) a *proton magnetometer* towed behind a survey vessel, so as to detect iron and steel objects which distort the earth's magnetic field; (2) *sidescan sonar* that transmits sound waves in a fan-shaped beam to produce a graphic image of surface features on the sea-bed; (3) a *sub-bottom profiler* that emits sound pulses which bounce back from features and objects buried beneath the sea floor. (Chapter 3)

Uniformitarianism The principle that the stratification of rocks is due to processes still going on in seas, rivers, and lakes; i.e. that geologically ancient conditions were in essence similar to or "uniform with" those of our own time. (Chapter 1)

uranium series dating A dating method based on the *radioactive decay* of isotopes of uranium. It has proved particularly useful for the period before 50,000 years ago, which lies outside the time range of *radiocarbon dating.* (Chapter 4)

varves Fine layers of alluvium sediment deposited in glacial lakes. Their annual deposition makes them a useful source of dating. (Chapter 4)

Wheeler box-grid An excavation technique developed by Mortimer Wheeler from the work of Pitt-Rivers, involving retaining intact baulks of earth between excavation grid squares, so that different layers can be correlated across the site in the vertical profiles. (chapter 3)

world system A term coined by the historian Wallerstein to designate an economic unit, articulated by trade networks extending far beyond the boundaries of individual political units (nation states), and linking them together in a larger functioning unit. (Chapter 9)

X-ray diffraction analysis A technique used in identifying minerals present in artifact raw materials; it can also be used in geomorphological contexts to identify particular clay minerals in sediments, and thus the specific source from which the sediment was derived. (Chapter 6)

X-ray fluorescence spectrometry (XRF) A method used in the analysis of artifact composition, in which the sample is irradiated with a beam of X-rays which excite electrons associated with atoms on the surface. (Chapter 9)

XTENT modeling A method of generating settlement hierarchy, that overcomes the limitations of both *central place theory* and *Thiessen polygons*; it assigns territories to centers based on their scale, assuming that the size of each center is directly proportional to its area of influence. Hypothetical political maps may thus be constructed from survey data. (Chapter 5)

Y-chromosome Sex chromosome present in males; unlike other *nuclear DNA*, the DNA in the Y-chromosome is not formed by recombination but is passed on exclusively in the male line. (Chapters 5 & 11)

zooarchaeology See *archaeozoology*.

Notes and Bibliography

Note: References for the box features are listed separately at the end of the respective chapter references.

Chapter 1: The Searchers: The History of Archaeology (pp. 19–48)

General references Bahn 1995, 1996; Daniel 1967, 1975, 1980; Gräslund 1987; Grayson 1983; Heizer 1969; Hood 1998; Schnapp 1996; Trigger 1989a. Autobiographical retrospectives include Willey 1974; Daniel & Chippindale 1989. **Europe** Klindt-Jensen 1975 (Scandinavia); Sklenár 1983 (Central Europe); Laming-Emperaire 1964 (France). **New World** Alcina 1995; Kehoe 1998; Willey & Sabloff 1974, 1993; Meltzer & others 1986; Fagan 1977; Bernal 1980 (Mexico). **Australia** Horton 1991. **Africa** Clark 1970; Robertshaw 1990. **India** Chakrabarti 1988.

p. 19 **Alternative, non-Western views of the past** Bahn 1996; Schnapp 1996.
p. 21 **Teotihuacán** Schávelzon 1983; **Huaca de Tantalluc** Alcina 1995, p. 16.
p. 30 **Layard** Lloyd 1980; Waterfield 1963. **Schliemann** Traill 1995.
p. 34 **Childe** Trigger 1980.
p. 35 **Ecological approach** Steward 1955; Clark, J.G.D. 1952.
pp. 35–36 **Archaeological science** Brothwell & Higgs 1969.
pp. 38–40 **The New Archaeology** Binford 1968; Clarke, D.L. 1968 & 1972.
pp. 40–41 **World archaeology** Braidwood & Howe 1960; MacNeish 1967–1972; Adams 1965; Leakey, M. 1984; Clark, J.D. 1970; Mulvaney & Kaminga 1999; Gould 1980; McBryde 1985.
pp. 46–47 **Feminist archaeology** Conkey & Spector 1984; Diaz-Andreu & Stig-Sørensen 1998; Gimbutas 1991; Nelson 1997.

Box Features

pp. 22–23 **Pompeii** Grant 1971; Corti 1951; Raper 1977; Maiuri 1970; Ling 1987.
pp. 26–27 **Evolutionary Thought** Harris 1968; Steward 1955; White 1959.
pp. 28–29 **19th-Century Pioneers** Willey & Sabloff 1993; Fagan 1977.
pp. 31–33 **Field Techniques** Bowden 1991 (Pitt-Rivers); Drower 1985 (Flinders Petrie); Hawkes 1982; Wheeler 1955 (Wheeler); Davies & Charles 1999 (Garrod).
pp. 36–37 **Women Pioneers** Claassen 1994; Diaz-Andreu & Stig-Sørensen 1998.
p. 39 **Processual Archaeology: Key Concepts** Binford 1968; Clarke, D.L. 1968
pp. 42–43 **Interpretive or Postprocessual Archaeologies.** In general: Hodder 1985, 1991; Shanks & Tilley 1987a and 1987b; Leone 1982; and Preucel and Hodder 1996. For discussion of some of the philosophical influences (Levi-Strauss, Ricoeur, Barthes, Derrida, Foucault etc.) see Tilley 1990; also Bapty and Yates 1990; and Preucel 1991. For critiques of these approaches see Binford 1987; Trigger 1989b; Peebles 1990; Bell 1994; Bintliff 1991; Cowgill 1991, and the criticisms following Shanks & Tilley 1989. For "interpretive" rather than "postprocessual" see Dark 1995; Hodder & others 1995. For phenomenological and praxis approaches see Embree 1997; Cassirer 1944; Tilley 1994; Treherne 1995; Thomas 1996; Barrett 1994.
pp. 44–45 **Interpretive Archaeologies at Çatalhöyük** Mellaart 1967; Hodder 1996 and 1999; see also Hodder 1997 and Hassan 1997; Meskell 1998; also consult websites: http://catal.arch.cam.ac.uk and Mysteries of Çatalhöyük: http://www.smm.org/catal/

Bibliography

ADAMS, R. McC. 1965. *The Land Behind Baghdad; A History of Settlement on the Diyala Plains.* Univ. of Chicago Press.

ALCINA FRANCH, J. 1995 *Arqueólogos o Anticuarios. Historia antigua de la Arqueología en la América Española.* Ediciones del Serval: Barcelona.

BAHN, P.G. (ed.). 1995. *The Story of Archaeology. The 100 Great Discoveries.* Barnes & Noble: New York; Weidenfeld & Nicolson: London.

BAHN, P.G. (ed.). 1996. *The Cambridge Illustrated History of Archaeology.* Cambridge Univ. Press.

BAPTY, I. & YATES, T. (eds.). 1990. *Archaeology after Structuralism.* Routledge: London.

BARRETT, J.C. 1994. *Fragments from Antiquity, an Archaeology of Social Life in Britain, 2900–1200 BC.* Blackwell: Oxford.

BELL, J.R. 1994. *Reconstructing Prehistory: Scientific Method in Archaeology.* Temple University Press: Philadelphia.

BERNAL, I. 1980. *A History of Mexican Archaeology.* Thames & Hudson: London & New York.

BINFORD, L.R. 1968. Post-Pleistocene adaptations, in *New Perspectives in Archaeology* (S.R. Binford & L.R. Binford eds.), 313–41. Aldine Press: Chicago.

——1987. Data, relativism and archaeological science, *Man* 22, 391–404.

BINTLIFF, J. 1991. Post-modernism, rhetoric and scholasticism at TAG: the current state of British archaeological theory. *Antiquity* 65, 274–78.

BOWDEN, M. 1991. *Pitt Rivers.* Cambridge Univ. Press.

BRAIDWOOD, R.J. & HOWE, B. 1960. *Investigations in Iraqi Kurdistan.* Studies in Ancient Oriental Civilization, No. 31. Oriental Institute of the Univ. of Chicago.

BROTHWELL, D.R. & HIGGS, E.S. (eds.). 1969. *Science in Archaeology.* (2nd ed.) Thames & Hudson: London; Praeger: New York.

CASSIRER, E. 1944. *An Essay on Man. Introduction to the Philosophy of Human Culture.* Yale University Press: New Haven.

CHAKRABARTI, D.K. 1988. *A History of Indian Archaeology from the Beginning to 1947.* Munshiram Manoharlal: New Delhi.

CLAASSEN, C. (ed.). 1994. *Women in Archaeology.* Pennsylvania Univ. Press: Philadelphia.

CLARK, J.D. 1970. *The Prehistory of Africa.* Thames & Hudson: London; Praeger: New York.

CLARK, J.G.D. 1952. *Prehistoric Europe: The Economic Basis.* Methuen: London.

CLARKE, D.L. 1968. *Analytical Archaeology.* Methuen: London.

——(ed.). 1972. *Models in Archaeology.* Methuen: London.

CONKEY, M. & SPECTOR, J. 1984. Archaeology and the study of gender, in *Advances in Archaeological Method and Theory 7* (M.B. Schiffer ed.), 1–38. Academic Press: New York & London.

CORTI, E.G. 1951. *The Destruction and Resurrection of Pompeii and Herculaneum.* Routledge & Kegan Paul: London.

COWGILL, G. 1991. Beyond criticizing New Archaeology. *American Anthropologist* 95, 551–73.

DANIEL, G.E. 1967. *The Origins and Growth of Archaeology.* Pelican: Harmondsworth.

——1975. *150 Years of Archaeology.* Duckworth: London.

——1980. *A Short History of Archaeology.* Thames & Hudson: London & New York.

——(ed.). 1981. *Towards a History of Archaeology.* Thames & Hudson: London.

——**& RENFREW, A.C.** 1988. *The Idea of Prehistory.* (Rev. ed.) Edinburgh Univ. Press; Columbia Univ. Press: New York.

DANIEL, G.E. & CHIPPINDALE, C. (eds.). 1989. *The Pastmasters.* Thames & Hudson: London & New York.

DARK, K.R. 1995. *Theoretical Archaeology.* Duckworth: London.

DAVIES, W. & CHARLES, R. (eds.). 1999. *Dorothy Garrod and the Progress of the Palaeolithic. Studies in the Prehistoric Archaeology of the Near East and Europe.* Oxbow Books: Oxford.

DIAZ-ANDREU, M. & STIG SØRENSEN, M.L. (eds.). 1998. *Excavating Women. A History of Women in European Archaeology.* Routledge: London.

DROWER, M. 1985. *Flinders Petrie.* Gollancz: London.

EMBREE, L. (ed.). 1997. *Encyclopedia of Phenomenology.* Kluwer: Dordrecht.

FAGAN, B. 1977. *Elusive Treasure. The Story of Early Archaeologists in the Americas.* Scribners: New York.

GIMBUTAS, M. 1991. *The Civilisation of the Goddess: the World of Old Europe.* Harper and Row: San Francisco.

GOULD, R.A. 1980. *Living Archaeology.* Cambridge Univ. Press.

GRANT, M. 1971. *Cities of Vesuvius: Pompeii and Herculaneum.* Michael Grant: London.

GRÄSLUND, B. 1987. *The Birth of Prehistoric Chronology.* Cambridge Univ. Press.

GRAYSON, D.K. 1983. *The Establishment of Human Antiquity.* Academic Press: New York & London.

HARRIS, M. 1968. *The Rise of Anthropological Theory.* Thomas Y. Crowell: New York.

HASSAN, F. 1997. Beyond the surface: comments on Hodder's "reflexive excavation methodology". *Antiquity* 71, 1020–25.

HAWKES, J. 1982. *Mortimer Wheeler: Adventurer in Archaeology.* Weidenfeld & Nicolson: London.

HEIZER, R.F. 1969. *Man's Discovery of His Past – A sourcebook of original articles.* Peek: Palo Alto.

HODDER, I. 1985. Postprocessual archaeology, in *Advances in Archaeological Method and Theory* (M.B. Schiffer ed.) 8, 1–26.

——1991. *Reading the Past.* (2nd ed.) Cambridge Univ. Press.

——(ed.). 1996. *On the Surface: Çatalhöyük 1993–5.* McDonald Institute, Cambridge.

——1997. 'Always momentary, fluid and flexible' towards a reflexive excavation methodology. *Antiquity* 71, 691–700.

——(ed.). 2000. *Towards Reflexive Method in Archaeology: The Example of Çatalhöyük.* McDonald Institute: Cambridge.

——, **SHANKS, M., ALEXANDRI, M., BUCHLI, V., CARMAN, J., LAST, J. & LUCAS, G.** 1995. *Interpreting Archaeology.* Routledge: London.

HOOD, R. 1998. *Faces of Archaeology in Greece: Caricatures by Piet de Jong.* Leopard's Head Press: Oxford.

HORTON, D. 1991. *Recovering the Tracks. The Story of Australian Archaeology.* Aboriginal Studies Press: Canberra.

KEHOE, A.B. 1998. *The Land of Prehistory. A Critical History of American Archaeology.* Routledge: New York & London.

KLINDT-JENSEN, O. 1975. *A History of Scandinavian Archaeology.* Thames & Hudson: London.

LAMING-EMPERAIRE, A. 1964. *Origines de l'Archéologie Préhistorique en France.* Picard: Paris.

LEAKEY, M. 1984. *Disclosing the Past.* Weidenfeld & Nicolson: London.

LEONE, M. 1982. Some opinions about recovering mind. *American Antiquity* 47, 742–60.

LING, R. 1987. A New Look at Pompeii, in *Origins* (B. Cunliffe ed.), 148–60. BBC Books: London.

LLOYD, S. 1980. *Foundations in the Dust.* (2nd ed.). Thames & Hudson: London & New York.

MACNEISH, R.S. & others (eds.). 1967–1972. *The Prehistory of the Tehuacán Valley.* Univ. of Texas Press: Austin.

MAIURI, A. 1970. *Pompeii.* Instituto Poligrafico dello Stato: Rome.

MCBRYDE, I. (ed.). 1985. *Who Owns the Past?* Oxford Univ. Press: Melbourne.

MELLAART, J. 1967. *Çatal Hüyük, a Neolithic Town in Anatolia.* Thames & Hudson: London & New York.

MELTZER, D.J., FOWLER, D.D. & SABLOFF, J.A. (eds.). 1986. *American Archaeology Past and Future.* Smithsonian Institution Press: Washington D.C.

MESKELL, L. 1998. Twin Peaks: the archaeologies of Çatalhöyük, in *Ancient Goddesses* (L. Goodison & C. Morris eds.), 46–62. British Museum Press: London.

MULVANEY, J. & KAMMINGA, J. 1999. *Prehistory of Australia.* Smithsonian Institution Press: Washington D.C. & London.

NELSON, S.M. 1997. *Gender in Archaeology. Analyzing Power and Prestige.* Altamira Press: Walnut Creek.

PEEBLES, C.S. 1990. From history to hermeneutics: the place of theory in the later prehistory of the Southeast. *Southeastern Archaeology* 9, 23–34.

PREUCEL, R.W. (ed.). 1991. *Processual and Postprocessual Archaeologies: Multiple Ways of Knowing the Past.* Center for Archaeological Investigation: Southern Illinois University at Carbondale.

——**& HODDER, I.** 1996. *Contemporary Archaeology in Theory. A Reader.* Blackwell: Oxford.

RAPER, R.A. 1977. The analysis of the urban structure of Pompeii: a sociological examination of land use, in *Spatial Archaeology* (D.L. Clarke ed.), 189–222. Academic Press: London.

ROBERTSHAW, P. (ed.). 1990 *A History of African Archaeology.* Currey: London; Heinemann: Portsmouth, N.H.

SCHAVELZON, D. 1983. La primera excavación arqueológica de América. Teotihuacán en 1675. *Anales de Antropología* (Mexico) 20, 121–34.

SCHNAPP, A. 1996. *Discovery of the Past.* British Museum Press: London.

SHANKS, M. & TILLEY, C. 1987a. *Social Theory and Archaeology.* Polity Press: Cambridge.

SHANKS, M. & TILLEY, C. 1987b. *Reconstructing Archaeology: Theory and Practice.* Cambridge Univ. Press.

——**& others.** 1989. Archaeology into the 1990s. *Norwegian Archaeological Review* 22, 1–54.

SKLENÁŘ, K. 1983. *Archaeology in Central Europe: the first 500 years.* Leicester Univ. Press; St Martin's: New York.

STEWARD, J.H. 1955. *Theory of Culture Change, the Methodology of Multilinear Evolution.* Univ. of Illinois Press: Urbana.

TAYLOR, W.W. 1948. *A Study of Archaeology.* American Anthropological Association Memoir 69.

THOMAS, J. 1996. *Time, Culture and Identity.* Routledge: London.

TILLEY, C. (ed.). 1990. *Reading Material Culture.* Blackwell: Oxford.

——1994. *A Phenomenology of Landscape.* Berg: Oxford.

TRAILL, D. 1995 *Schliemann of Troy: Treasure and Deceit.* John Murray: London.

TREHERNE, P. 1995. The warrior's beauty: the masculine body and self-identity in Bronze Age Europe. *Journal of European Archaeology* 3.1, 105–44.

TRIGGER, B.G. 1980. *Gordon Childe.* Thames & Hudson: London.

——1989a. *A History of Archaeological Thought.* Cambridge Univ. Press.

——1989b. Hyperrelativism, responsibility and the social sciences. *Canadian Review of Sociology and Anthropology* 26, 776–91.

TYLOR, E.B. 1871. *Primitive Culture.* Henry Holt: New York.

WATERFIELD, G. 1963. *Layard of Nineveh.* John Murray: London.

WHEELER, R.E.M. 1955. *Still Digging.* Michael Joseph: London.

WHITE, L.A. 1959. *The Evolution of Culture.* McGraw-Hill: New York.

WILLEY, G.R. (ed.). 1974. *Archaeological Researches in Retrospect.* Winthrop: Cambridge, Mass.

——**& PHILLIPS, P.** 1958. *Method and Theory in American Archaeology.* Univ. of Chicago Press.

——**& SABLOFF, J.A.** 1974. *A History of American Archaeology.* Thames & Hudson: London (3rd ed. W.H. Freeman: New York, 1993).

Chapter 2: What is Left? The Variety of the Evidence (pp. 49–70)

pp. 52–53 **Formation processes** Schiffer 1996; Nash & Petraglia 1987; Binford 1981; Brain 1981.

pp. 53–54 **Cultural formation processes** Schiffer 1976; Cockburn & others 1998 (mummies); Redford 1984 (destruction of Akhenaten's monuments).

p. 59 **Organic materials** Lister & Bahn 1994 (La Brea tarpits); Bowman 1983, 1994 (Vindolanda writing tablets); Sheets 1992, 1994 (Cerén).

pp. 63–64 **Dry environments** Sheets 1984 (El Salvador); Jennings 1953 (Danger Cave); Lynch 1980; Zimmerman & others 1971 (Aleutian mummy); Cockburn & others 1998 (mummies in general).

pp. 64–68 **Cold environments** Lister & Bahn 1994; Guthrie 1990 (frozen mammoths); Rudenko 1970 (Pazyryk); Hart Hansen & others 1991 (Qilakitsoq); Beattie & Geiger 1987 (the British Sailors).

pp. 68–70 **Waterlogged environments** In general: Coles, B. & J. 1989; Coles, B. 1992; Coles, J. 1984, 1986; Coles, J. & B. 1996; Purdy 1988; and the journal *Newswarp*. Coles & Lawson 1987 (European sites); Coles, B. & J. 1986 (Somerset Levels); Purdy 1991 (Florida); Glob 1969, 1973 (Danish bodies); Bocquet 1979, 1994; Bocquet & others 1982 (lake sites).

Box Features

p. 53 **Experimental Archaeology** Bell & others 1996; Ashbee & Jewell 1998.

pp. 60–61 **Ozette** Gleeson & Grosso 1976; Kirk & Daugherty 1974.

pp. 62–63 **Tutankhamun** Carter 1972; Reeves 1990.

p. 65 **Barrow Site** Dekin 1987; Lobdell & others 1987.

pp. 66–67 **The Iceman** Bahn 1995; Fleckinger & Steiner 1998; Spindler 1994.

Bibliography

ASHBEE, P. & JEWELL, P. 1998. The Experimental Earthworks revisited. *Antiquity* 72, 485–504.

BAHN, P.G. 1995. Last days of the Iceman. *Archaeology* May/June, 66–70.

——(ed.). 1996. *Tombs, Graves and Mummies.* Weidenfeld & Nicolson: London; Barnes & Noble: New York.

BEATTIE, O. & GEIGER, J. 1987. *Frozen in Time.* Bloomsbury: London.

BELL, M., FOWLER, P.J. & HILLSON, S.W. (eds.). 1996. *The Experimental Earthwork Project 1960–1992.* Research Report 100, Council for British Archaeology: York.

BINFORD, L.R. 1981. *Bones – Ancient Men and Modern Myths.* Academic Press: New York & London.

BOCQUET, A. 1979. Lake bottom archaeology. *Scientific American* 240 (2), 48–56.

——1994. Charavines il y a 5000 ans. *Les Dossiers d'Archéologie* 199, Dec.

——& others. 1982. La vie au Néolithique. Charavines, un village au bord d'un lac il y a 5000 ans. *Dossiers de l'Archéologie* No. 64, June.

BOWMAN, A.K. 1983. *Roman Writing Tablets from Vindolanda.* British Museum Publications: London.

——1994. *Life and Letters on the Roman Frontier: Vindolanda and its People.* British Museum Publications: London.

BRAIN, C.K. 1981. *The Hunters or the Hunted? An Introduction to African Cave Taphonomy.* Univ. of Chicago Press.

CARTER, H. 1972. *The Tomb of Tutankhamen.* Sphere: London.

COCKBURN, T.A., COCKBURN, E. & REYMAN, T.A. (eds.). 1998. *Mummies, Disease and Ancient Cultures.* (2nd ed.) Cambridge Univ. Press.

COLES, B. (ed.). 1992. *The Wetland Revolution in Prehistory.* Prehist. Soc./WARP: Exeter.

——& COLES, J. 1986. *Sweet Track to Glastonbury. The Somerset Levels in Prehistory.* Thames & Hudson: London & New York.

——&——1989. *People of the Wetlands.* Thames & Hudson: London & New York.

COLES, J. 1984. *The Archaeology of Wetlands.* Edinburgh Univ. Press.

——1986. Precision, purpose and priorities in Wetland Archaeology. *The Antiquaries Journal* 66, 227–47.

——& COLES, B. 1996. *Enlarging the Past. The Contribution of Wetland Archaeology.* Society of Antiquaries of Scotland, Monograph Series 11: Edinburgh.

——& LAWSON, A.J. (eds.). 1987. *European Wetlands in Prehistory.* Clarendon Press: Oxford.

DEKIN, A.A. 1987. Sealed in time: ice entombs an Eskimo family for five centuries. *National Geographic* 171, (6), 824–36.

FLECKINGER, A. & STEINER, H. 1998. *The Iceman.* Folio: Bolzano; South Tyrol Museum of Archaeology.

GLEESON, P. & GROSSO, G. 1976. Ozette site, in *The Excavation of Water-saturated Archaeological Sites (wet sites) on the Northwest Coast of North America* (D.R. Croes ed.), 13–44. Mercury Series 50: Ottawa.

GLOB, P.V. 1969. *The Bog People. Iron-Age Man Preserved.* Faber: London.

——1973. *The Mound People. Danish Bronze Age Man Preserved.* Faber: London.

GUTHRIE, R.D. 1990. *Frozen Fauna of the Mammoth Steppe.* Univ of Chicago Press.

HART HANSEN, J.P., MELDGAARD, J. & NORDQVIST, J. (eds.). 1991. *The Greenland Mummies.* British Museum Publications: London.

JENNINGS, J.D. 1953. *Danger Cave.* Univ. of Utah Anth. Papers, No. 27: Salt Lake City.

KIRK, R. & DAUGHERTY, R.D. 1974. *Hunters of the Whale.* Morrow: New York.

LISTER, A. & BAHN, P.G. 1994. *Mammoths.* Macmillan: New York; Boxtree: London.

LOBDELL, J.E., DEKIN, A.A. & others. 1984. The Frozen Family from the Utqiagvik Site, Barrow, Alaska. *Arctic Anthropology* 21 (1), 1–154.

LYNCH, T.F. (ed.). 1980. *Guitarrero Cave. Early Man in the Andes.* Academic Press: New York & London.

MONTLUÇON, J. 1986. L'électricité pour mettre à nu les objets archéologiques. *La Recherche* 17, 252–55.

NASH, D.T. & PETRAGLIA, M.D. (eds.). 1987. *Natural Formation Processes and the Archaeological Record.* British Arch. Reports, Int. Series 352: Oxford.

PURDY, B.A. 1991. *The Art and Archaeology of Florida Wetlands.* CRC Press: Boca Raton.

——(ed.). 1988. *Wet Site Archaeology.* Telford Press: Caldwell.

REDFORD, D.B. 1984. *Akhenaten, the Heretic King.* Princeton Univ. Press.

REEVES, N. 1990. *The Complete Tutankhamun.* Thames & Hudson: London & New York.

RUDENKO, S.I. 1970. *Frozen Tombs of Siberia: The Pazyryk burials of Iron Age horsemen.* Dent: London; Univ. of California Press: Berkeley.

SCHIFFER, M.B. 1976. *Behavioral Archaeology.* Academic Press: New York & London.

——1996. *Formation Processes of the Archaeological Record.* Univ. of Utah Press: Salt Lake City.

SHEETS, P.D. (ed.). 1984. *Archaeology and Volcanism in Central America.* Univ. of Texas Press: Austin.

——1992. *The Ceren Site. A prehistoric village buried by volcanic ash in Central America.* Harcourt Brace Jovanovich: Fort Worth.

——1994. Tropical time capsule: An ancient village preserved in volcanic ash yields evidence of Mesoamerican peasant life. *Archaeology* 47, 4, 30–33.

SPINDLER, K. 1994. *The Man in the Ice: The preserved body of a Neolithic man reveals the secrets of the Stone Age.* Weidenfeld & Nicolson: London.

ZIMMERMAN, M.R. & others. 1971. Examination of an Aleutian mummy. *Bull. New York Acad. Medicine* 47, 80–103.

Chapter 3: Where? Survey and Excavation of Sites and Features
(pp. 71–116)

p. 72 **Accidental discovery** Cotterell 1981 (China's first emperor).

p. 73 **Ground reconnaissance: documentary sources** Much information, including an account of Schliemann's work, can be obtained from the books by Glyn Daniel on historical archaeology (Chapter 1 above). Ingstad 1977 (L'Anse aux Meadows); Pritchard 1987 (biblical archaeology); Matthiae 1980 (Tell Mardikh); Wainwright 1962, Carver 1987 (place-name evidence).

pp. 74–79 **Reconnaissance survey** In general: Ammerman 1981; Bintliff & Snodgrass 1988; Heizer & Graham 1967; Nance 1983; Plog, Plog & Wait 1978; Redman & Watson 1970; Schiffer & others 1978. Dunnell & Dancey 1983, Lewarch & O'Brien 1981 (off-site studies); Isaac 1981, Foley 1981, Bower 1986 (Africa); Keller & Rupp 1983 (especially article by Cherry) (Mediterranean).

p. 79 **Extensive survey** Adams 1981, Redman 1982 (Mesopotamia); Flannery 1976, Blanton & others 1982 (Mesoamerica); Cherry 1983. **Intensive survey** Lehner 1985, 1997 (Giza); for Teotihuacán, see box feature references below.

pp. 79–84 **Aerial reconnaissance** General books include: Bradford 1957; Deuel 1973; Maxwell 1983; Riley 1987; Saint Joseph 1966; Wilson 1975; the Aerial Archaeology Research Group has produced the journal *AARGnews* since 1990. In French: Chevallier 1965, 1971; Dassie 1978; and *Dossiers de l'Archéologie* Nos. 1 (1973), 22 (1977), and 43 (1980). In German, Scollar 1965. Connah & Jones 1983 (Australia); Darling 1984 (Africa); Jones 1994 (New Zealand); Kunow 1995, Gojda 1997 (Central & Eastern Europe); Palmer & Cox 1993 (recent developments); Palmer 1984 (Danebury); Wilson 1982 (air-photo interpretation); Stoertz 1997 (Yorkshire Wolds). Palmer 1977 (computer methods for transcribing information from photographs). O'Brien & others 1982 (digital enhancement); Scollar & others 1990 (computer image processing); Gumerman & Neely 1972 (color infrared photography).

pp. 84–86 **Remote sensing from high altitude** Allen & others 1990 (GIS); Fowler 1996 (Stonehenge); Barisano & others 1986; Ebert 1984; El-Baz 1997; Holcomb 1992; Lyons & Mathien 1980; McManamon 1984; Sheets & McKee 1994. Maya archaeology: Adams, R.E.W. 1980, 1982; Adams, R.E.W. & others 1981 (radar).

pp. 87–89 **Geographic Information Systems** Aldenderfer & Maschner 1996; Allen, Green & Zubrow 1990; Burrough & McDonnell 1998; Gaffney & van Leusen 1995; Heywood & others 1998; Jones 1997; van Leusen 1993; Lock and Stančič 1995; Maschner 1996. Warren 1990 (predictive modeling).

pp. 89–92 **Site surface survey** Flannery 1976, 51–52 (Oaxaca survey by Hole). Pracchia & others 1985 (Mohenjodaro).

p. 94 **Subsurface detection: probes** Thomas 1988 (St Catherine's Island); Lerici 1959 (Etruscan tombs); Holden 1987, El-Baz 1988, 1997 (second boat pit at Giza); Dormion & Goidin 1987, Kérisel 1988 (French and Japanese work inside the Great Pyramid).

pp. 94–99 **Ground-based remote sensing** In general: Clark 1996. GPR (radar) Conyers & Goodman 1997; Goodman & others 1995; Conyers & Goodman 1999 (incl. Forum Novum); Goodman & Nishimura 1993 (Japan); White & Barker 1998 (Wroxeter). Also, specialized journals contain important articles, e.g. *Archaeometry* (since 1958), *Archaeological Prospection* (since 1994), and *Prospezioni Archeologiche* (Fondazione Lerici, Rome since 1966). French work in this field can be consulted in *Dossiers de l'Archéologie* No. 39, 1979, as well as in Hesse 1966. An excellent German summary, particularly of geophysical and geochemical methods, in Rottländer 1983.

pp. 99–103 **Resistivity** Atkinson 1963; Clark, A. 1969, 1975a (the latter also focuses on fluxgate gradiometers), 1996; Weymouth 1986 (concerns radar and other methods too).

pp. 103–04 **Magnetic methods** Among the many general references are: Aitken 1969; Clark, A. 1975b, 1996; Scollar 1969; Steponaitis & Brain 1976; Tite & Mullins 1970, 1971; Colani 1966; Foster & Hackens 1969. David 1998 (Stanton Drew). Underwater applications: Clausen & Arnold 1976; Foster 1970; Hall 1966. Applications in Australia: Stanley 1983.

p. 104 **Neutron scattering** Alldred & Shepherd 1963. **Geochemical methods** Clark, A. 1977; Cook & Heizer 1965. Work in Virginia: Solecki 1951. **Phosphate analysis** Craddock & others 1985; Eidt 1977, 1984; Proudfoot 1976; Sjöberg 1976; and at Cefn Graeanog, Conway 1983.

p. 105 **Dowsing** Graves 1980 (for believers; see review in *Antiquity* 58, 1984, 231–32); Bailey & others 1988 (medieval churches); van Leusen 1998. Rigorous tests on dowsers are discussed by Aitken 1959; Randi 1982, 307–25.

pp. 106–14 **Excavation** In general: Barker 1986, 1993; Hester & others 1997; Joukowsky 1980; McIntosh 1999; Spence 1990; Tite 1972. It is still rewarding to look at Wheeler's best account of his approach and methods: Wheeler 1954. Connah 1983 (Australia). **Stratigraphy** Harris 1989.

p. 114 **Computer classification** Plog, F. & Carlson 1989.

Box Features

p. 75 **Melos Survey** Cherry, in Renfrew & Wagstaff 1981; Cherry, Davis & Mantzanouri 1991.

p. 76–77 **Sampling Strategies** Among the most important general books are: Mueller 1974, 1975; Cherry & others 1978. Articles include Binford 1964; Nance 1983; Plog 1976, 1978; Plog & others 1978; South & Widmer 1977. Sampling applications in Mesoamerica, including the work of Winter: Flannery 1976; for Turkey, Redman & Watson 1970. The procedure followed by Redman and Watson in generating their stratified unaligned systematic sample is slightly different from that advocated by Haggett (1965: 197). According to Haggett it is termed stratified systematic unaligned and the selection of a square from a grid block is not fully random. The special problems of sampling in forests are covered by Chartkoff 1978 and Lovis 1976 (North America).

pp. 80–81 **Archaeological Aerial Reconnaissance** See main text references.

pp. 90–91 **Teotihuacán** Cabrera Castro & others 1982; Millon 1967, 1972/73, 1981; Manzanilla & others 1994.

pp. 92–93 **Abu Salabikh** Postgate 1982; 1987.

p. 95 **Underwater Archaeology** Good general works include Bass 1972, 1988; Delgado 1997; Muckelroy 1978; Throckmorton 1987. Also of interest, though somewhat outdated, is Taylor 1965. Many useful articles can be found in the *International Journal of Nautical Archaeology*, *American Journal of Archaeology*, and *National Geographic*. On new explorations at great depths, Ballard 1998, Hecht 1995, Stone 1999.

pp. 96–97 **Red Bay Wreck** Grenier 1988.

pp. 100–01 **Geophysical Survey at Wroxeter** White & Barker 1998.

p. 102 **Measuring Magnetism** Clark, A. 1996; Rowley & Davies 1973; and see main text references.

p. 104 **Controlled Archaeological Test Site** Isaacson & others 1999.

Bibliography

ADAMS, R.E.W. 1980. Swamps, canals, and the locations of ancient Maya cities. *Antiquity* 54, 206–14.

———1982. Ancient Maya canals. Grids and lattices in the Maya jungle. *Archaeology* 35 (6), 28–35.

———**BROWN, W.E. & CULBERT, T.P.** 1981. Radar mapping, archaeology, and ancient Maya land use. *Science* 213, 1457–63.

ADAMS, R.M. 1981. *Heartland of Cities: Surveys of Ancient Settlement and Land Use on the Central Floodplain of the Euphrates.* Univ. of Chicago Press.

AITKEN, M.J. 1959. Test for correlation between dowsing response and magnetic disturbance. *Archaeometry* 2, 58–59.

———1969. Magnetic location, in *Science in Archaeology* (D.R. Brothwell & E.S. Higgs eds.), 681–94. (2nd ed.) Thames & Hudson: London.

———1974. *Physics and Archaeology.* (2nd ed.) Oxford Univ. Press.

ALDENDERFER, M. & MASCHNER, H.D.G. (eds.). 1996 *Anthropology, Space and Geographic Information Systems.* Oxford Univ. Press: New York.

ALLDRED, J.C. & SHEPHERD, A. 1963. Trial of neutron scattering for the detection of buried walls and cavities. *Archaeometry* 6, 89–92.

ALLEN, K.M.S., GREEN, S.W. & ZUBROW, E.B.W. (eds.). 1990. *Interpreting Space: GIS and Archaeology.* Taylor & Francis: London/New York.

AMMERMAN, A.J. 1981. Surveys and archaeological research. *Annual Review of Anth.* 10, 63–88.

ATKINSON, R.J.C. 1963. Resistivity Surveying in Archaeology, in *The Scientist and Archaeology* (R. Pyddoke ed.), 1–30. Phoenix House: London.

BAILEY, R.N., CAMBRIDGE, E. & BRIGGS, H.D. 1988. *Dowsing and Church Archaeology.* Intercept: Wimborne, Dorset.

BALLARD, R.D. 1998. High-tech search for Roman shipwrecks. *National Geographic* 193(4), April, 32–41.

BARISANO, E., BARTHOLOME, E. & MARCOLONGO, B. 1986. *Télédétection et Archéologie*. CNRS: Paris.

BARKER, P. 1986. *Understanding Archaeological Excavation*. Batsford: London.

——1993. *Techniques of Archaeological Excavation*. (3rd ed.) Routledge (Batsford): London.

BASS, G.F. 1968. New tools for undersea archaeology. *National Geographic* 134, 402–23.

——1972. *Archaeology Under Water*. (Rev. ed.) Penguin: Harmondsworth.

——(ed.). 1988. *Ships and Shipwrecks of the Americas: A History Based on Underwater Archaeology*. Thames & Hudson: London & New York.

BINFORD, L.R. 1964. A consideration of archaeological research design. *American Antiquity* 29, 425–41.

BINTLIFF, J.L. & SNODGRASS, A.M. 1988. Mediterranean survey and the city. *Antiquity* 62, 57–71.

BLANTON, R.E. & others. 1982. *Ancient Mesoamerica: A Comparison of Change in Three Regions*. Cambridge Univ. Press.

BOWER, J. 1986. A survey of surveys: aspects of surface archaeology in sub-Saharan Africa. *The African Arch. Review* 4, 21–40.

BRADFORD, J.S.P. 1957. *Ancient Landscapes: Studies in Field Archaeology*. Bell & Sons: London.

BURROUGH, P.A. & MCDONNELL, R.A. 1998. *Principles of Geographical Information Systems*. Oxford Univ. Press.

CABRERA CASTRO, R. & others. 1982. *Teotihuacán 1980–82. Primeros Resultados*. Instituto Nac. de Antrop. e Historia: Mexico City.

CARVER, M. 1987. *Underneath English Towns. Interpreting Urban Archaeology*. Batsford: London.

CHARTKOFF, J.L. 1978. Transect interval sampling in forests. *American Antiquity* 43, 46–53.

CHERRY, J.F. 1983. Frogs round the pond: Perspectives on current archaeological survey projects in the Mediterranean region, in *Archaeological Survey in the Mediterranean Area* (D.R. Keller & D.W. Rupp eds.), 375–416. British Arch. Reports, Int. Series 155: Oxford.

——& others. (eds.). 1978. *Sampling in Contemporary British Archaeology*. British Arch. Reports, Int. Series 50: Oxford.

——, DAVIS, J.L. & MANTZANOURI, E., 1991. *Landscape Archaeology as Long Term History, Northern Keos in the Cycladic Islands*. Univ. of California Press: Los Angeles.

CHEVALLIER, R. 1965. *L'Avion à la Découverte du Passé*. Fayard: Paris.

——1971. *L'Archéologie aérienne*. U2: Paris.

CLARK, A. 1969. Resistivity surveying, in *Science in Archaeology* (D.R. Brothwell & E.S. Higgs eds.), 695–707. (2nd ed.) Thames & Hudson: London.

——1975a. Archaeological prospecting: a progress report. *Journal of Arch. Science* 2, 297–314.

——1975b. Geophysical surveying in archaeology. *Antiquity* 49, 298–99.

——1977. Geophysical and chemical assessment of air photographic sites. *Arch. Journal* 134, 187–93.

——1996. *Seeing Beneath the Soil: Prospecting Methods in Archaeology*. (2nd ed.) Routledge (Batsford): London.

CLAUSEN, C.J. & ARNOLD, J.B. 1976. The magnetometer and underwater archaeology. *Int. Journal of Nautical Arch.* 5, 159–69.

COLANI, C. 1966. A new type of locating device. 1: The instrument. *Archaeometry* 9, 3–8.

CONNAH, G. (ed.). 1983. *Australian Field Archaeology. A Guide to Techniques*. Australian Institute of Aboriginal Studies: Canberra.

——& JONES, A. 1983. Photographing Australian prehistoric sites from the air, in *Australian Field Archaeology. A Guide to Techniques* (G. Connah ed.), 73–81. AIAS: Canberra

CONWAY, J.S. 1983. An investigation of soil phosphorus distribution within occupation deposits from a Romano-British hut group. *Journal of Arch. Science* 10, 117–28.

CONYERS, L.B. & GOODMAN, D. 1997. *Ground-Penetrating Radar: An Introduction for Archaeologists*. Altamira Press: Walnut Creek.

——& ——1999. Archaeology looks to new depths. *Discovering Archaeology* 1 (1), Jan/Feb, 70–77.

COOK, S.F. & HEIZER, R.F. 1965. *Studies on the Chemical Analysis of Archaeological Sites*. Univ. of California Publications in Archaeology: Berkeley.

COTTERELL, A. 1981. *The First Emperor of China*. Macmillan: London; Holt, Rinehart & Winston: New York.

CRADDOCK, P.T. & others. 1985. The application of phosphate analysis to the location and interpretation of archaeological sites. *Arch. Journal* 142, 361–76.

DARLING, P.J. 1984. *Archaeology and History in Southern Nigeria: the ancient linear earthworks of Benin and Ishan*. Cambridge Monographs in African Archaeology. British Arch. Reports Int. Series 215: Oxford.

DASSIE, J. 1978. *Manuel d'Archéologie Aérienne*. Technip: Paris.

DAVID, A. 1998. Stanton Drew. *Past* (Newsletter of the Prehistoric Society) 28, April, 1–3.

DELGADO, J.P. (ed.). 1997. *British Museum Encyclopedia of Underwater and Maritime Archaeology*. British Museum Press: London; Yale Univ. Press: New Haven.

DEUEL, L. 1973. *Flights into Yesterday*. Pelican: Harmondsworth.

DORMION, G. & GOIDIN, J-P. 1987. *Les Nouveaux Mystères de la Grande Pyramide*. Albin Michel: Paris.

DUNNELL, R.C. & DANCEY, W.S. 1983. The siteless survey: a regional data collection strategy, in *Advances in Archaeological Method and Theory* (M.B. Schiffer ed.) 6, 267–87. Academic Press: New York & London.

EBERT, J.I. 1984. Remote sensing applications in archaeology, in *Advances in Archaeological Method and Theory* (M.B. Schiffer ed.) 7, 293–362. Academic Press: New York & London.

EIDT, R.C. 1977. Detection and examination of anthrosols by phosphate analysis. *Science* 197, 1327–33.

——1984, *Advances in Abandoned Site Analysis*. Univ. of Wisconsin Press.

EL-BAZ, F. 1988. Finding a Pharaoh's funeral bark. *National Geographic* 173 (4), 512–33.

——1997. Space Age Archaeology. *Scientific American* 277 (2), 40–45.

FLANNERY, K.V. (ed.). 1976. *The Early Mesoamerican Village*. Academic Press: New York & London.

FOLEY, R. 1981. *Off-site Archaeology and Human Adaptation in Eastern Africa*. British Arch. Reports, Int. Series 97: Oxford.

FOSTER, E.J. 1970. A diver-operated underwater metal detector. *Archaeometry* 12, 161–66.

FOSTER, E. & HACKENS, T. 1969. Decco metal detector survey on Delos. *Archaeometry* 11, 165–72.

FOWLER, M.J.F. 1996. High-resolution satellite imagery in archaeological application: a Russian satellite photograph of the Stonehenge region. *Antiquity* 70, 667–71.

GAFFNEY, V. & VAN LEUSEN, P.M. 1995. Postscript – GIS environmental determinism and archaeology, in Lock and Stančič 1995, 367–82.

GOJDA, M. 1997. *Aerial Archaeology in Bohemia*. Czech Acad. Sciences: Prague.

GOODMAN, D. & NISHIMURA, Y. 1993. A ground-radar view of Japanese burial mounds. *Antiquity* 67, 349–54.

——, ——& ROGERS, J.D. 1995. GPR time-slices in archaeological prospection. *Archaeological Prospection* 2, 85–89.

GRAVES, T. (ed.). 1980. *Dowsing and Archaeology*. Turnstone Books: Wellingborough.

GRENIER, R. 1988. Basque Whalers in the New World: The Red Bay Wreck, in *Ships and Shipwrecks of the Americas* (G. Bass ed.), 69–84. Thames & Hudson: London & New York.

GUMERMAN, G.J. & NEELY, J.A. 1972. An archaeological survey of the Tehuacán Valley, Mexico: A test of color infrared photography. *American Antiquity* 37, 520–27.

HAGGETT, P. 1965. *Locational Analysis in Human Geography*. Edward Arnold: London.

HALL, E.T. 1966. The use of the proton magnetometer in underwater archaeology. *Archaeometry* 9, 32–44.

HARRIS, E. 1989. *Principles of Archaeological Stratigraphy*. (2nd ed.) Academic Press: New York & London.

HECHT, J. 1995. 20,000 tasks under the sea. *New Scientist*, 30 Sept., 40–45.

HEIZER, R.F. & GRAHAM, J.A. 1967. *A Guide to Field Methods in Archaeology*. National Press: Palo Alto, Ca.

HESSE, A. 1966. *Prospections géographiques à faible profondeur. Applications à l'Archéologie*. Dunod: Paris.

HESTER, T.N., SHAFER, H.J. & FEDER, K.L. 1997. *Field Methods in Archaeology*. (7th ed.) Mayfield: Palo Alto, Ca.

HEYWOOD, I., CORNELIUS, S. & CARVER, S. 1998. *Introduction to Geographical Information Systems*. Addison-Wesley: Reading, Mass.; Longman: London.

HOLCOMB, D.W. 1992. Shuttle imaging radar and archaeological survey in China's Taklamakan Desert. *Journal of Field Arch.* 19, 129–38.

HOLDEN, C. 1987. A quest for ancient Egyptian air. *Science* 236, 1419–20.

INGSTAD, A.S. 1977. *The Discovery of a Norse Settlement in America. Excavations at L'Anse aux Meadows, Newfoundland, 1961–1968*. Oslo, Bergen, Tromsø.

ISAAC, G. 1981. Stone Age visiting cards: approaches to the study of early land use patterns, in *Pattern of the Past. Studies in Honour of David Clarke* (I. Hodder, G. Isaac & N. Hammond eds.), 131–55. Cambridge Univ. Press.

ISAACSON, J. & others. 1999. A Controlled Archaeological Test Site Facility in Illinois: training and research in Archaeogeophysics. *Journal of Field Archaeology* 26, 227–36.

JONES, C. 1997. *Geographical Information Systems and Computer Cartography*. Longman: London.

JONES, K. 1994. *Nga Tohuwhenua Mai Te Rangi: A New Zealand Archaeology in Aerial Photographs*. Victoria Univ. Press: Wellington.

JOUKOWSKY, M. 1980. *A Complete Manual of Field Archaeology*. Prentice-Hall: Englewood Cliffs, N.J.

KELLER, D.R. & RUPP, D.W. (eds.). 1983. *Archaeological Survey in the Mediterranean Area*. British Arch. Reports, Int. Series 155: Oxford.

KERISEL, J. 1988. Le dossier scientifique sur la pyramide de Khéops. *Archéologia* 232, Feb., 46–54.

KUNOW, J. (ed.). 1995. *Luftbildarchäologie in Ost- und Mitteleuropa*. Forschungen zur Archäologie im Land Brandenberg 3.

LEHNER, M. 1985. The development of the Giza necropolis: The Khufu Project. *Mitteilungen dt. archäol. Inst. Abt. Kairo* 41, 109–43.

———1997. *The Complete Pyramids*. Thames & Hudson: London & New York.

LERICI, C.M. 1959. Periscope on the Etruscan Past. *National Geographic* 116 (3), 336–50.

VAN LEUSEN, M. 1993. Cartographic modelling in a cell-based GIS, in *Computing the Past. Computer Applications and Quantitative Methods in Archaeology, CAA92* (J. Andresen, T. Madsen & I. Scollar, eds.), 105–24. Aarhus Univ. Press.

———1998. Dowsing and Archaeology. *Archaeological Prospection* 5, 123–38.

LEWARCH, D.E. & O'BRIEN, M.J. 1981. The expanding role of surface assemblages in archaeological research, in *Advances in Archaeological Method and Theory* (M.B. Schiffer ed.) 4, 297–342.

LOCK, G. & STANCIC, Z. (eds.). 1995. *Archaeology and Geographical Information Systems: a European perspective*. Taylor & Francis: London & Bristol, Penn.

LOVIS, W.A. 1976. Quarter sections and forests: an example of probability sampling in the northeastern woodlands. *American Antiquity* 41, 364–72.

LYONS, T.R. & MATHIEN, F.J. (eds.). 1980. *Cultural Resources: Remote Sensing*. U.S. Govt. Printing Office: Washington D.C.

MANZANILLA, L. & others. 1994. Caves and geophysics: an approximation to the underworld of Teotihuacán, Mexico. *Archaeometry* 36 (1), 141–57.

MASCHNER, H.D.G. (ed.). 1996. *New Methods, Old Problems: Geographic Information Systems in Modern Archaeological Research*. Center for Archaeological Investigations: Southern Illinois Univ.

MATTHIAE, P. 1980. *Ebla: An Empire Rediscovered*. Doubleday: New York.

MAXWELL, G.S. (ed.). 1983. *The Importance of Aerial Reconnaissance to Archaeology*. Council for British Arch. Research Report 49: London.

MCINTOSH, J. 1999. *The Practical Archaeologist*. (2nd ed.) Facts on File: New York; Thames & Hudson: London .

MCMANAMON, F.P. 1984. Discovering sites unseen, in *Advances in Archaeological Method and Theory* (M.B. Schiffer ed.) 7, 223–92. Academic Press: New York & London.

MILLON, R. 1967. Teotihuacán. *Scientific American* 216 (6), 38–48.

———(ed.). 1972/3. *Urbanization at Teotihuacán*. 2 vols. Univ. of Texas Press: Austin.

———1981. Teotihuacán: city, state and civilization, in *Archaeology (Supplement to the Handbook of Middle American Indians)* (J.A. Sabloff ed.), 198–243. Univ. of Texas Press: Austin.

MUCKELROY, K. 1978. *Maritime Archaeology*. Cambridge Univ. Press.

MUELLER, J.W. 1974. *The Use of Sampling in Archaeological Surveys*. Memoirs of the Soc. for American Arch. No. 28.

———(ed.). 1975. *Sampling in Archaeology*. Univ. of Arizona Press: Tucson.

NANCE, J.D. 1983. Regional sampling in archaeological survey: the statistical perspective, in *Advances in Archaeological Method and Theory* (M.B. Schiffer ed.) 6, 289–356. Academic Press: New York & London.

O'BRIEN, M.J. & others. 1982. Digital enhancement and grey-level slicing of aerial photographs: techniques for archaeological analysis of intrasite variability. *World Arch.* 14, 173–90.

PALMER, R. 1977. A computer method for transcribing information graphically from oblique photographs to maps. *Journal of Arch. Science* 4, 283–90.

———1984. *Danebury: an aerial photographic interpretation of its environs*. RCHM Supp. Series 6: London.

———& COX, C. 1993. *Uses of Aerial Photography in Archaeological Evaluations*. IFA Technical Paper 12.

PLOG, F. & CARLSON, D.L. 1989. Computer applications for the All American Pipeline Project. *Antiquity* 63, 258–67.

PLOG, S. 1976. Relative efficiencies of sampling techniques for archaeological surveys, in *The Early Mesoamerican Village* (K.V. Flannery ed.) 136–58. Academic Press: New York & London.

———1978. Sampling in archaeological surveys: a critique. *American Antiquity* 43, 280–85.

———, **PLOG, F. & WAIT, W.** 1978. Decision making in modern surveys, in *Advances in Archaeological Method and Theory* (M.B. Schiffer ed.) 1, 383–421.

POSTGATE, N. 1982. Abu Salabikh, in *Fifty Years of Mesopotamian Discovery. The Work of the British School of Archaeology in Iraq, 1932–82* (J. Curtis ed.), 48–61. British School of Arch. in Iraq.

———1987. Excavations at Abu Salabikh 1985–86. *Iraq* 49, 91–119.

PRACCHIA, S., TOSI, M. & VIDALE, M. 1985. On the type, distribution and extent of craft activities at Mohenjo-daro, in *South Asian Archaeology 1983* (J. Schotsmans & M. Taddei eds.). Istituto Universitario Orientale: Naples.

PRITCHARD, J.B. (ed.). 1987. *The Times Atlas of the Bible*. Times Books: London.

PROUDFOOT, B. 1976. The analysis and interpretations of soil phosphorus in archaeology, in *Geoarchaeology* (D.A. Davidson & M.L. Shackley eds.), 93–113. Duckworth: London.

RANDI, J. 1982. *Flim-Flam! Psychics, ESP, Unicorns and other Delusions*. Prometheus: Buffalo.

REDMAN, C.L. 1982. Archaeological survey and the study of Mesopotamian urban systems. *Journal of Field Arch.* 9, 375–42.

———& WATSON, P.J. 1970. Systematic intensive surface collection. *American Antiquity* 35, 279–91.

RENFREW, C. & WAGSTAFF, J.M. (eds.). 1981. *An Island Polity: The Archaeology of Exploitation on Melos.* Cambridge Univ. Press.

RILEY, D.N. 1987. *Air Photography and Archaeology.* Duckworth: London.

ROTTLÄNDER, R.C.A. 1983. *Einführung in die Naturwissenschaftlichen Methoden in der Archäologie.* Verlag Arch. Venatoria, Band 6. Institut für Vorgeschichte der Univ. Tübingen.

ROWLEY, T. & DAVIES, M. 1973. *Archaeology and the M40 Motorway.* Oxford Univ. Press.

SAINT JOSEPH, J.K. 1966. *The Uses of Air Photography.* A. & C. Black: London.

SCHIFFER, M.B. & others. 1978. The design of archaeological surveys. *World Arch.* 10, 1–28.

SCOLLAR, I. 1965. *Archäologie aus der Luft.* Landesmuseum: Bonn.

———1969. Some techniques for the evaluation of archaeological magnetometer surveys. *World Arch.* 1, 77–89.

———, **TABBAGH, A., HESSE, A. & HERZOG, I.** (eds.). 1990. *Remote Sensing in Archaeology.* Cambridge Univ. Press.

SHEETS, P. & MCKEE, B.R. (eds.). 1994 *Archaeology, Volcanism and Remote Sensing in the Arenal Region, Costa Rica.* Univ. of Texas Press: Austin.

SJÖBERG, A. 1976. Phosphate analysis of anthropic soils. *Journal of Field Arch.* 3, 447–54.

SOLECKI, R.S. 1951. Notes on soil analysis and archaeology. *American Antiquity* 16, 254–56.

SOUTH, S. & WIDMER, R. 1977. A subsurface sampling strategy for archaeological reconnaissance, in *Research Strategies in Historical Archaeology* (S. South ed.), 119–50. Academic Press: New York & London.

SPENCE C. (ed.). 1990. *Archaeological Site Manual.* (2nd ed.) Museum of London: London.

STANLEY, J.M. 1983. Subsurface survey: the use of magnetics in Australian archaeology, in *Australian Field Archaeology. A Guide to Techniques* (G. Connah ed.), 82–86. AIAS: Canberra.

STEPONAITIS, V.P. & BRAIN, J.P. 1976. A portable Differential Proton Magnetometer. *Journal of Field Arch.* 3, 455–63.

STOERTZ, C. 1997. *Ancient Landscapes of the Yorkshire Wolds.* RCHME: Swindon.

STONE, R. 1999. Researchers ready for the plunge into deep water. *Science* 283, 929.

TAYLOR, J. DU P. (ed.). 1965. *Marine Archaeology.* Hutchinson: London.

THOMAS, D.H. 1988. *St. Catherine's Island: An Island in Time:* Georgia Endowment for the Humanities: Atlanta.

THROCKMORTON, P. (ed.). 1987. *The Sea Remembers: Shipwrecks and Archaeology.* Weidenfeld: New York (published in Britain as *History from the Sea: Shipwrecks and Archaeology*; Mitchell Beazley: London).

TITE, M.S. 1972. *Methods of Physical Examination in Archaeology.* Seminar Press: London & New York.

———**& MULLINS, C.** 1970. Electromagnetic prospecting on archaeological sites using a soil conductivity meter. *Archaeometry* 12, 97–104.

———1971. Enhancement of the magnetic susceptibility of soils on archaeological sites. *Archaeometry* 13, 209–19.

WAINWRIGHT, F. 1962. *Archaeology, Place-Names and History.* Routledge & Kegan Paul: London.

WARREN, R.E. 1990. Predictive Modelling of Archaeological Site Location: a case study in the Midwest, in *Interpreting Space: GIS and Archaeology* (K.M.S. Allen, S.W. Green & E.B.W. Zubrow eds.), 201–15. Taylor and Francis: London & New York.

WEYMOUTH, J.W. 1986. Geophysical methods of archaeological site surveying, in *Advances in Archaeological Method and Theory* (M.B. Schiffer ed.) 9, 311–95. Academic Press: New York & London.

WHEELER, R.E.M. 1954. *Archaeology from the Earth.* Oxford Univ. Press (Penguin Books: Harmondsworth).

WHITE, R. & BARKER, P. 1998. *Wroxeter: Life and Death of a Roman City.* Tempus: Stroud.

WILSON, D.R. (ed.). 1975. *Aerial Reconnaissance for Archaeology.* Council for British Arch. Res. Rep. 12: London.

———1982, *Air Photo Interpretation for Archaeologists.* Batsford: London.

Chapter 4: When? Dating Methods and Chronology (pp. 117–170)

pp. 118–20 **Stratigraphy** See references for Chapter 3; Lyell 1830. **Bone age** Weiner 1955 (Piltdown hoax).

pp. 120–24 **Typological sequences** Montelius 1903 (classic example of artifact typologies constructed and used); Petrie 1899 (contextual seriation); Brainerd 1951; Robinson 1951; Kendall 1969; Dethlefsen & Deetz 1966 (frequency seriation).

p. 124 **Linguistic dating** Swadesh 1972.

pp. 125–26 **Pleistocene chronology** Klein 1999; Sutcliffe 1985; also Brothwell & Higgs 1969; Oakley 1964; Shackleton & Opdyke 1973; Zeuner 1958. Recently there have been suggestions that the dating for the Pleistocene should be revised: see Bassinot & others 1994.

p. 126 **Deep-sea cores** See references for Chapter 6. **Ice cores** Lorius & others 1985; Jouzel & others 1987.

p. 127 **Pollen dating** See references for Chapter 6. **Faunal dating** Klein 1999; Gowlett 1993; Pitts & Roberts 1997.

pp. 129–32 **Calendars etc.** In general: Tapsell 1984. Baines & Malek 1980 (Egypt); Coe & others 1986 (Maya).

pp. 133–34 **Varves** Zeuner 1958; Kitigawa & van der Plicht 1998.

pp. 134–37 **Tree-ring dating** In general: Baillie 1982, 1995; Eckstein 1984; Weiner 1992; Hillam & others 1990; Kuniholm & others 1996; Schweingruber 1988; Kuniholm & Striker 1987 (Aegean). For the early work in the American Southwest: Douglass 1919–1936.

pp. 137–45 **Radiocarbon dating** In general: Bowman 1990, 1994; Mook & Waterbolk 1983; also Ralph 1971; Tite 1972; Fleming 1976. Specific: Libby 1952; Taylor 1987 (history of method); Renfrew 1973, 1979; Pearson 1987; Stuiver & Pearson 1986, 1993; Stuiver & Reimer 1993; Becker 1993; Kromer & Spurk 1998; Stuiver & others 1998; Bronk Ramsey 1994 (calibration); Bard & others 1990, 1993 (calibration via Barbados coral); Buck & others 1994; Allen & Bayliss 1995; Bayliss & others 1997 (Bayesian methods); Hedges 1981 (accelerator mass spectrometry).

pp. 145–50 **Potassium-argon** Aitken 1990; Dalrymple & Lanphere 1969; Schaeffer & Zähringer 1966; McDougall 1990; Walter & others 1991. **Argon-argon** Renne & others 1997; Wintle 1996. **Uranium-series** Schwarcz 1982, 1993; McDermott & others 1993; Grün & Thorne 1997; Rink & others 1995. **Fission-track** Aitken 1990; Wagner & Van den Haute 1992. Bishop & Miller 1982 provide examples of the results obtained by these methods.

pp. 150–52 **Thermoluminescence** Good accounts: Aitken 1985, 1989, 1990; Fleming 1979; Wagner 1983; McKeever 1985; Aitken & Valladas 1993.

pp. 152–54 **Optical dating** David & others 1997; Rees-Jones & Tite 1997; Aitken 1989, 1998; Smith & others 1990; Roberts & others 1994; for Jimnium: Fullagar & others 1996; Spooner 1998; Roberts & others 1998; Wintle 1996.

pp. 154–55 **Electron spin resonance** Aitken 1990; Schwarcz & others 1989; Grün & Stringer 1991; Schwarcz & Grün 1993; Grün & others 1996; Wintle 1996.

pp. 155–59 **Calibrated relative methods** Aitken 1990; Brothwell & Higgs 1969; Weiner 1955. Specific methods: Michels & Bebrich 1971; Michels & Tsong 1980; Shackley 1998 (obsidian hydration); Bada 1985; Fleming 1976; Kimber & Hare 1992 (amino-acid racemization); Miller & others 1993 (isoleucine epimerization); Whitley & Dorn 1987 (cation-ratio); Bednarik 1992, Watchman 1993 (rock art dating); Bucha 1971, see also Bahn & Vertut 1997 (Chapter 5), Bahn 1998 (Chapter 6). For Côa, Zilhao 1995; Phillips & others 1997. For the Carthaginian stela, see Web news from the "Virtual Archaeometry Laboratory" rchleo@bluewin.ch; Phillips & others 1996, 1997 (Chlorine-36); Tarling 1983 (archaeomagnetism).

pp. 161–62 **Chronological correlations**
Kittleman 1979. Case studies: Harris &
Hughes 1978 (New Guinea): Sheets 1979
(Central America).
pp. 162–69 **World chronology** Scarre 1988;
Fagan 1990, 1995; Gowlett 1993.

Box Features

pp. 130–31 **Maya Calendar** Coe 2000; Coe &
others 1986.
pp. 137–41 **Radioactive Decay/The Publication
of Radiocarbon Dates/How to Calibrate** See
main text references.
pp. 148–49 **Dating Our African Ancestors** Klein
1999; Lewin 1987, 1989; Gowlett 1993;
Leakey 1981; Aitken & others 1993.
pp. 160–61 **Thera Eruption** Discussed by
various specialists in Doumas 1978, and
by Renfrew 1979; and the date by
Hammer & others 1987. Baillie & Munro
1988; Hardy & Renfrew 1991; Kuniholm
& others 1996; Renfrew 1996; Barber &
others 1997. For tephra in Greenland ice
core Zielenski & Germani 1998.

Bibliography

AITKEN, M.J. 1985. *Thermoluminescence
Dating*. Academic Press: London & New
York.
——1989. Luminescence dating: a guide
for non-specialists. *Archaeometry* 31,
147–59.
——1990. *Science-Based Dating in
Archaeology*. Longman: London & New
York.
——1998. *Introduction to Optical Dating*.
Oxford Univ. Press
——, STRINGER, C.B. & MELLARS, P.A. (eds.).
1993. *The Origin of Modern Humans and
the Impact of Chronometric Dating*.
Princeton Univ. Press.
——& VALLADAS, H. 1993. Luminescence
dating, in *The Origin of Modern Humans
and the Impact of Chronometric Dating*
(M.J. Aitken & others eds.), 27–39.
Princeton Univ. Press.
ALLEN, M.J. & BAYLISS, A. 1995. The
radiocarbon dating programme, in
*Stonehenge in its Landscape: Twentieth-
Century Excavations* (R.M.J. Cleal, K.E.
Walker & R. Montague), 511–35. English
Heritage: London.
BADA, J.L. 1985. Aspartic acid racemization
ages of California Paleoindian skeletons.
American Antiquity 50, 645–47.
BAHN, P.G. 1998. *The Cambrige Illustrated
History of Prehistoric Art*. Cambridge
Univ. Press.
——& VERTUT, J. 1997. *Journey through
the Ice Age*. Weidenfeld & Nicolson:
London; Univ. of California Press:
Berkeley.
BAILLIE, M.G.L. 1982. *Tree-ring Dating and
Archaeology*. Croom Helm: London;
Univ. of Chicago Press.
——1995. *A Slice through Time:
Dendrochronology and Precision Dating*.
Routledge (Batsford): London.

——& MUNRO, M.A.R. 1988. Irish tree rings,
Santorini and volcanic dust veils. *Nature*
332, 344–46.
BAINES, J. & MALEK, J. 1980. *Atlas of Ancient
Egypt*. Phaidon: Oxford; Facts on File:
New York.
BARBER, P.C., DUGMORE, A.J. & EDWARDS, K.J.
1997. Bronze Age myths? Volcanic
activity and human response in the
Mediterranean and North Atlantic
regions. *Antiquity* 71, 581–93.
BARD, E., ARNOLD, A., FAIRBANKS, G. & HAMELIN, B.
1993. ^{230}Th- ^{234}U and ^{14}C ages obtained by
mass spectrometry on corals.
Radiocarbon 35, 191–99.
——, HAMELIN, B., FAIRBANKS, R.G. & ZINDLER, A.
1990. Calibration of the ^{14}C timescale
over the past 30,000 years using mass
spectrometric U-Th ages from Barbados
corals. *Nature* 345, 405–10.
BASSINOT, F.C. & others. 1994. The
astronomical theory of climate and the
age of the Brunhes–Matuyama magnetic
reversal. *Earth and Planetary Science
Letters* 126, 91–108.
BAYLISS, A., BRONK RAMSEY, C. & MCCORMAC, F.G.
1997. Dating Stonehenge, in *Science and
Stonehenge* (B. Cunliffe & C. Renfrew
eds.), 39–60. British Academy: Oxford.
BECKER, B. 1993. An 11,000-year German
oak and pine dendrochonology for
radiocarbon calibration. *Radiocarbon* 35,
201–13.
BEDNARIK, R.G. 1992. Developments in rock
art dating. *Acta Archaeologica* 63:
141–55.
BISHOP, W.W. & MILLER, J.A. (eds.). 1982.
Calibration of Hominoid Evolution.
Scottish Academic Press: Edinburgh.
BOWMAN, S. 1990. *Radiocarbon Dating*.
British Museum Publications: London.
——1994. Using radiocarbon: an update.
Antiquity 68, 838–43.
BRAINERD, G.W. 1951. The Place of
Chronological Ordering in
Archaeological Analysis. *American
Antiquity* 16, 301–13.
BRONK RAMSEY, C. 1994. *OxCal Radiocarbon
Calibration and Stratigraphic Analysis
Program*. Research Laboratory for
Archaeology: Oxford.
BROTHWELL, D.R. & HIGGS, E.S. (eds.). 1969.
Science in Archaeology. (2nd ed.)
Thames & Hudson: London; Praeger:
New York.
BUCHA, V. 1971. Archaeomagnetic Dating,
in *Dating Techniques for the
Archaeologist* (H.N. Michael & E.K.
Ralph eds.), 57–117. Massachusetts Inst.
of Technology: Cambridge, Mass.
BUCK, C.E., LITTON, C.D. & SCOTT, E.M. 1994.
Making the most of radiocarbon dating:
some statistical considerations. *Antiquity*
68, 252–63.
COE, M.D. 2000. *The Maya*. (6th ed.)
Thames & Hudson: London & New York.
——, SNOW, D., & BENSON, E. 1986. *Atlas of
Ancient America*. Facts on File: New
York & Oxford.

DALRYMPLE, G.B. & LANPHERE, M.A. 1969.
*Potassium-Argon Dating. Principles,
Techniques and Applications to
Geochronology*. W.H. Freeman & Co: San
Francisco.
DAVID, B., ROBERTS, R., TUNIZ, C., JONES, R. &
HEAD, J. 1997. New optical and
radiocarbon dates for Ngarrabullgan
Cave, a Pleistocene archaeological site in
Australia. *Antiquity* 71, 183–88.
DETHLEFSEN, E. & DEETZ, J. 1966. Death's
Heads, Cherubs, and Willow Trees:
Experimental Archaeology in Colonial
Cemeteries. *American Antiquity* 31,
502–10.
DORN, R.I. & others. 1986. Cation-ratio and
Accelerator Radiocarbon Dating of rock
varnish on Mojave artifacts and
landforms. *Science* 231, 830–33.
DOUGLASS, A.E. 1919, 1928 & 1936. *Climatic
cycles and tree growth*. 3 vols. Carnegie
Institution of Washington: Washington.
DOUMAS, C. (ed.). 1978. *Thera and the
Aegean World*. Thera Foundation:
London.
ECKSTEIN, D. 1984. *Dendrochronological
Dating*. European Science Foundation:
Strasbourg.
EVANS, J. 1875. The Coinage of the Ancient
Britons and Natural Selection.
*Proceedings of the Royal Institution of
Great Britain* 7, 476–87.
FAGAN, B.M. 1990. *The Journey from Eden:
The Peopling of Our World*. Thames &
Hudson: London & New York.
—— 1995. *People of the Earth: An
Introduction to World Prehistory*. (8th ed.)
HarperCollins: New York & Glasgow.
FLEMING, S. 1976. *Dating in Archaeology. A
Guide to Scientific Techniques*. J.M. Dent:
London; St Martin's Press: New York.
——1979. *Thermoluminescence
Techniques in Archaeology*. Oxford Univ.
Press: Oxford & New York.
FULLAGAR, R.L.K., PRICE, D.M. & HEAD, L.D. 1996.
Early human occupation of northern
Australia: archaeology and
thermoluminescence dating of Jinmium
rock-shelter, Northern Territory.
Antiquity 70, 751–53.
GOWLETT, J. 1993. *Ascent to Civilization: The
Archaeology of Early Humans*. (2nd ed.)
McGraw-Hill: London & New York.
GRÜN, R. & STRINGER, C.B. 1991. Electron spin
resonance and the evolution of modern
humans. *Archaeometry* 33, 153–99.
—— & THORNE, A. 1997. Dating the
Ngandong humans. *Nature* 276, 1575.
—— & others. 1996. Dating of Florisbad
hominid. *Nature* 382, 500–01.
HAMMER, C.U., CLAUSEN, H.B., FRIEDRICH W.L. &
TAUBER, H. 1987. The Minoan eruption of
Santorini in Greece dated to 1645 BC?
Nature 328, 517–19.
HAMMOND, N. 1982. *Ancient Maya
Civilization*. Cambridge Univ. Press.
HARDY, D. & RENFREW, C. (eds.). 1991. *Thera
and The Aegean World III, Vol. 3.
Chronology*. Thera Foundation: London.

HARRIS, E.C. & HUGHES, P.J. 1978. An early agricultural system at Mugumamp Ridge, Western Highlands Province, Papua New Guinea. *Mankind* 11, 437–44.

HEDGES, R.E.M. 1981. Radiocarbon dating with an accelerator: review and preview. *Archaeometry* 23, 3–18.

HILLAM, J. & others. 1990. Dendrochronology of the English Neolithic. *Antiquity* 64, 210–20.

JOUZEL, J. & others. 1987. Vostok ice core: a continuous isotope temperature record over the last climate cycle (160,000 years). *Nature* 329, 403–08.

KENDALL, D.G. 1969. Some problems and methods in statistical archaeology. *World Arch.* 1, 68–76.

KIMBER, R.W.L. & HARE, P.E. 1992. Wide range of racemization of amino acids in peptides from fossil human bone and its implication for amino acid racemization dating. *Geochimica et Cosmochimica Acta* 56, 739–43.

KITAGAWA, H. & VAN DER PLICHT, J. 1998. Atmospheric radiocarbon calibration to 45,000 yr B.P.: late glacial fluctuations and cosmogenic isotope production. *Science* 279, 1187–89.

KITTLEMAN, L.R. 1979. Geologic methods in studies of Quaternary tephra, in *Volcanic Activity and Human Ecology* (P.D. Sheets & D.K. Grayson eds.), 49–82. Academic Press: New York & London.

KLEIN, R.G. 1999. *The Human Career.* (2nd ed.) Univ. of Chicago Press.

KROMER, B. & SPURK, M. 1998. Revision and tentative extension of tree-ring based ^{14}C calibration, 9200–11,855 cal BP. *Radiocarbon* 40, 1117–26.

KUNIHOLM, P.I. & STRIKER, C.L. 1987. Dendrochronological investigations in the Aegean and neighbouring regions 1983–1986. *Journal of Field Arch.* 14, 385–98.

————**& others.** 1996. Anatolian tree rings and the absolute chronology of the eastern Mediterranean, 2220–718 BC. *Nature* 381, 780–83.

LEAKEY, R.E. 1981. *The Making of Mankind.* Michael Joseph: London.

LEWIN, R. 1987. *Bones of Contention: Controversies in the Search for Human Origins.* Simon & Schuster: New York; Penguin: Harmondsworth 1989.

————1989. *Human Evolution.* (2nd ed.) Blackwell Scientific Publications: Oxford & Cambridge, Mass.

LIBBY, W.F. 1952. *Radiocarbon Dating.* Univ. of Chicago Press.

LORIUS C. & others. 1985. A 150,000 year climatic record from Antarctic ice. *Nature* 316, 591–96.

LYELL, C. 1830–33. *Principles of geology, being an attempt to explain the former changes of the earth's surface by reference to causes now in operation.* 3 vols. John Murray: London.

MCDERMOTT, F., GRÜN, R., STRINGER, C.B. & HAWKESWORTH, C.J. 1993. Mass-spectrometric U-series dates for Israeli Neanderthal/early modern hominid sites. *Nature* 363, 252–54.

MCDOUGALL, I. 1990. Potassium-argon dating in archaeology. *Science Progress* 74, 15–30.

MCKEEVER, S.W.S. 1985. *Thermoluminescence of Solids.* Cambridge Univ. Press.

MICHELS, J.W. 1973. *Dating Methods in Archaeology.* Seminar Press: New York.

————**& BEBRICH, C.A.** 1971. Obsidian Hydration Dating, in *Dating Techniques for the Archaeologist* (H.N. Michael & E.K. Ralph eds.), 164–221. Massachusetts Institute of Technology: Cambridge, Mass.

————**& TSONG, I.S.T.** 1980. Obsidian Hydration Dating: A Coming of Age, in *Advances in Archaeological Method and Theory* 3 (M.B. Schiffer ed.), 405–44. Academic Press: London & New York.

MILLER, G.H., BEAUMONT, P.B., JULL, J.T. & JOHNSON, B. 1993. Pleistocene geochronology and palaeothermometry from protein diagenesis in ostrich eggshells: implications for the evolution of modern humans, in *The Origin of Modern Humans and the Impact of Chronometric Dating* (M.J. Aitken & others eds.), 49–68. Princeton Univ. Press.

MONTELIUS, O. 1903. *Die Typologische Methode.* Stockholm.

MOOK, W.G. & WATERBOLK, H.T. 1983. *Radiocarbon Dating.* European Science Foundation: Strasbourg.

OAKLEY, K.P. 1964. *Frameworks for Dating Fossil Man.* Weidenfeld & Nicolson: London; Aldine Publishing Co: Chicago.

PEARSON, G.W. 1987. How to cope with calibration. *Antiquity* 60, 98–104.

————**& STUIVER, M.** 1993. High-precision bidecal calibration of the radiocarbon timescale, 500–2500 BC. *Radiocarbon* 35, 25–33.

PETRIE, W.M.F. 1899. Sequences in prehistoric remains. *Journal of the Anthropological Institute* 29, 295–301.

PHILLIPS, F.M., ZREDA, M.G., ELMORE, D. & SHARMA, P. 1996. A reevaluation of cosmogenic ^{36}Cl production rates in terrestrial rocks. *Geophysical Research Letters* 23 (9), 949–52.

————**, FLINSCH, M., ELMORE, D. & SHARMA, P.** 1997. Maximum ages of the Côa valley (Portugal) engravings measured with Chlorine-36. *Antiquity* 71, 100–04.

PITTS, M. & ROBERTS, M. 1997. *Fairweather Eden: Life in Britain half a million years ago as revealed by the excavations at Boxgrove.* Century: London.

RALPH, E.K. 1971. Carbon-14 Dating, in *Dating Techniques for the Archaeologist* (H.N. Michael & E.K. Ralph eds.), 1–48. Massachusetts Institute of Technology: Cambridge, Mass.

REES-JONES, J. & TITE, M.S. 1997. Optical dating of the Uffington White Horse, in *Archaeological Sciences 1995* (A. Sinclair, E. Slater & J. Gowlett eds.), 159–62. Oxbow: Oxford (Monograph 64).

RENFREW, C. 1973. *Before Civilisation.* Jonathan Cape: London; Knopf: New York (Pelican: Harmondsworth).

————1979. The Tree-ring Calibration of Radiocarbon: An Archaeological Evaluation, in *Problems in European Prehistory* (C. Renfrew), 338–66. Edinburgh Univ. Press: Edinburgh; Cambridge Univ. Press: New York.

————1996. Kings, tree rings and the Old World. *Nature* 381, 733–34.

RENNE, P.R. & others. 1997. $^{40}Ar/^{39}Ar$ dating into the historical realm: calibration against Pliny the Younger. *Science* 277, 1279–80.

RINK, W.J., SCHWARCZ, H.P., SMITH, F.H. & RADOVCIC, J. 1995. ESR ages for Krapina hominids. *Nature* 393, 358–62.

ROBERTS, R.G. & others. 1994. The human colonisation of Australia: Optical dates of 53,000 and 60,000 years bracket human arrival at Deaf Adder Gorge, Northern Territory. *Quaternary Geochronology (Quaternary Science Reviews)* 13, 575–83.

————**& ————**1998. Optical and radiocarbon dating at Jinmium rock shelter in northern Australia. *Nature* 393, 358–62.

ROBINSON, W.S. 1951. A method for chronologically ordering archaeological deposits. *American Antiquity* 16, 293–301.

SCARRE, C. (ed.). 1988. *Past Worlds: The Times Atlas of Archaeology.* Times Books: London; Hammond: Maplewood, N.J.

SCHAEFFER, O.A. & ZÄHRINGER, J. (eds.). 1966. *Potassium-Argon Dating.* Springer Verlag: Berlin & New York.

SCHWARCZ, H.P. 1982. Applications of U-series dating to archaeometry, in *Uranium Series Disequilibrium: Applications to Environmental Problems* (M. Ivanovich & R.S. Harmon eds.), 302–25. Clarendon Press: Oxford.

————1993. Uranium-series dating and the origin of modern man, in *The Origin of Modern Humans and the Impact of Chronometric Dating* (M.J. Aitken & others eds.), 12–26. Princeton Univ. Press.

————**& GRÜN, R.** 1993. ESR dating of the origin of modern man, in *The Origin of Modern Humans and the Impact of Chronometric Dating* (M.J. Aitken & others eds.), 40–48. Princeton Univ. Press.

————**& others.** 1989. ESR dating of the Neanderthal site, Kebara Cave, Israel, *Journal of Arch. Science* 16, 653–59.

SCHWEINGRUBER, F.G. 1988. *Tree Rings. Basics and applications of dendrochronology.* D. Reidel: Dordrecht & Lancaster.

SHACKLETON, N.J. & OPDYKE, N.D. 1973. Oxygen isotope and paleomagnetic stratigraphy of equatorial Pacific core V28-238. *Quaternary Research* 3, 39–55.

SHACKLEY, M.S. 1998. *Archaeological Obsidian Studies.* Plenum: New York.

SHEETS, P.D. 1979. Environmental and cultural effects of the Ilopango eruption in Central America, in *Volcanic Activity and Human Ecology* (P.D. Sheets & D.K. Grayson eds.), 525–64. Academic Press: New York & London.

SMITH, B.W., RHODES, E.J., STOKES, S., SPOONER, N.A. & AITKEN, M.J. 1990. Optical dating of sediments: initial quartz results from Oxford. *Archaeometry* 32, 19–31.

SPOONER, N.A. 1998. Human occupation at Jinmium, northern Australia: 116,000 years ago or much less? *Antiquity* 72, 173–78.

STUIVER, M. & PEARSON, G.W. 1986. High-precision calibration of the radiocarbon time scale, AD 1950–500 BC, in *Radiocarbon* 28 (2B), calibration issue: Proc. of the Twelfth International Radiocarbon Conference, 1985, Trondheim, Norway (M. Stuiver & R.S. Kra eds.).

————**& PEARSON, G.W.** 1993. High-precision bidecal calibration of the radiocarbon timescale, AD 1950–500 BC and 2500–6000 BC. *Radiocarbon* 35, 1–23.

————**& REIMER, P.J.** 1993. Extended ^{14}C data base and revised CALIB 3.0 ^{14}C calibration program. *Radiocarbon* 35, 215–30.

————**, ————& others.** 1998. INTCAL98 radiocarbon age calibration, 24,000–0 cal BP. *Radiocarbon* 40, 1041–84.

SUTCLIFFE, A.J. 1985. *On the Track of Ice Age Mammals.* British Museum (Natural History): London.

SWADESH, M. 1972. *The Origin and Diversification of Language* (J. Scherzer ed.). Routledge & Kegan Paul: London; Aldine: Atherton, Chicago.

TAPSELL, R.F. 1984. *Monarchs, Rulers, Dynasties and Kingdoms of the World.* Thames & Hudson: London & New York.

TARLING, D.H. 1983. *Palaeomagnetism.* Chapman & Hall: London.

TAYLOR, R.E. 1987. *Radiocarbon Dating: An Archaeological Perspective.* Academic Press: New York & London.

————**& AITKEN, M.J.** (eds.). *Chronometric Dating in Archaeology.* Plenum Press: New York.

TITE, M.S. 1972. *Methods of Physical Examination in Archaeology.* Seminar Press: London & New York.

WAGNER, G.A. 1983. *Thermoluminescence Dating.* European Science Foundation: Strasbourg.

————**& VAN DEN HAUTE, P.** 1992. *Fission-Track Dating.* Enke, Stuttgart/Kluwer: Norwell, MA.

WALTER, R.C. & others. 1991. Laser-fusion ^{40}Ar/^{39}Ar dating of Bed 1, Olduvai Gorge, Tanzania. *Nature* 354, 145–49.

WATCHMAN, A. 1993. Perspectives and potentials for absolute dating prehistoric rock paintings. *Antiquity* 67, 58–65.

WEINER, J. 1992. A bandkeramik wooden well of Erkelenz-Kückhoven. *Newsletter of the Wetland Archaeology Research Project* 12, 3–12.

WEINER, J.S. 1955. *The Piltdown Forgery.* Oxford Univ. Press: London & New York.

WHITLEY, D.S. & DORN, R.I. 1987. Rock art chronology in eastern California. *World Arch.* 19, 150–64.

WINTLE, A.G. 1996. Archaeologically-relevant dating techniques for the next century. *Journal of Arch. Science* 23, 123–38.

ZEUNER, F.E. 1958. *Dating the Past.* (4th ed.) Methuen: London.

ZIELINSKI, G.A. & GERMANI, M.S. 1998. New ice core evidence opposing a 1620s BC date for the Santorini 'Minoan' eruption. *Journal of Arch. Science* 25.

ZILHAO, J. 1995. The age of the Côa Valley (Portugal) rock art: validation of archaeological dating to the Palaeolithic and refutation of "scientific" dating to historic or protohistoric times. *Antiquity* 69, 883–901.

Chapter 5: How Were Societies Organized? Social Archaeology (pp. 173–224)

pp. 174–78 **Classification of societies, ranking, and inequality** Service 1971; Sanders & Marino 1970; also Redman 1978; Johnson & Earle 1987; Hastorf 1993; Wason 1994.

pp. 178–82 **Central Place Theory** Christaller 1933. **XTENT model** Renfrew & Level 1979.

pp. 182–86 **Middle Range Theory** Binford 1977, 1983. **Written records** *Archaeological Review from Cambridge* 1984, especially Postgate article. **Oral tradition** Wood 1985.

pp. 186–88 **Ethnoarchaeology** Yellen 1977; Hodder 1982; Binford 1983; Whitelaw 1983; Arnold 1985; Dragadze 1980; Renfrew 1993, 1994; Shennan 1989. Recent work is providing helpful insights into the Leroi-Gourhan/Binford debate: see Audouze 1987 and Valentin 1989.

pp. 190–91 **Investigation of activities** at an early hominid site is the subject of Kroll & Isaac 1984.

pp. 191–93 **Territories in mobile societies** Foley 1981 discusses the problems and potential of off-site archaeology.

pp. 194–95 **Settlements in sedentary societies** Binford & others 1970 (Hatchery West); Hill 1970 (Broken K Pueblo); Longacre 1970 (Carter Ranch Pueblo); Whitelaw 1981 (Myrtos).

pp. 195–96 **Ranking from burials** Shennan 1975 (Branč); Tainter 1980 (Middle Woodland burials); Bietti Sestieri 1993; Morris 1987; Whitley 1991.

pp. 196–200 **Collective works** Renfrew 1973, 1979 (Wessex and Orkney); Barrett 1994; Bradley 1993; Thomas 1991.

pp. 200–01 **Cumulative viewshed analysis** Wheatley 1995.

pp. 203–05 **Chiefdoms and states** see box feature references.

pp. 205–09 **Functions of the center** Kemp 1984–87 (Amarna); Hammond 1982 (Tikal); Millon 1981, Millon & others 1973; Cowgill & others 1984 (Teotihuacán); Biddle 1975 (Winchester). Fieldwork techniques used at Abu Salabikh: Postgate 1983.

pp. 209–11 **Social ranking** Freidel & Sabloff 1984 (Cozumel); Kemp 1989; Lehner 1985 (pyramids); Sabloff 1989 (Pacal); Cotterell 1981 (China's first emperor); Biel 1985 (Hochdorf).

pp. 211–15 **Economic specialization** Morris & Thompson 1985 (Huánuco Pampa): Tosi 1984 (Shahr-i-Sokhta).

pp. 215–17 **The archaeology of the individual and of identity** Renfrew 1994; Sofaer Derevenski 1997; Moore & Scott 1997; Hall 1997; Jones 1997; Gamble 1998. Bourdieu 1977; Thomas 1996; Gilchrist 1994; Meskell 1998a, 1999; Hodder 1986 (*Habitus*). For Foley Square and African-American cemetery: Harrington 1993; Yamin 1997a, 1997b; Fairbanks & Mullins-Moore 1980; Yentsch 1994.

pp. 218–22 **Investigating gender** Gimbutas 1989; Hodder 1991; Ucko 1968; Meskell 1995; Billington & Green 1996; Marler 1997; Goodison & Morris 1998 (archaeology of the goddess); Arnold 1991 (Vix princess); Claassen 1992, 1994; Conkey 1991; Conkey & Spector 1984; di Leonardo 1991; du Cros & Smith 1993; Gero & Conkey 1991; Gimbutas 1989; Hodder 1991; Robb 1994; Sørensen 1991 (Danish burials); Ucko 1968; Walde and Willows 1991; Wright 1996; Meskell 1998 a, b, c, 1999; Claassen & Royce 1997; Conkey & Gero 1997; Treherne 1995.

pp. 222–24 **Molecular genetics** Thomas & others 1998; Torroni & others 1994; Stone & Stoneking 1998, 1999; Poloni & others 1997.

Box Features

pp. 181–82 **Settlement Patterns in Mesopotamia** Johnson 1972.

p. 189 **Ancient Ethnicity and Language** Renfrew 1987, 1993; Marcus 1983a; Dragadze 1980; Marcus & Flannery 1996; Hall 1997; Jones 1997.

p. 193 **Space and Density** Yellen 1977; Whitelaw 1983.

p. 197 **Factor Analysis & Cluster Analysis** Binford & Binford 1966; Hill 1970; O'Shea 1984; Doran & Hodson 1975.

pp. 198–99 **Early Wessex** Renfrew 1973; Barrett 1994; Bradley 1993; Thomas 1991; Parker Pearson & Ramilisonina 1998; Cunliffe & Renfrew 1997.

p. 205 **Maya Territories** Coe 1993; Marcus 1983b; Mathews 1991; Martin & Grube 1995; Renfrew & Cherry 1986 (relations between polities); de Montmollin 1989.

pp. 206–07 **Multi-Dimensional Scaling** Cherry 1977; also Renfrew & Sterud 1969; Kruskal 1971.

pp. 212–13 **Moundville** Peebles 1987; Peebles & Kus 1977.

pp. 220–21 **Gender Relations in Early Intermediate Period Peru** Gero 1992, 1995.

Bibliography

ARNOLD, B. 1991. The deposed princess of Vix: the need for an engendered European prehistory, in *The Archaeology of Gender* (D. Walde & N.D. Willows eds.), 366–74. Archaeological Association: Calgary.

ARNOLD, D.E. 1985. *Ceramic Theory and Cultural Process.* Cambridge Univ. Press.

AUDOUZE, F. 1987. Des modèles et des faits: les modèles de A. Leroi-Gourhan et de L. Binford confrontés aux résultats récents. *Bull. Soc. Préhist. française* 84, 343–52.

BARRETT, J. 1994. *Fragments from Antiquity.* Blackwell: Oxford.

BIDDLE, M. 1975. Excavations at Winchester 1971. *Antiquaries Journal* 55, 295–337.

BIEL, J. 1985. *Der Keltenfürst von Hochdorf.* Konrad Theiss Verlag: Stuttgart.

BIETTI SESTIERI, A.M. 1993. *The Iron Age Community of Osteria dell'Osa.* Cambridge Univ. Press.

BILLINGTON, S. & GREEN, M. (eds.). 1996. *The Concept of the Goddess.* Routledge: London.

BINFORD, L.R. (ed.). 1977. *For Theory Building in Archaeology.* Academic Press: New York.

——1983. *In Pursuit of the Past.* Thames & Hudson: London & New York.

——, BINFORD, S.R., WHALLON, R. & HARDIN, M.A. 1970. *Archaeology at Hatchery West.* Memoirs of the Society for American Archaeology No. 24: Washington D.C.

BINFORD, S.R. & BINFORD, L.R. 1966. A preliminary analysis of functional variability in the Mousterian of Levallois facies, *American Anthropologist* 68, 238–95.

BOURDIEU, P. 1977. *Outline of a Theory of Practice.* Cambridge Univ. Press.

BRADLEY, R. 1993. *Altering the Earth – the Origins of Monuments in Britain and Continental Europe.* Edinburgh Univ. Press.

CHERRY, J.F. 1977. Investigating the Political Geography of an Early State by Multidimensional Scaling of Linear B Tablet Data, in *Mycenaean Geography* (J. Bintliff ed.), 76–82. British Assoc. for Mycenaean Studies: Cambridge.

CHRISTALLER, W. 1933. *Die Zentralen Orte in Süddeutschland.* Karl Zeiss: Jena.

CLAASSEN, C. (ed.). 1992. *Exploring Gender through Archaeology, Selected papers from the 1991 Boone Conference.* Monographs in World Archaeology 11. Prehistory Press: Madison.

——(ed.). 1994. *Women in Archaeology.* Pennsylvania Univ. Press: Philadelphia.

—— & ROYCE, E.A. (eds.). 1997. *Women in Prehistory: North America and Mesoamerica.* Univ. of Pennsylvania Press: Philadelphia.

COE, M.D. 2000. *The Maya.* (6th ed.). Thames & Hudson: London & New York.

CONKEY, M. 1991. Does it make a difference? Feminist thinking and archaeologies of gender, in *The Archaeology of Gender* (D. Walde & N.D. Willows eds.), 24–33. Archaeological Association: Calgary.

——& GERO, J.M. 1997. Programme to practice: gender and feminism in archaeology. *Annual Review of Archaeology* 26, 411–37.

——& SPECTOR, J. 1984. Archaeology and the study of gender, in *Advances in Archaeological Method and Theory 7* (M.B. Schiffer ed.), 1–38. Academic Press: New York & London.

COTTERELL, A. 1981. *The First Emperor of China.* Macmillan: London; Holt, Reinhart & Winston: New York.

COWGILL, G.L., ALTSCHUL, J.H. & SLOAD, R.S. 1984. Spatial analysis of Teotihuacán: a Mesoamerican metropolis, in *Intrasite Spatial Analysis in Archaeology* (H.J. Hietala ed.), 154–95. Cambridge Univ. Press.

CUNLIFFE, B. & RENFREW, C. (eds.). 1997. *Science and Stonehenge.* British Academy: Oxford.

DORAN, J.E. & HODSON, F.R. 1975. *Mathematics and Computers in Archaeology.* Edinburgh Univ. Press.

DRAGADZE, T. 1980. The place of "ethnos" theory in Soviet anthropology, in *Soviet and Western Anthropology* (E. Gellner ed.), 161–70. Duckworth: London.

DU CROS, H. & SMITH, L. (eds.). 1993. *Women in Archaeology, A Feminist Critique.* Occ. Papers in Prehistory 23. Research School of Pacific Studies, Australian National Univ.: Canberra.

FAIRBANKS, C.H. & MULLINS-MOORE, S.A. 1980 How did slaves live? *Early Man* 2.2, 2–7.

FLANNERY, K.V. 1999 Process and agency in early state formation. *Cambridge Archaeological Journal* 9(1), 3–21.

FOLEY, R. 1981. *Off-site archaeology and human adaptation in Eastern Africa.* British Arch. Reports: Oxford.

FREIDEL, D. & SABLOFF, J.A. 1984. *Cozumel: Late Maya Settlement Patterns.* Academic Press: New York.

GAMBLE, C. 1998. Palaeolithic society and the release from proximity: a network approach to intimate relations. *World Arch.* 29, 426–49.

GERO, J.M. 1992. Feasts and Females: gender ideology and political meals in the Andes. *Norwegian Arch. Review* 25, 15–30.

——1995. La Iconografía Recuay y el Estudio de Genero. *Gaceta Arqueológica Andina* 25/26.

——& CONKEY, M.W. (eds.). 1991. *Engendering Archaeology.* Blackwell: Oxford & Cambridge, Mass.

GILCHRIST, R. 1994. *Gender and Material Culture: the Archaeology of Religious Women.* Routledge: London.

GIMBUTAS, M. 1989. *The Language of the Goddess.* Harper and Row: New York.

GOODISON, L. & MORRIS, C. (eds.). 1998. *Ancient Goddesses.* British Museum Press: London.

HALL, J.M. 1997. *Ethnic Identity in Greek Antiquity.* Cambridge Univ. Press.

HARRINGTON, S.P.M.H. 1993. New York's great cemetery imbroglio. *Archaeology* March/April, 30–38.

HASTORF, C.A. 1993. *Agriculture and the Onset of Political Inequality before the Inka.* Cambridge Univ. Press.

HILL, J.N. 1970. *Broken K Pueblo: Prehistoric social organisation in the American Southwest.* Anthropological Papers of the Univ. of Arizona No. 18.

HODDER, I. 1982. *Symbols in Action.* Cambridge Univ. Press.

——1986. *Reading the Past. Current Approaches to Interpretive Archaeology.* Cambridge Univ. Press.

——1991. Gender representation and social reality, in *The Archaeology of Gender* (D. Walde & N.D. Willows eds.), 11–16. Archaeological Association: Calgary.

JOHNSON, A.W. & EARLE, T. 1987. *The Evolution of Human Societies: from Foraging Group to Agrarian State.* Stanford Univ. Press.

JOHNSON, G.A. 1972. A test of the utility of Central Place Theory in Archaeology, in *Man, Settlement and Urbanism* (P.J. Ucko, R. Tringham & G.W. Dimbleby eds.), 769–85. Duckworth: London.

JONES, S. 1997. *The Archaeology of Ethnicity. Constructing Identities in the Past and Present.* Routledge: London.

KEMP, B.J. 1984–87. *Amarna Reports I-IV.* Egypt Exploration Society: London.

——1989. *Ancient Egypt: Anatomy of a Civilization.* Routledge: London & New York.

KROLL, E.M. & ISAAC, G.L. 1984. Configurations of artifacts and bones at early Pleistocene sites in East Africa, in *Intrasite Spatial Analysis in Archaeology* (H.J. Hietala ed.), 4–31. Cambridge Univ. Press.

KRUSKAL, J.B. 1971. Multi-dimension scaling in archaeology: time is not the only dimension, in *Mathematics in the Archaeological and Historical Sciences* (F.R. Hodson, D.G. Kendall & P. Tautu eds.), 119–32. Edinburgh Univ. Press.

LEHNER, M. 1985. The development of the Giza necropolis: The Khufu Project. *Mitteilungen dt. archäol. Inst. Abt. Kairo* 41, 109–43.

DI LEONARDO M. (ed.). 1991. *Gender at the Crossroads of Knowledge: Feminist Anthropology in the Postmodern Era.* Univ. of California Press: Berkeley.

LONGACRE, W.A. 1970. *Archaeology as anthropology: a case study.* Anthropological Papers of the Univ. of Arizona No. 17.

MARCUS, J. 1983a. The genetic model and the linguistic divergence of the Otomangueans, in *The Cloud People* (K.V. Flannery & J. Marcus eds.), 4–9. Academic Press: New York & London.

——1983b. Lowland Maya Archaeology at the Crossroads. *American Antiquity* 48 (3), 454–88.

——& FLANNERY, K.V. 1996. *Zapotec Civilization. How Urban Society Evolved in Mexico's Oaxaca Valley*. Thames & Hudson: London & New York.

MARLER, J. (ed.). 1997. *From the Realm of the Ancestors: an anthology in honor of Marija Gimbutas*. Knowledge, Ideas and Trends Press: Manchester, Conn.

MARTIN, S. & GRUBE, N. 1995. Maya Superstates. *Archaeology* 48(6), 41–46.

MATHEWS, P. 1991. Classic Maya Emblem Glyphs, in *Classic Maya Political History* (T. Patrick Culbert ed.), 19–29. Cambridge Univ. Press.

MESKELL, L. 1995. Goddesses, Gimbutas and "New Age" archaeology. *Antiquity* 69, 74–86.

——1998a. Running the gamut: gender, girls and goddesses. *American Journal of Archaeology* 102, 181–85.

——1998b. An archaeology of social relations in an Egyptian village. *Journal of Archaeological Method and Theory* 5, 208–41.

——1998c. Intimate archaeologies: the case of Kha and Merit. *World Arch.* 29 (3), 363–79.

——1999. *Archaeologies of Social Life: Age, Sex, Class etc. in Ancient Egypt*. Blackwell: Oxford.

MILLON, R. 1981. Teotihuacán: City, state and civilization, in *Archaeology (Supplement to the Handbook of Middle American Indians)* (J.A. Sabloff ed.), 198–243. Univ. of Texas Press: Austin.

——, DREWITT, R.B. & COWGILL, G.L. 1973. *Urbanization at Teotihuacán, Mexico. Vol. 1: The Teotihuacán Map*. Univ. of Texas Press: Austin.

DE MONTMOLLIN, O. 1989. *The Archaeology of Political Structure: Settlement Analysis in a Classic Maya Polity*. Cambridge Univ. Press.

MOORE, J. & SCOTT, E. (eds.). 1997. *Invisible People and Processes: Writing Gender and Childhood into European Archaeology*. Leicester Univ. Press: London.

MORRIS, C. & THOMPSON, D. 1985. *Huánuco Pampa: An Inca City and its Hinterland*. Thames & Hudson: London & New York.

MORRIS, I. 1987. *Burial and Society. The Rise of the Greek City-State*. Cambridge Univ. Press.

O'SHEA, J. 1984. *Mortuary Variability, An Archaeological Investigation*. Academic Press: New York & London.

PARKER PEARSON, M. & RAMILISONINA. 1998. Stonehenge for the ancestors: the stones pass on the message. *Antiquity* 72, 308–26.

PEEBLES, C.S. 1987. Moundville from 1000–1500 AD in *Chiefdoms in the Americas* (R.D. Drennan & C.A. Uribe eds.), 21–41. Univ. Press of America: Lanham.

——& KUS, S. 1977. Some archaeological correlates of ranked societies. *American Antiquity* 42, 421–48.

POLONI, E.S., SEMINO, O. PASSARINO, G. & others. 1997. Human genetic affinities for Y-chromosome haplotypes show strong correspondence with linguistics. *American Journal of Human Genetics* 61, 1015–35.

POSTGATE, J.N. (ed.). 1983. *The West Mound surface clearance (Abu Salabikh Excavations Vol. 1)*. British School of Arch. in Iraq: London.

REDMAN, C. 1978. *The Rise of Civilization*. W.H. Freeman: San Francisco.

RENFREW, C. 1973. Monuments, mobilization and social organization in neolithic Wessex, in *The explanation of culture change: models in prehistory* (C. Renfrew ed.), 539–58. Duckworth: London.

——1979. *Investigations in Orkney*. Society of Antiquaries: London.

——1984. *Approaches to Social Archaeology*. Edinburgh Univ. Press.

——1987. *Archaeology and Language*. Jonathan Cape: London.

——1993. *The Roots of Ethnicity: Archaeology, Genetics and the Origins of Europe*. Unione Internazionale degli Istitute di Archeologia, Storia e Storia dell'Arte in Roma: Rome.

——1994. The archaeology of identity, *The Tanner Lectures on Human Values* 15, (G.B. Peterson ed.), 283–348. Univ. of Utah Press: Salt Lake City.

——& CHERRY, J.F. (eds.). 1986. *Peer Polity Interaction and Socio-Political Change*. Cambridge Univ. Press.

——& LEVEL, E.V. 1979. Exploring dominance: predicting polities from centers, in *Transformations. Mathematical Approaches to Culture Change* (C. Renfrew & K.L. Cooke eds.), 145–67. Academic Press: New York & London.

——& STERUD, G. 1969. Close proximity analysis: a rapid method for the ordering of archaeological materials. *American Antiquity* 34, 265–77.

ROBB, J. 1994. Gender contradictions, moral coalitions, and inequality in prehistoric Italy, *Journal of European Archaeology* 2 (1), 20–49.

SABLOFF, J.A. 1989. *The Cities of Ancient Mexico*. Thames & Hudson: London & New York.

SANDERS, W.T. & MARINO, J. 1970. *New World Prehistory*. Prentice-Hall: Englewood Cliffs.

SERVICE, E.R. 1971. *Primitive Social Organization. An Evolutionary Perspective*. (2nd ed.) Random House: New York.

SHENNAN, S.J. 1988. *Quantifying Archaeology*. Edinburgh Univ. Press.

——(ed.). 1989. *Archaeological Approaches to Cultural Identity*, Unwin Hyman: London.

SHENNAN, SUSAN. 1975. The Social Organisation at Branč. *Antiquity* 49, 279–88.

SOFAER DEREVENSKI, J. 1997. Engendering children, engendering archaeology, in *Invisible People and Processes: Writing Gender and Childhood into European Archaeology* (J. Moore & E. Scott eds.), 192–202. Leicester Univ. Press: London.

SØRENSEN, M.L.S. 1991. The construction of gender through appearance, in *The Archaeology of Gender* (D. Walde & N.D. Willows eds.), 121–29. Archaeological Association: Calgary.

STONE, A.C. & STONEKING, M. 1998. mtDNA analysis of a prehistoric Oneota population: implications for the peopling of the New World. *American Journal of Human Genetics* 62, 1153–70.

——& —— 1999. Analysis of ancient DNA from a prehistoric Amerindian cemetery. *Philosophical Trans. Royal Society of London, Series B* 354, 153–59.

TAINTER, J.A. 1980. Behavior and status in a Middle Woodland mortuary population from the Illinois valley. *American Antiquity* 45, 308–13.

——& CORDY, R.H. 1977. An archaeological analysis of social ranking and residence groups in prehistoric Hawaii. *World Arch.* 9, 95–112.

THOMAS, J. 1991. *Rethinking the Neolithic*. Cambridge Univ. Press.

——1996. *Time, Culture and Identity*. Routledge: London.

THOMAS, J.G., SKORECKI, K., BEN-AMI, H., PARFITT, T., BRADMAN, N. & GOLDSTEIN, D.B. 1998. Origins of Old Testament priests. *Nature* 394, 138–39.

TORRONI, A., CHEN, Y.-S., SEMINO, O. & others. 1994. Mitochondrial DNA and Y-chromosome polymorphisms in four native American populations from southern Mexico. *American Journal of Human Genetics* 54, 303–18.

TOSI, M. 1984. The notion of craft specialization and its representation in the archaeological record of early states in the Turanian Basin, in *Marxist Perspectives in Archaeology* (M. Spriggs ed.), 22–52. Cambridge Univ. Press.

TREHERNE, P. 1995. The warrior's beauty: the masculine body and self-identity in Bronze Age Europe. *Journal of European Archaeology* 3(1), 105–44.

UCKO, P.J. 1968. *Anthropomorphic Figurines*. Royal Anthropological Institute Occ. Paper No. 24: London.

VALENTIN, B. 1989. Nature et fonctions des foyers de l'habitation No 1 à Pincevent. *Nature et Fonction des Foyers Préhistoriques*. Actes du Colloque de Nemours 1987, Mémoires du Musée de Préhistoire de l'Ile de France, 2, 209–19.

WALDE, D. & WILLOWS, N.D. (eds.). 1991. *The Archaeology of Gender*. Proc. of 22nd Annual Conference of the Archaeological Association, Univ. of Calgary.

WASON, P.K. 1994. *The Archaeology of Rank*. Cambridge Univ. Press.

WHEATLEY, D. 1995. Cumulative viewshed analysis: a GIS-based method for investigating intervisibility, and its archaeological application, in *Archaeology and Geographical Information Systems: a European perspective* (G. Lock and Z. Stančič eds.), 171–85. Taylor & Francis: London & Bristol, Penn.

WHITELAW, T.M. 1981. The settlement at Fournou Korifi, Myrtos and aspects of Early Minoan social organisation, in *Minoan Society: Proceedings of the Cambridge Colloquium 1981* (O. Krzyszkowska & L. Nixon eds.), 323–46. Bristol Classical Press: Bristol.

——— 1983. People and space in hunter-gatherer camps: a generalising approach in ethnoarchaeology. *Archaeological Review from Cambridge* 2 (2), 48–66.

WHITLEY, J. 1991. *Style and Society in Dark Age Greece*. Cambridge Univ. Press.

WOOD, M. 1985. *In Search of the Trojan War*. BBC Books: London.

WRIGHT, R.P. (ed.). 1996. *Gender and Archaeology*. Univ. of Pennsylvania Press: Philadelphia.

YAMIN, R. 1997a. New York's mythic slum. *Archaeology* March/April, 44–53.

———1997b Lurid tales and homely stories of New York's Notorious Five Points, in *Archaeologists as Storytellers*, A. Praetzellis & M. Praetzellis (eds.), *Historical Archaeology* 32.1, 74–85.

YELLEN, J.E. 1977. *Archaeological Approaches to the Present*. Academic Press: New York & London.

YENTSCH, A.E. 1994. *A Chesapeake Family and their Slaves: A Study in Historical Archaeology*. Cambridge Univ. Press.

Chapter 6: What Was the Environment? Environmental Archaeology (pp. 225–268)

p. 225 General studies in **environmental archaeology** include Evans 1978; Fieller & others 1985; Delcourt & Delcourt 1991; Roberts 1998; Bell & Walker 1992; Goudie 1992; Simmons 1989; Mannion 1991; and *Environmental Archaeology* since 1995. Pleistocene environments: Bradley 1985; Lowe & Walker 1997; Sutcliffe 1985; Williams & others 1998. Holocene climates: Harding 1982. Climatic change in general is covered in special issues of the journals *World Archaeology* 8 (2), 1976; and *Dossiers de l'Archéologie* No. 93, 1985.

pp. 226–27 **Sea cores** Butzer 1983; Sancetta & others 1973; Shackleton, N.J. 1967; Shackleton, N.J. & Turner 1967; Chappel & Shackleton, N.J. 1986; Shackleton, N.J. 1987. Emiliani 1969 is still a useful, if outdated, introduction to core extraction. Also Thunell 1979 (east Mediterranean work); Brassell & others 1986 (fatty lipids). **Ice cores** Johnsen & others 1992; Alley & Bender 1998; Dahl-

Jensen & others 1998; Charles 1997 (tropical data), Thompson & others 1995, 1998 (Andean cores). **Ancient winds** Wilson & Hendy 1971; Parkin & Shackleton, N.J. 1973 (on W. Africa).

pp. 229–32 **Coastlines** In general: van Andel 1989; Masters & Flemming 1983; Thompson 1980. Work on Beringia: Elias & others 1996; West 1996; Dawson & others 1990 (tsunami). **Submerged land surfaces** at Franchthi: van Andel & Lianos 1984; Shackleton, J.C. & van Andel 1980, 1986. **Raised beaches** Koike 1986 (Tokyo Bay middens); Giddings 1966, 1967 (Alaskan beaches). **Coral reefs** Bloom & others 1974 (New Guinea); Dodge & others 1983. **Rock art** Chaloupka 1984, 1993 (Australia). The CLIMAP work is described in CLIMAP 1976.

pp. 232–33 **Studying the landscape** In general: Cornwall 1969; Gladfelter 1977; Hassan 1979; Pyddoke 1961; Rapp & Gifford 1982; Shackley 1975; Sutcliffe 1985; Vita-Finzi 1969, 1973; and *Geoarchaeology: an International Journal* (from 1986).

pp. 233–35 **Rivers** Dales 1965 (Indus); Fisk 1944 (Mississippi); Adamson & others 1980 (Blue & White Niles); Sneh & Weissbrod 1973 (Nile Delta).

p. 235 **Cave sites** Collcutt 1979. Laville 1976; Laville & others 1980; Schmid 1969; Sutcliffe 1985.

pp. 235–38 **Sediments and soils** Clarke 1971; Courty 1990 (soil micromorphology). Courty & others 1990; Spence 1990 (assessment in the field). Orliac 1975 (latex technique); van Andel & others 1986; Pope & van Andel 1984; van Andel & others 1990; Runnels 1995; Jameson & others 1995 (Argolid). **Loess** Bordes 1953 (Paris Basin): Kukla 1975 (Central Europe); 1987 (Central China). **Buried land surface** Street 1986 (Miesenheim forest); Stine 1994 (relict tree stumps).

p. 224 **Tree-rings and climate** Fritts 1976; Pearce 1996; Lara & Villalba 1993 (Chilean tree rings); Stahle & others 1998 (Jamestown); Grinsted & Wilson 1979 (isotopic analysis of tree-rings).

pp. 239–44 **Microbotanical remains** Good general works on **pollen analysis** are Traverse 1988; Faegri & others 1989; Dimbleby 1985, 1969; Moore, Webb & Collinson 1991; Bryant & Holloway 1983; Edwards 1979; Wilkinson 1971. Also Bonnefille 1983 (Omo-Hadar pollen); Raikes 1984 (Raikes' controversial opinions); Palmer 1976 (grass cuticles). Introductions to **phytoliths** include Piperno 1988; Pearsall 1982; Rovner 1971, 1983; Rapp & Mulholland 1992. For extraction from teeth, Armitage 1975; Middleton & Rovner 1994. Also Anderson 1980 (phytoliths on stone tools); Piperno 1985 (Panama work). **Diatom analysis** In general: Battarbee 1986; Mannion 1987. Also Bradbury 1975 (Minnesota work);

Voorhips & Jansma 1974 (Netherlands). **Rock varnishes** Dorn & DeNiro 1985. **DNA** Poinar & others 1998.

pp. 244–47 **Macrobotanical remains** General articles on **flotation** are Watson 1976, Williams 1973; also Pearsall 1989. Froth flotation: Jarman, H.N. & others 1972. Plant remains from frozen mammoths: Lister and Bahn 1994; from bog bodies: van der Sanden 1996, chapter 8. **Wood and charcoal** Western 1969; Minnis 1987; also Deacon 1979 (Boomplaas Cave).

pp. 247–50 **Microfauna** Andrews 1991 (owl pellets); Klein 1984 (dune mole rat); Evans 1972, 1969; Sparks 1969 (land molluscs); Koike 1986 (Tokyo Bay marine molluscs). General studies of **insects**: Buckland 1976; Elias 1994; Osborne 1976; Levesque & others 1997 (midge larvae). Also Coope 1977; Coope & others 1971 (beetles); Atkinson & others 1987 (British Pleistocene work); Girling & Greig 1985; Perry & Moore 1987 (Dutch elm disease); Addyman 1980; Addyman & others 1976; Buckland 1976, 388–91 (York Roman sewer).

pp. 250–53 **Macrofauna** Good introductions include Davis 1987; Chaplin 1971; Cornwall 1974. **Big-game extinctions** Martin & Klein 1984; Miller & others 1999; and papers in special volume of *Advances in Vertebrate Paleobiology* 1999. For the "combined explanation" of the extinctions: Owen-Smith 1987. For the epidemic theory, MacPhee & Marx 1997. See also Lister & Bahn 1994.

pp. 253–55 **New techniques: isotopes** Zeder 1978; Heaton & Lee 1986. **Other evidence** *Dossiers de l'Archéologie* 90, 1985 (tracks); Leakey 1987 (Laetoli tracks); Mead & others 1986 (fossil dung).

pp. 255–56 **Human environment** Burch 1971 (nonempirical). **Fire** Shahack-Gross & others 1997 (identification on bones); Brain & Sillen 1988 (Swartkrans); Schiegl & others 1996 (Israeli caves); Weiner & others 1998 (China). Legge 1972 (cave climates); Leroi-Gourhan 1981 (plant mattresses); Rottländer & Schlichtherle 1979, 264–66 (animal hides).

pp. 257–65 **Gardens** Leach 1984 (Maori); Cunliffe 1971 (Fishbourne); Jashemski 1979, 1986 (Pompeii); Farrar 1998 (Roman); Wiseman 1998; Lentz & others 1996 (Céren); see also *Garden History* since 1972, and *Journal of Garden History* since 1981. Also Miller & Gleason 1994. **Pollution** Addyman 1980 (York pollution); Hong & others 1994, 1996; Renberg & others 1994, Shotyk & others 1998 (lead pollution). **Land management** In general: Aston 1997. Flannery 1982 (Maya ridged fields); Bradley, R. 1978 (British field systems); Miyaji 1995 (paddy fields); Coles & Coles 1996, 140; Weiner 1992 (well). **Plow marks** under mounds: Fowler & Evans 1967; Rowley-Conwy 1987. **Woodland and vegetation** Coles

& Coles 1986 (Somerset Levels); Piggott 1973 (Dalladies mound); Rue 1987 (Copán pollen analysis); Hallam 1975; Clark 1983 (Australian fire-stick farming: the Lake George controversy is argued in Singh & Geissler 1985 and Wright 1986). Kershaw 1993 & debate in *Quaternary Australasia* 12 (2), Nov. 1994, 21–33 (Queensland evidence). Betancourt & van Devender 1981 (Chaco Canyon clearance). Betancourt & others 1991 (packrats, hyraxes, and Petra).

pp. 265–68 **Island environments** Environmental destruction in general: Diamond 1986. Transformation and extinctions are discussed in Kirch 1982 (Hawaii), 1983 (Polynesia); Anderson 1989 (New Zealand); Steadman 1995. **Easter Island** Bahn & Flenley 1992.

Box Features

p. 227 **Sea and Ice Cores** See main text references above.

p. 228 **Climatic Cycles: El Niño** Kerr 1996; Rodbell & others 1999; Sandweiss & others 1996; Fagan 1999. Huaca de la Luna: Bourget 1996.

pp. 234–35 **Cave Sediments** Magee & Hughes 1982 (Colless Creek); Guillien 1970 (freeze-thaw effects); Gascoyne 1992; Bar-Matthews & others 1997 (speleothems).

pp. 240–41 **Pollen Analysis** Langford & others 1986 (automated pollen identification); Behre 1986 (human effects on pollen diagrams); Greig 1982 (pollen from urban sites).

pp. 254–55 **Elands Bay Cave** Parkington 1981; Buchanan 1988.

pp. 258–59 **Site Catchment Analysis** General: appendix in Higgs 1975 (223–24); Higgs & Vita-Finzi 1972. Applications: Bailey & Davidson 1983; Findlow & Ericson 1980; Jarman, M.R. 1972; Jarman & others 1982; Flannery 1976. Critiques can be found in Flannery 1976, especially 91–95; Roper 1979; Dennell 1980.

pp. 259–60 **Cahokia and GIS** Milner 1990.

pp. 262–63 **Kuk Swamp** Golson 1976, 1977, 1990; Bayliss-Smith & Golson 1992; Hope & Golson 1995.

Bibliography

ADAMSON, D.A. & others. 1980. Late Quaternary history of the Nile. *Nature* 287, 50–55.

ADDYMAN, P.V. 1980. Eburacum, Jorvik, York. *Scientific American* 242, 56–66.

————**& others.** 1976. Palaeoclimate in urban environmental archaeology at York, England. *World Arch.* 8 (2), 220–33.

ALLEY, R.B. & BENDER, M.L. 1998. Greenland Ice Core: Frozen in Time. *Scientific American* 278 (2), 66–71.

VAN ANDEL, T.H. 1989. Late Quaternary sea level changes and archaeology. *Antiquity* 63 (241) 733–45. Also 1990, 64, 151–52.

————**& LIANOS, N.** 1984. High-resolution seismic reflection profiles for the reconstruction of post-glacial transgressive shorelines: an example from Greece. *Quaternary Research* 22, 31–45.

————, **RUNNELS, C.N. & POPE, K.O.** 1986. Five thousand years of land use and abuse in the Southern Argolid, Greece. *Hesperia: Journal of the American School of Classical Studies at Athens* 55 (1), 103–28.

————, **ZANGGER, E. & DEMITRACK, A.** 1990. Land use and soil erosion in prehistoric and historical Greece. *Journal of Field Arch.* 17, 379–96.

ANDERSON, A. 1989. *Prodigious Birds: Moas and Moa-Hunting in New Zealand.* Cambridge Univ. Press.

ANDERSON, P.C. 1980. A testimony of prehistoric tasks: diagnostic residues on stone tool working edges. *World Arch.* 12, 181–94.

ANDREWS, P. 1991. *Owls, Caves and Fossils.* Univ. of Chicago Press.

ARMITAGE, P.L. 1975. The extraction and identification of opal phytoliths from the teeth of ungulates. *Journal of Arch. Science* 2, 187–97.

ASTON, M. 1997. *Interpreting the Landscape* (3rd ed.) Routledge: London.

ATKINSON, T.C., BRIFFA, K.R. & COOPE, G.R. 1987. Seasonal temperatures in Britain during the past 22,000 years, reconstructed using beetle remains. *Nature* 325, 587–92.

BAHN, P. & FLENLEY, J. 1992. *Easter Island, Earth Island.* Thames & Hudson: London & New York.

BAILEY, G.N. & DAVIDSON, I. 1983. Site exploitation territories and topography: Two case studies from Palaeolithic Spain. *Journal of Arch. Science* 10, 87–115.

BAR-MATTHEWS, M. & others. 1997. Late Quaternary paleoclimate in the Eastern Mediterranean region from stable isotope analysis of speleothems at Soreq Cave, Israel. *Quaternary Research* 47, 155–68.

BATTARBEE, R.W. 1986. Diatom analysis, in *Handbook of Holocene Palaeoecology and Palaeohydrology* (B.E. Berglund ed.), 527–70. Wiley: London.

BAYLISS-SMITH, T. & GOLSON, J. 1992. Wetland agriculture in New Guinea Highlands, in *The Wetland Revolution in Prehistory* (B. Coles, ed.), 15–17. Prehist. Soc/WARP: Exeter.

BEHRE, K.-E. (ed.). 1986. *Anthropogenic Indicators in Pollen Diagrams.* Balkema: Rotterdam & Boston.

BELL, M. & WALKER, M.J.C. 1992. *Late Quaternary Environmental Change. Physical and Human Perspectives.* Longman: London.

BETANCOURT, J.L. & VAN DEVENDER, T.R. 1981. Holocene vegetation in Chaco Canyon, New Mexico. *Science* 214, 656–58.

————, **VAN DEVENDER, T.R. & MARTIN, P.S.** (eds.). 1991. *Packrat Middens. The last 40,000 years of biotic change.* Univ. of Arizona Press: Tucson.

BLOOM, A.L. & others. 1974. Quaternary sea level fluctuations on a tectonic coast: New 230Th/234U dates from the Huon Peninsula, New Guinea. *Quaternary Research* 4, 185–205.

BONNEFILLE, R. 1983. Evidence for a cooler and drier climate in the Ethiopian uplands towards 2.5 Myr ago. *Nature* 303, 487–91.

BORDES, F. 1953. *Recherches sur les limons quaternaires du bassin de la Seine.* Archives de l'Institut de Paléontologie Humaine, No. 26: Paris.

BOURGET, S. 1996. *Proyecto Arqueológico Huaca de la Luna: Informe Técnico 1995,* Vol. I Textos (S. Uceda & R. Morales eds.), 52–61. Universidad Nacional de La Libertad-Trujillo: Trujillo.

BRADBURY, J.P. 1975. Diatom stratigraphy and human settlement in Minnesota. *Geol. Soc. of America, Special Paper* 171, 1–74.

BRADLEY, R. 1978. Prehistoric field systems in Britain and north-west Europe: a review of some recent work. *World Arch.* 9, 265–80.

BRADLEY, R.S. 1985. *Quaternary Paleoclimatology: Methods of Paleoclimatic Reconstruction.* Allen & Unwin: Boston & London.

BRAIN, C.K. & SILLEN, A. 1988. Evidence from the Swartkrans cave for the earliest use of fire. *Nature* 336, 464–66.

BRASSELL, S.C. & others. 1986. Molecular stratigraphy: a new tool for climatic assessment. *Nature* 320, 129–33.

BRYANT, V.M. & HOLLOWAY, R.G. 1983. The role of palynology in archaeology, in *Advances in Archaeological Method and Theory* 6 (M.B. Schiffer ed.), 191–224. Academic Press: London & New York.

BUCHANAN, W.F. 1988. *Shellfish in prehistoric diet. Elands Bay, S.W. Cape Coast, South Africa.* British Arch. Reports, Int. Series 455: Oxford.

BUCKLAND, P.C. 1976. The use of insect remains in the interpretation of archaeological environments, in *Geoarchaeology* (D.A. Davidson & M.L. Shackley eds.), 369–96. Duckworth: London.

BURCH, E.S. 1971. The nonempirical environment of the Arctic Alaskan Eskimos. *Southwestern Journal of Arch.* 27, 148–65.

BUTZER, K.W. 1983. Global sea-level stratigraphy: an appraisal. *Quaternary Science Reviews* 2, 1–15.

CHALOUPKA, G. 1984. *From Palaeoart to Casual Paintings.* Northern Territory Museum of Arts and Sciences, Darwin. Monograph 1.

————1993. *Journey in Time.* Reed: Chatswood, NSW.

CHAPLIN, R.E. 1971. *The Study of Animal Bones from Archaeological Sites.* Seminar Press: London & New York.

CHAPPELL, J. & SHACKLETON, N.J. 1986. Oxygen isotopes and sea level. *Nature* 324, 137–40.

CHARLES, C. 1997. Cool tropical punch of the ice ages. *Nature* 385, 681–83.

CLARK, R. 1983. Pollen and charcoal evidence for the effects of aboriginal burning on the vegetation of Australia. *Archaeology in Oceania* 18, 32–37.

CLARKE, G.R. 1971. *The Study of Soil in the Field*. (5th ed.) Oxford Univ. Press.

CLIMAP Project Members. 1976. The Surface of the Ice-Age Earth. *Science* 191, 1131–37.

COLES, B. & COLES, J. 1986. *Sweet Track to Glastonbury: The Somerset Levels in Prehistory*. Thames & Hudson: London & New York.

COLES, J. & COLES, B. 1996. *Enlarging the Past. The Contribution of Wetland Archaeology*. Soc. of Antiquaries of Scotland Mono. Series 11: Edinburgh.

COLLCUTT, S.N. 1979. The analysis of Quaternary cave sediments. *World Arch.* 10, 290–301.

COOPE, G.R. 1977. Quaternary coleoptera as aids in the interpretation of environmental history, in *British Quaternary Studies: Recent Advances*. (F.W. Shotton ed.), 55–68. Oxford Univ. Press.

——, **MORGAN, A. & OSBORNE, P.J.** 1971. Fossil coleoptera as indicators of climatic fluctuations during the last glaciation in Britain. *Palaeogeography, Palaeoclimatology, Palaeoecology* 10, 87–101.

CORNWALL, I.W. 1969. Soil stratification and environment, in *Science in Archaeology* (D.R. Brothwell & E.S. Higgs eds.), 124–34. (2nd ed.) Thames & Hudson: London.

——1974. *Bones for the Archaeologist*. Phoenix House: London.

COURTY, M.-A. 1990. Soil micromorphology in archaeology, in *New Developments in Archaeological Science* (A.M. Pollard ed.), 39–59. Proc. of British Academy 77, Oxford Univ. Press.

COURTY, M.-A. & others. 1990. *Soils and Micromorphology in Archaeology*. Cambridge Univ. Press.

CUNLIFFE, B.F. 1971. *Fishbourne*. Thames & Hudson: London.

DAHL-JENSEN, D. & others. 1998. Past temperatures directly from the Greenland Ice Sheet. *Science* 282, 268–71.

DALES, G.F. 1965. Civilization and floods in the Indus valley. *Expedition* 7, 10–19.

DAVIS, S.J.M. 1987. *The Archaeology of Animals*. Batsford: London; Yale Univ. Press: New Haven.

DAWSON, A.G., SMITH, D.E. & LONG, D. 1990. Evidence for a Tsunami from a Mesolithic site in Inverness, Scotland. *Journal of Arch. Science* 17, 509–12.

DEACON, H.J. 1979. Excavations at Boomplaas Cave: a sequence through the Upper Pleistocene and Holocene in South Africa. *World Arch.* 10 (3), 241–57.

DELCOURT, H.R. & DELCOURT, P.A. 1991. *Quaternary Ecology. A Palaeoecological Perspective*. Chapman & Hall: London.

DENNELL, R. 1980. The use, abuse and potential of Site Catchment Analysis, in *Catchment Analysis: Essays on prehistoric resource space* (F.J. Findlow & J.E. Ericson eds.), 1–20. Anthropology UCLA 10.

DIAMOND, J.M. 1986. The environmentalist myth. *Nature* 324, 19–20.

DIMBLEBY, G. 1969. Pollen analysis, in *Science in Archaeology* (D.R. Brothwell & E.S. Higgs eds.), 167–77. (2nd ed.) Thames & Hudson: London.

——1978. *Plants and Archaeology*. Paladin: London.

——1985. *The Palynology of Archaeological Sites*. Academic Press: London & New York.

DODGE, R.E. & others. 1983. Pleistocene sea levels from raised coral reefs of Haiti. *Science* 219, 1423–25.

DORN, R.I. & DENIRO, M.J. 1985. Stable carbon isotope ratios of rock varnish organic matter: a new palaeoenvironmental indicator. *Science* 227, 1472–74.

EDWARDS, K.J. 1979. Palynological and temporal inference in the context of prehistory, with special reference to the evidence from lake and peaty deposits. *Journal of Arch. Science* 6, 255–70.

ELIAS, S.A. (ed.). 1994. *Quaternary Insects and their Environments*. Smithsonian Institution Press: Washington & London.

—— **& others.** 1996. Life and times of the Bering land bridge. *Nature* 382, 60–63.

EMILIANI, C. 1969. The significance of deep-sea cores, in *Science in Archaeology* (D.R. Brothwell & E.S. Higgs eds.), 109–17. (2nd ed.) Thames & Hudson: London.

EVANS, J.G. 1969. Land and freshwater mollusca in archaeology: chronological aspects. *World Arch.* 1, 170–83.

——1972. *Land Snails in Archaeology*. Seminar Press: London.

——1978. *An Introduction to Environmental Archaeology*. Paul Elek: London.

FAEGRI, K., EKALAND, P. & KRZYWINSKI, K. (eds.) 1989. *Textbook of Pollen Analysis*. (4th ed.) Wiley: London.

FAGAN, B. 1999. *Floods, Famines, and Emperors: El Niño and the Fate of Civilizations*. Basic Books: New York.

FARRAR, L. 1998. *Ancient Roman Gardens*. Sutton Press: Stroud.

FIELLER, N.R.J., GILBERTSON, D.D. & RALPH, N.G.A. (eds.). 1985. *Palaeoenvironmental Investigations: Research Design, Methods and Data Analysis*. British Arch. Reports, Int. Series 258: Oxford.

FINDLOW, F.J. & ERICSON, J.E. (eds.). 1980. *Catchment Analysis: Essays on prehistoric resource space. Anthropology UCLA 10*. Los Angeles.

FISK, H.N. 1944. *Summary of the geology of the lower alluvial valley of the Mississippi River*. Mississippi River Commission: War Dept., US Army.

FLANNERY, K.V. (ed.). 1976. *The Early Mesoamerican Village*. Academic Press: New York & London.

——(ed.) 1982. *Maya Subsistence*. Academic Press: New York & London.

FOWLER, P.J. & EVANS, J.G. 1967. Plough marks, lynchets and early fields. *Antiquity* 41, 289–301.

FRITTS, H.C. 1976. *Tree Rings and Climate*. Academic Press: New York & London.

GASCOYNE, M. 1992. Paleoclimate determination from cave calcite deposits. *Quaternary Science Reviews* 11, 609–32.

GIDDINGS, J.L. 1966. Cross-dating the archaeology of northwestern Alaska. *Science* 153, 127–35.

——1967. *Ancient Men of the Arctic*. Knopf: New York.

GIRLING, M.A. & GREIG, J. 1985. A first fossil record for *Scolytus scolytus* (F.) (elm bark beetle): Its occurrence in elm decline deposits from London and the implications for Neolithic elm disease. *Journal of Arch. Science* 12, 347–51.

GLADFELTER, B.G. 1977. Geoarchaeology: the geomorphologist and archaeology. *American Antiquity* 42, 519–38.

GOLSON, J. 1976. Archaeology and agricultural history in the New Guinea Highlands, in *Problems in Economic and Social Archaeology* (G. Sieveking & others, eds.), 201–20. Duckworth: London.

——1977. No room at the top: agricultural intensification in the New Guinea Highlands, in *Sunda and Sahul* (J. Allen, J. Golson & R. Jones eds.), 601–38. Academic Press: New York & London.

——1990. Kuk and the development of agriculture in New Guinea: retrospection and introspection, in *Pacific Production Systems. Approaches to Economic Prehistory* (D.E. Yen & J.M.J. Mummery eds.), 139–47. Occ. Papers in Preh. 18, Research School of Pacific Studies, Australian National Univ.: Canberra.

GOUDIE, A. 1992. *Environmental Change. Contemporary Problems in Geography*. (3rd ed.) Oxford Univ. Press: Oxford & New York.

GREIG, J. 1982. The interpretation of pollen spectra from urban archaeological deposits, in *Environmental Archaeology in the Urban Context* (A.R. Hall & H.K. Kenward eds.), 47–65. Council for British Arch., Research Report 43: London.

GRINSTED, M.J. & WILSON, A.T. 1979. Variations of 13C/12C ratio in cellulose of *Agathus australis* (kauri) and climatic change in New Zealand during the last millennium. *New Zealand Journal of Science* 22, 55–61.

GUILLIEN, Y. 1970. Cryoclase, calcaires et grottes habitées. *Bull. Soc. Préhist. française* 67, 231–36.

HALLAM, S.J. 1975. *Fire and Hearth*. Australian Inst. of Aboriginal Studies: Canberra.

HARDING, A. (ed.). 1982. *Climatic Change in Later Prehistory*. Edinburgh Univ. Press.

HASSAN, F. 1979. Geoarchaeology: the

geologist and archaeology. *American Antiquity* 44, 267–70.

HEATON, T.H.E. & others. 1986. Climatic influence on the isotopic composition of bone nitrogen. *Nature* 322, 822–23.

HIGGS, E.S. (ed.). 1975. *Palaeoeconomy.* Cambridge Univ. Press.

——— **& VITA-FINZI, C.** 1972. Prehistoric economies, a territorial approach, in *Papers in Economic Prehistory* (E.S. Higgs ed.), 27–36. Cambridge Univ. Press.

HONG, S. & others. 1994. Greenland ice evidence of hemispheric lead pollution two millennia ago by Greek and Roman civilizations *Science* 265, 1841–43.

——— **&** ——— 1996. History of ancient copper smelting pollution during Roman and medieval times recorded in Greenland ice. *Science* 272, 246–49.

HOPE, G. & GOLSON, J. 1995. Late Quaternary Change in the Mountains of New Guinea. *Antiquity* 69, 818–30.

JAMESON, M., RUNNELS, C.N. & VAN ANDEL, T.H. 1995. *A Greek Countryside. The Southern Argolid from Prehistory to the Present Day.* Cambridge Univ. Press.

JARMAN, H.N., LEGGE, A.J. & CHARLES, J.A. 1972. Retrieval of plant remains from archaeological sites by froth flotation, in *Papers in Economic Prehistory* (E.S. Higgs ed.), 39–48. Cambridge Univ. Press.

JARMAN, M.R. 1972. A territorial model for archaeology, in *Models in Archaeology.* (D.L. Clarke ed.), 705–33. Methuen: London.

——— **& BAILEY, G.N. & JARMAN, H.N.** (eds.) 1982. *Early European Agriculture: its Foundations and Development.* Cambridge Univ. Press.

JASHEMSKI, W.F. 1979. *The Gardens of Pompeii, Herculaneum and the villas destroyed by Vesuvius.* Vol. 1. Caratzas Brothers: New Rochelle. 1994 Vol. 2.

———1986. L'archéologie des jardins de Pompéi. *La Recherche* 17, 990–91.

JOHNSEN, S.J. & others. 1992. Irregular glacial interstadials recorded in a new Greenland ice core. *Nature* 359, 311–13.

KERR, R.A. 1996. Ice rhythms: core reveals a plethora of climate cycles. *Science* 274, 499–500.

KERSHAW, A.P. 1993. Palynology, biostratigraphy and human impact, *The Artefact* 16, 12–18. (See also papers in *Quaternary Australasia* 12 (2), Nov. 1994, 21–33.)

KIRCH, P.V. 1982. The impact of the prehistoric Polynesians on the Hawaiian ecosystem. *Pacific Science* 36, 1–14.

——— 1983. Man's role in modifying tropical and subtropical Polynesian ecosystems. *Archaeology in Oceania* 18, 26–31.

KLEIN, R.G. 1984. The large mammals of southern Africa: Late Pliocene to Recent, in *Southern Africa: Prehistory and Palaeoenvironments* (R.G. Klein ed.), 107–46. Balkema: Rotterdam & Boston.

——— **& CRUZ-URIBE, K.** 1984. *The Analysis of Animal Bones from Archaeological Sites.* Univ. of Chicago Press.

KOIKE, H. 1986. Jomon shell mounds and growth-line analysis of molluscan shells, in *Windows on the Japanese Past: Studies in Archaeology and Prehistory* (R.J. Pearson & others eds.), 267–78. Center for Japanese Studies, Univ. of Michigan.

KUKLA, G.J. 1975. Loess stratigraphy of Central Europe, in *After the Australopithecines* (K.W. Butzer & G.L. Isaac eds.), 99–188. Mouton: The Hague.

——— 1987. Loess stratigraphy in Central China. *Quaternary Science Reviews* 6, 191–219.

LANGFORD, M., TAYLOR, G. & FLENLEY, J.R. 1986. The application of texture analysis for automated pollen identification, in *Proc. Conference on Identification and Pattern Recognition,* Toulouse, June 1986, vol. 2, 729–39. Univ. Paul Sabatier: Toulouse.

LARA, A. & VILLALBA, R. 1993. A 3620-year temperature record from *Fitzroya cupressoides* tree rings in southern South America. *Science* 260, 1104–06.

LAVILLE, H. 1976. Deposits in calcareous rock shelters: analytical methods and climatic interpretation, in *Geoarchaeology* (D.A. Davidson & M.L. Shackley eds.), 137–57. Duckworth: London.

———, **RIGAUD, J-P. & SACKETT, J.** 1980. *Rock shelters of the Périgord. Geological stratigraphy and archaeological succession.* Academic Press: London & New York.

LEACH, H. 1984. *1,000 Years of Gardening in New Zealand.* Reed: Wellington.

LEAKEY, M. 1987. Animal prints and trails, in *Laetoli, a Pliocene site in northern Tanzania* (M. Leakey & J.M. Harris eds.), 451–89. Clarendon Press: Oxford.

LEGGE, A.J. 1972. Cave climates, in *Papers in Economic Prehistory,* (E.S. Higgs ed.), 97–103. Cambridge Univ. Press.

LENTZ, D.L. & others. 1996. Foodstuffs, forests, fields and shelter: a paleoethnobotanical analyis of vessel contents from the Cerén site, El Salvador. *Latin American Antiquity* 7 (3), 247–62.

LEROI-GOURHAN, A. 1981. Pollens et grottes ornées, in *Altamira Symposium* (1980), 295–97. Madrid.

LEVESQUE, A.J. & others. 1997. Exceptionally steep north–south gradients in lake temperatures during the last deglaciation. *Nature* 385, 423–26.

LIMBREY, S. 1975. *Soil Science and Archaeology.* Academic Press: London & New York.

LISTER, A. & BAHN, P. 1994. *Mammoths.* Macmillan: New York; Boxtree: London.

LOWE, J.J. & WALKER, M.J.C. 1997. *Reconstructing Quaternary Environments.* (2nd ed.). Longman: Harlow.

MACPHEE, R.D. & MARX, P.A. 1997. The 40,000 year plague: humans, hyperdisease, and first contact extinctions, in *Natural Change and Human Impact in Madagascar* (S.M. Goodman & B.D. Patterson, eds.), 169–217. Smithsonian Institution Press: Washington D.C.

MAGEE, J.W. & HUGHES, P.J. 1982. Thin-section analysis and the geomorphic history of the Colless Creek archaeological site in Northwestern Queensland, in *Archaeometry: An Australian Perspective* (W. Ambrose & P. Duerden eds.), 120–28. Australian National Univ.: Canberra.

MANNION, A.M. 1987. Fossil diatoms and their significance in archaeological research. *Oxford Journal of Arch.* 6, 131–47.

———1991. *Global Environmental Change.* Longman: London.

MARTIN, P.S. & KLEIN, R.G. (eds.). 1984. *Quaternary Extinctions: A Prehistoric Revolution.* Univ. of Arizona Press.

MASTERS, P.M. & FLEMMING, N.C. (eds.). 1983. *Quaternary Coastlines and Marine Archaeology.* Academic Press: London & New York.

MEAD, J.I. & others. 1986. Dung of *Mammuthus* in the Arid Southwest, North America. *Quaternary Research* 25, 121–27.

MIDDLETON, W. & ROVNER, I. 1994. Extraction of opal phytoliths from herbivore dental calculus. *Journal of Arch. Science* 21, 469–73.

MILLER, G.H. & others 1999. Pleistocene extinction of *Genyornis newtoni.* Human impact on Australian megafauna. *Science* 283, 205–08.

MILLER, N.F. & GLEASON, K.L. (eds.). 1994. *The Archaeology of Garden and Field.* Pennsylvania Univ. Press: Philadelphia.

MILNER, G. 1990. The late prehistoric Cahokia cultural system of the Mississippi valley: foundations, florescence, and fragmentation. *Journal of World Prehistory* 4, 1–43.

MINNIS, P.E. 1987. Identification of wood from archaeological sites in the American Southwest. *Journal of Arch. Science* 14, 121–32.

MIYAJI, A. 1995. Ikejima-Fukumanji site at Osaka, Japan. *NewsWARP* (Newsletter of Wetland Archaeol. Research Project) 17, May, 6–11.

MOORE, P.D., WEBB, J.A. & COLLINSON, M.E. 1991. *Pollen Analysis* (2nd ed.) Blackwell Scientific: Oxford.

ORLIAC, M. 1975. Empreintes au latex des coupes du gisement magdalénien de Pincevent: technique et premiers résultats. *Bulletin de la Soc. Préh. française* 72, 274–76.

OSBORNE, P.J. 1976. Evidence from the insects of climatic variation during the Flandrian period: a preliminary note. *World Arch.* 8, 150–58.

OWEN-SMITH, N. 1987. Pleistocene extinctions: the pivotal role of mega-herbivores. *Paleobiology* 13, 351–62.

PALMER, P. 1976. Grass cuticles: a new paleoecological tool for East African lake sediments. *Canadian Journal of Botany* 54, No. 15, 1725–34.

PARKIN, D.W. & SHACKLETON, N.J. 1973. Trade winds and temperature correlations down a deep-sea core off the Saharan coast. *Nature* 245, 455–57.

PARKINGTON, J. 1981. The effects of environmental change on the scheduling of visits to the Elands Bay Cave, Cape Province, South Africa, in *Pattern of the Past. Studies in Honour of David Clarke* (I. Hodder & others eds.), 341–59. Cambridge Univ. Press.

PEARCE, F. 1996. Lure of the rings. *New Scientist*, 14 December, 38–42.

PEARSALL, D.M. 1982. Phytolith analysis: applications of a new paleo-ethnobotanical technique in archaeology. *American Anthropologist* 84, 862–71.

——1989. *Paleoethnobotany*. Academic Press: New York & London.

PERRY, I. & MOORE, P.D. 1987. Dutch elm disease as an analogue of Neolithic elm decline. *Nature* 326, 72–73.

PIGGOTT, S. 1973. The Dalladies long barrow: NE Scotland. *Antiquity* 47, 32–36.

PIPERNO, D.R. 1985. Phytolithic analysis of geological sediments from Panama. *Antiquity* 59, 13–19.

——1988. *Phytolith Analysis: An Archaeological and Geological Perspective*. Academic Press: New York & London.

POINAR, H.N. & others. 1998. Molecular coproscopy: dung and diet of the extinct Ground Sloth *Nothrotheriops shastensis*. *Science* 281, 402–06.

POPE, K.O. & VAN ANDEL, T.H. 1984. Late quaternary alluviation and soil formation in the Southern Argolid: its history, causes, and archaeological implications. *Journal of Arch. Science* 11, 281–306.

PYDDOKE, E. 1961. *Stratification for the Archaeologist*. Phoenix House: London.

RAIKES, R.L. 1984. *Water, Weather and Prehistory*. Raikes: Wales; Humanities Press: N.J.

RAPP, G. & GIFFORD, J.A. 1982. Archaeological geology. *American Scientist* 70, 45–53.

—— **& MULHOLLAND, S.C.** (eds.). 1992. *Phytolith Systematics: emerging issues*. Vol. 1. Advances in Archaeological and Museum Science. Plenum: New York.

RENBERG, I., PERSSON, M.W. & EMTERYD, O. 1994. Pre-industrial atmospheric lead contamination detected in Swedish lake sediments. *Nature* 368, 323–26.

RENFREW, J. 1973. *Palaeoethnobotany*. Methuen: London.

ROBERTS, N. 1998. *The Holocene: An Environmental History*. (2nd ed.). Blackwell: Oxford.

RODBELL, D.T. & others. 1999. An ~15,000-year record of El Niño-driven alluviation in Southwestern Ecuador. *Science* 283, 516–20.

ROPER, D.C. 1979. The method and theory of site catchment analysis: a review, in *Advances in Archaeological Method and Theory* 2 (M.B. Schiffer ed.), 119–40. Academic Press: New York & London.

ROTTLÄNDER, R.C.A. & SCHLICHTHERLE, H. 1979. Food identification of samples from archaeological sites. *Archaeo Physika* 10, 260–67.

ROVNER, I. 1971. Potential of opal phytoliths for use in paleoecological reconstruction. *Quaternary Research* 1, 343–59.

——1983. Plant opal phytolith analysis: major advances in archaeobotanical research, in *Advances in Archaeological Method and Theory* 6 (M.D. Schiffer ed.), 225–66. Academic Press: New York & London.

ROWLEY-CONWY, P. 1987. The interpretation of ard marks. *Antiquity* 61, 263–66.

RUE, D.J. 1987. Early agriculture and early Postclassic Maya occupation in western Honduras. *Nature* 326, 285–86.

RUNNELS, C.N. 1995. Environmental degradation in ancient Greece. *Scientific American* 272, 72–75.

SANCETTA, C., IMBRIE, J. & KIPP, N. 1973. Climatic record of the past 130,000 years in North Atlantic deep-sea core V23-82; correlation with the terrestrial record. *Quaternary Research* 3, 110–16.

VAN DER SANDEN, W. 1996. *Through Nature to Eternity. The Bog Bodies of Northwest Europe*. Batavian Lion International: Amsterdam.

SANDWEISS, D.H. & others. 1996. Geoarchaeological evidence from Peru for a 5000 years B.P. onset of El Niño. *Science* 273, 1531–34.

SCHIEGL, S. & others. 1996. Ash deposits in Hayonim and Kebara Caves, Israel: macroscopic, microscopic and mineralogical observations, and their archaeological implications. *Journal of Arch. Science* 23, 763–81.

SCHMID, E. 1969. Cave sediments and prehistory, in *Science in Archaeology* (D.R. Brothwell & E.S. Higgs eds.), 151–66. (2nd ed.) Thames & Hudson: London.

SHACKLETON, J.C. & VAN ANDEL, T.H. 1980. Prehistoric shell assemblages from Franchthi Cave and evolution of the adjacent coastal zone. *Nature* 288, 357–59.

—— **&** —— 1986. Prehistoric shore environments, shellfish availability, and shellfish gathering at Franchthi, Greece. *Geoarchaeology: an International Journal* 1 (2), 127–43.

SHACKLETON, N.J. 1967. Oxygen isotope analyses and pleistocene temperatures re-assessed. *Nature* 215, 15–17.

——1987. Oxygen isotopes, ice volume and sea level. *Quaternary Science Reviews* 6, 183–90.

—— **& TURNER, C.** 1967. Correlation between marine and terrestrial pleistocene successions. *Nature* 216, 1079–82.

SHACKLEY, M. 1975. *Archaeological Sediments*. Butterworth: London.

——1982. *Environmental Archaeology*. Allen & Unwin: London.

SHAHACK-GROSS, R. & others. 1997. Black-coloured bones in Hayonim Cave, Israel: differentiating between burning and oxide staining. *Journal of Arch. Science* 24, 439–46.

SHOTYK, W. & others. 1998. History of atmospheric lead deposition since 12,370 ^{14}C yr BP from a peat bog, Jura Mountains, Switzerland. *Science* 281, 1635–40.

SIMMONS, I.G. 1989. *Changing the Face of the Earth. Culture, Environment, History*. Blackwell: Oxford.

SINGH, G. & GEISSLER, E.A. 1985. Late Cainozoic history of vegetation, fire, lake levels and climate at Lake George, New South Wales, Australia. *Phil. Trans. Royal Soc. London* B 311, 379–447.

SNEH, A. & WEISSBROD, T. 1973. Nile Delta: The defunct Pelusiac branch identified. *Science* 180, 59–61.

SPARKS, B.W. 1969. Non-marine mollusca and archaeology, in *Science in Archaeology* (D.R. Brothwell & E.S. Higgs eds.), 395–406. (2nd ed.) Thames & Hudson: London.

SPENCE, C. (ed.). 1990. *Archaeological Site Manual*. (2nd ed.) Museum of London.

STAHLE, D.W. & others. 1998. The Lost Colony and Jamestown Droughts. *Science* 280, 564–67.

STEADMAN, D.W. 1995. Prehistoric extinctions of Pacific island birds: Biodiversity meets Zooarchaeology. *Science* 267, 1123–31.

STINE, S. 1994. Extreme and persistent drought in California and Patagonia during mediaeval times. *Nature* 369: 546–49.

STREET, M. 1986. Un Pompéi de l'âge glaciaire. *La Recherche* 17, 534–35.

SUTCLIFFE, A.J. 1985, *On the Track of Ice Age Mammals*. British Museum (Natural History): London.

THOMPSON, F.H. (ed.). 1980. *Archaeology and Coastal Change*. Soc. of Antiquaries, Occasional Paper, New Series 1.

THOMPSON, L.G. & others. 1995. Late Glacial stage and Holocene tropical ice core records from Huascarán, Peru. *Science* 269, 46–50.

—— **&** —— 1998. A 25,000-year tropical climate history from Bolivian ice cores. *Science* 282, 1858–64.

THUNELL, R.C. 1979. Eastern Mediterranean Sea during the last glacial maximum: an 18,000 years B.P. reconstruction. *Quaternary Research* 11, 353–72.

TRAVERSE, A. 1988. *Paleopalynology*. Unwin Hyman: Boston.

VITA-FINZI, C. 1969. Fluvial geology, in *Science in Archaeology* (D.R. Brothwell & E.S. Higgs eds.), 135–50. (2nd ed.) Thames & Hudson: London.

————1973. *Recent Earth History.* Macmillan: London.

————1978. *Archaeological Sites in their Setting.* Thames & Hudson: London & New York.

VOORHIPS, A. & JANSMA, M.J. 1974. Pollen and diatom analysis of a shore section of the former Lake Wevershoof. *Geologie en Mijnbouw* 53, 429–35.

WATSON, P.J. 1976. In pursuit of prehistoric subsistence: a comparative account of some contemporary flotation techniques. *Mid-Continental Journal of Archaeology* 1, 77–99.

WEINER, J. 1992. The Bandkeramik wooden well of Erkelenz-Kückhoven. *NewsWARP* (Newsletter of the Wetland Arch. Research Project) 12, 3–11 (also 16, 1994, 5–17).

WEINER, S. & others. 1998. Evidence for the use of fire at Zhoukoudian, China. *Science* 281, 251–53.

WEST, F.H. (ed.). 1996. *American Beginnings. The Prehistory and Palaeoecology of Beringia.* Univ. of Chicago Press: Chicago & London.

WESTERN, A.C. 1969. Wood and charcoal in archaeology, in *Science in Archaeology* (D.R. Brothwell & E.S. Higgs eds.), 178–87. (2nd ed.) Thames & Hudson: London.

WILKINSON, P.F. 1971. Pollen, archaeology and man. *Arch. & Physical Anth. in Oceania* 6, 1–20.

WILLIAMS, D. 1973. Flotation at Siraf. *Antiquity* 47, 288–92.

WILLIAMS, M. & others. 1998. *Quaternary Environments.* (2nd ed.). Edward Arnold: London.

WILSON, A.T. & HENDY, C.H. 1971. Past wind strength from isotope studies. *Nature* 234, 344–45.

WISEMAN, J. 1998. The art of gardening. Eating well at a Mesoamerican Pompeii. *Archaeology* 51 (1), 12–16.

WRIGHT, R. 1986. How old is zone F at Lake George? *Arch. in Oceania* 21, 138–39.

ZEDER, M.A. 1978. Differentiation between the bones of caprines from different ecosystems in Iran by the analysis of osteological microstructure and chemical composition, in *Approaches to Faunal Analysis in the Middle East* (R.M. Meadow & M.A. Zeder eds.), 69–84. Peabody Museum of Arch. & Ethnol., Bull. No. 2.

Chapter 7: What Did they Eat? Subsistence and Diet (pp. 269–310)

pp. 269–82 **Paleoethnobotany** In general: Renfrew 1973, 1991; van Zeist & Casparie 1984; Greig 1989; Pearsall 1989; Hastorf & Popper 1989; Brooks & Johannes 1990; Dimbleby 1978; for the New World, Ford 1979; Gremillon 1997, Smith 1992, van Zeist & others 1991; Lentz & others (1996) Cerén.

pp. 270–74 **Macrobotanical remains**, especially in an urban context: Hall, A. 1986; Greig 1983; Dennell 1974 (internal evidence), 1976. Hillman 1973, 1984a & b, 1985; Jones 1984 (external analysis using ethnographic models or archaeological experiments); Miller 1996 (seeds from dung).

pp. 274–76 **Microbotanical remains** Fujiwara 1979, 1982 (rice phytoliths); Hillman & others 1993 (chemicals in plants).

pp. 276–78 **Plant processing** Dennell 1974, 1976; Hubbard 1975, 1976. Also Hillman 1981 (charred remains); Jones & others 1986 (crop storage). **Plant residues** In general: Hill & Evans 1987. In particular: Grüss 1932 (early work); Samuel 1996 (Egyptian bread & beer); Loy & others 1992; Piperno & Holst 1998 (starch grains); Rottländer & Schlichtherle 1979 (Neolithic sherds); Rottländer & Hartke 1982 (Roman sherds); Rottländer 1986 (Heuneburg); Hather 1994 (new techniques): McGovern 1998; McGovern & others 1996a, 1996b (early wine); Hastorf & DeNiro 1985 (isotopic analysis); Evershed & others 1991 (pot-fabric analysis).

pp. 278–79 **Plant domestication** In general: Zohary & Hopf 1993; Hillman & others 1989a; Ucko & Dimbleby 1969. In particular: Jarman 1972 (cereals); Hillman & Davies 1990 (domestication rates); Smith 1984 (*Chenopodium* work); Butler 1989 (legumes). Phytoliths and maize domestication: Piperno & others 1985; Pearsall 1978 (Ecuador maize); Piperno & Pearsall 1998 (Panama maize and Ecuador squash). Ubuka Bog, Japan: Tsukuda & others 1986. Wheat DNA: Brown & others 1993; Heun & others 1997.

p. 279 **Cookery and electron spin resonance** Hillman & others 1985. Lindow Man work: Stead & others 1986.

pp. 279–82 **Plant evidence from literate societies** Crawford 1979, Darby & others 1977, Saffirio 1972 (Egypt); Davies 1971 (Roman military diet); Garnsey 1988, Forbes & Foxhall 1978, Foxhall & Forbes 1982 (Graeco-Roman world); UNESCO 1984, 86 (T'ang granaries).

pp. 282–305 **Animal resources** In general: Reitz & Wing 1999; Davis 1987; Grayson 1984; Hesse & Wapnish 1985; Meadow 1980; Lyman 1982, 1994. A specialized journal began in 1987: *Archaeozoologia*.

pp.283–86 **Human exploitation of animals** In general: Clutton-Brock & Grigson 1983; Blumenschine 1986; Blumenschine & Cavallo 1992. The Olduvai/Koobi Fora work is described in Bunn 1981; Bunn & Kroll 1986; Potts & Shipman 1981; Shipman & Rose 1983; Potts 1988. See also papers in Clutton-Brock & Grigson 1983, and in *Journal of Human Evolution* 15 (8), Dec. 1986. Trampling of bones: Behrensmeyer & others 1986; Olsen & Shipman 1988.

pp. 287 **Cannibalism** Arens 1979; Russell

1987 (Krapina); for Fontbrégoua see Villa & others 1986; against Fontbrégoua, Pickering 1989; Peter-Röcher 1994 (Europe); for Anasazi cannibalism, White 1992; Turner & Turner 1999; against, Bahn 1992, Bullock 1998.

p. 287 **Macrofaunal assemblage** Speth 1983 (Garnsey).

pp. 287–90 **Age, sex, and seasonality** Hesse 1978, 1984; Silver 1969; Wilson & others 1982. Star Carr: Legge & Rowley-Conwy 1988. Sika deer: Koike & Ohtaishi 1985, 1987.

pp. 290–95 **Animal domestication** In general: Bökönyi 1969; Clutton-Brock 1981; Collier & White 1976; Crabtree 1993; Davis 1987; Hemme 1990; Higgs & Jarman 1969; Jarman & Wilkinson 1972; Olsen 1979. Meadow 1996 (Mehrgarh cattle); Ryder 1969 (work on skins); Reigadas 1992; Bahn 1994 (camelid hair); Bahn 1978 (control of Ice Age animals); Chaix & others 1997 (muzzled bear). Disease and deformity: Baker & Brothwell 1980. Telarmachay camelids: Wheeler 1984. Loftus & others 1994; Bradley & others 1996 (cattle DNA). Loreille & others 1997 (sheep/goat DNA).

pp. 295–99 **Small fauna: Birds** Anderson, A. 1989 (moa sites, Hawksburn in particular). **Fish** Casteel 1974a; Brinkhuizen & Clason 1986; Wheeler & Jones 1989; and on fish-meat weights, Casteel 1974b. **Microfauna and insects** Aumassip & others 1982/3 (locusts); Hall, R.A. & Kenward 1976 (York granaries). **Molluscs** Claassen 1998; Meighan 1969; Shackleton 1969; Bailey 1975; Kirch & Yen 1982 (Tikopia); Stein 1992.

p. 299 **Seasonality studies** Monks 1981. Oronsay fish otoliths: Mellars & Wilkinson 1980. Mollusc seasonality in general: Sheppard 1985.

pp. 301–03 **Exploitation of animal resources: Fishing and hunting** Andersen 1986, 1987 (Tybrind Vig boat); Noe-Nygaard 1974, 1975 (wounds on animal bones); Keeley & Toth 1981 (microwear analysis). **Blood residues** Loy 1983, 1987, 1993; Loy & Wood 1989; Loy & Hardy 1992; Eisele & others 1995; Newman & others 1996. **Fat residues** Rottländer & Schlichtherle 1979 (Geissenklösterle & Lommersum); Brochier 1983 (cave-herding); Schelvis 1992 (mites); Bull & others 1999 (manure). **Residues in vessels** Grüss 1933; Dudd & Evershed 1998 (milk); Rottländer & Hartke 1982 (Michelsberg); Rottländer & Schlichtherle 1979; Patrick & others 1985 (Kasteelberg). **Animal tracks** Leakey 1987 (Laetoli); Roberts & others 1996 (Mersey); Price 1995 (Sweden).

pp. 303–04 **Secondary Products Revolution** Sherratt 1981; Bogucki 1986 (LBK dairying).

p. 304 **Art and literature** Jett & Moyle 1986 (Mimbres fish).

pp. 304–05 **Individual meals** Hall 1974 (Chinese lady's tomb).

pp. 305–06 **Human remains: Individual meals** Anasazi colon: Reinhard & others 1992; stomach contents of bogmen: Brothwell 1986; van der Sanden 1996, chapter 8. Lindow man: Hillman 1986; Stead & Turner 1985; Stead & others 1986. **Fecal material** Identification as human: Bethell & others 1994. In general: Bryant & Williams-Dean 1975; Callen 1969; Reinhard & Bryant 1992. Tehuacán: Callen 1967; Callen & Cameron 1960. Nevada: Heizer 1969. Bearsden work: Knights & others 1983. Cesspits in general: Greig 1982; Worcester latrine: Greig 1981. The survival properties of organic residues through the human digestive system are listed in Calder 1977.

pp. 306–07 **Teeth** Puech 1978, 1979a, 1979b; Puech & others 1983; Fine & Craig 1981; Larsen 1983 (Georgia). **Phytoliths** Lalueza & Pérez-Pérez 1994.

pp. 307–10 **Isotopic methods: bone collagen** Price 1989. **Carbon isotope analyses** Tauber 1981 (Denmark); Chisholm & others 1982, 1983 (British Columbia); Sponheimer & Lee-Thorp 1999 (Australopithecines); van der Merwe & others 1981 (Venezuela); Schwarcz & others 1985 (Ontario); Sealy 1986; Sealy & van der Merwe 1986 (SW Cape); Ambrose & DeNiro 1986 (E. & S. Africa). **Nitrogen isotopes** Schoeninger & others 1983; Dorozynski & Anderson 1991 (Neanderthals); Svitil 1994 (Nubians). **Strontium analysis** Sillen 1994; Schoeninger 1981 (Near East); Schoeninger 1979 (Chalcatzingo); Schoeninger & Peebles 1981 (molluscs). See *Journal of Arch. Science* 18 (3), May 1991 (diet issue).

Box Features

pp. 272–73 **Paleoethnobotany** Wendorf & others 1980; Hillman & others 1989b; Hillman 1989 (Wadi Kubbaniya).

pp. 274–75 **Butser** Reynolds 1979.

pp. 280–81 **Rise of Farming in Near East** Bar-Yosef & Belfer-Cohen 1989; Bar-Yosef 1998; Harris 1996; Cowan & Watson 1992; Braidwood & Howe 1960; Hole & others 1969; Mellaart 1967; Binford 1968; Flannery 1965; Higgs & Jarman 1969; Renfrew, J. 1973; Vita-Finzi & Higgs 1970; Nadel & Hershkovitz 1991; Nesbitt 1995; Smith 1995; Bender 1978; Kislev & others 1992 (Ohalo); Bar-Yosef & Meadow 1995; Cauvin 1997; Heun & others 1997.

pp. 284–85 **Taphonomy** In general: Lyman 1994; Weigelt 1989; Behrensmeyer & Hill 1980; Bahn 1983; Noe-Nygaard 1977, 1987; Gifford 1981. Also Brain 1981 (S. African work); Binford 1981; Binford & Bertram 1977 (N. American work); Speth 1983 (Garnsey site).

pp. 288–89 **Quantifying Animal Bones** Problems: Grayson 1979, 1984.

Estimation of meat weight: Lyman 1979; Smith 1975. Butchery studies: White 1953, 1953/4. Moncin: Harrison & others 1994.

p. 291 **Teeth** In general: Hillson 1986. Klein & Cruz-Uribe 1984 (tooth-wear); Singer & Wymer 1982 (Klasies River Mouth Cave); Fisher 1984 (Michigan mastodons); Bourque & others 1978 (tooth sectioning technique); Spiess 1979 (Abri Pataud work); Lieberman & others 1990 (computer enhancement).

pp. 292–93 **Bison Drive Sites** Kehoe 1967 (Boarding School). Kehoe 1973 (Gull Lake). Other drive sites: Speth 1983 (Garnsey) and Wheat 1972 (Olsen-Chubbuck).

pp. 296–97 **Farming Origins: Abu Hureyra** Moore 1975, 1979; Hillman & others 1989a; Legge & Rowley-Conwy 1987.

pp. 300–01 **Shell Midden Analysis** Growth lines: Koike 1986 (Kidosaku); Koike 1979, 1980 (Natsumidai). Mollusc seasonality from oxygen isotopes: Bailey & others 1983; Killingley 1981; Shackleton 1973.

Bibliography

AMBROSE, S.H. & DENIRO, M.J. 1986. Reconstruction of African human diet using bone collagen carbon and nitrogen isotope ratios. *Nature* 319, 321–24.

ANDERSEN, S.H. 1986. Mesolithic dug-outs and paddles from Tybrind Vig, Denmark. *Acta archaeologica* 57, 87–106.

————1987. Tybrind Vig: a submerged Ertebolle settlement in Denmark, in *European Wetlands in Prehistory* (J.M. Coles & A.J. Lawson eds.), 253–80. Clarendon Press: Oxford.

ANDERSON, A. 1989. *Prodigious Birds: Moas and Moa-hunting in New Zealand.* Cambridge Univ. Press.

ARENS, W. 1979. *The Man-Eating Myth.* Oxford Univ. Press.

AUMASSIP, G., BETROUNI, M. & HACHI, S. 1982/3. Une structure de cuisson de sauterelles dans les dépôts archéologiques de Ti-n-Hanakaten (Tassili-n-Ajjer, Algérie). *Libyca* 30/31, 199–202.

BAHN, P.G. 1978. The "unacceptable face" of the West European Upper Palaeolithic. *Antiquity* 52, 183–92.

————1983. The case of the clumsy cave-bears. *Nature* 301, 565.

————1992. Review of "Prehistoric Cannibalism" by T.D. White. *New Scientist* 11 April, 40–41.

————1994. Time for a change. *Nature* 367, 511–12.

BAILEY, G.N. 1975. The role of molluscs in coastal economies: the results of midden analysis in Australia. *Journal of Arch. Science* 2, 45–62.

————, **DEITH, M.R. & SHACKLETON, N.J.** 1983. Oxygen isotope analysis and seasonality determinations: limits and potential of a new technique. *American Antiquity* 48, 390–98.

BAKER, J. & BROTHWELL, D. 1980. *Animal Diseases in Archaeology.* Academic Press: New York & London.

BAR-YOSEF, O. 1998. On the nature of transitions: the Middle to Upper Palaeolithic and the Neolithic Revolution. *Cambridge Arch. Journal* 8 (2), 141–63.

————**& BELFER-COHEN, A.** 1989. The origins of sedentism and farming communities in the Levant. *Journal of World Prehistory* 3, 447–98.

————**& MEADOW, R.H.** 1995. The origins of agriculture in the Near East, in *Last Hunters, First Farmers: New Perspectives on the Prehistoric Transition to Agriculture* (T.D. Price & A.B. Gebauer, eds.), 39–94. School of American Research Press: Santa Fe.

BEHRENSMEYER, A.K., GORDON, K.D. & YANAGI, G.T. 1986. Trampling as a cause of bone surface damage and pseudo-cutmarks. *Nature* 319, 768–71.

————**& HILL, A.P.** (eds.). 1980. *Fossils in the Making, Vertebrate Taphonomy and Paleoecology.* Univ. of Chicago Press.

BENDER, B. 1978. Gatherer hunter to farmer: a social perspective. *World Arch.* 10, 204–22.

BETHELL, P.H. & others. 1994. The study of molecular markers of human activity: the use of coprostanol in the soil as an indicator of human faecal material. *Journal of Arch. Science* 21, 619–32.

BINFORD, L.R. 1968. Post-Pleistocene adaptations, in *New Perspectives in Archaeology* (S.R. & L.R. Binford eds.), 313–41. Aldine: Chicago.

————1981. *Bones: Ancient Men and Modern Myths.* Academic Press: New York & London.

————**& BERTRAM, J.B.** 1977. Bone frequencies and attritional processes, in *For Theory Building in Archaeology* (L.R. Binford ed.), 77–153. Academic Press: New York & London.

BLUMENSCHINE, R.J. 1986. *Early Hominid Scavenging Opportunities.* British Arch. Reports, Int. Series 283: Oxford.

————**& CAVALLO, J.A.** 1992. Scavenging and human evolution. *Scientific American,* 267 (4), 70–76.

BOGUCKI, P. 1986. The antiquity of dairying in temperate Europe. *Expedition* 28 (2), 51–58.

BÖKÖNYI, S. 1969. Archaeological problems and methods of recognizing animal domestication, in *The Domestication and Exploitation of Plants and Animals* (P.J. Ucko & G.W. Dimbleby eds.), 219–29. Duckworth: London.

BOURQUE, B.J., MORRIS, K. & SPIESS, A. 1978. Determining the season of death of mammal teeth from archaeological sites: a new sectioning technique. *Science* 199, 530–31.

BRADLEY, D.G. & others. 1996. Mitochondrial diversity and the origins of African and

European cattle. *Proc. Nat. Acad. Science USA* 93, 5131–35.

BRAIDWOOD, R.J. & HOWE, B. 1960. *Prehistoric Investigations in Iraqi Kurdistan*. Oriental Institute: Chicago.

BRAIN, C.K. 1981. *The Hunters or the Hunted? An Introduction to African Cave Taphonomy*. Univ. of Chicago Press.

BRINKHUIZEN, D.C. & CLASON, A.T. (eds.). 1986. *Fish and Archaeology. Studies in Osteometry, Taphonomy, Seasonality and Fishing*. British Arch. Reports, Int. Series No. 294: Oxford.

BROCHIER, J.-E. 1983. Combustion et parcage des herbivores domestiques. Le point de vue sédimentologique. *Bull. Soc. Préhist. française* 80, 143–45.

BROOKS, R.R. & JOHANNES, D. 1990. *Phytoarchaeology*. Leicester Univ. Press.

BROTHWELL, D. 1986. *The Bog Man and the Archaeology of People*. British Museum Publications: London.

———& BROTHWELL, P. 1997. *Food in Antiquity: A Survey of the Diet of Early Peoples*. Johns Hopkins Univ.: Baltimore.

BROWN, T.A., ALLABY, R.G., BROWN, K.A. & JONES, M.K. 1993. Biomolecular archaeology of wheat: past, present and future. *World Arch.* 25, 64–73.

BRYANT, V.M. & WILLIAMS-DEAN, G. 1975. The coprolites of man. *Scientific American* 238, 100–09.

BULL, I.D. & others. 1999. Muck 'n' molecules: organic geochemical methods for detecting ancient manuring. *Antiquity* 73, 86–96.

BULLOCK, P.Y. (ed.). 1998. *Deciphering Anasazi Violence*. HRM Books: Santa Fe.

BUNN, H.T. 1981. Archaeological evidence for meat-eating by Plio-Pleistocene hominids from Koobi Fora and Olduvai Gorge. *Nature* 291, 574–77.

———& KROLL, E.M. 1986. Systematic butchery by Plio/Pleistocene hominids at Olduvai Gorge, Tanzania. *Current Anth.* 27, 431–52.

BUTLER, A. 1989. Cryptic-anatomical characters as evidence of early cultivation in the gram legumes (pulses), in *Foraging and Farming: The evolution of plant exploitation* (D.R. Harris & G.C. Hillman eds.). Unwin & Hyman: London.

CALDER, A.M. 1977. Survival properties of organic residues through the human digestive tract. *Journal of Arch. Science* 4, 141–51.

CALLEN, E.O. 1967. Analysis of the Tehuacán coprolites, in *The Prehistory of the Tehuacán Valley, 1: Environment and Subsistence* (D.S. Byers ed.), 261–89. Austin: London.

———1969. Diet as revealed by coprolites, in *Science in Archaeology* (D.R. Brothwell & E.S. Higgs eds.), 235–43. (2nd ed.) Thames & Hudson: London.

———& CAMERON, T.W.M. 1960. A prehistoric diet revealed in coprolites. *New Scientist* 8, 35–40.

CASTEEL, R.W. 1974a. *Fish Remains in Archaeology and Paleo-environmental Studies*. Academic Press: New York & London.

———1974b. A method for estimation of live weight of fish from the size of skeletal elements. *American Antiquity* 39, 94–98.

CAUVIN, J. 1997. *Naissance des divinités, naissance de l'agriculture: la révolution des symboles au néolithique*. (2nd ed.). Centre National de la Recherche Scientifique: Paris.

CHAIX, L. & others. 1997. A tamed brown bear (*Ursus arctos L.*) of the Late Mesolithic from la Grande-Rivoire (Isère, France)? *Journal of Arch. Science* 24, 1067–74.

CHISHOLM, B.S., NELSON, D.E. & SCHWARCZ, H.P. 1982. Stable carbon isotope ratios as a measure of marine versus terrestrial protein of ancient diets. *Science* 216, 1131–32.

———1983. Marine and terrestrial protein in prehistoric diets on the British Columbia coast. *Current Anth.* 24, 396–98.

CLAASSEN, C. 1998. *Shells*. Cambridge Univ. Press.

CLUTTON-BROCK, J. 1981. *Domesticated Animals from Early Times*. Heinemann/British Museum (Natural History): London.

———& GRIGSON, C. (eds.). 1983. *Animals and Archaeology, Vol. 1*. British Arch. Reports, Int. Series 163: Oxford.

COLLIER, S. & WHITE, J.P. 1976. Getting them young? Age and sex inferences on animal domestication in archaeology. *American Antiquity* 41, 96–102.

COWAN, C.W. & WATSON, P.J. (eds.). 1992. *The Origins of Agriculture. An international perspective*. Smithsonian Institution Press: Washington D.C.

CRABTREE, P.J. 1993. Early animal domestication in the Middle East and Europe, in *Archaeological Method and Theory 5* (M. Schiffer, ed.), 201–45. Univ. of Arizona Press: Tucson.

CRAWFORD, D.J. 1979. Food: Tradition and change in Hellenistic Egypt. *World Arch.* 11, 136–46.

DARBY, W.J., GHALIOUNGI, P. & GRIVETTI, L. 1977. *Food: The Gift of Osiris*. 2 vols. Academic Press: New York & London.

DAVIES, R.W. 1971. The Roman military diet. *Britannia* 3, 122–42.

DAVIS, S. 1987. *The Archaeology of Animals*. Batsford: London; Yale Univ. Press: New Haven.

DENNELL, R.W. 1974. Botanical evidence for prehistoric crop processing activities. *Journal of Arch. Science* 1, 275–84.

———1976. The economic importance of plant resources represented on archaeological sites. *Journal of Arch. Science* 3, 229–47.

DIMBLEBY, G. 1978. *Plants and Archaeology*. Paladin: London.

DOROZYNSKI, A. & ANDERSON, A. 1991. Collagen: a new probe into prehistoric diet. *Science* 254, 520–21.

DUDD, S.N. & EVERSHED, R.P. 1998. Direct demonstration of milk as an element of archaeological economies. *Science* 282, 1478–81.

EISELE, J.A. & others. 1995. Survival and detection of blood residues on stone tools. *Antiquity* 69, 36–46.

EVERSHED, R.P., HERON, C. & GOAD, L.J. 1991. Epicuticular wax components preserved in potsherds as chemical indicators of leafy vegetables in ancient diets. *Antiquity* 65, 540–44.

FINE, D. & CRAIG, G.T. 1981. Buccal surface wear of human premolar and molar teeth: a potential indicator of dietary and social differentiation. *Journal of Human Evolution* 10, 335–44.

FISHER, D.C. 1984. Mastodon butchery by North American Paleo-Indians. *Nature* 308, 271–72.

FLANNERY, K.V. 1965. The ecology of early food production in Mesopotamia. *Science* 147, 247–55.

FORBES, H.A. & FOXHALL, L. 1978. "The Queen of all Trees". Preliminary notes on the Archaeology of the Olive. *Expedition* 21, 37–47.

FORD, R.I. 1979. Paleoethnobotany in American Archaeology, in *Advances in Archaeological Method and Theory 2* (M.B. Schiffer ed.), 285–336. Academic Press: New York & London.

FOXHALL, L. & FORBES, H.A. 1982. Sitometreia: The role of grain as a staple food in classical antiquity, *Chiron* 12, 41–90.

FUJIWARA, H. 1979. Fundamental studies in plant opal analysis (3): estimation of the yield of rice in ancient paddy fields through quantitative analyses of plant opal. *Archaeology and Natural Sciences* 12, 29–42 (in Japanese, with English summary).

———1982. Fundamental studies in plant opal analysis. Detection of plant opals in pottery walls of the Jomon period in Kumamoto Prefecture. *Archaeology and Natural Sciences* 14, 55–65 (in Japanese, with English summary).

GARNSEY, P. 1988. *Famine and Food Supply in the Graeco-Roman World*. Cambridge Univ. Press.

GIFFORD, D.P. 1981 Taphonomy and Paleoecology: a critical review of Archaeology's sister disciplines, in *Advances in Archaeological Method and Theory 4* (M.B. Schiffer ed.), 365–438. Academic Press: New York & London.

GRAYSON, D.K. 1979. On the quantification of vertebrate archaeofaunas, in *Advances in Archaeological Method and Theory 2* (M.B. Schiffer ed.), 199–237. Academic Press: London & New York.

———1984. *Quantitative Zooarchaeology. Topics in the analysis of archaeological faunas*. Academic Press: New York & London.

GREIG, J. 1981. The investigation of a

medieval barrel-latrine from Worcester. *Journal of Arch. Science* 8, 265–82.

——1982. Garderobes, sewers, cesspits and latrines. *Current Arch.* 8 (2), No. 85, 49–52.

——1983. Plant foods in the past: a review of the evidence from northern Europe. *Journal of Plant Foods* 5, 179–214.

——1989. *Archaeobotany.* Handbooks for Archaeologists 4. European Science Foundation: Strasbourg.

GREMILLION, K.J. (ed.). 1997. *People, Plants, and Landscapes: Studies in Paleoethnobotany.* Univ. of Alabama Press: Tuscaloosa.

GRÜSS, J. 1932. Die beiden ältesten Weine unserer Kulturwelt. *Forschungen und Fortschritte* 8, 23–24.

——1933. Über Milchreste aus der Hallstattzeit und andere Funde. *Forschungen und Fortschritte* 9, 105–6.

HALL, A. 1986. The fossil evidence for plants in mediaeval towns. *Biologist* 33 (5), 262–67.

HALL, A.J. 1974. A lady from China's past *National Geographic* 145 (5), 660–81.

HALL, R.A. & KENWARD, H.K. 1976. Biological evidence for the usage of Roman riverside warehouses at York. *Britannia* 7, 274–76.

HARRIS, D.R. (ed.).1996. *The Origins and Spread of Agriculture and Pastoralism in Eurasia.* UCL Press: London.

HARRISON, R.J., MORENO-LOPEZ, G. & LEGGE, A.J. 1994. *Moncin: un poblado de la Edad del Bronce (Borja, Zaragoza).* Collection Arqueologia No. 16, Gobierno de Aragon: Zaragoza, Cometa.

HASTORF, C.A. & DENIRO, M.J. 1985. Reconstruction of prehistoric plant production and cooking practices by a new isotopic method. *Nature* 315, 489–91.

——& POPPER, V.S. (eds.). 1989. *Current Palaeoethnobotany: Analytical Methods and Cultural Interpretations of Archaeological Plant Remains.* Univ. of Chicago Press.

HATHER, J.G. (ed.). 1994. *Tropical Archaeobotany.* Routledge: London.

HEIZER, R.G. 1969. The anthropology of prehistoric Great Basin human coprolites, in *Science in Archaeology* (D.R. Brothwell & E.S. Higgs eds.), 244–50. (2nd ed.) Thames & Hudson: London.

HEMME, R.H. 1990. *Domestication.* Cambridge Univ. Press.

HESSE, B. 1978. *Evidence for Husbandry from the Early Neolithic Site of Ganj Dareh in Western Iran.* University Microfilms: Ann Arbor.

——1984. These are our goats: the origins of herding in West Central Iran, in *Animals and Archaeology, Vol. 3: Early Herders and their Flocks* (J. Clutton-Brock & C. Grigson eds.), 243–64. British Arch. Reports, Int. Series 202: Oxford.

——& WAPNISH, P. 1985. *Animal Bone*

Archaeology: From objectives to analysis. Taraxacum: Washington.

HEUN, M. & others. 1997. Site of einkorn wheat domestication identified by DNA fingerprinting. *Science* 278, 1312–14. (See also 279, pp. 302 & 1433.)

HIGGS, E.S. & JARMAN, M.R. 1969. The origins of agriculture: a reconsideration. *Antiquity* 43, 31–41.

HILL, H.E. & EVANS, J. 1987. The identification of plants used in prehistory from organic residues, in *Archaeometry: Further Australasian Studies* (W.R. Ambrose & J.M.J. Mummery eds.), 90–96. Australian National Univ.: Canberra.

HILLMAN, G.C. 1973. Crop husbandry and food production: modern basis for the interpretation of plant remains. *Anatolian Studies* 23, 241–44.

——1981. Reconstructing crop husbandry practices from charred remains of crops, in *Farming Practice in British Prehistory* (R. Mercer ed.), 123–62. Edinburgh Univ. Press.

——1984a. Interpretation of archaeological plant remains: the application of ethnographic models from Turkey, in *Plants and Ancient Man* (W. van Zeist & W.A. Casparie eds.), 1–41. Balkema: Rotterdam.

——1984b. Traditional husbandry and processing of archaic cereals in modern times: part 1, the glume wheats. *Bull. of Sumerian Agriculture* 1, 114–52.

——1985. Traditional husbandry and processing of archaic cereals in modern times: part 2, the free-threshing cereals. *Bull. of Sumerian Agriculture* 2, 21–31.

——1986. Plant foods in ancient diet: the archaeological role of palaeofaeces in general and Lindow Man's gut contents in particular, in *Lindow Man. The Body in the Bog* (I.M. Stead & others eds.), 99–115. British Museum Publications: London.

——1989. Late palaeolithic plant foods from Wadi Kubbaniya in Upper Egypt: dietary diversity, infant weaning and seasonality in a riverine environment, in *Foraging and Farming: the Evolution of Plant Exploitation* (D.R. Harris & G.C. Hillman eds.), 207–39. Unwin Hyman: London.

——, COLLEDGE, S.M. & HARRIS, D.R. 1989a. Plant-food economy during the Epi-Palaeolithic period at Tell Abu Hureyra, Syria: Dietary diversity, seasonality and modes of exploitation, in *Foraging and Farming: The Evolution of Plant Exploitation* (D.R. Harris & G.C. Hillman eds.) 240–68. Unwin Hyman: London.

——, MADEYSKA, E. & HATHER, J. 1989b. Wild plant foods and diet at Late Palaeolithic Wadi Kubbaniya: Evidence from charred remains, in *The Prehistory of Wadi Kubbaniya. Vol. 2: Studies in Late Palaeolithic Subsistence* (F. Wendorf & others eds.). Southern Methodist Univ. Press: Dallas.

——& DAVIES, M.S. 1990. Measured domestication rates in wild wheats and barley under primitive cultivation and their archaeological implications. *Journal of World Prehistory* 4, 157–222.

——& others. 1985. The use of Electron Spin Resonance Spectroscopy to determine the thermal histories of cereal grains. *Journal of Arch. Science* 12, 49–58.

——& others. 1993. Identifying problematic remains of ancient plant foods: A comparison of the role of chemical, histological and morphological criteria. *World Arch.* 25, 94–121.

HILLSON, S. 1986. *Teeth.* Cambridge Univ. Press.

HOLE, F., FLANNERY, K.V. & NEELY, J.A. 1969. *Prehistory and Human Ecology of the Deh Luran Plain.* Museum of Anthropology: Ann Arbor.

HUBBARD, R.N.L.B. 1975. Assessing the botanical component of human palaeoeconomies. *Bull. Inst. Arch. London* 12, 197–205.

——1976. On the strength of the evidence for prehistoric crop processing activities. *Journal of Arch. Science* 3, 257–65.

JARMAN, H.N. 1972. The origins of wheat and barley cultivation, in *Papers in Economic Prehistory* (E.S. Higgs ed.), 15–26. Cambridge Univ. Press.

JARMAN, M.R. & WILKINSON, P.F. 1972. Criteria of animal domestication, in *Papers in Economic Prehistory* (E.S. Higgs ed.), 83–96. Cambridge Univ. Press.

JETT, S.C. & MOYLE, P.B. 1986. The exotic origins of fishes depicted on prehistoric Mimbres pottery from New Mexico. *American Antiquity* 51, 688–720.

JONES, G.E.M. 1984. Interpretation of archaeological plant remains. Ethnographic models from Greece, in *Plants and Man* (W. van Zeistand & W.A. Casparie eds.), 43–61. Balkema: Rotterdam.

JONES, G. & others. 1986. Crop storage at Assiros. *Scientific American* 254, 84–91.

KEELEY, L.H. & TOTH, N. 1981. Microwear polishes on early stone tools from Koobi Fora, Kenya. *Nature* 293, 464–65.

KEHOE, T.F. 1967. *The Boarding School Bison Drive Site.* Plains Anthropologist, Memoir 4.

——1973. *The Gull Lake Site: a prehistoric bison drive site in southwestern Saskatchewan.* Publications in Anth. & History No. 1: Milwaukee Public Museum.

KILLINGLEY, J.S. 1981. Seasonality of mollusc collecting determined from 0–18 profiles of midden shells. *American Antiquity* 46, 152–58.

KIRCH, P.V. & YEN, D.E. 1982. *Tikopia: the Prehistory and Ecology of a Polynesian Outlier.* Bishop Museum Bull. 238: Honolulu.

KISLEV, M.E., NADEL, D. & CARMI, I. 1992.

Epipalaeolithic (19,000 BP) cereal and fruit diet at Ohalo II, Sea of Galilee, Israel. *Review of Palaeobotany and Palynology* 73, 161–66.

KLEIN, R.G. & CRUZ-URIBE, K. 1984. *The Analysis of Animal Bones from Archaeological Sites*. Univ. of Chicago Press.

KNIGHTS, B.A. & others. 1983. Evidence concerning Roman military diet at Bearsden, Scotland, in the 2nd century AD. *Journal of Arch. Science* 10, 139–52.

KOIKE, H. 1979. Seasonal dating and the valve-pairing technique. *Journal of Arch. Science* 6, 63–74.

———1980. *Seasonal dating by growth-line counting of the clam,* Meretrix lusoria. *Toward a reconstruction of prehistoric shell-collecting activities in Japan*. Univ. Museum Bull. 18, Univ. of Tokyo.

———1986. Prehistoric hunting pressure and paleobiomass: an environmental reconstruction and archaeozoological analysis of a Jomon shellmound area, in *Prehistoric Hunter-Gatherers in Japan – New Research Methods* (T. Akazawa & C.M. Aikens eds.), 27–53. Univ. Museum Bull. 27, Univ. of Tokyo.

———& ——— 1985. Prehistoric hunting pressure estimated by the age composition of excavated Sika Deer (*Cervus nippon*) using the annual layer of tooth cement. *Journal of Arch. Science* 12, 443–56.

———& OHTAISHI, N. 1987. Estimation of prehistoric hunting rates based on the age composition of sika deer (*Cervus nippon*). *Journal of Arch. Science* 14, 251–69.

LALUEZA, C.J.J. & PÉREZ-PÉREZ, A. 1994. Dietary information through the examination of plant phytoliths on the enamel surface of human dentition. *Journal of Arch. Science* 21, 29–34.

LARSEN, C.S. 1983. Behavioural implications of temporal change in cariogenesis. *Journal of Arch. Science* 10, 1–8.

LEAKEY, M. 1987. Animal prints and trails, in *Laetoli, a Pliocene site in northern Tanzania* (M. Leakey & J.M. Harris eds.), 451–89. Clarendon Press: Oxford.

LEGGE, A.J. & ROWLEY-CONWY, P.A. 1987. Gazelle killing in Stone Age Syria. *Scientific American* 257 (2), 76–83.

———& ———1988. *Star Carr Revisited: a Reanalysis of the Large Mammals*. Birkbeck College, Centre for Extra-Mural Studies: London.

LENTZ, D.L. & others. 1996. Foodstuffs, forests, fields and shelter: a paleoethnobotanical analysis of vessel contents from the Cerén site, El Salvador. *Latin American Antiquity* 7 (3), 247–62.

LIEBERMAN, D.E., DEACON, T.W. & MEADOW, R.H. 1990. Computer image enhancement and analysis of cementum increments as applied to teeth of *Gazella gazella*. *Journal of Arch. Science* 17, 519–33.

LOFTUS, R.T. & others. 1994. Evidence for two independent domestications of cattle. *Proc. Nat. Acad. Sci. USA* 91, 2757–61.

LOREILLE, O. & others. 1997. First distinction of sheep and goat archaeological bones by the means of their fossil DNA. *Journal of Arch. Science* 24, 33–37.

LOY, T.H. 1983. Prehistoric blood residues: detection on tool surfaces and identification of species of origin. *Science* 220, 1269–71.

———1987. Recent advances in blood residue analysis, in *Archaeometry: Further Australasian Studies* (W.R. Ambrose & J.M.J. Mummery eds.), 57–65. Australian National Univ.: Canberra.

———1993. The artifact as site: an example of the biomolecular analysis of organic residues on prehistoric tools. *World Arch.* 25, 44–63.

———& HARDY, B.L. 1992. Blood residue analysis of 90,000-year-old stone tools from Tabun Cave, Israel. *Antiquity* 66, 24–35.

———& WOOD, A.R. 1989. Blood residue analysis at Çayönü Tepesi, Turkey. *Journal of Field Arch.* 16, 451–60.

———, SPRIGGS, M. & WICKLER, S. 1992. Direct evidence for human use of plants 28,000 years ago: starch residues on stone artefacts from the northern Solomon Islands. *Antiquity* 66, 898–912.

LYMAN, R.L. 1979. Available meat from faunal remains: a consideration of techniques. *American Antiquity* 44, 536–46.

———1982. Archaeofaunas and subsistence studies, in *Advances in Archaeological Method and Theory* 5 (M.B. Schiffer ed.), 331–93. Academic Press: New York & London.

———1994. *Vertebrate Taphonomy*. Cambridge Univ. Press.

MCGOVERN, P.E. 1998. Wine for eternity/wine's prehistory. *Archaeology* 51 (4), July/August, 28–34.

———, FLEMING, S. & KATZ, S. (eds.). 1996a. *The Origins and Ancient History of Wine*. Gordon & Breach: New York.

———& others. 1996b. Neolithic resinated wine. *Nature* 381, 480–01.

MEADOW, R.H. 1980. Animal bones: problems for the archaeologist together with some possible solutions. *Paléorient* 6, 65–77.

———1996. The origins and spread of agriculture and pastoralism in northwestern South Asia, in *The Origins and Spread of Agriculture and Pastoralism in Eurasia* (D.R. Harris ed.), 390–412. UCL Press: London.

MEIGHAN, C.W. 1969. Molluscs as food remains in archaeological sites, in *Science in Archaeology* (D.R. Brothwell & E.S. Higgs eds.), 415–22. (2nd ed.) Thames & Hudson: London.

MELLAART, J. 1967. *Çatal Hüyük*. Thames & Hudson: London.

MELLARS, P.A. & WILKINSON, M.R. 1980. Fish otoliths as evidence of seasonality in prehistoric shell middens: the evidence from Oronsay (Inner Hebrides). *Proc. Prehist. Soc.* 46, 19–44.

VAN DER MERWE, N.J., ROOSEVELT, A.C. & VOGEL, J.C. 1981. Isotopic evidence for prehistoric subsistence change at Parmana, Venezuela. *Nature* 292, 536–38.

MILLER, N.F. 1996. Seed eaters of the ancient Near East: Human or herbivore? *Current Anth.* 37 (3), 521–28.

MONKS, G.M. 1981. Seasonality studies, in *Advances in Archaeological Method and Theory* 4 (M.B. Schiffer ed.), 177–240. Academic Press: New York & London.

MOORE, A.M.T. 1975. The excavation of Tell Abu Hureyra in Syria: a preliminary report. *Proc. Prehist. Soc.* 41, 50–77.

———1979. A pre-Neolithic farmers' village on the Euphrates. *Scientific American* 241, 50–58.

NADEL, D. & HERSHKOVITZ, I. 1991. New subsistence data and human remains from the earliest Levantine Epipalaeolithic. *Current Anth.* 32, 631–35.

NESBITT, M. 1995. Plants and people in ancient Anatolia. *Biblical Archaeologist* 58: 2, 68–81.

NEWMAN, M.E. & others. 1996. The use of immunological techniques in the analysis of archaeological materials – a response to Eisele; with report of studies at Head-Smashed-In buffalo jump. *Antiquity* 70, 677–82.

NOE-NYGAARD, N. 1974. Mesolithic hunting in Denmark illustrated by bone injuries caused by human weapons. *Journal of Arch. Science* 1, 217–48.

———1975. Two shoulder blades with healed lesions from Star Carr. *Proc. Prehist. Soc.* 41, 10–16.

———1977. Butchering and marrow-fracturing as a taphonomic factor in archaeological deposits. *Paleobiology* 3, 218–37.

———1987. Taphonomy in Archaeology. *Journal of Danish Arch.* 6, 7–62.

OLSEN, S.J. 1979. Archaeologically, what constitutes an early domestic animal?, in *Advances in Archaeological Method and Theory* 2 (M.B. Schiffer ed.), 175–97. Academic Press: New York & London.

———& SHIPMAN, P. 1988. Surface modifications on bone: trampling versus butchering. *Journal of Arch. Science*, 15, 535–53.

PATRICK, M., DE KONING, A.J. & SMITH, A.B. 1985. Gas liquid chromatographic analysis of fatty acids in food residues from ceramics found in the Southwestern Cape, South Africa. *Archaeometry* 27, 231–36.

PEARSALL, D.M. 1978. Phytolith analysis of archaeological soils: evidence for maize cultivation in Formative Ecuador, *Science* 199, 177–78.

———1989. *Paleoethnobotany*. Academic Press: New York & London.

PETER-RÖCHER, H. 1994. *Kannibalismus in der prähistorischen Forschung*. Universitätsforschungen zur

Prähistorischen Archäolgie, Band 20. Rudolf Habelt GmbH: Bonn.

PICKERING, M.P. 1989. Food for thought: an alternative to Cannibalism in the Neolithic. *Australian Arch.* 28, 35–39.

PIPERNO, D.R. 1984. A comparison and differentiation of phytoliths from maize and wild grasses: uses of morphological criteria. *American Antiquity* 49, 361–83.

——& HOLST, I. 1998. The presence of starch grains on prehistoric stone tools from the humid neotropics: indications of early tuber use and agriculture in Panama. *Journal of Arch. Science* 25, 765–76.

——& PEARSALL, D.M. 1998. *The Origins of Agriculture in the Lowland Neotropics.* Academic Press: Orlando.

——& others. 1985. Preceramic maize in Central Panama: Phytolith and pollen evidence. *American Anthropologist* 87, 871–78.

POTTS, R. 1988. *Early hominid activities at Olduvai.* Aldine de Gruyter: New York.

——& SHIPMAN, P. 1981. Cutmarks made by stone tools on bones from Olduvai Gorge, Tanzania. *Nature* 291, 577–80.

PRICE, N. 1995. Houses and horses in the Swedish Bronze Age: recent excavation in the Mälar Valley. *Past* (Newsletter of the Prehist. Soc.) 20, 5–6.

PRICE, T.D. (ed.). 1989. *The Chemistry of Prehistoric Human Bone.* Cambridge Univ. Press.

PUECH, P.-F. 1978. L'alimentation de l'homme préhistorique. *La Recherche* 9, 1029–31.

——1979a. The diet of early man: evidence from abrasion of teeth and tools. *Current Anth.* 20, 590–92.

——1979b. L'alimentation de l'homme de Tautavel d'après l'usure des surfaces dentaires, in *L'Homme de Tautavel, Dossiers de l'Arch.* 36, 84–85.

——, PRONE, A. & KRAATZ, R. 1980. Microscopie de l'usure dentaire chez l'homme fossile: bol alimentaire et environnement. *Comptes rendus Acad. Sciences* 290, 1413–16.

REIGADAS, M.C. 1992. La punta del ovillo: determinación de domesticación y pastoreo a partir del análisis microscópico de fibras y folículos pilosos de camélidos. *Arqueología* (Buenos Aires) 2, 9–52.

REINHARD, K.J. & BRYANT, V.M. 1992. Coprolite analysis, in *Archaeological Method and Theory* 14 (M. Schiffer, ed.), 245–88. Univ. of Arizona Press: Tucson.

——& others. 1992. Discovery of colon contents in a skeletonized burial: soil sampling for dietary remains. *Journal of Arch. Science* 19, 697–705.

REITZ, E.J. & WING, E.S. 1999. *Zooarchaeology.* Cambridge Univ. Press.

RENFREW, J. 1973. *Palaeoethnobotany.* Methuen: London; Columbia: New York.

——(ed.). 1991. *New Light on Early Farming. Recent developments in Palaeoethnobotany.* Edinburgh Univ. Press.

REYNOLDS, P.J. 1979. *Iron Age Farm. The Butser Experiment.* British Museum Publications: London.

ROBERTS, G. & others. 1996. Intertidal Holocene footprints and their archaeological significance. *Antiquity* 70, 647–51.

ROTTLÄNDER, R.C.A. 1986. Chemical investigation of potsherds of the Heuneburg, Upper Danube, in *Proc. 24th Int. Archaeometric Symposium* (J.S. Olin & M.J. Blackman eds.), 403–05. Smithsonian Institution Press: Washington D.C.

——& HARTKE, I. 1982. New results of food identification by fat analysis, in *Proc. 22nd Symposium on Archaeometry* (A. Aspinall & S.E. Warren eds.), 218–23. Univ. of Bradford.

——& SCHLICHTHERLE, H. 1979. Food identification from archaeological sites. *Archaeo-Physika* 10, 260–07.

RUSSELL, M. 1987. Mortuary practices at the Krapina Neanderthal site. *American Journal of Phys. Anth.* 72, 381–97.

RYDER, M.L. 1969. Remains derived from skin, in *Science in Archaeology* (D.R. Brothwell & E.S. Higgs eds.), 539–54. (2nd ed.) Thames & Hudson: London.

SAFFIRIO, L. 1972. Food and dietary habits in ancient Egypt. *Journal of Human Evolution* 1, 297–305.

SAMUEL, D. 1996. Investigation of ancient Egyptian baking and brewing methods by correlative microscopy. *Science* 273, 488–90.

VAN DER SANDEN, W. 1996. *Through Nature to Eternity. The Bog Bodies of Northwest Europe.* Batavian Lion International: Amsterdam.

SCHELVIS, J. 1992. The identification of archaeological dung deposits on the basis of remains of predatory mites (Acari; Gamasida). *Journal of Arch. Science* 19, 677–82.

SCHOENINGER, M.J. 1979. Diet and status at Chalcatzingo: some empirical and technical aspects of Strontium analysis. *American Journal of Phys. Anth.* 51, 295–310

——1981. The agricultural "revolution": its effect on human diet in prehistoric Iran and Israel. *Paléorient* 7, 73–92.

——& PEEBLES, C.S. 1981. Effect of mollusc eating on human bone strontium levels. *Journal of Arch. Science* 8, 391–97.

——, DENIRO, M.J. & TAUBER, H. 1983. Stable nitrogen isotope ratios of bone collagen reflect marine and terrestrial components of prehistoric human diet. *Science* 220, 1381–83.

SCHWARCZ, H.P. & others. 1985. Stable isotopes in human skeletons of Southern Ontario: reconstructing palaeodiet. *Journal of Arch. Science* 12, 187–206.

SEALY, J.C. 1986. *Stable Carbon Isotopes and Prehistoric Diets in the South-Western Cape Province, South Africa.* British Arch. Reports, Int. Series No. 293: Oxford.

——& VAN DER MERWE, N.J. 1986. Isotope assessment and the seasonal mobility hypothesis in the Southwestern Cape of South Africa. *Current Anth.* 27, 135–50.

SHACKLETON, N.J. 1969. Marine molluscs in archaeology, in *Science in Archaeology* (D.R. Brothwell & E.S. Higgs eds.), 407–14. (2nd ed.) Thames & Hudson: London.

——1973. Oxygen isotope analysis as a means of determining season of occupation of prehistoric midden sites. *Archaeometry* 15, 133–43.

SHEPPARD, R.A. 1985. Using shells to determine season of occupation of prehistoric sites. *New Zealand Journal of Arch.* 7, 77–93.

SHERRATT, A. 1981. Plough and pastoralism: aspects of the secondary products revolution, in *Pattern of the Past, Studies in Honour of David Clarke* (I. Hodder & others eds.), 261–305. Cambridge Univ. Press.

SHIPMAN, P. & ROSE, J.J. 1983. Early hominid hunting, butchering and carcass-processing behaviours: approaches to the fossil record. *Journal of Anth. Arch.* 2, 57–98.

SILLEN, A. 1994. L'alimentation des hommes préhistoriques. *La Recherche* 25, 384–90.

SILVER, I.A. 1969. The ageing of domestic animals, in *Science in Archaeology* (D.R. Brothwell & E.S. Higgs eds.), 283–302. (2nd ed.) Thames & Hudson: London.

SINGER, R. & WYMER, J. 1982. *The Middle Stone Age at Klasies River Mouth in South Africa.* Univ. of Chicago Press.

SMITH, B.D. 1975. Towards a more accurate estimation of the meat yield of animal species at archaeological sites, in *Archaeozoological Studies* (A.T. Clason ed.), 99–106. North-Holland: Amsterdam.

——1984. *Chenopodium* as a prehistoric domestate in Eastern North America: Evidence from Russell Cave, Alabama. *Science* 226, 165–67.

——1992. *Rivers of Change. Essays on early agriculture in Eastern North America.* Smithsonian Institution Press: Washington D.C.

——1995. *The Emergence of Agriculture.* W.H. Freeman: London; Scientific American Library: New York.

SPETH, J.D. 1983. *Bison Kills and Bone Counts: Decision Making by Ancient Hunters.* Univ. of Chicago Press.

SPIESS, A.E. 1979. *Reindeer and Caribou Hunters: An Archaeological Study.* Academic Press: New York & London.

SPONHEIMER, M. & LEE-THORP, J. 1999. Isotopic evidence for the diet of an early hominid, *Australopithecus africanus. Science* 283, 368–70.

STEAD, I.M., BOURKE, J.B. & BROTHWELL, D. (eds.). 1986. *Lindow Man. The Body in the Bog.* British Museum Publications: London.

————& TURNER, R.C. 1985. Lindow Man. *Antiquity* 59, 25–29.

STEIN, J. (ed.). 1992. *Deciphering a Shell Midden.* Academic Press: New York.

SVITIL, K.A. 1994. What the Nubians ate. *Discover*, June, 36–37.

TAUBER, H. 1981. 13C evidence for dietary habits of prehistoric man in Denmark. *Nature* 292, 332–33.

TSUKUDA, M., SUGITA, S. & TSUKUDA, Y. 1986. Oldest primitive agriculture and vegetational environments in Japan. *Nature* 322, 632–64.

TURNER, C.G. & TURNER, J.A. 1999. *Man Corn. Cannibalism and Violence in the Prehistoric Southwest.* Univ. of Utah Press: Salt Lake City.

UCKO, P.J. & DIMBLEBY, G.W. (eds.). 1969. *The Domestication and Exploitation of Plants and Animals.* Duckworth: London.

UNESCO. 1984. *Recent Archaeological Discoveries in the People's Republic of China.*

VILLA, P. & others. 1986. Cannibalism in the Neolithic. *Science* 233, 431–37.

VITA-FINZI, C. & HIGGS, E.S. 1970. Prehistoric economy in the Mount Carmel area of Palestine: site catchment analysis. *Proc. Prehist. Soc.* 36, 1–37.

WEIGELT, J. 1989. *Recent Vertebrate Carcasses and their Palaeobiological Implications.* Univ. of Chicago Press.

WENDORF, F., SCHILD, R. & CLOSE, A. (eds.). 1980. *Loaves and Fishes. The Prehistory of Wadi Kubbaniya.* Southern Methodist Univ. Press: Dallas.

WHEAT, J.B. 1972. *The Olsen-Chubbuck Site: a Paleo-Indian bison kill.* Soc. for American Arch., Memoir No. 26.

WHEELER, A. & JONES, A.K.G. 1989. *Fishes.* Cambridge Univ. Press.

WHEELER, J.C. 1984. On the origin and early development of camelid pastoralism in the Andes, in *Animals and Archaeology 3: Herders and their Flocks* (J. Clutton-Brock & C. Grigson eds.), 395–410. British Arch. Reports, Int. Series 202: Oxford.

WHITE, T.D. 1992. *Prehistoric Cannibalism.* Princeton Univ. Press.

WHITE, T.E. 1953. A method of calculating the dietary percentage of various food animals utilized by aboriginal peoples. *American Antiquity* 18, 393–99.

————1953/4. Observations on the butchering techniques of some Aboriginal peoples. *American Antiquity* 19, 160–4, 254–64.

WILSON, B., GRIGSON, C. & PAYNE, S. (eds.). 1982. *Ageing and Sexing Animal Bones from Archaeological Sites.* British Arch. Reports, Int. Series 109: Oxford.

VAN ZEIST, W. & CASPARIE, W.A. (eds.). 1984. *Plants and Ancient Man: Studies in Palaeoethnobotany.* Balkema: Rotterdam & Boston.

————& others. 1991. *Progress in Old World Palaeoethnobotany.* Balkema: Rotterdam.

ZOHARY, D. & HOPF, M. 1993. *Domestication of Plants in the Old World* (2nd ed.). Clarendon Press: Oxford.

Chapter 8: How Did They Make and Use Tools? Technology (pp. 311–350)

p. 311 **Industrial archaeology** Hudson 1963, 1979, 1983; *World Archaeology* 15 (2) 1983; and the journals *Industrial Arch.* (since 1964) and *Industrial Arch. Review* (since 1976). **Experimental archaeology** Ascher 1961; Coles 1973, 1979; Ingersoll & others 1977. See also *Dossiers de l'Archéologie* 46 (1980), 126 (1988), and 216 (1996).

p. 312 **Wood pseudomorphs** Castro-Curel & Carbonell 1995.

pp. 312–13 **Recognition of human agency** Barnes 1939; Patterson 1983; McGrew 1992; Toth & others 1993 (chimps). Calico Hills objects: Patterson & others 1987 ("for"); Haynes 1973 ("against"); Pakistan, Rendell & others 1989.

p. 313 **Ethnographic analogy** Bray 1978, p. 177 (Tairona pendant).

pp. 315–16 **Mines and quarries** In general: Shepherd 1980; *World Archaeology* 16 (2), 1984. Sieveking & Newcomer 1987 (flint mines); Bosch 1979 (Rijckholt); Jovanovic 1979, 1980 (Rudna Glava); Protzen 1986, 1993 (Incas); Alexander 1982 (salt); Bahn & Flenley 1992 (Easter Island).

p. 316 **Stone transportation** Protzen 1986 (Inca); Thom 1984 (Brittany menhirs). In general: Cotterell & Kamminga 1990.

pp. 316–19 **Construction work** Coulton 1977 (Greece); Haselberger 1985 (Didyma temple); Haselberger 1995 (Pantheon).

pp. 319–23 **Stone tool manufacture** Schick & Toth 1993; Boëda & others 1996 (hafting). Ethnographic studies: Gould 1980; Gould & others 1971; Hayden 1979a (Australia); Hayden 1987 (Maya); Toth & others 1992 (New Guinea). Egyptian depictions of flint knife production: Barnes 1947. **Replication studies** Crabtree 1970; Sieveking & Newcomer 1987; Toth 1987. Clovis point: Frison 1989. Folsom point: Crabtree 1966; Flenniken 1978. **Heat treatment** of stone tools: Domanski & Webb 1992; Gregg & Grybush 1976; Robins & others 1978; Rowlett & others 1974. Florida chert: Purdy & Brooks 1971. Solutrean: Bordes 1969; Collins 1973. Analysis by **thermoluminescence** Melcer & Zimmerman 1977. **Refitting** Cahen & Karlin 1980; Olive 1988; Cziesia & others 1990. For a cautionary view: Bordes 1980. Etiolles example: Pigeot 1988.

pp. 323–26 **Microwear** Hayden 1979b; Meeks & others 1982; Vaughan 1985. Russian work: Semenov 1964; Phillips 1988. Tringham's work: Tringham & others 1974. Keeley's work: Keeley 1974, 1977, 1980; Keeley & Newcomer 1977. Boomplaas experiment: Binneman &

Deacon 1986. Japanese work: Akoshima 1980; Kajiwara & Akoshima 1981. Vance 1987 covers **microdebitage**; Fischer & others 1984 (Danish projectile point tests). For projectile point experiments and function, Knecht 1997

p. 326 **Identifying function** Pitts & Roberts 1997, chapter 41 (handaxes); de Beaune 1987a, 1987b (Paleolithic lamps); Haury 1931 (Arizona beads).

pp. 326–27 **Technology of Stone Age art** Bahn & Vertut 1997; Bahn 1990; Clottes 1993. Thomas 1983 (Monitor Basin); Marshack 1975 (Marshack's work); Lorblanchet 1980, 1991 (Pech Merle experiments); Pales & de St Péreuse 1966 (technique of making relief-imprints); d'Errico 1987 (varnish replicas); d'Errico 1996 (surface profiling).

pp. 327–29 **Technology of animal products** General introduction: Macgregor 1985. Johnson 1985; Olsen 1989; d'Errico 1993a (natural or artificial bone tools); Francis 1982 (Indian shell experiments); d'Errico 1993b (microscopic criteria). **Manufacture** Smith & Poggenpoel 1988 (Kasteelberg); Campana 1987. **Function** Thompson 1954; Arndt & Newcomer 1986; Knecht 1997; Pokines 1998 (bone point experiments); Bahn 1976 (perforated batons); Campana 1979 (Natufian shoulder-blade); d'Errico & others 1984a, 1984b (varnish replicas); Coles 1962 (leather shield experiment).

pp. 329–33 **Wood technology** General introduction: Noël & Bocquet 1987. Particular reference to Britain: Coles & others 1978. Beaver marks: Coles & Orme 1983; Coles & Coles 1986 pl. 25. **Wheeled vehicles**: Piggott 1983. **Watercraft** Steffy 1994; Bass 1972, 1988; Hale 1980; Jenkins 1980 (Cheops ship); Welsh 1988 (trireme).

pp. 333–34 **Plant and animal fibers** Basketry: Adovasio 1977. Cordage impressions: Hurley 1979. Dyeing at York: Hall & Tomlinson 1984; Tomlinson 1985. **Textiles** Barber 1991 (general); Anton 1987; Amano 1979 (Peru); Dwyer 1973 (Nazca); Broadbent 1985 (Chibcha). Egyptian: Lucas & Harris 1962; Cockburn & others 1998. Hochdorf: Körber-Grohne 1987, 1988; Adovasio & others 1996 (Pavlov).

p. 334 **Fiber microwear** Cooke & Lomas 1987.

pp. 335–49 **Synthetic materials** Singer & others 1954. General works on scientific analysis: Tite 1972; Rottländer 1983; and *Dossiers de l'Archéologie* 42, 1980 (L'analyse des objets archéologiques).

pp. 335–36 **Pyrotechnology** Good general introduction: Perlès 1977. Thermal shock: Vandiver & others 1989.

pp. 336–38 **Pottery** General works: Anderson 1984; Barnett & Hoopes 1995; Bronitsky 1986; Gibson & Woods 1990; Matson 1969; Millet 1979; Orton & others 1993; Rice 1982, 1987; Rye 1981;

Shepard 1985; Van der Leeuw & Pritchard 1984. Also *World Archaeology* vols. 15 (3), 1984 (Ceramics); 21 (1), 1989 (Ceramic Technology). **Pot tempers** Bronitsky & Hamer 1986. **Firing of pots** Tite 1969. Kingery & Frierman 1974 (Karanovo sherd); Burns 1987 (kilns in Thailand); DeBoer & Lathrap 1979 (Shipibo-Conibo).

pp. 338–39 **Faience** Aspinall & others 1972. **Glass** Frank 1982; also Biek & Bayley 1979; Smith 1969; Bimson & Freestone 1987; Tait 1991. Green & Hart 1987 (Roman glass). Sayre & Smith 1961 (glass analyses); Henderson 1980; Hughes 1972 (British Iron Age).

pp. 339–42 **Archaeometallurgy** General works: Tylecote 1962, 1976; Lamberg-Karlovsky 1970. See also *World Archaeology* 20 (3), 1989. Coghlan 1951 (Old World); Tylecote 1987 (Europe); Tylecote 1986 (Britain); Benson 1979; Bray 1978 (S. America).

p. 342 **Alloying** Budd & others 1992 (arsenic); Eaton & McKerrell 1976. Hendy & Charles 1970 (Byzantine coins).

pp. 343–46 **Casting** Long 1965; Bray 1978 (lost-wax method). Bruhns 1972 (preserved molds); Rottländer 1986 (residues). Barnard & Tamotsu 1965; Barnard 1961 (Chinese metallurgy).

pp. 346–49 **Silver** Blanco & Luzon 1969 (Rio Tinto). **Fine metalwork** Alva & Donnan 1993. Shimada & Griffin 1994; Wulff 1966 (traditional methods). Grossman 1972 (goldwork). **Plating** La Niece & Craddock 1993; Lechtman 1984; Lechtman and others 1982 (Loma Negra work). **Iron** Coghlan 1956.

Box Features

p. 314 **Artifacts or "Geofacts" at Pedra Furada?** Parenti & others 1990; Guidon & Arnaud 1991; Meltzer & others 1994; Guidon & others 1996; Parenti 2000.

p. 318 **Raising Large Stones** Pavel 1992, 1995; see also Scarre 1999.

pp. 324–25 **Refitting and Microwear Studies** Meer site: Cahen & Keeley 1980; Cahen & others 1979; van Noten 1978; van Noten & others 1980.

pp. 330–31 **Woodworking in the Somerset Levels** Coles & Coles 1986.

p. 341 **Metallographic Examination** Thompson 1969.

pp. 344–45 **Copper Production in Peru** Shimada & others 1982; Merkel & Shimada 1988; Shimada & Merkel 1991; Burger & Gordon 1998.

p. 348 **Early Steelmaking** Ethnoarchaeology in general: Kramer 1979. Haya of Tanzania: Schmidt & Avery 1978; van Noten & Raymaekers 1988; Schmidt 1996.

Bibliography

ADOVASIO, J.M. 1977. *Basketry Technology. A Guide to Identification and Analysis.* Aldine: Chicago.

————— & **others.** 1996. Upper Palaeolithic fibre technology: interlaced woven finds from Pavlov I, Czech Republic, *c.* 26,000 years ago. *Antiquity* 70, 526–34.

AKOSHIMA, K. 1980. An experimental study of microflaking. *Kokogaku Zasshi* (Journal of the Arch. Soc. of Nippon) 66, 357–83 (English summary).

ALEXANDER, J. 1982. The prehistoric salt trade in Europe. *Nature* 300, 577–78.

ALVA, W. & DONNAN, C. 1993. *Royal Tombs of Sipán.* Fowler Museum of Cultural History, Univ. of California: Los Angeles.

AMANO, Y. 1979. *Textiles of the Andes.* Heian/Dohosa: San Francisco.

ANDERSON, A. 1984. *Interpreting Pottery.* Batsford: London.

ANTON, F. 1987. *Ancient Peruvian Textiles.* Thames & Hudson: London.

ARNDT, S. & NEWCOMER, M. 1986. Breakage patterns on prehistoric bone points: an experimental study, in *Studies in the Upper Palaeolithic of Britain and NW Europe* (D.A. Roe ed.), 165–73. British Arch. Reports, Int. Series 296: Oxford.

ASCHER, R. 1961. Experimental archaeology. *American Anthropologist* 63, 793–816.

ASPINALL, A. & others. 1972. Neutron activation analysis of faience beads. *Archaeometry* 14, 27–40.

BAHN, P.G. 1976. Les bâtons percés . . . réveil d'une hypothèse abandonnée. *Bull. Soc. Préhist. Ariège* 31, 47–54.

—————1990. Pigments of the imagination. *Nature* 347, 426.

————— & **FLENLEY, J.** 1992. *Easter Island, Earth Island.* Thames & Hudson: London & New York.

————— & **VERTUT, J.** 1997. *Journey through the Ice Age.* Weidenfeld & Nicolson: London; Univ. of California Press: Berkeley.

BARBER, E.J.W. 1991. *Prehistoric Textiles. The Development of Cloth in the Neolithic and Bronze Ages.* Princeton Univ. Press.

BARNARD, N. 1961. *Bronze Casting and Bronze Alloys in Ancient China.* Australian National Univ.: Canberra.

————— & **TAMOTSU, S.** 1965. *Metallurgical Remains of Ancient China.* Nichiosha: Tokyo.

BARNES, A.S. 1939. The differences between natural and human flaking on flint implements. *American Anthropologist* 41, 99–112.

—————1947. The technique of blade production in Mesolithic and Neolithic times. *Proc. Prehist. Soc.* 13, 101–13.

BARNETT, W.K. & HOOPES, J.W. (eds.). 1995. *The Emergence of Pottery. Technology and Innovation in Ancient Societies.* Smithsonian Institution Press: Washington D.C.

BASS, G. (ed.) 1972. *A History of Seafaring based on Underwater Archaeology.* Thames & Hudson: London.

—————(ed.) 1988. *Ships & Shipwrecks of the Americas.* Thames & Hudson: London & New York.

DE BEAUNE, S. 1987a. *Lampes et godets au*

Paléolithique. Supplément à Gallia Préhistoire.

—————1987b. Paleolithic lamps and their specialization: a hypothesis. *Current Anth.* 28, 569–77.

BENSON, E.P. (ed.). 1979. *Pre-Columbian Metallurgy of South America.* Dumbarton Oaks Research Library: Washington D.C.

BIEK, L. & BAYLEY, J. 1979. Glass and other vitreous materials. *World Arch.* 11, 1–25

BIMSON, M. & FREESTONE, J.C. (eds.). 1987. *Early Vitreous Materials.* British Museum Occasional Paper 56. British Museum: London.

BINNEMAN, J. & DEACON, J. 1986. Experimental determination of use wear on stone adzes from Boomplaas Cave, South Africa. *Journal of Arch. Science* 13, 219–28.

BLANCO, A. & LUZON, J.M. 1969. Pre-Roman silver miners at Riotinto. *Antiquity* 43, 124–31.

BOEDA, E. & others. 1996. Bitumen as a hafting material on Middle Palaeolithic artifacts. *Nature* 380, 336–38.

BORDES, F. 1969. Traitement thermique du silex au Solutréen. *Bull. Soc. Préhist. française* 66, 197.

—————1980. Question de contemporanéité: l'illusion des remontages. *Bull. Soc. Préhist. française,* 77, 132–33; see also 230–34.

BOSCH, P.W. 1979. A Neolithic flint mine. *Scientific American* 240, 98–103.

BRAY, W. 1978. *The Gold of El Dorado.* Times Newspapers Ltd: London.

BROADBENT, S.M. 1985. Chibcha textiles in the British Museum. *Antiquity* 59, 202–05.

BRONITSKY, G. 1986. The use of materials science techniques in the study of pottery construction and use, in *Advances in Archaeological method and Theory* 9 (M.B. Schiffer ed.), 209–76. Academic Press: New York & London.

————— & **HAMER, R.** 1986. Experiments in ceramic technology. The effects of various tempering materials on impact and thermal-shock resistance. *American Antiquity* 51, 89–101.

BRUHNS, K.O. 1972. Two prehispanic *cire perdue* casting moulds from Colombia. *Man* 7, 308–11.

BUDD, P. & others. 1992. The early development of metallurgy in the British Isles. *Antiquity* 66, 677–86.

BURGER, R.L. & GORDON, R.B. 1998. Early Central Andean metalworking from Mina Perdida, Peru. *Science* 282, 1108–11.

BURNS, P.L. 1987. Thai ceramics: the archaeology of the production centres, in *Archaeometry: Further Australasian Studies* (W.R. Ambrose & J.M.J. Mummery eds.), 203–12. Australian National Univ.: Canberra.

CAHEN, D. & KARLIN, C. 1980. Les artisans de la préhistoire. *La Recherche* 116, 1258–68.

————— & **KEELEY, L.H.** 1980. Not less than two,

not more than three. *World Arch.* 12, 166–80.

——, **KEELEY, L.H. & VAN NOTEN, F.** 1979. Stone tools, tool-kits and human behaviour in prehistory. *Current Anth.* 20, 661–83.

CAMPANA, D.V. 1979. A Natufian shaft-straightener from Mughuret El Wad, Israel: an example of wear-pattern analysis. *Journal of Field Arch.* 6, 237–42.

——1987. The manufacture of bone tools in the Zagros and the Levant. *MASCA Journal* 4 (3), 110–23.

CASTRO-CUREL, Z. & CARBONELL, E. 1995. Wood pseudomorphs from Level I at Abric Romani, Barcelona, Spain. *J. Field Arch.* 22, 376–84.

CLOTTES, J. 1993. Paint analyses from several Magdalenian caves in the Ariège region of France. *Journal of Arch. Science* 20, 223–35.

COCKBURN, T.A., COCKBURN E., & REYMAN, T.A. (eds.). 1998. *Mummies, Disease and Ancient Cultures.* (2nd ed.). Cambridge Univ. Press.

COGHLAN, H.H. 1951. *Notes on the Prehistoric Metallurgy of Copper and Bronze in the Old World.* Pitt Rivers Museum: Oxford.

——1956. *Notes on Prehistoric and Early Iron in the Old World.* Pitt Rivers Museum: Oxford.

COLES, B. & J. 1986. *Sweet Track to Glastonbury. The Somerset Levels Project.* Thames & Hudson: London.

COLES, J.M. 1962. European bronze shields. *Proc. Prehist. Soc.* 28, 156–90.

——1973. *Archaeology by Experiment.* Hutchinson: London.

——1979. *Experimental Archaeology.* Academic Press: New York & London.

——, **HEAL, S.V.E., & ORME, B.J.** 1978. The use and character of wood in prehistoric Britain and Ireland. *Proc. Prehist. Soc.* 44, 1–46.

——**& ORME, B.J.** 1983. *Homo sapiens* or *Castor fiber? Antiquity* 57, 95–102.

COLLINS, M.B. 1973. Observations on the thermal treatment of chert in the Solutrean of Laugerie-Haute, France. *Proc. Prehist. Soc.* 39, 461–66.

COOKE, W.D. & LOMAS, B. 1987. Ancient textiles – modern technology. *Archaeology Today* 8 (2), March 21–25.

COTTERELL, B. & KAMMINGA, J. 1990. *Mechanics of Pre-Industrial Technology.* Cambridge Univ. Press.

COULTON, J.J. 1977. *Greek Architects at work: problems of structure and design.* Cornell Univ. Press.

CRABTREE, D.E. 1966. A stoneworker's approach to analyzing and replicating the Lindenmeier Folsom. *Tebiwa* 9, 3–139.

——1970. Flaking stone with wooden implements. *Science* 169, 146–53.

CZIESIA, E. & others (eds.). 1990. *The Big Puzzle. International Symposium on Refitting Stone Artefacts.* Studies in Modern Archaeology, Vol. 1, Holos-Verlag: Bonn.

DEBOER, W.R. & LATHRAP, D.W. 1979. The making and breaking of Shipibo-Conibo ceramics, in *Ethnoarchaeology: Implications of Ethnography for Archaeology* (C. Kramer ed.), 102–38. Columbia Univ. Press: New York.

DOMANSKI, M. & WEBB, J.A. 1992. Effect of heat treatment on siliceous rocks used in prehistoric lithic technology. *Journal of Arch. Science* 19, 601–14.

DWYER, J.P. 1973 *Paracas and Nazca Textiles.* Museum of Fine Arts: Boston.

EATON, E.R. & McKERRELL, H. 1976. Near Eastern alloying and some textual evidence for the early use of arsenical copper. *World Arch.* 8, 169–91.

D'ERRICO, F. 1987. Nouveaux indices et nouvelles techniques microscopiques pour la lecture de l'art gravé mobilier. *Comptes rendus de l'Acad. Science Paris* 304, série II, 761–64.

——1993a. Criteria for identifying utilised bone: the case of the Cantabrian "tensors". *Current Anth.* 34. 298–311.

——1993b. La vie sociale de l'art mobilier paléolithique. Manipulation, transport, suspension des objets en os, bois de cervidés, ivoire. *Oxford Journal of Arch.* 12, 145–74.

——1996. Image analysis and 3-D optical surface profiling of Upper Palaeolithic mobiliary art. *Microscopy and Analysis,* January, 27–29.

——, **GIACOBINI, G. & PUECH, P-F.** 1984a. Varnish replicas: a new method for the study of worked bone surfaces. *Ossa. International Journal of Skeletal Research* 9/10, 29–51.

——1984b. Les répliques en vernis des surfaces osseuses façonnées: études expérimentales. *Bull. Soc. Préhist. française* 81, 169–70.

FISCHER, A. & others. 1984. Macro and micro wear traces on lithic projectile points. Experimental results and prehistoric examples. *Journal of Danish Arch.* 3, 19–46.

FLENNIKEN, J.J. 1978. Reevaluating the Lindenmeier Folsom: a replication experiment in lithic technology. *American Antiquity* 43, 473–80.

FORBES, R.J. (series) *Studies in Ancient Technology.* E.J. Brill: Leiden.

FRANCIS, P. JR. 1982. Experiments with early techniques for making whole shells into beads. *Current Anth.* 23, 13–14.

FRANK, S. 1982. *Glass and Archaeology.* Academic Press: New York & London.

FRISON, G.C. 1989. Clovis tools and weaponry efficiency in an African elephant context. *American Antiquity* 54, 766–78.

GIBSON, A. & WOODS, A. 1990. *Prehistoric Pottery for the Archaeologist.* Leicester Univ. Press.

GOULD, R.A. 1980. *Living Archaeology.* Cambridge Univ. Press.

——, **KOSTER, D.A. & SONTZ, D.A.** 1971. The lithic assemblages of the Western Desert Aborigines of Australia. *American Antiquity* 36, 149–69.

GREEN, L.R. & HART, F.A. 1987. Colour and chemical composition in ancient glass: an examination of some Roman and Wealden glass by means of Ultraviolet-Visible-Infra-red Spectrometry and Electron Microprobe Analysis. *Journal of Arch. Science* 14, 271–82.

GREGG, M.L. & GRYBUSH, R.J. 1976. Thermally altered siliceous stone from prehistoric contexts: intentional vs unintentional. *American Antiquity* 41, 189–92.

GROSSMAN, J.W. 1972. An ancient gold worker's toolkit: the earliest metal technology in Peru. *Archaeology* 25, 270–75.

GUIDON, N. & ARNAUD, B. 1991. The chronology of the New World: two faces of one reality. *World Arch.* 23, 167–78.

——**& others.** 1996. Nature and the age of the deposits in Pedra Furada, Brazil: reply to Meltzer, Adovasio & Dillehay. *Antiquity* 70, 408–21.

HALE, J.R. 1980. Plank-built in the Bronze Age. *Antiquity* 54, 118–27.

HALL, A.R. & TOMLINSON, P.R. 1984. Dyeplants from Viking York. *Antiquity* 58, 58–60.

HASELBERGER, L. 1985. The construction plans for the temple of Apollo at Didyma. *Scientific American* 253, 114–22.

——1995. Deciphering a Roman blueprint. *Scientific American* 272 (6), 56–61.

HAURY, E.W. 1931. Minute beads from prehistoric pueblos. *American Anthropologist* 33, 80–87.

HAYDEN, B. 1979a. *Palaeolithic Reflections. Lithic technology and ethnographic excavations among Australian Aborigines.* Australian Inst. of Aboriginal Studies: Canberra.

——(ed.). 1979b. *Lithic Use-wear Analysis.* Academic Press: New York & London.

——(ed.). 1987. *Lithic Studies among the Contemporary Highland Maya.* Univ. of Arizona Press: Tucson.

HAYNES, C.V. 1973. The Calico Site: Artifacts or Geofacts? *Science* 181, 305–10.

HENDERSON, J. 1980. Some new evidence for Iron Age glass-working in Britain. *Antiquity* 54, 60–61.

HENDY, M.F. & CHARLES, J.A. 1970. The production techniques, silver content and circulation history of the twelfth-century Byzantine Trachy. *Archaeometry* 12, 13–21.

HUDSON, K. 1963. *Industrial Archaeology.* John Baker: London.

——1979. *World Industrial Archaeology.* Cambridge Univ. Press.

——1983. *The Archaeology of the Consumer Society.* Heinemann: London.

HUGHES, M.J. 1972. A technical study of opaque red glass of the Iron Age in Britain. *Proc. Prehist. Soc.* 38, 98–107.

HURLEY, W.M. 1979. *Prehistoric Cordage.*

Identification of Impressions on Pottery. Taraxacum: Washington.

INGERSOLL, D., YELLEN, J.E. & MACDONALD, W. (eds.). 1977. *Experimental Archaeology.* Columbia Univ. Press: New York.

JENKINS, N. 1980. *The Boat beneath the Pyramid.* Thames & Hudson: London; Holt, Rinehart & Winston: New York.

JOHNSON, E. 1985. Current developments in bone technology, in *Advances in Archaeological Method and Theory* 8 (M.B. Schiffer ed.), 157–235. Academic Press: New York & London.

JOVANOVIC, B. 1979. The technology of primary copper mining in South-East Europe. *Proc. Prehist. Soc.* 45, 103–10.

——1980. The origins of copper mining in Europe. *Scientific American* 242, 114–20.

KAJIWARA, H. & AKOSHIMA, K. 1981. An experimental study of microwear polish on shale artifacts. *Kokogaku Zasshi* (Journal of the Arch. Soc. of Nippon) 67, 1–36 (English summary).

KEELEY, L.H. 1974. Technique and methodology in microwear studies: a critical review. *World Arch.* 5, 323–36.

——1977. The function of Palaeolithic stone tools. *Scientific American* 237, 108–26.

——1980. *Experimental determination of stone tool uses. A microwear analysis.* Univ. of Chicago Press.

——& NEWCOMER, M.H. 1977. Microwear analysis of experimental flint tools: a test case. *Journal of Arch. Science* 4, 29–62.

KINGERY, W.D. & FRIERMAN, J.D. 1974. The firing temperature of a Karanovo sherd and inferences about South-East European Chalcolithic refractory technology. *Proc. Prehist. Soc.* 40, 204–05.

KNECHT, H. (ed.). 1997. *Projectile Technology.* Plenum Press: New York.

KÖRBER-GROHNE, V. 1987. Les restes de plantes et d'animaux de la tombe princière d'Hochdorf, in *Trésors des Princes Celtes.* Exhibition catalog, Min. de la Culture: Paris.

——1988. Microscopic methods for identification of plant fibres and animal hairs from the Prince's Tomb of Hochdorf, Southwest Germany. *Journal of Arch. Science* 15, 73–82.

KRAMER, C. 1979. *Ethnoarchaeology: Implications of Ethnography for Archaeology.* Columbia Univ. Press: New York.

LAMBERG-KARLOVSKY, C.C. 1970. Historical continuity, stage and process: the development of a metallurgical technology. *Zbornik Narodnog Muzeja u Beogradu* (Recueil du Musée National de Beograde) 6, 349–60.

LA NIECE, S. & CRADDOCK, P.T. 1993. *Metal Plating and Patination.* Butterworth Heinemann: London.

LECHTMAN, H. 1984. Pre-Columbian surface metallurgy. *Scientific American* 250, 38–45.

——, ERLIJ, A. & BARRY, E.J. 1982. New perspectives on Moche metallurgy: Techniques of gilding copper at Loma Negra, Northern Peru. *American Antiquity* 47, 3–30.

VAN DER LEEUW, S.E. & PRITCHARD, A. (eds.). 1984. *The Many Dimensions of Pottery.* Univ. of Amsterdam.

LONG, S.V. 1965. Cire-perdue casting in pre-Columbian America: an experimental approach. *American Antiquity* 30, 189–92.

LORBLANCHET, M. 1980. Peindre sur les parois des grottes, in *Revivre la Préhistoire,* Dossiers de l'Archéologie 46, 33–39.

——1991. Spitting images: replicating the spotted horses of Pech Merle. *Archaeology* 44, Nov/Dec, 24–31.

LUCAS, A. & HARRIS, J.R. 1962. *Ancient Egyptian Materials and Industries.* Arnold: London.

MACGREGOR, A. 1985. *Bone, Antler, Ivory and Horn Technology.* Croom Helm: London.

MCGREW, W.C. 1992. *Chimpanzee Material Culture. Implications for Human Evolution.* Cambridge Univ. Press.

MARSHACK, A. 1975. Exploring the mind of Ice Age man. *National Geographic* 147, 62–89.

MATSON, F.R. 1969. Some aspects of ceramic technology, in *Science in Archaeology* (D.R. Brothwell & E.S. Higgs eds.), 592–602. (2nd ed.) Thames & Hudson: London.

MEEKS, N.D. & others. 1982 Gloss and use-wear traces on flint sickles and similar phenomena. *Journal of Arch. Science* 9, 317–40.

MELCER, C.L. & ZIMMERMAN, D.W. 1977. Thermoluminescent determination of prehistoric heat treatment of chert artifacts. *Science* 197, 1359–62.

MELTZER, D.J., ADOVASIO, J.M. & DILLEHAY, T.D. 1994. On a Pleistocene human occupation at Pedra Furada, Brazil. *Antiquity* 68, 695–714.

MERKEL, J. & SHIMADA, I. 1988. Arsenical copper smelting at Batán Grande, Peru. *IAMS* (Institute for ArchaeoMetallurgical Studies) No. 12, June, 4–7.

MILLET, M. (ed.). 1979. *Pottery and the Archaeologist.* Institute of Arch.: London.

NOEL, M. & BOCQUET A. 1987. *Les Hommes et le Bois: Histoire et Technologie du Bois de la Préhistoire à Nos Jours.* Hachette: Paris.

VAN NOTEN, F. 1978. *Les Chasseurs de Meer.* Dissertationes Archaeologicae Gandenses 18. De Tempel: Bruges.

——, CAHEN, D. & KEELEY, L.H. 1980. A Palaeolithic campsite in Belgium. *Scientific American* 242, 44–51.

——& RAYMAEKERS, J. 1988. Early iron smelting in Central Africa. *Scientific American* 258 (6), 84–91.

ODELL, G.H. 1975. Micro-wear in perspective: a sympathetic response to Lawrence H. Keeley. *World Arch.* 7, 226–40.

OLIVE, M. 1988. *Une Habitation Magdalénienne d'Etiolles, l'Unité P15.* Mémoire 20 de la Soc. Préhist. française.

OLSEN, S.L. 1989. On distinguishing natural from cultural damage on archaeological antler. *Journal of Arch. Science* 16, 125–35.

ORTON, C., TYERS, P., & VINCE, A. 1993. *Pottery in Archaeology.* Cambridge Univ. Press.

PALES, L. & DE ST PÉREUSE, M.T. 1966. Un cheval-prétexte: retour au chevêtre. *Objets et Mondes* 6, 187–206.

PARENTI, F. 2000. *Le Gisement Quaternaire de la Pedra Furada (Piauí, Brésil). Stratigraphie, chronologie, évolution culturelle.* Editions Recherches sur les Civilisations: Paris.

——, MERCIER, N. & VALLADAS, H. 1990. The oldest hearths of Pedra Furada, Brazil: thermoluminescence analysis of heated stones. *Current Research in the Pleistocene* 7, 36–38.

PATTERSON, L.W. 1983. Criteria for determining the attributes of man-made lithics. *Journal of Field Arch.* 10, 297–307.

——& others. 1987. Analysis of lithic flakes at the Calico Site, California. *Journal of Field Arch.* 14, 91–106.

PAVEL, P. 1992. Raising the Stonehenge lintels in Czechoslovakia. *Antiquity* 66, 389–91.

——1995. Reconstruction of the *moai* statues and *pukao* hats. *Rapa Nui Journal* 9(3), Sept. 69–72.

PERLES, C. 1977. *Préhistoire du Feu.* Masson: Paris.

PHILLIPS, P. 1988. Traceology (microwear) studies in the USSR. *World Arch.* 19 (3), 349–56.

PIGEOT, N. 1988. *Magdaléniens d'Etiolles: Economie de Débitage et Organisation Sociale.* Centre National de la Recherche Scientifique: Paris.

PIGGOTT, S. 1983. *The Earliest Wheeled Transport.* Thames & Hudson: London.

PITTS, M. & ROBERTS, M. 1997. *Fairweather Eden. Life in Britain half a million years ago as revealed by the excavations at Boxgrove.* Century: London.

POKINES, J.T. 1998. Experimental replication and use of Cantabrian Lower Magdalenian antler projectile points. *Journal of Arch. Science* 25, 875–86.

PROTZEN, J-P. 1986. Inca Stonemasonry. *Scientific American* 254, 80–88.

——1993. *Inca architecture and construction at Ollantaytambo.* Oxford Univ. Press: Oxford & New York.

PURDY, B.A. & BROOKS, H.K. 1971. Thermal alteration of silica materials: an archaeological approach. *Science* 173, 322–25.

RENDELL, H.M. & others. 1989. *Pleistocene and Palaeolithic Investigations in the Soan Valley of Northern Pakistan.* British Arch. Reports Int. Series S544: Oxford.

RICE, P.M. (ed.). 1982. *Pots and Potters: Current Approaches to Ceramic*

Archaeology. State College: Pennsylvania State Univ. Press.

——1987. *Pottery Analysis: A Sourcebook*. Chicago Univ. Press.

ROBINS, G.V. & others. 1978. Identification of ancient heat treatment in flint artefacts by ESR spectroscopy. *Nature* 276, 703–4.

ROTTLÄNDER, R.C.A. 1983. *Einführung in die naturwissenschaftlichen Methoden der Archäologie*. Verlag Arch. Venatoria, Band 6: Tübingen.

——1986. Chemical investigation of potsherds of the Heuneburg, Upper Danube, in *Proc. 24th Int. Archaeometry Symposium* (J.S. Olin & M.J. Blackman eds.), 403–5. Smithsonian Institution Press: Washington D.C.

ROWLETT, R.M., MANDEVILLE, M.D. & ZELLER, R.J. 1974. The interpretation and dating of humanly worked siliceous materials by thermoluminescence analysis. *Proc. Prehist. Soc.* 40, 37–44.

RYE, O.S. 1981. *Pottery Technology*. Taraxacum: Washington.

SAYRE, E.V. & SMITH, R.W. 1961. Compositional categories of ancient glass. *Science* 133, 1824–26.

SCARRE, C. (ed.). 1999. *The Seventy Wonders of the Ancient World. The Great Monuments and How they were Built*. Thames & Hudson: London & New York.

SCHICK, K.D. & TOTH, N. 1993. *Making Silent Stones Speak*. Simon & Schuster: New York; Weidenfeld & Nicolson: London.

SCHMIDT, P. & AVERY, D.H. 1978. Complex iron smelting and prehistoric culture in Tanzania. *Science* 201, 1085–89.

SCHMIDT, P.R. (ed.). 1996. *The Culture and Technology of African Iron Production*. Univ. Press of Florida: Gainesville.

SEMENOV, S.A. 1964. *Prehistoric Technology*. Cory, Adams & McKay: London.

SHEPARD, A.O. 1985. *Ceramics for the Archaeologist*. Carnegie Institute.

SHEPHERD, R. 1980. *Prehistoric Mining and Allied Industries*. Academic Press: New York & London.

SHIMADA, I., EPSTEIN, S. & CRAIG, A.K. 1982. Batán Grande: a prehistoric metallurgical center in Peru. *Science* 216, 952–59.

——& MERKEL, J.F. 1991. Copper-alloy metallurgy in Ancient Peru. *Scientific American* 265 (1), 62–68.

——& GRIFFIN, J.A. 1994. Precious metal objects of the Middle Sicán. *Scientific American* 270 (4), 60–67.

SIEVEKING, G. & NEWCOMER, M.H. (eds.). 1987. *The Human Uses of Flint and Chert*. Cambridge Univ. Press.

SINGER, C., HOLMYARD, E.J. & HALL, A.R. 1954. *A History of Technology: I*. Clarendon Press: Oxford.

SMITH, A.B. & POGGENPOEL, C. 1988. The technology of bone tool fabrication in the South-western Cape, South Africa. *World Arch.* 20 (1), 103–15.

SMITH, R.W. 1969. The analytical study of glass in archaeology, in *Science in Archaeology* (D.R. Brothwell & E.S. Higgs

eds.), 614–23. (2nd ed.) Thames & Hudson: London.

STEFFY, J.R. 1994. *Wooden Ship Building and the Interpretation of Shipwrecks*. Texas A&M Univ. Press: College Station.

TAIT, H. 1991. (ed.) *Five Thousand Years of Glass*. British Museum Press: London.

THOM, A. 1984. Moving and erecting the menhirs. *Proc. Prehist. Soc.* 50, 382–84.

THOMAS, D.H. 1983. *The Archaeology of Monitor Valley: Gatecliff Shelter*. Anth. Papers of the American Museum of Natural History, New York, vol. 59.

THOMPSON, F.C. 1969. Microscopic studies of ancient metals, in *Science in Archaeology* (D.R. Brothwell & E.S. Higgs eds.), 555–63. (2nd ed.) Thames & Hudson: London.

THOMPSON, M.W. 1954. Azilian harpoons. *Proc. Prehist. Soc.* 20, 193–211.

TITE, M.S. 1969. Determination of the firing temperature of ancient ceramics by measurement of thermal expansion. *Archaeometry* 11, 131–44.

——1972. *Methods of Physical Examination in Archaeology*. Seminar Press: London & New York.

TOMLINSON, P. 1985. Use of vegetative remains in the identification of dye plants from waterlogged 9th–10th century AD deposits at York. *Journal of Arch. Science* 12, 269–83.

TOTH, N. 1987. The first technology. *Scientific American* 256 (4), 104–13.

——, CLARK, D. & LIGABUE, G. 1992. The last stone ax makers. *Scientific American* 267 (1), 66–71.

——& others. 1993. Pan the tool-maker: investigations into the stone tool-making and tool-using capabilities of a Bonobo (*Pan paniscus*). *Journal of Arch. Science* 20, 81–92.

TRINGHAM, R. & others. 1974. Experimentation in the formation of edge damage: a new approach to lithic analysis. *Journal of Field Arch.* 1, 171–96.

TYLECOTE, R.F. 1962. *Metallurgy in Antiquity*. Arnold: London.

——1976. *A History of Metallurgy*. Metals Soc.: London.

——1986. *The Prehistory of Metallurgy in the British Isles*. Institute of MetalsL London.

——1987. *The Early History of Metallurgy in Europe*. Longman: London & New York.

VANCE, E.D. 1987. Microdebitage and archaeological activity analysis. *Archaeology* July/Aug., 58–59.

VANDIVER, P.B., SOFFER, O., KLIMA, B. & SVOBODA, J. 1989. The origins of ceramic technology at Dolní Věstonice, Czechoslovakia. *Science* 246, 1002–8.

VAUGHAN, P. 1985. *Use-wear Analysis of Flaked Stone Tools*. Univ. of Arizona Press: Tucson.

WELSH, F. 1988. *Building the Trireme*. Constable: London.

WULFF, H.E. 1966. *The Traditional Crafts of Persia*. MIT Press: Cambridge, Mass.

Chapter 9: What Contact Did They Have? Trade and Exchange
(pp. 351–384)

pp. 351–357 **Study of interaction** Exchange, economic and ethnographic background: Mauss 1925; Polanyi 1957; Sahlins 1972; Thomas 1991; Wallerstein 1974 & 1980; Gregory 1982; Appadurai 1986. Kula exchange network: Malinowski 1922; also Leach & Leach 1983. **Primitive valuables** Dalton 1977; Renfrew 1978 & 1986; and especially Clark, J.G.D. 1986.

pp. 358–67 **Characterization** of traded materials: Tite 1972; Peacock 1982; Harbottle 1982; Brothwell & Higgs 1969; Catling & Millett 1965. Sourcing of marble: Craig 1972; Herz & Wenner 1981. Jones 1986 (ceramics); Herz 1992, Barbin & others 1992 (marble); Beck & Shennan 1991 (amber); Kelley & others 1994 (Ar-Ar dating); Warashina 1992 (ESR).

pp. 367–73 **Distribution** patterns of traded items: Hodder & Orton 1976; Renfrew & Shackleton 1970; Scarre & Healy 1993. Stone axes: Cummins 1974; Clark 1965. Obsidian: Renfrew 1969; Renfrew & Dixon 1976; Renfrew, Dixon & Cann 1968; Cauvin 1998; Tykot & Ammerman 1997; Brooks & others 1997; Bradley & Edmonds 1993. Roman pottery: Peacock 1982. Prehistoric pottery: Peacock 1969; Ardika & others 1993. Wreck sites, with maritime trading patterns: Muckelroy 1980.

pp. 373–77 **Production** Torrence 1986; and Renfrew & Wagstaff 1982 (Melos); Singer 1984; Leach 1984 (Colorado Desert); Kohl 1975 (chlorite bowls); Peacock 1982 (Roman Britain).

pp. 377–78 **Consumption** Sidrys 1977 (Maya obsidian).

pp. 378–84 **Exchange: complete system** Renfrew 1975 and Pires-Ferreira 1976 (Mexico); Hedeager 1978 (buffer zone); Renfrew 1975 (trade and rise of the state); Wallerstein 1974 & 1980; Kohl 1987; Rowlands & others 1987; Wolf 1982 ("world system"); Wells 1980; Frankenstein & Rowlands 1978 (early Iron Age society); Rathje 1973 (Maya trade); Helms 1988 (exotic knowledge). See also Hodges 1982 (early medieval Europe); Earle & Ericson 1977; and *World Arch.* 5(2), 6(2/3), 11(1), 12(1).

Box Features

p. 354 **Modes of Exchange** Polanyi 1957; Sahlins 1972.

pp. 356–57 **Materials of Prestige Value** Clark, J.G.D. 1986.

pp. 360–61 **Analysis of Artifact Composition** Tite 1972; Harbottle 1982.

pp. 364–65 **Lead Isotope Analysis** Gale & Stos-Gale 1982 & 1992; Gale 1991; Budd & others 1993.

p. 369 **Trend Surface Analysis** Cummins 1974, 1979.

p. 370 **Fall-off Analysis** Peacock 1982.

pp. 374–75 **Distribution: the Uluburun Wreck** Bass 1987; Bass & others 1984, 1989; Pulak 1994.

p. 376 **Production: Greenstone Artifacts in Australia** McBryde 1979, 1984; McBryde & Harrison 1981.

p. 383 **Interaction Spheres: Hopewell** Brose & Greber 1979; Seeman 1979; Struever & Houart 1972; Braun 1986.

Bibliography

APPADURAI, A. (ed.). 1986. *The Social Life of Things*. Cambridge Univ. Press.

ARDIKA, I.W. & others. 1993. A single source for South Asian exported quality Rouletted Ware. *Man and Environment* 18, 101–10.

BARBIN, V., & others. 1992. Cathodoluminescence of white marbles: an overview. *Archaeometry* 34, 175–85.

BASS, G.F. 1987. Oldest Known Shipwreck Reveals Splendors of the Bronze Age. *National Geographic*, 172 (December) 693–732.

——, FREY, D.A. & PULAK, C. 1984. A Late Bronze Age Shipwreck, at Kaş, Turkey. *Internat. Journal of Nautical Arch.* 13 (4), 271–79.

——, PULAK, C., COLLON, D. & WEINSTEIN, J. 1989. The Bronze Age Shipwreck at Ulu Burun: 1986 Campaign. *American Journal of Arch.* 93, 1–29.

BECK, C. & SHENNAN, S. 1991. *Amber in Prehistoric Britain*. Oxbow: Oxford.

BRADLEY, R. & EDMONDS, M. 1993. *Interpreting the Axe Trade*. Cambridge Univ. Press.

BRAUN, D.P. 1986. Midwestern Hopewellian exchange and supralocal interaction, in *Peer Polity Interaction and Socio-Political Change* (C. Renfrew and J.F. Cherry eds.), 117–26. Cambridge Univ. Press.

BROOKS, S.O. & others. 1997. Source of volcanic glass for ancient Andean tools. *Nature* 386, 449–50.

BROSE, D. & GREBER, N. (eds.). 1979. *Hopewell Archaeology: The Chillicothe Conference*. Kent State Univ. Press.

BROTHWELL, D.R. & HIGGS, E. (eds.). 1969. *Science in Archaeology*. (2nd ed.) Thames & Hudson: London.

BUDD, P. & others. 1993. Evaluating lead isotope data: further observations. *Archaeometry* 35, 241–63.

CATLING, H.W. & MILLETT, A. 1965. A Study of the Inscribed Stirrup-jars from Thebes. *Archaeometry* 8, 3–85.

CAUVIN, M.-C. (ed.). 1998. *L'obsidienne au Proche et Moyen Orient*. British Arch. Reports Int. Series 738: Oxford.

CLARK, J.G.D. 1965. Traffic in Stone Axe and Adze Blades. *Economic History Review* 18, 1–28.

——1986 *Symbols of Excellence: precious materials as expressions of status*. Cambridge Univ. Press.

CRAIG, H. & V. 1972. Greek marbles: determination of provenance by isotopic analysis. *Science* 176, 401–3.

CUMMINS, W.A. 1974. The neolithic stone axe trade in Britain. *Antiquity* 68, 201–05.

——1979. Neolithic stones axes – distribution and trade in England and Wales, in *Stone Axe Studies* (T.H. Clough & W.A. Cummins eds.), 5–12. CBA Research Report No. 23: London.

DALTON, G. 1977. Aboriginal Economies in Stateless Societies, in *Exchange Systems in Prehistory* (T.K. Earle & J.E. Ericson eds.), 191–212. Academic Press: New York & London.

EARLE, T.K. & ERICSON, J.E. (eds.). 1977. *Exchange Systems in Prehistory*. Academic Press: New York & London.

FRANKENSTEIN, S. & ROWLANDS, M.J. 1978. The internal structure and regional context of Early Iron Age society in south-western Germany. *Bulletin of the Institute of Arch.* 15, 73–112.

GALE, N.H. (ed.). 1991. *Bronze Age Trade in the Mediterranean*. (Studies in Mediterranean Archaeology 90). Åström: Göteborg.

——& STOS-GALE, Z.A. 1982. Bronze copper sources in the Mediterranean: A new approach. *Science* 216, 11–20.

——&——1992. Lead isotope studies in the Aegean (The British Academy Project), in *New Developments in Archaeological Science* (A.M. Pollard ed.). Proc. of the British Academy 77, Oxford Univ. Press.

GREGORY, C.A. 1982. *Gifts and Commodities*. Cambridge Univ. Press.

HARBOTTLE, G. 1982. Chemical Characterization in Archaeology, in *Contexts for Prehistoric Exchange* (J.E. Ericson & T.K. Earle eds.), 13–51. Academic Press: New York & London.

HEDEAGER, L. 1978. A Quantitative Analysis of Roman Imports in Europe North of the Limes (0–400 A.D.), and the Question of Roman-Germanic Exchange, in *New Directions in Scandinavian Archaeology* (K. Kristiansen & C. Paluden-Müller eds.), 191–216. National Museum of Denmark: Copenhagen.

HELMS, M.W. 1988. *Ulysses' Sail*. Princeton Univ. Press.

HERZ, N. 1992. Provenance determination of Neolithic to Classical Mediterranean marbles by stable isotopes. *Archaeometry* 34, 185–94.

——& WENNER, D.B. 1981. Tracing the origins of marble. *Archaeology* 34 (5), 14–21.

HODDER, I. & ORTON, C. 1976. *Spatial Analysis in Archaeology*. Cambridge Univ. Press.

HODGES, R.J. 1982. *Dark Age Economics. The origins of towns and trade AD 600–1000*. Duckworth: London.

JONES, R.E. 1986. *Greek and Cypriot Pottery, A review of scientific studies*. Occasional Paper of the Fitch Laboratory 1, British School at Athens.

KELLEY, S., WILLIAMS-THORPE, O. & THORPE, R.J. 1994. Laser argon dating and geological provenancing of a stone axe from the Stonehenge environs. *Archaeometry* 36, 209–16.

KOHL, P.L. 1975. Carved chlorite vessels. *Expedition* 18, 18–31.

——1987. The use and abuse of World Systems theory. *Advances in Archaeological Method and Theory* 11 (M.B. Schiffer ed.), 1–36. Academic Press: New York & London.

LEACH, H.M. 1984. Jigsaw: reconstructive lithic technology, in *Prehistoric Quarries and Lithic Production* (J.E. Ericson & B.A. Purdy eds.), 107–18. Cambridge Univ. Press.

LEACH, J.W. & LEACH, E. (eds.). 1983. *The Kula. New Perspectives on Massim Exchange*. Cambridge Univ. Press.

MALINOWSKI, B. 1922. *Argonauts of the Western Pacific*. Dutton: New York; Routledge: London.

MAUSS, M.G. 1925. *The Gift*. Routledge: London.

MCBRYDE, I. 1979. Petrology and prehistory: lithic evidence for exploitation of stone resources and exchange systems in Australia, in *Stone Axe Studies* (T. Clough & W. Cummins eds.), 113–24. Council for British Arch.: London.

——1984. Kulin greenstone quarries: the social contexts of production and distribution for the Mount William site. *World Arch.* 16, 267–85.

——& HARRISON, G. 1981. Valued good or valuable stone? Considerations of some aspects of the distribution of greenstone artefacts in south-eastern Australia, in *Archaeological Studies of Pacific Stone Resources* (F. Leach & J. Davidson eds.), 183–208. British Arch. Reports: Oxford.

MUCKELROY, K. (ed.). 1980. *Archaeology Under Water. An Atlas of the World's Submerged Sites*. McGraw-Hill: New York & London.

PEACOCK, D.P.S. 1969. Neolithic pottery production in Cornwall. *Antiquity* 63, 145–49.

——1982. *Pottery in the Roman World: an ethnoarchaeological approach*. Longman: London & New York.

PIRES-FERREIRA, J.W. 1976. Obsidian Exchange in Formative Mesoamerica, in *The Early Mesoamerican Village* (K.V. Flannery ed.), 292–306. Academic Press: New York & London.

POLANYI, K. 1957. The economy as instituted process, in *Trade and Market in the Early Empires* (K. Polanyi, M. Arensberg & H. Pearson eds.). Free Press: Glencoe, Illinois.

PULAK, C.M. 1994. 1994 excavation at Uluburun: The final campaign. *The INA Quarterly* 21 (4), 8–16.

RATHJE, W.L. 1973. Models for mobile Maya: a variety of constraints, in *The Explanation of Culture Change*

(C. Renfrew ed.), 731–57. Duckworth: London.

RENFREW, C. 1969. Trade and culture process in European prehistory. *Current Anth.* 10, 151–69.

——1975. Trade as action at a distance, in *Ancient Civilizations and Trade* (J. Sabloff & C.C. Lamberg-Karlovsky eds.), 1–59. Univ. of New Mexico Press: Albuquerque.

——1978. Varna and the social context of early metallurgy. *Antiquity* 52, 199–203.

——1986. Varna and the emergence of wealth in prehistoric Europe, in *The Social Life of Things* (A. Appadurai ed.), 141–48. Cambridge Univ. Press.

——& DIXON, J.E. 1976. Obsidian in western Asia: a review, in *Problems in Economic and Social Archaeology* (G. de G. Sieveking, I.H. Longworth & K.E. Wilson eds.), 137–50. Duckworth: London.

——, DIXON, J.E. & CANN, J.R. 1968. Further analysis of Near Eastern obsidians. *Proc. Prehist. Soc.* 34, 319–31.

——& SHACKLETON, N. 1970. Neolithic trade routes realigned by oxygen isotope analyses. *Nature* 228, 1062–65.

——& WAGSTAFF, J.M. (eds.). 1982. *An Island Polity: the archaeology of exploitation in Melos.* Cambridge Univ. Press.

ROWLANDS, M., LARSEN, M. & KRISTIANSEN, K. (eds.). 1987. *Centre and Periphery in the Ancient World.* Cambridge Univ. Press.

SAHLINS, M.D. 1972. *Stone Age Economics.* Aldine: Chicago.

SCARRE, C. & HEALY, F. (eds.). 1993. *Trade and Exchange in Prehistoric Europe.* Oxbow Monograph 33: Oxford.

SEEMAN, M.L. 1979. *The Hopewell Interaction Sphere: the evidence for interregional trade and structural complexity.* Prehistory Research Series, Vol. 5 no.2. Indiana Historical Society: Indianapolis.

SIDRYS, R. 1977. Mass-distance measures for the Maya obsidian trade, in *Exchange Systems in Prehistory* (T.K. Earle, & J.E. Ericson eds.), 91–108. Academic Press: New York & London.

SINGER, C.A. 1984. The 63-kilometer fit, in *Prehistoric Quarries and Lithic Production* (J.E. Ericson & B.A. Purdy eds.), 35–48. Cambridge Univ. Press.

STRUEVER, S. & HOUART, G.L. 1972. An analysis of the Hopewell interaction sphere, in *Social Exchange and Interaction* (Univ. of Michigan Museum of Anthropology Anthropological Papers 46) (E.N. Wilmsen ed.), 47–79. Univ. of Michigan Museum of Anthropology: Ann Arbor.

THOMAS, N. 1991. *Entangled Objects.* Harvard Univ. Press.

TITE, M.S. 1972. *Methods of Physical Examination in Archaeology.* Academic Press: London.

TORRENCE, R. 1986. *Production and exchange of stone tools: prehistoric obsidian in the Aegean.* Cambridge Univ. Press.

TYKOT, R.H. & AMMERMAN, A.J. 1997. New directions in central Mediterranean obsidian studies. *Antiquity* 71, 1000–06.

WALLERSTEIN, I. 1974 & 1980. *The Modern World System.* 2 vols. Academic Press: New York & London.

WARASHINA, T. 1992. Allocation of jasper archaeological implements by means of ESR and XRF. *Journal of Arch. Science* 19, 357–73.

WELLS, P.S. 1980. *Culture contact and culture change: Early Iron Age central Europe and the Mediterranean world.* Cambridge Univ. Press.

WOLF, E.R. 1982. *Europe and the People without History.* Univ. of California Press: Berkeley.

Chapter 10: What Did They Think? Cognitive Archaeology, Art, and Religion (pp. 385–420)

pp. 385–87 **Theory and method** Philosophy of science: Bell 1994; Braithwaite 1953; Hempel 1966; Popper 1985. Cognitive archaeology: Gardin & Peebles 1992; Renfrew & others 1993; Renfrew & Zubrow 1994; Renfrew & Scarre 1998; Lock & Peters 1996; see also references to box feature **Interpretive and postprocessual archaeologies** in Chapter 1. Methodological individualism: Bell 1994; Renfrew 1987.

pp. 387–91 **Evolution of human symbolizing faculties and language** Donald 1991; Mellars & Gibson 1996; Pinker 1994; Noble & Davidson 1996; Isaac 1976 (Paleolithic stone tools). Self-consciousness and the mind: Dennett 1991; Penrose 1989; Searle 1994; Barkow & others 1992; Mithen 1990, 1996. **Chaîne opératoire** and production sequence: Perlès 1992; van der Leeuw 1994; Karlin and Julien 1994; Schlanger 1994. **Organized behavior** of early hominids: Binford 1981. Opposing views on variability in Mousterian assemblages: Binford 1973; Binford & Binford 1966; Bordes & de Sonneville-Bordes 1970; Mellars 1969, 1970. Gamble 1986 provides a good general view of the European Paleolithic.

pp. 391–97 **Written sources** Diringer 1962; Robinson 1995. Early proto-writing of the Vinča culture: Renfrew 1973 (Ch. 9); Winn 1981; Fischer 1997 (Easter Island). Oracle bones: Chou 1979. **Conceptualizing warfare** Chase 1991; Chase & Chase 1998; Sharer 1994, chapter 5; Webster 1998. **Literacy in Classical Greece** Cook 1987; Camp 1986.

pp. 397–99 **Establishing place: the location of memory** Éliade 1965, 22; Fritz 1978; Hodder 1990; Wheatley 1971; Tilley 1994; Chatwin 1987; Polignac 1984; Aveni 1990. The Neo-Wessex school and Neolithic monuments: Bradley 1998; Barrett 1994; Tilley 1994; Thomas 1991; Gosden 1994; Edmonds 1999; Richards 1994; Richards & Thomas 1984; Whittle & Pollard 1995. Chaco Canyon: Lekson &

others 1988; Marshall 1997; Sofaer 1997; Stein & Lekson 1992; Vivian & others 1978. Nazca lines: Aveni 1990.

pp. 399–401 **Units of time** Heggie 1981 (Thom's work); Aveni 1980, 1982, 1988 (Americas). **Units of length** Heggie 1981. **Units of weight** Mohenjodaro: Wheeler 1968; Renfrew 1985a.

pp. 402–03 **Planning** O'Kelly 1982 (Newgrange); Wheatley 1971; Ward-Perkins 1974 (town planning); Lauer 1976 (Step Pyramid).

pp. 404–05 **Symbols of value** In general: Clark, J.G.D. 1986; Shennan 1986. Mainfort 1985 (Fletcher cemetery); Renfrew 1978 (Varna gold).

pp. 406–12 **Archaeology of religion** Durkheim 1912; Rappaport 1971, 1999; Renfrew 1985b (Phylakopi sanctuary), 1994; Parker Pearson 1984 (metal hoards in Scandinavian bogs); Tozzer 1957 (*cenote* at Chichén Itzá); Coe 1978 (Popol Vuh); Marcus & Flannery 1994. Early cult deposits: Garfinkel 1994; Rollefson 1983; Bradley 1990.

p. 412 **Archaeology of death** Morris 1987; Whitley 1991.

pp. 412–19 **Art and representation** Case for mother-goddess cult argued by Gimbutas 1989, 1991; opposed by Ucko 1968. *Danzante* figures: see Chapter 13. Symmetry analysis: Washburn & Crowe 1989; Washburn 1983. Myth and philosophy in ancient societies: Frankfort & others 1946; Lévi-Strauss 1966.

pp. 419–20 **Aesthetic questions** Taylor & others 1994; Carpenter 1959; Morphy 1989, 1992; Pfeiffer 1982; Bourdieu 1984; Renfrew 1992.

Box Features

p. 390 **Indications of Early Thought** Arsuaga & others 1993; Atapuerca 1999; Bahn 1996; Cervera & others 1999 (Atapuerca); Marshack 1997 (Berekhat Ram); Kajiwara 1999 (Kamitakomori).

pp. 392–93 **Paleolithic Cave Art** Most up-to-date review: Bahn & Vertut 1997. Structuralist interpretation: Leroi-Gourhan 1968. Also: Leroi-Gourhan 1982. Chauvet & others 1996 (Chauvet).

p. 394 **Paleolithic Portable Art** Counting and notations: Marshack 1972a. See also Marshack 1972b, 1975, 1991; d'Errico 1989; d'Errico & Cacho 1994.

p. 401 **Megalithic Yard** Thom 1967. Critical assessment: Heggie 1981.

pp. 407–08 **Maya Symbols of Power** Political symbolism of Maya art: Marcus 1974; Schele & Miller 1986. Hammond 1982 discusses "the Maya mind."

pp. 411–12 **Cult Activity at Chavin** Burger 1984, 1992; Saunders 1989.

pp. 414–15 **Individual Artists in Ancient Greece** Beazley 1965; Boardman 1974. Cycladic figurines: Getz-Preziosi 1987. General problems of attribution: Hill & Gunn 1977.

pp. 416–17 **Conventions in Egyptian Art** Schafer 1974; Robins 1986, 1994.

p. 418 **Interpreting Swedish Rock Art** Tilley 1991; Patrik 1985.
p. 419 **Questions of Style** Washburn 1983; Wiessner 1983; Wobst 1977; Plog 1980; Sackett 1973.

Bibliography

ARSUAGA, J-L. & others. 1993. Three new human skulls from the Sima de los Huesos Middle Pleistocene site in Sierra de Atapuerca, Spain. *Nature* 362, 534–37.

ATAPUERCA: NUESTROS ANTECESSORES 1999. Exhibition catalogue. Museu Nacional de Ciencias Naturales: Madrid.

AVENI, A.F. 1980. *Skywatchers of Ancient Mexico.* Univ. of Texas Press: Austin.

——(ed.). 1982. *Archaeoastronomy in the New World.* Cambridge Univ. Press.

——(ed.). 1988. *World Archaeoastronomy.* Cambridge Univ. Press.

——(ed.). 1990. *The Lines of Nazca.* Univ. of Pennsylvania Press: Philadelphia.

BAHN, P.G. 1996. The Treasure of the Sierra Atapuerca. *Archaeology,* Jan./Feb., 45–48.

——**& VERTUT, J.** 1997. *Journey through the Ice Age.* Weidenfeld & Nicolson: London; Univ. of California Press: Berkeley.

BARKOW, J.H., COSMIDES, L. & TOOBY, J. (eds.). 1992. *The Adapted Mind: Evolutionary Psychology and the Generation of Culture.* Oxford Univ. Press.

BARRETT, J.C. 1994. *Fragments from Antiquity, an Archaeology of Social Life in Britain, 2900–1200 BC.* Blackwell: Oxford.

BEAZLEY, J. 1965. *Attic Black Figure Vase Painters.* Oxford Univ. Press.

BELL, J.A. 1994. *Reconstructing Prehistory: Scientific Method in Archaeology.* Temple Univ. Press: Philadelphia.

BINFORD, L.R. 1973. Interassemblage variability – the Mousterian and the "functional" argument, in *The Explanation of Culture Change* (C. Renfrew ed.), 227–54. Duckworth: London.

——1981. *Bones, Ancient Men and Modern Myths.* Academic Press: New York & London.

BINFORD, S.R. & BINFORD, L.R. 1966. A preliminary analysis of functional variability in the Mousterian of Levallois facies. *American Anthropologist* 68, 238–95.

BOARDMAN, J. 1974. *Athenian Black Figure Vases.* Thames & Hudson: London & New York.

BORDES, F. & DE SONNEVILLE-BORDES, D. 1970. The significance of variability in Paleolithic assemblages. *World Arch.* 2, 61–73.

BOURDIEU, P. 1984. *Distinction: A Social Critique of the Judgement of Taste.* Routledge: London.

BOYER, P. 1994. *The Naturalness of Religious Ideas. A Cognitive Theory of Religion.* Univ. of California Press: Berkeley.

BRADLEY, R. 1990. *The Passage of Arms: an Archaeological Analysis of Prehistoric Hoards and Votive Deposits.* Cambridge Univ. Press.

——1998. *The Significance of Monuments.* Routledge: London.

BRAITHWAITE, R.B. 1953. *Scientific Explanation.* Cambridge Univ. Press.

BURGER, R.L. 1984. *The Prehistoric Occupation of Chavín de Huántar, Peru.* Univ. of California Publications in Anthropology Vol. 14. Univ. of California Press: Berkeley.

——1992. *Chavín and the Origins of Andean Civilization.* Thames & Hudson: London & New York.

CAMP, J.M. 1986. *The Athenian Agora.* Thames & Hudson: London & New York.

CARPENTER, R. 1959. *The Esthetic Basis of Greek Art.* Univ. of Indiana Press: Bloomington.

CERVERA, J. & others. 1999 *Atapuerca. Un millón de años de historia.* Plot Ediciones/Editorial Complutense: Madrid.

CHASE, A. 1991. Cycles of Time: Caracol in the Maya Realm, in *Sixth Palenque Round Table, 1986* (M. Greene & V.M. Fields eds.), 32–42. Univ. of Oklahoma Press: Norman.

CHASE, D.Z. & CHASE, A.F. 1998. Settlement patterns, warfare and hieroglyphic history at Caracol, Belize. Paper presented at the 97th Annual Meeting of the American Anthropological Association, Philadelphia, Dec. 3, 1998.

CHATWIN, B. 1987. *The Songlines.* Johnathan Cape: London.

CHAUVET, J.-M. & others. 1996. *Chauvet Cave. The Discovery of the World's Oldest Paintings.* Thames & Hudson: London; Abrams: New York.

CHOU, H. 1979. Chinese oracle bones. *Scientific American* 240 (4), 100–09.

CLARK, J.G.D. 1986. *Symbols of Excellence: precious materials as expressions of status.* Cambridge Univ. Press.

COE, M.D. 1978. *Lords of the Underworld: Masterpieces of Classic Maya Ceramics.* Princeton Univ. Press.

COOK, B.F. 1987. *Greek Inscriptions.* British Museum Publications: London.

DENNETT, D.C. 1991. *Consciousness Explained.* Viking: London.

DIRINGER, D. 1962. *Writing.* Thames & Hudson: London.

DONALD, M. 1991. *Origins of the Modern Mind: Three Stages in the Evolution of Culture and Cognition.* Harvard Univ. Press: Cambridge, Mass.

DURKHEIM, E. 1912. *The Elementary Forms of the Religious Life.* Transl. by J.W. Swain. Free Press: New York 1965.

EDMONDS, M. 1999. *Ancestral Geographies of the Neolithic.* Routledge: London.

D'ERRICO, F. 1989. Paleolithic lunar calendars: a case of wishful thinking? *Current Anth.* 30, 117–18.

——**& CACHO, C.** 1994. Notation versus decoration in the Upper Palaeolithic: A case-study from Tossal de la Roca, Alicante, Spain. *Journal of Arch. Science* 21, 185–200.

ÉLIADE, M. 1965. *Le sacré et le profane.* Paris.

FISCHER, S.R. 1997. *Rongorongo. The Easter Island Script. History, Traditions, Texts.* Clarendon Press: Oxford.

FRANKFORT, H., FRANKFORT, H.A., WILSON, J.A. & JACOBSEN, T. 1946. *Before Philosophy.* Penguin: Harmondsworth.

FRITZ, J.M. 1978. Palaeopsychology today: ideational systems and human adaptation in prehistory, in *Social Archaeology, Beyond Subsistence and Dating* (C.L. Redman ed.), 37–61. Academic Press: New York.

GAMBLE, C. 1986. *The Palaeolithic Settlement of Europe.* Cambridge Univ. Press.

GARDIN, J.-C. & PEEBLES, C.S. (eds.). 1992. *Representations in Archaeology.* Univ. of Indiana Press: Bloomington.

GARFINKEL, Y. 1994. Ritual burial of cultic objects: the earliest evidence. *Cambridge Archaeological Journal* 4, 159–88.

GETZ-PREZIOSI, P. 1987. *Early Sculptors of the Cyclades.* Univ. of Michigan: Ann Arbor.

GIMBUTAS, M. 1989. *The Language of the Goddess.* Harper & Row: New York.

——1991. *The Civilisation of the Goddess: the world of Old Europe.* Harper & Row: San Francisco.

GOSDEN, C. 1994. *Social Being and Time.* Blackwell: Oxford.

HAMMOND, N. 1982. *Ancient Maya Civilization.* Rutgers Univ. Press, N.J.; Cambridge Univ. Press.

HEGGIE, D.C. 1981. *Megalithic Science. Ancient Mathematics and Astronomy in Northwest Europe.* Thames & Hudson: London & New York.

HEMPEL, C.G. 1966. *Philosophy of Natural Science.* Prentice-Hall: Englewood Cliffs, N.J.

HERRMANN, F.-R. & FREY, O.-H. 1996. *Die Keltenfürsten vom Glauberg.* Archäologische Gesellschaft in Hessen: Wiesbaden.

HILL, J.N. & GUNN, J. (eds.). 1977. *The Individual in Prehistory.* Academic Press: New York & London.

HODDER, I. 1990. *The Domestication of Europe.* Blackwell: Oxford.

ISAAC, G. 1976. Stages of cultural elaboration in the Pleistocene: possible archaeological indications of the development of language capabilities, in *Origins and Evolution of Language and Speech* (S.R. Harnad, H.D. Stekelis & J. Lancaster eds.), 275–88. Annals of the New York Acad. of Sciences, Vol. 280.

KAJIWARA, H. KAMADA, T., FUJIMURA, S. & YOKOYAMA, Y. The Oldest Stone Tool Cache:

The Kamitakamori site. Japan Abstract of the 64th Annual Meeting, Society for American Archaeology, 156, Chicago.

KARLIN, C. & JULIEN, M. 1994. Prehistoric technology: a cognitive science?, in *The Ancient Mind: Elements of Cognitive Archaeology* (C. Renfrew & E.B.W. Zubrow eds.), 152–64. Cambridge Univ. Press.

LAUER, J.-P. 1976. Saqqara. Thames & Hudson: London.

LECKSON, S.H. & others. 1988. The Chaco Canyon community. *Scientific American* 259.1 (July), 100–09.

VAN DER LEEUW, S. 1994. Cognitive aspects of "technique", in *The Ancient Mind: Elements of Cognitive Archaeology* (C. Renfrew and E.B.W. Zubrow eds.), 35–142. Cambridge Univ. Press.

LEROI-GOURHAN, A. 1968. *The Art of Prehistoric Man in Western Europe.* Thames & Hudson: London.

——1982. *The Dawn of European Art.* Cambridge Univ. Press.

LÉVI-STRAUSS, C. 1966. *The Savage Mind.* Weidenfeld & Nicolson: London; Univ. of Chicago Press.

LOCK, A. & PETERS, C.R. (eds.). 1996. *Handbook of Human Symbolic Evolution.* Oxford Univ. Press.

MAINFORT, R.C. 1985. Wealth, Space and Status in a Historic Indian Cemetery. *American Antiquity* 50, 555–79.

MARCUS, J. 1974. The iconography of power among the Classic Maya. *World Arch.* 6, 83–94.

——& FLANNERY, K.V. 1994. Ancient Zapotec ritual and religion: an application to the direct historical approach, in *The Ancient Mind: Elements of Cognitive Archaeology* (C. Renfrew and E.B.W. Zubrow eds.), 55–75. Cambridge Univ. Press.

MARSHACK, A. 1972a. *The Roots of Civilization: the cognitive beginnings of man's first art, symbol and notation.* McGraw-Hill: New York; Weidenfeld & Nicolson: London. (2nd ed. 1991, Moyer Bell: New York).

——1972b. Cognitive aspects of Upper Paleolithic engraving. *Current Anth.* 13, 445–77. Also 15 (1974), 327–32; 16 (1975), 297–98.

——1975. Exploring the mind of Ice Age man. *National Geographic* 147 (1), 64–89.

——1991. The Taï plaque and calendrical notation in the Upper Palaeolithic. *Cambridge Archaeological Journal* 1, 25–61.

——1997. The Berekhat Ram figurine: a late Acheulian carving from the Middle East. *Antiquity* 71, 327–37.

MARSHALL, M.P. 1997. The Chacoan roads – a cosmological interpretation, in *Anasazi – Architecture and American Design* (B.H. Morrow & V.B. Price eds.), 6–74. Univ. of New Mexico Press: Albuquerque.

MELLARS, P.A. 1969. The Chronology of Mousterian Industries in the Perigord region of South-West France. *Proc. Prehist. Soc.* 35, 134–71.

——1970. Some comments on the notion of 'functional variability' in stone tool assemblages. *World Arch.* 2, 74–89.

——& GIBSON, K. 1996. *Modelling the Early Human Mind.* McDonald Institute: Cambridge.

MITHEN, S. 1990. *Thoughtful Foragers: A Study of Prehistoric Decision Making.* Cambridge Univ. Press.

——1996. *The Prehistory of the Mind.* Thames & Hudson: London & New York.

MORPHY, H. 1989. From dull to brilliant: the aesthetics of spiritual power among the Yolnyu. *Man* 24, 21–40.

——1992. Aesthetics in a cross-cultural perspective: some reflections on Native American basketry. *Journal of the Anthropological Society of Oxford*, 23, 1–16.

MORRIS, I. 1987. *Burial and Ancient Society: the Rise of the Greek City State.* Cambridge Univ. Press.

NOBLE, W. & DAVIDSON, I. 1996. *Human Evolution, Language and Mind.* Cambridge Univ. Press.

O'KELLY, M.J. 1982. *Newgrange.* Thames & Hudson: London & New York.

PARKER PEARSON, M. 1984. Economic and ideological change: cyclical growth in the pre-state societies of Jutland, in *Ideology, Power and Prehistory* (D. Miller & C. Tilley eds.), 69–92. Cambridge Univ. Press.

PATRIK, L.E. 1985. Is there an archaeological record?, in *Advances in Archaeological Method and Theory* 8 (M.B. Schiffer ed.), 27–62. Academic Press: New York.

PENROSE, R. 1989. *The Emperor's New Mind.* Oxford Univ. Press.

PERLES, C. 1992. In search of lithic strategies: a cognitive approach to prehistoric stone assemblages, in *Representations in Archaeology* (J.C. Gardin & C.S. Peebles eds.), 223–47. Univ. of Indiana Press: Bloomington.

PFEIFFER, J. 1982 *The Creative Explosion: An Inquiry into the Origins of Art and Religion.* Harper and Row: New York.

PINKER, S. 1994. *The Language Instinct.* William Morrow: New York.

PLOG, S. 1980. *Stylistic Variation in Prehistoric Ceramics: Design Analysis in the American Southwest.* Cambridge Univ. Press.

POLIGNAC, F. DE. 1984. *La naissance de la cité grecque.* La découvertes: Paris.

POPPER, K.R. 1985. *Conjectures and refutations: the growth of scientific knowledge.* (4th ed.) Routledge & Kegan Paul: London.

RAPPAPORT, R.A. 1971. Ritual, Sanctity, and Cybernetics. *American Anthropologist* 73, 59–76.

——1999. *Ritual and Religion in the Making of Humanity.* Cambridge Univ. Press.

RENFREW, C. 1973. *Before Civilization. The Radiocarbon Revolution and Prehistoric Europe.* Johnathan Cape: London.

——1978. Varna and the Social Context of Early Metallurgy. *Antiquity* 52, 199–203.

——1985a. *Towards an Archaeology of Mind.* Cambridge Univ. Press.

——1985b. *The Archaeology of Cult. The Sanctuary at Phylakopi.* British School of Archaeology at Athens Supplementary Vol. No. 18: London.

——1987. Problems in the modelling of socio-cultural systems. *European Journal of Operational Research* 30, 179–92.

——1992. *The Cycladic Spirit.* Thames & Hudson: London; Abrams: New York.

——& others. 1993. What is cognitive archaeology? *Cambridge Archaeological Journal* 3, 247–70.

——1994. The archaeology of religion, in *The Ancient Mind: Elements of Cognitive Archaeology* (C. Renfrew & E.B.W. Zubrow eds.), 47–54. Cambridge Univ. Press.

——& SCARRE, C. (eds.). 1998. *Cognition and Material Culture: the Archaeology of Symbolic Storage.* McDonald Institute: Cambridge.

——& ZUBROW, E.B.W. (eds.). 1994. *The Ancient Mind: Elements of Cognitive Archaeology.* Cambridge Univ. Press.

RICHARDS, C.C. & THOMAS, J.S. 1984. Ritual activity and structured deposition in later Neolithic Wessex, in *Neolithic Studies* (R.J. Bradley & J. Gardiner eds.), 189–218. British Arch. Reports, 13: Oxford.

RICHARDS, J. 1994. The development of the Neolithic landscape in the environs of Stonehenge, in *Neolithic Studies* (R.J. Bradley & J. Gardiner eds.), 177–88. British Arch. Reports, 13: Oxford.

ROBINS, G. 1986. *Egyptian Painting and Relief.* Shire: Aylesbury.

——1994. *Proportion and Style in Ancient Egyptian Art.* Thames & Hudson: London; Univ. of Texas Press: Austin.

ROBINSON, A. 1995. *The Story of Writing.* Thames & Hudson: London & New York.

ROLLEFSON, G.O. 1983. Ritual and ceremony at neolithic 'Ain Ghazal (Jordan). *Paléorient* 9(2), 29–38.

SACKETT, J.R. 1973. Style, function and artifact variability in palaeolithic assemblages, in *The Explanation of Culture Change* (C. Renfrew ed.), 317–28. Duckworth: London.

SAUNDERS, N. 1989. *People of the Jaguar.* Souvenir Press: London.

SCHAFER, H. 1974. *Principles of Egyptian Art.* Clarendon Press: Oxford (first published 1919).

SCHELE, L. & MILLER, M.E. 1986. *The Blood of Kings, Dynasty and Ritual in Maya Art.* Kimbell Art Museum: Fort Worth; Thames & Hudson: London.

SCHLANGER, N. 1994. Mindful technology: unleashing the *chaîne opératoire* for an archaeology of mind, in *The Ancient Mind: Elements of Cognitive Archaeology* (C. Renfrew & E.B.W. Zubrow eds.), 143–51. Cambridge Univ. Press.

SEARLE, J.R. 1994. *The Rediscovery of the Mind*. MIT Press: Cambridge, MA.

SHARER, R.J. 1994. *The Ancient Maya*. 5th ed. Stanford Univ. Press: Stanford.

SHENNAN, S. 1986. Interaction and change in third millennium western and central Europe, in *Peer-polity Interaction and Socio-political Change* (C. Renfrew & J.F. Cherry eds.), 137–48. Cambridge Univ. Press.

SOFAER, A. 1997. The primary architecture of Chaco Canyon, in *Anasazi – Architecture and American Design* (B.H. Morrow & V. Price eds.), 88–132. Univ. of New Mexico Press: Albuquerque.

STEIN, J. & LEKSON, S. 1992. Anasazi ritual landscapes, in *Anasazi Regional Organization and the Chaco System* (D. Doyel ed.), 87–100. Maxwell Museum of Anthropology: Albuquerque.

TAYLOR, T. & others. 1994. Is there a place for aesthetics in archaeology? *Cambridge Archaeological Journal* 4, 249–69.

THOM, A. 1967. *Megalithic Sites in Britain*. Clarendon Press: Oxford.

THOMAS, J. 1991. *Rethinking the Neolithic*. Cambridge Univ. Press.

TILLEY, C. 1991. *Material Culture and Text: The Art of Ambiguity*. Routledge: London.

———1994. *A Phenomenology of Landscape*. Berg: Oxford.

TOZZER, A.M. 1957. *Chichen Itza and its Cenote of Sacrifice*. Peabody Museum Memoirs 11 & 12.

UCKO, P.J. 1968. *Anthropomorphic Figurines*. Royal Anthropological Institute Occasional Paper No. 24: London.

VIVIAN, R.G. & others. 1978. *Wooden Ritual Artefacts from Chaco Canyon in New Mexico*. Univ. of New Mexico Press: Tucson.

WARD-PERKINS, J.B. 1974. *Cities of Ancient Greece and Italy: planning in classical antiquity*. Sidgwick & Jackson: London.

WASHBURN, D.K. 1983. Symmetry analysis of ceramic design: two tests of the method on Neolithic material from Greece and the Aegean, in *Structure and Cognition in Art* (D.K. Washburn ed.), 138–63. Cambridge Univ. Press.

———& CROWE, D. 1989. *Symmetries of Culture*. Univ. of Washington Press: Seattle & London.

WEBSTER, D. 1998. Warfare and status rivalry: Lowland Maya and Polynesian comparisons, in *Archaic States* (G.M. Feinman & J. Marcus eds.), 311–52. School of American Research Press: Santa Fe.

WHEATLEY, P. 1971. *The Pivot of the Four Quarters: A preliminary enquiry into the origins and character of the ancient Chinese city*. Edinburgh Univ. Press.

WHEELER, R.E.M. 1968. *The Indus Civilization*. (3rd ed.) Cambridge Univ. Press.

WHITLEY, J. 1991. *Style and Society in Dark Age Greece: the Changing Face of Pre-literate Society 1100–700 BC*. Cambridge Univ. Press.

WHITTLE, A. & POLLARD, J. 1995. Windmill Hill causewayed enclosure: the harmony of symbols, in *Social Life and Social Change: Papers in the Neolithic of Atlantic Europe* (M. Edmonds & C. Richards eds.). Cruithne Press: Glasgow.

WIESSNER, P. 1983. Style and social information in Kalahari San projectile points. *American Antiquity* 48, 253–76.

WINN, S.M.M. 1981. *Pre-Writing in Southeastern Europe: the Sign System of the Vinca Culture c. 4000 BC*. Western Publishers: Calgary.

WOBST, M. 1977. Stylistic behavior and information exchange, in *For the Director: Research Essays in Honor of James B. Griffin* (C.E. Cleland ed.), 317–42. Museum of Anthropology, Univ. of Michigan Papers 61.

Chapter 11: Who Were They? What Were They Like? The Archaeology of People (pp. 421–460)

pp. 421–22 Useful introductions to archaeological aspects of **human remains:** Mays 1998; Brothwell 1972, 1981, 1986; Ubelaker 1984; Houghton 1980; Boddington & others 1987; White 1991. Race and physical anthropology: Gill & Rhine 1990. Human evolution: Klein 1999; Durant 1989. Cremations: Gejvall 1969. Mummies and bogbodies: Cockburn & others 1998; Brothwell 1986; Coles & Coles 1989; van der Sanden 1996. Egyptian mummies: David & Tapp 1984; David 1986; El Mahdy 1989. Scythian bodies: Rudenko 1970. Danish bodies: Glob 1973 (Bronze Age), 1969 (Iron Age). Pompeii & Herculaneum: Maiuri 1961; Gore 1984. Sutton Hoo inhumations: Bethell & Carver 1987. Placenta: Bahn 1991.

pp. 422–24 **Which sex?** In general: Genoves 1969a. Pales & de St Péreuse 1976 (La Marche portraits); Iscan & Miller-Shaivitz 1984 (tibia method). DNA method: Stone & others 1996; Faerman & others 1998 (Ashkelon); DNA from coprolites: Sutton & others 1996; Gremillion & Sobolik 1996.

pp. 424–28 **How long did they live?** In general: Genoves 1969b; Zimmerman & Angel 1986. Taung child: Bromage & Dean 1985; Dean 1985; Beynon & Dean 1988. Holly Smith's work: Smith 1986. For a skeptical view: Lampl & others 1991. **Computed tomography** application: Conroy & Vannier 1987. Gibraltar Child: Dean & others 1986. Root dentin: Bang 1993. Determining age from **bone microstructure:** Kerley 1965; Pfeiffer 1980. Chemical method of Shimoyama & Harada: *New Scientist* 2 May 1985, 22. **Interpreting age at death** Chilean mummies: Arriaza 1995. Problems in assessing age/sex data from cemeteries: Masset 1975.

pp. 428–31 **Height and weight** In general: Wells, L.H. 1969. Calculation from long bones: Trotter & Gleser 1958. **Facial characteristics** In general: Jordan 1983; Tattersall 1992. Cotterell 1981 (terracotta army); Puech & Cianfarani 1985, 32 (Janssens and tomb of Marie de Bourgogne); Harris & others 1978 (Tiye and Thuya); Nedden & others 1994 (Iceman); Zollikofer & others 1995 (Gibraltar skull).

pp. 431–32 **How related?** Radio-immunoassay of fossils: Lowenstein 1985. Human blood residues: Loy 1987; Cattaneo & others 1990. Blood group of Tutankhamun and Smenkhkare: Connolly & others 1969; Harrison & Abdalla 1972. DNA studies: Brown & Brown 1992; Ross 1992; Pääbo 1993; Hagelberg 1993/4; Herrmann & Hummel 1994. DNA from Egyptian mummies: Pääbo 1985. Florida brains: Doran & others 1986; Benditt 1989; Pääbo 1989; Doran 1992. DNA from bone: Hagelberg & others 1989; Hagelberg 1993.

pp. 433–34 **Walking** In general: Robinson 1972. Lucy in the trees: Stern & Susman 1983; Lucy as a biped: Latimer & others 1987; Johanson & Edgar 1996; Clarke & Tobias 1995 (Little Foot). Computed axial tomography: Pahl 1980; Spoor & others 1994. **Footprints** Laetoli: Leakey 1979; Day & Wickens 1980; Leakey & Harris 1987, 490–523; Tuttle & others 1990. Fossil prints in general: Duday & Garcia 1986. Pales's work, and the Niaux prints: Pales 1976; Roberts & others 1996 (Mersey).

pp. 434–35 **Handedness** In general: Babcock 1993; Corballis 1991. In Ice Age art: Bahn & Vertut 1997. See also Davidson 1986 (Nabataean); Puech 1978 (Mauer jaw); Bay 1982 (evidence from tools). Toth's work: Toth 1985.

pp. 435–37 **Speech** Endocasts: Holloway 1983; Falk 1983. Stone tools as evidence for speech: Isaac 1976; an opposite view: Dibble 1989. **Vocal tract** Neanderthal: Lieberman 1998; Lieberman & Crelin 1974; an opposing view: Carlisle & Siegel 1974. Hyoid bone: Arensburg & others 1989. Skull-base analyses: Laitman 1986. See also *Science* 256, 1992, 33–34, & 260, 1993, 893; Kay & others 1998 (Hypoglossal).

pp. 437–38 **Other behavior** Larsen 1997 (general). **Teeth** Smith 1983 (Neanderthal teeth as a third hand); Frayer & Russell 1987 (Neanderthal toothpicks). Puech & Cianfarani 1985, 32–33 (King Christian). **Hands** Susman 1994 (and see *Science* 268, 1995, 586–89, and 276, 1997, 32); Musgrave 1971; Oberlin & Sakka 1993 (Neanderthal dexterity). **Skeletal stress**

Trinkaus 1975 (Neanderthal squatting); Houghton 1980 (New Zealand); Hedges 1983 (Isbister); Molleson 1989, 1994 (Tell Abu Hureyra); Dutour 1986 (Niger/Mali). **Sexuality** Kauffmann-Doig 1979 (Peruvian pottery).

p. 438 **Paleopathology** In general: Aufderheide & Rodríguez-Martín 1998; Brothwell & Sandison 1967; Goldstein 1969; Hart 1983; Janssens 1970; Ortner & Aufderheide 1991; Ortner & Putschar 1985; Roberts & Manchester 1995; Rothschild & Martin 1992; Wells, C. 1964. Also two journals: *Dossiers de l'Archéologie* 97, Sept. 1985, "Les Maladies de nos Ancêtres"; and *World Archaeology* 21 (2)(1989), "The Archaeology of Public Health."

pp. 438–42 **Soft tissue** Vlcek 1952 (prehistoric fingerprints). For Greek pots, see *Science* 275, 1997, 1425. Mutilated hand stencils: Groenen 1988; Bahn & Vertut 1997; Sueres 1991. Artistic representations of pathologies: e.g. *Dossiers de l'Archéologie* 97, Sept 1985, 34–41. Monte Albán figures: Marcus, in Flannery & Marcus 1983.

p. 442 **Parasites and viruses** Patrucco & others 1983 (Peru); Bouchet & others 1996 (Arcy); Rothhammer & others 1985 (Chagas' Disease). Salo & others 1994 (Tuberculosis).

pp. 442–47 **Skeletal evidence** Grimaldi skeleton: Dastugue & de Lumley 1976, 617. Little Big Horn: Scott & Connor 1986; Scott & others 1989. Cranial deformation: Trinkaus 1982 (Neanderthalers); Brown 1981 (Australian Aborigines). Shanidar man: Trinkaus 1983. Skull of Bodo: *New Scientist* 9 Sept. 1982, 688. **Disease from bone evidence** Fennell & Trinkaus (Neanderthal); Anon 1994. Harrison & others 1979 (Tutankhamun's tomb); Frayer & others 1988 (Paleolithic dwarf); Murdy 1981 (Olmec "were-jaguar"); Mays 1985 (Harris lines); Capasso 1994 (Iceman). **Toxic poisoning** In general: Ericson & Coughlin 1981; Molleson & others 1985 (Poundbury lead analysis); Beattie & Geiger 1987 (frozen sailors); Aufderheide and others 1985 (lead analysis of Colonial Americans).

p. 447 **Teeth** In general: Hillson 1986; Alt & others 1998. Campbell 1981/2 (Aboriginal tooth avulsion); Davidson 1986 (Nabateaens); Crubézy & others 1998 (false tooth); d'Errico & others 1988 (Isabella d'Aragona).

p. 450 **Medical knowledge** Alt & others 1997; Lillie 1998 (early trepanation); Molleson & Cox 1988 (infant); Prematillake 1989 (hospital); Urteaga-Ballon & Wells 1986 (Peruvian medical kit).

pp. 451–52 **Nutrition** In general: Brothwell 1969; Cohen & Armelagos 1984. Higham & Thosarat 1998 (Thailand). Evidence in teeth: Hillson 1979 & 1986; Smith, P. 1972. **Chemical analysis of bone** Lambert &

others 1979 (Middle & Late Woodland sites); Lallo & Rose 1979 (Dickson Mounds); Larsen 1981 (Georgia).

pp. 452–55 **Population** In general: Hassan 1978, 1981; Masset 1975. Naroll 1962 (Naroll's equation); Milisauskas 1972 (LBK estimates); Casselberry 1974 (Casselberry's formula); Fox 1983 (Maori example). Other population estimates: Brothwell 1972 (Britain); Dobyns 1966 (America); Storey 1997 (Rome).

pp. 455–59 **Ethnicity and evolution: Genes** Polynesia: Hill & Serjeantson 1989; Hagelberg & Clegg 1993; Hagelberg 1993/4. Y chromosome work: Hammer 1995. Chromosome mapping: Wainscoat & others 1986. Mitochondrial work and "Eve" theory: Cann & others 1987; Templeton 1992; Thorne & Wolpoff 1992; series of papers in *American Anthropologist* 95, 1993, 9–96; Krings & others 1997; Ward & Stringer 1997. Possible problems with recombining mtDNA: Eyre-Walker & others 1999; Hagelberg & others 1999; Strauss 1999. Recent surveys of origins of modern humans: Mellars & Stringer 1989. For opposing views on evolution: Aitken & others 1993; Bräuer & Smith 1992; Johanson & Edgar 1996; Leakey & Lewin 1992; Nitecki & Nitecki 1994.

Box Features

p. 426 **Spitalfields: Determining Biological Age at Death** Adam & Reeve 1991; Molleson & Cox 1993. On inherent problems in age estimation, see Aykroyd & others 1999.

p. 430 **How to Reconstruct the Face** Gerasimov 1971. Philip of Macedon: Prag & others 1984; Prag & Neave 1997.

pp. 440–41 **Looking Inside Bodies** Egyptian mummies: Cockburn & others 1998; David & Tapp 1984; David 1986; El Mahdy 1989; Goyon & Josset 1988; Harris & Weeks 1973.

pp. 444–45 **Life and Death Among the Inuit** Hart Hansen & others 1985, 1991.

pp. 448–49 **Lindow Man** Stead & others 1986; Brothwell 1986; Turner & Scaife 1995.

pp. 454–55 **Genetics and Languages** Cavalli-Sforza & others 1994; Sims-Williams 1998; Renfrew 1992; McMahon & McMahon 1995; Excoffier & others 1987; Bertranpetit & others 1995; Barbujani & Sokal 1990; Blench & Spriggs 1997; Poloni & others 1997. For macrofamilies Dolgopolsky 1998; Greenberg 1963, 1987; Renfrew 1991; Renfrew & Nettle 1999; Barbujani & Pilastro 1993; Ruhlen 1991.

p. 458 **Studying the Origins of New World Populations** In general: Crawford 1998. Greenberg & others 1986; Greenberg 1987; Torroni & others 1992; Bateman & others 1990 (review of linguistic, dental and genetic evidence); Gibbons 1996 (recent genetic data).

Bibliography

ADAM, M. & REEVE, J. 1991. Excavations at Christ Church, Spitalfields, 1984–1986. *Antiquity* 61, 247–56.

AITKEN, M.J., STRINGER, C.B. & MELLARS, P.A. (eds.). 1993. *The Origin of Modern Humans and the Impact of Chronometric Dating.* Princeton Univ. Press.

ALT, K.W. & others. 1997. Evidence for Stone Age cranial surgery. *Nature* 387, 360.

——— **& others.** (eds.). 1998. *Dental Anthropology. Fundamentals, Limits and Prospects.* Springer: Berlin.

ANON. 1994. At Tell Abraq, the earliest recorded find of Polio. *Research, The University of Sydney,* 1994, 20–21.

ARENSBURG, B. & others. 1989. A middle palaeolithic human hyoid bone. *Nature* 338, 758–60.

ARRIAZA, B.T. 1995. *Beyond Death. The Chinchorro Mummies of Ancient Chile.* Smithsonian Inst. Press: Washington D.C. See also *National Geographic* 187 (3), March 1995, 68–89.

AUFDERHEIDE, A.C. & others. 1985. Lead in bone III. Prediction of social correlates from skeletal lead content in four colonial American populations. *American Journal of Phys. Anth.* 66, 353–61.

——— **& RODRIGUEZ-MARTIN, C.** (eds.). 1998. *The Cambridge Encyclopedia of Human Paleopathology.* Cambridge Univ. Press.

AYKROYD, R.G. & others. 1999. Nasty, brutish, but not necessarily short: a reconsideration of the statistical methods used to calculate age at death from adult human skeletal and dental age indicators. *American Antiquity* 64, 55–70.

BABCOCK, L.E. 1993. The right and the sinister. *Natural History* July, 32–39.

BAHN, P.G. 1991. Mystery of the placenta pots. *Archaeology* 44 (3), 18–19.

——— **& VERTUT, J.** 1997. *Journey through the Ice Age.* Weidenfeld & Nicolson: London; Univ. of California Press: Berkeley.

BANG, G. 1993. The age of a stone age skeleton determined by means of root dentin transparency. *The Norwegian Arch. Review* 26, 55–57.

BARBUJANI, G. 1991. What do languages tell us about human microevolution?, *Trends in Ecology and Evolution* 6 (5), 151–56.

——— **& SOKAL, R.R.** 1990. Zones of sharp genetic change in Europe are also linguistic boundaries, *Proceedings of the National Academy of Sciences of the U.S.A.* 87, 1816–19.

——— **& PILASTRO, A., DE DOMENICO S. & RENFREW, C.** 1994. Genetic variation in North Africa and Eurasia: neolithic demic diffusion versus paleolithic colonisation, *American Journal of Physical Anthropology* 95, 137–54.

——— **& PILASTRO, A.** 1993, Genetic evidence on origin and dispersal of human populations speaking languages of the Nostratic macrofamily, *Proceedings of the*

National Academy of Sciences of the USA 90, 4670–73.

BATEMAN, R. & others. 1990. Speaking of Forked Tongues, *Current Anth.* 31, 1–24.

BAY, R. 1982. La question du droitier dans l'évolution humaine. *Bull. Soc. d'Etudes et de Recherches Préhistoriques des Eyzies* 32, 7–15.

BEATTIE, O. & GEIGER, J. 1987. *Frozen in Time. The Fate of the Franklin Expedition.* Bloomsbury: London.

BENDITT, J. 1989. Molecular Archaeology. *Scientific American* 26, 12–13.

BERTRANPETIT, J., SALA, J., CALAFELL, F., UNDERHILL, P.A., MORAL, P. & COMAS, D. 1995. Human mitochondrial DNA variation and the origin of the Basques. *Annals of Human Genetics* 59, 63–81.

BETHELL, P.H. & CARVER, M.O.H. 1987. Detection and enhancement of decayed inhumations at Sutton Hoo, in *Death, Decay and Reconstruction* (A. Boddington & others eds.), 10–21. Manchester Univ. Press.

BEYNON, A.D. & DEAN, M.C. 1988. Distinct dental development patterns in early fossil hominids. *Nature* 335, 509–14.

BLENCH, R. & SPRIGGS, M. (eds.). 1997. *Archaeology and Language I: Theoretical and Methodological Orientations.* Routledge: London.

BODDINGTON, A., GARLAND, A.N. & JANAWAY, R.C. (eds.). 1987. *Death, Decay and Reconstruction.* Manchester Univ. Press.

BOUCHET, F. & others. 1996. Paléoparasitologie en contexte pléistocène: premières observations à la Grande Grotte d'Arcy-sur-Cure (Yonne), France. *Comptes rendus Acad. Sci. Paris* 319, 147–51.

BRÄUER, G. & SMITH, F.H. (eds.). 1992. *Continuity or Replacement: Controversies in* Homo sapiens *Evolution.* Balkema: Rotterdam.

BROMAGE, T.G. & DEAN, M.C. 1985. Re-evaluation of the age at death of immature fossil hominids. *Nature* 317, 525–27.

BROTHWELL, D.R. 1969. Dietary variation and the biology of earlier human populations, in *The domestication and exploitation of plants and animals* (P.J. Ucko & G.W. Dimbleby eds.), 531–45. Duckworth: London.

——1972. Palaeodemography and earlier British populations. *World Arch.* 4, 75–87.

——1981. *Digging up Bones. The excavation, treatment and study of human skeletal remains.* (3rd ed.) British Museum (Natural History): London; Oxford Univ. Press: Oxford.

——1986. *The Bog Man and the Archaeology of People.* British Museum Publications: London.

——& SANDISON, A.T. (eds.). 1967. *Disease in Antiquity.* C.C. Thomas: Springfield, Illinois.

BROWN, P. 1981. Artificial cranial deformation: a component in the variation in Pleistocene Australian Aboriginal crania. *Archaeology in Oceania* 16, 156–67.

BROWN, T.A. & BROWN, K.A. 1992. Ancient DNA and the archaeologist. *Antiquity* 66, 10–23.

CAMPBELL, A.H. 1981/82. Tooth avulsion in Victorian Aboriginal skulls. *Arch. in Oceania* 16/17, 116–18.

CANN, R.L., STONEKING, M. & WILSON, A.C. 1987. Mitochondrial DNA and human evolution. *Nature* 325, 31–36

CAPASSO, L. 1994. Ungueal morphology and pathology of the human mummy found in the Val Senales (Easter Alps, Tyrol, Bronze Age). *Munibe* 46, 123–32.

CARLISLE, R. & SIEGEL, H. 1974. Some problems in the interpretation of Neanderthal speech capabilities. *American Anthropologist* 76, 319–22.

CASSELBERRY, S.E. 1974. Further refinement of formulae for determining population from floor area. *World Arch.* 6, 116–22.

CATTANEO, C. & others. 1990. Blood in ancient human bone. *Nature* 347, 339.

CAVALLI-SFORZA, L.L. 1991. Genes, peoples and languages. *Scientific American* 265 (5), 72–78.

——, MENOZZI, P. & PIAZZA, A. 1994. *The History and Geography of Human Genes.* Princeton Univ. Press.

CLARKE, R.J. & TOBIAS, P.V. 1995. Sterkfontein Member 2 foot bones of the oldest South African hominid. *Science* 269, 521–24.

COCKBURN, T.A., COCKBURN, E. & REYMAN, T.A. (eds.). 1998. *Mummies, Disease and Ancient Cultures* (2nd ed.). Cambridge Univ. Press.

COHEN, M.N. & ARMELAGOS, G.J. (eds.). 1984. *Palaeopathology at the Origins of Agriculture.* Academic Press: New York & London.

COLES, B. & J. 1989. *People of the Wetlands: Bogs, Bodies and Lake-Dwellers.* Thames & Hudson: London & New York.

CONNOLLY, R.C. & others. 1969. Kinship of Smenkhkare and Tutankhamen affirmed by serological micromethod. *Nature* 224, 325–26.

CONROY, G.C. & VANNIER, M.W. 1987. Dental development of the Taung skull from computerized tomography. *Nature* 329, 625–27.

CORBALLIS, M.C. 1991. *The Lopsided Ape.* Oxford Univ. Press.

COTTERELL, A. 1981. *The First Emperor of China.* Macmillan: London.

CRAWFORD, M.H. 1998. *The Origins of Native Americans. Evidence from anthropological genetics.* Cambridge Univ. Press.

CRUBÉZY, E. & others. 1998. False teeth of the Roman world. *Nature* 391, 29 (& 394, 534).

DASTUGUE, J. & DE LUMLEY, M-A. 1976. Les maladies des hommes préhistoriques du Paléolithique et du Mésolithique, in *La Préhistoire française* Vol. 1:1 (H. de Lumley ed.), 612–22. CNRS: Paris.

DAVID, R. (ed.). 1986. *Science in Egyptology.* Manchester Univ. Press.

——& TAPP, E. (eds.). 1984. *Evidence Embalmed: Modern medicine and the mummies of Egypt.* Manchester Univ. Press.

DAVIDSON, E. 1986. Earliest dental filling shows how ancients battled with "tooth worms," *Popular Archaeology* Feb., 46.

DAY, M.H. & WICKENS, E.H. 1980. Laetoli Pliocene hominid footprints and bipedalism. *Nature* 286, 385–87.

DEAN, M.C. 1985. Variation in the developing root cone angle of the permanent mandibular teeth of modern man and certain fossil hominids. *American Journal of Phys. Anth.* 68, 233–38.

——, STRINGER, C.B. & BROMAGE, T.G. 1986. Age at death of the Neanderthal child from Devil's Tower, Gibraltar, and the implication for studies of general growth and development in Neanderthals. *American Journal of Phys. Anth.* 70, 301–9.

DIBBLE, H.L. 1989. The implications of stone tool types for the presence of language during the Lower and Middle Palaeolithic, in *The Human Revolution* (P. Mellars & C. Stringer eds.), 415–32. Edinburgh Univ. Press.

DOBYNS, H.F. 1966. Estimating Aboriginal American population. *Current Anth.* 7, 395–449.

DOLGOPOLSKY, A. 1998. *The Nostratic Macrofamily and Linguistic Palaeontology.* McDonald Institute: Cambridge.

DORAN, G.H. 1992. Problems and potential of wet sites in North America: the example of Windover, in *The Wetland Revolution in Prehistory* (B. Coles, ed.), 125–34. Prehist. Soc/WARP: Exeter.

——& others. 1986. Anatomical, cellular and molecular analysis of 8,000-yr-old human brain tissue from the Windover archaeological site. *Nature* 323, 803–06.

DUDAY, H. & GARCIA, M. 1986. La paléoichnologie humaine (études des empreintes fossiles). *Bull. Soc. Anth. Sud-Ouest* 21, 43–54.

DURANT, J.R. (ed.). 1989. *Human Origins.* Clarendon Press: Oxford.

DUTOUR, O. 1986. Enthesopathies (lesions of muscular insertions) as indicators of the activities of Neolithic Saharan populations. *American Journal of Phys. Anth.* 71, 221–24.

EL MAHDY, C. 1989. *Mummies, Myth and Magic in Ancient Egypt.* Thames & Hudson: London & New York.

ERICSON, J.E. & COUGHLIN, E.A. 1981. Archaeological toxicology. *Annals of the New York Academy of Sciences* 376, 393–403.

D'ERRICO, F., VILLA, G. & FORNACIARI, G. 1988. Dental esthetics of an Italian Renaissance noblewoman, Isabella d'Aragona. A case of chronic mercury intoxication. *Ossa* 13, 207–28.

EXCOFFIER, L., PELLEGRINI, B., SANCHEZ-MASAS, A., SIMON, C. & LANGANEY, L. 1987. Genetics and the history of sub-Saharan Africa. *Yearbook of Physical Anth.* 30, 151–94.

EYRE-WALKER, A. & others. 1998. How clonal are human mitochondria? *Philosophical Trans. of the Royal Society of London Series B* 266, 477–83.

FAERMAN, M. & others. 1998. Determining the sex of infanticide victims from the late Roman era through ancient DNA analysis. *Journal of Arch. Science* 25, 861–65.

FALK, D. 1983. Cerebral cortices of East African early hominids. *Science* 221, 1072–74.

FENNELL, K.J. & TRINKAUS, E. 1997. Bilateral femoral and tibial periostitis in the La Ferrassie 1 Neanderthal. *Journal of Arch. Science* 24, 985–95.

FLANNERY, K.V. & MARCUS, J. 1983. *The Cloud People: Divergent Evolution of the Zapotec and Mixtec Civilizations.* Academic Press: New York & London.

FORSTER, P. & others. 1996. Origin and evolution of native American mtDNA variation: a re-appraisal. *American Journal of Human Genetics* 59, 935–45.

FOX, A. 1983. Pa and people in New Zealand: an archaeological estimate of population. *New Zealand Journal of Archaeology* 5, 5–18.

FRAYER, D.W. & RUSSELL, M.D. 1987. Artificial grooves in the Krapina Neanderthal teeth. *American Journal of Phys. Anth.* 74, 393–405.

——**& others.** 1988. A case of dwarfism in the Italian late Upper Paleolithic. *American Journal of Phys. Anth.* 75, 549–65.

GEJVALL, N.-G. 1969. Cremations, in *Science in Archaeology* (D. Brothwell & E.S. Higgs eds.), 468–79. (2nd ed.) Thames & Hudson: London.

GENOVES, S. 1969a. Sex determination in earlier man, in *Science in Archaeology* (D. Brothwell & E.S. Higgs eds.), 429–39. (2nd ed.) Thames & Hudson: London.

——1969b. Estimation of age and mortality, in *Science in Archaeology* (D. Brothwell & E.S. Higgs eds.), 440–52. (2nd ed.) Thames & Hudson: London.

GERASIMOV, M.M. 1971. *The Face Finder.* Hutchinson: London.

GIBBONS, A. 1996. The peopling of the Americas. *Science* 274, 31–33.

GILL, G.W. & RHINE, S. (eds.). 1990. *Skeletal Attribution of Race.* Anth. Paper 4, Maxwell Museum of Anthropology: Albuquerque.

GLOB, P.V. 1969. *The Bog People.* Faber: London.

——1973. *The Mound People. Danish Bronze Age man preserved.* Faber: London.

GOLDSTEIN, M.S. 1969. The palaeopathology of human skeletal remains, in *Science in Archaeology* (D. Brothwell & E.S. Higgs eds.), 480–89. (2nd ed.) Thames & Hudson: London.

GORE, R. 1984. The dead do tell tales at Vesuvius. *National Geographic* 165 (5), 556–613.

GOYON, J-C. & JOSSET, P. 1988. *Un Corps pour l'Eternité. Autopsie d'une Momie.* Le Léopard d'Or: Paris.

GREENBERG, J.H. 1963. *The Languages of Africa.* Stanford Univ. Press.

——1987. *Language in the Americas.* Stanford Univ. Press.

——**, TURNER, C.G. & ZEGURA, S.L.** 1986. The settlement of the Americas: a comparison of the linguistic, dental and genetic evidence. *Current Anth.* 27, 477–97.

GREMILLION, K.J. & SOBOLIK, K.D. 1996. Dietary variability among prehistoric forager-farmers of eastern North America. *Current Anth.* 37, 529–39.

GROENEN, M. 1988. Les représentations de mains négatives dans les grottes de Gargas et de Tibiran. *Bull. Soc. Royale Belge d'Anth. et de Préhist.* 99, 81–113.

HAGELBERG, E. 1993. DNA from archaeological bone. *The Biochemist* Aug/Sept 17–22.

——1993/4. Ancient DNA studies. *Evolutionary Anthropology* 2, 199–207.

——**& CLEGG, J.B.** 1993. Genetic polymorphisms in prehistoric Pacific islanders determined by analysis of ancient bone DNA. *Proc. Royal Soc. London B* 252, 163–70.

——**, SYKES, B. & HEDGES, R.** 1989. Ancient bone DNA amplified. *Nature* 342, 485.

——**, GOLDMAN, N., LIO, P. & others.** 1999. Evidence of mitochondrial DNA recombination in a human population of island Melanesia. *Philosophical Trans. of the Royal Society of London Series B* 266 485–92.

HAMMER, M.F. 1995. A recent common ancestry for human Y chromosomes. *Nature* 378, 376–78.

HARRIS, J.E. & WEEKS, K.R. 1973. *X-Raying the Pharaohs.* Macdonald: London.

——**& others.** 1978. Mummy of the 'Elder Lady' in the tomb of Amenhotep II. *Science* 200, 1149–51.

HARRISON, R.G. & ABDALLA, A.B. 1972. The remains of Tutankhamun. *Antiquity* 46, 8–14.

——**& others.** 1979. A mummified foetus from the tomb of Tutankhamen. *Antiquity* 53, 19–21.

HART, G.D. (ed.), 1983. *Disease in Ancient Man.* Clarke Irwin: Toronto.

HART HANSEN, J.P., MELDGAARD, J. & NORDQVIST, J. 1985. The mummies of Qilakitsoq. *National Geographic* 167 (2), 190–207.

——**, —— & ——**(eds.). 1991. *The Greenland Mummies.* British Museum Press: London.

HASSAN, F.A. 1978. Demographic archaeology, in *Advances in Archaeological Method and Theory 1* (M.B. Schiffer ed.), 49–103. Academic Press: New York & London.

——1981. *Demographic Archaeology.* Academic Press: New York & London.

HEDGES, J.W. 1983. *Isbister: A chambered tomb in Orkney.* British Arch. Reports, Int. Series 115: Oxford.

HERRMANN, B. & HUMMEL, S. (eds.). 1994. *Ancient DNA.* Springer-Verlag: New York.

HIGHAM, C. & THOSARAT, R. 1998. *Prehistoric Thailand, from Early Settlement to Sukhothai.* River Books: Bangkok; Thames & Hudson: London.

HILL, A.V. & SERJEANTSON, S.W. (eds.). 1989. *The Colonisation of the Pacific: a Genetic Trail.* Oxford Univ. Press.

HILLSON, S.W. 1979. Diet and dental disease. *World Arch.* 11, 147–61.

——1986. *Teeth.* Cambridge Univ. Press.

HOLLOWAY, R.L. 1983. Cerebral brain endocast pattern of *Australopithecus afarensis* hominid. *Nature* 303, 420–22.

HOUGHTON, P. 1980. *The First New Zealanders.* Hodder & Stoughton: Auckland.

HURTADO DE MENDOZA, D. & BRAGINSKI, R. 1999. Y chromosomes of Native American Adam. *Science* 283, 1439–40.

ISAAC, G.L. 1976. Stages of cultural elaboration in the Pleistocene: possible archaeological indicators of the development of language capabilities, in *Origins and Evolution of Language and Speech* (S.R. Harnad & others eds.), 276–88. Annals of the New York Acad. of Sciences 280.

ISCAN, M.Y. & MILLER-SHAIVITZ, P. 1984. Determination of sex from the tibia. *American Journal of Phys. Anth.* 64, 53–57.

JANSSENS, P. 1970. *Palaeopathology.* Humanities: New Jersey.

JOHANSON, D. & EDGAR, B. 1996. *From Lucy to Language.* Simon & Schuster: New York.

JORDAN, P. 1983. *The Face of the Past.* Batsford: London.

KAUFFMANN-DOIG, F. 1979. *Sexual Behaviour in Ancient Peru.* Lima.

KAY, R.F. & others. 1998. The hypoglossal canal and the origin of human vocal behavior. *Proceedings of the National Academy of Sciences USA* 95, 5417–19.

KERLEY, E.R. 1965. The microscopic determination of age in human bone. *American Journal of Phys. Anth.* 23, 149–64.

KLEIN, R.G. 1999. *The Human Career* (2nd ed.). Univ. of Chicago Press.

KRINGS, M., STONE, A., SCHMILTZ, R. & others. 1997. Neanderthal DNA sequences and the origin of modern humans. *Cell* 90, 19–30.

LAITMAN, J.T. 1986. L'origine du langage articulé. *La Recherche* 17, No. 181, 1164–73.

LALLO, J.W. & ROSE, J.C. 1979. Patterns of stress, disease and mortality in two prehistoric populations from North America. *Journal of Human Evolution* 8, 323–35.

LAMBERT, B., SZPUNAR, C.B. & BUIKSTRA, J.E. 1979. Chemical analysis of excavated human bone from Middle and Late

Woodland sites. *Archaeometry* 21, 115–29.

LAMPL, M. & others. 1991. L'émail dentaire: une horloge controversée. *La Recherche* 236, 1225–27.

LARSEN, C.S. 1981. Skeletal and dental adaptations to the shift to agriculture on the Georgia coast. *Current Anth.* 22, 422–23; see also 24 (1983) 225–26.

———1997. *Bioarchaeology: Interpreting Behaviour from the Human Skeleton.* Cambridge Univ. Press.

LATIMER, B., OHMAN, J.C. & LOVEJOY, C.O. 1987. Talocrural joint in African hominoids: implications for *Australopithecus afarensis*. *American Journal of Phys. Anth.* 74, 155–75.

LEAKEY, M.D. 1979. Footprints in the ashes of time. *National Geographic* 155 (4), 446–57.

———**& HARRIS, J.M.** (eds.). 1987. *Laetoli, a Pliocene Site in Northern Tanzania.* Clarendon Press: Oxford.

LEAKEY, R. & LEWIN, R. 1992. *Origins Reconsidered. In search of what makes us human.* Little, Brown: Boston.

LIEBERMAN, P. 1998. *Eve Spoke.* Picador/Macmillan: London.

———**& CRELIN, E.S.** 1974. Speech and Neanderthal Man. *American Anthropologist* 76, 323–25.

LILLIE, M.C. 1998. Cranial surgery dates back to the Mesolithic. *Nature* 391, 854.

LOWENSTEIN, J.M. 1985. Molecular approaches to the identification of species. *American Scientist* 73, 541–47.

LOY, T.H. 1987. Recent advances in blood residue analysis, in *Archaeometry, further Australasian studies* (W.R. Ambrose & J.M.C. Mummery eds.), 57–65. Dept of Prehistory, Australian National Univ.: Canberra.

MCMAHON, A.M.S. & MCMAHON, R. 1995. Linguistics, genetics and archaeology: internal and external evidence in the Amerind controversy. *Trans. of the Philological Society* 93, 123–225.

MAIURI, A. 1961. Last moments of the Pompeians. *National Geographic* 120 (5), 650–69.

MASSET, C. 1975. La mortalité préhistorique. *Cahiers du Centre de Recherches Préhistoriques* 4 (Paris), 63–90.

MAYS, S.A. 1985. The relationship between Harris Line formation and bone growth and development. *Journal of Arch. Science* 12, 207–20.

———1998. *The Archaeology of Human Bones.* Routledge: London.

MELLARS, P. & STRINGER, C.B. (eds.). 1989. *The Human Revolution.* Edinburgh Univ. Press.

MERRIWETHER, D.A. 1999. Freezer anthropology: new uses for old blood. *Philosophical Trans. Royal Society of London, Series B* 354, 3–5.

MILISAUSKAS, S. 1972. An analysis of Linear culture longhouses at Olszanica BI, Poland. *World Arch.* 4, 57–74.

MOLLESON, T.I. 1989. Seed preparation in the Mesolithic: the osteological evidence. *Antiquity* 63, 356–62.

———1994. The eloquent bones of Abu Hureyra. *Scientific American* 271 (2), 60–65.

———**& COX, M.** 1988. A neonate with cut bones from Poundbury Camp, 4th century AD, England. *Bull. Soc. royale belge Anthrop. Préhist.* 99, 53–59.

———**&**———1993. *The Spitalfields Project.* Vol. 2, The Anthropology. Council for British Arch. Research Report 86: York.

———**, ELDRIDGE, D. & GALE, N.** 1985. Identification of lead sources by stable isotope ratios in bones and lead from Poundbury Camp, Dorset. *Oxford Journal of Arch.* 5, 249–53.

MURDY, C.N. 1981. Congenital deformities and the Olmec were-jaguar motif. *American Antiquity* 46, 861–71.

MUSGRAVE, J.H. 1971. How dextrous was Neanderthal Man? *Nature* 233, 538–41.

NAROLL, R. 1962. Floor area and settlement population. *American Antiquity* 27, 587–89.

NEDDEN, D. & others. 1994. Skull of a 5,300-year-old mummy: reproduction and investigation with CT-guided Stereolithography. *Radiology* 193, 269–72.

NICHOLS, J. 1992. *Linguistic Diversity in Space and Time.* Univ. of Chicago.

NETTLE, D. 1999. Linguistic diversity of the Americas can be reconciled with a recent colonization. *Proc. Nat. Acad. Sci. USA* 96, 3325–29.

NITECKI, M.H. & NITECKI, D.V. (eds.). 1994. *Origins of Anatomically Modern Humans.* Plenum: New York & London.

OBERLIN, C. & SAKKA, M. 1993. Le pouce de l'homme de Néanderthal, in *La Main dans la Préhistoire, Dossiers d'Archéologie* 178, 24–31.

ORTNER, D.J. & PUTSCHAR, W.G.J. 1985. *Identification of Pathological Conditions in Human Skeletal Remains.* (2nd ed.) Smithsonian Contribs. to Anth. No. 28: Washington D.C.

———**& AUFDERHEIDE, A.C.** (eds.). 1991. *Human Paleopathology: Current syntheses and future options.* Smithsonian Institution Press: Washington D.C.

PÄÄBO, S. 1985. Preservation of DNA in ancient Egyptian mummies. *Journal of Arch. Science* 12, 411–17.

———1989. Ancient DNA. Extraction, characterization, molecular cloning and enzymatic amplification. *Proc. Nat. Acad. of Sciences USA* 86, 1939–43.

———1993. Ancient DNA. *Scientific American* 269, 60–66.

PAHL, W.M. 1980. Computed tomography — a new radiodiagnostical technique applied to medico-archaeological investigation of Egyptian mummies. *Ossa* 7, 189–98.

PALES, L. 1976. *Les empreintes de pieds humains dans les cavernes.* Archives de l'Institut de Paléontologie Humaine No. 36. Masson: Paris.

———**& DE ST PÉREUSE, M.T.** 1976. *Les Gravures de la Marche. II: Les Humains.* Ophrys: Paris.

PATRUCCO, R. & others. 1983 Parasitological studies of coprolites of pre-Hispanic Peruvian populations. *Current Anth.* 24, 393–94.

PFEIFFER, S. 1980. Bone-remodelling age estimates compared with estimates by other techniques. *Current Anth.* 21, 793–94; and 22, 437–38.

POLONI, E.S., SEMINO, O. PASSARINO, G. & others. 1997. Human genetic affinities for Y-chromosome haplotypes show strong correspondence with linguistics. *American Journal of Human Genetics* 61, 1015–35.

PRAG, A.J.N., MUSGRAVE, J.H. & NEAVE, R.A.H. 1984. The skull from tomb II at Vergina: King Philip of Macedon. *Journal of Hellenic Studies* 104, 65–68.

———**& NEAVE, R.** 1997. *Making Faces, Using Forensic and Archaeological Evidence.* British Museum Press: London.

PREMATILLAKE, P. 1989. A Buddhist monastic complex of the mediaeval period in Sri Lanka, in *Domination and Resistance* (D. Miller & others eds.), 196–210. Unwin Hyman: London.

PUECH, P.-F. 1978. L'alimentation de l'homme préhistorique. *La Recherche* 9, 1029–31.

———**& CIANFARANI, R.** 1985. La Paléodontologie: étude des maladies des dents, in *Les Maladies de nos Ancêtres. Dossiers de l'Archéologie* 97, Sept., 28–33.

RENFREW, C. 1991. Before Babel: speculations on the origins of linguistic diversity. *Cambridge Archaeological Journal* 1(1), 3–23.

———1992. Archaeology, genetics and linguistic diversity, *Man* 27, 445–78.

———**& NETTLE, D.** (eds.). 1999. *Nostratic – Examining a Linguistic Macrofamily.* McDonald Institute: Cambridge.

ROBERTS, C. & MANCHESTER, K. 1995. *The Archaeology of Disease* (2nd ed.). Alan Sutton: Stroud; Cornell Univ. Press: Ithaca.

ROBERTS, G., GONZALEZ, S. & HUDDART, D. 1996. Intertidal Holocene footprints and their archaeological significance. *Antiquity* 70, 647–51.

ROBINSON, J.T. 1972. *Early Hominid Posture and Locomotion.* Univ. of Chicago Press.

ROSS, P.E. 1992. Eloquent remains. *Scientific American* 266 (5), 72–81.

ROTHHAMMER, F. & others. 1985. Chagas' Disease in Pre-Columbian South America. *American Journal of Phys. Anth.* 68, 495–98.

ROTHSCHILD, B.M. & MARTIN, L. 1992. *Palaeopathology. Disease in the fossil record.* CRC Press: Boca Raton.

RUDENKO, S.I. 1970. *The Frozen Tombs of Siberia.* Dent: London.

RUHLEN, M. 1991. *A Guide to the World's Languages I.* Stanford Univ. Press.

SALO, W.L. & others. 1994. Identification of *Mycobacterium tuberculosis* DNA in a pre-Columbian Peruvian mummy. *Proc. Natl. Acad. Sci. USA* 91, 2091–94.

VAN DER SANDEN, W. 1996. *Through Nature to Eternity. The Bog Bodies of Northwest Europe.* Batavian Lion International: Amsterdam.

SANTOS, F.R., PANDYA, A., TYLER-SMITH, C. & others. 1999. The central Siberian origin for native American Y chromosome. *American Journal of Human Genetics* 64, 6199–628.

SCOTT, D.D. & CONNOR, M.A. 1986. Post-mortem at the Little Bighorn. *Natural History* June, 46–55.

——, FOX, R.A., CONNOR, M.A. & HARMON, D. 1989. *Archaeological Perspectives on the Battle of the Little Bighorn.* Univ. of Oklahoma Press: Norman.

SIMS-WILLIAMS, P. 1998. Genetics, linguistics and prehistory: thinking big and thinking straight. *Antiquity* 72, 505–27.

SMITH, B.H. 1986. Dental development in *Australopithecus* and early *Homo. Nature* 323, 327–30.

SMITH, F.H. 1983. Behavioral interpretation of change in craniofacial morphology across the archaic/modern *Homo sapiens* transition, in *The Mousterian Legacy* (E. Trinkaus ed.), 141–63. British Arch. Reports, Int. Series 164: Oxford.

SMITH, P. 1972. Diet and attrition in the Natufians. *American Journal of Phys. Anth.* 37, 233–38.

SOKAL, R.R., ODEN, N.L. & WILSON, A.C. 1991. New genetic evidence supports the origin of agriculture in Europe by demic diffusion, *Nature* 351, 143–44.

——, ——& THOMSON, B.A. 1992. Origins of Indo-European: genetic evidence. *Proc. the Nat. Acad. of Sciences of the USA* 89, 7669–73.

SPOOR, F., WOOD, B. & ZONNEVELD, F. 1994. Implications of early hominid labyrinthine morphology for evolution of human bipedal locomotion. *Nature* 369, 645–48.

STEAD, I.M., BOURKE, J.B. & BROTHWELL, D. (eds.). 1986. *Lindow Man.* British Museum Publications: London.

STERN, J.T. & SUSMAN, R.L. 1983. The locomotor anatomy of *Australopithecus afarensis. American Journal of Phys. Anth.* 60, 279–317.

STONE, A.C., MILNER, G. & PÄÄBO, S. 1996. Sex determination of ancient human skeletons using DNA. *American Journal of Phys. Anth.* 99, 231–38.

——& STONEKING, M. 1999. Analysis of ancient DNA from a prehistoric Amerindian cemetery. *Philosophical Trans. of the Royal Society of London, Series B* 354, 153–59.

STOREY, G.R. 1997. The population of ancient Rome. *Antiquity* 71, 966–78.

STRAUSS, E. 1999. Can mitochondrial clocks keep time? *Science* 283, 1435–38.

SUERES, M. 1991. Les mains de Gargas: approche expérimentale et statistique du problème des mutilations. *Travaux de l'Institut d'Art Préhistorique de Toulouse* 33, 9–200.

SUSMAN, R.L. 1994. Fossil evidence for early hominid tool use. *Science* 265, 1570–73.

SUTTON, M.Q., MALIK, M. & OGRAM, A. 1996. Experiments on the determination of gender from coprolites by DNA analysis. *Journal of Arch. Science* 23, 263–67.

TATTERSALL, I. 1992. Evolution comes to life. *Scientific American* 267 (2), 62–69.

TEMPLETON, A.R. 1992. Human origins and analysis of mitochondrial DNA sequences. *Science* 255, 737.

THORNE, A.G. & WOLPOFF, M.H. 1992. The multiregional evolution of humans. *Scientific American* 266 (4), 76–83.

TORRONI, A. & others. 1994. Mitochondrial DNA and Y-chromosome polymorphisms in four native American populations from southern Mexico. *American Journal of Human Genetics* 54.

——& others. 1992. Native American mitochondrial DNA analysis indicates that the Amerind and Nadene populations were founded by two independent migrations, *Genetics* 130, 153–62.

TOTH, N. 1985. Archaeological evidence for preferential right-handedness in the lower and middle Pleistocene, and its possible implications. *Journal of Human Evolution* 14, 607–14.

TRINKAUS, E. 1975. Squatting among the Neanderthals: a problem in the behavioural interpretation of skeletal morphology. *Journal of Arch. Science* 2, 327–51.

——1982. Artificial cranial deformation in the Shanidar 1 and 5 Neanderthals. *Current Anth.* 23, 198–99.

——1983. *The Shanidar Neanderthals.* Academic Press: New York & London.

TROTTER, M. & GLESER, G.C. 1958. A reevaluation of estimation of stature based on measurements of stature taken during life and of long bones after death. *American Journal of Phys. Anth.* 16, 79–123.

TURNER, R.C. & SCAIFE, R.G. (eds.). 1995. *Bog Bodies. New Discoveries and New Perspectives.* British Museum Press: London.

TUTTLE, R., WEBB, D. & WEIDL, E. 1990. Further progress on the Laetoli trails. *Journal of Arch. Science* 17, 347–62.

UBELAKER, D.H. 1984. *Human Skeletal Remains.* (Rev. ed.) Taraxacum: Washington.

URTEAGA-BALLON, O. & WELLS, C. 1968. Gynaecology in Ancient Peru. *Antiquity* 42, 233–34.

VLCEK, E. 1952. Empreintes papillaires d'un homme paléolithique. *L'Anthropologie* 56, 557–58.

WAINSCOAT, J.S. & others. 1986. Evolutionary relationship of human populations from the analysis of nuclear DNA polymorphisms. *Nature* 319, 491–93; see also p. 449.

WARD, R. & STRINGER, C. 1997. A molecular handle on the Neanderthals. *Nature* 388, 225–26.

WELLS, C. 1964. *Bones, Bodies and Disease.* Thames & Hudson: London.

WELLS, L.H. 1969. Stature in earlier races of mankind, in *Science in Archaeology* (D. Brothwell & E.S. Higgs eds.), 453–67. (2nd ed.) Thames & Hudson: London.

WHITE, T. 1991. *Human Osteology.* Academic Press: New York.

ZIMMERMAN, M.R. & ANGEL, J.L. (eds.). 1986. *Dating and age determination of biological materials.* Croom Helm: London.

ZOLLIKOFER, C.P.E. & others. 1995. Neanderthal computer skulls. *Nature* 375, 283–85.

Chapter 12: Why Did Things Change? Explanation in Archaeology
(pp. 461–496)

p. 461 **Historical analysis** Braudel's three levels: Braudel 1972.

p. 462 **The individual** Methodological individualism: Bell 1994; Renfrew 1987a. Structuration theory: Giddens 1984; Bourdieu 1977; Barrett 1994.

pp. 463–65 **"Traditional" explanation** Culture = people hypothesis first set out in English: Childe 1929; its history traced: Trigger 1978, 1989. Renfrew 1969 & 1973a (Ch.5) discusses Childe's Vinča/Troy diffusionist link; 1982. Lapita: Green 1979; Bellwood 1987. Spread of alphabet: Gelb 1952. Issue of local innovation versus diffusion: Renfrew 1978a.

pp. 465–72 **Processual approach** Flannery 1967; Binford 1972, 1983. **Applications** Clark, J.G.D. 1952 (Swedish megaliths). Binford 1968 (origins of agriculture), and see now Binford 1999; Bender 1978 (alternative model).

p. 472 **Marxism** and human society: Childe 1936. **Marxist archaeology:** Gilman 1976, 1981; Friedman & Rowlands 1978; Frankenstein & Rowlands 1978; Spriggs 1984. Structural Marxism: Friedman 1974.

pp. 472–74 **Evolutionary archaeology** Dawkins 1989, but see Lake 1999; for Cultural Virus theory Cullen 1993. For evolutionary psychology: Tooby & Cosmides 1990; Barkow & others 1992; also Mithen 1996; Sperber 1996. For neo-evolutionary thought in the US and beyond: Dunnell 1980, 1995; Durham 1991; Cavalli-Sforza & Feldman 1981; Boyd & Richerson 1985; Maschner 1996; O'Brien 1996; Lyman & O'Brien 1998; Bintliff 1999.

pp. 474–75 **Universal laws** in the natural sciences: Hempel 1966. Other accounts of scientific reasoning: Braithwaite 1960; Popper 1985. Application of universal laws to archaeology: Watson, LeBlanc & Redman 1971, criticized by Flannery 1973 and Trigger 1978. Collingwood 1946 and Hodder 1986 cover the contrasting idealist-historical standpoint.

pp. 476–83 **Origins of the state** Alternative theories: Wittfogel 1957; Diakonoff 1969; Carneiro 1970, 1978; Renfrew 1972; Johnson & Earle 1987; Marcus 1990; Morris 1987. Agricultural intensification: Boserup 1965. Greg Johnson's work: Johnson 1982. Rathje's Maya work: Rathje 1971. Systems approach to origins of Mesoamerican agriculture: Flannery 1968. **Simulation** Chadwick's work: Chadwick 1979. Systems Dynamic Modeling: Zubrow 1981 (ancient Rome). Gilbert & Doran 1994; Mithen 1990. Multi-agent simulation: Drogoul & Ferber 1994.

pp. 483–86 **Postprocessual explanation** Structuralist approaches: Glassie 1975; Arnold 1983 examines a recent case study. See also Ch. 1.

pp. 486–91 **Critical Theory** Hodder 1986 and Shanks & Tilley 1987a, 1987b. **Neo-Marxist thought** Leone 1984 (Paca). Miller 1980 (Third World).

pp. 491–95 **Cognitive-processual archaeology** Good examples are found in Flannery & Marcus 1983; Schele & Miller, 1986; Conrad & Demarest 1984; Freidel 1981; Renfrew & Zubrow 1994; Earle 1997; Feinman & Marcus 1998; Blanton 1998; Rappaport 1999; Mann 1986; Flannery 1999. **Punctuated equilibria:** Gould & Eldredge 1977. Rise of Minoan palaces: Cherry 1983, 1984, 1986. **Catastrophe theory** is analyzed by Thom 1975; Zeeman 1977; Renfrew 1978a, 1978b. **Self-organization in non-equilibrium systems** Prigogine 1979, 1987; Prigogine & Stengers 1984; Allen 1982; van der Leeuw & McGlade 1997.

Box Features

pp. 464–65 **Great Zimbabwe** Garlake 1973.

p. 467 **Language Families and Language Change** Mallory 1989; Ruhlen 1991; Renfrew 1987b, 1990, 1991, 1992, 1994, 1996, 1998; Philipson 1977; Bellwood 1991, 1996; Diamond 1997.

pp. 468–69 **Molecular Genetics and Population Dynamics** Cavalli-Sforza & others 1994; Richards & others 1996; Sykes 1999; Malaspina & others 1998; Torroni & others 1998.

p. 471 **Origins of Farming** Binford 1968.

p. 473 **Marxist Archaeology** See main text references above.

pp. 478–79 **Origins of the State 1: Peru** Carneiro 1970.

pp. 480–81 **Origins of the State 2: The Aegean** Renfrew 1972. Utility of systems theory in archaeology: Salmon 1978.

pp. 484–85 **Classic Maya Collapse** Culbert 1973; Hosler & others 1977; Renfrew 1979; Doran 1981; Lowe 1985. Recent studies of state collapse: Tainter 1988; Yoffee & Cowgill 1988. Drought: Hodell & others 1995.

pp. 488–89 **European Megaliths** Different interpretations: Renfrew 1976 and Chapman 1981 (functional-processual); Tilley 1984 (neo-Marxist); Hodder 1984; Whittle 1996 (postprocessual): for the "Neo-Wessex school" see biblio. for Chapter 10, p. 397–99.

pp. 492–93 **The Individual as an Agent of Change.** Robb 1994; Mithen 1990; Barrett 1994; Flannery 1999.

Bibliography

ALLEN, P.M. 1982. The genesis of structure in social systems: the paradigm of self-organization, in *Theory and Explanation in Archaeology* (C. Renfrew, M.J. Rowlands & B.A. Segraves eds.), 347–74. Academic Press: New York & London.

ARNOLD, D.E. 1983. Design structure and community organization in Quinua, Peru, in *Structure and Cognition in Art* (D.K. Washburn ed.), 40–55. Cambridge Univ. Press.

BARKOW, J.H., COSMIDES, L. & TOOBY, J. 1992. *The Adapted Mind: Evolutionary Psychology and the Generation of Culture.* Oxford Univ. Press.

BARRETT, J.C. 1994. *Fragments from Antiquity,* Oxford: Blackwell.

BELL, J.A. 1994. *Reconstructing Prehistory: Scientific Method in Archaeology.* Temple University Press: Philadelphia.

BELLWOOD, P. 1987. *The Polynesians* (Rev. ed.) Thames & Hudson: London & New York.

——1991. The Austronesian dispersal and the origins of language. *Scientific American* 265, 88–93.

——1996. The origins and spread of agriculture in the Indo-Pacific region: gradualism and diffusion or revolution and colonization, in the *Origin and Spread of Agriculture and Pastoralism in Eurasia* (D.R. Harris, ed.), 465–98. UCL Press: London.

BENDER, B. 1978. Gatherer-hunter to farmer: a social perspective. *World Arch* 10, 204–22.

BINFORD, L.R. 1968. Post-Pleistocene adaptations, in *New Perspectives in Archaeology* (S.R. Binford & L.R. Binford eds.), 313–41. Aldine: Chicago.

——1972. *An Archaeological Perspective.* Seminar Press: New York & London.

——1983. *In Pursuit of the Past.* Thames & Hudson: London & New York.

——1999. Time as a clue to cause? *Proceedings of the British Academy* 101.

BINTLIFF, J. (ed.). 1999. *Structure and Contingency: Evolutionary Processes in Life and Human Society.* Leicester Univ. Press: London.

BLANTON, R. 1998. Beyond centralization: steps towards a theory of egalitarian behavior in archaic states, in *Archaic States* (G.M. Feinman & J. Marcus eds.). School of American Research Press: Santa Fe.

BOSERUP, E. 1965. *The Conditions of Agricultural Growth.* Aldine: Chicago.

BOURDIEU P. 1977. *Outline of a Theory of Practice.* Cambridge Univ. Press.

BOYD, R. & RICHERSON, J. 1985. *Culture and Evolutionary Process.* Univ. of Chicago Press.

BRAITHWAITE, R.B. 1960. *Scientific Explanation.* Cambridge Univ. Press.

BRAUDEL, F. 1972. *The Mediterranean and the Mediterranean World in the Reign of Philip II.* Collins: London.

CARNEIRO, R.L. 1970. A theory of the origin of the state. *Science* 169, 733–38.

——1978. Political expansion as an expression of the principle of competitive exclusion, in *Origins of the state: the anthropology of political evolution* (R. Cohen & E.R. Service eds.), 205–23. Institute for the Study of Human Issues: Philadelphia.

CAVALLI-SFORZA, L.L. & FELDMAN, M. 1981. *Cultural Transmission and Evolution: A Quantitative Approach.* Princeton Univ. Press.

——, MENOZZI, P. & PIAZZA, N. 1994. *The History and Geography of Human Genes.* Princeton Univ. Press.

CHADWICK, A.J. 1979. Settlement simulation, in *Transformations. Mathematical Approaches to Culture Change* (C. Renfrew & K.L. Cooke eds.), 237–55. Academic Press: New York & London.

CHAPMAN, R. 1981. The emergence of formal disposal areas and the "problem" of megalithic tombs in prehistoric Europe, in *The Archaeology of Death* (R. Chapman, I. Kinnes & K. Randsborg eds.), 71–81. Cambridge Univ. Press.

CHERRY, J.F. 1983. Evolution, revolution, and the origins of complex society in Minoan Crete, in *Minoan Society. Proceedings of the Cambridge Colloquium 1981* (O. Krzyszkowska & L. Nixon eds.). Bristol Classical Press: Bristol.

——1984. The emergence of the state in the prehistoric Aegean. *Proceedings of the Cambridge Philological Society* 30, 18–48.

——1986. Polities and palaces: some problems in Minoan state formation, in *Peer polity interaction and socio-political change* (C. Renfrew & J.F. Cherry eds.), 19–45. Cambridge Univ. Press.

CHILDE, V.G. 1929. *The Danube in Prehistory.* Clarendon Press: Oxford.

——1936. *Man Makes Himself.* Watts: London.

CLARK, J.G.D. 1952. *Prehistoric Europe: the Economic Basis.* Methuen: London.

COLLINGWOOD, R.G. 1946. *The Idea of History.* Oxford Univ. Press.

CONRAD, G.W. & DEMAREST, A.A. 1984. *Religion and Empire. The Dynamics of Aztec and Inca Expansion.* Cambridge Univ. Press.

CULBERT, T.P. (ed.). 1973. *The Classic Maya Collapse*. Univ. of New Mexico Press: Albuquerque.

CULLEN, B. 1993. The Darwinian resurgence and the cultural virus critique. *Cambridge Archaeological Journal*, 3, 179–202.

DAWKINS, R. 1989. *The Selfish Gene*. Oxford Univ. Press.

DIAKONOFF, I.M. 1969. The rise of the despotic state in Ancient Mesopotamia, in *Ancient Mesopotamia: socio-economic history* (I.M. Diakonoff ed.). Moscow.

DIAMOND, J. 1997. The language steamrollers. *Nature* 389, 544–46.

DORAN, J. 1981. Multi-actor systems and the Maya collapse, in *Coloquio: Manejo de Datos y Metodos Matemáticos de Arqueología* (G.L. Cowgill, R. Whallon & B.S. Ottaway eds.), 191–200. UISPP: Mexico City.

DROGOUL, A. & FERBER, J. 1994. Multi-agent simulation as a tool for studying emergent processes in societies, in *Simulating Societies: the Computer Simulation of Social Phenomena* (N. Gilbert & J. Doran eds.), 127–42. UCL Press: London.

DUNNELL, R.C. 1980. Evolutionary theory and archaeology, in *Advances in Archaeological Method and Theory* 3 (M.B. Schiffer ed.), 38–99. Academic Press: New York & London.

——1995. What is it that actually evolves? in *Evolutionary Archaeology: Methodological Issues* (P.A. Teltser ed.), 33–50. University of Arizona Press: Tucson.

DURHAM, W.H. 1990. Advances in evolutionary culture theory. *Annual Review of Anthropology* 19, 187–210.

——1991. *Coevolution: Genes, culture and human diversity*. Stanford Univ. Presss: Palo Alto.

EARLE, T. 1997. *How Chiefs Come to Power, the Political Economy in Prehistory*. Stanford Univ. Press.

FEINMAN, G.M. & MARCUS, J. (eds.). 1998. *Archaic States*. School of American Research Press: Santa Fe.

FLANNERY, K.V. 1967. Culture history vs. cultural process: a debate in American archaeology. *Scientific American* 217, 119–22.

——1968. Archaeological Systems Theory and Early Mesoamerica, in *Anthropological Archaeology in the Americas* (B.J. Meggers ed.), 67–87. Anthropological Society of Washington.

——1973. Archaeology with a capital 'S', in *Research and Theory in Current Archaeology* (C.L. Redman ed.), 47–53. Wiley: New York.

——1999. Process and agency in early state formation. *Cambridge Archaeological Journal* 9(1), 3–21.

——& MARCUS, J. 1983. *The Cloud People: Divergent Evolution of the Zapotec and Mixtec Civilizations*. Academic Press: New York & London.

FRANKENSTEIN, S. & ROWLANDS, M.J. 1978. The internal structure and regional context of Early Iron Age Society in south-western Germany. *Bulletin of the Institute of Archaeology* 15, 73–112.

FREIDEL, D. 1981. Civilization as a state of mind: the cultural evolution of the Lowland Maya, in *The Transition to Statehood in the New World* (G.D. Jones & R.R. Kautz eds.), 188–227. Cambridge Univ. Press.

FRIEDMAN, J. 1974. Marxism, structuralism and vulgar materialism. *Man* 9, 444–69.

——& ROWLANDS, M.J. 1978. Notes towards an epigenetic model of the evolution of "civilisation," in *The Evolution of Social Systems* (J. Friedman & M.J. Rowlands eds.), 201–78. Duckworth: London.

GARLAKE, P.S. 1973. *Great Zimbabwe*. Thames & Hudson: London; McGraw-Hill: New York.

GELB, I.J. 1952. *A Study of Writing*. Univ. of Chicago Press.

GIDDENS, A. 1984. *The Constitution of Society*. Univ. of California Press: Berkeley.

GILBERT, N. & DORAN, J. (eds.). 1994. *Simulating Societies: the Computer Simulation of Social Phenomena*. UCL Press: London.

GILMAN, A. 1976. Bronze Age dynamics in south-east Spain. *Dialectical Anthropology* 1, 307–19.

——1981. The development of social stratification in Bronze Age Europe. *Current Anth.* 22, 1–23.

GLASSIE, H. 1975. *Folk Housing in Middle Virginia*. Univ. of Tennessee Press: Knoxville.

GOULD, S.J. & ELDREDGE, N. 1977. Punctuated equilibria: the tempo and mode of evolution reconsidered. *Palaeobiology* 3, 115–51.

GREEN, R.C. 1979. Lapita, in *The Prehistory of Polynesia* (J.D. Jennings ed.), 27–60. Harvard Univ. Press: Cambridge, Mass.

HEMPEL, C.G. 1966. *Philosophy of Natural Science*. Prentice-Hall: Englewood Cliffs, N.J.

HODDER, I. 1984. Burials, houses, women and men in the European Neolithic, in *Ideology, Power and Prehistory* (D. Miller & C. Tilley eds.), 51–68. Cambridge Univ. Press.

——1986. *Reading the Past*. Cambridge Univ. Press.

HODELL, D.A., CURTIS, J.H. & BRENNER, M. 1995. Possible role of climate in the collapse of Classic Maya civilization. *Nature* 375, 391–94.

HOSLER, D.H., SABLOFF, J.A. & RUNGE, D. 1977. Simulation model development: a case study of the Classic Maya collapse, in *Social Processes in Maya Prehistory* (N. Hammond ed.), 553–90. Academic Press: New York & London.

JOHNSON, A.W. & EARLE, T. 1987. *The Evolution of Human Societies: from Foraging Group to Agrarian State*. Stanford Univ. Press.

JOHNSON, G.A. 1982. Organizational Structure and Scalar Stress, in *Theory and Explanation in Archaeology* (C. Renfrew, M.J. Rowlands & B.A. Segraves eds.). Academic Press: New York & London.

LAKE, M. 1999. Digging for memes: the role of material objects in cultural evolution, in *Cognition and Material Culture: the Archaeology of Symbolic Storage* (C. Renfrew & C. Scarre eds.), 77–88. McDonald Institute: Cambridge.

VAN DER LEEUW, S. & MCGLADE, J. (eds.). 1997. *Time, Process and Structured Transformation in Archaeology*. Routledge: London.

LEONE, M. 1984. Interpreting ideology in historical archaeology: using the rules of perspective in the William Paca Garden in Annapolis, Maryland, in *Ideology, Power and Prehistory* (D. Miller & C. Tilley eds.), 25–35. Cambridge Univ. Press.

LOWE, J.W.G. 1985. *The dynamics of apocalypse: a systems simulation of the Classic Maya collapse*. Univ. of New Mexico Press: Albuquerque.

LYMAN, R.L. & O'BRIEN, M.J. (eds.). 1998. The goals of evolutionary archaeology: history and explanation. *Current Anthropology* 39, 615–52.

MALASPINA, P., CRUCIANI, F., CIMINELLI, B.M. & others. 1998. Network analyses of Y-chromosome types in Europe, Northern Africa and Western Asia reveal specific patterns of geographic distribution. *American Journal of Human Genetics* 63, 847–60.

MALLORY, J.P. 1989. *In Search of the Indo-Europeans*. Thames & Hudson: London.

MANN, M. 1986. *The Sources of Social Power*. Cambridge Univ. Press.

MARCUS, J. (ed.). 1990. *Debating Oaxaca Archaeology*. Univ. of Michigan: Ann Arbor.

MASCHNER, H.D.G. (ed.). 1996. *Darwinian Archaeologies*. Plenum: New York.

MILLER, D. 1980. Archaeology and development. *Current Anth.* 21, 726.

MITHEN, S.J. 1990. *Thoughtful Foragers: a Study of Prehistoric Decision Making*. Cambridge Univ. Press.

——1996. *The Prehistory of the Mind*. Thames & Hudson: London & New York.

MORRIS, I. 1987. *Burial and Ancient Society: The Rise of the Greek City State*. Cambridge Univ. Press.

O'BRIEN, M. (ed.). 1996. *Evolutionary Archaeology*. Univ. of Utah Press: Salt Lake City.

PHILLIPSON, D.W. 1977. The spread of the Bantu languages, *Scientific American* 236, 106–14.

POPPER, K.R. 1985. *Conjectures and Refutations: the growth of scientific knowledge*. (4th ed.) Routledge & Kegan Paul: London.

PRIGOGINE, I. 1979. *From Being to Becoming*. Freeman: San Francisco.

——1987. Exploring complexity. *European Journal of Operational Research* 30, 97–103.

——**& STENGERS, I.** 1984. *Order out of chaos: man's new dialogue with nature.* Heinemann: London.

RAPPAPORT, R. 1999. *Ritual and Religion in the Makeup of Humanity.* Cambridge Univ. Press.

RATHJE, W.L. 1971. The Origin and Development of Lowland Classic Maya Civilisation. *American Antiquity* 36, 275–85.

RENFREW C. 1969. The Autonomy of the South-East European Copper Age. *Proc. Prehist. Soc.* 35, 12–47.

——1972. *The Emergence of Civilisation. The Cyclades and the Aegean in the Third Millennium BC.* Methuen: London.

——1973a. *Before Civilisation.* Jonathan Cape: London; Pelican: Harmondsworth.

——(ed.). 1973b. *The Explanation of Culture Change: Models in Prehistory.* Duckworth: London.

——1976. Megaliths, Territories and Populations, in *Acculturation and Continuity in Atlantic Europe (Dissertationes Archaeologicae Gandenses XVI)* (S.J. de Laet ed.), 298–320.

——1978a. The anatomy of innovation, in *Social Organisation and Settlement* (D. Green, C. Haselgrove & M. Spriggs eds.), 89–117. British Arch. Reports: Oxford.

——1978b. Trajectory discontinuity and morphogenesis, the implications of catastrophe theory for archaeology. *American Antiquity* 43, 203–44.

——1979. System collapse as social transformation, in *Transformations. Mathematical Approaches to Culture Change* (C. Renfrew & K.L. Cooke eds.), 481–506. Academic Press: New York & London.

——1982. Explanation revisited, in *Theory and Explanation in Archaeology* (C. Renfrew, M.J. Rowlands & B.A. Segraves eds.), 5–24. Academic Press: New York & London.

——1987a. Problems in the modelling of socio-cultural systems. *European Journal of Operational Research* 30, 179–92.

——1987b. *Archaeology and Language, the Puzzle of Indo-European Origins.* Jonathan Cape: London.

——1990. Models of change in language and archaeology. *Transactions of the Philological Society* 87, 103–78.

——1991. Before Babel: speculations on the origins of linguistic diversity. *Cambridge Archaeological Journal* 1, 3–23.

——1992. World languages and human dispersals: a minimalist view, in *Transition to Modernity, Essays on Power, Wealth and Belief* (J.A. Hall & I.C. Jarvie eds.), 11–68. Cambridge Univ. Press.

——1994. World linguistic diversity. *Scientific American* 268, 104–10.

——1996. Language families and the spread of farming, in *The Origin and Spread of Agriculture and Pastoralism in Eurasia* (D.R. Harris ed.), 70–92. UCL Press: London.

——1998. The origins of world linguistic diversity: an archaeological perspective, in *The Origin and Diversification of Language* (N.G. Jablonski & L.C. Aiello eds.), 171–92. California Academy of Sciences: San Francisco.

——**& ZUBROW, E.B.W.** (eds.). 1994. *The Ancient Mind: Elements of Cognitive Archaeology.* Cambridge Univ. Press.

——**& SCARRE, C.** (eds.). 1998. *Cognition and Material Culture: the Archaeology of Symbolic Storage.* McDonald Institute: Cambridge.

RICHARDS, M.R., CORTE-REAL, H., FORSTER, P. & others. 1996. Palaeolithic and neolithic lineages in the European mitochondrial gene pool. *American Journal of Human Genetics* 59, 185–203.

ROBB, J. 1994. Gender contradictions, moral coalitions, and inequality in prehistoric Italy. *Journal of European Archaeology* 2 (1), 20–49.

RUHLEN, M. 1991. *A Guide to the World's Languages.* Stanford Univ. Press.

SALMON, M. 1978. What can systems theory do for archaeology? *American Antiquity* 43, 174–83.

——1982. *Philosophy and Archaeology.* Academic Press: New York & London.

SCHELE, L. & MILLER, M.E. 1986. *The Blood of Kings. Dynasty and ritual in Maya art.* Kimbell Art Museum: Fort Worth; 1992 Thames & Hudson: London.

SHANKS, M. & TILLEY, C. 1987a. *Re-constructing Archaeology.* Cambridge Univ. Press.

——1987b. *Social Theory and Archaeology.* Polity Press: Oxford.

SPERBER, D. 1996. *Explaining Culture: a Naturalistic Approach.* Oxford Univ. Press.

SPRIGGS, M. (ed.). 1984. *Marxist Perspectives in Archaeology.* Cambridge Univ. Press.

SYKES, B. 1999. The molecular genetics of human ancestry. *Philosophical Trans. of the Royal Society of London Series B* 354, 185–203.

TAINTER, J.A. 1988. *The Collapse of Complex Societies.* Cambridge Univ. Press.

THOM, R. 1975. *Structural Stability and Morphogenesis.* Benjamin: Reading, Mass.

TILLEY, C. 1984. Ideology and the legitimation of power in the Middle Neolithic of Sweden, in *Ideology, Power and Prehistory* (D. Miller & C. Tilley eds.), 111–46. Cambridge Univ. Press.

TOOBY, J. & COSMIDES, J. 1990. The past explains the present: emotional adaptations and the structure of ancestral environments. *Ethology and Sociobiology* 10, 29–49.

TORRONI, A., BANDELT, H.-G., D'URBINO, L. & others. 1998. mtDNA analysis reveals a major Late Paleolithic population expansion from Southwestern to Northeastern Europe. *American Journal of Human Genetics* 62, 1137–52.

TRIGGER, B. 1978. *Time and Tradition.* Edinburgh Univ. Press.

——1989. *A History of Archaeological Thought.* Cambridge Univ. Press.

WATSON, P.J., LEBLANC, S.A. & REDMAN, C.L. 1971. *Explanation in Archaeology. An Explicitly Scientific Approach.* Columbia Univ. Press: New York & London.

WHITTLE, A. 1996. *Europe in the Neolithic, the Creation of New Worlds.* Cambridge Univ. Press.

WITTFOGEL, K. 1957. *Oriental Despotism, a Comparative Study of Total Power.* Yale Univ. Press: New Haven.

YOFFEE, N. & COWGILL, G.L. (eds.). 1988. *The Collapse of Ancient States and Civilizations.* Univ. of Arizona Press: Tucson.

ZEEMAN, E.C. 1977. *Catastrophe Theory, Selected Papers 1972–77.* Addison-Wesley: Reading, Mass.

ZUBROW, E.B.W. 1981. Simulation as a heuristic device in archaeology, in *Simulations in Archaeology* (J.A. Sabloff ed.), 143–88. Univ. of New Mexico Press: Albuquerque.

Chapter 13: Archaeology in Action
(pp. 499–532)

Bibliography

ADDYMAN, P.V. 1974. Excavations in York, 1972–3. First Interim Report. *Antiquaries Journal* 54, 200–32.

ARUP, OVE & UNIVERSITY OF YORK. 1991. *York Development and Archaeology.* English Heritage and City of York Council: York.

BAYLEY, J. 1992. *Non-Ferrous Metalworking from Coppergate.* Fasc. 17/7. York Archaeological Trust.

BLANTON, R.E. 1978. *Monte Albán: Settlement Patterns at the Ancient Zapotec Capital.* Academic Press: New York.

——**& KOWALEWSKI, S.A.** 1981. Monte Albán and after in the Valley of Oaxaca, in *Archaeology. Supplement to the Handbook of Middle American Indians I* (J.A. Sabloff ed.), 94–116. Univ. of Texas Press: Austin.

BUCKLAND, P.C. 1976. *The Environmental Evidence from the Church Street Roman Sewer System.* Fasc. 14/1. York Archaeological Trust.

FLANNERY, K.V. (ed.). 1976. *The Early Mesoamerican Village.* Academic Press: New York & London.

——(ed.). 1986. *Guilá Naquitz: Archaic Foraging and Early Agriculture in Oaxaca, Mexico.* Academic Press: New York.

——**& MARCUS, J.** (eds.). 1983. *The Cloud People: Divergent Evolution of the*

Zapotec and Mixtec Civilizations. Academic Press: New York.

——, MARCUS, J. & KOWALEWSKI, S.A. 1981. The Preceramic and Formative of the Valley of Oaxaca, in *Archaeology. Supplement to the Handbook of Middle American Indians I* (J.A. Sabloff ed.), 48–93. Univ. of Texas Press: Austin.

FLOOD, J. 1995. *Archaeology of the Dreamtime.* (3rd ed.). Angus & Robertson: Sydney, London & New York.

HIGHAM, C. & THOSARAT, R. 1994. *Khok Phanom Di. Prehistoric adaptation to the world's richest habitat.* Harcourt Brace College Publishers: Fort Worth.

JONES, R. (ed.). 1985. *Archaeological Research in Kakadu National Park.* Australian National Parks and Wildlife Service, Special Publication No. 13. Australian National Univ.: Canberra.

KEALHOFER, L. & PIPERNO, D.R. 1994. Early agriculture in southeast Asia: phytolith evidence from the Bang Pakong Valley, Thailand. *Antiquity* 68, 564–72.

MARCUS, J. & FLANNERY, K.V. 1996. *Zapotec Civilization. How Urban Society Evolved in Mexico's Oaxaca Valley.* Thames & Hudson: London & New York.

ORDNANCE SURVEY. 1988. *Roman and Anglian York, Historical Map and Guide.* Ordnance Survey: Southampton.

——1988. *Viking and Medieval York, Historical Map and Guide.* Ordnance Survey: Southampton.

ROBERTS, R.G. & others. 1994. The human colonisation of Australia: optical dates of 53,000 and 60,000 years bracket human arrival at Deaf Adder Gorge, Northern Territory. *Quaternary Geochronology (Quaternary Science Reviews)* 13, 575–83.

SCHRIRE, C. 1982. *The Alligator Rivers: Prehistory and Ecology in Western Arnhem Land.* Terra Australis 7, Australian National Univ.: Canberra.

SMITH, B.D. 1997. The initial domestication of *Cucurbita pepo* in the Americas 10,000 years ago. *Science* 276, 932–34.

THOMPSON, G.B. (ed.). 1996. *The Excavation of Khok Phanom Di, a Prehistoric Site in Central Thailand. Vol. IV. Subsistence and Environment: the Botanical Evidence.* Society of Antiquaries: London.

TWEDDLE, D. 1992. *The Anglian Helmet from Coppergate.* Fasc. 17/8. York Archaeological Trust.

Chapter 14: Whose Past? Archaeology and the Public (pp. 533–564)

General introductions to the topic of **archaeological ethics** and public relations: Green 1984; King 1983; McGimsey 1972; Smith 1974; Vitelli 1996. Archaeology and politics: Ucko 1987; Garlake 1973 discusses Great Zimbabwe in particular. Regional approaches: *World Archaeology* 1981/2, 13 (2 & 3).

pp. 533–34 **The meaning of the past** Bintliff 1988; Layton 1989a, 1989b.

pp. 534–36 **Ideology and nationalism** Díaz-Andreu & Champion 1996; Graves-Brown & others 1996; Jones 1997; Kohl & Fawcett 1995; Shnirelman 1996; China: Pearson 1976; Olsen 1987. Israel: Yadin 1966; Shay 1989; Silberman 1989.

pp. 536–42 **Who owns the past? Return of cultural property** Greenfield 1996; McBryde 1985; Mturi 1983. Particular reference to the Elgin Marbles: Hitchens 1987; St. Clair 1998, 1999. **Should we disturb the dead?** Bahn 1984; Bahn & Paterson 1986; Layton 1989b; Morell 1995 (Mungo, Tasmania, Jews, & Native American hair); Jones & Harris 1998. **Australian aborigines** Ucko 1983; **American Indians** Rosen 1980; Talmage 1982; Price 1991; Anyon & Ferguson 1995 (Zuni Pueblo); Swidler & others 1997.

pp. 542–44 **Virtual archaeology** Forte & Siliotti 1997; Davis 1997. **Economic lessons from the past** In general: Ford 1973. Desert agriculture: Evenari & Koller 1956; Evenari & others 1971; Agarwal 1977. Andes, Cusichaca project: Kendall 1984. Bolivian raised fields: Kolata & Ortloff 1989; Straughan 1991. Seismic archaeology: Guo Zhan 1985 (China); Nur 1991 (Near East); Stiros & Jones 1996.

pp. 546–49 **Conservation and destruction** Burns 1991, Holloway 1995. Salvage (rescue) archaeology: Chamberlin 1979; Gumerman & Schiffer 1977; Rahtz 1974. Approaches to the archaeological heritage: Cleere 1984; Darvill 1984; Darvill & others 1978. Conservation and legislation in Australia & New Zealand: Mulvaney 1981; McKinlay & Jones 1979.

pp. 549–53 **Damage by developers** Rose theater, England: Fagan 1990; Wainwright 1989. Japanese rescue: Tanaka 1984. Franklin dam affair: Kiernan & others 1983; Lewin 1982. Chinese dam: Childs-Johnson & Sullivan 1996. Mexico City: Matos Moctezuma 1980, 1988.

pp. 553–57 **Damage from looting** Chamberlin 1983; Hamblin 1970; Hess 1974; Meyer 1973. Egypt: Fagan 1975. American Southwest: Basset 1986; Monastersky 1990. China: *Newsweek* August 22 1994, 36–41; Afghanistan: Ali & Coningham 1998. Looting and the market in illicit antiquities: Tubb 1995; O'Keefe 1997; Watson 1997; Renfrew 1999; Prott 1997 (UNIDROIT); Ali & Coningham 1998 (Pakistan); Sanogo 1999 (Mali); Schmidt & McIntosh 1996 (Africa); Watson 1999 (Peru).

pp. 557–58 **Care of protected sites** Egypt: Toufexis 1985; McDonald 1996 (Nefertari); *New Scientist* 21 April 1988, 65. Mohenjodaro: Naqvi 1985. General: Young 1996.

pp. 558–59 **Who interprets the past?** Bintliff 1984; Kaplan 1994; Merriman 1991; Pearce 1992; Prentice 1993; Stocking 1985.

pp. 559–63 **Publish or be damned** Callow 1985; editorials in *Antiquity* 31, 1957 (121–22) & 47, 1973 (261–62). For Israel, Shanks 1994. Dead Sea scrolls: Silberman 1995. Wheeler's comment: Wheeler 1968.

p. 563 **The wider audience** Evans & others 1981 (especially 191–229); Fagan 1984. Japanese site presentation: Kiyotari 1987, 100.

pp. 563–64 **World archaeology** Cult- and pseudo-archaeology in general: Adam 1975; Cole 1980; Sabloff 1982; Stiebing 1984; Story 1976, 1980; White 1974; Wilson 1972, 1975. See also special issue Vol. 29 (2), 1987, of *Expedition* on "Archaeological Facts and Fantasies." For von Däniken himself: Ferris 1974 as well as the above works. Many excellent articles on this topic can be found in the journal *The Skeptical Inquirer.*

Box Features

p. 535 **The Politics of Destruction 1: The Bridge at Mostar** Chapman 1994; Halpern 1993.

p. 537 **The Politics of Destruction 2: The Mosque at Ayodhya** Mandal 1993; Frawley 1994; Sharma 1995; Sharma & others 1992.

pp. 544–45 **Applied Archaeology** Raised field project: Erickson 1985, 1988; Garaycochea 1987.

p. 547 **The Practice of CRM** Tombigbee: Gumerman & Schiffer 1977. Jenkins & Krause 1986; Peebles 1981.

pp. 552–53 **The Great Temple of the Aztecs** Matos Moctezuma 1988.

p. 554 **Mimbres** LeBlanc 1983.

pp. 556–57 **Collectors are the Real Looters** Cook 1991; Elia 1993; Gill and Chippindale 1993; Haskell and Penny 1981; Hughes 1984; Messenger 1989; Meyer 1974 (p. 193); Nicholas 1994; Ortiz 1994; Pinkerton 1990; Renfrew 1993; UNESCO 1970; Vitelli 1984, 1996; ICOM 1994; True & Hamma 1994; Dorfman 1998; and the journal *Culture Without Context*, since 1996. "Weary Herakles": Rose & Acar 1995; von Bothmer 1990. Getty kouros: Kokkou 1993. Lydian Treasure: Kaye & Main 1995; Rose & Acar 1995. Sevso Treasure: Sotheby's 1990; Mango & Bennett 1994; Renfrew 1999. Aidonia Treasure: Rose 1993; Demakopoulou 1996. Salisbury Hoard: Stead 1998.

pp. 560–61 **Archaeology and the Internet** see box text for useful website addresses.

p. 562 **Archaeology at the Fringe** Castleden 1998; Peiser & others 1998.

Bibliography

ADAM, J-P. 1975. *L'Archéologie devant l'Imposture.* Laffont: Paris.

AGARWAL, A. 1977. Coaxing the barren deserts back to life. *New Scientist* 15, Sept., 674–75.

ALI, I. & CONINGHAM, R.A.E. 1998. Recording and preserving Gandhara's cultural heritage. *Culture Without Context* 3, 10–16.

ANYON, R. & FERGUSON, T.J. 1995. Cultural Resources Management at the Pueblo of Zuni, New Mexico, USA. *Antiquity* 69, 913–30.

BAHN, P.G. 1984. Do not disturb? Archaeology and the rights of the dead. *Oxford Journal of Arch.* 3, 127–39.

——— **& PATERSON, R.W.K.** 1986. The last rights: more on archaeology and the dead. *Oxford Journal of Arch.* 5, 255–71.

BASSET, C.A. 1986. The culture thieves. *Science* 86, July/Aug., 22–29.

BINTLIFF, J.L. 1984. Structuralism and myth in Minoan studies, *Antiquity* 58, 33–38.

——— (ed.). 1988. *Extracting Meaning from the Past.* Oxbow Books: Oxford.

VON BOTHMER, D. (ed.). 1990. *Glories of the Past: Ancient Art from the Shelby White and Leon Levy Collection.* Metropolitan Museum of Art: New York.

BURNS, G. 1991. Deterioration of our cultural heritage. *Nature* 352, 658–60.

CALLOW, P. 1985. An unlovely child: the problem of unpublished archaeological research. *Archaeological Review from Cambridge* 4, 95–106.

CASTLEDEN, R. 1998. *Atlantis Destroyed.* Routledge: London.

CHAMBERLIN, E.R. 1979. *Preserving the Past.* Dent: London.

———1983. *Loot! the Heritage of Plunder.* Thames & Hudson: London.

CHAPMAN, J. 1994. Destruction of a common heritage: the archaeology of war in Croatia, Bosnia and Hercegovina. *Antiquity* 68, 120–26.

CHILDS-JOHNSON, E. & SULLIVAN, L.R. 1996. The Three-Gorges Dam and the fate of China's southern heritage. *Orientations* 27 (7), 55–64.

CLEERE, H. (ed.). 1984. *Approaches to the Archaeological Heritage.* Cambridge Univ. Press.

COLE, J.R. 1980. Cult archaeology and unscientific method and theory, in *Advances in Archaeological Method and Theory* 3 (M.B. Schiffer ed.), 1–33. Academic Press: New York & London.

COOK, B.F. 1991. The archaeologist and the art market: policy and practice. *Antiquity* 65, 533–37.

DARVILL, T. 1987. *Ancient Monuments in the Countryside, an Archaeological Management Review.* English Heritage: London.

———, **PARKER PEARSON, M., SMITH, R.W. & THOMAS, R.M.** (eds.). 1978. *New Approaches to Our Past, an Archaeological Forum.* Dept. of Archaeology: Southampton.

DAVIS, B. 1997. The future of the past. *Scientific American*, August, 89–92.

DEMAKOPOULOU, K. 1996. *The Aidonia Treasure: Seals and Jewellery of the Aegean Late Bronze Age.* Ministry of Culture: Athens.

DÍAZ-ANDREU, M. & CHAMPION, T. (eds.). 1996. *Nationalism and Archaeology in Europe.*

UCL Press: London.

DORFMAN, J. 1998. Getting their hands dirty? Archaeologists and the looting trade. *Lingua franca* 8 (4), 28–36.

ELIA, R. 1993. A seductive and troubling work. *Archaeology* Jan–Feb 1993, 64–69.

ERICKSON, C.L. 1985. Applications of prehistoric Andean technology: experiments in raised field agriculture, Huatta, Lake Titicaca: 1981–2, in *Prehistoric Intensive Agriculture in the Tropics* (I.S. Farrington ed.), 209–32. British Arch. Reports, Int. Series. No. 232: Oxford.

———1988. Raised field agriculture in the Lake Titicaca Basin: Putting ancient agriculture back to work. *Expedition* 30 (3), 8–16.

EVANS, J.D., CUNLIFFE, B. & RENFREW, C. (eds.). 1981. *Antiquity and Man. Essays in Honour of Glyn Daniel.* Thames & Hudson: London.

EVENARI, M. & KOLLER, D. 1956. Ancient masters of the desert. *Scientific American* 194 (4), 39–45.

——— **& others.** 1971. *The Negev: The Challenge of a Desert.* Harvard Univ. Press.

FAGAN, B.M. 1975. *The Rape of the Nile.* Scribners: New York.

———1984. Archaeology and the wider audience, in *Ethics and Values in Archaeology* (E.L. Green ed.), 175–83. Free Press: New York.

———1990. The Rose Affair. *Archaeology* 43 (2), 12–14, 76.

FERRIS, T. 1974. *Playboy* Interview: Erich von Däniken. *Playboy* 21 (8), Aug., 51–52, 56–58, 60, 64, 151.

FORD, R.I. 1973. Archaeology serving humanity, in *Research and Theory in Current Archaeology* (C.L. Redman ed.), 83–93. Wiley: New York.

FORTE, M. & SILIOTTI, A. (eds.). 1997. *Virtual Archaeology.* Thames & Hudson: London; Abrams: New York.

FRAWLEY, D. 1994. *The Myth of the Aryan Invasion of India.* Voice of India: New Delhi.

GARAYCOCHEA, I. 1987. Agricultural experiments in raised fields in the Lake Titicaca Basin, Peru. Some preliminary considerations, in *Pre-Hispanic Agricultural Fields in the Andean Region* (W. Denevan & others eds.), 385–98. British Arch. Reports, Int. Series No. 359: Oxford.

GARLAKE, P. 1973. *Great Zimbabwe.* Thames & Hudson: London; McGraw-Hill: New York.

GILL, D.W.J. & CHIPPINDALE, C. 1993. Material and intellectual consequences of esteem for Cycladic figures. *American Journal of Archaeology* 97, 601–60.

GRAVES-BROWN, P., JONES, S. & GAMBLE, C. (eds.). 1996. *Cultural Identity and Archaeology.* Routledge: London.

GREEN, E.L. (ed.). 1984. *Ethics and Values in Archaeology.* Free Press: New York.

GREENFIELD, J. 1996. *The Return of Cultural Treasures.* (2nd ed.) Cambridge Univ. Press.

GUMERMAN, G. & SCHIFFER, M.B. (eds.). 1977. *Conservation Archaeology.* Academic Press: New York & London.

GUO ZHAN 1985. My Life as an Archaeologist. *Unesco Courier* July, 36–37.

HALL, R. 1984. *The Viking Dig.* Bodley Head: London.

HALPERN, J.M. 1993. Introduction. *Anthropology of East Europe Review* 11/1, 5–13.

HAMBLIN, D.J. 1970. *Pots and Robbers.* Simon and Schuster: New York.

HASKELL, F. & PENNY, N. 1981. *Taste and the Antique.* Yale Univ. Press: New Haven & London.

HESS, J.L. 1974. *The Grand Acquisitors.* Houghton Mifflin: Boston.

HITCHENS, C. 1987. *The Elgin Marbles: Should they be returned to Greece?* Chatto & Windus: London.

HOLLOWAY, M. 1995. The preservation of past. *Scientific American* 272 (5), 78–81.

HUGHES, R. 1984. Art and Money. *New York Review of Books* 31 (19), 20–27.

ICOM. 1994. International Council of Museums. *One Hundred Missing Objects: Looting in Africa.* UNESCO: Paris.

JENKINS, N.J. & KRAUSE, R.A. 1986. *The Tombigbee Watershed in Southeastern Prehistory.* Univ. of Alabama Press.

JONES, D.G. & HARRIS, R.J. 1998. Archaeological human remains. Scientific, cultural and ethical considerations. *Current Anth.* 39, 253–64.

JONES, S. 1997. *The Archaeology of Ethnicity.* Routledge: London.

KAPLAN, F.E.S. (ed.). 1994. *Museums and the Making of 'Ourselves'.* Leicester Univ. Press.

KAYE, L.M. & MAIN, C.T. 1995. The saga of the Lydian Hoard: from Ushak to New York and back again, in *Antiquities Trade or Betrayed. Legal, Ethical and Conservation Issues* (K.W. Tubb ed.). Archetype: London.

KENDALL, A. (ed.). 1984. *Current Archaeological Projects in the Central Andes.* British Arch. Reports, Int. Series. No. 210: Oxford.

KIERNAN, K., JONES, R. & RANSOM, D. 1983. New Evidence from Fraser Cave for glacial age man in SW Tasmania. *Nature* 301, 13, 28–32; see also Vol. 300 (1982), 679; Vol. 305 (1983), 354; & Vol. 306 (1983), 636, 726.

KING, T.F. 1983. Professional responsibility in public archaeology. *Annual Review of Anthropology* 12, 143–64.

KIYOTARI, T. (ed.). 1987. *Recent Archaeological Discoveries in Japan.* Center for E. Asian Cultural Studies/UNESCO.

KOHL, P.L. & FAWCETT, C. (eds.). 1995. *Nationalism, Politics and the Practice of Archaeology.* Cambridge Univ. Press.

KOKKOU, A. (ed.). 1993. *The Getty Kouros Colloquium.* N.P. Goulandris Foundation & J. Paul Getty Museum: Athens.

KOLATA, A.L. & ORTLOFF, C. 1989. Thermal analysis of Tiwanaku raised field systems in the Lake Titicaca Basin of Bolivia. *Journal of Arch. Science* 16, 233–63.

LAYTON, R. (ed.). 1989a. *Who Needs the Past? Indigenous Values and Archaeology.* Unwin Hyman: London.

——(ed.). 1989b. *Conflict in the Archaeology of Living Traditions.* Unwin Hyman: London.

LEBLANC, S.A. 1983. *The Mimbres People.* Thames & Hudson: London & New York.

LEWIN, R. 1982. Tasmanian Ice Age sites threatened by dam. *Science* 218, 988.

LOWENTHAL, D. 1985. *The Past is a Foreign Country.* Cambridge Univ. Press.

MCBRYDE, I. (ed.). 1985. *Who Owns the Past?* Oxford Univ. Press: Melbourne.

MCDONALD, J.K. 1996. *House of Eternity: The Tomb of Nefertari.* Getty Conservation Institute: Los Angeles; Thames & Hudson: London.

MCGIMSEY, C. 1972. *Public Archaeology.* Seminar Press: New York.

——& DAVIS, H.A. (eds.). 1977. *The Management of Archaeological Resources: the Airlie House Report.* Society for American Archaeology: Washington.

MCKINLAY, J.R. & JONES, K.L. (eds.). 1979. *Archaeological Resource Management in Australia and Oceania.* New Zealand Historic Places Trust: Wellington.

MANDAL, D. 1993. *Ayodhya: Archaeology after Demolition.* Orient Longman: New Delhi.

MANGO, M.M. & BENNETT, A. 1994. *The Sevso Treasure, Part One.* Journal of Roman Archaeology Supplementary Series 12: Ann Arbor.

MATOS MOCTEZUMA, E. 1980. Tenochtitlán: New finds in the Great Temple. *National Geographic* 158 (6), 766–75.

——1988. *The Great Temple of the Aztecs.* Thames & Hudson: London & New York.

MERRIMAN, N. 1991. *Beyond the Glass Case: the Past, the Heritage and the Public in Britain.* Leicester Univ. Press.

MESSENGER, P. MAUCH (ed.). 1989. *The Ethics of Collecting Cultural Property: Whose Culture? Whose Property?* Univ. of New Mexico Press: Albuquerque.

MEYER, K.E. 1973. *The Plundered Past.* Atheneum Press: New York/Hamish Hamilton: London (1974).

MONASTERSKY, R. 1990. Fingerprints in the sand. *Science News* 138, 392–94.

MORELL, V. 1995. Who owns the past? *Science* 268, 1424–26.

MTURI, A.A. 1983. The return of cultural property. *Antiquity* 57, 137–39.

MULVANEY, D.J. 1981. What future for our past? Archaeology and society in the eighties. *Australian Arch.* 13, 16–27.

NAQVI, W.Q. 1985. Mohenjodaro, threatened centre of an ancient civilization. *Unesco Courier,* July, 32–35.

NICHOLAS, L.H. 1994. *The Rape of Europa: the Fate of Europe's Treasures in the Third Reich and the Second World War.* Knopf: New York.

NUR, A. 1991. And the walls came tumbling down. *New Scientist* 6 July, 45–48.

O'KEEFE, P.J. 1997. *Trade in Antiquities: Reducing Destruction and Theft.* UNESCO & Archetype: London.

OLSEN, J.W. 1987. The practice of archaeology in China today. *Antiquity* 61, 282–90.

ORTIZ, G. 1994. *In Pursuit of the Absolute: Art of the Ancient World from the George Ortiz Collection.* Exhibition Royal Academy of Arts: London.

PEARCE, S.M. 1992. *Museums, Objects and Collections: a Cultural Study.* Leicester Univ. Press.

PEARSON, R.J. 1976. The social aims of Chinese archaeology. *Antiquity* 50, 8–10.

PEEBLES, C. (ed.). 1981. Excavations in the Lubbub Creek Archaeological Locality. Vol. 1. Report on file. Museum of Anthropology, Univ. of Michigan: Ann Arbor.

PEISER, B.J., PALMER, T. & BAILEY, M.E. (eds.). 1998. *Natural Catastrophes during Bronze Age Civilisation.* British Archaeological Reports, International Series 728: Oxford.

PINKERTON, L.F. 1990. Due diligence in fine art transactions. *Journal of International Law,* 22, 1–29.

PRENTICE, R. 1993. *Tourism and Heritage Attractions.* Routledge: London.

PRICE, H.M. 1991. *Disputing the Dead: US law on Aboriginal remains and grave goods.* Univ. of Missouri Press: Columbia.

PROTT, L.V. 1997. *Comment on the Unidroit Convention.* Institute of Art and Law: London.

RAHTZ, P. (ed.). 1974. *Rescue Archaeology.* Pelican: Harmondsworth.

RENFREW, C. 1993. Collectors are the real looters, *Archaeology* May/June 1993, 16–17.

——1999. *Loot, legitimacy and ownership: the ethical crisis in archaeology.* (The Kroon Lecture for 1999.) Foundation for Anthropology and Prehistory in the Netherlands: Amsterdam.

ROSE, M. 1993. Greece sues for Mycenaean gold. *Archaeology* 46(5), 26–30.

——& ACAR, O. 1995. Turkey's war on the illicit antiquities trade. *Archaeology* 48(2), 45–56.

ROSEN, L. 1980. The excavation of American Indian burial sites: a problem in professional responsibility. *American Anthropologist* 82, 5–27.

SABLOFF, J.A. 1982. Introduction, in *Archaeology: Myth and Reality. Readings from Scientific American,* 1–26. Freeman: San Francisco.

ST. CLAIR, W. 1998. *Lord Elgin and the Marbles.* (3rd ed.) Oxford Univ. Press.

——1999. The Elgin Marbles, questions of stewardship and accountability. *International Journal of Cultural Property* 8, 397–521.

SANOGO, K. 1999. The looting of cultural material in Mali. *Culture Without Context* 4, 21–25.

SCHMIDT, P.R. & MCINTOSH, R. (eds.). 1996. *Plundering Africa's Past.* Indiana Univ. Press: Bloomington.

SHANKS, H. 1994. Archaeology's dirty secret. *Biblical Archaeology Review* 20 (5), Sept./Oct., 63–64, 79.

SHARMA, R.S. 1995. *Looking for the Aryans.* Orient Longman: New Delhi.

SHARMA, Y.D. & others. 1992. *Ramajamna Bhumi: Ayodhya: New Archaeological Discoveries.* Historians' Forum: New Delhi.

SHAY, T. 1989. Israeli archaeology – ideology and practice. *Antiquity* 63, 768–72.

SHNIRELMAN, V.A. 1996. *Who Gets the Past? Competitions for Ancestors among Non-Russian Intellectuals in Russia.* Woodrow Wilson Center Press: Washington D.C.

SILBERMAN, N.A. 1989. *Between Past and Present. Archaeology, Ideology and Nationalism in the Modern Middle East.* Anchor/Doubleday: New York.

——1995. *The Hidden Scrolls: Christianity, Judaism and the War for the Dead Sea Scrolls.* Heinemann: London.

SMITH, R.H. 1974. Ethics in field archaeology. *Journal of Field Archaeology* 1, 375–83.

SOTHEBY'S. 1990. *The Sevso Treasure, a Collection from Late Antiquity.* Sotheby's (Auction Catalogue): Zurich.

STEAD, I. 1998. *The Salisbury Treasure.* Tempus: Stroud.

STIEBING, W.H. 1984. *Ancient Astronauts, Cosmic Collisions and other Popular Theories about Man's Past.* Prometheus: Buffalo.

STIROS, S. & JONES, R.E. (eds.). 1996. *Archaeoseismology.* Fitch Lab. Occ. Paper 7, British School at Athens.

STOCKING, G.W. (ed.). 1985. *Objects and Others, Essays on Museums and Material Culture.* Univ. Of Wisconsin Press: Madison.

STORY, R.D. 1976. *The Space-Gods Revealed.* New English Library: London.

——1980. *Guardians of the Universe?* New English Library: London.

STRAUGHAN, B. 1991. The secrets of ancient Tiwanaku are benefiting today's Bolivia. *Smithsonian* 21, February, 38–49.

SWIDLER, N. & others. (eds.). 1997. *Native Americans and Archaeologists. Stepping Stones to Common Ground.* Altamira Press: Walnut Creek.

TALMAGE, V.A. 1982. The violation of sepulture: is it legal to excavate human burials? *Archaeology* 35 (6), 44–49.

TANAKA, M. 1984. Japan, in *Archaeological Approaches to the Present* (H. Cleere ed.), 82–88. Cambridge Univ. Press.

TOUFEXIS, A. 1985. Egypt battles a sleeping devil. *Time*, 27 May, 42–43.

TRUE, M. & HAMMA, K. 1994. *A Passion for Antiquities, Ancient Art from the Collection of Barbara and Lawrence Fleischman*. J. Paul Getty Museum: Malibu.

TUBB, K.W. (ed.). 1995. *Antiquities Trade or Betrayed. Legal, Ethical and Conservation Issues*. Archetype: London.

UCKO, P.J. 1983. Australian academic archaeology: Aboriginal transformations of its aims and practices. *Australian Arch.* 16, 11–26.

———1987. *Academic Freedom and Apartheid: The story of the World Archaeological Congress*. Duckworth: London.

UNESCO. 1970. Convention on the Means of Prohibiting and Preventing the Illicit Import, Export and Transfer of Ownership of Cultural Property. United Nations Educational, Scientific, and Cultural Organisation, General Conference, 16th Session, November 14, 1970, Paris.

U.S. DEPARTMENT OF THE INTERIOR. 1979. *Archaeological and Historical Data Recovery Program*. National Park Service: Washington.

VITELLI, K.D. 1984. The international traffic in antiquities: archaeological ethics and the archaeologist's responsibility, in *Ethics and Values in Archaeology* (E.L. Green ed.), 143–55. Free Press: New York.

——— (ed.). 1996. *Archaeological Ethics*. Altamira Press: Walnut Creek.

WAINWRIGHT, G.J. 1989. Saving the Rose. *Antiquity* 63 (240), 430–35.

WATSON, P. 1997. *Sotheby's, the Inside Story*. Bloomsbury: London.

———1999. The lessons of Sipán: archaeologists and *huaqueros*. *Culture Without Context* 4, 15–19.

WHEELER, R.E.M. 1968. Review of *Hod Hill* by Ian Richmond & others. *Antiquity* 42, 149–50, 292–96.

WHITE, J.P. 1974. *The Past is Human*. Angus & Robertson: Sydney.

WILSON, C. 1972. *Crash Go the Chariots*. Lancer Books: New York. (Rev. ed. Master Books: San Diego, 1976).

———1975. *The Chariots Still Crash*. Signet/New American Library: New York.

YADIN, Y. 1966. *Masada. Herod's Fortress and the Zealots' Last Stand*. Weidenfeld & Nicolson: London.

YOUNG, P. 1996. Mouldering monuments. *New Scientist*, 2 November, 36–38.

Acknowledgments

The authors and publishers are indebted to many scholars. They include Peter Addyman, Cyril Aldred, Wal Ambrose, Tjeerd van Andel, Manolis Andronikos, Gina Barnes, George Bass, Sophie de Beaune, Peter Bellwood, Martin Biddle, Morris Bierbrier, Lewis Binford, John Boardman, Gerhard Bosinski, Sheridan Bowman, Warwick Bray, Cyprian Broodbank, Don Brothwell, James Brown, Peter Bullock, Susan Bulmer, Sarah Bunney, Richard Burger, John Camp, Martin Carver, Zaida Castro-Curel, George Chaloupka, John Cherry, Henry Cleere, Kathy Cleghorn, Michael Coe, John Coles, Malcolm Cooper, Ben Cullen, Ruth Daniel, Janette Deacon, Albert Dekin, Richard Diehl, David Drew, Philip Duke, Christiane Eluère, Clark Erickson, Francisco d'Errico, Kent Flannery, John Flenley, Robert Foley, Charles French, Yuriko Fukasawa, Clive Gamble, Ignacio Garaycochea, Michel Garcia, Joan M. Gero, Jack Golson, Mrs D.N. Goulandris, Stephen Green, James Greig, Robert Grenier, Niède Guidon, Erika Hagelberg, Richard Hall, Sylvia Hallam, Norman Hammond, Fekri Hassan, Douglas Heggie, Gordon Hillman, Stephen Hughes, Simon James, Martin Jones, Rhys Jones, Alice Kehoe, Thomas F. Kehoe, Patrick Kirch, Vernon James Knight, Hiroko Koike, Alan Kolata, Roy Larick, Arlette Leroi-Gourhan, Tony Legge, Michel Lorblanchet, Jim Mallory, Joyce Marcus, Alexander Marshack, Yvonne Marshall, Paolo Matthiae, Isabel McBryde, Alan Millard, Mary Ellen Miller, Jean-Pierre Mohen, Gerda Møller, Theya Molleson, John Mulvaney, Hans-Jürgen Müller-Beck, Yasushi Nishimura, J.P. Northover, F. van Noten, Michel & Catherine Orliac, Annette Parkes, John Parkington, Pavel Pavel, Christopher Peebles, Dolores Piperno, Stephen Plog, Mercedes Podestá, Nicholas Postgate, John Prag, Cemal Pulak, Jeffery Quilter, Carmen Reigadas, Paul Reilly, Jane Renfrew, Peter Reynolds, Julian D. Richards, John Robb, Peter Rowley-Conwy, Andrée Rosenfeld, Nan Rothschild, Rolf Rottländer, Makoto Sahara, Nicholas Saunders, Béatrice Schmider, Sue Scott, Payson D. Sheets, Brian Sheppard, Izumi Shimada, Pat Shipman, Elizabeth Somerville, Chris Stringer, Migaku Tanaka, Michael J. Tooley, Robin Torrence, Grahame Walsh, Fred Wendorf, David Wheatley, Todd Whitelaw, Gordon R. Willey, Roger Wilson, and Pat Winker.

Special thanks are due to Jeremy Sabloff, Chris Scarre, and Michael Tite for their contributions to many parts of the book. Glossary by James McGlade and index by Dr David E. Michael.

Illustration Credits

Abbreviations: a-above; b-below; c-center; l-left; r-right; t-top

Aerial Archaeology in Jordan Project, Photo: Bob Bewley 82r
Aerofilms 154
Africana Museum, Johannesburg (photo L. Fourie) 193b
R. Agache, Service des Fouilles 81ar
Cyril Aldred 169l
Agora Excavations, American School of Classical Studies at Athens 397
Manolis Andronikos 430c
Courtesy of Mrs Mary Allsebrook, Oxford 361
American Museum of Natural History, New York, Dept. of Library Services, photo J. Bird 79r
Antalya Museum 556a
Archaeological Survey of India 32bl
Associated Press Ltd 120, 537
ATA Stockholm 184br
Arthur Aufderheide, University of Minnesota, Duluth 442
Paul Bahn 314, 319b, 321, 394bl, 447 (courtesy Hideji Harunari), 492, 542, 551
M.G.L. Baillie 134a
George Bass/Cemal Pulak, Institute of Nautical Archaeology 15bl, 374, 375
Jen and Des Bartlett and Bruce Coleman Ltd. 37bl
Peter Bellwood 267b, 316
Martin Biddle 208t, 208b
Lewis Binford 14br, 52l, 52r, 109, 187a, 187bl, 187br (photo H. Steyn), 193b (photo L. Fourie), 285t, 285c
G. Bosinski 238
Museum of Fine Arts, Boston 556t
Steve Bourget 228l, 228r
British Library 185bl
Copyright British Museum 144, 185ar, 357ac, 389, 417l, 429l, 448l, 449, 556br
British Society for the Turin Shroud 144
British Tourist Authority 398l
Otto Braasch 81
Richard Burger 410b, 411bl
Butser Ancient Farm, E. Perry 274, 275
Cahokia Mounds State Historic Site (painting by W.R. Iseminger) 260
Cambridge University Collection of Air Photos 80–81 (photo J.K. St Joseph), 232
Canadian Parks Service 96t (photo Denis Pagé), 96c (photo Rock Chan, Denis Pagé), 96b (by P. Waddell & J. Farley)
Martin Carver 78
D.A. Casey, courtesy D.J. Mulvaney 41
Z. Castro-Curel 312
Courtesy of D.Z. Chase and A.F. Chase, Caracol Archaeological Project 395
Michael D. Coe 184cl, 412 (drawn by Diane Griffiths Peck), 507c, 553b (drawn by David Kiphuth)

John Coles 272 (drawn by R. Walker), 330 (photo G. Owen), 330a, 330b, 331
University of Colorado Museum 36r
Colorado Springs Fine Art Center - Taylor Museum Collection 554c
E. de Croisset 323
Danebury Trust 83 (from B. Cunliffe, *Danebury* 1983, fig. 64)
Richard D. Daugherty 60–61
Andrew David, English Heritage 102
H.J. Deacon 110b, 247l, 247r
C. Desroches-Noblecourt 15ar
Albert A. Dekin, State University of New York at Binghamton 65t
Richard A. Diehl 329r
P. Dorrell, Jericho Exploration Fund 37tl
Egypt Exploration Society 184ac
English Heritage 69
Clark Erickson 545
Eurelios/Ministère de la Culture, Paris (photo Jean Clottes) 393
Brian Fagan 322r
Kent V. Flannery 500, 501, 505ar
John Flenley 267a
Robert Foley 192
Werner Forman 357b, 357br, 383l, 554l, 554r
Irving Friedman, U.S. Geological Survey, Denver 156
Vince Gaffney, University of Birmingham Field Archaeology Unit, 99br, 100–01
Joan Gero 220l, 220r, 221ar
The J. Paul Getty Museum, Malibu, California 557
John Glover 401b
G. Goakimedes 160
Jack Golson 262, 263
David Golstein 223tl
Courtesy of Dean Goodman, Geophysical Archaeometry Laboratory, University of Miami, Japan Division 99tl
Mrs D.N. Goulandris 415a
U. Seitz-Gray, Frankfurt 405l
Stephen Green 146, 147
Griffith Institute, Oxford 63a, 63c
Salvador Guilliem Arroyo, courtesy the Great Temple Project 74, 552a, 552r, 553
Norman Hammond 87 (from Hammond, *Ancient Maya Civilization* 1982, 5.14, 5.15, drawn by Richard Bryant), 309
R.D.K. Hadden 464l
Chester Higgins 217b
Charles Higham 516, 517, 518, 522
Gordon Hillman 297
Hirmer Fotoarchiv 168b, 185al, 414a, 414b, 538, 558
Historic Annapolis Foundation 490 (drawn by Barbara Paca)
Ian Hodder 14-15a (Çatalhöyük Research Project, Cambridge), 45bl&c, 188r
Forschungsinstitut für Alpine Vorzeit, Universität Innsbruck (photo Anton Koler) 66
Institute of Archaeology, University College London 15br

Acknowledgments

Courtesy of Illinois State Museum 223br
Simon James 239b
Jet Propulsion Laboratory, National
    Aeronautics and Space Administration,
    California 86
Rhys Jones 509, 510, 511, 512
Hiroshi Kasiwara 390a
Thomas F. Kehoe 292–93
Irmgard Groth Kimball 169r
Vernon James Knight, Jnr 110al
Hiroko Koike 390l
Mary Leakey (photo Bob Campbell) 40
Tony Legge 288, 289
André Leroi-Gourhan 439l
Photos: Lewin/Holokwa 441
Wilfredo Loayzo L. 411br
Michel Lorblanchet 327
Luis Lumbreras 411r (drawn by Felix
    Caycho)
Isabel McBryde 376a, 376b
Joyce Marcus 507a, 507ar
© Alexander Marshack 394a
Paolo Matthiae 184bl
Dept. of Medical Illustration, Univ. of
    Manchester 430bcl, 430bcr, 430br
Lynn Meskell 222
Mary Ellen Miller 485, 508
René Millon 90-91
George R. Milner and James Oliver 261
Ministère de la Culture, Direction du
    Patrimoine, Université de Provence,
    Centre Camille Jullian – CNRS 73t
    (photo A. Chéné)
J.-P. Mohen 317
T. Molleson (British Museum, Natural
    History) 426a, 426cl, 426cr, 426b
Musée des Antiquités Nationales, St-
    Germain-en-Laye 357bl, 404
Musée National d'Histoire Naturelle 440r
Museo Archeologico del Castello
    Visconteo di Pavia 338
Museum of London 14bl, 112 (from C.
    Spence (ed.) Archaeological Site
    Manual 1990), 113, 439t, 550 (photo
    Andrew Fulgoni)
Museo Nacional de Antropología 356
Museum für Völkerkunde, Vienna 357al
J.H. Musgrave, courtesy M. Andronikos
    430bl
Naples Museum, Soprintendenza alle
    antichita della campania 450
Naples National Museum 23br
National Monuments Record, Swindon 38
Nationalmuseet, Copenhagen 429cr, 444l,
    444a (photos John Lee), 445r (photo E.
    Løytved Rosenløv)
National Air and Space Museum,
    Smithsonian Institution, Washington
    D.C., 47
National Archives of Zimbabwe, Harare
    465a
Netherlands Institute for the Near East,
    Leiden 305
The Principal and Fellows of Newnham
    College, Cambridge 36c
National Archaeological Museum, Athens
    357c
Novosti Press Agency 389
Oriental Institute, University of Chicago

53, 337
Michel Orliac 237l
John Parkington 254a
Pavel Pavel 318 (318b photo: ProFoto)
Courtesy the Peabody Museum, Harvard
    University 28a2ndl, 28a2ndr, 33c,
    37tc&tr, 383r
Christopher Peebles 204b, 547
Petrie Museum of Egyptian Archaeology,
    University College London 32a
Pitt-Rivers Museum, Univ. of Oxford 31ar
Karim Sahib/AFP 534
Nicholas Postgate 93
John Prag 430t
Princeton University Press & the
    University of Cincinnati 480 (painting
    by Piet de Jong)
Robert Rausch 14br
Carmen Reigadas 294l, 294r
Colin Renfrew 202 (drawn by Alec
    Daykin), 400r
Gordon Roberts and Silvia Gonzalez 303
Joan Root 434a
John G. Ross 332bl, 332r
Jeremy A. Sabloff 111b
The St. Louis Art Museum, Eliza
    McMillan Fund 29a
Salisbury and South Wiltshire Museum 562
Delwen Samuel 277
Schloss-Gothorp, Schleswig-Holsteinisches
    Landesmuseum 422r
Béatrice Schmider 323
Toni Schneiders 535
Izumi Shimada 15ac, 344
Pat Shipman & Richard Potts 283
Photo Edwin Smith 23bl, 168t, 536
Smithsonian Institution, National
    Anthropological Archives, Bureau of
    American Ethnology Collection,
    Washington D.C. 28a3rdl, 28a4thl, 28ar
Staatliches Museen zu Berlin,
    Preussischer Kulturbesitz, Museum für
    Völkerkunde 221al, 438
Staatliches Museum für Völkerkunde,
    Munich 429cl
Sutton Hoo Research Trust, photos Nigel
    Macbeth 108, 422l
Texas Antiquities Committee 58t&b
David Hurst Thomas & the American
    Museum of Natural History 143
Javier Trueba/Madrid Scientific Films
    390b
UCLA Fowler Museum of Cultural
    History, Los Angeles 347l
U.S. General Services Administration 217t,
    217 inset
U.S. Geological Survey 233r
U.S. National Park Service 84
University of Pennsylvania Museum,
    Philadelphia 131
By courtesy of the Board of Trustees of the
    Victoria & Albert Museum 185br, 304l,
    357ar
Virginia Division of Historic Landmarks,
    photo R. Adams 111a
By courtesy of the Trustee of the
    Marquess of Northampton 1987
    Settlement 556b
Grahame L. Walsh 312b

Bradford Washburn 233l
Jurgen Weiner 264
Todd Whitelaw 193t, 193c
Gordon Willey 35
Wiltshire Archaeological & Natural
    History Society 21
York Archaeological Trust 523, 524, 525,
    526, 527, 528, 529, 531

**The publishers would also like to
acknowledge the following illustrators:**

Igor Astrologo 12, 19, 26, 56 (after Tracy
    Wellman), 68 (after Coles & Lawson
    1987, fig. 10), 172 (after Annick
    Boothe), 175, 196 (after Shennan
    1975), 459 (after Krings & others 1997).
Annick Boothe 54 (adapted from W.
    Rathje & M.Schiffer, Archaeology 1982,
    fig. 4.11), 65b (after Dekin 1984), 76
    (after Winter in Flannery (ed.) 1976,
    fig. 3.5), 77 (after Flannery (ed.) 1976,
    figs. 3.2, 5.2), 81br (after Oxford
    Archaeological Unit), 82l (after Connah
    & Jones, in Connah 1983, p. 77), 95l
    (after The Courier, Unesco Nov. 1987,
    p. 16, drawing by M. Redknap), 95r
    (after National Geographic, supplement
    Jan. 1990), 107 (after M. Carver,
    Underneath English Towns 1987, fig.
    2), 110ar (after J. Coles, Field
    Archaeology in Britain 1972, fig. 61),
    115 (after J. Deetz, Invitation to
    Archaeology, Natural History
    Press/Doubleday & Co., New York
    1967), 121, 122 (after Rathje & Schiffer,
    Archaeology 1982, fig. 4.17), 130, 133
    (after Zeuner 1958), 137, 138 (138l
    after Hedges & Gowlett in Scientific
    American 254 (1), Jan. 1986, p. 84),
    142b (after Hedges & Gowlett 1986,
    p.88), 151l (after Scarre (ed.) 1988,
    p.25), 151r, 159 (after Aitken 1990,
    figs. 6.1, 6.7), 161a, 163 (adapted from
    R. Foley & R. Dunbar, New Scientist 14
    Oct. 1989, p. 40, with addition by P.
    Winton), 166 (adapted from K. Feder &
    M. Park, Human Antiquity 1989, figs.
    12.1, 13.1), 174, (after Scarre (ed.)
    1988, p. 78), 179, 180 (after Johnson
    1972), 184al (after Bowen), 188l (after
    Hodder), 195 (after Scarre (ed.) 1988,
    p. 30), 197 (after Peebles), 204 (after
    Page, and Renfrew), 209, 210 (after
    Lehner), 213a (after Peebles), 229 (after
    van Andel 1989), 230ar (after Sutcliffe
    1985, fig. 5.4), 230b (after Shackleton
    & van Andel 1980, fig. 1), 234 (after K.
    Butzer, Archaeology as Human Ecology
    1982, fig. 4.3), 240 (after Shackley
    1981, fig. 4.3), 241a (after Scarre (ed.)
    1988, p.107), 241b (after Sutcliffe 1985,
    fig. 6.4), 245 (after Hillman, and
    Pearsall 1989), 250 (after Davis 1987,
    figs. 2.10, 2.12, 1.8), 252 (after Davis
    1987, figs. 5.5, 5.11), 255 (after
    Parkington), 266b (after Anderson),
    271 (after J. Greig, Plant Foods in the
    Past, J. of Plant Foods 5 1983, 179-214),

285b(after Brain), 291 (after Klein 1989, fig. 6.29), 292 (after Davis 1987, fig. 6.13a), 315 (after Davis 1987, fig. 4.5), 301 (after Koike), 302 (after M. Jones, *England Before Domesday* 1986, fig. 30), 312br (after K. Oakley, *Man the Toolmaker* (6th ed.) 1972, fig. 4), 299 (after I. Longworth & J. Cherry (eds.), *Arch. in Britain since 1945* 1986, fig. 22), 319a (after J.P. Protzen, Inca Stonemasonry, *Scientific American* 254, Feb. 1986, 84), 320, 324 (after F. van Noten & others, A Paleolithic Campsite in Belgium, *Scientific American*, 258 (4), April 1980, 52, 55), 335 (after Hodges 1970, figs. 51, 52, 172), 342 (after Hodges 1970, fig. 139), 345 (after Shimada), 346 (after R. Tylecote, *Metallurgy in Archaeology*, fig. 15), 348 (after P. Schmidt & D.H. Avery in *Science* 201, Sept. 1978, 1087), 368 (after Renfrew), 369 (after Cummins 1979), 371 (after Renfrew), 378 (after Sidrys), 379 (after Pires-Ferreira in Flannery (ed.) 1976, fig. 10.16), 381 (after Renfrew), 386 (after Renfrew), 400al (after Morley), 401a (after Thom), 403bl (after O'Kelly), 410a, 411a (after Burger), 416r (after Shäfer), 417al (after Shäfer), 417bl, 417c, 417r (after Robins 1986), 423, 425b (after Brothwell 1981, fig. 3.4), 427, 432, 435 (after Toth), 436 (after R. Lewin, *In the Age of Mankind* 1988, p.181), 444br, 451, 453 (after R. Lewin, *Human Evolution* 1984, p. 95), 466a (after Kirch), 466b (after Gelb), 470 (after Clark), 481 (after Renfrew), 487 (after Arnold), 545 (after Jesus Raymundo).
Ian Bott 62–63
Sue Cawood 22br, 53, 445a (after *National Geographic*, Feb. 1985, 194).
Simon S.S. Driver 134b (information from Bannister & Smiley in *Geochronology*, Tucson 1955), 164-65, 175, 198 (after Renfrew), 322l, 456 (after Turner).
Aaron Hayden 388 (after Karlin and Julien in Renfrew and Zubrow (eds.), 1994, fig. 15.1).
ML Design 22bl, 39 (after Bulleid, and Clarke), 50–51 (after A. Sherratt (ed.) *Cambridge Encyc. of Arch.*, 1980, fig. 20.5), 75 (after Renfrew & Wagstaff (eds.) 1982, fig. 2.1), 123 (after K.L. Feder & M.A. Park, *Human Antiquity* 1989, fig. 4.11), 127(after Brothwell & Higgs 1969, fig. 28), 132 (after Renfrew), 161b (after Renfrew), 237r (after Butzer 1982, fig. 8.8), 254b (after Parkington), 258l (after Vita-Finzi 1978, ill. 12), 258r (after M. Jarman & others (ed.), *Early European Agriculture* 1982, fig. 87), 259 (after Flannery 1976, 4.6), 281 (after Zohary & Hopf 1988, with additions), 296b (after Legge & Rowley-Conwy), 353, 354, 367 (after Peacock 1982, fig. 80), 372 (after Renfrew), 374b (after Bass), 376c (after McBryde), 383, 392l, 465b (after

Garlake), 479a, 480a, 488, 502 (after Scarre 1988, 208), 503 (after Flannery).
Lucy Maw 152, 212a, 227l, 286, 376t, 402 (after Mellaart), 448.
Iva Ellen Morris 48l, 48r (courtesy Lewis R. Binford).
P.P. Pratt, after Ruz 211
Schelay Richardson 329l.
Andrew Sanigar 126 (after Stringer & Gamble 1993, p. 43), 153 (after Roberts & others 1994, p. 577), 288, 289 (from information supplied by T. Legge), 309 (after N. Hammond), 365 (from information supplied by Z. Stos-Gale), 426b (from information supplied by T. Molleson), 454 (after Renfrew 1992, 462), 458 (after Leakey 1994, fig. 5.2).
Maggi Smith 514–15 (after Rhys Jones).
Tracy Wellman 67, 88t, 88c, 191(after Isaac), 201 (after Wheatley 1995), 205l, 231 (after Chaloupka 1984), 347r (after Alva & Donnan 1993, p. 173, drawn by A. Gutiérrez), 352, 406 (after Rollefson 1983), 418 (after Tilley 1991, fig. 44), 425a (after Houghton 1980), 426t (after Molleson & Cox 1993, 1.13), 434 (after M.H. Day & E.H. Wickens in *Nature* 286, July 1980, 386–87), 489 (after Piggott), 507b (after Marcus), 534r.
Philip Winton 73c, 141 (after Chris Bronk Ramsey/Oxcal), 163, 199r (after Mike Parker Pearson and Ramilisonina, 1998, fig. 8), 205b (after Mathews 1991, fig. 2.6), 221b (after Gero 1992, fig. 1), 242 (after Piperno and Ciochon, *New Scientist* 10/11/90), 243, 261 (from information supplied courtesy of George R. Milner & James Oliver), 364 (after Z. Stos-Gale), 385, 398r, 405r (after Bartel, Frey and others, 1998), 447 (after Renfrew 1998); 468 (after Cavalli-Sforza & others 1994, 5.11.1); 469 Torroni and others 1998, fig. 4).

Other sources

20 W. Stukeley, *Avebury*, 1724.
25l Drawing by Magnus Petersen 1846.
27 *The London Sketchbook*.
30 F. Catherwood, *Views of Ancient Monuments in Central America, Chiapas and Yucatán*, London 1844
31 A. Pitt-Rivers, *Excavations in Cranborne Chase*, 1893–1898.
37tr T. Proskouriakoff, *An Album of Maya Architecture*, Washington
37br R. Hood, *Faces of Archaeology in Greece*, 1998 courtesy of The Knossos Trust.
44 & 45tr J. Mellaart, *Catal Hüyük*, 1967
45br Çatalhöyük Research Project
64 After Rudenko.
70 G.F. Macdonald & B.A. Purdy, Florida's wet sites, *Early Man* 4 (4) 1982, 4-12
72l Piranesi, *Vedute di Roma*, 1757.
79l From *Archaeologia* 1907, vol. 60.
103 after Stanley, in Connah 1983, p.86.
104 Isaacson and others, 1999, *Journal of Field Archaeology* 26, 227–36

119 Wheeler, *Ancient India* 3 Jan. 1947.
124 After F. Hole, K.V. Flannery & J. Neely, *Prehistory and Human Ecology of the Deh Luran Plain*, Univ. of Michigan Memoirs of the Museum of Anthropology, No.1, fig. 64.
136 After B. Arnold, *Cortaillod-Est* Editions du Ruau: Saint-Blaise (redrawn M. Rouillard in B. & J. Coles, *People of the Wetlands* 1989, 85).
140, 142t After Gordon Pearson.
149 After R. Klein, *The Human Career* 1989, fig. 3.9.
180 After C. Renfrew & E.V. Level in C. Renfrew & K.L. Cooke (eds.), *Transformations* 1979, figs.6.11, 6.12.
214 After Craig Morris.
218 From Gimbutas 1974, p. 163, drawing by Linda Mount-Williams.
230al After W.M. Davis 1933.
246 After C. Spence (ed.), *Archaeological Site Manual, Museum of London* 1990.
248 After J.G. Evans & others, in *Proc. Of Preh. Soc.* 51, 1985, p.306.
249 After A. Marshack, *The Roots of Civilization* 1972, fig. 78b.
251 Adapted from C. Spence (ed.) 1990.
261 After Fowler 1971, fig. 10.
265 Morgan, *Houses and House Life of the American Aborigines*, 1881, fig. 37.
266t From P. Bellwood, *The Polynesians* (Rev. ed.) 1987, ill. 1.
278 After Mangelsdorf.
325r After D. Cahen & L. Keeley in *World Arch.* 12(2), 1980, fig. 5.
328 After Zervos 1959.
340 After Renfrew 1979.
341 D. Brothwell & E. Higgs, *Science in Archaeology* 1969, pls. XXV, XXVI.
343 After J. Rawson, *Ancient China* 1980, ill. 43.
359 After R.B. Mason & E.J. Keall, Provenance and Petrography of Pottery from Medieval Yemen, *Antiquity* 62 (236), Sept. 1988, 452-463.
370 After Fulford & Hodder 1975, in Peacock 1982, figs. 86, 87.
392r After M. Ruspoli, *The Cave of Lascaux* 1987, p. 200.
394br F. d'Errico & C. Cacho 1994, fig. 2.
396l From J. Oates, *Babylon* 1979, ill. 6.
396r From A. Toynbee (ed.), *Half the World* 1973, p.27.
403 After K. Mendelssohn, *The Riddle of the Pyramids* 1974, fig. 9.
417ar From Layard 1853.
437a From E. Matos Moctezuma, *The Great Temple of the Aztecs* 1988, ill. 23.
439r From E. Hadingham, *Secrets of the Ice Age* 1979, p.147, after C. Barrière 1975, fig. 17.
443 After J. Flood, *Archaeology of the Dreamtime* 1983, fig. 4.3 (after Brown 1981).
466 From R.G. Harrison & others in *Antiquity* 53 (207), March 1979,pl. VII.
505l From B. Fagan, *In the Beginning* (6th ed.)1988, fig. 16.4 (after Winter in Flannery (ed.) 1976, fig 2.17).

Index

Page numbers in *italics* indicate illustrations
For individual animal and plant species, see under "animal species," "plant species"

Abbot, Charles 29
Aborigines, Australian 41, 264, 273, 312, 321, 332, 369, 376, 398, 424, 428, 447, 453, 509–10, 513, 539, 540, 541, 544, 548, 549, 562, 564
Abri Blanchard 394
Abri Pataud 291
Abric Romani 312
absolute dating 117, 121, 122, 124, 125, 128–55, 156, 161, 170, 336
Abu Dhabi 276
Abu Hureyra 274, 296–97, *297*, 438
Abu Salabikh 92, *93*, 109, 208
Abu Simbel 14, *169*, 558
Abydos 277
accounting systems 211
Acheulian *see* axes
Acropolis 533, 538
Adams, Richard 86
Adams, Robert 40, 79, 181, 205
Addyman, Peter 523, 524, 530, 559
adobe 55, 228, 504
administration 209, 214, 224; *see also* social organization
Admiralty Islands 362
adze 383, 512, 513, 520
Aegean 34, 131, 132, 137, 160, 162, 169, 219, 226, 332, 346, 365, 366, 367, 373, 480–81
aerial photography 40, 75, 79, 80, 82–86, 88, 89, 90, 100, 116, 194, 262, 399, 516, 544, 545
aerial survey 79–89, 90
aesthetics 419–20
Afar 433
Afghanistan 358, 557
Africa 16, 25, 36, 40, 41, 53, 74, 78, 98, 125, 145, 148–49, 150, 159, 163, 165, 169, 186, 226, 228, 242, 252, 275, 285, 295, 336, 349, 374, 388, 438, 454, 455, 458, 467, 564; East 37, 40, 106, 126, 127, 128, 145, 148, 149, 156, 162, 191, 242, 284, 308, 348, 434, 538; North 335, 347; South 46, 110, 128, 155, 157, 245, 247, 248, 252, 253, 256, 284, 291, 298, 303, 308, 324, 328, 335, 425, 433, 492; southern 41, 148, 176; West 226, 273, 355, 467; *see also* Congo; Egypt; Kenya; Nigeria; Rhodesia; Tanzania; Zimbabwe
Afroasiatic languages 455
age 173, 195, 196, 197, 215, 219, 287, 288, 290, 291, 294, 421, 424–28, 452, 459, 519; age range 142; *see also* calibration
aging 288, 425–27
agriculture 117, 183, 200, 202, 237, 243, 263, 264, 279, 451, 463, 508, 522, 542, 543, 545; agricultural communities 78; damage 553; intensification 546; Maya 86, 484; origins of 40, 272; swidden

243, 264; workers 176, 177; *see also* farming
Ai Bunar 315
Aidonia Treasure 557
'Ain Ghazal 281, 408, *408*
Aitken, Martin 105
Akhenaten 55, 131, 207, 374, 429, 431, 535
Akrotiri 160, 161, 162, 208, 238, 413
Alaska 11, 14, 64, 65, 186, 187, 229, 230, 231, 233, 235, 237, 256, 285, 445
Aleutian Caves 56; **Aleutian Islands** 64
Alexander the Great 129, 189, 430, 534
algae 243
Ali Kosh 280, 339, 371, 372
aliens 562, 564
Allen, P.M. 495
alloys 339, 340, 342, 344, 361
alpha: emissions 146, 155; particles 150, 151; radiation 146
Alps 68, 95, 362, 366, 492; Austrian 315
Altai 64
Altaic languages 455
Altamira 391
altars 69, *69*, 409
Althusser, Louis 418, 486
Alva, Walter 555
amber 356, 374
Amboseli 192
Ambrose, Stanley 308
America 56, 144, 163, 168, 169, 228, 292, 294, 314, 410, 438, 457, 555; Central 163, 169, 223, 373, 438, 484, 485, 555; Meso- 16, 36, 49, 79, 85, 90, 129, 168, 169, 182, 183, 189, 215, 257, 321, 354, 356, 366, 382, 395, 399, 403, 405, 410, 412, 413, 417, 420, 437, 462, 499, 502, 503, 504, 555; North 13, 28–29, 34, 35, 47, 59, 74, 89, 105, 133, 134, 163, 168, 212, 232, 243, 249, 260, 264, 286, 293, 308, 322, 328, 373, 404, 452, 472, 490, 541; *see also under names of individual countries*
American Antiquarian Society 28
American Indians *see* Native Americans
American Museum of Natural History 541
American Society for Conservation Archaeology 547
Americas 13, 16, 25, 168, 169, 314, 399, 454, 455, 456
Amerind languages 455, 456
amino-acid racemization 156–57, 253, 426
amino acids 157, 422, 426
amphorae 95, 277, 367, *367*, 373, 374
Anaktuvuk Pass 186
analogy 182
analytical electron microscopy 441
Anasazi 238, 264, 265, 287, 305, 553
Anatolia 137, 161, 218, 279, 349, 355, 363, 365, 370, 371, 372, 467, 468
Anbangbang 509, 510–12, 513
Andel, Tjeerd van 231, 237
Andernach 238
Anderson, Athol 295
Andes 213, 220, 226, 228, 277, 295, 344, 403, 410, 494, 543
androcentrism 47, 218, 559

Angkor 86, 403, 557
Anglo-Saxons 154, 183, 185, 211, 526–27
animals 11, 13, 44, 52, 59, 70, 78, 92, 138, 164, 167, 176, 225, 231, 232, 247–55, 282–305, 413, 502; age 287; animalian forms *554*; annelids 249; arthropods 249; behavior 53; bones 35, 50, 52, 53, 250, 282, 288–90, 301, 313, 388, 503, 506, 520, 540; camelids 294, 295, 334; carnivores 250, 283, 284, 285, 286, 288; coleoptera 249; crustaceans 228; echinoderms 298; exotic 355; extinct 232; grassland 255, 308; grazers 254, 261, 264; herbivores 243, 250, 251, 252, 254, 286; mammals 238, 253, 256, 288, 291, 298, 436, 512, 519; marsupials 232, 512; nematodes 249, 306; origins and development 24, 26; predatory 191; products 263; remains 297, 310, 512; rodents 225, 247–48, 286, 298, 299, 501, 502; scavenging 250; studies 38; symbolism 409; teeth 291–92, *291–92*; traction 303
animal species 133; alpacas 295, 334; antelope 253, 256; armadillos 309; aurochs 303; baboon 256; badger 303, 334; bandicoot 512, 519; bats 247–48; bears 250, *250*, 393; bees 528; beetles 249, 298, 520, 528; beavers 52, 255, 329, 404; bisons 287, 292, *292*, 293, 295; boar 292, 300, 301; brown bear 294; buffalo 245, 254, 295; Californian sealion 302; camel 252; Cape buffalo 254, 291; caribou 14, 65, 302; cats 290, 303; cattle 250, *250*, 295, 303, 304, 492; cave bear 251, 255, 390; caymans 411; chimpanzees 313, 387, 436, 437, 459; cottontail rabbit 306; cows 287, 289, 290; coyote 502; crab 519; crocodile 231, *231*, 232, 511, 519; crows 519; deer 287, 301, 309, 393, 505; Dexter cattle 275, *275*; dogs 64, 103, 250, *250*, 266, 285, 286, 287, 290, 300, 303, 387, 520; dune mole rat 248; earthworms 106, 249; echidna 511; eland 254, 328; elephants 128, 252, 253, 322, 356, 374; elk 290, 418; equids 254; *Fasciolopsis buski* 521; flies 249, 298, 528; fox 434, 502; frogs 298; gazelle 281, 296, *297*; geckos 266; *Genyornis* 252; giant beaver 252; giant buffalo 254; giant horse 254; giraffe 252; goats 165, 250, *250*, 253, 280, 281, 287, 290, 295, 297, 302, 303, 309, 329, 481; golden spider beetles 250; gophers 306; grain beetles 250, 298; grasshopper 249, *249*; grizzly bear 302; grubs 286, 309; grysbok 254; hartebeest 246, 328; hippopotamus 374; horses 64, 245, 252, 255, 283, 295, 303, 334; hyenas 244, 253, 283, 284, 285; hyraxes 265; ibex 251, 393; jaguars 409, 411, *411*, 412, *552*; kangaroo 511; leopards 284, 285; lizards 501; llamas 221, 295; mammoths 64, 244, 252, 255, 287, 389, 393; marine turtles 309, 511; mastodon 252, 291; moose 302;

mountain goats 255; oxen 295, 304, 493; packrats 265; panther 357; pigs 104, 128, 149, 250, *250*, 263, 266, 286, 302, 353, 356; polar bears 65, 355; Polynesian rat 266, 267; porcupines 284, 286, 519; rabbit 300, 469; rat 267; rattlesnakes 212, *212*; red deer 287, 290, 303; reindeer 251, 255, 302, 324; rhinoceroses 254, 255, 393; ringtailed cat 306; roach 257; rock lobsters 255; roe deer 287, 290, 298, 303, 326; *Scolytus scolytus* 249; seals 65, 185, *185*, 204, 209; sea urchins 298; shad 257; Shasta ground sloth 255; sheep 165, 250, *250*, 253, 280, 281, 287, 289, 290, 292, 295, 297, 302, 303, 309, 334, 480; sika deer 290, 300; sloth 244; Soay sheep 275; stags 493; *Sthenurus* 252; toads 298; turtles 266, 299, 519; vicuña 294, *294*, 334; wallaby 512; walrus 356; warthog 256; wasp 298; waterbuck 253; weasel 334; weevils 249; whales 60, 61; white-tailed deer 306, 502; wildebeeste 253; wolves 60, 285; woolly rhinoceros 59, 251; zebra 256
Annapolis 490, *490, 491*
annealing 335, 339, 340, 341
Antalya Museum 556
Antarctic 126, 162, 163, 226, 227
anthropology 11, 12, 36, 45, 174
antimony 338, 339
antler picks 315
antlers 283, 286, 287, 288, 290, 315, 323, 324, 325, 327–29, 394, 493
anvils 313, 517, 519, 520
Anyang 210
apatite 150, 308
Apicius 282
Apliki 365
applied archaeology 544–45
archaeoastronomy 399
archaeobotany 270; *see also* paleoethnobotany
archaeological heritage management 546
Archaeological Institute of America 560
Archaeological Resources Protection Act 548
Archaeological Survey of India 30
archaeology 11–16, 17, 19, 24, 27, 40–48; as history 12; as science 12–13; history of 16, 19–48; modern 24–48; nature of 39; of cult 406; of identity 215–22, 476, 533–36; postmedieval 13, 41; reasoning in 38; variety and scope of 13
archaeometallurgy 339–49
archaeozoology 280, 283, 291, *see also* zooarchaeology
archaeomagnetic dating 158–59
architecture 166, *167*, 202, 209, 213, 220, 256; Maya 37, *37*; stone 34; theory 43
Arctic 126, 282, 442
Arcy-sur-Cure 442
Ardèche 393
Ardipithecus 162
ards 261, 275, 546
Arens, William 286
Argentina 168, 294, 434
Argolid 237
argon 138, 145, 148, 149, 150, 159, 360
argon-argon dating 145

Arica, Chile 427, 437
Ariège 249
Arikamedu 32, *32*, 363
Arizona 82, 135, 158, 326
Army Corps of Engineers 541, 546
Arnold, Bettina 219
Arnold, Dean 486, *487*
arsenic 339, 342, 358
Arsuaga, Juan-Luis 390
art 11, 36, 232, 246, 269, 303–04, 310, 326–27, 385–420, 451, 493
Arthur, Paul 23
artifacts 11, 24, 25, 33, 38, 39, 41, 42, 49–50, 52, 58, 60, 66, 69, 70, 74, 78, 89, 92, 94, 95, 97, 104, 106, 107, 111, 116, 117, 118, 120, 122, 127, 129, 131, 152, 156, 178, 186, 190, 191, 192, 195, 197, 202, 205, 208, 209, 210, 212, 215, 276–78, 311–13, 325, 358, 360–61, 376, 386, 404, 415, 463, 488, 501, 543, 557; *see also* classification, typology
artifact scatters 192, *192*
artificial intelligence theory 504
artists 414–15
Aryans 537
ash 145, 148, 160, 195, 208, 232, 238, 243, 256, 257, 262, 451, 505, 520
Ashkelon 424
Asia 163, 169, 252, 337, 457; central 528; northeast 456; southeast 467, 499, 519, 520, 522, *522;* western 12, 16, 281, *281*
aspartic acid 157, 427
asphalt 59
Assyria 169, 355, 405; art 417, *417*
astronomical events 399, 562
astronomy 129, 394
Aswan 272, 316; Aswan Dam 14, 558
Atapuerca 390
Athens 189, 366, 397, 414, 538
Atlantis 562
atomic absorption spectrometry (AAS) 360, 362, 451
Attica 365, 455
attributes 114, 115, 116
attritional age profile 291
Atwater, Caleb 28
Auckland 453
Aufderheide, Arthur 442, 447
augers 94
Australia 12, 13, 16, 41, 153, 163, 173, 186, 227, 228, 231, 234, 244, 252, 253, 264, 273, 287, 312, 321, 361, 369, 373, 376, 382, 398, 434, 447, 452, 499, 509–15, 539, 541, 548, 551
Australian Archaeological Association (AAA) 540; Australian Heritage Commission 548
australopithecines 37, 162, 284, 285, 425, 429, 433, 436
Australopithecus: afarensis 162, 433, 437; *africanus* 308, 433; *(Paranthropus) boisei* 145; *robustus* 309
Austria 59, 66, 238, 315, 394
Austronesian languages 467
AutoCAD 87
Avdat 543
Avebury *20*, 199, 200, 201, 248
Aveni, Anthony 399
Avery, Donald 348
awls 511
axeheads 315, 383

axes 24, 121, *121,* 202, 212, 262, 312, 330, 351, 353, 358, 359, 367, 369, 405, 509, 512, 555; Acheulian 163, 319, 323, 326, 387, 438
Ayodhya 46, 536, 537
Azilian 329
Aztecs 20, 72, 74, 169, 257, 282, 321, 356, 357, 367, 418, 438, 450, 551
azurite 335

Baalbek 557
Babylon 20, 169, 183, 185, 439, 534
bacteria 59, 244
Baghdad 30, 180
Bahn, Paul 294
Baillie, Michael 135
Bali 363
Balkans 46, 340, 355, 365
Baltic 374
Baluchistan 165
Ban Chiang 516
bands 174, 177, 179, 192, 194
Bangkok 516
Bang Pakong Valley 516, 519
Bantu 424, 454; languages 467
Bapty, Ian 42
Barbados 231
Barda Balka 431
Barker, Philip 100, 108
Barrett, John 492
Barrow 56, 64, 65, 445
barrows 200, 201
barter 355
Barthes, Roland 418, 486
Bar-Yosef, Ofer 281
basalt 316
basketry 333, 334, 503
baskets 44, 49, 60, 61, *61,* 63, 64, 68, 95, 415
Basques 96, 97, 454, *454,* 455
Bass, George F. 33, 95, 98, 331, 373, 374
Batán Grande 14, *14,* 344, 346
batons 328, *328*
battleship curves 123, 124
baulks 108, 257
Bayesian statistics 140, 141, 142
beaches 229; raised 229, 230, *230,* 231
beads 338, 342, 374, 383, 389, 440, 506, 521
Beaker Folk 463
Bearsden 306
Beattie, Owen 68, 447
Beau's lines 446
Beazley, Sir John 414
Bechan Cave 255
Becker, Berndt 135
Beechey Island 68, 446–47
beer 213, 214, 220, 276, 277, 282, 302
Behrensmeyer 284
Behy 238
belief 11, 17, 50, 71, 189, 406, 407, 465, 486, 539
Belize 49, 87, 257, 308, 395
Bell, James 476
bellows 345, *345,* 346
Bender, Barbara 281, 470
Beni Hassan 321
Bent, J.T. 464
Berekat Ram 390
Beresovka 56, 64

Bering Strait 163, 229, 456
Beringia 229, *229*
Berlin Museum 538, 555
Bernal, Ignacio 501
beta particles 150, 151; emissions 155
Betancourt, Julio 264
Betatakin 135, 136
Bible 19, 21, 24, 30, 73, 419; Book of Exodus 162; Creation 418; Flood 24; New Testament 73; Old Testament 73, 418, 419; Plagues of Egypt 162; *see also* creation stories
biblical archaeology 73
Biel, Jorg 211
big-game extinctions *252,* 252–53
"Big Man" 353
Bilzingsleben 147
Binford, Lewis 13, 26, 27, 38, 40, 41, 42, 53, 182, 186, 187, 190, 193, 197, 281, 283, 285, 386, 388, 389, 469, 470, 472, 475, 476
Binford, Sally 197, 389
Binneman, Johan 324
Bintliff, John 559
biological anthropology 11, 172, 432
biostratigraphy 149; *see also* faunal dating
bipedalism 433
birds 59, 70, 238, 248, 251, 253, 266, 267, 286, 295–300, 306, 357, 501, 513, 519; mummified 295
bird species: broadbills 519; chickens 104, 268; cormorants 255, 519; cranes 303; ducks 254; eagles 411; flamingos 255; fowl 266; herons 519; kiwi 266, *266;* macaques 520; moa 266, *266,* 267, 295; ostrich 374; owls 248, 283; pelicans 255, 519; pigeons 305; quail 305; waterfowl 232
Birley, Robin 59
Bismarck Archipelago 263
bismuth 358, 361
bison drive sites 293, *293,* 328
Blackfoot 293
Black Patch 270
Black Sea 366, 374, 467
blades 121, 319, 324, 329, 342, 388, 449
Blanco, Antonio 346
Blanton, Richard 494, 500, 506, 507
Bleivik, Norway 425
blood 302, 324, 431, 454; **groups** 431, 454; **residues** 114, 244, 301–02, 431
Bloom, Arthur 231
blueprints 317, 319, 393
bluestones 316
Boarding School site 292, *292,* 293
Boas, Franz 26, 27, 34, 420
boat axe culture 470
boats 62, 94, 331, 332, 352, 385, 418, 521; *see also* ships, shipwrecks
bodies 240, 421, 422, 427, 516; *see also* bog bodies
body shape, retrieval of 22, *23,* 23
bog bodies 69, 127, 244, 279, 305, 429
bogs 68, 127, 240, 241, 257, 275, 276, 409
Bogucki, Peter 304
Bökönyi, Sandor 280
Bonampak 215
bone collagen studies 308–10
bones 13, 65, 68, 106, 120, 155, 156, 157, 186, 190, 191, 222, 239, 248, 253, 256, 278, 283, 284–86, 288–90, 306–10, 311, 323, 324, 325, 327–29, 394, 410, 424–29, 431, 447, 449, 450, 451, 504, 511, 516, 519, 539, 555; animal 35, 50, 52, 53, 59, 111, 148, 250, *250,* 251, 269, 282, 288–90, 301, 388, 503, 506; birds 295, 298; cattle 28, *288;* epiphyses 425; human 40, *40,* 59, 65, 269, 306–10, 390, 421, 424–29, 438, 442–47, 521, 522; marine animals 231; microstructure 425; *see also* skeletons
Bonnefille, Raymonde 242
boomerang 232, 312
Boomplaas Cave 110, *110,* 245–47, *247,* 324
Bordes, François 189, 238, 321, *321,* 389
Boserup, Esther 477, 478
Bosnia 535, 536
Boston Museum of Fine Arts 556
Botta, Paul Emile 27
"bottom-up" approach 215, 216, 224
Boucher de Perthes, Jacques 24, 28
Bougon 317, *317*
Boulanden 258
Boule, Marcellin 435
Bourdieu, Pierre 42, 215, 216, 486
Bowdler, Sandra 234
bows 301, 438
box grid 108, 109
Boxgrove 128, 326
Braasch, Otto 82
Bradbury, J.P. 243
Bradley, Daniel 295
Braidwood, Robert J. 40, 280, 472
Brain, C.K. 40, 53, 256, 284, 285
brain endocasts 435, 436
Brainerd, G.W. 123, 124
Branč 196
Brassell, Simon 226
Braudel, Fernand 461, 491
Braun, David 383
Brazil 163, 313, 314
bread 276, 277, 279, 304, 305, 335
brick 56, *56,* 104, 207, 240, 303, 349
bridges 331, 535
Britain 35, 36, 39, 84, 105, 106, 145, 159, 176, 182, 200, 209, 223, 226, 229, 248, 249, 353, 359, 369, 401, 463, 483, 548
British Columbia 302, 308
British Institute of Archaeology (Ankara) 245
British Museum 120, 407, 448, 538, 539, 555, 557
Brittany 20, 229, 316
Broadbent, S.R. 401
Broadbent's criterion 399, 400
Broken K. Pueblo 194, 195, *195,* 197
Bromage, Tim 424
Bronitsky, Gordon 336
bronze 25, 38, 56, 98, 114, 117, 121, 211, 244, 330, 336, 339, 340, 342, 346, 363, 374, 380, 388, 395, 402, 404, 555
Bronze Age 14, 25, 33, 36, 55, 69, 73, 75, 136, 243, 257, 270, 289, 303, 308, 311, 328, 330, 331, 338, 342, 346, 365, 366, 367, 373, 385, 415, 418, 467, 471, 482, 493, 563; Early 199, 237, 363, 480, 488, 492; Late 59, 75, 82, 92, 121, 136, 154, 160, 162, 204, 216, 218, 219, 253, 358, 365, 480
Brooks, H.K. 322
brothels 216, 424
Brothwell, Don 38, 305
Brown, Peter 443
Bruhns, Karen 344
Buddhism 118, 450, 516, 557
Buffelskloof 246
Bunn, Henry 284
Burch, Ernest 256
Bureau of American Ethnology 28, 29
bureaucracy 176, 177, 205, 211
Burger, Richard 410
burial 54, 55, 62, 69, 77, 90, 99, 104, 105, 116, 171, 174, 195–96, 199, 201, 202, 210–11, 219, 222, 224, 231, 232, 272, 358, 389, 390, 405, 408, 412, 462, 480, 484, 488, 492, 493, 506, 508, 516, 519, 529, 530, 539, 540; communal 195, 211, 412, 488, 492; customs 211; mounds 21, 55, 64, 69, 74, 80, 102, 108, 110, *110,* 198, 200, 261, *261,* 421; *see also* cemeteries; grave goods; graves
burins 319, 323, 324
burning 55, 286, 315
burrowing animals 77, 106, 118, 325
butchery 13, 92, 176, 192, 283, 289, 295, 298, 323, 326, 503
Butler, Ann 279
Butser Farm 274–75, *274–75,* 302, 542
butter 277, 302, 304
Butzer, Karl 236
Byzantine 137, 265, 342, 528

"cabinets of curiosities" 20
Caesarea 95
caesium magnetometer 100, 102
Cahen, Daniel 325
Cahokia 257, 260–61, *260, 261*
Calakmul 205
calcite 158, 203, 366
calcium 105, 157, 253, 309, 362, 446, 451
calcium carbonate 126, 143, 147, 152, 227, 235, 248
Caldwell, Joseph 382
calendars 129–31, 132, 144, 183
calibration 140–42, 517; calibrated relative methods 155–59; *see also* dating
calibration curve 140, *140,* 141, 142, 160
Calico Hills 313
California 157, 158, 228, 229, 230, 238, 244, 313, 541
California Indians 286, 307, 451
Cambodia 86, 398, 403, 555, 557
Campana, Douglas 328
Canada 68, 95, 223, 326, 339, 549
canals 79, 83, 86, 211, 257, 411, 501, 544, 545
Cango Valley 246
Cann, Rebecca 457
cannibalism 215, 287
Cape Gelidonya 33, 373
Cape Krusenstern 231
Caracol 205, 395
carbon 137, 138, 141–45, 244, 278, 307, 308, 309, 310, 348, 349, 361, 364, 365; arc 360; radical 360
carbohydrates 452, 502
carbonates 57, 340
carbon dioxide 94, 138, 307, 337
carburization (carburizing) 341, 349
Carnac 20, 398
Carlson, David L. 114

Carnegie Institution, Washington 406
Carneiro, Robert 478
carrying capacity 452, 477
Carter Ranch 195
cartouche 209, 210
Carter, Howard 34, 62
carts 68, 304, 329, 331
Carver, Martin 523
carvings 60, 157–58, 385, *385*, 389, 394, 413, 415, 418
Casas Grandes 399
Caso, Alfonso 500
Casselberry, Samuel 453
Cassirer, Ernst 486
casting 339, 340, 342, *342*, 343, 345
Castro, Rubén Cabrera 90
Çatalhöyük 14, *14*, 44–45, *45*, 71, 176, 218, 280, 339, 372, 402, 561
catastrophe theory 27, 495
catastrophic age profile 291, *291*
Catherwood, Frederick 30
cathodoluminescence 366
cation ratios 157–58
Caton-Thompson, Gertrude 36, *36*, 464
Caune de l'Arago 152
causewayed enclosures 200, 202
Cauvin, Jacques 281
Cavalli-Sforza, Luca 454, 468
cave art 11, 36, 251, 285, 326, 392–93, 413, 434, 486; *see also* rock art
Cave Bay Cave 234
caves 59, 63, 64, 98, 110, 111, 144, 146, 147, 152, 155, 158, 190, *234*, 234–35, 240, 253, 254, 255, 256, 284, 302, 326, 408, 413, 434, 446, 492, 501; *see also* rockshelters
Çayönü 334, 339
Cefn Graeneg 105
Celtic languages 467
Celts 154, 211, 334
cemeteries 64, 123, 194, 196, 203, 224, 428, 521, 527, 546, 555
cemetery analysis 197
Central Intelligence Agency 85
central place theory 178–79, *179*, 180, 181
centralized societies 104, 209, 211, 213, 214–15
centrifuge 277, 359
ceramics 36, 55, 56, 114, 151, 155, 212, 213, 220, 280, 304, 348, 409, 501, 520; Classic Maya 131, 410; stoneware 337
cereals 143, 241, 270–71, 276, 279, 280, 281, 282, 297, 298, 304, 309, 335, 545
ceremonial centers 176, 178, 506
ceremonial exchange 382
Cerén 63, 257, 270, 311
Cerra el Plomo 68
cesspits 249, 306, 442, 528
Chaco Canyon 84, *84*, 264, 265, 298, 398, 399, 463
Chadwick, A.J. 482, 483
Chadwick, John 207, *207*
chaîne opératoire 321, 388, *388*
Chalcatzingo 309
chalcedony 214
Chalchuapa 162
chalk 53, 59, 99, 158, 315
Chaloupka, George 231, 232, 509, 512
Champollion, Jean-François 27, 30, 183
chaos theory 495

Chapman, John 488, 535
Chappell, J.M.A 231
characterization 358–67, 372, 384, 388
Charavines 69
charcoal 141, 144, 245–46, 264, 267, 272, 279, 306, 325, 327, 338, 346, 348, 349, 501, 503, 505, 517, 519, 522
chariots 329, *329*, 331
Charles, J.A. 342, 343
charring 270, 274, 278, 281
Charsadda 32
Chase, Arlen 395
Chase, Diane 395
Chauvet Cave 144, 391, 393, *393*
Chavín de Huántar 169, 385, 410–11, 420
chemical dating 119, 120
chemical residues 276–77
Cheops (Khufu) 210; see also pyramids
Cherry, John 75, 204, 206
chert 322, 503, 512, 513
Chesterman, Judson 438
Chetro Ketl 399
Chevdar 271
Chibcha 334
Chichén Itzá 95, 409, 484, 485, *485*
chief 176, 186, 211, 216
chiefdom 169, 176, 177, 188, 200, 203–15, 478, 479, 507
childbirth 223, 438, *438*
Childe, V. Gordon 26, 34, 35, 171, 195, 280–81, 463, 471, 472
children 196, 212, 219, 424, 425, 432, 434, 443, 472
Chile 64, 239, 298, 309, 437, 442
Chimú period 169, 450
China 13, 49, 72, 85, 94, 129, 159, 165, 169, 173, 182, 210, 237, 238, 256, 257, 282, 304, 305, 335, 343, 345, 349, 354, 356, 398, 412, 429, 462, 476, 516, 521, 528, 536, 545, 551, 554, 558
chinampas 257
Chinchorro 56, 64, 427, 437
chisels 329, 342, 512, 513
Chisholm, Brian 308
chlorine-36 dating 158
cholesterol 306, 422
Chomsky, Noam 486
Christaller, Walter 178
Christianity 117–18, 145, 168, 228, 349, 351, 409, 484, 536
chromatograms 244, 277
chromatography 277, 302, 326, 333, 422
chronology 33, 34, 117–70, 212, 225, 239, 282; correlations 161–62; relative 160
Chukchi Sea 231
Chumash Indians 541
churches 73, 100, 101, 105, 408, 439, 527, 535
Circleville 28
Cirencester 427, 428, 446
cire perdue technique, *see* lost-wax method
cisterns 264, 543
city states 174, 182, 183, 381, *381*, 382, 399
civilizations 13, 20, 27, 30, 34, 167
Clacton 324
Clark, Grahame 35, 49, 283, 290, 353, 369, 470
Clark, J. Desmond 26, 41
Clark, J.R. 379
Clarke, David L. 26, 27, 39, 40, 42, 182

Classic period (Mayan) 85, 130, 346, 406, 462
classification 34, 35, 38, 114, *114*, 116, 219; of societies 174–77; *175*; of stone tools 247
clay 49, 50, 55, 56, 59, 74, 94, 103, 104, 133, 151, 152, 157, 159, 204, 234, 235, 236, 243, 259, 262, 276, 278, 298, 334, 335, 336, 338, 342, 343, 349, 358, 359, 413, 439, 517, 519, 520; *see also* clay tablets; writing; writing tablets
clay tablets 44, 182, 184, *184*, 206
Clegg, John 457
CLIMAP project 232
climate 59, 63–64, 70, 118, 125–28, 133, 144, 158, 225–53, 256, 262, 288, 462, 543, 545; cycles 227; records 227, *227*, 228; *see also* glaciation
cloning 432
clothing 62, 63, 64, 65, 67, 68, 69, 213, 214, 220, 269, 380, 431, 444, 493
Clovis projectile points 322, 456
cluster analysis 196, 197, 206, 212, 519
coast 229–32, 230, 252, 255, 253, 254, 304
Coates, J.F. 332
Cóa Valley 158
cobalt 338
Coca-Cola bottles 13
cocaine 309
codices 395, 438, 450
Coe, Michael 410, 412, 413
cofferdam 111, *111*
coffins 62, 63, 69, 331, 440
cognitive archaeology 385–420
cognitive maps 386, *386*, 387, 388, 395, 406, 412, 413, 476
cognitive-processual archaeology 39, 42, 384, 461, 471, 483, 491–95, 496, 508
cognitivist approach 215, 492
coherence approach 493
coins 25, 107, 131, 182, 184, *184*, 205, 342, 346, 362, 365, 366, 379, 380, 400, 404, 526, 528, *529*, 555
Coles, Bryony 261, 329, 330
Coles, John 68, 261, 329, 330
collagen 120, 307–10, 445
Colless Creek 234
Collingwood, R.G. 462, 474, 475, 476, 486
Cologne 553
Colombia 313, 333, 343
colonialist assumptions 559
colonization 163, 164, *164–65*, 264, 266, 467
Colorado 442, 553
Colorado Desert, California 373
Colorado River 233, *233*
colorimetry 339
Columbus 332
commodities 355–57, 382, 383
Common Era 118
communism 27, 494, 536
competition 215, 252, 382, 479, 484–85; *see also* exchange
competitive emulation 382, 383
computed axial tomography (CAT), *see* computerized tomography (CT)
computers 208, 503, 510, 525, 526, 543; computer-aided design (CAD) 87; computer-aided mapping (CAM) 87; computer-assisted reconstruction

431;computer-based mapping system 260; computer integrated finds record 525; computerization 33, 39, 44, 78, 83, 84, 98, 105, 109, 114, 135; computer modeling 482, 525; computer rectification 83; computer simulation 482–83, 496
computerized tomography (CT) 425, 431, 433, 440, *441*, 448
Congo 438
conjoining *see* refitting
Conkey, Margaret 47, 219
Connolly, Robert 431
Connor, Melissa 443
Conquistadors 316, 356, 407
conservation 70, 95, 114, 522, 525, 542, 546–58, 559; legislative basis of 546–49
consumption 281, 282, 299, 367, 377–78, 384
contamination 117, 142–45
context 50, 52, 106, 117, 283
contextual seriation 122–23, *123*
contract archaeology 546–48
Controlled Archaeological Test Site 104, *104*
Conway, J.S. 105
Cook, Captain James 246, 318
Cook, S.F. 453
cooking 114, 195, 271, 276, 277, 279, 282, 295, 298, 307, 452; zones 236
Copán 30, 131, 205, 210, 264
copper 38, 56, 59, 196, 220, 315, 335, 336, 339, 340, 341, *341*, 342, 344–47, 356, 357, 360, 363, 364, 365, 366, 373, 374, 383; axes 212, 343; origins of 340, *340*
Copper Age 218, 337, 343, 492
Coppergate, York 109, 523, *523*, 525, 526, 527, 528, 530
coppicing 261
coprolites 240, 244, 255, 269, 296, 306, 424, 442, 501
coprosterol 306
corals 228, 231, 308
cores: lake 268; sea 126, 162, 226, 227, 241, 264
correspondence approach 493
Cortaillod-Est 136
Cortés, Hernán 367, 552
Cosa 367
Cosmides, Leda 473
Cosquer Cave 72, 73, *73*, 393
cost-surface analysis 87
Costa Rica 86
Council for British Archaeology 560
County Sites and Monuments Record 549
Cowgill, George 208
Cox, Chris 85
Cozumel 111, 210
Crabtree, Donald 321, 322
craft 92, 176, 177, 336, 384, 480; production 203, 213; specialization 195, 203, 205, 207, 214; specialists 176, 177, 183, 203, 211, 213–14, 373; technology 480
Cranborne Chase 31, *31*
cranial capacity 424, 435, 452
Crawford, O.G.S. 82
creation stories 418, 419
Crelin, Edmund 436
Crete 34, 36, 126, 160, 195, 205, 208, 302, 364, 365, 367, 373, 374, 409, 419, 480, 488, 539, 559

critical theory 486, 490, 491, 533
CRM, *see* culture resource management
Croatia 148, 189, 286, 437, 535, 557
Croce, Benedetto 486
crop marks 79, 80, 83, 84, 85
crops *see* farming; plant species
cross dating 131, 132
Crowe, Donald 415
crucibles 345, 528
Cruz-Uribe, Kathryn 291
C-transforms *see* cultural formation processes
Cuello 308
Cuicuilco 208
Cullen, Ben 27, 473
cultivation 42, 79, 264, 274, 278, 279, 478, 517, 521, 522
cults 385, 391, 408, 410, 420
cultural anthropology 11, 173
cultural formation processes (C-transforms) 52, 53, 54, 70, 118, 119, 462, 483
cultural resource management (CRM) 33, 546, 547, 548, 549
culture 11, 25, 34, 35, 39, 89, 114, 171, 177, 188, 189, 214, 215, 379–80, 412, 414, 415, 418, 463, 469, 493, 538, 539; change 13, 25, 379–80; collapse 268; ecology 35; group 171; icons 493; heritage 12, 47, 558; history 39; process 39; replication 473; virus 27, 473
cuneiform tablets 30, 439; writing 27, 183, 185, 396
Cunningham, William 21
cupellation 346, 528
cutmarks 52, 53, 284, 286, 298, 313, 330, 388
Cuzco 55, 213, 319, 545
Cycladic Islands 413, 420, 553; sculptures 555
cylinder-seals 303
Cyprus 237, 278, 290, 364, 365, 372, 373, 374
Czech Republic 82, 238, 334, 335, 338, 413, 439

daggers 121, 280, 342, 343, 389, 492, 493, 557
Dalladies 264
Dalton, George 355
Dancey, William 74
Danebury 83, *83*, 84
Danger Cave, Utah 56, 63
Daniel, Glyn 83
Däniken, Erich von 562, 564
Danube 176, 345, 374
danzante figures 413, 439, 507, *507*, 508
Darling, Patrick 85
Darwin, Charles 24–25, 26, 27, *27*, 49, 120, 148, 471, 474
dating 12, 32, 33, 35, 38, 117–70, 184, 223, 239, 501, 510–11, 541; errors in 117, 139, 145; of human ancestors 148–49; *see also* absolute dating; archaeomagnetic dating; argon–argon dating; cation ratios; chemical dating; chronological dating; chronology; cross dating; faunal dating; fission track dating; geomagnetic dating; laser fusion argon-argon dating; linguistic dating; magnetic direction dating; optical

dating; paleomagnetic dating; potassium-argon dating; radiocarbon dating; relative dating; sequence dating; trapped electron dating; uranium-series dating, uranium-thorium dating
Daugherty, Richard 60, 61, *61*
David, Rosalie 441
Davis, Edwin 28
Davis, Simon 292
Dawkins, Richard 26, 27, 473
Day, Michael 433
Deacon, Hilary 245
Deacon, Janette 324
Dead Sea Scrolls 563
Deaf Adder Gorge 510
Dean, Christopher 424
Dean, Jeffrey 135
death 412, 424–29, 438–50; masks 429; *see also* paleopathology
De Beaune, Sophie 326
decoration 49, 56, 114, 115, 116, 120, 122, 188, 202, 205, 220, 326, 338, 366, 390, 393, 415, 416, 419, 463
deductive explanation 475; reasoning 39
Deetz, James 115
deforestation 236, 237, 243, 263, 266, 267, 268, 485
deformity 438–50
Deh Luran Plain 124, 280
Deir el-Medina 219, 222, *222*, 277
deities 183, 382, 408, 409
Dejarnette, D.L. 212
Dekin, Albert 65
democracy 395, 560–61
demography 281, 452–55, 472
dendrochronology 133, 134–37, 139, 264; *see also* tree ring chronology
DeNiro, Michael 244, 308
Denmark 69, 127, 219, 261, 274, 275, 278, 301, 305, 308, 422, 429, 443, 494, 548, 549, 553
Dennell, Robin 271
Dennett, Daniel 387
dental hygiene 437, 452, 521; dentistry 447; *see also* teeth
depiction 391, 412, 415, 416, 418–20, 422
d'Errico, Francesco 328, 394
Derrida, Jacques 486
desert 64, 82, 85, 193, 333
desiccation 63, 64, 65, 246, 270, 421, 428
design in tool manufacture 387–88
destruction 11, 55, 71, 499, 533, 535, 537, 545, 546–58, 559; *see also* looting
developers 41, 74, 549–53, 557
Devil's Tower Cave 425, 431
dexterity 437
Diakonoff, Igor 471, 476
diatoms 243, *243*, 359
Dickson Mounds 451
Didyma 317, 319
diet 63, 172, 251, 255, 261, 269–310, 336, 451–52, 501–02, 511–12, 520, 521
diffusion 214, 380, 463–65, *466*
diffusionist explanations 463–65, 488
Dilthey, Wilhelm 486
Diospolis Parva 122, 123
disease 249, 250, 291, 295, 438–50, 452, 459, 544; amoebic dysentery 442; anemia 521; anthracosis 65; anthrax 442; arterial disease 441; arthritis 67,

438; atherosclerosis 65; bilharzia 442; Calvé-Perthe's disease 444; caries 307; Chaga's disease 442; Down's syndrome 444; dwarfism 446; ear-canal pathology 544; eczema 439; leprosy 443; lung cancer 443; pneumoconiosis 441; pneumonia 65; tuberculosis 442, *442*; *see also* parasites
distribution 200–01, 367–73, 377
distribution maps 77, 194, 367, *367*, 369
ditches 50, 53, 80, 81, *81*, 84, 94, 98, 101, 104, 105, 106, 151, 198, 257, 262, 303, 306, 527, 545
Divostin 194
Diyala 180–81
DNA 222, 223, 224, 244, 276, 279, 295, 326, 442, 443, 455, 457, 458, 468, 469, 473; analysis 67, 277, 302, 424, 431, 432, 459
dolerite 316
Dolní Věstonice 238, 335, 413, 439
Domesday Book 526
domestication 278, 282, 286, 290, 292, 294–95, 472; *see also* agriculture; morphology
dominance 173, 179, 380, 382
domus 397
Donald, Merlin 387
Donnelly, Ignatius 562
Doran, Glen 432
Doran, J.E. 495
Dorn, Robert 157, 244
Douglass, A.E. 134, 135
Doumas, Christos 160
"down-the-line" exchange 369, 370, 371, 372
dowsing 105
Dravidian languages 455
Dreamtime 562
drop zone 186, 178
dry environments 63–64, 70, 311, 331, 452
Duisburg 303
dung 255, 302, 442
Dunnell, Robert 74
Dura Europus 379
Durango, Colorado 63
Durkheim, Emile 406
Durrington Walls 248
Dutch elm disease 249, 250
dyes 333, 334, 528

Earle, Timothy 46, 494
early state modules (ESMs) 379, 381, *381*
earth mother 413; *see also* mother goddess
earthquakes 267, 544
Earthwatch 559
East Anglia 85, 555
East Turkana 149, 150
Easter Island 200, 267–68, *268*, 315, 316, 318, *318*, 395
Eaton, E.R. 342
Ebla 73, 182, 184
Eccles, John 387
echo sounding 98, 230
ecofacts 49, 50, 225
ecofeminism 218
ecological approach 35, 39, 40, 48, 280, 470, 508
ecological determinism 462
economic organization 224
economic specialization 213, 214

Ecuador 228, 279, 346
egalitarian societies 195–96, 198
eggshell 65, 253, 295, 374
Egypt 14, 19, 27, 32, 33, 36, 38, 49, 55, 56, 63, 72, 85, 94, 98, 118, 123, 129, 132, 144, 162, 169, 173, 182, 210, 222, *222*, 282, 294, 304, 305, 333, 334, 339, 367, 374, 395, 400, 403, 413, 416–17, 419, 431, 446, 450, 476, 534, 535, 538, 539, 542, 543, 557–58; Predynastic 338; Upper 32, 122, 272
Egypt Exploration Society 43
Egyptians 63, *129*, 207, 209, 222, 277, 298, 302, 336, 367, 373, 416–17, 419, 432, 439, 440
Egyptology 13, 94, 129
Ein Mallaha 294
Eisley, Loren 321
Elands Bay Cave 231, 248, 254–55
electrical resistivity 99
electrolysis 57, 58
electromagnetic methods 98, 102
electronic distance measurer (EDM) 78
electron probe microanalysis 343, 361
electron spin resonance (ESR) 138, 147, 148, 150, 154–55, 279, 322, 367
electroplating 347
Elgin Marbles 538, *538*
Elia, Ricardo 556
Éliade, Mircea 397
El Niño 228
El Salvador 49, 63, 162, 257, 270, 311, 377
e-mail 560
emblems 209
emissary trading 369
enantiomers 157
endogamy 223
endoscope 94, 449
energy dispersive XRF (ED XRF) 360, 361
Engels, Friedrich 26, 27, 474, 558
England 59, 68, 69, 73, 80, 82, 105, 128, 136, 154, 183, 208, 257, 261, 312, 315, 316, 333, 334, 338, 409, 422, 432, 434, 550, 551, 555, 563
English Heritage 100, 523, 524, 525, 548, 551, 562, 563
engravings 154, 157–58, 249, 327, 346, 394, 434
Enlène 249
environment 16, 35, 225–68, 282, 486, 501
environmental archaeology 13; circumscription 476, 478; remains 49, 50; zones 19
Environmental Impact Statement 546, 547, 549
eoliths 312
Ephesus 229
epidemics 252, 291
Epipaleolithic period 296, 297, 325
Erickson, Clark 544
Er Lannic 229
erosion 59, 92, 200, 232, 233, 237, 243, 259, 268, 288, 485, 515
Eskimo 14, *14*, 64, 65, 190, 256, 326, 444–45; see also Inuit
Eskimo-Aleut languages 455, 456
estuary 255, 519, 520, 521
Ethiopia 85, 145, 162, 242, 433
ethnic cleansing 11, 46, 535, 536
ethnic group 171, 188, 389
ethnicity 189, 219, 384, 455–59, 536
ethnoarchaeology 11, 13, 14, *14*, 41, 174,

176, 182, 186, *187*, 187, 188, 189, 191, 209, 224, 271, 284, 313, 321, 337, 348, 349, 359, 459
ethnography 11, 27, 186, 286, 287, 313, 349, 350, 359, 376, 415, 453, 506, 509, 510, 521
ethnohistory 210, 213, 506
ethnology 11
ethnonym 189
Etiolles 323
Etruscans 94, 169, 346, 466, 553, 555
Euphrates 296
Eurasians 457
Europe 34, 43, 59, 105, 121, 129, 131, 133, 165, 168, 176, 178, 209, 218, 232, 237, 242, 252, 253, 299, 337, 340, 342, 349, 363, 413, 415, 457, *468*, 509; Central 82, 287; Eastern 82, 226, 287; Northern 56, 200, 374; Western 489
Evans, Sir Arthur 34, 36, 208, 559
Evans, John 24, 25, 26
Evans, John 248
"Eve" 457
Evershed, Richard 278
evolution 24–25, 26, 48, 120, 155, 162–70, 270, 455–59; of stone tools 320, *320*
evolutionary archaeology 27, 471–73
evolutionary psychology 27
excavation 21, 25, 30, 31, 32, 71, 74, 78, 80, 85, 89, 92, 105, 106–16, 170, 173, 194, 203, 208, 235, 349, 350, 363, 499, 501, 509, 533, 540–41, 545, 548; at Avebury 248; at Ayodhya 537; at Boomplaas Cave 110, *110*, 247, *247*, 324; at Çatalhöyük 44–45; at Khok Phanom Di 516, 521, *522*; at Moundville 212; at Ozette 60; at Tennessee–Tombigbee Waterway 547; at Wroxeter 100; at York 257, 522–32; in Wessex 198; methods 106, 107–11, *110*; of burials 539; open-area 108, *108*, 109; purposes 106; rescue 550; salvage 83, 109, 550, 551, *551*; selective 208; stratigraphic 33, 44, 124, 517; techniques 38, 40, 94, 95; underwater 95, 97, 331; *see also* classification
exchange 203, 351–84, 400, 469; modes of 354; *see also* trade
Excoffier, Laurent 454
Exekias 414
experimental archaeology 53, 200, 542
experimentation 326, 330, 349, 350
explanation 39, 461–96
extensive survey 79
external trade/exchange 352, 477, 480
extinctions 252–55

Fábrica San José 504
factor analysis 196, 197, 206
faience 336, 338–39, 356, 361
fall-off analysis 370, 371
Falk, Dean 436
famine 451
farmers 174, 176, 177, 194, 203, 241, 264, 278, 308, 443, 447, 451, 467, 506, 543, 557
farming 16, 32, 44, 51, *51*, 85, 165, 167, 168, 169, 174, 176, 177, 198, 200, 211, 216, 236, 238, 258, 260, 264, 279–82, 294, 329, 450, 454, 467, 470, 476, 489,

516–22, 544–45; methods 203; in Western Asia 280–81; origins 296–97, 472
fatty lipids 226, 276
fauna 225, 229, 247–55; faunal analysis 239; faunal dating 127–28, 148, 149
feasts 220, 281, 382, 470
feathers 65, 244, 295, 356, 444
featherwork 64, 504
feedback 479, 481, 494, 504
Feinman, Gary 500, 506
felt 64
feminist archaeology 42, 46–47, 218, 486, 559
fens 68, 85, 238
Ferguson, C. Wesley 135
Feyerabend, Paul 486
fiber-optic endoscope 440–41
fibers 59, 158, 244, 276, 294, *294,* 306, 333–34, 435, 511
field boundaries 71; laboratory 116, 510; survey 40, 508; systems 257; techniques 30, 31–33, 40, 71
Field Museum, Chicago 541
fields 84, 85, 86, 105, 183, 521, 544, *545*
fieldwork 71, 105, 111, 499
figurines 70, 220, 280, 335, 343, 346, 390, 413, 415, *415,* 492, 506
fingerprints 439
Finland 134
Fiorelli, Giuseppe 22
fire 70, 101, 236, 256, 264, 313, 315, 335, 503; controlled 256
firing 55, 56, 335–37, 359, 520
First Intermediate Period (Egyptian) 129
fish 228, 248, 255, 257, 260, 261, 268, 273, 282, 286, 295–300, 304, 305, 306, 442, 472, 511, 519, 520; anadromous 472; barramundi (giant perch) 231, *231,* 232; grayling 257; perch 257, 520; salmon 286; *see also* fishhooks; fishing; shellfish
Fishbourne 257
Fisher, Daniel 291
fishhooks 520, 521
fishing 260, 281, 282, 301, 307, 452, 520
fishing equipment 60; fish traps 278
fission-track dating 137, 148, 149, 150, 363, 366
Five Points 216, 217
Fladmark, Knut 326
Flag Fen 330, 563
flakes 262, 312, 321, 322, 323, *323,* 325, 388, 503, 513, 520; *see also* stone, tools
Flannery, Kent 26, 27, 40, 46, 178, 215, 259, 280, 465, 469, 475, 476, 477, 481, 483, 492, 494, 499, 500, 501, 503, 504, 505, 506, 508
Flenley, John 267
Fletcher Site 404
flint 92, 106, 151, 152, 155, 203, 311, 313, 315, 324, 325, 326, 335, 358, 359, 377, 383, 388, 390, 419; knappers 322, *322; see also* tools
floating chronology 129, 136–37
floodplain 260, 261, 465, 510
floods 80, 118, 231, 232, 238, 250, 268, 272, 291, 521, 543, 557
Flores Magón 85
Florida 11, 49, 56, 69, 70, 432, 455, 546

flotation 244, 245, *245, 270,* 272, 280, 296, 305, 326, 377, 505, 511, 512, 519 flour 276, 277
fluorine 119, 120
fluxgate gradiometer 102; magnetometer 102
Foley, Robert 192
Folsom points 321
Fontanet 256, 431, 434
Fontbrégoua cave 286, 302
food 35, 54, 62, 64, 71 *167,* 176, 177, 199, 211, 213, 240, 258, 269–310, 335, 353, 355, 409, 447, 451, 470, 477, 502, 503, 527; chains 239; plant 270–82; preparation 504; processing 270–71, 388; procurement 504; production 164, 203, 213, 462, 503; residues 12, 49, 114, 336, 449; *see also* cereals; diet
food-sharing hypothesis 388–89
footprints 59, 295, 422, 431, 434, *434,* 439
foragers 504; marine 308
foraminifera 226, 227, 238
Ford, James A. 34, 124
forest 42, 77, 207, 238, 242, 243, 262, 263, 264, 470, 501, 519, 546; prehistoric 63
formation processes 13, 52, 53
Formative period 76, 378, 500, 501, 503
Forrester, Jay 483
fortifications 205, 480
fortress 524, *524,* 526, 534, 539, 543
Forum Novum 98, *99*
Forum (Rome) 72, *72*
fossil: cuticles 242; dung 255
fossils 40, *40,* 149, 157, 233, 235, 249, 256, 279, 283, 359, 431, 435; coral reefs 231; hominid 46, 85, 148, 436; *see also* animal, remains; bones; human, remains
Foucault, Michel 486
Fowler, Martin 85
France 24, 59, 68, 72, 81, 144, 152, 186, 188, 197, 219, 249, 256, 258, 274, 286, 291, 294, 302, 308, 317, 326, 327, 357, 367, 388, 393, 394, 413, 434, 442, 469, 488
Franchthi Cave 230, *230,* 231, 252, 372
Francis, Peter 328
Frankenstein, Susan 380, 471
Frankfort, Henri 418
Frankfurt School 486
Frayer, David 437
Freidel, David 210, 215
frequency seriation 122, *123,* 123–24, *124*
frescoes 14, 161, *161,* 280, 413, 543
Friedman, Irving 156, 471
Frierman, Jay 337
fringe archaeology 562
Frison, George 322
fruits 59, 244, 246, 296, 304, 305, 309, 543
fuel 258, 269, 274
Fujiwara, Hiroshi 274, 513
functionalism 39, 470, 474, 488
functional-processual phase 39, 470, 488, 489, 494, 495
funeral rites 210, 409, 412
funerary monuments 199; practice 196, 305, 409
fungi 238, 249
fur 63, 404
furnaces 338, 344, *344,* 345, 346, 348, 349
furniture 245, 329
Furumark, Arne 121, 131

Gadamer, Hans-Georg 418
Gale, Noel 365
Gamble, Clive 215
gamma rays 150, 151
Ganj Dareh Tepe 287, 303
Garaycochea, Ignacio 544
gardens 257, 262–63, 490–91
Garfie, Salvatore 207
Gargas 434, 439
Garnsey 287
Garrod, Dorothy 32, *32,* 218, 281
gas liquid chromatograpy 276, 303
Gatecliff Shelter, Nevada 119, 143, *143,* 144
Gatun Basin 243
Geiger counter 139
Geissenklösterle 256, 302
gender 42, 173, 215, 216, 218–22, 224, 493
gender-specific terminology 47
genes 432, *432,* 455, 457–59
genetics 222–24, 421, 431, 442, 454–55, 456, 458, 459, 473, 481
genocide 535
geochemical analysis 105, 116
Geographic Information Systems (GIS) 81, 83, 84, 87–89, 116, 198, 200, 257, 258, 260, 268, 525, 526, 549, 551
Geographic Resources Analysis Support Systems (GRASS) 549
geomagnetic dating 148
geomagnetic reversals 126, 149, 159
geomorphology 75, 225, 230–31, 235, 259, 261, 297, 510
geophysical sensing 94, 95, 101, 116
geophysical survey 88, 90, 100–01, 105
Gerasimov, Mikhail 430
Germanic languages 467
Germany 63, 68, 81, 82, 84, 92, 121, 135, 136, 147, 211, 226, 238, 256, 258, 274, 379, 380, 405, 422, 431, 459, 535, 536, 553
Gero, Joan 220
Getty Conservation Institute 557; Museum 556
Getz-Preziosi, Patricia 415
Gibbon, Edward 484
Gibraltar 425, 434
Giddens, Anthony 42, 398, 486
Giddings, J. Louis 231
Gilchrist, Roberta 216
Gilman, Antonio 471
Gimbutas, Marija 44, 46–47, 218, 413
Giza 62, 210, 332; *see also* pyramids
"glacial man" 28
glacial maximum 229
glacials 125, 126, 225
glaciation 226, 232
glaciers 125, 133, 227, 229, 232, 233, *233*
glass 148, 150, 156, 214, 336, 338–39, 356, 361, 374, 380; blowing 338, 339
Glassie, Henry 486
Glastonbury 68, 182
Glauberg 405
glauconite 59
global positioning system (GPS) 88, 89
Glory, André 328
glottochronology 124, 189, 456
Glozel 562
glyphs (Mayan) 130, 183, 205, 395, *395,* 406, 407
gods 215, 410, 412
Gojda, Martin 82

gold 56, 62, 63, 210, 211, 315, 339, 340, 342, 345, 346, 347, 356, 357, 374, 380, 400, 402, 404–05, 412, 419, 480, 528, 555
Goldman, Hetty 37
Goldstein, David 223
Golson, Jack 262
Gombrich, Ernst 419
Gönnersdorf 238
Gorman, Chester 516
Göttweig 238
Gould, Richard 41, 321
Gould, Stephen J. 26
Gournia 36
Grace, Virginia 37
gradiometer survey 100, 101
granaries 50, 250, 282, 298
Grand Menhir Brisé 316
granite 316
granulometry 235
graphite 337
grasses 105, 168, 240, 242, 243, 244, 256, 262, 275, 276, 307, 308, 513, 520
grassland 248, 263, 264
Grauballe Man 306, 422, 442
grave goods 33, 55, 62, 64, 195, 196, 197, 199, 210, 211, 212, 309, 404, 405, 492, 493, 517, 519, 520, 539
gravel 50, 99, 234, 235, 303
graves 32, 55, 64, 86, 98, 122, 123, 196, 197, 219, 224, 389, 412, 506, 516, 520, 539; *see also* burials; cemeteries
Great Lakes 228, 232
Great Orme 315
Great Temple of the Aztecs, Tenochtitlan 20, 72, 409, 551, 552–53, *553*
Great Wall of China 49, 72, *72*, 209
Great Zimbabwe 36, 41, 463, 464, *464*, 465, 533; *see also* Zimbabwe
Greece 13, 19, 20, 30, 36, 38, 121, 131, 169, 172, 173, 182, 183, 189, 204, 206, 211, 215, 230, 237, 294, 304, 332, 339, 349, 354, 365, 367, 372, 373, 374, 379, 382, 395, 397, 405, 410, 414–15, 420, 425, 430, 439, 446, 450, 455, 467, 480, 481, 482, 488, 534, 542, 553, 555, 557
Greeks 129, 182, 204, 282, 317, 319, 331, 335, 354, 359, 382, 399, 402, 419, 429, 466, 474, 538, 555
Greenberg, Joseph 455, 456
Greenland 64, 68, 126, 161, 162, 226, 227, 228, 257, 306, 307, 355, 444–45
Greenland Ice Core Project 226
Greig, James 240
Grenier, Robert 96, *96*
grid 105, 108; lines 110
grid-square excavation method 32
Grimes Graves 203, 289, 315, 377
Grotte du Taï 394
ground-based remote sensing 94–105
ground-penetrating radar (GPR) 98, 99, 100
ground reconnaissance 72–79
growth lines 300, 301, *301*
Grüss, Johannes 276, 302
Guatemala 156, 377, 410, 412
Guidon, Niède 314
Guilá Naquitz 279, *501*, 501–04
Guillien, Yves 234
Gull Lake site 293, *293*
gypsum 326

Habermas, Jürgen 486
habitus 42, 199, 216, 219
Hadar 145, 162, 242, 433
Hadrian 429, *429*
Hadrian's Wall 59, 282
Hadza 176
Hag Ahmed Youssef 332
Hagasa 432
Hagelberg, Erika 457
Haghia Triadha 364, 365
hair 65, 309, 511, 520; styles 63, 422, 429
Haiti 231
Hajji Firuz Tepe 277
half-life 137, 146
Hallstatt 59, 315, 344
Halpern, J.M. 535
Hambledon Hill 144
Hamer, Robert 336
hammering 328, 335, 339, 340, 342, 343
hammers 313, 315, 319, 345
hammerstones 316, 317, 319, 321, 325, 435
Hammond, Norman 308
Hancock, Graham 562
hand-axes 24, 121, 163, 319, 323, 326, 387, 438; *see also* axes
hand prints 439; stencils 439, *439*
Harada, Kaoru 427
Harappa 32, 182, 208
harbors 95, 96
Haroun al-Rashid 355
harpoons 65
Harris, Edward 162
Harris, James 431
Harris lines 446, 451
harvesting 272, 274, 452, 472
Haselberger, Lothar 317
Hastorf, Christine 277
Hatchery West 194
Haury, Emil 326
Haven, Samuel 28, *28*
Hawaii 267, 492, 494
Hawes, Harriet Boyd 36, *36*
Hawkes, Christopher 172
Hawksburn, Al 295
Haya 348
Hayden, Brian 321
headdresses 64, 357, *357*, 383
health 310, 421, 438–52, 521
hearths 50, 60, 103, 159, 187, 190, 193, 234, 243, 256, 324, 346, 408, 453
Heaton, Tim 253
Hebrew 466
Hebron 281
Hedeager, Lotte 379, 380, *380*
Hegira 118
Heidegger, Martin 42, 398, 486
height 428–29, 448, 459
Heizer, Robert 306, 453
Helbaek, Hans 280, 305
Helladic, Late 131, 482; Middle 482
hemoglobin 302
Hempel, Carl 475
Hendy, M.F. 342
Hengistbury Head 106
herbal medicines 304
Herculaneum 22, 49, 162, 230, 238, 438, 447, 451, 555
heritage industry 542; studies 11–12
hermeneutic (interpretational) approach 42, 418, 486

Hesiod 20
Hesse, Brian 287
Hesses, Dr Albert 99
Heun, Manfred 279
Heuneburg 277
Hidaka 276
hides 303, 323, 324, 380
hierarchical society 202, 207, 405, 477
hieroglyphs 27, 37, 183, 204, 205, 395, 406, 466, 481, 506
Higgs, Eric 38, 257, 258, 280, 283
Higham, Charles 451, 499, 516, 517, 522
Hill, Adrian 457
Hill, James 194, 195, 197
hillforts 32, 83
Hillman, Gordon 245, 272, 279, 296
Hindus 46, 185, 537
Hippodamus 402
Hissarlik 30; *see also* Troy
historical chronologies 129, 131–32, 139, 144
historical particularism 26
Hitler, Adolf 467, 536, 555
Hittite 304, 349
Hizbollah 557
hoards 55, 373
Hoare, Richard Colt 21
Hochdorf 211, 334, 405
Hodder, Ian 42, 43, 44, 71, 188, 195, 202, 218, 397, 475, 476, 483, 489, 490, 491, 560
Hole, Frank 89, 92, 124, 280
Holm, Bill 420
Holme-next-the-Sea 56, 69
Holmes, William Henry 28, 29, 34
Holocene 126, 127, *127*, 239, 244, 314, 373, 434, 443, 501
holograms 5443
Homer 30, 73, 186, 204
home range 191
hominids 46, 85, 145, 147, 148, 149, 155, 159, 190, 256, 284, 285, *285*, 387, 388, 421, 429, 431, 433, 436
Homo erectus 145, 148, 163, 307, 313, 387, 390, 436, 437, 443, 457, 458
Homo habilis 145, 149, 162, 163, 387, 388, 435, 436, 437
Homo sapiens 390, 437, 443
Homo sapiens neanderthalis 152, 163; *see also* Neanderthals
Homo sapiens sapiens 16, 32, 163, 387, 389, 413, 457
Hopewell 382, 383
Hopi Indians 538
horizontal stratigraphy 106, 108, 116, 231
horticulture 162
Hoving, Thomas 556
Hoxne 324
Huaca de Tantalluc 21
Huang Ho valley 165
Huánuco Pampa 213, 214, *214*
Hudson Bay 65
Huggin Hill 112, *113*
Hughes, Philip 162
Hughes, Robert 556
humans: ancestry 16, 19, 24, 25, 40, 162–70, *163*; antiquity of 24, 25, 48; agency 283; action 42, 74, 119, 286; behavior 41, 54, 55, 437–38, 465; beliefs 11, 17, 50, 71, 189, 406, 407, 465; environment 255–68; exploitation

of animals in Paleolithic 283–84, 286; feet 250; impact on island environments 265–68; interference in soil deposits 236; manure 302; origins 12, 40, 155, 162–70, 314, 421, 456, 564; remains 32, 33, 38, 62, 69, 155, 157, 195, 269, 305–10, 313, 421–24, 440–41, 488, 525, 539, 540, 541, 542; representation of in art 416, *416;* sites 145, 146, 190; teeth 306–07, 437, 521
hunter-gatherers 13, 16, 78, 168, 172, 173, 174, *174,* 176, 178, 186, 191, 192, 193, 253, 258, 259, 272, 279, 310, 336, 382, 442, 443, 451, 452, 453, 470, 472, 473, 509–15, 522; camps 193, *193;* mobile 176, 177, 190–92, 224; techniques for study 190–92
hunters 16, 52, *52,* 282, 283, 284, 286, 492
hunting 40, 53, 60, 65, 172, 195, 281, 293, 301, 307, 308, 438, 450, 451, 493, 511
Huon peninsula 229, 231
Hussein, Saddam *534*
Hutton, James 24
Huxley, Thomas 473
hydraulic hypothesis 476
hydrology 242
hydroxyapatite 155
hyperdisease 253
hypothetico-deductive approach 475, 495

Iberia 241, 340, 468
Ica 64
ice 125, 126, 133, 228, 230, 233; cores 126, 133, 161, 162, 226, 227, 228, 239, 241, 257; sheets 228, 229; wedges 233
Ice Age 35, 37, 41, 118, 125–26, 133, 134, 164, 188, 226, 231, 239, 241, 244, 245, 246, 248, 249, 251, 252, 254, 262, 292, 294, 303, 329, 392, 393, 394, 422, 431, 433, 434, 435, 439, 462, 472
Iceland 355
Iceman 56, 66–67, *66–67,* 68, 431, 446
iconography 43, 210, 221, 403, 407, 410, 411
ideas 12, 19, 384, 486
ideology 221, 412, 465, 488, 490–91, 494, 536, 542, 558–59
Ikejima-Fukumanji site 257
Iliad 30, 186, 204
illicit antiquities market 553, 555–58
Ilopango volcano 49, 162
Incas 55, 68, 173, 184, *184,* 209, 213, 214, 220, 257, 316, 317, 319, 344, 478, 544, 545; garments 220, *220;* quarries 316
India 49, 185, 186, 228, 328, 363, 415, 467, 469, 476, 537
Indo-European languages 455, 467
inductive reasoning 39
inductively coupled plasma emission spectrometry (ICPS) 362
Indus 30, 119, 169, 182, 208, 233, 385, 400, 403, 476, 537
industrial archaeology 311
Industrial Revolution 331, 339
inference 12, 43, 115
"influences" 38, 39, 214, 464
infrared: absorption spectroscopy 366; film 84, 85, 86; linescan (IRLS) 84; radiation 256, 366; spectroscopy 276, 277
ingots 95, 345, 364, 365, 374, 528

Ingstad, Anne Stine 73
Ingstad, Helga 73
inorganic materials 55, 105, 151
inscriptions 12, 184, *184,* 185, *185,* 222, 395, 397, 406, 508, 539
insects 59, 225, 240, 247, 249–50, 286, 298, *298,* 299; 527–28, *554*
Institute of Archaeology (London) 14, 272, 296
Institute of Archaeology and History (INAH) (Mexico) 90
Institute of Field Archaeologists 563
Institute of Nautical Archaeology (Texas) 95, 332, 374
interaction spheres 382, 383
interactions 378–84, 480, 481
internal exchange 352
Internet 543, 560–61, 563
interpretation 11, 42–43, 47, 48, 262–63, 363, 365, 366, 384, 386, 418, 427
interpretive archaeology 16, 42–46
interpretive explanation 483–91
Inuit 11, 65, 444–45; see also Eskimo
ion beam analysis 361
Ipiutak 231
Iran 82, 124, 214, 253, 277, 280, 287, 295, 303, 336, 339, 340, 371, 377
Iraq 11, 32, 40, 92, 169, 179, 205, 208, 210, 280, 282, 390, 405, 431, 443, 555
Ireland 68, 238, 329, 402
iron 57, 68, 95, 104, 114, 117, 157, 159, 336, 341, *341,* 344, 347, 349, 366, 451; ore 378; oxide 103, 244, 326, 349
Iron Age 25, 41, 59, 64, 68, 69, 80, 83, 101, 154, 182, 219, 243, 274–75, 277, 305, 311, 344, 349, 380, 409, 422, 429, 443, 448, 471, 493
irrigation 86, 203, 211, 232, 257, 259, 478, 508, 544, 545, 558
Isaac, Glynn 40, 190, 191, 387, 388
Isbister 438
Iscan, Yasar 424
Islam 118, 169
Israel 95, 147, 155, 223, 235, 239, 244, 256, 257, 279, 280, 281, 294, 302, 328, 390, 419, 424, 435, 437, 442, 443, 447, 534, 539, 545, 564
isochrons 340
isopachs 161, *161*
isostatic uplift 230, *230*
isotopes 126, 137, 145, 146, 148, 150, 155, 226, 227, 229, 231, 235, 239, 244, 253, 277, 307, 308, 309, 310, 358, 361, 363–66, 373, 374, 384
isotopic analysis 307–10, 363–66, 445
Italy 22, 68, 92, 94, 208, 237, 238, 365, 367, 415, 443, 446, 492, 493, 544, 555
ivory 65, 356, 366, 389, 413

jade 309, 356, 366, 395, 409, 412, 419, 506, 552
Jamaica 95
Jamestown 13, 239
Janssens, Paul 429
Japan 56, 99, 133, 134, 257, 274, 276, 279, 290, 302, 303, 321, 367, 390, 426, 434, 438, 447, 551, 563
Jarmo 280, 372
Java 148

Jefferson, Thomas 21, 24
Jemaa head 152, *152*
Jericho 36, 280, 281
Jett, Stephen 304
jewelry 62, 63, 210, 211, 361, 366, 431, 517, 521; *see also* ornamentation
Jews 222, 223, 539
Jinmium 153, 154
Jinzhou 429
Johanson, Donald 433
Johnson, Gregory 180, 181, 205, 477
Jomon period 231, 248, 274, 276, 290, 300, 303, 447
Jones, Rhys 41, 264, 499, 509, *512,* 514
Jones, Sir William 467
Jong, Piet de 37, *37,* 480
Jordan 265, 279, 280, 281, 408
Jorvik Viking Centre 500, 522, 523, 527, 530, 531, *531,* 542
Judaism 539
Julien, Michèle 388

Kabul Museum 557
kachinas 538
Kachiqhata 316
Kahun 334
Kakadu National Park 499, 500, 509–15
Kalahari Desert 191, 193, 328, 419, 453
Kaminaljuyu 156
Kamitakomuri 390, *390*
Karanovo 337
Karlin, Claudine 388
Kartvelian languages 455
Kaş 331, 374
Kasteelberg 303, 328
KBS tuff controversy 149, 150
Kebara 152, 155, 256, 437
Keeley, Lawrence 301, 323, 324, 325
Kehoe, Thomas 293
Kemp, Barry 210
Kendall, Anne 543
Kendall, D.G. 401
Kennewick Man 457, 541
Kenniff Cave 41
Kenya 149, 150, 162, 188, 190, 191, 192, 301, 388, 435
Kenyon, Kathleen 36, *37,* 280
Keros 555
Kershaw, Peter 264
Khok Phanom Di 499, 500, 516–22
Khorsabad 405
Kidder, Alfred 33, *33,* 34, 82
Kidosaku 290, 300, *300,* 301, *301*
kilns 103, 104, 105, 159, 203, 335, *335,* 337, 367, 370, 377
Ki'na 513
Kingery, W.D. 337
kings 215; Maya 183; kingship 205, 216
kinship 173, 176, 218, 376; distance 193
Kirch, Patrick 266
kivas 399
Klasies River 157, 291
Klein, Richard 248, 291
Knorosov, Yuri 406
Knossos 37, 208, 367, 419
Kogi Indians 313
Kohl, Philip 377
Koike, Hiroko 231, 248, 300
Kolata, Alan 544
Konya Plain 44, 280

Koobi Fora 162, 190, 191, 284, 301, 321, 388, 435
Kosovo 536
Koster, Illinois 109, *109*
Kow Swamp 443, 540
Kowalewski, Stephen 500, 506
Krapina 148, 286, 437
Krings, Matthias 432, 459
Krzemionki 315
Kückhoven 136, 264, *264*
Kuk Swamp 162, 257, 262–63, *263*
kula 353, 355
Kültepe 355
!Kung San 41, 191, 176, 193, 328, 419, 453, 477
Kuniholm, Peter 137
Kushan period 557
Kuwait 85
Küyünjik 30
Kyrenia 331
Kythnos 373

labor 198, 199, 200, 203, 210, 213, 218, 220, 263, 437, 485, 545; division of 503, 511–12
Labrador 95
La Brea 59
La Chapelle aux Saints 435
La Cotte de St Brelade 286
lacquer 236, 304
Laetoli 37, 253, 428, 433, 558; footprints 434, *434*
La Ferrassie 258, 435, 443
Laitman, Jeffrey 436, 437
Lake: Arenal 86; Baringo 188; Chichancanab 485; Constance 302; George 264; Mungo 540; Neuchâtel 82; Ontario 95; Pallcacocha 228; Suigetsu 134; Titicaca 542, 544, 545; Turkana 190; Wevershoof 243; Zeribar 280
lake dwellings 69–70
lakes 68, 69, 133–34, 233, 239, 260
Lal, B.B. 537
Lallo, John 451
La Marche 294, 327, 422
Lamb, Winifred 37
Laming-Emperaire, André 393
lamps 326, 409, 445
land bridges 229
land management 257, 261
landmines 86
LANDSAT 84, 85, 86
landscape 199, 225, 232–39, 398, 399; glaciated 232–33
landscape archaeology 42, 71, 89, 398
land use 78, 79, 89, 203, 549
Langdale axe 369
language 124, 182, 183, 189, 384, 386, 387, 406, 454–55, 467; *see also* speech
language families 455, 467
language replacement 467
L'Anse aux Meadows 73
lapis lazuli 214, 356, 358
Lapita culture 373, 465, 466, 467
La Quina 435
Larsen, Clark 307, 452
Lascaux 19, 59, 72, 256, 326, 391, 435, 543
laser-fusion argon-argon dating 145, 149, 367
Late Formative 506
Late Woodland 451

latex 97, 236, 237; molding 158
Lathrap, Donald 337
Latimer, Bruce 433
latrines 111, 270, 306, 539
Laurion 365, 373
La Venta 316
laws 11, 99, 106, 176, 183, 185, 499, 541, 543, 547, 546–49
Layard, Austen Henry 27, 30
lead 56, 257, 339, 340, 346, 361, 364, 365, 366, 373, 374; poisoning 446–47
Leakey, Louis 40, 148
Leakey, Mary 37, *37*, 40, 148, 433
Leakey, Richard 149
leather 53, 59, 63, 64, 67, 68, 214, 244, 327–29, 444, 525
Lebanon 82, 279, 280, 557
LeBlanc, Steven 475, 548, 554
Lechtman, Heather 347
Lee, Richard 41
left-handedness 434, 435
Legge, Tony 290, 297
Lehner, Mark 210
Lehringen 335
length 399–400, 401
Leonardo da Vinci 447
Leone, Mark 42, 483, 490
Lerici, Carlo 94
Leroi-Gourhan, André 187, 188, 323, 393, 486
Leroi-Gourhan, Arlette 256
Lesbos 37
Lespugue 357
Levallois technique 319
Lévi-Strauss, Claude 418, 420, 486
Lewin, Peter 441
lexicostatistics 124
Lianos, Nikolaos 231
Libby, William 35, 138, 139
Lieberman, Philip 436
life expectancy 452
light detection apparatus (lidar) 86
Lima 33
limestone 59, 146, 147, 210, 235, 405, 543
Lincolnshire 369
Lindbergh, Charles 82
Lindner rockshelter 510, 512, *512*, 515
Lindow Man 279, 306, 334, 428, 437, 441, 448, *448*, 449, *449*
lineage 176, 220, 222–24, 473
Linearbandkeramik 136, 238, 304, 453
linear uptake (LU) model 155
Ling, Roger 23
linguistic dating 124
linguistics 456, 457, 486
lintels 318, 395, 407
literacy 124, 132, 174, 182, 186, 204, 222, 279, 282, 395–97, 407
litharge 346
Little Big Horn 443
Little Ice Age 226, 227, 267
Little Salt Spring Bog 432
living floors 388–89
loan words 124
loess 237–38, 335
Loma Negra 347
Lommersum 302
London 13, 14, 69, 111, 112, 159, 272, 296, 439, 523, 550
Longacre, William 195
long barrows 198, 200, 201

long houses 60, 109
looms 333
looting 11, 13, 50, 52, 54, 55, 59, 533, 543, 548, 553, 555–58
Lorblanchet, Michel 327, *327*
Los Angeles 59, 157, 250
Los Gavilanes 442
Lost Tribes of Israel 564
lost-wax casting 339, 340, 342, *342*, 343, 346, 402
Louvre 538, 555, 556
Lovelock Cave, Nevada 56, 63, 306, 424, 442
Lowe, John 484
Lowenthal, David 533
Loy, Thomas 302, 431
Lubbock, John 24, 27
Lubbub Creek 547, *547*
"Lucy" 429, 433
Lukacs, György 486
Lumbreras, Luis 410, 411
Lundelius, Ernest 252
Luoyang 282
Luxor 543
Luzón, J.M. 346
Lydian Hoard 538, 556
Lyell, Charles 24, 26, 286

Macedonia 534
Machu Picchu 543
McBryde, Isabel 376
McGrew, William 313
McKern, W.C. 34
McKerrell, Hugh 342
MacNeish, Richard 40, 306
McPherron, Alan 194
macrobotanical remains 244–46, 270–74
macrofamilies 455
macrofauna 250–55, 287
macrofossils 333
macroremains 264, 286, 306
Madagascar 199
Magdalenian 324, 328, 388, 392
magnesium 105, 253, 339
magnetic direction dating 159, *159*
magnetic resonance imaging 441
magnetic survey methods 103–04, 105
magnetism 102, 103–04, 126, 149, 159
magnetometer 90, 95, 99, 102
Maiden Castle 32, 80, *80*, 432, 442
Mainfort, Robert 404
Maiuri, Amedeo 23
Makah Indians 60, 61, *61*
Malaspina, Patrizia 468, 469
Malaysia 273
Mali 555
Malinowski, Bronislaw 353
malnutrition 450, 452, 459
Maloney, Bernard 519
Malta 398, 402, 413
Malthus, Thomas 26, 477
Mammoth Cave 424
manganese 157, 243, 339; dioxide 326
Mann, Michael 494
manuports 388
manure 274, 275, 302, 528
Manzanilla, Linda 90
Maori 257, 453, 540, 541, 549
mapping 75, 80, 86–87, 89, 90–91, 98, 182, 204, 208, 260–61, *292*, 373, 457
maps 73, 74, 77, 86, 87, 88, 89, 98, 161,

178, 198, 204, 207, 208, 260, 376, *379*, 385, 396, 402, 412; contour 103; cumulative viewshed 201, *201*; distribution 77, 194, 367, *367*, 369, *369*; dot density 103; gray scale 103; photogrammatic 83; planimetric 87; rainfall 280; topographic 87, 91, 207, 208; vegetation 280; viewshed 200; *see also* cognitive maps
marble 359, 366
Marcus, Joyce 40, 189, 407, 413, 494, 500, 501, 503, 505, 508
Marcuse, Herbert 486
Marinatos, Spyridon 160
marine resources 231, 252
Marino, Joseph 177
market exchange 354, 369, 384
marriage 202, 218, 223, 352
Marsangy 323
Marshall, Sir John 30
Marshack, Alexander 390, 394
Martin, Paul 252, 253, 255
Marx, Karl 26, 27, 406, 418, 474, 558
Marxism 35, 461, 470, 489, 490–91
Marxist archaeology 471, 474
Masada 534
Mask 186, 187
masks 62, 70, 281, 356, *356*, 357, *357*, 409, 412, 429
Massachusetts Institute of Technology 483
mass spectrometry 145, 227, 360, 364; accelerator mass spectrometry (AMS) 141, 144, 145, 157, 158, 302; gas chromatography mass spectrometry 276, 326; gas source mass spectrometers 364; thermal ionization mass spectrometry (TIMS) 146, 147, 364, 366
material culture 11, 12, 48, 188, 202, 216, 483, 486, 491; prestige 356–57, 404
matrilines 220
matrilocal residence 223
matrix 50, 59, 142
Matson, Fred 280
Matthews, Wendy 236
Maudslay, Alfred 34, 407, 539
Mauer 307, 435
Mauraki site 302
Maurillac 308
Mauss, Marcel 353
Maya 19, 30, 33, 34, 37, 49, 63, 85, 86, 87, 94, 111, 123, 129, 130–31, 169, 173, 183, 184, 204, 205, 207, 209, 210, 257, 264, 321, 377, 380, 382, 395, 399, 400, 409, 412, 413, 450, 476, 483, 499, 539; Classic 205, 380, 462, 477, 484–85, 505; calendar 129, 130–31; kings 183, 205; lowlands 205, 398, 477; Preclassic 308; Postclassic 505; stelae 405, 406, 555; symbols of power 406–07; temples 200; warfare 215, 395, 521
Mead, Jim 255
Meadow, Richard 292
Meadowcroft Rockshelter 87, 269
meals 269, 279, 305–06, 310; *see also* diet, food
Meare 68
measurement 391, 399–401
meat 203, 220, 266, 267, 276, 282, 294, 295, 298, 303, 306–10, 323, 324, 325, 335, 388, 512, 520; weight 287, 289

Mecca 118
medical knowledge 450
medieval period 131, 137, 185, 209, 226, 229, 240, 241, 243, 347
Mediterranean 95, 160, 163, 226, 230, 235, 237, 292, 309, 338, 339, 355, 365, 366, 373, 374, 380, 402, 471, 472, 488, 495
Meer site 324, *324*, 325
megafauna 252
megaherbivores 253
megalithic 398, 470; rings 401; yard 400, 401, 402, 420; megaliths 199, 200, 488–89
Mehrgarh 165, 292
Melanesia 168, 353, 355, 356, 466, 521
Melanesians 307, 443, 457
Mellaart, James 44, 280
Mellars, Paul 299, 389
Melos 75, 77, 78, 160, 372, 373; *see also* Phylakopi
memes 27, 473
Mendel, Gregor Johann 473
Mercer, Roger 377
mercury 447
Merriwether, Andrew 456
Mersey 434
Merwe, Nikolaas van der 308
Merzien 81, *81*
Mesa Verde 135, 446, 463
Meshed 377
Meskell, Lynn 218, 222
Mesolithic (Middle Stone Age) 32, 106, 198, 230, 291, 296, 299, 301, 308, 309, 311, 321, 325, 329, 455, 470
Mesopotamia 27, 30, 34, 40, 79, 85, 92–93, 144, 169, 179, 180, 181, 183, 185, 205, 294, 303, 304, 335, 336, 338, 342, 374, 395, 396, *396*, 410, 412, 420, 471, 476
Messenia 482, 483
metal 55, 56–58, 62, 102, 103, 214, 311, 313, 329, 330, 339–49, 358, 362, 365, 373, 384, 480; non-ferrous 339–42, 346, 360
metal detectors 102, 103–04
metallographic examination 340, 341, 342
metallurgy 42, 177, 336, 337, 345, 349, 352, 480
metal ores 59, 257, 336, 340, 349
metalworking 203, 528
meteorites 148, 161
meteors 562
methodological individualism 215, 386, 461, 491
Metropolitan Museum, New York 538, 556
Meyer, Karl 556
Mexico 16, 19, 29, 30, 40, 49, 55, 59, 74, 76, 82, 85, 89, 95, 111, 168, 210, 228, 259, 306, 309, 316, 367, 373, 378, 446, 463, 476, 484, 500, 534, 542, 552, 557
Mexico City 72, 74, 79, 90, 203, 551, 552, 555
Mezhirich 286
mica 59, 150, 383, *383*
Michel, Mark 548
Michels, Joseph 156
Michelsberg 302
microbotanical remains 239–44, 274, 276
microclimates 234, 248, 256
microdebitage 326
microfauna 225, 247–51, 298, 501

microfossils 226, 227, 243
microliths 311, 321
micromorphology 14, 45, 234, 235–36, 327
micro-retouch 314
microscope 340, 341, 425, 427
microscopic analysis 256, 277, 294, 295, 302, 342, 359, 384, 390
microwaves 155
microwear analysis 276, 301, 323–26, 328, 334, 349
middens 194, 231, 248, 255, 265, 298, 299
Middle East 244, 543
Middle Formative period 378, 506
Middle Kingdom (Egyptian) 129
middleman 369, 371
Middle Range Theory 12, 182
Middle Stone Age *see* Mesolithic
Middle Woodland 196, 451
Midwestern Taxonomic System 34
Miesenheim 63, 238
migrationist explanations 463, 464, 465, 488
migrations 200, 296, 456, *456*, 463, 465, 466, *466*, 468
Milisauskas, Sarunas 453
milk 203, 302, 303, 304
Miller, Mary Ellen 407
Miller, Paul 526
Miller-Shaivitz, Patricia 424
Millon, René 90
Milner, George 257, 260
Mimbres 50, 52, 304, 419, 463, 553, 554, *554*
Mindel 125
minerals 148, 150, 152, 153, 238, 244, 256, 270, 338, 347, 359, 365, 383, 505
mines 289, 315–16, 344, 373, 377, 384; *see also* Grimes Graves; Great Orme
minimum number of individuals (MIND) 270, 289
Minoans 34, 36, 126, 160, 169, 195, 205, 302, 365, 367, 373, 400, 419, 480, 495, 539, 559
mirror 64, 221, 280
missing link 120
Mississippian 212, 310, 357, 547
Mississippi River 21, 233,237, 260
Mithen, Steven 387, 473, 483, 492
mitochondrial DNA (mtDNA) 222, 223, 432, 454, 455, 457, 459, 468, 469
Mitterberg 315
Mixtec 189
mobiliary art 394, 413
Moche 169, 228, 333, 346, 347, 429, 438, 555
Moctezuma, Eduardo Matos 552
models 95, 385, 496
modularity of mind 473
Mohenjodaro 30, 83, 92, 208, 233, 400, 403, *403*, 558
molds 97, 339, 343–45, 528
molecular clocks 458
molecular genetics 222–24, 279, 459, 467, 468–69
Molleson, Theya 438
molluscs 133, 228, 231, 238, 267, 295–300, 310, 356, 519; barnacles 519; clams 300, 301, *301*; cockles 298, 299, 520; freshwater 257, 513; land 248; marine 248–50; mussels 511, 513; oysters 298, 299; snails 225, 238, 248, 501, 519; spiny oyster 220

Moncin 288, 289
money 380, 404
Monitor Basin 326
monocausal explanations 477
Monte Albán 413, 439, 500, 506, 507–08, *508*
Montelius, Oscar 25, 26, 34, 121
monuments 41, 42, 50, 55, 69, *69*, 79, 82, 123, *168–69*; 169, 176, 194, 198, 199, 201–02, 210, 224, 256, 359, 385, 391, 395, 397, 398, 399, 407, 484, 485, 488, 508, 535; burial 210; public 200, 203; ritual 202
Moore, Andrew 296
Moore, C.B 212
Moore, Elisabeth 86
Morgan, Lewis Henry 26, 27, 34, 474
Morley, Frances R. 413
Morley, Sylvanus G. 413
morphology 226, 270, 276, 277–78, 282, 442; dental 431
Morris, Craig 213, 214
Morrison, J.S. 332
mortality 452, 521
Mössbauer spectroscopy 366, 378
Mostar 535
Motecuhzoma II 357, 367
"mother goddess" 44, *45*, 46, 218, 219, 413, 552
Moundbuilders 21, 28, 29, 30
mounds 28, 86, 92, 119, 196, 198, 199, 212, 257, 261, 297, 300, 516
Moundville, Alabama 176, 197, 211, 212–13
Mount: Arenal 86; Carmel 32; Hagen 162; Hymettos 366; Pendeli 366; Vesuvius 22, 162, 438; William 376, *376*
Mousterian period 152, 186, 189, 389; *see also* Paleolithic, Middle
Moyle, Peter 304
"Mrs Ples" 433
mud brick 56, *56*, 207, 240, 276, 303, 335
Mugharet El Wad 328
Mugumamp Ridge 162
Muldbjerg 278
multicollector mass spectrometer (ICP-MSS) 364
multi-dimensional scaling (MDSCAL) 193, 204, 206–07, *207*, 519
multiplier effect 480
multiregional hypothesis 457, 458, *458*
multi-spectral sensors 85
multivariate explanations 477, 479, 481–82
multivariate statistics 197, 206, 519
Mulvaney, John 41, *41*
mummies 62, 64, 222, 240, 295, 305, 306, 309, 311, 334, 421, 422, 429, 431, 432, 433, 437, 439, 440, 442, 444, 539, 555
mummification 55, 63, 295, 298, 428, 441, 446
Munsell Soil Color Charts 236
Murdy, Carson 446
Murray River 376, 540
Museum: of African and African-American History (New York) 217; of London 112; of Tenochtitlan Project 552
museums 60, 538–42, 559
Museums' Association 555
Musgrave, Jonathan 437
music 409
musical instruments 221; panpipes 220, 383
Muslims 189, 535, 537

mutilation 439, *439*
Mycenae 30, 121, 122, 131, 169, 172, 182, 186, 206, 211, 356, 374, 446, 480, *480*
Mycenaeans 34, 169, 204, 412
Myrtos 195
myth 204, 412, 415, 418–19

Nabataeans 543
Nabonidus 20
Na-Dene languages 455, 456
Nakano, Masuo 302–03
Namibia 253
Nämforsen 418
Naples Museum 555
Napoleon I (Bonaparte) 27, 555, 556
Naqada cemetery 32
Nara 257
Naranjo 412
Narita 427
Naroll, Raoul 452, 453, 504
NASA 85, 86
Natal Province 253
National Archaeological Record 549
National Historic Preservation Act 546
National Institute of Anthropology and History 552
nationalism 534–36
National Library of Air Photographs 82
National Museum of Anthropology, Mexico City 555
National Parks Service 83, 546, 545
National Register of Historic Places 546
National Science Foundation 548, 559
Native American Graves Protection and Repatriation Act (NAGPRA) 541, 548
Native Americans 28, 34, 41, 109, 186, 456, 457, 489, 540–42, 548, 564; Navajo 418; Northwest Coast 382
Natufian culture 32, 280, 281, 472
natural formation processes (N-transforms) 52, 53, 55–57, 70, 118, 562
Nauwalabila I 153, *153*
Navajo 418
Naxos 366
Nazca 64, 334, 399
Neanderthals 32, 147, 148, 152, 155, 286, 307, 308, 389, 390, 425, 427, 431, 432, 435, 436, 443, 459
Neander Valley 459
Near East 19, 32, 34, 36, 40, 50, 55, 56, 73, 92, 109, 121, 129, 164, 169, 173, 182, 236, 280, 295, 296, 303, 335, 336, 340, 342, 346, 347, 349, 354, 367, 371, 372, 377, 382, 419, 462, 472, 544
Neave, Richard 430, *430*
Nefertiti 374, 538
negative feedback 479, 494
Negev Desert 244, 435, 447, 539, 543
Nelson Bay 157
neodymium 364
Neolithic (New Stone Age) 25, 36, 59, 69, 80, 81, 111, 136, 182, 195, 216, 218, 229, 236, 237, 238, 248, 249, 250, 255, 261, 264, 270, 271, 277, 278, 281, 292, 296, 297, 300, 302, 308, 330, 351, 353, 359, 363, 366, 369, 418, 462, 468, 471, 488, 492, 509; Early 198, 199, 200, 238, 258, 297, 304, 311, 335, 371, 438, 453; Group VI 369; lake dwellings 277; Late 67, 176, 194, 198, 200; long houses

109; mines 289, 315, 377; pre-pottery 281; Revolution 35, 280, 281, 471; temples 402; town 44; vase 218, *218*; villages 136, 372
neo-Marxism 42, 471, 474, 486, 488, 489, 490–91
Neo-Wessex school 199, 216, 398, 489
Netherlands 89, 243, 274, 315
Nettle, Daniel 456
neutron activation analysis (NAA) 150, 338, 339, 361, 362, 363, 372, 378
neutron scattering 104
Nevada Test Site 13
"New Archaeology" 27, 38–43, 47, 48, 71, 385, 461, 463, 469, 470, 471, 472, 474, 475, 483, 491, 493, 495, 496
New Delhi 46
Newfoundland 73, 230
Newgrange 398, 402, 403, *403*
New Guinea 162, 229, 231, 257, 262, 321, 353, 356, 373, 457, 465, 466, 477, 493
New Kingdom (Egyptian) 129, 184, 282
New Mexico 33, 82, 285, 287, 298, 304, 463, 542
New World 21, 27, 40, 84, 207, 210, 229, 252, 253, 255, 282, 308, 313, 314, 331, 332, 333, 336, 343, 345, 349, 442, 450, 453, 463; origins of population 456; pottery 36
New York 69, 216–17
New Zealand 227, 239, 257, 266, 295, 427, 437, 453, 516, 517, 539, 540, 548–49
Ngarrabullgan Cave 153
Niaux 326, 434
Nicholas II, Tsar 429
Nichols, Johanna 456
Niger 438
Nigeria 85, 152
Nile 233, 374, 476, 558 ; Valley 63, 557
Nineveh 30, 439; *see also* Layard, A.H.
Nishimura, Yasushi 94
nitrogen 119, 120, 138, 253, 277, 308, 309, 361, 364
Nixon, Richard 546
Njemps 188
Noe-Nygaard, Nanna 301
Nohmul, Belize 76, *76*
Nok 152
Noksakul, Damrongkiadt 516
nomothetic explanation 475
non-artifactual remains 49, 50
"non-cultural phenomena" 469
non-destructive techniques 440–41
Non Nok Tha 516
Nong No 517, 521–22
non-probabilistic sampling 76
Norman Conquest 523
Normans 522, 526
Norris Farms 223
North Pole 149
Norton Priory 295
Norway 69, 425
Noten, Francis van 325
Novelletto, Andrea 468
N-transforms *see* natural formation processes
nuclides 158
number of identified specimens (NISP) 289
Nunamiut 13, 41, 186, 187, 190
nutrition 310, 451–52; *see also* diet; food; health

nuts 304, 516, 543
Nyerup, Rasmus 19

Oaxaca 40, 76, 89, 92, 259, 366, 373, 378,
413, 499, 500, *500*, 502, 503, 504, 505,
505, 506, 508; *see also* Monte Albán;
San José Mogote
obelisk (Aswan) 316
obsidian 44, 150, 156, 214, 321, 324, 332,
356, 362, 366, 370, 371–73, *372*, *373*,
377, 378, 383, 384, 552; hydration 156,
156; scarcity (OS) 378; volcanic glass
203
ocher 154, 325, 327, 512
oestradiol 422, 424
oestrone 422
Ohalo II 281
Ohtaishi, Noriyuki 290
Okazaki, Satomi 324
Okeechobee burial platform 70, *70*
Old Copper culture 339
"Old Europe" 46, 218
Old Kingdom (Egyptian) 129, 169
Oldowan 163; tools 319
Old Stone Age 13, 19, 25, 29, 52, 53, 55; *see
also* Paleolithic
Olduvai Gorge 19, 37, 40, 145, 148, 149,
150, 162, 163, 283, 284, 319, 388, 538
Old World 27, 30, 34, 48, 117, 211, 272,
282, 303, 321, 329, 332, 339, 343, 349,
358, 455
Oliver, James 284
Ollantaytambo 316
Olmec 169, 309, 446, 499; head 169, *169*,
359; stelae 316
Olorgesailie 388, 538
Olympic Games 129, 215, 382
Omaha Plains Indians 197
Oman 85
Omo Valley 242
Ontario 95, 308
onyx 356
Oplontis 257
optical dating 138, 150, 153–54, 510, 512
optical emission spectometry (OES) 339, 340,
360, 362, 363
optically stimulated luminescence (OSL) 153,
154
oral histories 12, 534
oral tradition 174, 182, 186, 418, 441
Ordnance Survey 549
ores 59, 257, 336, 340, 349, 364, 365
organic materials 55–70, 141, 143, 144, 157,
158, 243, 244, 279, 333, 510, 513, 516,
523
organic remains 49, 50, 68–70, 104, 119, 239
Oriental Institute, Chicago 280, 418
Orkney 59, 195, 201, 398, 438; *see also*
Skara Brae
Orliac, Michel 236
ornamentation 63, 171, 188, 220, 231, 383,
383, 389, 493, 504, 506, 516, 519; *see
also* jewelry
Oronsay 299
Oseberg 69
O'Shea, John 197
osteoarthritis 446, 448, 452
Ostia 82, 455, 519
ostrakon (ostraka) 397; *see also* potsherds
otoliths 299, *299*

Ötzi *see* Iceman
"Out of Africa" model 458, 459
ovens 104, 159, 269, 271, 276, 295, 335
overexploitation 299
Overton Down 53
Owen-Smith, Norman 253
oxbow lake 520
oxidization 337, 346
Oxpemul 85
oxygen 59, 126, 226, 227, 229, 231, 248,
349, 358, 361, 362, 364, 365, 485
oxygen isotope technique 226, 227, 235, 238,
366, 485
Ozette 56, 59, 60–61, *60–61*, 94

Pääbo, Svante 431, 432, 459
Paca, William 490, 491
Pachacamac 33, *33*, 34
Pacific Ocean 126, 163, 168, 169, 200, 226,
227, 228, 266, *266*, 373, 465
paddy fields 257, 274, 276, 434
Page, Denys 204
paintings 43, 55, 73, 144, 215, 282, 326,
342, *342*, 373, 392, 413, 414, 418, 434,
512, 554; *see also* art; cave art
Pakistan 80, 92, 119, 208, 233, 292, 313,
400, 467, 557, 558
palaces 50, 182, 184, 205, 209, 405, 527
Palaikastro 205
Palenque 205, 210
paleoclimatic studies 232, 280
paleoclimatologists 125
paleodemography 452
paleoenvironmental work 513
paleoethnobotany 269, 272–73, 280, 297
Paleo-Indians 87, 291, 322, 446, 456, 501
Paleolithic (Old Stone Age) 13, 25, 46, 52,
53, 107, 111, 118, 121, 125, 150, 157,
158, 176, 177, 187, 190, 215, 229, 237,
238, 251, 272, 283, 311, 321, 327, 388,
413, 538, 558; art 13, 390, 391, 392–94,
455, 462, 486; human exploitation of
animals in 283–84, 286; Lower 120,
121, 145, 152, 159, 163, 170, 283, 284,
298, 302, 306, 312, 324, 326, 387, 536,
553; Middle 32, 152, 156, 163, 186,
197, 258, 286, 309, 312, 335, 387, 389,
390; pottery 336; tools 47, 311, 419;
Upper 59, 73, 121, 144, 158, 236, 238,
256, 272, 291, 294, 295, 299, 302, 319,
322, 326, 327, 328, 329, 335, 356, 357,
388, 389, 390, 392–94, 399, 413, 429,
431, 439, 443, 468; *see also* Mousterian;
Cave Art
"paleoliths" 29, *29*
paleomagnetic dating 158, 227, 238; *see also*
archaeomagnetic dating
paleontology 291
paleopathology 438, 450
Pales, Léon 327, 433
Palestine 32, 36, 280, 371, 374
Palmer, Patricia 242
Palmer, Roger 83
palynologists 127, 280
palynology 239–42, 243, 266
Panama 243, 277
Panhellenic Games 189, 215
Pantheon (Rome) 319
Papua New Guinea 162, 231
papyrus 62, 182, 184, 450

parasites 442; *Ascaris* 442; fleas 528; lice
442, 528; maw worm 448; midges 249;
mites 249, 302, 442; pinworm 442;
roundworm 442; tapeworm
(*Diphyllobothrium*) 442; ticks 442;
thorny-headed worm 442; trichinosis
65; whipworm (*Trichuris*) 442, 448
Parenti, Fabio 314
Paris 13, 159, 236, 319, 323, 324, 440,
447, 553; Basin 188, 238
Parkington, John 254
Parks Canada 95, 97
Paros 366
Parry, J.T. 85
Parthenon 536, 538
particle-induced gamma-ray emission (PIGME,
PIGE) 361
pastoralism 237, 281, 308
Patagonia 238
Patrik, Linda 418
Patrucco, Raul 442
Paudorf 238; Loess Formation 238
Pavel, Pavel 318
Pavlov 238, 334, 335, 413
Pawnee 197
Pazyryk 49, 56, 64, 65
Peacock, David 359
Pearsall, Deborah 279
Pearson, Mike Parker 199
peat 68, 69, 70, 240, 241, 243, 257, 275,
276, 303, 448, 513
Pech Merle 326
Pecos Pueblo 34
Pecos Ruin 33
pedologist 237
Pedra Furada 163, 313, 314, *314*
Peebles, Christopher 197
peer polities 214, 382, 383, 384
Pennsylvania University Museum 334
Penrose, Roger 387
permafrost 64, 233, 250, 442
Persia 185
Perticarari, Luigi 553
Peru 14, 21, 33, 34, 35, 49, 55, 56, 64, 74,
168, 173, 214, 220, 220–21, 228, 295,
304, 309, 316, 333, 334, 337, 343,
344–47, 385, 398, 410, 438, 442, 450,
478–79, 486, *487*, 534, 543, 544–45,
555, 557
Peter-Röche, Heidi 287
Petexbatun 485
Petra 265
Petrie, Sir William Flinders 30, 32, *32*, 33,
34, 122, 123, 131, 334
petroglyphs 157, 158
petrographic analysis 36, 341, 353
petrographic thin section 358
petrography 235
petrology 358, 359, 369, 376
pharynx 436
phenomenological approach 42, 215, 398, 476
Philadelphia Declaration 555
Philae 558
Philip (II) of Macedon 25, 189, 405, 425, 430,
430, 431, 534, *534*
Phillips, Philip 38, 39, 469, 475
philosophy of science 38–39, 42, 491–93
Phoenicians 95, 257, 374, 464, 466
Phoenician script 466
phosphate: residues 302; tests 105, 302

phosphorus 105, 302
photogrammetry 433, 525
photography 111, 233, 246, 499, 542; aerial 40, 75, 79, 80, 82–86, 88, 89, 90, 100, 116, 194, 262, 399, 516, 543, 545; color 108; oblique 80, 83; rectified 525; steroscopic 525; vertical 83
photosynthesis 143, 307
Phylakopi 75, 160, 409
physical anthropology 11, 12, 421, 438; *see also* biological anthropology
phytoliths *242*, 242–43, 264, 267, 274, 276, 279, 307, 324, 513, 519, 521
pictograms 303
Piedras Negras 37
pigments 158, 276, 326, 336, 338, 359, 361, 365, 448
Piltdown man 120, *120*, 562
Pincevent 187, 188, 236, 237, 295, 323, 324
Piperno, Dolores 243, 279
Piranesi, Gimabattista 72
Pires-Ferreira, Jane 378, 379
Pirika 302
pits 32, 64, 77, 84, 92, 94, 102, 103, 104, 106, 118, 119, 151, 300, 348, 408, 504, 506, 509, 528
Pittioni, Richard 38, 362
Pitt-Rivers, General Augustus 25, 26, 30, 31, *31*, 32, 71, 108
planning 391, 402–03; time 388
plans 88, 104
plantations 217, 546
plant impressions 276
plant macroremains 264–65
plants 13, 60, 85, 138, 164, 167, 176, 226, 231, 232, 239–47, 255, 269–82, 309, *467*, 501, 505, 511, 513; groups 307; management of 278; non-woody 323; origin and development 13, 26; remains/residues 35, 44, 50, 55, 244–47, 261, 264–66, 276–78, 280, 310, 502, 512, 522, 527, *527*; studies 38, 239–47, 252
plant species: *Acacia karroo* 246, 247, *247*; acorns 307, 502; agave 257, 311, 502; arrowroot 277; bamboo 304, 511; bananas 262; barley 80, 165, 276, 279, 280, 281, 481; beans 168, 481, 502, 505; bottle gourd 278; bracken 59; brushwood 143; buckwheat 279; cabbage 278; cacti 503; *Chenopodium* 278; Chilean wine palm 267; chili peppers 257, 505; clubmoss 333; corn 257, 307, 410, 481; dóm palm 272; einkorn 275, 279, 296; emmer 275, 305; ferns 60, 519; grain 63, 84, 160, 183, 269, 271, 276, 308, 526; grapes 145, 244, 543; grass 63; greenweed 333; hackberry 503; *Indigofera articulata* 334; knotgrass 270; lilies 232; madder 528; maize 63, 64, 168, 213, 243, 257, 260, 264, 279, 307, 308, 451, 452, 481, 502, 505, 506; mangrove 519; manioc 168, 277, 308; marsh elder 279; millet 168; mint 205, 244; mountain sorrel 306; mustard seeds 63; nabk berries 305; olives 374, 480, 543; palms 273; *Pandanus* 262; peppers 168; plums 528; *Polygonum aviculare* 270; potatoes 168, 213, 278; prickly pears

502, 505; sloes 528; spelt 275; reeds 62, 333, 503, 511, 513; rice 86, 165, 232, 274, 276, 513, 516–22; rhinoceros bush 245; rushes 333; rye 296; sorghum 168; squashes 63, 168, 278, 279, 502, 505; straw 276, 336; sunflowers 63, 279; taro 262, 263, 276, 520; tobacco 279; vines 145, 480; watermelon 305; wheat 80, 145, 165, 168, 275, 276, 280, 281, 305, 481, 543; wild nutgrass 272; woad 333, 528; yams 104, 262, 263; yucca 244
plaster 59, 243, 244, 257, 280, 311, 422; relief 44
plating 347
platinum 346
Plato 562
Playa de los Gringos, Chile 298
Pleistocene 133, 158, 238, 248, 250, 251, 253, 255, 314, 443, 472, 473, 501, 510; chronology 125–26; Late 230, 244, 292; Lower 126, 312; Middle 126, 130, 190; Upper 126
Pliny: the Elder 246; the Younger 21
Plog, Fred 114
Plog, Stephen 77, 419, 506
plowing 54, 55, 81, *81*, 92, 105, 200, 203, 211, 248, 257, 261, 304, 492
plows 80, 261, 294, 546
Poidebard, Father Antoine 82
Pokot 188
Poland 59, 82, 315, 453
Polanyi, Karl 354
polish 276, 301, 328, 520
pollen 127, 225, 233, 238, 239, 240–41, 243, 247, 248, 249, 257, 263, 267, 276, 279, 306, 390, 470, 485, 501, 506, 519, 521; analysis 240–41, 256, 262, 264, 448, *448*; diagram 240, 264; sequences 280; zones 127, 239
pollution 257, 409, 538, 558
polyandry 218
polygamy 218
polymerase chain reaction 432
Polynesia 144, 163, 186, 227, 252, 265, 267, 354, 356, 412, 465, 466, 467, 468
Polynesians 424, 457, 467
Pompeii 21, 22–23, *22–23*, 49, 56, 63, 162, 182, 208, 230, 238, 257, 276, 304, 349, 395, 422, 438, 450, 455, 543, 555
Pontnewydd Cave *146*, 147, *147*
Popol Vuh 410
Popper, Karl 386, 387, 475, 476
population 515; density 515; dynamics 222, 472; history 454; increase 228, 478; pressure 281, 484, 504; size 74, 191, 192, 195, 300; structure 452; studies 452–55; trends *453*
population-specific polymorphism 223, 454, 455
portraits 429
Port Royal 95
Portugal 158, 340, 393, 488
positive feedback 481, 494
positivism 42, 461, 490, 491
Post, Lennart von 239
Postclassic period 407, 484, 501; Late 156
Postgate, Nicholas 92, 183
postglacial epoch 127, 156, 225, 239, 242; pollen core 241, *241 see also* Holocene
postholes 50, 59, 104, 274

postmodernism 16, 42, 43
post-positivism 42, 486
postprocessual archaeology 16, 42–44, 46, 47, 48, 199, 215, 385, 398, 399, 418, 461, 462, 471, 482, 483–91, 494, 495, 496, 562
post-structuralism 42, 486, 496
potassium 145, 150, 157, 339; iodide 277
potassium-argon dating 138, 145, 148, 149, 150, 159, 433
potlach 355, 382
pots 11, 12, 34, 50, 56, 115, 120, 151, 171, 188, 244, 276, 336–37, 346, 355, 388, 422
potsherds 86, 90, 92, 104, 194, 244, 276, 277, 303, 336, 338, 359, 397, 519
Potterne 59
potters 338, 367, 439, 554
pottery 49, 53, 56, 59, 68, 95, 104, 105, 114, 121, 122, *122*, 123, *123*, 124, 150, 151, 152, 159, 177, 178, 189, 194, 199, 212, 214, 242, 243, 244, 276, 277, 280, 293, 302, 313, 335, 336–38, 341, 359, 361, 362, 377, 384, 395, 410, 419, 446, 463, 480, 486, 508, 517, 520, 521; aboriginal 29; decorated 202, 415; Han dynasty; 257; Indian 34; Minoan 160; Mycenaen 131; Recuay-style 220; ; tempers 36, 336, 338, 359; thin section 359, *359*; typology *122*, 122–24, 131; *see also* clay; firing
Potts, Dan 443
Potwar Plateau, Pakistan 313
Poundbury 446, 450
Poverty Point, Louisiana 79, *79*
Powell, John Wesley 28, *28*, 29
power 209, 215, 221, 404–05, 406–07, 494
Prag, John 430
praxis 42, 219
pre-Columbian 210, 264, 331, 333, 336, 349, 438, 442, 443; *see also* American Indians; Paleo-Indians
predators 252, 283, 286, 298
predictive models 89
Predynastic period 63, 122, 123
prehistory 12, 13, 19, 24, 34, 36, 132, 164, 198, 231, 404–05, 499
preservation 60–61, 62, 65–67, 114, 462; *see also* conservation
prestige 173, 176
Prestwich, Joseph 24
Prigogine, Ilya 26, 495
primary centers 203–05, 209, 214
"Princess of Vix" burial 219
probabilistic sampling 76, 77
processual archaeology 15, 39, 42, 380, 386, 461, 464, 465, 469, 482, 483, 489, 490, 491; key concepts 39
production 373–77, 384
Proskouriakoff, Tatiana 37, *37*, 406
protein 120, 157, 302, 451, 452, 502, 504
proto-Indo-European 467
proton-induced X-ray emission (PIXE) 361, 362
proton precession magnetometer 95, *95*, 102, 194
Protzen, Jean-Pierre 316, 317, 319
Pseira 302
pseudoarchaeology 562
Ptolemaic period 282
puberty 219

public archaeology 16, 43, 497, 522–32, 533–64
publication 71, 139, 559, 560–61, 563
Pueblo Bonito 135, 265, *265*, 298
Pueblo Indians 121, 135, 194, 554
pueblos 326
Pueblo Tapado 343
Puech, Pierre-François 306, 328, 435
Pulak, Cemal 374
pulsed induction meter 99
pumice 145, 150
punctuated equilibrium 27, 494–95
Purdy, Barbara 322
Putnam, Frederic *28*, 29
Pylos 204, 206, 207, 367, *480*
pyramids 21, 49, 55, 62, 72, 79, 94, 98, 200, 210, *210*, *332*, 403, *403*, 442
Pyrenees 232, 326, 335
pyrotechnology 313, 335, 346, 356, 480

Qafzeh 148, 152, 155
Qilakitsoq 56, 68, 444
Quanterness 201, 202, *202*
quarries 54–55, 156, 203, 315, 316, *316*, 366, 373, 376, 384, 520
quartz 153, 154, 314, 338, 356, 359, 383, 512, 513
quartzite 512, 513
Quechua 545
Queensland 153, 158, 234, 264
Queyash Alto 220, 221, *221*
Quimbaya 343
Quinua 486, *487*
quipu 184
Qumran, Palestine 563

race 189, 421, *465*, 488
radar 86, 98
radiation 85, 86, 138, 146, 150, 155, 158, 162, 360, 361, 366; counter 151
radioactive: clocks 117, 125, 137–50, 148, 150; decay 137, 138, 145, 146, 150, 155
radioactivity 104, 118, 151, 152
radiocarbon dating 12, 35, 38, 41, 66, 119, 121, 126, 127, 132, 134, 135, 137, *138*, 138–45, 146, 150, 152, 153, 156, 157, 158, 160, 162, 163, 170, 212, 227, 231, 238, 245, 265, 280, 293, 302, 314, 340, 348, 421, 463, 488, 501, 503, 508, 513, 516, 517, 519, 541; calibration of 140–42, 161; contamination 142–44; impact of 144–45
radioimmunoassay 431
Raikes, Robert 242
rain 59, 125, 135, 194, 228, 235, 242, 246, 248, 264, 275, 280, 543, 545
rainforests 59, 78, 85, 262
raised fields 544
Ramesses II 440, *440*, 447, 558; temples 14, *14*, 98
Ramesses V 441
Rancho la Brea 250
random stratified sampling 178, 194
rank 173, 183, 195, 202, 212, 506
ranked societies 169, 176, 463
ranking 177, 195–96, 198, 209–11, 212
Rano Raraku 315
Rappaport, Roy 406, 493–94
Rathje, William L. 13, 380, 477
Rawlinson, Henry 30

Rayleigh waves 94
Real Alto, Ecuador 279
reciprocity 353–55, 354, 369, 384
reconstruction 13, 430, 436, 544
recording 86–87, 94, 111, 112, 114, 116, 211, 549, 559
Red Bay wreck, Canada 95, *96*, 96–97
Redford, Donald 55
redistribution 205, 211–13, 354, 369, 384
Redman, Charles 77, 475
Reed, Charles A. 280
refitting 321, 322–23, 325
regional survey 71, 75, 77
Reigadas, Carmen 294
Reinecke, Paul 121
relative dating 117, 118–28, 161, 170
relativism 43, 44, 490, 491
religion 189, 200, 207, 219, 280, 385–420, 494, 506, 508, 539
remote sensing 71, 84–86, 94–105, 116, 194, 549
Renaissance 20, 169, 338, 347, 555
Renfrew, Colin 75, 371, 404, 480, 488
Renfrew, Jane 277
repetitive strain injury 438
replication 321–22
representation 389, 391, 410, 412, 415, 418–20; in Egyptian art 416–17
rescue archaeology 209, 216, 217, 522, 550; *see also* salvage archaeology
research design 71
residues 12, 49, 114, 244–45, 276–78, 301–03, 306, 336, 344, 431, 449
resistivity 99
resistivity surveys 90, 100, 104, 105
Reynolds, Peter 274, 275
Reynolds, Robert G. 504
rhesus negative gene 454, *454*, 468
Rhodes, Cecil 464
Rhodesia 36
Ricoeur, Paul 418, 486
Richards, Julian D. 526
Richards, Martin 468, 469
Richmond, Ian 562
Rift Valley 85, 126, 145
right-handedness 435
Rijckholt 315
Ring of Brodgar 398, *398*
Rio Tinto 346
Riparo del Romito 446
ritual 173, 176, 203, 205, 215, 220, 221, 222, 261, 286, 335, 383, 389, 398, 399, 408–09, 410, 411, 412, 488, 493–94, 506
rivers 89, 233, 238, 259, 260, 261, 298, 521
river action 55, 78, 259–61
roads 73, 87, 209, 224; Roman 209, *209*, 526; *see also* tracks
Robb, John 492
Robinson, W.S. 123, 124
Robins, Gay 416
rock art 36, 44, 73, 154, 157–58, 160, 215, 231–32, 252, 312, *312*, 314, 327, 385, 415, 493, 509, *509*; Swedish 418, *418*, 492
rocks 24, 85, 104, 145–48, 150, 151, 154, 157–58, 233, 336, 359, 383; varnishes 243
rockshelters 63, 158, 234, 235, 256, 298, 312, 413, 501, *501*, 509, 510, 511, 515; *see also* caves

Romans 11, 21, 22–23, 59, 69, 75, 82, 95, 98, 100, 101, 104, 105, 111, 129, 131, 162, 169, 182, 204, 229, 237, 241, 253, 255, 257, 294, 298, 302, 303, 304, 306, 333, 334, 338, 339, 346, 357, 359, 370, 373, 379, 380, 424, 427, 429, 443, 448, 474, 526, 529, 534, 539, 551; army 282; glass 338, *338*, 339, 357, *357*; towns 209, 240, 241, 250, 466
Rome 13, 20, 72, *72*, 74, 98, 159, 169, 183, 319, 450, 455, 484, 539
rongo-rongo script 395
Roosevelt, Anna 308
rope 184, 318, 435
Rose, Jerome 451
Rose theater, London 523, 548, *548*
Rosetta Stone 27
Rottländer, Rolf 256, 277, 302, 344
Rowlands, Michael 380, 471
Rowley-Conwy, Peter 290, 297
Royal Commission on the Historical Monuments of England (RCHME) 522, 524, 549
Royal Ontario Museum, Toronto 441
rubbish pits 118, 200, 303
Rudenko, Sergei 64
Rudna Glava 315
Rue, David 264
Rumiqolqa 316
Runnels, Curtis 237
running sections 109
Russell, Mary 286, 437
Russell Cave, Alabama 278
Russia 49, 85, 528
Rutherford backscattering 361
Rwanda 438
Ryder, Michael 292

Sabloff, Jeremy 34, 172, 210, 483, 485, 564
Sackett, James 419
sacrifices 215, 507
Sahara 25, 66, 165, 252
Sahlins, Marshall 26, 203, 354
St. Catherine's Island, Georgia 94
St Lawrence Island 64
salinity 226, 227, 243
Salisbury Hoard 557
salt mines 59
salvage archaeology 14, 43, 72, 73–74, 87, 109, 209, 550, 551, *551*, 552
Samoa 465, 466
sampling 39, 40, 74, 75, 76–78, 89, 111, 208, 209
sampling strategies 76–77
Samuel, Delwen 277
San 50, 52, 63, 69, 153, 230, 231, 234, 235, 336, 442, 451, 513; *see also* !Kung San
San Diego 157
Sanders, William T. 74, 177
sandstone 314, 325, 510, 513, 515, 520
San Francisco 229, 230
San José Mogote 259, 505, 506, 507, 508
Sanskrit 467
Santo Domingo Tomaltepec 504, 506
Santorini 160, 208; *see also* Thera
Saqqara 184, 304, 305, 403, 451
Sardinia 373
Saskatchewan 293
satellites 85, 88
Saudi Arabia 85

Saxe, Arthur 200, 488
Saxons 431; towns 209
Sayre, E.V. 339
scaffolding 326
scale 173, 174, 177–78, 200, 215
Scandinavia 133, 134, 161, 230, 233, 385, 409, 523
scanning electron microscope (SEM) 240, 242, 247, 277, 283, 295, 326, 327, 328, 334, 337, 361, 394, 424, 431, 437, 448, 520
scavengers 16, 40, 52, *52*, 53, 283, 285, 286, 308
scepters 210, 374
Schäfer, Heinrich 416
Schedule of Ancient Monuments 548, 553
Schiffer, Michael 52, 462, 483
Schele, Linda 406
schist 325
Schliemann, Heinrich 30, 34, 74, 210, 357, 555
Schmidt, Erich 82
Schmidt, Peter 348
Schoeninger, Margaret 309
Schrire, Carmel 509, 512
Schulman, William E. 135
Schutkowski, Helgar 424
"scientism" 39, 42, 43, 475, 482
Scotland 84, 230, 299, 338, 367
Scott, Douglas 443
Scozzari, Rosaria 468
scrapers 303, 319, 321
screening (sieving) 30, 111, *111*, 244, 247, 248, 377, 505, 510
sculptures 43, 210, 392, 410, 411, 413, 557; Assyrian 30
scurvy 447, 451
sea levels 125, 225, 229, *229*, 230, 232, 252, 472
sealings 209, 367
Searle, John 387
seasonality 278, 283, 286, 288, 298, 502
season of death 288, 290
Secondary Products Revolution 303
Second Radiocarbon Revolution 132, 141
sectioning 110, *110*
sediment 50, 95, 98, 127, 133–34, 142, 147, 153, 226, 227, 232, 233, 234, 235–38, 240, 243, 244, 248, 252, 256, 258, 262, 270, 281, 422, 442, 485, 512, 515
sedimentation 126, 520
sedimentology 235
seeds 59, 244, 245, 246, 257, 271, 272, 275, 296, 297, 306, 506, 519, 520, 527, *527*
Segesta, Sicily 317
segmentary societies 168, 176, 177, 178, 194–96, 198, 200–03, 488
seismic: archaeology 544; methods 94, 98, 100, 230; reflection profiling 230
self-organizing systems 27, 495
Semenov, Sergei 323
"sequence dating" 32, 120–24, 125, 126, 135
Serbs 189, 535
seriation 32, 33, 122
Serpent Mound 50
Service, Elman 26, 174, 177
settlement 79, 80, 85, 87, 89, 176, 181, 182, 198, 200, 231, 237, 260, 371, 452, 504; central place 371; hierarchy 176, 177, 178, 508
settlement patterns 89, 174, 178–82, 212, *212*, 237; studies 87

Sever, Thomas 86
Sevso Treasure 556, *556*
sewers 11, 241, 250, 298, 306, 424, 526
sex 195, 196, 197, 215, 218, 219, 222, 290, 293, 294, 421, 422, *423*, 424, 428, 429, 448, 452, 459; identification 223, 287
sexual dimorphism 287
Shaft Graves 211, 412
Shahr-i-Sokhta 214, 377
Shakespeare, William 523, 550
shamanism 411, *411*, 418
Shamash 183, 185, *185*
Shang civilization 169, 345, 487
Shang dynasty 173, 210, 343, 396, 412
Shanidar Cave 390, 443
Shanks, Michael 42, 46, 483, 490
shape 114, 115, 116, 120, 122
Shaugh Moor 303
Shear, Josephine 37
Sheets, Payson 63, 86
shellfish 254, 266, 299, 308, 434, 519, 520, 521, 522; *Meretrix lusoria* 300; *Spondylus gaederopus* 220, 355, 366
shell midden analysis *103*, 300–01
shell mounds 297, 300, 509
shells 126, 133, 157, 221, 226, 227, 231, 244, 248, 255, 286, 298, 300, 327–29, 336, 353, 355, 356, 358, 378, 388, 504, 505, 506, 511, 513, 516, 520
Shennan, Susan 196
Shepard, Anna O. 36, *36*
Sherratt, Andrew 303, 304
Shield Trap Cave 284
Shimada, Izumi 344
Shimoyama, Akira 427
Shipibo-Conibo Indians 337
ships 69, 331, 332, 373; trireme 332; warships 332
shipwrecks 11, 13, *14*, 33, 58, *58*, 59, 72, 95, 97, 111, 225, 373, 374, 450, 548; *see also* boats; ships
Shona 463
shorelines 230, 231–32, 248
Siberia 64, 226, 229, 335, 418, 456
Sicán 346
sickles 274, 276, 326, 329
sickle sheen 276
sidescrapers 324, 503
sideways-looking airborne radar (SLAR) 86
Sidrys, Raymond 377, 378
sieving 30, 111, *111*, 247, 248, 270, 289, 304, 306, 377; *see also* screening
significance testing 39, 201
Silbury Hill 198, 199, 200
Silchester 303
silica 242, 243, 442
Sillen, Andrew 256, 309
silt 97, 234, 236, 238, 513, 521
silting 233, 268
silver 56, 64, 257, 315, 339, 340, 341, *341*, 342, 345, 346, 356, 365, 373, 380, 383, 400, 404, 480, 528
Sima de los Huesos 390
simple random sample 76, *76*, 77, *77*
simulation models 452
Singer, C.A. 373
Singh, Gurdip 264
Sipán 346, 555
Siphnos 365
Sitagroi 270

site catchment 505; analysis (SCA) 257, 258–59, 281
site exploitation territory analysis 257, 258
site notebooks 111
sites 49, 50, 51, 71, 80, 83, 86–87, 89–105, 116, 145, 149, 174, 179, 190, 192, 193, 199, 240, 268, 270, 277, 510; abandoned 207–08; analysis 256; cave 235, 240; coastal 230; early hominid 148, *148*, 159; hierarchy 176, 177, 179, 180, 204, 224; hunter gatherer 176, 257; Japanese 257, 434; kiln 337; Minoans 195; Mycenaean 374; occupied 208–09; Palaeolithic 251; protected 558; recording of new 549; size 203; threats to 549–58
site surface survey 89, 92, 205, 336
Skara Brae 59, 195
skeletons 59, 69, 133, 147, 148, 152, 195, 218, 223, 228, 301, 302, 305, 307, 308, 309, 389, 421, 422, *423*, 424, 425, 426, 427, 429, 435, 437, 438, 442–43, 446–47, 452, 457, 485, 539, 540, 541, 552, 564
Skhūl 148, 155
skins 49, 63, 69, 256, 283, 284, 289, 292, 309, 333, 376
skulls 120, 157, 280, 287, 293, 421, 425, 426, *426*, 429, 430, *430*, 341, 432, 433, 434, 436, 438, 441, 443, 447, *447*, 448, 450, 519, 521
slag 344, 345, 346, 348, 349
slaughter pattern 287
slavery 258
smelting 336, 338, 339, 340, 344, 349, 358, 365, 366
Smenkhkare 431
Smith, Bruce 278
Smith, Cyril 340
Smith, Holly 425
Smith, Robert L. 156
Smith, R.W. 339
Smithsonian Institution 28, 48, 541
Sneferu 210
social anthropology 11, 173, 215; *see also* cultural anthropology
social archaeology 173–224
social organization 16, 39, 51, 164, 172, 174, 182–88, 198, 199, 202, 209, 215, 224, 503, 508, 517, 519, 526–27
social subsystem 39
Society for American Archaeology 541
Society of Professional Archaeologists (SOPA) 547, 563
soil 50, 51, 52, 56, 57, 59, 70, 80, 84, 89, 94–105, 111, 116, 151, 194, 200, 235–38, 239, 240, 241, 256, 259, 260, 261, 263, 264, 268, 280, 284, 298, 302, 358, 377, 422, 482, 484, 513, 545; chalk 200; development 236; profile 236–37, *237*; samples 274; *see also* phosphate tests; screening
soil marks 80, 81, 83
soldering 346, 361, 446
Solea 365
Solecki, Ralph 105
Solomon Islands 266, 276
Solutrean culture 322, 392
Somerset Levels 68, 127, 136, 255, 261, 330–31, 546

Somme River 24, 28
sonar 98
Sorenson, Marie Louise Stig 219
Sotheby's 555
South Street 261, *261*
space shuttle 86
Spain 158, 210, 251, 252, 257, 288, 312, 326, 329, 340, 346, 367, 390, 391, 393, 413, 434, 450, 454, 488, 558
Spanish 213, 545; Conquest 331, 544; language 467; Levantine 413; Main 373
species diversity 245
Spector, Janet 47
speech 435–37; *see also* language
speleothems 235, 239
Sperber, Dan 473
Speth, John 285, 287
Sphinx of Giza 538, 558, *558*
Spiess, Arthur 291
spina bifida 446
spinning 220
Spitalfields 424, 426, 427
Sprengel's deformity 446, *446*
Spurk, Marco 135
Spurrell, F.C.J. 323
Squier, Ephraim 28, *28*
Sri Lanka 185, 363, 398, 450
stalactites 235
stalagmites 147, 152, 235, 246
standing stones 199, 401
standing wave technology 94
stanols 302
Star Carr 35, 290, 329
Starunia 59
State Historic Preservation Offices 548, 551
states 169, 177, 178, 179, 188, 203–15, 477, 479, 508; early 176–77; origins of 478–79, 480–81, 508
statistical methods 76, 135, 142, 196
statues 62, 168, 183, 200, 281, 316, 318, *318*, 405, 407, 556
status 173, 195, 196, 209, 210, 504, 505
Stead, Ian 557
steel 95, 341, 347, 349; steelmaking 348
Steffy, J. Richard 332
stelae 30, *30*, 131, 158, 185, 316, 395, 399, 405, 406, 493, 544
stencils 73, *73*, 392, 439
Stephens, John Lloyd 30
Steponaitis, Vincas 212
step trenching 109
Sterkfontein 433
Stern, Jack 433
Steward, Julian 26, 27, 35
Stine, Scott 238
Stockholm 303
stomach contents 305, 310
Stone, Anne 459
stone 64, 74, 114, 117, 121, 152, 195, 315–27, 338, 359, 376, 384, 394, 395, 504, 513; axes 202, 326, 330, 353, 358, 359, 413; blocks 55; chipped 24, 311, 362, 370, 372, 503; colored 359; cubes 400, *400*; extraction 315–16; quarries 54–55, 315, 316, *316*, 520; picks 316; raising 318; tombs 73; tools 47, 49, 50, 53, 54, 56, 114, 121, 162, 192, 197, 214, 220, 243, 244, 247, 255, 276, 283, ´6, 301, 311, 315–17, 318–27, 336, ´, 348, 349, 362, 370, 372, 388, 389,

390, 435, 436, 510, 511; transportation 316; walls 80, 102, 319, *319*; working and fitting 317, 319
Stone Age 25, 28, 29, 52, 301, 311, 318
Stone, Anne 223
Stonehenge 19, 50, 79, *79*, 85, 141, 142, 172, 176, 198, 199, 200, 201, 316, 318, 359, 367, 543, 562, 564
Stoneking, Mark 223, 457, 459
stones 106, 191, 199, 412; raising 318, *318*
storage 54, 114, 194, 195, 205, 211–13, 236, 270, 271, 274, 278, 282, 297, 338, 388, 453, 504
Stos-Gale, Zofia 365
Strabo 282, 451
strata 77, 106, 118, 156
stratification 24, 77, 78, 106, 107, 118, *119*, 126, 478
stratified random sampling 77, *77*, 178
stratified unaligned systematic sampling 77, *77*
stratigraphy 21, 33, *33*, 36, 44, 98, 106, 107, 110, 118–20, 124, 125, 142, 143, 144, 148, 149, 190, 227, 231, 337, 501, 509, 522
Stringer, Chris 425
strontium 309, 310, 358, 364, 366, 451
structuralism 461, 496
structural Marxism 471, 490
structuration theory 42, 398, 462, 486
Stuiver, Minze 142
Stukeley, William 20; journal of *21*
style 120, 122, 202, 413, 415, 419
submerged land surfaces 230–31
subsistence 16, 39, 253, 269–310, 470–71, 515
subsoil 80, 104, 151
Sukhothai 337
sulphur 344, 364
Sumer 183, 413
Sumerians 34, 183, 205, 210, 303, 377, 402, 476
Summers, R. 464
Sungir 389
supernatural 385, 391, 398, 406, 410, 412
surface: attributes 114; sampling 208; survey 71, 78, 79, 90, 92, 116, 178, 336, 549
surgical equipment 450, *450*
survey 71, 77, 78, 79, 90, 102, 178, 501, 509
survey grid 78, 90
surveying equipment 78, *78*, 112, *113*
survivorship curve 287
Susa 336
Susman, Randall 433, 437
Sutton Hoo 105, 108, *108*, 211, 311, 422, 529
Swadesh, Morris 124
swamps 49, 68, 136, 238, 243, 262, 513
Swarcz, Henry 308
Swartkrans Cave 256, 285, *285*, 298, 335
Sweden 105, 131, 134, 184, 257, 303, 415, 418, *418*, 431, 488, 492
Sweet Track 330, *330*
swidden agriculture 243, 264; *see also* agriculture; farming
Switzerland 49, 68, 82, 95, 136, 233, 257
swords 210, 329, 342, 405, 493
Sykes, Brian 468, 469
symbolic exchange 380–82, 384

symbolic systems 508
symbolism 16, 39, 43, 281
symbols 215, 382, 385, 387, 389, 391, 404–12, 486, 536; of organization and power 404–05; for other world 406–12, 493–94
symmetry analysis 415
synthetic materials 313, 335–39
syphilis 447
Syracuse 536
Syria 73, 82, 182, 274, 280, 321, 374, 379, 438
systematic random sample 75
systematic sampling 77, *77*
systematic surface survey 78
systems approach 479–82
synostosis 425, *425*

Tabun 147, 155, 302
Tainter, Joseph A. 196
Tairona Indians 313
Taklamakan Desert 85
Taku 321
tannin 69, 307
Tanzania 19, 7145, 150, 162, 176, 253, 319, 348, 388, 428, 433, 558
taphonomy 52, 191, 247, 283, 284–86
Tasmania 41, 158, 227, 234, 434, 540, 551
tattoos 64, *64*, 67, 68, 445, *445*
Tauber, Henrik 308
Taung 425
Tautavel 302
taxation 176, 177, 211, 213
Taxila 30, 32
Tayles, Nancy 519, 521
Taylor, Walter W. 38
technology 16, 35, 38, 39, 84, 106, 117, 172, 177, 203, 213, 225, 232, 238, 259, 332, 338, 339, 440, 452, 474, 503, 511–12, 515, 543; *see also* computers; metallurgy; tools
tectonic movements 230, 231
teeth 147, 148, 155, 250, 253, 276, 283, 286, 287, 290, 291–92, *291–92*, 293, 306–07, 310, 383, 424, 425, 429, 447, 450, 451, 456, 519, 521
Tehuacán Valley 40, 306
tektites 148
Telamarchay 295
teleconnections 161
Tel Haror 539
tell 50, 92, 109, 119
Tell el-Amarna 131, 207, 282, 338–39, 367, 402, 403
Tell Mardikh 73, 182, 184; *see also* Ebla
Tello, Julio 183, 410
temperate climates 59, 135, 235, 304
temperature 59, 120, 125, 126, 135, 156, 225, 226, 227, 230, 231, 232, 249, 251, 253, 256, 300, 302, 335, 336, 337, 339, 345, 349
Temple of the Inscriptions 210, 211, *211*
Temple of the Sun (Cuzco) 55
temples 50, 86, 176, 177, 200, 205, 207, 317, 399, 408, 411, 508, 516, 536, 558; Greek 319
Templeton, Alan 457, 458
Templo Mayor *see* Great Temple of the Aztecs
Teotihuacán 20, 21, 72, 79, 89, 90–91, *91*, 92, 178, 203, 207, 208, 399

Tepe Ali Kosh 340
Tepe Gawra 336
Tepe Yahya 377
tephra 160, 161, 162
tephrachronology 162
terracing 203, 220, 231, 236, 257, 259, 478, 543
terracotta: figures 44, 72, 94, 152, 210, 335, 413, 429; head 152, *152*; sculptures 552; statues 281; wall cones 205
terrorism 543
test excavations 210
test pits 92, 116
textiles 44, 49, 59, 64, 68, 69, 214, 311, 333–34, 356, 410, 503, 528; *see also* clothing; fabrics; fibers
texts 211, 246, 310, 450
Thailand 16, 85, 337, 450, 499, 516, 522
Thames 409, 429, 439
Thebes 55, 62, 98, 282, 329, 334, 373, 429, 431, 539, 558
thematic mapper (TM) 85
theodolite 112, *113*
Thera 126, *160,* 160–61, 208, 238, 413
thermal prospection 105
Thermi 37
thermoluminescence (TL) 138, 145, 150, *151,* 151–52, 153, 154, 155, 322
thermoremament magnetism (TRM) 103, 159
Thiessen polygons 179, 200
thin section 359, 369, 384, 520
"third wave" feminism 218, 219
Thom, Alexander 399, 400, 401
Thom, René 26, 495
Thomas, Cyrus 28, *28,* 29, 34
Thomas, David Hurst 94, 143
Thomas, Julian 216
Thomas, Mark 223
Thompson, Sir Eric 406
Thompson, Jill 519
Thompson, M.W. 329
Thomsen, C.J. 25, *25,* 114, 117, 311
thorium 146, 150, 155, 365
Thosarat, Rachanie 516, 517, 522
Three Age System 25, 48, 114
Thule 65, 231
Thunell, Robert 226
Tibet 226
tidal waves 161, 230
Tierras Largas 76, 505, *505*
Tikal 131, 205, 207, 395
Tikopia 266, 299
Tilley, Christopher 42, 46, 418, 483, 488, 490
timber circles 68, 69, 199, 400
timber 55, 94, 97, 135, 136, 137, 239, 245, 265, 275, 331, 332, 452, 503, 525; *see also* wood
time slices 98, 100
Timna Valley 244
tin 152, 336, 338, 339, 342, 364, 374, 528
Titanic 13, 57
titanium 157
Tiye, Queen 62, 429, 431
Tobias, Phillip 436
Tokyo Bay 231, 248
Tollund Man 69, 306, 429, *429*
Toltecs 20, 169
tomb paintings 342, 373
tombs 73, 94, 98, 200, 202, 240, 277, 282,

397, 402, 412, 429, 446, 488, 489, 539, 555, 557; chambered 201, 202, *202*
Tooby, John 473
toolkits 163, 389
toolmarks 284, 329
tools 11, 28, 29, 52, 54, 55–56, 71, 117, 172, 186, 188, 203, 258, 286, 294, 301–04, 311–50, 388, 394, 435, 436, 501, 512, 545; at Barrow 65; at Çatalhöyük 44; at Mount Arenal 86; bone 55–56, 324; bronze 117, 121, 330, 339, 360, 374, 388, 555; design 387–88; evolution of stone 320, *320*; flake 163, 322, 323, *323*; flint 152, 311, 315, 322, 324, 335, 388, 390, 419; for plant processing 276; function 323; iron 117; Iron age 274; metal 53, 122, 330; obsidian 16, 324, 358; Oldowan 319; pebble 163, 314, *314*, 387; stone 47, 49, 50, 53, 54, 55–56, 114, 117, 121, 122, 162, 192, 197, 220, 243, 244, 247, 255, 276, 283, 286, 301, 311, 315–17, 318–27, 336, 337, 348, 349, 362, 370, 372, 388, 389, 390, 435, 436, 510, 511; traditional 545; wooden 55–56, 315
"top-down" approach 215, 216
Torihama 291
Torrence, Robin 373
Torroni, Antonio 223, 456, 468
Tosi, Maurizio 214
toss zone 186, 187
Tossal de la Roca 394, *394*
Toth, Nicholas 321, 435
tourism 44, 534, 542–43, 546, 558
town planning 256
towns 179, 180, 181, 206, 209, 280
toys 329
trace-element analysis 38, 162, 340, 362–63, 366, 374, 384
trackways 68
tracks 253, 303
trade 16, 38, 71, 182, 184, 205, 351–84, 404, 477, 480, 488, 505–06, 511, *528;* *see also* exchange
transects *75,* 77, 98, 178
transport 52, 86, 199, 388, 499, 501
transported landscapes 268
trapped electron dating 150–51
travertine 146, 147, 152, 235
tree-rings 69, 127, 133–37, *134, 136,* 140–41, 142, 143, 155, 160, 161, 162, 170, 228, 238–39
trees 243, 261, 275, 285, 307, 408; prehistoric 238, *238*
tree species: ash 162; beech 127; birch 59, 127; bristlecone pine 135, 160; cedar 60, 61, *61,* 63, 94; Douglas fir 135; elm 249, 250, 462; eucalyptus 264; fir 264, 265; hazel 278; Irish oak 161; juniper 265; lemon 257; lime 249; oak 69, 135, 142, 240, 249, 330, 470, 501; palm 63; pine 127, 240, 264, 501, 503; piñon pine 135, 265; ponderosa pine 265; spruce 265; terebinth 374; thorn 501; willow 238, 278; yew 335, 435
Treherne, Paul 219
trend surface analysis 369
trepanation 450
Trianda 160
tribal society 198, 200

tribes 176, 177, 182, 189, 202, 222
Trigger, Bruce 483
Tringham, Ruth 323
Trinkaus, Erik 443
Troy 30, 37, 73, 210, 555
tsunamis 161, 230
Tuck, James A. 96
Turin Royal Canon 129
Turin Shroud 141, 144, *144,* 145
Turkey 14, 33, 44, 59, 77, 95, 98, 176, 218, 229, 279, 280, 295, 317, 331, 334, 339, 373, 374, 402, 538, 555, 556
Turner, Christy 456
Tutankhamun 19, 34, 62–63, 71, 117, 210, 331, 405, 428, *428,* 431, 446, 539, 557
tuyères 344, 345, 528
Tweddle, Dominic 529
Tybrind Vig 301
Tykot, Robert H. 308
Tylor, Edward 11, 26, 27, 34
typological sequences 120–24, 509
typology 25, 39, 49, 114, 116, 118, 120–24, 125, 132, 336
Tyre 82

Uaxactún 399, 400
Ubar 85
Ucko, Peter 218, 413
Uhle, Max 33, 34
Ullunda 303
Uluburun 14, 59, 95, 331, 365, 373, 374–75, *374, 375*
ultrasonic cleaning 303
Umm el-Tlel 321
underwater archaeology 13, 14, *14,* 33, 68, 69, 70, 95–97, 102, 331, 559
UNESCO 551, 557
"uniformitarianism" 24
Union Internationale des Sciences Pré- et Protohistoriques 46
United States 13, 29, 34, 38, 41, 42, 43, 46, 87, 94, 186, 215, 244, 257, 260, 306, 339, 382, 383, 421, 451, 473, 483, 539, 546, 547, 549, 551, 554, 557
United States Corps of Engineers 549
University Museum, Philadelphia 555, 556
unsystematic surface survey 78
Ur 34, 169, 208, 210, 304, 311, 402
Uralic languages 455
uranium 119, 120, 146, 148, 150, 155, 365, 366
uranium-series dating 126, 138, 146–48, 227
uranium-thorium dating 142, 158, 235
Uruk 169, 180, 303
Utqiagvik 65
Uttar Pradesh 46, 537
Uxmal 484

Val Camonica 415, 492
Valladas, Hélène 152
Valley of the Kings (Thebes) 98, 219, 222, 405
valleys 478, 479; U-shaped 232
valuables 355–57, 382
value 216, 400, 404; intrinsic 356
Vanuatu 362–63
Varna 216, 404–05
varnish 157, 158, 244, 327
varves *133,* 133–34, 142, 155, 161, 233, 238
vegetation 59, 77, 78, 80, 81, 85, 88, 105,

127, 225, 238–51, 253, 255, 260, 264, 280, 462, 501, 513; management of 261, 264–65, 267; *see also* plants; plant species
Velikovsky, Immanuel 562
Venezuela 308
Venus de Milo 538
"Venus" figurines 390, 394
Veracruz 329, 378
Verberie 324
Vergina 405, 425, 430, 534
Verlorenvlei estuary 254, *254*
vertical stratigraphy 106, 108, 116, 231
Vesuvius 63, 145
veterinary medicine 304
Vidra, Romania 218
viewshed 89, 200, 201
Vikings 69,73, 184, 227, 250, 292, 332, 333, 334, 419, 431, 522, 525, 527, 528, 529, 530
Villa, Paola 286
Vinča culture 395
Vindolanda 59, 282, 334
Virgil 282
virtual reality 543
Virú Valley 35, 74
visual examination 234, 358
Vita-Finzi, Claudio 257, 258, 281
vocal tract 436–37
Vogel, John 308
volcanic activity 21–23, 52, 59, 63, 64, 86, 126, 145, 160, 161, 162, 232, 238, 250, 267, 270, 291, 545; *see also* ash; Herculaneum; Pompeii
Vostok core 126, 226

Wade-Gery, Vivian 37
Wadi Kubbaniya 272, 273, *273*
Wadi Mamed 432
wagons 211, 331, 380
Wahgi Valley 262
Waidelich, Dietmar 422
Wainscoat, James 457
Wales 315, 367
walking 433
Wallace, Douglas 456
Wallerstein, Immanuel 352, 353, 382
wall paintings 44, 73, 160, 215, 312, *312*, 314, 374, 417, 555, 558
Walsh, Grahame 312
Ward, Michael 557
warehouses 213, 214, 298, 526
warfare 42, 55, 214, 215, 268, 287, 382, 477, 478, 479, 493
Warren, Peter 195
warriors 42, 211, 218
Washburn, Dorothy 415
Watchman, Alan 376, *376*
water 59, 69, 80, 86, 89, 111, 120, 142, 147, 155, 190, 225, 226, 227, 228, 232, 233, 234, 243, 255, 257, 264, 377, 407, 409, 505, 545; *see also* floods; sea
watercraft 60, 331–33; *see also* boats, ships
waterlogged conditions 63, 68–70, 107, 114, 142, 238, 244, 246, 249, 261, 311, 333, 334, 452, 525, 527
Watson, Patty Jo 77, 475
wavelength dispersive XRF 360–61, 363

wealth 195, 196, 199, 210, 216, 219, 409, 521
weapons 11, 42, 55, 65, 121, 221, 232, 329, 438, 449; metal 34, 49, 122, 342, 429, 480
weathering 235, 240, 250, 256, 284, 286
weaving 333, 334, 407, 511; equipment 60, 213
Webster, Graham 100
Weeks, Kent 98
weight 400, 428–29, 448, 459
weights and measures 209, 385
Wellcome, Sir Henry 82
wells 95, 264, *264*
Wells, Calvin 427
Wendorf, Fred 272
Wessex 74, 76, 186, 198–99, 200, 399
West Kennet barrow 200
wetlands 49, 56, 68, 85, 232, 260, 261, 511; *see also* Coles, Bryony; Coles, John; peat bogs; bog bodies
Wetwang 311
Wharram Percy 435
Wheatley, David 200
Wheatley, Paul 398
wheel 329, *329*, 336, 337, *337*
Wheeler box grid 108
Wheeler, Jane 295
Wheeler, Sir Mortimer 32, *32*, 36, 71, 109, 119, 208, 363, 443, 563
White Horse of Uffington 154, *154*
Whitehouse, Ruth 492
Whitelaw, Todd 193, 195
White, Leslie 26, 27
White, Shelby 556
White, Theodore 283
White, Tim 443
Whittle, Alasdair 489
Wickens, E. 433
Wiessner, Polly 419
Wilkinson, Paul 299
Willey, Gordon 34, 35, *35*, 38, 39, 74, 172, 469, 475, 485
Wilson, Allan 457
Wilson, Daniel 27
Wilson, Thomas 29
Winchester 208, *208*, 209
Winckelmann, Johann Joachim 22
Wind, Jane 433
Windeby 422
Windover Pond 432
winds 227, 240, 275, 374; ancient 226
wine 277, 302, 304, 367
Winter, Marcus 76
Wittfogel, Karl 476, 477
Wobst, Martin 419
wood 44, 49, 59, 61, *61*, 63, 64, 65, 67, 68, 103,135, 141, 143, 256, 257, 276, 311, 323, 324, 326, 329–33, 335, 346, 503, 511, 525; desiccated 246; firewood 505; remains of 245–46; waterlogged 246; woodcutting 265, 331; wooden artifacts 44, 104; wooden piles 69;wooden tools 55–56, 315; *see also* timber
Woodhenge 248
woodlands 201, 248, 308, 519, 528; management of 261, 264–65
woodworking 52, 68, 330–31

wool 203, 303, 334, 528
Woolley, Leonard 34, 311
World Archaeological Congress (WAC) 46, 537
World Heritage List 551
world system 352–53, 382
World War I 82
World War II 13, 48, 83, 117, 125, 133, 137, 138, 236, 283, 401, 421, 455, 535, 536, 548, 555
WorldWideWeb 560–61
worms 249–50
Wounded Knee 541, 542
Wright, Henry 46
Wright, Herbert R. Jr 280
Wright, Richard 264
writing 304, 385, 387, 391, 395, 396
writing tablets 55, 73, 182, 282, 367, 529, *529*
written records 12, 38, 174, 182–86, 204, 411, 418
Wroxeter 98–99, *99*, 100–01, *100–01*, 346

xeroradiography 440, 449
X-ray diffraction 366
X-ray fluorescence analysis (XRF) 339, 340, 342, 360–61, 362, 422
X-rays 239, 287, 326, 349, 429, 431, 433, 439, 440, 443, 444, 446, 447
XTENT modeling technique 178, 179–80, *180*, 182

Yadin, Yigael 535
Yangzi 165, 521, 522, 551
Yates, Tim 42
Yaxchilán 407, 539
Y-chromosomes 222, 223
Yellen, John 193
Yemen 359
York 11, 16, 250, 255, 257, 298, *298*, 333, 334, 431, 500, 522–32, 563; Roman 526; Anglo-Saxon 526–27; Viking 527
York Archaeological Trust (YAT) 500, 522, 523, 524, 525, 526, 530; laboratory 525, *525*
Yorktown, Virginia 111
Yucatán 30, 82, 85, 123, 210, 409
Yugoslavia 46, 189, 194, 315, 419, 438, 535, 536

Zagros Mountains 280, 371
Zapotec 169, 189, 356, 500, 501, 506, 508; mask *356;* workmen *505*
Zeder, M.A. 253
Zeist, W. van 280
Zeeman, C. 26
Zhoukoudian Cave 256, 536
Zias, Joe 447
Zinjanthropus boisei 37
Zimbabwe 150, 463, 534; *see also* Great Zimbabwe
zircon 150, 359
Zonneveld, Frans 433
zooarchaeology 250, 269, 283, 292, 301; *see also* archaeozoology
Zubrow, Ezra 483
Zulus 492
Zuni Pueblo 542